THE
IMMIGRATION HISTORY
RESEARCH CENTER

THE
IMMIGRATION HISTORY
RESEARCH CENTER

A Guide to Collections

Compiled and Edited by
SUZANNA MOODY
and
JOEL WURL

*Production Coordinated by Judith Rosenblatt
and Anne Bjorkquist Ng*

FOREWORD BY RUDOLPH J. VECOLI

Bibliographies and Indexes in American History,
Number 20

GREENWOOD PRESS
New York • Westport, Connecticut • London

Library of Congress Cataloging-in-Publication Data

University of Minnesota. Immigration History Research Center.
    The Immigration History Research Center : a guide to collections /
compiled and edited by Suzanna Moody and Joel Wurl ; production
coordinated by Judith Rosenblatt and Anne Bjorkquist Ng.
        p.   cm.—(Bibliographies and indexes in American history,
    ISSN 0742-6828 ; no. 20)
    Includes bibliographical references and index.
    ISBN 0-313-26832-0 (alk. paper)
        1. Minorities—United States—History—Sources—Bibliography—
Catalogs.   2. Immigrants—United States—History—Sources—
Bibliography—Catalogs.   3. United States—Emigration and
immigration—History—Sources—Bibliography—Catalogs.
4. University of Minnesota.   Immigration History Research Center—
Catalogs.   I. Moody, Suzanna.   II. Wurl, Joel.   III. Title.
IV. Series.
Z1361.E4U58   1991
[E184.A1]
016.973—dc20   91-16262

British Library Cataloguing in Publication Data is available.

Copyright © 1991 by Immigration History Research Center

Library of Congress Catalog Card Number: 91-16262
ISBN: 0-313-26832-0
ISSN: 0742-6828

First published in 1991

Greenwood Press, 88 Post Road West, Westport, CT   06881
An imprint of Greenwood Publishing Group, Inc.

Printed in the United States of America

The paper used in this book complies with the
Permanent Paper Standard issued by the National
Information Standards Organization (Z39.48-1984).

10 9 8 7 6 5 4 3 2 1

Copyright Acknowledgment

"The Immigration History Research Center: A Historical Profile
and Prospective Glimpse," adapted and reprinted by permission of
the editor, Lubomyr R. Wynar, from the same-titled article by Joel
Wurl in *Ethnic Forum* 8:1, 1988.

Contents

Foreword

The publication of this guide represents the culmination of a quarter century of work on the part of the Immigration History Research Center (IHRC), dedicated to documenting the immigrant experience. As such, it is a benchmark whereby we can gauge not only what has been achieved, but also what remains to be done. Had the IHRC not come into existence when it did, one wonders what would have happened to the materials described in this guide. Would they have ended up in a dump or bonfire as happened to so much of the documentation created by the immigrants?

The following profile of the IHRC by Joel Wurl describes the Center's establishment in 1965. It is astounding today to think that no systematic effort had previously been made to gather the historical records of that epochal period of immigration, from the 1880s to the 1920s, when arrivals reached an all time high. American libraries and archives, suffering from cultural myopia, simply had not regarded the newspapers, the archives, the manuscripts of those newcomers as having significant historical value. If it was not written or printed in English, the assumption was that it was not worth saving. As a result, vast amounts of those records were destroyed. The IHRC (joined by other institutions since the seventies) has been gathering the fragments which amazingly survived decades of neglect.

It had been an assumption of mainstream institutions, shared by most historians, that the immigrants had been inarticulate, if not illiterate, and had left no significant written records. But once we began to scour the country for such materials, we found stacks and files of manuscripts, books, ledgers, newspapers, and magazines piled high in attics and basements, garages and barns, lodge halls and churches, printing shops and business offices. How many tons of such records we have packed and shipped to the IHRC, God only knows.

Major credit for their preservation belongs to the ethnic institutions and individuals who had the foresight to save these materials when no one else seemed to care about them and who were now willing to have them sent off to distant Minnesota so that they might be preserved for the sake of history. It needs to be said that practically all of these materials have come as gifts to the University of Minnesota. On behalf of present and future generations of students of American history, we express our deepest gratitude to the literally thousands of donors who gave *their* records to the IHRC.

Clearly the founding and development of the IHRC was itself expressive of the new social history that emerged from the social and political traumas of the sixties. Variously described as "history from the bottom up" and "history from the inside out," it sought to give voices and faces to those anonymous elements of society, racial minorities, workers, women, and immigrants, who had been traditionally excluded from the history of the United States as written and taught. The IHRC collections, which document the experiences of some twenty-four ethnic groups, make it possible to bring within American history the many millions of immigrants and their descendants. Through the texts of *their* newspapers, letters, diaries, and archives, the internal histories of their lives and their communities can be reconstructed.

The diary of an Italian priest, the minute book of a Slovak lodge, the records of a Finnish cooperative, the letters of a Syrian scholar, the memoir of a Croatian miner, these are among the documents that have been gathered at the IHRC and are described in this guide. Contrary to the prejudice that immigrants were illiterate and inarticulate, they left extensive written records of their thoughts, feelings, and actions. These documents enable us to see America through their eyes, to experience their joys and hardships, and to share their aspirations and despair as they struggled to make new lives for themselves and their children in this new land.

An enterprise such as that of the IHRC must rely upon the encouragement and assistance of many friends. Our mother institution, the University of Minnesota, which nurtured the Center over the years, is to be commended for its steadfast support. In the private sector, the Center's first and most constant patron has been the Northwest Area Foundation (formerly the Louis W. and Maud Hill Family Foundation). A timely grant from the Rockefeller Foundation in the seventies underwrote a major expansion of the IHRC's activities. Equally important has been the funding from the National Endowment for the Humanities and the National Historical Publications and Records Commission. An NEH Challenge Grant in the early eighties placed the Center on a solid footing.

However, it has been our friends in the ethnic communities who have been our most loyal and generous supporters over the years. We are particularly grateful to the ethnic organizations, including the Polish National Alliance, the United Fund for Finnish American Archives, the Ukrainian National Association, the Theodore Saloutos Memorial Fund for Greek American Studies, the Philip K. Hitti Memorial Fund (for Near Eastern American Studies), and the Order Sons of Italy in America, which have supported important indexing, microfilming, and archival projects. To these and all the other ethnic groups and individuals who have given us their generous help, we take this opportunity to express our deepest appreciation.

The preparation of this guide itself has been a major undertaking which has consumed a great deal of IHRC staff time and effort over the last several years. A grant from the Northwest Area Foundation underwrote the basic costs of the project, and for this we are most thankful. But it was the talents, skills, and dedication of the IHRC staff which, when all is said and done, determined the quality of this guide. Their contributions are appropriately acknowledged elsewhere in the volume. I wish to particularly cite the leadership of Joel Wurl, Curator of the IHRC, who got this project off the ground, kept it airborne during critical stages of flight, and brought it to a safe landing.

Rudolph J. Vecoli
Professor of History
Director, Immigration History Research Center

Acknowledgments

When we embarked upon this publication project, we guessed it might require just over a year of our time and would intrude on the routines of only a few other IHRC staff. Needless to say, the complexity of the task went far beyond our expectations. Without the support, dedication, and skill of those identified below, this book simply would not have been produced. Our appreciation is endless.

The Northwest Area Foundation furnished the primary financial assistance for this effort, making possible the full-time employment of Project Director Suzanna Moody. Credit for obtaining that grant belongs to IHRC Director Rudolph Vecoli, whose role as the principal architect in developing the Center's research collections is discussed in the historical profile segment of this book. The following pages are, as much as anything, a testament to his untiring efforts over the past 20 years to preserve and promote the history of American immigrants. His encouragement, patience, and counsel were central to this publication project.

Nearly everyone at the IHRC shared in piecing the guide together. No one devoted more time and energy to the project than Anne Bjorkquist Ng, who managed word processing and formatting efforts, and Judith Rosenblatt, who shepherded the publication through the final stages of editing, selection of graphics, and manuscript design.

An extraordinary amount of research went into the descriptions of manuscript collections, monographs, and periodicals. The work of reviewing individual manuscript collections and producing draft essays for monograph holdings was assigned to a staff research team that included Louise Martin, Halyna Myroniuk, Timo Riippa, Linda Watson, and ourselves. In addition, the labor-intensive task of verifying and modifying information on the ca. 4,000 newspaper and serial listings fell to Halyna Myroniuk, Becky Hall, and Peggy O'Neill Bakko.

Other contributions by staff members included the following: Becky Hall, word processor data entry; Halyna Myroniuk, data verification, selection and captioning of illustrations, and translations of Byelorussian, Russian, and Ukrainian; Wendy Smiley, research and clerical assistance; Stephanie Cain Van D'Elden, proofreading, selection of illustrations, and coordination of publication production. We hope these individuals will, with an awareness of our deep gratitude, take pride in the results of their efforts.

Translations found throughout the guide were supplied in some cases by the source material itself but more often by staff and friends of the Center. Staff members, along with some named above, who assisted in this work were graduate students Anna Jaroszyńska-Kirchmann, Babs Boter, and John Wrathall; *Svoboda* Index Project Coordinator Walter Anastas, Jr.; and Anastas's assistant Teresa Mlekodaj. Those from outside the IHRC who kindly volunteered their language expertise included: Nicholas Berkholtz (Latvian), Van

Cardashian (Armenian), John Gera (Rusin), Jean Hanna (Arabic), Hans Kalitzki (German, Yiddish), Zeyra Avsar Keye (Turkish), Kalju Kubits (Estonian), John Matlon (Slovak), Rev. Ilie Motu (Romanian), Paul Rupprecht (Hungarian), Vanča Schrunk (Croatian, Serbian, Slovenian), Karleen Sheppard (Czech), Andris Straumanis (Latvian), Birute and Kestutis Tautvydas (Lithuanian), Dimitri Tselos (Greek), and Linda Watson (Italian). Their service is typical of the generous support the Center has received over the years from private organizations and individuals and is greatly appreciated.

In conclusion, we wish to acknowledge collectively all who have contributed the documents, photographs, organizational records, scrapbooks, publications, and other historical treasures described in the following chapters. The IHRC is a thriving research repository only because hundreds of individual immigrants and their descendants have entrusted it with preserving their heritage. In a sense, these people are the real "authors" of this guide, and it is to them that the publication is dedicated.

Joel Wurl
Curator

Suzanna Moody
Project Director

The landing at the Battery in New York City, ca. 1906; from *Aliens or Americans?* by Howard B. Grose, Dayton, OH, Missionary Society of the United Brethren Church, 1906.

The Immigration History Research Center: A Historical Profile and Prospective Glimpse

The publication of this guide coincides with a milestone in the evolution of the University of Minnesota's Immigration History Research Center (IHRC). It was approximately twenty-five years ago that the first historical document was acquired by the then "Immigrant Archives." More than simply an interesting case study of a major resource collection and educational program, the story of the IHRC's establishment and development furnishes a microcosmic sketch of the immigration history field over the past two and one-half decades. For instance, the list of scholars who have conducted research at the Center, served on its advisory boards, or studied in its reading room en route to a University of Minnesota Ph.D. includes many of the most recognizable contributors to ethnic historiography.

Born of the "New Social History" movement, the IHRC and its research holdings have helped shape, and have clearly been shaped by, the course of scholarship and the burgeoning academic and general public interest in the history of European ethnic groups.[1] This symbiotic relationship is perhaps best seen in the evolution of the Center's archival and library collections. Early acquisition efforts of the Immigrant Archives and its companion Center for Immigration Studies reflected the research community's crusade to fill a void in historical literature, and material was broadly solicited and liberally accepted. As the corpus of writing grew and new understandings of ethnic societies and their institutions emerged, a process to which the Archives contributed significantly, collecting activity became more directed, targeting fraternal organizations, journalists and publishing houses, consumer enterprises, social service agencies, and more.

Recently, acquisition decisions and initiatives have been influenced by the appearance of studies in increasing numbers examining immigration and ethnicity at the community level and exploring more closely the roles of women, children, and family units. Meanwhile, the collections in hand have themselves prompted researchers to form new questions and recognize new methodological strategies. Probably the greatest challenge lying ahead for the IHRC is sustaining this vital inter-relationship with research interests and directions, not only through its work in preserving and making available historical materials, but in its education and outreach programming as well.

Formative Years

The IHRC's "charter" consists of a series of correspondence between University of Minnesota administrators and members of the history department between 1963 and 1965. The initial idea for a program to collect immigrant documentation crystallized just prior to this in the course of a special research project conducted by historians Timothy Smith, Hyman Berman, William Wright, and Clarke Chambers exploring the history of education in Minnesota's Iron Range communities.[2] The research team discovered that analyzing social institutions in these regions required an understanding of the several ethnic cultures found there.   In the search for relevant evidence, the historians uncovered significant documents in private hands while confronting a serious lack of such material in libraries and archives.   Recognizing that this was not simply a regional phenomenon, organizers set out to build a national repository to begin compensating for the apparent widespread neglect of ethnic documentation.

In early 1963, the University formed an Immigrant Archives Committee, chaired by Timothy Smith, and provided basic support through the library for "a modest program to collect archives and publications of recent immigrants to America from Central, Eastern, and Southern Europe."[3] Early seed money was obtained from the Fund for the Advancement of Education, and the University allocated funds for a full-time curator; but fund raising soon became a primary agenda item for the Immigrant Archives Committee (and it has remained so throughout the IHRC's history).   The Committee also worked to establish an administrative base for the various unfolding activities.   The Committee's "Proposal for the Establishment of a Center for Immigration Studies" won the approval of University administration in September, 1965.   This document called for the new Center to be established within the College of Liberal Arts, working coordinately with the University Library in the development and maintenance of the research collections.[4] In the summer of 1966, the Center for Immigration Studies (renamed the IHRC in 1974) formally began operation, and William Wright was appointed director for a period of one year.

It is clear from early files that those associated with the Immigrant Archives project were casting a very wide net in their search for collections. Along with carrying through on collecting opportunities that had surfaced during the previous Iron Range research project, Timothy Smith and his colleagues began to contact numerous individuals and organizations and to travel extensively (including to Europe). In addition, they enlisted the help of field work "associates" from other universities, including Victor Greene, then at Kansas State University, A. William Hoglund of the University of Connecticut, and Rudolph Vecoli of the University of Illinois, who in 1967 would become the Center's director.[5] This activity yielded results that exceeded expectations; initial acquisitions of South Slavic manuscripts and publications were soon augmented by the receipt of Ukrainian, Hungarian, Finnish, and Italian materials and more, including microfilm of collections held by European repositories.   As Rudolph Vecoli later wrote, "It soon became apparent that we had stumbled on a virgin field, which indeed at times appeared to be quicksand threatening to engulf us by our very success."[6]

Library and Archives

In the process of amassing this material in the early years, a rough definition of collecting boundaries emerged which continues to be operative today. Influenced in part by the concentration of ethnic groups encountered in the Iron Range project, by a desire to avoid overlapping the collecting missions of some other repositories, and by the prospect of limited staff and facilities, organizers confined their interests to immigrants chiefly from eastern, central, and southern Europe and the Near East--those associated with the "second wave" of migration of the decades just before and after 1900. While by no means entirely homogeneous, these "new" immigrants did share a number of characteristics, including in most cases a working-class background that was brought to bear on America's industrializing economy.[7] A list soon materialized of twenty-four ethnic groups deemed to be within the archives' collecting sphere. Within this sphere, few other constraints were imposed on accepting or soliciting material: artifacts were not (and still are not) generally considered appropriate, and the information had to relate in some way to the experiences of immigrants and their descendants or to the process and causes of migration. In addition, the geographic coverage took on national dimensions, indeed international as exemplified in the microfilmed emigration-related records from the Austrian and Hungarian national archives.[8]

The collection that has grown from this broad mission is today arguably the richest available for the study of America's eastern, southern, and central European ethnic groups. Over 4,000 linear feet of manuscript materials (880 individual collections) are joined by approximately 25,000 books and pamphlets and 4,000 newspaper and serial titles. A thorough description of the strengths of these holdings is beyond the purpose of this article; however, some general characterizations can be made here. Manuscript materials break down into six major types: 1) records of ethnic organizations, e.g. fraternals, churches, publishing houses, social and cultural societies, political and labor associations, and consumer cooperatives; 2) papers of ethnic community or organization leaders; 3) papers of ordinary immigrants or descendants of immigrants; 4) records of social service agencies established *for* immigrants; 5) papers of leaders of these service agencies; and 6) papers of historians, social scientists, creative writers, artists, and performers.[9] Books and pamphlets are predominantly publications of the ethnic communities themselves and include literary works, church anniversary albums, and organizational reports of various kinds. Also contained is a significant number of publications about immigrants, such as scholarly and popular historical accounts and U.S. government reports, and materials produced for immigrants, including grammar and citizenship books. The newspapers and serials generated by a multitude of ethnic presses constitute an outstanding source of information on the concerns and perspectives of ethnic communities. Also among the periodicals are scholarly journals and newsletters as well as publications of various voluntary service organizations and multiethnic cultural agencies.

The primary contribution in shaping the nature of the Center's holdings has come from Rudolph Vecoli, director of the institution since 1967. Vecoli's early recognition of the value and potential abundance of records emanating from the organizational lifeblood of ethnic communities gave rise to special collecting and preservation initiatives in the 1970s.[10] With grant support from the National Endowment for the Humanities, the IHRC conducted a four-year Ethnic Fraternal Project beginning in 1977 designed to acquire records for the Center, promote acquisition by other archives, and facilitate management and preservation of records by the fraternals themselves. Among the IHRC's several fraternal collections are the records of the National Slovak Society, the Slovenian National Benefit Society (Slovenska Narodna Podporna Jednota), and the Serb National Federation.[11]

The IHRC, in conjunction with the Center for Research Libraries in Chicago, also embarked upon two successful national newspaper microfilming efforts, the Carpatho-Ruthenian Microfilm Project and the Polish Microfilming Project. In both cases, files of newspapers dispersed throughout the country were located and brought together for filming; the Carpatho-Ruthenian project resulted in the microfilming of virtually the entire available output of that ethnic group's press.[12]

Another intensive collecting program was launched in 1977, directed at the several international institutes located in municipalities throughout the country. Funded by the National Historical Publications and Records Commission (NHPRC), the International Institutes Project attracted to the IHRC collections of those organizations from Boston, St. Louis, and St. Paul and made possible the microfilming of others from Baltimore, Buffalo, New Haven, and more.[13]

More recently, the Center worked with members of the Minnesota Finnish American Historical Society to generate documentation on the everyday life of a regional ethnic population. The Minnesota Finnish American Family History Collection, containing oral history recordings along with autobiographical and genealogical material, provides an outstanding opportunity for researchers to apply a microanalytical approach in examining social history from the participants' perspectives.[14] Currently, the IHRC is engaged in two additional newspaper microfilming projects focusing on the Finnish and Italian groups; and it has completed a three-year program to survey, acquire, and describe the records of the Order Sons of Italy in America, the nation's largest and oldest Italian fraternal organization.[15]

Research and Outreach

Technically, the IHRC was not directly responsible for the resource material collected until recently. Library and archival operations were, up to 1985, administratively the province of the university library system, which funded the position of curator. In practice, however, the director and other staff of the IHRC played an integral role in the development and maintenance of the collections. But the chief mission of the IHRC, and previously the Center for Immigration Studies, was the promotion of research activity and interest in the history of immigration and ethnicity, accomplished through various conferences, publications, research grants, public outreach programs, and involvement in the instructional life of the university. The IHRC today is responsible for this type of programming as well as the management of the research holdings.

Some of the most ambitious manifestations of the Center's work in furthering research have been the conferences and symposia it has sponsored. The list includes programs devoted to Finnish migration, Italians in rural and small town America, the Slovenian American leader Louis Adamic, Minnesota's ethnic language schools, and Arabic-speaking immigration to North America.[16]   The high point of the Center-sponsored conferences occurred in 1986 with the international symposium "A Century of European Migrations, 1830-1930: Comparative Perspectives." Approximately forty-five of the leading scholars in immigration studies from ten countries gathered to review current research and look ahead to future directions.

Proceedings from several of these conferences have been (or, in the case of the 1986 symposium, will be) published with the IHRC's assistance. In addition to facilitating the production and distribution of these volumes, the Center has developed a modest publication program of its own consisting largely of bibliographies and descriptions of its collections.[17] The newsletter *Spectrum*, published since 1975, has received acclaim for its helpful essays relating the Center's holdings to key topical areas of ethnic research. Within the past few years, the IHRC's collections, along with those of other archives and libraries, have contributed to two important microfilm publications of primary sources: Research Publications' "Immigrant in America" series, consisting of thousands of ethnic imprints, and University Publications of America's "immigration history" series, thus far including previously unpublished immigrant autobiographies.

From its inception, the Center has viewed its enterprise in an international context and has worked toward building relations with interested parties abroad. Recent years have witnessed heightening levels of research activity devoted to emigration studies among scholars in European and Near Eastern nations. Research institutions serving as bases for this activity now exist in several countries, and include the Institute of Migration in Turku, Finland; the Polonia Research Institute at the Jagiellonian University in Krakow, Poland; and the Centro Studi Emigrazione in Rome, Italy. With these counterpart operations and with individual scholars, the IHRC has arranged or facilitated exchanges of research material and researchers, collaborated on conference programming, and participated in cooperative microfilming efforts. Some examples of this include the Finnish American Newspaper Microfilming Project mentioned above, administered jointly by the IHRC and Helsinki University Library along with Suomi College in Michigan; the two-part symposium honoring Louis Adamic, held in St. Paul and in Ljubljana, Yugoslavia; and the recent exchange of personnel between the University of Minnesota and Marie-Curie Skłodowska University in Lublin, Poland, enabling the IHRC to enlist the services of a professionl archivist with native language fluency.   Such relationships have contributed a great deal to the development of the Center's holdings, as in the case of the collection of 14,000 "America Letters" located and microfilmed in Finland and made available to the IHRC and other institutions.

The IHRC's successes in attracting research materials have largely been a factor of its diligence in cultivating links with the ethnic communities it serves. A major step toward that end occurred in 1977 with the establishment of the Friends of the IHRC. Made up of people affiliated with the various ethnic groups whose history the Center documents, this organization serves to strengthen channels of communication with the general public. Close rapport with ethnic communities has proven integral not only to identifying acquisition opportunities but to amplifying fundraising efforts as well. Although the IHRC has prospered substantially from government and foundation support,[18] donations from individuals and ethnic organizations have accounted for a sizable portion of the over $2 million in non-University of Minnesota funding obtained since 1963. Recent initiatives supported by private monies include the above-mentioned Sons of Italy Archives project (funded by the Order Sons of Italy in America along with NHPRC), the production of an extensive index to the Ukrainian American newspaper *Svoboda* (ongoing, funded by the Ukrainian National Association), and the processing of Greek American manuscript collections, including the papers of the eminent historian Theodore Saloutos (funded by many individual donations from the Greek community).

As the IHRC moves into its second twenty-five years, a number of important issues will require attention: improved physical facilities, increased outreach to potential researchers and collection donors, a more focused collection development program, and greater resources and effort to arrange, describe, and preserve materials.

A common thread runs through nearly all of these major goals: interaction and coordination with other repositories and with the research community. During the past twenty-five years since the Center's establishment, the number of people and institutions involved in "doing" ethnic history has risen at a staggering rate.[19] Regrettably, communication among these parties is sporadic and unstructured. The Immigration History Society provides a vehicle for organized dialogue, but its membership includes too few archival, museum, and library professionals, and nothing else along these lines exists to serve the particular concerns of these ethnic resource specialists. The IHRC is hopeful that the time is now right for building some type of network of ethnic repositories, a vision held by many in the past. In part toward that end, the IHRC is coordinating a 1990 conference of researchers and archivists to evaluate the state of ethnic documentation nationally, and the prospects and strategies for strengthening coordination in the future.

Given the number of organizations like ours with overlapping interests and the lack of human and financial resources available to most of us, is it logical for anyone to face alone the large amount of work that remains to be done in preserving and promoting ethnic history? The IHRC's future goals and activities will be predicated on the belief that the answer to this question is clearly "no" and that other institutions are prepared to explore more concerted, imaginative approaches to collective action. If these presumptions prove accurate, the next twenty-five years should be a fruitful and exciting time for the IHRC and, one hopes, for ethnic repositories generally.

Notes

1. For previously published descriptions of the IHRC and its history see Rudolph J. Vecoli, "The Immigration Studies Collection of the University of Minnesota," *American Archivist* 32 (April 1969): 139-145; Nicholas V. Montalto, "The Challenge of Preservation in a Pluralistic Society," *American Archivist* 41 (October 1978): 399-404; Rudolph J. Vecoli, "Diamonds in Your Own Backyard: Developing Documentation on European Immigrants to North America," *Ethnic Forum* 1 (September 1981): 2-16; and Susan Grigg, "A World of Repositories, a World of Records: Redefining the Scope of a National Subject Collection," *American Archivist* 48 (Summer 1985): 286-295.

2. Vecoli, "Immigration Studies Collection," 142-143 and Grigg, "World of Repositories," 289. The project generated five unpublished essays, completed in 1963: Hyman Berman, "Education for Work and Labor Solidarity: The Immigrant Miners and

Radicalism on the Mesabi Range"; Clarke A. Chambers, "Social Welfare Policies and Programs on the Minnesota Iron Range, 1880-1930"; and Timothy L. Smith, "Educational Beginnings, 1884-1910," "Factors Affecting the Social Development of Iron Range Communities," and "School and Community: The Quest of Equal Opportunity, 1910-1921."

3. "University of Minnesota Immigrant Archives Project," proposal for foundation support, November 26, 1964, 7 pp.

4. "Proposal for the Establishment of a Center for Immigration Studies," July 1965, 2 pp. This proposal went through a number of drafts and was reviewed by several administrators before formal approval in September 1965.

5. Timothy Smith, "The University of Minnesota, Immigrant Archives: A Progress Report, and a Review of Policy, December 31, 1965," 6 pp.

6. Vecoli, "Immigration Studies Collection," 143.

7. Vecoli, "Diamonds in Your Own Backyard," 4.

8. These collections are labeled at the IHRC as: "Austria. Staatsarchiv" and "Hungary. Országos Levéltár."

9. Grigg, "A World of Repositories," 292.

10. See Vecoli, "Immigration Studies Collection," for discussion of the importance of fraternal, church, and newspaper documentation.

11. The project resulted in a guide to fraternal records at the IHRC and elsewhere, *Records of Ethnic Fraternal Benefit Associations in the United States: Essays and Inventories* (St. Paul: IHRC, 1981). See also Montalto, "Challenge of Preservation," 400-402.

12. Project descriptions and listings of microfilmed titles are contained in Frank Renkiewicz, comp., *The Carpatho-Ruthenian Microfilm Project: A Guide to Newspapers and Periodicals* (St. Paul: IHRC, 1979), and Frank Renkiewicz and Anne Bjorkquist Ng, comp., *A Guide to Polish American Newspapers and Periodicals in Microform* (St. Paul: IHRC, 1988).

13. For more complete information on the objectives and accomplishments of this project see Nicholas V. Montalto, comp., *The International Institute Movement: A Guide to Records of Immigrant Service Agencies in the United States* (St. Paul: IHRC, 1978). See also Montalto, "Challenge of Preservation," 402-404.

14. This collection is described in Mary Koske, comp., Suzanna Moody, ed., *Guide to the Minnesota Finnish American Family History Collection* (St. Paul: IHRC, 1985). Procedural guidance for producers/donors of family history materials was provided in Carl Ross and Velma Doby, *Handbook for Doing Finnish American Family History* (Minneapolis: Minnesota Finnish American Family History Project and Minnesota Finnish American Historical Society, 1980, second printing 1988).

15. John Andreozzi, comp., *Guide to the Records of the Order Sons of Italy in America* (St. Paul: IHRC, 1989). The Sons of Italy Archives Project resulted in the accessioning of over 600 linear feet of records at the IHRC.

16. Publications resulting from conferences have included: Michael G. Karni, Matti E. Kaups, and Douglas J. Ollila, Jr., eds., *The Finnish Experience in the Western Great Lakes Region: New Perspectives* (Turku, Finland: Institute for Migration, in cooperation

with IHRC, 1975); Betty Ann Burch, ed., *Minnesota's Ethnic Language Schools: Potential for the 80s* (St. Paul: IHRC, 1983); Rudolph Vecoli, ed., *Italian Immigrants in Rural and Small Town America: Essays from the Fourteenth Annual Conference of the American Italian Historical Association* (Staten Island: American Italian Historical Association, 1987); and Eric G. Hooglund, ed., *Crossing the Waters: Arabic-speaking Immigrants to the United States Before 1940* (Washington and London: Smithsonian Institution Press, 1987).

17. Many of these are cited in the publications appendix of this guide.

18. Major contributors to the IHRC over the years have included the Northwest Area Foundation, the Rockefeller Foundation, the Minnesota State Legislature, the Minnesota Humanities Commission, the National Historical Publications and Records Commission, and the National Endowment for the Humanities.

19. See Lubomyr Wynar and Lois Buttlar, *Ethnic Museums, Libraries, and Archives in the United States* (Kent State University Press, 1978) and *A Directory of International Migration Study Centers, Research Programs, and Library Resources* (Staten Island: Center for Migration Studies, 1987).

Introduction

What This Guide Is and Is Not

This book attempts to furnish a thorough summary of the archival and library holdings of the Immigration History Research Center. Its purpose is to assist researchers in determining the usefulness of the IHRC's collections and to explain the procedures for gaining access to them. Although the material described in this guide is obviously of most direct value to those researching subjects relating to immigration and ethnicity, the IHRC should not be overlooked as a potential resource for studies on labor, women, religion, journalism, education, and other areas of American social and cultural history. In addition to facilitating research work, this publication will, we hope, serve to remind people of the need to ensure the preservation of organizational records, personal papers, books, newspapers, and other material similar to that described in the following pages.

Every time an archival or special collections repository generates a product like this, it reinforces the truism that a guide is technically obsolete even before it appears in print. The IHRC's experience is certainly no exception. A good deal of material has arrived at the IHRC since we began work on this guide, and we wish it could all have been listed. However, information on recent acquisitions can be obtained upon request, and many of these items are regularly highlighted in the IHRC's newsletter, referred to in the publications appendix.

Comprehensiveness is another elusive accomplishment for repository guides. We can fairly characterize the extent of descriptive information contained here as "thorough," but we make no pretense that the coverage is all-embracing. This guide, like many of its ilk, was conceived as an introduction and orientation to the sources and services of the IHRC. More detailed information, such as inventories for manuscript collections or catalog records for books and periodicals, is available on site or upon request for much of the material presented in the following chapters.

One other potential presumption we want to dismiss from the outset is the notion that this volume is in any way definitive with regard to ethnic group designations and the categorization of material within particular groups. In order to make resources accessible, a repository must identify and organize them in some manner. Throughout its history, the IHRC has made a conscious effort to avoid the appearance of "defining" ethnicity through its handling of the collections it receives. While decisions regarding the arrangement and description of material are made with the intent of objectivity, we recognize that some of the information in this guide might suggest that the Center promotes particular interpretations of issues for which consensus is currently lacking. We wish to make clear again that such choices are not made for the purpose of presenting a given viewpoint on history; this is a role more appropriately reserved for the users of our collections.

The remainder of this introduction is intended to explain how this guide was put together and can be most effectively used. Information in the appendixes will acquaint readers with the IHRC's research services and procedures as well as some of the Center's other publications. As with the other portions of the book, additional information on these topics is available from the Center.

Evolution of the Guide: The How and Why of the Information Included

The seed for this publication was planted in 1984 when the IHRC received $20,000 from the Northwest Area Foundation to update and expand upon the Center's "Guide to Manuscript Holdings," printed in 1976. Early planning for the new guide led to the decision to include much more information on monograph and periodical materials than had been presented in the previous booklet, and it revealed the need for substantial work to improve the level of consistency and quality in existing catalog descriptions for manuscript collections. In part to facilitate the latter, the Center elected to embark upon a project to automate its manuscript collections catalog, with the dual objectives of developing effective descriptions for the printed guide and further increasing access to the material through computerized searching capabilities. This course of action transformed the publication project into something much broader and more labor intensive, but the impact of applying new technology to the endeavor proved to be positive and far reaching in terms of the administration and research use of the IHRC's holdings generally.

The effort to prepare the guide and develop the computer database for manuscript collections began in earnest in early 1987, when Suzanna Moody was hired to direct the project. Her work as a professional indexer--a key product being the book-length index of the reference volume *Women's History Sources* (Andrea Hinding, ed., New York: R. R. Bowker, 1979)--coupled with her library and archival experience enabled the project to get off the ground quickly and effectively. Moody was assisted throughout the project by a research team of IHRC staff members, identified individually in the acknowledgments section of this book. These staff members, whose regular duties involved other IHRC projects or functions, played major roles in producing the manuscript collection descriptions and, particularly, the monograph collection essays in this guide.

Manuscript Collection Descriptions. The project's first focus was on developing the manuscript collection entries. Information about manuscript collections was entered in the IHRC's new microcomputer system consisting of Zenith hardware and the MicroMARC:amc software package, developed at Michigan State University for the specific purpose of administering archival cataloging information. Along with its flexibility in meeting a variety of in-house needs for enhancing access to collections, the software enabled the Center to adopt the MARC-AMC format for description of archival and manuscript material (a practice becoming increasingly conventional in archival repositories) and to anticipate the eventual sharing of its database electronically through national bibliographic networks or with other archives and researchers individually.

The computer records created for each manuscript collection consisted chiefly of information derived from existing catalog cards, inventories, accession registers, and relevant correspondence. However, as mentioned above, these sources varied considerably in quality and inclusiveness, depending often on the extent to which a given collection had been professionally arranged and described. In cases where available finding aids were lacking essential information, the staff research team was assigned to analyze the collections to furnish additional details. Although time consuming, this process contributed a significant amount of new and valuable information to the IHRC's descriptive database for manuscript collections.

Upon production of the MicroMARC:amc record for each manuscript collection, selected components were edited and formatted on word processing equipment to generate entries for the guide. The entry was crafted with the intent that it serve as a concise overview of the collection sufficient to enable researchers to infer the potential relevance or usefulness of the documents. Readers will note some variance in the amount and type of information given for collections. Again, this often correlates with the extent of archival processing work carried out for the materials.

Essays on Monograph Holdings. To convey information about the Center's extensive monograph holdings, we decided to prepare essays synthesizing the strengths of the collection for each ethnic group and highlighting exemplary titles. Members of the staff research team were requested to draft the essays based on their analysis of the books in the context of what they already knew or were able to learn about the universe of available publications by, for, or about their assigned immigrant groups. Although such an approach undoubtedly resulted in some specific, deserving titles being omitted, the alternatives of listing every volume or of completely disregarding the book collections would have been either unwieldy or unacceptable.

The authors of these essays were given a difficult task: to evaluate the Center's holdings without pronouncing judgment on the quality of particular publications. In other words, the essays were intended to be mainly *descriptive*, not *prescriptive*. Determining which areas or topics covered by the monograph collections could be considered "strengths" was often a delicate matter and one that could not escape subjectivity. We fully expect that researchers who use these materials will formulate some different opinions on the level of coverage for various topics, and we welcome feedback on such observations.

Newspaper and Serial Listings. For the IHRC's newspaper and serial holdings, we concluded that listing each title was the most helpful alternative, from the researcher's standpoint, and that this could be accomplished far more readily than it could be for monographs. The goal was to furnish a simple compilation, based on the Center's existing card catalog, which would incorporate only the most essential information about each title. This goal was indeed met, but it proved to be not as simple as we thought. While in-house cataloging records have served researchers well over the years, the attempt to adapt them for a major publication exposed the fact that none of the Center's ca. 4,000 periodicals has ever been *formally* cataloged. Thus, as with the other sections of the guide chapters, a considerable amount of research was needed to enhance the quality and completeness of the newspaper and serial listings. Even with this investment of staff time, however, absolute consistency and accuracy were not within grasp and could only have been attained through detailed analysis of nearly every file. All too common title changes, the fragility of some of the material, and the lack of staff expertise for certain languages compounded matters.

Translations. Translations of foreign-language titles of monographs, newspapers, and serials were supplied in a number of ways. The IHRC's in-house catalog carried translations for many of the titles, and these were repeated in the guide. Other translations were taken from several published bibliographies and guides to the ethnic press, such as Lubomyr R. Wynar and Anna T. Wynar's *Encyclopedic Directory of Ethnic Newspapers and Periodicals in the United States* (1976); *The Ethnic Press in the United States: A Historical Analysis and Handbook*, edited by Sally M. Miller (1987); and *The Immigrant Labor Press in North America, 1840's-1970's*, edited by Dirk Hoerder (3 volumes, 1987). The remainder of titles were translated directly by staff members and associates of the Center with relevant language skills (see acknowledgments). English translations or subtitles that appear on the mastheads or nameplates of the publications themselves were used when available; the guide does not indicate those titles to which this applies.

Final Production Process. The copy editing, proofreading, selection and placement of photographs, and indexing of this publication were carried out by IHRC staff over the course of a year. The Center also produced the camera-ready text using microcomputer equipment and an Apple LaserWriter II NT printer. The photographs that appear throughout the volume were selected from the IHRC's holdings, representing a small cross section of the types of images and materials found in many of the Center's manuscript collections and print holdings.

Organization of Information

The organization of chapters in this guide—i.e., by ethnic group (in alphabetical order)—reflects the organization of collections and finding aids at the IHRC. Each chapter comprises descriptions of manuscript, monograph, newspaper, and serial holdings for an individual ethnic group.

In each chapter, entries for the four types of holdings are arranged in the following order: 1) manuscript descriptions, 2) an overview essay on monograph holdings, 3) listing of newspapers, and 4) listing of serials. For each subsection except the monograph essays, individual entries are arranged alphabetically.

Some country names associated with cities of birth (manuscripts section) or of publication (newspapers and serials) have changed over the years as a result of wars or treaties that transferred territory. The countries are listed as they would have been at the time of birth or publication, whenever it was possible to ascertain this. For example, with regard to periodicals published in German cities, Germany is listed as the place of publication for years before 1948; East or West Germany is used for later dates. However, modern English spelling has been used for place names as much as possible.

Manuscript Collections. Descriptions of manuscript collections include the following elements for *all* collections: main entry (a personal or corporate name, or a collection title, in English, followed by original language if other than English); birth and death dates for individuals, if known; type of collection (papers, records, collection); span dates of the collection, or, if the dates are not known, the abbreviation "n.d."; the size of the collection, in linear inches or feet (rounded), or number of microfilm reels or sound recordings; and description of the contents of the collection. *Optional* collection description elements include a historical or biographical sketch; the language(s) of the material if *other* than the language of the homeland of the ethnic group; a note on the availability of an inventory; indication of access restrictions; a location note on originals if the collection is in microfilm or photocopy form; and a note on related collections, if any. "In OSIA Guide" is appended to descriptions of those Italian American collections included in the Sons of Italy Archives at the IHRC. These collections are described more fully in the IHRC's *Guide to the Records of the Order Sons of Italy in America* (see reference in the publications index).

Example:

Main entry (birth and death dates).
Type of collection, span dates. Size.

Historical or biographical sketch.
Description of the contents of the collection. *Language. Availability of inventory. Access restrictions. Location of originals. Related collections.*

Monograph Essays. Monograph essays consist of an evaluative overview of holdings for each ethnic group. They do not list all holdings by title. The essays highlight the strengths and, in some cases, weaknesses of each monograph collection. Each essay considers holdings that reflect important areas of the immigrant experience, such as the migration process, acculturation, literature, organizations, religion, politics, education, and work.

Newspapers. Newspaper holdings are listed alphabetically by title. The following is provided when known: title translation; sponsoring organization; alternate title(s), including previous title(s) and information on mergers and predecessor or successor publications; place(s) of publication; frequency of publication; years of holdings; and format (if microfilm), followed by years of microfilm holdings. Listing a particular year means the IHRC holds one or more issues, but not necessarily all issues, of that year. If the city of publication is unknown, the country is in brackets. Language(s) of publication may be listed if other than the language of the group's homeland.

Serials. Like the newspapers, serial holdings are listed alphabetically by title. The entries include, when known, the same elements as those for newspapers.

Example of newspaper or serial entry:

Title (translation of title; organization, alternate title[s]), place of publication
(previous place[s] of publication). Frequency (previous frequency):
years. (Microfilm: years). Language(s).

Abbreviations. Standard U.S. Postal Service abbreviations have been used for states. Other abbreviations used are:

b.	=	born	ft.	=	feet
ca.	=	circa	in.	=	inches
d.	=	died	n.d.	=	no date (date unknown)

A group of Russian Jewish immigrants anticipating life in the New World, ca. 1900; from *On the Trail of the Immigrant*, by Edward A. Steiner, New York, Fleming H. Revell Co., 1906.

IHRC Guide to Collections

General Collection

Manuscript Collections

Adler, Selig.
Papers, 1933. 2 linear in.

Papers of Adler consist of a photocopy of his notes for Marcus Lee Hansen's immigration history course. *In English. Original forms part of Selig Adler papers, University Archives, State University of New York at Buffalo, Buffalo, NY.*

Alliance of Transylvania Saxons, Series I (Cleveland, Ohio).
Records, 1902-1981. 1 microfilm reel.

The Alliance is a fraternal and insurance organization. It was founded in 1902 and is open to Americans of Transylvanian Saxon descent. It has forty-three branches and approximately 10,000 members. Its weekly publication is the *Volksblatt*.
Records include convention minutes. *In German. Related collections: Alliance of Transylvania Saxons, Series II (Cleveland, OH); Alliance of Transylvania Saxons, Series III (Cleveland, OH).*

Alliance of Transylvania Saxons, Series II (Cleveland, Ohio).
Records, 1957-1981. 1 microfilm reel.

Records consist of minutes of the grand officers' meetings. Minutes of 1970-1980 restricted. *In English. Related collections: Alliance of Transylvania Saxons, Series I (Cleveland, OH); Alliance of Transylvania Saxons, Series III (Cleveland, OH).*

Alliance of Transylvania Saxons, Series III (Cleveland, Ohio).
Records, 1923-1981. 35 microfilm reels.

Records consist of application files Nos. 42-23958. *Restricted. In English. Related collections: Alliance of Transylvania Saxons, Series I (Cleveland, OH); Alliance of Transylvania Saxons, Series II (Cleveland, OH).*

American Council for Emigres in the Professions (New York, New York).
Records, ca. 1938-1979. 475 linear ft.

Founded in 1945, the American Council for Emigres in the Professions (ACEP) was a service organization aiding professional émigrés in all aspects of resettlement. The ACEP was formerly the American Committee for Refugee Scholars, Writers and Artists. In 1963, it absorbed the National Committee for Resettlement of Foreign Physicians. The ACEP provided counseling, English tutoring, evaluation and interpretation of foreign credentials, and job retraining and placement as well as specialized help such as studios for music practice, art exhibitions, and radio broadcasts.

Records consist of case records and administrative files of the Council and its predecessors. Included are history, medical, and research files, annual reports, board records, meeting records, language instruction materials, placement reports, employment seminar programs, career information files, correspondence, and lists of the board of directors. *Mainly in English. Preliminary inventory available. Restricted.*

American Council for Nationalities Service (New York, New York).
Records, 1918- . 180 linear ft.

The Council had its origins during World War I in the United States Committee on Public Information, Division of Work with the Foreign Born. After several brief nongovernmental affiliations, the Division became independent in 1921 as the Foreign Language Information Service (FLIS). The main purpose of the FLIS was education; it also provided service to immigrant organizations. The FLIS was disbanded in 1939, succeeded by the Common Council for American Unity (CCAU), which continued the educational mission of the FLIS. The CCAU was responsible for release of information to the foreign language press, operated a radio service, published *Common Ground*, and worked with the government to help with activities such as alien registration and foreign language publicity. In 1959, the CCAU merged with the American Federation of International Institutes (AFII) under the new name American Council for Nationalities Service (ACNS). The ACNS carried on most of the projects and activities of its predecessor organizations, including work with the foreign language press and radio, nationality groups, and the United States government. It has played an important role in resettlement of Cuban and Southeast Asian refugees.

Records of the ACNS contain records and publications of its predecessors, FLIS, CCAU, and AFII. The collection records

the activities of the Council, which has been interested in all aspects of immigration and resettlement, including educational services, ethnic presses and radio, social services, and immigration legislation. *In multiple languages. Preliminary inventory available. Related collection: Josephine Roche.*

Assembly of Captive European Nations (New York, New York).
Records, 1954- . 60 linear ft. and 13 scrapbooks.

The Assembly was founded in 1954 by exiled democratic leaders, diplomats, trade unionists, and intellectuals from captive European nations. Its purpose is political action aimed at the restoration of freedom and independence for the nations of Albania, Bulgaria, Czechoslovakia, Estonia, Hungary, Latvia, Lithuania, Poland, and Romania. Committees of the ACEN include Cultural-Information, Economic-Social, and Political-Legal.

Records include internal organizational materials of delegations to various nations; information on the General Committee and its members; information on working committees; records of the plenary assemblies; minutes; lists of national and international member organizations, consultative organizations, and associate-member organizations; information on the United Nations and Council of Europe; and information on relations with and correspondence with various governments, including that of the United States. *In multiple languages. Inventory available.*

Austria. Main Government Archives (Allgemeines Verwaltungs-archiv) (Vienna).
Records, 1910-1913. 1 microfilm reel.

Records consist of reports and correspondence from Austro-Hungarian consulates in the United States pertaining to immigration. Topics include the Greek Catholic Church; pan-Slavic nationalist agitation; immigration from Galicia; Hungarian, Slovak, and Slovene American newspapers; conditions of Slovak workers in Pennsylvania; political activity of immigrants; the Hungarian Reformed

Church in New York; Slovene and Hungarian American organizations; and Croats and Serbs. Correspondents include Archbishop John Ireland of St. Paul, MN, and Monsignor Falconio. *In German. Inventory available (in German only).*

Austria. Foreign Affairs Ministry (Ministerium des Aussern) (Vienna).
Records, 1895-1914. 2 microfilm reels.

Records consist of selected consular reports and correspondence dealing with immigrants to the United States from the Austro-Hungarian Empire. Included are reports from Austrian consuls in Pittsburgh, PA; information on the Greek Catholic Church and the Catholic Church, Latin Rite, in the United States; reports on Slovak and Galician immigration; Slovak American newspapers; and information on Russian Orthodoxy. Correspondents include Archbishop John Ireland of St. Paul, MN. *In German. Inventory available (in German only).*

Austria. Royal and Imperial Foreign Ministry (k.u.k. Ministerium des k.u.k. Hauses des Aussern).
Records, ca. 1874-1918. 2 microfilm reels.

Records of this Austrian archives include a booklet on churches and church schools of the Helvetic Confession in Bohemia; information on the Polish people (1874-1877), including a copy of *Dziennik Warsawski*; and files pertaining to the Uniate Church in Galicia (1885-1891, 1914-1915, 1918) and Vatican-ustro-Hungarian relations. Also included is an index to Austrian files pertaining to the Hungarian Prime Ministry's American Action; the files themselves are not included. *Mainly in German; some items in French, Italian, and Polish.*

Austria. State Archives (Staatsarchiv) (Vienna).
Records, 1848-1918. 32 microfilm reels.

Records consist of consular dispatches, telegrams, police reports, and correspondence pertaining to emigrants from the Austro-Hungarian Empire.

Included are communications and annual immigration reports from the Austro-Hungarian consulates in Canada, Germany, Latin American, the South Slav lands, the United States, and European cities. Reports and correspondence contain information on a wide variety of topics, including (but not limited to) immigrants' political activity, radical political groups, espionage, immigration legislation, natural disasters and relief efforts, return migration, and Austrian immigrant groups. Annual migration reports (1906-1909) are broken down by regions and states. The reports detail immigrants' living conditions, wages, working conditions, shipping reports, and size and flow of immigrant groups from Austria-Hungary. Reports from the years 1904 to 1916 include the above as well as Magyar consular reports, descriptions of climate and geography of various regions, and investigations of steamship companies. Reports concentrate on Austro-Hungarian immigrants in the Southern States. *In German. Partial inventory available (in German and English).*

Banater Benefit Society (Cleveland, Ohio).
Records, 1911-1959. 2.5 linear ft.

A mutual aid organization originally known as the Erster Deutsch-Ungarischer Unterstützungs Verein (EDUUV), the Society was established in Cleveland, OH, in 1911. Membership consisted primarily of Roman Catholic German immigrants from Banat, in what is now Yugoslavia and Romania. The Banaters were descendants of Swabians who had settled in the Banat area in the 16th and 17th centuries and began coming to the United States in the late 1800s.

Records include minutes, membership, and financial records of the Society and related groups, including the Banater Athletic Club (1922-1930), the Banater Civic League, the Banater Damen-chor, the Banater Männer-chor, the Banater Frauen Verein, the Banater Hall Gesellschaft, and the Banater Sewing Circle. Also included are records of the Central Ohio Sänger Verein; the Cleveland Soccer League; the Deutsch-

Canadian Verband (German-Canadian
Home Society, Regina, Saskatchewan);
the Deutscher Stadtverband (German-
American Civic League); the Greater (or
German) Beneficial Union, Districts 70
and 258; materials pertaining to other
German American organizations; and
papers of Matthias Bohr. *In German (old
and Roman script), and English.
Inventory available.*

**Bureau for Intercultural Education
(New York, New York).**
Records, ca. 1940-1960. Ca. 1.5
linear ft.

The Bureau was founded ca. 1940
after reorganization of its predecessors,
the Service Bureau for Education in
Human Relations and the Service Bureau
for Intercultural Education. Rachel
DuBois had founded the former to help
teachers and school administrators in the
New York area set up intercultural
programs. In 1937, the Service Bureau
became the "Commission on Intercultural
Education" of the Progressive Education
Association; in 1938 it was renamed the
Service Bureau for Intercultural
Education. DuBois resigned in 1940, and
the organization then became the Bureau
for Intercultural Education. Its first
director was Stewart Cole, who was
succeeded by H. H. Giles. The group
established field centers in cities such as
Detroit, MI, led workshops for educators,
and conducted scientific research. It
ceased to operate in 1954.

Records include correspondence,
articles, interviews, minutes, publications,
and reports. Also included are tapes and
transcriptions of tapes of Stewart Cole.
*In English. Inventory available. Related
collections: Stewart Cole; Rachel Davis
DuBois.*

**Chicago Foreign Language Press
Survey (Chicago, Illinois).**
Records, ca. 1861-1938. 67 microfilm
reels.

Organized in 1936, the Survey
translated and classified selected news
articles that appeared in the foreign
language press of Chicago during the past
century. The project was under the

auspices of the Works Projects
Administration and the Chicago Public
Library.

Organized by topic--including
education, mores, social and economic
organization, politics, and war--files of
translated articles include materials for the
following ethnic groups in Chicago:
Albanian, Bohemian, Chinese, Croatian,
Danish, Dutch, Filipino, German, Greek,
Hungarian, Italian, Jewish, Lithuanian,
Norwegian, Polish, Russian, Serbian,
Slovak, Slovene, Spanish, Swedish, and
Ukrainian. *In English. Inventory
available. Negatives held by Chicago
Public Library.*

**Citizens Committee on Displaced
Persons (New York, New York).**
Records, 1946-1953. 5 linear in.

The Committee was formed in 1946,
initiated by the American Council of
Voluntary Agencies and the National
Committee on Immigration Policy. Its
objective was to seek temporary
legislation suspending immigration quotas
and allowing displaced persons to enter
the United States. The CCDP aroused
public concern through local committee
groups, publications, films, etc., and also
lobbied directly for passage of the desired
bills. Though unsuccessful in obtaining
passage of the Stratton Bill (HR2910) and
Wiley Bill (S2242), the CCDP played
some role in passage of the Displaced
Persons Act of 1948, and in its
amendment in 1950. The Committee
disbanded after the adoption of this
amendment.

Records include correspondence,
financial records, and minutes. Most
correspondence is of Nathan W. Levin,
who was involved in financial supervision
of the Committee. *In English. Inventory
available.*

Cole, Marie Chase.
Papers, ca. 1936-1949. 1 linear in.

Cole was Executive Secretary of the
YWCA of New York City. Papers
comprise reports, bulletins, and brochures
of the YWCA and the International
Institute of New York. Materials pertain
particularly to work with displaced

persons. Also included are an international cookbook, and the 1936 Christmas issue of the *Woman's Press*. *In English.*

Cole, Stewart G. (1892-).
Papers, ca. 1937-1979. Ca. 1 linear ft.

An educator and author, Cole was educated at McMaster University (Toronto, Canada), and the University of Chicago. He taught at various schools and colleges and published extensively.

Papers highlight Cole's career and his leadership in various organizations. Included are correspondence, reports, book reviews, manuscripts, publications, photographs, and honorary plaques. Materials pertain to his involvement in Anytown, U.S.A., the Service Bureau for Intercultural Education, the National Conference of Christians and Jews, religion, and education. *In English. Inventory available. Related collections: Bureau for Intercultural Education; Rachel Davis DuBois.*

Cotton, Thomas L. (1891-1964).
Papers, ca. 1925-1937. 6 linear in. and 1 oversize portfolio.

A public relations specialist and community leader with an interest in adult education, Cotton was born in Cumberland, IA. He began work with the YMCA while attending Dartmouth College, later worked with the Boston Naval YMCA, and in 1917 went to Russia to organize YMCA activities among the armies of the eastern front. Upon his return to the United States, he worked for the New York YMCA (Foreign Born Division), the International Community Center, the American-Russian Chamber of Commerce, the Foreign Language Information Service, the Folk Festival Council, the Temporary Emergency Relief Administration, and the Works Projects Administration. In 1948, he founded Thomas L. Cotton Associates, a public relations firm, and later served on the New York State Citizens Council.

Cotton's papers include biographical information, personal correspondence, organizational reports, writings, and materials pertaining to educational

organizations, adult education, Lithuanian Americans, Polish Americans, and miscellaneous published material. Correspondents include Eleanor Roosevelt and Anna Roosevelt Dall. Other materials pertain to Cotton's YMCA work, the International Community Center, the Foreign Language Information Service, the Folk Festival Council, the Croatian Fraternal Union, Dania, and ethnic events in the Chicago and New York areas. *In English. Inventory available.*

DuBois, Rachel Davis (1892-).
Papers, ca. 1932-1957. 15.5 linear ft.

DuBois was born in Clarkesboro, NJ, the daughter of Quaker farmers. She attended Bucknell University, and taught in the schools of Glassboro, NJ, until 1920. From 1920 to 1924, she was active in the peace movement. Subsequently, improvement of racial and ethnic group relations and development of greater appreciation for American society's diverse cultural strains became her life's work. She helped develop the assembly program technique, which combined assembly programs on contributions of various ethnic or racial groups to American life with classroom follow-up. After moving to New York City in 1929, DuBois initiated and participated in a series of intercultural curriculum experiments in schools in Washington, DC; Philadelphia, PA; and Englewood, NJ. She received her doctorate in educational sociology from NYU. In 1934, she founded the Service Bureau for Education in Human Relations, later identified as the Service Bureau for Intercultural Education.

In 1941, DuBois founded the Intercultural Education Workshop, which in 1946 was incorporated as the Workshop for Cultural Democracy. It remained in existence until about 1958. In 1951, the State Department sent DuBois to West Germany to aid in post-war reconstruction. When she returned, the Workshop focused its efforts on programs to train "leaders of leaders" on a nationwide basis. After its dissolution, she was invited by the Southern Christian Leadership Conference to lead a program to lessen race tensions in the South. Her lifetime activities as teacher, author, lecturer, and organizational leader earned her many commendations and distinctions. Papers include both personal papers and organizational records documenting much of DuBois's life and career, and are comprised of correspondence, minutes, reports, publications, and curricular materials. *In English. Inventory available. Related collections: Bureau for Intercultural Education; Stewart G. Cole.*

Flynn, Elizabeth Gurley (1890-1964).
Papers, 1917-1923. 1 microfilm reel.

A labor activist, Flynn was born in Concord, NH, daughter of Irish immigrant revolutionaries. In 1906 she joined the Industrial Workers of the World (IWW) and was active in textile strikes in Lawrence, MA (1912), and Paterson, NJ (1913), as well as in the Minnesota Mesabi Range iron miners strike and the Passaic, NJ, strike (both 1916). She was organizer for the Workers Defense Union between 1917 and 1923. She was a founding member of the American Civil Liberties Union in 1920. In 1937 she joined the Communist Party; she was jailed from 1955 to 1957 for advocating the violent overthrow of the U.S. government. She died in Moscow.
Correspondence and miscellaneous papers pertain to Flynn's efforts to secure justice for labor leaders, anarchists, IWW members, and others deprived of their civil rights during the "Great Red Scare." *Originals held by Wisconsin State Historical Society.*

Graff, George.
Papers, ca. 1931-1947. Ca. 5 linear in. and 1 tape cassette.

Graff, an educational administrator, was associated with the Service Bureau for Intercultural Education. Papers comprise correspondence, minutes, newspaper clippings, reports, newsletters, and miscellany pertaining to the Service Bureau and to intercultural education. The tape contains an interview with Graff. Correspondents include Rachel Davis DuBois, Margaret Mead, E. C. Lindemann, Mordecai Soltes, and Stewart

G. Cole. Newspaper clippings pertain to Blacks and to treatment of Jews in the 1930s. Also included are papers by DuBois, the *Interracial Newsletter*, issues of *Intercultural Education News*, and materials on the radio program "Americans All--Immigrants All" and the American Institute of Intercultural Arts. *In English. Inventory available. Related collection: Rachel Davis DuBois.*

Hansen, Conrad.
Papers, 1920-1976. Ca. 1 linear in. and 1 cassette tape.

Papers of Hansen comprise a photocopied memoir by him of his work as Americanization secretary for the YMCA in St. Paul, MN, and a cassette tape of an interview of Hansen conducted by Rudolph Vecoli. *In English.*

Hughes, Langston.
Papers, 1932-1953. 1 linear in.

Papers of Hughes consist of correspondence to him from M. Margaret Anderson, editor of *Common Ground*, magazine of the Common Council for American Unity. Included are three letters from Louis Adamic. *In English. Restricted: available for reference use only; permission for reproduction and publication must be obtained from Yale University Library. Available as photocopies only. Originals held by Yale University Library, New Haven, CT.*

Hungarian Ministry of Religion and Public Instruction (Budapest).
Records, 1901-1906. 1 microfilm reel.

Records of the Ministry (Orszagos Leveltar, Minisz Terelnoksegi Leveltar) pertain to Slovak nationalism, pan-Slavism, and Czech-Slovak activities in Europe and the United States. Also included are Hungarian county and church officials' reports, a few Slovak publications, and a few village school statistics from Szepes County. *Mainly in Hungarian.*

International Center of Baltimore (Maryland).
Records, 1922-1976. 1 microfilm reel.

The Center originated in 1888 with establishment of the Baltimore YWCA's "Helping Hand Society." In 1911, the YWCA appointed a "Foreign Communities Secretary," and an International Institute Building was opened in 1919. In 1929, the Institute became independent of the YWCA; it did not prosper, however, and an effort was made to revive the YWCA's nationality group program. In 1935, the East Baltimore Center was renamed the International Center of the YWCA, and in 1970, the Center moved to the central YWCA building in Baltimore.

Records include minutes, annual reports, monthly reports on agency activities and services rendered (1936-1943, 1957-1968), financial reports, directors' correspondence (1928-1970), and related records. Also included is a history of the YWCA and the Baltimore International Center. *Mainly in English. Inventory available. Related collection: American Council for Nationalities Service.*

International Institute of Biddeford-Saco (Maine).
Records, 1916-1941. 1 microfilm reel.

The Institute was established by the York County, ME, YWCA in 1919. It was closed in 1936 due to lack of funds and the illness of its director.

Records include annual association meetings of the York County YWCA, records of the Institute (1924-1935), bylaws, and reports of the Institute (ca. 1933-1934). *In English. Inventory available. Originals held by York County YWCA, Saco, ME. Related collection: American Council for Nationalities Service.*

International Institute of Boston (Massachusetts).
Records, 1924-ca. 1955. 25 linear ft.

The Institute had its inception in 1923, and opened in 1924. Described as a "service bureau for foreign-speaking people," it sought to provide information, education, and personal service to clients. The Institute published a monthly newsletter, the *Beacon*, beginning in 1933, and sponsored several annual social events. In addition, community and nationalities studies were done. The Institute severed its ties with the YWCA in 1935 and became autonomous. It subsequently became a member of the Boston Council of Social Agencies, the Greater Boston Community Fund, and the National Institute for Immigrant Welfare (the umbrella organization for independent international institutes--later the American Federation of International Institutes). In 1959, it merged with the American Council for Nationalities Service. During the late 1940s, the Institute struggled to maintain its services and provided aid to war victims and recreational facilities to enlisted men. Throughout the 1950s, it continued to work with both immigrant and international communities in Boston.

Records of the Institute substantially document its first thirty years and consist of case files, administrative records, files on activities, resources, memorabilia, and information on related organizations. *Mainly in English. Inventory available. Case files closed. Related collection: American Council for Nationalities Service.*

International Institute of Buffalo (New York).
Records, 1917-1936. 1 microfilm reel.

The Institute was established under the auspices of the Buffalo YWCA in 1918. It separated from the YWCA in 1934 and is still in existence.

Records include Board minutes, correspondence, evaluation studies, narrative and miscellaneous reports, lists, notes, and brochures. *In English. Inventory available. Originals held by Buffalo YWCA. Related collection: American Council for Nationalities Service.*

International Institute of Jersey City (New Jersey).
Records, 1926-1938. 1 microfilm reel.

Records of the Institute consist of minutes, correspondence, and reports pertaining to its separation from the YWCA. *Mainly in English. Related collection: American Council for Nationalities Service.*

International Institute of Lewiston (Maine).
Records, 1917-1944. 1 microfilm reel.

The Institute had its beginnings in 1917, when the Lewiston-Auburn YWCA appointed an immigration secretary. In 1919, the Institute was formally established. For several years, it retained semi-autonomous status but by 1941 had been reorganized as a Foreign Community Department. The Department was discontinued in 1946.

Records consist of minutes of the Institute Committee (1937-1941), annual reports (1918-1944), monthly narrative reports (1917-1943), miscellany, and National Board Statistical Reports (1928-1930). *In English. Inventory available. Related collection: American Council for Nationalities Service.*

International Institute of McKeesport (Pennsylvania).
Records, 1922-1940. 1 microfilm reel.

The Institute was organized by the McKeesport YWCA in 1918. It occupied rental quarters until 1926, when it was moved into the main YWCA building. In 1940, the Institute separated from the YWCA and merged with the American Service Institute of Allegheny County.

Records include annual reports, annual statistical reports to the national board (1927-1939), scrapbooks of newspaper clippings pertaining to Institute publicity and activities (1923-1940), background on the foreign born (ca. 1936-1937), photographs (1921-1923), and miscellany. *Mainly in English. Inventory available. Originals held by McKeesport YWCA. Related collection: American Council for Nationalities Service.*

International Institute of Minnesota.
Records, ca. 1920-1971. 42 linear ft. and 1 microfilm reel.

The Institute had its beginnings in 1919, under the auspices of the YWCA. During the 1920's, it offered English and citizenship classes, casework services, and activities for St. Paul ethnic communities. The first executive director, Alice J. Sickels, came in 1931. Under her direction, the Institute expanded and also began sponsoring the Festival of Nations. In 1938, the Institute broke from the YWCA, the result of expanding programs in casework and folk art, inclusion of men in programs, and increased service to non-Protestants. During the years prior to World War II, casework emphasized naturalization and resolution of immigrant legal problems. During and after World War II, services centered on resettlement of displaced persons. The Institute has continued, in various ways, to help the foreign born adjust to American life while retaining their cultural heritage.

Records of the Institute include music, travel literature, case files, correspondence, photographs, minutes of the membership council and board of directors (on microfilm), administrative records, educational program information, department records, documentation of group services and activities, material on special programs, publications, publicity, and miscellany. *Mainly in English. Inventory available. Case files closed. Related collection: American Council for Nationalities Service.*

International Institute of New Bedford (Massachusetts).
Records, 1919-1939. 1 microfilm reel.

The Institute was organized by the New Bedford YWCA in 1918. It was retained as a separate branch until 1931, when it was moved to the main building of the Association and reorganized as the "International Department." It was discontinued in 1942.

Records consist of bylaws, monthly and annual narrative statistical reports, minutes of the International Institute Committee, and miscellaneous financial materials. *In English. Inventory available. Originals held by YWCA of New Bedford. Related collection: American Council for Nationalities Service.*

International Institute of New Castle (Pennsylvania).
Records, 1929-1960. 1 microfilm reel.

The Institute was established in 1923. Until 1933, it was housed in rental quarters in an area of heavy immigrant concentration; a financial crisis then forced it to move into the central YWCA building. The Institute continued to operate until ca. 1950, when it was merged with the Adult Program Department. Until the late 1950s, a few of the Institute's clubs, such as the Italian Mothers Club and the Polish Mothers Club, remained in existence.

Records consist of minutes and attendance lists of the International Institute Committee and records of the Italian Mothers Club. *In English. Inventory available. Originals held by New Castle YWCA. Related collection: American Council for Nationalities Service.*

International Institute of New Haven (Connecticut).
Records, 1928-1933. 1 microfilm reel.

The Institute was established in 1919 under the auspices of the YWCA. It separated from the YWCA in 1932, and in September of that year closed because of financial problems.

Records consist of minutes and reports of the Institute's Committee, correspondence and monthly reports, and miscellany including a "Study of Services for the Foreign-Born" done by the New Haven Council of Social Agencies. *In English. Inventory available. Originals held by YWCA of New Haven. Related collection: American Council for Nationalities Service.*

International Institute of Niagara Falls (New York).
Records, 1918-1925. 1 microfilm reel.

The Institute was established in 1919 under the auspices of the YWCA. It separated from the YWCA in 1933 and became known as the International Center and Girls Club. Its work was discontinued in 1970.

Records of the Institute consist of correspondence, monthly reports, and newspaper clippings. *In English. Inventory available. Originals held by YWCA of Niagara Falls. Related collection: American Council for Nationalities Service.*

International Institute of St. Louis (Missouri).
Records, 1919-1960. 17 linear ft.

The Institute was established in 1919 under the direction of Letitia Fyffe; it was under the auspices of the YWCA from 1920 until 1923, when it became an agency of the St. Louis Community Fund. The Institute provided casework, education, and recreation services. During the Depression, cooperative efforts between the Institute and ethnic communities were manifested by Christmas folk festivals, international arts and crafts exhibits, and the International Folk Festival of 1934. From 1935 to 1937, a branch was active in the Italian American section of Fairmont Hill. During World War II and the years following, efforts were concentrated on resettlement of refugees and war brides. Between 1950 and 1960, recreational group activities figure prominently in records of the Institute. In 1955, the Institute became affiliated with the American Council for Nationalities Service.

Records of the Institute include historical overviews, bylaws, constitutions, articles of incorporation, and administrative minutes; monthly and annual reports and records of annual meetings; statistical reports on services; membership materials; financial records; programs and projects; materials pertaining to specific ethnic groups; English and citizenship classes; community agencies and resources; publicity materials; photographs; and case records. *Mainly in English. Inventory available. Case records closed. Related collection: American Council for Nationalities Service.*

Kenyon, Mildred Adams.
Papers, 1936-1976. 1 linear in.

An author and translator, Kenyon began her career writing for *Woman's Journal* in New York. She soon became a feature writer for the *New York Times* and contributed to many other magazines. She often was on assignment in Europe and witnessed historic events such as Russia's admittance to the League of Nations and the making of the Spanish constitution in 1931. She also reported on the Spanish Civil War and became involved with relief efforts and work with refugee immigrants. She continued her work during World War II, aiding refugees from the Nazi regime. Kenyon specialized in interviewing such notables as Huey Long, Henry A. Wallace, and Calvin Coolidge.

Papers pertain mostly to her work with Spanish Civil War refugees and relief organizations. Included are correspondence to and from various persons and committees concerning relief work (1939-1942), organizational and special reports (1940-1942), publications, press releases, personal notes, and a diary. *In English. Inventory available.*

Lutheran Church Archives (Budapest, Hungary).
Records, ca. 1880-1889. 1 microfilm reel.

Records of the Church consist of minutes of the Lutheran Superintendent of Sáros-Zemptén's official visits in 1883 to churches and their filial congregations: Hanusfalva (Hanu-Šovce), Mernyik (Merník), Kladzćhyny (Kladzany), Ujklenóc (Novy Klenovec), Pazdics (Poszišovce), Rank (Rankovce), Ofalva (Opina), Zsegnye (Žegňa), Budamér (Budzimir), Akos (Obyšovce), Kassa (Košice). Minutes contain budget and leadership data; vital statistics are excluded. *In Hungarian. Originals held by the Lutheran Church Archives (Budapest, Hungary).*

Lutheran World Federation Service to Refugees (Geneva, Switzerland).
Records, 1947-1949. 1 microfilm reel.

The Federation was originated by Howard Hong, a Norwegian Lutheran and director of refugee work for the Lutheran World Convention and the World Council of Churches. He also was associated with the YWCA in its work with World War II prisoners of war.

Records of the Service include a report edited by Hong, with contributions by leaders of Lutheran churches in exile and by Service staff. The report includes information on the origins of the Service; various Lutheran churches and groups including Estonians, Hungarians, Latvians, Lithuanians, Poles, and Ukrainians; educational, institutional, and youth work; and refugees in Germany after World War II. Also included are correspondence from pastors, financial records, publicity materials, and photographs. *In English. Inventory available. Originals held by Howard Hong, St. Olaf College (Northfield, MN).*

Malkovsky, Kyra (1894-   ).
Papers, ca. 1939-1949. Ca. 4 linear in.

A social case worker with Russian immigrants, Malkovsky was born in Minsk and came to the United States in 1917. After five years as an employee of the Russian embassy in New York, she began a long career as a social worker with the International Institute of New York City. She was also co-founder in 1925 of the Children's Welfare Society and worked for the Tolstoy Foundation in Austria, Italy, and the United States.

Papers comprise journals; case work and statistical reports; photographs and other materials of the International Institute of New York City; and miscellaneous correspondence, publications, and materials pertaining to the YWCA Summer School at Fletcher Farm (Proctorville, VT). *In English. Inventory available.*

Minneapolis Public Schools.
   Multi-Ethnic Role-Playing Activities
   Project.
Records, 1979-1980. 5 linear in.

Records of the Project include
role-playing activities developed for
secondary school students by the school
system's Ethnic Cultural Center.
Activities include "Immigration Quotas,"
"Hard Times," "Mining of the
Reservation," "Malloy Island," "Molly
McGuires," and "HydroFarm Plan." Also
included is correspondence to the
Advisory Committee and two drafts of a
final report. *In English.*

Minnesota Project on Ethnic America.
Records, 1975-1979. 2 linear in.

Records of the Project consist of
bylaws, incorporation papers,
correspondence and memoranda, and
minutes of the board of directors. *In
English.*

Mitchell, Ruth Crawford.
Papers, 1916-1978. 2 microfilm reels and
   1 tape cassette.

Mitchell was assistant and field
secretary to Edith Terry Bremer, national
secretary of the YWCA National Board,
Immigration and Foreign Community
Work.
   Papers consist of a diary (1916-1917)
and a taped interview (1978) discussing
her association with the YWCA and the
Institute movement. The diary details her
training in New York under Bremer's
direction. *In English.*

New York City P.S. 20 Alumni
   Association.
Records, ca. 1958-1972. 1 linear in.

Public School 20 served the Jewish
Lower East Side of New York City. Its
graduates include Edward G. Robinson,
Paul Muni, Sen. Jacob Javits, and George
and Ira Gershwin. It is the only
elementary school in New York with an
alumni association.
   Records include newspaper clippings,
photographs, lists of alumni, routine
correspondence, invitations, programs, and
other records as well as miscellaneous
publications. *In English.*

Rempel, Dietrich D. (b. ca. 1886).
Papers, 1985. 2 linear in.

A physician, Rempel was born in
Ukraine in the Mennonite village of
Gnadenfeld, near the Azov Sea. He was
educated at the University of Dorpat, in
Estonia, and earned his MD in 1913. He
served as a medical officer in 1914 in the
Russian Army and later in the White
Army, until he and his wife fled in 1920
following the Revolution. Rempel's
siblings were deported to Siberia and
remained in concentration camps there.
The Rempels eventually came to the
United States in 1922 and settled in
Minneapolis, MN. Dr. Rempel practiced
in the Mennonite community of
Brownton, MN.
   Papers consist of an unpublished typed
manuscript of memoirs entitled "Holy
Cross to the Hammer and Sickle." The
memoirs relate events during the Russian
Revolution of 1917. *In English.*

Restore Ellis Island Committee.
Records, 1974-1980. Ca. 1 linear in.

The records consist of photocopies of
correspondence, speeches, and press
releases of Peter Sammartino related to
his service as chairman of the Committee.
In English.

Roche, Josephine Aspinwall (1886-1976).
Papers, 1913-1923. 2 microfilm reels.

Director of the Foreign Language
Information Service (later the American
Council for Nationalities Service), Roche
was educated at Vassar College and
Columbia University, where she
developed an interest in social work.
Before coming to the FLIS, she was chief
probation officer and director of girls'
work in the Denver, CO, Juvenile Court,
inspector of amusements and
policewomen in Denver, and special
investigator for the National Consumers'
League. During World War I, she did
relief work in Belgium. From 1934 to
1937, she served as assistant secretary of

the U.S. Treasury, from 1934 to 1940 as a representative on the President's Cabinet Committee on Economic Security, and also as chair of an interdepartmental committee for health and welfare services of the federal government.

Roche's papers include personal letters and reminiscences of immigrants, such as one from a Lithuanian steel worker; materials pertaining to the immigrants and to the problems they faced, with excerpts from the immigrant press; and information on various aspects of immigrant life, including health, organizations, work, legal problems, and women's lives. Also included are budget statements, copies of the *Immigrant* and the *Bulletin*, correspondence of Roche and George Creel, and pamphlets on the FLIS. Among groups represented are Czech, Hungarian, Slovak, Ukrainian, and Yugoslav Americans. *Mainly in English. Related collection: American Council for Nationalities Service.*

Trieste State Archives (Italy).
Records, 1863-1922. 6 microfilm reels.

Records consist of consular reports, correspondence, emigration statistics, statistics on return migration, shipping information, passenger regulations, information on epidemics and diseases, letters to officials of the Austro-Hungarian Empire, and information pertaining to the Canadian Pacific Rail Road and to the Hamburg America Line. *Mainly in German and Italian; some French and English.*

United States. Immigration and Naturalization Service.
Records, 1919-1932. 8 microfilm reels.

Records of the INS, files 71-42 and No. 54809-general, largely consist of correspondence of the Service regarding deportation proceedings against radicals, anarchists, and communists during the Palmer Raids of 1919-1920, and particularly to the cases of Carlo Tresca, Vincenzo Vacirca, and Pietro Allegra.

Included are correspondence of J. Edgar Hoover; Anthony Caminetti of the Immigration Commission of the Department of Labor, and the Italian

Ambassador to the Department of State; directives to INS local offices; lists of aliens under investigation; transcripts of hearings; membership lists from the Union of Russian Workers; and excerpts from the Russian press, the *Worker, Daily Worker, Moscow News,* and the *International Sea-Transport Worker.* Also included are publications and correspondence of the American Civil Liberties Union and newspaper clippings on cases (especially from the *Tampa Tribune* [FL]). Materials mainly concern Italian-, Russian-, and Spanish-speaking aliens. *Mainly in English; some Russian and Spanish. Originals held by National Archives and Records Service, Washington, DC.*

United States Committee on Public Information, Division of Work with the Foreign Born.
Records, 1916-1919. 1 microfilm reel.

During World War I, the United States Committee on Public Information, Division of Work with the Foreign Born, published and disseminated materials intended to inform persons of foreign origin residing in the United States of their rights and obligations. Records include correspondence, newspaper clippings from American and foreign newspapers, and miscellaneous publications. *In multiple languages. Preliminary inventory available. Microfilm negatives held by National Archives and Records Service, Washington, D.C.*

Watson, Annie Clo (1891-1960).
Papers, 1934-1960. 3 linear in.

A social worker, Watson began her career at the Flint, MI, YWCA in the early 1920s; during that time she was also associated with the New York School of Social Work. In 1928, she began a long association with the American Federation of International Institutes when she became executive director of the International Institute of San Antonio, TX. She later worked with the International Institute of San Francisco, CA.

Watson was active in developing the Fellowship Church for All People and in founding the Council for Civic Unity. She also served on the board of the American Civil Liberties Union; was active with the International House of Berkeley, CA; and assisted ethnic groups including Chinese Americans, Japanese Americans, and Mexican Americans. She was a president of the National Association of Social Workers (Golden Gate Chapter), and winner of the prestigious Koshland Award for Social Work.

Papers consist of biographical information, correspondence, personal publications, and other publications. Included are newspaper clippings and photographs pertaining to her career, articles and speeches, publications dealing with customs and costumes of other cultures, and information regarding establishment of the Annie Clo Watson Scholarship for Social Workers. Correspondence largely pertains to efforts to relocate war refugees following World War II. *In English. Inventory available.*

Wilson, Elizabeth.
Papers, 1956-1978. Ca. 1 linear in.

Wilson was Executive Director of the International Institute (Gary, IN) from 1945 to 1965. Papers include correspondence, newspaper clippings, and memoirs pertaining to her career in the immigrant service movement. *In English.*

Young Men's Christian Association.
  International Committee (New York, New York).
Records, ca. 1903-1936. 5 microfilm reels.

In 1907, the YMCA established a comprehensive immigration program to assist immigrants at embarkation and debarkation points, in transit, and after arrival in the United States. This service program included bureaus of information, employment, legal aid, medical aid, banking advice, courses in English, citizenship and naturalization procedures, and related services. A YMCA agent was appointed for Ellis Island.

Selected records of the YMCA consist of documents pertaining to immigrants and immigration as well as U.S. immigration policy and law. Included are minutes, reports, and correspondence of the Industrial Department; materials pertaining to the General Committee of Immigration Aid at Ellis Island; records of the YMCA of Greater New York containing information on the National Liberal Immigration League, the Immigrant Education Society, and the International Committee of the YMCA; and miscellaneous publications and autobiographical materials. *Mainly in English. Inventory available.*

Young Women's Christian Association of Greater Lansing (Michigan). Nationality Communities Department.
Records, 1916-1941. 1 microfilm reel.

The Department was established in 1924 and was the first such department organized by the YWCA. Records include annual reports (1926-1949), a scrapbook of programs, club announcements, newsletters (1926-1931), records of the Thistle Club (ca. 1928-1951), membership lists, and photographs. Also included are programs of the Caledonian Club, the Foreign Students Night School, the German Dramatic Club, the Mothers Club, the Syrian Sisterhood, and the Young Phoenician Society. *In multiple languages. Inventory available. Originals held by YWCA of Greater Lansing.*

Monographs

Over 850 volumes comprise the IHRC's General collection. These include both primary publications and secondary studies of a thematic or multi-ethnic nature. The collection is especially useful for researchers interested in immigration history broadly or in specific topics or issues. It should be noted also, however, that many of these publications contain useful material for the study of particular immigrant groups, including those for which the IHRC maintains separate collections.

Secondary studies include most of the major books written by recent scholars of immigration and ethnic history. Among these authors are John Bodnar, Joshua Fishman, Victor Greene, Oscar Handlin, John Higham, Maxine Seller, and Phillip Taylor. Also included are key works by earlier scholars such as Theodore Blegen, John R. Commons, Emily Greene Balch, Marcus Lee Hansen, Robert Park, Joseph Roucek, and George Stephenson.

Along with general analyses of immigration, the collection contains numerous book-length treatments of more specific themes as they pertain to the immigrant experience. Among these are education, literature, the arts, refugee migration, assimilation, women, children, and politics. Particularly well represented are religion, labor and labor activism, language, the ethnic press, and immigration law and its impact. The collection is also strong in its coverage of published research on immigrant life in particular states and cities.

Primary publications cover the same wide range of subjects dealt with in secondary studies. These include books and pamphlets produced for or about immigrants by various secular and religious organizations and individuals. A major example is the large number of citizenship manuals and guidebooks distributed by the federal government as well as private publishers. Organizations whose literature on immigrants and immigration can be sampled through the collection include the American Committee for the Protection of the Foreign Born, the American Council for Nationalities Service (and its predecessor agencies, the Foreign Language Information Service and the Common Council for American Unity), the Young Men's Christian Association and Young Women's Christian Association, the American Immigration and Citizenship Conference, the Industrial Workers of the World, the International Ladies Garment Workers Union, and the International Refugee Organization. Included also are the writings of several noted participant-observers of and commentators on American immigration and ethnicity. Among them are Jacob Riis, Rachel Davis DuBois, Peter Roberts, Kenneth D. Miller, Daniel P. Moynahan, Nathan Glazer, and Michael Novak.

Publications of the U.S. government form a substantial component of the collection. Many of these are documents of the Immigration and Naturalization Service providing information on immigration law or registration rules. Also contained are late-1800s documents of the U.S. Treasury Department as well as reports from numerous congressional committees including the Committee on Immigration and Naturalization, the Committee of the Judiciary, and the Committee on Un-American Activities. In addition, the IHRC holds on microfilm the entire set of reports produced by the U.S. Immigration Commission (Dillingham Commission), 1907-1910.

An important compilation of primary publications preserved on microfilm and pertaining to several ethnic groups is "The Immigrant in America" collection produced by Research Publications, Inc. This collection, filmed from the holdings of several libraries, including the IHRC, contains over 4,000 imprints (most of them scarce) from thirty-seven European immigrant groups from ca. 1820 to 1929. Among the groups covered in this extensive microfilm series are Albanians, Bulgarians, Carpatho-Rusins, Croatians, Czechs, Finns, Greeks, Hungarians, Italians, Jews, Latvians, Lithuanians, Poles, Romanians, Russians, Serbians, Slovaks, Slovenians, and Ukrainians. There is also a segment on "general immigration."

Newspapers

Chicago Record, Chicago, IL. Weekly: 1977. English, Spanish, and Ukrainian.

The Dawn, Miami, FL. Monthly: 1979-date. English.

Ethnic America, Pittsburgh, PA. Frequency varies: 1973-1974. English.

Ethnic American News, Pittsburgh, PA. Monthly: 1976-1977. English.

Heritage Review, New Jersey. Bi-monthly: 1971-1972. English.

Justice, Jersey City, NJ. Semi-monthly (frequency varies): 1919, 1924-1958. English.

Michigan Slav, Detroit, MI. Monthly: 1942-1943. English.

Miners' Bulletin, Hancock, MI. Weekly: 1913-1914. English.

Minnesota Labor (previously titled **Timber Worker; Midwest Labor**), Minneapolis, MN (previously published in Duluth, MN). Weekly: 1937, 1939-1941, 1943-1944, 1946-1947. English.

The Minnesota Leader, St. Paul, MN. Irregular: 1938-1942. (Includes an issue of **Minnesota Union Advocate**, 1941). English.

National Co-operative News, Chicago, IL. Weekly: 1919-1920. English.

Northwest Ethnic News, Seattle, WA. Monthly: 1984-1986. English.

The Orthodox Church, Syosset, NY. Monthly: 1970, 1974, 1976-1986. English.

Our Sunday Visitor, Marquette, MI. Weekly (?): 1953. English.

Pick & Axe, Bessemer, MI. Weekly: 1976-1977. English.

Richardson Family Researcher and Historical News, Broken Bow, NE. Quarterly: 1980. English.

Saxon News Volksblatt, Cleveland, OH. Weekly. (Microfilm: 1954-1980).

The Wanderer, St. Paul, MN. Weekly: 1962. English.

Serials

AAASS Newsletter (American Association for the Advancement of Slavic Studies), Columbus, OH. Frequency varies: 1975-1978. English.

ACEN News (Assembly of Captive European Nations), New York, NY. Frequency varies: 1955-1956, 1960, 1962, 1965-1971. English.

ACNS Newsletter (American Council for Nationalities Service), New York, NY. Quarterly: 1982. English.

Acontecer Migratorio (Migration Occurring; Centro de Estudios de Pastoral y Asistencia Migratoria), Caracas, Venezuela. Quarterly: 1978-1981. Spanish.

Alliance of Friendship, Chicago, IL. Frequency varies (bi-annual?): 1970, 1979. English.

American Association for Southeast European Studies Newsletter, Columbus, OH. Frequency varies: 1975-1977, 1979. English.

American Council for Nationalities Service Reports (previously titled **The World of ACNS**), New York, NY. Frequency varies: 1971-1973. English.

American Council for Nationalities Service Interpreter Releases, New York, NY. Frequency varies: 1940, 1971-1982. (Holdings also contain miscellaneous releases). English.

American Immigration and Citizenship Conference Legislative Bulletins, New York, NY. Frequency varies: 1969-1978. English.

American Immigration and Citizenship Conference News, New York, NY. Frequency varies: 1968-1982. English.

American Institute for Marxist Studies Newsletter, New York, NY. Bi-monthly: 1975-1985. English.

The American Leader, New York, NY. Monthly: 1916. English.

American Review of Eastern Orthodoxy, New York, NY. Monthly: 1955-1967, 1970. English.

The American Slav, Pittsburgh, PA. Monthly: 1939-1947, 1957, 1961, 1967. English.

Americans for Congressional Action to Free the Baltic States News Bulletin, Los Angeles, CA. Frequency varies: 1963-1966, 1970. English.

AREO Quarterly (Eastern Orthodox Catholic Church in America; merged with **American Review of Eastern Orthodoxy** in 1957), New York, NY. Quarterly: 1956. English.

Association for the Advancement of Baltic Studies Newsletter, Mahwah, NJ (previously published in Brooklyn, NY). Semi-annual: 1976-1977, 1979-1985. English.

Association of Immigration and Nationality Lawyers Immigration Journal, New York, NY. Bi-monthly: 1980. English.

Association of Immigration and Nationality Lawyers Newsletter, New York, NY. Bi-monthly: 1978-1979. English.

Association of Immigration and Nationality Lawyers Reports, Memorandums & Bulletins, New York, NY. Frequency varies: 1963-1964, 1975-1979. English.

Balkan Arts Traditions, New York, NY. Annual: 1977. English.

Baltic Bulletin, Los Angeles, CA. Bi-monthly: 1982-1984. English.

Baltic Events (previously titled **Estonian Events**), West Hill, Ontario, Canada, and Irvine, CA. Bi-monthly: 1970-1975. English.

Baltic Forum, Gothenburg-Stockholm, Sweden. Quarterly: 1984. English.

The Baltic Review, New York, NY (previously published in Stockholm, Sweden). Frequency varies: 1945-1949, 1953-1971. English.

Baltic University Contributions of Baltic University, Hamburg, Germany. 1946. German, Lithuanian and English.

Baltimore's Ethnic Identity, Baltimore, MD. Bi-monthly: 1976-1979. English.

BATUN (Baltic Appeal to the United Nations; United Baltic Appeal Information Service News Release), Bronx, NY. Frequency varies: 1967-1982. English.

The Beacon (previously titled **The International Beacon**), Boston, MA. Monthly: 1959-1961, 1967, 1973-1974. (Microfilm: 1973-1974). English.

Benedictine Bulletin, Cleveland, OH. Frequency varies: 1971. English.

Building Blocks (National Center for Urban Ethnic Affairs), Washington, DC. Quarterly: 1973-1976, 1981-1983, 1985. English.

Canada Manpower and Immigration Publications, Ottawa, Ontario, Canada. Annual: 1974-1976. English and French.

Canadian Association of Slavists Newsletter, Toronto, Ontario, Canada. Monthly (?): 1962. English.

Canadian Ethnic Studies; Études Ethniques au Canada, Calgary, Alberta, Canada. Bi-annual: 1969-date. English.

Canadian Ethnic Studies Association (Société Canadienne d'Études Ethniques) Bulletin, Toronto, Ontario, Canada. Frequency varies: 1974-date. English and French.

CEESSA News (Central and East European Studies Society of Alberta), Edmonton, Alberta, Canada. Bi-monthly (?): 1977. English.

Center for Migration Studies Newsletter, Staten Island, NY. Monthly: 1973-1980, 1983. English.

Central Europe Journal, Bonn, West Germany. Monthly: 1966, 1968-1971. English.

The Central European Federalist, Jackson Heights, NY. Semi-annual: 1953-1958, 1962-1971. English.

Central European Newsletter, New York, NY. Bi-monthly: 1957. English.

The Challenge, Detroit, MI. Bi-weekly: 1980, 1986. English.

Citizen, Ottawa, Ontario, Canada. Published five times per year: 1963. English and French.

Cokato Historical Society Newsletter, Cokato, MN. Quarterly: 1984-date. English.

Colorado State University Information Bulletin; Germans from Russia in Colorado Study Project, Fort Collins, CO. Annual (?): 1977-1979. English.

Common Ground, New York, NY. Quarterly: 1940-1949. English.

Concern (Orthodox Christian Education Commission), New York, NY. Quarterly: 1969. English.

Cross-Cultural Southwest Ethnic Study Center Bulletin, El Paso, TX. Frequency varies: 1973, 1975-1976. English.

Cultural Columns, Harrisburg, PA. Bi-monthly: 1982-1984. English.

Cultures Canada, Toronto, Ontario, Canada. Monthly: 1980. English and French.

East and West; Facts from behind the Iron Curtain, London, England. 1947-1948. English.

East Europe (previously titled **News from behind the Iron Curtain**), New York, NY. Monthly: 1956-1957, 1960, 1962.

The Emigrant Institute Information, East Moline, IL. 1960, 1977-1978. English.

Emigration Digest (previous title of **International Migration Digest** and **International Migration Review**), Staten Island, NY. Annual: 1955-1957. English.

EMPAC Newsletter (Ethnic Millions Political Action Committee), Bayville, NY. Bi-monthly: 1975-1976. English.

Ethnic Affairs, New York, NY. Frequency varies: 1973-1974. English.

Ethnic American News, Pittsburgh, PA. Quarterly: 1977. English.

The Ethnic and Minority Scene in Wisconsin, Stevens Point, WI. Monthly: 1972. English.

Ethnic and Racial Studies, Henley-on-Thames, England. Quarterly: 1978-date. English.

Ethnic Arts Quarterly, St. Paul, MN. Quarterly: 1983. English.

Ethnic Forum, Kent, OH. Frequency varies: 1981-date. English.

Ethnic Heritage Studies Project Newsletter, Providence, RI. Frequency varies: 1972, 1974. English.

Ethnic Newsletter, Washington, DC. Bi-monthly: 1974-1977. English.

Ethnic Philadelphia, Philadelphia, PA. Frequency varies: 1970-1972. English.

Ethnicity: An Interdisciplinary Journal of the Study of Ethnic Relations, New York, NY. Quarterly: 1974-1981. English.

Ethos, Buffalo, NY. Monthly: 1974-1976. English.

Expressions (The Urban Tradition Newsletter), Chicago, IL. Quarterly: 1985-date. English.

Face to Face (Anti-Defamation League of B'nai B'rith), New York, NY. Quarterly: 1975-1979, 1981-date. English.

The Folio, Philadelphia, PA. Quarterly: 1959, 1961. English.

Folk-News, New York, NY. Bi-weekly: 1932-1939. English.

Forum (National Clearinghouse for Bilingual Education), Rosslyn, VA. Bi-monthly: 1984. English.

Fraternal Monitor, Indianapolis, IN. Monthly: 1970-date. English.

Fraternity, New York, NY. Monthly: 1929-1930. English.

Freedom's Facts against Communism (All American Conference to Combat Communism), Washington, DC. Frequency varies: 1952-1959, 1961, 1967. English.

Friends of the Immigration History Research Center Newsletter (previously titled News from the Friends of IHRC), St. Paul, MN. Frequency varies: 1979, 1981-date. English.

Friendship Universal, Washington, DC. Quarterly: 1964-1965. English.

GOP Nationalities News, Washington, DC., Frequency varies: 1972-1974, 1976. English.

GOP Nationalities Reporter, Minneapolis, MN. Monthly: 1967, 1969. English.

Heritage, Chicago, IL. Quarterly: 1980-date. English.

Heritage Language Bulletin, Toronto, Ontario, Canada. Quarterly: 1987. French and English.

Heritage News, Milwaukee, WI. Monthly: 1980-1981. English.

IHRC News, St. Paul, MN. Frequency varies: 1980, 1986-date. English.

Immigrant's Protective League Annual Report, Chicago, IL. Annual: 1917, 1930. English.

Immigration History Newsletter, Philadelphia, PA (previously published in St. Paul, MN. Semi-annual: 1968-date. English.

Immigration Research Digest, Philadelphia, PA (previously published in New York, NY). Semi-annual: 1960-1969. English.

In Review Bulletin (American Committee for Protection of Foreign Born), New York, NY. Frequency varies: 1935-1937.

In Their Own Words, Venice, Italy. Bi-annual: 1986. English.

Jerome B. Ingber and Associates Newsletter, Minneapolis, MN. Quarterly: 1980-1981. English.

Intercommunity Arts Newsletter, Washington, DC. Monthly: 1976-1978. English.

Intergovernmental Committee for Migration Monthly Dispatch, Geneva, Switzerland. Monthly: 1981-1983, 1985-date. English.

International Institute of Milwaukee Newsletter, Milwaukee, WI. Ten issues per year: 1978-1981. English.

International Institute of Minnesota Festival of Nations, St. Paul, MN. Annual: 1934, 1936, 1939, 1942, 1947, 1949, 1952, 1955, 1958, 1961, 1964, 1967, 1976. English.

International Institute of Minnesota Newsletter (title varies: **Nationality News** until 1970), St. Paul, MN. Monthly: 1953, 1957, 1958, 1960-1967, 1969-1979. English.

International Migration (preceded by **Migration**), Geneva, Switzerland. Quarterly: 1963-1965, 1968-1969, 1972, 1975, 1978, 1982-1987. English, Spanish and French.

The International Migration Digest (previously titled **Emigration Digest**, succeeded in 1966 by **International Migration Review**), Staten Island, NY. Semi-annual: 1964-1966. English.

International Migration Review (preceded by **International Migration Digest**), Staten Island, NY. Quarterly: 1964-date. Cumulative index 1964-1976. English.

International Peasant Union Bulletin, Washington, DC.- New York, NY. Monthly: 1951, 1971. English.

International Rescue Committee Annual Report, New York, NY. Annual: 1961-1962, 1964-1969, 1971-1975. English.

The Interpreter (Foreign Language Information Service; titled **The Bulletin** for 1922), New York, NY. Monthly: 1922-1930. English.

Invandrar Rapport (Migration Report), Borås, Sweden. 1977. Swedish and various languages.

Jacob's Well (Orthodox Church in America), Binghamton, NY. Quarterly: 1986. English.

Journal of American Ethnic History, New Brunswick, NJ. Semi-annual: 1981-date. English.

Journal of Baltic Studies (previously titled **Bulletin of Baltic Studies**), Brooklyn, NY. Quarterly: 1970-1981. English.

The Journal of Ethnic Studies, Bellingham, WA. Quarterly: 1973-date. English.

Journal of Intercultural Studies, Concord, MA. Tri-annual: 1980. English.

Journal of Mennonite Studies, Winnipeg, Manitoba, Canada. Annual: 1983. English.

Journal of the Polish-Hungarian World Federation, Chicago, IL. Semi-annual: 1970. English.

Kaleidoscope Canada (title varies: **Focus on Immigration, Manpower and Immigration Information Service; Ethnic Kaleidoscope Canada**), Ottawa, Ontario, Canada. Quarterly: 1973-1983. French and English.

Łącznik Polsko-Ukraïns'kyï Zv'iazkovyï (Polish-Ukrainian Ties), New York/Munich, West Germany. Frequency varies: 1984. Polish and Ukrainian.

The Lamp (American Committee for Protection of Foreign Born), New York, NY. Monthly: 1944. English.

Light of Orthodoxy (United Movement of Orthodox Youth), New York, NY. Bi-monthly: 1953-1954. English.

The Manitoba Multicultural Resources Centre Bulletin, Winnipeg, Manitoba, Canada. Bi-annual: 1986-date. English.

Migration (succeeded by International Migration), Geneva, Switzerland. Quarterly: 1961-1962. English.

Migration Review (previously titled Immigration Review), Washington, DC. Quarterly: 1967-1971. English.

Migration Today (newspaper format before 1976), Staten Island, NY. Bi-monthly: 1973-1976. English.

Minnesota Genealogist, St. Paul, MN. Quarterly: 1983-1984. English.

Mosaic (Institute for Intercultural Relations and Ethnic Studies), New Brunswick, NJ. Quarterly (monthly): 1975-1977, 1979-1980. English.

Mosaic Church Growth, Atlanta, GA. Quarterly: 1977-1979. English.

Multiculturism (Ministry of Culture & Recreation of Ontario), Toronto, Ontario, Canada. Quarterly: 1977. English.

Multi-Ethnic Heritage Studies Center Newsletter, Vineland, NJ. Monthly: 1981.

Multi Ethnic Horizon (Ann Arbor Public Schools), Ann Arbor, MI. Weekly: 1975. English.

Multi News (Department of the Secretary of State), Ottawa, Ontario, Canada. Bi-monthly: 1976-1977. French and English.

National Association of Interdisciplinary Ethnic Studies, La Crosse, WI. Semi-annual: 1976-1977. English.

National Confederation of American Ethnic Groups News (NCAEG), Washington, DC. Every six weeks: 1958-1961. English.

National Coordinating Assembly on Ethnic Studies Newsletter, Washington, DC. Frequency varies: 1972-1973. English.

National Ethnic Studies Assembly Newsletter, Detroit, MI. Semi-annual: 1974-1975, 1977. English.

National Ethnic Studies Assembly Newsletter, Washington, DC. Monthly: 1973. English.

National Fraternal Congress of America Annual Meeting, Chicago, IL. Annual: 1974, 1976-1977. English.

National Museum of Man; Canadian Centre for Folk Culture Studies Newsletter. Ottawa, Ontario, Canada. Annual: 1968-1972. English.

Nationalities Papers, Charleston, IL. Quarterly: 1973-1974, 1977-date. English.

Nationalities Service Center Annual Report, Philadelphia, PA. Annual: 1977-1978. English.

Nationalities Services Center News Bulletin, Cleveland, OH. Monthly: 1959, 1961, 1963. English.

A New America (newsletter of Ethnic Millions Political Action Committee), Bayville, NY. Bi-monthly: 1975-1977. English.

New Dimensions (The Balch Institute for Ethnic Studies), Philadelphia, PA. Bi-annual: 1982-date. English.

The New Jersey Heritage (The New Jersey Tercentenary Commission), Trenton, NJ. 1963. English.

New Jersey Mosaic, Jersey City, NJ. Quarterly: 1979, 1987. English.

The New Review, Toronto, Ontario, Canada. Quarterly: 1961-1971. English.

Newcomer, Los Angeles, CA. Quarterly: 1965. English.

Newsbox, Omaha, NE. Quarterly: 1974-1975. English.

Newsletter from behind the Iron Curtain, Stockholm, Sweden. Quarterly (?) (weekly): 1947-1949, 1971-1972. English.

Northern Mosaic, Thunder Bay, Ontario, Canada. Bi-monthly: 1975, 1986-1987. English.

The Novak Report on the New Ethnicity, Washington, DC. 1979-1981. English.

Ohio Slavic and East European Newsletter, Columbus, OH. Bi-monthly: 1973. English.

The One Big Union Monthly (Industrial Workers of the World), Chicago, IL. Monthly: 1937-1938. English.

Oral History of the American Left Newsletter, New York, NY. Annual: 1978-1979. English.

Original Works, Victoria, British Columbia, Canada. Quarterly: 1969-1971. Various languages.

Orthodox Theological Society in America Bulletin, Annapolis, MD. Monthly: 1975-1979. English.

Our Life, Württemberg, Germany. Monthly: 1948. German.

Pennsylvania Ethnic Studies Newsletter, Pittsburgh, PA. Quarterly (bi-monthly): 1975-1978, 1984-date. English.

The Persecuted Church, Springville, CA. Quarterly: 1975-date. English.

Polyphony, Toronto, Ontario, Canada. Bi-annual: 1977-date. English.

Problems of Communism, Washington, DC. Monthly: 1953. English.

Quo Vadimus, New York, NY. Bi-monthly: 1980-1981. English.

Ragusan Research Bulletin, San Carlos, CA. Quarterly: 1983-date. English.

Range History, Gilbert, MN. Quarterly: 1976-1981. English.

Range History News (Iron Range Historical Society), Gilbert, MN. Quarterly: 1978, 1981. English.

Refugee Abstracts (International Refugee Integration Resource Center), Geneva, Switzerland. Quarterly: 1982, 1984. English.

Refugees (Public Information Section of the United Nations High Commissioner for Refugees), Geneva, Switzerland. Monthly: 1985-date. English.

Saskatchewan Multicultural Magazine, Regina, Saskatchewan, Canada. Monthly: 1985-1986. English.

Scoop, Minneapolis, MN. Bi-monthly: 1976. English.

The Slavonic Monthly, New York, NY. Frequency varies: 1941-1946. English.

Sophia, Newton Centre, MA. Bi-monthly: 1986. English.

Southeast Minnesota Historical Center News, Winona, MN. Quarterly: 1977. English.

Spectrum (Immigration History Research Center), St. Paul, MN. Frequency varies: 1975-date. English.

Statistics of Fraternal Benefit Societies, Chicago, IL. Annual: 1966-1982. English.

Synaxis, Chilliwhack, British Columbia, Canada. Monthly: 1975-1976. English.

Texas People, San Antonio, TX. Monthly: 1976-1977. English.

The Tlingit Herald, Chilliwhack, British Columbia, Canada. Monthly: 1975, 1977. English.

United Cooperative Farmers Supplement for the Twenty-fifth Anniversary (supplement to The Cooperative Farmer), Fitchburg, MA. Special issue: 1955. English.

U.S. Bureau of Immigration Annual Report, Washington, DC. Annual: 1892, 1896-1905, 1907-1909, 1912-1918, 1920-1931. English.

U.S. Catholic Historical Society News and Notes, Yonkers, NY. Quarterly: 1976-1978. English.

U.S. Commissioner of Naturalization Annual Report, Washington, DC. Annual: 1923, 1924, 1926-1932. English.

U.S. Committee for Refugees Issue Papers, Washington, DC. Monthly: 1984-date. English.

U.S. Department of Justice Immigration and Naturalization Services Annual Report, Washington, DC. Annual: 1952-1953, 1955-1967, 1972-1974. English.

U.S. Treasury Department Quarterly Report of the Chief of the Bureau of Statistics relative to Imports, Exports, Immigration and Navigation of the United States. Quarterly: 1890-1893. English.

Upper Midwest Folklife Newsletter, Madison, WI. Four times per year: 1978. English.

The Vigil (Diocese of the Midwest Orthodox Church in America), Hinsdale, IL. Bi-monthly: 1982, 1984-1986. English.

The Village Interpreter, Moorehead, MN. Quarterly: 1982-date. English.

Viltis: A Folklore Magazine, Denver, CO (previously published in Chicago, IL; Norwalk, CT; and San Diego, CA). Bi-monthly: 1945-1961, 1968-date. English.

Voice of the American Slav, New York, NY (previously published in Pittsburgh, PA). Frequency varies: 1942, 1944. English.

Wayne State University Ethnic Studies Newsletter, Detroit, MI. Annual: 1986-1987. English.

Wayne State University Folklore Archive Annual Report, Detroit, MI. Annual: 1969-1970. English.

World Refugee Survey (American Council for Nationalities Service, U.S. Committee for Refugees), New York, NY. Annual: 1981, 1984-1985. English.

WZAK The Ethnic Voice of Cleveland (WZAK Radio), Cleveland, OH. Bi-weekly (weekly): 1972-1975. English.

Young Life (Orthodox Christian Education Commission of the Standing Conference of Orthodox Bishops in the Americas), Nyack, NY. Monthly: 1966. English.

Your Diocese Alive (The Diocese of Philadelphia and Eastern Pennsylvania), South Canaan, PA. Bi-monthly: 1984. English.

Západ (The West), Toronto, Ontario, Canada. Bi-monthly: 1982. Czech and Slovak.

Albanian American Collection

Monographs

Albanian American monograph holdings consist of approximately thirty-five volumes. Two subject areas--Albanian Orthodoxy and politics--constitute the strengths of the collection. Useful materials also exist in the areas of Albanian American literature, history, migration, and the ethnic press.

Of the three religions traditional to the Albanian American community--Eastern Orthodoxy, Islam, and Roman Catholicism--the IHRC collections highlight the first. Sources on the Albanian Orthodox Church in America, founded in New York in 1908, include works by Fan S. Noli, a composer and politician as well as the Church's first ordained priest (later its Metropolitan), and the *Fiftieth Anniversary Book of the Albanian Orthodox Church in America, 1908-1958* (1960). Primary sources are also available pertaining to the Albanian Orthodox Diocese of America, founded after World War II. Writings of Bishop Mark Lipa include *Informative and Progress Report of Our Diocese*, an essay pamphlet with a lay council's report (1961), and *Divine Liturgy of St. John Chrysostom* (1964); there is also an album marking the consecration of a church in Chicago (*Consecration of the Saint Nicholas Albanian Orthodox Church, Oct. 10, 1971*, 1971).

The continuing interest of Albanian Americans in the mother country is apparent in IHRC holdings reflecting political activity. The organization most fully represented is the Pan-Albanian Federation of America, founded in Boston in 1912 to promote Albanian nationalism. Available publications of "Vatra" (The Hearth), as the organization is popularly known, include Fehime Pipa's *Elementary Albanian: Filltar i shqipes* (1900) and albums commemorating its forty-fifth and fiftieth anniversaries. Other political works in the IHRC holdings include *The Background of the Italian-Greek Conflict* (1940), a pamphlet by the activist Faik Konitza presenting an Albanian view. Postwar opposition both to the platform of Vatra and to that of Shqipëria e Lirë (Free Albania Organization) is expressed in Glenn A. McLain's *Albanian Exposé: Communism Versus Liberation for Albania* (1952), published by the Albanian American Literary Society (Quincy, MA).

The IHRC holds a small selection of literature in Albanian. World literature translated by Fan Noli, among others, is present, as well as poetry of Ramiz Harxhi (*Ndjenjat e zemres: vjersha*, 1917) and Arshi Pipa (*Libri i burgut* [The Book of Prison], 1959). The collection also includes fiction, *Dasmë në shtëpi të vançit* (n.d.), and one-act plays, *Kthimi në krujë* (1964) and *Skënderbeu* (Scanderbeg, 1972), all by Vasil D. Alarupi.

General history on Albanian Americans can be found in Constantine A. Demo's full-length study of the early migration, *The Albanians in America: The First Arrivals* (1960). On the background of Albanian migration, works on Albanian history by Fan Noli (*Historia e skénderbeut: Kryezolit té arbérise [1405-1468]*, 1950) and Faik Konitza (1957) are available. Finally, the ethnic Albanian press is represented by the sixtieth anniversary album (1969) of the Boston weekly newspaper *Dielli* (The Sun), since 1912 the official organ of Vatra.

Newspapers

The Albanian American, Boston, MA. Monthly: 1954-1958.

Dielli (The Sun), Boston, MA. Monthly (weekly): 1965-date. Includes English.

Drita E Vertete (True Light), Boston, MA. Monthly: 1965, 1969-1982.

Liria (Liberty), Boston, MA. Weekly: 1964-1986. Includes English.

Skënderbeu (Scanderbeg), Boston, MA. Monthly: 1951. Includes English.

Serials

Adriatic Review, Boston, MA. Monthly: 1918-1920. Includes English.

Vreshta (The Vineyard), Boston, MA. Quarterly: 1970. English.

Yll'i Mëngjezit (The Morning Star), Boston, MA. Semi-monthly: 1917-1918. Includes some English and French.

Armenian American Collection

Monographs

The Armenian American monograph collection is not extensive (ca. 140 volumes), but it furnishes a useful cross section of that group's culture and history. Particular strengths lie in the areas of literature and poetry, autobiographical accounts, religious publications, and writings on Armenia and its history. Also included are general historical studies of Armenian Americans, works dealing with Armenians in particular regions of the United States, and publications of and about secular Armenian American organizations.

Little in the way of scholarly monograph-length research exists for this immigrant group. The IHRC holds the important study authored by Robert Mirak, *Torn Between Two Lands: Armenians in America, 1890 to World War I* (1983), an adaptation of his PhD dissertation written in 1965. Also included are earlier works by M. Vartan Malcolm (*The Armenians in America*, 1919) and James Tashijian (*The Armenians of the United States and Canada; A Brief Study*, 1970). In addition, the collection includes the recent overview *Armenians in America: Celebrating the First Century*, published by the Armenian Assembly of America (1987). These general histories are supplemented by a small number of regional studies, chiefly dealing with Armenians in Massachusetts and California, areas heavily settled by this ethnic group. Among these are *The Armenians in Massachusetts*, by the Federal Writers' Project, Massachusetts (1937); Charles Mahakian's *History of the Armenians in California* (1974); and Aram Serkis Yeretzian's *A History of Armenian Immigration to America with Special Reference to Conditions in Los Angeles* (1974; reprint of 1923 thesis). A helpful source of general information on Armenian American institutions and activities is the *Armenian American Almanac*, edited by Hamo Yassilian (1985) and found in the IHRC's reference section.

Armenian American literature and poetry are represented in the works of several authors. The IHRC holds a good sampling of the writings of William Saroyan, including *My Name Is Aram* (1940), *Not Dying* (1963), and *Human Comedy* (1943). Others included are A. A. Bedikian, Mihran Azhderian, David Kherdian, and playwrights Haig Baronian and Gabriel Soundoukian. In addition, the collection contains anthologies of Armenian poetry and short stories, including *Armenian-American Poets: A Bilingual Anthology*, compiled and translated by Garig Basmadjian (1976) and *Arveste II: An Anthology of Short Stories* (1962).

Several works relating to the history and culture of Armenia furnish useful information on the forces of migration within the homeland and on the value system brought to America by Armenian immigrants.   Among these are Hagop Andonian's *Modern Armenian* (1966); Vahan M. Kurkjian's *A History of Armenia* (1959); and *Tales from the Armenian: Antranig Antreassian, Vahe Haig, Sooren Manuelian, Peniamin Noorigian*, translated by Jack Antreassian (1955).   Also included are commentaries on Armenian-Turkish adversarial relations, such as *Turkey, Author of Genocide: The Centenary Record of Turkey, 1822-1922* by James Tashjian (1965) and *Martyrdom and Rebirth: Fateful Events in the Recent History of the Armenian People*, published by the Armenian Church in America (1965).

Publications on religion relate almost exclusively to the Armenian Apostolic Church, the dominant church for this immigrant group.   Many of these deal with the history and practices of the church generally, though some are focused on its development in the United States.   Some key examples of this material include Rev. Oshagan Minassian's *A Brief History of the Armenian Church* (1961); the Armenian National Apostolic Church of America's *Crisis in the Armenian Church: Text of a Memorandum to the National Council of the Churches of Christ in the United States of America* (1958); Archbishop Khoren Narbey's *A Catechism of Christian Instruction, According to the Doctrine of the Armenian Church* (1955); and *Commemorative Album; Issued on the Occasion of the Holy Consecration of the Armenian Apostolic Church of Greater Boston, October 19-20, 1957*.

The goals and activities of the Armenian General Benevolent Union, the major fraternal organization for Armenian Americans, are substantially reflected in its published bylaws and reports as well as in historical studies.   Among these are Bedros Norehad's *The Armenian General Benevolent Union; Its History and Purpose* (1966?); *Campaign Report of the Emergency Relief Fund of the Armenian General Benevolent Union and a List of Contributors* (1943-1944); and *Treasured Armenian Recipes* (1973 edition, copyright 1949).   Other organizations represented to a lesser degree include the Armenian National Union of America, the National Association for Armenian Studies and Research, and the Armenian Students' Association of America.

The collection includes several autobiographies of Armenian immigrants; most of these were published during the past three decades.   Examples of these are George M. Mardikian's *Song of America* (1956); Avedis Nakashian's *A Man Who Found a Country* (1940); James K. Sutherland's *The Adventures of an Armenian Boy* (1964); Ralph G. Darian's *My Safaris via Inferno: Life and Thoughts of an Armenian-American Lawyer* (1959); and Peter Najarian's *Voyages* (1971).   The monograph collection as a whole contains mainly English language materials, though for earlier years there are several works written in Armenian, such as *K'ristap'or Mik'ayēlian* by A. Ayaronian (1926) and *P'arlament'akan kanonner ev zhoghovavarowt'iwn* (Parliamentary Regulations and Democracy) by Hakob G. Derdzakian (1912).

Newspapers

The Armenian Mirror-Spectator, Watertown, MA. Weekly: 1960-1961, 1963-date. English.

The Armenian Reporter, Flushing, NY. Weekly: 1967-1968, 1970-1980. English.

Armenian Weekly, Boston, MA. Weekly: 1970-1976, 1978-1981. English.

Asbarez (Arena), Glendale, CA. Daily: 1983-date. Includes English.

Asbarez (Arena; English edition), Glendale, CA. Daily: 1983-date. English.

Baikar (Struggle), Watertown, MA. Daily: 1956, 1961, 1963, 1965-1967, 1969-date.

Hairenik (Fatherland), Boston, MA. Daily: 1963-1965, 1969, 1971-1976.

Lraper (The Armenian Herald), Los Angeles, CA (previously published in New York, NY). Weekly (semi-weekly): 1965-date. Includes English.

Massis Weekly, Pasadena, CA. Weekly: 1983-1987.

Nor Ashkar (The New World), New York, NY. Weekly: 1964-1966, 1968-1969, 1971-1972. Includes English.

Nor Or (New Day), Los Angeles, CA. Semi-weekly: 1972.

Serials

AMAA News (Armenian Missionary Association of America), Paramus, NJ. Quarterly: 1983-1984. English.

Amerika-Hay Hanragitak Taregirk' (American Armenian Encyclopedic Almanac), Boston, MA. Annual: 1925-1926.

ANCA Washington Report (Armenian National Committee of America), Washington, DC. Monthly: 1985-date. English.

Ararat, New York, NY. Quarterly: 1960-date. English.

Armenian Affairs, New York, NY. Quarterly: 1949-1950. English.

Armenian Assembly Journal (previously titled **Armenian Assembly of America Newsletter**), Washington, DC. Quarterly: 1974-1982, 1984-date. English.

The Armenian Church (English version of **Hayastanyaitz Yegeghetzy**), New York, NY. Monthly (except July and August): 1970-1971, 1976. English.

Armenian Cultural Organization of Minnesota Newsletter, Minneapolis, MN. Monthly: 1980-date. English.

The Armenian Guardian, New York, NY. Monthly: 1958-1968. English.

The Armenian Horizon, Los Angeles, CA. Bi-annual: 1980-1983. English.

Armenian National Council of America Teghekatow, New York, NY. Monthly (?): 1949-1950.

The Armenian Review, Boston, MA. Quarterly: 1981-1982. English.

Giligia (Cilicia; periodical of the prelacy of the Armenian Apostolic Church of America), New York, NY. Quarterly: 1966. Includes English.

The Gotchnag, New York, NY. Monthly: 1965-1968.

Hairenik Monthly, Boston, MA. Monthly: 1936-1937, 1939-1941.

Hakhtanag (Victory; Holy Martyrs Ferrahian Armenian High School), Encino, CA. 1968. Includes English.

Hayastanyaitz Yegeghetzy (The Armenian Church), New York, NY. Quarterly (previously published monthly, except July and August): 1948, 1951, 1962-1970, 1974, 1976.

Hoosharar (The Prompter), New York, NY. Semi-monthly (except July and August): 1956, 1962-1971, 1974. Includes English.

Nor Serowndin: Patkerazard Tarets'oyts'e (New Generation: Illustrated Almanac), Boston, MA. Annual: 1916.

Nshooyl (Ray of Light; St. Paul's Armenian Apostolic Church), Syracuse, NY. Quarterly: 1974-1976. Includes English.

Title page of the Armenian-language *Amerika-Hay Hanragitak Taregirk'* (Armenian [American] Encyclopedic Almanac), Boston, MA, 1925.

Bulgarian and Macedonian American Collections

Monographs

For the purposes of this guide, publications relating to Bulgarian Americans and Macedonian Americans are described together below. This is not meant in any way to blur distinctions between Macedonians and Bulgarians. It is done simply in recognition of the fact that due to historical circumstances and migration patterns too involved to relate here, sources useful for the study of one group are often relevant for the other.

General works are a strong point of the small Bulgarian and Macedonian American monograph collection, totaling ca. thirty volumes. Other topics for which materials are present range from bibliographic compilations through volumes depicting the ethnic press, religion, and literary activity.

The collection includes Nikolay Altankov's *The Bulgarian-Americans* (1979), the first book-length study devoted entirely to the Bulgarians in the United States. Also available is a collection of newspaper articles entitled *Macedonians in North America: An Outline Published by the Coordinating Committee of the Youth Sections with the Macedonian Patriotic Organizations of the United States and Canada* (1960). The book *Bulgaria, A Bibliographic Guide* by Marin V. Pundeff (1965), found in the reference section, covers topics pertaining to the motherland. Other useful accounts of Bulgarian and Macedonian immigration history are contained in some of the works referred to in the final paragraph below and in the IHRC's general collection.

An assortment of socialist pamphlets gives primary evidence of labor activity among Bulgarian Americans. Suiuznata Sots. Knizharnitsa i Pechatnitsa (Federated Socialist Bookstore and Printery, Granite City, IL) issued pamphlets with tracts by E. V. Debs and others (1917-1918). Pamphlets published by Industrialnitie Rabotnitsi na Svieta (Industrial Workers of the World, Chicago) between 1920 and 1924 include *Shto e I.R.S.?* (What is the I.W.W.?).

On the subject of the ethnic press, the IHRC has an undated catalog of books issued by the press of the newspaper *Naroden Glas* (National Herald). Published in Granite City from 1907 to 1950, *Naroden Glas* at its height was the most influential Bulgarian American newspaper.

A primary source for the study of the Bulgarian Eastern Orthodox Mission (later a diocese) for the United States and Canada is the manual of bylaws of the St. Stefan

Bulgarian Orthodox Church (Indianapolis, IN), printed in 1929 at the press of the *Makedonska Tribuna* (Macedonian Tribune) in the same city.

Literary publications in the collection feature works by the two best-known Bulgarian American writers. By Peter Demetroff Yankoff there is a fictionalized autobiographical account, *Peter Menikoff: The Story of a Bulgarian Boy in the Great American Melting Pot* (1928). By Stoyan Christowe there are both factual and fictionalized autobiographies, *This Is My Country* (1938), *My American Pilgrimage* (1947), and *The Eagle and the Stork* (1976), as well as a fictional treatment of Ali Pasha of Jannina, *The Lion of Yanina* (1941).

Researchers interested in Macedonian and/or Bulgarian Americans are encouraged to consult also the small collection of books (ca. eighty volumes) shelved and classified as "Yugoslav." Included here are works dealing with more than one of the South Slavic groups. Predominant among these are secondary studies (many of them key publications) such as *Americans from Yugoslavia*, by Gerald G. Govorchin; *South Slavic Immigration in America*, by George Prpic (1978); *Yugoslav Migrations to America*, by Branko Colakovic (1973); *The Yugoslavs in America: 1880-1918*, by L. Blaisdell; and several studies by Adam Eterovich and others on South Slavic people in particular states or regions.

Newspapers

Makedonska Tribuna (Macedonian Tribune), Indianapolis, IN. Weekly: 1963-date. Includes English.

Yugoslav

Jugoslavenski Glasnik (Yugoslav Herald), Chicago, IL/Calumet, MI/New York, NY. Weekly: 1938-1945. Serbian and/or Croatian.

Jugoslovenski Obzor (Yugoslav Observer), Milwaukee, WI. Semi-monthly: 1933-1945. Slovenian.

Serials

American Bulgarian Review, Mount Vernon, NY. Frequency varies: 1957, 1960. Includes English.

Balkania, St. Louis, MO. Quarterly: 1967-1973. English.

Bulgarian Studies Association Newsletter, Gary, IN. Quarterly: 1980. English.

Bulgarian Studies Group Newsletter, Gary, IN. Quarterly: 1978-1979. English.

Yugoslav

Balkan and Eastern European American Genealogical and Historical Society, San Francisco, CA. Frequency varies: 1964-1966. English.

The Florida State University Center for Yugoslav-American Studies Proceedings and Reports (previously titled **The Florida State University Slavic Papers**), Tallahassee, FL. Annual: 1972-1977. English.

The Florida State University Joint Yugoslav-American Advisory Council Proceedings and Reports, Tallahassee, FL. Annual: 1978-1979. English.

Jugoslav Review, New York. Monthly. (Microfilm: 1923). Serbian and/or Croatian, Slovenian.

Jugoslaven (The Yugoslav), Västerås, Sweden. Quarterly: 1979. Croatian and English.

Jugoslavia Kalendar (Yugoslavia Calendar), Chicago, IL. Annual: 1939. Slovenian and English.

Kolo, New York, NY. Monthly: 1924. Slovenian.

Medunarodni Problemi (International Problems), Belgrade, Yugoslavia. Quarterly: 1982. Serbian and/or Croatian.

Naš Kalendar (Our Calendar), Toronto, Ontario, Canada. Annual: 1958. Slovenian.

Sokolski Vesnik (Sokol Herald), Milwaukee, WI. Quarterly: 1967-1975, 1980-1984. Serbian, Croatian, and Slovenian.

T & T (formerly **Today and Tomorrow**), Milford, NJ. Bi-monthly: 1945-1948, 1950. English.

The Tamburitzan, Pittsburgh, PA. Bi-monthly: 1959-1961, 1976. English.

That's Yugoslavia (supplement to **Hrvatska Domovina**), Hamburg, West Germany. Monthly: 1982. English.

United Committee of South-Slavic Americans Bulletin, New York, NY. Frequency varies: 1943-1946. English.

United Yugoslav Relief Fund of America News Bulletin (previously titled Yugoslav News Bulletin), New York, NY. Frequency varies: 1941-1945. English.

Yugoslav-American Academic Association of the Pacific Bulletin, Palo Alto, CA. Quarterly: 1977. English.

Yugoslav-American Society Newsletter, Minneapolis, MN. Bi-monthly: 1987-date. English.

Yugoslav Facts and Views, New York, NY. Monthly: 1975-1981. English.

Yugoslavia Ministarstvo Socijalne Politike Iseljenički Odsek Iseljenička Služba: Izveštaj Narodnoj Skupštini (Yugoslav Ministry of Social Policy Emigration Department Emigration Service: Report to National Assembly), Belgrade, Yugoslavia. Bi-annual: 1925-1927. Serbian and/or Croatian.

Byelorussian American Collection

Monographs

The Byelorussian American monograph collection is very small, numbering only a dozen titles. However, these publications are useful for studying the history of this ethnic group in America. There is no one major work documenting the Byelorussian experience in the United States. The two significant studies to date are the work by Vitaut Kipel, "Byelorussians in New Jersey," in *The New Jersey Ethnic Experience*, edited by Barbara Cunningham (1977), and the brief essay, "The Byelorussian Community of Cleveland," in *Ethnic Communities of Cleveland*, edited by Michael S. Papp (1973). Both are available in the IHRC's general section. Byelorussian settlement in Canada is documented in John Sadouski's *History of the Byelorussians in Canada* (1981).

The Byelorussian community included a small group of émigré writers, among whom were such poets as Mikhas Kavyl' and Uladzimir Hlybinny. Kavyl's works in the collection include his poems in *Pad zorami belymi; Vershy* (Beneath the White Stars; Poems, 1954) and sonnets in *Tsiazhkiia dumy; Saniety* (Heavy Thoughts; Sonnets, 1961). Hlybinny's *Na beragokh pad sontsam* (On the Shores beneath the Sun, 1964) consists of Byelorussian stories and also a bibliography of his writings abroad.

The formation of the Byelorussian Autocephalic Orthodox Church can be traced in I. Kasiak's general history of the Byelorussian Orthodox Church entitled *Z historyi pravaslaŭnaĭ tsarkvy Belaruskaha narodu* (From the History of the Orthodox Church of the Byelorussian Nation, 1956). In addition, there is V. Panucevič's *Bieraściejskaja Vunija* (Union of Brest, 1972), a lecture given on the 375th anniversary of the Brest Union.

Finally, the collection includes a general history by Nicholas P. Vakar entitled *Belorussia: The Making of a Nation* (1956).

Newspapers

Belarus (Byelorussia), New York, NY. Weekly: 1953, 1956-1957.

Belaruskae Slova (The Byelorussian Word), Germany. Monthly: 1954-1956.

Belaruskae Slova (The Byelorussian Word), South River, NJ. Monthly: 1956-1958.

Belaruskaia Tr'ibuna (Byelorussian Tribune), Garfield, NJ. Monthly: 1953.

Belaruski Emigrant (Byelorussian Emigrant), Toronto, Ontario, Canada. Monthly: 1953.

Belaruski Holos (Byelorussian Voice), Toronto, Ontario, Canada. Monthly: 1965-date.

Byelarus (Byelorussia), Jamaica, NY. Monthly: 1958, 1967, 1969, 1975-1977.

Serials

Baiavaia Üskalos' (Kernels of Struggle), Toronto, Ontario, Canada. Frequency varies: 1962, 1969-1974, 1976-1977, 1979.

Belarus u Amèrytsy (Byelorus in America), South River, NJ. Monthly: 1948.

Belaruskayia Dumka (Byelorussian Thought), Milltown, NJ. Bi-annual: 1969-1970. Includes English.

Belaruskayia Moladz' (Byelorussian Youth), Jamaica, NY. Quarterly: 1959-1963, 1972-1979.

Belaruski Èmigrant (Byelorussian Emigrant), Toronto, Ontario, Canada. Monthly: 1948-1949.

Belaruskim Shliakham (Byelorussian Pathway), Chicago, IL. 1955.

Holas Tsarkvy (Voice of the Church), New York, NY. Frequency varies: 1961, 1965, 1971-1974, 1976-1977.

Litva (Lithuania), Chicago, IL. Frequency varies: 1967, 1970, 1973.

Narodnym Shliakham (People's Pathway), Toronto, Ontario, Canada. 1954.

Siaŭbit (The Sower), Fort Edward, NY. Bi-monthly: 1964, 1968.

Uzdym (Bridle; Organ of Byelorussian Activity in Exile), Cleveland, OH. Monthly: 1964-1965.

Veda (Knowledge), Brooklyn, NY. Monthly: 1951-1954. Includes some English.

Vialitva (Great Lithuania), East Brunswick, NJ. Annual: 1975. Includes English.

Zapisy (Annals of the Byelorussian Institute of Arts and Sciences), New York, NY. Quarterly: 1952-1954.

Carpatho-Rusin American Collection

Manuscript Collections

Guzy, Anne.
Papers, n.d. Ca. 1 linear in.

Papers consist of an account of family life in Velkrop, Austria-Hungary (now in Czechoslovakia), in the late 1800s. Guzy discusses agriculture, the role of the churches, marriage customs, housing, folk medicine, foods, clothing, funerals, holidays, and child care. *In English.*

Holy Ghost Greek Catholic Church (Cleveland, Ohio).
Records, 1909-1967. 1 microfilm reel.

Church records consist of marriage registers. *In Latin and English.*

Monographs

The Carpatho-Rusin American monograph collection numbers some 120 titles. Its strengths lie in the areas of old world history, general history of the immigrant group, religion, and language and literature.

Among the more comprehensive works on the history of Carpatho-Rusins in the Old World and in the United States are Paul R. Magocsi's *Our People: Carpatho-Rusyns and Their Descendants in North America* (1984); Keith P. Dyrud's *The Rusin Question in Eastern Europe and in America, 1890-World War I* (unpublished thesis, 1976); Filipp I. Svistun's "Prikarpatskaia Rus' pod vladieniem Avstrii (1850-1896)" (Subcarpathian Ruthenia Under Austrian Reign) and Peter Kohanik's "Nachalo istorii Amerikanskoi Rusi" (Early History of Rusins in America), these two works reprinted in one volume (1970); Simeon Pysh's *A Short History of Carpatho-Russia* (1973); and Frantisek Nemec's *The Soviet Seizure of Subcarpathian Ruthenia* (1955). There are also numerous individual works that deal with specific aspects of Carpatho-Rusin history, such as Magocsi's "The Ruthenian Decision to Unite with Czechoslovakia," in *Slavic Review* (34:2) and "The Political Activity of Rusyn-American Immigrants in 1918," in *East European Quarterly* (10:3); Walter K. Hanuk's *The Subcarpathian-Ruthenian Question:*

1918-1945 (1962); and Michael Yuhasz's *Wilson's Principles in Czechoslovak Practice; The Situation of the Carpatho-Russian People Under the Czech Yoke* (1929).

Research interest in the Carpatho-Rusins as a distinct ethnic group has grown in recent years. An important manifestation of this is *Proceedings of the Conference on Carpatho-Ruthenian Immigration, 8 June 1974* edited by Richard Renoff and Stephen Reynolds (1975).

Religion plays a central part in the lives of Carpatho-Rusins, and the group's religious development in the homeland and in the United States is well represented in the collection. Relevant titles include a survey by Walter C. Warzeski, *Byzantine Rite Rusins in Carpatho-Ruthenia and America* (1971), Rev. A. Pekar's *Our Past and Present: Historical Outlines of the Byzantine Ruthenian Metropolitan Province* (1974), and John Slivka's two substantial works, *Historical Mirror: Sources of the Rusin and Hungarian Greek Rite Catholics in the United States of America 1884-1963* (1978), and *The History of the Greek Rite Catholics in Pannonia, Hungary, Czechoslovakia and Podkarpatska Rus' 863-1949* (1974). Among the more prolific of the learned priests who wrote on Carpatho-Rusin religious history was Rev. Basil Shereghy. His works include *The Greek-Catholic Church* (1948), *Vospitanije Podkarpato-Ruskoho svjascenstava; The Training of Carpatho-Ruthenian Clergy* (1951), and *What are Greek Catholics?* (1948). In addition to the above, there are many parish jubilee and anniversary booklets.

Early literary works by Carpatho-Rusins are to be found mainly in immigrant newspapers, almanacs, and periodicals. Most Carpatho-Rusin writers tended to be from the learned clergy. One of these was the Rev. Emilij A. Kubek (1859-1940), whose four-volume collection of short stories and poems, *Narodny povisti i stichi* (Folk Tales and Poems, 1922-1923) is available at the IHRC. A general overview of Carpatho-Rusin literature in America can be found in Paul R. Magocsi's *Subcarpathian Immigrant Literature* (1975). The subject of language is dealt with in Charles E. Bidwell's *The Language of Carpatho-Ruthenian Publications in America* (1971) and Magocsi's *The Language Question Among the Subcarpathian Rusyns* (1979) and *Let's Speak Rusyn* (1976).

Fraternal societies and brotherhoods have also played an important part in the lives of Carpatho-Rusin Americans. Among the oldest and largest of these is the Greek Catholic Union of Rusyn Brotherhoods, founded in Wilkes-Barre, PA, in 1892. Other fraternals include the United Societies of the Greek Catholic Religion of the United States of America and the Greek Catholic Russian Orthodox Brotherhood of America. The monograph collection contains constitutions, bylaws, and convention programs of those organizations.

Finally, the collection includes several significant reference works: *Carpatho-Ruthenica at Harvard: A Catalog of Holdings*, compiled by Paul R. Magocsi and Olga K. Mayo (1983, second printing); Magocsi's *An Historiographical Guide to Subcarpathian Rus* (1974); and Edward Kasinec's *The Carpatho-Ruthenian Immigration in the United States: A Note on Sources in Some U.S. Repositories* (1975). Also included is James M. Evans's *Guide to the Amerikansky Russky Viestnik* (American Russian Messenger, 1979), an index to the major weekly newspaper. This first volume covers the years 1894-1914 and is a good tool for locating literary writings and historical information.

Newspapers

American Russian Falcon (previously titled **Sokol Sojedinenija**), Homestead, PA. Weekly. (Microfilm: 1914-1919, 1921-1936).

Amerikánsky Russky Viestnik (American Russian Messenger; succeeded by **Greek Catholic Union Messenger**), Homestead, PA. Weekly: 1943. (Microfilm: 1894-1896, 1901-1904, 1906-1952). Includes English.

The **Byzantine Catholic World**, Pittsburgh, PA. Bi-monthly (weekly): 1957, 1959-1962, 1965-date. (Microfilm: 1956-1974). English.

The **Carpatho-Russian American**, Yonkers, NY. Monthly: 1968-1969. (Microfilm: 1968-1969). English.

Cerkovnaja Nauka (Church Advisor), Johnstown, PA. Weekly. (Microfilm: 1903, 1951-1952, 1954-1955, 1967, 1969, 1982-1984).

Cerkovnyj Vistnik (Church Messenger), McKees Rocks and Pittsburgh, PA; Pemberton, NJ. Weekly (semi-monthly): 1982-1984. (Microfilm: 1946-1975). Includes English.

Den (The Day), New York, NY. Daily (weekly). (Microfilm: 1923-1926).

Eastern Catholic Life, Passaic, NJ. Weekly: 1975-date. (Microfilm: 1965-1974). English.

The **Eastern Observer**, Homestead, PA. Bi-weekly. (Microfilm: 1942-1943). English.

Golos Naroda (Voice of the People), New York, NY. Weekly: 1919.

Golos Pravdy (The Voice of Truth), New York, NY. Semi-monthly (monthly). (Microfilm: 1938-1945). Includes English.

Greek Catholic Union Messenger (continuation of **Amerikansky Russky Viestnik**), Homestead, PA. Weekly: 1972, 1975-date. (Microfilm: 1953-1975). English.

Karpato-Russkoe Slovo (Carpatho-Russian Word), New York, NY. Bi-weekly: 1935. (Microfilm: 1935-1938).

Karpatska' Rus (Carpathian Rus'), Yonkers, NY. Weekly: 1939, 1952, 1955, 1960-1962, 1965-1971, 1974-1978.

Karpats'ka Zoria (Carpathian Star), New York, NY. Monthly: 1952. (Microfilm: 1951-1952).

Lemko-Karpatska Rus' (Lemko-Carpathian Rus'), Yonkers, NY. Weekly. (Microfilm: 1928-1969).

Prikarpatskaia Rus' (Carpathian Rus'; supersedes **Sien Otechestva**), New York, NY. Weekly (semi-weekly). (Microfilm: 1918-1920).

Prosvita (The Enlightenment), Pittsburgh and McKeesport, PA. Weekly: 1977-date. (Microfilm: 1917-1975). Includes English.

Rusin (The Ruthenian), Philadelphia and Pittsburgh, PA. Weekly. (Microfilm: 1910-1916).

Russian Messenger (previously titled **Russkij Vistnik**), Pittsburgh, PA. Frequency varies. (Microfilm: 1933-1943). Includes English.

Vistnik (Messenger), McKees Rocks, PA. Monthly: 1942-1943, 1946, 1956, 1961, 1963. Includes English.

Vistnik (Messenger), Pittsburgh, PA. Weekly. (Microfilm: 1941-1955).

Vostok (The East), Perth Amboy, NJ. Semi-monthly (monthly). (Microfilm: 1927, 1930-1933, 1935-1950).

Serials

The A.C.R.Y. Annual (The Youth of the American Carpatho-Russian Orthodox Greek Catholic Diocese), Pittsburgh, PA. Annual: 1954, 1966-1968, 1970-1972, 1974-1977, 1980. Includes English.

The A.C.R.Y. Guardian (Eastern Seaboard of the American Carpatho Russian Youth), New York, NY. Quarterly: 1957-1958. English.

American Carpatho-Russian Youth, Pittsburgh, PA. Annual. (Microfilm: 1949-1954, 1956, 1958-1962, 1964-1973). Includes English.

Amerikansko-Russkiĭ Kalendar' (American Russian Calendar), Philadelphia, PA. Annual: 1911, 1919, 1936-1938, 1940, 1941-1943, 1950, 1956. (Microfilm: 1911, 1923, 1925, 1928-1933, 1940, 1943, 1950). Includes English.

Amerikanskiĭ Russkiĭ Miesiatsoslov (American Russian Almanac; previously titled Amerikansky Russko-Slovensky Kalendar), Homestead, PA. Annual: 1912, 1916, 1920-1921.

The Apostle (Newsletter of the Western States Deanery of the Byzantine Catholic Eparchy of Parma, Ohio), Anaheim, CA. Monthly: 1977. English.

Bratstvo (Brotherhood), Cleveland, OH. Monthly: 1945. (Microfilm: 1940-1952). Russian and English.

The Carpathian, Pittsburgh, PA. Monthly: 1943. (Microfilm: 1941-1943). English.

Carpathian Observer, Rochester, NY. Quarterly: 1976. English.

Carpatho-Russian Echoes, Ft. Lauderdale, FL. Monthly: 1984-date. English.

The Carpatho-Russian Youth, Bridgeport, CT. Monthly. (Microfilm: 1938-1941). English.

Carpatho-Rusyn American, Fairview, NJ. Quarterly: 1978-date. English.

Cerkvi Pokrova Prečistoj D'ivy Marii Vykaz Prijemu i Vydaju (Church of the Protection of the Virgin Mary Income and Expense Reports), Chicago, IL. Annual: 1929-1930, 1932-1933.

Chranitel' (Guardian), Johnstown, PA. Monthly. (Microfilm: 1920-1921).

The Chrysostom, Granville, NY. Monthly. (Microfilm: 1935-1938). English.

Dushpastyr (Shepherd of Souls), New York, NY. Monthly. (Microfilm: 1909-1910).

GCU Messenger (Greek Catholic Union), Munhall, PA. Bi-weekly: 1984. English.

The Greek Catholic Sower, Joliet and Lisle, IL. Monthly. (Microfilm: 1949-1950). English.

Greek Catholic Union Yearbook, Homestead, PA. Annual: 1976-1978, 1980-1982. (Microfilm: 1912-1937, 1939-1943, 1945-1977). Includes English.

Holos Vostočnej Cerkvi (The Voice of the Eastern Church), Perth Amboy, NJ. Monthly. (Microfilm: 1941-1945). Includes English.

Jedinstvo (Unity), Gary, IN. Monthly. (Microfilm: 1942-1943). Includes some English.

Kalendar' Amerikanskaho Russkaho Sokola Sojedinenija (American Russian Sokol Union Almanac; previously titled Kalendar' Uhro-Russkaho Sokola Sojedinenija), Homestead, PA. Annual. (Microfilm: 1919, 1921-1936). Includes English.

Kalendar' Greko Kaftoličeskaho Sojedinenija v U.S.A. (Almanac of the Greek Catholic Union of the U.S.A.; previously titled **Amerikansky Russko-Slovensky Kalendar** and **Amerikanskiĭ Russkiĭ Miesiatsoslov**), Munhall, PA. Annual: 1925-1930, 1935-1938, 1940, 1942, 1967. Includes English.

Kalendar' Organizacii Svobody (Almanac of the Freedom Organization), Perth Amboy, NJ. Annual. (Microfilm: 1925-1929, 1933-1940). Includes some English.

Kalendar "Sobranija" ("Alliance" Almanac; previously titled **Kalendar' Prosvity**), McKeesport, PA. Annual. (Microfilm: 1918-1919, 1921-1932, 1935-1938). Includes English.

Karpatorusskiĭ Kalendar' "Lemko" (Carpatho-Russian Lemko Almanac), Philadelphia. PA. Annual: 1922, 1930.

Karpatorusskiĭ Kalendar' Lemko-Soiuza (Carpatho-Russian Almanac of the Lemko Uinon), Yonkers, NY. Annual: 1932, 1937-1938, 1940-1971. (Microfilm: 1930-1971).

Karpatorusskij Narodnyj Kalendar' (Carpatho-Russian National Almanac), Perth Amboy, NJ. Annual. (Microfilm: 1944-1946). Includes English.

Karpatorusskije Novosti (Carpatho-Russian News), New York, NY. Monthly, bi-weekly. (Microfilm: 1943-1945). Includes English.

Listok (Leaflet), Uzhgorod, Ukraine. Semi-monthly. (Microfilm: 1885-1903).

The Marian, Whiting, IN. Monthly (except July and August): 1954-1956. English.

Narodna Obrana (National Defense), Homestead, PA. Weekly. (Microfilm: 1917).

Nauka (Doctrine), Uzhgorod, Ukraine. Bi-weekly, weekly. (Microfilm: 1897-1921).

Nebesnaja Carica (Queen of Heaven), McKeesport, PA. Monthly. (Microfilm: 1927-1955). Includes English.

Niva (The Sown Field), Yonkers, NY (previously published in Homestead, PA). Monthly. (Microfilm: 1911, 1916).

Pravoslavije (Orthodoxy), Nicholson, PA. Monthly. (Microfilm: 1941). Includes some English.

Pravoslavnyĭ Amerikanskiĭ Viestnik (Russian Orthodox American Messenger), New York, NY. Semi-monthly. (Microfilm: 1896-1897). Includes English.

Prolom (The Breach), New York, NY. Monthly (irregular). (Microfilm: 1919-1921).

Proroczeskoe Svitlo (The Prophetic Light), Proctor, VT. Monthly, bi-monthly: 1921-1953. (Microfilm: 1921-1953).

Rusin-Ruthenian, New York, NY. Monthly. (Microfilm: 1952-1960). Includes some English.

Russkiĭ Pravoslavnyĭ Kalendar' (Russian Orthodox Calendar), Pittsburgh, PA. Annual: 1929, 1931-1932, 1934, 1941. (Microfilm: 1929, 1931, 1934). Includes some English.

Russko-Amerikanskiĭ Pravoslavnyĭ Kalendar' (Russian American Orthodox Calendar), Wilkes-Barre, PA. Annual. (Microfilm: 1906, 1910(?), 1912, 1914-1917, 1921-1923, 1925-1927, 1929-1930, 1932-1933, 1937, 1947, 1950). Includes some English.

Rusyny Newsletter, McKeesport, PA. Monthly: 1980. English.

The Seminarian, Johnstown, PA. Annual: 1969, 1971-1972, 1974. English.

Slovo k Narodu (A Word to the People), Pittsburgh, PA. Monthly. (Microfilm: 1943-1944). Includes some English.

Svit D'itej (Children's World), Homestead, PA. Semi-monthly. (Microfilm: 1921-1973). Includes English.

Svoboda (Liberty), New York, NY. Weekly: 1944. (Microfilm: 1944).

Svobodnoe Slovo Rusi (Free Word of Rus'; title varies: **Svobodnoe Slovo; Svobodnoe Slovo Karpatskoi Rusi**), Mt. Vernon, NY (previously published in Newark, NJ). Bi-monthly (monthly): 1959-1961, 1967-1968, 1971-date. (Microfilm: 1959-1964).

Učitel' (Educator), McKeesport, PA. Monthly. (Microfilm: 1932). Includes some English.

UROBA Messenger (United Russian Orthodox Brotherhood of America), Pittsburgh, PA. 1982-1984. English.

Vechernii Zvon (Evening Bells), Chicago, IL (Northfield, CT). Monthly: 1958, 1960.

Visnyk Karpats'koho Soiuza (Bulletin: Carpathian Alliance), New York, NY. Quarterly. (Microfilm: 1970-1973).

The Voice of Mount St. Macrina, Uniontown, PA. Monthly, bi-monthly, quarterly. (Microfilm: 1948-1977). Includes English.

Vozhd' (Leader), Lakewood, OH. Monthly. (Microfilm: 1929-1930). Includes English.

Croatian American Collection

Manuscript Collections

Balokovič, Zlatko (1895-1965).
Papers, 1942-1955. 2.5 linear ft.

A world-renowned violinist and activist for Yugoslav nationalism, Balokovič was born in Zagreb. During the 1920's and 1930's, he and his American wife, Joyce Borden, toured extensively in Europe; but during World War II they settled in Camden, ME. Balokovič became deeply involved with many wartime committees; and in 1946, the couple visited Yugoslavia as official representatives of the American Committee for Yugoslav Relief. There, he became personally acquainted with Marshall Tito, Milovan Djilas, and others. In 1947, Zlatko and Joyce Balokovič returned to America for a coast-to-coast speaking tour telling of their experiences. As a result of these activities, they were investigated by the U.S. House Committee on Un-American Activities; they were subsequently cleared. Until the 1960s, Balokovič continued to give concerts. He died in 1965 and was buried in Zagreb.

Papers include an autobiography, correspondence, diaries, contracts, handbills, manuscripts, newspaper clippings, published articles, speeches, photographs, and tour itineraries of or collected by the Balokovičes. Papers relate chiefly to Balokovič's musical career and to his involvement with Yugoslav and Croatian organizations such as the American Committee for Yugoslav Relief (ca. 1946-1950), the National Council of Americans of Croatian Descent (1943-1948), the United Committee of South Slavic Americans, and the United Yugoslav Relief. Correspondents include Louis Adamic, James Brunot, U.S. Atty. Gen. Tom Clark, Mirko G. Kuhel, Hilton H. Railey, Eleanor Roosevelt, Ivan Subašic, Thomas J. Watson, and various newspaper editors. *Mostly in English. Inventory available.*

Croatian Fraternal Union of America. Lodge 530 (Melcher, Iowa).
Records, 1896-1971. 1 ledger and 1 envelope.

A fraternal benefit association, the Union was organized in Pittsburgh, PA, in 1894 as the Croatian Union. The Union encourages programs promoting the history and heritage of Croats and maintains scholarship and old age benefit funds.

Records include an account book, life insurance records, miscellaneous lists of names and addresses, correspondence with members, and transfers and membership payments from the Pittsburgh headquarters to members in Iowa. A few personal items of Frank Sepich are also included. *Includes English. Partial inventory available.*

Devich, Andrew (1896-).
Papers, 1976. 16 pages.

Devich was born in Krasno, Croatia. He left Croatia for the United States in 1913. In Minnesota, he joined two of his brothers, who later remigrated. Devich worked in a lumber camp, in mines, and on North Dakota farms. After the war, Devich was naturalized and continued to work in the mines and, when they closed, at various jobs.

Devich's papers consist of an autobiography in which he discusses his early life in Croatia and the process of immigration and settlement in Buhl, MN, his bachelor life, his wedding preparations, life during the Depression, and mining. *In English.*

Dramatski Zbor "Nada" (Chicago, Illinois).
Collection, ca. 1923-1938. 26 linear ft.

Dramatski Zbor "Nada," a Croatian American dramatic society, was formed in 1923 with ties to the Yugoslav Educational Federation, an immigrant organization that also published the newspaper *Novi Svijet* (later *Znanje*). The plays the society performed fell into three categories: great Croatian historical plays such as August Šenoa's *Zlatarevo Zlato* (The Goldsmith's Gold); classics like Gogol's *Revizor* (The Inspector General); and proletarian plays such as *Osloboditelji* (The Liberators).

The collection includes approximately 250 manuscript and typescript plays, performance announcements, posters, and sheet music of the society. *Includes English. Inventory available.*

Kerhin, Zlatko Ivan (1881-1968).
Papers, 1910-1976. 14 linear ft.

Kerhin was born in Sisak, Croatia, and left ca. 1898 for Chicago, IL. There he married Ana Pepich, sister of Stephen Pepich, a popular Yugoslav singer and musician. The Kerhins lived in Chicago, Pueblo, CO, and Pittsburgh, PA, but finally settled in Gary, IN. Kerhin was active in civic affairs, and particularly in the development and promotion of Croatian singing and music societies. He helped found the Singing Zora Society in Chicago and the Society Javor in Pittsburgh. Kerhin was also active in Croatian American activities nationally, helping to organize two singers' alliances (or župe), the Mihanovič (in Chicago), and Faller (in Pittsburgh). In 1949, these župe became part of the national American-Croatian Singers Federation (Američko-Hrvatski Pjevački Savez); Kerhin served as its president off and on during the 1950's and 1960's.

Papers of Kerhin include correspondence, genealogical information, programs and other materials of Croatian American musical societies, sheet music for Croatian songs, reminiscences by Kerhin's daughter, Zora, and scrapbooks. *Includes English. Preliminary inventory available.*

Kraja, Josip (1891-).
Papers, ca. 1915-1965. Ca. 5 linear ft.

Kraja, an editor and publisher, was born in Dubrovnik and immigrated to the United States in 1907. He settled in Youngstown, OH, where he owned a printing company and published several foreign language newspapers. He was editor of *Hrvatska Stampa* and served several times as president of the National Croatian Circle.

Kraja's papers include correspondence; records of the National Croatian Circle; business records of the United Printing Company (Youngstown, OH); notebooks; newspaper clippings; periodicals; photographs; and other personal, professional, and organizational papers. *Includes some English. Preliminary inventory available.*

Lupis-Vukić, Ivo. F. (1876-).
Papers, ca. 1912-1957. 17 microfilm reels.

Lupis-Vukić was a Croat who occasionally lived in and travelled in Croatian communities in the United States between 1891 and 1930. He was the author of *Medju Našim Narodom u Americi* (Among Our People in America).

His papers consist mainly of correspondence, an autobiography, articles (some with English translations), and typescripts. Correspondents include Louis Adamic, Pjoder Aranicki, and others. *Includes English. Inventory available.*

Preveden, Francis Ralph (1890-1959).
Papers, 1821-1959. 10.5 linear ft.

Preveden was born in Kamenica, Croatia. In 1922, he immigrated to the United States and in 1927 received his PhD from the University of Chicago. Preveden taught linguistics and classics at DePaul and Duquesne universities. From 1942 to 1959, he served as a translator for various government agencies, including the Department of Defense. Preveden's major work was his *History of the Croatian People* (1955-1962).

Papers relate mainly to his *History* and to disputes with the Croatian Fraternal Union over its publication. The resulting correspondence provides substantial information on the political and cultural activities of Croatian Americans during the 1940's and 1950's. Also included are dictaphone records and transcriptions, photographs, and correspondence between author and publisher. *Includes English. Inventory available.*

Rukavina Family History.
Papers, 1983. 1 linear in.

The Rukavina family history and genealogy documents the family of Thomas Rukavina, who came to Chicago, IL, in 1900, where he joined his brother and other Croats from the Lika area. He eventually became a successful saloon keeper in Chicago. In 1913, he married Lucy Basič (1885-1929) and moved to the Iron Range of Minnesota, where he worked as a miner.

The bound typescript, "The Rukavina Family History" details the family's experiences in Chicago and on Minnesota's Iron Range. *In English.*

St. Mary's Roman Catholic Church (Rankin, Pennsylvania).
Records, 1896-ca. 1967. Ca. 1.5 linear ft.

Records of St. Mary's Roman Catholic Church of Rankin, PA, one of the oldest and largest Croatian parishes in the United States, include minutes, financial records, membership lists (1917, 1927), anniversary booklets from other Croatian Catholic churches in the United States, miscellany, and personal items of the Rev. Basiljko Bekavac. *Includes English. Inventory available.*

Splivalo, Joseph (1900-   ).
Papers, 1922-1988. 5.5 linear in.

Papers of Splivalo include translations of Yugoslav poetry, articles about his family, and articles about Dalmatian seamen. Also included is a typescript of his autobiography, "Bread with Seven Crusts," photographs of Dalmatia and family members, and correspondence. *Includes English and Italian. Inventory available.*

Tomašić, Dinko A. (1902-1975).
Papers, n.d. 6 linear in. (1 microfilm reel).

Tomašić was born in Smokvica, Croatia. He studied sociology at the Universities of Zagreb and Paris. He taught in Zagreb and, after his immigration to the United States ca. 1943, at Indiana University. Tomašić also worked for the United States Air Force and for Radio Free Europe. He was the author of numerous publications on the sociology of international relations.

Papers consist of a typescript of Tomašić's book, *Americans for Croatia. In English. Also on microfilm. Access to original manuscript is restricted for preservation purposes.*

Union of Canadian Croatians (Savez Kanadskih Hrvata).
Records, ca. 1940's-1950's. 10 linear in.

The Savez Kanadskih Hrvata was a socialist, pro-Tito group advocating a postwar Yugoslavia of united ethnic

minorities. The drama and music
sections of the organization produced
plays and music reflecting these interests
in their themes of socialist and worker
education, peasant life, and partisan
battles and struggles.

Collection includes playscripts and
sheet music of the organization's drama
and music sections. Also included are a
few poems and a speech of Josef Tito
from the newspaper *Rijeckilist*. *Inventory
available.*

Monographs

Croatian American monograph holdings are small in number (ca. 200 volumes) but
cover a variety of subject areas and include several key works. Only a handful of
substantive historical overviews of this ethnic group has emerged. Of these studies, the
IHRC holds George J. Prpic's *The Croatian Immigrants in America* (1971); Frances
Kraljic's *Croatian Migration to and from the United States, 1900-1914* (1978); and Ivan
Čizmić's *Hrvati u životu Sjedinjenih Američkih Država; doprinos u ekonomskom,
političkom i kulturnom životu* (Croats in the Life of the United States of America; Their
Contributions in Economic, Political, and Cultural Life, 1982).

In addition to his considerable writings on Croatian American history, George Prpic
has also compiled bibliographies of Croatian source materials and literature. Included in
the IHRC's collection are his *Croatia and the Croatians: A Selected and Annotated
Bibliography in English* (1982) and *The Croatian Publications Abroad after 1939: A
Bibliography* (1969). Other useful reference tools available include Nada Kesterčanek's
Croatian Newspapers and Calendars in the United States (1952 and 1971) and
biographical directories of Croatian Americans and Croatian Canadians by Francis
Eterovich and Vladimir Markotic.

The holdings contain a good selection of regional and local studies of Croats in
various parts of the United States. Along with works dealing with Croats in areas of
most numerous settlement, such as Stephen Gazi's *Croatian Immigration to Allegheny
County, 1882-1914* (1956), Carl Kasunic's *Croatian Immigrants in the Greater Cleveland
Area* (1964), and Croatian Franciscan Fathers' *The Life and Work of the Croatian People
in Chicagoland: Centennial 1848-1948/49* (1949), the collection documents activity of
this ethnic group in Michigan's Upper Peninsula, Iowa, St. Louis, and Eagle River, WI.

In part a reflection of the strong concern held by Croatian Americans for affairs in
their homeland, a number of volumes have been published in North America chronicling
the history of Croatia and Yugoslavia and the historical relationships between Croats and
other South Slavic people. Among those to be found at the IHRC are Francis Ralph
Preveden's *A History of the Croatian People: From Their Arrival on the Shores of the
Adriatic to the Present Day, with Some Account of the Gothic, Roman, Greek, Illyrian,
and Prehistoric Periods of the Ancient Illyricum and Pannonia* (1955-1962); Francis H.
Eterovich's *Croatia: Land, People, Culture* (1964-1970); Dominik Mandić's *Bosna i
Hercegovina; povjesno-kritička istraživanja* (Bosnia and Herzegovina; A Critical
Historical Study, 1960-1962 [volumes one and two]); and N. Dinko Suljak's *Croatia's
Struggle for Independence: A Documentary History* (1977). Conversely, the collection
contains a small number of items, both primary and secondary, published in Croatia
dealing with migration issues from the perspective of the homeland, including Ivan F.
Lupis-Vukić's *Medju našim narodom u Americi* (Among Our People in America, 1929),
Večeslav Holjevac's *Hrvati izvan domovine* (Croats Outside Their Homeland, 1968), and
Stjepan Lojen's *Uspomene jednog iseljenika* (Memories of an Emigrant, 1963).

The development of religious institutions and practices (predominantly Roman
Catholic) in Croatian American communities is well represented through various parish
histories and jubilee albums. Included are publications from localities in Ohio,
Pennsylvania, Illinois, New York, and Wisconsin. The collection contains a smaller
number of monographs reflecting the activities of secular organizations, such as fraternal
or cultural societies. Among these are the Croatian Fraternal Union of America's *Kratki*

pregled povijesti hrvatske bratske zajednice, 1894-1949 (A Short Review of the History of the Croatian Fraternal Union, 1949), a study of the largest Croatian fraternal organization; and the Croatian Republic Peasant League's *50 godišnica hrvatskog republikanskog kluba HRSS, 1924-1974* (Fiftieth Anniversary, 1924-1974, Croatian Republic Club, Croatian Republic Peasant League, Los Angeles, California, Sunday, June 23, 1974; 1974).

Croatian American involvement in the performing and visual arts is manifested in scattered works on music, drama, and other artistic endeavors. Among these are Branimir Marić's *Glasovi domovine: Hrvatski narodni pjevnik* (Voices of the Homeland: Croatian National Songbook, 1954); Rudolf Matz's *Hrvatska narodna pjesma* (Croatian National Song, 1951); and *Hrvatski šalivdžija: zbirka šale i satire, anegdota i pričica* (Croatian Joke-Maker: Collection of Jokes and Satire, Anecdotes and Fables, 191?). Examples of poetry and fiction written by, for, and about Croats in the United States emerge through writings by Ante Kadić, Nada Kesterčanek, and others. The collection also includes language education publications directed at Croatian Americans, such as the Educational Committee of the Croatian Fraternal Union of America's *Čitanka za hrvatsku i ostalu jugoslavensku djecu u Sjedinjenim Državama* (A Reader for Croatian and Other Yugoslav Children in the United States, 1923), along with a citizenship book for Croats produced by the National Catholic Welfare Conference.

Researchers interested in this ethnic group are encouraged to consult also the small collection of books (ca. eighty volumes) shelved and classified as "Yugoslav." Included here are works dealing with more than one of the South Slavic nationality groups. Predominant among these are secondary studies (many of them key publications) such as *Americans from Yugoslavia*, by Gerald G. Govorchin; *South Slavic Immigration in America*, by George Prpic; *Yugoslav Migrations to America*, by Branko Colakovic; *The Yugoslavs in America: 1880-1918*, by L. Blaisdell; and several studies by Adam Eterovich and others on Yugoslavs in particular states or regions. Also included in this section are books and pamphlets concerning the formation of the Yugoslav nation, primarily written from the perspective of Yugoslav immigrants, and published in many cases by the United Committee of South Slavic Americans.

Newspapers

Američki Hrvat (The American Croat), Pittsburgh, PA. Weekly: 1945. (Microfilm: 1946).
   Includes English.

Američki Hrvatski Glasnik (American Croatian Herald), Chicago, IL. Weekly: 1955-1956.

Chicago, Chicago, IL. Weekly. (Microfilm: 1893-1894).

The Croatian Times, Omaha, NE. Monthly: 1977-1978. English.

Danica (The Morning Star), Chicago, IL. Weekly: 1947, 1953-1965, 1968-1973.

Domovina (Homeland), New York, NY. Weekly. (Microfilm: 1916-1917).

Hrvatska Država (The Croatian State), Munich, West Germany. Bi-monthly: 1962-1965, 1967-1968, 1970-1977.

Hrvatska Vila (The Croatian Fairy), Trinidad, CO. Weekly: 1912.

Hrvatska Zastava (Croatian Flag), Chicago, IL. Daily. (Microfilm: 1905-1917).

Hrvatski Glas (Croatian Voice; merged with Hrvatski Glas of Acton, Ontario, Canada), Nanaimo, British Columbia, Canada (previously published in Sudbury and Hamilton, Ontario, Canada). Weekly: 1979-date. Includes English.

Hrvatski Glas (Croatian Voice; merged with **Hrvatski Glas** of Sudbury, Ontario, Canada), Acton, Ontario, Canada (previously published in Winnipeg, Manitoba, Canada). Weekly: 1939, 1940, 1954, 1959-1980. Includes English.

Hrvatski Glas (Croatian Voice; Croatian Peasant Party), Vancouver, British Columbia, Canada. Monthly: 1981-date. Includes English.

Hrvatski Glasnik (Croatian Herald), Allegheny, PA. Weekly. (Microfilm: 1908-1919).

Hrvatski List and Danica Hrvatska (The Croatian Gazette and the Croatian Morning Star), New York, NY. Tri-weekly. (Microfilm: 1922-1928, 1930-1941).

Hrvatski Svijet (Croatian World), New York, NY. Three times per week: 1939, 1941, 1942, 1945, 1955, 1956.

Hrvatski Svijet (Croatian World), New York, NY. Daily. (Microfilm: 1914).

Hrvatski Tjednik Danica (The Croatian Weekly Morning Star), Chicago, IL. Weekly: 1977-date.

Jadran (The Adriatic), San Francisco, CA. Weekly. (Microfilm: 1908-1910, 1915).

Jugoslovenska Zastava (Yugoslav Flag), Chicago, IL; New York, NY; St. Louis, MO; and Pittsburgh, PA. Weekly. (Microfilm: 1919). Includes English.

Jugoslovenski Svijet (The Southern Slav World; title varies: **Hrvatski Svijet**), New York, NY. Daily. (Microfilm: 1908-1920).

Križ (Cross), Gary, IN. Monthly: 1945, 1953-1957. Includes English.

Napredak (Progress), Allegheny City, PA. Weekly: 1896-1908.

Narodni Glasnik (People's Herald), Chicago, IL. Weekly: 1946, 1965-1973.

Narodni List (The National Gazette), New York, NY. Daily. (Microfilm: 1898-1920).

Narodni List (The National Gazette), New York, NY. Daily. (Microfilm: 1903).

Naš Svijet (Our World), Sarajevo, Yugoslavia. 1966.

Naša Nada (Our Hope), Gary, IN. Frequency varies: 1954-date. Includes English.

Naše Novine (Our Newspaper), Toronto, Ontario, Canada. Weekly: 1973-date.

New Yorski Tjednik (New York Weekly), New York, NY. Weekly: 1973.

Novi Svijet (The New World; title changes to **Znanje**), Chicago, IL. Weekly: 1924-1931.

Radnička Borba (The Workers' Struggle), Cleveland, OH. Monthly (weekly): 1963-1970.

Vijesnik Hrvatske Katoličke Zajednice (Bulletin of the Croatian Catholic League), Gary, IN. 1921.

Zajedničar (The Fraternalist), Pittsburgh, PA (previously published in Allegheny, PA). Weekly: 1944, 1952, 1955, 1959, 1961-date. (Microfilm: 1907-1940). Includes English.

Znanje (Knowledge; previously titled **Novi Svijet**), Chicago, IL. Weekly: 1935-1939.

Zpravodaj (Reporter), Chicago, IL. Monthly: 1962, 1965-1966, 1972.

Yugoslav

Jugoslavenski Glasnik (Yugoslav Herald), Chicago, IL/Calumet, MI/New York, NY. Weekly: 1938-1945. Serbian and/or Croatian.

Jugoslovenski Obzor (Yugoslav Observer), Milwaukee, WI. Semi-monthly: 1933-1945. Slovenian.

Serials

American Croat, Arcadia, CA. Frequency varies: 1971, 1977, 1978. Includes English.

American Croatian Academic Club Bulletin, Cleveland, OH. Frequency varies: 1965-1971. Includes English.

The American-Croatian Historical Review, Youngstown, OH. Monthly: 1946. English.

The American Croatian Pioneer, Cleveland, OH. Monthly: 1963. English.

Ave, Buenos Aires, Argentina. Monthly: 1955.

Ave Maria (Hail Mary), McKeesport, PA (previously published in Pittsburgh, PA). Monthly: 1943-1946, 1953-1955. Includes English.

Croatia Press, New York, NY (previously published in Cleveland, OH). Quarterly (bi-monthly): 1954, 1956, 1958-1980. Croatian or English.

Croatian-American Academic Association of the Pacific Quarterly Bulletin, San Carlos, CA. Quarterly: 1979. English.

Croatian Catholic Union of the U.S.A. Constitution and By-laws, Gary, IN. Irregular: 1921-1922, 1932, 1939, 1950, 1962. Includes English.

The Croatian Courier, Detroit, MI. Monthly: 1955-1956. Includes English.

Izvješća; Glavnih Odbornika, Odbora i Časnika Hrvatske Bratske Zajednice u Americi (Reports of the Main Committee-Members, Committees, and Officers of the Croatian Fraternal Union of America), Pittsburgh, PA. Every four years (previously published triennially): 1932, 1935, 1939, 1943, 1947, 1951, 1955, 1959. Includes English.

Croatian Fraternal Union of America Summary Audit Report, Pittsburgh, PA. Every four years: 1943, 1947, 1951, 1955, 1959. English.

Croatian Fraternal Union of America Lodge 14 Vijesnik, Cleveland, OH. Quarterly: 1965-1966. Includes English.

Croatian Fraternal Union of America By-laws, Pittsburgh, PA. Every four years (previously published triennially): 1918, 1926, 1929, 1932, 1935, 1939, 1943, 1947, 1951, 1963, 1971. Includes English.

Croatian Fraternal Union of America Zapisnik Konvencije, Pittsburgh, PA. Every four years (previously published triennially): 1900, 1906, 1926, 1929, 1932, 1935, 1939, 1947, 1951, 1959. Includes English.

Croatian Historical Society of Western Canada Newsletter, Calgary, Alberta, Canada. Semi-annual: 1982-date. Includes English.

Croatian Review; Hrvatska Smotra, Philadelphia, PA. Semi-annual: 1931. Includes English.

Croatian Information Service, Arcadia, CA. Monthly: 1978. English.

Crveni Kalendar (Red Calendar), Chicago, IL. Annual: 1920-1924.

Danica Hrvatska Koledar (The Croatian Morning Star Almanac), New York, NY. Annual: 1922.

Hrvatska Revija (Croatian Review), Munich, West Germany (previously published in Buenos Aires, Argentina). Quarterly: 1955-date.

Hrvatski Domobran Godišnjak (Croatian Home Defenders Almanac), Pittsburgh, PA. Annual: 1938, 1940.

Hrvatski Glas Kalendar za Godinu (Croatian Voice Calendar for the Year), Winnipeg, Manitoba, Canada. Annual: 1940, 1945, 1956, 1960, 1964-1969, 1971, 1975-1976, 1980.

Hrvatski Godišnjak (Croatian Almanac; see also **Ave Maria**), McKeesport, PA. Annual: 1947-1950. Includes English.

Hrvatski Iseljenik (Croatian Emigrant), Zagreb, Yugoslavia. Monthly: 1940.

Hrvatski Kalendar (Croatian Almanac), Chicago, IL. Annual: 1944-1950, 1965, 1970.

Hrvatski Katolički Glasnik (Croatian Catholic Messenger), Chicago, IL. Monthly: 1945, 1948-1950, 1953, 1956-1957, 1968-date.

Hrvatski List & Danica Hrvatska Koledar (The Croatian Gazette and the Croatian Morning Star Almanac), New York, NY. Annual: 1926, 1928, 1930-1944.

Izbor (Selections), Buenos Aires, Argentina. Monthly: 1954-1955. Includes some Spanish.

Journal of Croatian Studies, New York, NY. Annual: 1960-1983. English.

Junior Magazine (Croatian Fraternal Union Junior Order Department), Pittsburgh, PA. Bi-monthly: 1956-1976. Includes English.

Kalendar Narodnoga Lista (National Gazette Calendar), New York, NY. Annual: 1917.

Kalendar Novi Svijet (New World Calendar), Chicago, IL. Annual: 1928.

Kronika Zavoda za Književnost i Teatrologiju JAZU (Chronicle of the Institute for Literature and Theater Arts), Zagreb, Yugoslavia. Bi-annual: 1984.

Mali Hravtski Kalendar (Little Croatian Calendar), Buenos Aires, Argentina. Annual: 1950.

Matica, Zagreb, Yugoslavia. Monthly: 1952-1975, 1977-date. Includes English.

Matica Iseljenički Kalendar (Emigrant Matica Calendar), Zagreb, Yugoslavia. Annual: 1955-1970, 1972-1973, 1977-1983, 1985-date. Includes English.

Migracije (Migrations; previously titled **Bilten**), Zagreb, Yugoslavia. Monthly: 1972-1983.

Migracijske Teme (Migration Themes), Zagreb, Yugoslavia. Quarterly: 1985-date. Includes English summary.

Narod (The Nation), San Francisco, CA. Monthly: 1945-1946.

Narodni Kalendar (The People's Almanac), Chicago, IL. Annual: 1964-1967.

Narodni Kalendar (The People's Almanac), Pittsburgh, PA. Annual: 1945.

Naša Nada Kalendar (Our Hope Almanac), Chicago, IL. Annual: 1927-1928, 1932, 1946-1949. Includes English.

Naše More (Our Sea), Dubrovnik, Yugoslavia. Bi-monthly: 1955-1956, 1959, 1961, 1963-1967, 1972-1979.

North American Council for Independence of Croatia; Vjesnik Vijeća, Windsor, Ontario, Canada. 1972. Includes English.

Nova Jugoslavija (New Yugoslavia), New York, NY. Semi-monthly: 1942.

Nova Jugoslavija (New Yugoslavia), Montevideo, Uruguay. Semi-monthly (?). (Microfilm: 1944).

Osoba i Duh (Person and Spirit), Albuquerque, NM. 1955.

Petrica Kerempuh, Chicago, IL. (Microfilm: 1983).

Radnički Kalendar (Workers' Calendar), Pittsburgh, PA. Annual: 1939.

Rasprave o Migracijama (Discussions on Migration), Zagreb, Yugoslavia. Quarterly: 1981-1983.

Republika Hrvatska (Croatian Republic), Buenos Aires, Argentina. Bi-monthly: 1958-1959. Includes English.

Slavjanska Sloga (Slavic Unity), San Francisco, CA. Daily (?). (Microfilm: 1895).

St. Nicholas Roman Catholic Church; Mjesečni Vijesnik (Monthly News), Pittsburgh, PA. Monthly: 1932.

Socijalistički Radnički Kalendar (Socialist Workers' Almanac), Cleveland, OH. Annual: 1964-1965. Includes English.

Sokol (American Sokol Messenger), St. Louis, MO. Monthly. (Microfilm: 1933-1934). Includes English.

Svjetlo (The Light), Chicago, IL. Monthly: 1911.

The Tamburitzan, Pittsburgh, PA. Bi-monthly: 1959-1960. English.

The Trumpeter, Borger, TX. Quarterly: 1981. Croatian and English.

United American Croats Bulletin, New York, NY. Frequency varies: 1965-1970. Includes English.

Vinculum Caritatis (Chain of Charity), Chicago, IL. 1965.

Zdravlje (Health), Detroit, MI. Monthly: 1929.

Yugoslav

Balkan and Eastern European American Genealogical and Historical Society, San Francisco, CA. Frequency varies: 1964-1966. English.

The Florida State University Center for Yugoslav-American Studies Proceedings and Reports (previously titled The Florida State University Slavic Papers), Tallahassee, FL. Annual: 1972-1977. English.

The Florida State University Joint Yugoslav-American Advisory Council Proceedings and Reports, Tallahassee, FL. Annual: 1978-1979. English.

Jugoslav Review, New York, NY. Monthly. (Microfilm: 1923). Serbian and/or Croatian, Slovenian.

Jugoslaven (The Yugoslav), Västerås, Sweden. Quarterly: 1979. Croatian and English.

Jugoslavia Kalendar (Yugoslavia Calendar), Chicago, IL. Annual: 1939. Slovenian and English.

Kolo, New York, NY. Monthly: 1924. Slovenian.

Medunardoni Problemi (International Problems), Belgrade, Yugoslavia. Quarterly: 1982. Serbian and/or Croatian.

Naš Kalendar (Our Calendar), Toronto, Ontario, Canada. Annual: 1958. Slovenian.

Sokolski Vesnik (Sokol Herald), Milwaukee, WI. Quarterly: 1967-1975, 1980-1984. Serbian, Croatian, and Slovenian.

T & T (formerly **Today and Tomorrow**), Milford, NJ. Bi-monthly: 1945-1948, 1950. English.

The Tamburitzan, Pittsburgh, PA. Bi-monthly: 1959-1961, 1976. English.

That's Yugoslavia (supplement to **Hrvatska Domovina**), Hamburg, West Germany. Monthly: 1982. English.

United Committee of South-Slavic Americans Bulletin, New York, NY. Frequency varies: 1943-1946. English.

United Yugoslav Relief Fund of America News Bulletin (previously titled **Yugoslav News Bulletin**), New York, NY. Frequency varies: 1941-1945. English.

Yugoslav-American Academic Association of the Pacific Bulletin, Palo Alto, CA. Quarterly: 1977. English.

Yugoslav-American Society Newsletter, Minneapolis, MN. Bi-monthly: 1987-date. English.

Yugoslav Facts and Views, New York, NY. Monthly: 1975-1981. English.

Yugoslavia Ministarstvo Socijalne Politike Iseljenički Odsek Iseljenička Služba: Izveštaj Narodnoj Skupštini (Yugoslav Ministry of Social Policy Emigration Department Emigration Service: Report to National Assembly), Belgrade, Yugoslavia. Bi-annual: 1925-1927. Serbian and/or Croatian.

Czech American Collection

Manuscript Collections

American Fund for Czechoslovak Refugees (New York, New York).
Records, 1948-1968. 25 linear ft.

The American Fund for Czechoslovak Refugees was formed in 1948 by Ján Papánek and others to help refugees of the Communist coup with their immediate needs, their resettlement, and adjustment to their new homes. Its first chairman was Dr. James T. Shotwell of the Carnegie Endowment for International Peace. The American Fund for Czechoslovak Refugees established working relationships with other organizations, such as the International Refugee Organization, and was recognized by the U.S. Department of State as a voluntary agency. It was staffed mostly by volunteers and assisted by organizations such as the Czechoslovak National Council of America. It was active in a number of states and also had offices abroad.

Records of the Fund are comprised of case files. *Includes English. Inventory available. Restricted.*

American Sokol Organization. Western District.
Records, 1975-1978. 1 linear in.

The American Sokol Organization (ASO) was founded in 1865 by Czech Americans. It endeavors to teach sportsmanship through competitions, particularly in gymnastics. The organization also sponsors folk dancing, language classes, schools, camps, and other cultural activities.

Records of the organization's Western District consist of a photocopy of a scrapbook containing clippings and printed ephemera documenting Sokol and Czech community activities in Nebraska, Iowa, and Minnesota. *In English.*

Bergman, Marion.
Papers, 1975. 7 linear in.

Papers of Bergman, a Czech American author, consist of the manuscript of her book, "America's Slavic Legacy." *In English.*

Czech-American Dramatic Society of Chicago (Illinois).
Records, n.d. Ca. 7 linear ft.

Collection consists of play scripts and musical scores used by the Society.

Kassal, Monsignor Edward (1876-1975).
Papers, 1924-1965. 4 linear in.

Monsignor Kassal was born in Polna, Bohemia, and came to the United States in 1905. He served for sixty years in Slavic Catholic settlements near Dickinson, ND; in Jackson, Owatonna, and Winona, MN; and in Eastman, WI.

His papers consist mainly of commemorative pamphlets and photographs. *In English. Inventory available.*

Kucera, Adolf.
Papers, 1949-1976. Ca. 1 linear in.

Kucera was a post-World War II displaced person and a pre-World War II officer in the Czechoslovakian army. Papers comprise correspondence between Kucera and other Czech displaced persons, and a short autobiography of Kucera from *Archer* magazine.

Lerando, Leo Z.
Papers, ca. 1890-1936. 5 linear ft.

Lerando was a Czech American professor of Romance languages and literature. He came to the United States in 1916 and taught at various places, including St. Theresa's College (Winona, MN).

Papers include correspondence, photographs, scrapbooks, newspaper clippings, publications, and memorabilia documenting his teaching and research pursuits as well as his involvement in Czech American activities. *Includes English and a few items in German.*

Miller, Rev. Kenneth Dexter (1887-1968).
Papers, 1910-1969. 1.5 linear ft.

Miller, a Presbyterian minister, was a leader in interdenominational efforts to makes churches responsive to the needs of urban dwellers, especially ethnic minorities. He was educated at Princeton University and Union Theological Seminary, then participated in a study program in Bohemia to prepare him for work among Czech immigrants in the United States. While living in Bohemia,

he became acquainted with Thomas Garrigue Masaryk, who became president of Czechoslovakia. After his return to the United States, Miller continued his work with Czech immigrants. He directed the Jan Hus Neighborhood House (New York, NY), worked for the YMCA War Work Council (1917-1919), marched across Siberia with Czech troops during World War I, worked with the Presbyterian Board of Home Missions assisting Slavic immigrants, and served as executive secretary of the Presbytery of Detroit. In 1937, he was a founding member of the Masaryk Institute of New York; he also served as head of the New York Mission Society. He was European director of the American Fund for Czechoslovak Regugees, Inc., until his retirement.

Miller's papers consist of correspondence; drafts, reviews, and advertisements for his articles and books; a stamp collection; memorabilia; personal journals from his time in Bohemia, including discussions of religious attitudes of Bohemians and the story of his Siberian trek; personal scrapbooks; and photographs. Also included is correspondence of his wife, Ethel P. Miller. *Includes English. Inventory available. Restricted.*

Pavlíček, Joseph (1890-1986).
Papers, ca. 1923-1959. Ca. 4 linear ft.

Pavlíček was born in Rozsochy, Moravia (Czechoslovakia). He immigrated to the United States ca. 1908 and lived in St. Paul, MN. Pavlíček was a long-time member and officer of the St. Paul Sokol Gymnastic Society, served as president of the Northern District of the American Sokol Union, and was a chief promoter of the Sokol summer camp in Pine City, MN. He was also a representative for the International Institute of Minnesota (St. Paul), relief worker for Czechoslovakia during World War II, and member of the Czech Society of America and Lodge Orel (St. Paul, MN) of the Western Bohemian Fraternal Association.

Papers of Pavlíček pertain mainly to his activities in various Czech American organizations. Included are biographical information, correspondence, newspaper clippings, financial records, and scrapbooks. *Includes English. Inventory available.*

Roucek, Joseph (1902-1984).
Papers, 1931-1984. 88.5 linear ft.

Roucek was born in Prague and came to the United States in 1921. He studied at Occidental College in Los Angeles, CA, supporting himself as a concert pianist, lecturer, and silent movie actor. He also was featured in vaudeville on western circuits and entertained in the summer camps of the Yellowstone Park Camps Company. Roucek later received his PhD from New York University and taught sociology at numerous American, Canadian, and European colleges and universities. He was a prolific author of books and articles and founder of Delta Tau Kappa, an international social science honorary society. His contributions to international understanding were recognized by the royal governments of Romania and Yugoslavia.

Roucek's papers contain articles and manuscripts, newspaper clippings, correspondence, photographs and photograph albums, and scrapbooks. Materials pertain mainly to ethnic and minority groups, religion, Delta Tau Kappa, immigration, human rights, the "race question," and education. *In English. Inventory available.*

Rypka, Zdenka (1894-1975).
Papers, ca. 1863-1953. 1 linear ft.

A teacher and housewife active in Czech American organizations, Rypka was born in Washington, IA. She became a teacher in the area of Osage and St. Ansgar, IA, and later moved to Owatonna, MN. She worked in a dry goods store until she retired at age seventy-five. During the 1920's, Rypka was active in the Western Fraternal Life Association (Západní Česko-Bratrská Jednota) and was involved in Czech home talent plays. During the 1930's, she was active as a 4-H Club leader.

Papers include clippings, correspondence, diaries, notebooks, photograph albums, and scrapbooks; notebooks contain her poems. Collection also includes her handwritten transcriptions of Czech folk songs along with published programs and other materials of Czech home talent associations such as Vzdělávací Odbor Západní Česko-Bratrské Jednoty. *Includes English. Inventory available.*

Vyskocil, Charles H.
Papers, n.d. 1 linear in.

Papers of Vyskocil contain a manuscript essay on Czechs in Kewaunee, WI, a series of articles from *Hospodář* on Czechs in Manitowoc County, WI, and translations of these writings by Vyskocil. *Includes English.*

Zajíček, Oldřich (1925-1975).
Papers, ca. 1949-1973. 10 linear in.

Papers of Zajíček comprise correspondence, essays, and publications of the National Committee for a Free Europe, the Christian Democratic Union of Central Europe, the Czechoslovak Foreign Institute in Exile, and other organizations in which he was active. Also included is a poem he wrote. *Includes English.*

Západní Česko-Bratrská Jednota.
 Lodge No. 44 (Freeborn County, Minnesota).
Records, 1850-1984. Ca. 1 linear in.

Records of the Lodge consist of photocopied documents and newspaper clippings pertaining to the lodge. Also included is a photocopy of a historical essay by John R. Lukas entitled "The Bohemian Settlement." *In English.*

Monographs

The Czech American monograph collection, numbering ca. 1,020 volumes, effectively documents several aspects of the Czech experience in the United States, including migration; settlement; cultural, community, and religious life; the press; and business and labor. These strengths are complemented by miscellaneous works such as recipe books, grammars and textbooks, agricultural works, and citizenship primers.

General works on Czech immigration include Thomas Capek's *The Czechs (Bohemians) in America* (1920), Kenneth D. Miller's *The Czecho-Slovaks in America* (1922), Joseph Roucek's *The Czechs and Slovaks in America* (1967), Jan Habenicht's *Dějiny Čechův Amerických* (History of Czech Americans, 1910), and the Czechoslovak National Council in America's *Panorama: A Historical Review of America* (1970). Among the relevant bibliographies found in the IHRC's reference section are Esther Jerabek's *Czechs and Slovaks in North America: A Bibliography* (1976), and Stanley B. Kimball's *Slavic American Imprints: A Classified Catalog of the Collection at the Lovejoy Library* (1972). There are also bibliographies pertaining to imprints from Czechoslovakia, including Rudolf Sturm's *Czechoslovakia: A Bibliographic Guide* (1967).

Most major locations of Czech settlement in the United States are well represented by both early accounts and more contemporary studies. Titles include Daniel D. Droba's *Czech and Slovak Leaders in Metropolitan Chicago* (1934), Josef Cermak's *Dějiny občanské války, s připojením zkušeností českých vojínů* (History of the [U.S.] Civil War, Including Experiences of the Czech Soldiers, 1889), Vladimir Kucera's *Czechs and Nebraska* (1967), Robert I. Kutek's *The Story of a Bohemian Village* (1970), Josef A. Dvorak's *Dějiny Čechů ve státu South Dakota* (History of the Czechs in the State of South Dakota, 1920), and the Institute of Texan Cultures's *The Czech Texans* (1972). Numerous other local and regional histories are available.

The collection reflects the experiences and practices of both Protestant and Catholic Czech Americans. Among the Protestant groups, the Czech Baptists are best represented. Titles relating to religion include Vaclav Vojta's *Czechoslovak Baptists* (n.d.), Joseph Cada's *The Czech-American Catholics, 1850-1920* (1964), Josef Hessoun's *Krátké dějiny a seznam českokatolických osad ve. Spoj. Státech Amerických* (A Short History and Register of Czech Catholic Settlements in the United States of America, 1890), Guido Kisch's *In Search of Freedom, A History of American Jews from Czechoslovakia*, as well as numerous local histories, such as Jan Habenicht's *History of the Parish of St. Wenceslaus in New Prague, Minnesota* (1956). Church and parish histories are available from Chicago, Kansas, Missouri, Nebraska, New York, North Dakota, and Wisconsin.

Czech American community life centered on various organizations such as fraternal, benevolent, gymnastic, musical, and women's societies. The IHRC has an excellent collection of books dealing with this aspect of Czech American life. Among these are Karel M. Prchal's *Sokol Ideals* (n.d.), Jarka Jelinek's *Sokol and the Sokol Idea* (1957), Josef Martínek's *Století jednoty Č.S.A., 1854-1954: Dějiny jednoty Československých Spolků v Americe* (One Hundred Years of the C.S.A.: The History of the Czechoslovak Society of America, 1955), and Anna Machovska's *Dějiny Jednoty českých dam ve Spojených Státech severní Ameriky* (History of the Unity of Czech Ladies in the United States of North America, 1895).

The collection contains a good concentration of poetry and fiction, including works by Josef Martinek, Bedrich Moravec, and Josef Tomanek. Works on music include songbooks of the Lyra Czech Singing Society (Chicago) and Alice G. Masaryk's *Hudba ve Spillville* (Music in Spillville, 1963). General works on Czech cultural contributions to American life include Miloslav Rechcigl, Jr.'s, *The Czechoslovak Contribution to World Culture* (1964), and Eva E. Rechcigl's *Biographical Directory of the Members of the Czechoslovak Society of Arts and Sciences in America* (1972).

Several volumes provide information on Czech involvement in the American work force. Among these are Joseph Z. Schneider's *Some Recollections of My Fifty Professional Years* (1967), and Thomas Capek's *The Czechs and Slovaks in American Banking* (1921). The history and output of the Czech American press can be researched in Thomas Capek's *Padesát let českého tisku v Americe* (Fifty Years of the Czech Press in America, 1911), Vojtech Nevlud's *Czech and Slovak Periodical Press Outside Czechoslovakia as of 1968* (1968), and his *Czech and Slovak Periodicals Outside Czechoslovakia* (1978).

Newspapers

Americké Listy (American Letters), Perth Amboy, NJ. Weekly: 1962-1966, 1968-date.

Bohemia, Munich, West Germany. 1953-1957.

Catholic Workman, New Prague, MN. Monthly: 1963, 1972-date. English.

Čechoslovák (The Czechoslovak), London, England. Weekly: 1944-1945, 1953-1955, 1957-1958, 1960-1967.

České Slovo (Czechoslovak), Munich, West Germany. Monthly: 1955, 1959-1975.

Chicagské Listy (Chicago Newspaper), Chicago, IL. Semi-weekly (?). (Microfilm: 1893).

Denní Hlasatel (Daily Bohemian Herald), Chicago, IL. Daily: 1941, 1971, 1973. (Microfilm: 1891-1941).

Evropská Federace (European Federation), Toronto and Queenstown, Ontario, Canada. Quarterly: 1963-1965.

Hlas Exilu (The Voice of Exile), Munich, West Germany. Monthly: 1955.

Hlas Národa (The Voice of the Nation), Chicago, IL. Weekly: 1976-date. Includes English.

Hlasatel (Bohemian Herald), Cicero, IL. Semi-weekly: 1941, 1944-1945, 1947-1949, 1953-1956, 1965-1972, 1979.

Hlasatel (Bohemian Herald), Chicago, IL. Semi-weekly. (Microfilm: 1902-1912).

Katolík (The Catholic), Chicago, IL. Weekly: 1962, 1971-1975.

Kewaunské Listy (Kewaunee Newspaper), Kewaunee, WI. Weekly. (Microfilm: 1892-1917).

Minnesotské Noviny (Minnesota News), St. Paul, MN. Weekly: 1906-1907, 1911-1912.

Národ (The Nation), Chicago, IL. Weekly (daily until 1944): 1944, 1955, 1960-1963, 1969-1975.

Naše Hlasy (Our Voices), Toronto, Ontario, Canada. Weekly: 1955, 1959-1962, 1964-1967, 1969-1976, 1978.

Nedělní Svornost (Sunday Concord; supplement of Svornost), Chicago, IL. Weekly: 1942, 1950, 1957.

New Yorské Listy (New York Newspaper), New York, NY. Daily: 1962.

Nový Domov (New Home), Toronto, Ontario, Canada. Weekly: 1966, 1968, 1972.

Nový Svět (The New World), Cleveland, OH. Weekly (daily until 1973): 1966-date.

Práce (Work; Amalgamated Clothing Workers of America), New York, NY/Chicago, IL. Bi-weekly (weekly and semi-monthly). (Microfilm: 1925-1927).

Právo (Justice), Cleveland, OH. Weekly. (Microfilm: 1912-1916).

Právo Lidu (The Rights of the People), Chicago, IL. Daily. (Microfilm: 1893-1894).

Slávie (Slavia), Racine, WI. Weekly. (Microfilm: 1861-1862, 1865, 1870-1918).

Spravedlnost (Justice), Chicago, IL. Daily (weekly): 1932. (Microfilm: 1903, 1913).

Svoboda (Liberty), El Campo and La Grange, TX. Weekly (semi-weekly): 1960.

Telegram, Edmonton, Alberta, Canada. Semi-monthly: 1971-1975.

Vlastenec (Patriot), La Crosse, WI. Weekly. (Microfilm: 1903-1909, 1927).

Serials

Agrární Politika; Ústřední List Československé Republikánské Strany v Zahraničí (Agrarian Politics; Central Daily of the Czechoslovak Republic Abroad), New York, NY. 1954-1955.

The American Bi-Monthly, Chicago, IL. Bi-monthly: 1914-1915. English.

The American Bulletin, Cicero, IL. Monthly: 1957-date. English.

The American-Czechoslovak Fellowship, Chicago, IL. Quarterly: 1942. English.

American Czechoslovak Flashes, Chicago, IL. Monthly: 1946-1949. English.

American Sokol, Berwyn, IL. Monthly: 1898-1901, 1903, 1911, 1917, 1921, 1923, 1933-1934, 1940-1941, 1943-1946, 1948-1956, 1958-1959, 1963-1981. English.

Americký Sborník Sokolský (American Sokol Almanac), Chicago, IL. Annual: 1929-1930.

Amerikán Národní Kalendář (The American National Calendar), Chicago, IL. Annual: 1897, 1899, 1904, 1910-1911, 1914-1957.

The Bohemian Review, Chicago, IL. Monthly: 1917. English.

The Bohemian Voice, Omaha, NE. Monthly: 1893. English.

Boletín Católico Checoslovaco (Catholic Czechoslovak Bulletin), New York, NY. Frequency varies: 1941-1946. Spanish.

Boletín Checoslovaco (Czechoslovak Bulletin; previously titled **Nuevas Llegadas Desde Checoslovaquia Bajo La Dominación Nazi**), New York, NY. Bi-weekly: 1940-1946. Spanish.

Brázda (The Furrow), Hamilton, Ontario, Canada. Monthly: 1962.

Brko Sokolí (Sokol Quill), Chicago, IL. Monthly: 1935.

Čas (Time), London, England; Chicago, IL; New York, NY; and Berkeley, CA (place of publication varies). Bi-monthly: 1951-1954, 1958-1960. Includes English.

České Osady v Americe (Czech Settlements in America), Hamburg, Germany. Monthly: 1888-1889.

Česko-Americký Sborník Sokolský; Kalendář (Czech-American Sokol Almanac; Calendar), Chicago, IL. Annual: 1917.

Československá Akademie Věd. Komise Pro Dějiny Krajanů Čechů a Slováků v Zahraničí (Czechoslovak Academy Head Committee for the History of Czech and Slovak Countrymen Abroad), Prague, Czechoslovakia. Frequency irregular: 1963-1969.

Československé Noviny (Czechoslovak News), New York, NY. Monthly: 1955-1957.

Československý Den (Czechoslovak Day), Chicago, IL. Annual: 1953-1954, 1956-1957, 1959-1964, 1974. Includes English.

Československý Přehled (Czechoslovak Overview), New York, NY. Monthly: 1954-1958.

Československý Sociálně Demokratický Časopis (Czechoslovak Social Democratic Journal), New York, NY. 1956. Includes English.

Československý Sokol v Zahraničí (Czechoslovak Sokol Abroad), Toronto, Ontario, Canada. Monthly: 1951-1952, 1964, 1968, 1971-1972.

Československý Svět (Czechoslovak World), Prague, Czechoslovakia. Bi-weekly: 1971-date. Includes English.

Československý Svět Kalendář (Czechoslovak World Calendar), Prague, Czechoslovakia, Annual: 1980, 1984-date.

Český Amerikán Národní Kalendář (Czech American National Calendar), Chicago, IL. Annual: 1958.

Český Odd Fellow (Czech Odd Fellow), Berwyn, IL. Monthly: 1952-1960, 1962-1968. Includes English.

Čin (Action; Independent Czechoslovak Monthly), New York, NY. Monthly: 1964. Includes English.

Council of Free Czechoslovakia Zpravodaj (Reporter), New York, NY (previously published in Washington, DC). 1949-1952, 1954.

Cyrilometodějská Liga v Kanadě (SS. Cyril and Methodius League in Canada), Hamilton, Ontario, Canada. 1958. Includes some English.

Czech Slovak Protective Societies Orgán Bratrstva Č.S.P.S. (Brotherhood Organ), Berwyn, IL. Monthly: 1929, 1933-1934. Includes English.

The Czechoslovak American (American YMCA in Czechoslovakia), Kinsky Palace, Prague, Czechoslovakia. Annual (?): 1921. English.

Czechoslovak Free Enterprise Middle Class Party in Exile in Canada Zprávy ŽOS (News of ŽOS), Toronto-Hamilton, Ontario, Canada. 1960.

Czechoslovak Free Trade Union Federation Information Bulletin, Long Island, NY. 1959. English.

Czechoslovak Newsletter (Council of Free Czechoslovakia), Washington, DC. Monthly (?): 1976.

Czechoslovak Press Survey (Research Departments of Radio Free Europe). 1964. English.

Czechoslovak Republican Party in Exile Central Committee. Zprávy ŽOS (News of ŽOS), Bronx, NY. 1965.

The Czechoslovak Review, Chicago, IL. Monthly: 1919. English.

Czechoslovak Society of America Journal (previously titled **Orgán Československých Spolků v Americe**), Cicero, IL. Monthly: 1934, 1937-1942, 1944-1947, 1964, 1968-date. Includes English.

Czechoslovak Society of America Junior Magazine, Cicero, IL. Monthly: 1962-1964. English.

Czechoslovak Society of Arts and Sciences in America Los Angeles Chapter. SVU Bulletin, Van Nuys, CA. Frequency varies: 1971-1979. English.

Czechoslovak Society of Arts and Sciences in America. Zprávy SVU (News of SVU), New York, NY. Monthly: 1960, 1962-1979.

Czechoslovak Sources and Documents, New York, NY. Quarterly: 1943. English.

The Czechoslovak Specialist (The Czechoslovak Philatelic Society of North America), Chicago, IL. Monthly: 1947, 1963. English.

Demokracie a Socialismus (Democracy and Socialism), London, England. 1954-1955.

Doklady a Rozpravy (Facts and Conversations), London, England. 1953, 1956.

Domácnost (The Household), Milwaukee, WI. Semi-weekly, weekly: 1891-1892. (Microfilm: 1883, 1885, 1897-1905, 1908-1930).

Duch Času (Spirit of the Times), Chicago, IL. Weekly: 1890-1891, 1904-1905, 1909-1910, 1916-1917, 1925-1927, 1930-1933, 1942-1945. (Microfilm 1892-1903, 1912-1916, 1918, 1920-1939).

Frankfurtský Kurýr (Frankfurt Courier), Frankfurt am Main, West Germany. Monthly: 1971-1972.

Fraternal Herald; Bratrský Věstník (Western Bohemian Fraternal Association), Omaha, NE. Monthly: 1952-date. Includes English.

Hlas Československa (Voice of Czechoslovakia), New York, NY (previously published in Washington, DC). Monthly: 1951-1952, 1955.

Hlas Jednoty (Voice of Unity; official organ of the Unity of Czech Ladies and Men), Berwyn, IL. Monthly: 1952, 1954, 1972. Includes English.

Hlas; Kalendář pro České Katolíky v Americe (The Voice; Calendar for Czech Catholics in America), St. Louis, MO. Annual: 1917, 1919, 1922, 1928-1932.

Hlas Nových (Voice of the Newcomers), Toronto, Ontario, Canada. Semi-monthly: 1970-1973.

Hlasatel Kalendář (The Herald Almanac), Chicago, IL. Annual: 1910, 1918, 1921, 1924-1926, 1928, 1930-1967.

Hlídka (Guard Watch), Chicago, IL. Monthly: 1920-1922.

Horkého Národní Kalendář (National Calendar of Horky), New York, NY. Annual: 1917, 1919.

Hospodář (Farmer), West, TX (previously published in Omaha, NE). Semi-monthly: 1894, 1896-1903, 1905, 1907-1914, 1916-1939, 1941-1947, 1949-1982.

Husův Lid (People of Hus), Chicago, IL. Monthly: 1940-1941, 1947-1965.

Jednou za Čas (Once in a While; Bohemia Arts Club of Chicago), Chicago, IL. Frequency varies: 1925.

Kalendář Československého Světa (Calendar of the Czechoslovak World), Prague, Czechoslovakia. Annual: 1973-1977, 1981.

Kalendář Povídkář (Calendar of Stories), Chicago, IL. Annual: 1941-1943, 1960-1962.

Kalendář Vlast (Calendar of the Homeland), Berwyn, IL. Annual: 1947-1948.

Kanadské Listy (Canadian Journal), Toronto, Ontario, Canada. Monthly: 1974-1975, 1977.

Katolický Dělník (Catholic Workman), Dodge, NE. Monthly: 1948. Includes English.

Knihovna Americká (American Library), Omaha, NE. Semi-monthly: 1895-1898.

Krajanský Kalendář (Countrymen's Calendar), Prague, Czechoslovakia. Annual: 1965, 1970-1971.

Křestánská Demokracie Zprávy (Czech Christian Democratic Movement Bulletin), New York, NY. Bi-monthly: 1954, 1956. Includes English.

Křestanské Listy a Husův Lid (Christian Journal and the People of Hus), Chicago, IL. Monthly: 1959-1965.

Květy Americké (American Flowers), Omaha, NE. Semi-monthly: 1885-1887.

Listy (Journal), Rome, Italy. Monthly: 1971-1972.

Malé Noviny (Brief News), Washington, DC. Frequency varies: 1971.

Maria; Kalendář pro Lid Katolický (Maria; Calendar for Catholics), New York, NY. Annual: 1903, 1906, 1909, 1911.

Mladá Republikánská Generace v Exilu (Czechoslovak Young Republican Generation in Exile), Hamilton, Ontario, Canada. 1954.

Mladé Proudy (Small Streams), Stuttgart, West Germany (previously published in London, England). Monthly: 1949-1950.

Modrá Revue (Blue Review), Rotterdam, The Netherlands. Monthly: 1955-1958, 1961.

Moravan (The Moravian), Chicago, IL. Monthly: 1955-1959.

Moravský Den (Moravian Day), Chicago, IL. Annual: 1945, 1947, 1949-1950, 1953-1954, 1958-1959, 1963, 1969-1970, 1972, 1974.

Most (All American Czechoslovak Monthly), Chicago, IL. Monthly: 1931. Includes English.

Národ (The Nation), London, England. Monthly: 1951.

Národ; Česko-Americký Katolický Kalendář (The Nation; Czech American Catholic Calendar; previously titled **Katolik Kalendář**), Chicago, IL. Annual: 1895, 1908, 1915-1918, 1921-1922, 1924-1927, 1929-1974.

Národní Demokrat (National Democrat), Berwyn, IL. Monthly: 1954.

Národní Střed (National Center), Washington, DC. Quarterly: 1956-1957.

Náš Směr (Our Direction), New York, NY. Bi-monthly: 1952-1953.

Naše Cesta (Our Path), Vienna, Austria (previously published in Paris, France). Frequency varies: 1952, 1954-1955.

Naše Dějiny (Our History), Hallettsville, TX. Bi-monthly: 1986-date. English.

Naše Hlasy Kalendář (Our Voices Calendar), Toronto, Ontario, Canada. Annual: 1974.

Naše Snahy (Our Trends), Chicago, IL. Bi-monthly: 1965, 1971-1972, 1975-1976. One 1975 issue in English.

Naši v Holandsku (Our People in Holland), Rotterdam, Holland. Monthly: 1954-1955.

News Flashes from Czechoslovakia Under Nazi Domination, Chicago, IL. Weekly: 1940-1946. English.

Nová Éra (The New Era), New York, NY. Weekly: 1915-1916.

Nové Obzory (New Horizons), New York, NY. Bi-monthly: 1953.

Novina (News), Cleveland, OH (previously published in Paris, France; Chicago, IL; and Northbrook, IL). Frequency varies: 1949-1950, 1965, 1967, 1972-1973. Includes some French and English.

Nový Život (New Life), Rome, Italy. Monthly: 1955-1956, 1958-1959, 1961-1962, 1964-1966, 1968.

Obrana Narodny Kalendář (The People's Defense Almanac), Scranton, PA. Annual: 1922.

Odborář (Union Man; supplement of the Revue Syndicale Tchecoslovaque), New York, NY/Paris, France. 1959.

Orel (Eagle), Chicago, IL. Monthly: 1954-1955, 1957.

Osvobozeni (Liberation), London, England. 1953, 1956.

Our Gardens; Naše Zahrádky, Berwyn, IL. Monthly: 1972. Includes English.

Palachův Hlasatel (The Palach Herald), Toronto, Ontario, Canada. Monthly: 1973-1978.

Památník Osady Sv. Prokopa (Memorial of the Community of St. Procopius; St. Procopius Roman Catholic Church), Chicago, IL. Annual: 1910, 1915-1916.

Pečírkův; Národní Kalendář (National Calendar of [Dr. Jaromir] Pecirka), Prague, Czechoslovakia. Annual: 1924, 1927-1928.

Perspektivy (Perspectives), New York, NY. Irregular: 1961-1962.

Pionýr; Česko-Americký Kalendář (Pioneer; Czech American Calendar), Omaha, NE. Annual: 1917-1918.

Pokrok (Progress), Berwyn, IL. Monthly: 1960-1961, 1963; one undated issue.

Posel (The Messenger; Czech Catholic Union), Cleveland, OH. Quarterly: 1950-1959, 1962-1976, 1978. Includes English.

Pravda (The Truth), Berwyn, IL. Monthly: 1928.

Pravda a Slavná Naděje (Truth and Glorious Hope), Chicago, IL. Monthly: 1930, 1961, 1967, 1969. Includes Slovak.

Přítel Dítek; Časopis pro Česko-Americkou Mládež a Přátele Její (The Children's Friend; Magazine for Czech-American Youth and Their Friends), Chicago, IL. Weekly: 1945-1947.

The Procopian (St. Procopius College), Lisle, IL. Annual: 1932-1933. English.

The Procopian (St. Procopius Club), Chicago, IL. Monthly: 1923. Includes English.

Proměny (Metamorphoses), New York, NY. Quarterly: 1964-1974, 1976-1980. Includes Slovak.

Reflektor (Reflector), Chicago, IL. Monthly: 1946-1947. Includes some English.

Rencontres; Revue Litteraire (Encounters; Literary Review), Paris, France. Quarterly: 1962-1965. French.

Rieger (Rieger [Political] Clubs in the United States), Berwyn, IL. Monthly: 1919, 1938-1941.

Ročenka Amerických Dělnických Listů (Yearbook of American Workers Journal), Cleveland, OH. Annual: 1927.

Rodina (The Family), Racine, WI. Weekly: 1885-1890, 1892-1894, 1906-1907.

Rozpravy (Conversations), Brussels, Belgium. Monthly: 1951-1953. Includes some French and English.

SVU Publications Occasional Papers (Czechoslovakia Society of Arts and Science in America), Washington, DC. Annual: 1976-1978. Includes English.

Sborník Bohemia (Bohemia Almanac), Cologne-Ehrenfeld, West Germany. Monthly: 1957, 1960.

Sborník Sokolský; Kalendář (Sokol Almanac; Calendar), Kolín, Bohemia. Annual: 1891, 1893-1895.

Sdruženi Českých Výpomocných Spolku v Chicagu Věstník (League of Helping Societies in Chicago Bulletin), Chicago, IL. 1918 (?).

Severův Český Kalendář a Domácí Lékař (Czech Calendar of [Václav] Severa and Family Doctor), Cedar Rapids, IA. Annual: 1917.

Sklizeň: Nezávislá Kulturní Revue (Harvest: Independent Cultural Review), Hamburg, West Germany. Monthly: 1953-1962, 1964-1965.

Sklizeň Svobodné Tvorby: Sborník (The Harvest of Free Literary Work), Norman, OK. 1959.

Skutečnost (Reality), Geneva, Switzerland. Monthly: 1949-1954.

Slovo (The Word), St. Paul, MN. Monthly: 1976-date. English.

Sokol Americký (American Sokol), Berwyn, IL. Monthly: 1964. English.

Sokol Detroit News, Detroit, MI. Monthly (?): 1961. English.

Sokol San Francisco Bulletin (previously titled San Francisco Sokolský Věstník), San Francisco, CA. Quarterly: 1963-1967. Includes English.

Sokolská Župa Serverovýchodní Věstník (Northeastern District, American Sokol Union Bulletin), Bedford, OH. Monthly: 1949-1951. Includes English.

Sokolský Věstník (Sokol Bulletin), San Mateo, CA. Monthly: 1974. Includes English.

Studie (Studies), Rome, Italy. Frequency varies: 1960, 1966, 1968-1969.

Svatá Rodina; Kalendář pro Lid Katolický (Holy Family; Calendar for Catholics), New York, NY. Annual: 1902.

Svědectví (Testimony), New York, NY-Paris, France. Quarterly: 1956-1960, 1962-1966. Includes Slovak.

Svobodná Škola (Free Thinking School), Oak Park, IL. Monthly (bi-monthly and weekly): 1911-1917, 1919-1926, 1939-1940, 1942-1943, 1947-1948, 1950.

Svobodné Československo (Free Czechoslovakia; succeeded by Věk Rozumu), Chicago, IL. Monthly: 1939-1968, 1972-1977.

Svojan (Myself; Freethinkers Community of Chicago), Chicago, IL. Monthly: 1894-1920, 1922-1924.

Tribuna (Tribune), Chicago, IL. Monthly: 1967.

Věk Rozumu (Age of Reason), Berwyn, IL. Monthly (bi-monthly during July and August): 1977-1978, 1981-date.

Velký Národní Kalendář pro Čas a Věčnost (Great National Calendar for Time and Eternity), New York, NY. Annual: 1904-1905.

Věstník (Herald; official organ of the Bohemian Roman Catholic First Central Union in the United States), Chicago, IL. Monthly: 1917.

Věstník (Herald; Czechoslovak National Council of America), Cicero, IL. Monthly: 1958-date.

Věstník (Herald; Official Organ of the Slavonic Benelovent Order of the State of Texas), West, TX. Weekly: 1979-date. Includes English.

Věstník Česko-Americké Jednoty (Herald of the Česko-Americka Jednota), Lyons, IL. Monthly: 1930, 1936-1939. Includes English.

Věstník; Československých Spolků v Montreale (Herald; Czechoslovak Societies in Montreal), Montreal, Quebec, Canada. 1968.

Vezmi a Čti (Take and Read), Chicago, IL. Quarterly: 1914-1917.

Vinice (The Vineyard), Winnipeg, Manitoba, Canada. Five times a year: 1962-1964, 1966.

The Voice of Freedom (supplement to Revoluční Výzva), New York, NY. Monthly: 1916. English.

Volné Listy (Freedom Pages), Brooklyn, NY. Monthly: 1906. (Photocopy).

Všedělnický Kalendář (All Labor Calendar), Chicago, IL. Annual: 1910-1911, 1921, 1927-1928.

Vůdce (Leader; Order of Czech Benedictines), Chicago, IL. Monthly: 1926-1927, 1942-1950, 1952-1966.

Zábavné Listy (Entertainment Pages), Cleveland, OH. Semi-monthly: 1897-1898.

Zápisník (Notebook), New York, NY. Bi-monthly: 1958-1962.

Zprávda o Československu (Report about Czechoslovakia), New York, NY. Monthly (semi-monthly): 1950-1953.

Zpravodaj (Reporter; Alliance of Czechoslovak Exiles in Chicago), Chicago, IL. Monthly: 1959-1962, 1965-1966, 1969-1975.

Zpravodaj (Reporter; Bulletin of the Council of Free Czechoslovakia), Washington, DC. Monthly: 1949-1951.

Zpravodaj Čechů a Slováků ve Švýcarsku (Reporter of Czechs and Slovaks in Switzerland), Zurich, Switzerland. Semi-monthly: 1971.

Zpravodaj (Reporter; Central Czech National Alliance in America), Chicago, IL. Monthly: 1943.

Zvon (Bell), New Rochelle, NY. Monthly: 1972-1977.

Estonian American Collection

Manuscript Collection

**Estonian Association of Minnesota
(Minnesota Eesti Selts) (Minneapolis).**
Records, ca. 1955-1978. Ca. 1 linear ft.

Records of the Association contain
organizational and commemorative material
from the Association and its Estonian
House (Eesti Maja) in Minneapolis, MN.
Also included is information on the
Estonian House in Chicago, IL. *Includes
English.*

Monographs

The Estonian American monograph collection, comprising ca. 165 volumes, reflects
two distinct phases of immigration to the United States. The collection is especially
strong in materials relating to organizational activities that mirror the cultural and social
needs of the post-World War II Estonian communities. Many of these items relate to
specific, significant events such as World Congresses, regional festivals, and scouting
jamborees. The collection contains comparatively little on the earlier phase of Estonian
immigration, occurring around the turn of the century.

The IHRC holds no comprehensive bibliography of the Estonian immigrant
experience in the United States. Marju Parming and Tõnu Parming's *A Bibliography of
English Language Sources on Estonia* (1974) deals with published material on Estonia
itself and the Estonian diaspora throughout the world. The same is true of J. Balys and
Uno Teemant's *Estonian Bibliographies: A Selected List*, a listing of bibliographies that
appears in *Lituanus* (Fall 1973), found in the Lithuanian American serials collection.
The Estonians in America 1627-1975: A Chronology and Fact Book, by Jann Pennar et
al. (1975), includes a brief bibliographical essay that essentially refers the researcher to
Estonian American periodicals.

The Estonians in America 1627-1975 is the only general history of Estonian
Americans in the monograph collection. A brief historical and sociological analysis of

the pre-World War II community can be found in Joseph Roucek's "The American Estonians," in Francis Brown and Joseph Roucek's *One America* (1952), shelved in the general collection. Another brief history of the Estonians in America can be found in *Uue Ilma Juubeli Album 1909-1934*, a twenty-fifth anniversary album of the Estonian American Communist newspaper *Uus Ilm*. T. Parming's essay, *The Estonian-American Workers Movement* (ca. 1976) also contains information on early Estonian migration.

The bulk of the collection contains publications relating to the organizational life of post-World War II Estonian Americans. These consist of materials published by national and regional associations that fostei .d the associational life of Estonian American communities. The collection contains a number of Estonian Association anniversary booklets like *Long Islandi Eesti Selts XV* (Long Island's Estonian Association, 1967?) and *20 Aastat Connecticuti Eesti Seltsi 1950-1970* (Twenty Years of Connecticut's Estonian Association, 1970). The monograph collection also contains numerous jubilee albums of Lutheran churches founded by the émigrés. Typical of these are *EELK Lakewoodi Pühavaimu Kogudus 1949-1964* (Estonian Evangelical Lutheran Church [EELK] Holy Spirit Congregation in Lakewood [NJ], 1964) and *EELK Patersoni Pauluse Kogudus 1950-1970* (EELK St. Paul's Congregation of Paterson [NJ], 1970). There are no similar materials pertaining to Estonian Baptist congregations or to Estonian Greek Orthodox Catholic parishes in the collection.

Especially prominent are publications relating to Estonian international and regional festivals. The 1976 World Congress in Baltimore, Maryland, for example, is represented by numerous programs and booklets from concerts, art exhibits, and other cultural and sports events. These include *Esto '76 Kunst* (Esto '76 Art, 1976); *Muusikalised Üritused. II Ülemaailmsetel Eesti Päevadel* (Musical Events. II World Estonian Festival, 1976); and *Tuulemaa* (Land of Wind, 1976), a folk-dance instruction guide. Regional festivals are documented by programs like *Lääneranniku Eestlased* (West Coast Estonians, 1959), *Kesklääne Eestlaste Suvepäevad* (Midwest Estonians Summer Festival, 1967), and *Idaranniku Eestlased* (East Coast Estonians, 1967). The popularity of song festivals, a tradition going back to Estonia, is reflected in monographs such as *I Eesti Laulupäev USA Idarannikul, Lakewoodis* (First Estonian Song Festival, American East Coast, in Lakewood; 1963), a program for the first nationwide music festival in 1963. Another illustration of the role of music is the Estonian Learned Society's *Estonian Music for Children's and Youth Choruses and Orchestras* (1976).

The Estonian Scouting Movement can be researched through guide books and camp newsletters from the annual jamborees as well as a general history, *Estonian Scouting 1912-1962*. Items relating to the 1967 World Jamboree in Lakewood, New Jersey, attended by Estonian Scouts from throughout the world, include *Suurlager "Koguja" Kutse* (Jamboree Gathering Call, 1967) and *Suurlager Koguja Ameerika Ajakirjanduses* (Jamboree Call in the American Press, 1967).

The collection has a large number of books dealing with Estonia's historical and political situation. Among these are *Estonians in the Free World* (1960), published by the Estonian National Council, and *Estonia: Highlights on History, Independence, and Soviet Occupation* (1964?), issued by the Estonian World Council.

The Estonian American collection is strong in the area of literature. Especially well represented is the post-World War II fiction and poetry published in Canada and Sweden and written by some of Estonia's leading writers. Among the writers are émigré novelists and poets such as Marie Under and Bernard Kangro. Publications of the Estonian Learned Society in America include Viktor Koressaar and Aleksis Rannit's *Estonian Poetry and Language: Studies in Honor of Ants Oras* (1965), a festschrift to the eminent Estonian scholar. The collection also contains Professor Oras's literary histories, *A Survey of Estonian Literature* (1957?) and *Estonian Poetry* (n.d.).

Newspapers

Eesti Post (Estonian Post), Geislingen, West Germany. Weekly: 1949-1950.

Eesti Rada (Estonian Trail), Augsburg, West Germany. Weekly: 1949-1950.

Meie Elu (Our Life), Toronto, Ontario, Canada. Weekly: 1965-date.

Pildipost (Illustrated Post), Geislingen, Germany. Weekly (?): 1949.

Uus Ilm (The New World), Monroe, NY. Weekly: 1912, 1919-1921, 1923-1927, 1930.

Vaba Eesti Sõna (Free Estonian Word), New York, NY. Weekly: 1949-date.

Vaba Eestlane (Free Estonian), Toronto, Ontario, Canada. Semi-weekly: 1952-1955, 1973-1974.

Vabadusvõitlus (The Struggle for Freedom), New York, NY. 1954.

Serials

Aja Kaja (The Echo of Time), Albany, NY. Frequency varies: 1965-1970.

Baltimore'i Eesti Organisatsioonide Bülletään (Baltimore Estonian Organizations' Bulletin), Baltimore, MD. Monthly: 1973-1977.

Eesti Ev. Luteri Usu Kiriku Teated (Estonian Evangelical Lutheran Church Newsletter), New York, NY. Monthly (?) 1950.

Eesti Kalendar (Estonian Almanac), Detmold, Germany. Annual: 1949.

Eesti Kirik (The Estonian Church), Uppsala, Sweden. Monthly: 1954-1959, 1970, 1974.

Eesti Kirik Vabaduses (Estonian Church in Freedom; Yearbook of the Estonian Evangelical Lutheran Church), Toronto, Ontario, Canada. Annual: 1958-1959.

Eesti Male (Estonian Chess), Ozone Park, NY. 1974-1975.

Eesti Seinekalendar (Estonian Wall Calendar), New York, NY. Annual: 1960, 1963.

Estonian League of the West Coast Bülletään, Vancouver, British Columbia, Canada. Frequency varies (?): 1976, 1977.

Kirikuleht (Church Newsletter), Geislingen, West Germany. Monthly: 1948-1950, 1952-1955 [supplements to Kirikuleht: Meie Lastele, 1948, 1952-1955, three undated issues; Meie Noortele, 1952-1955, three undated issues].

Kodukolle (Home Hearth), Montreal, Quebec, Canada. Monthly: 1952-1954.

Kultuuriside; Eesti Kultuurfondi Teataja (Cultural Ties; The Estonian Cultural Fund Newsletter), New York, NY. Semi-annual: 1969-1971, 1973-1974, 1976-1977.

Los Angelese Eesti Seltsi Teataja (Los Angeles's Estonian Association Newsletter), Los Angeles, CA. 1968.

Meie Elu Tähtraamat (Our Life Almanac), Toronto, Ontario, Canada. Annual: 1962-date.

Meie Tee (Our Path), New York, NY. Bi-monthly: 1935-1938, 1941-1942, 1944-1946, 1948-1979.

Minnesota Postimees (Minnesota Courier), Minneapolis, MN. Irregular: 1952-1954, 1957-1977.

Mötteid (Thoughts), Chicago, IL. Monthly and bi-monthly: 1965-1966. Includes English.

New Yorgi Eesti Ev.-Luteri Usu Kirik (The New York Estonian Evangelical Lutheran Church), New York, NY. Bi-monthly: 1952-1954.

N.Y. Eesti Filatelistide Selts Bülletään (NY Estonian Philatelist Society Bulletin), New York, NY. Bi-annual: 1971-1973, 1976, 1978-1980. Includes English.

Noorte Sõna (The Word of Youth), New York, NY. Monthly: 1957-1965, 1967, 1970-1971.

Oma Kirik (Our Church), Brooklyn, NY. Monthly: 1969, 1972.

Põhja-Ameerika IV Eesti Päevade Teataja (North American IV Estonian Festival Newsletter), New York, NY. 1968.

Põhjamaa Tähistel (On the Northland Signs; supplement to newspaper Eesti Rada), Augsburg, Germany. Weekly: 1946-1948.

Rahvuslaste (Nationalists), Islington, Ontario, Canada. Bi-monthly: 1967-1968, 1971.

Tulimuld; Eesti Kirjanduse ja Kultuuri Ajakiri (Fire and Earth; The Magazine of Estonian Literature and Culture), Lund, Sweden. Frequency varies: 1950-1960.

Ühispanga Uudised (The Co-op Bank News), Toronto, Ontario, Canada. Annual: 1957-1966, 1969, 1977.

Usk ja Elu (Faith and Life), Toronto, Ontario, Canada. Bi-monthly: 1968-1977, 1979-1982.

Usu Sõna (Word of Faith), Chicago, IL. 1950.

Uus Ilm (The New World; successor to newspaper Uus Ilm), Monroe, NY. Monthly: 1984.

Vaba Eestlase Tähtraamat (The Free Estonian's Almanac), Toronto, Ontario, Canada. Annual: 1966, 1968, 1970-1972, 1974.

Väliseestlase Kalendar (The Calendar for the Estonian Abroad), New York, NY. Annual: 1950-1979, 1982.

Viiking (Viking), Brooklyn, NY. 1961, 1966.

Viimasel Minutil (At the Last Minute), Lakewood, NJ. Three issues only for 1967 Estonian Scout Jamboree.

Võitlev Eesti (Fighting Estonia), New York, NY. Frequency varies: 1952-1954, 1956.

Finnish American Collection

Manuscript Collections

Aamunkoitto Temperance Society (Brooklyn, New York).
Records, 1887-1901. 1 microfilm reel.

Records consist of membership lists and minutes.

Ahlbeck, Karl (1881-1954).
Papers, 1978-1982. Ca. 1 linear in.

Papers of Ahlbeck consist of translations by his daughter, Lila A. (Ahlbeck) Lindgren, of his manuscript, "A Short History of the Finnish Settlement of Isabella, Minnesota." The two translations are dated 1978 and 1982; the second has documentation with it. *In English.*

Aho, John E.
Papers, 1905-1907. 1 notebook.

Papers of John E. Aho consist of an income and expense ledger for the Source of Light Temperance Society (Valon Lähdeof) of Eveleth, MN. *Includes English.*

America Letters: Etelä-Pohjanmaa, Finland.
Collection, 1890-1960. 16 microfilm reels.

Collection consists of 4,000 letters sent by Finnish immigrants in Canada and the United States to friends and family in the Etelä-Pohjanmaa area of Finland. *Inventory available. Negatives held by Turku University, Turku, Finland. Related collections: America Letters, Satakunta, Finland; America Letters, Varsinais Suomi, Finland.*

America Letters: Satakunta, Finland.
Collection, 1890-1964. 25 microfilm reels.

The collection contains 6,000 letters sent by Finnish immigrants in the United States and Canada to the Satakunta area. The letters discuss a multitude of subjects including family news, economic conditions, living and working conditions, weather, and moves in search of employment. Also included are family photographs. *Inventory available. Negatives held by Turku University, Turku, Finland. Related collections: America Letters, Etelä-Pohjanmaa, Finland; America Letters, Varsinais Suomi, Finland.*

**America Letters: Varsinais Suomi,
Finland.**
Collection, 1885-1960.   16 microfilm
reels.

The collection contains 4,000 letters
written by Finnish immigrants to relatives
and friends in the Varsinais Suomi area
of Finland.   *Inventory available.
Negatives held by Turku University,
Turku, Finland.   Related collections:
America Letters, Etelä-Pohjanmaa,
Finland; America Letters, Satakunta,
Finland.*

**Amerikan Uutiset (American News)
(New York Mills, Minnesota).**
Collection, n.d.   1 linear in.

Collection consists of manuscripts and
typescripts of articles published in
Amerikan Uutiset by George Latvala, Matt
Kantola, Paavo A. Kairanen, and Elina
Becka.

**Bethel Evangelical Lutheran Church
(Ishpeming, Michigan).**
Records, 1897-1970.   1 microfilm reel.

The Church was founded as the
Finnish Evangelical Lutheran Church of
Ishpeming and was affiliated with the
Finnish Evangelical Lutheran Church in
America, Suomi Synod.   Records of the
congregation include baptism, con-
firmation, communion, and funeral
registers.

Blomquist Family.
Collection, 1897-1987.   1 linear in.

Collection consists of a genealogy of
the Blomquist Family from St. Paul, MN.
In English.

Carlson, Curt.
Papers, 1978.   1 folder.

Papers of Carlson consist of
genealogical information on the
Haapalahti and Carlson families of
Sweden and Finland and a brief history
of Finnish migration to Sweden, Norway,
and the United States.   *In English.*

**Central Cooperative Wholesale
(Superior, Wisconsin).**
Records, ca. 1916-1962.   13 linear ft.

The organization was originally part of
the Cooperative Central Exchange, formed
in 1917.   It functioned as a marketing
and purchasing agency for farm produce.
The Exchange developed its own line of
merchandise during the 1920s, while its
membership and sales continued to grow.
In the late 1920s, however, as a result of
the split between Communist and non-
Communist members, the non-Communist
faction, which retained control, changed
the organization's name to the Central
Cooperative Wholesale.   During the
1930s, while the Cooperative prospered,
the membership and the operation became
more Americanized.   In 1956, the name
was changed to Central Cooperatives,
Inc.; it continued to operate until the
early 1960s and merged with Midland
Cooperatives in 1963.

Records include correspondence,
minutes, memoranda, district meeting
plans, reports, newspaper clippings,
pamphlets, registration lists, and a large
number of photographs.   The records
contain substantial correspondence with
and information on other cooperatives in
the area.   *In English.   Inventory available.
Related collections: Walter Harju; Edith
Koivisto.*

**Cooperative Trading Association (New
York, New York).**
Records, 1928-1930.   1 folder.

Records of the Cooperative Trading
Association consist of a membership
certificate and a stock certificate.   *In
English.*

Davis, Lionel B.
Papers, 1966-1971.   2 linear in.

Papers of Lionel B. Davis consist of a
typescript of a master's degree paper and
another college paper on Finnish
American dance music (waltzes).   Also
included is sheet music in manuscript,
with Finnish titles, of schottische dance
tunes.   *Includes English.*

Doby, Velma (Hakkila) (1923-   ).
Papers, 1975-1977. 1 linear in.

Doby was born in Brule, WI, of Finnish immigrant parents. She worked for the Peace Research Institute (Washington, DC), Wayne State University (Detroit, MI), the Minneapolis, MN, public schools, and the Immigration History Research Center. She has been active in Finnish American organizations, especially the Minnesota Finnish-American Historical Society, FinnFest U.S.A., and the Finnish genealogy section of the Minnesota Genealogy Society.

Doby's papers consist largely of college papers on Finnish Americans and Finnish American life written for classes at the University of Minnesota. Also included is a background study of Finnish American women, interviews with Mary Hakkila and Kaisa Maki, an English translation of Helmi Mattson's handwritten autobiography, a poem, and miscellaneous articles. *In English.*
Related collection: Helmi Dagmar Mattson.

Enkel, Kenneth J. (1916-   ).
Papers, 1947-1958. 8 linear in.

Enkel received his law degree in 1941 from the University of Minnesota. During the McCarthy Era he defended aliens in the Minnesota region who faced deportation under the McCarran-Walter Act. Enkel's papers consist of legal briefs, documents, and correspondence relating to deportation proceedings in the McCarthy Era with regard to the following seven persons or cases: Taisto A. Elo, Knut E. Heikkinen, Mrs. Vera Hathaway, Harry Roast, Charles Rowoldt, *Lopez-Hernandez v. Brownell,* and *Heikkila v. Barber.* The materials on the Knut Heikkinen case are incomplete. Mr. Enkel undertook these cases at the behest of the Minnesota Committee for the Protection of the Foreign Born. *In English. Inventory available.*

Erickson, Eva Helen (1912-   ).
Papers, 1929-1938. Ca. 1 linear in.

Papers consist of memoirs entitled "As a Kid in Wisconsin," along with a photograph album of the Labor Sports Union Training School (Loon Lake, MI). *In English.*

Erickson, Hilma (Bockman) (1887-1968).
Papers, 1931-1968. 2 linear ft.

Erickson was born in Merikarvia, Finland, and came to America with her brother in 1905; two of her sisters and another brother also immigrated. She worked in a boarding house and hospital in Ishpeming, MI, and married Ilmari Erickson, a miner, in 1914. In 1916, the family moved to Waukegan, IL, because Ilmari had been blacklisted for refusing to testify on behalf of the mines when a work partner was killed because of unsafe work conditions. Both Hilma and Ilmari became active members of the Workers Hall in Waukegan, and he served on the Board of Directors for the Waukegan Cooperative Trading Company. Hilma's papers consist of letters written to her daughter Eva Helen Erickson. *Includes English translations.*

Farmers Cooperative Mercantile Association (Kettle River, Minnesota).
Records, 1918-1931. 2 microfilm reels.

Records are minutes of the board of directors for 1918-1924 and 1927-1931, and financial records from 1923 and 1931.

FinnFest U.S.A. (Owatonna, Minnesota).
Records, 1982-1988. 3.5 linear ft.

FinnFest U.S.A. is a national organization that sponsors an annual celebration (of the same name) of Finnish culture in the United States. Records consist of correspondence, newspaper articles, tape recordings, publicity materials, and other items pertaining to FinnFest U.S.A. celebration. *In English.*

Finnish American League for Democracy (Fitchburg, Massachusetts).
Records, 1944-1962. 2 microfilm reels.

The League was the successor to the Finnish Socialist Federation, a language federation of the Socialist Party of America. Founded in 1940, it was modeled after Finland's Social Democratic Party and stood for parliamentary socialism.

Records include treasurer's minute books and other minute books.

Finnish American Trade Unionists (New York, New York).
Collection, 1943. 1 folder.

Collection includes conference proceedings, a pamphlet, memoranda, and correspondence relating to Finnish American activities denouncing Finland's participation as an Axis ally during World War II. *In English.*

Finnish Apostolic Lutheran Church (New York Mills, Minnesota).
Records, 1874-1977. 1 microfilm reel.

Records of the Church comprise birth, baptism, confirmation, marriage, burial, and financial records of the congregation.

Finnish Dramatic Scripts.
Collection, n.d. 1 linear in.

Collection of Finnish dramatic scripts includes the following titles: *Kostina, Ajan Laulu, Ananiaksen Ehtoollinen,* and *Kaksi Varasta.*

Finnish Evangelical Lutheran Congregation (Republic, Michigan).
Records, 1916. 1 microfilm reel.

Records of the Congregation comprise baptism, confirmation, communion, marriage, and funeral registers.

Finnish Luther Congregational Church (Milwaukee, Wisconsin).
Records, 1930-1975. Ca. 2 linear ft.

In 1930, a group of Finns in Milwaukee, WI, sought to establish their own church, the Finnish Lutheran Church of Milwaukee. In March of 1932, the congregation voted to affiliate with the Congregational denomination, and the name was changed to Finnish Luther Congregational Church. The church maintained an active congregational life and also participated in community affairs. During World War II, the church coordinated the Finnish relief effort in the Milwaukee area. In the 1960s, membership declined; the congregation was officially disbanded in 1969.

Records of the Church include minutes of the Ladies Aid; financial records; registers of baptisms, confirmations, marriages and deaths; and sermons. Also included are materials on the Finnish Relief Effort (1935-1952). *Inventory available.*

Finnish Sick and Accident and Benefit Association of Menessen, Pennsylvania and Monongahela Valley.
Records, 1927-1929. Ca. 1 linear in.

Records of the Association consist of the organization's constitution and a letter from the Finnish Evangelical Lutheran Church of America (Hibbing, MN, pastorate). *Includes English.*

Finnish Socialist Federation Chapter, Astoria, Oregon.
Records, 1912-1915. 1 folder.

The Astoria, OR, chapter of the Finnish Socialist Federation was founded in 1904. In a few years its membership numbered between three and four hundred. The club founded the socialist newspaper *Toveri*, which became one of three major newspapers of the Finnish Socialist Federation, together with *Työmies* and *Raivaaja*. The club's many activities included an active and large theater group.

The photocopies of the chapter's records consist of minutes of the board of

directors. The minutes deal mostly with
business affairs, and indirectly reflect
much of the cultural activity in the
Finnish American community at this time.
Inventory available.

**Finnish Socialist Federation Chapter,
Ely, Minnesota.**
Records, 1905-1966. 1 microfilm reel.

The organization was founded ca. 1910
as a chapter of the Finnish Socialist
Federation. In the Socialist-Communist
split of 1920, the Ely group went with
the Communists and became a chapter of
the Finnish Workers Federation.
Records consist of meeting minutes.

**Finnish Socialist Federation Chapter,
Markham, Minnesota.**
Records, 1911-1931. 1 linear ft.

The Markham, MN, chapter belonged
to the Midwestern district of the Finnish
Socialist Federation. The Federation
broke up in 1920, but some of its local
chapters, like the Markham group,
continued to carry their old name for
years after the split in the parent
organization.
Records consist of minutes of the
Markham chapter.

**Finnish Socialist Federation. National
Executive Committee (Chicago,
Illinois); Eastern District Committee
(Fitchburg, Massachusetts).**
Records, 1913-1925. 2 ledgers.

The Finnish Socialist Federation
(Suomalainen Sosialistijärjestö) was
founded in Hibbing, MN, in August of
1906. It was the first successful attempt
to unite all Finnish Socialists into one
national organization. At its peak
strength (1912-1914) it had an average
membership of 13,000 and was the
largest foreign language federation in the
Socialist Party of the United States. The
Federation was organized into three
districts: the Western, Midwestern, and
Eastern. Each had its own newspaper,
the *Toveri, Työmies,* and *Raivaaja,*
respectively. There were 273 local
chapters. The Federation broke up in

1920 over the general question of
affiliating with the Third International and
over the specific issue of whether or not
to remain in the Socialist Party of
America. The resulting reorganized
federations continued, however, to refer to
themselves as the Finnish Socialist
Federation even after their split.
Records include minutes of the Eastern
District Committee (1913-1920) and the
National Executive Committee (1915-
1925). *Inventory available.*

**Finnish Socialist Organizations--West
Coast Chapters.**
Collection, 1904-1967. 2.5 linear ft.

The collection consists of financial
records, correspondence, minutes,
membership records, stock certificates,
and playscripts from ten Finnish Socialist
organizations active in California and
Oregon. The organizations are: Berkeley
(CA) Finnish Comrade Association
(Berkeley Suomalainen Toveri Yhdistys);
Berkeley (CA) Finnish Cultural Club;
International Workers' Organization
(Berkeley, CA); the Finnish American
Historical Society; the Fort Bragg (CA)
Toveri Club; the Portland, OR, Finnish
Comrade Association (Toveri Yhdistys);
the Rocklin (CA) Labor Temple
Association; the Socialist Party of
America (West Berkeley, CA); the Toveri
Yhdistys (West Berkeley, CA); and the
West Berkeley Finnish Socialist Chapter
(West Berkeley [CA] Suomalainen
Sosialisti Osasto). *Includes English.
Inventory available.*

**Finnish Workers' Federation of the
United States (New York, New
York).**
Records, ca. 1910-1967. 1.5 linear ft.

The Finnish Workers' Federation of
the United States was organized in 1927
and incorporated in New York City in
1932. It was the political, cultural, and
educational organization of the Finnish
American Communists and actively
supported militant labor unions, farmers'
organizations, the cooperative movement,
and the unemployed movement. In 1941,
the Federation joined the International
Workers' Order as the Finnish American

Mutual Aid Society. When the IWO was dissolved in the early 1950s, Federation activity continued under leadership of district committees.

Records of the Federation include minutes, corporate documents, correspondence, financial records, and reference material. Also included are constitutions and bylaws of Finnish associations in Illinois, a commemorative scrapbook of the Finnish People's Democratic Organizations, correspondence regarding the deportation of William Lahtinen, financial statements of the Pacific Development Society (Astoria, OR) and of the People's Voice Cooperative Publishing Company (New York Mills, MN), and various Socialist Party publications. *Includes English. Inventory available.*

Finnish Workers' Society "Kehitys" Archive (Cloquet, Minnesota).

Records, 1911-1939. 4 microfilm reels.

The Finnish Workers' Society "Kehitys" of Cloquet, MN, was founded in 1903 and in 1906 joined the Socialist Party and the Finnish Socialist Federation. During the 1914 Socialist-Industrial Workers of the World schism the group withdrew from all national organizations and became an independent workers' society. Although both "Wobblies" and Socialists participated in its activities, the group was never part of the IWW.

Records of the Society consist of financial records, minutes, membership lists, and play scripts.

Fitchburg, Massachusetts, Finnish Evangelical Mission Church (Fitchburgin Lähetysseurakunnan Arkisto).

Records, 1892-1909. 1 ledger (1 microfilm reel).

The Fitchburg, MA, Finnish Evangelical Mission Church was associated with the Massachusetts Congregational Conference. In 1960, the church changed its name to Elm Street Congregational Church. Records consist of the church's baptism register. *In English.*

Gardner, Massachusetts, Finnish Socialist Chapter Archive.

Records, 1905-1966. 4 microfilm reels.

The Gardner, MA, Finnish Socialist Chapter was founded in 1905 as an independent workers' club. Shortly thereafter, it joined the Finnish American Workers' League, Imatra, a short-lived nationwide movement patterned after the Imatra Society of New York. The League promoted mutual aid and cultural activities. The Gardner group left the Imatra League in 1906, joined the Socialist Party, and became a Finnish Socialist chapter. The Gardner chapter included a drama society, band, choir, lending library, sewing circle, young people's league, and gymnastics group.

Records of the chapter consist of chapter minutes and minutes of the chapter's suborganizations. *Inventory available (in Finnish).*

Halonen, Arne.

Papers, 1939-1986. 2 linear in.

Papers of Halonen comprise newspaper clippings pertaining to him and his wife, Irene; the Finnish Relief Drive in Minnesota; and Finnish organizational activities in Minnesota and California; along with clippings of a newspaper column written by Halonen. Also included are a booklet he wrote, entitled "Minnesota's Help to Finland," and photographs of him and a Minneapolis choral group directed by Irene Halonen. *Includes English.*

Harju, Earl M.

Papers, ca. 1960-1986. Ca. 1 linear in.

Papers of Harju, a journalist, comprise personal and general correspondence; photocopies of his articles in *Between Ourselves*, the *San Francisco Chronicle*, and *People's World*; newspaper clippings; and telegrams congratulating Walter A. Harju on his sixtieth birthday. Subjects include the Spanish Civil War, Jack London Club, Finns in California, and American-Soviet Friendship Society. *In English.*

Harju, Walter A. (1900-).
Papers, ca. 1929-1973. 1.5 linear ft. and 17 tapes.

A writer, carpenter, and historian, Harju was born in Brown County, SD. During the 1930s, he was employed by the WPA Federal Writers' Program; his *History of Meeker County, Minnesota* and *History of Wright County, Minnesota* were based upon studies begun while he worked for the WPA. He wrote many articles on the Finns in America and Minnesota, on cooperativism, particularly the left-wing faction, and on trade unionism. He wrote under the pseudonymns "John Carpenter" and "Vincent Ignatius" as well as his own name. Harju worked for the Cooperative Central Exchange (later the Central Cooperative Wholesale) in Superior, WI, served as California correspondent for the *Työmies-Eteenpäin* (Superior, WI), and was active in the Centennial of Finnish Immigration (1963-1964) and the Fiftieth Anniversary of Finnish Independence (1967). He also collected numerous oral histories of Finnish American "pioneers" who describe their early days in the United States.

Papers include correspondence, speeches, articles, photographs of early Finnish American social life in California, oral histories, newspaper clippings, an autobiography of Henry Ahlgren, and letters to editors. Included is information by or about the Cooperative Central Exchange, cooperatives, *Työmies-Eteenpäin*, the Workers and Farmers Cooperative Unity Alliance (Superior, WI), and other persons and organizations. *Mainly in English. Inventory available. Related collections: Central Cooperative Wholesale.*

Heikkila, William (1906-1960).
Papers, ca. 1947-1962. Ca. 3 linear ft.

William Heikkila was born in Vihti, Finland. His father was a Finnish citizen residing in Minnesota and his mother, a native of Finland, was a naturalized American citizen. Heikkila lived in the United States but was never naturalized. For this reason and because of his activities in the Communist Party during the 1930s, deportation proceedings were instituted against him in 1947. The trials and appeals continued until 1958, but in the end he remained in the United States.

His papers consist of legal files relating to his deportation case and press clippings about the case. *In English. Inventory available. Related collection: Kenneth J. Enkel.*

Hibbing Finnish Workers' Club (Minnesota).
Records. 1935-1974. 2 linear in.

Records of the Club consist of minutes and a ledger of accounts. *Includes English.*

Hippaka, Lembi.
Papers, n.d. 1 linear ft.

Papers of Hippaka, a second generation Finnish American, consist of three scrapbooks containing articles on Finland and the Finns, Hippaka's travelogue of her first trip to Finland in 1937, the Delaware Tercentenary Celebration of the Swedes and Finns in Delaware (1939), and the Russo-Finnish War of 1939-1940. *In English.*

Holy Trinity Lutheran Church (Hibbing, Minnesota).
Records, 1901-1936. 1 microfilm reel.

Founded as the Hibbing Finnish Evangelical Lutheran Church, the church's name was soon changed to Holy Trinity Lutheran Church. The congregation was independent of any national Lutheran synods.

Records of the Church include baptism, confirmation, communion, marriage, and funeral registers.

Hurula, Kaisa Maria.
Papers, ca. 1890. Ca. 1 linear in.

Hurula was born in Karunki, Finland. Papers consist of a brief recollection of her first day in church in America. *Includes English translation.*

Idän Uutiset (Eastern News) Publishing Company (Fitchburg, Massachusetts).
Records, 1896-1899. 1 microfilm reel.

During its formation, the publishing company of the early Finnish American newspaper *Idän Uutiset* was referred to in its minutes as both the National Publishing Company and the Finnish Newspaper Company. In 1897, it became known as the *Idän Uutiset* Publishing Company.

Records consist of proceedings of the board of directors and monthly meetings of the newspaper staff. Minutes also document the formation of the Finland-Swedish publication *Finska Amerikanaren* (now *The Norden*).

Imatra Society (Brooklyn, New York).
Records, 1896-1961. 9 microfilm reels.

The Society was a Finnish American social club founded in 1890 in New York City. It provided mutual aid for its members and sponsored social and cultural activities such as dances, plays, lectures, concerts, and picnics. The Society had its own hall, which housed a theater, gymnasium, restaurant, pool hall, reading room, bar, and sauna. Subgroups of the Society included a band, choir, theatrical group, and folk dancing ensemble.

Records of the Society consist of proceedings, membership lists, and publications. *Inventory available in Finnish.*

Jackson, Alex.
Papers, n.d. (ca. 1910). 2 linear in.

Papers of Alex Jackson consist of a manuscript of his novel, "Viuluni Itkee."

Järven Kukka Temperance Society (Sparta and Gilbert, Minnesota).
Records, 1897-1921. 9 ledgers.

Formed in 1897 in Sparta, MN, the Society was transferred in 1909 to Gilbert, MN, when the town of Sparta was moved to allow development of new iron ore mines. In 1898, the Society built its own hall in Sparta; the Society also built a hall in Gilbert. By 1921, debts had forced the Society to give up its assets, and it apparently ceased to exist at about that time.

Records include minutes, membership lists, and account books. *Inventory available.*

Jokinen, Walfrid J. (1915-1970).
Papers, ca. 1952-1964. Ca. 1.5 linear ft.

A college professor and historian, Jokinen was born in Hibbing, MN, of Finnish immigrants. After graduating from high school, he worked as a reporter for *Industrialisti* (Duluth, MN). He served in the Air Force from 1942 to 1946, then attended the University of Minnesota. He received his PhD from Louisiana State University in 1955; subsequently, he taught there and became chairman of the Sociology Department and assistant dean of the graduate school. Jokinen's great interest was the Finns. He was contributing editor to H. R. Wasastjerna's *Minnesotan Suomalaisten Historia* (History of the Finns in Minnesota), which he had intended to revise and translate, using material from his own doctoral dissertation.

Jokinen's papers consist of biographical material; correspondence mainly regarding translation of Wasastjerna's book and disputes about it; a manuscript, "The Finns in Minnesota: A Social History"; and research reports. *Includes English. Inventory available. Related collections: Alex Kyykhynen.*

Kajastus Finnish Laborers' Association (Milford, New Hampshire).
Records, 1913-1966. Ca. 1 linear in.

The Kajastus Finnish Laborers' Association (Milford, NH) was founded in 1908 to promote socialism and educational and spiritual development of Finnish workers in the area. The Association joined the Finnish Socialist Federation and the American Socialist Party. During the 1920 split within the Finnish Socialist Federation, the Association also split; the left-wing faction went to the Finnish Socialist Federation, and the right wing remained in the Finnish Federation of the American Socialist Party. A few years later, the

Kajastus Association joined the Finnish American League for Democracy.

Records of the Kajastus Association comprise the official papers and bylaws; and clippings and articles on New England Finnish Americans. *Includes English. Inventory available.*

Kaleva, Nuoriso Chapter (Ely, Minnesota).
Records, 1937-1944. 1 folder.

Records of this Finnish American young people's organization include minutes and miscellaneous memoranda. Material of the Junior Kaleva Lodge is also included. *Includes English. Inventory available.*

Kantola, Matt.
Papers, 1978. 1 folder.

Papers of Kantola, of Lake Worth, FL, consist of a letter and a poem.

Karni, Ina (Laukala).
Papers, ca. 1904, 1978. 1 linear in.

Papers of Karni comprise a typescript family history, two ledgers of the Finnish Day Committee, and miscellaneous items. *Includes English.*

Kätkä, Terttu.
Papers, 1950-1976. 1 linear ft.

Papers of author and poet Kätkä include two novels, poetry, and articles from magazines and newspapers.

Kattainen, Adam.
Papers, ca. 1930-1935. 1 linear in.

Papers of Kattainen, a Finnish American temperance advocate, consist of poems and speeches. Also included are minutes (1942-1943) of the Alango-Field, MN, Red Cross Chapter.

Kendall, Erick.
Papers, 1950. 2 linear in.

Papers of Kendall, one of the leading second generation figures in the Finnish

American Cooperative movement, consist of an autobiographical work in manuscript entitled "We Conquered Communism," which concerns the Cooperative-Communist split. *In English. Restricted.*

Ketonen, John E.
Papers, 1975. 2 linear in.

Papers of Ketonen consist of a manuscript of his book, *Finnish American Horizons.* The material consists of more than one hundred short articles, poems, songs, reminiscences, and biographies of Finnish Americans. *In English. Inventory available.*

Klemi, A. L. (1874-1924).
Papers, ca. 1977-1980. 3 music scores.

Klemi was born in Iitti, Finland. He received musical training early in life and attended three years of college. After college, he worked as a railroad telegrapher and station master in Russia and Finland, and he composed several musical pieces. He subsequently immigrated to the United States where he continued to compose music. He also worked as a translator at Ellis Island and as a motorman-conductor for a trolley line and later worked in a music store.

Klemi's papers consist of music scores. *In English.*

Koivisto, Edith (Laine) (1888-1981).
Papers, 1903-1981. 12 linear ft.

Koivisto was born in Kuusankoski, Finland, and immigrated to Spokane, WA, in 1910. In 1912, she moved to Smithville, MN, where she worked at and attended Työväen Opisto (Work People's College). In 1913, she married Arvid Koivisto (d. 1964); they lived in Duluth, MN, and Quincy, MA, before settling in Hibbing, MN, where Arvid worked for the Hibbing Co-op and Central Cooperative Wholesale. In Hibbing, Edith was active in numerous choral and theatrical groups. She also published articles frequently in the Hibbing newspapers and wrote numerous plays in Finnish and English as well as histories of Finnish Americans in the Hibbing area.

She remained deeply involved in cultural activities of the Hibbing area until her death.

Papers include biographical material on her and other Finnish Americans in Minnesota, art materials, diaries, creative works such as plays and newspaper articles, historical works and research notes, photographs, scrapbooks, and material relating to her activities in Finnish American organizations. Also included are records of and other information on the Finnish-American Historical Society, the Northern Minnesota Finnish Midsummer Festival, the Sovinto, Tapio and Totuuden Etsijä temperance societies (Hibbing, MN), the Work People's College (Työväen Opisto), Ladies of Kaleva, Central Cooperative Wholesale (Superior, WI), Hibbing Art Center, and other cultural groups in the Hibbing area. Also included are correspondence and other papers of Arvid Koivisto and of the Koivistos' daughter Armida (Koivisto) Caird (1922-1972). A supplement, donated by Armida Caird's family, continues many series described in the original collection. *Includes English. Inventory available. Related collection: Minnesota Finnish American Family Histories.*

Koivulehto, Lauri.
Papers, n.d. 1 linear in.

Papers of Koivulehto consist of newspaper clipings of an article by Koivulehto on frontier life in Minnesota.

Korhonen, John P. (1874-1958).
Papers, 1906-1958. 1 linear in.

Papers of Korhonen consist of photographs, correspondence, mortgages, stocks, and a declaration of intent for American citizenship. Also included is a funeral memorial folder for Korhonen. *Includes English.*

Koski, Ernest Theodore (1908-1989).
Papers, ca. 1950-1983. 2 linear in.

Papers of Koski consist of a scrapbook containing newspaper clippings, correspondence, photographs, and

memorabilia. Included is a series of articles entitled "Juuret Suomessa Elämä Amerikassa" (Finnish Roots--American Life) which Koski wrote for *Työmies-Eteenpäin* (1982-1983) and material on the Työmies Society and *Työmies-Eteenpäin*. *Related collection: Minnnesota Finnish American Family Histories.*

Koski, Henry Gust.
Papers, 1980. Ca. 1 linear in.

Papers consist of a typed manuscript describing Finnish American pioneer life in northern Idaho.

Kyyhkynen, Alex (1888-1984).
Papers, ca. 1940s-1970s. Ca. 18 linear ft.

Kyyhkynen was born in Kemijärvi, Finland. In 1910, he immigrated to Duluth, MN, where he opened the Dove Clothing Store and became active in Finnish American organizations. He was a founder and president of the Minnesota Finnish-American Historical Society and a member of the Finnish American fraternity Kaleva Lodge and the Messiah Lutheran Church (Duluth). He also served as Finnish consul for northern Minnesota and was given the First Class Knight of the White Rose Order of Finland in 1965.

Kyyhkynen's papers consist of personal material and records of Finnish American organizations in Minnesota, particularly the Minnesota Finnish-American Historical Society. *Includes English. Inventory available. Related collection: Walfrid Jokinen; Edith Koivisto; Minnesota Finnish American Family Histories.*

Lahtinen, William.
Papers, 1954-1967. 6 linear in.

Papers of Lahtinen, a political activist, consist of testimony and transcripts from his deportation trial. *In English.*

Miners from the Mesabi Range, northern Minnesota, 1908.

Finnish American student participants in the Central Cooperative Wholesale's co-op courses, Superior, WI, 1924.

Laurila, Emil.
Papers, 1935-1940. Ca. 1 linear in.

Papers of Laurila consist of farm
records, correspondence, and photographs
of a pioneer homestead farm near
Markham, MN. Correspondents include
John E. Aho. *Includes English.*

Lehtinen, Kaarle Hjalmar.
Papers, ca. 1924-1955. 6 linear in.

Papers of Lehtinen consist primarily of
correspondence to him from the Wayne
Produce Association and the Fairfield
Cooperative Farm Association
(Suomalainen Osuusfarmi) of Jesup, GA,
as well as from friends in the Jesup area.
Also included are photographs, postcards,
and miscellaneous printed material.

Lipponen, Maija.
Papers, ca. 1964-1968. 2.5 linear in.

Lipponen was a Minnesota Finnish
radical activist who spent her retirement
in Lake Worth, FL. Her papers consist
of three scrapbooks containing typescripts,
newspaper clippings of her poems, and
newspaper clippings of articles (some by
Lipponen) about the Finnish Workers'
Education Club (Lake Worth, FL) and
other radical Finnish interests and
activities.

Luoma, Frank O.
Papers, 1985. Ca. 1 linear in.

Papers of Luoma consist of a
handwritten history of the Finnish people
of Wawina Township, MN. *In English.*

Mäkelä, Oscar.
Papers, 1906. Ca. 1 linear in.

Papers of Mäkelä consist of a
notebook of poetry and popular songs,
some by Mäkelä himself.

Mäkelä, Reino (1915-1977).
Papers, 1958-1981. Ca. 1 linear in.

Mäkelä was born in Ishpeming, MI,
the son of immigrant parents. In 1931,
the entire family migrated to Karelia in
the Soviet Union, where Reino married
and worked most of his life as a
lumberjack. Several family members,
including Reino's youngest brother and
his father-in-law, were imprisoned during
the Russo-Finnish conflict of 1939-1940.
Mäkelä's papers consist of letters he
wrote to Eva Helen Erickson. *In English.*

Maki, Aino (1905-   ).
Papers, 1920-1973. 1 linear in.

Papers of Maki consist of photographs
of key figures in the Cooperative Central
Exchange (later the Central Cooperative
Wholesale) of Superior, WI, as well as
cooperative training classes from the
1920s and 1930s. Also included is an
addition to Maki's family history, which
is part of the Minnesota Finnish
American Family Histories collection. *In
English. Related collection: Central
Cooperative Wholesale; Minnesota Finnish
American Family Histories.*

Matsen, William.
Papers, 1985. Ca. 1 linear in.

Papers of William Matsen consist of a
typescript of the William Matsen family
history entitled "And the Last Shall Be
First." *In English.*

**Mattson, Helmi Dagmar (Lampila)
(1890-1974).**
Papers, 1916-1974. 3 linear ft.

An author and journalist, Mattson was
born in Multia, Finland. She immigrated
to Canada in 1911 and married William
Mattson in 1913. The couple became
U.S. citizens in 1914 and lived at various
times in Minnesota, New York, and
Oregon. From her arrival in the United
States, Helmi was a prolific contributor of
poetry, articles, and serialized novels to
the *Toveritar* newspaper. She also took
an active interest in Finnish American
theater and wrote full-length plays. In
spring 1920, she became editor of the
Toveritar, a position she held for ten
years. In later years, she was a frequent
contributor of articles and poetry to the
Työmies-Eteenpäin and *Naisten Viiri*
newspapers. She was one of the founders

of the Northwest Finnish American Historical Society in 1961 and edited the organization's memorial album in 1965.

Papers include an autobiography, correspondence, diaries, and memorabilia; handwritten and typescript articles, poetry, plays, and books; records and papers relating to the Northwestern Finnish American Historical Society; minutes of meetings of the Mt. Solo Washington Finnish Club; bylaws of the Finnish Workers Association (Portland, OR); photographs and photograph albums; and scrapbooks. *Includes some materials in English. Inventory available. Related collection: Velma (Hakkila) Doby.*

Miettunen, Ina.
Papers, 1931-1960. 1 linear in.

Papers of Miettunen include minutes (1931-1954) of the Minnesota Finnish-American Historical Society, Virginia, MN, Chapter; photographs; records of the Messiah Lutheran Church (Mountain Iron, MN); and correspondence. *Includes English.*

Milford Finnish Relief Committee (Milford, New Hampshire).
Records, 1939-1941. Ca. 1 linear in.

The Committee was formed in 1939 when the local club of the Finnish American League for Democracy elected a committee to begin war relief efforts on behalf of Finland. The Milford chapter raised over $1100 by sponsoring coffee parties, dances, and collection drives.

Records of the Milford Committee contain correspondence, lists of contributors, receipts, and miscellaneous newspaper clippings on the relief effort. Correspondents include Herbert Hoover; Oskari Tokoi; the Finnish consulate in New York; the Finnish legation in Washington, DC; the Finnish Relief Fund, Inc.; and New Hampshire senators. *Includes English. Inventory available.*

Minnesota Federation of Finnish Civic Clubs (Virginia, Minnesota).
Records, ca. 1934-1973. 2 linear ft.

The Federation was organized in 1934 at Mountain Iron, MN, with the purpose of educating its members, providing program events and public festivals, and furthering the political and economic well-being of its members. It has various branches, the central one in Virginia, MN.

Records include correspondence, constitution and bylaws, photographs, proceedings, and minutes of the Federation and two of its member clubs (the American Finnish Civic Club, Virginia, MN, and the North Star Civic Club, Kinney, MN). *Inventory available.*

Minnesota Finnish American Family Histories.
Collection, ca. 1860-1984. Ca. 4 linear ft. and 154 cassette tapes.

Begun in 1979, the Minnesota Finnish American Family History Project undertook to document the personal histories and experiences of Minnesota Finnish Americans. The Project was sponsored by the Minnesota Finnish-American Historical Society and the Iron Range, St. Louis County, and Otter Tail County historical societies.

Materials gathered for the Project range from brief genealogies to extensive family history narratives relating the experiences of several generations. Collections include documents, photographs, and oral histories. The collection offers a wealth of primary material with special strengths in women's, regional, and family studies, as well as political and social events important to the area's Finnish Americans. The collection also provides a reliable tool for genealogical research, as it includes documents such as birth and death certificates. *Includes English. Published inventory and detailed index to the collection available (including individual names of donors and participants). Some materials restricted.*

Modern Woodmen of America, Angora Branch (Angora, Minnesota).
Records, 1921. 1 ledger.

Founded in 1883, the Woodmen is a fraternal benefit organization. The Minnesota branch was founded in 1921.

Records are minutes and a membership ledger. *In English.*

Moon, Miriam M.
Papers, ca. 1908-1975. 5 linear in.

Papers of Moon, a Finnish American actress, consist of correspondence, photographs, and newspaper clippings relating to her theatrical career. *Includes English.*

Mt. Iron-Kinney-Cherry Parish (Suomi Synod; Mountain Iron, Minnesota).
Records, 1939-1960. 6 linear in.

Records include parish board correspondence, a ledger of parish board minutes, and Sunday Church bulletins.

Nashwauk Finnish Socialist Chapter and Related Organizations (Nashwauk, Minnesota).
Records, 1906-1953. 2.5 linear ft.

In 1905, Finnish workers in the mining community of Nashwauk, MN, organized a local Finnish Socialist Club, which in 1906 became the Nashwauk Finnish Socialist Federation Chapter, affiliated with the Finnish Socialist Federation. The Chapter continued to use the Finnish Socialist Federation name until 1924, when its name was changed to the Nashwauk Workers' Party Chapter. In 1925, the Workers' Party abolished its ethnic chapters and the Nashwauk Finns founded a local Finnish Workers' Association. In 1932, the name was changed again to the Finnish Workers' Educational Society and continued under that name until its termination in 1952. The hall built by the original group in 1907 had been used throughout and was eventually incorporated as the Finnish Hall Corporation. In 1908, the women of the original Socialist Club organized a sewing circle, which existed as a women's auxiliary throughout the various

name changes of the parent organization. In 1929, the auxiliary became the Nashwauk Finnish Women's Cooperative Guild, which existed until 1953.

Records consist of twenty-two ledgers reflecting Finnish organizational activity in Nashwauk. Included are minutes, membership ledgers, and financial records. *Inventory available.*

Nelson, Arvid (1890-1967).
Papers, 1889-1967. 3 linear ft.

Nelson was born in Whitesboro, CA, the son of Finnish immigrants. A journalist and editor of Finnish American publications, he was also very active in Finnish socialist, fraternal, cooperative, and relief organizations.

Nelson worked for *Toveri* in Seattle, WA, and Astoria, OR, between 1913 and 1915. In 1917, he moved with his family to Superior, WI, where he edited *Työmies* until 1926. While in Superior, he also helped organize the Workers' Mutual Savings Bank and was active in the Cooperative Central Exchange. Eventually, the Nelsons returned to California, where he continued to be active in Finnish organizations such as the Berkeley Finnish Brotherhood and the Berkeley Consumers Cooperative. In 1942, he worked as a translator for the U.S. Department of War Information preparing materials in Finnish for broadcast on the Voice of America. He soon left to edit *Raivaaja* (Fitchburg, MA), returning in 1943 to California.

Nelson's papers include correspondence, brochures, financial records, manuscripts, newspaper clippings. notebooks, and membership cards. *Includes English. Inventory available.*

Northern States Cooperative Guilds and Clubs (Superior, Wisconsin).
Records, ca. 1930-1969. Ca. 4 linear ft.

The Northern States Cooperative Guilds and Clubs was organized in 1930 in Superior, WI, as the Northern States Women's Cooperative Guild. The Guild was a federation of local women's cooperative groups in the Central Cooperative Wholesale area and functioned as an auxiliary to it. It organized summer youth camps, promoted the cooperative movement with fair booths and other projects, and served as a contact between homemakers and the Cooperative's commodity program. In the early 1930s up to seventy guilds were affiliated with it, but in the 1940s membership began to decline. The organization was disbanded in 1969.

Records include scrapbooks, financial records, minutes, newsletters, correspondence, and bylaws. *In English. Inventory available.*

North Hurley Cooperative Association (Wisconsin).
Records, 1930-1939; 1972. 2 linear in.

Records of the North Hurley Cooperative Association consist of minutes, including those of the organizational meeting.

Orr Farmers' Cooperative Trading Company (Orr, Minnesota).
Records, 1953-1966. 1 ledger.

The Farmers' Cooperative Trading Company of Orr, MN, was established in 1919 and was affiliated with the Central Cooperative Wholesale based in Superior, WI. Records of the Company consist of monthly minutes of the board of directors. *In English.*

Paananen, Tuulikki.
Papers, ca. 1930-1970. 1 linear ft.

Paananen was a dancer and film actress. Papers contain correspondence, newspaper clippings, photographs, and scrapbooks relating to her career in Finland and the United States. Also included is some material relating to Fanny Bay Runo, Paananen's mother. Photographs include some taken in Finland and the United States of Fanny Bay Runo's family and friends, numerous photographs of Paananen, and autographed studio photographs given to her by Finnish, Swedish, and American actors and actresses. *Includes English. Inventory available.*

Paddock Bethany Lutheran Church (Sebeka, Minnesota).
Records, 1914-1977. 9 linear in.

Records of the Church include records of the Ladies Aid Society. Church records consist of constitution and bylaws of the congregation, annual reports, model constitutions of major American Lutheran church bodies, miscellaneous religious publications, photographs of early Finnish American church leaders, and two sixty-minute cassette tapes. Records of the Ladies Aid Society include minutes of monthly meetings, issues of the *Lutheran Counselor* magazine, and miscellaneous pamphlets. *Includes English. Inventory available.*

Pelto, Matti.
Papers, 1908-1910. Ca. 1 linear in.

Papers of Pelto consist of an autobiography, translated by Vienna Maki, describing life in a mining community and work in the mines at the turn of the century. *In English.*

Pohjan Leimu Temperance Society (Soudan, Minnesota).
Records, 1886-1925. 1 microfilm reel.

The Pohjan Leimu was the first Finnish temperance society in Minnesota, originally belonging to the International Order of Good Templars. In 1888, the Pohjan Leimu and four other lodges resigned from the Good Templars and joined the National Finnish Temperance Brotherhood in America.

Records of the Pohjan Leimu Temperance Society consist of correspondence and minutes.

***Raivaaja* Publishing Company (Fitchburg, Massachusetts).**
Records, 1896-1966. 1 microfilm reel.

The *Raivaaja* Publishing Company was begun in 1905. In 1906 *Raivaaja* became the newspaper of the Finnish Socialist Federation Eastern District; and since 1940 it has been the newspaper of the Finnish American League for Democracy.

Records of the Company include proceedings of the board of directors. *Inventory available in Finnish.*

Raunio, Pentti.
Papers, 1938. 1 linear in.

Raunio came to the United States in the late 1930s at the invitation of the Finnish Workers' Federation to direct drama and theater courses in various Finnish communities. His papers consist of a manuscript of his unpublished novel, "Isä."

Rautio, Tyyne.
Papers, ca. 1947-1970. Ca. 1 linear ft.

Papers of Rautio consist of a scrapbook of newspaper clippings relating to historical events in the Finnish American community nationally, such as anniversary celebrations of organizations, newspapers, and societies; biographies and obituaries of noted Finnish American leaders; and a potpourri of articles on Finnish American musicians, actors, actresses, and artists.

Redgranite Finnish Socialist Club (Wisconsin).
Records, 1908-1911. 1 linear in.

Records of the Club consist of a minute book along with a two-page manuscript titled "Brief History of the Finn Hall, Redgranite, Wisconsin." *Manuscript in English.*

Riihimäki, Leander.
Papers, n.d. 1 notebook.

Papers of Riihimäki, of Quincy, OR, consist of a notebook and a photograph.

Roivanen, Cedric (1942-).
Papers, n.d. 1 linear in.

Papers of Roivanen consist of a family genealogy. *In English.*

Ross, Carl (1913-).
Papers, 1935-1976. 1.5 linear in.

Ross is an independent scholar, historian, and author who has written extensively on Finnish Americans and Finnish American history. Born in Hancock, MI, of immigrant parents, Ross was a leader in the early 1940s of Communist Party youth work and a Party leader. From 1930 to 1934, he was secretary of the Midwest district of the Labor Sports Union, a radical, mostly Finnish organization, and editor of *Työmies* and, later, of *Clarity.* In 1946, he became secretary of the Communist Party of the Minnesota-Dakotas district and a leader of Communist labor activity in Minnesota. Ross left the Communist Party in 1957. In the 1970s, he retired from business for a life of scholarship and became executive secretary of the United Fund for Finnish-American Archives.

Ross's papers include newspaper clippings of his articles on the history of the Finns in America and two books on communism. *In English.*

Saari, Hilja.
Papers, 1915-1983. Ca. 1 linear in.

Saari was active in the Finnish American community in Minnesota. Her papers consist of a brief history of the Palisade Finn Hall (typescript and handwritten), founded in 1913; a copy of the articles of incorporation under the name "Taisto" Hall; and four photographs and two negative prints. *Includes English.*

Saari, Onni (b. 1887).
Papers, ca. 1900-1965. Ca. 3 linear ft.

Saari was born in Finland and attended secondary school before coming to the United States. He studied at the Work People's College in Duluth, MN, and later at the Cass Technical High School in Detroit, MI. He served at various times as editor of the Finnish American and Finnish Canadian newspapers *Raivaaja, Työmies, Sosialisti, Eteenpäin,* and *Vapaus.* He co-edited an English-Finnish dictionary with S. Nuorteva and translated numerous books from English into Finnish. In his later years, he made his home in Ashburnham, MA, remaining active in cooperative activities and writing on labor and political issues for various Finnish newspapers.

Saari's papers consist of personal correspondence, including letters to his first wife, Aino Saari; materials on Finnish Americans and their activities; materials on the Finnish American press; histories of Finns in Troy (NH), and Friberg, Westminister, and Worcester (MA); and writings and materials on the Ashburnham (MA) Farmers' Club, the United Cooperative Farms, and other cooperative activities. *Includes English. Inventory available.*

Saima Workers' Society (Fitchburg, Massachusetts).
Records, ca. 1914-1964. 3 microfilm reels.

The Saima Workers' Society was founded in 1894 as a Finnish workers' organization. In 1905, it joined the Finnish Socialist Federation, and by 1924-1925 it was the largest such chapter in the country, with over 500 members. The Saima became a chapter of the Finnish American League for Democracy in 1940. In 1946, second generation Finns organized the Finnish American Club of Saima to carry on the activities of the original organization.

Records of the Society include board of directors minutes, correspondence, economic committee reports, proceedings, and property inventories. *Inventory available.*

St. Louis County Rural Schools (Minnesota).
Collection, 1935-1940. 1 folder.

Collection consists of agricultural extension information and publications.

St. Mark's Evangelical Lutheran Church (Waukegan, Illinois).
Records, 1953-1958. 1 microfilm reel.

Records consist of minutes of quarterly, special, and annual congregational meetings. *In English.*

St. Paul's Finnish Evangelical Lutheran Church (Alango-Field, Minnesota).
Records, ca. 1930-1961. 3 microfilm reels.

Records of the Church consist of membership lists, financial records, minutes of the church council meetings, and miscellany. *Inventory available.*

Salmi, Sofia.
Papers, n.d. 1 notebook.

Salmi's papers consist of a notebook containing poetry and drawings.

Sebeka Cooperative Creamery Association (Sebeka, Minnesota).
Records, 1908-1973. Ca. 1 linear ft.

Records of the Association consist of bylaws, articles of incorporation, and minutes. *Inventory available.*

Selvä Temperance Society (Hutten, Minnesota).
Records, 1931-1937. Ca. 1 linear ft.

Records of the Society contain correspondence, financial records, and minutes. Also included is a scrapbook of newspaper clippings about the Russo-Finnish War and World War II.

Seppamaki, Johan and Fiina.
Papers, 1977. Ca. 1 linear in.

Papers consist of a photocopy of a typed family history. *In English.*

Star of Hope Temperance Society (Toivon Tähti Raittiusseura) (Duluth, Minnesota).
Records, 1915-1918. 5 linear in.

Records consist of one minute book. Officers were Antti Mannisto, Evert Torkko, A. Lundquist, and Kalle Ruuttila.

Stohl, Frank.
Papers, 1882-1987. Ca. 3.5 linear in.

Papers of Stohl consist of a photocopy of an essay entitled "The Eureka

(California) Brotherhood Lodge History"
by Hilma Siikarla, translated by Stohl; a
register of Finnish Americans in Reedley,
CA (including those Finnish pioneers still
living in 1955) compiled for a fiftieth
anniversary celebration of the Finnish
settlement in the area; and photocopies of
manuscripts by Stohl entitled "Finnish
Women of Reedley, California," and "The
History of the Reedley Finnish
Brotherhood Lodge No. 20, 1909-1987."
Also included are photocopied records of
the Reedley Finnish Relief Committee,
including financial ledgers, correspondence, and minutes. *Mainly in
English.*

Strom, Rora.
Papers, n.d. 1 folder.

Papers of Strom consist of poems and
a letter.

Torkko, Rev. Evert E. (b. 1901).
Papers, 1925-1966. Ca. 5 linear ft.

Torkko was born in Soudan, MN. He
was ordained at Messiah Lutheran Church
(then the Finnish Lutheran Church) of
Duluth, MN, and served in Suomi Synod
parishes of Cloquet and Duluth, MN;
Astoria, OR; Monessen, PA; Los Angeles,
CA; and Newberry, MI.

His papers consist of correspondence,
birth, baptismal, and marriage records,
and church bulletins. *Partial inventory
available.*

Törmä-Silvola Family.
Papers, ca. 1901-1979. Ca. 9 linear ft.

Fred Törmä (b. 1888) was born in
Kihniö province, Finland, and came to
Nashwauk, MN, in 1906, where he
married Hilma Lempeä. He was involved
in formation of the Elanto Cooperative
(Nashwauk, MN) in 1908 and was a
board member of the Central Cooperative
Wholesale. He was also active in the
Minnesota Finnish-American Historical
Society.

Richard H. Silvola (b. 1899) was born
in Soudan, MN. He served in the armed
forces and was a member of the
Minnesota House of Representatives for
ten years. In 1932, he married Sylvia
Törmä, daughter of Fred and Hilma
Törmä. Silvola was active in many
organizations, including the Finlandia
Foundation, Suomi Seura, and the
Finnish-American Historical Society, as
well as cooperative organizations.

The Törmä-Silvola family papers
consist largely of scrapbooks,
photographs, and organizational materials
from various Finnish American groups.
Includes English. Inventory available.

Tuomi, Karin.
Papers, 1950-1976. Ca. 3 linear in.

Tuomi was a Finnish American author
who lived in Palo Alto, CA. Papers
include a manuscript of her novel, "Pelli
ja Perhe Siirtolaisena," poetry, and
personal papers.

Työmies Society (Superior, Wisconsin).
Records, 1903-1970. 18 linear ft. and
1 microfilm reel.

A Finnish American Socialist, later
Communist, publishing company, the
Työmies Society was founded in 1903.
Records include minutes of annual
meetings and minutes of the executive
committee and board of directors. Also
included are personal papers of Andrew
Roine of Angora, MN; unpublished
proletarian plays; and sheet music from
the lending library. *Inventory available.
Supplement, board of directors minutes,
available only on microfilm.*

Väänänen, Joseph.
Papers, 1935-1983. Ca. 1 linear in.

Väänänen came to the United States in
1903. He wrote articles for the Finnish
American newspaper *Työmies* and was
active in the Finnish American socialist
movement.

His papers consist mostly of family
correspondence; a photograph of
Väänänen is also included.

Väinö Temperance Society (Ishpeming, Michigan).
Records, 1889-1901. 2 microfilm reels.

Records consist of minutes and membership lists.

Valon Lähde Temperance Society.
Records, 1909. 1 ledger.

Ledger contains financial records of the Society.

Valontuote Temperance Society (Virginia, Minnesota).
Records, 1893-1968. 5 linear ft.

The Valontuote Temperance Society was organized in 1893. It was affiliated with the Finnish National Temperance Brotherhood in America, the central organization of local temperance societies, but in 1897 left the national organization because of a dispute over a rule against dancing. The Society remained in existence until 1966.
Records of the Society consist of bylaws, constitutions, correspondence, membership books, and minutes. *Inventory available.*

Vermillion Range Cooperative Park Association (Ely, Minnesota).
Records, 1937-1954. 6 linear in.

Incorporated in 1932 for the purpose of providing a park with buildings and picnic facilities for the recreational use of its members, the Association was disbanded in 1955, and the park land was divided up and sold. Records consist of correspondence, financial records, and minutes of the Association. *In English.*

Vesi Temperance Society (Ely, Minnesota).
Records, 1894-1942. 2 microfilm reels.

Records on microfilm consist of proceedings of the board of directors.

Virginia Cooperative Society (Virginia, Minnesota).
Records, ca. 1911-1962. Ca. 1 linear ft.

The Virginia Cooperative Society was established in 1909 as the Virginia Work People's Trading Company. By 1931, the cooperative had about 1,000 members, mostly Finnish, and consisted of two stores and a service station. In 1936, the name was changed to the Virginia Cooperative Society; it continued to exist until the early 1970s.
Records of the cooperative consist of a history of the Society until 1939, financial records, records relating to the closely allied Range Co-op Federation (MN), and publications relating mostly to the cooperative movement. *Includes English. Inventory available.*

Virginia, Minnesota, Suomi-Synod Evangelical Lutheran Congregation.
Records, 1901-1950. 1 microfilm reel.

Records consist of baptism, confirmation, marriage, and funeral registers as well as financial records.

Virtanen, Tyyne.
Papers, 1924-1925. 1 notebook.

Virtanen was a student at Suomi College, Hancock, MI. Papers consist of a notebook of poetry. *In English.*

Waasa Threshing and Milling Company (Waasa Township, Minnesota).
Records, 1917-1934. 1 ledger.

Records consist of minutes.

Wargelin, Raymond Waldemar (1911-).
Papers, 1986. 3 linear in.

Wargelin, a Lutheran clergyman and educator, was born in Republic, MI. He served Suomi Synod Lutheran congregations in Berkeley and Reedley, CA and Fairport Harbor; was president of Suomi Synod; was president of Suomi College (Hancock, MI), where he also taught theology; and was editor-in-chief of the *Lutheran Counselor.*

Papers consist of unpublished writings including "Suomi Synod Ministerium, 1876-1972"; "When the Suomi Synod Was Served by Pastors From Finland"; and "Social and Theological Profiles of the Suomi Synod Ministerium." Also included is a listing of Suomi Synod congregations. *In English.*

Waukegan Cooperative Trading Company (Waukegan, Illinois).
Records, ca. 1930-1937. Ca. 1 linear in.

Collection consists of correspondence concerning the activities of cooperatives and general information on their work. *In English.*

Wayne County Producers' Association (McKinnon, Georgia).
Records, ca. 1922-1966. Ca. 1 linear ft.

Originally the Fairfield Cooperative Association, the organization was founded in the early 1920s as a Finnish American cooperative farm. Records include financial records, membership lists, minutes, payroll records, and miscellaneous items. *Inventory available.*

Westerback, Rev. M. N.
Papers, 1950-1962. Ca. 1 linear in.

Papers of Rev. Westerback, a Finnish American clergyman and author from Clearwater, FL, consist of correspondence and writings. *Includes English.*

Wiita, Duane.
Papers, 1936-1970. Ca. 1 linear in.

Papers of Wiita consist of photocopies of his birth certificate and his parents' marriage certificates. *In English.*

Wiita, John (1888-   ).
Papers, 1975-1984. Ca. 1 linear in.

Wiita was born in Ylistaro, Finland. After attending folk school he came to the United States at the age of seventeen. He settled in Superior, WI, where he worked as a longshoreman and railroad car repairman and was active in the

Superior Chapter of the Finnish Socialist Federation. He was also associated with the Work People's College of Duluth, MN. In 1916, he moved to Detroit, MI, and subsequently to various places, always remaining active in socialist organizations, particularly with the Finnish American and Finnish Canadian labor press, including *Toveri, Sosialisti, Työmies, Vapaus,* and *Eteenpäin.* After the 1920 split within the Finnish Socialist Federation, Wiita remained with the Finnish Federation and Workers' Party of America; however, by 1945, when he moved to Brooklyn, CT, he had dropped his Communist Party membership.

Wiita's papers include his correspondence with Michael G. Karni, an autobiography, and short sketches on Finnish American labor history and biographies of Finnish Americans. *Inventory available.*

Women's Association "Striver" (Naisyhdistys Pyrkijä) (Brooklyn, New York).
Records, 1923-1972. Ca. 1 linear ft.

The Naisyhdistys Pyrkijä was a women's mutual aid organization, established in 1893 for women who worked as domestics.

Records include two printed pamphlets giving the history of the organization until 1953 and a copy of *Suomen Säveltäjiä: Kudentoista Vuosisadan Ajalta* (Finnish Composers: From the Sixteenth Century, edited by Suho Ranta). *Includes English. Inventory available.*

Workers' Publishing Company (Duluth, Minnesota).
Records, ca. 1915-1975. Ca. 4 linear ft.

In 1914, Finnish supporters of industrial unionism founded the Socialist Publishing Company in Duluth, MN, and began publication of the *Sosialisti,* a daily paper. In 1916, its name was changed to *Teollisuustyöläinen* (The Industrial Worker); a law suit was brought against it, and it ceased publication later that year. In 1917, it reappeared as the *Industrialisti,* published by the newly formed Workers' Socialist Publishing Company, which also published annuals such as the *Industrialistin Joulu* and *Työväen Taskukalenteri*, as well as books by leaders within the Finnish IWW movement. The Workers' Socialist Publishing Company was closely allied to the Work People's College in Duluth. In 1954, the publishing company's name was again changed, to the Workers' Publishing Company. In 1975, the *Industrialisti*, one of the last foreign-language IWW newspapers published in the United States, ceased publication.

Records of the Workers' Publishing Company contain correspondence, financial records, and office files. Also included are items relating to the Work People's College (Duluth, MN) and the Finnish American Athletic Club. *Includes English. Inventory available. Related collection: Work People's College (Duluth, MN).*

Work People's College (Duluth, Minnesota).
Records, 1904-1962. 5 linear ft. and 1 microfilm reel.

The Work People's College had its beginnings in 1903, when leaders of the Finnish National Lutheran Church of America opened the Finnish People's College and Theological Seminary (Suomalainen Kansan Opisto ja Teologinen Seminaari) in Minneapolis, MN, to provide training for clergy and a liberal education for Finnish Americans in general. Financed by the sale of stock shares, the institution was open to all but soon failed and was moved to the Duluth suburb of Smithville, where more Finnish Americans had settled. Finnish American Socialists were strong supporters of the school and by 1908 had gained control of it. It was renamed the Work People's College (Työväen Opisto) and religion was dropped from the curriculum. During the next few years, the school was the pride of the Finnish Socialist Federation, but when the Federation split in 1914 over the issue of industrial unionism, the Work People's College became a labor school of the Industrial Workers of the World. It continued so until it ceased holding classes in 1940.

Records of the College contain correspondence, financial records, stock certificates, student club minutes, student rosters, and lists of and photocopies of proletarian plays. *Includes English. Inventory available. Plays available as photocopies only. Related collection: Workers' Publishing Company (Duluth, MN).*

Monographs

The Finnish American monograph collection, numbering ca. 1,475 volumes, is one of the IHRC's largest. As a whole, it constitutes a representative cross section of all aspects of Finnish American life, particularly organizational activity. Because the church, the temperance societies, the labor and cooperative movements, and the fraternal organizations played such important roles in Finnish American history, the historical record emerges to a large degree from their publications. Consequently, much of the material in the collection takes the form of organizational guidebooks, bylaws, proceedings of conventions, texts on basic principles and issues, and autobiographies by organizational leaders.

The collection contains all of the major Finnish American bibliographies. John Kolehmainen's *The Finns in America; A Bibliographical Guide to Their History* (1947) is still considered an indispensible source. It is supplemented by Olavi Koivukangas and S. Toivonen's *A Bibliography on Finnish Emigration and Internal Migration* (1978) and K. Kotiranta's *Union Catalog of American Finnish Literature* (1970). Newspapers are dealt with in A. William Hoglund's *Union List of Finnish Newspapers Published by Finns in the United States and Canada, 1876-1985* (1985) and his *Finnish Immigrants in America, 1880-1920* (1960).

An excellent selection of general histories of Finnish immigration is available in the collection. The most complete study is the above-mentioned *Finnish Immigrants in America, 1880-1920* by Hoglund. Carl Ross's *The Finn Factor in American Labor,*

Culture and Society (1977) provides a Midwestern, labor perspective. Significant sources of data on early Finnish American communities are Salomon Ilmonen's *Amerikan suomalaisten historia, Vols. I, II, and III* (The History of Finns in America; 1918, 1923, 1926) as well as his *Amerikan suomalaisten sivistyshistoria* (The Cultural History of Finns in America, 1931). A key history of the Finland-Swedes is Anders Myhrman's *Finlandssvenskarna i Amerika* (Finland-Swedes in America, 1972). The recent publication *Women Who Dared: The History of Finnish American Women*, edited by Carl Ross and K. Marianne Wargelin-Brown, represents an important examination of the contributions and experiences of Finnish immigrant women.

The collection also includes the major overviews of Finnish American migration, history, and culture that have appeared as collections of essays, notably, Turku University's *Old Friends--Strong Ties* (1976); *Finnish Diaspora II: The United States*, edited by Michael Karni (1981), and *The Finns in America: A Social Symposium*, edited by Ralph Jalkanen (1972). Important studies by Finnish writers include Akseli Järnefelt's *Suomalaiset Amerikassa* (The Finns in America, 1899), Rafael Engleberg's *Suomi ja Amerikan suomalaiset* (Finland and the Finns in America, 1944) and Reino Kero's *Suuren lännen suomalaiset* (Finns in the Great, Vast West, 1978). The migration process is dealt with in depth in Kero's *Migration from Finland to North America* (1974) and Keijo Virtanen's *Settlement or Return; Finnish Emigrants (1860-1930) in the International Overseas Return Migration Movement* (1979).

State and regional histories that cover the primary areas of Finnish settlement in the United States are well represented. These include Hans Wasastjerna's *Minnesotan suomalaisten historia* (The History of the Finns in Minnesota, 1957), Armas Holmio's *Michiganin suomalaisten historia* (The History of the Finns in Michigan, 1967), Esa Arra's *Illinoisin suomalaisten historia* (The History of the Finns in Illinois, 1971), and John Kolehmainen's *A Haven in the Woods: The Story of Finns in Wisconsin* (1951) as well as his *From Lake Erie's Shores to the Mahoning and Monongahela Valleys: A History of the Finns in Ohio, Western Pennsylvania and West Virginia* (1977). Finnish American activities on the East Coast are described in histories of organizations, such as *The History of Finnish Organizations in Greater New York*, edited by Katri Ekman (1976); and Liisa Liedes's *The Finnish Imprint* (1982) for New England. For over a decade the Finnish American Historical Society of the West has been publishing the history of West Coast Finns in its *Finnish Emigrant Studies Series*, located in the Finnish American serials collection.

The various aspects of Finnish American religious life are thoroughly covered in the IHRC holdings. This is particularly true of the Finnish American Evangelical Lutheran Church, Suomi Synod, whose publications range from sermon compilations, hymnals, prayer-books, and children's ABC books to histories of the church like V. Rautanen's *Amerikan suomalainen kirkko* (The Finnish Church in America, 1911) and examinations of the church's role in immigrant life such as *The Faith of the Finns*, edited by Ralph Jalkanen (1972). Also well represented in the collection are works dealing with the Apostolic Lutheran Church. Primary among these are Uuras Saarnivaara's *The History of the Laestadian or Apostolic Lutheran Movement in America* (1947) and recent studies from Finland like Pekka Raittila's *Lestadiolaisuus pohjois-Amerikassa vuoteen 1885* (Laestadianism in North America to 1885, 1982) and his *Lestadiolaisuuden bibliographia* (Bibliography of Laestadianism, 1967).

Fewer materials have been published about the Finnish American National Evangelical Lutheran Church. Its history is documented in *Amerikan Suomalaisen Evankeelisen Luterilaisen Kansalliskirkkokunnan 25 vuotis Juhla-albumi, 1898-1923* (The Twenty-fifth Anniversary Memorial Album of the Finnish American National Evangelical Lutheran Church, 1923) and J. E. Nopola's *Our Three-Score Years: A Brief History of the National Evangelical Church* (1958). Also represented to a lesser degree is the Evangelical Mission Society (also known as the Finnish American Free Church Congregationalists), whose history is described in *Muistoja 30 vuotisesta lähetystyöstä* (Remembrances of Thirty Years of Mission Work, 1936). The collection includes the autobiographies of two prominent ministers: Väinö Välkiö's *Silta atlannin yli* (Bridge

Over the Atlantic, 1953) and Fanny Heino's *Siirtolaistytön kohtalo* (An Immigrant Girl's Destiny, 1954?).
The IHRC's Finnish American holdings are very strong for all three factions of the Finnish American labor movement: the Socialists, Communists, and Syndicalists. Particularly noteworthy are the proceedings of the national and district conventions of the Finnish Socialist Federation (1906-1923), which are supplemented by numerous manuscript holdings for individual local Socialist chapters. The monograph collection contains several major labor histories: F. J. Syrjälä's *Historia-aiheita amerikan suomalaisesta työväenliikkeesta* (Historical Essays on the Finnish American Labor Movement, 1925), Elis Sulkanen's *Amerikan suomalaisen työväenliikkeen historia* (History of the Finnish American Labor Movement, 1951), Leo Mattson's *40 vuotta* (Forty Years, 1946) and Walter Lahtinen's *50 vuoden varrelta* (Memories from Fifty Years, 1953). Included also are early theoretical works like Alex Halonen's *Sosialismin perusteet* (The Foundations of Socialism, 1908) and Leo Laukki's *Teolliseen yhteiskuntaan* (Toward an Industrial Society, 1917), as well as autobiographies by noted figures from the Finnish American labor movement such as Martin Hendrickson's *Muistelmia 10-vuotisesta raivaajatyöstäni* (Reminiscences of My Ten-Year Pioneer Work, 1908) and Oskari Tokoi's *Sisu: Even Through a Stone Wall* (1957). Numerous doctoral dissertations in the collection, among them Auvo Kostiainen's *The Forging of Finnish American Communism, 1917-1919* (1978), cover various phases of the Finnish American labor movement. The collection also contains an array of books and pamphlets on political theory, bylaws and rules of order for local chapters, party platforms, and numerous songbooks.

Monograph holdings on the Finnish American cooperative movement are also very strong. However, this area is covered in greater depth in the serials, newspaper, and manuscript collections; for example, available serials include the yearbooks of the Cooperative League of the USA, the Northern States Cooperative League, and the Cooperative Central Exchange (later the Central Cooperative Wholesale and finally the Central Cooperatives, Inc.). In the monograph collection the history of the Cooperative Central Exchange is described in Erick Kendall's *And into the Future: A Brief Story of the Central Cooperative Wholesale's 25 Years of Building Towards a Better Tomorrow* (1945), A. J. Hayes's *The CCW Story* (1950), and in greater depth in Michael Karni's dissertation *Yhteishyvä--For the Common Good* (1975). Among primary materials dealing with the CCE's break with the Communist Party are William Marttila's *Osuustoiminta ja sen merkitys luokkataistelussa* (Cooperativism and Its Significance to the Class Struggle, 1930) and George Halonen's *Taistelu osuustoimintarintamalla* (Battle on the Cooperative Front, 1932). The collection contains major texts such as V. S. Alanne's *Fundamentals of Consumer Cooperatism* (1932) and *Manual for Cooperative Directors* (1938) as well as published guidebooks, bylaws, and songbooks for local cooperatives. Although much of the material covers Midwestern cooperatives, East Coast cooperatives are described in Frank Aaltonen's *Maynard Weavers: The Story of the United Cooperative Society of Maynard* (1941) and in other histories such as the Sulkanen labor history already cited. The collection has very little on Finnish American cooperatives on the West Coast.

Just as the cooperative holdings reflect a Midwestern emphasis, so also do the IHRC holdings on the temperance movement. Most of the materials deal with the Midwestern Finnish National Temperance Brotherhood, one of five regional temperance leagues. The Brotherhood's twenty-five-year history is detailed by Salomon Ilmonen in *Juhlajulkaisu Suomalaisen Kansallis Raittius Veljeysseuran 25 vuotisen toiminnan muistoksi* (Commemorative Album Celebrating Twenty-five Years of Work by the Finnish National Temperance Brotherhood, 1912). The collection also contains another standard source, *Rauhankokous ja pääpiirteitä amerikan suomalaisten raittiustyön historiasta* (The Peace Conference and Main Features in the History of Finnish American Temperance Work), edited by J. W. Lilius (1908). A history of the Eastern Finnish Temperance Association is found in *50 vuotis juhlajulkaisu, 1895-1945* (Fifty Year Commemorative Album), published by the Alku Temperance Society of Maynard, MA.

The monograph collection holds relatively little on the two Finnish American fraternal organizations, the national Knights and Ladies of Kaleva and the West Coast-centered United Finnish Kaleva Brothers and Sisters. *Kalevaisten, Kalevan Ritarien ja Kalevan Naisten, Viisikymmenenvuotis muistojulkaisu, 1898-1948* (Fifty Year Commemorative Album of the Knights and Ladies of Kaleva, 1948) is one of the few extant organizational histories. The story of the Ladies of Kaleva is described in *Kalevan Naisten historian ääriviivoja, 1904-1954* (A Historical Outline of the Ladies of Kaleva, 1954). The collection contains organizational guidelines, bylaws, a songbook and several anniversary albums of individual lodges. Articles of a historical nature frequently appear in the annual periodical, the *Kalevainen.* The history of the United Finnish Kaleva Brothers and Sisters is described in *50-vuotis historia* (Fifty Year History, 1937). Their quarterly magazine, the *Veljeysviesti* (The Message of Brotherhood), is available in the Finnish American serials collection. The collection also contains very little on the Finland-Swedes' International Order of Runeberg, whose history is documented in the seventy-year jubilee album *Memorabilia "Minnesskrift" of the International Order of Runeberg 1898-1968* (n.d.).

A general history of the ethnic press is found in Taisto Niemi's dissertation *The Finnish Lutheran Book Concern, 1900-1950: A History and Developmental Study* (1960) as well as in John Kolehmainen's *Sow the Golden Seed* (1955). The collection also contains articles by Kolehmainen on Finnish newspapers in Michigan and Ohio. Among the anniversary books for individual newspapers are *Amerikan Suometar: Muistojuhla* (*Amerikan Suometar*: Commemorative Celebration, 1915), *Toveritar Kymmenenvuotias, 1911-1921, Muistojulkaisu* (*Toveritar* Ten Years, Commemorative Album, 1921), and *Työmies, Raivaaja, Toveri, 10 vuotta* (*Työmies, Raivaaja, Toveri*, 10 Years, 1913, 1915, 1917). Detailed histories of individual newspapers also appear in special anniversary editions of the given newspapers.

The monograph collection contains a substantial and representative selection of creative literature that was read by the Finnish immigrants. This includes translations of authors like Tolstoy, Zola, Hall Caine, Conan Doyle, and H. Rider Haggard. Of particular interest are original works by Finnish American writers, of whom Sara Röyhö and her *Petetyn naisen kosto* (A Betrayed Woman's Revenge, 1908) and Kalle Potti with his *Iloinen harbori* (The Happy Harbor, 1924) represent the popular, romantic style of the day. Aku Päiviö's *Sara Kivistö* (1913), Richard Pesola's *Sorretun poluilla* (On the Paths of the Oppressed, 1909) and Helmi Mattson's *Aavikon vaeltajat* (Wanderers of the Prairie, 1928) are typical of Finnish American proletarian fiction.

Newspapers

Amerikan Kaiku (American Echo), Duluth, MN (previously published in Brooklyn, NY). Semi-weekly: 1906.

Amerikan Sanomat (American Tidings), Ashtabula, OH. Weekly: 1898, 1912.

Amerikan Sanomat (American Tidings), Calumet, MI. Weekly: 1959-1960.

Amerikan Suomalainen (Finnish American; previously titled American Suomalainen Lehti), Calumet, Red Jacket, and Hancock, MI; Chicago, IL. Weekly: 1897-1898. (Microfilm: 1879-1894).

Amerikan Suometar (The American Finn), Hancock, MI. Tri-weekly: 1904, 1906-1907, 1909-1911, 1916, 1925, 1932, 1935-1936, 1938-1941, 1944-1947, 1949-1962.

Amerikan Uutiset (The American News), Calumet, MI. Semi-weekly: 1901-1903, 1905-1906.

Amerikan Uutiset (The American News; previously titled Minnesotan Uutiset), Lantana, FL (previously published in New York Mills, MN). Semi-weekly: 1946-1947, 1949, 1951, 1953-1954, 1956-1986. (Microfilm: 1933, 1935-1973).

Finnish American family of Henry Luttisen, Paulsba, WA; from *Amerikan Albumi*, Brooklyn, NY, 1904.

Auttaja (The Helper), Ironwood, MI. Weekly: 1918, 1926, 1931, 1947-1948, 1950-1951, 1953-1964.

Canadan Uutiset (The Canadian News), Thunder Bay, Ontario, Canada. Weekly: 1952, 1974-date. (Microfilm: 1931-1975).

Cooperative Builder, Superior, WI. Weekly: 1931-1934, 1936-1943, 1945-1946, 1953, 1957, 1960-1961, 1965, 1972-1982. English.

Copper Country News, Calumet, MI. Weekly: 1959. English.

Eteenpäin (Forward; superseded by **Työmies-Eteenpäin** after 1950), New York, NY (previously published in Worchester, MA). Daily: 1925, 1932. (Microfilm: 1922-1929, 1931-1932, 1934-1935, 1938, 1946, 1948, 1950).

Finlandia, Brooklyn, NY. Semi-monthly: 1940.

Finnish American Weekly, Duluth, MN. Weekly: 1937. English.

Fitchburgin Sanomat (The Fitchburg Tidings), Fitchburg, MA. Weekly: 1937.

Industrialisti (Industrialist), Duluth, MN. Weekly: 1918-1919, 1926-1929, 1931-1940, 1942, 1950-1973, 1975.

Isien Usko (Faith of Our Fathers), Thunder Bay, Ontario, Canada. Monthly: 1953-1957, 1959-1962, 1965-1977.

Keskilännen Sanomat (The Midwestern Tidings), Duluth, MN. Semi-weekly: 1949-1956.

Keskusosuuskunnan Tiedonantaja (The Central Cooperative Exchange Messenger), Superior, WI. Weekly: 1929.

Lännen Suometar (The Western Finn), Astoria, OR. Twice weekly: 1939-1942.

Lännetär (The Westerner), Astoria, OR. Weekly: 1900-1901.

Leading Star, Seattle, WA. Monthly: 1969, 1976. English and Swedish.

Loimaan Lehti (Loimaa News), Loimaa, Finland. Weekly. (Microfilm: 1934).

Naisten Viiri (Women's Banner), Superior, WI. Weekly: 1952-1978.

New Yorkin Lehti (New York News), New York, NY. Tri-weekly. (Microfilm: 1891-1893).

New Yorkin Uutiset (Finnish New York News), Brooklyn, NY. Semi-weekly (daily): 1951-1954, 1957-1961, 1965, 1969, 1973-1986. (Microfilm: 1912-1915, 1917-1919).

Norden, Brooklyn, NY. Weekly: 1935-1937, 1939, 1941-1948, 1950-1957, 1959, 1962-1964, 1966-1970, 1974-date. Swedish and English.

Opas (The Guide), Calumet, MI. Semi-weekly: 1934, 1945-1947, 1953-1957. Includes some English.

Päivälehti (The Daily Journal), Duluth, MN-Calumet, MI. Daily: 1903-1904, 1906, 1930, 1935-1943, 1945-1948. (Microfilm: 1908-1948).

Pohjan Tähti (The North Star), Fitchburg, MA. Daily: 1916, 1918, 1925.

Pohjolan Sanomat (Northland News), Calumet, MI. Weekly: 1957-1959.

Raivaaja (The Pioneer), Fitchburg, MA. Daily (weekly, tri-weekly): 1948, 1950, 1952, 1955-1957, 1960, 1965, 1967-date. (Microfilm: 1905-1965).

Sankarin Maine (The Hero's Fame; previously titled **Swen Tuuwa**), Houghton and Hancock, MI. Weekly. (Microfilm: 1878-1881).

Siirtolainen (The Emigrant; previously titled **Lännetar**; superseded by **Finnish-Am Weekly**), Duluth, MN (previously published in Brooklyn, NY, and Kaleva, MI). Weekly. (Microfilm: 1917-1925).

Sirpale (The Splinter), Oulu, Finland. Weekly. (Microfilm: 1933).

Sosialisti (The Socialist; title changes to **Teollisuustyöläinen** in 1916), Duluth, MN. Daily: 1915-1916. (Microfilm: 1914-1916).

Totuus (The Truth), Fitchburg, MA. Weekly (?): 1900.

Toveri (The Comrade), Astoria, OR. Weekly: 1921, 1926.

Toveritar (The Woman Comrade), Astoria, OR. Weekly: 1914, 1918-1919, 1925. (Microfilm: 1915-1930).

Työläisnainen (The Working Woman), Superior, WI. Weekly: 1930-1931.

Työmies (The Worker), Ishpeming, MI. Weekly. (Microfilm: 1889-1893).

Työmies-Eteenpäin (Worker Forward; previously titled **Työmies**), Superior, WI. Semi-weekly: (frequency varies): 1913-1914, 1938-1941, 1945, 1950-date. (Microfilm: 1909-1950). Includes English.

Työväen Osuustoimintalehti (The Workers' Cooperative Journal), Superior, WI. Weekly: 1930-1931, 1933-1964. (Microfilm: 1930-1965).

Uusi Kotimaa (The New Homeland), New York Mills, MN. Weekly (tri-weekly): 1897, 1902, 1904, 1906, 1912, 1914, 1928-1930, 1932-1934.

Valwoja (The Guardian), Calumet, MI. Three times per week: 1940, 1943, 1946-1957.

Vapaa Sana (Free Speech), Toronto, Ontario, Canada. Semi-weekly: 1957, 1961-1962, 1966-1967, 1970-1972, 1974.

Vapaus (Freedom), Sudbury, Ontario, Canada. Tri-weekly: 1923, 1925, 1961, 1965-1968, 1970.

Viikkolehti (The Weekly), Fitchburg, MA. Weekly: 1939.

Viikkosanomat (The Weekly News), Toronto, Ontario, Canada. Weekly: 1974-date. Includes English.

Serials

Ahjo (The Forge), Duluth, MN. Quarterly: 1916-1922.

Aika (Era), Sointula, British Columbia, Canada. Semi-monthly. (Microfilm: 1903-1904).

Aikamme (Our Era), Vancouver, British Columbia, Canada. Bi-monthly: 1984-date. Includes English.

Airue (The Guide), Thunder Bay, Ontario, Canada. Annual: 1910-1911.

Airut (The Herald), Monessen, PA. 1917.

Almanakka (Almanac), Hancock, MI. Annual: 1913, 1916, 1925, 1928, 1932, 1937, 1940, 1942-1945, 1947-1948, 1951-1954, 1956-1964.

Amerikan Suomalaisten Taskukalenteri (Finnish American Pocket Calendar), Superior, WI. Annual: 1943-1945, 1947.

Amerikan Suomalaisen Kansallis-ja Raittiusmielisen Väestö. Joulu (Christmas Annual of Nationalistic and Temperance-Minded Finnish Americans), Duluth, MN. Annual: 1915.

Amerikan Suomalaisten Osoitekalenteri (Finnish American Address Calendar), Ironwood, MI. Annual: 1903.

Amerikan Suomalaisten Vapaamieliset Julkaisut (Publications of the Finnish American Free-Thinkers), Duluth, MN. Three times per year: 1958, 1961.

Amerikan Yhdistyneet Suomalaiset Sosialistiset Kustannusyhtiöt Kalenteri (The United Finnish American Socialist Publishing Company Calendar), Fitchburg, MA. Annual: 1914-1917, 1919-1921.

Apostolic Lutheran Church of America Minutes and Financial Statements of the Annual Meeting, place of publication varies. Annual: 1923, 1927, 1932-1936, 1951-1952, 1956, 1958-1959, 1961-1963, 1965, 1967-1972, 1974-1975, 1977, 1980, 1983.

Apostolic Lutheran Missionary Association Eastern Branch Financial Statement. Annual: 1977. English.

Armonsanoma (The Message of Grace), Kemi, Finland. Monthly: 1911.

Aura (The Plow), Hancock, MI. Monthly: 1914-1919.

Between Ourselves, Berkeley, CA. Irregular: 1947-1980. English.

The Bridge (Suomi Alumni Bulletin), Hancock, MI. Quarterly: 1958, 1963-date. English.

Canadan Viesti (The Canadian Messenger), Winnipeg, Manitoba, Canada (previously published in Toronto, Ontario, Canada). Monthly: 1954, 1959, 1963, 1971-1972. Includes English.

Central Cooperative Wholesale Financial and Operating Statements, Superior, WI. Annual: 1924-1930, 1932, 1934-1940. Includes English.

Central Cooperative Wholesale Weekly Bulletin, Superior, WI. Weekly: 1939. English.

Central Cooperatives, Inc. Yearbook, Superior, WI. Annual: 1919-1920, 1922-1964. (Anniversary issue: 1937; annual reports: 1947-1962). Includes English.

Children's Friend, Ironwood, MI. Monthly: 1938. English.

Christian Monthly (English edition of **Kristillinen Kuukauslehti**), New York Mills, MN (previously published in Calumet and Laurium, MI, and Esko, MN). Monthly: 1949-1984. English.

Cooperation, New York, NY. Monthly: 1921, 1925-1927, 1929-1930, 1932-1934. English.

Co-operative Central Exchange Catalog, Superior, WI. Monthly: 1930. English.

The Cooperative League of the U.S.A. Yearbook, New York, NY. Frequency varies: 1930, 1932, 1936, 1939, 1950-1954. English.

Cooperative Publishing Association Annual Report, Superior, WI. Annual: 1943, 1945, 1948, 1952-1953, 1955-1957. Includes English.

The Cooperative Pyramid Builder, Superior, WI. Monthly: 1926-1931. English.

Cooperative Wholesale Society The People's Yearbook, Manchester, England. Annual: 1939, 1944. English.

Eloa (Life), Hancock, MI. Frequency varies: 1919-1920, 1944.

Eteenpäin Kalenteri Kansalle (Forward: Calendar for the People), Tampere, Finland. Annual: 1906, 1908.

Etsijä (The Seeker), Duluth, MN. Quarterly: 1929.

Evankelinen Lähetysyhdistys Jouluviesti (The Evangelical Mission Society Christmas Message), Fitchburg, MA. Annual: 1926-1927.

Evankelis-Luterilaisen Kansalliskirkon Vuosikirja ja Kalenteri (The National Evangelical-Lutheran Church Yearbook and Calendar), Ironwood, MI. Annual: 1904, 1908, 1952, 1954, 1959-1960.

FACS Newsletter (Finnish American Club of Saima), Fitchburg, MA. Monthly: 1978-date. English.

FCA Directory (Finnish Center Association), Farmington Hills, MI. Annual: 1980-date. English.

FCA Newsletter (Finnish Center Association), Farmington Hills, MI. Monthly (bi-monthly): 1970-1974, 1978-date. English.

Finland Review, New York, NY. Monthly: 1919. English.

The Finland Sentinel, New York, NY. Monthly: 1918. English.

Finlandia Foundation Newsletter, Santa Monica, CA. Frequency varies: 1967, 1970-1971, 1973. English.

Finnam Newsletter (Finnish American Historical Society of the West), Portland, OR. Frequency varies: 1974-1977. English.

Finn Focus, Hancock, MI. Quarterly: 1984. English.

The Finnish-American Blue-White Book, New York, NY. Annual: 1963-1968. Includes English.

Finnish American Cultural Activities, Minneapolis/St. Paul, MN. Monthly: 1984-date. English.

The Finnish American Heritage (previously titled Finnish American Society, Inc., News and Views), Minneapolis, MN. Monthly: 1979-date. English.

Finnish American Society, Inc. News and Views (title changed to The Finnish American Heritage in 1979), Minneapolis, MN. Monthly: 1972-1979. Includes English.

Finnish American Society of Santa Clara County Newsletter, Cupertino, CA. Monthly: 1985-date. English.

Finnish Americana, New Brighton, MN. Annual: 1978-1984. English.

Finnish Connection, Vancouver, British Columbia, Canada. Bi-monthly: 1986. English.

Finnish Cultural Center Newsletter, Fitchburg, MA. Quarterly: 1987. English.

Finnish Emigrant Studies Series (previously titled Finnam Newsletter), Portland, OR. Quarterly: 1969-1977. English.

Finnish Evangelical Lutheran Church of America or Suomi Synod Directory, Hancock, MI. Annual: 1955-1962. English.

Finnish Evangelical Lutheran Church of America or Suomi Synod Yearbook, Hancock, MI. Annual: 1936-1937, 1939, 1941-1962. Includes English.

Greater Chicago Finnish Yearbook, Chicago, IL. Annual: 1932, 1940-1941. Includes English.

The Greater N.Y. Finnish Bicentennial Planning Committee Newsletter, New York, NY. Bi-monthly: 1975-1976. English.

Greater New York Finnish Directory and General Information, New York, NY. Annual: 1932. Includes English.

Greetings of Peace (English edition of **Rauhan Tervehdys**), Calumet, MI. Monthly: 1948-1949, 1951-1957, 1968-1974. English.

Hengelliseltä Taistelutantereelta (From the Spiritual Battlefield), Fitchburg, MA. Frequency varies: 1910.

Herää Valvomaan (Rise on Guard), Helsinki, Finland. 1960.

Heritage Preservationist, Minneapolis, MN. Quarterly: 1983-1984. Includes English.

Idän Suomalaisen Raittius-Kansan Liiton Joulujulkaisu (Eastern Finnish Temperance Organization's Christmas Publication), Fitchburg, MA. Annual: 1919, 1926-1927.

Idän Suomalaisen Raittius-Kansan Liiton Kesäjulkaisu (Eastern Finnish Temperance Organization's Summer Publication), Brooklyn, NY. Annual: 1933.

Industrialistin Joulu (Industrialist Christmas; previously titled **Sosialistin Joulu**), Duluth, MN. Annual: 1914-1928, 1946-1960.

Institute of History General History University of Turku Studies Publications, Turku, Finland. Irregular: 1971-1977. Includes English, French, and German.

Joulu (Christmas), Superior, WI, and Sudbury, Ontario, Canada. Annual: 1930, 1939-1940, 1943-1948, 1950-1970, 1972-1974, 1977.

Jouluviesti (Christmas Message), Fitchburg, MA. 1957.

Kalenteri Amerikan Suomalaiselle Työväelle (Calendar for Finnish American Workers), Fitchburg, MA. Annual: 1914-1921.

Kalevainen (The Kalevan), Virginia, MN (previously published in Brooklyn, NY; Hancock, MI; and Duluth, MN). Annual (monthly): 1916-1921, 1923-1930, 1933-1934, 1936-1946, 1948-1979. Includes English.

Kalevan Kansa (Kaleva's People), Fairport Harbor, OH (previously published in Duluth, MN). Frequency varies: 1931-1933.

Kanadan Suomalaisten Kalenteri (Canadian Finnish Calendar), Thunder Bay, Ontario, Canada. Annual: 1962-1964.

Kansalliskirkon Juhlajulkaisut (The National Church Holiday Publications), Ironwood, MI. Quarterly: 1913, 1915, 1918, 1927, 1930.

Kansan Ääni Raittiusmielisten Kevät-Albumi (The Voice of the People Temperance Spring Album), Hancock, MI (previously published in Rock Springs, WY). Annual: 1899-1902.

Kansan Henki (Spirit of the People), Duluth, MN. Quarterly: 1916-1919, 1921-1922.

Kansan Huumori (Popular Humor), New York, NY. Semi-monthly: 1936-1938.

Kansan Kalenteri (The People's Calendar), Helsinki, Finland. Annual: 1906-1908, 1911.

Kansan Toveri (The People's Comrade), New York Mills, MN. Bi-weekly: 1897-1898. (Microfilm: 1897-1898).

Kansanvalistusseuran Kalenteri (The People's Enlightenment Society Calendar), Helsinki, Finland. Annual: 1895-1898, 1900-1903, 1905-1913, 1936-1938.

Kevät (Spring), Superior, WI (previously published in Sudbury, Ontario, Canada). Annual: 1948, 1951-1952, 1971-1978.

Kevät-Albumi (Spring Album), Hancock, MI. 1902.

Kevätsoihtu (Spring Torch), Duluth, MN. 1942.

Kirkko (The Church), Hibbing, MN. Annual (?): 1934.

Kirkollinen Kalenteri (The Church Calendar), Hancock, MI. Annual: 1903-1979, 1981. Includes English.

Kirkonkello (The Church Bell), Duluth, MN. Frequency varies: 1932-1937.

Kodin Joulu (Christmas at Home), New York Mills, MN. Annual: 1958-1964.

Koitto (Daybreak), Duluth, MN. Monthly: 1919.

Koti (Home), Duluth, MN, and Hancock, MI. Monthly: 1922-1924. Includes English.

Kotilähetys-Ystävä (The Home Mission Friend), Hancock, MI. 1922, 1938, 1943.

Kotimatkalla (Homeward Bound), Helsinki, Finland. Annual: 1923.

Köyhälistön Nuija (The Hammer of the Proletariat), Hancock, MI. Annual: 1907-1912.

Kristillinen Kuukausilehti (Christian Monthly Paper), Laurium, MI (previously published in Blind Slough, OR; Astoria, OR; and Calumet, MI). Monthly: 1916-1922, 1924-1940, 1942-1962.

Kultainen Aika (The Golden Age), Duluth, MN. Weekly: one undated issue.

Kuuluttaja (Commentator), Duluth, MN. Monthly: 1939-1941, 1944-1945(?).

Lähetysyhdistyksen Jouluviesti (Mission Society Christmas Message), Fitchburg, MA. Annual: 1946-1947.

Lapatossu (The Shoepack), Superior, WI. Semi-monthly: 1911-1913, 1916, 1918-1920.

Laskiainen Yearbook (The Shrovetide Yearbook), Virginia, MN. Annual: 1940. English.

Lasten Joulu (The Children's Christmas), Astoria, OR. Annual: 1918-1922.

Lasten Kevät (The Children's Spring), Astoria, OR. Annual: 1918, 1920, 1922.

Lukemista Kaikille (Reading for Everyone), Duluth, MN. Frequency varies: 1958-1961.

Luokkataistelu (The Class Struggle), New York, NY. Monthly: 1919.

Lutheran Counselor, Hancock, MI. Semi-monthly (monthly): 1944-1947, 1949, 1956-1958, 1962. English.

The Lutheran Voice, Ironwood, MI. Monthly (except July-August): 1950. English.

The Lutheran Youth, Ironwood, MI. Monthly: 1941. English.

The Messenger (previously titled Lasten Lehti), Hancock, MI. Monthly, Sept.-May: 1910, 1912, 1914, 1916, 1927-1928, 1936, 1938-1939, 1954-1961. Includes English.

Michiganin Suomalainen (The Michigan Finn), Detroit, MI. Annual: 1961-1963.

Minnesota Finnish-American Bicentennial Committee Duluth Branch Minutes of Meetings, Duluth, MN. 1976. English.

Minnesota Finnish American Historical Society, Minneapolis/St. Paul, MN. Monthly: 1977-1980. English.

Minnesotan Raittiusliiton Juhlajulkaisu (Minnesota Temperance League Holiday Publication), Duluth, MN. Annual: 1932.

Minnesotan Suomalaisten Juhannusjuhla (Minnesota Finns' Midsummer Festival), place of publication varies. Annual: 1905-1906, 1908-1909, 1912-1914, 1918-1919, 1929-1931, 1935-1936, 1939-1941, 1947, 1951, 1953-1971. Includes English.

New Yorkin Lehden Kalenteri (Calendar of the New York Journal), New York, NY. Annual: 1893.

New Yorkin Uutiset Jouluviesti (Christmas Message of the Finnish New York News), New York, NY. Annual: 1918-1919, 1921, 1927, 1952, 1955.

New Yorkin Uutiset Juhannus-Viesti (Midsummer Tidings of the Finnish New York News), New York, NY. Annual: 1921.

Northern States Cooperative League Yearbook (continued in 1930 by the Cooperative League of the U.S.A.), Minneapolis, MN. Annual: 1925-1928. English.

Northern States Co-operator, Minneapolis, MN. Bi-monthly: 1925. English.

Nuori Suomi (Young Finland), Duluth, MN (previously published in Brooklyn, NY). Annual: 1903-1904, 1907.

Nuorison Joulu (Young People's Christmas), Hämeenlinna, Finland. 1916, 1920.

Nuorison Paimen (Shepherd of Youth), Ironwood, MI. Monthly: 1924-1926. Includes English.

Nuorten Kesä (Young People's Summer), Helsinki, Finland. 1917.

Nuorten Ystävä (Friend of Youth), Hancock, MI. Monthly: 1916-1921, 1925-1926, 1930, 1932, 1934-1936. Includes English.

Nykyaika (Modern Age), Fitchburg, MA. Monthly (semi-monthly): 1921-1924, 1929-1930, 1934.

Paimen-Sanomia (The Shepherd's Tidings), Hancock, MI. Semi-monthly (weekly and monthly): 1889, 1902, 1910-1913, 1915-1916, 1920-1922, 1925, 1927-1929, 1933, 1936, 1939-1941, 1943-1950, 1952-1962.

Päivälehti Publishing Company. Joulu (Christmas), Duluth, MN. Annual: 1928, 1930.

Päivälehti Publishing Company. Juhannus (Midsummer Day), Duluth, MN. Annual: 1941, 1943.

Päivälehti Publishing Company. Kevät (Spring), Duluth, MN. Annual: 1945.

Palvelija (The Servant), New York Mills, MN. Monthly: 1949-1950, 1955, 1957, 1961, 1966-date. Includes English.

Pelto ja Koti (Farm and Home), Superior, WI (previously published in Hancock, MI). Weekly (semi-monthly and monthly): 1913-1920.

Punainen Kalenteri (The Red Calendar), Helsinki, Finland. Annual: 1926-1927.

Punainen Soihtu (The Red Torch), Duluth, MN. Annual: 1916-1927, 1938-1939, 1941.

Punatähti (The Red Star), New York, NY. Annual: 1930, 1933, 1936-1939.

Punikin Joulu (Red's Christmas Annual), Helsinki, Finland. Annual: 1921.

Punikki (Red), Brooklyn, NY (published in Superior, WI until 1931). Semi-monthly: 1922, 1924-1936.

Pyhän Matteuksen Suomalainen Ev.-Luterilainen Seurakunta. Seurakuntalehti (St. Matthew's Finnish Ev. Lutheran Church Newsletter), Sudbury, Ontario, Canada. Quarterly: 1977-1980.

Raitis Joulu (Temperate Christmas), Duluth, MN. Annual: 1932-1936, 1938-1939.

Raitis Juhannus (Temperate Midsummer), Duluth, MN. Annual: 1935, 1937.

Raittius Kalenteri (Temperance Calendar), Michigan. Annual: 1920.

Raittiuskansan Kalenteri (Calendar of the Temperance-Minded), Hancock, MI (place of publication varies until 1945). Annual: 1897, 1899-1932, 1934-1936, 1943-1947, 1949-1971.

Raittiuskansan Kesäjulkaisu (Summer Publication of the Temperance-Minded), Hancock, MI. Annual: 1919, 1921.

Raittiuslehti (Temperance News), Hancock, MI (previously published in Ishpeming, MI; New York Mills, MN; Superior, WI; New York, NY; Calumet, MI; and Kaleva, MI). Monthly: 1892-1913.

Raivaajan Joulu (The Pioneer's Christmas), Fitchburg, MA. Annual: 1951-1952.

Raivaajan Työvainiolta (From the Prioneer's Work Field), Fitchburg, MA. Annual: 1905, 1907-1911.

Rauhan Sana (The Word of Peace), Rovaniemi, Finland. Monthly: 1935-1940, 1947, 1949-1951.

Rauhan Tervehdys (Greetings of Peace; combined with English edition in 1972), Calumet, MI. Monthly: 1922-1925, 1927, 1944-1957, 1966-1974, 1977.

Reunion of Sisters, Minneapolis, MN. Frequency varies: 1984, 1987. English.

Ribbon, New York, NY. 1952. Includes English.

Säkeniä; Sosialistinen Kuukausijulkaisu (Sparks; Socialist Monthly Publication), Fitchburg, MA. Monthly: 1909-1921.

Salolampi Sanomat (Woodland Pool Tidings), Minneapolis, MN. Quarterly: 1980-1984. English.

Sanomia Siionista (Tidings from Zion), Oulu, Finland. Monthly: 1894-1896.

Seuranlehti (Society News), Fergus Falls, MN (Minneapolis, MN). 1978-date. English.

Siionin Lähetyslehti (Zion's Mission News), Oulu, Finland. Monthly: 1921-1923, 1925, 1927, 1947.

Siirtokansan Kalenteri (Immigrants' Calendar), New York Mills, MN (previously published in Duluth, MN). Annual: 1918-1978. Includes English.

Siirtolaisuus (Migration), Turku, Finland. Quarterly: 1975-1985. Includes English.

Sisu (Courage), Duluth, MN. Frequency varies: one undated issue.

Soihtu (The Torch), Chicago, IL. Monthly: 1906.

Sorretun Kevät (Springtime of the Oppressed), Astoria, OR. Annual (?): 1908.

Suomalainen (The Finn), Hancock, MI. Monthly: 1962-1964.

Suomalainen Almanakka ja Kalenteri (Finnish Almanac and Calendar), New York, NY. Annual: 1908, 1917-1918, 1923-1924, 1928, 1933.

Suomalainen Kalenteri (Finnish Calendar), New York, NY. Annual: 1917-1919, 1921-1923, 1925.

Suomalaisen Kansallis-Raittius-Veljeysseura. Pöytäkirja Vuosikokouksessa (Finnish National Temperance Brotherhood Annual Meeting Minutes), Fitchburg, MA. Annual: 1909.

Suomen Silta (Finland's Bridge), Helsinki, Finland. Bi-monthly: 1937, 1952-1953, 1955, 1957-1959, 1961-1965, 1967, 1974-date. Includes English.

Suomen Yleinen Kalenteri (Finland's General Calendar), Helsinki, Finland. Annual: 1921-1923.

Suomenkielinen Puhelinluettelo (Directory of the Finnish Speaking Population in Florida), Lake Worth, FL. Annual: 1961-1962. Includes English.

Suomi College Alumni Directory, Hancock, MI. Annual: 1963. English.

Suomi College Bulletin (previously titled **Suomi-Opiston Juhlajulkaisut**), Hancock, MI. Quarterly: 1912, 1914-1916, 1918, 1922, 1924-1930, 1932-1937, 1939-1941, 1943-1962, 1973-1975. Includes English.

Suomi College Finnish American Bicentennial U.S.A. Newsletter, Hancock, MI. 1975. English.

Suomi College and Theological Seminary General Catalogue and Announcements, Hancock, MI. Annual: 1910-1911, 1913-1914, 1916-1917, 1929-1930, 1932-1937, 1939-1941, 1948-1956. Includes English.

Suomi College and Theological Seminary Yearbook (title varies: Fennia, Suomi and Suomian), Hancock, MI. Annual: 1915, 1919-1922, 1924, 1926, 1931-1932, 1950, 1952, 1961-1962. Includes English.

Suomi-Finland. U.S.A., Helsinki, Finland. 1976. Includes English.

Suomi-Opiston Viesti (Tidings from Suomi College), Hancock, MI. Quarterly: 1963-1971, 1973-1975, 1977.

Suomi Theological Seminary Good News from Suomi, Hancock, MI. Annual: 1956-1958. English.

Sydänkesä (The Heart of Summer), Fitchburg, MA. Annual: 1950-1951.

Taistelun Viiri (Banner of Struggle), Sudbury, Ontario, Canada. Annual: 1933, 1935.

Taskukalenteri (Pocket Calendar), Canada. Annual: 1940, 1952-1953.

Teosofian Valo; Suomalainen Teosofinen Kuukausilehti Amerikassa (The Light of Theosophy; The Finnish Theosophical Monthly in America), Cleveland, OH. 1913.

Tie Vapauteen (Road to Freedom), Duluth, MN (place of publication varies). Monthly (frequency varies until 1921): 1919-1937.

Tietokalenteri (Informational Calendar), Helsinki, Finland. Annual: 1910-1913, 1919.

Tietokäsikirja (Informational Handbook), Fitchburg, MA. Annual: 1912-1913.

Totuuden Todistaja (The Witness of the Truth), New York, NY. Monthly: 1936-1937, 1939, 1949, 1951, 1955-1956, 1968.

Totuus (The Truth), Duluth, MN. Frequency varies: 1920-1924.

Turun Yliopisto (Turku University), Turku, Finland. Frequency varies: 1967, 1969-1976. Includes English summaries.

Työkansan Kalenteri; Kanadan Suomalaisen Työväestön Vuosijulkaisu (The Work People's Calendar; Canadian Finnish Workers' Yearbook), Thunder Bay, Ontario, Canada. Annual: 1913.

Työläisen Taskukalenteri (The Workers' Pocket Calendar), Duluth, MN. Annual: 1924-1925, 1927, 1932, 1934-1935, 1938, 1946-1948, 1950, 1952.

Työmiehen Joulu (The Workers' Christmas), Superior, WI. Annual: 1907-1914, 1916-1929.

Työmiehen Kalenteri (The Workers' Calendar), Helsinki, Finland. Annual: 1922-1923.

Työmies (The Worker), Ishpeming, MI. Weekly. (Microfilm: 1889-1893).

Työmies Society Liikkeenhoitajan Tili-ja Liikekertomus ja Johtokunnan Toimintakertomus (Työmies Society Manager's Financial and Business Report and Report from the Board of Directors), Superior, WI. Annual: 1927-1928.

Työmies Society Vuosikokouksen Pöytäkirja (Työmies Society's Annual Meeting Minutes; previously titled **Pöytäkirja Tehty Työmies Kustannusyhtion Vuosikokouksesta**), Superior, WI. Annual: 1913-1927, 1930.

Työmies Societyn Tili-ja Tomintakertomukset (Työmies Society's Financial and Activities Reports), Superior, WI. Annual: 1930.

Työn Kalenteri (Work Calendar), Helsinki, Finland. Annual: 1925.

Työväen Kalenteri (The Workers' Calendar), Hancock, MI. Annual: 1905-1906.

Työväen Kalenteri (The Workers' Calendar), Helsinki, Finland. Annual: 1909-1911, 1913-1915.

Työväen Kalenteri (The Workers' Calendar), Duluth, MN. Annual: 1955-1956.

Työväen-Opiston Kevätjulkaisu (Work People's College Annual), Duluth, MN. Annual: 1938-1940. Includes English.

Työväen Tasku-Kalenteri (The Workers' Pocket Calendar), Duluth, MN. Annual: 1932, 1934, 1937, 1946-1950, 1952, 1954-1955.

Työväen Vappu (Workers' May Day), Helsinki, Finland. Annual: 1933.

Urheilu-Viesti (Sports Tidings), Hancock, MI. Annual: 1909-1910.

Uuden Ajan Joulu (The New Era's Christmas), Duluth, MN. Annual: 1937-1945.

Uudenajan Soihtu (The New Era's Torch), Hancock, MI. Annual: 1914.

Uusi Aika (The New Era), Brooklyn, NY. Monthly: 1914.

Väkäleuan Kalenteri (The Barbed Chin Calendar), Thunder Bay, Ontario, Canada. Annual: 1913.

Vallankumous; Työväen Opiston Toverikunnan Julkaisu (Revolution; Publication of the Work People's College Fraternity), Hancock, MI. Annual: 1909-1915.

Valoa (Light), Hancock, MI. Annual: 1943-1968. Includes English.

Valoa; The Ohio Pennsylvania and West Virginia Temperance Council (Light), Fairport, OH. Annual: 1933-1934, 1939.

Valon Sirpaleita (Shards of Light), New York Mills, MN. Annual: 1935. Includes English.

Valon Soihtu (The Torch of Light), Ishpeming, MI. Monthly: 1916.

Vapauden Viiri (Freedom's Banner), Sudbury, Ontario, Canada. Quarterly (?): 1938.

Vappu (May Day), Sudbury, Ontario, Canada (place of publication varies). Annual: 1906-1934, 1938-1943, 1945-1949, 1951-1967.

Veljeysviesti (The Message of Brotherhood), Astoria, OR. Monthly: 1927, 1932-1935, 1938-date. Includes English.

Viesti (Tidings), Brooklyn, New York. Monthly: 1930-1936.

Vuosikirja (Yearbook), Superior, WI. Annual: 1926, 1927.

Yhteishyvä (Commonwealth), Rock, MI. Monthly: 1939.

Zion Evangelical Lutheran Church of Virginia, Minnesota Annual Report, Virginia, MN. Annual: 1954. English.

Greek American Collection

Manuscript Collections

Argoe, Kostis Tamias (191?-1982).
Papers, 1930-1969. 3 linear ft.

Argoe (originally Argyropoulos) was a Greek American journalist and community leader in Chicago, IL. His papers include published and unpublished articles, one-act plays, records of Greek American cultural organizations in Chicago, and correspondence and printed material related to the Cyprus issue. Articles include those written for the *Greek Press* by Argoe under his pseudonym Tzimis Brouklis and clippings from the *United Community Echo*. Records include those of the Hellenic Cultural Circle of Chicago and the Peloponnesian Study Society of Chicago. Materials on the Cyprus issue include correspondence and leaflets of the Justice for Cyprus Committee, Cypriot government publications, and clippings from major newspapers. *Mainly in English. Inventory available.*

Callimachos, Demetrios P. (1879-1963).
Papers, ca. 1876-1963. Ca. 20 linear ft.

Callimachos, a journalist, priest, and author, was born in Madytos, Turkey. He was educated in Istanbul, Smyrna, and Athens, and came to the United States in 1914. He was active in many Greek and Greek American associations and other organizations, including the Greek American Progressive Association (GAPA), the Clergy Club, the Greater New York Federation of Churches, the New York Academy of Political Science, the Institute Egyptien, the XVI International Congress of Orientalists, and the Honorary Institute of Byzantine Music. During his career, he lectured for the Panhellenic Union of America and edited the daily *Ethnikos Keryx* (National Herald, New York, NY), *National Renaissance* (a Greek American monthly), *Eleutheros Typos* (Free Press, Chicago, IL), and *Vima tes GAPA* (Tribune of GAPA, Pittsburgh, PA). He also served as the priest of St. Constantine's Church (Brooklyn, NY) and taught at St. Athanasius Seminary. His publications in English include *Powerful Modern Greek Characters* (N. J. Cassavetes, trans., n.d.).

Papers include biographical information, correspondence, writings and speeches, resources, legal documents, memorabilia, collected ephemera, and photographs. The many correspondents include the American Committee for Armenian and Syrian Relief, the Cyprian National Federation of America, George Demeter, George E. Phillies, Theodore Saloutos, and many other organizations and persons. Topics represented in the resources series include research in the religious archives of Patmos and Alexandria, the Greek American press, Greek American organizational life, editorial drafts, the Greek Orthodox Archdiocese of North and South America, relief causes, Greek politics, and manuscripts by other authors. Photographs document Greek American life, especially in the New York area. *Includes some English. Inventory available. Related collection: Theodore Saloutos. Collection is closed until 1997.*

Donus, George B. (1905-   ).
Papers, n.d. 1 linear in.

Papers of Donus, a prominent Greek American poet, author, artist, and educator, consist of miscellaneous published materials by and about him. Also included are biographical sketches and reminiscences along with samples of his creative writing. *In English.*

Fergis, Sophia (Chakiris) (1909-   ).
Papers, 1984. 1 linear in.

Papers consist of an autobiographical manuscript entitled "Escape to a New Dawn: Based on a True Story." The story describes her family's suffering in their hometown of Platiano, Turkey, beginning in 1913; their immigration to Thessalonika in 1914 and to the United States in 1915-1916; and their life in Cincinnati, OH. Also included is a photograph of Fergis ca. 1924. *In English.*

Greek Community Council of Marysville (California).
Records, 1931-1935. Ca. 1 linear in.

Records of the Marysville Council, a local kinotis (a kind of governing body for immigrant Greek communities) consist of a ledger showing dues, donations, expenditures, and other financial records. *Includes English.*

Greek Orthodox Archdiocese of North and South America, Department of Laity (New York, New York).
Records, ca. 1950-1981. Ca. 41.5 linear ft.

Records of the Department include correspondence, financial records, photographs, press releases, subject files, and print materials. Much of the collection relates to activities of the Greek Orthodox Youth Association, the Biennial Clergy-Laity Congress, individual parishes, relations with other denominations, and relations with religious and secular social action groups. *Includes English. Inventory available.*

Holter, April.
Papers, n.d. Ca. 1 linear in.

Papers of Holter consist of a term paper entitled "The Greeks of Minneapolis" and related notes of interviews. *In English.*

Mantis, Mary.
Papers, 1953-date. Ca. 1.5 linear ft.

Papers of Mantis comprise newspaper clippings, brochures, newsletters, reports, and bulletins pertaining to Greek Americans and Greek American organizational activity. Included are a guide and questionnaire to an oral history collection project entitled "Arete: The Memories of Greek American Women"; correspondence, reports, and minutes of the St. Paul (MN) chapter of the Order of AHEPA (American Hellenic Educational Progressive Association); miscellaneous AHEPA publications; books, pamphlets, and newsletters about the political situation in Cyprus; correspondence of the Daughters of Penelope chapters in Hibbing and St. Paul, MN; and miscellaneous newspaper clippings, postcards, and photographs relating to Greece and Greek Americans. *Mainly in English.*

**Minnesota Friends of Cyprus
(Minneapolis-St. Paul).**
Records, 1967-1981. 3.5 linear ft. and
1 cassette tape.

The Minnesota Friends of Cyprus was
founded in 1974 as the Minnesota Cyprus
Committee. Its purposes are related to
the Cyprus problem: to contribute to its
just solution, to provide information, and
to aid refugees. The organization lobbies
with the U.S. government, holds public
discussions and other events, and has
published a newsletter (1977-1979).
Members have participated in regional,
national, and international events,
including the 1975 Women Walk Home
(Cyprus). As of 1987, the MFC was
inactive but still extant.

Records consist of organizational
papers and financial records,
correspondence, print and near-print
materials, newspaper clippings, maps,
posters, ephemera, and photographs.
Included is correspondence with U.S.
government officials and representatives,
including President Gerald Ford, Hodding
Carter III, Rep. Donald M. Fraser, Sen.
Hubert H. Humphrey, Rep. Joseph E.
Karth, Sen. Walter F. Mondale, Rep.
Albert H. Quie, Sen. Paul S. Sarbanes,
Secy. of Defense James R. Schlesinger,
and Rep. Bruce F. Vento. Private
correspondents include Andrew A.
Athens, Kostis T. Argoe, N. G. Dimitriou,
Phoebus J. Dhrymes, Archbishop Iakovos,
Leon P. Stavrou, and Patroklos Stavrou.
Mainly in English. Inventory available.

**Minnesotans for Democracy in Greece
(Minneapolis-St. Paul).**
Records, 1964-1979. 7 linear in.

Records consist of correspondence,
clippings, minutes, reports, and published
materials of the organization. *In English.*

Order of AHEPA (Washington, D.C.).
Records, 1925-1981. 79 microfilm reels.

A social, cultural, and fraternal
organization, the Order of AHEPA
(American Hellenic Educational
Progressive Association) was founded in
1922. The Order has about 50,000
members, with 440 local branches and

500 auxiliaries for women and children.
It helps newly arrived Greeks adapt to
American life, encourages the
dissemination of Hellenic ideas and
culture, provides financial assistance to
various charities, sponsors tours to
Greece, grants college scholarships, and
encourages the study of Greek language
and culture.

Records include supreme convention
minutes (1929-1980), convention summary
minutes (1925-1981), yearbooks (1936-
1981), the AHEPAN magazine (1927-
1981), and death benefit records (1956-
1971). *In English.*

Papademetriou, Constantine G.
Papers, 1947-1977. 2 linear in.

Papers relate chiefly to
Papademetriou's activities as a priest.
Included are a membership account book
of Saint George Greek Orthodox Church
(Moline, IL); outgoing letters and other
papers from Saint Anthony's Greek
Orthodox Church (Clairton, PA); and
mementos of the fiftieth anniversary of
his ordination. *Inventory available.*

Poletis, N. A.
Papers, ca. 1920-1942. Ca. 1 linear in.

The papers of Poletis consist of letters
from Greek American organizations;
newspaper clippings from Fort Dodge, IA,
about Greek war relief efforts; a
mimeographed report to the convention of
the Fourteenth District of the Order of
AHEPA; and photographs. *Includes
English.*

Saloutos, Theodore (1910-1980).
Papers, ca. 1887-1982. Ca. 45 linear ft.

An eminent historian of Greek
American studies and of agrarian politics
and reform movements, Saloutos was
born in Milwaukee, WI, son of immigrant
parents from Peloponnisos. Saloutos
taught at the University of Wisconsin,
Oberlin College, and UCLA. While at
Oberlin College he began work on Greek
immigration which ultimately resulted in
publication of *The Greeks in the United
States* (1964). He was deeply involved in

Greek community affairs, participating in
organizations such as the Sons of Pericles
(Milwaukee), the Order of AHEPA, the
Hellenic University Club of Southern
California, and the Save Cyprus Council
of Southern California. Saloutos wrote
several major works and numerous
articles, and was a frequent speaker.

Papers of Saloutos include personal
and professional correspondence; research
notes; documentation of organizational,
teaching, and political activities;
photographs; diaries; and memorabilia.
Correspondents include but are not
limited to, Louis Adamic, Frank P.
Agnost, Dean Alfange, O. Fritiof Ander,
Costas Athanasiades, Charles Bookidis,
George Christy, Nicholas C. Culolias,
Julius C. C. Edelstein, Kimon Friar,
James A. Geroulis, Oscar Handlin,
Andrew T. Kopan, Peter T. Kourides,
George J. Leber, Charles C. Moskos,
Helen Z. Papanikolas, George E. Phillies,
Paul S. Sarbanes, Spyros P. Skouras,
George C. Vournas, Basil J. Vlavianos,
James S. Vlasto, Speros Vryonis, Carl
Wittke, and Elias Ziogas. The collection
contains a vast amount of information on
various Greek American organizations and
individuals. *Includes English and some
German. Published inventory available.*

Tselos, Dimitri (1899-   ).
Papers, ca. 1927-1975. Ca. 1 linear ft.

Dimitri Tselos was a professor of art
history at the University of Minnesota,
with specialties in Byzantine, early
medieval, and modern art. His papers
consist of his writings on art and
architecture, book reviews, and articles in
the Greek American press. *In English.
Inventory available.*

**United States. Department of State.
Decimal files 868 and 711.68.**
Records, 1910-1929. 48 microfilm reels.

Records of the Department relate to
internal affairs of Greece and to political
relations between Greece and the United
States. The bulk of the records is
instructions to and dispatches from
diplomatic and consular officials. Also
included are notes between the
Department and foreign diplomatic
representatives in the United States,
memoranda prepared by Department
officials, and correspondence with
officials of other government departments
and with private firms and individuals.
*In English. Originals held by the
National Archives and Records
Administration, Washington, DC.*

Monographs

The recent addition of historian Theodore Saloutos's personal library to the IHRC
augmented holdings already strong in the area of religion and created new areas of strength
in general works; Greek emigration policy and the background to the migration, and Greek
American organizations, political activities, geographical distribution, ethnic press, and
literature. Topics such as assimilation, education, and the family are represented to a lesser
degree.

Among the IHRC books are the key secondary works about Greek Americans
(including bibliographies), as well as a variety of directories, biographies, and guides.
Available overviews, in addition to Saloutos's *They Remember America* (1956) and *Greeks
in the United States* (1964), include Henry Pratt Fairchild's *Greek Immigration to the United
States* (1911); Thomas Burgess's *Greeks in America* (1913); Andreas M. Andreadis's *He
Hellenike metanasteusis* (The Greek Migration, 1917); Seraphim G. Canoutas's *Ho
Hellenismos en Amerike* (Hellenism in America, 1918); J. P. Xenides's *The Greeks in
America* (1922); *The Greek American Community in Transition*, edited by Harry J.
Psomiades and Alice Scourby (1982); Charles Moskos's *Greek Americans: Struggle and
Success* (1980); and others. Also present are the two extant bibliographies: Michael
Cutsumbis's *Bibliographic Guide to Materials on Greeks in the U.S., 1890-1968* (1970) and
Evangelos Vlachos's *Annotated Bibliography of Greek Migration* (1966).

The IHRC has biographies and autobiographies of such figures as Michael Anagnos and Spyros Skouras, among others; these supplement directories of Greek Americans in higher learning (1974) and in business (1979). Primary sources from the early twentieth century include publications intended for newly arrived Greek immigrants such as guides, advice manuals, and primers of English.

On the subject of religion, most items are publications of the Orthodox Christian Educational Society or the Greek Orthodox Archdiocese of North and South America and its parishes. Publication dates range from the 1910s to the present, with the period since World War II having fullest coverage. Among the archdiocesan publications are bylaws, catechisms, and liturgies; ecumenical guidelines and discussions (1960s); a 1955-1956 catalog of the Holy Cross Theological School in Brookline, Massachusetts; and yearbooks, anniversary albums, and commemorative albums (such as those marking national assemblies). Also present are publications of the Greek Orthodox Youth Association (GOYA). A number of pamphlets published by the Church or by others pertain to controversies of the 1940s through the 1970s; among these works by John Papas, Constantine Dukakis, Demetrios Callimachos, and others, are discussions of Holy Cross Seminary. Numerous other religious sources highlight particular localities, as for example the fiftieth anniversary album of a San Diego church community (1977). Also included are secondary studies, such as a biography of Patriarch Athenagoras I by George Papaioannou (1976) and a history by Nicon D. Patrinacos, *The Aims and Program of Archdiocesan Education* (1976).

The migration of Greeks to the United States is treated at length in the general works listed above. Questions of emigration and emigration policy are the subjects of Greek works dating from the pre-World War I period and later. Some aspects of the background to the post-World War II migration are reflected in studies by Irwin Sanders (*Village Social Organization in Greece*, 1953) and Scott McNall (*The Greek Peasant*, 1974) describing peasant life in the modern Greek village.

Greek immigrants, like others, formed numerous fraternal organizations, mutual benefit societies, and relief societies, often established by people from the same original village or region. The IHRC has commemorative albums of mutual benefit societies of former Samians (1923), Arahovans of Laconia (1950), Lacedaemonians (1952), Thracians (1962), and Arcadians (1956 and 1964), among others. In addition there are primary materials from two broad Greek American organizations: the American Hellenic Educational Progressive Association (AHEPA) and the Greek American Progressive Association (GAPA). Order of AHEPA publications among the IHRC holdings include a history by its long-time executive secretary George Leber (1972) as well as extensive primary sources documenting the organization and its auxiliaries. At the national level there are books by AHEPA leaders V. I. Chebithes and George C. Vournas as well as manuals (including manuals of bylaws), yearbooks, and an annual report (1976). Commemorative publications comprise anniversary albums and convention publications (albums, summaries of minutes, and informational publications about the Greek heritage and prominent individuals). Publications of AHEPA auxiliary organizations are also present: from the Daughters of Penelope, the senior women's auxiliary, there is a fiftieth anniversary album (1979), and from the Sons of Pericles, the junior men's auxiliary, there is a manual containing its constitution and bylaws (1926). Sources at the IHRC relating to GAPA extend to publications of individual GAPA lodges as well as annual national convention albums (1930 and 1931) and an undated manual supplying texts of a constitution and bylaws for women's lodges.

In the area of politics the IHRC holdings contain assorted primary sources on Greek American involvement in foreign and domestic political issues. Many are publications issued by organizations. These include pamphlets of the Pan-Epirotic Union in America (1919) and of the Dodecanesian League of America (1942). The Panhellenic Union, influential in the recruitment of immigrants for Greece during the Balkan wars of 1912-1913, is represented by a yearbook from 1920. From a later period there are publications of organizations concerned with the Cyprus issue (1960s-present). In the 1970s, domestic concerns are evident in a publication by HANAC (Hellenic American

Neighborhood Action Committee, Inc.), *The Needs of the Growing Greek-American Community in the City of New York.*

Most arriving Greeks settled in the cities of the northeastern and north-central states. The IHRC has wide-ranging primary sources in the form of local communities' commemorative albums marking fiftieth anniversaries (Astoria, NY [1977]; central Ohio [1962]; and Baltimore [1946]) and other events (Brooklyn [1920], Chicago [1937 and 1982], and Atlanta [1975]). Regional professional directories for the western states (n.d.) and Illinois (1975) are also present. Many secondary works at the IHRC treat the Greek American history of a selected city, greater urban area, county, or state. States discussed wholly or in part include California (Demitra Georgas's *Greek Settlement of the San Francisco Bay Area*, 1974), Florida (Helen Halley's *A Historical Functional Approach to the Study of the Greek Community of Tarpon Springs*, 1952), Massachusetts (George T. Eliopoulos's *Greek Immigrants in Springfield, Massachusetts, 1884-1944*, 1967), Minnesota (Karen Anne Bruce's *The Social Organization of the Greek Community in Minneapolis*, 1961), Ohio (Angelos Nikolaou Alexopoulos's *The Greek Story of Canton, Ohio, 1898-1973*, 1974), Texas (*The Greek Texans* by the Institute of Texan Cultures, 1974), and Utah (Helen Papanikolas's *Toil and Rage in a New Land: The Greek Immigrants in Utah*, 1970).

On the subject of the Greek American press, the royalist *Atlantis* (1894-1973) is represented by such publications as a poetry anthology. Regarding the rival *Ethnikos Keryx* (National Herald), the IHRC holds publications such as yearbooks from the 1920s and 1930s and a *National Herald* book catalog (*Genikos timokatalogos* [General Price Catalog], 1930).

From among the arts the IHRC holdings feature literary works written by Greek Americans or dealing with Greek themes. The collection includes novels by Tiffany Thayer, Konstantinos P. Rhodokanakes, Albert Isaac Bezzarides, Mary Vardoulakis, Roxane Cotsakis, Warren Tute, Harry Mark Petrakis, and Elia Kazan. Poetry is present by Anesti I. Ganotaki and by George B. Donus.

Greek American educational materials at the IHRC reflect that community's emphasis on the use of Greek parochial schools to replace or supplement public schooling. A major secondary study is Andrew Kopan's dissertation *Education and Greek Immigrants in Chicago, 1892-1973: A Study in Ethnic Survival* (1974). The broad range of primary sources available includes, among others, an instructional manual for teachers in Church schools (Georgios Alexandros's *Hodegos tou didaskontos prosopikou ton Hellenikon Katekhetikon Scholeion* [Guide for the Teaching Staff in Greek Sunday Schools], 1930), a Greek-language anthology for Greek American girls (Mene Dimitriou's *Prote Helleno-Amerikanike paidike anthologia dia ta Hellenopoula tes Amerikes* [First Greek-American Children's Anthology for the Greek Children of America], 1935), Greek language primers for Greek American children (E. Wesander's *Modern Greek Reader*, 1943), and a dedication album for the Hellenic-American School in Lowell, MA (1959).

The assimilation or acculturation of Greek Americans is the subject of several volumes available at the IHRC. These include *The Social Adjustment of the Greeks in Spartanburg, South Carolina*, by Rosamonde Ramsey Boyd (1948); a compilation of sociological surveys of Greeks abroad, *Enquêtes sociologiques sur les émigrants grecs* (Sociological Research on the Greek Emigrants), by Elias Demetras (1971); and a dissertation, *Upward Mobility, Assimilation, and the Achievements of the Greeks in the United States with Special Emphasis on Boston and Philadelphia*, by Dimitrios Ioannis Monos (1972). Studies are also present dealing specifically with language assimilation (Gregorios D. Androutsopoulos's *Skepseis Tines peri diatereseos tou Hellenismou tes Amerikes* [Thoughts on the Preservation of Hellenism in America], 1955) or retention (Paul D. Seaman's *Modern Greek and American English in Contact*, 1972).

Newspapers

Akropolis (The Acropolis), Westminster, British Columbia, Canada. Monthly (?): 1981-1982. Includes English.

AHEPAN (American Hellenic Educational Progressive Association), Washington, DC. Monthly: 1976-1977. English. (See also "Order of AHEPA" entry in manuscript collections section of this chapter.)

Anagennesis (Rebirth), Montreal, Quebec, Canada. Weekly: 1972.

Athenai (The Detroit Athens), Detroit, MI. Weekly: 1956, 1965, 1980.

Athena, Chicago, IL. Weekly: 1910.

Atlantis, New York, NY. Daily and Sunday: 1947-1967, 1969.

The Chicago Pnyx, Glenview, IL. Monthly: 1955, 1968-1974. English.

Demokratia (Democracy), New York, NY. Monthly: 1974. English.

Drasis (Drasis), Montreal, Quebec, Canada. Monthly: 1972.

Eirenikos (The Pacific), San Francisco, CA. Weekly: 1911.

Eleutheros Typos (Free Press), Chicago, IL. Semi-monthly: 1945-1946, 1963-1965, 1972.

Ellenika Nea (Hellenic News), New York, NY. Weekly: 1963-1970. Includes English.

Ellenike Echo (Hellenic Echo), Vancouver, British Columbia, Canada. Bi-weekly: 1971-1973. Includes English.

Ellenike Phone (Hellenic Voice), Astoria, NY. Semi-weekly: 1974, 1978.

Ellenismos tes Amerikes (Hellenism in America), Ulster Park, NY. Monthly: 1976-1977.

Ellinikos Ilios (The Hellenic Sun), Montreal, Quebec, Canada. Monthly: 1972.

Epicheirematika Nea (Business News), New York, NY. 1977.

Epirus United (Panepirotic Federation of America), New York, NY. Monthly: 1962. Includes English.

Ethnikon Vima (National Greek Tribune; previously titled **Vima**), Detroit, MI. Weekly: 1965-1981, 1983-date. (Microfilm: 1934-1980). Includes some English.

Ethnikon Vima (National Tribune), Sydney, Australia. Weekly: 1963.

Ethnikos Keryx (The National Herald), New York, NY. Daily: 1945-1946, 1948, 1950, 1952-1957, 1961-1967, 1969-1981. Includes English.

The Greek-American, Lowell, MA. Weekly: 1948.

Greek American, New York, NY. Semi-monthly: 1969-1971. Includes English.

Greek-American News, Los Angeles, CA. Weekly: 1975. English.

The Greek Press, Chicago, IL. Weekly: 1929, 1957-1960, 1963-date. English.

The Greek Star, Chicago, IL. Weekly: 1949, 1956, 1961, 1963, 1966-date. Includes English.

Greek Sunday News, Boston, MA. Weekly (except last two weeks in July): 1963-1983. Includes English.

The Hellenic American, New York, NY. Bi-monthly: 1964-1965, 1967. English.

The Hellenic Chronicle, Boston, MA. Weekly: 1961-1962, 1964-date. English.

The Hellenic Journal, San Francisco, CA. Bi-monthly: 1975-date. Includes English.

Hellenic Review, St. Louis, MO. Weekly: 1920.

Hellenic Times, New York, NY. Weekly: 1973-1981. English.

Hellenic View, Vancouver, British Columbia, Canada. Semi-monthly: 1973.

The Hellenic Voice (previously titled The Voice), Cleveland, OH. Bi-monthly: 1976-date. English.

Hellenikon Vema (Hellenic Tribune), Toronto, Ontario, Canada. Weekly: 1965.

Hellenikos Tachydromos (Hellenic Express), Montreal, Quebec, Canada. Weekly: 1967-1970.

Hellenikos Typos (Greek Press), Chicago, IL. Weekly. (Microfilm: 1942-1945). Includes English.

Hellenokanadikon Vima (Greek Canadian Tribune), Montreal, Quebec, Canada. 1965, 1967.

Fanos (The Lantern), New York, NY. 1964. Includes some English.

Chronos (The Greek Times), San Francisco, CA. Weekly: 1918.

The Illuminator, Pittsburgh, PA. Monthly: 1980-1982. English.

Kampana (The Bell), New York, NY. Frequency varies: 1956, 1964-date.

Kopanos (The Big Stick), New York, NY. Weekly: 1917.

Kypros (Cyprus Greek-American Review), New York, NY. 1962, 1965.

Loxias (The Blade), Chicago, IL. Weekly: 1917. Includes English.

Makedonia (Macedonia), New York, NY. Bi-monthly: 1965. Includes English.

The Mercury, Berkeley, CA. Bi-monthly: 1927. English.

The National Herald, New York, NY. Daily: 1956-1957. English.

Nea Kalifornia (The New California), San Francisco, CA. Weekly: 1957-1958, 1962, 1964-1977.

Nea Poreia (The New Course), New York, NY. Monthly: 1975.

The Omogenia, New York, NY. Monthly: 1969-1974.

Orthodox Observer, New York, NY. Semi-monthly: 1971-1982. Includes English.

Penhellenios (The Panhellenic), Ontario, Canada. Monthly: 1972.

Parnassus (Hellenic Newspaper of the Western States), Los Angeles, CA. Semi-monthly: 1951. Includes English.

Phone ton Apodemon (The Voice of the Migrants), Athens, Greece. 1963-1964, 1971-1972, 1976-1978.

Phos (The Light), Astoria, NY. Monthly: 1964, 1966-1967.

Proini (Morning News), New York, NY. Daily: 1977-1978, 1980.

Thessalonike (Thessalonica), Chicago, IL. Weekly: 1928. Includes English.

Velouchi (The Velouchi. Bulletin of the Evrytanian Association "Velouchi"), Charlotte, NC. Quarterly: 1966.

The Voice, Cleveland, OH. Bi-monthly: 1980. Includes English.

Weekly Review Proini, New York, NY. Weekly: 1985, 1986. English.

The Western Hellenic, San Francisco, CA. Weekly: 1975. English.

Serials

Akademia (Academy of St. Basil), Garrison, NY. Annual: 1967. English.

AHEPA (American Hellenic Educational Progressive Association, Annual District Convention, Grainfield District No. 14 [Iowa, Minnesota, North Dakota, South Dakota]), place of publication varies. Annual: 1953-1956, 1974-1975, 1983. English.

AHEPA (National Convention), Washington, DC. Annual: 1955. English.

AHEPA Beacon (Grainfield District No. 14), Mason City, IA. Quarterly: 1949-1951. English.

The AHEPA Fez (Grainfield District No. 14), Waterloo, IA. Monthly: 1959-1983. English.

AHEPA Messenger, New York, NY. Semi-monthly: 1932. English.

The AHEPAN, Washington, DC. Frequency varies: 1929-1953, 1955-65, 1968-1978, 1980, 1983-date. English.

AHEPAN Newsletter, Washington, DC. Quarterly: 1982-1983. English.

American Review of Eastern Orthodoxy, Fern Park, FL. Monthly (except July and August): 1973. English.

American Society for Neo-Hellenic Studies, Inc. Newsletter, New York, NY. 1969. English.

Annunciation Herald, Baltimore, MD. 1972. Includes English.

Argus, Milwaukee, WI. Monthly: 1964-1966. Includes English.

Ascension Bulletin, Oakland, CA. Monthly: 1983-date. English.

Athene, Chicago, IL. Quarterly: 1957, 1959, 1962-1963, 1965. English.

The Basilian, Stockton, CA. Quarterly: 1985-date. English.

Byzantina Metabyzantina (The Society for the Promotion of Byzantine and Modern Greek Studies), New York, NY. Frequency varies: 1949. Includes English.

Byzantium, New York, NY. 1971. Includes English.

Cathedral Echo, San Francisco, CA. Monthly (?): 1972. Includes English.

The Christian Orthodox, Richmond, VA. Quarterly: 1964. English.

Daughters of Penelope Convention Yearbook, Washington, DC (?). Annual: 1954-1955, 1974. English.

Diakonia, Los Angeles, CA. Bi-monthly: 1954. Includes English.

The Diocesan Voice, San Francisco, CA. Monthly: 1983-1984. English.

Ecclesia (Church), Pittsburgh, PA. Frequency varies: 1969-1976. Includes English.

Echo tou Kathedrikou (Cathedral Echo), New York, NY. Monthly: 1938-1940. Includes English.

Edict, Detroit, MI. 1965. English.

Ellenoamerikanikos Telephonikos Katalogos Meizonos Neas Yorkes (Greek American Telephone Directory--Greater New York), New York, NY. Annual: 1977-1978.

The Epistle, Hempstead, NY. Frequency varies: 1971-1972, 1974. Includes English.

Fone tes Ellados (The Voice of Greece), New York, NY. Monthly: 1966-1968. Includes English.

The GOYAN (Greek Orthodox Youth of America), New York, NY. Quarterly: 1953-1956, 1958, 1961, 1963, 1968. Includes English.

The Greek American, New York, NY. Weekly: 1986-date. English.

Greek Orthodox Archidiocese of North and South America Financial Statements, New York, NY. Annual: 1955, 1964. English.

Greek Orthodox Archdiocese of North and South America News Bulletin, New York, NY. Frequency varies: 1970. English.

Greek Orthodox Archdiocese of North and South America Regulations and Uniform Parish Bylaws, New York, NY. Biennial: 1955, 1960, 1962, 1964-1965. Includes English.

Greek Orthodox Archdiocese of North and South America Yearbook, New York, NY. Annual: 1955, 1960-1963, 1976, 1978-1980, 1982, 1986-1987. Includes English.

Greek Orthodox Archdiocese of North and South America Decisions of the 19th Clergy-Laity Congress of the Greek Orthodox Archdiocese of North and South America in Athens, July 20-27, 1968. New York, NY. Special issue. Includes English.

Greek Orthodox Teachers' Benevolent Association of the Greek Archdiocese Yearbook, New York, NY. Annual: 1964. Includes English.

The Greek Orthodox Theological Review, Brookline, MA. Semi-annual: 1954, 1956-1964, 1966-1970, 1972, 1974, 1977, 1979. English.

Greek Orthodox Youth of America Choir Director's Manual, New York, NY. Annual: 1964, 1970-1971, 1973. Includes English.

Greek Orthodox Youth of America International Conference Proceedings, New York, NY. Annual: 1956-1959, 1961-1966, 1968. English.

Greek Orthodox Youth of America, Diocese 1, District 1, District Conference Proceedings, Haines Falls, NY. Annual: 1961. English.

Greek World, New York, NY. Bi-monthly: 1976-1978. English.

The Hellenic American, Detroit, MI. Monthly: 1965. English.

Hellenic Calendar, Fountain Valley, CA. Quarterly: 1979-1981, 1984. English.

The Hellenic News, Philadelphia, PA. Monthly: 1964. Includes English.

Hellenic Newsletter, Phoenix, AZ. Monthly: 1972. English.

Hellenic Review, Forest Hills, NY. Monthly: 1963-1967. English.

Hellenism, Chicago, IL. Monthly: 1968-1970. English.

Hemerologion tes Ekklesias tes Hellados (Calendar of the Greek Church), Athens, Greece. Annual: 1970, 1973.

Holy Cross Greek Orthodox Theological School Hemerologiake Epeteris, Brookline, MA (previously published in Pomfret Center, CT). Annual: 1941, 1944, 1948, 1951, 1953, 1962-1965. Includes English.

Journal of the Hellenic Diaspora, New York, NY. Quarterly: 1974-1985. English.

Koimesis Theotokou (Dormition of the Virgin), Brooklyn, NY. Monthly: 1972-1975. Includes English.

Koinonia (Communion), Brookline, MA. Bi-annual: 1978-1980. English.

Logos, Long Island City, NY. 1969. Includes English.

The Logos, Fort Wayne, IN. Monthly: 1968-1972. English.

Maids of Athena, Daughters of Penelope Junior Women's Auxiliary Convention Yearbook, Washington, DC (?). Annual: 1975. English.

Message (St. Paraskevi Greek Orthodox Church), Greenlawn, NY. Monthly: 1966-1972, 1974-1979. English.

National Forum for Greek Orthodox Church Musicians Liturgical Guide Book, Englewood, CO. Annual: 1984-1986. Includes English.

Nea Hellas (New Greece), Montreal, Quebec, Canada. Monthly: 1970.

Nea Yorke (New York; Greek American Monthly Review), Clifton, NJ. Monthly: 1976-date. Includes English.

Neolea News, Brooklyn, NY. Bi-monthly: 1969. English.

Neo-Hellenic Studies Bulletin (Center for Neo-Hellenic Studies), Austin, TX. Frequency varies: 1967, 1969-1970. English.

Nike (Victory), New York, NY. Weekly: 1913.

Order of AHEPA Platograms, Charleston, SC. Frequency varies: 1977. English.

The Orthodox Herald, London, England. Monthly: 1970. English.

Orthodox Light (St. George Greek Orthodox Church), Passaic, NJ. Semi-annual (?): 1967-1970. Includes English.

Orthodox Observer; Orthodoxos Pareretes, New York, NY. Monthly (bi-weekly): 1934-1936, 1960-1961, 1964-1971. Includes English.

Penelopean Echo, Washington, DC. Quarterly: 1985. English.

The Philhellene (American Friends of Greece), New York, NY. Bi-annual: 1942-1950. English.

Philoptochos Informer, Grand Rapids, MI. Three times per year: 1968-1974. Includes English.

Pilgrimage, Wheaton, IL. Monthly: 1975-1976. Includes English.

Pneuma (The Spirit), Brooklyn, NY. Semi-annual (?): 1976-1977. Includes English.

The Progress, Bloomfield Hills, MI (previously published in Jamestown, NY). Monthly: 1963-1970. Includes English.

Prometheus; "The Only Greek Almanac in America," New York, NY. Annual: 1913.

Saint Andrew, Chicago, IL. Monthly: 1965, 1968-1976. Includes English.

The Saint Demetrios Echo, Chicago, IL. Bi-monthly: 1983-date. Includes English.

Saint George Forum, Bethesda, MD. Bi-monthly: 1969-1970. (Photocopies). Includes English.

St. George Greek Orthodox Church Sunday Bulletin, St. Paul, MN. Weekly (?): 1969. English.

The Saint George Herald, Bethesda, MD. Quarterly: 1972-1973, 1975-1982. English.

Satyros, New York, NY. Frequency varies: 1925-1952.

The United Community Echo, Chicago, IL. Monthly: 1957-1968, 1972-1982. Includes English.

Voice of the Annunciation, Memphis, TN. Frequency varies: 1966-1971. English.

 Candy Store, 166-168 Second St., North of Grand Ave., Phone Grand 1259, Milwaukee.

Postcard of the Greek American candy store "Rigas," Milwaukee, WI, n.d.

Hungarian American Collection

Manuscript Collections

Ablonczy, Pál.
Papers, 1963. 1 linear in. and
1 microfilm reel.

Ablonczy was a Hungarian immigrant
who was active in labor organizations
during the 1920s and 1930s. Papers
consist of a manuscript of his
autobiography. *Microfilm is duplicate of
manuscript.*

**Association of Hungarian Students in
North America (Cambridge,
Massachusetts).**
Records, 1956-1967. Ca. 4 linear ft.

The Association was formed in 1957
by university students who were refugees
from the 1956 Hungarian Revolution.
The group assisted Hungarian refugee
students in Canada and the United States
and conducted an exchange program
between American and Hungarian
students. The Association is a charter
member of the United Federation of
Hungarian Students, an international
organization.
Records of the Association consist
mostly of correspondence. *Includes
English.*

Balogh, Dezsö De A.
Papers, 1938-1965. 2.5 linear ft.

Papers of Balogh, a member of the
editorial board of the periodical *Képes
Magyar Magazin* in New York City,
consist of journals, pamphlets, and
newspaper clippings on communism and
Hungary. *Includes English.*

**Baross Gábor Social and Sick Benefit
Society (St. Pauli Baross Gábor
Társas és Segély Égylet) (St. Paul,
Minnesota).**
Records, ca. 1892-1970. 1.5 linear ft.

The Society, an insurance and fraternal
organization founded in 1892, was active
until the early 1970s.
Records comprise ledgers containing
meeting minutes, financial records, and
membership lists. Also included are
textbooks published in Hungary and used
in Barossi Hungarian American School.
Inventory available.

Egri, Lajos, 1888-1967.
Papers, ca. 1917-1968. 1 linear ft.

Egri was born in Eger, Hungary, and
came to the United States in 1908. He
was a playwright for the Hungarian

radical theater in New York City at the
end of World War I, founder in the
mid-1930s of the Egri school of writing,
and author of *The Art of Creative Writing*
and other works on writing. Many of
Egri's plays were printed in *Elöre*, the
magazine of the Hungarian Federation of
the Socialist Party, and were performed
by small theater groups affiliated with the
Hungarian section of the Communist
Party and a Hungarian workingmen's
association in New York City. Egri
joined the Elöre Group of Players, an
amateur theatrical group, and later became
one of its directors. He also worked as a
journalist, edited an illustrated Hungarian
weekly published in New York City,
edited plays for the Columbia Broadcasting System, and wrote television
scripts.

His papers consist of his early plays,
poetry, an autobiographical sketch,
correspondence, miscellany, and an
interview with his widow by Jozsef
Kovacs. *Inventory available.*

Fenyes, Maria.
Papers, ca. 1949-1977. 4 linear in.

Papers consist of flyers, programs,
photographs, and miscellany relating to
the activities of Hungarians in California.
Includes English.

**First Hungarian Day (Fairmont, West
    Virginia).**
Records, 1939-1960. 1 ledger.

The First Hungarian Day was an
annual event held by a group of
Hungarian Americans. Records include
minutes of meetings, texts of speeches,
lists of names, and translations of
newspaper articles.

Gracza, Elizabeth.
Papers, n.d. 1 folder.

Gracza was a Hungarian immigrant.
Papers contain letters, photographs, travel
information, and documents for Elizabeth
and Suzanne Gracza, as well as flyers
about Hungarian films, artist Bela Petheo,
and the scouting group Magyar
Cserkészszövetség. *Includes English.*

Hokky, Károly (1883-).
Papers, 1954-1970. Ca. 1 linear ft.

An educator and politician, Hokka was
born in Abaujszepesi, Hungary, and was
educated at the Universities of Budapest
and Kolozsvár. He taught school, served
in the military during World War I,
organized the Christian Social Party in
Carpathian Ruthenia, and served in the
Parliaments of Hungary and
Czechoslovakia. Following World War
II, he came to the United States as a
refugee.

Hokky's papers include correspondence, especially with Maria Ugron
Podhorsky, along with miscellaneous
papers and writings. *Includes English.*
Inventory available.

**Hungarian Evangelical Reformed
    Conventus Archives (Budapest,
    Hungary).**
Records, ca. 1904-1915. 29 microfilm
    reels.

The Hungarian Evangelical Reformed
Churches in the United States had strong
ties to the homeland, fostered by the
American Action plan devised by the
Hungarian government in 1903. The
American Action program operated
through the churches (Catholic as well as
Protestant) to protect emigrants from
assimilation into American society and to
encourage their return to Hungary. By
joining the homeland church, the
Hungarian congregations in America
received financial and spiritual assistance
from the General Conventus of the
Reformed Church of Hungary.

The records document the most
successful period of the American Action
program. Included are correspondence,
reports, registers, and publications relating
to Hungarian Evangelical Reformed
Churches in the United States and
Canada.

Hungarian Postcards.
Collection, n.d. Ca. 1 linear in.

The Hungarian American postcard
collection includes cards from Hungary
and of the Bethlen Home for the Aged in
Ligonier, PA. *Includes English.*

**Hungarian Reformed Church
(Cleveland, Ohio).**
Records, 1890-1944. 1 microfilm reel.

Records of this Protestant church
include baptism records and financial and
minute books. *Inventory available.*

Hungarian Scrapbook.
Ca. 1936-1942. 1 linear in.

The Hungarian scrapbook contains
newspaper clippings from Hungarian
American newspapers including *Új Előre*
(Cleveland, OH). Clippings consist of
poetry, socialist and communist articles,
and pictures.

Hungarians in Elk River, Minnesota.
Collection, 1868-1948. 1 linear in.

Collection, assembled by Betty
Belanger, consists of letters from
Hungary, Romania, and Canada, to
residents of Elk River, MN.

**Hungarians in Toronto (Ontario,
Canada).**
Collection, 1955-1975. Ca. 1 linear in.

Collection consists of newspaper
clippings, programs, postcards, and
leaflets documenting the Toronto
Hungarian community. *Includes English.*

**Hungarian Prime Minister's Office
(Országos Levéltár
Miniszterelnökségi Levéltár).**
Records, 1895-1917. 66 microfilm reels.

Records include information on the
Greek Catholic Church in the United
States; on Slovak nationalism in Slovakia
and its impact on Slovaks in the United
States and Argentina; on remigrated
Ruthenians who converted to Orthodoxy;
on Slovak political activity in the United
States, and that of remigrated Slovaks;
and on the number of remigrated Slovaks.
Also included is information on
Hungarians in the United States and
Canada; Slovak and Hungarian American
newspapers; political activity of
Hungarian Americans and Croatian
Americans; Slovenian and Dalmatian

political activity in the United States,
Canada, and South America; German-U.S.
relations; the Catholic Church in
Pennsylvania; and the Hungarian
Reformed Church in the United States.
Other materials pertain to Hungarian
emigration policy and matters concerning
emigration. *In multiple languages.*
Inventory available.

**Hungarian Scouts Association (Magyar
Cserskéz Szövetség) (Garfield, New
Jersey).**
Records, 1965-197?. Ca. 4 linear in.

In 1951, Ferenc Beodray and Ede
Császár organized the first Hungarian Boy
Scout troop in the United States. In the
same year, the international headquarters
of the Hungarian Scouts Association was
moved from West Germany to Garfield,
NJ. There are scouting troops among
Hungarian immigrants in the United
States, Canada, Latin America, Europe,
and Australia.

Records of the Magyar Cserskéz
Szövetség consist of correspondence and
organizational material of the central
administration and of Troop No. 6 "Gábor
Aron" (Passaic, NJ). *Includes English.*
Inventory available.

**Hungarian Theatre Posters (Los
Angeles, California).**
Collection, 1964-1971. 1 folder.

The collection consists of posters and
programs for Hungarian-language plays
performed in the Los Angeles area.

Huzianyi, Stephen.
Papers, n.d. Ca. 4 linear in.

Huzianyi was active in Hungarian
American organizations in the Chicago,
IL, area. During the 1930s and 1940s, he
was a member and officer of the Chicago
Hungarian Young People's Club (later
renamed the Verhovay Chicago Branch
503, a branch of Verhovay Fraternal
Insurance Association). Huzianyi wrote a
column in *Verhovay Journal* during
World War II on Hungarian Americans in
the armed forces and, following the war,
served as Secretary of the American

Hungarian Relief, Inc., Chapter 20 (Chicago).

His papers consist of correspondence, newspaper clippings, photographs, and publications. *Includes English.*

International Institute of Minnesota. Special File on Hungarians (St. Paul).
Collection, ca. 1928-1957. 2 linear in.

This file from the International Institute of Minnesota relates mainly to resettlement of Hungarian refugees following the Hungarian Revolution of 1956. Included are photocopies of related news articles from local newspapers and some materials on activities of Hungarians in the Twin Cities. *In English.*

Jánossy-Johnson Family.
Papers, 1920-1978. 4 linear in.

The Jánossys are a musical Hungarian American family. Gustav S. Jánossy, his four brothers, and his sister, Olga, were encouraged in music as children because their mother, Helen, had been denied music lessons as a child. The children were presented with musical instruments and lessons on their tenth birthdays. Olga later went into business, but her five brothers all pursued musical careers, two as double bass players, two as violinists, and one as a violincellist. They organized a Hungarian orchestra in 1934. It was disbanded in 1938, when Gustav joined the Minneapolis Symphony Orchestra, for which his brother William also played. Gustav later was a member of the Los Angeles Philharmonic, and Henry played in the West Point Military Band before going into a career in industry.

Papers include newspaper clippings, manuscripts, photographs, programs, and miscellaneous papers documenting the musical careers of family members. *In English.*

Jobbágy, Domokos.
Papers, 1964-1968. Ca. 3 linear in.

Jobbágy was a Hungarian American author. Papers consist of manuscripts for two of his novels, "Spies, Counterspies, Traitors" and "I Was Their Prisoner." *In English.*

Lazar, Ferencz (Frank).
Papers, n.d. 1 folder.

Papers of Lazar, a Hungarian immigrant and resident of St. Paul, MN, include letters, naturalization documents, photographs, a military pass, membership documents for the Hungarian Aid Association of America, and religious miscellany. *Includes English.*

Los Angelesi Magyar Munkás Mükedvelö Kör (Los Angeles, California).
Records, 1920-1922. Ca. 1.5 linear in.

Records of this Hungarian American workers' organization consist of minutes of the organization and of its subsidiary, Los Angelesi Munkás Datarada.

Macker, Julius.
Papers, ca. 1947-1971. Ca. 2 linear ft.

Papers of Macker include correspondence, newspaper clippings, minutes, and annual statements and miscellany relating to his service as president of the William Penn Association, the largest Hungarian American fraternal and benefit association. *Includes English.*

Minnesota Hungarians (Minneapolis, Minnesota).
Records, ca. 1961-1972. 4 linear in.

Formed ca. 1957 by Hungarian immigrants in the Minneapolis-St. Paul area, the organization held parties and banquets and brought in Hungarian American speakers and entertainers. In addition, the group raised funds for relief purposes.

Records consist of correspondence, membership lists, invitations, posters, and material on the Hungarian American actress Zita Szeletszky. *Includes English. Inventory available. Substantial parts of this collection are available only as photocopies; originals returned to donors.*

Moor, Peter.
Papers, n.d. Ca. 1 linear in.

Papers of Moor, a Hungarian-born journalist and poet, include photocopies of published poems and short stories and typescripts of a tableau and two short stories. *Includes English.*

Nyiregynazy, Pál V. (1888-1973).
Papers, 1952-1975. 4 linear in.

Nyiregynazy was a Hungarian Canadian who had been a mayor in Hungary before coming to Canada. He wrote a popular weekly column for the newspaper *Kanadai Magyarság* and was prominent in the Hungarian community in Toronto.

His papers include personal correspondence, newspaper clippings, photographs, and collections of Hungarian poems, including original unpublished verse of György Hornik.

Papp, Gaspar.
Papers, 1922. Ca 1 linear in.

Papers consist of two Hungarian passports, one for Papp and one for his wife, Lidia (Kato) Papp. Also included is a notebook of Hungarian songs about life in America.

Petofi Club, Inc. (Detroit, Michigan).
Records, 1961-1965. Ca. 1 linear in.

The Petofi Club was a Hungarian American social and cultural organization founded in 1961. Records consist of a ledger of minutes.

Puskás, Julianna.
Papers, n.d. 1 linear in.

Papers of Puskás, a Hungarian historian, consist of typescripts of her writings pertaining to Hungarians and

Hungarian American organizations. Also included is a list of Hungarian American newspapers, churches, political groups, and organizations.

Radwany, Emery.
Papers, ca. 1937. Ca. 2 linear in.

Radwany was born into a prominent family in the small town of Rozsyno (now in Czechoslovakia) and grew up in Budapest. He came to the United States in 1931 and was naturalized five years later.

His papers consist of his manuscript, "Kingdom Lost," relating personal and family reminiscences of Hungarian life and customs, with related episodes from Hungarian history, 1840-1936. *In English.*

Sopron School of Forestry, University of British Columbia (Vancouver, Canada).
Collection, n.d. 1 linear in.

Following the Hungarian Revolution of 1956, almost all of the student body and half the staff of Sopron School of Forestry escaped to Austria. Many emigrated from there to British Columbia, where lectures were resumed, in Hungarian, at the University of British Columbia. Most graduates of the school settled in Canada and the United States and found work in the fields of forestry and engineering.

The collection consists of reprints of forestry articles, newspaper clippings, and letters. *Includes English.*

Szathmary, Louis.
Collection, 1947-1965. 5 linear in.

Collection consists of typescripts and drafts of speeches Melchior Chonto gave on topics including world peace, European politics, communism, Americanism, and the Hungarian revolt of 1956. Also included are correspondence, newspaper clippings, and magazine articles on the 1956 revolt, Hungarian relief, and the placement of Hungarian refugees. *Includes English. Restricted.*

Turmezeí, Rev. Francis C.
Papers, ca. 1950-1977. 6 linear ft.
(including 20 rolls of film and two
inches of picture postcard records).

Papers of Turmezeí, a Hungarian
American priest and educator, consist of
personal papers, writings, poetry, films,
and a box of Hungarian picture postcards
that are 45-rpm recordings. Turmezeí
taught education at the College of St.
Thomas (St. Paul, MN). *Includes
English.*

**United Hungarian Fund (Egyesült
Magyar Alap) (Toronto, Ontario,
Canada).**
Records, 1968-1976. 2 linear in.

The United Hungarian Fund, a cultural
organization, was part of the Hungarian
Canadian Federation based in Toronto,
Canada. The organization raised money
to support schools, the New Horizon
Handycraft Guild, scouting groups, and
other activities and groups.

Records of the Fund consist of
correspondence, pamphlets, and other
publicity material.

**Workingmen's Sick Benevolent and
Education Federation (International
Workers' Order Hungarian Section,
Branch 116) (Avenel, New Jersey).**
Records, 1924-1942. Ca. 6 linear in.

Records of this labor-oriented
Hungarian American society consist of
minutes and financial records.

Monographs

The Center's Hungarian American monograph collection includes approximately 760
volumes. Its strengths lie in the areas of religion, literature, and material on refugees of
World War II and the 1956 Hungarian revolution.

In addition to the bibliography by Joseph Széplaki based on the Center's own
collection, *Hungarians in the United States and Canada: A Bibliography* (1977), the IHRC
has several other general and specialized Szeplaki bibliographies. For example, *The
Hungarians in America 1583-1974: A Chronology and Fact Book* (1975) includes important
dates and documents relating to the Hungarian experience in America as well as
bibliographical references. Also available is an annotated bibliography by Ilona Kovács, *The
Hungarians in the United States* (MLS thesis, Kent State University, 1975) as well as the
article "Historical, Literary, Linguistic, and Ethnographic Research on Hungarian Americans"
by Steven B. Várdy and A. Huszár Várdy in the journal *Hungarian Studies* (1985).

Historical works on Hungarian Americans include Emil Lengyel's *Americans from
Hungary* (1948), still considered an important account of pre-World War II Hungarian
immigration. Another general work is László Könnyü's *Hungarians in the United States:
An Immigration Study* (1967). The experience of the large numbers of Hungarians who
immigrated after the 1956 revolution in Hungary is examined by S. Alexander Weinstock
in *Acculturation and Occupation: A Study of the 1956 Hungarian Refugees in the United
States* (1969). A more recent contribution to the field is S. B. Várdy's *The Hungarian-
Americans* (1985). In addition, Joshua Fishman's *Hungarian Language Maintenance in the
United States* (1966) focuses on the social psychology of language retention. Sociologist
John Kósa explores immigrant kinship systems among Hungarian Canadians in *Land of
Choice: The Hungarians in Canada* (1957).

Much of the significant scholarship in Hungarian American studies is in the form of
unpublished doctoral dissertations. The Center holds more than twenty of these, on such
topics as religious and cultural organizations, acculturation, and specific Hungarian
communities in the United States. Joseph Széplaki's *Doctoral Dissertations Related to
Hungary* (1974), is a useful guide.

The Center's collection of works on religion includes histories and commemorative
publications for more than a hundred Hungarian American churches of various
denominations, as well as scholarly books and dissertations. An example of the latter is

Aladár Komjáthy's dissertation, *The Hungarian Reformed Church in America: An Effort to Preserve a Denominational Heritage* (1962).
Scholars in Hungary have contributed significantly to the body of research on the Hungarian experience in America. This scholarship has essentially been concerned with economic, social, and demographic aspects of emigration. The Center's collection includes two recent works in Hungarian, Miklós Szántó's *Magyarok Amerikaban* (Hungarians in America, 1984) and Julianna Puskás's *Kivandorlo magyarok az Egyesült Államokban 1880-1940* (Hungarian Emigrants in the United States, 1982), a comparative analysis of emigration and the development of Hungarian settlements in America. The Center also has the condensed and translated version of Puskás's work, *From Hungary to the United States, 1880-1914* (1982). A recent compilation of Hungarian documentation is the two-volume *"Valahol túl, meseországban . . ." Az amerikás magyarok 1895-1920* ("Somewhere in a Distant Fabled Land . . ." American Hungarians 1895-1920), edited by Albert Tezla (1987).
The IHRC's collection of Hungarian American literature is extensive, containing the works of Erzsébet Kisjókai, György Kemény, László Könnyü, László Szabó, Albert Wass, and many others. Hungarian Canadian authors are also well represented. In writings about Hungarian American literature and writers, László Könnyü's *History of American Hungarian Literature: Presentation of American Hungarian Authors of the Last 100 Years and Selections from Their Writings* (1962) focuses primarily on Hungarian language publications, and includes biographical sketches. Also useful is Enikö Molnár Basa's chapter on Hungarian American literature in *Ethnic Perspectives in American Literature: Selected Essays on the European Contribution*, edited by Robert J. Di Pietro and Edward Ifkovic (1983), found in the IHRC's general collection.

Newspapers

Akroni Magyar Hirlap (Akron Hungarian Journal), Akron, OH. Weekly: 1957, 1960.

Alkotó Magyar (Creative Hungarian), New York, NY. Monthly: 1973. Includes English.

Amerikai Magyar Élet (American Hungarian Life), Chicago, IL. Weekly: 1965-1968, 1972-1978, 1980.

Amerikai Magyar Népszava (American Hungarian People's Voice), Cleveland, OH. Daily: 1943.

Amerikai Magyar Népszava (American Hungarian People's Voice), New York, NY. Frequency varies: 1966, 1972, 1974-1975, 1979-1980.

Kanadai Amerikai Magyar Szó (Hungarian Word), New York, NY. Weekly: 1965-1973, 1975-date.

Amerikan Magyar Világ (American Hungarian World), Cleveland, OH. Weekly: 1971, 1973-1975.

Bérmunkás (Industrial Workers of the World), Cleveland, OH. Weekly: 1947. (Microfilm: 1921-1946).

Californiai Magyarság (California Hungarians), Los Angeles, CA. Weekly: 1928-1932, 1936-date.

Chicago és Környéke (Chicago and Vicinity), Chicago, IL. Weekly: 1967, 1972-date.

Detroiti Magyar Ujság (Detroit Hungarian News; previously titled **Detroiti Ujság**; merged with **Az Ujság**), Wyondette, Detroit, MI-Cleveland, OH. Weekly: 1935, 1943-1975. Includes English.

Donau-Bote (Danube Herald; German edition of **Nemzetör**), Zurich, Switzerland. Monthly: 1975. Includes German.

Eletünk (Our Life), St. Gall, Switzerland. Monthly: 1975.

Fighter (English edition of Szittyakürt), Cleveland, OH. Monthly: 1976-1980. English.

A Hét (The Week), Cleveland, OH. Weekly: 1965. Includes English.

Interest, Chicago, IL. Weekly: 1935-1939.

Kanadai Magyar Ujság (Canadian Magyar News), Winnipeg, Manitoba, Canada. Weekly: 1965-1976.

Kanadai Magyarság (Canadian Hungarians), Toronto, Ontario, Canada. Weekly: 1964, 1970, 1974-1976, 1979-1981. (Microfilm: 1951-1974).

Katolikus Magyarok Vasárnapja (Catholic Hungarians' Sunday), Youngstown, OH. Weekly: 1963, 1965-1983.

Kis Dongo (Little Bumblebee; previously titled Dongo), Detroit, MI. Semi-monthly: 1909, 1919, 1924-1928, 1932, 1941-1948, 1950-1963, 1965-1966.

Kivándorlási Ellenör (Emigration Controller; Bulletin for Settlement and Social Issues of Emigrants and Returnees), Budapest, Hungary. Bi-weekly. (Microfilm: 1908).

Kivándorló (The Emigrant), Budapest, Hungary. Weekly. (Microfilm: 1904-1905). Includes German.

Krónika (The Chronicle), New York, NY. Monthly: 1958, 1959.

Külföldi Magyarság (Hungarians Overseas), Budapest, Hungary. Semi-monthly. (Microfilm: 1920-1925).

Magyar Banyászlap (Hungarian Miners' Journal), Detroit, MI. Frequency varies: 1939, 1954.

Magyar Élet (Hungarian Life), Toronto, Ontario, Canada. Weekly: 1967-1970, 1972, 1974-date.

Magyar Hiradó (Magyar Herald), Metuchen, NJ. Weekly: 1975.

Magyar Hirek (Hungarian News), Budapest, Hungary. Bi-weekly: 1962, 1968-1979.

Magyar Hirlap (Hungarian Newspaper), Buenos Aires, Argentina. Weekly: 1972-1975.

Magyar Hirlap (Hungarian Newspaper), Toronto, Ontario, Canada. Weekly: 1967-1968, 1971.

Magyar Holnap (Hungarian Tomorrow), New York, NY. Monthly: 1976-1978. Includes English.

Magyar Jövő (Hungarian Future), New York, NY. Tri-weekly: 1941. Includes some English.

Magyar Szabadság (Magyar Freedom), Passaic, NJ. Semi-weekly: 1965-1966.

Magyar Tribune, Chicago, IL. Weekly: 1930, 1932, 1934.

Magyar Ujság (Hungarian News; emerged from coalition of Detroit Magyar Ujság and Az Ujság) Cleveland, OH. Weekly: 1976-1980.

Magyarországi Melleklet (Hungarian Supplement; supplement to the Reformed Hungarian Americans' Journal), Budapest, Hungary. Semi-weekly. (Microfilm: 1938).

Magyarság (Hungarian People), Pittsburgh, PA. Weekly: 1969, 1971-1977.

Napjaink (Our Days), Toronto, Ontario, Canada. Monthly: 1975-1977.

Napló (Diary), New York, NY. Weekly: 1976.

Nemzeti Figyelö (National Observer), Garfield, NJ. Frequency varies: 1972-1973.

Nemzetör (National Guard), Munich, West Germany. Monthly: 1968-1970, 1972-1977, 1980, 1981.

Népszabadság (People's Freedom), Budapest, Hungary. 1975, 1978.

New Yorki Napló (New York Diary), New York, NY. Semi-monthly: 1975-1976.

Norwalki Hirlap (Newspaper of Norwalk), Norwalk, CT. Weekly: 1926-1927.

Otthon (American Home), Chicago, IL. Weekly: 1935, 1944-1945.

Pátria (Fatherland), Lakewood, OH. Quarterly: 1974. Includes English.

Philadelphia-i Függetlenség-Independence (Independence of Philadelphia), Philadelphia, PA. Weekly: 1924-1925.

Reformatusok Lapja (Calvin Synod Herald), Columbus, OH. Monthly (bi-monthly, June-September): 1966. Includes English.

St. Louis és Vidéke (St. Louis and Vicinity), St. Louis, MO. Bi-weekly: 1952, 1964-1969.

Sporthiradó (Sports Journal), Toronto, Ontario, Canada. Weekly: 1958, 1960.

Szabad Magyarság (Free Hungarians), New York, NY. Weekly: 1958-1962.

Szabadság (Liberty), Cleveland, OH. Daily: 1944, 1966.

Szabadságharcos Magyar (Magyar Freedom Fighters), Baltimore, MD. Frequency varies: 1970.

Számadás (Responsibility), Toronto, Ontario, Canada. Quarterly: 1975, 1977.

Szittyakürt (Scytha-Call), Cleveland, OH. Monthly: 1966, 1970-1971, 1976-date.

A Tény (The Fact), Los Angeles, CA. Frequency varies: 1947-1951, 1954, 1968, 1970.

Új Elöre (New Forward), New York, NY. Daily: 1924 (?), 1930, 1932, 1935-1936, one undated issue.

Új Magyar Hang (New Hungarian Voice; previously titled Lorain és Videke), Lorain, OH. Semi-monthly (frequency varies until 1968): 1965-1981.

Új Vilag (New World), Los Angeles, CA. Weekly: 1974-1977.

Az Ujság (Hungarian News; merged with Detroit Magyar Ujság to form Magyar Ujság), Cleveland, OH. Weekly: 1973-1975.

Verhovayak Lapja (Verhovay Journal), Detroit, MI. Weekly: 1936-1942, 1944-1945. Includes English.

William Penn (previously titled Verhovayak Lapja, Rakoczi Szemle), Detroit, MI. Monthly: 1961-1963. Includes English.

Wisconsini Magyarság (Wisconsin Hungarians), Milwaukee, WI. Weekly: 1964-1972. (Microfilm: 1929, 1943-1973).

Serials

Álarc (Mask), Chicago, IL. Monthly: 1959-1961.

American Hungarian Educator (American Hungarian Educators' Association Newsletter), Silver Spring, MD. Triennial: 1979-1984. English.

American Hungarian Foundation Bulletin (previously titled American Hungarian Studies Foundation Bulletin), New Brunswick, NJ. Annual: 1966-1975. English.

American-Hungarian Radio News, Toledo, OH. Frequency varies: 1952.

The American Hungarian Review, St. Louis, MO. Quarterly: 1963, 1965-1967, 1970-1973. Includes English.

Amerikai Magyar Élet Évkönyve (American Hungarian Life Yearbook), Chicago, IL. Annual: 1965-1966.

Amerikai Magyar Hang (American Hungarian Voice), New York, NY. Bi-monthly: 1950-1951.

Amerikai Magyar Naptár (American Hungarian Calendar), Cleveland, OH (previously published in New York, NY). Annual: 1940, 1943-1944, 1946-1947, 1952, 1955-1956, 1958.

Amerikai Magyar Református Naptár (American Hungarian Reformed Calendar), Philadelphia, PA. Annual: 1920.

Amerikai Magyarok Évkönyv Naptára (American Hungarians' Almanac Calendar), New York, NY. Annual: 1953.

Awakener (Center for Southern Hungarian and Balkan Studies), Cleveland, OH. Quarterly: 1973. English.

Bajtársi Levél (Veteran's Letter; Veteran's Association of the former Royal Hungarian Gendarmerie), Calgary, Alberta, Canada. Monthly: 1971, 1973-1979.

Baltimore-i Értesítö (Baltimore Bulletin), Baltimore, MD. 1973. Includes English.

Barataínknak a Magyar Jezsuitak (Hungarian Jesuits to Our Friends), Toronto, Ontario, Canada (previously published in New York, NY). Annual: 1972-1974, 1976-1980.

Bérmunkás Naptár (Wage Earner Calendar), Cleveland, OH. Annual: 1944-1952, 1954.

Bethlen Naptár (Bethlen Almanac), Ligonier, PA. Annual: 1943-1951, 1953-1970, 1972-1975.

Bridgeport Hungarian Evangelical and Reformed Church Annual Report, Bridgeport, CT. Annual: 1952-1954, 1956, 1966. Includes English.

Bukfenc (Somersault), Cleveland, OH. Semi-monthly: 1919.

Californiai Magyar Zseb Telefonkönyv (és) Naptár (Californian Hungarian Pocket Phone Book and Calendar), Los Angeles, CA. Annual: 1973-1980. Includes English.

Calvin Synod--United Church of Christ Conference Proceedings (previously Magyar Synod of the Evangelical and Reformed Church), New Brunswick, NJ. Annual: 1940-1943, 1946, 1948-1949, 1952 (separate English and Hungarian editions), 1953-1955, 1957-1960, 1962-1967. Includes English.

Calvin Synod Herald, Perth Amboy, NJ. Frequency varies: 1974-1975. Includes English.

Calvin United Church of Christ Annual Report (previously Hungarian Reformed Church of Toledo), Toledo, OH. Annual: 1949, 1959, 1962-1964. English.

Calvin's Chimes, Toledo, OH. Frequency varies: 1965-1966. Includes English.

Caribi Ugság (Caribbean News), Caracas, Venezuela. Weekly: 1974-1975, 1977-1979.

Carpathian Observer, Rochester, NY. Semi-annual: 1973-1975. English.

Crusader (Hungarian Turul Society, Inc.), West Hill, Ontario, Canada. Quarterly: 1975. English.

Csendes Percek (Quiet Moments; Hungarian edition of **The Upper Room**), Lethbridge, Alberta, Canada. Bi-monthly: 1958-1959, 1967-1968.

Delamerikai Magyar Hirlap Évkönyve (Calendar of the South American Hungarian Journal), São Paulo, Brazil. Annual: 1945, 1953, 1955-1956, 1964.

Diariuma; Diario de los Amigos de los Libros Hungaros (Diary of the Friends of Hungarian Books), Buenos Aires, Argentina. Frequency varies: 1952-1953.

Egyetértés (Concord), Homestead, PA. Monthly: 1928.

Elöre (Forward), New York, NY. Weekly: 1917.

Erdély Védelmében (In the Defense of Transylvania), New York, NY. 1978-1979, 1982.

Erös Vár (Mighty Fortress), Cleveland, OH. Monthly: 1967, 1973-1974.

Értesítö (Bulletin), New York, NY. Monthly: 1955, 1977-1978.

Északi Vártán (On the Northern Sentry Duty), Long Island City, NY. Quarterly: 1978-1982, 1984.

Európai Magyar Irók Kongresszusa Kalendárium (Calendar of the European Hungarian Writers' Congress), Munich, West Germany. Annual: 1960.

Evangeliumi Vilagszolgalat (Evangelical World Service), Buffalo, NY. Monthly: 1951-1956.

Évi Historias Kalendáriuma (Annual Historical Calendar), Youngstown, OH. Annual: 1951-1952, 1957-1977.

Evkönyv (Yearbook), Los Angeles, CA. Annual: 1976-1980.

A Fáklya (The Torch), Warren, OH. Bi-monthly: 1960-1961, 1963-1966, 1970-1976.

A Fatimai Kálvária Hirei (News of the Fatima Calvary), Youngstown, OH. Frequency varies: 1956-1962.

First Hungarian Evangelical and Reformed Church Yearbook, Los Angeles, CA. Annual: 1969-1971. Includes English.

First Hungarian Reformed Church Yearbook, Cleveland, OH. Annual: 1926-1927, 1929, 1937-1965. Includes English.

First Hungarian Reformed Church Report, Pittsburgh, PA. Annual: 1965. Includes English.

Fraternity (Hungarian Reformed Federation of America), Ligonier, PA. Quarterly (monthly): 1956-1957, 1959, 1961, 1964-1984. Includes English.

Független Magyar Hírszolgálat (Independent Hungarian News Service Bulletin), Falls Church, VA. Bi-weekly: 1977-1980.

Gesta (Accomplishments), Stuttgart, West Germany. Frequency varies: 1964-1966, 1968.

The Guardian of Liberty (English edition of the newspaper **Nemzetör**), Munich, West Germany. Bi-monthly: 1972-1977. English.

Hadak Utján; A Magyar Harcosok Bajtársi Közösségének Tájékoztatója (On the Triumphal March; Bulletin of the Hungarian Soldiers' Fraternal Community), Munich, West Germany. Bi-monthly (?): 1970-1971, 1973-1975.

Hazai Tudositasok (Information from Home), Budapest, Hungary. Semi-monthly: 1981-1982.

A Hét (The Week), New York, NY. Weekly (?): 1924.

Hidfö (Bridgehead), London, England. Bi-monthly: 1967-1971, 1973-1974, 1976-1978.

Hidfö Könyvtár (Bridgehead Library), Munich, West Germany. Quarterly (?): 1968-1969, 1971-1972, 1974.

Hidverök Évkönyve (Bridge Builders' Yearbook), Neumarkt-St. Veit, West Germany. Annual: 1954.

Híradó (Hungarian Information Bulletin), Cleveland, OH. Monthly: 1956.

Híradó (Bulletin; Hungarian Scout Association), Toronto, Ontario, Canada. Daily during summer camp (Aug. 14-23): 1975.

Humoros Nyugat (Humorous West), Los Angeles, CA. Monthly: 1975-1979.

A Hungária Hontalan Magyarok Hetilapja Naptára (Hungaria Calendar--Stateless Hungarians' Weekly), Bad Wörishofen, West Germany. Annual: 1951.

A Hungária Naptára (Hungaria Calendar), Munich, West Germany. Annual: 1954.

Hungarian Calendar, Washington, DC. Annual: 1960. English.

The Hungarian Digest, Lancaster, MA. Bi-monthly: 1966. English.

Hungarian Evangelical and Reformed Church Annual Report, Chicago, IL. Annual: 1935-1938, 1942, 1952, 1958, 1961-1965. Includes English.

Hungarian Folk Museum News, Passaic, NJ. Monthly (?): 1981-1982. Includes English.

Hungarian Heritage Review (previously titled The Eighth Hungarian Tribe), Union, NJ (previously published in Ligonier, PA). Monthly: 1974-date. English.

The Hungarian Quarterly, New York, NY. Quarterly: 1961-1963. English.

Hungarian Reformed Federation of America By-laws, Ligonier, PA. Every four years (?): 1936, 1940, 1956. Includes English.

Hungarian Studies Newsletter, New Brunswick, NJ. Frequency varies: 1973-1982. English.

Hungarian Studies Review (previously titled The Canadian-American Review of Hungarian Studies), Toronto, Ontario, Canada. Semi-annual: 1974-date. English.

Hungarian United Presbyterian Church Annual Report, Youngstown, OH. Annual: 1965-1967. Includes English.

International Workers' Order Hungarian Section Naptár, New York, NY. Annual: 1940.

Itt-Ott (Here-There; title varies: Itt-Ott Szeminárium in 1972), Ada, OH (Hereford, PA in 1972). Five issues per year: 1969-1980. (Index: 1967-1977). Includes English.

John Calvin Magyar Reformed Church Yearbook, Perth Amboy, NJ. Annual: 1967. Includes English.

Kanadai-Magyar Naptar (Canadian-Hungarian Calendar), Winnipeg, Manitoba, Canada. Annual: 1948-1949.

Kanadai Magyar Ujság Naptára (Canadian Hungarian News Yearbook), Winnipeg, Manitoba, Canada. Annual: 1950, 1955-1968.

Kapocs (Bond), Vancouver, British Columbia, Canada. Annual (semi-annual): 1965-1967, 1971, 1973, 1975.

Karikázó (Round Dance; Hungarian folklore newsletter), New Brunswick, NJ. Quarterly: 1975-date. English.

Kárpát (The Carpathian), Cleveland, OH. Frequency varies: 1958-1959, 1964-1965, 1970-1973.

Katolikus Értesítö (Catholic Bulletin), Caracas, Venezuela. Monthly (?): 1979-1980.

Katolikus Magyarok Vasárnapja Kalendar (Calendar of Catholic Hungarians' Sunday; title varies: **Béke-Naptára, Képes Naptára, Histórias Kalendárium, Magyar Kéve** and **Halkuló Harangok**), Youngstown, OH. Annual: 1942, 1946-1947, 1949, 1951, 1952, 1954-1980, 1981-1984.

Katolikus Szemle (Catholic Review), Rome, Italy. Quarterly (?): 1963, 1966-1974. Includes English summaries.

Képes Magyar Magazin (Illustrated Hungarian Magazine), New York, NY. Monthly: 1956-1958.

Képes Magyar Újság (Illustrated Magyar News), Detroit, MI/Cleveland, OH. Monthly: 1976.

Képes Magyar Világhíradó (Illustrated Hungarian World Review), Twinsburg, OH. Monthly: 1972, 1974-1977.

Képes Világhíradó (Illustrated World Review), Toronto, Ontario, Canada. Monthly: 1959-1969.

Kerecsen (Falcon), Ann Arbor, MI. Frequency varies: 1975.

Kivándorlási Értesítö (Emigration Bulletin), Budapest, Hungary. Semi-monthly. (Microfilm: 1903-1907).

The Kossuth Foundation Bulletin, New York, NY. Frequency varies: 1966. English.

Krónika; A Kanadi Magyar Kultúrközpont Híradója (Chronicle; Journal of the Canadian Hungarian Cultural Center), Toronto, Ontario, Canada. Monthly: 1975-date.

Küldetés (Mission), Toronto, Ontario, Canada. Monthly: 1975-1976.

Lármafa (Alarm Pole), Lienz, Austria. Quarterly: 1956-1966.

Lármafa Erdélyi Évkönyv (Alarm Pole Transylvanian Yearbook), Lienz, Austria. Annual: 1967-1968.

Láthatár (Horizon), Budapest, Hungary. Monthly. (Microfilm: 1936-1944).

Latóhatár (Horizon), Munich, West Germany. Monthly: 1953, 1958.

Lehel Kürtje (Lehel's Bugle), Toronto, Ontario, Canada. Monthly: 1967.

Los Angelesi Értesítö (Bulletin of Los Angeles), Los Angeles, CA. Irregular: 1974-1975.

Ludovikas Hirado (Ludovika [Military Academy] Journal), Munich, West Germany. Bi-monthly: 1977-1978.

Magyar Bányász Naptár (Hungarian Miner's Guide and Yearbook), New York, NY. Annual: 1918. Includes some English.

Magyar Család (Hungarian Family), Surrey, England. Quarterly: 1967-1973.

Magyar Csendörök Családi Közössége (Hungarian Gendarmes' Family Community), Cleveland, OH. Irregular: 1973.

Magyar Cserkész (Hungarian Scout Magazine; Hungarian Boy Scout Association), Garfield, NJ. Frequency varies: 1953, 1958-1961, 1966-1982, 1984.

Magyar Egyház (Magyar Church), Ligonier, PA. Monthly (except June-September): 1942, 1968, 1970-1975. Includes English.

Magyar Élet (Californian's Hungarian Life), Glendale, CA. Weekly: 1958.

Magyar Evangelical and Reformed Church Annual Report, Elyria, OH. Annual: 1956. Includes English.

Magyar Évkönyv (Hungarian Yearbook), New York, NY. Annual: 1986-1987.

Magyar Faluszövetség Vasárnap (Hungarian Rural Association's Sunday), New York, NY. Annual: 1960-1970.

Magyar Gyermekek (Hungarian Children), Munich, West Germany. Monthly: 1956-1957, 1960.

Magyar Hirek (Hungarian News), Budapest, Hungary. Frequency varies (bi-monthly): 1980-date.

Magyar Hirek Kincses Kalendárium (Treasure Calendar of the Hungarian News), Budapest, Hungary. Annual: 1962, 1964-1977, 1979-date.

Magyar Kalendárium (Hungarian Calendar), Stuttgart, Germany. Annual: 1948.

Magyar Könyvbarátok (Hungarian Book Lovers), Cologne, West Germany. Quarterly: 1959.

Magyar Magazin (Hungarian Magazine), Toronto, Ontario, Canada. Monthly: 1965.

Magyar Naptár (Hungarian Calendar; 1956 issue titled **Mindentudó Kalendárium**), New York, NY. Annual: 1956, 1958, 1962-1966, 1968, 1970, 1972-1977.

Magyar Naptára (Hungarian Calendar), São Paulo, Brazil. Annual: 1951.

Magyar Nök (Hungarian Women), Munich, West Germany. Quarterly (monthly): 1956, 1960-1968.

A Magyar Otthon Egyesület Évkönyve (The Hungarian Home Society Yearbook), Toronto, Ontario, Canada. Annual: 1968.

Magyar Szabadságharcos (Hungarian Freedom Fighter), Union City, NJ (previously published in Pittsburgh, PA). Monthly: 1969-1970.

Magyar Tájékoztató (Hungarian Bulletin), Montreal, Quebec, Canada. Frequency varies: 1956 (?).

Magyar Találkozó Krónikája (Chronicles of the Hungarian Reunion; Proceedings of the Annual Congress of the Hungarian Literary and Artistic Association), Cleveland, OH. Annual: 1962, 1966-1974, 1976, 1978-1981.

Magyar Történelmi Szemle (Hungarian Historical Review), New York, NY. Quarterly: 1969-1970. Includes English, French and German.

Magyarok Világlapja (Hungarians' World News), Budapest, Hungary. Monthly. (Microfilm: 1938).

Mindszenty Népe (Mindszenty's People), Cleveland, OH (?). Monthly: 1954-1955.

The Mindszenty Report, St. Louis, MO. Monthly: 1974-1981. English.

A Nap Fiai (Sons of the Sun), Buenos Aires, Argentina. Monthly: 1971-1975, 1977.

Napotthon Naptára (Sun Home Calendar), Sandusky, OH. Annual: 1970.

Nemzetör Évkönyv (National Guard Yearbook), Munich, West Germany. Annual: 1970.

Nemzetvédelmi Tájékoztató (Information about Defense of Nation), Hollywood, CA. Monthly: 1971.

Nevessünk (Let's Laugh), Flint, MI. Monthly (?): 1919.

News from Hungary: Magyarországi Hirek, New York, NY. Frequency varies: 1965-1973.

Nök Világa (Women's World), New York, NY. Monthly: 1954, 1956-1957, 1959, 1964-1970.

Nyelvünk és Kultúránk: As Anyanyelvi Konferencia Védnökségének Tájékoztátója (Our Language and Culture: Bulletin of the Mother Tongue Conference's Sponsorship; previously titled A Magyar Nyelvért és Kultúráért), Budapest, Hungary. Quarterly: 1971-date.

Nyugati Magyarság (Western Hungarians), Montreal, Quebec, Canada. Monthly: 1953-1954.

Ösi Gyökér (Ancient Roots), Buenos Aires, Argentina. Bi-monthly: 1973-1978.

Ötágú Sip: Magyar Folyóirat (Ocarina: Hungarian Journal), New Brunswick, NJ. Bi-monthly: 1974-1975.

Pannonia-Kör (Pannonia Circle), Montreal, Quebec, Canada. Monthly (?): 1975. Includes some French and English.

Parázs (Embers), Wheeling, IL (previously published in Chicago, IL). Monthly: 1977-1982. Includes some English.

Párduc (Panther), Buenos Aires, Argentina. Bi-monthly: 1977.

Pásztortűz (Shepherd's Campfire), Cologne, West Germany. Monthly (?): 1962.

Pax Romana (Roman Peace), Munich, West Germany. Semi-annual: 1964-1970, 1972, 1976.

A Perth Amboyi Hiradó Naptára (Perth Amboy Herald Almanac), Perth Amboy, NJ. Annual: 1946.

Piszkafa (Poker), New York, NY. Weekly: 1923, 1924, 1937, 1938. Includes some English.

Postakürt: A Délafrikai Magyar Egyesület Folyóirata (Postilion Horn: Journal of the South African Hungarian Society), Johannesburg, South Africa. Monthly: 1971-1974.

Református Hirek (Reformed News), New York, NY. Bi-monthly: 1974-1980.

Reformátusok Lapja (Hungarian Reformed Religious Paper), Perth Amboy, NJ. Monthly (bi-monthly June-September): 1969. Includes English.

St. Joseph's Hungarian Catholic Church, New York, NY. Monthly: 1974-1975.

St. Michael's Greek Catholic Church Annual Report, Lorain, OH. Annual: 1958. Includes English.

Studies for a New Central Europe, Cleveland, OH. Frequency varies: 1963-1964, 1966-1969. English with French and German resumes.

Sumir Hiradó (Magyar Newsletter), Cupertino, CA. Tri-annual: 1973-1975 and undated issue.

Szabad Magyar Tájékoztató (Free Hungarian Information Service), New York, NY. Frequency varies: 1974-1975.

Szabadságharos Hiradó (Freedom Fighter News), Los Angeles, CA. Frequency varies: 1976-1978.

Szabadság Naptára (Freedom Calendar), Cleveland, OH. Annual: 1930-1931.

Szabadulás (Liberation), Audubon, PA. Monthly (?): 1979.

Székely Nép (Szekely People), Rochester, NY/Cleveland, OH. Frequency varies: 1975-1979.

Szemle (Review), Brussels, Belgium. Quarterly: 1959-1963.

Szemle (Review; Associated Hungarian Teachers), Toronto, Ontario, Canada. Monthly: 1962-1963.

Szent Erzsébet Rozsái (Roses of St. Elizabeth), Staten Island, NY. Monthly (?): 1939.

Szinházi Ujság (Hungarian Theatre News), Chicago, IL. Monthly: 1926.

A Szív (The Heart), Hamilton, Ontario, Canada (previously published in Budapest, Hungary; and Shrub Oak, NY). Monthly: 1938, 1954, 1961-1965, 1968-1981.

A Szív Nagy Képesnaptára (The Heart's Illustrated Large Calendar), Buffalo, NY/Cleveland, OH. Annual: 1955, 1957.

Szivárvány (Rainbow), Montreal, Quebec, Canada. Monthly: 1961.

Szolgálat (Service), Eisenstadt, Austria. Quarterly: 1969, 1971-1972, 1974.

Tájékoztató (Information; World Federation of Hungarian Jews), New York, NY. Monthly: 1961-1964.

Tanú (Witness), Toronto, Ontario, Canada. Monthly: 1979.

Toronto és Ontario Magyar Cimtara és Naptára (Hungarian Directory and Calendar of Toronto and Ontario; title varies: Toronto és Ontario Magyar Cimtara és Évkönyve), Toronto, Ontario, Canada. Annual: 1969-1970, 1973.

Transsylvania (American Transylvanian Federation), New York, NY. Quarterly: 1967-1969, 1973-1975.

True Hungary, New York, NY. Quarterly: 1956-1957, 1965. Includes English.

Tudósitó (Reporter; Hungarian Catholic League of America), New York, NY. Monthly: 1955-1956.

Turán (Turanian), Buenos Aires, Argentina. 1964-1966.

Új Élet (New Life), Toronto, Ontario, Canada. Monthly: 1959-1960, 1967-1968.

Új Európa (New Europe), Munich, West Germany. Monthly: 1968.

Új Idö (New Era), Lakewood, OH. Monthly: 1982, 1984-date.

Új Látóhatár (New Horizon), Munich, West Germany. Monthly: 1961-1964. Includes English summary.

Új Magyar Út (New Hungarian Way), Washington, DC. Monthly: 1950-1955.

Út és Cél (Way and Goal), Brussels, Belgium. Monthly: 1953-1954, 1971, 1976.

Utitárs (Traveling Companion), Innsmola, Norway. Monthly: 1966-1967.

Üzenet (Message), Caracas, Venezuela. Monthly: 1978.

Vagyunk (We Are), Munich, West Germany. Monthly: 1974-1976.

Vasárnapi Levél Kulturélet (Sunday Cultural Life Letter), Vienna, Austria. Monthly: 1962-1963, 1968.

Vezetök Lapja (Leader's Magazine; Hungarian Scout Leader magazine), Garfield, NJ. Quarterly: 1969, 1971-1984.

Vigilia (Vigil), Budapest, Hungary. Monthly: 1966-1968, 1970, 1972-1975, 1977-1979.

Virrasztó (Awakener), Long Island City, NY. Frequency varies: 1970-1975.

Washingtoni Krónika (Washington Chronicle), Washington, DC. Quarterly: 1977.

William Penn Life (William Penn Fraternal Association), Pittsburgh, PA. Quarterly: 1969. Includes English.

Zsebnaptár (Pocket Calendar), New York, NY. Annual: 1923

Italian American Collection

Manuscript Collections

Abbate, Paolo L. (1884-1973).
Papers, 1919-1973. 1 linear in.

An internationally renowned sculptor as well as an ordained minister, teacher, and author, Abbate was born in Villa Rosa, Italy. He came to the United States in 1903 and worked in New York City. President of the International Fine Arts League and a member of the National Sculptors' Council, the Artists Council, Inc., and the Connecticut Artists and Writers Society, Abbate also founded the Torrington UNICO Club, an Italian American service organization.

Papers consist of a scrapbook of items about his sculpture and newspaper clippings about him and his works. *Includes English.*

Ambrosino, Simone J.
Papers, 1956-1986. Ca. 2.5 linear ft.

Ambrosino was Grand Venerable of the Order Sons of Italy in America (OSIA), Delaware Grand Lodge (1974-1979). Collection includes state membership lists, convention records, correspondence, constitution and bylaws, and materials pertaining to individual OSIA lodges. Included are OSIA Supreme Convention books and correspondence; President Jimmy Carter's resolution declaring June 22, 1980, National Italian-American Day in honor of OSIA's seventy-fifth anniversary; and materials on national fundraising and relief activities. *In English. In OSIA Guide.*

America-Italy Society (New York, NY).
Records, 1925-1959. 2.5 linear ft.

The Society, a cultural and social organization (established in 1918 as the Italy-America Society) was incorporated in 1935. It was inactive during World War II because of Italy's alliance with the Axis powers and was dissolved in 1948. In 1949, it was reestablished under its present name. The organization has as its purpose promotion of friendship, based on mutual understanding, between Italy and the United States.

Records of the America-Italy Society include correspondence, minutes, financial records, brochures, corporate documents, and photographs. Included is information regarding the Italy-America Society's dissolution, with correspondence of founder Luigi Criscuolo. Records also contain correspondence of or with Ellsworth Bunker, Thomas McKittrick, John Astor, and Clare Boothe Luce. *Includes English. Inventory available.*

American Committee for Italian War Relief (St. Paul, Minnesota).
Records, 1943-1948. 1 linear in.

Records of the Committee, organized to aid war victims in Italy and composed of representatives of Italian American organizations and Catholic churches, include minutes, correspondence, newspaper clippings, and articles of incorporation. *Includes English.*

American Committee on Italian Migration (ACIM), Chicago Chapter (Illinois).
Records, 1954-1967. 2.5 linear ft.

The Chicago chapter of ACIM was formed in 1952, the same year that the national organization was founded. The purposes of ACIM were to study the problem of overpopulation in Italy; to publicize the need for Italian emigration; to promote legislation permitting Italians to enter the United States, including revision of the McCarran-Walter Act; to cooperate with the Roman Catholic Bishops' Resettlement Council; to raise funds for Italian resettlement; and to publish a monthly bulletin.
Records include a brief history, correspondence, organizational papers, souvenir journals and symposia, photographs and newspaper clippings, and special events information.
Correspondents include U.S. senators, church dignitaries, the Italian ambassador and consuls, and other figures in the Italian government. Included is correspondence with Lyndon B. Johnson, Birch Bayh, Frank Annunzio, Everett M. Dirksen, Jacob K. Javits, Edward M. Kennedy, and Mayor Richard Daley of Chicago. *Includes English. Inventory available.*

American Italian Historical Association. Stella del Nord Chapter (Upper Midwest).
Records, ca. 1976-1985. 3 linear ft.

Records of the Association consist of organizational minutes, correspondence, and financial materials as well as photographs and oral history tapes gathered to document the history of Italian Americans in the Upper Midwest, mainly Minnesota. *In English.*

American Italian Historical Association Conference, 1972 (Boston, Massachusetts).
Tapes and transcripts. Ca. 1 linear in.

Tapes and partial transcript relate to the conference topic "Italian American Radicalism: Old World Origins and New World Developments." *In English.*

Andreozzi, John.
Collection, 1885-1905. 2 linear in.

Collection comprises U.S. Census record summaries of Italians living in Cumberland, WI. Summaries are taken from 1885, 1895, 1900, and 1905 censuses. *In English.*

Angeletti, Edward J.
Papers, 1959-1977. Ca. 1 linear ft.

A judge, Angeletti served as First Assistant Grand Venerable of OSIA Maryland Grand Lodge (1975-1977), and as Grand Orator (1971-1975). Collection consists of materials pertaining to the Maryland Grand Lodge. Included are Grand Council minutes; officers' lists; and correspondence relating to various members of the Maryland Grand Council, to schisms within the Lodge, and to committees and activities, including Baltimore City Fair, Italian Festival, Mortuary Fund, and the tax status of the Lodge. *In English. In OSIA Guide.*

Anzalone, Charles (1888-1959).
Papers, ca. 1937-1970. 1 microfilm reel.

A businessman and Louisiana politician, Anzalone was born in Cefalidina, Sicily. He came to the United States with his parents in 1896, worked for six years as a laborer on Louisiana sugar plantations, and then in 1902 moved to Independence (Tangipahoa Parish), LA. He became a farmer and leader in the strawberry industry and prominent in business and civic affairs. A devoted follower of Huey Long, he was active in politics, serving as alderman and mayor of Independence, and then state representative.

Papers include biographical information, correspondence, and newspaper clippings pertaining to Anzalone's political career; materials pertaining to legislation; and a seminar paper by John V. Baramonte, Jr. *Includes English. Inventory available.*

Artoni, Gioacchino (1866-1937).
Papers, ca. 1915-1942. Ca. 1 linear in.

Artoni was born in Pieve (Reggio Emilia), Italy. After coming to the United States, he worked as a miner in Pennsylvania, as a farmer, and in the silk industry in Paterson, NJ. A socialist, he wrote for the socialist press, was a manager of cooperative stores, and was an organizer for the Amalgamated Clothing Workers of America. He was known with great affection by his colleagues as "Papa Artoni."

Papers consist primarily of newspaper clippings about him. *Includes English.*

Ascoli, Max (1898-1978).
Papers, ca. 1935-1968. 2 microfilm reels.

An Italian Jewish intellectual and author, Ascoli held the chair of Philosophy of Law at the University of Rome. Opposed to Mussolini's regime, he left Fascist Italy in 1932 and came to the United States on a Rockefeller Foundation scholarship. He was active in the Mazzini Society, an antifascist organization founded in 1939 by Italian émigrés and other Italians.

Papers include correspondence, minutes, publications, reports, and newspaper clippings relating to the activities of the Mazzini Society and its officers. *Includes English. Originals held by Boston Public Library.*

Augusto, Emilio.
Papers, 1931-1972. 2 linear in.

Augusto was publisher and editor of an Italian newspaper of Paterson, NJ, *La Voce Italiana* (formerly *La Vedetta Coloniale*). Papers of Augusto consist of photographs of Fascist Italy and

prominent Italian American socialists, as well as miscellaneous personal and business correspondence, some pertaining to his newspapers. *Includes English.*

Baciagalupi, James Augustus (1882-1950).
Papers, ca. 1926-1950. Ca. 1 linear in.

Baciagalupi was president of Transamerica Corporation and the Bank of America. He grew up in California, the son of Italian immigrant parents, and received a law degree from Hastings College of Law.

His papers consist of correspondence and obituaries from two San Francisco newspapers. *In English.*

Bambace, Angela (1898-1975).
Papers, ca. 1938-1976. 6 linear in.

A labor organizer and vice-president of the International Ladies' Garment Workers Union, Bambace was born in Santos, Brazil, of Italian parents. The family came to the United States when Angela was six. She grew up in East Harlem, NY, and began work in the garment industry when she was seventeen. An advocate of women's rights, she founded the first women's local of the ILGWU in 1936; she was the only woman on the ILGWU executive board in 1956. She helped organize the Amalgamated Clothing Workers' Union strike in Elizabeth, NJ, in 1932, and the walkout of 75,000 dressmakers in New York City in 1933.

Papers include personal correspondence and correspondence related to union work, political and labor speeches, clippings related to labor and Bambace's union work, interviews with Bambace, clippings and letters related to Bambace's death, and photographs of Bambace with political and labor notables. *Includes English. Preliminary inventory available.*

Barolini, Helen.
Papers, ca. 1967-1979. 1.5 linear ft.

Papers of Helen Barolini, an Italian American author, consist of manuscripts and proofs of her novel *Umbertina* and other manuscripts of her poems, articles, and stories. *In English.*

Beck, R. Merrill.
Papers, 1975-1987. Ca. 1 linear ft.

Beck served the OSIA Virginia Grand Lodge as Grand Venerable (1983-1987). Collection consists of souvenir books and minutes of Virginia Grand Lodge conventions; Grand Lodge correspondence, officer lists, and materials relating to various committees and programs, including the Virginia Chapter of the Commission for Social Justice; and records of local Virginia lodges. *In English. In OSIA Guide.*

Benvegar, Charles.
Papers, 1941-1987. 1 linear in.

Collection consists of materials pertaining to Benvegar's life; newspaper clippings, poetry, and miscellaneous newsletters relating to Luigi Scialdone Lodge No. 2221 (OSIA, Baltimore, MD); "A Footnote to American History," detailing Benvegar's work as a government employee during and after World War II; and other writings. *In English. In OSIA Guide.*

Berardinelli, Nicola (b. 1894).
Papers, ca. 1912-1976. 6 linear in.

Berardinelli, a composer and opera baritone, was born in Castel di Sangro, Italy. In 1910 he came to the United States, where he taught voice, composed music, and performed. He was director and teacher at the Berardinelli School of Music and conductor of and singer with the Illinois Opera Company, the Conti Light Opera Company, and the Chicago Popular Opera Company. He was on the faculty of the Chicago Conservatory and the Chicago School of Music, and the author of *Secrets of Singing* (1971).

Berardinelli's papers consist of photographs, sheet music, playbills, programs, and newspaper clippings. Most materials pertain to his activities in Chicago, Denver, and New York. *Includes English. Inventory available.*

Bonadio, Maria Butera (b. 1882).
Papers, 1905-1986. 1 linear in.

Papers of Bonadio, an Italian immigrant residing in Kenosha, WI, consist of photographs and newspaper clippings (1858-1986) and one document in Italian, mostly biographical information on Bonadio, who came from Italy in 1905. *Mainly in English.*

Broccolino, Arnold.
Papers, 1971-1974. 22 linear ft.

Broccolino served the Maryland Grand Lodge of OSIA as Grand Venerable (1969-1974), First and Second Assistant Grand Venerable (1959-1969), and Grand Trustee. Collection consists of OSIA Supreme Lodge and Grand Lodge records along with records of non-OSIA Italian American organizations and events. Supreme Lodge records include Anti-Defamation Commission materials and correspondence regarding arbitration cases in Maryland. Records of the Maryland Grand Lodge include a ledger listing state officers and delegates; Grand Convention minutes; Grand Council minutes, correspondence, reports, and arbitration case documents; and reports of local lodges. *Mainly in English. In OSIA Guide.*

Buccieri, Martin R.
Papers, 1938-1986. 2 linear ft.

Buccieri served as Supreme Delegate of OSIA (1971-1973) and as Grand Venerable of the Illinois Grand Lodge (1965-1971, 1975-1977). Collection includes correspondence of the Illinois Grand Lodge and Columbus Day celebration programs; the 1938 Chicago Park Board's plans of the ship Santa Maria; materials on the Chicago Columbus Day parade, Boys Town of Italy, and the Santa Rita Foster Parents Association; and the Parish Directory of St. Vincent Ferrer Church. Also included are award banquets and program booklets relating to Illinois OSIA local lodge No. 1974. *In English. In OSIA Guide.*

Cacchiola, Carmine.
Papers, 1920-1988. Ca. 1.5 linear ft.

Cacchiola was a founder of the Glen Cove (NY) Lodge No. 1016 (OSIA). He is active in the New York Grand Lodge and has served OSIA as the National Deputy to New Jersey. He is also a member of Alpha Phi Delta, a fraternity of Italian American men.

Papers include materials pertaining to national and state lodges of OSIA; booklets, reports, bylaws, and a newsletter of the Alpha Phi Delta fraternity; and photographs of the Glen Cove lodge. Local OSIA materials also include program pamphlets, membership information, and information about New York local lodges. *Includes English. Inventory available. In OSIA Guide.*

Caira, Aldo A.
Papers, 1945-1987. Ca. 8.5 linear ft.

Caira held several national leadership positions in OSIA, serving as national President from 1981 to 1985. At the state level (Massachusetts) he held several offices beginning in 1969, culminating with the state presidency (1969-1973).

Collection contains OSIA Supreme correspondence, records, minutes, brochures of Supreme Conventions, and Supreme Council minutes; Caira's speeches; "On the Move" columns from OSIA *News*; and materials on numerous OSIA committees and projects. State level records include Massachusetts Grand Lodge convention records, Grand Council minutes, correspondence, and records of a wide variety of committees and projects. Also included is information on Massachusetts districts and local lodge activities. *Mainly in English. Inventory available. In OSIA Guide.*

Caira, Michael A.
Papers, 1981-1988. 18 linear ft.

Caira was born in Wilmington, MA, where he now lives. He served OSIA as Grand Trustee of Massachusetts (1979-1981), National Deputy (1983-1985), and National Executive Director (1985-1988).

Papers include national convention minutes, reports, and booklets; council minutes and correspondence; speeches of national officers; information on many committee activities and charitable efforts; financial records; correspondence pertaining to regional conferences and with state lodges; a film script entitled "The Italians and Jews in Occupied Europe"; and a portrait of Frank Montemuro. Speeches are those of Supreme Venerables Aldo Caira, Bruno Giuffrida, and Frank Montemuro and his own. *In English. Inventory available. In OSIA Guide.*

Cama, Anthony.
Papers, 1960-1980. 2 linear in.

Cama is a teacher and writer who lives in Lynn, MA. He has been active in OSIA and has served as president of Riunite Lodge No. 889.

Papers consist of a Junior Division ritual book, correspondence and Columbus Day Committee minutes from the Riunite Lodge, a Columbus Day proclamation by Governor John Volpe, a resumé of Paul Lazzaro, newspaper clippings about the Lynn, MA, OSIA lodges and the Massachusetts Grand Lodge, and photographs of local lodge activities. *In English. Inventory available. In OSIA Guide.*

Candela, Elisabeth (Colicchio).
Papers, 1967-1987. 1 linear in.

Elisabeth Candela served in various offices in the Ohio Grand Lodge of OSIA, and as Venerable of the OSIA Anita Garibaldi Lodge No. 722. Collection includes the directory of the Ohio Grand Lodge; report of the Grand Trustees; miscellaneous material relating to the 1967 Grand Convention held in Ashtabula; and resumés, correspondence, and newspaper clippings pertaining to Candela. Also included are Columbus Day programs of Anita Garibaldi Lodge. *In English.*

Cappello, Rosemary.
Papers, 1974-1976. Ca. 1 linear in.

Cappello, a writer, was born in Llanerch, PA. Her articles appeared in the *Camden Catholic Star Herald*, the *Nola Express*, and other publications.

Papers consist of articles and poetry; included are her reminiscences of her father, an Italian immigrant shoemaker. *In English. Articles are photocopies.*

Capraro, Anthony (Nino) (1891-1975).
Papers, ca. 1896-1975. Ca. 15 linear ft.

Born in Sciacca, Sicily, Capraro came to the United States as a child, settling with his family in New York in 1902. As a teenager Capraro joined a group of Italian American anarchists inspired by Errico Malatesta. Arrested in 1908 in connection with his political activities, Capraro spent three years in jail. After his release, he became one of the major organizers of the Amalgamated Clothing Workers of America and a collaborator of labor activists Sidney Hillman and August Bellanca. While directing the 1919 strike of textile workers in Lawrence, MA, Capraro was kidnapped and beaten. At that time he was also a correspondent for the *New York Call*, a Socialist daily newspaper. Later he edited his own newspaper, *Utopia*, in Rochester, NY. During the 1920s, Capraro was active in the effort to save the lives of Sacco and Vanzetti. In the 1940s, as a member of the Mazzini Society, he became a spokesman for antifascism among Italian Americans. As an arbiter in labor disputes, he founded the Greater Clothing Contractors Association in New York City in 1932.

Papers include extensive correspondence, clippings, and materials relating to the Lawrence textile strike; correspondence with notable labor and socialist activists, including Carlo Tresca, Augusto Bellanca, Pietro Allegra, Jacob Potofsky, and Arturo Giovannetti; correspondence and materials relating to *Alba Nuova*, *Il Nuovo Mondo*, and the Mazzini Society; clippings on labor, fascism, communism, and socialism; and extensive personal and family correspondence. *Includes English. Inventory available.*

Caradonna, Nino (1898-1980).
Papers, 1911-1980. Ca. 6 linear ft.

A poet and publisher in Cleveland, OH, and St. Louis, MO, Caradonna immigrated to the United States in 1921. More than ten volumes of his poetry have been published and several have been translated into various languages.

His papers consist primarily of correspondence, much of it with other notable Italian and Italian American writers. Also included are manuscripts of his writing and that of other poets, and photographs. *Includes English. Preliminary inventory available.*

Caselli, Alberico.
Papers, 1918-1947. 6 linear in.

Caselli was one of the founders of the first Sezione Socialista Italiana in Chicago. Papers consist of two scrapbooks and one package of newspaper clippings. The clippings, many from *Stampa Libera* of New York (formerly *Il Nuovo Mondo*), relate chiefly to Italian fascism, World War II, and socialism. Some clippings relate to Filippo Turati, Italo Balbo, Errico Malatesta, Carlo Sforza, and Pietro Nenni. Also included are antifascist cartoons from the American press, postcard portraits of famous socialists, and photographs and articles on the Vienna Commune, the interim social-democratic government that ended with suppression of the worker uprising in Vienna in 1934. *Includes English. Inventory available.*

Castagnola, Salvatore.
Papers, 1893-1909. 1 linear in.

Papers of Castagnola consist of a photocopied typescript of his autobiography, Part I, telling of his childhood in Sicily and life in Brooklyn, NY. *In English.*

Celli, Fred.
Papers, ca. 1926-1972. Ca. 5 linear ft.

Papers consist of personal correspondence; and correspondence, minutes, miscellany, reports, and publications of socialist and antifascist organizations. Among organizations represented are the Italian Socialist Federation; the Socialist Party of America and its Italian Section; the Matteoti League; the Mazzini Society; the Fratellanza Italo-Americana, Abraham Lincoln (New York); Italian American publishing companies; and the International Workers' Order. *Includes English. Inventory available.*

Cernuto, Joseph (1898-1973).
Papers, 1929-1967. 5 linear in.

Cernuto served OSIA as Supreme Treasurer (1949-1969) and Supreme Trustee (1939-1949) and in several offices at the state and local levels. Collection consists of OSIA Supreme Convention books, a copy of the General Laws of the Order, Pennsylvania Grand Convention books, miscellaneous Pennsylvania Grand Lodge testimonial dinner programs, the program for the dedication of the building for Loggia Nuova Camillo Benso Di Cavour No. 874 (Mt. Pleasant, PA), and newspaper clippings. *Mainly in English. In OSIA Guide.*

Chenet, Albert.
Collection, 1941-1978. 3 linear in.

Chenet served as chairman of the Mortuary Fund Committee of OSIA Pennsylvania Grand Lodge (1939-1941) and as Third and First Assistant Grand Venerable (1967-1977). Collection includes Grand Convention books, Grand Council minutes and correspondence, testimonial dinner booklets, photographs of flood damage in Italy, and newspaper clippings. *Includes English. Inventory available. In OSIA Guide.*

Christopher Columbus Society (Calumet, Michigan).
Records, ca. 1935. 1 linear in.

Materials pertaining to the Society include a poster memorializing club members who died between 1923 and 1935 and miscellaneous forms of the Italian American Federation of the Upper Peninsula. *Includes English.*

Ciccotelli, Mario.
Papers, 1936-1987. 7 linear in.

Ciccotelli was born in the Marches and came to the United States in 1947. He has served OSIA as Illinois Grand Trustee (1967-1973, 1985-1987) and has been president of Chicago Heights Lodge No. 1430, formerly called Luce e Gloria Lodge.

Collection consists of records of the OSIA Luce e Gloria Lodge No. 1430, including minutes, financial records, correspondence, bulletins, medical certificates for sickness benefits awarded, and other materials. Also included are a photograph of the 1965 Grand Convention, minutes and reports of the 1985 and 1987 conventions, Grand Council minutes for 1986, Supreme Lodge resolutions ratified by the Grand Lodge in 1955, and Supreme Lodge records from the 1950s including national president reports. *Includes some records in English. In OSIA Guide.*

Circolo Culturale Italiano di Baltimora (Baltimore, Maryland).
Records, ca. 1940-1970. 1 linear ft.

This organization was founded in 1955 by Dr. Raffaele Canevaro, Mrs. George Knipp, and Regina Soria for those interested in Italian culture. Records consist of correspondence, financial records, membership lists, flyers, and announcements. Also included are correspondence and newspaper clippings relating to the Italian-American Committee of the National War Fund. *Includes English. Inventory available.*

Ciresi, Rose (1908-1988).
Papers, ca. 1930-1976. 9 linear in.

Ciresi, an Italian American from St. Paul, MN, was a member of the Columbus Memorial Association of St. Paul, Inc., and was instrumental in making Columbus Day a state holiday in Minnesota. Her other activities included membership in the Summer School of Catholic Action; and Holy Redeemer, St. Paul, Archdiocesan Sodality Council.

Papers contain numerous clippings on Holy Redeemer Church in St. Paul, MN, and correspondence, clippings, and programs from the Columbus Memorial Association of St. Paul, Inc. *In English. Related collection: Columbus Memorial Association of St. Paul, Inc.*

Clemente, Egidio (b. 1899).
Papers, ca. 1925-1970. 2.5 linear ft.

Clemente was born in Trieste and came to the United States in 1920 after being imprisoned during World War I for pro-Italian sympathies. In New York and Pittsburgh, he was active in the Italian Socialist Federation of the Socialist Party of America. A printer and journalist, he worked in Chicago for *La Parola del Popolo*, the organ of the Italian Socialist Federation, and for the antifascist *Il Nuovo Mondo*. Clemente was active in the Chicago movement to free Sacco and Vanzetti and was a founding member of the Chicago section of the Mazzini Society. He continued to work in the socialist movement and in labor organizing and antifascist activities; during World War II, he served in United States intelligence operations in Algeria, Sicily, and Rome. After the war Clemente renewed publication of *La Parola del Popolo* as a private venture, serving as editor and publisher.

Clemente's papers relate mostly to *La Parola del Popolo*. Included is correspondence from the 1960s with prominent Italians and Italian Americans relating to the socialist movement in the United States and Italy, the Vietnam War, and other topics. Correspondents include Angelo Cordaro, Costantino Lazzari, Norman Thomas, and Nino Caradonna. *Includes English. Inventory available.*

Columbus Memorial Association of St. Paul (Minnesota).
Records, 1935-1965. 1 linear ft.

Founded in 1929 as the St. Paul Chapter of the Columbus Memorial Association, the organization became incorporated in 1945 as the Columbus Memorial Association of St. Paul (MN). Its main objectives are ". . . to maintain, perpetuate, and, if necessary, defend the historical accomplishments of Christopher Columbus, Discoverer of America." The principal focus of the organization has become the annual banquet in honor of Columbus. The organization also seeks to maintain October 12 as an official holiday and supports local events celebrating Columbus. Membership consists of St. Paul residents who are Italian or of Italian descent, as well as representatives from other Italian organizations in Minnesota.

Records of the organization include bylaws, constitution, membership records, minutes, financial records, correspondence, and a scrapbook. *In English and Italian. Inventory available.*

Consiglio, Antonio (1890-1967).
Papers, 1926-1959. 3 linear in.

Consiglio founded the OSIA Delaware Grand Lodge in 1923 and served as Grand Venerable (1927-1948). He was an OSIA Supreme Trustee (1946-1947 and 1949-1959).

Papers include OSIA Supreme Convention booklets, general laws, telegrams, programs from national and state lodge and non-OSIA testimonial dinners, and correspondence. Also included are a publicity kit issued by American Relief for Italy, Inc., and photographs taken at Order Sons of Italy in America national and state conventions and banquets. *In English. In OSIA Guide.*

Cornetta, Martin V.
Papers, 1922-1987. Ca. 2.5 linear ft.

Cornetta served the OSIA Virginia Grand Lodge as Grand Venerable (1979-1983), Assistant Grand Venerable (1977-1979), and Grand Trustee (1975-1977). Collection consists of records of the Virginia Grand Lodge, which was founded in 1922, dissolved in the early 1940s, and reactivated in 1949. Grand Lodge records include correspondence and reports; Grand Convention and Council records; financial ledgers; photographs, including one of the Grand Council; and photocopies of a letter from Governor Trinkle to the Grand Venerable and an insurance policy issued by Unione Italiana

Umberto I. *Mainly in English. In OSIA Guide.*

Costa, Eugene.
Papers, 1973-1974. 1 linear in.

Costa served the West Virginia Grand Lodge (OSIA) as Grand Venerable (1971-1975), First Assistant Grand Venerable (1965-1971), and Second Assistant Grand Venerable (1963-1965). Collection consists of correspondence, Costa's Grand Venerable report to the 1974 West Virginia Grand Convention, and a legal document relating to the Christopher Columbus Lodge No. 1199 hall. *In English. In OSIA Guide. Related collection: OSIA Christopher Columbus Lodge No. 1199.*

Costa, Louis (1890-1976).
Papers, ca. 1925-1969. 1 linear in.

Costa was born in Caulonia, Italy, and came to West Virginia at the age of fourteen. He served the West Virginia Grand Lodge (OSIA) as First Assistant Grand Venerable (1973-1975), Grand Orator (1935-1941), Grand Trustee (1933-1935), and President of the Mortuary Fund (1948-1969).
Collection consists of a booklet of the West Virginia Grand Convention, and photographs of Grand Lodge activites. *Includes English. In OSIA Guide.*

Crescenzo, Roy.
Papers, ca. 1926-1938. 2 items.

A resident of Duluth, MN, Crescenzo was a member of Duluth Local Lodge Principe Ereditario Umberto II No. 992 of OSIA. Papers consist of an affadavit and a copy of a protest against Italy's treatment of Jews. *Includes English.*

Crisafi, Michelangelo (1893-1972).
Papers, 1918-1972. 6 linear ft.

A poet and author, Crisafi was born in the province of Palermo, Sicily. He left Italy in 1912 and settled in New Haven, CT, where for forty-five years he labored for the Tilo Roofing Company. In 1916 he took the pseudonym of Germoglino

Saggio, under which he wrote prolifically, contributing to numerous periodicals in Italy and the United States and authoring several published volumes. In later years, Crisafi aided the founding of a library in his hometown of Caletta, Sicily, and also assisted in the collection of Italian and Italian American publications for the Immigration History Research Center.
Crisafi's papers include extensive correspondence with Italian-American literary figures, among them Riccardo Cordiferro, Angelo M. Virga, Nino Caradonna, Pietro Greco, Luigi Roberto Burgo, Giuseppe Incalicchio, and Antonino Crivello. Scrapbooks and notebooks of his poetry and prose and reviews of his writing, as well as his critical judgments about the efforts of other Italian American writers, form a major part of the collection. Another section is devoted to collections of poetry and prose by other Italian American writers. *Includes English. Inventory available.*

Crivello, Antonino (1888-1969).
Papers, ca. 1939-1965. 5 linear ft.

Crivello was born in Palermo, Sicily, and immigrated to the United States at the age of fifteen. He became active in union organizing of tailors and dressmakers in New York. He was principal founder of the Circolo Libertario Pensiero ed Azione in New York. In 1917 he was hired as the Italian representative in the Education Department of International Ladies' Garment Workers' Union Local 25; and later he became manager of ILGWU Local 144 (Newark, NJ). Crivello belonged to numerous labor and antifascist groups, among them the Camera del Lavoro Italiana di New York, the Anti-fascist Alliance of North America, and the Italian Labor Education Bureau. He was also a poet and held membership in various literary academies in the United States and Italy. He was well-known for his antiwar writings during World War I.
Crivello's papers consist primarily of notebooks, clippings, and manuscript copies of his poetry and song lyrics, and of translations he made of other poets'

works. Business correspondence with various members of the ILGWU and minutes of ILGWU Local 144 Executive Board meetings are also included. *In English and Italian. Inventory available.*

Cupelli, Alberto (b. 1905).
Papers, ca. 1933-1973. 5 linear ft.

Cupelli was born in Lago (Cosenza), Italy, and came to the United States in 1923 to escape fascism; he was naturalized in 1944. Cupelli was active in the Italian antifascist movement in the United States and was associate editor of *Il Mondo* in New York from 1938 to 1946. Following World War II, he served as the Italian consular agent in New Haven, CT. Cupelli was co-author of *Gli Italiani di New York*, a publication of the Federal Writers Project.

Cupelli's papers relate mainly to his involvement in the Italian antifascist movement and his role as consular agent. Included in the collection are substantial files of newspaper clippings pertaining to Italian fascism in the United States and correspondence with leaders of the antifascist movement, including Gaetano Salvemini, Don Luigi Sturzo, Alberto Tarchiani, and Walter Toscanini. Additional files contain materials and correspondence relating to labor figures such as Luigi Antonini, Girolamo Valenti, Giuseppe D. Procopio and Vincenzo Vacirca. Typescripts of Cupelli's writings on Italian immigration and the history of his village and family are also included, as are radio scripts for weekly commentaries on various New Haven radio stations and newspaper columns he wrote for the New Haven *Glimpse.* Correspondence and materials relating to Cupelli's work as consular agent comprise another large portion of the collection. *Includes English. Inventory available.*

D'Agostino, Paul A. (1901-1966).
Papers, 1927-1963. Ca. 1.5 linear ft.

D'Agostino was an OSIA Supreme Trustee (1947-1953), Grand Venerable of Massachusetts (1959-1961), and Chairman of the OSIA Committee on Immigration and Naturalization (1950). Papers consist of an OSIA Supreme Convention book

and books containing the Supreme Constitution and bylaws; Massachusetts Grand Lodge convention books, constitution and bylaws; materials of various committees and projects such as revision of the bylaws, regulation of the death fund and life insurance program, membership drives, and scholarship fund; material relating to D'Agostino's legal career; photographs; and a scrapbook of newspaper clippings. *Mainly in English. In OSIA Guide.*

D'Alfonso, Dominic and Dante.
Collection, n.d. 1 linear in.

The D'Alfonso collection consists of a banner from OSIA G. Marconi Lodge No. 165 (PA) and three photographs of local Philadelphia, PA, OSIA lodges. *Includes English. In OSIA Guide.*

D'Ariano, Regina and Roy.
Papers, ca. 1938-1970. 2 linear in.

Regina and Roy D'Ariano were Italian American authors who came to the United States in 1912. Their papers consist of manuscripts of three short stories and books written by them: "David and Ruth"; "La Piccola Cantatrice"; and "The Princess Under Seven Veils." *Includes English.*

Darin, Grace.
Papers, 1981-1984. 1 linear in.

Grace Darin's papers consist of family histories, including "The Darin Family: A Century Chronicle;" "The Darin Family: A Supplement"; "The Rileys of Iron Belt: A Family Memoir"; and "The Darin Family: Looking Toward the Future-A New Generation." *In English.*

De Ciampis, Pasquale Mario (b. 1894).
Papers, ca. 1920-1989. 6.5 linear ft.

De Ciampis was born in Morcone, Italy. He was active in the labor movement in Naples and continued this activity after coming to the United States in 1912 where he worked as a furrier. A syndicalist, he associated himself with the Italian newspaper *Il Proletario* and served as its editor in 1922-1933 and 1936-1937. When the paper ceased publication in 1946, De Ciampis began gathering materials to write a history of it, abstracting each issue.

The bulk of De Ciampis's papers consists of drafts for his history of *Il Proletario*, the first draft of which is in excess of 4,000 pages. De Ciampis also did research on the history of his own family and that of his hometown of Morcone. Included are drafts and extensive notes on *Il Proletario* and its editors, family photographs, a funeral book of Mrs. De Ciampis, personal correspondence and notes, genealogical research material and correspondence, maps, and an autographed clipping and medallion of De Ciampis by sculptor P. S. Abbate. *Some items in English. Inventory available.*

De Lalla, Vincenzo (b. 1882).
Papers, 1927-1964. 6 linear in.

De Lalla, a pharmacist, was born in Tolve, Italy, and came to the United States in 1898. He graduated from Columbia University College of Pharmacy in 1904 and later owned a pharmacy in Utica, NY. De Lalla had a long-standing acquaintance with important Italian American poets and writers.

Papers of de Lalla consist of correspondence with poets and authors Nino Caradonna, Cesare Crespi, Arturo Giovannitti, Onorio Ruotolo, and others. Also included are six poems by de Lalla. *Includes English. Inventory available.*

De Ore, Anthony L.
Papers, 1952-1977. 8 linear in.

Anthony De Ore served as Grand Treasurer (1969-1971) and Grand Trustee (1957-1967) of the OSIA Pennsylvania Grand Lodge. Collection includes Columbus Day and testimonial dinner programs of OSIA, Pennsylvania District 12 (Fayette County), the bulletin of the Trivento Diocese in Italy, newspaper clippings, and photographs pertaining to OSIA District 12. *All but one item in English. In OSIA Guide.*

De Russo, Rocco (1914-1975).
Papers, ca. 1938-1971. 2.5 linear ft.

De Russo began acting in and writing plays in Naples and Rome at a young age. He toured in the United States with his company "Arte Vera," and his career was covered in Italian American newspapers. He became a very popular comedian in the Italian American theater and also recorded songs and skits. Later in life, De Russo also published poetry and composed music.

Papers consist of transcripts, reviews, and souvenir programs of forty-nine plays De Russo wrote as well as his unpublished autobiography, "Brani della carriera artistica del Comm. Rocco Dé Russo." *Mainly in Italian. Inventory available.*

De Santis, Frank J.
Papers, 1981-1986. 10 linear in.

De Santis has served as First Assistant Grand Venerable of the OSIA California Grand Lodge (1987-1989). He also served the lodge as Second Assistant Grand Venerable (1985-1987), Grand Trustee (1979-1981), and Grand Orator (1983-1985). Papers include correspondence with twenty-five local California lodges. *In English. In OSIA Guide.*

De Santis, Peter J.
Papers, 1929-1985. 3 linear ft.

De Santis served OSIA as Grand Venerable of the California Grand Lodge (1967-1971), National Foundation Commission Trustee (1975-1984), and Fifth Assistant National President (1987-). Collection includes California Grand Convention books, Supreme Lodge meeting reports and minutes, and some material on the California chapter of the Commission for Social Justice. Also included are several dinner dance programs for the Pugliese Lodge No. 1375 (Los Angeles, CA) and several booklets of statutes and regulations for the state lodge Hospitalization Fund and Mortuary Fund. *Mainly in English. In OSIA Guide.*

Delfino, Diego (1874-1926).
Papers, 1912-1929. 1.5 linear in.

Papers of Delfino, an Italian immigrant physician who lived in Ohio, West Virginia, and New Jersey, consist of original and translated letters to his uncle and daughter in Reggio Calabria, Italy. Also included are papers relating to settlement of Delfino's estate, a translation and biographical sketch by his grandson Diego Cassone, a photograph of Delfino and his daughter, and newspaper clippings about his death. *Includes English.*

Della Noce, Frank (b. 1894).
Papers, 1920-1971. Ca. 1.5 linear ft.

Della Noce was born in Penna Sant'Andrea, Italy, and arrived in the United States at the age of seventeen. He helped to organize the first OSIA local lodge in Maryland in 1913. He served the OSIA Maryland Grand Lodge as Grand Orator (1944-1950), Grand Recording Secretary (1920-1944), and Grand Trustee (1971-1974).

Collection contains OSIA Supreme Lodge correspondence and booklets, bylaws books, and OSIA Supreme Convention and Council minutes and booklets. The bulk of material is from the OSIA Maryland Grand Lodge and includes Council and Convention minutes and reports, correspondence, financial reports, lists of grand officers and delegates, assorted reports on activities, and photographs. *A few items in English. In OSIA Guide.*

DeLuca, Angelo (b. 1904).
Papers, ca. 1904-1983. 3.5 linear ft.

DeLuca, born in New York City to immigrant Italians, is known primarily for his poetry, although he has also written newspaper articles and lyrics. Most of DeLuca's poetry has been published by Great Society Press, of which DeLuca is the publisher.

Papers consist of his poems, articles and lyrics, both in draft and published form, and related reviews and correspondence. DeLuca's personal correspondence and the correspondence of other DeLuca family members forms another section of this collection. Also included is artwork and correspondence of Meyer Bernstein, an artist and friend of DeLuca. *Includes English. Inventory available.*

Di Donato, Pietro.
Papers, n.d. 1 linear in.

Papers of Italian American author Di Donato consist of a photocopy of the manuscript for his play "Moro." *In English.*

Di Giulio, Palmer (1898-1959).
Papers, 1931-1959. 1 linear in.

Di Giulio was an attorney and chairman of the Immigration and Naturalization Commission of the Supreme Lodge of OSIA. Papers include OSIA programs from testimonial dinners of his local OSIA lodge, Abruzzi No. 1376; correspondence; and an Illinois Grand Lodge resolution honoring Di Giulio at his death. Also included are a tape of a 1958 Columbus Day speech by Di Giulio, several poems, a paper titled "Questions and Answers About Naturalization," a 1938 Chicago Post Office directive on citizenship, correspondence regarding naturalization, miscellaneous published materials, and photographs and newspaper clippings. *All but one item in English.*

Di Silvestro, Giovanni M. (1879-1958).
Collection, 1909-1954. Ca. 5.5 linear ft.

A lawyer, Di Silvestro was born in Abruzzo, Italy, and immigrated to Philadelphia in 1903. He was very active in Italian American civic life and served OSIA as its longest tenured Supreme Venerable (1921-1935).

Collection consists of Supreme Convention records, grand lodge records, and non-OSIA materials. Letters and telegrams detail the ongoing communications of Di Silvestro during his terms as Supreme Venerable. Other documents, including materials of officers and lodges and newspaper clippings, describe the activities of grand lodges. Newspaper clippings describe OSIA banquets, meetings, pilgrimages to Italy, events in Italy, and the Italo-Ethiopian War. Other documents concern OSIA opposition to the 1924 immigration law, the Italian World War I debt, Lega Italiana, the Sacco-Vanzetti case, and the Dante Orphanage (Concordville, PA). Included is a great deal of non-OSIA correspondence with many civic leaders, scholars, and Italian American organizations. *Includes English. In OSIA Guide.*

Donato, Geno and Lou.
Papers, 1979-1987. 10 linear in.

Geno Donato served the OSIA Indiana Grand Lodge as Grand Venerable (1983-1989); he was also Assistant Grand Venerable (1979-1983) and Grand Trustee (1977-1979). His wife, Lou Donato, was the Grand Recording Secretary (1983-1989).

Collection includes Supreme Lodge Commission for Social Justice correspondence, minutes and delegate materials of Indiana Grand Lodge meetings, and some Grand Lodge correspondence. *In English. In OSIA Guide.*

Donnaruma, Caesar L. (b. 1900).
Papers, ca. 1928-1974. 2 linear ft.

Donnaruma, a journalist and editor, was born in Boston, MA, son of James V. and Florence Donnaruma. He began his apprenticeship in journalism with his father's Italian American newspaper, *La Gazzetta del Massachusetts* (later the *Post-Gazette*), and after his father's death in 1953 became its editor and publisher. He retired in 1971.

Papers consist mostly of records and correspondence relating to publication of the newspapers. Of special interest is correspondence with political figures, including John F. Kennedy. *Includes English. Inventory available. Related collection: James V. Donnaruma.*

Donnaruma, James V. (1874-1953).
Papers, 1897-1962. Ca. 3 linear ft.

Donnaruma came to the United States from Italy in 1886 and settled in Boston, MA. Donnaruma was the founder, publisher and editor of one of the most influential and successful Italian language newspapers in New England, *La Gazzetta del Massachusetts*, published in Boston since August 1903. (The newspaper continues being published today as an English language weekly, the *Post-Gazette.*)

Papers consist mostly of business files relating to publication of Donnaruma's newspaper. Papers of his son and successor Caesar L. Donnaruma and correspondence with prominent Italian Americans are also included. *Includes English. Related collections: Caesar L. Donnaruma; Fortune Gallo.*

Errigo, Joseph A. L.
Papers, 1882-1982. Ca. 2.5 linear ft.

Errigo served as Grand Venerable of the OSIA Delaware Grand Lodge (1948-1952, 1964-1966). At the national level, he served as Supreme Recording Secretary (1957-1961), Third Assistant Supreme Venerable (1961-1963), cochair of the Immigration and Naturalization Commission, and chair of the Anti-Defamation Commission.

Collection comprises records of various OSIA committees of the national lodge, Delaware Grand Lodge, and local Delaware lodges, along with personal papers of Errigo. Materials pertain to the national commissions he led, the Supreme Convention, and the Delaware Grand Convention. Also included are speeches, correspondence, historical notes, an officers list of the Caesar Rodney Lodge No. 2359 (Wilmington, DE) and a Delaware Grand Lodge Venerables list. Personal papers of Errigo include materials relating to his family history, legal career, and miscellaneous events pertaining to Delaware, and consist of manuscripts of plays, histories and other writings, and photographs. *Includes English. In OSIA Guide.*

Ets, Marie Hall (b. 1895).
Papers, ca. 1930s-1960s. 1.5 linear ft.

An author, Ets was born in North Greenfield, WI. She received her doctorate from the University of Chicago and studied art at the Art Institute of Chicago. She is best known for her award-winning career as a writer and illustrator of children's books. In 1918, she journeyed to Chicago and became a social worker at the Chicago Commons settlement house. There she met "Rosa Cassettari," an Italian immigrant who related many stories of her childhood in Italy. Mrs. Ets used this material to write *Rosa, the Life of an Italian Immigrant* (Minneapolis, University of Minnesota Press, 1970).

Papers of Ets comprise research notes and manuscript drafts of Rosa's oral memoir as well as a collection of folktales as told to Ets by Rosa. *Mainly in English with some titles in Italian. Inventory available.*

Falco, Josephine M.
Papers, 1940-1981. 6 linear in.

Falco served as Supreme Recording Secretary of the Order Sons of Italy in America (1985-1989). She also served as Second Assistant Grand Venerable of the OSIA Massachusetts Grand Lodge (1977-1983) and in several other state leadership positions beginning in 1961.

Collection consists of books on grand lodge statutes, rituals, and constitution and supreme laws. Also included are Massachusetts Grand Lodge Convention books, miscellaneous correspondence and materials pertaining to Grand Lodge projects, and photographs. *Mainly in English. In OSIA Guide.*

Fay, Joseph E.
Collection, 1972-1977. 3 linear in.

Fay served as New York Grand Venerable of OSIA from 1975 to 1977, as Supreme Trustee from 1979 to 1981, and Supreme Treasurer from 1985 to 1987. Collection consists of OSIA New York Grand Convention books and minutes, Grand Council minutes, a list of Grand Lodge officers, and miscellaneous Grand Lodge correspondence and brochures. *In English. In OSIA Guide.*

Felice, John.
Collection, 1969-1985. 1 linear in.

Felice was elected Grand Venerable of the Virginia Grand Lodge of OSIA (1987) and has served as Assistant Grand Venerable (1983-1985). Collection includes convention booklets and minutes of the Virginia Grand Lodge, financial reports, miscellaneous officer lists and correspondence, and a Supreme Convention booklet. Also included are minutes and other materials pertaining to several Virginia local lodges. *In English. In OSIA Guide.*

Ferrari, Robert (b. 1886).
Papers, ca. 1912-1965. Ca. 5 linear ft.

Ferrari was born in Salerno, Italy, and came to the United States, where he completed his studies for a law degree at Columbia University in 1910. In addition to practicing law, Ferrari was a lecturer for the Scholastic Council of New York, a criminology instructor at New York University, and an assistant director for the journal *Criminal Law and Criminology*. He later taught criminology at John Marshall College of Law in New York. His prolific writings on law appeared in numerous legal journals.

Papers include correspondence; drafts of Ferrari's autobiography; articles on law; and other works; as well as miscellaneous maps, tourist brochures, and travel guides pertaining to Italy and the United States. *Includes English. Inventory available.*

First Italian Presbyterian Church (Chicago, Illinois).
Records, 1891-1940. 1 microfilm reel.

Records consist of minutes of the official meetings ("sessions") of church elders to discuss church business, examine and admit new members, and discuss charges of un-Christian conduct and other matters. *Includes English.*

Flynn, Elizabeth Gurley (1890-1964).
Papers, ca. 1922-1944. 1 microfilm reel.

A labor activist, Flynn was born in Concord, NH, daughter of Irish immigrant revolutionaries. In 1906, she joined the Industrial Workers of the World and was active in textile strikes in Lawrence, MA (1912), and Paterson, NJ (1913), as well as in the Minnesota Mesabi Range iron miners strike (1916) and the Passaic, NJ, strike (1916). She was organizer for the Workers Defense Union between 1917 and 1923. She was a founding member of the American Civil Liberties Union in 1920. In 1937, she joined the Communist party; she was jailed from 1955 to 1957 for advocating the violent overthrow of the United States government. She died in Moscow.

Papers selected from the Flynn collection relate to Carlo Tresca, efforts to secure justice for political prisoners, labor, and fascism. *Includes English. Related collection: Carlo Tresca.*

Fornari, Harry D.
Papers, ca. 1941-1976. 1 linear in.

An Italian Jew, Fornari came to the United States in the late 1930s, following the adoption of "racial laws" by Fascist Italy. Papers of Fornari, a historian and business executive, include newspaper clippings, programs, and speeches documenting his work as chairman of the Council of Immigrant Youth and with the Immigrants' Conference. The Council was organized after the United States entered World War II to show solidarity with the new homeland and to work for the Civilian Defense Volunteer Office as requested. It was affiliated with the Conference, a patriotic coalition of various immigrant groups. *Includes English and German.*

Forte, Felix (1895-1975).
Papers, 1927-1975. Ca. 1 linear in.

The son of Italian immigrants, Forte was born in Boston's North End. He received a law degree from Boston University in 1916 and was a long-time member of its faculty. In 1930, he was appointed to the Somerville District Court and in 1939 was named to the superior court bench; he presided at the Brinks robbery trial in 1956. Forte served OSIA as Supreme Venerable (1940-1947), Assistant Supreme Venerable (1939-1940), Grand Venerable of Massachusetts (1933-1937), and Assistant Grand Venerable (1923-1925). He was the first American-born leader of the Order.

Papers include biographical sketches, a speech entitled "What Makes America Tick," and 1947 convention materials from OSIA, including a telegram from President Harry S. Truman. *In English. Inventory available. In OSIA Guide.*

Fortunato, Rev. John B. (1880-1967).
Papers, ca. 1898-1967. Ca. 1 linear in.

Rev. Fortunato was a minister in the United Presbyterian Church and pastor of an Italian American congregation in Pittsburgh, PA. Papers are photocopies of correspondence, newspaper clippings, and publications. *Includes English.*

Fucilla, Joseph.
Papers, n.d. Ca. 1 linear in.

Fucilla was a professor of Italian language and literature at Northwestern University for many years. Papers of Fucilla consist of a photocopy of his autobiography. *In English. Original held by Northwestern University, Chicago, IL.*

Gallo, Fortune (1878-1970).
Papers, ca. 1930-1960. 1 linear ft.

Gallo was born in Torremaggiore, Italy, and came to the United States in 1895. He was an impresario and manager of opera companies, founding the San Carlo Grand Opera Company, the Fortune Gallo Concern Company, Fortune Gallo Enterprises, and Fortune Gallo Musical Company. Gallo's auto-biography, *Lucky Rooster*, was published in 1967 by Exposition Press (NY).

Papers consist of his "personal books," programs, and newspaper clippings and opera directories describing the work of his company. *Mainly in English. Inventory available. Related Collection: James V. Donnaruma.*

Gay, Peter B. (1915-).
Papers, 1939-1987. Ca. 2.5 linear ft.

A Taunton, MA, attorney, Gay served in the Massachusetts House of Representatives from 1948 to 1958. He was National President of OSIA (1973-1975) after serving as Third, Second, and First Assistant Supreme Venerable (over the years 1963-1973).

Collection consists of OSIA convention records, committee reports, officers' correspondence of the Supreme Lodge, materials pertaining to nineteen state lodges, Gay's speeches, press releases, and newspaper clippings. *In English. In OSIA Guide.*

Giaccone, Francis X. (b. 1886).
Papers, 1921-1976. 4.5 linear ft.

Giaccone was New York State Human Rights Commissioner and Supreme Court justice. He was Grand Venerable of the New York State Lodge of OSIA from 1943 to 1951 and is credited with bringing a dissident group back into the state lodge in 1943.

Collection consists of personal papers and materials pertaining to the Order. Personal papers consist of published articles and speeches by Giaccone, newspaper clippings, and correspondence. OSIA material consists of information on testimonial dinners honoring Giaccone, a souvenir booklet from the New York Grand Convention, and some New York Grand Lodge correspondence. *Mainly in English. In OSIA Guide.*

Gimino, Maria.
Papers, ca. 1926-1950. Ca. 1 linear in.

Gimino was a lecturer, language teacher, and authority on Italian costumes, historical data, and habits. She worked at the International Institute of Pittsburgh, PA (ca. 1919), and was a member of the board of directors for the International Institute of Jersey City, NJ (ca. 1930s-1950s).

Papers include newspaper clippings, photographs of her, and various opera programs. *In English.*

Giovannitti, Arturo
Papers, ca. 1959. Ca. 1 linear in.

Papers of Giovannitti consist of his typescript play entitled "The Alpha and the Omega (In Memory of a Very Rich Holy Man)." *In English.*

Giuffrida, Bruno S.
Collection, 1964-1987. Ca. 1.5 linear ft.

Giuffrida served as National President of OSIA (1985-1987) and as Grand Venerable of the California Grand Lodge (1963-1967) after holding other leadership posts at both levels. Collection consists of materials on Supreme conventions, Supreme correspondence, information relating to various OSIA committees and programs, material on the 1985 California Grand Convention, and the New York and Connecticut Grand Conventions. Photographs and newspaper clippings are also included. *In English. In OSIA Guide.*

Gorrasi, Joseph (1909-1981).
Collection, 1926-1987. Ca. 1 linear ft.

An attorney, Gorrasi was an Associate Justice of the Boston Municipal Court from 1963 until his retirement in 1972. Gorassi served OSIA as Supreme Venerable (1957-1961) and as Grand Venerable of the Massachusetts Grand Lodge (1937-1946) after holding lower positions at both levels.

Collection consists of national lodge records and correspondence, and Massachusetts Grand Lodge records, including Grand Convention records, miscellaneous copies of Grand Council minutes, miscellaneous material relating to the Lodge during World War II, and transcripts of radio speeches. Also included are newspaper clippings and photographs. *Mainly in English. In OSIA Guide.*

Gralton, Olga (Vecoli).
Papers, ca. 1933-1936. Ca. 1 linear ft.

The Gralton collection consists of seven scrapbooks of newspaper clippings, one describing the flight of General Italo Balbo and his air armada to the United

States in 1933. The six remaining scrapbooks contain clippings pertaining to the Italo-Ethiopian War and to Italian notables. *Includes English. Inventory available.*

Grandinetti, Emilo (1882-1964).
Papers, 1910-1960. 1 linear ft.

A labor organizer, Grandinetti was born in Catanzaro, Italy. Before coming to America in 1907, he was active in newspaper work and socialist agitation. A leader of the Chicago garment workers strike of 1910, Grandinetti became an organizer for the Amalgamated Clothing Workers of America (ACWA) from ca. 1914 until he retired in 1948. His union activities were centered in Cleveland, OH, but he was also active in strikes and organization in Chicago, IL, and St. Louis, MO. In addition to his union work, Grandinetti was a publicist and author. After retiring, he contributed to *La Parola del Popolo* (Chicago).

Papers include personal correspondence, largely relating to his union activities and affiliation with the Mazzini Society and the Democratic Party, Foreign Language Division. Also included are union handbills and pamphlets as well as newspaper clippings pertaining to the ACWA (especially in Chicago, Cincinnati and St. Louis), to the Chicago Tailors Strike of 1910, and to organization of the Curlee Clothing Company in St. Louis. Many of the articles were taken from *Il Lavoro*, the Italian-language organ of the ACWA, and the *Advance*, its English language newspaper. Also included are articles from *La Parola del Popolo* and typescripts highlighting Grandinetti's opposition to fascism, as well as speeches and photographs. *Includes English. Inventory available.*

Greco, Francesco (1898-1966?)
Papers, ca. 1925-1966. 2.5 linear ft.

Greco was a poet, born in Savelli (Catanzaro), Italy, in 1898. He came to the United States in 1923, worked as a carpenter, then in the real estate business. He was one of several well known poets who wrote in the Calabrian dialect.

Papers consist of his typescript poems, newspaper clippings, correspondence, and his published works. Among them is his *L'Anima Allo Specchio; liriche* (1964). *Includes English and Portuguese.*

Grieco, Rose.
Papers, ca. 1956-1974. 1 linear in.

Grieco was an author, playwright, dance instructor, authority on Italian folklore, and founder and director of the Italian Folklore Group of Montclair (NJ). She studied dance and music as a child, and later graduated from the American Academy of Dramatic Arts (Feagin School) and La Sevilla School of Dancing.

Papers consist of a typescript of her comedy "Anthony on Overtime," several published articles on Italian and Italian American themes, photographs, and newspaper clippings about her. *Includes English.*

Grillo, Clara (Corica).
Papers, ca. 1928-1977. 1 linear ft.

Nationality secretary at the Nationalities Services Center (formerly the International Institute) in Cleveland, OH, Grillo was born in Cleveland of Sicilian parents. She graduated from Ohio State University with a major in education and received a master's degree from Western Reserve University. In 1934, she married Dominic Grillo, a theater impresario. While nationality secretary of the Cleveland International Institute (1926-1928) she wrote a thesis (1928) entitled "A Study of Survivals of Customs of Italians and How They Conflict with Attitudes in America."

Papers include newspaper clippings; a transcript of an interview with her; correspondence between her husband, Dominic Grillo, and Eduardo Migliaccio (Farfariello); articles on Italians in Cleveland and the International Institute of Cleveland; and correspondence, playbills, and financial records pertaining to theater, films, and vaudeville. *Includes English and Spanish. Inventory available.*

Italian Americans from St. Paul working on a railroad section, Dilworth, MN, 1919.

Peter LaNasa and Joe Inserra's fruit wagon at a parade in St. Paul, MN, 1922.

Gualtieri, Humbert L.
Papers, ca. 1938. 2.5 linear in.

Gualtieri was a prominent anti-communist, antifascist, and socialist, born in Calabria, Italy. He edited several Italian-language publications, including *Il Proletario* (under the pseudonym Enotrio Greco), *La Stampa Libera*, *Il Mondo*, and *Nazioni Unite*. He wrote a book on the labor movement in Italy. He was also an officer of the Bakery and Confectionary Workers International Union of America, AFL, Local 102.

Papers consist of a typescript of his study, *Origin and Growth of the Italian Labor Movement (1860-1904)*, and copies of newspaper articles written at the time of his death. *Includes English.*

Harkness, Wayne.
Papers, 1930-1987. 5 linear in.

Harkness served as Grand Recording Secretary (1983-1987) and First Vice President (1987-) for OSIA Northwest Grand Lodge. (The Lodge includes Idaho, Montana, Washington, and portions of Oregon and was founded in 1929.)

Collection includes Northwest Grand Convention minutes and scattered Grand Council minutes. *In Italian and English.*

Iannuzzi, Joseph.
Papers, 1922. 1 linear in.

Iannuzzi is a member of OSIA Per Sempre Lodge No. 2344 (Rosedale, NY). His father, Enrico, was born in Avellino (Campania), Italy, and became a member of OSIA Prima Italia Lodge No. 10 (New York City) after coming to the United States.

Papers of Joseph Iannuzzi consist of a Fondo Unico Mortuario certificate signed by Dr. Vincent Sellaro, founder of the Order. *Inventory available. In OSIA Guide.*

International Ladies Garment Workers' Union (ILGWU), Local 48, Italian Cloak, Suit and Skirt Makers' Union (New York).
Records, 1920-1965. 5 microfilm reels.

Local 48 was second in size to Local 89 in Italian membership. Eduardo

Molisani was the longtime business manager and he was succeeded by his son, E. Howard Molisani. Records of the Union consist of minutes of the Executive Board. *Related collection: Papers of E. Howard Molisani.*

Italian Actors Union (New York, New York).
Records, ca. 1938-1969. 6 linear in. and 1 microfilm reel.

The Union was founded in 1938 as a branch of the Associated Actors and Artistes of America, and was affiliated with the AFL. Records comprise constitution and bylaws, membership lists, correspondence, scripts, speeches and essays concerning the Italian theater in New York, contracts, memoranda, financial records, materials pertaining to the Italian Recreation Center (New York), and, on microfilm only, the minutes of the Union's Executive Council. *Includes English.*

Italian American Club of Duluth (Minnesota).
Records, 1927-1943. 2 linear in.

Records of the Club consist of constitution and bylaws, papers of incorporation, financial ledger and savings account passbook, membership lists, minutes of meetings, and miscellaneous organizational papers. In addition, the collection contains correspondence and minutes of meetings of the Minnesota State Federation of Italian Americanization Clubs. *In English.*

Italian American Ephemera.
Collection, n.d. 1 folder.

Collection includes sheet music entitled "Valorosi Emigranti," along with postcards; frontispieces from *La Morte di Francisco Ferrer*; a calling card of Anthony Caminetti, Commissioner

General of Immigration; and Italian Canadian centennial decals.

Italian-American Federation of the Upper Peninsula (Calumet, Michigan).
Records, 1908-1925. 1 linear ft.

The Federation was founded in 1909 with the purpose of uniting the various Italian mutual benefit societies in the area within one organization. Records include applications and other forms. Also included are correspondence, financial records, and photographs. *Includes English. Inventory available.*

Italian American Miscellaneous.
Records, ca. 1913-1946. 1 microfilm reel.

Records include correspondence, photographs, and newspaper clippings pertaining to Elizabeth Gurley Flynn and correspondents (Arturo Giovanetti, Nicolo Sacco, Bartolomeo Vanzetti, and Carlo Tresca); materials relating to fascist activities in the United States, including those of the Lictor Association (formerly federation); and Italian American labor pamphlets. *Includes English. Negatives held by Biblioteca Americana, Istituto di Studi Americani, University of Florence, Italy. Related collection: Carlo Tresca.*

Italian Evangelical Movement (Wisconsin).
Records, ca. 1928-1969. Ca. 1 linear in.

The Evangelical Association, a missionary church among Italian immigrants, was founded in 1916. It merged with the United Evangelical Church in 1922, and the name was changed to Evangelical Church.

Records consist of essays, correspondence, newspaper clippings, and programs concerning the Movement and its leaders, Rev. G. Busacca, Rev. A. Germanotta, and Rev. August Giuliani. Rev. Busacca was the first pastor in charge of evangelical work among Italians in Racine, Wisconsin (1914-1922). Rev. Giuliani, a converted Italian Catholic priest, came to Milwaukee in 1911 to begin evangelical missionary work. In 1913, he opened a branch mission in Racine. *Mainly in English.*

Italian Flood Relief Committee (St. Paul, Minnesota).
Records, 1952. 11 items.

The Committee was created to raise funds for aid of Po River flood victims and was composed of representatives of St. Paul Italian organizations and Catholic churches. Records include correspondence, minutes, and news releases. *In English and Italian.*

Italians in Chicago-Oral History Project.
Collection, n.d. Ca. 2.5 linear ft. and seven videotape cassettes.

The Italians in Chicago Project was a two-year program based at the History Department of the University of Illinois at Chicago Circle; its purpose was to document the Italian American experience in Chicago. Oral history interviews with 113 Italian Americans living in the Chicago area were one component of the project. Men and women from three generations were interviewed regarding such topics as work, leisure, neighborhoods, family life, religion, interethnic events, and other special events. People from the following neighborhoods and towns were interviewed: Belmont-Cragin, Bridgeport, Chicago Heights, Grand Avenue, Highwood, Kensington-Pullman-Roseland, Melrose Park, Near North, Twenty-Fourth and Oakley Avenue, and the Near West Side. Each of the 113 transcripts includes a biographical questionnaire, a legal release form, and record keeping information. Among the videotapes is an interview with Egidio Clemente and scenes, ca. 1920s, from a Melrose Park Our Lady of Mt. Carmel Feast. *Includes English. Inventory available. Transcripts are copies; originals held by the University of Illinois at Chicago Circle, Chicago, IL.*

Italy. Legation in the United States.
Records, 1861-1906. 22 microfilm reels.

Records include volumes and official communications from officials of the Italian Legation to the Department of State, telegrams and cables, memoranda prepared by State Department officials commenting on the Italian notes, memoranda of conversations between Legation officials and the Department of State, communications from White House officials, and copies of speeches delivered by Italian ministers and ambassadors. Correspondence includes letters or copies of letters from the King of Italy to the President of the United States, claims of Italians against the government or citizens of the United States, lists of officials and employees of the Italian Legation, copies of communications from Italian consulates in the United States to the Legation, and pamphlets, newspapers, and other printed material. *Includes French and English. Negatives held by National Archives, Washington, DC.*

Italy. Office of the Commissioner of Emigration (Commissariato Generale dell' Emigrazione).
Records, 1901-1927. 18 microfilm reels.

Records of the office pertain to emigration and immigration legislation (Italian and foreign), office activities, office personnel, and field offices in border towns and port cities. *Inventory available (in Italian only). Negatives held by Centro Studi Emigrazione, Rome. Originals in Archivio Storico Diplomatico, Ministero degli Affari Esteri, Roma.*

Jackson, Harold E.
Papers, 1952-1986. 3 linear ft.

Jackson, who lives in Seattle, WA, has held several leadership positions in the OSIA Northwest Grand Lodge, including Supreme Venerable (1979-1983). He was also a Supreme Trustee (1983-1987).

The collection consists of records of the OSIA national lodge and the Northwest Grand Lodge. National records are of committee activities and correspondence. Records of the Northwest Grand Lodge include

Convention and Council materials and Grand Venerable invitations. Also included are miscellaneous banquet and award booklets. *In English. In OSIA Guide.*

Kelley, Mary.
Papers, 1930's-1985. 8 linear in.

Kelley immigrated with her family to Indiana in 1929. She has served the OSIA Indiana Grand Lodge as Grand Venerable (1977), Assistant Grand Venerable (1975-1977), and Grand Trustee (1973-1975).

Collection includes OSIA Supreme Constitution and General Laws and Indiana Grand Lodge meeting minutes and booklets. Also included are miscellaneous award and banquet booklets and a photograph. *All except one item in English. In OSIA Guide.*

La Capria, Vincent (1899-ca. 1965).
Papers, ca. 1952-1971. 1 linear in.

La Capria was born in Palmi, Italy, and came to the United States in 1905. He was a vice-president of the Amalgamated Clothing Workers of America and was also active in civic and charitable organizations, such as the American Committee on Italian Migration and Boys Town of Italy.

His papers contain correspondence, newspaper clippings, speeches, and photographs. *Includes English.*

Lamont, Michael.
Papers, 1904-1976. 1 linear in.

Papers of Lamont (or Michaelangelo Lomanto) consist of an unpublished autobiography relating his childhood experiences in the coal-mining regions of West Virginia and Ohio as well as life in Cleveland's Little Italy. *In English.*

Landi, P. Vincent.
Papers, 1929-1984. Ca. 2 linear ft.

Landi is a lawyer who has served OSIA as Supreme Treasurer (1977-1982), New York Grand Venerable (1969-1973), First Assistant Grand Venerable (1967-

1969), Second Assistant Grand Venerable (1965-1967), and Grand Trustee (1937-1939). Collection consists of OSIA Supreme Lodge records including convention materials, reports of the Garibaldi-Meucci museum, resolutions regarding the media and Italian Americans, and reports on charitable activities. Also included are OSIA New York Grand Lodge Convention and Council records, brochures from various events, a large selection of documents of the Committee Against Bias, Bigotry, and Prejudice (which Landi chaired), speeches, correspondence, and photographs. *In English. In OSIA Guide.*

Liberatore, Frank W.
Papers, 1932-1976. 5 linear in.

Liberatore was OSIA Massachusetts Grand Financial Secretary (1959-1963) and Supreme Trustee of OSIA (1955-1959). Collection includes a Massachusetts Grand Lodge convention program, miscellaneous Massachusetts Grand Lodge brochures, local lodge program booklets, photographs, and artifacts. *In English. In OSIA Guide.*

Liberti, Armand.
Papers, 1940-1983. 1 linear ft.

Liberti served as Grand Venerable of the OSIA Delaware Grand Lodge (1981-1985), and as First Assistant Grand Venerable (1976-1979). Collection consists of minutes, correspondence, and materials pertaining to Columbus Day celebrations, the March of Dimes Campaign, and local lodges, as well as to the Supreme Council plenary session of 1974 and the 1967 Supreme Convention. *Includes English. In OSIA Guide.*

Licari, Thomas.
Papers, 1980. Ca. 1 linear in.

The Licari family originally came from Montelebre, Sicily, and settled first in New York City and then in Biwabik, MN, in 1902. Papers consist of photographs and a magazine article on the Licari family reunion, as well as

background information on family members. *In English.*

Ligouri, Louis.
Papers, 1951-1972. 5 linear in.

Ligouri served as Venerable of the Order Sons of Italy in America, Gabriele D'Annunzio Lodge No. 22 (Paterson, NJ), and also as Grand Treasurer of the OSIA New Jersey Grand Lodge (1970-1975). Collection includes minutes and dinner programs of the Gabriele D'Annunzio Lodge, along with some correspondence regarding the Sons of Italy Archives project, photographs, and artifacts. *Includes English. In OSIA Guide.*

Locke, Octavia Capuzzi Waldo (1929-).
Papers, ca. 1973-1983. 7 linear in.

An author and artist, Locke received her BA from Temple University (Philadelphia, PA), and was awarded a Fulbright Fellowship to the Academy of Fine Arts (Rome, Italy). Papers of Locke consist of two published stories she wrote; a typescript and galley proofs of her first novel, *A Cup of the Sun* (written under the name Octavia Waldo); photocopies of newspaper and magazine articles; and a copy of a literary magazine containing her short story "The Collection." *In English.*

Lucarini, Umberto (1892-1965).
Papers, 1927-1960. 6 linear in.

Lucarini was born in Italy and arrived in the United States in 1920. He organized the Madera Consumers Cooperative in Madera, CA, in 1927 and managed it until 1951. Papers comprise records of the cooperative, pamphlets and bulletins written by Lucarini, personal correspondence, travel diaries, and newspaper clippings about Albert Einstein. *Includes English. Inventory available.*

Manzardo, Mario.
Papers, ca. 1967-1977. 10 linear in.

Manzardo was a labor activist born in Italy and raised in Chicago and Pullman,

IL. Papers consist of articles on Pullman, Roseland, and Kensington, IL (ca. 1920s and 1930s); articles on labor history (ca. 1890-1930s); book reviews; and ephemera from labor, political, and community activities in Chicago (ca. 1960s-1970s). Many articles are typescript; clippings are mainly from the *South End Reporter* (Chicago), and *Hyde Park Herald*. *In English.*

Marchello, Maurice R. (1902-1973).
Papers, ca. 1922-1972. 2 linear ft.

Marchello was born in Coal City, IL, son of the first Italian immigrants to that city. He began work in the mines and the railroads, but continued his education, earning a law degree in 1926 and spending a year in Rome on a scholarship. He practiced law in Chicago, served as attorney for the state of Illinois at various state agencies, and was active in the Democratic Party. In 1961, he began a second career as a journalist and author, writing for the Italian American Chicago papers *Fra Noi* and *La Tribuna*, and authoring several books, including *Crossing the Tracks* and *Black Coal for White Bread*.

Papers include personal correspondence; materials relating to Marchello's literary, journalistic, and legal careers and his political activities; and miscellany, including photographs, newspaper clippings, ephemera, and travel mementos. Included are manuscripts of articles written for *Fra Noi*, scripts of radio broadcasts, speeches, lectures, short stories, and manuscripts of *Crossing the Tracks* and *Black Coal for White Bread*. *In English. Inventory available.*

Marinelli, Anne V. and Angela.
Papers, ca. 1975. Ca. 1 linear in.

Anne and Angela Marinelli had distinguished careers as librarian and teacher, respectively. Daughters of John and M. Concetta (Varriano) Marinelli, who immigrated to the United States from Campobasso, Italy, the sisters grew up in Hibbing, Minnesota. Angela received an MA from Columbia University and traveled and taught extensively. She developed statewide programs for the Minnesota Department of Education. Anne was educated at the University of Wisconsin, Columbia University, and the University of Illinois and worked at various college libraries.

Papers consist of articles about, and photographs of, the Marinelli sisters. *In English. Restricted.*

Martello, Nicholas J.
Papers, 1930-1987. 6 linear in.

Martello served as OSIA Supreme Trustee (1987-) and Grand Venerable of the Ohio Grand Lodge (1983-1987), after holding other local and state offices. Collection consists of records of OSIA Ashtabula (OH) Lodge No. 1169, correspondence and miscellaneous reports of the Ohio Grand Lodge, miscellaneous correspondence and information on the activities of various local lodges throughout Ohio, newspaper clippings, and photographs. *Includes English. In OSIA Guide.*

Martinelli, Phylis.
Papers, 1977-1987. 5 linear in.

Phylis Martinelli is a sociologist, author of works on Italian Americans and a member of the American Italian Historical Association. Her husband, Philip Martinelli, was Financial Secretary of OSIA Arizona Grand Lodge. Collection consists of materials pertaining to the OSIA Scottsdale, AZ, Lodge No. 2335 and includes membership lists, lodge newsletters, and a series of raffle tickets, newspaper clippings, and correspondence. *In English. In OSIA Guide.*

Marzani, Carl.
Papers, ca. 1970-1974. 3 linear in.

Marzani came to the United States as a child from Italy. He became an employee of the U.S. Department of State and was later accused of Communist Party membership. He authored a novel, *The Survivor*, about this experience and became a publisher.

Papers of Marzani consist of photocopies of manuscript prologue and seven chapters from his autobiography; a photocopied manuscript of his essay "Watergate and American Neo-Fascism"; and two pamphlets written by him entitled "Withdraw! From an Indochina War that Dishonors Our Country and Threatens Nuclear Disaster" and "The Threat of American Neo-Fascism." *In English.*

Massari, Vincent (1898-1976).
Papers, 1895-1976. Ca. 5 linear ft.

Massari, a labor organizer, editor, and antifascist, was born in Luco nei Marsi (Aquila), Italy, and came to the United States in 1915, following his parents to Pueblo, CO. His father was a coal miner and union organizer involved in the 1914 Ludlow Massacre. Vincent was active in organizing Colorado mine workers and served in the Columbian Federation (as officer, as well as editor and publisher of the Federation's newspaper, *L'Unione* for more than 25 years). He also edited and published other newspapers, including *La Voce del Popolo*, founded by him in 1920. He was a notary public, and proprietor of the Massari Travel Agency. Elected to the Colorado House of Representatives and then to the state Senate, he was instrumental in the establishment of the University of Southern Colorado.

Papers include biographical materials as well as correspondence relating to Massari's civic activities, his travel agency, his work as legislator, the Columbian Federation, *L'Unione*, the Ludlow massacre of 1914, and his work as a notary public. Also included are scrapbooks, newspaper clippings, and correspondence and records relating to the newspaper *L'Abbruzzo-Molise*, which he edited and published, and Lega Patriottica Italo Americana. Correspondents include Frank Mancini, Giovanni Massari, Ettore Chiariglione, Gaetano Venditti, Zopito Valentini, Egidio Clemente, Girolamo Valenti, Carmelo Zito, Alberto Tarchiani, and Giovanni Schiavo. *Includes English. Inventory available.*

Massaro, Dominic R.
Papers, 1923-1987. Ca. 17.5 linear ft.

Massaro has served OSIA as National Historian, National Deputy, and in numerous other appointive offices. He was appointed a New York State Supreme Court Justice in 1987.

Collection consists of records and minutes of OSIA Supreme Conventions and Supreme Council; correspondence of Massaro as Director of Public Relations, Chairman of the Membership and Expansion Committee, and as National Historian; correspondence and reports of various OSIA committees; convention material, council minutes, correspondence, committees, and activities of the OSIA New York Grand Lodge; and records of other state and local lodges, particularly Northwest Bronx Lodge 2091. In addition, there is a large amount of material pertaining to non-OSIA activities relating to Italian Americans and general ethnic issues and programs in New York, along with newspaper clippings, photographs, and artifacts. *Mainly in English. Inventory available. In OSIA Guide.*

Maurino, Ferdinando D.
Papers, ca. 1963-1972. Ca. 1 linear in.

Papers of Maurino, a professor of Italian at the University of Tennessee, include several of his articles on Italian and Italian American writers. *Includes English.*

Meduri, Danny (1885-1976).
Papers, 1910-1976. 1 linear in.

Meduri was an opera singer from New York. Papers include photographs, newspaper clippings, sheet music, programs, and playbills from his performances. *In English.*

Migliaccio, Eduardo "Farfariello" (1882-1946).
Papers, ca. 1909-1958. 9 linear ft.

A character actor in theater, known for his ability to portray a wide range of human types, Migliaccio was born in Cava dei Tirreni (Salerno), Italy, and came to the United States in 1897 with his family. He worked for a time at the Sandolo Bank (Hazelton, PA) and then became involved in theater, using the name "Farfariello." He wrote verses and music for his sketches, and soon became well known both in the United States and in Italy for his "macchiette," or character studies, many based on his acute observation of immigrant life.

Papers consist of correspondence; some 2,500 pieces of manuscript and published sheet music, the majority written by him; 150 manuscript plays in Neapolitan dialect; photographs, playbills, and scrapbooks of memorabilia. *Includes English. Inventory available.*

Mitrione, Mary.
Papers, 1953-1985. 10 linear in.

Now State Historian, Mitrione previously served the OSIA Indiana Grand Lodge as Recording Secretary for most years from 1953 to 1979 and as Grand Trustee (1961-1963, 1965-1966, and 1981-1983). Collection consists of Indiana Grand Convention and Council minutes and reports, correspondence, and treasurers' reports. Also included are some records of local lodges. *Mainly in English. In OSIA Guide.*

Molinari, Alberico (1876-1948).
Papers, n.d. Ca. 1 linear in.

A physician and socialist, Molinari was founder and editor of *L'Ascesa del Proletariato* (Wilkes-Barre, PA) in 1907, and editor of *La Parola del Popolo* (Chicago, IL), 1911-1920. In 1921, he returned to Italy where, as an antifascist, he was imprisoned a number of times.

Papers consist of typescripts of Molinari's play "I Martiri di Chicago," a four-act historical drama. *Includes English.*

Molisani, E. Howard (1911-1987).
Papers, 1920-1987. 5 linear ft.

A labor leader, Molisani served the OSIA Supreme Lodge as a member of the National Foundation and of the Garibaldi-Meucci Museum Commission.

Collection consists of records of the OSIA Supreme Lodge, the New York Grand Lodge, and materials pertaining to labor and labor organizations, along with personal papers. Records of the OSIA Supreme Lodge include Convention, Council, and National Foundation minutes; materials of the Garibaldi-Meucci Museum Commission; and materials pertaining to the National Italian American Coordinating Committee. A large part of the collection pertains to Italian American labor and labor organizations. Represented are the Italian American Labor Council, and the Italian Labor Center (New York City). Also included are materials pertaining to the American Committee for Italian Migration, the AFL-CIO, ILGWU Local No. 48, AMICO, Boys Town of Italy, the Federal Advisory Committee on Immigration, and the Catholic Interracial Council of New York. Personal papers include materials on trips Molisani took to Italy to visit labor, government, church, and earthquake relief groups, and photographs. *Mainly in English. In OSIA Guide. Related collection: ILGWU Local No. 48.*

Montemarano, Joseph A. (1932-1987).
Papers, 1971-1987. Ca. 11.5 linear ft.

Montemarano served OSIA as Grand Venerable (1981-1985), First Assistant Grand Venerable (1977-1981), and Grand Recording Secretary (1973-1977) of the New York Grand Lodge. Collection consists of OSIA Supreme Lodge, New York Grand Lodge, and other OSIA and non-OSIA materials. Included are Supreme Convention and Council records, foundation documents, reports of the Garibaldi-Meucci Museum and of the Commission for Social Justice, and records of the 1981 visit to the Italian earthquake region. New York Grand Lodge records include meeting documents, committee records and reports; materials from awards dinners, credit union, and state foundation; membership reports; resolutions; and lists of Grand Venerable activities. Also included are several local New York lodge histories. Non-OSIA materials pertain to the Columbus Citizens Club

(New York), St. Francis Hospital (New York), and the Coalition of Italian American Associations. *Mainly in English. In OSIA Guide.*

Montemuro, Frank J., Jr. (1925-   ).
Papers, 1938-1985. 13 linear ft.

Montemuro, a lawyer, was appointed to the bench of the Superior Court of Pennsylvania in 1980. He has participated actively in many civic and professional organizations. Montemuro served OSIA as Supreme Venerable (1977-1981), and as Grand Venerable of the Pennsylvania Grand Lodge (1969-1977).

Collection includes records of OSIA Supreme Conventions, materials relating to various OSIA officers, and materials on various OSIA committees and programs. Records of the Pennsylvania Grand Lodge include Executive Committee and Grand Council minutes, committee and fund reports as well as material relating to local lodges in Pennsylvania and other state lodges. Also included are photographs, along with information on non-OSIA programs and activities. *In English. Inventory available. In OSIA Guide.*

Morabito, Gregorio (1895-   ).
Papers, 1921-1983. 1 linear in.

Morabito served as Grand Recording Secretary of OSIA New York Grand Lodge (1928-1973). Collection includes music and lyrics to the "OSIA Anthem" and the "Song of the Sons of Italy"; miscellaneous certificates and acknowledgements of Morabito's service as a public accountant and 50-year member of OSIA; correspondence regarding the New York War Fund Campaign; miscellaneous correspondence from various people, including New York Mayor Fiorello La Guardia and Thomas E. Dewey, governor of New York; newspaper clippings; photographs; and an Italian passport. *Mainly in English. In OSIA Guide.*

Morganti, Cesare.
Papers, ca. 1863-1964. 7 linear ft.

Morganti was a portrait photographer and journalist. Papers consist mainly of newspaper clippings on Italian, Italo-American, and American topics. Also included are photographs, correspondence, and materials relating to Denver, CO, where Morganti worked. *Includes English. Inventory available.*

Negovetti, John.
Papers, 1923-1985. Ca. 1.5 linear ft.

Negovetti was Grand Venerable (1977-1979) and Grand Orator (1985-1987) of the Order Sons of Italy in America, Indiana Grand Lodge. Collection consists of OSIA Constitution and General Laws, ritual books, Supreme Laws and Judicial Code, and the Review of Ritual conducted at the 1961 Supreme Convention. Also included are Illinois Grand Lodge convention booklets, program booklets honoring Negovetti as "Man of the Year," and records of the Maggio 11, 1860 Lodge No. 1065 (East Chicago, IN). Other materials include newspaper clippings and artifacts. *In English. In OSIA Guide.*

Novaco, James (1899-1973).
Papers, 1924-1968. 2 linear in.

Novaco held the OSIA offices of Grand Trustee (1925-1929), Grand Treasurer (1929-1933), and Grand Financial Secretary (1933-1969) in the Connecticut Grand Lodge. Collection consists of photographs, letters, local lodge records, badges and ribbons, and a minute book. *In OSIA Guide.*

Odone, Father Nicolo Carlo (1868-1947).
Papers, 1895-1947. 17 linear ft.

Odone was born in Sestri Ponente, Italy. He was ordained into the priesthood in 1889 and came to America, where he performed priestly functions. After a short stay in Coal City, IL, he returned to Italy in 1897, but in 1899 again came to America, invited by Archbishop Ireland to come to St. Paul,

MN, to establish a church for the Italians. He served the Italian community as pastor of the Holy Redeemer Church until 1910. Subsequently, he became chaplain at the House of the Good Shepherd in St. Paul. From 1924 to 1927, he had a number of short-term clerical appointments, and in 1927 he took up various duties at Margaret Barry House, a mission facility for Italians in Minneapolis, MN. In 1934, he retired in Stillwater, MN.

Papers include a 90-volume personal diary, containing sketches, correspondence, financial records, and newspaper clippings. Materials relate to his activities as pastor of Holy Redeemer Congregation, Margaret Barry House, and House of the Good Shepherd. Also included are records of the Holy Redeemer Congregation. *Includes English. Inventory available.*

Order Sons of Italy in America. Alabama Grand Lodge.
Records, 1923-1987. 7 linear in.

The Alabama Grand Lodge of the Order Sons of Italy in America was founded in 1929. Records consist of booklets, financial records, membership lists, statutes and regulations, and photographs. Included are a Supreme Convention book, a "Demand for Dispensation" from a local lodge, Grand Lodge Columbus Day booklets, records of Bessemer (AL) Lodge No. 1497, bylaws of the Società Italiana Femminile Corona Regina Elena (Bessemer), photocopies of the Silver Anniversary booklet of the Italian Society of U.S.P.P. (Umberto di Savoia Principe di Piemonte), and photographs. *Includes English. In OSIA Guide.*

Order Sons of Italy in America. Americo Vespucci Lodge No. 1722 (Kankakee, Illinois).
Records, 1937-1970. 3 linear in.

The OSIA Americo Vespucci Lodge No. 1722 was founded in 1934. Records include a dues payment ledger, several copies of the General Laws of the Grand Lodge of Illinois and its mortuary fund, and copies of the Supreme Lodge ritual book. *In OSIA Guide.*

Order Sons of Italy in America. Arizona Grand Lodge.
Records, 1976-1985. Ca. 1.5 linear ft.

The OSIA Arizona Grand Lodge was founded in 1977. Records include Grand Convention and Council materials, reports of activities and fund-raising, and correspondence. Also included are correspondence with local lodges, local lodge officer directories, Supreme Convention material, and Supreme correspondence. *In English. In OSIA Guide.*

Order Sons of Italy in America. Blue Island Lodge No. 1659 (Blue Island, Illinois).
Records, 1937-1981. 2 linear in.

The OSIA Blue Island Lodge No. 1659 was founded in 1933. Records include a minute book, a booklet titled "The History of Saint Donatus Parish," and photographs and other information pertaining to the Lodge. *Includes English. In OSIA Guide.*

Order Sons of Italy in America. California Grand Lodge.
Records, 1925-1986. 9.5 linear ft.

The OSIA California Grand Lodge was founded in 1925. Records include California Grand Convention and Council books, minutes, and reports. Also included are an OSIA soccer club booklet, a 10K "runathon" entrants' book and expense book, Grand Lodge transfer cards, Hospitalization Fund applications and payments for forty-five local lodges, Grand Lodge membership applications, and materials relating to the Mortuary Fund. *Mainly in English. Inventory available. In OSIA Guide.*

Order Sons of Italy in America. Camelia-Colombo Lodge No. 1294 (Klamath Falls, Oregon).
Records, 1924-1977. 2 linear in.

The OSIA Cristoforo Colombo Lodge No. 1294, was organized as a men's chapter in Klamath Falls, OR, under jurisdiction of the Grand Lodge of California. In 1937, a women's lodge, Camelia Lodge No. 1802, was founded in the city; the lodges merged in 1964 to become Camelia-Colombo No. 1294.

Records include a statement of Supreme Venerable Stefano Miele and correspondence of the National lodge (1936-1937); meeting minutes, membership, and officer lists of the Cristoforo Colombo No. 1294 and Camelia No. 1802 lodges; newsclippings pertaining to the combined lodge; and a 1937 photograph of members and officers of both lodges. *Includes English. Inventory available. In OSIA Guide.*

Order Sons of Italy in America. Christopher Columbus Lodge No. 1199 (Charleston, West Virginia).
Records, 1922-1977. 5 linear ft.

The OSIA Christopher Columbus Lodge No. 1199 was founded in 1923. Records consist of membership applications, financial records, Mortuary Fund membership cards, House Committee and lodge meeting minutes, individual insurance policies, correspondence, and Grand Convention records. *Includes English. In OSIA Guide. Related collection: Eugene Costa.*

Order Sons of Italy in America. Cristoforo Colombo-Cesare Battisti Lodge No. 861 (Michigan).
Records, 1918-1986. Ca. 1.5 linear ft.

The Lodge was founded in 1918 and dissolved and reorganized in 1929. Records include minutes, financial records, and booklets of annual Columbus Day dances. Also included are Supreme and Grand Lodge correspondence and Grand Council and Grand Convention minutes. *Includes English. In OSIA Guide.*

Order Sons of Italy in America. Cristoforo Colombo Lodge No. 1033 (Hartford, Connecticut).
Records, 1925-1936. 4 linear in.

The OSIA Cristoforo Colombo Lodge No. 1033 was founded in 1920. Records include two ledgers containing minutes of meetings, and pages from a membership ledger book. *In OSIA Guide.*

Order Sons of Italy in America. Cristoforo Colombo Lodge No. 1719 (Nebraska).
Records, 1968-1986. 2 linear in.

The Lodge was founded in 1934. Records consist of minutes. *Includes English. In OSIA Guide.*

Order Sons of Italy in America. Delaware Grand Lodge.
Records, 1925-1985. 8 linear in.

The Delaware Grand Lodge was the eleventh state lodge chartered by OSIA (1923). Records include state membership applications, a scholarship ball booklet, Grand Lodge incorporation papers, booklets about the Rose Parade float, and a ritual book. Also included are correspondence of the St. Gabriel lodge (DE), a "History of Italians in Newcastle," correspondence of the Prince of Piedmont lodge (DE), a photograph of the Stella D'Italia No. 1273 (DE), and *Pockets of Settlement: The Italian-American Experience in Delaware. In English. Inventory available. In OSIA Guide.*

Order Sons of Italy in America. Elena di Savoia Regina D'Italia Lodge No. 1486 (Nebraska).
Records, 1935-1940. 1 linear in.

The Lodge was founded in 1927. Records consist of minutes. *In OSIA Guide.*

Order Sons of Italy in America. Fede e Amore No. 1505 (Southington, Connecticut).
Records, 1936-1969. 2 linear in.

The OSIA Fede e Amore Lodge No. 1505 was founded as a women's lodge in 1928. In 1971, it merged with Cesare Battisti Lodge No. 622, a men's lodge, and became Southington Lodge No. 622.

Records consist of a minute book. *Includes English. In OSIA Guide.*

Order Sons of Italy in America.
Florida Grand Lodge.
Records, 1923-1987. 10 linear ft. and 52
cassette tapes.

The OSIA Florida Grand Lodge was
founded in 1953. Records include OSIA
national Convention and committee
reports; Grand Convention records; and
Grand Lodge correspondence, financial
receipts and disbursements, and committee
reports on activities and charities. Also
included are OSIA membership applications, some dating from the 1920's and
1930's; lists of officers; charter
applications; tapes of Florida Grand
Council meetings; per capita reports and
records of numerous Florida local lodges;
and photographs. *Mainly in English.*
Inventory available. In OSIA Guide.

Order Sons of Italy in America.
Garibaldi-Meucci Museum (Staten
Island, New York).
Records, 1987. 1 videotape.

In 1914, the Order Sons of Italy in
America acquired the Antonio Meucci
home and has maintained it as a museum
since that time in honor of the Italian
inventor and his coworker in the 1950s,
Giuseppe Garibaldi. Records consist of a
videotape depicting the house and its
contents. *In English. In OSIA Guide.*

Order Sons of Italy in America. Glen
Cove Lodge No. 1016 (New York).
Records, 1924-1988. Ca. 1.5 linear ft.

The OSIA Glen Cove Lodge No. 1016
was founded in 1920, the first OSIA
lodge founded on Long Island, NY.
Records include correspondence,
members' dues payments, financial
ledgers, certificates of illness, various
bylaws and ritual books, officers' lists,
and minutes of the Glen Cove Benevolent
Association. Also included are OSIA
New York Grand Convention papers,
officers' lists, and reports. *Includes*
English. In OSIA Guide.

Order Sons of Italy in America.
Gorizia Lodge No. 704 (North
Adams, Massachusetts).
Records, 1925-1963. 7 linear in.

The OSIA Gorizia Lodge No. 704 was
chartered in 1917 in North Adams, MA.
In 1969, it merged with North Adams
Lodge No. 1417.
Collection consists of meeting minutes.
Includes English. In OSIA Guide.

Order Sons of Italy in America.
Guglielmo Marconi Lodge No. 1140
(Clarksburg, West Virginia).
Records, 1923-1973. Ca. 1 linear ft.

The Guglielmo Marconi Lodge No.
1140 was founded in 1922. Records
comprise mortuary fund applications and
policies, membership applications, bylaws
booklets, financial receipt books, and
correspondence, along with brochures
from the West Virginia Labor Federation,
AFL-CIO. *In English and Italian. In*
OSIA Guide.

Order Sons of Italy in America.
Hartford Lodge No. 333
(Connecticut).
Records, 1939-1971. 3 linear in.

The OSIA Hartford (CT) Lodge No.
333 was founded in 1915 as Fratellonza
Lodge No. 333 and changed its name in
1939. Records consist of a minute book,
a certificate citing the lodge for attaining
its membership quota, a 1940 edition of
the bylaws booklet, information on the
OSIA National Home drive, several
decals, and banners. *Includes English. In*
OSIA Guide.

Order Sons of Italy in America.
Illinois Grand Lodge.
Records, 1924-1987. 4 linear ft.

The OSIA Illinois Grand Lodge was
founded in 1924. Records include Illinois
Grand Convention minutes, Columbus
Day banquet programs, scholarship
awards, and Grand Lodge and local lodge
officer lists. Also included are materials
relating to activities and programs of the
lodge, such as the mortuary fund
insurance policies and benefits records. In

addition, there are local lodge membership applications and lists, photographs, and films. *Mainly in English. In OSIA Guide.*

Order Sons of Italy in America. Joseph Franzalia Lodge No. 2422 (West Walton Beach, Florida). Records, 1977-1986. 7 linear in.

Joseph Franzalia, a native of West Virginia, organized an OSIA lodge in Fort Walton Beach that took the name Northwest Florida Lodge No. 2422. Later the members honored him by changing its name to Joseph Franzalia Lodge No. 2422.

Records consist of a historical sketch; State Convention and Council materials, Grand Venerable reports, and officers directory; a list of Florida local lodge venerables; and correspondence, bylaws, financial reports, guest book, membership lists, minutes, and other materials of Lodge No. 2422. *In English. Inventory available. In OSIA Guide.*

Order Sons of Italy in America. La Colomba Lodge No. 2439 (Glendale, Arizona). Records, 1979-1983. 1 linear in.

The OSIA La Colomba Lodge No. 2439 was founded in 1979 in Glendale, AZ. Records include minutes, committee records, bylaws, and membership lists. *In English. In OSIA Guide.*

Order Sons of Italy in America. Maria Cristina Di Savoia Lodge No. 1752 (Kankakee, Illinois). Records, 1935-1976. Ca. 1.5 linear ft.

The OSIA Maria Cristina Di Savoia Lodge No. 1752 was founded in 1935. Records include minutes, dues payment ledgers, disbursement ledgers, and bank statements. Also included are photographs, a framed copy of the Lodge charter, and a large banner. *Includes English. In OSIA Guide.*

Order Sons of Italy in America. Maryland Grand Lodge. Records, 1925-1987. 19.5 linear ft.

The OSIA Maryland Grand Lodge was founded in 1920. Records consist of OSIA Supreme Lodge records, convention and council materials, and committee and charity reports. Grand Lodge records consist of convention and council minutes and reports, district meeting minutes, reports of charity committees, information on the Italian Festival and other social activities, state lodge ledgers and financial reports, Mortuary Fund record, and Ameritan Awards programs. Local lodge records include membership and officers lists, and correspondence. Also included are photographs, and information on non-OSIA Italian American leaders and organizations. *Mainly in English. Inventory available. In OSIA Guide.*

Order Sons of Italy in America. Massachusetts Grand Lodge. Records, 1919-1987. 26.5 linear ft.

The OSIA Massachusetts Grand Lodge was chartered in 1914. Records consist of local and national OSIA materials. Included are OSIA Supreme Convention records, and reports on committees, including the Immigration and Naturalization Commission. Massachusetts Grand Lodge materials include minutes, correspondence, financial records, officer lists, local lodge charters, information on charities and activities, photographs, and motion picture films. *Mainly in English. Inventory available. In OSIA Guide.*

Order Sons of Italy in America. Monmouth County-Mt. Carmel Lodge No. 1215 (New Jersey). Records, 1940-1987. 5 linear in.

The Lodge was founded in Asbury Park, NJ, in 1925, expanded to include Mt. Carmel in 1927, and expanded again in 1985 to include Monmouth County. Records include building certificates, a financial ledger, bylaws, souvenir booklets, miscellaneous certificates, photographs, and a flag. *In English and Italian. In OSIA Guide.*

**Order Sons of Italy in America.
National Office.**
Records, ca. 1941-1987. 47 linear ft.

The Order Sons of Italy in America
was founded in New York City in 1905.
Its national office remained in Manhattan
until the mid 1950s, when it was moved
to Philadelphia. In 1981 the office was
relocated in a new building in
Washington, DC. The Order is the
largest and oldest Italian fraternal
organization in the United States.

Records of the OSIA National Office
include records of Supreme Conventions,
the Supreme Council, and the National
Foundation; correspondence of financial
officers; financial ledgers of the Supreme
Lodge and National Foundation; and
records of the Garibaldi-Meucci Museum,
the Immigration and Naturalization
Commission, the Anti-Defamation
Commission, *OSIA News*, and a multitude
of other committees and projects. Per
capita reports and correspondence with all
grand lodges and local lodges compose a
large section of these records. Fraternal
pacts with local lodges in Bermuda and
the Grand Bahamas are present, as well
as materials pertaining to charities such as
those for birth defects and relief for
earthquake victims in Italy. *Mainly in
English. Inventory available. In OSIA
Guide.*

**Order Sons of Italy in America.
Nebraska Grand Lodge.**
Records, 1930-1987. 4 linear in.

The OSIA Nebraska Grand Lodge was
founded in 1935. Records include deeds
of property, mortgages, licenses,
promissory notes, articles of
incorporation, and other legal and
financial records of the Lodge. Also
included are materials pertaining to Lodge
contributions to Monte Cassino Orphanage
Fund, Columbus Day banquet programs,
miscellaneous correspondence, newspaper
clippings, photographs including a large
one of OSIA members, and minutes of
meetings of the Italian Community
Center. *In English. In OSIA Guide.*

**Order Sons of Italy in America. New
Jersey Grand Lodge.**
Records, 1920-1987. 2.5 linear ft.

The OSIA New Jersey Grand Lodge
was chartered in 1911, the second lodge
in OSIA. In 1923, the Lodge opened an
orphanage in Nutley, NJ, which
functioned until 1970.

Records consist of Grand Convention
records, Grand Council minutes, per
capita records, financial reports, bylaws,
orphanage records, banquet booklets, state
and local lodge officer and member lists,
photographs, newspaper clippings, and a
scrapbook. *Includes English. In OSIA
Guide.*

**Order Sons of Italy in America. New
York Grand Lodge (New York, New
York).**
Records, ca. 1910-1987. 17 linear ft.

The New York Grand Lodge of OSIA
was chartered in 1911, the first of the
Order's twenty-two grand lodges. During
the early years, it was the largest of the
OSIA grand lodges; in 1925, its membership numbered about 30,000. In 1915, a
death insurance fund was established, and
a Welfare Department was added in the
early 1920's. The Grand Lodge also
maintained a representative at Ellis Island,
granted scholarships to high school
students, and contributed to relief efforts
in Italy during and after World War I.
During the 1960's, the Grand Lodge
began a period of rapid growth and
encouraged efforts to uphold a positive
image of Italian Americans. It also
established a foundation, built a senior
citizen housing complex, and set up its
headquarters in Great Neck, Long Island.

Records of the New York Grand
Lodge pertain to national, state, district,
and local OSIA activities and non-OSIA
groups and activities and also include
photographs and artifacts. National
records (1959-1987) include material on
the supreme (national) conventions, the
Cassino Memorial Orphanage, the
Garibaldi-Meucci Museum, the nationwide
OSIA campaign to award Anthony
Casamento a Medal of Honor for his
World War II service, and the National
Insurance program. State materials
comprise correspondence and lists of

officers; lists of delegates, minutes, and reports of conventions; minutes of the Grand Council; and records of committee activities. District records include lists of deputies who acted as representatives of the Grand Venerable and minutes of district meetings attended by the presidents of local lodges. Local records comprise lists of officers, correspondence, and activity booklets. Collection also includes a non-OSIA report on Italian Cultural Organizations in North America (1977). *Mainly in English. Inventory available. In OSIA Guide.*

Order Sons of Italy in America. Ohio Grand Lodge.
Records, 1923-1987. 14.5 linear ft.

The OSIA Ohio Grand Lodge was founded in 1915. Records include Grand Convention and Council minutes and reports; correspondence; membership, financial, and Benefit Insurance Commission records; and typescripts of Grand and local lodge histories. Also included are Supreme Convention and activity reports, reports and correspondence of many state lodge committees and non-OSIA organizations, miscellaneous newspaper clippings, OSIA officer directories, and photographs. *Includes English. Inventory available. In OSIA Guide.*

Order Sons of Italy in America. Ontario Grand Lodge (Canada).
Records, 1926-1987. 5 linear in.

The OSIA Grand Lodge of Ontario was founded in 1924. Records include incorporation documents, minutes of Grand Conventions, a list of subor-dinate lodges, miscellaneous correspondence, bylaws of the Grand Order of Italo-Canadians, a ritual book, and constitution and bylaws. Also included are convention books, a summary of membership in various local lodges, and newspaper clippings. *Mainly in English. In OSIA Guide.*

Order Sons of Italy in America. *OSIA News* Office.
Records, 1946-1987. 14.5 linear ft.

The *OSIA News* was initiated in 1946 with A. Alfred Maniello as its director. Al Maino began as a staff member in 1946 and assumed the director's position in 1963.

Records consist of Supreme Lodge records, including *OSIA News* reports, mailing lists, convention reports of various committees, Supreme Council minutes, and correspondence of national officers. The bulk of documents are those of the National Public Relations Committee, which was very active in combating bigotry and defamation in the 1950s and early 1960s. Included are letters, newspaper clippings, reports on Mafia charges, and an exchange of memoranda between the Committee and grand lodges on how to combat national and local slurs against Italians. Correspondents include Walter Winchell, producers of the television program "The Untouchables," various politicians, and state and local lodges. *Mainly in English. Inventory available. In OSIA Guide.*

Order Sons of Italy in America. Peninsula Italian-American Lodge No. 2145 (Hampton, Virginia).
Records, 1961-1987. 2 linear in.

The OSIA Peninsula Italian-American Lodge No. 2145 was founded in 1964. Records consist of a Virginia Grand Lodge Convention Souvenir book, Lodge Council meeting minutes, lists of officers and members, and a recipe book produced by the Lodge. Also included are miscellaneous correspondence, brochures, and newspaper clippings. *In English. In OSIA Guide.*

Order Sons of Italy in America. Pennsylvania Grand Lodge.
Records, 1916-1987. 120 linear ft. and 47 microfilm reels.

The OSIA Pennsylvania Grand Lodge was founded in 1913 and has been the largest of the twenty-two grand lodges since the 1920s. Records include OSIA Supreme Convention and Council records and many activity reports; Grand Convention and Council documents; membership applications; correspondence and reports on the Dante Orphanage (Concordville, PA); and information on the Sons of Italy Savings and Loan Association, Columbus Day celebrations, and other projects. Composing over half the collection are insurance records, including fifty-five feet pertaining to members enrolled in the Mortuary Fund. Financial records include ledgers offering details on members' deaths, case information on death claims, and other financial reports. Other materials include officers' correspondence, files on local lodges, souvenir booklets, and hundreds of photographs. *Includes English. Inventory available. In OSIA Guide.*

Order Sons of Italy in America. Quebec Grand Lodge (Canada).
Records, 1952-1987. 5 linear in.

The OSIA Grand Lodge of Quebec was founded in 1923. Records include Grand Lodge financial reports, Grand Executive Council minutes, materials relating to the Italian Festival, and a book celebrating the 50th anniversary of the Piave Lodge. *Includes French and English. Inventory available. In OSIA Guide.*

Order Sons of Italy in America. Renaissance-Alliance Lodge No. 1966 (Rhode Island).
Records, 1947-1975. 2 linear ft.

The OSIA Renaissance-Alliance Lodge No. 1966 was founded in 1947. Records include a Rhode Island OSIA Grand Convention book, lodge minutes, ritual books, bylaws, correspondence, membership applications and lists, financial records, booklets, correspondence concerning various lodge social functions, and photographs. *In English. In OSIA Guide. Related collection: Vincent Ragosta.*

Order Sons of Italy in America. Rhode Island Grand Lodge.
Records, 1918-1988. 2.5 linear ft.

The OSIA Rhode Island Grand Lodge was founded in 1915. Records include Rhode Island Grand Convention and Council records, Grand Lodge correspondence and membership lists, financial ledgers, quarterly reports of district lodges, financial contributions, and officer lists. Also included are records of the Italian-American Youth Lodge and several local lodges, clippings, and photographs. *Includes English. In OSIA Guide.*

Order Sons of Italy in America. Roma Lodge No. 1196 (Racine, Wisconsin).
Records, 1924-1964. Ca. 5.5 linear ft.

Records of the OSIA Roma Lodge No. 1196 include minutes of meetings, membership applications, ledgers, program booklets, correspondence, and minutes of the Italo-Americano Cittadino Club. *Includes English. In OSIA Guide.*

Order Sons of Italy in America. Sacra Famiglia Lodge No. 2456 (Saginaw, Michigan).
Records, 1979-1987. 1 linear in.

The Lodge was founded in 1980. Records consist of minutes. *In English. In OSIA Guide.*

Order Sons of Italy in America. Uguaglianza Lodge No. 83 (Bronx, New York).
Records, 1915-1983. 3.5 linear ft.

The OSIA Uguaglianza Lodge No. 83 was founded in the Bronx, NY, in 1911. Led by labor leader Luigi Antonini, the Lodge joined the schismatic group, Sons of Italy Grand Lodge, Inc., 1925 to 1943, after which it returned to the Order.

Records consist of minutes, financial records, dues payment ledgers, register of loans, correspondence, and booklets of the annual dinner-dance. Also included are the New York Grand Lodge bylaws book, ritual book, and the equivalent items from the Sons of Italy Grand Lodge, Inc.

(1933). *Includes English. In OSIA Guide.*

Order Sons of Italy in America. Veturia Romana Lodge No. 1200 (Salem, Massachusetts).
Records, 1923-1966. 8 linear in.

The OSIA Veturia Romana Lodge No. 1200 was founded in 1923 as a women's lodge. It became a mixed lodge in 1974.

Records include minutes, a scrapbook, and photographs. Also included are several national and state records and certificates, a brochure on the Junior Division, clippings, photographs, and artifacts. *Includes English. In OSIA Guide.*

Order Sons of Italy in America. Victor Emanuel Lodge No. 1646 (Haverhill, Massachusetts).
Records, 1892-1963. 3 linear in.

The Vittorio Emanuele II Society was founded in Haverhill in 1891. In 1920, the organization joined OSIA as Vittorio Emanuele Lodge No. 1041. It withdrew from the Order during the 1920s but rejoined in 1932, when it became Vittorio Emanuele Lodge No. 1646. By 1935, the name had been changed to Victor Emanuel and in later years was changed again to the Haverhill Mixed Lodge No. 1646.

Records consist of state and local OSIA records, along with newspaper clippings, photographs, and artifacts. State records include convention and council records, and a ritual book for installation of local lodge officers. Local records include a history of the lodge, correspondence, and mortuary fund materials. Records also include newspaper clippings about the opening of the lodge hall and presentation of a statue of Dante by the lodge, photographs, and artifacts. *Mainly in English. Inventory available. In OSIA Guide.*

Order Sons of Italy in America. Vittoria Colonna Lodge No. 1355 (Racine, Wisconsin).
Records, 1941-1987. 3 linear in.

The OSIA Vittoria Colonna Lodge No. 1355 was founded in 1925. Records include Supreme Convention and National Lodge materials, Lodge correspondence, miscellaneous receipts, bylaws, ritual booklets, and a program for the 50th anniversary of the Lodge's founding. *Mainly in English. In OSIA Guide.*

Order Sons of Italy in America. West Virginia Grand Lodge.
Records, 1929-1987. 4 linear ft.

The OSIA West Virginia Grand Lodge was founded in 1923. The bulk of the collection pertains to the Grand Lodge Mortuary Fund, including applications, reports, claim records, receipt books, general ledgers, and correspondence. Also included are Grand Convention and Council records, Grand Lodge financial reports, records of local lodges, and photographs. *Includes English. In OSIA Guide.*

Orsini, Louis A. (1918-   )
Papers, 1924-1987. Ca. 3.5 linear ft.

Orsini was the State President of the Order Sons of Italy in America, Michigan Grand Lodge (1949-1959), and Supreme Deputy (1960-1961). Collection consists of Grand Convention and Council minutes, speeches, Grand Lodge correspondence, and bylaws. *Includes some English. In OSIA Guide.*

Ossanna, Fred A. (b. 1893).
Papers, ca. 1927-1972. Ca. 3 linear in.

Ossanna, a successful lawyer in Minneapolis after his graduation from the University of Minnesota Law School, was active in political and civic affairs. He became a national as well as state leader in various Italian American organizations.

Papers consist largely of material pertaining to UNICO, a social and civic organization, and to the National Italian American Civic League (of which he was president from 1933 to 1938), including photographs. *Includes English. Inventory available.*

Ottaviano, John, Jr. (1917-)
Collection, 1927-1987. 2 linear ft.

Ottaviano was the Order Sons of Italy in America National President (1961-1965) after holding several Connecticut and National Lodge offices, including Grand Venerable (1951-1953). Collection consists of OSIA Supreme Convention and Council materials, committee reports (twenty-one activities), correspondence, legal and financial records, and correspondence with twelve state and several local lodges. Non-OSIA organization material and OSIA photographs are also included. *In English. In OSIA Guide.*

Our Lady of Mt. Carmel Church.
  Ladies Society (Kenosha, Wisconsin).
Records, 1948-1983. 8 linear in.

Records of the Society consist of financial materials, membership rosters, and general administrative records as well as registers of two women's organizations in the parish, the Mt. Carmel Society and the St. Therese Society. Also included are a typescript of "The Italians in Milwaukee" by Salvatore Tagliavia, a booklet of the Italians in Milwaukee County, newsletters of Our Lady of the Holy Rosary Society, and a dedication book. *In English. Inventory available. Related collection: Anita M. Petermark. Typescript available as photocopy only.*

Pascarelli, Anne M.
Papers, 1948-1987. Ca. 1 linear ft.

Pascarelli served the Order Sons of Italy in America as Supreme Trustee (1969-1973), and chair of the Birth Defects Committee (charitable activity) after holding several Massachusetts state lodge offices. Collection contains scattered state lodge convention booklets, reports, and program mementos. Many records pertain to the Dorchester (No. 1848), Deledda (No. 1783), and Quincy (No. 1295), MA, lodges. *Mainly in English. In OSIA Guide.*

Pasqualicchio, Leonard (1886-1975).
Papers, ca. 1945-1972. 4 linear in.

Pasqualicchio was the Order Sons of Italy in America Supreme Delegate (1942-1952) and acted as the Order's lobbyist in Washington, DC. He was also founder and president of the National Council for American-Italian Friendship.
Collection consists of a copy of the OSIA constitution and bylaws, miscellaneous photographs, correspondence, and personal papers of Pasqualicchio. Personal papers include his notes for a book; newspaper clippings, brochures, and other material on Constantino Bromidi, the architect of the United States Capitol building; Pasqualicchio's speeches; invitations to presidential inaugurations; and correspondence from other political figures such as Hubert H. Humphrey and J. Edgar Hoover. *Mainly in English. In OSIA Guide.*

Petermark, Anita M.
Papers, 1974-1983. 2.5 linear in.

Papers of Petermark (or Pietromartire) comprise a genealogy, church bulletins, newspaper clippings, and miscellany concerning the Italian community in Kenosha, WI. Also included are membership information and printed materials from Our Lady of Mt. Carmel Church Ladies Society and an Italian phone directory. *Mainly in English. Inventory available. Related collection: Our Lady of Mt. Carmel Church, Ladies Society (Kenosha, WI).*

Petta, Richard V.
Papers, 1959-1987. Ca. 4.5 linear ft.

Petta was the Order Sons of Italy in America Supreme Trustee (1981-1985), served on the National Council's Bylaws and Ritual Revision Committee, and was Virginia Grand Venerable (1973-1977). Collection consists of OSIA Supreme Lodge convention minutes and reports, officer directories, financial reports, and records of the National Foundation. Reports of the National Membership Committee are also included, as are extensive documents of the committee to revise national bylaws and ritual.

Virginia Grand Lodge records include correspondence and reports, Grand Convention records, membership statistics, and OSIA wall calendars. There are also materials pertaining to local lodges, including a large volume of minutes and correspondence from George Washington Lodge No. 2038 (Vienna, VA). *In English. In OSIA Guide.*

Piacenza, Aldobrando (1888-1976).
Papers, 1951-1973.   Ca. 1 linear in.

A poet, painter, and folk artist, Piacenza was born in Sant'Anna Pelaso, Italy, and came to the United States in 1902.   He lived in Chicago and Highwood, IL, and worked as a gardener, store clerk, bakery employee, and owner of an ice cream parlor.   He also created elaborate bird houses.

Papers contain articles about his art work and a short autobiography. *Includes English.*

Pioletti, Monsignor Louis F.
   (1887-1972).
Papers, 1908-1972.   5 linear ft.

Pioletti was born in Corio, Italy. Drawn to the priesthood from earliest youth, he studied at the Theological Seminary of Turin and received his DD degree in 1910.   Concerned by the spiritual and cultural difficulties of Italian immigrants in foreign countries, he was sent to St. Paul, MN, to minister to the needs of Italians there.   In 1925, he was appointed pastor of Holy Redeemer Church and its mission parish of St. Ambrose, in St. Paul.   Under his care, the parishes were soon thriving.   Pioletti became a monsignor in 1957.   He was active in many Italian American organizations, especially the Columbus Memorial Association.   In the 1960s, Pioletti led his parish in an unsuccessful effort to prevent destruction of the parish house and church for freeway construction.   He retired in 1968, a year after Holy Redeemer Church was demolished.

Papers comprise correspondence, diaries, and biographical information; sermons and notes of his Italian pastorate; sermons, notes, awards, and newspaper clippings from his pastorate at Holy Redeemer Church and St. Ambrose Parish; and publications and photographs.

Included are parish records from Holy Redeemer Church and correspondence and information pertaining to Italian American organizations, among them the Columbus Memorial Association and UNICO. *Includes English. Inventory available. Related collections: John Aloysius Vannelli; Holy Redeemer Church.*

Pitea, Francesco.
Papers, ca. 1910-1965.   Ca. 1 linear in.

Pitea worked in Paterson, NJ, textile mills and was also a poet.   Much of his poetry takes the form of political satire and was published in *La Scopa* and other antifascist publications.

Papers consist of manuscripts and typescripts of his poetry.

Pittaro, Vito (1864-1951).
Papers, ca. 1891-1952.   Ca. 4 linear ft.

Pittaro, a prominent business and civic leader in the Stamford, CT, Italian community, was born in San Fele (Potenza), Italy.   He graduated from the University of Naples and came to the United States when he was twenty-six. He was editor of several Italian American serials and newspapers and was cofounder, with Pietro P. Vescio, of *La Tribuna* (Stamford, CT).   He also founded La Società Operaia and the Istituto Italiano di Stamford and was author of a history of the Italians in Stamford.   Pittaro was also a banker, taught night school classes, was the first Italian notary public in Stamford, and was active in the Italian Cooperative and Commercial Company there.

Papers include biographical materials, correspondence, notary papers, memorabilia, newspaper clippings, photographs, typescripts, and writings. Also included are records and other materials pertaining to the Italian Cooperative and Investment Company, the Stamford Italo-American Historical Society, La Società Operaia, and the Società Italiana di Mutuo Soccorso Vittorio Emanuele III. *Includes English. Inventory available.*

Procopio, Giuseppe D. (b. 1889).
Papers, ca. 1933-1961. Ca. 3 linear ft.

Born in Calabria, Italy, Procopio came to the United States in 1904. An Italian American labor leader, Procopio was active in the Confederazione Italo Americano del Lavoro and the United Shoe Workers of America and was manager of Local 563 of the Shoe Service Union and vice-president of International Wholesale and Department Store Unions. He was co-editor and publisher of *Il Corriere de Popolo*, founder and editor of *Prometeo*, and editor of *L'Independence*, as well as a writer for many other publications. He was an important member of American Aid to Calabria and president of its successor organization, the Calabrian Social Center of New York, after World War II.

Papers comprise articles and clippings about Procopio's union activities. *Includes English. Temporarily closed.*

Procopio, Vincenzo (1873-1943).
Papers, 1895-1943. 3 linear in.

Procopio was born in San Vito Sullo Ionio (Calabria), Italy, trained as a lawyer, and came to New York City in the late 1890s. He worked as a lawyer, banker, and steamship agent and then moved to West Virginia, where he was a co-editor of *La Sentinella*. He served the Order Sons of Italy in America as the first Grand Venerable of the West Virginia Grand Lodge (1923-1929) and as Supreme Trustee (1935-1939).

Collection includes miscellaneous personal papers of Procopio and materials relating to OSIA. The latter include newspaper clippings, photographs depicting Grand and Supreme lodge functions, artifacts, and regalia for Supreme Trustee and Grand Venerable. *Includes English. In OSIA Guide.*

Puglisi, George.
Papers, 1955-1975. Ca. 5 linear in.

Puglisi, a director of multimedia and library services for the Stratford, CT, public schools, has been a member and officer of UNICO National. Papers include newspaper clippings, programs, minutes, and miscellany of Italian Americans and Italian American organizations and celebrations in the Bridgeport, CT, area. Included are minutes of the Italian Community Center of Greater Bridgeport, programs of the Trinacria Mutual Aid Society, programs from the Gran Carnevale, and miscellany. *In English. Inventory available.*

Quilici, George Lancelot (1897-1969).
Papers, 1934-1969. 2 linear ft. and 16 scrapbooks.

A lawyer and judge, Quilici was born in Chicago, IL. He obtained his law degree from DePaul University and practiced labor law with Arthur Goldberg in the Chicago area. In 1940, he was elected municipal court judge; he was reelected until 1962, when he was elected to the superior court. He also made an unsuccessful bid for appointment to the federal bench in 1943. He was an early supporter of the National Lawyers Guild, civil rights for minorities, and antifascism. During World War II, he helped organize and lead the Italian-American Victory Council. He also participated in government-sponsored radio broadcasts to Italy and supported the movement to erase the name of the Fascist General Italo Balbo from Chicago streets and parks.

Papers reveal Quilici's career as a judge and antifascist activist. Included are briefs and newspaper clippings on Cook County (Chicago) election fraud cases; materials pertaining to his election campaigns, controversial cases, antifascist activities, and work on civil rights publications; and miscellaneous biographical information. Correspondence relates to the Chicago Bar Association-Judicial Poll, the Italian-American Victory Council, Chicago Italian American Day, and Italian Relief. Other correspondence, speeches, and clippings pertain to Quilici's antifascist radio work and to the Balbo affair. Also included are materials of the National Lawyers Guild, news releases, and newspaper clippings and publications by and about the U.S. House Un-American Activities Committee. *Mainly in English. Inventory available.*

Ragosta, Vincent A. (1924-   ).
Papers, 1923-1986.   4 linear ft.

Ragosta served the Order Sons of Italy in America as Supreme Trustee (1979-1983) and Rhode Island Grand Venerable (1971-1979).   Collection includes OSIA Supreme Convention and Council materials, and constitution and general laws booklets.   Rhode Island Grand Lodge records include Grand Convention books, correspondence, and Grand Venerable correspondence.   Also included are Lodge minutes, officer lists, membership applications, correspondence of Renaissance-Alliance Lodge No. 1966, newspaper clippings, and photographs. *Mainly in English. In OSIA Guide. Related collection: Order Sons of Italy in America. Renaissance-Alliance Lodge No. 1966 (Rhode Island).*

Riley, Jenny P.
Papers, 1952-1985.   2 linear in.

Papers of Riley consist of materials collected for an undergraduate research paper pertaining to the St. Paul, MN, Italian community.   (The manuscript of "The Upper Levee and the Holy Redeemer Church" may be found with other unpublished essays in the IHRC's collection.)   Papers include interviews with residents; newspaper clippings; and copies of documents from the Housing and Redevelopment Authority, the Department of Highways and the Archdiocese of St. Paul.   *In English.*

Rivisto, Michael A. (1909-   ).
Collection, 1957-1986.   2 linear in.

Rivisto was an OSIA Supreme Trustee (1967-1969) and State President of the Northwest Lodge (1965-1967).   (The Northwest Lodge, founded in 1929, includes Idaho, Washington, Montana, and portions of Oregon.)
Collection includes information on OSIA Supreme and Grand Lodge committees regarding scholarship and cultural programs, lodge formation, membership, federation, fundraising to fight Cooley's Anemia and birth defects, and immigration reform.   Non-OSIA records pertain to the National Federation of Italian American Organizations.   *In English. In OSIA Guide.*

Romano, Mary.
Papers, 1921-1987.   1 linear in.

Romano held the office of Connecticut Grand Trustee in the Order Sons of Italy in America (1945-1975).   Collection consists of correspondence and charter application of OSIA Gloria Lodge No. 1117 (New London, CT); Connecticut Grand Lodge reports and correspondence; a booklet for the 1939 Silver Jubilee dinner of the Grand Lodge; and booklets from Columbus Day dances.   Supreme Lodge records focus on Italian World War II prisoners, aid to Italian war victims, and a resolution urging that Italy be involved in the founding of the United Nations.   Also included are artifacts and two photographs.   *Mainly in English. In OSIA Guide.*

Rubini, Rudy.
Papers, 1796-1956.   Ca. 2.5 linear ft.

The Rubini collection consists of materials pertaining to the Order Sons of Italy in America, Cristoforo Colombo Lodge, formerly Society.   The Society was organized in Wilmington, DE, in 1909 and became Lodge No. 1125 in 1927.   It disbanded in 1956.
Records include minutes, ledgers on membership dues collection, financial records, sickness and death benefit payments, bylaw and ritual books, and records of the lodge hall dating back to 1796; the hall was purchased in 1928. Other materials include the OSIA Delaware Grand Lodge bylaws, officers' regalia, and a paper embosser.   *Includes English. In OSIA Guide.*

Ruotolo, Onorio (1888-1966).
Papers, ca. 1915-1966.   2.5 linear ft.

A sculptor and poet, Ruotolo was born in Cervinara, Italy, in 1908.   The struggle and poverty he observed in New York City engendered in him a concern for society, which he expressed in cartoons, poetry, and sculpture.   During World War I, he produced a number of sculptures showing the horrors of war. In 1914, he and Arturo Giovannitti became co-directors of *Il Fuoco*, a magazine of art and politics. After an ideological split between them, Ruotolo began *Minosse*, a socio-literary publication. He also worked during this time to found the Leonardo Da Vinci Art School. In the 1940s and 1960s, he turned his efforts to poetry and prose, and from 1950 to 1957 he served as an aide of the Amalgamated Clothing Workers of America.

Papers include biographical information, organizational records and correspondence of the Leonardo Da Vinci Art School, photographs, illustrations, poetry and prose works, articles and criticisms of Ruotolo's work, and works of and about other individuals. Correspondents include Helen Keller, Fiorello La Guardia, Arturo Giovannitti, Alberto Viviani, Armando Mazza, Dorothy Caruso, Rosita Carotti Leopardi di Pesparo, and many others. *Includes English. Inventory available.*

Sacco and Vanzetti Case.
Collection, ca. 1922-1926. 2 linear in.

Collection includes typescripts and published copies of briefs, arguments, etc. presented in the case of Sacco and Vanzetti by defense counsel William G. Thompson. *In English.*

St. Anthony of Padua Roman Catholic Church (Cleveland, Ohio).
Records, 1887-1912. 1 microfilm reel.

Records include a marriage record book and baptismal records with index. *Mainly in Latin. Originals held by St. Anthony of Padua Roman Catholic Church, Parma, OH.*

St. Charles Borromeo Church. Holy Name Society (St. Louis, Missouri).
Records, ca. 1944-1960. 1.5 linear in.

Records contain minutes of meetings and financial reports. The Holy Name Society assisted the parish in maintaining the church and its surroundings. *In English.*

Saladino, John A. (1940-).
Papers, 1965-1987. 7.5 linear ft.

Saladino served OSIA as National Recording Secretary (1981-1985), National Deputy (1973-1981), Massachusetts Grand Recording Secretary (1977-1981), and Grand Trustee (1975-1977). Collection consists of OSIA Supreme Lodge records, including convention and council minutes and correspondence; National Foundation minutes and reports; and reports of numerous activities. Massachusetts Grand Lodge records include convention and council records, correspondence, reports of the Organization and Education Commission and other committees, and Benefit Insurance Commission minutes and reports. Also included are records of Medford (MA) Lodge No. 1359 and other local lodges, along with newspaper clippings, photographs, artifacts, and regalia. *In English. Inventory available. In OSIA Guide.*

Sarcone, Antonio L. (1884-1964).
Papers, ca. 1904-1964. Ca. 1 linear ft.

Sarcone was born in Crucoli, Italy, and came to the United States in 1906. He settled in Des Moines, IA, and became editor of *Il Risveglio* (later the *American Citizen*). His activities included civic, political, and organizational work in numerous capacities with particular emphasis on Americanization of immigrants.

Papers include correspondence, citations, scrapbooks, newspaper clippings, and photographs documenting Sarcone's life and the Italian community in Des Moines. Included are constitutions and bylaws of various Italian American organizations, correspondence and clippings regarding his work with the Italian Welfare Society, materials pertaining to *Il Risveglio*, and miscellany. *In English. Inventory available.*

Saudino, Domenico (1888-1964).
Papers, 1927-1961. 2 linear ft.

Saudino was born in Drusacco (Piedmont), Italy, son of a tailor. He came to the United States in 1912, where he became a writer, antifascist, publicist for socialist and anticlerical causes, and long-time contributor to *La Parola del Popolo* (Chicago, IL) and *Il Corriere del Popolo* (San Francisco, CA). After Mussolini's rise to power, Saudino became an outspoken critic of fascism. His most famous book was *Sotto il Segno del Littorio: La Genesi del Fascismo*, which was translated into Greek and occasioned a diplomatic protest by the Italian government. Saudino was a member of the National Council of the Italian Socialist Federation in the United States as early as 1924 and continued to be active in the organization for many years. During the 1930s and 1940s, he published widely in Italian newspapers in the United States, Argentina, Italy, and Mexico.

Papers, largely in manuscript form, include publications, books, essays, and newspaper articles. Also included are a diary of a trip to Europe, a typescript of a work on American fascism published in two special issues of *La Parola del Popolo* (1959, 1961), and miscellany. *Includes English. Inventory available.*

Scafetta, Joseph, Jr.
Papers, 1973-1987. 1.5 linear ft.

Scafetta served the OSIA Virginia Grand Lodge as Grand Orator (1983-1987) and Grand Financial Secretary (1987-). State lodge records consist of correspondence of the West Virginia Grand Orator, records of the Ritual Revision committee, amended versions of the Virginia Grand Lodge bylaws, and "Guidelines for Drafting Bylaws for Local Lodges," along with Grand Convention and Council materials, and reports regarding arbitration issues of the Grand Lodge of Maryland. Records of the local lodge Avanti Italiani No. 2381, of which Scafetta was president (1981-1983), are also available. *In English. In OSIA Guide.*

Scarpaci, Jean Vincenza.
Papers, ca. 1970. 1 linear ft. and 1 microfilm reel.

Papers include an annotated bibliography and biographical information on the history of Italians in Louisiana ca.

1890-1910, contained on index cards. Also included is a microfilm copy of the Donaldsville, LA, *Daily Times* (June 1897 through May 1898). *In English. Restricted.*

Scigliano, George A. (1874-1906).
Papers, ca. 1874-1907. Ca. 1 linear in.

An attorney active in local and state government, Scigliano was born in Boston, MA. He was city councilman (1901-1903) for the 6th Ward, the first Boston Italian elected to public office. From 1904 to 1906, he was a state representative. He was considered an anti-Mafia crusader and an opponent of corruption generally.

Papers consist of photocopies of newspaper clippings concerning Scigliano's activities. *Includes English.*

Sisca, Alessandro (1875-1940).
Papers, 1893-1968. 6 linear ft.

Sisca, also known as Riccardo Cordiferro, was born in San Pietro in Guarano, Italy. He came to America in 1892 and in 1893 founded the literary journal *La Follia di New York* with his father, Francesco, and brother, Marziale (b. 1878). He remained its director until 1909; he continued to work on the editorial board and published his works under many pseudonyms. He was imprisoned several times for his socialist and anticlerical views. During the Sacco and Vanzetti case, he served as official spokesman for the Utica, NY, pro Sacco and Vanzetti committee. A frequent speaker on literary as well as social subjects, Sisca was, in addition, a popular playwright; and he wrote many songs, some of which were introduced to the public by Enrico Caruso.

Papers include personal correspondence, untitled works, and notes; notebooks of clippings; published works by other writers; correspondence, records, receipts, contracts, poetry, short stories, and clippings pertaining to *La Follia di New York*; and correspondence, published materials, and miscellany of Marziale Sisca. Correspondents of Marziale Sisca include Thomas Dewey, Fiorello La Guardia, Enrico Caruso, and Presidents

Taft and Eisenhower. *Includes some English. Inventory available.*

Smith, Dwight C., Jr.
Collection, ca. 1890-1979. 10 linear ft.

Collection consists of books, articles, computer analyses, and games collected by Smith for studies on the treatment of the Mafia and Italian Americans in American culture. *In English. Preliminary inventory available.*

Sola, Anthony.
Papers, 1950-1983. 9 linear in.

Anthony "Bud" Sola served as Grand Recording Secretary of the OSIA California Grand Lodge (1979-1983), as Grand Treasurer (1969-1973), and as Grand Trustee (1967-1969). Collection consists of California Grand convention booklets and minutes, scholarship award booklets, and several historical publications. *In English. In OSIA Guide.*

Spatuzza, George J. (1896-1979).
Papers, 1924-1979. 6.5 linear ft.

Spatuzza was born in Sicily and came to the United States in 1908. He became a lawyer and served the Order Sons of Italy in America as Supreme Venerable (1947-1957) and as Grand Venerable of Illinois (1926-1928, 1931-1947).
Collection includes records of the OSIA Supreme Lodge and of the Illinois Grand Lodge. Supreme Lodge records include correspondence, convention records, committee reports such as those from the Immigration and Naturalization Commission, reports of Washington lobbyist Leonard Pasqualicchio, and occasional Supreme Council minutes. Materials of the Illinois Grand Lodge feature convention records, correspondence, booklets from OSIA and other Italian events such as Italo Balbo's 1933 reception, memoranda on visits to local lodges, and various reports. There are many drafts of speeches given by Spatuzza, a large collection of newspaper clippings relating to many topics, photographs, and artifacts. *Includes English. Inventory available. In OSIA Guide.*

Spatuzza, John G. (1925-).
Papers, 1937-1985. 7 linear ft.

Spatuzza, son of George Spatuzza, served as OSIA Supreme Venerable (1975-1977), and Grand Venerable of Illinois (1963-1965). Collection includes OSIA Supreme Lodge records, Illinois Grand Lodge records, and other OSIA materials. Supreme Lodge records include convention and council documents, many committee reports, and correspondence. Illinois Grand Lodge materials include Grand Convention books and reports, correspondence, scholarship and committee reports, and brochures from a variety of OSIA events. Correspondence and reports from many local lodges, and miscellaneous newsclippings are also included. Non-OSIA records include those of the Justinian Society, the Joint Civic Committee of Italian Americans, and political organizations. *Mainly in English. Inventory available. In OSIA Guide.*

Speranza, Gino.
Papers, ca. 1901-1923. 2 microfilm reels.

A lawyer from New York City, Speranza served as secretary of the Society for the Protection of Italian Immigrants. Papers include correspondence relating to the Society, reports, speeches, and clippings and statistics pertaining to Italian immigrants. *Includes English. Negatives held by Biblioteca Nazionale Centrale, Florence, Italy.*

Spinelli, Grace Billotti (b. 1907?).
Papers, ca. 1928-1969. 2 linear in.

Spinelli was born in the province of Enna, Italy, and came to the United States in 1917. From 1930 to 1937 she was Italian nationality worker at the Jersey City International Institute; she ran for mayor of Jersey City in 1940. She was associated with the YWCA for much of her life and became industrial secretary of the Passaic, NJ, YWCA in 1946. Her husband, Marcos Spinelli, a Brazilian of Tuscan background, became a well known writer in the United States.
Papers include a typescript of memoirs; papers and reports relating to

the International Institute, including a 1934 report relating to the foreign-born in New Jersey; text of a lecture given by Edward Corsi in 1931; and a scrapbook with clippings on Spinelli, her activities, and the YWCA. *Includes English.*

Strollo, Joanne L.
Papers, 1946-1986. 7 linear in.

Strollo, the first woman to become a line officer of OSIA's Supreme Council, has served the Order as Third Assistant Supreme Venerable (1987-), Fourth Assistant Supreme Venerable (1985-1987), and Supreme Financial Secretary (1981-1985). Her father, Ernest M. Strollo, was a leading figure in OSIA Giuseppe Giusti Lodge No. 683 (Germantown, PA) and the Pennsylvania Grand Lodge.

Collection consists of Pennsylvania Grand Lodge records including correspondence, officers' lists and convention minutes; correspondence, officers' lists, minutes, and a recipe book of the Women's Division Council of the Lodge; a Supreme Convention book; correspondence, bylaws, banquet programs, and activity booklets relating to Lodge No. 683; and correspondence and newspaper clippings pertaining to Ernest M. Strollo. *Mainly in English. In OSIA Guide.*

Susi, Americo.
Papers, 1923-1935. Ca. 1 linear in.

Susi was an Italian American laborer originally from Introdacqua (Aquila), Italy. Papers consist of his membership booklets for "Club Introdacquese" (Youngstown, OH) and for "Società Italiana di M. S. Generale Gustavo Fara" (Sharpsville, PA).

Teresi, Matteo (b. 1875).
Papers, 1914-1968. 4 linear in.

An editor and lawyer, Teresi was born in Alia (Palermo), Italy, and came to the United States in 1907 after completing his education. Teresi was editor of *L'Araldo* (Cleveland, OH) and author of many books and articles.

Papers include typescripts of published and unpublished writings on social issues. *Includes English. Inventory available.*

Thomas, Norman (1884-1968).
Papers, ca. 1943-1955. 1 microfilm reel.

A socialist, Thomas was also an antiwar activist during World War I and World War II. He was a candidate for several New York offices and for U.S. president in the elections from 1928 to 1944. He was also involved in the Passaic, NJ, textile workers' strike of 1919 and in the 1930s strikes of the Southern Tenant Farmers Union. He was a founder of the American Civil Liberties Union. He was chairman of the Carlo Tresca Memorial Committee, which published a pamphlet in 1945 discussing the case and demanding that the murder be solved.

Papers relate to the Committee. Included are pamphlet page proofs, press releases, newspaper clippings, and correspondence relating to the Tresca case. *Includes English.*

Tino, Edmond N.
Papers, 1916-1987. Ca. 2 linear ft.

Tino, a native of Torrington, CT, has held various offices in OSIA including Supreme Trustee (1977-1981), Grand Venerable of Connecticut (1973-1977), and Grand Financial Secretary (1969-1973). Collection consists of records of national, state, and local OSIA lodges. National records include Supreme Convention documents, Supreme Council minutes, correspondence, reports on the Cassino Orphanage and other projects. State lodge documents include Grand Convention minutes, booklets, Grand Council minutes, correspondence, and information on Columbus Day and other activities. *Mainly in English. In OSIA Guide.*

Todesco, Clementine (b. 1903).
Papers, n.d. Ca. 1.5 linear in.
(photocopies).

Todesco and her family came to
America from Faller, Italy, in 1930; they
settled in Detroit, MI. Papers consist of
folktales from northern Italy. The stories
were collected and translated into English
in 1940-1941 by Bruna Todesco,
Clementine's daughter. *In English.
Restricted: not to be reproduced without
permission of Wayne State University
Folklore Archives, which holds the
originals.*

Tognotti-Martin, Franca.
Papers, 1966-1987. 2 linear in.

Tognotti-Martin was born in Tuscany,
Italy, and eventually settled in Charleston,
WV, after coming to the United States.
She served the OSIA West Virginia
Grand Lodge as Grand Recording
Secretary (1977-1987).

Collection consists of OSIA West
Virginia Grand Lodge correspondence,
Grand Convention materials, local lodge
correspondence, and lists of officers and
members. Also included are a Supreme
Lodge directory and a Public Relations
Commission report. *In English. In OSIA
Guide.*

Toro, Anthony.
Collection, 1943-1980. 5 linear in.

Toro lived in Hartford, CT, and held
the office of Supreme Trustee in OSIA
(1957-1959, 1961-1965). Collection
consists of lists of officers, Grand Lodge
Convention information, miscellaneous
materials on Grand Lodge activities, and
correspondence. *Mainly in English. In
OSIA Guide.*

Tresca, Carlo (1879-1943).
Papers, n.d. 1 microfilm reel.

Tresca, an anarcho-syndicalist and
antifascist, was born in Salmona (Aquila),
Italy. He was active in the socialist
movement in Italy and in 1904 came to
the United States to avoid a prison
sentence. He was editor of *Il Proletario,
La Plebe, L'Avvenire,* and *Il Martello,*

and was a member of the Mazzini
Society. In 1912 he associated with the
Industrial Workers of the World (IWW)
in organizing the Lawrence textile
workers' strike. He continued that
association until 1916 when IWW leader
"Big Bill" Haywood accused him of
negotiating an improper deal with Iron
Range, MN, authorities to be released
from a homicide charge during the
Mesabi Iron Strike. Tresca was
imprisoned several times over the years
as he continued a passionate militancy
against Stalinism and Fascism. He was
assassinated in New York City in 1943.
The IHRC holds part one of a manuscript
biography of Tresca by Max Nomad,
*Carlo Tresca, Rebel without Uniform; The
Seed and the Seedling.*

Papers consist of an autobiography. *In
English. Related collections: Elizabeth
Gurley Flynn; Italian American,
Miscellaneous; and Norman Thomas.
Autobiography forms part of Tresca
Memorial Papers, New York Public
Library, Manuscript Division.*

Tummolillo, Ernesto (1879-1916).
Papers, ca. 1902-1977. Ca. 1 linear in.
(photocopies).

Tummolillo was a noted Neapolitan
playwright who came to the United States
in 1901. He also worked at the Ellis
Island Immigration Office in New York.

Papers consist of photocopies of a
biography written by his great grandson,
Gennaro Dispigno; correspondence;
photographs; Neapolitan songs; a play
written by Tummolillo; and newspaper
clippings. *Includes English; songs,
poetry, and play in Neapolitan dialect.*

Turco, Rev. Luigi (b. 1890).
Papers, ca. 1938-1968. Ca. 2 linear in.

Turco was born in Riesi, Sicily. He
came to the United States in 1913,
worked in shoe factories in Boston and
Wakefield, MA, and in 1915 converted to
the Italian Baptist Church. He attended
Colgate Theological Seminary and served
as pastor of Italian Baptist churches in
Passaic (NJ), Buffalo (NY), and Meriden
(CT). In the 1950s, Turco became
involved in the New Thought movement,

particularly Devine Science and Religious Science; he intended to start a church in Meriden based on New Thought principles.

Papers consist primarily of typed articles, manuscripts, and sermons pertaining to religion, philosophy, and other topics. *The Spiritual Autobiography of Luigi Turco*, edited, with an introductory memoir by Lewis Turco, is in the IHRC's Italian American book collection. *Includes English.*

Unity, Nobility and Ambition Society (Brooklyn, New York).
Records, ca. 1912-1935. 1 linear in.

The Society, a cultural organization, was founded in 1929 by a group of young second-generation Italian Americans to develop knowledge and appreciation of Italian culture. Records consist of a scrapbook of clippings, contracts, tickets, programs, essays, and issues of the Society's publication, *Nik Naks*. *Mainly in English.*

Valenti, Girolamo (1892-1958).
Papers, ca. 1904-1960. 2 microfilm reels.

Valenti was born in Valguarnera, Sicily, and came to the United States in 1911. A labor organizer for the Amalgamated Clothing Workers in the East, Valenti was also editor of several Italian American publications. In addition to labor activities, he edited the antifascist daily *Il Nuovo Mondo* (1925-1931), *La Stampa Libera*, *La Parola del Popolo* (New York), and *Parola dei Socialisti*, and also worked for the Italian American radio station WHAY (CT).

Papers include correspondence and published items, cartoons and caricatures by Fort Velona; photographs; newspaper clippings on fascism, socialism, and World War I; and materials pertaining to Arturo Giovannitti and New York politicians. *Includes English. Negatives in the Tamiment Library, New York University, which holds the Gerolamo Valenti papers.*

Vannelli, John Aloysius.
Papers, ca. 1923-1982. 4 linear ft.

Vannelli grew up in St. Paul, MN, and Scranton, PA. He was employed at the Zinsmaster Bakery in St. Paul and served in various union activities. In 1949, he became vice-president of the Bakers' Union. After retirement, he became a member of the Senior Citizens League and an active member of Stella del Nord chapter of the American Italian Historical Association.

Papers reflect Vannelli's avocation as a historian and collector of Italian Americana. Included are newspaper clippings pertaining to Italian American history, especially in Minnesota; annual reports, programs, and miscellany from Holy Redeemer Parish (St. Paul, MN); notebooks, including a biography of Vannelli's parents; a biography of Monsignor Louis Pioletti, poetry and historical research notes on the Italians in Minnesota; and a small quantity of personal material. *Mainly in English. Inventory available. Related collections: Monsignor Louis F. Pioletti; Holy Redeemer Church.*

Varalla, Charles R.
Papers, 1981-1987. 8 linear in.

Varalla has served the OSIA Florida Grand Lodge as Grand Venerable (1985-1987) and Grand Orator (1983-1985). Collection consists of materials pertaining to the OSIA Florida Grand Convention and Council, correspondence, notes and reports of the State Orator, and records committees and charities. Also included are records of two local Florida lodges. *In English. In OSIA Guide.*

Vecoli, Rudolph J.
Papers, ca. 1965-1980. 4 linear ft.

Personal and professional papers of Vecoli, director of the Immigration History Research Center since 1967, pertain significantly to the American Italian Historical Association. Also included are files on ethnic organizations, institutions, and conferences. *Mainly in English. Restricted: access requires written permission of donor.*

Velona, Fort (1893-1965).
Papers, 1919-1962. 8 linear in.

A prominent Italian American socialist active in the Amalgamated Clothing Workers of America, Velona was also well known for his caricatures and political cartoons. Papers contain correspondence, photographs, newspaper clippings, articles, cartoons, and publications. The bulk of the collection consists of originals of caricatures and cartoons dealing with domestic and international labor and politics. Issues of and clippings from *La Parola del Popolo* are also included. *Includes English.*

Viani, Angelo (1893-1974).
Papers, 1923-1970. 2 linear ft.

Viani was born in Bagnolo, Italy. He served OSIA as Grand Recording Secretary (1933-1955) and Grand Venerable (1953-1967) of the West Virginia Grand Lodge.
Collection includes financial records of the Mountaineer Building and Loan Association and OSIA materials including a national ritual book; correspondence, membership applications, and incorporation papers of the OSIA West Virginia Grand Lodge; and local officers' regalia. *Includes English. In OSIA Guide.*

Yarusso, Gentille R.
Papers, ca. 1977. Ca. 1 linear in.

Yarusso grew up in the Swede Hollow area of St. Paul, MN. He was a boys' adviser for the Christ Child Community Center and a rifle instructor in the Minnesota Small Arms Rifle Training Program.
Papers consist of autobiographical vignettes of his early life in Swede Hollow. *In English.*

Yellam, Michael.
Papers, 1967-1987. 4 linear in.

Yellam served as Grand Venerable of the OSIA Northwest Grand Lodge (1975-1979). Collection consists of OSIA Supreme Convention and Council material and commission reports; Northwest Grand Lodge convention books, constitution and bylaws, and materials relating to various Grand Lodge committees. Also included are booklets concerning activities of several local lodges. *In English. In OSIA Guide.*

Yona, David and Anna.
Papers, ca. 1971. 1 linear in.
(photocopies only).

David Yona (1901-1971) was born in Ivrea, in northern Italy; he and Anna were married in 1932 in Turin. They came to the United States in 1940, and lived in New York City. He was a civil engineer by profession and a frequent contributor of articles to the Italian American magazine *Controcorrente* during and after World War II.
Papers consist of two typed manuscripts of memoirs. David's memoirs cover his childhood in an Italian Jewish family through 1932; Anna's cover 1932-1945. Also included is a list of David's articles that appeared in *Controcorrente. In English.*

Zappulla, Giuseppe (b. 1901).
Papers, ca. 1927-1973. 1 linear ft.

Zappulla was born in Buccheri, Italy, and came to the United States in 1921. He edited and published several Italian American newspapers and magazines and wrote plays, essays, and speeches. He worked for *La Sicilia* (NY), *Il Corriere Italiano* (Wilkes-Barre, PA), *Corriere d'America* (NY), *Italamerican Magazine* (NY), and other newspapers.
Papers consist of Zappulla's writings in both published and manuscript form. Also included are reviews of his works, correspondence with prominent Italians and Italian Americans, and poems by Joseph Zappulla. Correspondents include Nino Caradonna, Arturo Giovannitti, and Joseph Tusiani. *Includes English. Inventory available. Related collection: Nino Caradonna.*

Wedding of Nick and Amelia Corbo, St. Paul, MN, 1913.

Primary school attended by Joseph Dellago, Virginia, MN, ca. 1900s.

Zattoni, Albino.
Papers, ca. 1930-1947. 3 linear in.

Zattoni was an antifascist. His papers contain correspondence and newspaper clippings pertaining to his fighting in the Spanish Civil War and to his volunteer work during World War II, when he re-educated captured Italian soldiers. Also included is a file of correspondence referring to the Mazzini Society. *Includes English and Spanish.*

Zuzolo, Peter R.
Papers, 1960-1987. 10 linear ft.

Zuzolo has been Second Assistant Supreme Venerable (1987-), Third Assistant Supreme Venerable (1985-1987), Supreme Treasurer (1981-1985), and New York Lodge Grand Venerable (1977-1981) of OSIA. Collection contains National Convention, Council and Foundation records and New York Grand Lodge Convention and Council materials, including reports of committees. Also included is correspondence relating to numerous local OSIA lodges in New York and particularly to Arturo Toscanini Lodge No. 2107 (East Northport, NY). Other materials relate to non-OSIA organizations, including the American Committee for Italian Migration, AMITA, the New York City Board of Education, and numerous other ethnic and heritage groups. *In English. In OSIA Guide.*

Monographs

The Italian American collection is one of the IHRC's largest, with ca. 1,400 items. Standard works in the field of Italian American immigration history are well represented; in addition to monographs, the collection includes a good number of unpublished dissertations. Books, tracts, and pamphlets, often issued by immigrant presses and in Italian, make up the larger part of the collection. They span a range of genre and subjects: autobiographies; plays; poetry; novels; and works dealing with politics and religion, often of a polemical nature. Among these are rare items such as Camillo Cianfarra's *Il diario di un emigrante* (The Diary of an Immigrant, 1904); Giuseppe Gaja's *Ricordi d'un giornalista errante* (Memoirs of a Wandering Journalist, ca. 1900); Luigi Carnevale's *Il giornalismo degli emigranti italiani nel Nord America* (The Journalism of the Italian Emigrants in North America, 1909); and biographical directories of Italians in Philadelphia, New Orleans, central New York State, and Connecticut (1907-1912), compiled by A. Frangini.

General bibliographies on Italian immigration include Centro Studi Emigrazione's *Primo Catalogo Generale della biblioteca del Centro Studi Emigrazione* (First General Catalog of the Library of the Center for Emigration Studies, 1967); Francesco Cordasco's Italian Americans: A Guide to Information Sources (1978) and Vittorio Briani and Francesco Cordasco's *Italian Immigrants Abroad: A Bibliography* (1979). These works include Italian-language sources. There are also specialized bibliographies noted below on religion, literature and the press.

Older studies include Robert F. Foerster's *The Italian Emigration of Our Times* (1919); Antonio Mangano's *Sons of Italy: a Social and Religious Study of the Italians in America* (1917); and Antonio Stella's Some Aspects of Italian Immigration to the United States (1924). In addition, the Center holds the published writings of the pioneer historian of Italian Americans, Giovanni E. Schiavo, including *The Italians in America before the Civil War* (1934); *Italian American History* (two volumes, 1947, 1949); and *Four Centuries of Italian-American History* (1958). Schiavo also compiled the *Italian-American Who's Who*, of which the IHRC has scattered volumes (I, 1935-XXI, 1966). More recent works include Leonard Covello's *The Social Background of the Italo-American School Child* (1967); Richard Gambino's *Blood of My Blood: The Dilemma of the Italian Americans* (1974); Luciano Iorizzo and Salvatore Mondello's *The Italian Americans* (1980); as well as volumes of collected essays: *Perspectives in Italian Immigration and Ethnicity* (1977), edited by Silvano M. Tomasi; *Italian Americans: New Perspectives in Italian Immigration and Ethnicity*, edited by Lydio F. Tomasi (1985); and the first volume (of three) of Fondazione Giovanni Agnelli's *EuroAmericani; La popolazione di origine italiane negli Stati Uniti* (The Population of Italian Origin in the United States, 1987).

In addition, the Center holds a full set of the published proceedings of conferences of the American Italian Historical Association; among these are *The Italian Immigrant Woman in North America* (1978); *Pane e Lavoro: The Italian American Workingclass* (Bread and Work, 1980); and *Italian Immigrants in Rural and Small Town America* (1987). Selections of documentary materials are contained in Wayne Moquin and Charles Van Doren's *A Documentary History of the Italian Americans* (1974); *WOP: A Documentary History of Anti-Italian Discrimination in the United States* (1973), compiled by Salvatore J. LaGuimina; and *The Italians: Social Backgrounds of an American Group* (1974), edited by Francesco Cordasco and Eugene Bucchioni.   Photographic histories include *A Portrait of the Italians in America* (1982), edited by Vincenza Scarpaci; and *Images: A Pictorial History of Italian Americans* (1981), from the Center for Migration Studies.

The majority of Italian immigrants settled in urban areas, and scholarship in the field reflects this. The collection contains numerous studies on the Italian experience in such cities as New York, Philadelphia, Chicago, Boston, and San Francisco. A collaborative work covering various cities is *Little Italies in North America* (1981), edited by Robert F. Harney and J. Vincenza Scarpaci. Among recent works are Dino Cinel's *From Italy to San Francisco: The Immigrant Experience* (1982); Donna Gabaccia's *From Sicily to Elizabeth Street* (1984); and Gary Mormino's *Immigrants on the Hill: Italian Americans in St. Louis, 1882-1982* (1986).

The press, although it has received relatively little attention from scholars, was a vital part of the Italian American community. The collection includes a comprehensive guide to Italian American periodicals, Pietro Russo's "Catalogo Collettivo della Stampa Periodica Italo-Americana, 1836-1980" (The Collective Catalog of the Italo-American Periodical Press, unpublished); as well as an overview of the Italian press abroad, Vittorio Briani's *La stampa italiana all'estero dalle origine ai nostri giorni* (The Italian Press Abroad from Its Origins to Our Times, 1977). Leonardo Bettini's *Bibliografia Dell'Anarchismo* (Bibliography of Anarchism, volume I, toma 1-2, 1972, 1976) and *The Immigrant Labor Press in North America, 1840s-1970s: An Annotated Bibliography*; volume three, *Migrants from Southern and Western Europe* (1987), edited by Dirk Hoerder, provide bibliographical data and locations of extant files of the anarchist, socialist, and labor press. In addition, the IHRC holds the personal papers of a number of newspaper editors and publishers as well as extensive files of newspapers and serials that reflect a broad spectrum of ideologies and interests. The role of Italian immigrants in labor and radical movements is the subject of *Gli italiani fuori d'Italia: Gli emigrati italiani nei movimenti operai dei paesi d'adozione, 1880-1940* (The Italians Outside of Italy: The Italian Emigrants in the Labor Movements of their Adopted Countries, 1982), edited by Bruno Bezza. Recent works are Gary R. Mormino and George Pozzetta's *The Immigrant World of Ybor City: Italians and their Latin Neighbors in Tampa, 1885-1985* (1987); and Donna Gabaccia's *Militants and Migrants: Rural Sicilians Become American Workers* (1988).

Labor and radical publications are a particular strength of the collection, which includes works by Armando Borghi, Luigi Galleani, Errico Malatesta, Arturo Giovannitti, Carlo Tresca, Vincenzo Vacirca, and Flavio Venanzi.   A major resource is the voluminous personal library of labor activist Anthony Capraro. These publications complement the Center's Italian American manuscript holdings and newspaper and serial collections, which are also rich in materials on labor, radical politics, and anti-Fascism. Works on Fascism and anti-Fascism include Gaetano Salvemini's *Italian Fascist Activities in the United States* (1977) and John P. Diggins's *Mussolini and Fascism: The View from America* (1982).

Literary works, in both Italian and English, comprise a substantial part of the collection. Italian Americans have been prolific writers of autobiographies, novels, and especially poetry.   Major authors represented include Nino Caradonna,   Riccardo Cordiferro, Jerre Mangione, and Pietro Di Donato. The Center's collection also includes many hard-to-find works that were published in limited editions, often by the authors themselves. Of particular interest are the farces in the Sicilian dialect about the character "Nofrio" by Giovanni De Rosalia, a noted humorist. Also available are secondary studies on Italian American writings: Olga Peragallo's annotated bibliography, *Italian American Authors and Their Contributions to American Literature* (1949), and Rose Basile Green's *The Italian American Novel; A Document of the Interaction of the Two Cultures* (1974). A useful collection is *The Dream Book: An Anthology of Writings by Italian American Women* (1985), edited by Helen Barolini.

Many of the publications are concerned with religion. A guide to this literature is *Italian Americans and Religion: An Annotated Bibliography* (1978), compiled by Silvano M. Tomasi and Edward Stibili. Missionary work among the Italians is well documented, particularly the activities of the Scalabrini fathers. A valuable selection of documents from the Order's archives are in *Storia della Congregazione Scalabriniana* (History of the Scalabrini Order, five volumes, 1969, 1973, 1973, 1974, 1975), edited by Mario Francesconi. Devotional works and catechisms complement the papers of several Italian priests. In addition, there is a sizable collection of jubilee and commemorative albums of Italian parishes. Protestant evangelism among the Italians is represented by a number of autobiographies and commentaries. Other publications, especially tracts, express the widespread anticlericalism among the immigrants.

As with other immigrant groups, fraternal organizations were an important part of Italian American community life. The collection holds a considerable number of constitutions of mutual aid societies as well as the minute books of several. Works on the history of the Order Sons of Italy in America (OSIA) include Baldo Aquilano's *L'Ordine Figli D'Italia in America* (The Order Sons of Italy in America, 1925) and Ernest Biagi's *The Purple Aster* (1961). The IHRC recently acquired more than 600 linear feet of archival material documenting this organization (see "Manuscript Collections"). These materials are described in *Guide to the Records of the Order Sons of Italy in America*, compiled by John Andreozzi (1989).

The Center's collection also includes numerous studies that look at the mass migration from Italy's point of view. The subject of remigration has been addressed by Francesco P. Cerase's *L'emigrazione di ritorno: innovazione o reazione?* (Return Migration: Innovation or Reaction? 1971) and Betty Boyd Caroli's *Italian Repatriation from the United States, 1900-1914* (ca. 1973). An especially important sourcebook for Italian emigration is Gianfausto Rosoli's *Un Secolo di Emigrazione Italiana, 1876-1976* (A Century of Italian Emigration, 1976). A documentary history of Italian emigration is A. Ciuffoletti and M. Degl'Innocenti's *L'Emigrazione nella Storia d'Italia, 1868-1975* (Emigration in the History of Italy, 1978). Francesco Cordasco's *Italian Mass Emigration: The Exodus of a Latin People* (1980) is a bibliographical guide to the *Bolletino dell'Emigrazione* (Emigration Bulletin), an important source of information published by Italy's Commissariato Generale dell'Emigrazione from 1902 to 1927. Also useful to the scholar are older periodicals such as *L'Emigrato Italiano* (The Italian Emigrant) and *Italica Gens* (Italic People) as well as current journals such as *Affari Sociali Internazionali* (International Social Affairs) and *Studi Emigrazione* (Emigration Studies), all listed in the serials section of this chapter.

Newspapers

Abruzzo-Molise, Rochester, NY (previously published in Pueblo, CO). Weekly (semi-weekly): 1926. (Microfilm: 1918-1923, 1926).

L'Adunata dei Refrattari (Gathering of the Recalcitrants), New York, NY. Monthly (semi-monthly, weekly): 1922-1971.

L'Agenda (The Agenda; previously titled **The National Italian American News**), Brooklyn, NY. Weekly (bi-weekly): 1971-1980, 1985. Includes English.

Alba Nuova (The New Dawn), New York, NY. Semi-monthly: 1922.

Albania, New York, NY. Monthly: 1936, 1938-1939.

America, St. Louis, MO. Monthly: 1942-1943. Includes English.

The American Citizen (previously titled **Il Risveglio**), Des Moines, IA. Weekly: 1923-1924, 1926-1972. Includes English.

The American Citizen, Memphis, TN. Weekly: 1934. Includes English.

The American Citizen, Omaha, NE. Semi-monthly: 1937, 1952, 1975, 1977-date.

L'Araldo (The Herald), Cleveland, OH. Weekly: 1948.

L'Araldo Italiano (The Italian Herald), New York, NY. Daily: 1912-1914.

L'Ascesa del Proletariato (The Rise of the Proletariat), Scranton, PA (previously published in Wilkes-Barre, PA). Frequency varies: 1908-1910. (Microfilm: 1908-1910).

L'Asino (The Donkey), New York, NY. Weekly: 1908-1910.

L'Aurora (The Dawn), Paterson, NJ. Bi-weekly. (Microfilm: 1899-1930).

L'Avvenire (The Future), Steubenville, OH. Weekly. (Microfilm: 1910).

L'Avvenire (The Future), New York, NY. Weekly. (Microfilm: 1916-1917).

L'Avvenire (The Future), Utica, NY. Weekly. (Microfilm: 1900-1905).

L'Azione (Action), New York, NY. Bi-weekly: 1941-1942.

Il Bollettino (Bulletin), New York, NY. Monthly: 1945-1951.

Bollettino della Sera (Evening Bulletin; merged with **Il Popolo**), New York, NY. Daily: 1923.

Bollettino dello Sciopero dei Sarti (The Tailors' Strike Bulletin), Chicago, IL. Weekly (?). (Microfilm: 1910).

The Boston Free Press, Boston, MA. Quarterly (monthly): 1960-1967. English.

The Bulletin, Middletown, CT. Weekly: 1948-1949. Includes English.

La Calabria (Calabria), New York, NY. Weekly: 1938.

La Capitale (Capital), Sacramento, CA. Weekly: 1938.

The Challenge, New York, NY. Irregular: 1970-1974. English.

Il Cittadino (The Citizen), New York, NY. Weekly: 1916. (Microfilm: 1915-1919).

The Colorado Leader, Denver, CO. Weekly: 1974-date. English.

Columbus, Denver, CO. Monthly: 1928-1929.

Il Commerciante Italiano (The Italian Merchant), New York, NY. Weekly: 1936, 1938.

The Connecticut Italian Bulletin, Hartford, CT. Monthly: 1972-1974. Includes English.

La Cooperazione (Cooperation), Barre, VT. Semi-monthly. (Microfilm: 1911).

Corriere Commerciale (Commercial Courier), New York, NY. Weekly: 1936.

Corriere d'America (American Courier), New York, NY. Daily: 1923-1940.

Il Corriere del Berkshire (The Berkshire Courier), Pittsfield, MA. Bi-monthly (weekly): 1969-1974.

Il Corriere di Chicago (The Chicago Messenger), Chicago, IL. Semi-monthly (weekly). (Microfilm: 1907, 1917).

Corriere Canadese (Canadian Courier), Toronto, Ontario, Canada. Daily (weekly): 1964-1971. Supplements Il Guerin Sportivo, 1970 and Il Tempo, 1965-1969.

Corriere de Trinidad (Trinidad Courier), Trinidad, CO. Weekly: 1919, 1934, 1941. Includes English.

Il Corriere del Popolo (The People's Messenger; absorbed L'Unione, Pueblo, CO), San Francisco, CA. Monthly (semi-weekly, weekly): 1935-1936, 1938-1940, 1942-1945, 1947-1954, 1957-1959, 1961-1962, 1965. (Microfilm: 1916-1962).

Corriere del Wisconsin (Wisconsin Courier), Milwaukee, WI. Weekly: 1927. Photocopy. Includes some English.

Corriere Illustrato (Illustrated Courier), Toronto, Ontario, Canada. Weekly: 1964-1969. Includes English.

Corriere Illustrato Il Tempo (Illustrated Courier, The Times; included as a supplement to Corriere Illustrato), Rome, Italy. Daily: 1965-1968.

Il Corriere Italiano (The Italian Courier), Milwaukee, WI. Monthly: 1938-1940.

Corriere Libertario (The Libertarian Courier), Barre, VT. Weekly. (Microfilm: 1914-1915).

Corriere Siciliano (Sicilian Courier), New York, NY. Weekly: 1938.

Il Crociato (The Crusader), Brooklyn, NY. Weekly: 1962-1973. Includes English.

La Cronaca Illustrata (The Illustrated Chronicle), New York, NY. Weekly: 1945.

Cronaca Sovversiva (The Subversive Chronicle), Lynn, MA. Weekly. (Microfilm: 1903-1919, 1933).

Il Diritto (The Right), New York, NY. Frequency varies. (Microfilm: 1918-1919).

La Donna Italiana (The Italian Woman), New York, NY. Monthly: 1937-1938.

The Echo (previously titled The Italian Echo), Providence, RI. Weekly: 1961, 1965-1968, 1971, 1974, 1978, 1984-1985, 1987-date. English.

L'Eco d'Italia (Echo of Italy; merged with L'Italo-Americano, Los Angeles, CA), San Francisco, CA. Weekly: 1968-1970, 1974.

L'Eco d'Italia (Echo of Italy), New York, NY. Weekly. (Microfilm: 1862-1894).

L'Era Nuova (New Age), Paterson, NJ. Weekly. (Microfilm: 1908-1909).

La Fiaccola (The Torch), Buffalo, NY. Weekly. (Microfilm: 1909-1912).

Florida Italian Bulletin, Fort Lauderdale, FL. Monthly: 1973-1974. Includes English.

La Follia di New York (The New York Folly), New York, NY. Monthly (bi-weekly): 1907-1911, 1914-1924, 1926-1928, 1934-1954. (Microfilm: 1907-1911, 1914-1924, 1926-1928, 1934-1946). Includes English.

The Forum, Baltimore, MD. Monthly (bi-monthly): 1973-1988. English.

Forze Nuove (New Forces), Downsview, Ontario, Canada. Bi-weekly: 1976. Includes English.

Fra Noi (Between Us), Chicago, IL. Monthly: 1960-date. English.

La Frusta (The Whip), Denver, CO. Weekly: 1920-1922. Includes English.

La Gazzetta (The Gazette), Windsor, Ontario, Canada. Bi-weekly: 1979-date. Includes English.

La Gazzetta Italiana (The Italian Gazette), Salt Lake City, UT. Weekly: 1913.

Gazzetta Italiana (Italian Gazette), Seattle, WA. Weekly: 1947-1952.

Gazzetta del Massachusetts (Massachusetts Gazette), Boston, MA. Weekly. (Microfilm: 1903-1905, 1907-1911, 1915-1960).

Il Gazzettino (The Little Gazette), Boston, MA. Monthly: 1929.

Germinal! Messina, Italy. (Microfilm: 1906).

Il Giornale di Chicago (The Chicago Journal), Chicago, IL. Daily. (Microfilm: 1916).

Il Giornale Italiano (The Italian Journal), New York, NY. Monthly: 1910-1912.

Il Giornale di Toronto (The Toronto Journal), Toronto, Ontario, Canada. Weekly: 1967. (Microfilm: 1967-1975). Includes English.

Giornale L'Italia (Italy Journal), San Francisco, CA. Daily: 1908.

Giovinezza (Youth), Boston, MA. Weekly: 1924.

Giuseppe Garibaldi, Philadelphia, PA. 1907. (Microfilm: 1907).

Giustizia (Justice), Jersey City, NJ (New York, NY). Monthly (weekly): 1930-1935, 1938, 1957-1958, 1968, 1974. (Microfilm: 1919-1946).

La Giustizia (Justice), Reggio Emilia, Italy. Weekly: 1954.

La Giustizia (Justice), Rome, Italy. Daily: 1954.

La Gogna (The Pillory), Kensington, IL. Monthly (?): 1909. (Microfilm: 1909).

Golden Lion, Bethpage, NY. Bi-monthly: 1964-1965, 1970-1988. English.

Grand Ledger, Flint, MI. Quarterly: 1983-1987. English.

Il Grido del Popolo (The Cry of the People), Denver, CO., and Rock Springs, WY. Weekly: 1907.

Il Grido della Folla (The Cry of the Crowd), Milan, Italy. Weekly: 1905. (Microfilm: 1905).

Il Grido della Folla (The Cry of the Crowd), New York, NY. Semi-monthly. (Microfilm: 1916).

Il Grido della Stirpe (The Cry of the Ancestry), New York, NY. Weekly: 1923-1925, 1934-1936, 1940.

Hill 2000, St. Louis, MO. Monthly: 1973-1984. English.

Incontro (Meeting), Boston, MA. Monthly: 1972-1976.

L'Independente (The Independent), Hancock, MI. Weekly: 1917.

L'Internazionale (The International), Boston, MA. Weekly. (Microfilm: 1917).

Intesa Libertaria (Libertarian Alliance), New York, NY. Weekly: 1939.

Iron County News (previously titled **La Nostra Terra**), Hurley, WI. Weekly. (Microfilm 1904-1950). Includes English.

L'Italia (Italy), Chicago, IL. Weekly, tri-weekly, daily: 1957, 1959-1960, 1963. (Microfilm: 1886-1899, 1901-1918).

L'Italia Letteraria (Literary Italy), New York, NY. Weekly: 1908.

L'Italia Libera (Free Italy), New York, NY. Monthly: 1943, 1945-1946.

L'Italia Nostra (Our Italy), Brooklyn, NY. Weekly. (Microfilm: 1915-1916).

Italian-American Digest, New Orleans, LA. Quarterly: 1981-1982. English.

The Italian Bulletin, Hartford, CT. Monthly: 1978, 1980-1981. Includes English.

The Italian News, Boston, MA. Weekly: 1921-1923, 1925-1965. English.

The Italian Observer, Rome, Italy. Weekly: 1948. Includes English.

Italian Press, Utica, NY. Weekly. (Microfilm: 1930-1931). Includes English.

The Italian Times, Milwaukee, WI. Monthly: 1979-1980, 1982-1984, 1986-date. Includes English.

Italian Tribune News (previously titled **Italian Tribune**) Newark, NJ. Weekly: 1941-1957, 1965-1974. English.

The Italian Tribune of America (previously titled **La Tribuna Italiana de America**), Detroit, MI. Weekly: 1965-1970. Includes English.

The Italian Weekly, Rochester, NY. Weekly: 1947-1949.

L'Italiano (The Italian), Denver, CO. Weekly: 1912.

L'Italo-Americano (The Italian American), New Orleans, LA. Daily. (Microfilm: 1899). Includes English.

L'Italo-Americano (The Italian American; merged with **L'Eco d'Italia**), San Francisco, CA. Weekly: 1957, 1959, 1962-1965, 1967-1970, 1974, 1978-1980, 1982-date.

Italo-American Times, Bronx, NY. Bi-monthly: 1964-1977. English.

Il Lavoratore (The Worker), Chicago, IL. Daily: 1924. (Microfilm: 1924-1925).

Il Lavoratore (The Worker), New York, NY. Weekly: 1924-1927.

Il Lavoratore (The Worker), Toronto, Ontario, Canada. Semi-monthly. (Microfilm: 1935-1938).

Il Lavoratore del Mare (The Seaman), New York, NY. Monthly: 1945-1946.

Il Lavoratore Italiano (The Italian Worker), Pittsburg, KS. Weekly, tri-monthly, semi-monthly: 1908-1909. (Microfilm: 1906-1928).

Il Lavoratore Italiano (The Italian Worker), Trinidad, CO. Weekly: 1904. (photocopy)

Il Lavoro (Labor), New York, NY. Weekly: 1922-1924. (Microfilm: 1917-1932).

La Legione (The Legion), New York, NY. Semi-monthly: 1942-1943.

Il Leone (The Lion), San Francisco, CA. Monthly: 1969-1978. (Microfilm: 1929-1930, 1932, 1934-1988).

La Libera Parola (Free Word), Philadelphia, PA. Weekly: 1923, 1940-1941, 1945-1949. Includes English.

Il Libertario (The Libertarian), La Spezia, Italy. Weekly: 1903, 1905. (Microfilm: 1903).

The Lion's Roar, Cleveland, OH. Bi-annual (3 times a year, annual): 1974-1986. English.

La Lotta (The Struggle), New York, NY. Weekly: 1909. (Microfilm: 1909).

Lotta di Classe (Class Struggle), New York, NY. Weekly: 1927. (Microfilm: 1912, 1914-1918).

La Luce (The Light; title varies: **La Luce Il Pensiero**), Utica, NY. Weekly. (Microfilm: 1901-1921).

Le Madonie, Castelbuono, Italy. Semi-monthly: 1950-1953.

Il Martello (The Hammer), New York, NY. Bi-weekly. (Microfilm: 1922-1925, 1927, 1935-1946).

Mastro Paolo (Master Paolo), Philadelphia, PA. Weekly. (Microfilm: 1903).

Il Messaggero (The Messenger), Utica, NY. Weekly: 1925.

Il Messaggiero dell'Ordine (The Messenger), Utica, NY. Weekly. (Microfilm: 1936-1948).

The Messenger (previously titled **Il Piccolo Messaggero, Il Messaggero**), Kansas City, KS. Bi-monthly, monthly. (Microfilm: 1926-1965). Includes English.

Il Minatore Italiano (The Italian Miner), Laurium and Calumet, MI. Daily. (Microfilm: 1915-1916).

Il Mondo (The World), New York, NY. Daily: 1941. Includes English page.

Il Movimento (The Movement), Chicago, IL . Weekly. (Microfilm: 1916).

Nazioni Unite (The United Nations), New York, NY. Semi-monthly: 1940, 1943-1946. Includes English.

Northwest Italian News, Seattle, WA. Monthly: 1970-1971, 1973, 1977-1988. (Microfilm: 1961-1988). English.

La Notizia (The News), Boston, MA. Daily: 1950. (Microfilm: 1916-1918).

La Nuova Capitale (The New Capital), Trenton, NJ. Monthly: 1969-1975.

Il Nuovo Mondo (The New World), New York, NY. Daily: 1927, 1931.

Il Nuovo Vessillo (The New Flag), New York, NY. Weekly (?): 1923, 1925, 1944.

'O Scugnizzo (Little Rascal), New York, NY. Weekly: 1938.

L'Operaia (The Working Woman), New York, NY. Weekly. (Microfilm: 1913-1919).

L'Operaio Italiano (The Italian Worker), Paris, France. Monthly: 1935-1936, 1938-1939.

L'Opinione della Domenica (The Sunday Opinion), Philadelphia, PA. (Microfilm: 1916-1918).

Ordine Figli d'Italia in America Bollettino Ufficiale (Official Bulletin of the Order Sons of Italy in America; changed to magazine format in 1922), New York, NY. Monthly (weekly): 1916-1917. (Microfilm: 1918, 1920).

Ordine Nuovo (The New Order), New York, NY. Bi-weekly (?): 1941. Includes English.

Ordine Nuovo (The New Order), Philadelphia, PA. Weekly: 1936-1941, 1946-1947, 1957.

OSIA News (official organ of the Supreme Lodge, Order Sons of Italy in America), Webster and Worcester, MA. Monthly: 1948, 1952, 1972-1988. (Microfilm: 1947-1971). Includes English.

Il Paese (The Country), Philadelphia, PA. Monthly: 1939-1940.

La Parola (The Word; title changes to La Parola del Popolo (The Word of the People) and paper assumes magazine format in 1951), New York, NY (previously published in Chicago, IL). Weekly: 1922, 1933, 1936, 1938-1940.

La Parola degli Italiani in America (The Word of the Italians in America), Los Angeles, CA. Weekly: 1938, 1940-1941.

La Parola dei Socialisti (The Socialists' Word), Chicago, IL. Weekly: 1908-1911, 1913.

La Parola Proletaria (The Proletarian Word), Chicago, IL. Weekly. (Microfilm: 1916-1917).

Il Pensiero (The Thought), St. Louis, MO. Semi-monthly: 1926, 1929, 1933, 1943, 1947, 1952, 1974-date. Includes English.

Il Pensiero Italiano (Italian Thought; title changes to La Colonia, 1927), Utica, NY. Weekly. (Microfilm: 1914-1929). Includes English.

La Plebe (The Populace), Philadelphia, PA. Weekly. (Microfilm: 1907-1908).

Il Popolo (The People), New York, NY. Weekly (?): 1922, 1938. Includes English.

Il Popolo (The People; Italian Independent Newspaper), Philadelphia, PA. Weekly: 1905-1906. (Microfilm: 1905-1906).

Il Popolo Italiano (The Italian People), Atlantic City, NJ (previously published in Philadelphia, PA). Monthly (weekly, daily): 1939, 1947, 1958, 1963-1966, 1969-date. Includes English.

Post Gazette (supersedes La Gazetta del Massachusetts), Boston, MA. Weekly. 1944-1945, 1947-1952, 1969-date. (Microfilm: 1903-1905, 1907-1911, 1915-1960). English.

Il Progresso Italo-Americano (Italian-American Progress), New York, NY. Daily: 1915-1930, 1932-1934, 1943, 1947-1951, 1961, 1965-1966, 1969-1977, 1979, 1981-1982.

Il Proletario (The Proletarian), Boston, MA. Weekly. (Microfilm: 1918).

Il Proletario (The Proletarian; title varies: La Difesa; Il Nuovo Proletario), Chicago, IL (previously published in New York, NY). Weekly (irregular): 1899-1946. (Microfilm: 1899-1946).

La Propaganda (Propaganda), Chicago, IL. Weekly. (Microfilm: 1908).

La Questione Sociale (The Social Question), Paterson, NJ. Bi-weekly. (Microfilm: 1895-1916).

Il Ribelle (The Rebel), New York, NY. 1939.

Il Rinnovamento (The Renewal), Nyack, NY. Bi-monthly: 1925.

Il Riscatto (Redemption), Chicago, IL. Semi-monthly. (Microfilm: 1914).

Il Risveglio (The Awakening), Denver, CO. Weekly: 1906-1911, 1914-1915, 1917, 1920-1924, 1927-1936, 1938-1939, 1941, 1949. (Microfilm: 1915-1917).

Il Risveglio (The Awakening), Dunkirk, NY. Weekly: 1935-1938.

Roma (Rome), Denver, CO. Weekly: 1908-1910, 1913-1915, 1921.

La Scopa (The Broom), Paterson, NJ. Weekly. (Microfilm: 1926-1928).

Secolo Nuovo (New Century), San Francisco, CA. Weekly. (Microfilm: 1903).

La Sentinella (The Sentry), Bridgeport, CT. Weekly: 1940, 1947.

Il Sole (The Sun), Toronto, Ontario, Canada. Weekly: 1970.

Il Sole Illustrato (The Illustrated Sun; merger of **Il Sole** and **Corriere Illustrato**), Toronto, Ontario, Canada. Weekly: 1970.

Sons of Italy Herald, Cherry Hill, NJ. Bi-monthly: 1974, 1976-1977, 1980-1988. English.

Sons of Italy News, Boston, MA. Monthly: 1929.

Sons of Italy Times, Philadelphia, PA. Weekly: 1964-date. (Microfilm: 1960-1965, 1967-1974). Includes English.

La Stampa (The Press), Salt Lake City, UT. Weekly: 1926. Includes English.

La Stampa Libera (The Free Press), New York, NY. Daily: 1931-1938.

La Stampa Unita (The United Press), Rochester, NY. Weekly. (Microfilm: 1923-1933).

La Stella (The Star), Utica, NY. Weekly. (Microfilm: 1932-1933). Includes English.

Sunshine News, St. Petersburg, FL. Monthly: 1971, 1973-1974, 1981. English.

Lo Svegliarino (The Little Alarm Clock), Seattle, WA. Monthly: 1959-1962, 1965-1968. (Microfilm: 1947-1961). English.

La Terra (The Earth), Stockton, CA. Weekly. (Microfilm: 1907).

La Tribuna (The Tribune), Stamford, CT. Monthly: 1947, 1950-1952.

La Tribuna del Popolo (The People's Tribune), Boston, MA. Weekly. (Microfilm: 1915).

La Tribuna del Popola (The People's Tribune; previously titled **La Tribuna Italiana d'America**, and **La Tribuna Italiana del Michigan**), Detroit, MI. Weekly: 1947-1952, 1970-1977. (Microfilm: 1909-1911, 1913-1921, 1923-1969).

La Tribuna di Utica (The Utica Tribune), Utica, NY. Weekly. (Microfilm: 1912).

La Tribuna Italiana (The Italian Tribune), Milwaukee, WI. Monthly. (Microfilm: 1941-1967). Includes English.

La Tribuna Italiana Transatlantica (The Transatlantic Italian Tribune), Chicago, IL. Weekly: 1907, 1923.

Il Tribuno (The Tribune), Newark, NJ. Weekly. (Microfilm: 1908).

The Trumpet (La Tromba), Denver, CO. Weekly: 1935-1942. English.

Unione (Union), Pittsburgh, PA. Weekly: 1972.

L'Unione (Union), Pueblo, CO. Weekly: 1907-1908, 1014, 1922, 1924-1926, 1934-1935, 1937-1938, 1940-1947. (Microfilm: 1897-1900, 1916-1917, 1921-1927, 1931-1934).

L'Unione Mondiale (The Worldwide Union), Rome, Italy. Semi-monthly: 1947.

L'Unità (Unity), New York, NY. Monthly: 1971-1972.

L'Unità Operaia (Working-class Unity; continues as a serial, 1938), New York, NY. Semi-monthly: 1935-1938.

L'Unità del Popolo (Unity of the People), New York, NY. Monthly, weekly: 1939-1949. (Microfilm: 1940-1951). Includes English.

University Press (previously titled **The West Des Moines Press**), Des Moines, IA. Weekly: 1936-1969. English.

Vaco 'e Pressa (In a Hurry), New York, NY. Weekly: 1935.

Il Vallo (The Rampart), Salerno, Italy. Monthly: 1947.

La Vera Redenzione (The True Redemption), Bridgeport, CT. Frequency varies. (Microfilm: 1917).

Il Vesuvio (Vesuvius), Philadelphia, PA. Weekly. (Microfilm: 1896).

Il Vindice (The Avenger; changes to magazine in 1927), Pueblo, CO. Weekly: 1907-1909, 1911, 1913-1915, 1917, 1919-1920, 1922-1924, 1927-1928. Includes English after 1926.

Vita Nuova (New Life), Rock Springs, WY. Weekly: 1908-1909.

La Vittoria (Victory), New York, NY. 1940.

La Vittoria (Victory), Toronto, Ontario, Canada. Weekly. (Microfilm: 1942-1943). Includes English section.

La Voce (The Voice), Newington, CT (Harwinton, CT). Monthly: 1973-1974. Includes English.

La Voce (The Voice), Rincón, Argentina. Monthly: 1956.

La Voce del Popolo (The Voice of the People), Dearborn, MI. Weekly: 1964, 1969-1970. Includes English.

La Voce del Popolo (The Voice of the People), San Francisco, CA. Weekly, semi-weekly, daily. (Microfilm: 1868-1905).

La Voce del Popolo Italiano (The Voice of the Italian People), Cleveland, OH. Weekly, daily. (Microfilm: 1909-1922). Includes English section.

La Voce della Colonia (The Voice of the Colony), Philadelphia, PA. Weekly. (Microfilm: 1896).

La Voce dell'Emigrante (The Voice of the Emigrant), Kansas City, MO. Weekly: 1915. Includes English.

La Voce degli Italo-Canadesi (The Voice of Italian Canadians), Toronto, Ontario, Canada. Weekly. (Microfilm: 1938-1940).

La Voce d'Italia (The Voice of Italy), Brooklyn, NY. Weekly: 1947.

La Voce Indipendente (The Independent Voice), Philadelphia, PA. Monthly (?): 1938.

La Voce Italiana (The Italian Voice), Paterson, NJ. Weekly: 1982-date.

Voce Italiana (Italian Voice), Washington, DC. Monthly: 1975-1986. Includes English.

Voce Libertarià (Libertarian Voice), New York, NY. 1972.

The Voice of Italy, New York, NY. Weekly: 1935-1936. Includes English.

Serials

ACIM Dispatch (American Committee on Italian Migration), New York, NY. Frequency varies: 1952-1968, 1971-1973. English.

ACIM Newsletter (American Committee on Italian Migration), New York, NY. Frequency varies: 1969-1970, 1972-1976, 1978-date. English.

Affari Sociali Internazionali (International Social Relations), Milan, Italy. Quarterly: 1973, 1984-1987.

Alba Nuova (The New Dawn), New York, NY. Monthly: 1921.

L'Alba Sociale (The Social Dawn), Ybor City-Tampa, FL. Bi-weekly. (Microfilm: 1901).

L'Allarme (The Alarm), Sommerville, MA. Frequecy varies. (Microfilm: 1916).

Almanacco Enciclopedico Personeni (Encyclopedic Almanac Personeni), New York, NY/San Francisco, CA. Annual: 1930.

Almanacco Sociale Italo Americano (Italian American Social Almanac), Chicago, IL. Annual: 1924 (English section)-1925.

Almanacco Sovversivo (Subversive Almanac), Barre, VT. Annual: 1906-1907.

America (previously titled **La Frusta**), Denver, CO. Monthly: 1923-1924.

America, St. Louis, MO. Monthly: 1942-1943. Includes English.

America-Italy Newsletter, New York, NY. Quarterly: 1955-1978, 1983. English.

America-Italy Society Inc. Memo, New York, NY. Three issues per year: 1977-1978. English.

American Italian Historical Association (AIHA) Newsletter, Brooklyn, NY (place of publication varies). Frequency varies: 1967-1968, 1970, 1972-1975, 1977-1983, 1985 (one undated issue). English.

American-Italian Historical Association Central Jersey Chapter Newsletter, Princeton, NJ. Monthly: 1981. English.

American Italian Historical Association Central New York Chapter Newsletter, Morrisville, NY. Bi-monthly: 1985-date. English.

American Italian Historical Association Maryland, Washington, DC. Chapter Newsletter, Baltimore, MD. Quarterly (?): 1977. English.

American Italian Historical Association Midwest Regional Chapter Newsletter, Chicago, IL. Quarterly: 1980. English.

American Italian Historical Association Western Chapter Newsletter, San Franscisco, CA. Quarterly: 1978-date. English.

Americans of Italian Descent, Inc. (AID) News, New York, NY. Frequency varies: 1968-1969. English.

AMITA (American Italian Achievements), New York, NY. Annual: 1977, 1979, 1981. English.

L'Anarchia (Anarchy), New York, NY. Monthly (?): (Microfilm: 1918). Includes some English.

L'Anarchico (The Anarchist), New York, NY. Monthly. (Microfilm: 1888).

Antonion (Society of St. Anthony of Padua), St. Paul, MN. Frequency varies: 1983-date. English.

L'Appello (The Call), Cleveland, OH. Monthly. (Microfilm: 1917).

Arba Sicula; Sicilian Language Folklore and Literary Review, Brooklyn, NY. Annual: 1979-1980, 1983-1984, 1986. Includes English.

L'Asino (The Donkey), Rome, Italy. Weekly: 1901-1908, 1917, 1919-1922.

Association of Italian-Canadian Writers Newsletter, Edmonton, Alberta, Canada. Monthly: 1987. English.

Attenzione (Attention), New York, NY. Bi-monthly: 1979-date. English.

L'Aurora (The Dawn), Brooklyn, NY. Monthly: 1924.

L'Aurora (The Dawn), Utica, NY. Weekly, semi-monthly. (Microfilm: 1928-1929). Includes English.

L'Avvenire (The Future), New York, NY. Bi-weekly: 1943.

Balilla, Lynn, MA. Semi-monthly. (Microfilm: 1912).

The Beacon (previously titled The East Side Journal and The Mayfield Herald), Cleveland, OH. Monthly: 1933. Includes English.

Bollettino della Giunta Cattolica Italiana per L'Emigrazione (Bulletin of the Italian Catholic Committee for Emigration), Rome, Italy. Monthly: 1951-1952, 1964.

Il Bollettino Italiano (The Italian Bulletin), Chicago, IL. Monthly: 1957-1958. Includes English.

Bollettino Quindicinale dell'Emigrazione (Biweekly Emigration Bulletin), Milan, Italy. Bi-weekly: 1949-1953.

The Bridge, St. Paul, MN. Quarterly: 1944-1945. English.

Il Caffe (The Cafe), Sacramento, CA. Bi-monthly: 1981-1982.

Calendario Civile (Civic Calendar), Chicago, IL. Annual: 1954.

Il Carroccio (The Italian Review), New York, NY. Monthly: 1915-1916, 1920-1925, 1930-1932. Includes English.

Casa Italiana Newsletter (Columbia University), New York, NY. Frequency varies: 1966, 1971, 1975-1977. English.

Center of Italian-American Studies, Brooklyn, NY. Quarterly: 1980. English.

La Cisilute, Rexdale, Ontario, Canada. Quarterly (?): 1976.

Columbus (previously titled Corriere Italo-Americano), New York, NY. Monthly: 1917-1924, 1928. Includes English.

Columbus Day Souvenir Program, San Francisco, CA. Annual: 1971, 1973, 1976, 1978-1980. English.

Comitato Italiano per la Storia Americana Bollettino (Italian Committee for American History Bulletin), Florence, Italy. Annual: 1976.

Comparè, New York, NY. Monthly: 1976. English.

Il Compasso (The Compass), Chicago, IL. Monthly: 1954.

La Comune (The Commune), Philadelphia, PA. Monthly. (Microfilm: 1911-1915).

Congress of Italian-American Organizations, Inc. (CIAO) Reports, New York, NY. Frequency varies: 1972-1977. English.

Controcorrente (Countercurrent), Boston, MA. Monthly: 1938-1951. (English section 1939-1945).

Controcorrente: Rivista di Critica e di Battaglia (Countercurrent: Magazine of Criticism and Battle), Boston, MA. Bi-monthly: 1963-1964.

Il Contro-Pelo (Counterpoint), Barre, VT. Monthly. (Microfilm: 1911-1912).

Il Convito (The Banquet), Bronx, NY. Monthly: 1926-1927.

Il Co-operatore (The Cooperator; Official Organ of the Pueblo Cooperative Association Mercantile Co.), Pueblo, CO. Bi-monthly: 1918-1919. (Microfilm: 1918-1919).

Dante, New York, NY. Monthly: 1940. Includes English.

I Diritti dell'Uomo (The Rights of Man), Rome, Italy. Quarterly (?): 1952.

Divagando (Wandering), New York, NY. Weekly: 1952, 1955-1957.

Due Mondi (Two Worlds), New York, NY. Monthly: 1979.

East End Journal (previously titled **East Side Journal**; consolidated with **La Zotta** in 1939) Cleveland, OH. Monthly: 1933-1939. Includes English.

Eighth Annual Report of the Italian Culture Council, Inc., Newark, NJ. Annual: 1971.

L'Emigrato Italiano (The Italian Emigrant; previously titled **L'Emigrato Italiano in America** and **Le Missioni Scalabriniane**), Bassano del Grappa, Italy (previously published in Rome, Italy). Monthly: 1914-1920, 1944-1946, 1953, 1961-1977.

Fairmount News, St. Louis, MO. Monthly: 1939-1942. Includes English.

Fiori e Sorrisi Italici (Italic Flowers and Smiles), New York, NY. Semi-monthly: 1914.

Fioritura Nova (New Flowering), Brooklyn, NY. Weekly: 1919.

La Follia di New York (The New York Folly), New York, NY. Monthly: 1934-1935, 1939, 1955, 1958-1971, 1982-date. Includes English.

Fratellanza News, St. Louis, MO. Monthly: 1971-1975. English.

Friends of Danilo Dolci, Inc., Philadelphia, PA (previously published in New York, NY). Monthly: 1971-1973, 1975, 1983. English.

La Gazzetta Legale Italo-Americana (The Italo-American Legal Gazette; previously titled **La Gazzetta del Notaio Italo-Americano**), New York, NY. Monthly: 1951. Includes English.

Il Gazzettino (The Little Gazette), South San Francisco, CA. Frequency varies: 1973-1979. Includes English.

Germinal, Chicago, IL. Monthly. (Microfilm: 1913).

Il Giornalino (The Little Daily), Albuquerque, NM. Monthly: 1975, 1977-1979, 1981. Includes English.

Il Giornalino (The Little Daily), Middlebury, VT. Monthly: 1979-1983.

Giovinezza (Youth), New York, NY. Monthly: 1932.

Guardia Rossa (The Red Guard), New York, NY. Occasional: 1920.

Guida Pratica della Parrocchia Italiana del SS. Redentore (Practical Guide of the Italian Parish of the Holy Redeemer), St. Paul, MN. 1909. Includes English.

I-Am, New York, NY. Monthly: 1976-1977. Includes English.

L'Idea (The Idea), New York, NY. Semi-monthly: 1923.

Identity, New York, NY. Monthly: 1977. English.

L'Indipendente (Independent Order Sons of Italy), New York, NY. 1924.

L'Informatore per l'Emigrante (The Emigrant's Adviser), Rome, Italy. Monthly: 1922-1928.

International Lyric Courier, New York, NY. Monthly: 1949-1950. Includes English.

L'Internazionale (The International), Philadelphia, PA. Semi-monthly. (Microfilm: 1909).

Istituto di Studi Americani, Comitato di Coordinamenta per gli Studi di Storia Americana Bollettino (Bulletin of the Coordinating Committee for American History Studies, Institute of American Studies), Florence, Italy. Monthly (?): 1972.

Istituto Italiano di Cultura Newsletter (Italian Cultural Institute Newsletter), New York, NY. Quarterly: 1970-1978. English.

Italamerican, New York, NY. Monthly: 1954-1955, 1967-1968. Includes English.

The Italian, Miami, FL. Monthly: 1971, 1974. English.

Italian American Coalition Newsletter, New York, NY. Monthly: 1972. English.

Italian American Digest, New Orleans, LA. Quarterly: 1974-1983, 1987. English.

Italian American Family Scene, San Francisco, CA. Monthly: 1975-1976. Includes English.

Italian American Federation of the East Bay Columbus Celebration, Oakland, CA. Annual: 1979. English.

Italian American Review, Brooklyn, NY. Monthly: 1967, 1976. English.

Italian American Review, New York, NY. Weekly: 1921-1922. Includes English.

Italian Americana, Buffalo, NY. Semi-annual: 1975-1976, 1979, 1981. English.

Italian Canadiana, Toronto, Ontario, Canada. Quarterly (?): 1985. Includes French and English.

Italian Chamber of Commerce Bulletin, Chicago, IL. Bi-monthly, monthly: 1957-1959, 1968-1970. (Microfilm: 1908-1921). Includes English.

Italian Chamber of Commerce Almanac, New York, NY. Annual: 1932-1933. Includes English.

Italian Cultural Society, Sacramento, CA. Quarterly (?): 1982, 1985. English.

Italian Culture Council, Inc. Bulletin, New York, NY. Monthly: 1965-1972. English.

Italian Heritage Newsletter, Rowayton, CT. Monthly: 1969-1975. English.

Italian Intercollegiate Review, New York, NY. Monthly: 1923. English.

Italian Monthly (previously titled **Canale Tre**), New York, NY. Monthly: 1978-1980. English.

The Italian Times, Milwaukee, WI. Monthly: 1979, 1982. English.

The Italian Professional Man, New York, NY. Annual: 1937-1938. English.

Italian Social Science Center Newsletter, Flushing, NY. Frequency varies: 1973. English.

The Italian Young Folks League of America Bulletin, Brooklyn, NY. Monthly: 1925-1933. English.

Italiani nel Mondo (Italians in the World), Rome, Italy. Bi-weekly: 1945-1953, 1969.

Italica Gens (Italic People), Turin, Italy. Frequency varies: 1910-1916.

L'Italico (The Italic), Portland, OR. Weekly: 1913.

Italo American National Union (I.A.N.U.) Bulletin, Mount Morris, IL. Bi-monthly: 1967. English.

Italo American National Union Newsletter, Melrose Park, IL (previously published in Chicago, IL). Monthly: 1978-1985. English.

Italo Canadian Commercial Directory, Toronto, Ontario, Canada. Annual: 1967. Includes English.

Italy. Commisariato dell'Emigrazione. Bolletino dell'Emigrazione (Office of the Commissioner of Emigration. Emigration Bulletin), Rome, Italy. Monthly. (Microfilm: 1902-1927).

Italy. Ministero degli Affari Esteri. Direzione Generale dell'Emigrazione. Notiziario dell'Emigrazione (Ministry of Foreign Affairs. General Directorate of Emigration. Emigration News), Rome, Italy. 1953.

Italy. Ufficio Centrale per l'Emigrazione Italiana Bollettino (Bulletin of the Central Office for Italian Emigration), Rome, Italy. Monthly: 1968.

Italy America Monthly, New York, NY. Monthly: 1934-1935. English.

Italy and Us, Washington, DC. Bi-monthly: 1979-1980. English.

Italy Italy, Long Island City, NY. Monthly: 1984. English.

Joint Civic Committee of Italian Americans Update (previously titled **Joint Civic Committee of Italian Americans Newsletter**), Chicago, IL. Frequency varies: 1975-1980, 1982-1983. English.

The Justinian Law Journal, Chicago, IL. Frequency varies: 1964-1974, 1976-1978. English.

Know Canada (Conoscere Il Canada). Windsor, Ontario, Canada. Weekly: 1984. Includes English.

Lantern, Boston, MA. Monthly: 1929. English.

Il Lavoratore Industriale (The Industrial Worker), San Francisco, CA. (Microfilm: 1912). Includes French.

Lavoro (Labor; American Italian Labor Alliance), New York, NY. Monthly: 1956.

La Libertà (Liberty), New York, NY. Frequency varies. (Microfilm: 1902).

Leonardo Da Vinci Art School Yearbook, New York, NY. Annual: 1924, 1937-1939. Includes English.

Libertas (Industrial Workers of the World), Brooklyn, NY. 1927.

Lucca Bolletino Economico (Lucca Economic Bulletin), Lucca, Italy. Bi-monthly: 1975.

La Lucerna (The Lamp), River Forest, IL (previously published in New York, NY). Monthly: 1946, 1950-1954, 1958.

Il Lupo (The Wolf), Omaha, NE. Monthly: 1925.

Il Martello (The Hammer), New York, NY. Bi-weekly: 1942-1943.

Mazzini News, New York, NY. Weekly: 1941-1942. English.

Mazzini-Verdi Club News, Chicago, IL. Monthly: 1971-1972. Includes English.

Le Mammole della Madre Cabrini (The Violets of Mother Cabrini), Rome, Italy. Quarterly: 1966.

Mazzuchelli Bulletin, Sinsinawa, WI. Frequency varies: 1965-1968, 1974-1976, 1978-1979. English.

Il Messaggero (The Messenger), Kansas City, MO. Monthly: 1958, 1965, 1967, 1975. Includes English.

Il Messaggero di Lucca (The Lucca Messenger), Lucca, Italy. Monthly: 1956, 1969-1984.

1900--29 Luglio--1901 (1900--29 July--1901), New York, NY. (Microfilm: 1901).

Le Missioni Scalabriniane (The Scalabrinian Missions), Rome, Italy. Bi-monthly: 1944-1946.

Il Momo; Satirical--Humorous--Critical, Philadelphia, PA. Semi-monthly: 1922.

Il Mondo (The World), New York, NY. Monthly: 1938-1946. Includes English.

Il Mondo Libero (The Free World), Dearborn, MI. Monthly: 1956-1959, 1961-1972. Includes English.

Mondo Nuovo (New World), Parlin, NJ. Monthly: 1972.

Mosaico (Mosaic), Downsview, Ontario, Canada. Monthly: 1975-1976. Includes English.

Mother Cabrini Messenger, Chicago, IL. Bi-monthly: 1952-1966, 1979-date. English.

The New Aurora (Italian Baptist Association), Upper Darby, PA. Monthly: 1963-1970. Includes English.

A New Day, Bloomfield, NJ. Annual: 1976. English.

News & Notes from Father Peter, Springfield, PA. Frequency varies: 1976-1978. English.

Notiziario Consolare (Consular Bulletin), Toronto, Ontario, Canada. Monthly: 1979.

Notiziario Emigrazione (Emigration News), Italy. Quarterly: 1982-1985.

Notiziario Internazionale del Movimento Sindicale Libero (International News of the Free Syndical Movement), New York, NY. Monthly: 1949, 1952.

Notizie dall'Italia (News from Italy), Turin, Italy. Quarterly: 1980-1981, 1983-date. English.

Notizie della Stella (Stella News), St. Paul, MN. Quarterly: 1977-date. English.

Novatore (The Innovator), New York, NY. Semi-monthly. (Microfilm: 1910-1911).

Nuovi Tempi (New Times), Paterson, NJ. Irregular. (Microfilm: 1918).

Ordine Figli d'Italia in America Bollettino Ufficiale (Official Bulletin of the Order Sons of Italy in America), New York, NY. Monthly: 1923-1924. (Microfilm: 1923-1929).

L'Organizzatore (The Organizer), Ybor City, FL. Weekly: 1920.

Pacis Romanae Ordo Filiorum (PROF) Magazine (Order of the Sons and Daughters of the Roman Peace), New York, NY. 1968. English.

Il Palcoscenico (The Stage), New York, NY. Monthly: 1936.

Panorama, New York, NY. Monthly: 1941.

La Parola del Medico (The Doctor's Word), New York, NY. Semi-monthly: 1916-1917.

La Parola del Popolo (The Word of the People; Italian Socialist Federation of the Socialist Party of U.S.A.), Chicago, IL. Monthly: 1937.

La Parola del Popolo (The Word of the People), Chicago, IL. Bi-monthly (new series 1951): 1951-1982. Includes some English.

La Pasqua dei Lavoratori (The Workers' Easter), New York, NY. (Microfilm: 1898).

Il Pensiero (The Thought), New York, NY. Quarterly: 1939.

Petrosino, Florence, Italy. Monthly: 1973.

Il Piccolo Scrivano (The Little Scribe; East High School), Rochester, NY. Frequency varies: 1936-1937, 1939-1940.

Il Piccone (The Pickax), Taylorville, IL. (Microfilm: 1909).

Pious Society of the Missionaries of St. Charles Borromeo Annuario Scalabriniano, Rome, Italy. Annual: 1965.

Pro Nobis (For Us; Knights of Romulus), Calumet, MI. Monthly: 1912.

Il Progresso Italo-Americano (The Italian American Progress), New York, NY. Bi-weekly: 1944.

Progresso Italo-Americano Calendario (Italian American Progress Calendar), New York, NY. Annual: 1907.

Prometeo (Prometheus; Amalgamated Clothing Workers), New York, NY. Annual (?): 1925, 1928. Includes English.

La Protesta Umana (Human Protest), Chicago, IL. Monthly. (Microfilm: 1902-1903).

La Protesta Umana (Human Protest), San Francisco, CA. Monthly, weekly. (Microfilm: 1900, 1903-1904). Italian; one 1904 issue with French supplement.

Quaderni Canadesi (Canadian Notebooks), Downsview, Ontario, Canada. Quarterly: 1978.

Quaderni Italiani (Italian Notebooks), New York, NY (previously published in Boston, MA). Quarterly: 1942, 1944.

Quaderno de Giustizia e Libertà (Notebook of Justice and Liberty), Paris, France. Bi-monthly: 1933-1935.

Red White Green Magazine (Italian American Sports Hall of Fame), Bensenville, IL. Quarterly: 1979. English.

Il Refrattario (The Recalcitrant), New York, NY. Monthly (?). (Microfilm: 1919).

Regnum Christi Insieme (Reign of Christ Without End; National Italian Center), Chicago, IL. Semi-annual: 1950, 1952, 1960-1975, 1980.

The Renewal; Il Rinnovamento (A Magazine of Christian Thought and Ethics), Jersey City, NJ. Bi-monthly: 1965. Includes English.

La Rinascenza (Renaissance), Stamford, CT. Bi-weekly: 1922.

La Riscossa (The Revolt), Brooklyn, NY. Monthly. (Microfilm: 1916-1917).

Risorgimento (Resurgence), Brooklyn, NY. 1919.

Rivista Italo-Americana (Italian-American Review), Denver, CO. Monthly: 1913-1914.

La Rivolta (The Revolt), Madison, IL. Monthly. (Microfilm: 1913-1914).

La Ronda (The Patrol), New York, NY. Monthly (?): 1945.

The Rubican, New York, NY. Monthly: 1944, 1954-1956. English.

Lo Scacciapensieri (The Pastime), Omaha, NE. Bi-weekly: 1933.

Scalabrinians, Staten Island, NY. Quarterly: 1979-date. English.

Selezione Centro Studi Emigrazione--Roma (Digest from the Emigration Studies Center, Rome), Rome, Italy. Monthly: 1966-1967, 1969-1972.

La Sentinella (The Sentry), Hoboken, NJ. Weekly. (Microfilm: 1907).

La Sentinella (The Sentry), Utica, NY. Weekly. (Microfilm: 1915).

Servizio Migranti (Migration Service), Rome, Italy. Monthly: 1973-date.

La Settimana (The Week), New York, NY. Weekly: 1936-1937. Includes some English.

Sicilia Parra; Newsletter of Arba Sicula, the International Sicilian Ethnic and Cultural Association, Brooklyn, NY. Quarterly: 1983-1984. English.

Il Solco (The Furrow), New York, NY. Monthly: 1927.

La Strada; Rivista Mensile di Cultura Popolare (The Street: A Monthly Review of Popular Culture), New York, NY. Monthly: 1937-1938.

Strenna Almanacco e Catalogo Generale della Libreria Banca Tocci (Gift Almanac and General Catalog of the Tocci Bookstore), New York, NY. Annual: 1913.

Studi Emigrazione (Emigration Studies), Rome, Italy. Quarterly: 1964-date. Includes French and English.

Studi Emigrazione (Emigration Studies; supplement), Rome, Italy. Semi-monthly (begins as new series monthly, 1969): 1966-1967, 1969.

Il Teatro; Rivista Mensile per il Mondo Artistico (The Theater; Monthly Review of the Artistic World), New York, NY. Monthly: 1943.

Trade with Italy, New York, NY. Monthly: 1967. English.

Tradizioni (Tradition; Italian Folk Art Federation of America), Philadelphia, PA. Bi-annual: 1984. English.

Il Tricolore - Italy Is (The Tricolor - Italy Is), Hollywood, CA. Monthly: 1974. Includes English.

Umanesimo (Humanism), Naples, Italy. Quarterly: 1967. Includes English.

Umberto & Bresci, New York, NY. (Microfilm: 1903). Includes French and English.

UNICO (title changed to UNICO National Magazine, 1976), Bloomfield, NJ. Bi-monthly: 1962, 1966-date. English.

UNICO Foundation Inc. Bulletin, Greenfield, WI. Monthly: 1977. English.

UNICO National Convention, United States (various cities). Annual: 1968-1980. English.

UNICO National St. Paul Chapter Annual Awards Dinner, St. Paul, MN. Annual: 1953, 1955, 1957, 1959, 1983. English.

The UNICO Newsletter, Bloomfield, NJ. Bi-monthly: 1983-date. English.

L'Unità Operaia (Working-class Unity; previously in newspaper format), New York, NY. Monthly: 1938.

United Italian American Labor Council Annual Conference, New York, NY. Annual: 1963-1964, 1966-1968, 1970, 1975. English.

Unity-Italiana, Milan, Italy. Bi-monthly: 1966-1967.

L'Uomo Nuovo (The New Man), New York, NY. Monthly (?). (Microfilm: 1916-1917).

Il Veltro (The Greyhound; Italian Chamber of Labor), New York, NY. Monthly: 1924-1925.

The Vigo Review, New York, NY. Monthly: 1938. Italian or English.

Vita (Life), New York, NY. Bi-weekly, monthly. (Microfilm: 1915).

Vita Parrocchiale (Parochial Life), Milwaukee, WI. Monthly: 1936-1937, 1939-1941. Includes English.

La Voce del Tipografo (The Printer's Voice; New York Italian Typographical Union), New York, NY. Monthly: 1936, 1938. Includes English.

La Voce dello Schiavo (The Slave's Voice), Tampa, FL. Frequency varies. (Microfilm: 1900-1901). Includes Spanish.

Voce Italiana (Italian Voice), Washington, DC. Monthly: 1971-1974. Includes some English.

Il Vomero (The Plowpoint), Philadelphia, PA. Monthly (?): 1940.

Washington Newsletter, Washington, DC. Monthly: 1977-date. English.

La Zotta (consolidated with **East End Journal**, 1939), St. Louis, MO. Bi-monthly: 1939-1940. Includes English.

Jewish American Collection

Manuscript Collections

Marmarosher Jewish Center (Cleveland, Ohio).
Records, 1911-1961. 1 microfilm reel.

Records include financial records, minute book, and miscellany. Included are minutes of the Marmarosher Young Men's Association (1943); minutes of board meetings (1949-1961); Marmarosher Jewish Center bulletins, banquet programs, an address book, and a dues book (1911-1913). *Includes Hebrew and English.*

Sherit Jacob Israel Synagogue (Cleveland, Ohio).
Records, 1919-1938. 1 microfilm reel.

Records of the Synagogue consist of financial records, minute book, membership lists, and miscellany. Included are membership lists and minutes of the Sharith Jacob Congregation Sisterhood, organized in 1932. *In Hebrew and English.*

Temple of the Heights (Cleveland, Ohio).
Records, 1891-1920. 1 microfilm reel.

Records consist of a minute book. *Includes German.*

Monographs

The IHRC's Jewish American collection, numbering ca. 330 volumes, is not large in relationship to the amount of writing produced by and about this group. However, it does include useful material for the study of East European Jews in America.

General histories of the Jewish experience in the United States include Henry L. Feingold's *Zion in America: The Jewish Experience from Colonial Times to the Present*

(1974), Max I. Dimont's *The Jews in America* (1978), and *The American Jewish Experience*, edited by Jonathan Sarna (1986). The collection also contains Moses Rischin's *Inventory of American Jewish History* (1954), a bibliographic survey of the primary and secondary sources available to scholars. Two other useful reference tools are Irving J. Sloan's *The Jews in America 1621-1970: A Chronology and Fact Book* (1971), and Morris V. Schappes' *A Documentary History of the Jews in the United States 1654-1875* (1971). In addition, the *American Jewish Yearbook*, published annually since 1900, chronicles the state of American Jewry through articles, biographical notes, and statistical information. The Center's collection includes volumes for 1911 through 1969.

Samuel Joseph's *Jewish Immigration to the United States from 1881-1910* (1914, 1969 reprint) is a useful early statistical and comparative study of the mass migration of East European Jews to the United States from the 1880s through World War I. A collection of documents, newspaper excerpts, and immigrant accounts of life in the United States is contained in Abraham J. Karp's *Golden Door to America: The Jewish Immigrant Experience* (1976). *The East European Jewish Experience in America; A Century of Memories: 1882-1982*, edited by Uri Herscher (1983), presents immigrant memoirs that illustrate the process of Americanization. Jewish society and culture are also the focus of a book of essays edited by Marshall Sklare, *The Jews: Social Patterns of an American Group* (1958, 1977 reprint).

Histories of individual Jewish communities have been written since the 1880s, by both amateur and professional historians. The IHRC's collection includes a variety of these works, particularly those of scholars and whose content relates to the large Jewish population of New York City. Included are Hyman B. Grinstein's *The Rise of the Jewish Community of New York, 1654-1860* (1945; reprint, 1976) and Arthur A. Goren's *New York Jews and the Quest for Community: The Kehillah Experiment, 1908-1922* (1970). There are a number of multi-ethnic studies on New York City that look at the Jewish experience. Two of these available in the IHRC's general collection are Thomas Kessner's *The Golden Door: Italian and Jewish Immigrant Mobility in New York City 1880-1915* (1977) and Nathan Glazer and Daniel Patrick Moynihan's *Beyond the Melting Pot: The Negroes, Puerto Ricans, Jews, Italians, and Irish of New York City* (1970).

Gerald Sorin's *The Prophetic Minority: American Jewish Immigrant Radicals, 1880-1920* (1985) documents activity in the labor movement and left-wing politics. In addition, the collection includes Melech Epstein's *Profiles of Eleven* (1965), containing biographies of such labor figures as Morris Hillquit and Sidney Hillman.

The history of Yiddish theater is the subject of Nahma Sandrow's *Vagabond Stars* (1977). The Center's collection also includes the popular play whose title became a catch phrase of Americanization, *The Melting Pot* (1909), by Israel Zangwill. Several other Zangwill plays dealing with Jewish immigrant life in the urban ghetto are also part of the collection. *The Literature of American Jews*, edited by Theodore L. Gross (1973), is an anthology of writing by Jewish Americans, including Michael Gold, Emma Lazarus, and Mary Antin. Perhaps the most famous Yiddish journalist of the time was Abraham Cahan, founder and editor of the *Jewish Daily Forward*. Excerpts from Cahan's work are contained in Moses Rischin's anthology *Grandma Never Lived in America: The New York Journalism of Abraham Cahan* (1985).

Literature on the Jewish experience in America cuts across many ethnic groups. Researchers may find useful material in other ethnic group collections, particularly those of East European immigrants.

Newspapers

American Jewish World, Minneapolis, MN. Weekly: 1971, 1981-date. English.

Jewish Journal, Brooklyn, NY. Weekly: 1977-1978. English.

Jewish Press, Brooklyn, NY. Weekly: 1977-1978. English.

Jewish Record, Elizabeth, NJ. Weekly: 1941. English.

The Jewish Week & The American Examiner, New York, NY. Weekly: 1977. English.

JIAS News, Montreal, Quebec, Canada. Quarterly: 1978-date. Includes English and some French.

Novy Americanetz (New American), Jersey City, NJ. Weekly: 1980. Russian.

Reform Judaism, New York, NY. Monthly: 1977. English.

Wisconsin Jewish Chronicle, Milwaukee, WI. Weekly: 1974. English.

Serials

AJHS Heritage (American Jewish Historical Society), Waltham, MA. Semi-annual: 1984. English.

American Jewish Archives, Cincinnati, OH. Quarterly: 1973-1982, 1984-date. English.

American Jewish Joint Distribution Committee Annual Report, New York, NY. Annual: 1940-1946. English.

American Jewish Life, New York, NY. Monthly (except July and August): 1951-1952. English.

American Judaism, New York, NY. Quarterly: 1954, 1962, 1965. English.

Bnai Yiddish Journal, New York, NY. Bi-monthly: 1975. Includes English.

Calumet (Canadian Council of Christians and Jews), Toronto, Ontario, Canada. Monthly: 1979. English.

Canadian Jewish Yearbook, Montreal, Quebec, Canada. Annual: 1959. English.

Dropsie College for Hebrew and Cognate Learning Register, Philadelphia, PA. Annual: 1928-1929. English.

Identity, Minneapolis, MN. Semi-annual: 1967-1984. English.

The Immigrant, New York, NY. Monthly: 1928. English.

Institute of Jewish Affairs Periodic Reports on the Jewish Position, New York, NY. Monthly: 1964. English.

Issues, New York, NY. Semi-annual: 1962-1965, 1967-1969. English.

Jewish Currents, New York, NY. Monthly: 1977-1978. English.

Jewish Family Almanac, New York, NY. Annual: 1943. English.

Jewish Information, Chicago, IL. Quarterly: 1962. English.

Jewish Life, New York, NY. Monthly: 1956. English.

Kultur un Lebn (Culture and Life), New York, NY. Bi-monthly: 1975. Includes English.

Leo Baeck Institute Yearbook XIII, London, England. Annual: 1968. English and German.

Modern Jewish Studies, Flushing, NY. Annual: 1977-1979. English.

New American (Committee for the Absorption of Soviet Emigres), Jersey City, NJ. Weekly: 1980. English and Russian.

The Record, Washington, DC. Semi-annual: 1968. English.

Search, Niles, IL. Quarterly: 1983-date. English.

Studies in American Jewish Literature, University Park, PA. Semi-annual: 1975-1979. English.

Tayerer Landsman (Dear Countrymen), Miami, FL. Monthly: 1987-date. English.

Unser Tsait (Our Time), New York, NY. Monthly: 1972-1979.

Yiddish Studies and MJS (Modern Jewish Studies) Newsletter, Flushing, NY. Quarterly: 1978-1979. Includes English.

YIVO News (previously titled **News of the YIVO;** YIVO Institute for Jewish Research), New York, NY. Quarterly: 1984-1987. Includes English.

Latvian American Collection

Manuscript Collections

**American Latvian Association
(Washington, D.C.).**
Records, ca. 1948-1974. 20 linear ft.

A cultural and social organization
founded in 1951, the Association
currently has about 10,000 members in
190 local groups. It "endeavors to unite
and represent the Latvians in the United
States . . ." and is comprised of four
bureaus: cultural affairs, information,
relief and assistance, and sports. Publications include *Kultūras Biroja Biļetens,
ALA Žurnāls, ALA Vēstis, Latvian News
Bulletin,* and Sunday school textbooks.
Records include correspondence,
organizational records, records of local
branches, and publications. *Inventory
available.*

Čaks, Raimunds.
Papers, ca. 1943-1980. 3 linear ft.

Čaks, a Latvian American journalist,
lives in West Allis, WI. Papers include
correspondence, programs, and publications, largely relating to the Latvian
scouting movement and to his affiliation
with the Latvian Welfare Association
(Daugavas Vanagi).

Dundurs, Erik A. (1922-1984).
Papers, 1949-1982. 4 linear ft.

An active member of the Twin Cities
Latvian community, Dundurs left his
native Latvia in 1944, just ahead of the
advancing Russian army. He fled to
Germany, where he worked for the
International Refugee Organization. In
1949, he and his wife, Biruta, immigrated
to Minnesota. Between 1949 and 1951,
Mr. and Mrs. Dundurs served as
managers of a St. Paul, MN, resettlement
home for displaced persons. Positions he
held after 1951 included radio talk show
host and (1971-1984) manager in the U.S.
Savings Bond division of the Treasury
Department's Minneapolis office.
Dundurs founded and served as president
of the Council for the Liberation of
Captive Peoples from Soviet Domination.
He was also an active member of the
Republican Party.
Papers consist of correspondence,
memorabilia, newspaper clippings,
speeches, scrapbooks, and files on various
organizations of which Dundurs was a
member. Also included are files
regarding a variety of subjects, mostly
dealing with Latvian Americans and U.S.
foreign policy. *In English. Preliminary
inventory available.*

Gulbis, Talivaldis.
Papers, ca. 1980. 1 linear in.

Photocopy of Gulbis's paper, "The Story of the Latvian Lutheran Immigrants in the United States of America." *In English.*

Jaremko, Christina.
Papers, 1981. Ca. 1 linear in.

Papers of Jaremko consist of oral history transcripts of interviews of fifteen former Latvian displaced persons. Included also are interviews with three non-Latvian DPs. *In English.*

Kauls Family.
Papers, 1981. Ca. 1 linear in.

Included is a manuscript entitled "Flight to Freedom," which traces the history of the Teodors (1872-1954) and Sara (1879-1959) Kauls family. The Kauls moved from Ukraine to Riga in 1910, and to Czechoslovakia in 1924. Following World War II, they migrated from a displaced persons camp in Würzburg, Germany, to Michigan and Minnesota. The story is told by Gloria Kauls. *In English. Restricted.*

Latvian Chorus Shield of Songs (Koris Dziesmu Vairogs) (Kalamazoo-Grand Rapids, Michigan).
Records, 1945-1980. 5 linear ft.

The group formed in the displaced persons camp at Groshabersdorf, Germany, in 1945. Most of the members resettled in Kalamazoo and Grand Rapids, MI. It continued in those cities until it was disbanded in 1981.
Records and papers include correspondence, minutes, history, programs, and memorabilia. *Preliminary inventory available.*

Latvian Relief Fund of America, Inc. (Amerikas Latviešu Palīdzības Fonds) (Philadelphia, Pennsylvania).
Records, 1955-1969. 1 notebook.

Amerikas Latviešu Palīdzības Fonds, founded in 1952, provides Latvian immigrants with life and health insurance plans through a mutual assistance foundation. It also provides welfare services to elderly and impoverished Latvian Americans.
Records of the Fund consist of a loose-leaf notebook with brochures explaining insurance plans and minutes and related materials of Fund board meetings. *Inventory available.*

Latvian Welfare Association, Hawks of the River Daugava in the United States (Daugavas Vanagi A.S.V.) (Chicago, Illinois).
Records, 1956-1968. 2.5 linear ft.

A welfare organization founded in 1945 in Belgium by Latvian war veterans, the Association has about 10,000 members, and includes youth organizations. It publishes *Daugavas Vanagu Mēnešraksts* and regional newsletters.
Records include correspondence, imprints, and miscellaneous papers documenting local activities and relations with national Latvian organizations. *Includes English. Preliminary inventory. Related collection: Latvian Welfare Association of Minnesota (Daugavas Vanagu Apvienība Minnesotā) (Minneapolis-St. Paul).*

Latvian Welfare Association of Minnesota (Daugavas Vanagu Apvienība Minnesotā) (Minneapolis-St. Paul).
Records, 1957-1980. 2.5 linear ft.

The Association was founded in the late 1940s in displaced persons camps in Germany and Austria. Its original purpose was to serve as a veterans' welfare organization, but over the years it has become more active politically. The Twin Cities, MN, branch is also engaged in arranging ethnic events, has a choir, and publishes an occasional bulletin.
Records of the Association include correspondence, material relating to other Latvian American organizations, newsletters, and miscellany. Included are materials of or relating to the Latvian Foundation, Inc., Latvian Truth Fund, Inc. (Patiesības Fonds), Latvian Heritage

Foundation (Latviska Mantojuma Fonds), the American Latvian Association, the World Federation of Free Latvians, and the national Daugavas Vanagi organization. *Preliminary inventory. Related collection: Latvian Welfare Association (Daugavas Vanagi A.S.V.) (Chicago, IL).*

Latvian Youth's Two-Times-Two (Latviešu Jaunatnes Divreizdivi). Records, 1966. 2 linear in.

The program is a one-week summer seminar for Latvian American youth. The 1966 gathering was at Camp Cavell, Lexington, KY.

Records of Latviešu Jaunatnes Divreizdivi include a workbook for discussions of Latvian history and culture and Latvian problems in American society, along with song sheets and brochures.

Rasiņš, Nikolajs (1915-). Papers, ca. 1954-1979. Ca. 2.5 linear ft.

Rasiņš was born near Ludza in Latvia, where he worked as a teacher and tax budget inspector until World War II. During the War, he fled to a displaced persons camp in Germany and in 1949 came to the United States. He worked in construction for a year in Colorado Springs, CO, and then for the Alexander Film Company there. Rasiņš remained active in Latvian cultural activities; helped found the Colorado Springs Latvian Society; prepared radio, television, and press material about Latvians; and aided resettlement of recently arrived Latvian displaced persons. In 1957, he moved to Minneapolis, MN, where he worked until his retirement at KTCA-TV, the local public television station. In Minneapolis, he chaired a committee in 1967-1968 to organize the local celebration of Latvia's fiftieth anniversary of independence, and helped organize the Latvian Credit Union and the Latvian House.

Papers include tape recordings, slides, newspaper clippings, correspondence, and financial records relating to Rasiņš's Latvian American broadcasting and other Latvian American community activities in Colorado Springs and in the Twin Cities.

Includes English. Preliminary inventory available.

Rozentāls, Magdalēna (1915-). Papers, ca. 1945-1980. Ca. 2 linear ft.

Rozentāls was born in Liepāja, Latvia. In 1940, she completed the history program at the University of Latvia and after coming to America received a master's degree in library science from Columbia University in New York. She relocated to Minneapolis, MN, where she worked in the University of Minnesota Libraries until her retirement. She has had numerous publications and is an editor of *Akadēmiska Dzīve*, an annual Latvian scholarly journal.

Papers relate mainly to material dealing with Latvian refugees throughout the world. Included are photo albums, serials, correspondence, theater programs, and miscellany. *Includes English. Inventory available.*

Slaucītājs, Leonīds (1899-1971). Papers, 1947-1969. 1 linear ft.

A geophysicist and mathematician, Slaucītājs was born in rural Latvia. In 1918, he served in the Russian Arctic fleet and later returned to independent Latvia, volunteered in the Latvian navy, and resumed his studies. He received a mathematics degree from the University of Latvia and in 1931 began to teach there. In 1940, he assumed directorship of the geophysics and meteorology institute at the University of Latvia; two years later, he completed a doctorate in mathematics. He fled in 1944 with his wife, Milda (Hartmans) Slaucītājs, and their two children to Germany, where he taught at Baltic University and worked at the German Sea Observatory. After World War II, they left for La Plata, Argentina, where Slaucītājs directed the Geophysics Department at the University of La Plata until 1968. He led three expeditions to Antarctica during that time. Slaucītājs pursued avocations in music and painting.

His papers, mainly about geomagnetism, include memoirs, biographical materials, publications, material on Latvian cultural affairs in Australia, and

materials relating to his activities in the
arts. *Includes English, German, and
Spanish. Inventory available.*

Tūters, Edvarts (1893-1984).
Papers, ca. 1922-1965.   1.5 linear ft.

Papers of Latvian American author and
poet Tūters consist of typescripts of
poetry and other writings, newspaper
clippings, correspondence, and several
publications.

Monographs

The Latvian American monograph collection, numbering ca. 900 volumes, reflects
the life, interests, and concerns of particularly the post-World War II Latvian refugees
who came to the United States. The primary strength of the collection is in materials
that mirror the extensive associational life in Latvian émigré communities not only in the
United States but throughout the world. It contains relatively little primary or secondary
material on Latvian immigrants who arrived in the United States at the turn of the
century.

Bibliographic information on Latvian American history is found in works
concentrating on the post-World War II period and reflecting the published output of
Latvian communities throughout the world. These include Zelma Ozols's *Latvia: A
Selected Bibliography* (1963) and Benjamiņš Jēgers's *Bibliography of Latvian
Publications Outside Latvia 1940-1960, Vols. I & II* (1968), which was followed by his
Bibliography of Latvian Publications Outside Latvia 1961-1970 (1977) and "A Survey of
Lettica in the Libraries of the Free World" in *The Journal of Baltic Studies* (No. 1,
1977). Jonas Balys has compiled two listings of bibliographies: "Bibliography of Baltic
Bibliographies" in *Lituanistikos Darbai* (Lithuanian Studies, Vol. 2, 1969) with updates
in *Naujoji Viltis* (New Hope, No. 2, 1971 and No. 4, 1972) in the Lithuanian American
serials collection; and "Latvian Bibliographies: A Selective List" in *The Journal of Baltic
Studies* (No. 4, 1973) in the IHRC general serials collection. A short bibliography is
also included in *The Latvians in America 1640-1973; A Chronology and Fact Book*, by
Maruta Kārklis et al. (1974). Available, too, is a 1929 bibliography of Latvian books in
the Chicago Public Library, *Čikagas publiskās bibliotekas latviešu grāmatas* (Chicago
Public Library's Latvian Grammar, 1929).

The IHRC has a good representation of general histories of Latvian immigration.
Among these are Osvaldš Akmentiņš's *Amerikas Latvieši 1888-1948; Fakti un apceres*
(American Latvians; Facts and Considerations, 1958) and his *Latvians in Bicentennial
America* (1976). The Kārklis book also provides a chronological overview, including
information on the early period of migration. Joseph Roucek's "Latvian Americans" in
Francis Brown and Joseph Roucek's *One America* (1945), located in the IHRC general
collection, is a short historical and sociological examination of Latvian American
communities. The monograph collection contains two academic papers by sociologist
Juris Veidemanis that examine Latvian settlement patterns, family life, and assimilation:
"The New Immigrant: A Challenge to an Older Theory" (1962) and "Profile of the
Latvian DP: Twelve Years in Wisconsin" (1962).

The large volume of printed matter published by cultural and educational
associations is richly represented in the IHRC's Latvian American collection. The
collection is especially strong on the American Latvian Association in the United States,
whose organizational records are also held by the IHRC. The monograph collection
includes a wide variety of publications issued by the Association's five bureaus, ranging

from books and bulletins on political issues to programs for concerts, music festivals, and art exhibits. Other organizations represented in the collection are the Daugavas Vanagi, a Latvian welfare organization founded by war veterans, and the Latvian Relief Fund, a mutual welfare organization.

The popularity of music is evident in the number of published materials that relate to choral groups and music festivals. These are typified by *Latvian DP Singing Festival*, edited by Jānis Poruks (1946), and Osvaldš Akmentiņš's *The Latvians Are Coming* (1978), which commemorates a Latvian choral festival in Boston, MA.

Religious activity is reflected in jubilee albums that document the history of Lutheran churches established in the early 1950s. These include *Bostonas un apkārtnes Latviešu Ev.-Lut. Trimdas Draudzes 10 Gadi* (Boston and Area Latvian Evangelical Lutheran Exile Congregation—Ten Years, 1961), and *Čikāgas Latviešu Ev.-Lut. Jāņa Draudzes 10 Gadi, 1951-1961* (Chicago Latvian Evangelical Lutheran John Congregation—Ten Years, 1961).

Among the items that deal specifically with pre-World War II Latvian immigrants to the United States is Osvaldš Akmentiņš's *Lielais Kurzemnieks Amerikā* (The Great Courlander in America, 1984), a biography of Jacob Sieberg, an Latvian American pioneer. Organizational activity of the early immigrants is reflected in commemorative albums of fraternal associations like the Illinois Latvian Benevolent Society's *70 Gadu Jubileja* (Seventy Year Anniversary, 1967) and the *Filadelfijas Brīvo Latvju Biedrība 90, 1892-1982* (Philadelphia Society of Free Letts, 1982). Jānis Eglīte's *Čikāgas Latviešu Ev.-Lut. Ciānas Draudzes 60 Gadi* (Chicago Latvian Ev.-Luth. Zion Congregation—Sixty Years, 1957) contains the history of Chicago's oldest Latvian congregation. The collection includes numerous books on various periods of Latvian history and aspects of culture. Typical of these are Alfreds Bilmanis's *A History of Latvia* (1951) and Arnolds Spekke's *History of Latvia; An Outline* (1951). The collection is rich in works by novelists, poets, and playwrights, many of them refugees like Anšlavs Eglītis, a Latvian writer and dramatist, whose literary output spans the war years, the displaced persons experience, and resettlement in the United States. Other works deal with folk art, dance, customs, and other aspects of folk culture, especially folk tales, whose popularity and cultural significance is mirrored in the fifteen-volume collection of Latvian legends and fairy tales, *Latviešu tautas teikas un pasakas* (Latvian Folktales and Stories), edited by Pēteris Šmits (1962-1970). Overviews of Latvian theater in the United States appear in Alfreds Straumanis's *Baltic Drama: A Handbook and Bibliography* (1981), located in the IHRC general collection.

Newspapers

Amerikas Latvietis (American Latvian), Boston, MA. Semi-monthly: 1960-1961, 1965-1976.

Amerikas Vēstnesis (American Herald), Boston, MA. Semi-weekly: 1955, 1958-1959, 1961.

Amerikas Westnesis (Amerikas Vēstnesis; American Herald), Boston, MA. Semi-monthly (previously published monthly): 1918. (Microfilm: 1897-1904).

Deewa Sweiksme (Dieva Sveiksme; Praise to the Lord), Boston (Roxbury), MA. Weekly: 1906. (Photocopy).

Dzimtene (The Homeland), Württemberg, Germany. Semi-weekly: 1945.

Dzimtenes Balss (Voice of the Homeland), Riga, Latvia. Weekly: 1959, 1961-1964, 1966-1968, 1971-1977, 1980-1983, 1985.

Grēvenas Zinas (Greven News), Greven, Germany. Weekly: 1946.

Jaunais Apskats (New Review), Toronto, Ontario, Canada. Weekly: 1955.

Laiks (Time), Brooklyn, NY. Semi-weekly: 1949-date.

Latviešu Vēstnesis (Latvian Herald), Dillingen, Germany. Weekly: 1945.

Latvija (Latvia), Augsdorf bei Detmold, West Germany. Semi-weekly: 1951.

Latvija Amerikā (Latvia in America; previously titled **Latvija Brīvā Balss**), Toronto, Ontario, Canada. Semi-weekly: 1951-date.

Latvju Balss (Latvian Voice; previously titled **Latviešu Balss**), Berlin, Germany. Semi-weekly: 1944-1945.

Par Atgriešanos Dzimtenē (About Returning Home), Berlin, East Germany. Weekly: 1955-1958.
Sporta Apskats (Sports Roundup), Toronto, Ontario, Canada. Semi-monthly: 1956-1957, 1959-1963, 1968.

Tālos Krastos (At the Distant Shores), Philadelphia, PA. Semi-monthly: 1948.

Tēvzeme (Fatherland; merged with **Dzimtenes Balss** in 1946), Hanau, Germany. Semi-weekly: 1945-1948.

Serials

ABN Informācija (ABN Information), Baden-Württemberg, West Germany. Monthly: 1950.

Aglonas Vēstis (News of Algona), Chicago, IL. Monthly: 1974, 1977, 1980-1983.

Akadēmiskā Dzīve (Academic Life), Minneapolis, MN. Annual: 1961-1981.

Amberland; "Dzimtenes Balss" (Motherland's Voice) Literary Supplement, Riga, Latvia. Frequency varies: 1968, 1973-1975. English.

ALA Kultūras Biroja Biļetens (American Latvian Association Bureau of Culture Bulletin), New York, NY. Semi-annual: 1959-1966.

American Latvian Association Latviešu Dzīves Archīva Valdes Apkārtraksts (ALA Latvian Life Archive Board Newsletter), Washington, DC. 1956.

ALA Vēstis (ALA News), Rockville, MD. Frequency varies: 1972-1974, 1976, 1978-1983.

ALA Žurnals (ALA Journal), Rockville, MD. Three times yearly: 1970-1981.

Amerikas Latviešu Apvienība (American Latvian Association), Washington, DC. 1966.

Amerikas Latviešu Jaunatnes Apvienība. Apkārtraksts (American Latvian Youth Organization. Bulletin), place of publication varies. Frequency varies: 1955, 1965, 1969, 1970.

Amerikas Latviešu Jaunatnes Apvienība. Pulcina Nodaļa. Biļetens (American Latvian Youth Organization. Group Section. Bulletin), Ann Arbor, MI. Quarterly (?): 1956.

Amerikas Lavtiešu Jaunatnes Apvienība. Zinas (American Latvian Youth Organization. News), place of publication varies. Quarterly (?): 1957-1958, 1966.

Amerikas Latviešu Jaunatnes Organizācijas Komitejas Izdevums Raksti (American Latvian Youth's Organizing Committee's Writings), Danville, PA. Bi-monthly (monthly): 1952-1953.

Amerikas Latviešu Katolu Apvienība Alkas Zinas (American Latvian Catholic Association ALKA News), place of publication varies. Frequency varies: 1975, 1980, 1984.

Amerikas Latviešu Palīdzības Fonda. Zinas (Latvian Relief Fund of America. News), Philadelphia, PA. Annual: 1956-1968, 1971.

Apskats (Review), Don Mills, Ontario, Canada. 1961, 1977, 1979.

Apvienības Jaunā Dzīve Raksti (Writings of the New Life Association), Chicago IL. 1955.

Architekts (The Architect; Society of Latvian Architects Abroad), Stockholm, Sweden. Frequency varies: 1960-1962, 1965. Latvian with English summary.

Archīvs (Archive), Elwood, Victoria, Australia. Annual: 1960-1964, 1967-1969, 1971-date.

ASV Ziemelrietumu Apkārtraksts (Northwest U.S.A. Newsletter), Portland, OR. 1968, 1970. Includes some English.

Atbalss (Echo), Riga, Latvia. Monthly: 1980-1981.

Atskaņas (Rhymes; Latvian Boy Scout and Girl Scout Magazine), St. Paul, MN. Frequency varies: 1961-1963, 1965.

Atstari (Reflections), Grand Rapids, MI. 1953.

Atvase (Offspring), Washington, DC. 1955-1956.

Atziņas un Pārdomas (Conclusions and Considerations), Riga, Latvia. Quarterly (?): 1974-1977.

Ausekļītis (The Little Morning Star), Toronto, Ontario, Canada. Annual (?): 1970.

Ausma (Dawn), Boston, MA. Monthly: 1941-1944.

Ausma (Dawn), Indianapolis, IN. Semi-monthly: 1952, 1954-1957.

Avots Prērīja (The Well in the Prairie), Minneapolis, MN (previously published in Sioux Falls, SD). Quarterly (?): 1952-1953, 1955.

A.V.V. Zinas (A.V.V. News), Quakertown, PA. 1973.

Āža Rags (The Billy Goat's Horn), Portland, OR. 1964.

The Baltic Peoples Want To Exist, Germany. Quarterly: 1950. English.

Baltiešu Ziņas Austrija (The Baltic News in Austria), Salzburg, Austria. Weekly: 1947-1948.

Bavārijas Latviešu Vēstnesis (Latvian News Bulletin in Bavaria; changed to newspaper Latvija in 1946), Munich, Germany. Weekly: 1945-1946.

The Beacon, Mount Vernon, NY. Monthly: 1944-1946, 1948. English.

Bitītes Kalendars (A Calendar for the Children), Esslingen am Neckar, West Germany. Annual: 1947, 1951-1953.

Bostonas Latviešu Ev.-Lut. Misijas Draudze (Boston Latvian Evangelical-Lutheran Mission Congregation), Jamaica Plain, MA. 1974.

Bostonas Latviešu Ev. Lut. Trīsvienības Draudze (Boston Latvian Evangelical-Lutheran Trinity Congregation), Roxbury, MA. Monthly: 1943, 1946, 1963.

Bostonas un Apkārtnes Ev.-Lut. Trimdas Draudze (Boston and Area Evangelical-Lutheran Exile Congregation), Brookline, MA. Frequency varies: 1980-date.

Brazilijas Latviešu Kalendars (Brazil's Latvian Calendar), Brazil. Annual: 1960.

Brīvais Vārds (The Free Word), Toronto, Ontario, Canada (place of publication varies). Annual: 1957, 1960, 1963, 1970-1971, 1975.

Brīvie Latvieši (Free Latvians), New York, NY. Monthly (?): 1941.

Ceļa Biedrs (Companion), Lincoln, NE (previously published in Minneapolis, MN). Monthly: 1956-date.

Ceļa Zīmes (Road Signs), London, England (previously published in Stockholm, Sweden). Frequency varies: 1948-1982.

Ceļi: Rakstu Krājums (Roads: A Collection of Writings), Lund, Sweden. Irregular: 1963, 1972, 1977, 1979. Includes German.

Ceļš; Gara Dzīves Mēnešraksts (The Road; A Monthly of the Soul), Würzburg, Germany. Monthly: 1947-1948.

Ciānas Vēstnesis (Zion Latvian Lutheran Church Newsletter; 1953 issues titled **Zvans Labai Vēstij**), Chicago, IL. Frequency varies (?): 1953, 1979-1983, 1985-date.

Čikāgas Latviešu Biedrība Informācijas Biletēns (Chicago Latvian Society Information Bulletin), Chicago, IL. Bi-monthly: 1955-1959.

Čikāgas Vējos (In Chicago's Winds), Chicago, IL. 1963.

Čikāgas Ziņas (Chicago News), Chicago, IL. Ten issues per year: 1976-date.

Čikāgas Ziņas (title varies: **Otto Krolla Mākslas Aģentūras Apkārtrakts, Čikāgas Latviešu Ziņas**), Chicago, IL. Bi-monthly: 1955, 1957-1961.

DV Report, London, England. Frequency varies: 1962, 1964. English.

Daba Raksti Dabaszinatnēm (Nature Writings for the Natural Sciences), Pinneberg, Germany. Quarterly: 1948.

Daugava, Stockholm, Sweden. Quarterly: 1947.

Daugavas Vanagu ASV Valde (Daugavas Vanagi--U.S.A. Board of Directors), Long Island City, NY. Frequency varies: 1954, 1965-1977, 1979-1982.

Daugavas Vanagu Apvienība ASV Ziemeļrietumos (Daugavas Vanagi--Northwestern U.S.A. Association), Longview, WA. Irregular (?): 1964-1970.

Daugavas Vanagu Apvienība Detroitas Informācijas Biļetens (Daugavas Vanagi--Detroit Association Information Bulletin), Farmington Hills, MI. Frequency varies: 1980, 1982.

Daugavas Vanagu Bostonas Apvienība (Daugavas Vanagi--Boston Association), Boston, MA. Monthly (?): 1980.

Daugavas Vanagu Britu Kolumbijas Nodaļa Apkārtraksts (Daugavas Vanagi--British Columbia Section's Newsletter), Vancouver, British Columbia, Canada. Quarterly: 1971.

Daugavas Vanagu Britu Kolumbijas Nodaļa Biļetens (Daugavas Vanagi--British Columbia Section's Bulletin), Vancouver, British Columbia, Canada. Semi-annual: 1971.

Daugavas Vanagu Čikāgas Apvienība Apkārtraksts (Daugavas Vanagi--Chicago Association's Newsletter; title changes to **Ziņas**), Chicago, IL. 1970, 1974.

Daugavas Vanagu Dienu Rīcības Komiteja (Daugavas Vanagi Days Organizing Committee), Chicago, IL. Monthly (?): 1966.

Daugavas Vanagu Dienvidkalifornijas Apvienība Vēstnesis (Daugavas Vanagi--Southern California Association Herald; previously titled **Informācijas Biļetens** and published in Los Angeles, CA), North Hollywood, CA. Monthly (?): 1964, 1970-1971, 1973, 1976-1977, 1980.

Daugavas Vanagu Filadelfijas Apvienība Apkārtraksts (Daugavas Vanagi--Philadelphia Association Newsletter), Philadelphia, PA. Bi-monthly: 1977, 1979-1980.

Daugavas Vanagu Kalamazū Apvienība Apkārtraksts (Daugavas Vanagi--Kalamazoo Association Newsletter), Kalamazoo, MI. 1956.

Daugavas Vanagu Klīvlandes Apvienība Apkārtraksts (Daugavas Vanagi--Cleveland Association Newsletter), Cleveland, OH. 1965, 1970.

Daugavas Vanagu Klīvlandes Apvienība Ziņotājs (Daugavas Vanagi--Cleveland Association Bulletin), Cleveland, OH. Quarterly (?): 1968-1969, 1974-1976, 1979-1981, 1983.

Daugavas Vanagu Kolorādo Apvienība (Daugavas Vanagi--Colorado Association), Evergreen, CO (previously published in Englewood, CO). Bi-monthly: 1969-1973, 1975-1977.

Daugavas Vanagu Mēnešraksts (Daugavas Vanagi Monthly), West Allis, WI (previously published in Augustdorf and Münster, Germany, and Toronto, Ontario, Canada). Bi-monthly: 1949, 1954-date.

Daugavas Vanagu Milvoku Apvienība Apkārtraksts (Daugavas Vanagi--Milwaukee Association Newsletter), Milwaukee, WI. Frequency varies: 1952-1974, 1976-1977.

Daugavas Vanagu Milvoku Vanadžu Kopa Apkārtraksts (Daugavas Vanagi--Milwaukee "Hens" Group Newsletter), Milwaukee, WI. Frequency varies: 1969.

Daugavas Vanagu Minesotas Apvienība Biļetens (Daugavas Vanagi--Minnesota Association Bulletin), Minneapolis, MN. Frequency varies: 1957, 1959, 1961, 1965-1966, 1980-1981.

Daugavas Vanagu Nujorkas Apvienība Apkārtraksts (Daugavas Vanagi--New York Association Newsletter), New York, NY. Frequency varies: 1965-1977, 1979-1980.

Daugavas Vanagu Vanadžu Kopas Priekšniece ASV Apkārtraksts (Daugavas Vanagi--U.S.A. "Hens" Group Chairwoman's Newsletter), Indianapolis, IN. Frequency varies: 1964, 1969-1970, 1980.

Daugavas Vanagu Vašingtonas, DC, Apvienība Apkārtraksts (Daugavas Vanagi--Washington, DC, Association Newsletter), Washington, DC. Frequency varies: 1976-1977.

Degpunkts (Limelight; Latvian School of Chicago, Inc.), Chicago, IL. Annual (?): 1980.

Deitonas Latviešu Ev.-Lut. Draudze. Draudzes Vēstis (Dayton Latvian Evangelical-Lutheran Congregation. Congregation Herald; previously titled Apkārtraksts), Dayton, OH. Quarterly: 1954-1957, 1960, 1963, 1966-1971, 1973-date.

Denveras Latviešu Klubs (Denver's Latvian Club), Denver, CO. Irregular (?): 1956, 1957.

Detmoldas Vēstis (Detmold Herald), Detmold, Germany. 1945.

Detroitas Ev. Lut. Latviešu Kristus Draudze (Detroit Evangelical-Lutheran Latvian Christ Church; previously titled Baznīcas Vēstis. Par Nacionālu un Demokrātisku Tautas Baznīcu Latviešiem Amerikā), Detroit, MI. Monthly: 1952-1958.

Detroitas Sv. Pavīla Ev. Lut. Draudze (Detroit St. Paul Evangelical-Lutheran Church), Detroit, MI. 1967.

Dienvidkalifornijas Latviešu Ev.-Lut Draudze Vēstnesis (Southern California Latvian Evangelical-Lutheran Church Herald), Glendale, CA (?). Monthly: 1954-1955, 1974.

Dienvidkalifornijas Latviešu Informācijas Biļetens (Southern California Latvian Information Bulletin), Los Angeles, CA. Monthly: 1951-1974.

Dievzemīte (God's Country), Ingolstadt, Austria. Weekly (?): 1945.

Drauga Vēsts (Friend's Message), New York, NY. Monthly: 1942-1945, 1947.

Dzelzceļnieks Trimdā (The Railroader in Exile), Sanford, FL (previously published in Bronx, NY). Annual: 1955-1957, 1973, 1977-1982.

Dziesmu Vairogs (Shield of Songs), Kalamazoo, MI. Annual: 1955-1966, one undated issue.

Dzimtene (The Homeland), New York, NY. Monthly (?): 1940, 1941.

Dzimtenes Balss (The Voice of the Homeland), Brooklyn, NY (previously published in Stockholm and Eskilstuna, Sweden; Chicago, IL; and Freeport, NY). Monthly: 1947, 1954-1955, 1961, 1964-1966.

Dzimtenes Kalendārs (Calendar of the Homeland), Västerås, Sweden. Annual: 1981.

Dzirkstele (The Spark), Brauweiler bei Cologne, Germany. Monthly: 1948-1949.

Dzīvais Vārds (The Living Word), Minneapolis, MN. Frequency varies: 1962-1965, 1972.

Eglājs (The Fir Grove), Winston-Salem, NC. 1945.

Fišbachas Latviešu Komiteja (Fischbach Latvian Committee; merged with Dienas Vēstis July 1, 1948), Fischbach, Germany. Daily (weekly before after July 1, 1948): 1948-1949.

Gaidu Kalendārs (Girl Scout Calendar), Toronto, Ontario, Canada. Annual: 1972.

Gaisma (The Light), Brussels, Belgium. Quarterly: 1969, 1971, 1973-1980.

Garezera Raksti (Writings from Long Lake; Lapa supplement for Latvian Scouts and Guides), Fischbach, Germany (previously published in Latvia). Annual (?): 1947-1948.

Garezera Ziņas (Garezera News), Three Rivers, MI. Frequency varies: 1965-1966, 1968, 1971-1972, 1974-1983.

Garezers, Grand Rapids, MI. 1965.

Grand Rapidas un Apkartnes Ev.-Lut. Latviešu Draudze (Grand Rapids and Area Evangelical-Lutheran Latvian Church), Grand Rapids, MI. Frequency varies: 1952-1953, 1955, 1971.

Grandrapidu Latviešu Ev. Lut. Vienības Draudze (Grand Rapids Latvian Evangelical-Lutheran Unity Church), Grand Rapids, MI. Monthly (?): 1953.

Gudrā Pūce (The Wise Owl), Milwaukee, WI. Annual (?): 1970, 1976, 1981.

Ierosmei (To Motivate), Flushing, NY. Annual: 1981-1982.

Ilustrētais Vārds (Illustrated Word), Augsburg, Germany. Monthly: 1946-1948. Includes some English.

Indianas Latviešu Biedrība (Indiana Latvian Society), Indianapolis, IN. 1953.

Intelekts (Intellect), Chicago, IL. Irregular: 1965.

Invalīdu Vēstis (War Invalids' Message), Memmingen, West Germany. 1971.

Jamaica Plain Luterānu Draudze (Jamaica Plain Lutheran Church), Jamaica Plain, MA. Monthly: 1980.

Jaunā Gaita (The New Course), Hamilton, Ontario, Canada. Bi-monthly: 1955-date. (Index: 1955-1974).

Jaunais Vārds (The New Word), Meerbeck, Germany. Monthly: 1946-1947.

Jaunās Balsis (The New Voices), Los Angeles, CA (previously published in Anaheim and North Hollywood, CA). Bi-monthly: 1954-1958.

Jaunatnei (For Youth; supplement to weekly newspaper **Latvju Domas**), Augsburg, Germany. Weekly: 1945-1946.

Jaunatnes Atbalss (Echo of Youth), Three Rivers, MI. Irregular: 1967, 1969-1970, 1973.

Jaunatnes Balss (Voice of Youth; supplement to **Svētrīta Zvani**), Minneapolis, MN. 1955.

Jaunatnes Balss (Voice of Youth), Toronto, Ontario, Canada. 1959.

Jaunatnes Ceļš (The Road of Youth), Lakewood, OH. Quarterly: 1970-1971, 1973.

Jaunie Zvani (New Bells), Grand Haven, MI. Bi-monthly (?): 1981-1982.

Jautra Maska (The Merry Mask), Milwaukee, WI. One time publication for the annual carnival sponsored by the Wisconsin Latvian Society: 1954.

Jersika, Neuötting, Germany. Bi-monthly (?): 1946.

Kadets (The Cadet), Toronto, Ontario, Canada. Frequency varies: 1969, 1972, 1975, 1977-1980.

Kalamazū Latviešu Biedrība (The Kalamazoo Latvian Society), Kalamazoo, MI. Bi-monthly (?): 1953.

Kanādas Daugavas Vanadzes (Daugavas Vanagi--Canadian "Hens"), Toronto, Ontario, Canada. Annual: 1971-1972.

Kanādas Latviešu Ev. Lut. Draudzēm un Mācitājiem. Apkārtraksts (Newsletter for Canadian Latvian Evangelical-Lutheran Churches and Ministers), Hamilton, Ontario, Canada. 1953.

Kaŗa Invalids (The War Invalid), Memmingen, West Germany. Annual: 1957-1968, 1970-1983.

Ķegums; Rakstu un Pārrunu Kopojums Skautu un Gaidu Vadības Darbam (Ķegums; Collection of Papers and Discussions for Use by the Leadership of the Boy Scouts and Girl Scouts), Grand Haven, MI. Annual: 1952, 1966, 1971-1972, 1974, 1977, 1980.

Klēts (The Barn; supplement to **American Latvian Humanities and Social Science Association Bulletin**), East Orange, NJ. 1958.

Klīvlandes Apvienotā Latviešu Ev.-Lut. Draudze; Draudzes Ziņas (Cleveland United Latvian Evangelical-Lutheran Church; Church News), Cleveland, OH. Bi-weekly: 1963-1973, 1980-1983.

Klīvlandes Latviešu Biedrība (Cleveland Latvian Society), Cleveland, OH. Frequency varies (?): 1954, 1957-1958, 1961, 1963-1964, 1966, 1968-1969, 1971-1972, 1981-1983.

Klīvlandes Latviešu Ev.-Lut. Draudze Apkārtraksts (Cleveland Latvian Evangelical-Lutheran Church Newsletter; succeeded by **Klīvlandes Apvienotā Latviešu Ev.-Lut. Draudze; Draudzes Ziņas**), Cleveland, OH. Monthly (?): 1954-1958, 1963.

Kolorado Vēstis (Colorado Message), Denver, CO. Semi-annual: 1973-1974.

Kontrapunkts (Musical Counterpoint), Kalamazoo, MI. Frequency varies: 1952-1982.

Krājējs (Collector), Brampton, Ontario, Canada. Frequency varies: 1976-1980. Includes some English.

Kristīgā Balss (Christian Voice), South Euclid, OH. Monthly: 1952, 1954-1958, 1960, 1968, 1973-1974, 1980-date.

Kristus Draudzes Vēstis (Christ Church Herald), Minneapolis, MN. Monthly: 1972-date.

Krusta Gaismā (In the Light of the Cross), Philadelphia, PA. Frequency varies: 1949-1968.

Labietis; Laikraksts Latvietību Dievtuŗu Sadraudzes Izdevums (Gentleman; Journal for Lettishness, Godholders' Fellowship Publication), Chicago, IL. Semi-annual: 1955-1983.

Lāčplesis (The Bear Slayer), Lancaster, PA. Frequency varies: 1956, 1966, 1969-1973, 1975-1976, 1978.

Laika Mēnešraksts (Time Monthly; supplement to the newspaper **Laiks**), Brooklyn, NY. Bi-monthly (monthly): 1955-1963.

Laikmets (The Era; previously titled **Latvju Sieviete**), Minneapolis, MN. Frequency varies: 1952-1956, 1958, 1960, 1962, 1968.

Laiks (The Time), Esslingen am Neckar, Germany. Monthly: 1946-1949.

Laiku Mijas (Changing Times), Grand Rapids, MI. Bi-monthly (?): 1980.

Lakeview Latviešu Ev.-Lut Draudze Apkārtraksts (Lakeview Latvian Evangelical-Lutheran Church Newsletter), Lakeview, NJ. Monthly: 1952.

Lankasteras un Apkārtnes Latviešu Biedrība Vēstis (Lancaster and Area Latvian Society Herald), Lancaster, PA. Irregular (?): 1956-1957.

Lāpa (Torch; Latvian Youth Magazine), Fischbach, Germany. Bi-weekly: 1946-1948.

Lāpa (Torch), Kalamazoo, MI. 1971.

LARA's Lapa (Sheet of LARA), Anaheim, CA (Madison, WI). Quarterly: 1974-1975, 1977.

Latvian Bulletin, New York, NY. Quarterly: 1951-1953. English.

The Latvian Collector (Latvian Philatelic Society), Albany, NY. Frequency varies (?): 1979-1980. English.

Latvian Foundation, Inc. Apkartraksts, Millis, MA. 1980.

Latvian Information Bulletin, Washington, DC. Quarterly: 1938-1946, 1952, 1954-date. Includes English.

Latvian News Digest, Rockville, MD. Bi-monthly: 1976-date. English.

Latvian Scout and Guide Global Jamboree Ziņas, Tannersville, NY. 1977. Includes English.

Latvia Today; Informative Literary Publication (Latvian Committee for Cultural Relations with Countrymen Abroad), Latvia. 1981-1983. English.

Latviešu Agronomu Biedrība ASV Apkārtraksts (Newsletter of the Association of Latvian Agronomists in the U.S.A.), New York, NY. Bi-monthly (?): 1954.

Latviešu Akadēmiskas Ziņas (Latvian Academic Review), New York, NY. Frequency varies: 1953-1957, 1960, 1974.

Latviešu Almanachs (Latvian Almanac), London, England, Annual: 1954-1958.

Latviešu Apvienība Minesotā Ziņas (Latvian Organization of Minnesota News), Minneapolis, MN. Frequency varies: 1952-1956, 1973.

Latviešu Ārstu un Zobārstu Apvienības Apkārtraksts (Latvian Physicians and Dentists Association Newsletter), Sedro Woolley, WA (previously published in Pendleton, OR). Quarterly: 1952, 1955-1966, 1968-1969, 1975.

Latviešu Balss Austrijā (Latvian Voice in Austria), Salzburg, Austria. Weekly: 1945-1947.

Latviešu Banku Kalendārs (Latvian Bank Calendar), Toronto, Ontario, Canada. Annual: 1960-1975.

Latviešu Biedrība Vašingtonas Štatā. Informācija (Washington State Latvian Society. Information), Seattle, WA. Monthly: 1952-1974.

Latviešu Biedrība Vašingtonas Štatā. Informācijas Biļetens (Washington State Latvian Society. Information Bulletin), Seattle, WA. 1951, 1953.

Latviešu Biedrību Sadarbības Centra Apkārtraksts (Latvian Society Collaboration Center Newsletter), Chicago, IL. 1966.

Latviešu Dziesmu Svētki Kanādā II (Latvian Song Festival in Canada II), Toronto, Ontario, Canada. 1956.

Latviešu Dziesmu Svētki Kanādā III (Latvian Song Festival in Canada III), Toronto, Ontario, Canada. 1961.

Latviešu Ev. Lut. Draudžu Apvienība Amerikā Pārvaldes Apkārtraksts (Latvian Evangelical-Lutheran Church Association in America, Administrative Newsletter), Washington, DC. Frequency varies: 1952-1957, 1963, 1965, 1967-1968, 1970-1972.

Latviešu Gada Gramata (Latvian Yearbook), Esslingen am Neckar, West Germany. Annual: 1947-1948, 1950.

Latviešu Inženieru Biedrība ASV Apkārtraksts (Latvian Engineers Society in America Newsletter), Bronx, NY. 1963.

Latviešu Jauniešu Biļetēns Austrumu Piekrastē (East Coast Latvian Youth Bulletin), Washington, DC. 1955.

Latviešu Kalendārs (Latvian Calendar), Augsburg, Germany. Annual: 1947.

Latviešu Kalendārs (Latvian Calendar), Copenhagen, Denmark. Annual: 1971.

Latviešu Kara Invalīdu Apvienība (Latvian War Invalids Organization), Brooklyn, NY. Monthly (?): 1959.

Latviešu Koru Apvienība A.S.V. Apkārtraksts (Latvian Choral Association in America, Newsletter), Cleveland, OH. 1971.

Latviešu Kreditsabiedrību Gada Grāmata (Latvian Credit Union Yearbook; previously titled **Latviešu Banku Kalendārs**), Toronto, Ontario, Canada. Annual: 1976-1979.

Latviešu Liberālu Apvienība Informācijas Biļetens (Latvian Liberal Association Information Bulletin), Washington, DC. 1957.

Latviešu Mežkopju un Meža Darbinieku Kopa ASV (Latvian Foresters and Forest Workers Group in America), Grand Rapids, MI. Bi-monthly: 1964, 1967.

Latviešu Nacionala Apvienība Kanada Ziņas (Canadian Latvian National Association News), Toronto, Ontario, Canada. 1953-1954.

Latviešu Preses B-Bas Gada Gramata (Latvian Press Society's Yearbook), Waverly, IA (?). Annual: 1952.

Latviešu Pretestĩbas Kustĩbas Dalĩbnieku Apvienĩba Informãcija (Latvian Resistance Movement Participants' Association Information), Detroit, MI (previously published in Greven, West Germany). 1956.

Latviešu Skautu Priekšnieks (Latvian Scout Leader), Grand Rapids, MI. Semi-annual: 1957-1958, 1963.

Latviešu Studentu Centrãlã Savienĩba Apkãrtraksts (Latvian Students' Central Union Newsletter), St. Paul, MN. 1961.

Latviešu Teãtru Apvienĩbas Ziemeļ-Amerikã Apkãrtraksts (North American Latvian Theater Association Newsletter), Cleveland, OH. Frequency varies: 1966-1979.

Latviešu Trimdinieku Kalendãrs (Latvian Exiles' Calendar), Fürth, Germany. Annual: 1948.

Latvietis Latvietim (A Latvian for a Latvian), Rockville, MD. 1974, 1977.

Latvija Šodien (Latvia Today), Washington, DC. Annual: 1972-1980.

Latvijas Brĩvĩbai (For Latvia's Freedom), New York, NY. Frequency varies: 1952-1961, 1967-1969, 1972.

Latvijas Ev.-Lut. Baznĩcas Gada Grãmata un Kalendãrs (Latvian Evangelical-Lutheran Church Yearbook and Calendar), Glenview, IL (previously published in Esslingen am Neckar, West Germany). Annual: 1952-1962, 1965, 1967, 1969-1970, 1972-1976, 1978-1983.

Latvijas Lakstĩgala (The Nightingale of Latvia), Minneapolis/St. Paul, MN. 1979.

Latvju Domas (Latvian Thoughts), Augsburg, Germany. Monthly: 1947.

Latvju Mãksla (Latvian Art), Rockville, MD. Annual: 1975-1983.

Latvju Mũzika (Latvian Music), Kalamazoo, MI. Annual: 1968-1983.

Latvju Sports (Latvian Sport), Lübeck, Germany. Weekly: 1945-1949.

Latvju Vieglatlẽts (Latvian Athletic Magazine), Fort Wayne, IN (later published in Milwaukee, WI). Annual: 1963-1966.

Latvju Zeltene; Rokdarbu Mẽnešraksts Latvju (Latvian Maiden; Needlework Monthly), Munich, Germany. Annual (?): 1948-1949.

Latvju Žurnãls (Latvian Journal), New York, NY. Frequency varies: 1951-1956.

Lĩbekas Vẽstnesis (Lübeck Herald), Lübeck, Germany. Daily: 1945-1946.

Linkolnas Vẽstnesis (Lincoln Herald), Lincoln, NE. Bi-weekly: 1953-1959.

Los Andželosas Dziesmu Svẽtku Ziņas (Los Angeles Song Festival News), Monterey Park, CA. Frequency varies: 1969-1970.

Mãjas Draugs (Friend of the Home), Chicago, IL. Monthly: 1949-1955.

Manas Draudzes Ziņotãjs (My Congregation's News; title changed to **Mana Draudze** after 1961), Boston, MA. Monthly: 1952-1958, 1960.

Mančesteras Latviešu Ev.-Lut. Draudzes Ziņas (Manchester Latvian Evangelical-Lutheran Church News), Manchester, CT. Frequency varies: 1956-1958, 1960-1964, 1966-1967, 1969-date.

Mazputniņš (Little Bird; Latvian Youth Literary Society), Willowdale, Ontario, Canada (previously published in Kalamazoo, MI). Monthly: 1959, 1961-1962, 1964-1969, 1971-1980.

Memmingenas Zinu Biļetens (Latvian News Bulletin in Memmingen), Memmingen, Germany. Weekly (?): 1948.

Mēs (We; previously titled **Ceļinieks**), Kalamazoo, MI (previously published in Winnipeg, Manitoba, Canada and Niagara Falls, NY), Frequency varies: 1960-1968.

Meža Vēstis (Forestry News; previously titled **Meža Darbinieku Vēstis**), Vallingby, Sweden (previously published in Fischbach, West Germany). 1964.

Mičiganas Sv. Jāna Ev.-Lut. Latviešu Draudze Ziņotājs (Michigan St. John's Evangelical-Lutheran Church News; title varies: **Ziņojumi Mičiganas Ev.-Lutera Draudzei; Ziņotājs; Dzimtenes Baznīcas Balss**), Kalamazoo, MI. Monthly (?): 1956, 1958.

Miera Draudzes Kalendārs (Peace Church Calendar), Los Angeles, CA. Annual: 1968.

Miera Draudzes Ziņas (Peace Church News; previously titled **Baznīcas Ziņas** and **Ziņas**), Los Angeles, CA. Monthly: 1970, 1972-1974, 1981-1982.

Milvoku Latviešu Ev. Lut. Sv. Jāna Draudze (Milwaukee Latvian Evangelical-Lutheran St. John Church; previously titled **Apkārtraksts**), Milwaukee, WI. Monthly: 1980-date.

Milvoku Latviešu Skolas Komitejas Prezidija Apkārtraksts (Milwaukee Latvian School Committee's Presidium Newsletter), Milwaukee, WI. 1961 (?).

Montreālas Latviešu Biedrības Ziņotājs (Montreal Latvian Society Bulletin), Montreal, Quebec, Canada. Monthly: 1950, 1978-1982.

Mūsu Domas (Our Thoughts), Toronto, Ontario, Canada. Monthly: 1951.

Mūsu Skola (Our School), Washington, DC (?). Monthly (?): 1964.

Mūsu Valodas (Our Languages), New York, NY. Annual: 1972.

Nebraskas Ziņotājs (Nebraska Messenger), Lincoln, NE. Monthly: 1960-1962.

The New Word (English version of **Jaunais Vards**), Meerbeck, Germany. Monthly: 1946-1947. English.

Nujorkas Latviešu Ev. Lut. Draudze Baznīcas Ziņas (New York Latvian Evangelical-Lutheran Church News), Brooklyn, NY. Monthly: 1952-1958, 1961, 1963-1964, 1966-1970, 1972-1974, 1977.

Omahas Latvietis (The Omaha Latvian), Omaha, NE. Annual: 1962-1963, 1965-1968, 1971-1972.

Oregonas Latviešu Biedrība Portlandes Nodaļa Apkārtraksts (Oregon Latvian Society--Portland Section Newsletter), Portland, OR. 1957.

Oregonas Latviešu Ev.-Lut. Draudze Apkārtraksts (Oregon Latvian Evangelical-Lutheran Church Newsletter), Portland, OR. Bi-Monthly: 1961-1963, 1978-1981.

Oregonietis (The Oregonian; previously titled **Oregonas Latviešu Beidrības Informācijas Biļetens**), Portland, OR. Monthly: 1958-1960, 1963-1965, 1967, 1969-date.

Paklau (Listen), Chicago, IL. Irregular: 1962.

Pēdējais Laiks (Recent Times), Toronto, Ontario, Canada. Frequency varies: 1981-1982.

Pie Svētavota (At the Holy Well), Heepen, West Germany. Quarterly: 1948-1950, 1959-1970, 1973.

Portlandes Latviešu Jaunatnes Pulciņš Apkārtraksts (Portland Latvian Youth Group Bulletin), Portland, OR. 1955.

Portlandes Oregonas Gada Atmiņas (Portland, Oregon, Annual), Portland, OR. Annual: 1971-1973, 1975, 1977-1981, 1983-1984.

Preses Pīle (Press Canard), Boston, MA-New York, NY. Frequency varies: 1957, 1959-1960, 1964.

Preses Pīle (Press Canard), Münster, West Germany. 1962.

Preses Pīle (Press Canard), Chicago, IL. 1963.

Preses Pīle (Press Canard), Toronto, Ontario, Canada. 1979.

Raina un Aspazijas Gada Gramata (The Rainis and Aspazija Yearbook), Västerås, Sweden. Annual: 1968, 1970, 1972, 1975-1981.

Rājums; Raksti Latviešu Valodas Kopšanai (Tilled Field; Contributions to the Preservation of the Latvian Language, Baltic Philology Association of Chicago), Chicago, IL. 1964.

Raksti (Writings), New York, NY. Monthly: 1952-1953.

Raksti (Writings; supplement to the newspaper **Latvija Amerika**, Toronto, Ontario, Canada), Bronx, NY. Weekly: 1973.

Rakstnieka Ceļi (Writers' Road), New York, NY. 1957.

Republikānis (The Republican), Los Angeles, CA. Irregular: 1958.

Rokas Grāmata un Gimenes Kalendārs (Handbook and Family Calendar), Brooklyn, NY. Annual: 1953, 1955-1957, 1959.

Sanfrancisko Dziesmu Svētku Ziņas (San Francisco Song Festival News), San Francisco, CA. 1967-1968.

Sauksme (Reveille), Kempten, Germany. Monthly: 1946-1948.

Saulainā Krasta Vēstis (The Sun Coast Herald), St. Petersburg, FL. Monthly: 1980-date.

Senatobijas Latviešu Ev. Lut. Draudze Ziņu Biļetens (Senatobia Latvian Evangelical-Lutheran Church News Bulletin), Senatobia, MS. Irregular (?): 1952-1953.

Sešikā; Pārkrievošana, Tautas Iznīcināšana Latvijā (Sešikā; Russification, National Destruction in Latvia), Toronto, Ontario, Canada. Monthly: 1972.

Sidnejas Latviešu Teātris (Sydney Latvian Theater), Sydney, Australia. 1972.

Sīkumi (Trifles), Toronto, Ontario, Canada. Annual: 1974.

Sirakūzu Latviešu Biedrības Biļetens (Syracuse Latvian Society Bulletin), Syracuse, NY. Quarterly: 1962-1963, 1965, 1970.

Sirakūzu Vēstis (Syracuse Herald), Syracuse, NY. Bi-monthly: 1973-date.

Skatuve (The Stage), Lakewood, OH. Annual: 1977, 1981-1982.

Skatuve un Dzīve (Stage and Life), Chicago, IL. Monthly: 1959.

Sporta Gada Gramata (Sports Yearbook), Hanau am Main, Germany. Annual: 1948.

Sporta Vēstis (Sports Herald), Minneapolis, MN. 1955.

Strēlnieks (The Rifleman), Chicago, IL. Annual: 1965-1972, 1974-1975.

Studiju Grupas Biļetens (Study Group Bulletin), Kalamazoo, MI. Irregular: 1967-1968, 1970.

Svešos Krastos (On the Unknown Shores), Philadelphia, PA. Quarterly: 1973-date.

Svešuma Balss (The Voice of a Foreign Land), Riga, Latvia. Quarterly: 1965, 1968, 1974-1976.

Svētcelnieks (The Pilgrim), Lincoln, NE. Irregular: 1972-1973.

Svētdienas Balss (Sunday Voice), South Euclid, OH. Monthly: 1955, 1961-1977.

Svētrīta Zvani (Holy Morning Bells), Minneapolis, MN. Monthly: 1954, 1956-date.

Teātru Apvienības Vēstule (Theater Association Letter), Cleveland, OH. Irregular: 1980-1981.

Technikas Apskats (Technical Review), Montreal, Quebec, Canada. Quarterly: 1954-1959, 1962-1980.

Tēvzemes Avīze (The Fatherland's Newspaper), Three Rivers, MI. Semi-weekly (?): 1967.

Tilts (The Bridge), Minneapolis, MN. Frequency varies: 1949-1976.

Toronto Centrā (In the Toronto Center), Toronto, Ontario, Canada. Frequency varies (?): 1978-date.

Toronto Latviešu Biedrība Apkārtraksts (Toronto Latvian Society Newsletter), Toronto, Ontario, Canada. Quarterly: 1966-1982.

Treji Vārti (Three Gates), Grand Haven, MI (previously published in St. Clair Shores, MI). Bi-monthly: 1967-1983.

Trimdas Skola (School in Exile), Solna, Sweden. Frequency varies: 1954-1959, 1961-1964.

Trīs Zvaignes (Three Stars), Neuötting (later Berchtesgaden-Strub), Germany. Monthly: 1946-1947.

Ugunskurs (Campfire; Magazine for Latvian Boy Scouts and Girl Guides in Exile), Milwaukee, WI (previously published in Hersbruck, Germany). Frequency varies: 1948, 1951-1953, 1955, 1957, 1959.

Universitas, New York, NY (previously published in Riga, Latvia; Stuttgart and Münster, Germany). Quarterly: 1954-1982.

Vaga (Furrow), Toronto, Ontario, Canada. Annual: 1981-1982.

Valdemārijas Vēstis (The Woldemar Herald), West Allis, WI. Quarterly (?): 1963-1971.

Vārds (Word), Chicago, IL. Irregular: 1957.

Vārti (The Gates), New York, NY. Monthly (?): 1952.

Vašingtonas Latviešu Biedrība Apkārtraksts (Washington Latvian Society Newsletter), Washington, DC. Monthly: 1952.

Vašingtonas Latviešu Ev.-Lut. Draudze Baznīcas Ziņas (Washington Latvian Evangelical-Lutheran Church News), Washington, DC. Monthly: 1952, 1955-1959, 1963-1968, 1972-1974.

Vēja Zvani (Wind Chimes), Chicago, IL. Monthly: 1979, 1981.

Vēstis (Tidings), Chicago, IL. 1980-1981.

Vēstis. Detroitas Latviešu Informācijas Biļetens (The Herald. Detroit Latvian Information Bulletin), Detroit, MI. Monthly: 1953-1959, 1961-1974.

Vēstnesis (Messenger), Boston, MA. Monthly: 1973, 1976-1984.

Vēstule Dzintrām (A Letter to the Sorority "Dzintra"), Minneapolis, MN. 1973.

Vidienes Balsis (Midwest Voices), Minneapolis, MN. Monthly: 1981-1984.

Vilnis (The Wave; previously titled **Apkārtraksts**), Salem, OR. Annual (?): 1963, 1973, 1975.

Vinipegas Latviešu Biedrības Izdevums Informators (Winnipeg Latvian Society Informer), Winnipeg, Manitoba, Canada. Monthly: 1983-date.

Viskonsinas Vēstis (Wisconsin Herald), Fond du Lac, WI. Monthly: 1954-1955, 1959, 1961-1972.

Vispārējo Latviešu Dziesmu Svētki ASV Rīcības Komiteja Apkārtraksts (General U.S.A. Latvian Song Festival Action Committee Newsletter), Cleveland, OH (?). Monthly: 1963, 1968.

Vita Nostra (Our Life), Bronx, NY. Irregular: 1967-1968, 1970.

Zelta Vārtu Vēstis (Golden Gate Herald), Los Gatos, CA. Monthly: 1952-1958, 1961, 1968-1969, 1971-1975, 1980-1982.

Zeme un Tauta (The Land and People), Grand Haven, MI (previously published in Lincoln, NE). Frequency varies: 1956, 1962, 1971-1972, 1975, 1979, 1981-1983.

Zemnieku Vienība (Peasant Union), New York, NY. 1960.

Ziemeļamerikas Latviešu Teātru Apvienības Apkārtraksts (North American Latvian Theater Association Newsletter), Lakewood, OH. Three times per year (?): 1970, 1973, 1977-1978.

Ziemeļkalifornijas Apskats (Review of Northern California), San Jose, CA. Monthly: 1959-1974, 1980-1983.

Zīle (Acorn), Washington, DC. Irregular: 1958.

Zintis (The Seer of Wisdom), Chicago, IL. Quarterly: 1961-1965. English.

Lithuanian American Collection

Manuscript Collections

Bimba, Anthony (1894-1982).
Papers, 1957-1976. 1 linear in.

Bimba was born in Užusieniai, Lithuania. After coming to the United States he became a journalist and historian; he was also active in politics as a member of the left wing of the Lithuanian American Socialists. He participated in the formation of the Lithuanian Communist League of America, which joined the Communist Party of America in 1919. Bimba served as editor of *Laisvè* (Liberty) from 1924 until 1973. From 1936 until his death, he was editor of the quarterly magazine *Šviesa*, the organ of the Lithuanian Literature Society. He wrote twenty-two books and pamphlets, most in Lithuanian (see monograph essay).

Papers consist of a copy of his autobiography and a typescript interview with him by Rudolph J. Vecoli. *Includes English.*

Čėsna, Jonas (1897-1975).
Papers, 1950-1974. Ca. 5 linear ft.

Čėsna was born in Lithuania and educated in Ukraine. He fought for Ukrainian independence after World War I, was captured by the Poles, and spent time in a prisoner of war camp. In 1922, he returned to Lithuania, where he attended military school and then became a captain in the cavalry. In 1940, when the Russians occupied Lithuania, he served in the 29th of October Territorial Corps until it was disbanded during the German occupation of Lithuania in 1941. In 1944 he escaped to Germany and in 1949 came to the United States with his family. He maintained close ties with the provisional Ukrainian Government in Exile and also preserved the historical archives of the Defense of the Fatherland Detachment (Tėvynės Apsaugos Rinktinė), with which he had fought. His final years were spent in St. Paul, MN, with his wife Kotryna and his daughter Liuda.

Papers include his own writings and material on Polish-Lithuanian disputes.

Jokūbaitis, Antanas Juozas (1887-).
Papers, ca. 1921-1973. Ca. 6 linear in.

Jokūbaitis, a poet, was born in Lithuania, arrived in the United States in 1913, and lived in Brookline, MA. His papers include correspondence, newspaper clippings, and copies of his works. Jokūbaitis used the pseudonym Anthony J. Jacobsen. *Includes English. Inventory available.*

Juras, Rev. Msgr. Francis (1891-).
Papers, ca. 1891-1978. 1 linear in.

Juras was born in Bridai, Lithuania. He was a pastor at St. Francis Church in Lawrence, MA, for nearly forty years.

Papers consist of an autobiographical scrapbook of newspaper clippings, photographs, certificates, and correspondence. Much of the material is photocopied. *Includes English.*

Žukauskas, Vitalis.
Papers, ca. 1949-1965. Ca. 5 linear ft.

A dramatist and author who also performed as a comedian in a topical one-man show called the Theater of One (staged for Lithuanian audiences in Canada, Australia, and the United States), Žukauskas was born in Lithuania and came to the United States after World War II. In 1951, he organized the Lithuanian Community Players in Brooklyn, NY.

Papers include announcements, bulletins, programs, and miscellany pertaining to Lithuanian American cultural activities. *Inventory available.*

Monographs

The Lithuanian American monograph collection is the largest of the IHRC's Baltic American holdings, numbering ca. 1,250 items. Both phases of large-scale immigration-- the first, which occurred from the late 1860s up to 1920, and the second, which took place after World War II--are clearly reflected; although materials relate more extensively to the post-World War II period.

Bibliographic information on the Lithuanian American immigrant experience can be found in Antanas Kučas's *Lithuanians in America* (1975), Adam Kantautas's *A Lithuanian Bibliography* (1975), and Algirdas Budreckis's *The Lithuanians in America 1651-1975* (1976).   William Wolkovich-Valkavičius has written an extensive critical overview of sources available in English in "Toward a Historiography of Lithuanian Immigrants to the United States," which appears in the *Immigration History Newsletter* (November 1983), located in the IHRC reference collection. Wolkovich-Valkavičius has also written numerous articles, some of which contain bibliographies, for the Lithuanian American journal *Lituanus*. A listing that concentrates primarily on the post-World War II period is Jonas Balys's "Lithuanian Bibliographies," part of an article, "Bibliography of Baltic Bibliographies," in *Lituanistikos Darbai* (Lithuanian Studies, Vol. 2, 1969); supplements to it appear in *Naujoji Viltis* (New Hope; No. 2, 1971, and No. 4, 1972). A major source of information on Lithuanian Americans is the six-volume *Encyclopaedia Lituanica* (Lithuanian Encyclopedia), of which the IHRC has the first volume.

The monograph collection contains several key general histories of Lithuanians in America. These include J. R. Jonas's *Lietuviai Amerikoj* (Lithuanians in America, 1899); Kazys Gineitis's *Amerika ir Amerikos Lietuviai* (America and American Lithuanians, 1925); Anastas Miliukas's *Amerikos Lietuviai XIX; Šimtmetyje, 1868-1900* (American Lithuanians in the Nineteenth Century, 1938); and Antanas Kučas's *Lithuanians in America* (1975). The collection also contains the Budreckis chronology, *The Lithuanians in America 1651-1975*, and Joseph Roucek's *American Lithuanians* (1940). All of these works, to varying degree, describe patterns of Lithuanian American migration, settlement, organizational life, and acculturation. Other similar analyses of the early period can be found in the journal *Lituanus*.

The collection is very strong on histories of specific Lithuanian American communities. Vladas Būtėnas examines Pennsylvania communities in *Pennsylvanijos Angliakasių Lietuva* (Lithuania of the Pennsylvania Miners, 1977).   Chicago is substantially dealt with in David Fainhauz's *Lithuanians in Multi-Ethnic Chicago* (1977) as well as Aleksas Ambrose's *Chicagos Lietuvių Istorija 1869-1959* (The History of Lithuanians in Chicago, 1967). Other histories that deal with Lithuanian centers of settlement include John Cadzow's *Lithuanian Americans and Their Communities of Cleveland* (1978); Jeronimas Cicenas's *Omahos Lietuviai* (The Lithuanians of Omaha, 1955); and Wolkovich-Valkavičius's *From the Nemunas to the Assabet; A History of the Lithuanians and Lithuanian Americans of Hudson, Massachusetts* (1966).

The history of the early Lithuanian Americans emerges to a large extent from immigrant biographies and autobiographies, published materials relating to organizational activities, and the extensive output of the Lithuanian American press. Reflections on early community life may be found in Vincas Ambroze's *Autobiografija. Vincas Ambrozevičius (75 metu sukakciai)* (Autobiography of Vincas Ambrozevičius [Up to the Age of Seventy-five], 1942); Vytautas Širvydas's *Juozas O. Širvydas, 1875-1931* (1941); and Aréjas Vitkauskas's *An Immigrant's Story* (1956). Wolkovich-Valkavičius's *Lithuanian Pioneer Priest of New England* (1980) describes religious life and the ideological schisms in the community. Dissension within the immigrant community is also dealt with in Victor Greene's *For God and Country: The Rise of Polish and Lithuanian Ethnic Consciousness in America* (1975).

The nationalist-clericalist struggle is documented in publications of the Lithuanian Alliance of America, which range from *Susivienijimo Lietuviŭ Amerikoje Istorija. Nuo 1886 iki 1951 metŭ* (The History of the Lithuanian Alliance in America, 1916) to numerous jubilee histories. Also found in the monograph collection are the Alliance's organizational materials, such as copies of the constitution and bylaws printed in both Lithuanian and English. There is comparatively little on the Lithuanian Roman Catholic Alliance of America, other than Antanas Kučas's *Lietuviŭ Romos Katalikŭ susivienijimas Amerikoje* (Alliance of the Lithuanian Roman Catholics in America, 1956) and articles that appear in church parish jubilee albums. These albums and histories, however, constitute a rich resource on Lithuanian Roman Catholic parishes throughout the country. Representative of these are Antanas Kučas's *The History of St. Peter's Lithuanian Parish, South Boston* (1956) and Povilas Abelkis's *Visŭ šventŭjŭ parapija Roselande 1906-1956* (All Saints Parish of Roseland, 1956), a history of Chicago's All Saints Parish. The collection also includes numerous theological works published by Lithuanian American religious publishing houses.

The extensive publishing activity of Lithuanian Americans is documented in Frank Lavinskas's *Amerikos Lietuviŭ Laikraščiai 1879-1955* (The Lithuanian Press in the United States, 1955). Descriptions in English of the Lithuanian American press are found in Balys's "The American Lithuanian Press" in *Lituanus* (Spring, 1976) and M. G. Slavenas's "Lithuanian Ethnic Press" in *The Ethnic Press in the United States*, edited by Sally Miller (1987), located in the IHRC general collection. The Lithuanian American monograph collection also has a number of self-education guides and books published by the various publishing houses for the immigrants. These include textbooks for learning English such as Joseph Laukis's *Rankvedis angliškos kalbos* (English Phrase Book, 1906) and S. Tananevicz's *Vienatinis savo ruŝies lietuviŝkai-angliŝkos kalbos rankvedis* (A Unique Lithuanian-English Phrase Book, 1912); self-help books like Jonas Kaŝkiaučius's *Darbininko sveikata* (Worker's Health, 1925) on health and hygiene; popularizations of the sciences and humanities such as Juozas Adomaitis's *Geografija arba žemés apraszymas* (Geography or a Description of the Earth, 1906) and John Szlupas's *Lietuviŭ pratéviai Mažojoje Aziojaje* (Lithuanian Forefathers in Asia Minor, 1915); and translations of popular fiction as well as classics from world literature.

Also well represented are books of a political and ideological nature such as translations of works by Marx, Lenin, Gorky, and Kautsky. All of these were published by *Laisvé*, the Socialist and, later, Communist newspaper. There are also numerous books and pamphlets by the labor activist, journalist, and writer, Anthony Bimba. These include works like his *Istorija klasiŭ kovos Amerikoje* (The History of Class Struggle in America, 1925) and *Religija ir piktadarystés* (Religion and Evil, 1925). Bimba's 1926 sedition trial is documented in Wolkovich-Valkavičius's *Bay State "Blue" Laws and Bimba* (1973). In addition, the IHRC holds Bimba's personal reading library, along with a copy of his autobiography.

Among the creative writings of Lithuanian Americans is poetry by immigrant writers, like Kazimieras Urbonaivičius's *Jono Kmito eilés* (Verses of John Kmitas, 1921).

The collection also contains a rich assortment of Lithuanian American plays, among them M. Grigonis's *Linksmos dienos* (Happy Days, 1913), K. S. Karpavičius's *Juozapas ir Zelbora ir paraono sapnas* (Joseph and Zelbora and the Pharaoh's Dream, 1923), and J. Steponaitis's *Už Vilnių!* (For Vilnius! 1934). The history of Lithuanian American dramatic activity appears in Bronius Vaškelis's "Lithuanian American Theatre" in *Ethnic Theatre in the United States*, edited by Maxine Seller (1983), and Alfreds Straumanis's *Baltic Drama: A Handbook and Bibliography* (1981), both located in the IHRC general collection.

Books such as *Lithuania and World War II* (1947) and *Lithuania, Country and Nation* (1946) reflect historical, political, and sociocultural events in Lithuania before, during, and following World War II and are among the large number of works produced by refugees who fled their homeland. Many of these were published in the displaced persons camps of Germany. The DP experience itself is represented in accounts like Juozas Pašilaitis's *Hearken, Then Judge; Sidelights on Lithuanian DPs* (1949?) and in refugee autobiographies such as Barbara Armonas's *Leave Your Tears in Moscow* (n.d.). Publications from this time period deal heavily with Lithuanian history, language, and literature. These are typified by works such as Pranas Čepėnas's *Naujųjų laikų Lietuvos istorija* (History of Lithuania in Modern Times, 1947); Alfred Senn's *The Lithuanian Language, a Characterization* (1942); and Vaclovas Biržiška's *Lietuvių rašytojų kalendorius* (Calendar of Lithuanian Writers, 1946). In particular, the many aspects of folk culture are dealt with in numerous books, among them Balys's *Lietuvių dainos Amerikoje* (Lithuanian Folk Songs in America, 1958 and 1977) and *The First Marian Reader; Folktales, Legends, and Short Stories* (1951). The collection is especially strong in poetry written by Lithuanian émigré poets throughout the world. Most of it appears in Lithuanian, although some has been translated; for example, Frank Yakstis's *Translation of Lithuanian Poetry* (1968).

An abundance of materials reflect the histories of émigré organizations. *Lietuvių Veteranų Sąjungos Ramovės pirmas dešimtmetis, 1950-1960* (The First Decade of the Lithuanian Veterans' Association "Ramovė"), for example, outlines the history of the Lithuanian Veterans Organization; Leonardas Šimutis's *Amerikos Lietuvių Taryba; 30 metų Lietuvos Laisvės kovoje, 1940-1970* (Lithuanian American Council; Thirty Year Struggle for Lithuanian Independence, 1970) describes the history of the Lithuanian American Council. The role of Lithuanian women in organizational activity is examined in *The Lithuanian Woman* (1968), a history of the Federation of Lithuanian Women's Clubs, edited by Birutė Novickis.

Newspapers

Akiračiai (Horizons), Chicago, IL. Monthly (except August and December): 1969-1970, 1986.

America, Brooklyn, NY. Weekly: 1946, 1948-1951.

Amerika, Brooklyn, NY. Weekly: 1949.

Amerikos Lietuvis (The American Lithuanian), Worcester, MA. Weekly: 1936, 1947, 1949, 1952, 1954.

Argentinos Lietuviu Balsas (The Voice of Argentinian Lithuanians), Buenos Aires, Argentina. Monthly: 1983.

Aušra (Dawn), Warsaw, Poland. Monthly (?): 1960-1962, 1966.

Darbas (Labor), New York, NY. Bi-weekly. (Microfilm: 1929-1930).

Darbininkas (Worker), Brooklyn, NY. Semi-weekly: 1947-1956, 1958-1968, 1970-date.

Dirva (The Field), Cleveland, OH. Frequency varies: 1949, 1954, 1959-date.

Draugas (The Friend), Chicago, IL. Daily: 1948-1949, 1951, 1953-1954, 1957, 1959-1968, 1970-date.

Europos Lietuvis (European Lithuanian), London, England. Weekly: 1985, 1986.

Floridos Lietuviai (Lithuanians in Florida), Gulfport, FL. Monthly: 1961-1964.

Garsas (The Echo), Wilkes-Barre, PA. Monthly: 1947, 1949, 1965, 1967-1968, 1973-1974, 1979-date. Includes English.

Gimtasis Krastas (Native Land), Vilnius, Lithuania. Weekly: 1977, 1979-1985.

Karys (Warrior), Berlin, Germany. Weekly (?): 1945.

Keleivis (Traveler), Boston, MA. Weekly: 1931, 1944, 1948-1949, 1951, 1953, 1955-1957, 1959-1962, 1965, 1967, 1969-1979.

Kultuvė (The Thrasher), Detmold, Germany. Weekly (?): 1947 (?)-1948.

Kultuvė (The Thrasher), Brooklyn, NY. Annual: 1951-1953.

Laikas (Time), Buenos Aires, Argentina. Monthly (?): 1985.

Laisvė (Liberty), Brooklyn, NY. Daily: 1929, 1938, 1940, 1942, 1946-1959, 1962, 1965-1966, 1974, 1976-1984.

Laisvoji Lietuva (Free Lithuania), Chicago, IL (previously published in Toronto, Ontario, Canada). Semi-weekly: 1950-1954, 1958-1962, 1965-1981, 1985.

Liaudies Balsas (The People's Voice), Toronto, Ontario, Canada. Weekly: 1949.

Lietuviai (The Lithuanians), Berlin, Germany. Semi-weekly: 1944, 1945.

Lietuvis (The Lithuanian), Dorverden, Germany. Bi-weekly (?): 1945.

Lietuvis (The Lithuanian), Memmingen, West Germany. Weekly (semi-weekly): 1949-1950.

Lietuviu Balsas (The Lithuanian Voice), Chicago, IL. Bi-monthly: 1987.

Lietuviu Kelias (The Lithuanian Pathway), Brooklyn, NY. Weekly: 1950.

Lietuviu Zinios (Lithuanians News), Pittsburgh, PA. Weekly: 1948.

Lietuviu Žodis (The Lithuanian Word), Detmold, Germany. Weekly: 1946-1949.

Lietuvos Pajūris (Lithuanian Seashore), Cleveland, OH. Quarterly: 1963-1967, 1969-1970, 1985.

Mintis (The Thought), Memmingen, Germany. Three times weekly (daily): 1946-1949.

Mūsu Kelias (Our Pathway), Dillingen, Germany. Semi-weekly (weekly): 1945-1948.

Mūsų Pąstogė (Our Shelter), Bankstown, Australia. Weekly: 1985, 1987.

Mūsų Viltis (Our Hope), Fulda, Germany. Weekly: 1945-1946.

Mūsų Žodis (Our Word; continuation of **A Z** and **Mūsų Žinios**), Greven, Germany. Weekly: 1946.

Naujienos (Lithuanian Daily), Chicago, IL. Daily: 1938, 1947, 1951, 1954, 1960, 1962, 1965, 1968-1985.

Nepriklausoma Lietuva (Independent Lithuania), Montreal, Quebec, Canada. Weekly: 1947-1949, 1958-1959, 1967, 1969, 1971-1975, 1979-1980, 1983-1985, 1987.

The Observer, Chicago, IL. Monthly: 1984-1985. English.

Rytas (Morning), South Boston, MA. Weekly: 1951-1952.

Rytas (Morning), Waterbury, CT. Weekly. (Microfilm: 1896-1898).

Sandara (The League), Chicago, IL. Weekly: 1949, 1966-1967, 1970, 1972-1974, 1980, 1982-1985, 1987. Includes English.

Saule (Sun), Mahannoy City, PA. Semi-weekly: 1948-1949, 1955, 1958.

Tėviškės Aidai (Echoes of the Homeland), Melbourne, Australia. Weekly: 1985, 1987.

Tėviškės Garsas (Sound of the Homeland), Schweinfurt, Germany. Weekly: 1945-1948.

Tėviškės Žiburiai (The Lights of the Homeland), Mississauga, Ontario, Canada (previously published in Toronto, Ontario, Canada.). Weekly: 1949-1951, 1957-date.

Tevyne (Motherland), New York, NY. Weekly: 1917, 1950-1951, 1956-1959, 1961-1968, 1970, 1972-1974, 1976, 1979-1980, 1983-1985, 1987. Includes English.

Tėvynės Balsas (Voice of the Homeland), Vilnius, Lithuania. Weekly: 1947-1948, 1965-1966.

Tiesa (Truth), Middletown, NY. Monthly: 1970-1980, 1983, 1985. Includes English.

Tremtis (The Exile), Memmingen, West Germany. Weekly: 1950-1951.

Už Sugrįžimą į Tėvynę (For the Return to the Motherland), Berlin, East Germany. Weekly (?): 1955, 1956.

Vaga (The Channel), Buenos Aires, Argentina. Semi-monthly: 1980.

Valio (Hurrah), Philadelphia, PA. Monthly: 1950.

Vienybe (Unity), Brooklyn, NY. Weekly: 1948-1949, 1951-1959, 1961-1984. Includes English.

Vilnis (The Surge), Chicago, IL. Daily: 1948, 1966, 1978-1984.

Žiburiai (Lights), Augsburg, Germany. Weekly (three issues weekly): 1945-1949. (Daily supplement: 1946).

Zinios; The Lithuanian Daily News, Brooklyn, NY. Daily (?): 1950.

Serials

Aidai (Echoes), Brooklyn, NY (previously published in Augsburg and Hochfeld, Germany; Baltic DP Camp, Schwäbisch Gmünd, Germany; DP Camp Hanau, Germany; Kennebunkport, ME). Quarterly: 1946-date.

Akečios (The Harrow; Lithuanian Magazine of Humor), Brooklyn, NY. Quarterly: 1965-1968.

Akiračiai (Horizons), Chicago, IL. Ten issues per year: 1968-1970, 1973, 1978.

Amerikos Lietuvių Bendruomene (American Lithuanian Community Bulletin), Chicago, IL. 1963.

Amerikos Lietuvių Katalikų Metraštis (American Lithuanian Catholic Annual), Chicago, IL. Annual: 1916.

Apreiškimo Parapijos Žinios Biuletenis (Visitation Parish News Bulletin), Brooklyn, NY. Weekly: 1965, 1978, 1980, 1982, 1984-1985, 1987. Includes English.

Apszvieta (Enlightenment), Shenandoah, PA (previously published in Plymouth, PA). Bi-monthly (?): 1892-1893.

Ateitis (The Future), Chicago, IL (previously published in Brooklyn, NY). Monthly (except July and August): 1947, 1949-1972, 1978-1985.

Ateitis (The Future), Pittsburgh, PA. Weekly. (Microfilm: 1900, 1901).

Atspindžiai (The Reflex), Chicago, IL. Frequency varies: 1952-1953.

Atžalėlės (Regrowth), Putnam, CT. 1964.

Bendradarbis (Co-Worker), Putnam, CT. Annual: 1963-1967, 1979-1980, 1984.

Bendrojo Amerikos Lietuvių Šalpos Fondo Astuntasis Seimas (Eighth Conference of the General American Lithuanian Welfare Fund), Chicago, IL-Brooklyn, NY. Bi-annual: 1956-1962.

Bishop's Brief (English edition of **Vyskupo Informacija**), Brooklyn, NY. Quarterly: 1985. English.
Bridges, Brooklyn, NY. Monthly: 1977-1978, 1980, 1982-date. English.

Chicago Lithuanian Engineer and Architect Society Bulletin, Chicago, IL. 1950.

Chronicle of the Catholic Church in Lithuania (translation of the original **Lietuvos Katalikus Bažnyčios Kronika**), Brooklyn, NY. Frequency varies: 1972-date. English.

Current News on the Lithuanian Situation, Washington, DC. Frequency varies: 1941-1957. English.

Darbas (Labor), Brooklyn, NY (previously published in Boston, MA). Quarterly: 1949, 1953-1958.

Darbininkas (The Worker), Brooklyn, NY. Semi-weekly: 1951, 1954.

Darbininkų Kalendorius (Workers' Almanac), Brooklyn, NY. Annual: 1928-1930, 1935-1936.

Eglutė (The Little Fir), Putnam, CT (previously published in Lawrence and Brockton, MA). Monthly: 1950-1967, 1984-1985.

ELTA Information Bulletin, Washington, DC. (previously published in New York, NY). Monthly: 1962, 1966, 1970, 1974, 1977-date. English.

Eltos Informacijos (Elta Information Bulletin), Washington, DC. Frequency varies: 1968-1972, 1974, 1976-1978, 1980-date.

The Epistle (Chicagoland Chapter Vatican Philatelic Society), Chicago, IL. 1964.

Evangelijos Šviesa (Light of Evangelism), Chicago, IL. Quarterly: 1964, 1966-1967, 1970-1972.

Evangelijos Žodis (Word of the Gospel), Chicago, IL. Monthly: 1951-1955.

Gabija, Brooklyn, NY. Frequency varies: 1951-1954.

Gairės (Landmarks; scouting publication), Chicago, IL. Undated issue.

Gimtinės Garsai (Sounds of the Native Land), Waterbury, CT. Monthly: 1947.

Gimtoji Kalba (The Native Language), Riverside, IL. Quarterly: 1958-1968.

Gintaras (Amber), Spakenberg, Germany. 1948.

Girios Aidas (Echo of the Forest), Chicago, IL. Quarterly: 1950-1953.

Į Laisvę; Lietuvių Politikos Žurnalas (Toward Freedom; Lithuanian Political Journal), Bakersfield, CA (previously published in Brooklyn, NY, Boston, MA, Chicago, IL, and Germany). Tri-annual: 1948, 1953-1965, 1967-date.

Institute of Lithuanian Studies Proceedings, Chicago, IL. Irregular: 1971, 1973, 1975.

Jaunimo Žygiai (Deeds of Youth), Cleveland, OH (previously published in Brooklyn, NY). Annual (semi-annual): 1955, 1957-1962.

Jaunoji Lietuva (Young Lithuania), Chicago, IL. Monthly (bi-monthly): 1914-1915.

Jonistų Balsas (Voice of the Johnist Fathers; St. John's Missionary Fathers), Chicago, IL. Monthly: 1946.

Kalifornijos Lietuvis (California Lithuanian; merged with Lietuvių Dienos, 1950), Los Angeles, CA. Monthly: 1946-1949. Includes English.

Kanados Lietuvių Sąjungos Biuletenis (Lithuanian League of Canada Bulletin), Montreal, Quebec, Canada. 1949.

Karys (Warrior), Brooklyn, NY. Monthly: 1950-date.

Kibirkštėlės (Little Sparklers), Putnam, CT. Weekly (summer only): 1952-1953, 1956, 1966.

Kimas, Boston, MA. Frequency varies: 1951-1958.

Knights of Lithuania Mid Atlantic District Bulletin, Bronx, NY. 1976.

Knygos Bičiulis (The Book's Friend), Brooklyn, NY. 1953 (one undated issue).

Knygų Lentyna (The Book Shelf), Danville, IL (previously published in Württemberg, West Germany). Irregular: 1951-1957, 1960-1966.

Kova (The Struggle; Lithuanian Socialist Federation of America), Philadelphia, PA. Weekly: 1911.

Kova (The Struggle), Philadelphia, PA. Monthly: 1920.

Krivūlė (The Elder's Staff), Bad Wörishofen, West Germany. Bi-annual: 1978, 1981, 1983, 1985.

Kronikos Balsas (Voice of the Chronicle), Chicago, IL. Annual: 1982-1983, 1985.

Kunigų Vienybės Forum (Priests' Unity Forum), Maspeth, NY (?). Monthly: 1935-1937.

Kurėjas (The Creator), Chicago, IL. Weekly. (Microfilm: 1900).

Labora (Labor), Manchester, MI. 1958.

Laiko Žodis (A Timely Word), Richmond Hill, NY. Quarterly: 1968, 1970.

Laiškai Lietuviams (Letter to Lithuanians), Chicago, IL. Monthly: 1950-date.

Laisvas Žodis (Free World), Toronto, Ontario, Canada. 1951.

Laisvasis Pasaulis (Free World), Woodhaven, NY. 1957, 1959. Includes English.

Laisvei (To Freedom), Vilnius, Lithuania/New York, NY. Annual: 1981.

Laisvoji Lietuva (The Free Lithuania), Chicago, IL. Monthly: 1951.

Laivas (The Ship; previously titled Kristaus Karaliaus Laivas), Chicago, IL. Monthly (weekly, bi-weekly): 1937, 1946, 1949, 1961-1973, 1985.

Liaudies Menas (People's Art; previously titled **Lietuvių Meno Sajunga**), Chicago, IL. Frequency varies: 1950-1951. Includes English.

Lietuva (Lithuania), Brooklyn, NY. Monthly: 1940-1941. Includes some English.

Lietuva Politikos Žurnalas (Lithuanian Political Journal), New York, NY. Semi-annual: 1952-1956. Includes English summaries.

Lietuviai Amerikos Vakaruose (Lithuanian in Western America), Los Angeles, CA. Monthly: 1964, 1979, 1983.

Lietuvis Teisininkas (The Lithuanian Lawyer), Detroit, MI. Annual: 1949-1952.

Lietuvis Žurnalistas (Lithuanian Journalist), Chicago, IL. Frequency varies: 1972.

Lietuviszkas Kningynas (Lithuanian Library; supplement to **Garsas**), Wilkes-Barre, PA. 1894 (?).

Lietuviškos Knygos Mėgėjas (Lithuanian Book Fan), Chicago, IL. Frequency varies: 1952-1954.

Lietuvių Atletų Klubo Zinios (Lithuanian Athletic Club News), New York, NY. 1978-1979.

Lietuvių Dienos (Lithuanian Days; merged with **Kalifornijos Lietuvis**, 1950), Hollywood, CA. Monthly: 1950-date. Includes English.

Lietuvių Gydytojų Biuletenis (Lithuanian Medical Bulletin), Chicago, IL. Quarterly: 1960-1970.

Lietuvių Jaunimas (Lithuanian Youth), Boston, MA. 1972. Includes English.

Lietuvių Katalikų Mokslo Akademija Suvaziavimo Darbai IV 1957 (Lithuanian Catholic Academy of Science Conference Proceedings IV 1957), Rome, Italy. 1961.

Lietuvių Namų Žinios (Lithuanian Home News), Toronto, Ontario, Canada. Monthly: 1983.

Lietuvių Naujienos (Lithuanian News), Philadelphia, PA. Monthly: 1949, 1953. Includes English.

Lietuvių Tautos Praeitis (Lithuanian Historical Review), Chicago, IL. Irregular: 1971.

Lietuvių Žinios (Lithuanian News; St. Casimir's Catholic Church), Los Angeles, CA. Semi-monthly: 1952-1953.

Lietuvos Katalikų Bažnyčios Kronika (Chronicle of the Catholic Church in Lithuania), Chicago, IL. Frequency varies: 1972-1975.

Lietuvos Pajūris (Lithuania's Coast), Montreal, Quebec, Canada. Quarterly: 1960-1968.

Lietuvos Ūkio Atstatymo Studijų Komisijos Darbai (Reports of the Commission for the Study of the Economic Reconstruction of Lithuania), Boston, MA. Frequency varies: 1951-1953.

Literatūra ir Menas (Literature and Art), Vilnius, Lithuania. Weekly: 1979.

Literatūra Metraštis (Yearbook of Lithuanian Literature, Art and Science), Chicago, IL. Annual: 1950.

Literatūros Lankai (Literature Review), Buenos Aires, Argentina. 1952-1953, 1955.

Lithuania Philatelic Society Bulletin, Chicago, IL. Frequency varies: 1948-1949, 1952-1954, 1962-1968. Includes English.

Lithuanian Bulletin, Chicago, IL (previously published in New York, NY). Frequency varies: 1943-1951, 1963. English.

Lithuanian Committee for Religious Congress Biuletenis (Bulletin), Brooklyn, NY. 1966.

Lithuanian Heritage Newsletter, Boston, MA. Annual (?): 1987. English.

Lithuanian Museum Review (previously titled **Museum Review**), Chicago, IL. Frequency varies: 1967-1985. Includes English.

Lithuanian Philatelic Society of New York Bulletin, Philadelphia, PA. Quarterly: Issues 43 and 45. English.

The Lithuanian Press Abroad Yearbook, Chicago, IL. Annual: 1966-1974.

Lithuanian Sports Review, Chicago, IL. 1965-1966. English.

Lituanica, Chicago, IL. 1951.

Lituanistikos Darbai (Lithuanian Studies), Arlington, MA (previously published in Chicago, IL). Annual: 1969, 1973. Includes English.

Lituanus, Chicago, IL. Quarterly: 1956-1985. (Cumulative index for 1954-1978). English.

Lux Christi (The Light of Christ), Putnam, CT. Quarterly: 1951-1966, 1968-1971.

Margutis (Easter Egg), Chicago, IL. Monthly (except August): 1938, 1948-1949, 1954-1965.

Maria, Chicago, IL. Annual: 1956, 1959, 1961-1963. English.

The Marian, Chicago, IL. Monthly (bi-monthly in July and August): 1965. English.

Medicina (Journal of the World Lithuanian Medical Association), New York, NY. Bi-monthly: 1971-1975, 1979, 1984.

Meilė (Love), Du Bois, PA. Monthly: 1920, 1922, 1924.

Metmenys (Patterns), Chicago, IL. Quarterly: 1959-1966, 1968, 1970, 1975-1978.

Metraštis (Annual; Journal of American Lithuanian Engineers and Architects), Brooklyn, NY. Annual: 1951.

Mintis (Thought), London, England. Frequency varies: 1971.

Mintis (Thought), Memmingen, Germany. Monthly (bi-monthly): 1946.

Mišios (The Mass), Putnam, CT. 1977, 1984, 1987.

Moteris (Woman; Lithuanian Women's Magazine), Toronto, Ontario, Canada. Frequency varies: 1955-1972, 1974, 1978-1982.

Moterų Balsas (The Women's Voice), Philadelphia, PA. Monthly: 1916-1922.

Moterų Dirva (Women's Field), Chicago, IL. Bi-monthly: 1942, 1951, 1965, 1979-date. Includes English.

Mūsų Dienos (Our Days), Rodney, Ontario, Canada. Weekly: 1951.

Mūsų Sparnai (Our Wings), Chicago, IL. Semi-annual: 1951-1955, 1959-1961, 1963-1969, 1971-1973, 1975.

Mūsų Vytis (Our Knight), Chicago, IL. Quarterly: 1951, 1954-1955, 1957, 1962, 1965, 1969-1970, 1974.

Mūsų Žinios (Our News), Chicago, IL. Monthly: 1972, 1975, 1980.

Muzika (Music), Brooklyn, NY-Philadelphia, PA. Monthly: 1916.

Muzikos Žinios (Music News), Chicago, IL (two 1967 issues published in Elizabeth, NJ). Quarterly (monthly): 1936, 1938-1943, 1946-1950, 1955-1956, 1963-1964, 1966-1968, 1971, 1975, 1977.

Naujasis Gyvenimas (The New Life), Munich, Germany. Frequency varies: 1945-1948.

Naujoji Aušra (New Dawn), Chicago, IL. Monthly: 1947-1949.

Naujoji Gadynė (The New Era), Philadelphia, PA. Monthly: 1916-1917.

Naujoji Viltis (The New Hope), Chicago, IL. Annual: 1970-1981.

Nemuno Kraštas (Nemunas Countryside), Witzenhausen, West Germany. Bi-monthly: 1965-1968, 1976-1977, 1980. Includes German.

Nemunas, Scranton, PA (previously published in Chicago, IL). Frequency varies: 1950-1951.

Nepriklausoma Lietuva (Independent Lithuania), Montreal, Quebec, Canada. Monthly (bi-monthly): 1946-1947.

Pasaulio Lietuvis (The World Lithuanian), Cleveland, OH. Bi-monthly: 1963-1985, 1987.

Pasaulio Lietuvių Bendruomenės (PLB) Seimo Vadovas (World Lithuanian Community's Conference Guide), New York, NY. Annual: 1958.

Pasaulio Lietuvių Jaunimas (Lithuanian World Youth), Chicago, IL. Bi-monthly: 1973. Includes English.

Paskutinis Trimitas (The Last Trumpet), Cicero, IL. Monthly (?): 1954.

Pažanga (Progress), Du Bois, PA. Monthly: 1934.

Pedsakai (Footprints), Wiesbaden, Germany. Monthly (bi-monthly): 1946-1947.

Peleda (The Owl; Lithuanian Humor Magazine), Chicago, IL. Monthly: 1951-1954.

Peleda (The Owl; Lithuanian Humor Magazine), Welland, Ontario, Canada. Quarterly: 1956.

Pensininkas (Pensioner), Chicago, IL. Monthly (?): 1986.

Philadelphijos Lietuvių Kalendorius (Philadelphia's Lithuanian Calendar), Philadelphia, PA. Annual: 1949. Includes English.

Philadelphijos Lietuvių Tremtinių Bendruomenė Mūsų Žinios (Philadelphia's Lithuanian Exile Community's Our News), Philadelphia, PA. 1951-1952.

Plukė (Anemone), Chicago, IL. 1953.

Rimbas (The Whip), Brooklyn, NY. 1947.

St. Anthony's High School Antonianum, Kennebunkport, ME. Annual: 1960, 1964. Includes some English in 1960 issue.

St. Mary of the Angels Church Parish Bulletin, Brooklyn, NY. Weekly: 1961, 1963-1966. Includes English.

Saleziečių Balsas (Voice of the Salesian Fathers), Rome, Italy (previously published in Turin and Asti, Italy). Four or five issues per year: 1950-1959, 1961-1969.

Šaltinis (The Spring), Nottingham, England. Bi-monthly: 1970-1973, 1985.

Sandaros Kalendorius (Sandara's Calendar), Boston, MA. Annual: 1924.

Santarvė (Accord), London, England/New Haven, Connecticut. Irregular: 1951-1958.

Savu Keliu (Our Way), Cleveland, OH. Frequency varies: 1949-1952.

Sėja (The Sowing), Chicago, IL. Quarterly: 1953-1977, (Index: 1953-1977).

Severos Lietuviškas Kalendorius (Severa's Lithuanian Calendar), Cedar Rapids, IA. Annual: 1926.

Šiluvos Balsas (Messenger of Our Lady of Šiluva), Crown Point, IN. 1957, 1959. Includes English.

Skautas (Scout), Rodney, Ontario, Canada. Monthly: 1949.

Skautų Aidas (Scout's Echo), Chicago, IL. Ten issues per year: 1946-1947, 1950, 1954-1957, 1961, 1963-1966, 1968-1970, 1984-1985.

Skautybė (Scouting; supplementary publication enclosed in **Skautų Aidas**), Oakville, CT. 1965-1966, 1968.

Smeigtukas (Lancet; Lithuanian Humor Magazine), New York, NY. Bi-monthly: 1958, one undated issue.

Sportas (Sport), Brooklyn, NY. Bi-monthly: 1959, 1961.

Sporto Žinios (Lithuanian Sports News), Chicago, IL (previously published in East Cleveland, OH). Monthly: 1957-1959.

Studentų Gairės (Students' Landmarks), Chicago, IL (previously published in Cleveland, OH). Monthly (?): 1953-1954, 1956-1957.

Studentų Varpas (Students' Bell), Chicago, IL. Annual (?): 1958, 1960.

Studentų Žodis (Students' Word), Brooklyn, NY. Monthly: 1942.

Susivienijimo Lietuvių Amerikoje Raportai ir Darbai (Lithuanian Alliance of America Report of Accomplishments), New York, NY. Biennial: 1936, 1938, 1942, 1946-1960, 1964, 1966.

SLA [Susivienijimo Lietuvių Amerikoje Jaunuolių] Atzalynas (Lithuanian Alliance of America Youth Journal), New York, NY. Bi-monthly: 1959-1960. Includes English.

Susivienijimo Lietuvių Amerikoje Kalendorius (Lithuanian Alliance of America Calendar), New York, NY. Annual: 1916.

Šv. Kazimiero Akademijos Aidai (St. Casimir Academy Echoes), Chicago, IL. Five issues per year: 1939-1953.

Šv. Pranciškaus Varpelis (The Bell of St. Francis), Kennebunkport, ME (previously published in Pittsburgh, PA). Monthly: 1943-1947, 1951, 1955-1958, 1964-date.

Svečias (The Guest), Bremen, West Germany. Bi-monthly: 1961, 1963-1965.

Šviesa (The Light), Ozone Park, NY. Quarterly: 1934-1937, 1940-1943, 1946-1958, 1962-1979.

Šviturys (The Beacon), Chicago, IL. Monthly: 1949.

Švyturys (The Beacon), Chicago, IL. Monthly: 1964-1965.

Švyturys (The Beacon), Vilnius, Lithuania. 1964.

Tarka (Grater), New York, NY. Monthly: 1911.

Tauta (The Nation), Brooklyn, NY. Monthly: 1936.

Tauta Budi; Kalendorius (The Nation Watches; Calendar), Toronto, Ontario, Canada. Annual: 1954.

Technikos Pasaulis (The World of Technology), Würzburg, Germany. 1946.

Technikos Žodis (The Engineering Word), Chicago, IL. Bi-monthly (monthly): 1951-1964, 1971-1972, 1976.

Teisininkų Žinios (Jurists' News), Chicago, IL. Quarterly: 1952-1958.

Tėvai Jėzuitai Čikagoje Mūsų Žinios (The Jesuit Fathers of Chicago Our News), Chicago, IL. Bi-weekly: 1972.

Tevai Pranciškonai Metraštis (The Franciscan Fathers Chronicle), Kennebunkport, ME. Annual: 1950.

Teviškele (Native Land; supplementary children's magazine of the newspaper **Dirva**), Chicago, IL. Monthly: 1952-1955.

Tėviškės Aidas (Native Land's Echo), Chicago, IL. 1952.

Tėvynės Atgarsiai (Motherland's Echoes), Chicago, IL. Bi-monthly (?): 1966.

Tėvynės Sargas (The Guardian of the Fatherland), Chicago, IL (previously published in Brooklyn, NY, and Reutlingen, Germany). Three issues per year: 1947-1949, 1951-1985, 1987.

Tiesos Kelias (Way of the Truth), Kaunas, Lithuania. Monthly: 1925-1932, 1934, 1938-1939.

Tremtinių Informacijos (Exiles' Information; Lithuanian Society of Former DPs), Waterbury, CT. Frequency varies: 1950-1952.

Tremtinių Mokykla (Exiles' School), Nürtingen, Germany. Frequency varies: 1946.

Užuolanka (Detour), Chicago, IL. Monthly: 1955, 1961.

Varpas (The Bell), Chicago, IL. Frequency varies: 1953-1977, 1980-1981.

Veidrodis (The Mirror), Chicago, IL. Monthly: 1914.

Vėpla (The Oaf; Lithuanian Humorous and Satirical Publication), Montreal, Quebec, Canada. Monthly: 1955-1958.

Vėtyklė (Winnowing Machine), Chicago, IL. One undated issue.

Vienybės Metraštis (Unity Chronicle), New York, NY (?), Annual (?): 1924.

Vilnies Kalendorius (The Wave's Calendar), Chicago, IL. Annual: 1942, 1945-1947, 1949, 1951-1952, 1954-1957, 1959-1963, 1965, 1971.

The Violation of Human Rights in Soviet Occupied Lithuania Reports, Glenside, PA. Annual: 1971-1977, 1979-1982. English.

Voice, Chicago, IL. Monthly: 1948, 1951. Includes English.

The Voice of Lithuanian Americans, Brooklyn, NY. Monthly: 1938. English.

Vyčių Kardas (The Knights of Lithuania Sword), Detroit, MI. Monthly: 1950-1952. Includes English.

Vyskupo Informacija (Lithuanian edition of **Bishop's Brief**), Brooklyn, NY. Quarterly: 1985.

Vytis (The Knight), Centerville, OH. Monthly (bi-monthly in June-September): 1946, 1948, 1950-1954, 1958, 1972-1976, 1981, 1985. Includes English.

Žiniaraštis (Register), Chicago, IL. Monthly (?): 1933.

Zinios ir Mintys (Information and Reflections; American Lithuanian Resistance Movement), Los Angeles, CA. Irregular: 1954-1955.

Žvaigždė (The Star), Chicago, IL (1945 and 1949 issues published in Boston, MA). Monthly: 1933, 1936, 1943-1945, 1947-1950, 1952, 1954, 1956, 1959-1967.

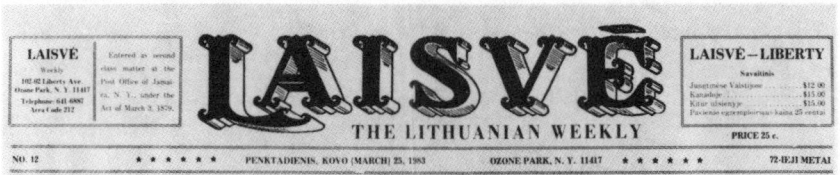

Nameplate from the Lithuanian American *Laisvė* (Liberty), Brooklyn, NY, 1983, edited by Lithuanian-born journalist and historian Anthony Bimba from 1924 until 1973.

Anthony Bimba, 1918.

Near Eastern American Collection

Manuscript Collections

Ahmed, Frank.
Papers, ca. 1917-1971. Ca. 1 linear in.

Papers of Ahmed, a Turkish American, include brief histories of Turks in America, newspaper clippings pertaining to Turkish Americans and to Turkish-Greek conflicts, and miscellany. *In English and Turkish.*

Ajami Family.
Family history, ca. 1952-1980. Ca. 1 linear in.

Papers of the Ajami family include letters, photographs, newspaper clippings, programs, and poetry. Much of the material pertains to Selma (Bojolad) Ajami, an opera singer, and to Jocelyn Ajami, an artist. Correspondence refers to Philip K. Hitti, and correspondents include Ambassador Fletcher Warren. *Includes English, Spanish, and German.*

Al Akl, F. M. (1903-1971).
Papers, ca. 1920-1971. 2 linear ft.

Al Akl was a surgeon, author, poet, photographer, inventor, and art collector.

He was born in Egypt, educated there, and received his MD from the American University of Beirut. After postgraduate training in London, Paris, and Vienna, he came to New York, where he practiced medicine and was active in Arab American affairs in addition to his other activities. He was decorated by the governments of Egypt, Syria, and Lebanon.

Papers consist of correspondence, photographs, writings, and other materials documenting Al Akl's various activities. *Mainly in English.*

American Arabic Association (Boston, Massachusetts).
Records, ca. 1969-1981. Ca. 1 linear in.

The Association is a nonsectarian cultural and charitable organization dedicated to improvement of relations between the United States and Arabic-speaking countries. Records consist mainly of program announcements for meetings. *In English.*

Ansara, James M.
Papers, ca. 1920-1982. Ca. 10 linear ft.

Ansara wrote extensively on migration of Arabic-speaking people in the United States and was active in Arab American organizations. He served as executive secretary and executive director of the Syrian and Lebanese American Federation of the Eastern States and as editor of the *Federation Herald* (later the *National Herald*), its monthly publication. In 1956, he moved to Boston and set up a consulting business on Middle Eastern and Arab relations, but he continued to be active in the National Association.

Papers include personal correspondence and records of organizations relating to Americans of Arab descent, including those of the National Association of Syrian-Lebanese American Federations. Also included are writings and notes; school notes and papers; newspaper clippings; photographs; and published materials, mainly pertaining to Middle East affairs. *Mainly in English. Partial inventory available.*

Arab Cultural Center (San Francisco, California).
Records, 1978-1981. 1 linear in.

Records of the Center consist of bylaws, objectives, press releases, flyers, etc. Also included are press releases of the American Federation of Ramallah Palestine and its founding. *Mainly in English.*

Association of Arab-American University Graduates, Twin Cities Chapter (Minneapolis, Minnesota).
Records, 1970-1987. Ca. 2 linear ft.

The Association of Arab-American University Graduates is a cultural, educational, and professional organization founded in 1967. It assists in development of the Arab world by donating the professional services of its members. It is nonprofit, nonsectarian, and nonpolitical and is open to university graduates of Arabic origin.

Records of the Twin Cities Chapter include resolutions, pamphlets, newspaper clippings, meeting announcements, and papers on Zionism. The records pertain to the national organization as well as to the Twin Cities Chapter. *Includes English.*

Couri, Joseph M.
Papers, ca. 1907-1980. Ca. 1 linear in.

Papers of Couri, a Lebanese American, include photographs, correspondence, and copies of citizenship documents for Najiba and Tony Ferris (originally Antonios Farès). Also included is a pamphlet on the Ladies Itoo Society (Peoria, IL). *Includes English. Photocopies only.*

Federation of Turkish American Societies, Inc. (New York, New York).
Records, ca. 1981-1984. 1 linear in.

Records consist of letters to U.S. senators, newspaper clippings, and mailing lists. Most materials pertain to Turkish-American relations. *In English and Turkish.*

Hamarneh, Sami K.
Papers, ca. 1960-1972. Ca. 1 linear in.

Hamarneh was a historian of Islamic medicine at the Smithsonian Institution (Washington, DC). Papers include correspondence and professional papers. *Includes English.*

Hitti, Philip Khuri (1886-1978).
Papers, ca. 1915-1976. Ca. 15 linear ft.

Hitti was born in Shimlan, Lebanon. He graduated from the American University of Beirut and taught there until he came to the United States in 1913. He received his PhD from Columbia University, where he taught in the Department of Oriental Languages. In 1920, he returned to the American University of Beirut as a history professor. From 1926 until his retirement in 1954, he taught at Princeton University in the Departments of Oriental Languages and Literatures and Near Eastern Studies. In the United States, Hitti was an authority on the cultures, history, religions, and languages of the Near East and worked to create among Americans an appreciation and understanding of Arabic and Islamic cultures. In 1945, he served as adviser to the Arab delegations to the United Nations organizational meeting in San Francisco. He also served as a consultant to American government agencies and corporations, was the author of numerous books, and trained generations of scholars.

Hitti's papers include personal and professional correspondence, lectures and speeches, book reviews, writings, personal memorabilia, and copies of U.S.-sponsored archaeological dig contracts. *Mainly in English. Inventory available. Restricted. Related collection: William H. Shehadi.*

Mokarzel, Mary.
Papers, ca. 1921-1972. Ca. 3 linear ft.

Papers of Mary Mokarzel, who succeeded her father as publisher of the Arab American newspaper *Al-Hoda* (The Guidance), consist of personal correspondence, business records, photographs, advertisements, and miscellany. Also included are subscription lists for the *Lebanese American Journal.* Correspondents include Sheikh Pierre Gemayel, William M. Kunstler, Khalil Habib Sayegh, Leonard S. Tack, Necib Trabulsi, and others. *Inventory available.*

Naff, Alixa.
Papers, 1962. Ca. 1 linear in.

Papers of Naff consist of a photocopied typescript pertaining to folklore and life histories collected from Christian Syrian Lebanese first generation immigrants in the United States. *In English.*

Najjar Family.
Papers, ca. 1975-1982. Ca. 1 linear in.

The Najjar family (originally Al-Balady) are Lebanese Americans and Orthodox Christians from Lebanon and Syria and later from New York and Montreal. The family history consists of a family chronicle and genealogy. *In English. Photocopy only.*

Rashid Family Club of America.
Papers, 1979-1980. 1 booklet.

The Rashids are a Lebanese American family, the first five members of which immigrated in 1896 and moved to the Midwest, settling in Detroit, Michigan; Iowa; and Illinois. Papers consist of a reunion booklet (1979) and newspaper clippings describing a reunion of the family. *In English.*

Shehadi, William H.
Papers, 1954-1957. Ca. 1 linear in.

Papers of William H. Shehadi contain correspondence, newspaper clippings, and photographs pertaining to activities in honor of Philip Khuri Hitti, in particular to the banquet given by the Alumni Association of the American University of Beirut in honor of Hitti's retirement in 1954. *In English.*

Soffa Family.
Papers, 1979. Ca. 1 linear in.

The history of the Syrian American Soffa family is a chronicle of the families of Amen (ca. 1873-1949), John (1897-), and Anna Soffa, and their respective spouses and spouses' families. Amen Soffa came to the United States in the late 1890s, and became a trader in Wisconsin and Minnesota. In 1901, he married Nazera Kimmel (originally Cammel), a Lebanese American, and they settled near Preston, MN. The family history consists of a photocopy of *The Family History Book: A Genealogical Record,* compiled by Barry Marshall Dahl. *In English.*

Syrian Ladies' Aid Society (Brooklyn, New York).
Records, 1908-1958. Ca. 1 linear in.

Records of this charitable society consist of bylaws, correspondence, newspaper clippings, photographs, and miscellany. *Includes English.*

Monographs

The IHRC collection of Near Eastern American monographs, although not large (ca. 180 volumes), is representative of the experiences of Arabic-speaking people in the United States. History, including settlement and assimilation, and religion are two areas of particular strength.

Available bibliographies on the history of Near Eastern immigrants include Philip Kayal's "An Arab-American Bibliography," in *Arabic Speaking Communities in American Cities*, edited by Barbara C. Aswad (1974); Ayad al-Qazzaz's *Women in the Arab World: An Annotated Bibliography* (1975); and George Dmitri Selim's *The Arabs in the United States: A Selected List of References* (1983).

The Arab American experience was the subject of an IHRC-sponsored conference in 1983, proceedings of which are published in *Crossing the Waters: Arabic-Speaking Immigrants to the United States before 1940*, edited by Eric Hooglund (1987). Other general works on Near Eastern Americans include the Aswad book mentioned above, Amer Ibrahim Al-Kindilchie's *Arab Immigrants in the United States* (1976), James Ansara's *The Immigration and Settlement of the Syrians* (thesis, 1931), Habib I. Katibah's *Arabic Speaking Americans* (1946), Philip K. Hitti's *The Arabs: A Short History* (1944), and Beverlee Turner Mehdi's *The Arabs in America, 1492-1977: A Chronology and Fact Book* (1978).

The origins and migration of Near Eastern groups can be researched in Frank Ahmed's *An Anatolian Odyssey: Early Turkish Migration to America, 1900-1924* (1984); *The Story of Lebanon and its Emigrants*, published by the Al-Hoda Press (1968); and Alixa Naff's *Becoming American: The Early Arab Immigrant Experience* (1985). Publications on particular communities with settlements of Near Eastern immigrants include John G. Moses' *From Mt. Lebanon to the Mohawk Valley: The Story of Syro-Lebanese Americans of the Utica Area* (1981); Lucius Hopkins Miller's *Our Syrian Population: A Study of the Syrian Communities of Greater New York* (1904); *Syrian and Lebanese Texans*, from the Institute of Texan Cultures (1974); and Mohammad Tavakoli-Yazdi's *Persian Assyrian Immigrants in the Metropolitan Chicago Area* (1970).

Of the various religious groups, three are well represented in the collection. They are Muslims, and Maronite and Orthodox Christians. Works on the former include Abdo A. Elkholy's *The Arab Moslems in the United States: Religion and Assimilation* (1966); Yahya Aossey, Jr.'s *Fifty Years of Islam in Iowa, 1925-1975* (1975); and Elkholy's *Religion and Assimilation in Two Muslim Communities in America* (1960). The Arab Christian experience in America is reflected in Mary C. Sengstock's *Kinship in a Roman Catholic Ethnic Group* (1975); Thomas J. McMahon's *The Irish of the East: The Maronites, Their History and Liturgy* (n.d.); May Ahdab-Yehia's "The Detroit Maronite Community" (in the Aswad anthology); and Pierre Gemayel's *A Call from Christian Lebanon* (1955). Also included are church histories, such as the *St. Nicholas Syrian Orthodox Church* (1957); *St. Nicholas Orthodox Church* (1973); and *Church of the Holy Family 50th Jubilee, 1918-1968* (1968).

The Arab Americans are vigorous organizers of clubs and societies, often connected with family and church. IHRC monographs on this aspect of Arab American life include *Membership Directory (1970, 1971)* of the Association of Arab-American University Graduates and a history of the group, *The First Decade, 1967-1977* (complemented by manuscript holdings); the *Constitution and By-Laws of the Arab National League* (n.d.); *The Nineteenth Annual Convention of the American Ramallah Federation* (1977); and the Risq G. Haddad Foundation's *Charter, Constitution, and By-Laws* (1943).

For some areas of Near Eastern American life, including political involvement, the press, education, and cultural works, the IHRC monograph collection contains only a few representative works. They include *Political Action Guide: You Can Make Your Opinion Heard in Congress* (1984); Al-Kindilchie's *Arab Immigrants in the United States* (1976); and "Research on Arab Child Bilinguals," in Aswad's book.

The IHRC holds a good sample of available literary works, many of them in Arabic. Included are Sargon Boulas's *Tigris* (n.d.); *Arab Writers in America: Critical*

Essays and Annotated Bibliography (1981); Fouad M. Al Akl's *Until Summer Comes* (1945); Eugene Paul Nassar's *Wind of the Land: Two Prose Poems* (1979); Na'um Makarzel's *Qissah* (1900); and many items, in Arabic and English, by Kahlil Gibran. Material relating to music includes Alexander Maloof's *Oriental Piano Compositions; Syrian Popular Songs* (1924); *Twelve Arabic Popular Songs* (1938); and *Syrian, Oriental and American Vocal and Instrumental Compositions* (1928).

Among the small number of biographies and autobiographies are Barbara Young's *A Study of Kahlil Gibran: This Man from Lebanon* (1931); Stanley E. Kerr's *The Lion of Marash: Personal Experiences with American Near East Relief, 1919-1922* (1973); Jean Gibran's *Kahlil Gibran, His Life and World* (1981); Michael A. Shadid's *A Doctor for the People* (1939); Salom Rizk's *Syrian Yankee* (1943); and Rev. Abraham Rihbany's *A Far Journey* (1914). A recent study of mainstream society's perceptions of Arabic people is Michael Suleiman's *Arabs in the Mind of America* (1988).

Newspapers

Action, New York, NY. Weekly: 1969-1982. English.

American University of Beirut News, New York, NY. Quarterly: 1973. English.

Arab Mirror (previously a section of **Voice of Masr**), Jersey City, NJ. Monthly: 1977-1978. Includes English.

Al-Bayan (The Explanation), Detroit, MI. Weekly: 1959, 1966.

Al Bedaya (The Beginning), Little Rock, AR. Monthly: 1981-1982. Includes English.

Belady (My Country), Glendale, CA. Monthly: 1974-1975. Includes English.

The Caravan, Brooklyn, NY. Weekly: 1953-1954, 1959, 1961. (Microfilm: 1953-1961). English.

Free Palestine, Washington, DC. Monthly: 1969-1972. English.

The Heritage, New York, NY. Weekly: 1968, 1970, 1972, 1974. English.

Al-Hoda (The Guidance), New York, NY. Weekly: 1960, 1966, 1973-date.

Al-Islaah (The Reform), New York, NY. Weekly: 1949, 1952, 1953, 1956, 1966, 1969-1983. (Microfilm: 1949-1958, 1962-1977). Includes English.

Meraat ul Gharb (Mirror of the West), Brooklyn, NY. Tri-weekly: 1950-1952, 1955-1959.

New Lebanese American Journal (previously titled **Lebanese American Journal**), New York, NY. Weekly: 1956-1978. English.

The News Circle (changed to serial format in 1980), Los Angeles, CA. Monthly: 1973-1980. English.

The Palestinian Voice, Los Angeles, CA. Semi-weekly: 1971-1976. Includes English.

El Ra-Ed News (The Pioneer), Staten Island, NY. Bi-monthly: 1975-1978. Includes English.

As-Sameer (The Entertainer), Brooklyn, NY. Daily (?): 1949-1951, 1953.

As-Sayeh (The Wanderer), New York, NY. Semi-weekly: 1947, 1953-1954.

The Source, Ottawa, Ontario, Canada (previously published in Edmonton, Alberta, and Vancouver, British Columbia, Canada). Semi-monthly: 1971-1978. Includes English.

Star News Pictorial, Los Angeles, CA. Monthly: 1961-1964. English.

The Tulsa Star, Tulsa, OK. Bi-weekly: 1972-1978. English.

Voice of Masr, Jersey City, NJ. Monthly: 1974, 1977. Includes English.

Al-Wafa (The Fulfillment), Lawrence, MA. Semi-weekly. (Microfilm: 1907-1910).

Serials

ADC Background Papers (American Arab Anti-Discrimination Committee Research Institute), Washington, DC. Frequency varies: 1982-1984. English.

ADC Issues (ADC Research Institute), Washington, DC. Frequency varies: 1981-1984. English.

ADC Times (previously titled **ADC Reports**), Washington, DC. Ten issues per year: 1980-date. English.

American-Arab Affairs, Washington, DC. Quarterly: 1982-1984. English.

American-Arab Affairs Council Special Report, Washington, DC. Quarterly (bi-monthly): 1982, 1983. English.

ANERA Newsletter (American Near East Refugee Aid, Inc.), Washington, DC. Bi-monthly: 1970-1973. English.

Arab Cultural Center Newsletter, San Francisco, CA. Frequency varies: 1973-1981. English.

The Arab News, Dearborn, MI. Monthly (?): 1979.

Arab Views, New York, NY. Monthly: 1969-1970. English.

The Arab World, New York, NY. Quarterly: 1944, 1946. English.

The Arab World (The Arab Information Center), New York, NY. Bi-monthly (monthly): 1958, 1965-1972. English.

Arab World Issues, Belmont, MA (Detroit, MI). Frequency varies: 1975-1977, 1980. English.

Association of Arab-American University Graduates Information Papers, North Dartmouth, MA. Frequency varies: 1970-1978. English.

Association of Arab-American University Graduates Membership Directory, Washington, DC. Annual: 1969-1971. English.

Association of Arab-American University Graduates, Inc. Newsletter, Belmont, MA (previously published in Shrewsbury, MA, and Detroit, MI). Frequency varies: 1968-date. English.

ATAA News Line (Assembly of Turkish-American Associations) Washington, DC. Quarterly: 1985-date. English.

ATA-USA (Bulletin of the Assembly of Turkish American Associations), Washington, DC. Quarterly: 1980-1985. English.

Ay Yildiz (Turkish Star; Turkish American Cultural Association of Georgia), Atlanta, GA. Monthly: 1985. English.

The Cedar Press, Long Beach, CA. Monthly: 1975. English.

The Copts "Christians of Egypt," Jersey City, NJ. 1977. English.

Egypt, Washington, DC. Quarterly: 1951-1952. English.

The Federation Herald (title changed to **The National Herald** in 1956), Washington, DC (previously published in Fitchburg, MA). Monthly: 1940-1943, 1948-1955. English.

Federation News (Federation of American Syrian-Lebanon Clubs), Columbus, OH. Monthly: 1952-1953. English.

Focus (National Association of Arab Americans), Washington, DC. Monthly: 1982. English.

Habibi, Mt. View, CA. Monthly: 1979. English.

Inside, Washington, DC. Monthly: 1983. English.

The Islamic Center Bulletin, Washington, DC. Quarterly: 1972-1975. English.

Islamic Center of Minnesota Newsletter, Minneapolis, MN. 1973. English.

Al-Khālidāt (The Eternals), Terre Haute, IN (place of publication varies). Monthly (except March and April): 1928, 1930-1931.

The Link, New York, NY. Bi-monthly: 1971-1976, 1979-1981. English.

The Middle East Newsletter, Beirut, Lebanon. Frequency varies: 1968-1971. English.

Mideast Monitor (previously titled **Middle East Focus**), Belmont, MA. Frequency varies: 1984-date. English.

MIM Newsletter, New York, NY. Weekly (?): 1986. Turkish and English.

Najda Newsletter (Women Concerned about the Middle East), Berkeley, CA. Monthly (bi-monthly): 1982-1983. English.

The National Herald (previously titled **The Federation Herald**), Washington, DC. Monthly: 1956-1959. English.

The News Circle (previously published as a newspaper), Glendale, CA. Monthly: 1980, 1982-1985. Includes English.

The News Circle Almanac, Los Angeles, CA. Annual: 1974-1975. English.

Notebook (Arab American Institute), Washington, DC. Quarterly: 1985. English.

The Official Bulletin, Houston, TX. Monthly: 1954, 1962. English.

Palestine Resistance Bulletin, Buffalo, NY. Monthly (?): 1971. English.

The South Florida Basilian, Hialeah, FL. Semi-annual (?): 1963-1964. English.

The Syrian Ark, Indianapolis, IN. Monthly: 1941, 1952-1954. English.

The Syrian World, New York, NY. Monthly, weekly: 1927-1928. (Microfilm: 1926-1935). English.

Toledo Archdiocesan Messenger (previously titled **Archdiocese Messenger**), Toledo, OH. Bi-monthly: 1962, 1964, 1969-1975. English.

Türk Birliği Bültemi (Journal of Turkish Unity; Federation of Turkish-American Societies Inc.), New York, NY. Monthly: 1984. Turkish and English.

The Turkish-American Gazette, Flushing, NY. Bi-monthly: 1985. English.

United Holy Land Fund Newsletter, Chicago, IL. Monthly: 1980-1981. English.

U.S. OMEN (United States Organization for Medical and Educational Needs), San Francisco, CA. Annual: 1967, 1973, 1975, 1979-1981. English.

Voice, Washington, DC. Monthly: 1982. English.

The Word, Englewood, NJ. Monthly: 1962-1963, 1965-1971, 1975. English.

Bashara Kalil Forzley's Dry Goods Store and delivery car, Worcester, MA, ca. 1925; from *An Autobiography of Bashara Kalil Forzley*, Worcester, MA, 1958.

Polish American Collection

Manuscript Collections

Alecks, Joseph.
Papers, 1938-1976. 1 linear ft.

Alecks began his career as a newspaper reporter. During the 1950s he was secretary to Boston mayors John B. Hynes and John Collins, and eventually he became Comptroller of the Commonwealth of Massachusetts. Alecks was a prominent member of the Polish American community and of Polish American organizations, including the Polish-American Veterans of Foreign Wars (Kościuszko Post, Dorchester, MA), the Polish-American Citizens Club of South Boston, and the Polish American Veterans Boston Post. He authored a Massachusetts state law commemorating Polish Constitution Day and was instrumental in naming the General Casimir Pulaski Skyway.

Papers include personal correspondence, newspaper clippings, pamphlets, and photographs. *Includes English.*

Alliance of Poles in America (Cleveland, Ohio).
Records, 1907-1932. 1 microfilm reel.

The Alliance, a regional, cultural, and fraternal insurance organization, was founded in 1895 as the Alliance of Poles in the State of Ohio. Its name was changed ca. 1917. The Alliance has ca. 17,000 members and eighty-three branches in Ohio, Michigan, and Pennsylvania. It provides life insurance to members, cooperates with other Polish American organizations in cultural activities, sponsors clubs for Polish youth, maintains a library, and provides scholarship funds.

Records include minutes of meetings of the Central Body (1917-1930) and its predecessor, the Alliance of Poles in the State of Ohio (1907-1917); lists of officers; minutes of conventions (1907-1932); and texts and revisions of constitutions. *Includes English.*

Alliance Publishing Company (Chicago, Illinois).
Records, ca. 1939-1961. Ca. 3 linear ft.

Alliance is the publisher of two prominent Polish American newspapers, the daily *Dziennik Związkowy* (1908-present), and the bi-weekly, *Zgoda* (1881-present). Records of the Company include correspondence, cartoons, newspaper clippings, editorial material, photographs, and material for the 1952 *Kalendarz Związkowy*, an annual publication. Also included are material on the American Star Congress of 1949 and a financial report for the Polish

American Congress. *Includes English.*
Inventory available.

American Committee for Resettlement of Polish Displaced Persons (Chicago, Illinois).
Records, ca. 1948-1968.   2 linear ft.

The Committee (ACRPDP) was formed in 1948 in affiliation with the Polish American Congress to aid in resettlement of Polish people then in European displaced persons camps. It represented several larger Polish American organizations. The ACRPDP had twenty-six state division committees, many local committees, and representatives in England and Germany. It continued to function after expiration in 1951 of the Displaced Persons Act (Public Law 774, June 1948), in cooperation with the National Catholic Welfare Conference. Its operations ceased in 1968.

Records include correspondence (1948-1964), financial records, information on fund drives, reports, and organizational papers including bylaws and articles of incorporation. Correspondents include the Travelers Aid Society of Chicago (IL), the Displaced Persons Commission, the Advisory Committee on Voluntary Foreign Aid, the American Council of Voluntary Agencies for Foreign Services, Inc., the Attorney General of the State of Illinois, and many Polish American organizations. *Includes English.*
Inventory available. Related collection: Polish American Congress (Chicago, IL).

American Council of Polish Cultural Clubs (Falls Church, Virginia).
Records, 1949-1982.   8 linear in.

The Council was founded in 1948, with headquarters in Falls Church, VA, to facilitate communication among Polish cultural clubs and to promote understanding of Polish culture in the United States. Records of the twenty-one branches of the Council consist of official convention records and publications of affiliated organizations. *Mainly in English.*

American Polish Civil War Centennial Commission (New York, New York).
Records, 1961-1965.   1.5 linear ft.

The Commission was affiliated with the Polish American Historical Society and was established to stimulate research into, and public awareness of, Polish participation in the Civil War. Records consist of correspondence, press releases, and publications. *Includes English.*

American Relief for Poland, District 33 (Chicago, Illinois).
Records, ca. 1941-1976.   4.5 linear ft.

The American Relief for Poland was organized in 1939 to aid Polish war victims and refugees. Funds were gathered in connection with drives for the National War Chest Fund and United War Fund, national clearinghouses for relief funds. In 1945 a delegation of the organization visited displaced persons camps in Germany. The organization helped sponsor and relocate these refugees, substantially aided by the National Catholic Welfare Conference--War Relief Services. Relief supplies were also sent to Poland after the Armistice and distributed through efforts of Caritas, a Catholic relief organization. In 1958, the ARP sponsored construction of an artificial limb factory in Poland and also, with the effort of Dr. C. Walton Lillihei, contributed to installation in Warsaw of surgical equipment for heart ailments. The ARP also sponsored a colony for Polish refugees, many of them children, in Santa Rosa, Mexico.

Records of the Chicago district include correspondence, organizational papers, financial documents, and applications of displaced persons for immigration to the United States. *Includes English.*
Inventory available.

Archacki, Henry (1907-).
Papers, ca. 1934-1979.   80 linear ft.

Archacki, a Polish American artist, journalist, publisher, and illustrator, was born in Warsaw, Poland. He came to the United States with his family. They settled in Chicago, IL, where Archacki showed an early proclivity for art and journalism. He worked as sports reporter for *Dziennik Związkowy* and in 1930 went to New York as head artist for the Brooklyn branch of the paper. In 1931, he began his "Czy wiecie że" (Do You Know) drawings, and became sports editor of *Poland* and *Czas* and, later, of *Nowy Świat*. He remained active in Polish American organizations, including the Reymont Literary Guild, the Polish American Athletic Club, the Polish American Tennis Club, and the General Krzyżanowski Memorial Committee.

Archacki's papers include correspondence, articles, newspaper clippings from Polish American newspapers, photographs, materials on sports, and publications. *Includes English. Inventory available.*

Augustyn, Stanley.
Papers, ca. 1969-1972. Ca. 1 linear in.

Augustyn's papers consist of correspondence, essays, newspaper clippings, postcards, and miscellany. Materials pertain to the National Shrine of Our Lady of Częstochowa, Holy Cross Parish (Maspeth, NY), World War II and Poland, Polish relief, and New York City's Northside neighborhood. *Includes English.*

Barańska, Janina Lewandowska.
Papers, ca. 1920-1975. Ca. 3 linear in.

A social worker by profession, Barańska acted for many years with the Polish Theater of Buffalo, NY. She was president of the Federation of Polish Women, Buffalo; an officer of the Polish Republican Women's Club of Erie County, NY; and active in Dom Polski Association, Service Men's Mothers Club, Kółko Polek Charitable Society, and Buflopole Women's Federation (Federacja Kobiet Buflopole). She received several awards and citations for her civic activities.

Her papers include newspaper clippings, scrapbooks, reminiscences, photographs, and theatrical programs. *Includes English. Inventory available.*

Białasiewicz, Józef F.
Papers, ca. 1919-1976. Ca. 1.5 linear ft.

Białasiewicz was a Polish American newspaper editor from Chicago, IL. Papers include correspondence, financial records, newspaper clippings, reports, and miscellany pertaining to the Polish American Book Company, *Polonia*, and *Ameryka-Echo*. *Includes English.*

Bristol, Helena Ogrodowska (1896-).
Papers, 1937-1966. 5 linear in.

An author and English teacher, Bristol was born in Żyrardów, Poland. Her family came to the United States in 1905 and settled in Philadelphia, PA. Helena was educated at the University of Pennsylvania and Columbia College of Music and for many years taught English at the Philadelphia High School for Girls. She married Wayne A. Bristol in 1926. She authored several books, including *House of Tuttle, After Thirty Years: Poland Revisited* (1939), and *Let the Blackbird Sing: A Novel in Verse* (1952).

Papers include a manuscript of "The God of Late Beginnings" and published writings. *Includes English.*

Brya, Stanley Michael (1887-).
Papers, ca. 1930- . 4 linear ft.

A self-taught historian, Brya was born near Nowy Targ, Poland, and came to the United States in 1904 to escape conscription in the army. He settled in Chicago, IL, where he worked in slaughterhouses and then moved to Pennsylvania to become a coal miner. In 1913, he settled in Minneapolis, MN, where he worked for Dayton Hudson Corporation. Brya devoted much time to popularizing the accomplishments of his fellow countrymen, and published numerous articles in the American press.

Papers comprise correspondence, newspaper clippings of articles he wrote, and a scrapbook. *Includes English. Preliminary inventory.*

Burandt, August.
Papers, 1900. 1 page.

Papers of Burandt (or Burant) consist of a letter he wrote from Poland to his brother, Bernard, a farmer in the Stevens Point, WI, area. In the letter, Burandt discusses his poor health and his religious faith.

Ciszewski, Mrs. Barbara.
Papers, ca. 1948-1970. Ca. 1 linear in.

Papers consist of newspaper clippings, correspondence, and student notebooks. Clippings pertain to Polish Americans, NATO, disarmament, communism, and other topics. *Includes English.*

Citizens Committee and Recruiting Centre #20 (Minneapolis, Minnesota).
Records, ca. 1913-1938. 2.5 linear in.

The Recruitment Committee for the Polish Army in France (Komitet Obywatelski w Minneapolis, Minnesota, i Komitet Rekrutacyjny dla Armii Polskiej we Francyi) was organized through efforts of the Polish Falcons Alliance in 1917. Its president was Julian Szajnert. Local citizens committees were organized to oversee organization of the Polish Army, listing names of those interested, preparing sendoffs of troops, and recruiting volunteers. Recruitment Centre No. 20 sent over 200 volunteers to fight in World War I. From 1919 to 1921, it collected funds on behalf of the Committee of the National Department in America (Komitet Wydziału Narodowego w Ameryce) for relief of Polish children.
Records of Centre #20 consist of correspondence and minutes. *Includes English.*

Czas Publishing Company (Brooklyn, New York).
Records, ca. 1925-1975. Ca. 2 linear ft.

Czas is a large East Coast Polish American publishing company. It formerly published the weekly newspaper *Czas* (until publication ceased in 1975).
Records consist chiefly of editorial correspondence and published material. *Includes English. Inventory available.*

Drzewieniecki, Walter M.
Papers, ca. 1970- . Ca. 7 linear in.

Drzewieniecki is an emeritus professor of history at SUNY-Buffalo. Papers consist of correspondence, newspaper clippings, and programs documenting his career and Polish American activities in Buffalo, NY. *Includes English.*

Fox, Rev. Paul J. (1874-1963).
Papers, ca. 1890-1961. 20 linear ft.

Fox was born in Kojkowice, Poland, came to the United States in 1896, was naturalized in 1904, and married in 1908. He was educated at Western Reserve University, Oberlin Theological Seminary, and Johns Hopkins University. He served as pastor of various Polish Presbyterian churches in Ohio, Maryland, New Jersey, and Illinois. Fox was editor of the Polish magazine *Advance* and author of *The Poles in America* and *The Polish National Catholic Church.* He was also associated with St. Paul's Polish Presbyterian Church (Baltimore, MD) and, as a social worker and director, with the Laird Neighborhood Community House in Chicago, IL.
Papers of Rev. Fox reflect his various activities in the United States and Poland. Included are manuscripts of his publications and press articles, many of them for *Przebudzenie* (Awakening); religious materials; college lecture notes and educational materials; documentation of the Laird Community House; records from his visit to Poland; newspaper clippings; and extensive correspondence. *Includes English. Inventory available.*

Friedel, Mieczyslaw.
Papers, n.d. Ca. 1 linear in.

Friedel was a Polish American journalist, actor, radio program director, and U.S. Army Combat Intelligence officer. Papers consist of a photocopy of his manuscript entitled "Unbookish and Undivulged Story about World War II." The manuscript consists of newspaper clippings of a diary Friedel wrote for the Polish American Daily *Kuryer Polski* (Milwaukee, WI). *In English.*

Friends of Polish Culture (Boston, Massachusetts).
Records, ca. 1945-1968. 6 linear in.

Records consist of financial records, membership lists, correspondence, and miscellany. *Includes English.*

Golaski, Walter M. (1913-).
Papers, ca. 1961-1972. Ca. 1 linear in.

Golaski is an industrial engineer, scientist, and inventor from Philadelphia, PA. Papers include a curriculum vitae, correspondence, and publications. *In English. Inventory available.*

Gottwald, John (1905-).
Papers, 1958-1976. Ca. 1 linear ft.

Gottwald was born in Mizun, Austria, and completed his veterinary medicine studies at the Academy of Veterinary Medicine in Poland. He worked as a veterinarian until 1940 in Nowogródek, Poland, and then in the Łódź area. From 1947 to 1951, he worked in occupied Austria for the French Army as garrison veterinarian. In 1951, he came to the United States, where he worked for the USDA as a veterinary medical officer.

Papers consist of correspondence with family and friends in Poland. *Includes some English and German.*

Hoinko, Thaddeus (1895-).
Papers, ca. 1920-1978. 12 linear ft.

Hoinko was a Polish diplomat active in Polish American organizations after he came to the United States. He was born in Ukraine, lived in Poland, and in 1922 came to America as an official of the First Polish Consulate. Through his position, he became familiar with Polish Americans in major U.S. cities. He was hired by the American Polish Chamber of Commerce (New York, NY) and became a U.S. citizen in 1938. He wrote the column "Polonica Americas" for the organization's magazine *Poland.* In 1941, he became executive secretary of the Polish-American War Relief Society, later renamed Polish War Relief; and in 1944 he was appointed to the Polish Information Center in New York. From

1945 to 1964, he worked for *Opportunity* magazine in Chicago, IL.

Hoinko's papers include correspondence, photographs, and materials pertaining to his organizational activities, particularly with the Polish American Council and the American Polish Chamber of Commerce. Also included are typescripts of lectures on Poland and international affairs and papers of his wife, Marjorie Pitman Hoinko. *Includes English.*

Janda, Victoria (d. 1961).
Papers, ca. 1934-1961. Ca. 6 linear in.

An author and social worker, Janda published three books of poetry, served as president of the Polanie Club of Minneapolis-St. Paul, MN, and was first executive secretary of the International Institute of St. Paul. She was also a member of the Minneapolis Poetry Society and the League of Minnesota Poets and was recipient of many literary and civic honors. Her books include *Singing Furrows* (1953), *Star Hunger* (1942), and *Walls of Space* (1945).

Papers include correspondence, literary manuscripts, typescripts of memoirs, speeches, stories, poems, Polish legends for young people, pencil drawings, collected articles about Poland, and photographs. *Includes English.*

Jaskólski, Alexandra (1918-).
Papers, ca. 1930-1979. Ca. 4.5 linear ft.

Papers of Jaskólski, a musician and music teacher (who as a soloist was known as Oleńka Nurczyńska Butylda), document her musical and journalistic career. Included are publications and administrative correspondence from the New England Conservatory of Music, Polish and Polish American music, diaries, miscellany, and materials pertaining to Jaskólski's work as editor of the Polish American *Gazeta Polonii. Includes English. Inventory available. Related collections: Walter Nurczyński and Valeria Wycke Nurczyńska; Karol T. Jaskólski.*

Jaskólski, Karol T. (1908-1972).
Papers, ca. 1939-1973. 107 linear ft.

Jaskólski was an editor of the Polish American newspaper *Kuryer Codzienny* and founder and editor of the *Gazeta Polonii*. He was born near Cracow, received a university education, and was a faculty member at the University of Lvov prior to World War II. After the war, he came to the United States and settled in Boston, MA. He was active in many Polish American organizations in Boston and for more than twenty years directed the "Polish Variety Hour" radio program. He also taped many programs for Voice of America.

Jaskólski's papers reflect his activities as editor of *Kuryer Codzienny* and *Gazeta Polonii* and his involvement with radio broadcasts of the "Polish Variety Hour" and Voice of America. Included in this rich collection are personal and professional correspondence, newspaper clippings, financial reports, diaries, publications, programs, announcements and advertising copy, receipts, programs for the Polish Variety Hour, information pertaining to performances of "Mazowsze" in Boston and to the Poznań Boys Choir, photograph albums and photographs, commemorative brochures, and awards. Correspondence and other materials pertain to Jaskólski's mother-in-law Valeria Nurczyński, to Walter Nurczyński, and to his wife, Alexandra. Correspondents include John F. Kennedy, Edward M. Kennedy, Hubert H. Humphrey, other government officials, and numerous prominent Polish Americans. *Includes English. Partial inventory available.*
Related collections: Walter Nurczyński and Valeria Wycke Nurczyńska; Alexandra Jaskólski.

Kiełkowski, Victor (1896-).
Papers, ca. 1949-1976. Ca. 3 linear ft.

A former army officer and career officer in the Polish gendarmerie, Kiełkowski was born in a village near Lipno, Poland. He was educated at a teachers' college in Wymślin. During World War I, he completed army infantry officers' training school. He fought the Bolsheviks and, when his regiment disbanded, returned to Poland. There he continued his career in the gendarmerie and in the army until he was compelled to emigrate because of unspecified difficulties concerning his position. Kiełkowski came to Chicago, IL, but no reference is made in his papers to his activities after his arrival there.

Papers consist of correspondence, biographical materials, personal papers, and some writings. *Includes some English and German. Inventory available.*

Kierońska, Henia.
Papers, ca. 1939-1969. Ca. 1 linear in.

Kierońska's papers consist of articles and newspaper clippings pertaining to Polish Americans and their history; articles, photographs, and cartoons regarding the German blitz in Poland in 1939; a family history of Anthony Sadowski (1661-1736), a Polish American pioneer in Pennsylvania; and a Polish American history by Frank A. Zabrosky. Most articles are from the *Philadelphia Inquirer* and *Zgoda*. *Includes English.*

Kosciolowski, Sophie (ca. 1903-).
Papers, ca. 1914-1971. Ca. 1 linear in. (transcript).

Kosciolowski was born in Poland and came to the United States with her parents in 1912. After returning to Poland for a year, she came back to the United States in 1914, and the family settled in Chicago, IL. She worked at Armour & Co. Dried Beef Packing Department from ages thirteen to fifteen, then again beginning in 1931. In 1938 she was elected steward, and eventually became vice president of Local 347 of United Packinghouse, Food, and Allied Workers, and served as a member of the Grievance Committee and National Armour Chain Bargaining Committee.

Transcript of oral interview covers her experiences as an immigrant in 1914, her work as a child in a meat packing plant, her membership in the United Packinghouse, Food and Allied Workers' Union, and her work as an employee of and labor organizer at Armour & Co., ca. 1914-1971. *In English.*

Kowalski, John.
Papers, ca. 1940-1970. Ca. 6 linear ft.

Papers of Kowalski, a prominent leader of the East Coast Polish American community, include materials pertaining to the Association of the Sons of Poland, the Polish American Congress, the Pulaski Association, Inc., the Józef Piłsudski Institute of America, and miscellany. Included are pamphlets, photographs, postcards, newspaper clippings, and brochures. *Includes English. Partial inventory available.*

Leszczyńska, Valeria.
Papers, 1939-1940. 1 linear ft.

Papers consist of three scrapbooks containing newspaper clippings from *Dziennik dla Wszystkich* (Buffalo, NY). The clippings pertain to World War II in Poland.

The Mazur Polish Dancers of Milwaukee, Inc. (Wisconsin).
Collection, ca. 1949-1978. 1 linear in.

Collection consists of photocopies of newspaper articles and of photographs, as well as some programs. *Mainly in English.*

Miciak, Lillian J. (Nemeroski).
Papers, ca. 1960-1976. 14 linear in.

Miciak, a lawyer, was active in Miami and Hollywood, FL, Polish organizations, including the Polish American Congress, both nationally and locally; the Millenium Culture Series; the Miami Polish American Club; and the Polish Roman Catholic Union of America, Soc. No. 753 (Cambridge, MA).
Papers contain correspondence, newspapers and newspaper clippings, photographs, reports, and scrapbooks pertaining to her activities and to the Polish community in the Hollywood, FL, area. *Includes English.*

Mischke, Angela (1905-).
Papers, ca. 1969. 14 pages.

Mischke arrived at Ellis Island with her family in 1913. They settled in Chicago, IL, joining her father who had come to the United States five years previously. After attending parochial schools through eighth grade, she left to work, first as a baste puller in the tailor shop where her father worked as a presser, then in a glove factory. She took evening business courses and started a series of office jobs; she also worked for the Polish National Alliance until her marriage. Mischke was active in a local Polish singing group, Chór Warszawski; Trinity Parish Literary Circle; and Holy Trinity Church choir.
Her papers consist of an autobiography. *In English.*

Nurczyński, Anthony.
Papers, 1930-1946. Ca. 1.5 linear ft.

Nurczyński was a community leader in Boston's Polish cultural life, particularly as organizer and director of its musical groups. He arranged music for the Shep Nolan Band and for Krakowiaki, who played live on the "Echoes of Poland" radio hour.
Papers consist primarily of published and mimeographed sheet music. *Includes some English. Related collections: Walter and Valeria Wycke Nurczyński; Alexandra Jaskólski.*

Nurczyński, Walter (ca. 1893-1962) and Valeria Wycke Nurczyńska (1897-1967).
Papers, 1936-1968. Ca. 4.5 linear ft.

A singer, Valeria (or Valerie) Nurczyńska was born in Łodź, Poland; she came to the United States as a child and studied voice. She became a United States citizen in 1920, after her marriage to Walter. During World War II, she was chair of the United Women's Society of Greater Boston (affiliated with Polish War Relief). She was a member of the Polish National Alliance (Chicago, IL), organizer of PNA Lodge 3008, and a founder of the Polish Singers' Alliance of New England and of Lira Chorus of

Boston. She gave concerts and recitals in many cities and also did opera and radio work.

Walter Nurczyński was also born in Poland. From ca. 1937 to 1944, he was producer of the Boston area radio program "Echoes of Poland," and ca. 1943 was president of the Polish War Relief Committee of Boston, MA.

Papers consist of clippings, correspondence, sheet music (mostly songs sung by Valeria), and radio scripts, as well as financial reports of the Polish War Relief Committee of Boston. Also included are correspondence and photographs of Alexandra Jaskólski and papers of Karol Jaskólski. *Includes English. Related collections: Alexandra Jaskólski; Karol T. Jaskólski; Anthony Nurczyński.*

Panek, Ludwik and Wanda.
Papers, ca. 1928-1971. 6 linear in.

Ludwik Panek (1884-) was born near Łańcut, Poland. After coming to the United States, he was active in Polish American organizations. He received a medal for recruiting for the Polish National Alliance (Chicago, IL), was Grand Marshal for the Polish Day parade in Chicago (1920), a member of Polish Falcons, and was president and founding member of the committee for aid to Polish American veterans of World War I.

Wanda Panek was a member and champion of Polish Falcons District No. 2 (in the 1920s); subchairperson of the Technical Committee, Polish Falcons Nest No. 2; and was in charge of athletic events for young female Sokół members in 1927.

Papers of the Paneks contain publications and ephemera from the Civic Committee of Polish National Relief Fund (1976-1977), the Polish National Alliance (ca. 1940), Polish Falcons of America (national headquarters and Nest No. 2), St. Stanislaus Parish (Chicago, IL), the Chicago Intercollegiate Council, and the Chicago Park District. *Includes some English.*

Paryski Publishing Company (Toledo, Ohio).
Records, ca. 1930-1960. Ca. 210 linear ft.

Founded in 1889 by Antoni A. Paryski (or Panek, 1865-1935), the Company was one of the most important Polish American publishing houses in the United States. Among its publications were several thousand books and pamphlets, primarily in Polish, and the popular newspaper, *Ameryka-Echo* (1889-1962). Publications covered the widest possible range, including religion, fiction, textbooks, and histories. Paryski was the first Polish publisher to employ American mass-marketing techniques.

Records consist of the vast business and editorial papers of the Company. Included are correspondence, advertisement orders, editorial materials, and a variety of financial records. *Includes English. Inventory available.*

Polish American Book Company (Chicago, Illinois).
Records, 1955-1972. Ca. 10 linear ft.

Records of the Company consist of correspondence, financial records, newspaper clippings, and press releases pertaining to the newspapers *Polonia* and *Ameryka-Echo*, the Independent Publishing Company, and to organizations such as the Polish American Congress. *Includes some English. Related collection: Polish American Congress (Chicago, IL).*

Polish American Congress (Chicago, Illinois).
Records, ca. 1940-1972. 52 linear ft.

A political, cultural, and social organization founded in 1944 in Chicago, IL, the Congress has as its purpose promotion of Polish culture in the United States, support of freedom and independence for the people of Poland, and sponsorship of social and cultural activities to unite Polish Americans. The organization publishes a quarterly newsletter, the *Polish American Congress Newsletter.*

Records consist of general administrative materials of the Congress along with questionnaires, correspondence, documents, and financial reports of the American Committee for the Resettlement of Polish Displaced Persons. *Includes English. Inventory available. Related collections: American Committee for the Resettlement of Polish Displaced Persons (Chicago, IL); Polish American Congress, Illinois Division (Chicago).*

Polish American Congress. Illinois Division (Chicago, Illinois).
Records, ca. 1944-1972. Ca. 8 linear ft.

PAC Illinois Division records consist of correspondence, member lists, donor lists, financial records, minutes, information on American citizens in Poland and on naturalized Poles, files pertaining to Polish immigration matters, correspondence of the Compensation Committee of the Polish American Congress (regarding compensation for Poles who were in German labor or prison camps during World War II), Illinois statutes and regulations, and photographs. *Includes English. Inventory available. Related collection: Polish American Congress (Chicago, IL).*

Polish Canteen for Servicemen (New York, New York).
Records, 1943-1975. 1 linear in. and 1 tape cassette.

The Canteen, or Świetlica, was organized in New York City in 1943 to provide persons in the armed services with a recreational facility. It was located in the Polish National Home and served refreshments, sponsored fundraisers such as dances, and maintained a library. When it closed in 1945, it had served more than 48,000 persons. In January 1946, the canteen was reorganized as the Polish Women's Service Club, a humanitarian organization working on behalf of Poles.

Records include a brief history, financial records, newspaper clippings, memorabilia, photographs, programs, and copies of a weekly newspaper column that described Canteen activities. Also included is limited material regarding the Polish Women's Service Club. *Includes English. Inventory available. History available also on cassette.*

Polish Centrale of Minneapolis, Minnesota (Centrala Polonii w Minneapolis).
Records, 1931-1938. Ca. 2 linear in.

Previously the Polish National Department (Minneapolis, MN), the Centrale coordinated the efforts of Polish Americans to aid the cause of Poland during World War I. The Minneapolis branch, founded ca. 1931, grew into an autonomous organization that represented the community's major organizations, initially Polish American and, later, also the VFW. It sponsored patriotic celebrations and local political activism such as resolutions supporting candidates for local offices.

Records consist of minutes. *Includes English.*

Polish Falcons of America (Sokół Polski) (Pittsburgh, Pennsylvania).
Records, 1912-1980. 9 microfilm reels.

The Falcons is a fraternal and cultural organization founded in 1887 and based in Pittsburgh, PA. The organization's major purpose is to provide insurance to members. In addition, it sponsors social and cultural activities, including summer camps, gymnastics, folklore, and sports; it has also provided scholarships to students of Polish descent. The organization was a leader in the movement to restore the Polish state during and after World War I.

Records consist of convention records, including minutes of "extraordinary congresses" and "plenum sessions." Major topics include unification of the two Unions of Polish Falcons in America, the constitution and purposes of the new union, the Falcons's administrative structure and programs, military instruction in the United States, and famine aid to Galicia. *Inventory available for supplement portion only. Originals held by Polish Falcons of America, 97 S. 18th St., Pittsburgh, PA 15219.*

Polish Library Society (Minneapolis, Minnesota).
Records, ca. 1901-1918. 1.5 linear in.

Records consist of two bound volumes. Included are a book of financial records with lists of library members from various local Polish National Alliance lodges and a book labeled "Minute Book of Polish Library of Minneapolis" containing minutes (1917-1918) and correspondence (1913-1921) of the Citizens Committee and Recruiting Centre #20 (Minneapolis).

Polish National Aid Association (Grand Rapids, Michigan).
Records, 1878-1976. Ca. 3 linear ft.

A cultural and mutual aid society, the Association (formerly Lodge 57 of the Polish National Alliance) was founded in 1878. It held annual celebrations marking Polish national holidays, built the first Polish hall in the United States (1885), and established a choir and drama circle. Other activities included aid to Polish orphans, local churches, organizations, and causes; political efforts in local elections and in national campaigns for Polish independence; recruiting for the Polish Army; and sale of Polish bonds.
Records comprise financial records, minutes, inventories, and membership records of the organization.

Polish National Alliance of the United States of North America (Związek Narodowy Polski) (Chicago, Illinois).
Records, ca. 1938-1961. Ca. 5 linear in.

Founded in 1880, the Alliance is the largest and second oldest Polish American fraternal organization, with membership of about 317,000 and 1,350 lodges in thirty-six states. Its activities include maintenance and promotion of Polish culture, art, and tradition, as well as exercising leadership in Polish American cultural life. The PNA supports Polish American scholarship and education; it owned and operated Alliance College in Cambridge Springs, PA. The organization also conducts relief and charitable work for Poland. It participated in efforts on behalf of free and independent Poland after World Wars I and II. The Alliance, with headquarters in Chicago, publishes its official organs *Zgoda, Polish Daily Zgoda,* and *Alliance Calendar.*
Records include annual reports, evaluation reports, and analyses of operations. *In English. Related collections: PNA, Lodge 1042 (Minneapolis, MN); PNA, Lodge 1530 (Minneapolis, MN); PNA, Lodge 22 (Minneapolis, MN); PNA, Council 23 (Chicago, IL); PNA; PNA Home (Minneapolis, MN); PNA, Council 20 (Minneapolis, MN); PNA Council 12 (Minneapolis, MN).*

Polish National Alliance of the United States of North America, Council 12 (Minneapolis, Minnesota).
Records, ca. 1884-1966. Ca. 2 linear ft.

Records of PNA Council 12 include minutes, ledgers of contributors' names, financial reports, membership lists, and financial ledgers. Also included are financial records of the Polish Library Society, and of Group 22. *Inventory available. Related collection: PNA (Chicago, IL).*

Polish National Alliance of the United States of North America, Council No. 20 (Minneapolis, Minnesota).
Records, 1916-1935. 1 microfilm reel.

Records of the PNA Minneapolis Council No. 20 include minutes of the Executive Committee. *Related collection: PNA (Chicago, IL).*

Polish National Alliance of the United States of North America, Council 23 (Chicago, Illinois).
Records, 1914-1918. 1 microfilm reel.

Records of PNA Council 23 consist of minutes of sessions, including those of the organizational session, and lists of officers and members. *Negatives held by the Center for Research Libraries, Chicago, IL. Related collection: PNA (Chicago, IL).*

Polish National Alliance of the United States of North America, General Casimir Pulaski Society Lodge No. 3155 (El Paso, Texas).
Records, ca. 1959-1972. Ca. 1 linear in.

Records consist of correspondence of founders Lt. Col. Francis C. and Virginia Kajencki, a history of the Lodge, photographs, and newspaper clippings. *In English. Related collection: PNA (Chicago, IL).*

Polish National Alliance of the United States of North America Home (Minneapolis, Minnesota).
Records, 1937-1974. Ca. 2 linear in.

Leaders of the Northeast Minneapolis, MN, Polish American community collaborated to incorporate, finance, and manage an institution to house major neighborhood activities. The Home was built before 1937.
Records consist of minutes of regular, annual, and special meetings of the Home's board of directors. The board was made up of members of various PNA lodges and the Polish National Alliance Commercial Club. *Related collection: PNA (Chicago, IL).*

Polish National Alliance of the United States of North America, Lodge No. 22 (Minneapolis, Minnesota).
Records, 1884-1916. Ca. 1 linear in.

Records of PNA Lodge 22 consist of a minute book, including minutes of the organizational meeting, regular, and extraordinary meetings. *Related collection: PNA (Chicago, IL).*

Polish National Alliance of the United States of North America, Lodge No. 1042 (Minneapolis, Minnesota).
Records, 1936-1954. Ca. 1 linear in.

Records of PNA Lodge 1042 include minutes of regular and annual meetings. *Related collection: PNA (Chicago, IL).*

Polish National Alliance of the United States of North America, Lodge No. 1530 (Minneapolis, Minnesota).
Records, 1914-1955. Ca. 2.5 linear in.

Records of PNA Lodge No. 1530 consist of minutes of regular, annual, and special meetings; membership lists; financial reports; and lists of officers. *Includes English. Related collection: PNA (Chicago, IL).*

Polish National Catholic Church, Central Diocese (Scranton, Pennsylvania).
Records, 1897-1967. 10 microfilm reels.

The Church was founded in 1897 in Scranton, PA, in response to the desire of some Polish Americans for a more active voice in their religious life. In Scranton, Polish miners and factory workers of the Sacred Heart Church requested lay representation in parish affairs. Their request was refused, but with the help of Bishop Franciszek Hodur, the group formed its own church, St. Stanislaus. The first PNCC Synod was held in 1904, in Scranton. By that time, there were two dozen parishes and 20,000 members in five states. The Church established the Savonarola Theological Seminary (Scranton, PA) in 1907, and an affiliated fraternal society, the Polish National Union of America (Spójnia), in 1908. The PNCC also sponsors many newspapers, publications, and a summer camp.
Records of the Diocese contain baptism, confirmation, marriage, and death records. *Includes English, Latin and Lithuanian. Restricted.*

Polish National Catholic Church. Western Diocese, Sacred Heart Church (Minneapolis, Minnesota).
Records, 1914-1965. 1 microfilm reel and ca. 1 linear in.

Records of the Church include baptism, marriage and death records, parish committee minutes, and financial reports. *Includes Latin; microfilm in Polish only.*

Polish American Savings and Loan Company, founded in 1923, Cleveland, OH, 1929.

Polish Roman Catholic Union, Circuit No. 22 (St. Paul, Minnesota).
Records, 1919-1939. Ca. 1 linear in.

Founded in 1873, the Union is a fraternal, cultural, recreational, and sports organization. It sponsors educational and religious tours to Canada and Europe, gives financial assistance to students, aids elderly and disabled members, and sponsors sports activities. The Union has ca. 129,000 members with branches in twenty-five states. It is headquartered in Chicago, IL, and publishes *Naród Polski*.
Records of Circuit No. 22 of St. Paul consist of a minute book of regular and annual meetings. *Related collections: Polish Roman Catholic Union, St. Jacob Apostle Society, Lodge No. 445 (St. Paul, MN); Polish Roman Catholic Union, St. Joseph Society, Lodge No. 893 (St. Paul, MN).*

Polish Roman Catholic Union, St. Jacob Apostle Society, Lodge No. 445 (St. Paul, Minnesota).
Records, 1919-1941. Ca. 2 linear in.

Records of PRCU Lodge No. 445 of St. Paul consist of a minute book of regular, semiannual, and annual meetings. *Related collections: Polish Roman Catholic Union, Circuit 22 (St. Paul, MN); Polish Roman Catholic Union, St. Joseph Society, Lodge No. 893 (St. Paul, MN).*

Polish Roman Catholic Union, St. Joseph Society, Lodge No. 893 (St. Paul, Minnesota).
Records, 1915-1920. Ca. 1 linear in.

Records of PRCU Lodge No. 893 of St. Paul, organized in 1915, consist of a minute book of monthly meetings. *Related collections: Polish Roman Catholic Union, Circuit 22 (St. Paul, MN); Polish Roman Catholic Union, St. Jacob Apostle Society, Lodge No. 445 (St. Paul, MN).*

Polish Union of America, Inc., Chapter 2 (St. Paul, Minnesota).
Records, 1986-1917. 1 linear in.

The Union, a fraternal, cultural, relief, and social organization, was founded as a result of schism within the Polish National Alliance in the late 1880s, and was led by Father Dominic Majer, a St. Paul, MN, priest and patriarch of Minnesota Polonia. Five lodges were organized in the Twin Cities and one each in Owatonna and Duluth, MN, but the locus of membership, power, and the office organ *Słońce* (Sun) shifted eastward by 1900. A series of reorganizations in the next decade led to the formation of the Polish Union of the United States with headquarters in Wilkes-Barre, PA, and the Polish Union of America in Buffalo, NY.
Records consist of three membership dues books.

Polish Union of the United States of North America (Wilkes-Barre, Pennsylvania).
Records, 1939-1971. Ca. 5 linear in.

The Union is a fraternal benefit and insurance society founded in 1890 in St. Paul, MN. After six years, it was moved to Buffalo, NY, and then to Wilkes-Barre, PA. It was incorporated in 1907 under the name Polish Union of America and took its present name by charter amendment in 1921. After World War II, the Union became a member of the Polish American Congress. The Union provides insurance, scholarships, and charitable support for Polish Americans.
Records of the Union include published materials, an audit, correspondence, materials pertaining to *The Polish Review*, and a jubilee album. Also included are correspondence, minutes, newspaper clippings, ledgers, and press releases of the Anthracite Relief Committee for Poland organized by the Union (Wilkes-Barre, 1939-1942); and correspondence, minutes, newsletters, and other materials pertaining to the American Red Cross, Community War Chests, Center of the Friends of the Polish Soldier (Centrum Przyjaciół Żołnierza Polskiego), the Polish National Alliance, the Polish YMCA work in the Middle

East, the Polish American Council, World War II, and refugees. *Includes English. Inventory available.*

Procanin, Anna (Barzyk).
Papers, ca. 1914-1915. 6 linear in.

Procanin lived in Chicago, IL, and was active in several Polish American and other organizations. Her memberships included the Polish National Alliance; Warehouse and Mail Order Employees Union, Local #743 (Chicago); and Klub Łęczan #1. The last, a charitable organization, was founded in Chicago in 1923; members were persons from Łęki Górne, Poland, who provided aid to those in the homeland.

Papers include business and personal correspondence, newspaper clippings, and photographs. *Includes English.*

Różański, Clement.
Papers, 1919-1969. 16 linear ft.

Różański was an attorney in New York City and Brooklyn, NY, for nearly fifty years. His clients included hundreds of Polish Americans and major local institutions such as the Polish National Alliance of Brooklyn and the Consulate General of Poland in New York.

Papers include legal files consisting of invoices, title examination reports, account files, endorsements, home insurance certificates, landlords' lease reports, and numbered card files of legal cases. Also included are financial records and business correspondence. *In English.*

Różański, Edward C. and Loda.
Papers, ca. 1940- . 43 linear ft.

An optometrist active in Polish American organizations, Edward Różański was born in Chicago, IL, in 1915. He served as president of the Polish American Congress, Illinois State Division, and as a director of the Polish National Alliance and was active in other organizations including the International Platform Association, Pi Tau Gamma Polish American Educators Club of Illinois, the Order of Lafayette, and the Kopernik Quincentennial Observance of

the Illinois Polish American Congress. He also served as general manager of Alliance Printers and Publishers and was named "Man of the Year" of United Polish Councils in 1970.

Loda, born in Chicago in 1918, has been active in numerous Polish American cultural and religious organizations, with a particular interest in preserving historical materials. The Société Historique et Littéraire Polonaise of Paris, France, honored her with the Krasinski Medallion for the Polonica-Americana Collection.

Papers of the Różańskis include correspondence (of both Edward and Loda), minutes, newspaper clippings, press releases, and organizational publications relating to Dr. Różański's activities in the Polish American community. Organizations represented in the collection include the Polish American Congress, the Polish National Alliance, the Polish Roman Catholic Union of America, the Polish Western Association of America, the Orchard Lake Schools, the Legion of Young Polish Women, the Chicago Society, Alliance College, the American Museum of Immigration, and the Polish Army Veterans of America. Also included are minutes of the Protokół Trzeciego Zjazdu Polskiej Rady Międzynarodowej (the Third Convention of the Polish International Council) and material pertaining to the Mikołaj Kopernik Observance Committee, Polish art, the Polish press in the United States, Radio Free Europe, the United States Bicentennial, the Polish Falcons of America, and displaced persons. *Includes English. Inventory available.*

Sadowski, Dr. Roman J. (1879-1965).
Papers, ca. 1919-1960. Ca. 3 linear in.

Dr. Sadowski was born in Płock, Poland, and came to the United States as a child. He graduated from the Detroit College of Medicine in 1903. Sadowski practiced in the Detroit area and was active in numerous Polish American and professional associations as well as being on the board of directors of several companies. He was a member and/or officer of the Polish American Congress, the Polish Roman Catholic Union, and the Medical and Dental Association of Americans of Polish Origin, and was a founder of Polish Falcons Nest #79 (Detroit). He also served on the Detroit City Plan Commission and was the recipient of many awards and honors.

Papers include correspondence, newspaper clippings (many pertaining to Sadowski's daughter), financial documents, and photographs. Also included are notes on ancestry, issues of medical society bulletins, and bulletins of Polish organizations. *Includes English.*

St. John Cantius Roman Catholic Church (Wilno, Minnesota).
Records, ca. 1883-1974. 5 microfilm reels.

St. John Cantius Church has been the center of one of Minnesota's oldest rural Polish settlements, founded ca. 1880 through the efforts of Rev. R. Byzewski of Winona and Archbishop John Ireland of St. Paul. Records include baptism, marriage, and death registers, parish committee minutes, financial records, photographs, and newspaper clippings. Also included are the research notes of parish historian Rose Parulski. *Includes Latin and English.*

Śmietana, Walter.
Papers, ca. 1970-1973. Ca. 2 linear in.

Śmietana served as acting president of Alliance College (Cambridge Springs, PA), as director of the Alliance College Student Teaching Committee, as chair of the Alliance College Teacher Education Committee, and as chair of the College's Department of Education and Psychology. He was also National Chair of the Polish American Congress Committee on Quincentennial of the Birth of Copernicus.

Papers consist of minutes of the Alliance College Teacher Education Committee; press releases from the college; newspaper clippings and academic bulletins; photographs; correspondence with Dr. Mieczysław Klimaszewski, Chancellor of Jagiellonian University (Cracow, Poland); materials pertaining to the Quincentennial Committee; and an Alliance College Convocation program. *Includes English.*

Świerczyński, Jan (1892-).
Papers, ca. 1912-1975. Ca. 3 linear in.

A longtime resident of Chicago, IL, Świerczyński was a member of the Polish Falcons of America (Pittsburgh, PA); the American Committee for Resettlement of Polish Displaced Persons; and the Polish Veterans in Exile Association, Circle #15 (Chicago). He was also a contributor to many Polish causes and organizations in the Midwest and abroad.

Papers consist of a manuscript on Polish folk music and musicians in Chicago in the late nineteenth and early twentieth centuries; correspondence; and ephemera from the Organizational Committee of the Free Poland Society of Pittsburgh, the Polish-Hungarian World Federation (Chicago), Polish Veterans in Exile Association (Chicago), Związek Polaków w Mendozie (Mendoza, Argentina), Union of Polish Invalids in Great Britain (war invalids), and numerous Polish American organizations in Chicago and the Midwest. Correspondents include Arthur C. Waldo of Polish Falcons of America, and W. Anders, Polish National Fund (London). Also included are photographs and newspaper clippings. *Includes English.*

Symans, Edward Alan.
Papers, 1971-1983. 2 linear ft.

Symans (originally Szymański) lived in Poland for many years as an employee of the U.S. Foreign Service. He has published three volumes of poetry and is a founder of the Polish Heritage Society of Grand Rapids, MI.

Papers include correspondence with his wife, Therese M. Symans; newspaper clippings, mostly from Grand Rapids, MI; and personal papers, research notes, and scrapbooks. Correspondence and clippings pertain to immigration, genealogy, and articles and poetry written by Symans. Also included are newsletters of the Polish Heritage Society. *Includes English and Spanish.*

Szcześniak, Boleslaw Boym.
Papers, 1948-1977. Ca. 1 linear ft.

Szcześniak, a medievalist and scholar of East Asian history, came to the United States soon after World War II. He taught at the University of Notre Dame, Department of History.

Papers consist largely of his and his family's personal correspondence. Also included are proceedings of the South Bend (IN) Polish Library (1914-1957), and a file pertaining to celebration of the Copernical Year (1973) in South Bend. *Includes English.*

Szewc, Rose G.
Papers, ca. 1916-1929. 1 linear ft.

Szewc, who served as Executive Secretary of the American Association for the Education of Foreign-Born Soldiers in the United States, was born in Warsaw, Poland. Her family came to the United States when she was a young child. She worked as a legal stenographer and as manager in the Ft. Wayne (IN) Department of Western Life Indemnity Company. She also contributed poetry to the *Indianapolis Star*. Around 1917, she became interested in teaching English and Americanization to foreign-born recruits at Ft. Benjamin Harrison near Indianapolis. In 1918, she moved to New York City, where she was associated with Ignacy Paderewski and the Polish National Committee. She also worked as secretary of the Mid-European Union in Washington, DC, in the late 1910s. During the 1920s and 1930s, she worked for Tatra Production Company of New York, NY.

Papers of Szewc consist of correspondence, newspaper clippings, and miscellany concerning her life in Indiana prior to 1918 and as secretary in the law firm of Clement Różański of New York City and Brooklyn, NY. Also included are engravings; short fiction drafts; invoices and financial records; photographs; correspondence with W. O. Górski of the Polish Victims' Relief Fund; a letter from Herbert A. Miller, director, Committee for the League of Nations of Eastern Europe; correspondence between Szewc and Gen. Edwin F. Glen; and artifacts. *Includes English and Russian (one item). Related collections: Clement Różański; Tatra Production Company (New York, NY).*

Szulak, Rev. Francis Xavier (1863-1903).
Papers, ca. 1869-1903. 1 microfilm reel.

Szulak was a Jesuit missionary born in Poland. After coming to the United States, he lived in Chicago, IL, and conducted missionary work in the surrounding states. He organized parishes in Michigan; Buffalo, NY; Nebraska; and Wisconsin; and also worked in Minnesota.

Papers consist of a diary. Volumes II-VI concern his activities in Minnesota and elsewhere in the Midwest. *Includes German (Gothic cursive script) and Latin.*

Tatra Production Company (New York, New York).
Records, 1919-1920. 1 linear ft.

The Company was created to produce a film based on the life of Ignacy Paderewski. Records consist of correspondence, minutes, and stock certificates. Also included are a photograph of Rose G. Szewc and a manuscript entitled "Reflections on Friendship" and signed "Różański." *Includes English. Related collections: Clement F. Różański; Rose G. Szewc.*

West Side Democratic and Civic Club (South Bend, Indiana).
Records, 1930-1961. Ca. 2 linear in.

Records of this Polish American organization consist of minutes of regular monthly and annual meetings. *Includes English (1951-1962). Available as photocopies only.*

Wiewióra, Joseph.
Papers, 1973-1979. Ca. 7 linear in.

Wiewióra, a journalist and writer, edited *Zgoda*, the official publication of the Polish National Alliance of the United States of North America (PNA). He was born and educated in Poland and began his journalistic career as a teenager with the now defunct *Dziennik Zjednoczenia* in

Chicago. In 1929-1930, he worked for *Gwiazda Polarna* with Wacław Gąsiorowski in Stevens Point, WI, but returned to *Dziennik Zjednoczenia* in 1930. He later left newspaper work to become a newscaster for Polish radio programs at Hammond, IN. After serving in the Southwest Pacific during World War II, he worked variously for the Conkey Publishing Company and as chief investigator of the Juvenile Court of Lake County, IN. In 1958, he became Chicago office director of the Polish American Congress and editor of *Dziennik Związkowy* and *Zgoda*.

Papers include drafts of articles pertaining to the U.S. Bicentennial and of other *Zgoda* articles and advertisements, background for articles including press releases from the PNA, PNA bylaws, a booklet on the Fourth Convention of Polonia Society, issues of *Zgoda*, a booklet entitled *In the Mainstream of American Life*, correspondence, and photographs. *Includes English.*

Wodarski, Rev. John P.
Papers, ca. 1962-1969. Ca. 1 linear in.

Wodarski's papers include mimeographed minutes, bylaws, constitution, and other items pertaining to the Association of Polish Priests of Connecticut and to Father Stephen Bartkowski. Also included is an anniversary booklet from Holy Cross Church (New Britain, CT). *Includes English.*

Wolny, Wilhelm A.
Papers, ca. 1938-1971. 1 linear ft. and 1 scrapbook.

Wolny, a leader in the Polish American communities in Detroit, MI, and San Francisco, CA, came to the United States after World War II. He and his wife moved first to Detroit, where Wolny was active in the Polish theater "Rozmaitości" and other cultural activities. The Wolnys then moved to San Francisco, where Wilhelm continued to be active in the Polish American community. He was elected president of the Polish National Alliance Council #4, served as a delegate of Polish American

Congress Lodge 7 (Daly City, CA), participated in the Ignacy Paderewski Club, and was a member of the Polish American Congress, California Division.

Papers include personal correspondence, minutes and records of Northern California Polish organizations, newspaper clippings, a scrapbook, and miscellany. Included are materials pertaining to the Polish Relief Committee of the United Polish Societies, the Polish National Alliance, the Ignacy Paderewski Club, Inc., and the Polish American Congress (all of San Francisco); Polski Teatr "Rozmaitości" (Detroit); the National Association of Polish Americans, Inc.; the Polish American Congress (California-Arizona Division); Polish-German relations; social activities of Polonia in California; and articles by Józef Sanocki. *Includes some English. Inventory available.*

Wołodkowicz, Andrzej (1928-).
Papers, 1964-1967. 6 linear in.

A specialist on Polish Canadian problems, Wołodkowicz was born in Warsaw. He lived and studied in England and France before immigrating to Canada in 1955, where he completed his education. He has been active in many Polish Canadian organizations, and has published on Polish Canadian problems.

Papers consist of correspondence, questionnaires, and newspaper clippings used in the compilation of Wołodkowicz's book, *Polish Contribution to Arts and Sciences in Canada* (1969). *Includes English and French. Inventory available.*

Zawistowski, Rev. Józef Lebiedzik (1884-1967).
Papers, ca. 1914-1967. 16.5 linear ft.

Zawistowski was born in the Polish area of Upper Silesia and came to the United States in 1914 to become a priest of the Polish National Catholic Church. He served parishes from Duluth, MN, to Schenectady, NY, and was one of the prominent leaders of the PNCC. During World Wars I and II, Rev. Zawistowski was active in relief efforts. He was also instrumental in stabilizing many parishes to which he was assigned and was a prolific writer.

Papers consist of correspondence; manuscripts of books, pamphlets, and articles written by Rev. Zawistowski; and newspaper clippings. The collection is especially rich in correspondence with Bishop Franciszek Hodur. Other correspondents include Bishop L. Grochowski, Rev. J. Kula, Bishop T. Zieliński, Bishop W. Faron, Bishop V. Gawrychowski, Bishop J. Leśniak, Bishop J. Sołtysiak, V. Rev. T. Czarkowski, and others. *Includes some English. Inventory available.*

Zieliński, Jaroslav de (1844-1922).
Papers, 1871-1922. 1 linear ft.

A pianist and teacher of voice and music, Zieliński was born in Lubycza Królewska and studied piano in Poland and other parts of Europe. He was wounded during his participation in the Polish uprising against tsarist Russia in 1863-1864. In 1864, he came to the United States, enlisting as a bugler in the Fourth Massachusetts Cavalry of the Union Army. After the Civil War, he resumed his musical career, publishing

piano music, appearing in concerts, and teaching piano and voice. He lived in Michigan, New York, and Los Angeles. In Los Angeles, he founded the Zielinski Trio Club and headed a school of music.

Papers consist of correspondence, handbills, manuscripts, programs, a scrapbook, and photographs. Also included are research notes of Robert C. Bryant and Edward A. Symans pertaining to Zieliński's life. Correspondence is predominantly with Zieliński's friend and pupil Edith V. Rann. *Mainly in English; includes some Polish, French, and German. Inventory available.*

Zorn, Otylia (Smocińska).
Papers, 1956-1977. Ca. 8 linear in.

Papers of Otylia "Tess" Zorn consist of a scrapbook containing correspondence, memorabilia, newspaper clippings, and photographs pertaining to the histories of the Zorn and Smociński families, the American Polish Club of Lake Worth, FL, the Polish-American Citizens' Club of Camden, NJ, and bylaws of the Polish-American Club (Polski Dom) of Palm Beach County, FL. *In English.*

Monographs

The Polish American monograph collection numbers over 4,000 books and pamphlets. Included are works on education, assimilation and interethnic relations, work, community life, migration, geographical distribution and influences, the ethnic press, the Polish American community in general (including general bibliographies), religion, politics, the arts, and folklore. Books from the library of the late Rev. Józef Zawistowski, an active figure in the Polish National Catholic Church movement in the United States, account for about half of the collection. The Zawistowski Collection contains hundreds of publications dealing with religion, philosophy, literature, politics, economics, and music, most published in Polish in the United States in the first half of this century.

General book-length treatments of American Polonia are represented at the IHRC by a total of over fifty historical or cultural overviews, biographies or autobiographies of famous persons, general bibliographies, and registers listing prominent individuals. The histories cover the entire period of the Polish presence in the United States and include works written either by American non-Poles or by Polish researchers in Poland, in addition to works treating the subject from the Polish American viewpoint. While most of the histories date from the 1930s or later, the earliest are from the first decade of this century. Works of note include *The Poles in America*, by Paul Fox (1977, reprint of 1922 edition); *America's Polish Heritage: A Social History of the Poles in America*, by Joseph Wytrwal (1961); *The Polish Americans: Whence and Whither*, by Theresita Polzin (1973); and *For God and Country*, by Victor Greene (1975). An important recent study is John Bukowczyk's *And My Children Did Not Know Me: A History of the Polish Americans* (1987).

Taking the Zawistowski Collection into account, books issued by church organizations constitute the largest single group in the IHRC Polish American monograph holdings. The Zawistowski library includes writings by and about Bishop Franciszek Hodur, founder of the Polish National Catholic Church, as well as works by Zawistowski himself, and contains many rare publications documenting non-Roman Catholic Polish religious activities. Available PNCC materials encompass both national publications, such as hymnals and educational/promotional pamphlets, and local parish publications, such as jubilee books and financial reports. Among the secondary works on the PNCC are a discussion of the church schism, Jan Czyżak's *Rozdział kościelny wśród polaków w Ameryce; Przycinek [przyczynek] do historyi emigracyi polskiej w Ameryce* (Church Division among Poles in America; Contribution to the History of Polish Emigration in America, 1927), and Hieronim Kubiak's *The Polish National Catholic Church in the United States of America from 1897 to 1980: Its Social Conditioning and Social Functions* (1982). The more predominant Roman Catholic presence among Polish immigrants is documented in several works, including Joseph John Parot's *Polish Catholics in Chicago, 1850-1920: A Religious History*. Primary materials on Polish Roman Catholics in the United States include local parish commemorative albums; also present is an edition of Jesuit missionaries' letters, Ludwik Grzebień's *Burzliwe lata Polonii amerykańskiej; Wspomnienia i listy misjonarzy jezuickich 1864-1913* (Stormy Years of American Polonia; Memoirs and Letters of Jesuit Missionaries, 1983). Also available are a number of Roman Catholic clergy biographies.

On the subject of education, the IHRC holdings contain both primary and secondary sources. Primary materials are of two types: jubilee volumes issued by Polish American preparatory schools and seminaries, and instructional books on Polish language and literature for children and for college students. Studies include Dorota Praszałowicz's *Amerykańska etniczna szkoła parafialna; Studium porównawcze trzech wybranych odmian intsytucji* (The American Ethnic Parochial School; Comparative Study of the Three Chosen Types of Institutions, 1986) and Józef Miąso's *The History of the Education of Polish Immigrants in the United States* (1977).

The question of assimilation (or, viewed conversely, of the maintenance of ethnic identity) is the subject of an American study, Walery J. Jasiński's *Teksty dotyczące asymilacji Polaków w Ameryce* (On the Assimilation of the Poles in America, 1941) and of several volumes published in Poland. The latter works include a collection of theoretical essays, *Założenia teorii asymilacji* (Assumptions of the Theory of Assimilation), edited by Hieronim Kubiak and Andrzej K. Paluch (1980); an anthropological monograph on cultural change, Aleksander Posern-Zieliński's *Tradycja a etniczność; Przemiany kultury Polonii amerykańskiej* (Tradition and Ethnicity; Transformations of American Polonia's Culture, 1982); and a discussion of the theoretical and methodological questions of assimilation, Grzegorz Babiński's *Więź etniczna a procesy asymilacji; Przemiany organizacji etnicznych: zagadnienia teoretyczne i metodologiczne* (Ethnic Bonds and Assimilation Processes; Transformations of Ethnic Organizations: Theoretical and Methodological Problems, 1986). Other American and Polish works characterize assimilation within a given geographical area, such as Ewa Morawska's *The Maintenance of Ethnicity: Case Study of the Polish American Community in Greater Boston* (1977). On interethnic relations, there are monographs on the Polish American stereotype, such as Andrzej Kapiszewski's *Stereotyp Amerykanów polskiego pochodzenia* (Stereotype of Americans of Polish Descent, 1978), and on assimilation and interethnic conflict, such as Kapiszewski's *Asymilacja i konflikt; Ž problematyki stosunków etnicznych w Stanach Zjednoczonych Ameryki* (Assimilation and Conflict; On the Problems of Ethnic Relations in the United States of America, 1984). A sociological analysis of Polish American community life is contained in Helena Znaniecki Lopata's *Polish Americans: Status Competition in an Ethnic Community* (1976).

Publications pertaining to the subject area of work include Polish and American studies treating industrialization, participation in labor unions, and strike actions in the mines. Among the latter monographs is *The Slavic Community on Strike: Immigrant*

Labor in Pennsylvania Anthracite (1968), by Victor Greene, found in the IHRC's general section.

Polish American organizations are represented by anniversary albums often incorporating historical overviews: examples are albums of two fraternal benefit societies, the Polish National Union (Spójnia), founded in Scranton, PA, in 1908, and the Polish Union of the United States of North America, established in Wilkes-Barre (PA) in 1890. Additional primary materials for such organizations are commemorative and descriptive brochures. Among secondary publications are reference works. Individual histories are available for a number of organizations. The IHRC has two histories (1913 and 1948) of the Polish Roman Catholic Union of America. For the Polish Falcons of America, a history from 1929 in English and a multivolume history from 1953 through 1974 in Polish by Arthur Waldo are present. There are also histories of the Polish Union of America (1930) and of the Polish Women's Alliance (1938).

The largest Polish American fraternal group, the Polish National Alliance of the United States of North America, is represented in the collection by Stanisław Osada's *Historya Związku Narodowego Polskiego i rozwój ruchu narodowego* (History of the Polish National Alliance and Development of the National Movement, a 1905 volume reprinted in 1957) and Adam Olszewski's *Historia Związku Narodowego Polskiego* (History of the Polish National Alliance, six volumes published between 1957 and 1963). The most recent study of this organization is Donald Pienkos's *PNA: A Centennial History of the Polish National Alliance of the United States of North America* (1985). Also numbered among the IHRC holdings are many organizational publications, constituting extensive primary documentation for Polish American events and activities.

Works in the collection discussing specific localities cover many of the areas with the largest Polish populations. There are descriptions of the sizeable communities of Chicago (*Poles of Chicago, 1837-1937; A History of One Century of Polish Contribution to the City of Chicago, Illinois*, n.a., ca. 1937), Detroit (Sister Mary Remigia Napolska's *The Polish Immigrant in Detroit to 1914*, 1946), Cleveland (John J. Grabowski's *Polish Americans and Their Communities of Cleveland*, 1976), and Philadelphia (Carol Ann Golab's *The Polish Communities of Philadelphia, 1870-1920: Immigrant Distribution and Adaptation in Urban America*, 1971); a guide to information on Buffalo's Polish population is W. M. Drzewieniecki's *Polonica Buffalonensis: Annotated Bibliography of Source and Printed Materials Dealing with the Polish-American Community in the Buffalo, New York, Area* (1976). For New York City there is a 1938 popularized description of Poles residing there in the seventeenth and eighteenth centuries.

The earliest Polish colony, a Silesian farming settlement established at Panna Maria, Texas, in 1854, is the subject of Andrzej Brożek's *Ślązacy w Teksasie; relacje o najstarszych osadach polskich w Ameryce* (Silesians in Texas; Reports about the Oldest Polish Settlements in America, 1972), among other works. Regarding California, works are available on Los Angeles (Neil C. Sandberg's *Ethnic Identity and Assimilation: The Polish-American Community; Case Study of Metropolitan Los Angeles*, 1974) as well as on the state as a whole. Additional works describe the Polish American experience in Virginia and Kentucky taken together, Connecticut, and Pennsylvania. A sociological study of a particular Polish American community is Arthur E. Wood's *Hamtramck [MI], Then and Now* (1955).

Secondary works on Polish migration from the homeland, many published in Poland, treat a wide range of topics. Some studies delimit the topic by period, such as Józef Okołowicz's *Wychodźtwo i osadnictwo polskie przed wojną światową* (Polish Immigration and Settlement before the World War, 1920), or by area within Poland, for example, in Krystyna Duda-Dziewierz's *Wieś małopolska a emigracja amerykańska; Studium wsi Babica powiatu rzeszowskiego* (Little Poland Countryside and American Emigration: Study of the Village Babica in Rzeszów Region, 1938). Contemporaneous views of the migration question date from the beginning of the twentieth century through the interwar period and include discussions of the ruling policies and of emigration as a social phenomenon. Return migration following the restoration of Polish independence in 1918 is also the subject of a monograph, Adam Walaszek's *Reemigracja ze Stanów Zjednoczonych do Polski po I wojnie światowej, 1919-1924* (Return Migration from the

United States to Poland after World War I, 1983). In relation to the history of ideas there is Benjamin P. Murdzek's *Emigration in Polish Social-Political Thought, 1870-1914* (1977). For background to the migration, the researcher may consult the seminal study *The Polish Peasant in Europe and America*, by William Thomas and Florian Znaniecki (1958, reprint of 1927 edition [second, revised edition of 1918 work]), and, more generally, Oscar Halecki's *History of Poland* (1956). Reports by Polish visitors to the United States include, among others, an English translation of newspaper accounts written by the famous novelist Henryk Sienkiewicz in 1876-1878, *Portrait of America; Letters*, edited and translated by Charles Morley (1959).

Ethnic press publications form a large component of the Polish American monograph collection. An extensive number of items bear the imprints of the Paryski Publishing Company of Toledo (OH) and the Czas Publishing Company of Brooklyn (NY). The collection includes secondary works describing the history of Polish American journalism such as Stanisław Osada's *Prasa i publicystyka polska w Ameryce; W treściwym referacie opracowanym z okazji dwóchsetnego jubileuszu prasy w Polsce i sześćdziesięciolecia w Ameryce* (Polish Press and Journalism in America; A Short Report Prepared for the 200 Year Anniversary of the Press in Poland and the Sixty-Year Anniversary in America, 1930). There are also bibliographies of recent Polish periodicals abroad, such as Jan Kowalik's *Bibliografia czasopism polskich wydanych poza granicami Kraju od wrzesnia 1939 roku* (World Index of Polish Periodicals Published Outside of Poland since 1939, 1976), and of Polish calendars abroad, such as *Bibliografia kalendarzy polonijnych 1838-1982* (Bibliography of Polonia Calendars), by Władysław Chojnacki and Wojciech Chojnacki (1984). An annotated bibliography by Jan Wepsiec lists Polish American serial publications from 1842 to 1966. On the subject of Polish Americans and politics, the IHRC monograph holdings include case studies of particular urban experiences: Edward R. Kantowicz's *Polish-American Politics in Chicago, 1888-1940* (1975) and *Ethnic Politics in Urban America: The Polish Experience in Four Cities*, edited by Angela T. Pienkos (1978).

Literature is represented by a wide variety of works by both Polish and Polish American writers. Among the latter are the poet and essayist Helen Ogrodowska Bristol; Antoni Jax, a writer of works for the stage; the poet Victoria Janda; Monica Krawczyk, author of stories; the novelist and poet Antoni Gronowicz; and the poet Edward Symans. (See manuscript collections for descriptions of papers of some of these individuals.) Songs by the Chicago composer Frank Przybylski are also available, as is a photographic album by the émigré painter Michael Rekucki. On the subject of folklore, the IHRC has folk and popular song anthologies published in the United States in this century as well as workbooks and popular histories.

Newspapers

Am-Pol Eagle, Buffalo, NY. Weekly: 1964-1966, 1973-1974, 1976-1980. English.

Ameryka-Echo (America-Echo), Chicago, IL (previously published in Toledo, OH). Weekly: 1926, 1955-1956, 1962-1964, 1966-1968.

Ameryka-Echo (America-Echo; Toledo Daily Mail Edition), Toledo, OH. Daily. (Microfilm: 1914-1931).

Ameryka-Echo (America-Echo; Toledo Daily Edition), Toledo, OH. Daily. (Microfilm: 1915-1933).

Ameryka-Echo (America-Echo; Toledo Weekly Edition), Toledo, OH. Weekly. (Microfilm: 1889-1971).

Ameryka-Echo (America-Echo; Toledo Weekly Mail Edition), Toledo, OH. Weekly. (Microfilm: 1914-1956).

Czas (Times), Brooklyn, NY. Weekly: 1931, 1948-1975. (Microfilm: 1906-1929, 1931-1975).

Czas (Polish Times), Winnipeg, Manitoba, Canada. Weekly: 1931, 1968-date.

Czerwone Maki (Red Poppy Seeds), Ludlow, MA. Bi-weekly: 1985. Includes English.

Dziennik Chicagoski (The Polish Daily News), Chicago, IL. Daily: 1921, 1927-1932, 1935, 1938-1947, 1951-1970.

Dziennik dla Wszystkich (Everybody's Daily), Buffalo, NY. Daily: 1943, 1955-1956. (Clippings, 1939-1940).

Dziennik Polski (Polish Daily News), Detroit, MI. Daily: 1975-1980. (Microfilm: 1904-1941; includes Sunday supplement 1936-1939).

Dziennik Polski (The Polish Daily), London, England. Daily: 1968.

Dziennik Zjednoczenia (The Union Daily News), Chicago, IL. Daily: 1933.

Dziennik Zjednoczenia (The Union Daily News), Chicago, IL. Daily (country edition). (Microfilm: 1922, 1927).

Dziennik Związkowy (Polish Daily Zgoda), Chicago, IL. Daily: 1940-1941, 1948-1950, 1954-1956, 1961-1962, 1964, 1966, 1970-date.

Dziennikarz (The Journalist), Chicago, IL. Monthly: 1937.

Echo Tygodnia (Echo Weekly), Toronto, Ontario, Canada. Weekly: 1984.

Gazeta Katolicka w Kanadzie (The Catholic Gazette in Canada), Winnipeg, Manitoba, Canada. Weekly: 1931, 1933.

Gazeta Polonii (Polish-American Gazette), Boston, MA. Weekly: 1964-1972.

Gazeta Polska Narodowa (Polish National Gazette; title varies: Gazeta Polska w Chicago, 1873-1914), Chicago, IL. Weekly, semi-weekly. (Microfilm: 1888, 1890, 1895, 1905-1907, 1909-1910, 1912-1917).

Gazeta Readingska (Reading Gazette), Reading, PA. Monthly: 1931, 1979. Includes English.

Głos Ludowy (The People's Voice), Detroit, MI. Weekly: 1966-1979. Includes English.

Głos Narodu (The Voice of the People), Jersey City, NJ. Weekly: 1932, 1951, 1953, 1961-1962, 1969, 1973, 1976-1978.

Głos Polek (The Women's Voice), Chicago, IL. Monthly (semi-monthly): 1960-1961, 1971, 1978. (Microfilm: 1902-1903, 1910-1973). Includes English.

Głos Polski (Polish Voice), Toronto, Ontario, Canada. Weekly: 1965-1972.

God's Field (previously titled Rola Boża), Scranton, PA. Semi-monthly (weekly): 1923-1937, 1941-1943, 1947, 1949-1959, 1961-date. (Microfilm: 1923-1975). Includes English.

Górnik (Miner; includes Górnik Codzienny and Niedzielny Górnik), Wilkes-Barre, PA. Daily: 1922. (Microfilm: 1922).

Gwiazda (The Star), Holyoke, MA. Weekly: 1950. Includes English.

Gwiazda (Polish Star), Philadelphia, PA. Weekly: 1964-date. Includes English.

Gwiazda Polarna (Northern Star), Stevens Point, WI. Weekly: 1931, 1949, 1968-1969, 1972-date. Includes English.

Hasło Polskie (Polish Slogan), Pittsburgh, PA. Weekly: 1917-1918.

Hilltopper, Cambridge Springs, PA. Monthly: 1984. English.

Jedność (Unity), Philadelphia, PA. Weekly: 1933-1934.

Jedność Polek (Unity of Polish Women), Cleveland, OH. Semi-monthly: 1931, 1972-date.

Jutro Polski (Polish Fortnightly "Poland of Tomorrow"), London, England. Monthly (semi-monthly): 1964-1965, 1969-date.

Jutrzenka (The Morning Star), Cleveland, OH (previously published in Pittsburgh, PA). Weekly: 1912. (Microfilm: 1893-1894).

Kometa (Comet), Cleveland, OH. Weekly: 1918.

Kronika (Chronicle), Newark, NJ. Weekly: 1948. Includes English.

Kronika Tygodniowa (Weekly Chronicle. People's Voice), Toronto, Ontario, Canada. Weekly: 1967, 1972-1973, 1976-1977, 1979.

Kurier Polski (The Polish Courier), Milwaukee, WI. Weekly. (Microfilm: 1966-1968). Includes English.

Kurier Polsko-Kanadyjski (The Polish-Canadian Courier; Independent Polish Weekly), Toronto, Ontario, Canada. Weekly: 1974-1979. Includes English.

Kurjer Polski (Polish Courier), Buenos Aires, Argentina. Weekly: 1933.

Kuryer (The Courier), Cleveland, OH. Weekly: 1931. Includes English.

Kuryer Polski (The Polish Courier), Milwaukee, WI. Daily. (Microfilm: 1888-1962; also miscellaneous issues 1911-1925).

Kuryer Zjednoczenia (The United Courier), Cleveland, OH. Semi-monthly: 1971-date. Includes English.

Na Antenie (On the Air, published on behalf of the Polish Broadcasting Department, Radio Free Europe), London, England (previously published in Munich, West Germany). Monthly: 1963-1971.

Naród Polski (Polish Nation), Chicago, IL. Semi-monthly: 1937, 1956, 1961-date. Includes English.

Narodowiec (The Nationalist; title varies: **Wiadomości Codzienne**), Cleveland, OH. Weekly: 1912-1919. (Microfilm: 1912-1919).

The New England Polish American Digest, Lynn, MA. Bi-monthly: 1977-1982. English.

The New World, Chicago, IL. 1971. English.

Niedziela (Sunday), Detroit, MI. Weekly. (Microfilm: 1891-1894, 1898-1902).

Nowiny (The Passaic News), Passaic, NJ. Weekly: 1931. Includes English.

Nowiny Minnesockie (Minnesota News), St. Paul/Minneapols, MN. Weekly: 1960, 1965-1978.

Nowy Dziennik (Polish Daily News), New York, NY. Daily: 1971-1980, 1982, Spec. Ed. 1975.

Nowy Świat (The New World), New York, NY. Daily: 1935-1936, 1945, 1948-1949, 1959, 1961-1966, 1968-1969, 1973.

Obywatel (The Citizen), Binghamton, NY. Weekly: 1933.

Title page from *Kalendarz Emigracyiny* (Emigration Calendar), published by the Polish Emigration Society in Warsaw; Warsaw, Poland, 1928.

Obywatel Amerykański (American Citizen), Jamesburg, NJ. Weekly: 1961-1963, 1978. Includes English.

Ognisko (Camp Fire), New York, NY. Semi-monthly. (Microfilm: 1887-1889).

Ognisko Domowe (Hearth), Detroit, MI. Weekly. (Microfilm: 1929-1930).

Orzeł Polski (The Polish Eagle), Union, MO (previously published in Washington and Krakow [St. Gertrude], MO). Three times a month. (Microfilm: 1870-1872).

Panorama, Chicago, IL. 1983.

Patryota (The Patriot), Philadelphia, PA. Weekly: 1931.

Pittsburczanin (The Pittsburgher), Pittsburgh, PA. Semi-monthly (weekly): 1970-1976.

Polak Amerykański (Polish American), Jamesburg, NJ. Weekly: 1961-1962, 1964, 1976-1979.

Polish American, Chicago, IL. Weekly: 1965-1967. English.

Polish American, Minneapolis/St. Paul, MN. Monthly: 1937, 1942. English.

Polish American Journal, Scranton, PA. Monthly: 1956-1963, 1965, 1967-1968, 1970-date. English.

Polish American Voice, Buffalo, NY. Monthly: 1983. English.

Polish-American World, Baldwin, NY. Weekly: 1959-1968, 1970, 1973-1980. English.

Polish Courier (previously titled **Kuryer Codzienny**), Boston, MA. Weekly (daily): 1914, 1948-1963.

Polish Daily News (English edition of **Dziennik Polski**), Detroit, MI. Daily: 1974-1978. English.

The Polish Express, Toronto, Ontario, Canada. Bi-weekly: 1986.

Polonia, Chicago, IL. Weekly: 1971-1976.

Polonia Reporter, Buffalo, NY. Bi-monthly: 1981-1982. English.

Polonia w Americe (Polonia in America), Cleveland, OH. Weekly. (Microfilm: 1905).

Post Eagle, Clifton, NJ. Weekly: 1963-1966, 1971-date. English.

Przebudzenie (The Awakening), Chicago, IL. Frequency varies: 1929-1931, 1937, 1946-1947, 1949-1951. (Microfilm: 1927-1933, 1935-1940, 1943-1946, 1948-1951, 1953-1954). Includes English.

Przemysłowa Demokracja (Industrial Democracy), Long Island City and New York, NY. Bi-weekly. (Microfilm: 1925-1926).

Przewodnik Katolicki (Catholic Leader), New Britain, CT. Weekly: 1962, 1964.

Przyjaciel Ludu (The People's Friend), Camden, NJ. Weekly: 1931.

Przyjaciel Wolności (The Polish Weekly Newspaper), Trenton, NJ. Weekly: 1931.

PUA Parade (Polish Union of America), Buffalo, NY. Monthly: 1984. English.

The Pulaski News, Pulaski, WI. Semi-monthly: 1976-date. English.

Republika-Górnik Pennsylwański (Republic-Pennsylvania Miner), Scranton, PA. Weekly: 1931, 1934.

Robotnik Polski (The Polish Workman), Brooklyn, NY. Monthly: 1943, 1946, 1961-1967. (Microfilm: 1907-1942).

Robotnik Polski (The Polish Workman), Chicago, IL. Weekly. (Microfilm: 1903-1906).

Rola Boża (God's Field), Scranton, PA. Bi-weekly. (Microfilm: 1923-1975). Includes English.

Rolnik (The Farmer), Stevens Point, WI. Weekly: 1931. (Microfilm: 1899, 1901, 1904-1960).

Siła Ludu (The People's Power), Cleveland, OH. 1922.

Słońce (The Sun), St. Paul, MN. Weekly. (Microfilm: 1898-1900).

Słowo Polskie (The Polish Word), Utica, NY. Weekly: 1963. (Microfilm: 1911-1914, 1922-1940).

Słowo-Solidarność (Word-Solidarity), Toronto, Ontario, Canada. Weekly: 1982.

Sokół Polski (Polish Falcon), Pittsburgh, PA. Semi-monthly: 1931, 1962, 1972-1986. (Microfilm: 1910-1967). Includes English.

Sprawa (The Common Cause), London, England. Semi-monthly (?): 1945. Includes English.

Stowarzyszeniec (Association Member), Milwaukee, WI. Monthly: 1924, 1945, 1948.

Straż (The Guard), Scranton, PA. Weekly: 1926, 1930-1931, 1935-1947, 1949, 1951, 1955-1957, 1963-1983, 1986-date. (Microfilm: 1897-1898, 1900-1907, 1910, 1913, 1917, 1919-1937). Includes English.

Świat (The Polish World), New York, NY. Weekly: 1934-1935.

Świt (The Dawn), New York, NY. 1943.

Sztandar Polski (The Polish Banner), Bay City, MI. Weekly. (Microfilm: 1917-1925).

Tydzień Polski (Polish Week; Sunday supplement to **Nowy Dziennik**), New York, NY. Daily: 1973, 1977.

Tygodnik Górniczy (Miner's Weekly), Shenandoah, PA. Weekly: 1931.

Tygodnik Polski (The Polish Weekly), New York, NY. Weekly: 1943.

Tygodnik Polski (The Polish Weekly; supersedes **Tygodniowy Przegląd Literacki Koła Pisarzy z Polski**), New York, NY. Weekly. (Microfilm: 1943-1947).

U.S.A. Polonia (previously titled **Tydzień**), New York, NY. Weekly: 1976-1982.

Wiadomości (News), London, England. Weekly: 1954-1972.

Wiadomości Codzienne (Polish Daily News), Cleveland, OH. Daily: 1961-1962. (Microfilm: 1916-1928).

Wiara i Ojczyzna (Faith and Fatherland), Chicago, IL. Twice weekly, weekly. (Microfilm: 1981, 1986).

Wiarus (Old Campaigner), Winona, MN. Weekly. (Microfilm: 1892-1893).

Wielkopolanin (The Great Pole), Pittsburgh, PA. Weekly: 1931, 1933.

Zgoda (Unity), Chicago, IL. Semi-monthly: 1961-date. Includes English.

Związkowiec (The Alliancer), Cleveland, OH. Semi-monthly: 1931, 1953, 1955, 1968-date. Includes English.

Związkowiec (The Alliancer), Toronto, Ontario, Canada. Semi-weekly: 1965-date.

Serials

Abstynent (Abstainer), Chicago, IL. Monthly: 1911.

Alatus (Alliance College Polish Club), Cambridge Springs, PA. Monthly: 1971. English.

Alliance College Bulletin, Cambridge Springs, PA. Frequency varies: 1958-1959, 1973-1975. English.

Alliance College Aquila, Cambridge Springs, PA. Annual: 1950, 1967-1969. English.

Alliance Report, Cambridge Springs, PA. Bi-annual: 1980. English.

Almanach Polonii (Polonia's Almanac), Warsaw, Poland. Annual: 1961, 1965-date.

American Council of Polish Cultural Clubs Newsletter, Detroit, MI. Quarterly (?): 1977-1980. English.

American Polish Monthly, Syracuse, NY. Monthly: 1939-1940. Chiefly English.

American Polish Society Centrala Newsletter, Minneapolis, MN. Frequency varies: 1975, 1977. English.

American Polonia Reporter, New York, NY. Quarterly: 1962-1963, 1965-1966, 1968. English.

American Relief for Poland Monthly, Chicago, IL. Monthly: 1946-1947. English.

Annual Statement of the Association of the Sons of Poland, Jersey City, NJ. Annual: 1971-1973. English.

Anuario Rural Kalendarz (Anuario Rural Calendar), Buenos Aires, Argentina. Annual: 1945. Spanish and English.

Apostoł (The Apostle), Detroit, MI. Monthly: 1926-1927, 1933-1934, 1936-1938. English.

Association for the Advancement of Polish Studies Newsletter, Cambridge Springs, PA. Quarterly: 1973. English.

Association for the Advancement of Polish Studies Bulletin, Cambridge Springs, PA. Quarterly: 1975-1978. English.

Ave Maria (Hail Mary), Buffalo, NY. Bi-monthly: 1931-1934, 1936-1964, 1966-1985.

Banku Polskiego Sprawozdanie (The Polish Bank Report), Warsaw, Poland. Annual: 1934.

Biały Orzeł (White Eagle), New York, NY. Monthly: 1944, 1952-1953, 1955. Includes some English.

Bi-Centennial Newsletter, Cambridge Springs, PA. Frequency varies: 1974-1975. English.

Bicz Boży (God's Whip), Chicago, IL. Weekly: 1912.

Bicz Boży (God's Whip), Chicago, IL. Weekly: 1927.

Biuletyn Polski Fundacji Pułaskiego (Polish Bulletin of the Pulaski Foundation), Newark, NJ. Monthly (?): 1944.

Books and Things, Cheshire, CT. Monthly: 1971-1974. English.

The Brooklynite, Brooklyn, NY. Monthly: 1950-1952. Includes English.

Bulletin of Polish Medical Science and History, Chicago, IL. Quarterly (?): 1967-1979. English.

Causes Unlimited Newsletter, Hamtramck, MI. Monthly (?): 1982. English.

Centrum Jana Pawła II Biuletyn (John Paul II Center Bulletin), Orchard Lake, MI. Bi-monthly: 1984-1987.

Chicago Society Forum, Chicago, IL. Monthly: 1966-1976. English.

Chicago Society News, Chicago, IL. Monthly: 1923. English.

The Cluck, Pittsburgh, PA. 1938. Includes English.

Comments on Polish Affairs, New York, NY. Frequency varies: 1944. English.

Contemporary Poland, Warsaw, Poland. Bi-weekly: 1973-1980. English.

Czeterolistna Koniczyna (The Four Leaf Clover), Jamaica, NY. Monthly: 1974-1975.

Czuj Duch (Polish Scouting Organization), New York, NY. Quarterly: 1978. Includes some English.

Czuwaj (Be Prepared), Ville de Laval, Quebec, Canada. Quarterly: 1968-1970. English.

Dom Polski Newsletter (Polish Home Newsletter), Flint, MI. Monthly: 1985. English.

Dzień Święty (The Holy Day), Chicago, IL. Weekly: 1884, 1891-1900, 1902, 1904, 1909-1910.

Dzwon (The Bell), Manitowoc, WI. Weekly: 1891-1892.

The Eagle, Orchard Lake, MI. Annual: 1946, 1948-1960, 1962, 1964-1967. English.

The Eaglet, Detroit, MI. Tri-annual: 1982-date. English.

East European Problems, New York, NY. Quarterly: 1956-1957. English.

Echo, Brooklyn, NY. Frequency varies: 1943. Includes English.

Echo, Chicago, IL. Bi-monthly: 1979. Includes English.

Echo z Afryki (Echo from Africa), St. Paul, MN (previously published in St. Louis, MO). Monthly: 1940-1942, 1946-1949, 1965-date.

Echo z Jadwigowa (Echo from Jadwigów), Detroit, MI. Monthly: 1942, 1944. Includes English.

Extension, Chicago, IL. Monthly: 1966. English.

Filaret, Pittsburgh, PA. Monthly: 1914, 1920, 1922-1923.

Flota Polska (The Polish Fleet), New York, NY. Monthly: 1920.

Franciscan Message, Pulaski, WI. Monthly: 1947-1962, 1964-1969. English.

Free Poland, Chicago, IL. Semi-monthly: 1915-1919. English.

Free Poland; Wolna Polska, New York, NY. Monthly: 1975-1976. Includes English.

Friends of Polish Art Newsletter, Southfield, MI. Quarterly: 1983-1985. English.

Głos Studencki (The Students' Voice), Cambridge Springs, PA. Bi-monthly: 1938. Includes English.

Gość Niedzielny (Sunday Guest), Chicago, IL. Weekly: 1928, 1931, 1933-1937, 1942, 1944, 1947-1948.

Gusto, Bronx, NY. Bi-monthly: 1979, 1980. English.

Harcerz Z.N.P. (The PNA Scout), Chicago, IL. Semi-monthly: 1935.

Hejnał (Trumpeter), Florissant, MO. Quarterly: 1979, 1981. Includes English.

Hejnał Mariacki (Marian Trumpeter), Warsaw, Poland. Monthly: 1972-1976, 1979-1980, 1983-1987.

Horyzonty (Horizons), Paris, France. Monthly: 1960-1961, 1964, 1970.

The Houston Sarmatian, Houston, TX. Quarterly: 1984-1985. Includes English.

Ilustrowany Kalendarz i Skorowidz Handlowy Nowego Świata (Polish American Yearbook and Classified Directory), New York, NY. Annual: 1942-1944, 1946, 1949, 1951-1952, 1954-1956.

The Immaculate, Kenosha, WI. Monthly (bimonthly June-July): 1966. English.

Information Bulletin (Society for Relations with Poles Abroad), Warsaw, Poland. Annual (?): 1979. English.

Informator (Business and Professional Directory), New York, NY. Annual: 1935, 1936.

Informator (Directory), Warsaw, Poland. Annual: 1980.

Informator Federacja Polek w Kanadzie (Directory of the Federation of Polish Women in Canada), Toronto, Ontario, Canada. Quarterly: 1983-1984.

Informator Spoleczny (Civic Directory), Brooklyn, NY. Bi-monthly: 1975-1979. Includes English summary.

Instytut Józefa Piłsudskiego w Ameryce Biuletyn (Piłsudski Institute of America for Research in the Modern History of Poland, Inc. Bulletin), New York, NY. Annual: 1960, 1963-1965, 1969-1970, 1973-1977, 1979-1983, 1985. Includes English.

Jaskółka (The Swallow), Stevens Point, WI. Monthly: 1927-1935.

Jasna Góra (Shrine of Our Lady of Częstochowa: Pauline Father's Monthly), Doylestown, PA. Monthly: 1960, 1965-1966, 1969-1970. Includes English.

Jedność (Unity), Montreal, Quebec, Canada. Monthly: 1951.

K.S. "Polonia" Greenpoint Biuletyn Klubowy (K.S. "Polonia" Greenpoint Club Bulletin), Brooklyn, NY. Monthly: 1973, 1975.

Kalendarz Czasu (Times Calendar), Winnipeg, Manitoba, Canada. Annual: 1949, 1956, 1958.

Kalendarz dla Ludu Polskiego w Emigracyi i Stanach Zjednoczonych (Calendar for the Polish People on Emigration and in the United States), Chicago, IL. Annual: 1906.

Kalendarz Emigracyjny (Emigration Calendar), Warsaw, Poland. Annual: 1928, 1931.

Kalendarz Franciszkański (Franciscan Almanac), Pulaski, WI. Annual: 1913-1915, 1918, 1921, 1923, 1925-1928, 1930-1936, 1938-1940, 1948-1949, 1952-1960, 1962-1969, 1972.

Kalendarz i Przewodnik (Calendar and Guidebook), Toledo, OH (?). Annual: 1914.

Kalendarz Kotwiczny (Anchor Calendar), Brooklyn, NY. Annual: 1926.

Kalendarz Krzyżowca (Crusader's Calendar), Washington, DC. Monthly: 1967.

Kalendarz Legjonów (Legions' Calendar), Chicago, IL. Annual: 1917.

Kalendarz Ludowy (People's Calendar), Chicago, IL. Annual: 1913-1915, 1923.

Kalendarz Mariański (Marian Calendar), Stockbridge, MA. Annual: 1969, 1972.

Kalendarz Marjański (Marian Calendar), Vimperk, Czechoslovakia. Annual: 1911-1919, 1927.

Kalendarz Polaka w Kanadzie (Calendar of the Pole in Canada), Winnipeg, Manitoba, Canada. Annual: 1950.

Kalendarz Polski (Polish Calendar), Brooklyn, NY. Annual: 1966.

Kalendarz Polski (Polish Calendar), Cedar Rapids, IA. Annual: 1915.

Kalendarz Polski (Polish Calendar), Erie, PA. Annual: 1942.

Kalendarz Polski (Polish Calendar), Philadelphia, PA. Annual: 1969-1976, 1981.

Kalendarz Rycerza Niepokalanej (Calendar of the Knight of the Immaculate), Rome, Italy. Annual: 1925, 1934, 1937-1939, 1973-1974, 1980.

Kalendarz Salwatora (Salvation Calendar), Gary, IN. Annual: 1946-1956, 1958, 1960-1961, 1964, 1966. Includes English.

Kalendarz Serca Jezusowego (The Sacred Heart Calendar), Cracow, Poland. Annual: 1927-1928, 1930-1934, 1939.

Kalendarz Słowa Bożego (The God's Word Calendar), Gorna Grupa, Pomorze, Poland. Annual: 1935, 1937-1939.

Kalendarz Świętego Michała (Saint Michael's Calendar), Chicago, IL. Annual: 1912-1913.

Kalendarz Św. Piotra Klawera (St. Peter Klawer's Calendar), St. Paul, MN. Annual: 1933, 1935-1939, 1960, 1965-1975.

Kalendarz Światowego Związku Polaków z Zagranicy (Calendar of the World Union of Poles from Abroad), Warsaw, Poland. Annual: 1938-1939.

Kalendarz Uniwersalny (Universal Calendar), Vimperk, Czechoslovakia. Annual: 1908, 1912, 1915, 1918-1919, 1923, 1925, 1928-1929.

Kalendarz Warszawski (Warsaw Calendar), Warsaw, Poland. Annual: 1946.

Kalendarz Wszechświatowy (All-World Calendar), Vimperk, Czechoslovakia. Annual: 1927.

Kalendarz Związkowy (Polish National Alliance Yearbook), Chicago, IL. Annual: 1912-1915, 1922, 1924, 1936, 1938, 1941, 1943-1944, 1946-1949, 1951-1980.

The Kantian, Erie, PA. Annual: 1954, 1960. English.

Kantowianin (The Kantowian), Indiana Harbor, IN. Monthly: 1929-1930. Includes some English.

The Kapustkan, Chicago, IL. Monthly: 1941. English.

Kazalnica (The Pulpit), New Castle, PA. Monthly: 1941, 1943-1945.

Kazalnica Popularna (The Popular Pulpit), Orchard Lake, MI. Quarterly: 1937-1939, 1943-1944.

The Keynote, South Bend, IN. Monthly: 1979. English.

Kombatant w Ameryce (Quarterly of the Polish Veterans of World War II), New York, NY. Quarterly: 1956-date. Includes some English.

Komitet Narodowy Amerykanów Pochodzenia Polskiego Biuletyn (National Committee of Americans of Polish Descent, Inc. Bulletin), New York, NY. Quarterly (?): 1945, 1948. Includes some English.

Konfederacja (Confederation), Irvington, NJ. Monthly: 1976-1978.

Kontakt (Contact), Paris, France. Monthly: 1985-1987.

Kopernik (Copernicus) Newsletter, Cambridge Springs, PA. Frequency varies: 1973-1974. English.

Kosciół Reformacyjny w Ameryce (The Church of the Reformation of America), Chicago, IL (Scranton, PA). Monthly. (Microfilm: 1906-1909).

The Kościuszko Foundation Newsletter, New York, NY. Monthly: 1946-1978. English.

Kościuszko Foundation Annual Ball, New York, NY. Annual: 1937-1939, 1945, 1947-1950, 1953, 1955, 1957, 1962-1966, 1969-1972, 1975-1978. English.

Kościuszko Foundation Presentation Ball, Boston, MA. Bi-annual: 1949, 1955, 1957, 1959, 1961, 1963, 1966-1967, 1969, 1971, 1973, 1976-1977, 1979, 1981. English.

Krajowa Agencja Informacyjna (Polish Information Agency), Warsaw, Poland. Weekly: 1971-1983.

Krajowa Agencja Informacyjna Supplement (Polish Information Agency Supplement), Warsaw, Poland. 1973-1977.

Kronika Seraficka (The Seraphic Chronicle), Detroit, MI (previously published in Buffalo, NY and Milwaukee, WI). Monthly: 1933-1950, 1954. Includes English.

Książka Roczna i Kalendarz "Ameryki-Echa" (Yearbook and Calendar of "America-Echo"; previously titled **Kalendarz Polski Ameryki-Echa**), Toledo, OH. Annual: 1924-1925, 1927-1936, 1939-1940, 1942-1944, 1946-1957, 1959.

Kultura (Culture), Paris, France. Monthly: 1953, 1961, 1968, 1970-1980.

Lake Oracle, Orchard Lake, MI. Monthly: 1946-1947. English.

The Lamplighter, Bayonne, NJ. Monthly (?): 1973. English.

Lekcje Biblijne dla Dorosłych do Użytku w Domu i w Szkole (Bible Lessons for Adults in Home and School), Pittsburgh, PA. Four undated issues. Includes English.

Liga (The League), Chicago, IL (previously published in Detroit, MI). Monthly: 1944-1946, 1948.

Listy do Polaków (Letters to the Poles), New Britain, CT. Monthly: 1971-1978.

The Massachusetts Federation of Polish Women's Clubs, Inc. Newsletter, Ludlow, MA. Annual: 1960, 1963, 1968, 1970, 1974-1976. English.

Memento, Detroit, MI. Monthly: 1931.

Merchant's Guide, New York, NY. Monthly: 1949. Includes English.

Miesięcznik Franciszkański (Franciscan Monthly), Pulaski, WI. Monthly: 1915-1916, 1922-1950, 1952-1973.

Miesięcznik Parafialny (St. Hedwig Parish Monthly), Trenton, NJ. Monthly: 1948. Includes English.

Migrant Echo, San Francisco, CA. Quarterly: 1972-1981. Includes English.

Minnesota Pol-Am Newsletter, Minneapolis, MN. Monthly: 1980-1983, 1985-1987. English.

Młody Polak Zagranicą (Young Pole Abroad), Warsaw, Poland. Bi-monthly: 1934-1935.

Młodzież Afrykańska (African Youth), St. Paul, MN. Monthly: 1969-1971.

Monthly American Polish, Syracuse, NY. Monthly: 1939-1940. English.

The Monthly Future (Friends of Poland Inc.), New York, NY. Monthly: 1939-1941. English.

Morze (The Sea), Chicago, IL. Quarterly (monthly): 1943, 1960, 1964-1965.

Mowa Radiowa (Radio Speech), Buffalo, NY. Weekly: 1931-1932.

Murzynek (The Negro Child), St. Louis, MO. Monthly: 1938-1942, 1945-1949.

Na Antenie (On the Air; published on behalf of the Polish Broadcasting Deparatment, Radio Free Europe), London, England. Monthly: 1969.

Nasz Świat (Our World Weekly), Detroit, MI. Weekly: 1942-1943, 1945.

Nasza Ojczyzna (Our Fatherland), Warsaw, Poland. Monthly: 1958, 1971. Includes English section.

Nasza Rodzina (Our Family), Paris, France. Monthly: 1971-1975.

Nasza Szkoła (Our School), Brooklyn, NY. Frequency varies: 1932.

Nasze Jutro (Our Future), Chicago, IL. Monthly: 1936. Includes some English.

Nasze Pisemko (Our Pamphlet), Detroit, MI. Monthly: 1924, 1928, 1930-1932, 1934-1948.

Nasze Sprawy (Our Matters), Los Angeles, CA. Monthly (?): 1969. Includes English.

National Committee of Americans of Polish Descent, Inc. Biuletyn Organizacyjny (Organizational Bulletin), New York, NY. Frequency varies: 1942-1948.

National Medical and Dental Association of America Bulletin (previously titled **The Medical and Dental Bulletin**), Chicago, IL. Monthly: 1929-1956, 1964. Includes English.

The National P.L.A.V. News (Polish Legion of American Veterans of the United States of America), Chicago, IL. Frequency varies: 1961, 1974-1978. English.

National Polish Committee of America, Chicago, IL. Semi-monthly (weekly): 1918-1921.

National United Choirs Newsletter, Scranton, PA. Bi-annual: 1983-1987. English.

Naukowy Instytut Emigracyjny i Kolonjalny Kwartalnik (Emigration and Colonial Science Institute Quarterly), Warsaw, Poland. Quarterly: 1926-1930.

The Nazareth, Philadelphia, PA. Five times per year: 1974, 1976-1977. English.

Neptun (Neptune), Philadelphia, PA. Monthly: 1940-1941.

The New American, Chicago, IL. Monthly: 1935-1939. English.

New Horizon, New York, NY. Monthly: 1975-1979, 1985. English.

New Life, New York, NY. Quarterly: 1969-1970. English.

The New Link (Association of Polish Engineers in Canada), Toronto, Ontario, Canada. Bi-monthly: 1983-1985. Includes English.

Niedziela (The Sunday), Detroit, MI. Weekly: 1897.

Niepokalana (The Immaculate), Paris, France. Monthly: 1959, 1971-1976.

Nowe Drogi (New Roads), Chicago, IL. Monthly: 1956.

"O" Publication of the Arts (previously titled **Echo**), Toronto, Ontario, Canada. Quarterly: 1970-1976. Includes English.

Odgłos Trójcowa (Holy Trinity Echo), Chicago, IL. Monthly: 1933.

Okno na Świat (Window of the World), Chicago, IL. Monthly: 1946-1947.

Okólnik Wydziału Narodowego Polskiego (Polish National Department Circular), Chicago, IL. Bi-weekly: 1919-1920.

The Old Courthouse News, South Bend, IN. Quarterly: 1968. English.

Orchard Lake Alumnus, Orchard Lake, MI. Quarterly: 1937-1950, 1952-1953, 1968. Includes English.

Orchard Lake Good News, Orchard Lake, MI. Frequency varies: 1980-1984. English.

Orka Biuletyn Informacyjny (Plowing--Information Bulletin), Chicago, IL. Monthly, irregular: 1955-1969.

Orlęta (Eaglets), Chicago, IL. Monthly: 1955.

Orzeł Biały (White Eagle), London, England. Monthly: 1967-1970, 1974.

Osa (The Wasp), New York, NY. Monthly: 1940-1941, undated sample copy. Includes some English.

PBA Bulletin (Professional & Businessmen's Association), Buffalo, NY. Monthly: 1981. English.

PNCC Studies (Polish National Catholic Church), Scranton, PA. Annual: 1980-1986. English.

The Paderewski Foundation Annual Banquet and Ball, New York, NY. Annual: 1962-1966. English.

Paduan (title varies: **San Francis Magazine; St. Francis Messenger**), Pulaski, WI. Monthly: 1925-1927, 1929-1935. English.

Pamiętnikarstwo Polskie (Polish Memoirs), Warsaw, Poland. Bi-monthly: 1971-1974.

Pan z Wami (The Lord Be with You), Orchard Lake, MI. Bi-monthly: 1971-1972, 1976.

Pancerniak (Tank Corpsman), Chicago, IL. 1973.

Panorama Polonii (Polonia's Panorama), Los Angeles, CA. Monthly: 1972.

Patron, Brooklyn, NY. Weekly: 1942-1944, 1946-1974, 1976-1980. Includes English.

Perspectives, Washington, DC. Bi-monthly (quarterly): 1971-date. English.

Płomyk (Little Flame; Youth Circle at Henryk Sienkiewicz School), Brooklyn, NY. Quarterly: 1940-1944, 1946, 1948. Includes English.

Po Prostu (Simply), Chicago, IL. Frequency varies: 1975-1976.

Pociecha Starości: Kalendarz (Comfort for Old Age: Calendar), Vimperk, Czechoslovakia. Annual: 1927.

Pokój (Peace; The Official Newsletter of the Polish American Folk Theatre), Detroit, MI. Monthly: 1973, 1975-1976, 1978. Includes English.

Polacy Zagranicą (Poles Abroad), Warsaw, Poland. Monthly: 1933-1934, 1936, 1939.

Polak w Kalifornii (The Polish Californian), San Francisco, CA. Monthly: 1952-1954.

Pol America, Los Angeles, CA. Quarterly: 1978, 1984. Includes English.

Polamerican Law Journal, Chicago, IL. Semi-annual: 1938-1941. English.

Poland. Główny Urząd Statystyczny Rzeczypospolitej Polskiej (The Main Statistical Agency of the Polish Republic), Warsaw, Poland. Quarterly: 1929, 1931. Includes French.

Poland. Główny Urząd Statystyczny Rzeczypospolitej Polskiej (The Main Statistical Agency of the Polish Republic), Warsaw, Poland. Annual: 1930. Includes French.

Poland. Główny Urząd Statystyczny (The Main Statistical Agency), Warsaw, Poland. Three issues per month: 1934-1935. Includes French.

Poland (American edition), Warsaw, Poland. Monthly: 1972, 1974-1977. English.

Poland America (previously titled **Poland**), Ware, MA. Monthly: 1923-1933. English.

Poland and Germany, London, England. Quarterly: 1960-1961, 1963-1972. English.

Poland Fights, New York, NY. Semi-monthly: 1941-1944. (Index 1941-1943). English.

Poland of Today, New York, NY. Monthly: 1946-1949. English.

Poland Today, Los Angeles, CA. Quarterly: 1984-1985. English.

The Polish American, Maynard, MA. Monthly: 1984-1985. Includes English.

Polish American Almanac, New York, NY. Annual: 1970. Includes English.

Polish American Congress Bulletin, Chicago, IL. Monthly (bi-monthly): 1945-1946. English.

Polish American Congress Newsletter, Chicago, IL. Quarterly: 1958, 1969-1973, 1976-1977, 1979, 1983-date. English.

Polish American Congress; Downstate New York Division, Biuletyn (Bulletin), New York, NY. Quarterly: 1972-1973. Includes English.

Polish American Congress; Illinois Division Newsletter, Harwood Heights, IL. Bi-monthly (?): 1972. English.

Polish American Congress; Michigan Division (KPA-PAC) Bulletin, Detroit, MI. Monthly: 1975. English.

Polish American Congress; New Jersey Division Biuletyn (Bulletin), Irvington, NJ. Quarterly: 1974-1975. Includes English.

Polish American Congress; New Jersey Division Newsletter, Perth Amboy, NJ. Monthly: 1979. Includes English.

Polish American Congress of Texas (previously titled **San Antonio Polonia News**), San Antonio, TX. Quarterly (?): 1970-1971. English.

Polish American Congress; Wisconsin Division Bulletin, Milwaukee, WI. Quarterly: 1984, 1986. English.

Polish American Educators Association Newsletter (PAEA), Chicago, IL. Monthly: 1973-1979. English.

Polish American Historical Association (PAHA) Bulletin (previously titled **Bulletin of the Commission for Research on Polish Immigration; Polish American Historical Commission Bulletin**), Chicago, IL (previously published in New York, NY, and Orchard Lake, MI): Quarterly (monthly): 1943-1983. English.

Polish American Immigration and Relief Committe Annual Charity Ball, New York, NY. Annual: 1950, 1957-1961, 1963, 1965, 1968-1969, 1971-1972, 1975. Includes English.

The Polish American Journal, Manchester, CT. Monthly: 1941, 1961. Includes English.

Polish American Librarians Association Newsletter, Hamtramck, MI. Frequency varies: 1976-1978. English.

Polish American Museum News Bulletin, Port Washington, NY. Quarterly: 1986. English.

Polish American News, Philadelphia, PA. Monthly: 1985-1986. English.

Polish American Patriot, Monessen, PA. Frequency varies: 1974, 1976. English.

Polish American Progress Association, Jersey City, NJ. 1976. English.

Polish American Review, Chicago, IL. Monthly: 1956. English.

Polish American Review, Chicago, IL (previously published in Cleveland, OH). Monthly: 1935-1936. English.

Polish American Studies, Chicago, IL (previously published in Orchard Lake, MI). Semi-annual: 1944-date. (Index for 1944-1973). English.

Polish American Voice, Buffalo, NY. Monthly: 1983. English.

Polish Art and Film, Hollywood, CA. Monthly: 1937-1938. Includes English.

Polish Arts and Culture Foundation Bulletin, San Francisco, CA. Bi-monthly: 1975-1977, 1980-1987. English.

Polish Arts Club Bulletin, Chicago, IL. Monthly: 1946, 1975-date. English.

Polish Assistance Inc. Bulletin, New York, NY. Quarterly: 1978. English.

The Polish Book Guild, Inc. Newsletter, River Edge, NJ. Quarterly: 1972, 1974. English.

The Polish Cause, Chicago, IL. Semi-monthly (irregular): 1915. English.

Polish Engineering Review, Montreal, Quebec, Canada. Quarterly: 1944-1945. English.

Polish Facts and Figures, New York, NY. Frequency varies: 1944-1945. English.

Polish Genealogical Society Bulletin, Chicago, IL. Quarterly: 1984-1986. English.

Polish Genealogical Society Newsletter, Chicago, IL. Semi-annual: 1979-1980, 1982, 1984-date. English.

Polish Heritage (title varies: **American Council of Polish Cultural Clubs Bulletin; Quarterly Review; The Quarterly Review of Polish Heritage**), place of publication varies. Quarterly: 1950-date. English.

Polish Heritage Society, Grand Rapids, MI. Semi-monthly: 1975-date. English.

Polish Information Bulletin, Washington, DC. Bi-monthly: 1939. English.

Polish Institute of Arts and Sciences in America Bulletin, New York, NY. Quarterly: 1942-1945. Includes English.

Polish Institute of Arts and Sciences in America Information Bulletin, New York, NY. Frequency varies: 1963, 1966-1973. English.

Polish Intercollegiate Club Gazette, Philadelphia, PA. Monthly: 1935-1936. Includes English.

Polish Museum of America Protokół Zjazdu Dyrekcji Polskiego Muzeum w Ameryce (Protocol of the Convention of the Board of Directors of the Polish Museum in America), Chicago, IL. Bi-annual: 1960-1964, 1966-1967.

Polish Museum of America Quarterly, Chicago, IL. Quarterly: 1972-1974, 1976-1978, 1980. English.

Polish National Alliance By-Laws, Chicago, IL. Irregular: 1963, 1967, 1971, 1975. English.

Polish National Alliance Constitution and By-Laws, Chicago, IL. Irregular: 1909, 1935, 1939, 1947. English.

Polish National Alliance Konstytucja i Ustawy (Convention Diary), Chicago, IL. Irregular: 1947, 1951, 1959, 1963, 1967, 1971.

Polish National Alliance Pamiętnik Sejmu (Officers' Report), Chicago, IL. Irregular: 1927, 1940, 1947, 1951, 1955, 1959, 1963, 1967, 1971, 1975, 1979. Includes English.

Polish National Alliance of Brooklyn Convention Minutes, Brooklyn, NY. Irregular: 1939, 1950, 1958, 1966.

Polish National Alliance of Brooklyn Sprawozdanie Urzedników, Brooklyn, NY. Tri-annual: 1939-1942, 1946-1961.

Polish News and Views, Warsaw, Poland. Bi-monthly (?): 1960-1961. English.

Polish Perspectives, Warsaw, Poland. Monthly: 1963, 1974-1977. English.

The Polish Review (Polish Institute of Arts and Sciences in America), New York, NY. Quarterly: 1956-1980. English.

Polish Review (Polish Information Center), New York, NY. Frequency varies: 1941-1945. English.

The Polish Review and East European Affairs (previously titled **Polish Review**), New York, NY. Monthly (weekly, bi-weekly): 1944-1949. English.

The Polish Student Bulletin, Chicago, IL. Monthly: 1932. English.

Polish Studies Center Newsletter, Bloomington, IN. Frequency varies: 1979-1980. English.

Polish Studies Newsletter, Brookville, MD. Monthly: 1985. English.

Polish War Relief, Chicago, IL. Frequency varies: 1943. English.

Polka (Polish Woman), Scranton, PA. Quarterly: 1935-1954, 1956-1959, 1961-1962, 1968-date. (Microfilm: 1935-1974). Includes English.

Polka Scene, Cleveland, OH. Monthly: 1982-1983. English.

Polonia; Almanach i Zbiór Faktów (Polish American Almanac and Book of Facts), Detroit, MI. Annual: 1945-1946. Includes English.

Polonia Catalogue Bulletin, Chicago, IL. Annual: 1976, 1978-1980. Includes English.

Polonian, San Francisco, CA. Bi-monthly: 1971-1973, 1984-1985. Includes English.

Polonus Philatelic Society Bulletin, Chicago, IL. Monthly: 1963, 1965, 1967-1977. English.

Polonus Philatelic Society Catalogue, Chicago, IL. Annual: 1962-1963, 1970-1971. English.

Polski Czerwony Krzyż Kalendarz (Polish Red Cross Calendar), London, England. Annual: 1941.

Polski Kalendarz Misyjny (Polish Missionary Calendar), Detroit, MI. Annual: 1939-1940.

Polski Przegląd Emigracyjny (Polish Emigration Review), Cracow, Poland. Frequency varies. (Microfilm: 1907-1911, 1914).

Polski Teatr Robotniczy Biuletyn Kółko Literackie (Polish Workers' Theatre Bulletin Literary Circle), New York, NY. Monthly: 1938.

Polskie Stronnictwo Ludowe Biuletyn (Polish Peasant Party Bulletin), Washington, DC. Monthly, frequency varies: 1981-1987.

Pope John Paul II Center Newsletter, Orchard Lake, MI. Bi-monthly: 1984-1987. English.

Posłaniec (Messenger), Newark, NJ. Weekly: 1923-1926.

Posłaniec Godziny Różańcowej (Messenger of the Rosary Hour), Buffalo, NY. Semi-monthly: 1932-1934.

Posłaniec Matki Boskiej Saletyńskiej (Messenger of Virgin Mary), Twin Lakes, WI (previously published in Ware, MA). Monthly (except July and August): 1925-1927, 1931-1952, 1971-1974, 1976.

Posłaniec Serca Jezusa (Polish Messenger of the Sacred Heart), Chicago, IL. Monthly: 1917-1951, 1970-1978.

Posłaniec Świętego Franciszka (St. Francis Messenger), Pulaski, WI. Monthly: 1915, 1917, 1922-1924.

The Post, East Lansing, MI. Quarterly (?): 1987. English.

Postęp (Advance), Baltimore, MD. Monthly: 1916-1920.

Problemy Polonii Zagranicznej (Problems of Polonia Abroad), Wrocław, Poland. Annual: 1960, 1966-1967, 1971-1974.

Promień (Sunbeam), Chicago, IL. Quarterly: 1943-1947, 1949-1955, 1957-1963, 1966-1976, 1978-1980. Includes English.

Przebudzenie (The Awakening), Chicago, IL. Weekly: 1929-31, 1947, 1949-51.

Przegląd Emigracyjny (Emigration Review), Warsaw, Poland. Quarterly. (Microfilm: 1926-1928; index to 1926-1927).

Przegląd Katolicki (The Catholic Review), Milwaukee, WI. Monthly: 1926-1936.

Przegląd Kościelny (Ecclesiastical Monthly), Milwaukee, WI. Monthly: 1915-1925.

Przegląd Polonii (Polonia Review), Glendale, CA. Monthly: 1975-1978. Includes some English.

Przegląd Polonijny (Polonia Review), Wrocław, Poland. Quarterly: 1975-date. Includes English summaries.

Przegląd Polski (Polish Review), Chicago, IL. Quarterly: 1974, 1976.

Przegląd Polski (Polish Review), St. Louis, MO. Monthly: 1973. Includes English.

Przegląd Polsko-Amerykański (Polish-American Literary Review), Chicago, IL. Monthly: 1911-1913. Includes some English.

Przegląd Powszechny (Polish Catholic Monthly), London, England. Monthly: 1967-1975.

Przegląd Wszechpolski (All-Poland Review; previously titled **Przegląd Emigracyjny**), Lvov, Poland. Semi-monthly. (Microfilm: 1892-1895).

Przewodnik Kupiecki (Merchants' Guide), Detroit, MI. Quarterly (monthly): 1936-1940, 1944-1946. Includes some English.

Przyjaciel Żołnierza Kalendarz (Soldier's Friends Calendar), Warsaw, Poland. Annual: 1916, 1921, 1923, 1926, 1929.

Przyszłość (Future), Chicago, IL. Monthly: 1943.

PS Arts, Randolph, NJ. Quarterly: 1977-1980. English.

Polish Union of America Parade, Buffalo, NY. Monthly: 1971, 1976-1979. Includes English.

Pulaski Day Parade, New York, NY. Annual: 1941, 1961-1964, 1966-1967, 1979. English.

Pulaski Foundation Bulletin, New York, NY. Monthly (?): 1961. Includes English.

Pulaski Foundation Bulletin, Newark, NJ. Monthly: 1942-1944. English.

Pulaski Magazine and Digest, Omaha, NE. Monthly: 1938. English.

Pulaski Memorial Banquet, New York, NY. Annual: 1969-1970, 1976-1977. English.

PWR Monthly (Polish War Relief of the U.S.A.), Chicago, IL. Monthly: 1945. English.

Quarterly of the Polish Western Association of America, Chicago, IL. Quarterly: 1960-date. Includes English.

Quo Vadis (Wherever You Go), New York, NY. Monthly (?): 1955-1957. Includes some English.

Relax, Chicago, IL. Weekly: 1984.

Report on Poland, New York, NY. Frequency varies: 1951-1952.

Rocznik Polonijny (Polonia Almanac), Lublin, Poland. Annual: 1980-1981.

Róże Maryi (Roses of Mary), Stockbridge, MA. Monthly: 1945, 1947, 1949-1969, 1972-1973, 1975.

Rozgłos Salezjański (Salesian Voice), Ramsey, NJ. Monthly: 1936, 1939-1941.

Rycerz Niepokalanej (The Knight of the Immaculate), Rome, Italy. Monthly: 1971-1978.

S.O.S. U.S.A., Ship of State, Salem, MA. Monthly: 1970-1972. English.

SPK w Kanadzie (Polish Combatants Association in Canada, Inc.), Toronto, Ontario, Canada. Quarterly: 1963.

Sacred Heart of Jesus News and Views, Minneapolis, MN. Monthly: 1966-1967. Includes English.

St. Adalbert Parish Directory Informator, Philadelphia, PA. Annual: 1966, 1968. Includes English.

St. Adalbert Parish Family, Elmhurst, NY. Weekly: 1976-1977. Includes English.

St. Stanislaus Catholic Church Bulletin, Ambridge, PA. Monthly: 1957, 1959-1960. Includes English.

The Sentinel, Meriden, CT. Monthly: 1940, 1942-1943. English.

Singers Bulletin, New York, NY. Quarterly: 1979. Includes English.

Skarb Rodziny (The Family Treasure), Erie, PA. Monthly (except August): 1917-1955. Includes English.

Skarb Rodzinny (The Family Treasure), Techny, IL. Monthly: 1939.

Słoneczko (Sun; Children's Weekly), Stevens Point, WI. Weekly (except July and August): 1941.

Słowo i Liturgia (Word and Liturgy), Orchard Lake, MI. Quarterly: 1986-date.

Sodalis-Polonia (previously titled **Sodalis Maryański**), Orchard Lake, MI. Frequency varies: 1922-1925, 1928-1934, 1940-1941, 1947-1949, 1966-1975.

Sokół; Przewodnik Gimnastyczny (Falcon; Gymnastic Guidebook), Chicago, IL. Monthly: 1908.

Społem (Together), Anaconda, MT. Annual (?): 1934 (?).

Stowarzyszenie Weteranów Armii Polskiej w Ameryce Sprawozdanie (Polish Veterans Association of America Reports), New York, NY. Tri-annual: 1955-1958, 1964-1967.

The Student Press, Scranton, PA. Quarterly: 1977-1979. Includes English.

Studia Polonijne (Polonia Studies), Lublin, Poland. Annual: 1976, 1978-1979, 1981. Includes English summaries.

Studium (News Abstracts), Chicago, IL. Quarterly: 1977-1980. English.

Survey of Poland, New York, NY. Bi-monthly: 1936-1939. English.

Św. Jadwiga Biuletyn (St. Hedwig's Church Bulletin), Chicago, IL. Monthly: 1936. Includes English.

Święta Rodzina Kalendarz (Holy Family Calendar), Warsaw, Poland. Annual: 1919.

Szaniec (The Rampart), Chicago, IL. Monthly: 1972-1973.

Szkolnictwo (Education; previously titled **Szkolnictwo Ludowe**), Nowy Sącz, Poland. Frequency varies. (Microfilm: 1891-1895).

Szlakiem Legjonów (The Legions' Path), Chicago, IL. Annual: 1914-1915.

Tatrzański Orzeł (Tatra Eagle), Passaic, NJ. Quarterly: 1950-date.

Technika Popularna (Technical Review), Chicago, IL. Monthly: 1920.

Tematy (Perspectives in Culture, Inc.), New York, NY/London, England. Quarterly: 1962-1967.

Towarzystwo Rozwoju Ziem Zachodnich: Biuletyn Komisji Polonii Zagranicznej (Association for the Development of the Western Territories: Commission of Polonia Bulletin), Warsaw, Poland. Weekly (?): 1963.

Tribune of Enslaved Nations, Salem, MA. Monthly: 1965. English.

Trumpeter (Polish Heritage Association of Maryland), Glen Burnie, MD. Bi-monthly: 1984. English.

Tygodnik Nowojorski (New York Weekly), Elmhurst, NY. Weekly: 1984-1986. Includes English supplement.

Tygodnik Polski (The Polish Weekly), New York, NY. Weekly: 1943-1947.

Tygodnik Powieściowo-Naukowy (Weekly of Novels and Science News), Chicago, IL. Weekly: 1884-1888, 1891-1897, 1899.

Tygodniowy Przegląd Literacki Koła Pisarzy z Polski (Weekly Literary Review of the Writers' Circle from Poland), New York, NY. Weekly. (Microfilm: 1941-1942).

Voice of Sarmatia, Cleveland, OH (?). Monthly: 1946.

Walka (Struggle), Chicago, IL. Monthly: 1961-1969.

Wesoły Towarzysz Ludu: Illustrowany Kalendarz (The Merry Companion of the People: Illustrated Calendar). Annual: 1931.

Weteran (Veteran), New York, NY (previously published in Cleveland, OH; Chicago, IL; and Detroit, MI). Monthly: 1926-1939, 1941-1944, 1946-1949, 1951-1953, 1956-1957, 1960-date.

Wiadomości Misyjne (Missionary News), Dearborn, MI. Monthly: 1923-1924.

Wiadomości-News, Chicago, IL. Monthly (?): 1966.

Wiadomości o Polsce (Report on Poland), New York, NY. Monthly: 1953.

Wiadomości Polskie (Polish News), Los Angeles, CA. Quarterly (monthly): 1972-1973, 1975.

Wiadomości Polskie (Polish News), Montreal, Quebec, Canada. Monthly: 1963-1967.

Wiadomości Wojskowe (Military News; previously titled **Biuletyn Informacyjny**), London, England. Frequency varies: 1950-1953.

Wici (Call to Arms), Chicago, IL. Weekly: 1916-1917, 1919.

Wieści. Polskie Stronnictwo Ludowe (News. Polish Peasant Party), Brussels, Belgium. Quarterly: 1983.

Wojciechowjanin (St. Adelbert's News), Chicago, IL. Monthly: 1925, 1935-1938. Includes English.

The World Polish Community, Rockville, CT. Quarterly (?): 1987. English.

Wspólnymi Siłami ku Wolnej Polsce Biuletyn (Mutual Effort for Independent Poland Bulletin), Chicago, IL. Monthly (?): 1962.

Wszystko Przez Serce Jezusa (Everything through the Sacred Heart), Manitowoc, WI. Weekly: 1888.

Wychodźca (Immigrant), Warsaw, Poland. Bi-weekly: 1935.

Wyzwolenie Ludu (Liberation of the People), Salem, MA. Monthly: 1957-1958. Includes English.

Zachodnia Agencja Prasowa (Western Press Agency), Warsaw, Poland. 1963.

Zbiór Materiałów Politycznych (Collection of Political Materials), Chicago, IL. Frequency varies: 1958-1960, 1962.

Zeszyty Naukowe Katolickiego Uniwersytetu Lubelskiego (Lublin Catholic University Studies), Lublin, Poland. Quarterly: 1974. Includes English summaries.

Zew Młodych (The Youth Call), Chicago, IL. Monthly: 1952-1954.

Zgoda (Unity), Chicago, IL. Monthly: 1943. Includes English.

Źródło (The Spring), Milwaukee, WI. Weekly: 1899.

Zrzeszenie Artystow Scen Polskich w St. Z.J. Newsletter (Newsletter of the Association of the Polish Actors in the United States), New York, NY. Monthly: 1974. English.

Zrzeszenie Przyjaciół Polskiego Żołnierza Biuletyn Informacyjny (Polish Soldier's Aid Association Information Bulletin; previously titled **Zrzeszenie Przyjaciół Żołnierza Polskiego**), New York, NY. Monthly: 1946-1947.

Romanian American Collection

Manuscript Collections

Iulu Maniu American Romanian Relief Foundation.
Records, 1953-1965. Ca. 1 linear ft.

The Foundation was a voluntary organization formed to assist Romanians in immigration and resettlement. Records consist of bylaws, annual reports, and various programs of meetings. *Includes English. Inventory available.*

Romanian Orthodox Episcopate in America.
Records, 1906-1975. Ca. 1 linear ft.

The Episcopate was officially established in 1929, although the first Romanian Orthodox parish in the United States was organized in 1904. The Romanian Orthodox Episcopate of America is the ecclesiastical center for about 50,000 Romanian Orthodox Christians in this country, with central offices located in Jackson, MI. Official relations with church authorities in Romania were severed in 1951; and from 1952 Bishop Valerian D. Trifa headed the church, which is now under jurisdiction of the Russian Orthodox Greek Catholic Church of North America.

Records contain minutes, programs of congresses, press releases, reports, and sample documents. *Includes English. Inventory available. Circular letters restricted.*

Union and League of Romanian Societies in America, Inc.
Records, 1900-1958. 19.5 linear ft.

The Union and League was established as the result of a merger of early Romanian American fraternal societies. In 1906, the "Vulturul" organization of Homestead, PA, and "Invierea" of Martins Ferry, OH, signed the Consolidation Act of the Union of the Romanian Beneficial and Cultural Societies. In 1928, the Union joined with the League of Romanian Beneficial and Cultural Societies, forming the present-named organization. The Union and League played an important role in development of Romanian American churches, parochial schools, and press.

Records of the Union and League include correspondence of the Cleveland, OH, headquarters; minutes and financial books of various branches throughout the United States; and membership registers. *Inventory available.*

Monographs

The Romanian American monograph collection, totaling ca. 175 volumes, provides substantial coverage for several subject areas: Romanian migration, the Romanian American community as a whole, acculturation, religion, organizations and associations, particular communities, arts and entertainment, and folklore.

There are two relatively recent book-length bibliographies on Romanian immigration: Radu Toma's *Romanii din America* (Romanians of America, 1978, covering emigration to World War II only); and Vladimir Wertsman's *The Romanians in America and Canada: A Guide to Information Sources* (1980). General works about the Romanians in America include Nicolae Iorga's *Scrisori către Românii din America, 1921-1924* (Writings about Romanians of America, n.d.); Serban Drutzu and Andrei Popovici's *Românii în America* (The Romanians in America, ca. 1925); Ion Iosif Şchiopul's *Românii din America* (Romanians of America, 1913); and Vladimir Wertsman's *The Romanians in America, 1748-1974: A Chronology and Fact Book* (1975). Also in the collection are two major books about acculturation of Romanian Americans: Alexandra Roceric's *Language Maintenance within an American Ethnic Community: The Case of Romanian* (1982), and Kenneth A. Thigpen's *Folklore and the Ethnicity Factor in the Lives of Romanian Americans* (1973). The collection also includes several histories of Romania.

Particular communities have been the subject of key studies: Christine Avghi Galitzi's *A Study of Assimilation Among the Roumanians in the United States* (1929, 1968 reprint); Josef J. Barton's *Peasants and Strangers: Italians, Rumanians, and Slovaks in an America City, 1890-1950* (1975); and Theodore Andrica's *Romanian Americans and their Communities of Cleveland* (1977).

On religious groups--the Romanian Orthodox Episcopate in America (ROEA), the Romanian Orthodox Missionary Episcopate of America (ROMEA), the Roman Catholic Church of the Byzantine Rite (Romanian Byzantine Rite), the Romanian Baptist Association of the U.S.A., small groups of Romanian Protestant Pentecostals, and a few independent Orthodox churches--the IHRC holdings include many publications on church music and on Orthodox liturgy, as well as works dealing with the individual denominations. Two histories of the ROEA are present: Vasile Hategan's *Fifty Years of the Romanian Orthodox Church in America* (1959); and the comprehensive study by Gerald Bobango, *The Romanian Orthodox Episcopate of America: The First Half-Century, 1929-1979* (1979). There is also a general treatment, Dimitrie Gazdaru's *Episcopatul Românesc din America* (The Romanian Episcopate of America, 1957), along with significant commemorative volumes. On the smaller ROMEA there is its self-published *The Romanian Orthodox Missionary Episcopate in America: A Short History* (1967). The Romanian Byzantine Rite is described in *Golden Jubilee, 1912-1962*, published by Most Holy Trinity Catholic Parish (1962).

Fraternal societies are well represented in the collection. The IHRC has the official twenty-five-year and fifty-year histories of the Union and League of Romanian Societies in America: *Istoria Uniunei şi Ligei Societăţilor Române de Ajutor şi Cultură din America, 1906-1931* (History of the Union and League of Romanian Societies of Help and Culture in America, 1931) and *Istoria Uniunii şi Ligii Societăţilor Româneşti din America* (History of the Union and League of Romanian Societies of America), edited by Sofron S. Fekett (1956). The earlier League of Roumanian-American Societies is represented by its constitution (1924).

Romanian American literary publications in the IHRC range from Ilie M. Selisteanul's undated history of America (*Istoria Americei*, two volumes) to the journal of the philosopher Mircea Eliade (*No Souvenirs*, 1977). Autobiographical works include Anisoara Stan's *They Crossed Mountains and Oceans* (1947). Fictional works by C. R. Pascu, Constantin Virgil Negoita, and Dominick Nicol are present, as are poetry by Vasile Posteuca and others and an anthology of verse, *Romania Is a Song*, edited by Eli Popa (1967). Romanian folklore publications at the IHRC include a book of Romanian folksongs and tunes, issued by the American Romanian Orthodox Youth Association.

Newspapers

America, Cleveland, OH (previously published in Detroit, MI). Semi-monthly (previously weekly, semi-weekly, daily, triweekly): 1972-date. (Microfilm: 1906-1966).

Comuniunea Românească (Romanian Community), Detroit, MI. Quarterly: 1973-1979, 1981-1982. Includes English.

Credinţa (The Faith), Detroit, MI. Monthly: 1966-date. Includes English.

Cuvântul Românesc (The Romanian Voice), Hamilton, Ontario, Canada. Monthly: 1976-date.

Dreptatea (Justice), New York, NY. Monthly: 1974-1985.

Drum (Path), Grosse Point Woods, MI. Quarterly: 1966-1974.

Ecouri Româneşti (Romanian Echoes), Toronto, Ontario, Canada. Monthly: 1974-1984.

Glasul Patriei (Voice of the Fatherland), Bucharest, Romania. Weekly: 1972.

Glasul Vremii (The Voice of the Time), Youngstown, OH. Weekly. (Microfilm: 1912).

Libertatea (Freedom), Woodside, NY (Detroit, MI). Monthly (weekly). (Microfilm: 1929-1930).

România, New York, NY. Monthly (?): 1968.

Românul (The Romanian), Youngstown, OH (previously published in Cleveland, OH). Weekly (daily, semi-weekly): 1928-1929. (Microfilm: 1906-1928).

Românul (The Romanian), Long Island, NY. Three times per year: 1960. Includes Spanish.

Românul American (The Romanian American), Detroit, MI. Weekly: 1939-1950, 1955-1960.

Solia (The Herald), Detroit, MI. Monthly (bi-weekly): 1936-1973. (Microfilm: 1936-1973). Includes English.

Steaua Noastră (Our Star), New York, NY. Bi-weekly. (Microfilm: 1912-1931).

Tribuna Româna (The Romanian Tribune), Detroit, MI. Weekly: 1930.

Tribuna României (Romania's Tribune), Bucharest, Romania. Semi-monthly: 1972-date. Includes English page.

Serials

American Romanian Review, Cleveland, OH. Bi-monthly: 1977-1980, 1985-date. English.

Asociaţia Română din Canada Buletinul (The Bulletin of the Romanian Association in Canada), Montreal, Quebec, Canada. Issue no. 45 (undated). Includes French.

Biblioteca Andreiu Şaguna (The Andrei Saguna Library), New York, NY. Monthly: 1950.

Boian News Service, New York, NY. Bi-weekly: 1972-date. Includes English.

Buletin de Informaţie Pentru Români în Exil (Information Bulletin for Romanians in Exile), Paris, France. Monthly: 1955-1957. Includes French.

Calendarul America (America Calendar), Detroit, MI (previously published in Cleveland, OH). Annual: 1912, 1916, 1920, 1922-1928, 1930, 1932-1974. Includes English.

Calendarul Bibliotecei Române (Romanian Library Calendar), New York, NY. Annual: 1917.

Calendarul Candela (Candle Calendar), Detroit, MI. Annual: 1957.

Calendarul Credinta ("The Faith" Calendar), Detroit, MI. Annual: 1966-1971, 1975-1978, 1983. (Microfilm: 1966-1971). Includes English.

Calendarul Solia (Solia Almanac), Jackson, MI. Annual: 1936-1978, 1981. Includes English.

Calendarul Viaţa Nouă (New Life Calendar), Detroit, MI. Annual: 1934-1935.

Calendarul Ziarului Deşteptarea (Newspaper Awakening Calendar), Detroit, MI. Annual. (Microfilm: 1922, 1927-1928, 1937-1938, 1946-1958, 1964).

Carpathian Observer, Rochester, NY. Semi-annual: 1976, 1978. English.

Chreştinul (The Christian), Cleveland, OH. Quarterly. (Microfilm: 1913-1914). Includes English.

La Coş (At the Wastebasket), Edwardsville, IL. Monthly: 1904. (Photocopy).

Cronica Romaneasca (Report on Romania), New York, NY. Monthly: 1955, 1957.

Curierul (The Courier), Santa Clara, CA. Quarterly (?): 1983.

Datini (Traditions), St. Paul, MN. 1986.

Fiii Daciei (Sons of Dacia), New York, NY. Quarterly: 1972-date.

Foaia Interesantă (Interesting Page; literary page of **Libertatea**), Cleveland, OH. Monthly. (Microfilm: 1917).

Holocaust Christian, New York, NY. Irregular: 1984-date. English.

Information Bulletin, Jackson, MI. Quarterly: 1983-date. English.

Lucruri Noi şi Vechi (New and Old Works), Glendale, CA. Monthly: 1985-date.

Lumea Liberă (The Free World; title varies: **Renasterea**), Cincinnati, OH. Monthly. (Microfilm: 1911-1914).

Luminatorul (The Illuminator), Cleveland, OH (previously published in Detroit, MI). Monthly: 1944, 1966-1974. Includes English.

Mioriţa (Young Lamb), Hamilton, New Zealand, and Rochester, NY. Bi-annual: 1977-1981, 1983. English.

The New Pioneer, Cleveland, OH. Quarterly: 1942, 1945, 1948. English.

New York Spectator, Brooklyn, NY. Quarterly: 1982-1984. Includes French and English.

Porunca Vremii (Master of the Times), New York, NY. Monthly: 1970-date.

Pribeagul (The Wanderer), New York, NY. Monthly. (Microfilm: 1911).

România Democrata (Democratic Romania), Woodside, NY. Frequency varies: 1972-1982.

România Muncitoare (Laboring Romania), Paris, France. Monthly: 1954.

Romanian American Ladies Association Newzette, Youngstown, VA. 1959. English.

Romanian Bulletin (Romanian Library), New York, NY. Monthly: 1972-1973, 1975-1979. English.

Romanian Orthodox Church News, Bucharest, Romania. Quarterly: 1973-1974, 1982. English.

Romanian Orthodox Episcopate of America Congresul Episcopiei Annual Report, Grass Lake, MI. Annual: 1974-1978. English.

Romanian Sources, Pittsburgh, PA. Semi-annual: 1975-date. English.

Roumania, Chicago, IL. Monthly. (Microfilm: 1917-1918). Includes English.

Roumanian Bulletin, New York, NY. Monthly. (Microfilm: 1932-1935). English.

Society for Romanian Studies Newsletter, Huntington, IN. 1980-1983, 1985. English.

Solia (The Herald; previously published as a newspaper), Detroit, MI. Monthly: 1974-date. Includes English.

Steaua Noastră şi România Nouă (Our Star and the New Rumania), New York, NY. Monthly: 1920. Includes English.

Ţara şi Exilul (Country and the Exile), Dominican Republic. Monthly: 1973-1975, 1983-1985.

Tribuna Noastră (Our Tribune), New York, NY. Quarterly: 1978-1979, 1981-date.

Tricolorul (The Tricolor), Toronto, Ontario, Canada. Monthly: 1980-date. Includes French and English.

Unirea (The Union), East Chicago, IN (previously published in Cleveland, OH). Monthly: 1950-date. Includes English.

Unirea Almanac (title varies: **Calendarul Bisericei Române Catolice, Romanian Catholic Church Almanac**), East Chicago, IN. Annual: 1943-1966, 1968-date. Includes English.

Title page from the Romanian calendar *Calendarul National Al Ziarului "America"* (National Awakening "America" calendar), Cleveland, OH, 1920.

Russian American Collection

Manuscript Collections

Alexeev, Wassilij.
Papers, n.d. Ca. 1 linear in.

Papers of Alexeev consist of a typescript of his work, "Russians in America." *In English.*

Eisenstadt-Jeleznov, Mikhail (1900-1970).
Papers, ca. 1940-1979. 10 linear in. and 1 scrapbook.

A writer and journalist, Eisenstadt-Jeleznov was born in Minsk, Russia, and came to New York in 1924. For many years, he worked for *Novoye Russkoye Slovo* (The New Russian World) as a humor and political columnist. Under his pseudonym of M. K. Argus, he wrote several books, including *Moscow-on-the-Hudson* (1951) and *A Rogue With Ease* (1953). He also contributed to *Saturday Review* and wrote several books in Russian.

Papers include biographical information, correspondence with publishers, manuscripts and typescripts of his work, clippings of his columns and articles, and notes on Greek mythology. *In English and Yiddish. Inventory available.*

Federated Russian Orthodox Clubs (Pittsburgh, Pennsylvania).
Records, 1943-1965. 2.5 linear ft.

Founded in Pittsburgh, PA, in 1927, the FROC is a religious, cultural, charitable, social, and athletic organization. It has 175 senior and 70 junior chapters in the United States and Canada. The organization maintains a scholarship fund, publishes the *Russian Orthodox Journal*, and supports St. Tikhon's Seminary (South Canaan, PA) and St. Vladimir's Orthodox Theological Seminary (New York City). It has also contributed to the Russian Orthodox Pro-Cathedral (New York City), to construction of the War Memorial Shrine (Washington, DC), and to local parishes.

Records consist of reports and minutes of executive board meetings and annual conventions. Also included are convention programs, manuals for membership drives, and standing rules and resolutions. *In English. Inventory available.*

Kniazeff, A. N.
Papers, ca. 1955-1965. 1.5 linear in.

Papers of Kniazeff are comprised of Russian American material from the San Francisco, CA, area. Materials pertain to

the Russian Community Club and to the
National Organization of Russian Scouts.
Includes English.

Russian Orthodox Church Archives.
  Alaska Diocese.
Records, ca. 1825-1966.   12 microfilm
  reels.

Archives of the Church (also known as
the Russian Orthodox Greek Catholic
Church of North America), Alaska
Diocese, contain correspondence, reports,
registers, and other Church records. The
bulk of the records concern the
Khvikhpak (Yukon) River Mission.
These cover the mission's history from its
founding in 1845 until 1959. Also
included are correspondence and parish
record books of the Khvikhpak Mission,
parish records of the various other
churches in Alaska, and an index to the
records of the Alaska church collection of
the Russian Orthodox Greek Catholic
Church of North America, which is held
at the Library of Congress. *Inventory
available. Originals of Diocese Archives
are held by St. Herman's Pastoral School,
Juneau, Alaska. Microfilm master held by
the Alaska State Library, Juneau, Alaska.*

**Russian Orthodox Greek Catholic
  Church of North America.**
Index to records, ca. 1733-1938.
  1 microfilm reel.

Records consist of an index to the
Alaska church collection of the Russian
Orthodox Greek Catholic Church of North
America. *The Russian Orthodox Greek
Catholic Church of North America
Collection and the original of the index to
it are held by the Library of Congress,
Washington, DC.*

Simirenko, Alex (1931-).
Papers, ca. 1961-1964. Ca. 1 linear ft.

Papers of Simirenko, a writer, consist
of a preliminary survey, notes,
photographs, and other material used in
writing his book, *Pilgrims, Colonists and
Frontiersmen: An Ethnic Community in
Transition* (1964). The book concerns
the Russians of Minneapolis, MN.
Includes English.

Monographs

The Russian American monograph collection consists of ca. 370 volumes. Its
strengths lie in general and regional history, religion, fraternal organizations, language
and citizenship, and literature.

General studies on the history of Russians in the United States are few; of these
the IHRC has a full representation. Jerome D. Davis's *The Russian Immigrant* (1922;
reprinted in 1969) remains a basic study. Complementing this earlier work is the more
current and comprehensive study of Russians in North America by Ivan K. Okuntsoff,
entitled *Ruskaia emigratsiia v Severnoi i Iuzhnoi Amerike* (Russian Emigration in North
and South America, 1967). A more recent but abbreviated attempt is the sociological
survey done by Nancy Eubanks, *The Russians in America* (1973). Soviet studies on
Russian immigration are represented by two recent works: L. A. Bagranov's *Immigranty
v S.Sh.A.* (Immigrants in the U.S.A., 1957); and L. N. Fursova's *Immigratsiia i
natsional'noe razvitie Kanady, 1946-1970 gg.* (Immigration and the National Development
of Canada, 1975).

The earliest settlements of Russians in North America can be traced back to 1741
in Alaska. The experiences and presence of the Fort Ross settlement are best recorded
in a recent work by Hector Chevigny, *Russian America: The Great Alaskan Venture,
1741-1867* (1965). Regional studies of Russians in the United States concentrate mainly
on Russians living in California. Such works include Emil Theodore Bunje's *Russian
California, 1805-1841* (1937); Clarence John Du Four's *The Russian Withdrawal from
California* (1933); and Robert A. Thompson's *The Russian Settlement in California*

Known as Fort Rosso, Founded 1812, Abandoned 1841: Why the Russians Came and Why They Left (1970, reprint of 1896 edition). Also available are Alex Simirenko's *Pilgrims, Colonists and Frontiersmen; An Ethnic Community in Transition* (1964); and *American-Russians in the Bridgeport Community*, by Lionel F. Orr, Jr. (1956). The early Russian settlers in Hawaii are documented in Richard A. Pierce's work, *Russian Hawaiian Adventure, 1815-1817* (1965).

The Russian American monograph collection strongly documents religion. A substantial work on the Russian Orthodox Church in America is Michael George Kovach's thesis, *The Russian Orthodox Church in America* (1957). Among other works on the history of the church are: *Russkaia pravoslavnaia tserkov' v' Sievernoi Amerike; Istoricheskaia spravka* (The Russian Orthodox Church in Northern America: Historical Study, 1954) and the brief sketch by Archbishop Ioann of San Francisco and the Western United States, *Pravoslavie v Amerike: Ekkleziologicheskii ocherk* (Orthodoxy in America: Ecclesiological Essay, 1963). Some of the political conflicts surrounding the Church can be found in Reverend Peter G. Kohanik's *The Austro-German Hypocrisy and the Russian Orthodox Greek Catholic Church* (1915). The collection also includes a substantial number of individual church histories (such as jubilee anniversary albums) which provide useful background for comparative research of the religious Russian community and its struggles to meet both spiritual and lay needs.

The Molokan sect of the Eastern Orthodox Church is chronicled in two works: John K. Berokoff's *Molokans in America* (1969); and an earlier work by Pauline V. Young, *The Pilgrims of Russian Town: The Community of Spiritual Christian Jumpers in America* (1932). The most current work on Molokans concerns oral traditions, Willard Bergese Moore's *Molokan Oral Tradition; Legends and Memorates of an Ethnic Sect* (1973). The Molokans' faith prevented them from participating in wars; to assist their members in this matter they published the *Handbook for Molokan Conscientious Objectors* (1969). The history of the largest Canadian Doukhobor community is contained in George Woodcock's *The Doukhobors* (1968).

Among the various Russian American fraternal organizations were the Russian Orthodox Catholic Mutual Aid Society, the Russian Brotherhood Organization, and the Russian Mutual Aid Society. The IHRC Collection has four substantial histories written about the Russian Orthodox Catholic Mutual Aid Society: *The Tenth Anniversary*, by Venedikt I. Turkevich, covering 1895 through 1905; Peter G. Kohanik's *Russkoe Pravoslavnoe kafol. obshchestvo vzaimopomoshchi v Siev.-Amerikanskikh Soedinennykh Shtatakh: K XX-lietnemu iubileiu, 1895-1915* (The Russian Orthodox Catholic Mutual Aid Society in the North American United States: Towards the Twentieth Jubilee, 1915); *Rus' i pravoslavie v' Sievernoi Amerikie* (Rus' and Orthodoxy in North America, 1920); and the more recent seventieth anniversary publication *Russkoe Pravoslavnoi obshchestvo vzaimo-pomoshchi* (The Russian Orthodox Mutual Aid Society, 1965). The women's branch of the Society is represented in a short history covering 1907 through 1926 written by Iona Miliasevich, *Kratkii istoricheskii ocherk zhizni Russakgo Pravoslavnago zhenskago obshchestva vzaimo-pomoshchi v S.Sh.A.* (A Brief Historical Sketch of the Life of the Russian Orthodox Women's Mutual Aid Society in the U.S.A., 1926). The Russian Mutual Aid Society, founded in 1927 in New York by politically active working class immigrants, is depicted in I. A. Elmer's *Russkie rabochie v Amerike: k piatnadtsatiletiiu Russkogo narodnogo obshchestva vzaimopomoshchi v Amerike* (Russian Workers in America: Towards the Fiftieth Anniversary of the Russian National Mutual Aid Society in America, 1935).

The collection includes a number of works dealing with language and citizenship. Among these are Nina Mart'ianova's *Russko-angliiskii razgovornik: A Conversation Guide for Russians in the United States* (194?); Ahapius Honcharenko's *Russko-anhliiskie razgovory; Russian and English Phrase Book, Specially Adapted for the Use of Traders, Travelers, and Teachers* (1868); *Kak pisat' angliiskie pis'ma delovyi i na raznye sluchai zhizni: rukovodstvo dlia russkikh v Amerike* (How to Write English Letters for Business and Everyday Life: Handbook for Russians in America, 1958?); and *Kak stat' grazhdaninom Soedinennykh Shtatov; Polnoe novoe rukovodstvo dlia zhelaiushchikh stat' grazhdanami Soedinennykh Shtatov* (How to Become a Citizen of the United States;

Complete New Guide for Those Who Want to Become Citizens of the United States, 1953).

Russian American literature is represented by biographies, memoirs, and novels. Included are Victor A. Yakhontoff's *Over the Divide: Impersonal Record of Personal Experiences* (1939); Paul Chavchavadze's *Family Album* (1949) and his *Marie Avinov: Pilgrimage through Hell* (1968); Alex Shoumatoff's *Russian Blood: A Family Chronicle* (1982); and Mark V. Vichniak's *Gody emigratsii, 1919-1969 Paryzh-Niu-Iork (vospominannia)* (Emigration Years, Paris-New York [Memories], 1970). One of the most popular authors whose writing appeared in newspapers and books was M. K. Argus, pseudonym of Mikhail Eisenstadt-Jeleznov. The Center has his works *Amerikia Smeetsia* (America Laughs), *Antologiia Amerikanskogo Iumora* (Anthology of American Humor, 1962), and *Drugaia zhiz'n i bereg da'lnii* (Second Life and Distant Shore, 1969); his autobiography *Moscow-on-the-Hudson* (1951); and his novels *A Rogue with Ease* (1953) and *Poluser'ezno, polusutia; satira, lirika* (Half Serious, Half Humorous; Satire, Lyrics, 1959). To complement these publications, the IHRC also holds his personal papers. Recent works that deal with Russian émigré literature include Temira Pachmuss's *A Russian Cultural Revival; A Critical Anthology of Émigré Literature before 1939*, and Ludmila A. Foster's two-volume *Bibliography of Russian Émigré Literature, 1918-1968* (1970).

Newspapers

Almanac-Panorama, Los Angeles, CA. Monthly: 1980.

Dyiia Posliedyiia Novosty (News of Recent Events), Paris, France. Daily: 1927.

Griadushchee (The Future), Sydney, Australia. Monthly: 1956-1957.

Kazak (Cossack), Neuilly-sur-Seine, France. Monthly: 1951-1953, 1955, 1957-1964, 1971-1976. Includes some French.

Light of Orthodoxy, Pittsburgh, PA. Monthly: 1962, 1964-1965, 1967-1968. English.

Lubov (Love), Mayfield, PA. Bi-monthly (monthly): 1924-1957. (Microfilm: 1924-1957).

Nashe Vremia (The Modern Time), San Francisco, CA. Weekly: 1953.

Nashi Dni (Our Days), Bryte, CA. Weekly: 1967-1969.

Novaia Zaria (New Dawn), San Francisco, CA. Daily: 1948, 1953, 1962.

Novoe Russkoe Slovo (New Russian Word), New York, NY. Daily: 1941-1944, 1951-1979.

Novyi Mir (New World; merged with **Russky Golos**), New York, NY. Daily, tri-weekly, weekly: 1911. (Photocopy). (Microfilm: 1911-1919, 1926-1938).

Orthodox America, Etna, CA. Monthly: 1984. English.

The Orthodox Church, New York, NY (previously published in Philadelphia, PA). Ten issues a year: 1965-1976. English.

Posliedniia Novosti (Latest News), Paris, France. Daily: 1927.

Possev (Sowing), Frankfurt am Main, West Germany. Weekly: 1947-1949, 1954, 1964.

Pravda (The Truth), Philadelphia, PA. Weekly, bi-weekly, monthly: 1943, 1945, 1952-1954, 1960-1961, 1963-date. (Microfilm: 1917-1975). Includes English.

Pravoslavnyi Amerikanskii Viestnik (Orthodox American Herald; title varies: Russsko-Amerikanskii Pravoslavnyi Viestnik), New York, NY. Semi-monthly. (Microfilm: 1896-1897). Includes English.

Rossiia Zagranitzei (Outside Russia), New York, NY. Quarterly (?): 1965. Includes English.

Rossiya (Russia), New York, NY. Semi-weekly: 1942-1943, 1952, 1955, 1958-1963, 1965-1973.

Russkaia Mysl'; La Pensée Russe (Russian Thought), Paris, France. Weekly: 1948, 1953, 1955-1957, 1961, 1963-1964, 1971.

Russkaia Zhizn' (Russian Life), San Francisco, CA. Daily (except Sundays, Mondays, and holidays): 1962, 1964-1975, 1977.

Ruskii Emigrant (The Russian Emigrant), New York, NY. Weekly: 1912-1914.

Russko-Amerikanskii Pravoslavnyi Viestnik (Russian American Orthodox Messenger; title varies: Pravoslavnyi Amerikanskii Viestnik), Jackson Heights, Long Island, NY. Semi-monthly. (Microfilm: 1896-1942). Includes English.

Russky Golos (Russian Voice), New York, NY. Weekly: 1945, 1963-date.

Svit (The Light), Wilkes-Barre, PA (previously published in Philadelphia, PA). Bi-monthly (weekly, bi-monthly): 1911-1915, 1917-1924, 1927-1928, 1931-1944, 1946-1947, 1958, 1965-date. (Microfilm: 1908, 1911-1924, 1927-1928, 1931-1944, 1946-1948, 1953-1954, 1965-1971, 1973-1975). Includes English.

Vestnik Russkago Studencheskago Khrystiankago Dvizheniia; Le Messager (Herald of the Russian Student Christian Movement), Paris, France. Monthly. (Microfilm: 1931).

Za Vozvrashcenie na Rodinu (For Return to the Motherland), Berlin, East Germany. Frequency varies: 1955-1960.

Serials

The Alaska Herald (previously titled Free Press and Alaska Herald), San Francisco, CA. Semi-monthly (weekly): 1868-1874. Includes English.

American Russian Cultural Association Annual Report, New York, NY. Annual: 1943-1947. English.

Amerikanskii Pravoslavnyi Viestnik' (Russian Orthodox American Messenger), New York, NY. Monthly: 1918. Includes some English.

The Archangel, Philadelphia, PA. Quarterly: 1952-1959, 1969. Includes English.

Association of Russian Imperial Officers in America Biulleten' (Bulletin), New York, NY. Triennial: 1955-1956.

Belyi Lotos (White Lotus), Santa Barbara, CA. Bi-annual: 1959, 1962-1963.

Bich (The Whip; Humor Magazine), New York, NY. 1938.

D.P. Satirikon, Augsburg, West Germany. Monthly (weekly): 1949-1950.

Delo Truda--Probuzhdenie (Cause of Labor--Awakening), New York, NY. Monthly (?): 1961.

Den' Russkago Rebenka (Day of the Russian Child), San Francisco, CA. Annual (?): 1954.

Detstvo vo Khriste (Childhood in Christ), Trenton, NJ. 1953-1954.

Dietstvo i Iunost' vo Khristie (Childhood and Youth in Christ), Mahopac, NY. Bi-monthly: 1955.

Edinaia Tserkov (One Church), New York, NY. Monthly: 1951-1954.

Eparkhial'niia Viedomosti (Diocesan Journal), New York, NY. Monthly: 1953-1954.

Evanhel'skii Vestnyk (Russian Gospel Messenger), Chicago, IL. Monthly: 1960.

Golos Truda (The Voice of Labor), New York, NY. Monthly: 1911. Microfilm print copy.

Holy Trinity Monastery, Jordanville, NY. Frequency varies: one undated issue, 1956, 1963, 1965. Includes some English.

Iezhegodnik Pravoslovnoi Tserkvy v Amerike (Annual of the Orthodox Church of America), Syosset, NY. Annual: 1975-1979.

Informatsiïnyï Biulleten' Russkogo Emigrantskogo Lageria v Shleïsgeïme (Information Bulletin of the Russian Emigrant Camp in Schleissheim), Schleissheim, Germany. Weekly: 1947-1948.

Informatsionnyi Biulleten' (Information Bulletin), Utica, NY. Annual: 1958, 1961-1963.

Kanadskyi Pravoslavnyi Kalendar (Canadian Greek Orthodox Calendar; title change 1973: Pravoslavnyi Tserkovnyi Kalendar), Toronto, Ontario, Canada. Annual: 1954-1964, 1966, 1968-1972.

Klich K' Molodoï Rossii (Call to Young Russia), San Francisco, CA. Frequency varies: 1933-1934.

Koster Razvedchika (Camp Fire Lighter), Oak Park, IL. Quarterly: 1964-1965, 1981.

Light of Orthodoxy, New York, NY. Monthly: 1953. English.

Luch (Ray), Iselin, NJ. Bi-monthly: 1960.

Medved' (The Bear), Cleveland, OH. Monthly: 1958-1959.

Metropolia News (Official Acts of the Russian Orthodox Church of America), New York, NY. Bi-monthly: 1964. English.

Miloserdnii Samarianin; Russkii Zhurnal v Kanade (Good Samartian; Russian Journal in Canada), Lethbridge, Alberta, Canada. Monthly: 1954. Includes English.

Molokanskoe Obozrenie (The Molokan Review; A Russian Molokan Annual Review), Los Angeles, CA. Annual: 1945, 1947, 1949. Includes English.

Morskiia Zapiski (The Naval Records; The Association of Russian Imperial Naval Officers in America, Inc.), New York, NY. Quarterly: 1955-1956, 1958.

Moskva (Moscow), Chicago, IL. Monthly: 1930-1931.

Nash Put' (Our Way), Chicago, IL. Monthly: 1950, 1952-1954.

Nashi Vesti (Our News), New York, NY. Monthly: 1957-1965, 1967-1972.

Niva (Cornfield), New York, NY. Bi-monthly: 1954-1955.

Novaia Rossiia (New Russia), Pittsburgh, PA. Bi-monthly: 1918.

Novyi Golos (New Herald), Chicago, IL. Monthly: 1951. Includes some English.

Novyi Put' (The New Road), New York, NY (previously published in Paris, France). 1947.

Novyĭ Zhurnal (The New Review), New York, NY. Quarterly: 1942, 1944-1953, 1955-date. (Index: 1942-1970).

Obzor (Digest; previously titled Obzor Inostrannoĭ Pechati), Munich-Feldmoching, Germany. Weekly: 1948.

Obzor Russkoĭ Pechati (The Russian Press Digest), New York, NY. Monthly: 1953, 1956.

One Church; Edinaia Tserkov, Youngstown, OH (previously published in New York, NY). Bi-monthly: 1952-1964, 1968-1980. English.

Opyt (Experience), London, Ontario, Canada. Annual (?): 1984.

Opyty (Experiences), New York, NY. Bi-annual: 1953-1958.

Orthodox Alaska, Kodiak, AK. Quarterly: 1979. English.

Orthodox Church in America Yearbook and Church Directory (previously titled Yearbook of the Russian Orthodox Greek Catholic Church in America), Syosset, NY. Annual: 1968-1973, 1975-1981. English.

Orthodox Education Day, Crestwood, NY. Annual: 1970-1972, 1977-1980. English.

The Orthodox Herald, Vestal, NY. Monthly: 1952-1985. English.

Orthodox Life, Jordanville, NY. Bi-monthly: 1950-date. English.

The Orthodox Word, Platina, CA (previously published in San Francisco, CA). Bi-monthly: 1965-date. English.

Pereklichka (Roll Call), New York, NY. Monthly: 1952-1954.

Po Stopam Khrista (Following the Steps of Christ; Orthodox Quarterly), Berkeley, CA. Quarterly (monthly): 1950-1979.

Pravoslavnaia Rus'; Tserkovno-Obshchestvennyĭ Organ (Orthodox Russia), Jordanville, NY. Bi-weekly: 1947-1948, 1951-date.

Pravoslavnaia Zhizn'; Ezhemiesiachnoe Prilozhenie k Zhurnalu (Orthodox Life), Jordanville, NY. Monthly: 1950-date.

Pravoslavnoe Obozrienie; Periodicheskiĭ Zhurnal Russkoĭ Pravoslavnoĭ M'isli (Orthodox Observer) Montreal, Quebec, Canada. Frequency varies: 1968.

Pravoslavnyĭ Khristianskiĭ Viestnik' (Orthodox Christian Herald), Cleveland, OH. Monthly: 1925.

Pravoslavnyĭ Prikhodskiĭ Listok' (Orthodox Parish Leaflet), New York, NY. Monthly: 1919.

Pravoslavnyĭ Put' (The Orthodox Pathway; supplement to Pravoslavnaia Rus'), Jordanville, NY. Annual: 1950-1953, 1955-1976, 1978-1984.

Pravoslavnyĭ Tserkovnyĭ Kalendar' (Orthodox Church Calendar; previously titled Kanadskyĭ Pravoslavnyĭ Kalendar), Montreal, Quebec-Toronto, Ontario, Canada. Annual: 1973, 1975-1977.

Pravoslavnyĭ Tserkovnyĭ Kalendar (Orthodox Church Calendar), USSR. Annual: 1961, 1964.

Prizyv (The Call), New York, NY. Monthly: 1950-1954.

Put'-ko-Khristu (The Way to Christ), Winnipeg, Manitoba, Canada. Monthly: 1923.

Put' Pravdy (The Way of Truth), Los Angeles, CA. 1954.

Revnitel' Pravoslaviia (Zealot of the Christian Orthodoxy), New York, NY. Semi-monthly: 1914-1915.

Rossiĭskaia Nezavisimost' (Russian Independence), Brooklyn, NY. Bi-weekly: 1963, 1964.

The Russian American, New York, NY. Frequency varies: 1976-1977, 1979-1985. English.

Russian Immigrants' Representative Association in America Information Bulletin, New York, NY. Monthly: 1958.

Russian National Society Bulletin, Columbus, NY. Weekly: 1921. English.

Russian Orthodox American Messenger (supplement to **Amerikanskiĭ Pravoslavnyĭ Viestnik'**), New York, NY. Monthly: 1902. English.

Russian Orthodox Catholic Church Yearbook, New York, NY. Annual: 1953-1954. Includes English.

Russian Orthodox Catholic Mutual Aid Society of U.S.A. Convention Reports, Wilkes-Barre, PA. Frequency varies: 1934, 1938, 1942, 1946, 1950, 1954, 1958. Includes English.

Russian Orthodox Church of Christ the Savior Parish Bulletin, New York, NY. Monthly: 1949.

Russian Orthodox Greek Catholic Church of America Yearbook and Church Directory, New York, NY. Annual: 1951-1954, 1956, 1958, 1960, 1962-1965, 1967. English.

Russian Orthodox Journal, Donora, PA (place of publication varies). Monthly (bi-monthly January-February and July-August): 1930-1984. English.

Russkiĭ Amerikanets (The Russian American), Long Island City, NY. Frequency varies: 1975-1976. Includes English.

Russkiĭ Kalendar (Russian Calendar), New York, NY. Annual: 1965.

Russkiĭ Nastol'nii Kalendar--Spravochnik (Russian Desk Calendar--Reference Book), New York, NY. Annual: 1952, 1955, 1960, 1964, 1966.

Russkiĭ Pravoslavnyĭ Kalendar i Bogosluzhebnyia Ukazaniia (Russian Orthodox Calendar and Divine Service Instructions), New York, NY. Annual: 1959.

Russkiĭ Vestnik (Russian Herald), New York, NY. Monthly: 1938-1942, 1947-1948, 1955, 1959-1961. Includes English.

Russko-Amerikanskiĭ Pravoslavnii Kalendar (Russian American Orthodox Calendar; previously titled **Pravoslavnyĭ Russko-Amerikanskiĭ Kalendar**), Wilkes-Barre, PA. Annual: 1902, 1910, 1912-1917, 1921-1923, 1925-1927, 1929-1930, 1932-1933, 1936-1937, 1947, 1950. Includes English.

Russko-Amerikanskiĭ Pravoslavni'ii Viestnik (The Russian American Orthodox Messenger), Sea Cliff, Long Island, NY. Monthly: 1938-1954, 1963-1964, 1966.

Russkoe Delo (Russian Cause), New York, NY. Monthly: 1959-1962, 1965-1967, 1970, 1972.

Russkoe Natsional'noe Obshchestvo. Biuleten' (The Russian National Society. Bulletin), New York, NY. Weekly: 1921.

Russkoe Obozrenie (Russian Review), Chicago, IL. Monthly: 1929. Includes some English.

Russkoe Studencheskoe Khristianskoe Dvizhenie (The Russian Student Christian Movement; previously titled **Viestnik Russkago Studencheskago Khrystyianskago Dvizheniia**), Paris, France. Quarterly (monthly). (Microfilm: 1926-1936).

Russkoe Studencheskoe Khristianskoe Dvizhenie. Vestnik (The Russian Student Christian Movement. Messenger), New York, NY-Paris, France. Quarterly: 1962-1963.

St. Herman Orthodox Calendar, Platina, CA. Annual: 1978. English

St. John's Russian Orthodox Church Yearbook, Passaic, NJ. Annual: 1938-1939. Includes English.

St. Mary's Russian Orthodox Church Bulletin, Minneapolis, MN. Monthly: 1952-1960, 1962-1963. English.

St. Vladimir's Orthodox Theological Seminary Newsletter, Crestwood, NY. Semi-annual: 1963-1964. English.

St. Vladimir's Theological Quarterly, Tuckahoe, NY. Quarterly: 1952-1954, 1957-1964, 1969-date. English.

Seiatel' Istin'i (The Sower of Truth; A Russian Christian Monthly), Ashford, CT (previously published in Hartford, CT). Monthly (except July): 1955, 1967-1968.

Skautënik; Zhurnal Ptenchikov i Volchat San Frantsiisskoï Druzhiny NORS-R (The Scout; Magazine of the San Francisco Troop Birds and Wolves of NORS-R), San Francisco, CA. Frequency varies: 1963-1965.

Soglasie (Agreement), Los Angeles, CA. Monthly: 1954, 1956-1960, 1973, 1976.

Staroe Vremia; Literaturno-Istoricheskie Tetradi (Old Times; Literary-Historical Notebook), New York, NY. Quarterly: 1954.

Strannik; Ofitsial'nïĭ Organ Russkoho Otdela Sobranii Bozhiikh (Pilgrim; Official Organ of the Russian Division of the Assemblies of God), Garfield, NJ. Quarterly: 1956.

Svobodnaia Rossiia (Free Russia), Los Angeles, CA. Bi-monthly: 1955.

Svobodnye Slovo (The Free Word), New York, NY. Monthly: 1915-1916.
The Tikhonaire, South Canaan, PA. Annual: 1957, 1960, 1963-1965, 1968, 1970, 1974, 1976-1979. English.

Tovarishch' Russkago Immigranta v' Amerikie (Friend of the Russian Immigrant in America), New York, NY. Annual: 1913.

Troitskiĭ Pravoslavnïĭ Russkiĭ Kalendar (Trinity Orthodox Russian Calendar), Jordanville, NY. Annual: 1951-1966.

Vechnaia Rossiia (Eternal Russia), New York, NY. Frequency varies: 1962.

Vera i Znanie (Faith and Knowledge), Kingston, NY. 1951.

Vestnik Pervopokhodnika (Society of First Campaign Combatants), Los Angeles, CA. Monthly: 1963, 1967-1970, 1975-1976.

Viestnik' Obshchestva Russkikh' Veteranov' Velikoĭ Voĭny (Messenger of the Russian Veterans of World War I), San Francisco, CA. Frequency varies: 1926-1965.

Vpered (Forward), San Francisco, CA. Monthly: 1959-1960.

Za Svobodu (For Freedom), New York, NY. Frequency varies (monthly through 1943): 1941-1943, 1945-1947.

Za Vashu i Nashu Svobodu. Biuleten' (For Your and Our Freedom. Bulletin), U.S.A.-Canada. Frequency varies: 1965.

Zhar-Ptitsa; Ezhemiesiachnyĭ Literaturno-Khudozhest-Vennyĭ Zhurnal (Firebird; Monthly Literary and Arts Magazine), San Francisco, CA. Monthly: 1952-1959.

Zlatotsviet; Ezhemiesiachnyĭ Literaturno-Khudo-Zhestvennyĭ Zhurnal (Asphodel; Monthly Literary and Arts Magazine), Burlingame, CA. Monthly: 1962.

Znamia Rossii (The Banner of Russia), New York, NY. Monthly: 1953-1954, 1959-1970, 1972-1973.

Serbian American Collection

Manuscript Collections

Dedijer, Stevan.
Papers, 1912-1983. Ca. 1 linear in.

Papers of Dedijer consist of photocopied manuscripts of two autobiographical essays, "Heracleitos, Me and 'A Damned Place Called Bastogne,'" and "Treasure Hunts in Alien Worlds." *In English.*

Palandech, John R.
Papers, 1919-1963. Ca. 1 linear in.

Palandech was a prominent Serbian American publisher. He published the *Ujedinjeno Srpstvo* (United Serbian, the leading Serbian American newspaper) and had his own agency, the John R. Palandech Agency (Foreign Language Newspaper Representatives, Advertising and Publicity Service). Palandech's papers include correspondence and pamphlets. *Includes English.*

Serb National Federation. Jedinstvo (Unity) (Cleveland, Ohio).
Records, 1923-1959. 1 microfilm reel.

Jedinstvo (Srpski Potporni Savez Jedinstvo) was founded in 1920 when two groups of lodges split from the group Sloga. Jedinstvo was formed by Srpsko Društvo Jedinstvo (Chicago, IL), Srpsko Društvo Sveti Sava (Cleveland, OH), and Srpsko Društvo Jedinstvo (Los Angeles, CA), with headquarters in Cleveland. The other group organized as Srpski Savez Svesna Srbadija, with headquarters in New York City. Jedinstvo was a social, educational, and mutual benefit society. In 1963, it merged with the Serb National Federation.

Records consist of rules and bylaws. *Includes English. Inventory available. Not to be reproduced without written permission from the Serb National Federation. Originals held by Serb National Federation, Pittsburgh, PA.*

Serb National Federation. National Office (Pittsburgh, Pennsylvania).
Records, 1925-1980. 10 microfilm reels.

The Serb National Federation was formed by the merger of various Serbian fraternal organizations, beginning in 1901 with the founding of the Serbian Orthodox Society. In 1929, the two largest associations, Srbobran-Sloga and Savez Sloboda, united to form the Federation. In 1960, the Federation merged with the independent society, Oblich. A final merger occurred in 1963 when the Serbian Beneficial Union (Jedinstvo) joined the Federation. The Federation is the largest Serbian

American benevolent society; it has over 21,000 members in the United States and Canada. Its purpose is to provide insurance, promote and preserve Serbian culture, and provide sports and educational activities. Its official organ, *American Srbobran* is the oldest currently published Serbian newspaper in the United States. (It was published in Pittsburgh as *Srbin* beginning in 1901; the name was changed in 1905.)

Records of the Federation include minute books of the Supreme Council, Executive Board, and Board of Directors (1929-1980); convention minutes (1931-1979); convention reports (1931-1979); calendars (from *American Srbobran*, 1925-1926, 1929, 1931-1967; from the Serbian Orthodox Church in the United States and Canada, 1967-1981). *Includes English. Inventory available. Not to be reproduced without written permission of the Serb National Federation. Originals held by Serb National Federation, Pittsburgh, PA.*

Serb National Federation. Oblich (Chicago, Illinois).
Records, 1940. 1 microfilm reel.

A Serbian cultural and mutual benefit organization, Oblich was founded in Chicago in 1938. It merged with the Serb National Federation in 1960.

Records consist of bylaws. *Inventory available. Not to be reproduced without written permission from the Serb National Federation. Originals held by Serb National Federation, Pittsburgh, PA.*

Serb National Federation. Sloboda (Pittsburgh, Pennsylvania).
Records, 1917-1929. 1 microfilm reel.

A fraternal and beneficial society, Sloboda was founded in 1917 when a group of lodges broke from the Serbian American group Srbobran and formed the Srpski Savez Sloboda. In 1928, it merged with Srbadija to form Savez Sloboda. In 1929, that organization merged with Srbobran-Sloga to form the Serb National Federation.

Records of Sloboda include rules and bylaws, charter, legal papers, minutes, convention minutes, convention reports,

and calendars. *Includes English. Inventory available. Not to be reproduced without written permission of the Serb National Federation. Originals held by Serb National Federation, Pittsburgh, PA.*

Serb National Federation. Sloga (New York, New York).
Records, 1916-1920. 1 microfilm reel.

Sloga (Federation of United Serbs-Unity) was founded in Cleveland, OH, by Michael Pupin when representatives of Srpski Pravoslavni Savez Srbobran, Prvi Srpski Dobrotvorni Savez (Chicago, IL), and Prvi Crnogorski Savez (Chicago) met in 1909 to form Savez Sjedinjenih Srba-Sloga. Its home office was established in New York City. In 1920, a group of lodges split from Sloga and formed the organization Srbadija (New York) and the organization Jedinstvo (Cleveland). Sloga merged with Srbobran to form Srbobran-Sloga in 1921 (Pittsburgh, PA); in 1929, it became part of the Serb National Federation.

Records consist of constitution, bylaws, legal papers, minutes, convention minutes, and convention reports. *Includes English. Inventory available. Not to be reproduced without written permission of the Serb National Federation. Originals held by Serb National Federation, Pittsburgh, PA.*

Serb National Federation. Srbadija (New York, New York).
Records, 1922. 1 microfilm reel.

Srbadija was a mutual benefit, educational, social, and religious organization. It was founded in 1920 when two groups of lodges split from the group Sloga to form Srpski Savez Svesna Srbadija and Srpski Potporni Savez Jedinstvo. In 1928, it united with Sloboda in Pittsburgh, PA, to form the Savez Sloboda. This organization merged with Srobran-Sloga to form the Serb National Federation.

Records of Srbadija consist of the constitution and bylaws. *Includes English. Inventory available. Not to be reproduced without written permission from the Serb National Federation. Originals held by Serb National Federation, Pittsburgh, PA.*

Serb National Federation. Srbobran (Pittsburgh, Pennsylvania).
Records, 1901-1920. 1 microfilm reel.

Serbian Orthodox Society (Srbobran) was founded in Pittsburgh in 1901 by Sava Hajden. It was a religious, educational, social, and beneficial organization. It strove to spread the Christian Orthodox religion in America, help in the construction of Serbian Orthodox churches and schools, and provide aid to its members in cases of sickness and death. Its headquarters was on Pittsburgh's South Side. The official organ of the Society was *Srbin*, which began publication in 1901. In 1917, the Sloboda Serb Society seceded from Srbobran and formed its own group. Srbobran then merged with Federation of United Serbs (Sloga) of New York to form United Society Srbobran-Sloga (Srbobran-Sloga) in 1921. In 1929, that group merged with Sloboda to form the Serb National Federation.

Records of Srbobran include the constitution; bylaws; combined minute book (executive board and convention); minutes, including those of the organizational meeting; reports of conventions and of the insurance examiner; and correspondence of the state insurance offices. *Includes English. Inventory available. Not to be reproduced without written permission of the Serb National Federation. Originals held by Serb National Federation, Pittsburgh, PA.*

Serb National Federation. Srbobran-Sloga (Pittsburgh, Pennsylvania).
Records, 1901-1928. 23 microfilm reels.

A fraternal, beneficial, and cultural organization, Srbobran-Sloga was founded in 1921 from the merger of Srpski Pravoslavni Savez Srbobran (founded in 1901) and Savez Sjedinjenih Srba-Sloga (founded in 1909). Its official organ was *American Srbobran*, which was first published as *Srbin* in Pittsburgh in 1901. In 1929, Srbobran-Sloga merged with Savez Sloboda to form the Serb National Federation.

Records consist of rules and bylaws, convention and executive board minutes, convention reports, membership applications, death claims, death notices from lodges, family information, correspondence, and miscellany. *Includes English. Inventory available. Not to be reproduced without written permission from the Serb National Federation. Originals held by Serb National Federation, Pittsburgh, PA.*

Serbian Orthodox Church (in America), New York Calendar of the Episcopal Correspondence.
Records, 1898-1925. 2 microfilm reels.

The Serbian Orthodox Church in America was under the jurisdiction of the Russian Archdiocese of North America and the Aleutian Islands. Records include materials on organization of the Serbian Church and its parishes, its background in Europe, Serbs in the United States, Serbian churches in New York City, and Serbian House in New York along with an index of priests and a chronological index of churches. *In English. Inventory available. Originals held by St. Nicholas Cathedral, New York, NY.*

Vaskov, Milan (1894-1970).
Papers, 1935-1970. Ca. 1.5 linear ft.

Vaskov was a Serbian American photoengraver who lived in several cities before settling in Pittsburgh, PA. He was born in Santa Clarya, Romania, and came to the United States in 1912.

His papers include personal and business correspondence, photographs, scrapbooks, and advertisements. Correspondence consists mainly of letters of family and of the Serbian newspaper *Slobodna Reč* (Pittsburgh, PA). Correspondents included Milan's daughter Olga Romano, his son Simon Vaskov, and his sister Beatrice Petkovič. *Includes English. Inventory available.*

Monographs

The Serbian American monograph collection consists of some 115 titles covering the spectrum of the social, political, and religious life of Serbian communities in America.

The collection contains a number of works chronicling the general history of the Serbian immigrant experience. Among them are B. Grahovac's *Srbi u Ameritsi* (Serbs in America, 1919), Milan Jevtić's *Mala Srbija: Srpsko useljeništvo u Americi* (Small Serbia: Serbian Immigration to America, 1916), Pero Slepčević's *Srbi u Americi* (Serbians in America, 1917), and Božidar Purić's *Naši iseljenici* (Our Emigrants, 1929). These are complemented by a more recent thesis in English, Bozidar Dragicevich's *American Serb* (1973). In addition, an overview of Serbian life in America can be drawn from the index to the largest and oldest Serbian American newspaper, the *American Srbobran*, entitled *American Srbobran; Selective Index, 1906-1976*, prepared by Milan M. Radovich and Robert P. Gakovich (1980). Other key reference tools include Gakovich and Radovich's *Serbs in the United States and Canada: A Comprehensive Bibliography* (1976), and Mirko and Danica Blesich's *The Serbian Who's Who: Biographic Directory of Americans and Canadians of Serbian Descent*.

Serbian immigrants tended to settle in the East and in Midwestern mining and factory cities as well as on the West Coast, mainly California. The collection includes several regional studies, such as Adam Eterovich's *The First Serbian Pioneers in America and Their Activities in California and the South* (1977), *Serbian Americans and Their Communities of Cleveland*, by Dragoslav Georgevich, et al. (1977); Vladimir N. Vucinich's *From the Adriatic to the Pacific: Serbs in the San Francisco Bay Area* (1983); and Luka M. Pejović's two early publications *Srbi na srednjem zapadu* (Serbs in the Midwest, 1936); and *Život i rad američkih Srba* (Life and Work of American Serbians, 1934), on Serbs in Michigan and St. Louis, MO, respectively.

The collection includes a number of volumes dealing with Serbian-Croatian relations. Among these are Lazo M. Kostić's *Obmane i izvrtanja kao podloga narodnosti: Srpsko-hrvatski odnosi poslednjih godina* (Illusions and Distortions as Basis of Nationality: Serbo-Croatian Relations in Recent Years, 1959), Laza M. Kostić's *Sporni predeli Srba i Hrvata* (Conflicting Areas of Serbs and Croats, 1957), and J. Z. Milosavljević's, *Srpsko-hrvatski spor i Neimari Jugoslavije* (Serbo-Croatian Conflict and the Builders of Yugoslavia, 1945).

Monographs reflecting Serbian and Serbian American affairs during and after World War II include both primary publications and secondary studies. Examples of these are *Ruth Mitchell, Chetnik, Tells the Facts about the Fighting Serbs, Mihailovich and "Yugoslavia"* (1943); Mihailo P. Minić's *Rasute kosti (1941-1945)* (Scattered Bones, 1965); Vaso Trivanovitch's *The Case of Drazha Mikhailovich; Highlight of the Evidence against the Chetnik Leader* (1946); and *Spomenica palih Srba vazduhoplovaca, 1941-1945* (Memorial to Fallen Serbian Pilots), edited by Milos K. Achin (1975).

The Serbian Orthodox Church has played an important part in the religious, social, and political life of the Serbian American community. During World War II, the church publicized its persecution and the victimization of Serbs in the homeland. Among the monographs dealing with this subject are *Martyrdom of the Serbs: Persecutions of the Serbian Orthodox Church and Massacre of the Serbian People* (1943), and Dionisije Milivojevich's *The Persecution of the Serbian Orthodox Church in Yugoslavia* (1945). In 1963 a schism occurred within the Serbian Orthodox Church in America. A sociological study of this schism is found in two brief works by Djuro J. and Frank J. Fahley: *Changes and Socio-Religious Conflict in an Ethnic Minority Group: The Serbian Orthodox Church in America* (1975), and *Structural Sources of Ethnic Factionalism* (reprinted from *Social Science*, 44:1, January 1969). In addition there are several substantial church anniversary books containing histories of individual parishes.

Serbian American literature first appeared primarily in the many newspapers and journals founded by fraternal mutual aid societies. Among the earliest poets was Proka Jovkić, whose volume about the land he left behind, *Poezija neba i zemlje* (Poetry of Sky and Earth, 1910), the IHRC holds. Another early poet, writer, and inventor was

Michael Pupin. His autobiography, *From Immigrant to Inventor* (1926), won him the Pulitzer Prize. Among the post-World War II poetry and writings included in the Serbian American monograph collection are Jovan Dučić's, *Staza pored puta/Moji saputnici/Jutra sa Leutara: Reči o čoveku* (The Path Beside the Road/My Cotravelers/Morning on the Leutara: Words About Man, 1951); Dragoslav Dragutinović's *Noć duža od snova; pripovetke* (Night Longer than Dreams; Stories, 1976) and *Pesnikova mladost i ljubav; roman* (Poet's Youth and Love; Novel, 1978); and Jovan Kontić's *Kroz oganj i suze; pripovetke* (Through Fire and Tears; Stories, 1946).

In addition there are a number of anniversary books and monographs containing the constitution or bylaws of the Serb National Federation, the largest Serbian fraternal organization in America.

Researchers interested in this ethnic group are encouraged to consult also the small collection of books (ca. eighty volumes) shelved and classified as "Yugoslav." Included here are works dealing with more than one of the South Slavic nationality groups. Predominant among these are secondary studies (many of them key publications) such as *Americans from Yugoslavia*, by Gerald G. Govorchin; *South Slavic Immigration in America*, by George Prpic; *Yugoslav Migrations to America*, by Branko Colakovic; *The Yugoslavs in America: 1880-1918*, by L. Blaisdell; and several studies by Adam Eterovich and others on Yugoslavs in particular states or regions. Also included in this section are books and pamphlets concerning the formation of the Yugoslav nation, primarily written from the perspective of Yugoslav immigrants, and published in many cases by the United Committee of South Slavic Americans.

Newspapers

American Srbobran (American Serb Defender), Pittsburgh, PA. Tri-weekly: 1942-1943, 1965-date. (Microfilm: 1906-1912, 1918-1940). Includes English.

Diocesan Observer, Libertyville, IL. Weekly: 1965-date. Includes English.

Glas Kanadskih Srba (Voice of Canadian Serbs), Windsor, Ontario, Canada. Weekly: 1971-date. Includes English.

Jugoslovenski Američki Glasnik (Yugoslav-American Herald), Monterey Park, CA. Monthly: 1961-1970. Includes English.

Kanadski Srbobran (The Canadian Srbobran [Serb Defender]), Hamilton, Ontario, Canada. Weekly: 1963-date.

Path of Orthodoxy (official organ of the Serbian Orthodox Church in the United States and Canada), Leetsdale, PA. Monthly: 1977-date. Includes English.

Sloboda (Liberty), Chicago, IL. Weekly: 1965-1982.

Slobodna Reč (Free Expression), Pittsburgh, PA. Weekly. (Microfilm: 1934-1948).

Srbadija (Serbia), New York, NY. Monthly (bi-monthly, weekly, bi-weekly). (Microfilm: 1921-1927).

Srpska Borba (The Serbian Struggle; format changes to a serial, 1982), Chicago, IL. Weekly: 1953-1981. Includes English.

Yugoslav

Jugoslavenski Glasnik (Yugoslav Herald), Chicago, IL/Calumet, MI/New York, NY. Weekly: 1938-1945. Serbian and/or Croatian.

Jugoslovenski Obzor (Yugoslav Observer), Milwaukee, WI. Semi-monthly: 1933-1945. Slovenian.

Serials

The American Serb, Chicago, IL. Monthly: 1944-1946. English.

American-Serb Life, Pittsburgh, PA. Monthly: 1948.

Amerikanski Srbobran; Srpski Pravoslavni Kalendar (American Serb Defender; Serbian Orthodox Calendar), Pittsburgh, PA. Annual: 1922-1923, 1926, 1941, 1943, 1962-1965. Includes English.

The Beacon, Alhambra, CA. Quarterly: 1965. English.

Bratstvo (Fraternity, Serbian Monthly Review), Toronto, Ontario, Canada. Monthly: 1965.

Cheshal' (The Comb), Cheswick, PA. Monthly: 1947. Includes English.

Danas; Mesečni Časopis (Today; Monthly Journal), Chicago, IL. Monthly: 1963-1964.

Eparhiski Glasnik (The Diocesan Herald), Libertyville, IL. Annual: 1964-1966. Includes English.

Jugoslaven (The Yugoslav), San Pedro, CA. Monthly: 1928. Slovenian.

Jugoslovenski Forum (The Yugoslav Forum), New York, NY. Monthly: 1926. Includes Slovenian.

Karadorde Srpski Narodni Kalendar (Karadorde Serbian National Calendar), Pittsburgh, PA. Annual: 1928.

Naša Omladina (Our Youth; special Christmas issue of the **American Srbobran**), Pittsburgh, PA. Frequency varies: 1931. English.

Pravoslavlje; Glasnik Srpske Pravoslavne Džrkve (Orthodoxy; Herald of the Serbian Orthodox Church), Libertyville, IL. Quarterly: 1960, 1964.

Ravna Gora (Flat Mountain), Windsor, Ontario, Canada. Monthly (?): 1949. Includes English.

Serb World, Milwaukee, WI. Quarterly: 1979-1983. English.

The Serbian Democratic Forum, Chicago, IL. Frequency varies: 1973, 1975. English.

Serbian Orthodox Church in the U.S.A. and Canada Calendar, Pittsburgh, PA. Annual: 1966, 1974. Includes English.

Serbian Orthodox Church of the United States of America and Canada Glasnik (Herald), Chicago, IL. Monthly: 1965. Includes English.

Serbian Orthodox Church in the United States of America and Canada Official News Digest, South Holland, IL. Semi-monthly: 1965-1982. Includes English.

The Serbian Orthodox Herald, Libertyville, IL. Quarterly: 1945. English.

Srpska Borba (The Serbian Struggle; previously published as a newspaper), Flushing, NY. Monthly: 1982-date.

Srpsko Istorijsko-Kulturno Društvo "Njegoš" u Americi Glasnik (Herald of the Serbian Historical and Cultural Association "Njegoš"), Chicago, IL. Semi-annual: 1974.

Srpska Tsrkva (The Serbian Church), Chicago, IL. Monthly: 1923.

Srpski Misionar; Duhovni Časopis (Serbian Missionary), Jordanville, NY. Frequency varies: 1962-1964. Includes some English.

Srpski Narodni Kalendar Amerika (Serbian People's Calendar America), Chicago, IL. Annual: 1959-1964.

Srpski Pravoslavni Kalendar Sveti Sava (Serbian Orthodox Calendar Saint Sava), Villa Lake, IL. Annual: 1971. Includes English.

The Tesla Journal, Lackawanna, NY. Annual: 1981-1983, 1986-1987. English.

World Magazine; Naučno-Zabavni Ilustrovani Mesečni Magazin (Illustrated Monthly Magazine in Serbian Language for Science, Culture, and World Affairs), Toronto, Ontario, Canada. Monthly: 1961.

Zavičaj (Homeland), Belgrade, Yugoslavia. Monthly: 1969, 1974-date.

Zavičaj Kalendar (Homeland Calendar), Belgrade, Yugoslavia. Annual: 1977.

Yugoslav

Balkan and Eastern European American Genealogical and Historical Society, San Francisco, CA. Frequency varies: 1964-1966. English.

The Florida State University Center for Yugoslav-American Studies Proceedings and Reports (previously titled **The Florida State University Slavic Papers**), Tallahassee, FL. Annual: 1972-1977. English.

The Florida State University Joint Yugoslav-American Advisory Council Proceedings and Reports, Tallahassee, FL. Annual: 1978-1979. English.

Jugoslav Review, New York. Monthly. (Microfilm: 1923). Serbian and/or Croatian, Slovenian.

Jugoslaven (The Yugoslav), Västerås, Sweden. Quarterly: 1979. Croatian and English.

Jugoslavia Kalendar (Yugoslavia Calendar), Chicago, IL. Annual: 1939. Slovenian and English.

Kolo, New York, NY. Monthly: 1924. Slovenian.

Medunardoni Problemi (International Problems), Belgrade, Yugoslavia. Quarterly: 1982. Serbian and/or Croatian.

Naš Kalendar (Our Calendar), Toronto, Ontario, Canada. Annual: 1958. Slovenian.

Sokolski Vesnik (Sokol Herald), Milwaukee, WI. Quarterly: 1967-1975, 1980-1984. Serbian, Croatian, and Slovenian.

T & T (formerly **Today and Tomorrow**), Milford, NJ. Bi-monthly: 1945-1948, 1950. English.

The Tamburitzan, Pittsburgh, PA. Bi-monthly: 1959-1961, 1976. English.

That's Yugoslavia (supplement to **Hrvatska Domovina**), Hamburg, West Germany. Monthly: 1982. English.

United Committee of South-Slavic Americans Bulletin, New York, NY. Frequency varies: 1943-1946. English.

United Yugoslav Relief Fund of America News Bulletin (previously titled Yugoslav News Bulletin), New York, NY. Frequency varies: 1941-1945. English.

Yugoslav-American Academic Association of the Pacific Bulletin, Palo Alto, CA. Quarterly: 1977. English.

Yugoslav-American Society Newsletter, Minneapolis, MN. Bi-monthly: 1987-date. English.

Yugoslav Facts and Views, New York, NY. Monthly: 1975-1981. English.

Yugoslavia Ministarstvo Socijalne Politike Iseljenički Odsek Iseljenička Služba: Izveštaj Narodnoj Skupštini (Yugoslav Ministry of Social Policy Emigration Department Emigration Service: Report to National Assembly), Belgrade, Yugoslavia. Bi-annual: 1925-1927. Serbian and/or Croatian.

Slovak American Collection

Manuscript Collections

Andic, Vojtech E.
Papers, ca. 1960-1968. Ca. 2 linear in.

Andic was a former secretary general of the Czechoslovak Society of Arts and Sciences in America. Papers consist of articles, speeches, and souvenir programs. *Includes English.*

Blaho, P. and V. Šrobar.
Papers, ca. 1906-1913. 1 microfilm reel.

Correspondence, including letters from Rev. Francis Škutil of SS. Cyril and Methodius Church, Boonton (NJ). *Originals held by Slovak Central Archives, Bratislava, Czechoslovakia.*

Canadian Slovak League. Branch 10 (Ft. William, Ontario, Canada).
Records, 1924-1943. 1 microfilm reel.

Records of the League include minutes, papers, and plays (1924-1935) of the Educational and Dramatic Society of Young Slovaks; membership information; and financial records. *Related collection: Educational and Dramatic Society of Young Slovaks (Ft. William, Ontario, Canada).*

Educational and Dramatic Society of Young Slovaks (Ft. William, Ontario, Canada).
Records, 1924-1935. 1 microfilm reel.

The Society was founded in 1924. Records contain minutes, plays, membership information, dues records, and miscellany. *Related collection: Canadian Slovak League, Branch 10 (Ft. William, Ontario, Canada).*

First Catholic Slovak Union (Cleveland, Ohio).
Records, 1890-1958. 40 linear ft.

The First Catholic Slovak Union (Prvá Katolícka Slovenská Jednota) was organized in 1890. It is the largest Slovak fraternal benefit society in North America and has over 700 local lodges in the United States and Canada. There is also a youth auxiliary and a sports club attached to the Union. The FCSU provides its members with life insurance and social and cultural activities, and it helps to perpetuate Slovak consciousness. It publishes a weekly newspaper, *Jednota*, two yearbooks (*Furdek* and *Kalendár Jednota*) and books on Slovak history and culture.

Records of the FCSU include correspondence, auditors' reports, convention minutes, registers of members, and membership and insurance applications. *Inventory available.*

First Catholic Slovak Union, SS. Cyril and Methodius Lodge No. 3 (Minneapolis, Minnesota).
Records, 1888-1902. 1 microfilm reel.

Records consist of minutes of the lodge. *Related collection: St. Cyril's Church (Minneapolis, MN).*

First Evangelical Slovak Society of the Holy Trinity (Cleveland, Ohio).
Records, 1892-1943. 1 microfilm reel.

Records of the Society include a membership book (1892-1898), minute book (1892-1897), and the birth, marriage, and death records (1894-1943) of the Holy Trinity Parish.

Matica Slovenská (Martin, Slovakia).
Collection, 1890-1947. 3 microfilm reels.

Records of this national institute in Slovakia consist of correspondence between Slovaks in the United States and Canada with leaders in Slovakia. Correspondents include representatives of the National Slovak Society of the United States and Slovaks in many states, including Ohio, Illinois, New Jersey, Wisconsin, New York, and Pennsylvania. Topics include correspondence of steamship and railroad companies, the Slovak American press, and businessmen. Also included is a listing of the institute's holdings pertaining to Slovak Americans.

National Slovak Society (Pittsburgh, Pennsylvania).
Records, ca. 1895-1976. 300 linear ft. and 200 microfilm reels.

A fraternal organization founded in 1890, the Society is the oldest Slovak society in the United States and has over 450 lodges. The Society publishes its official organ, the bi-weekly newspaper *National News* (Národný Noviny), and the annual *Národný Kalendár*.
Records include correspondence, financial and legal records, minutes, and a large quantity of insurance claim records. Correspondence includes that of national officers with local lodges, and of the Society's Young Folks' Circle with the national headquarters. Convention records (1937-1974) consist of reports, minutes, correspondence, delegates' lists, campaign literature, revised copies of bylaws, and the Society's constitution. Also included are records of the Supreme Assembly and Executive Committee (1934-1959); official referendum ballots from individual assemblies concerning district dues; materials of the office of Supreme Treasurer (1963) and the office of President (1954); pledge documents of elected officers (1913, 1916); a scrapbook of the Young Folks' Circle (1916-1917); and lists of 810 local assemblies and circles. *Includes English. Inventory available. Some legal records are restricted.*

Novak, Michael.
Papers, 1970-1976. Ca. 6 linear ft.

Novak is a syndicated columnist and resident scholar at the American Enterprise Institute (Washington, DC). He has authored many books, including *The Rise of the Unmeltable Ethnics*, and has also been a political speechwriter, antiwar and civil rights advocate, and consultant to government and business.
Papers consist of personal and professional materials including typescripts, newspaper clippings, publications, and correspondence. Materials pertain mostly to nationality groups, including Scandinavian and Slavic Americans, as well as to Catholics, education, and the Polish American Congress. *Mainly in English.*

Osuský, Štefan (1888-   ).
Papers, ca. 1914-1937. 1 linear ft.

A lawyer, Osuský was born in Slovakia and came to the United States after completing elementary school. He received a law degree from the University of Chicago and practiced law in Chicago. During World War I, he worked for creation of an independent Czechoslovak state. Following the war, he served in the diplomatic services of Great Britain and Switzerland, and from 1931 to 1938 he was the Czech ambassador to France. After the Munich Pact, he joined the Beneš government in London.

Papers contain personal and professional papers and writings, largely pertaining to the movement for Czech independence, negotiations of President Woodrow Wilson with Emperor Charles of Austria, relations between the Czech National Committee and French government, Hungarian involvement in World War I, Louis Kossuth, the economic situation in Austria-Hungary prior to World War I, and Michael Korolyi's visit to the United States. Also included are bulletins of the Slovak World Congress, and poetry. *Includes English and French.*

Podkrivacky, Adam.
Papers, ca. 1920-1965. 27.5 linear ft.

Papers of Podkrivacky, a former president of the First Catholic Slovak Union, consist of personal and organizational materials. Official documents of the FCSU constitute the bulk of the collection, including financial records, membership lists, and photographs. *Includes English. Related collection: First Catholic Slovak Union (Cleveland, OH).*

Rolík, Rev. Andrew.
Papers, 1919-1975. Ca. 3 linear in.

An Evangelical Lutheran minister, Rolík was ordained after coming to the United States in 1909. He served Slovak Lutheran churches in Pennsylvania, Ohio, and Michigan.

Papers consist of typescripts, poetry, various church publications (such as jubilee programs), and sheet music.

Church publications are from Evangelical Lutheran churches in Johnstown, PA, and Muskegon, MI, where Rolík was pastor. *Includes some English.*

St. Cyril's Church (Minneapolis, Minnesota).
Records, 1898-1910. 1 microfilm reel.

Records of the Church include membership lists, minutes, and financial records of the Parish Committee. *Related collection: First Catholic Slovak Union, SS. Cyril and Methodius Lodge No. 3 (Minneapolis, MN).*

St. Stephen's Roman Catholic Church (Streator, Illinois).
Records, 1884-1908. 1 microfilm reel.

St. Stephen's was the first Slovak Catholic parish established in America, founded ca. 1883. The affiliated St. Stephen's School, run by Franciscan Sisters, opened in the fall of 1888 and was the first Slovak school in the United States.

Records consist of baptism, marriage, and death records. *Mainly in English; some Latin.*

St. Wendelin's Parish (Cleveland, Ohio).
Records, 1911-1926. 1 microfilm reel.

Chancery records of the Parish include parish census material, records of various men's and women's societies associated with the Parish, a map of the parish, correspondence pertaining to construction of schools and purchase of land, and correspondence of Rt. Rev. J. P. Farrelly, Rev. Augustin Tomasek, and Rev. Joseph Bresnyak. *In English.*

Monographs

The IHRC Slovak American monograph collection numbers about 820 books and pamphlets. Religion, organizational activity, general and community history, migration, acculturation, and politics are all strongly represented. Also available are works on literature, education, art, music, the press, work, customs, and folklore. Among the relevant bibliographies in the IHRC's reference section are Esther Jerabek's *Czechs and Slovaks in North America* (1976), Joseph S. Roucek and Patricia Pinkham's *American*

Slavs: A Bibliography (1944), and Stanley B. Kimball's *Slavic-American Imprints: A Classified Catalog of the Collection at Lovejoy Library* (1972).

The importance of the church in the lives of Slovak immigrants and their descendants is reflected in works relating to both Catholics and Protestants. There are many jubilee and commemorative publications; these often contain important information about individuals and communities as well as about parishes. There are also hymn books, sermons, catechisms, and Lutheran and Catholic Bibles. George Dolak's *A History of the Slovak Evangelical Lutheran Church in the United States of America, 1902-1927* (1955), Richard Portasik's *Slovak Franciscans in America: History of Most Holy Savior Commissariat* (1966), Michael Lasko's *The Churches of the Eastern Rite in North America* (1964), Fedor Ruppeldt's *Slovenski evangelici v Amerike* (Slovak Lutherans in America, 1931), Sr. M. Martina Tybor's *Slovak American Catholics* (1976), and June Granatir Alexander's *The Immigrant Church and Community: Pittsburgh's Slovak Catholics and Lutherans, 1880-1915* (1987) are representative of the large number of writings on religion.

Organizational activities of Slovak Americans are represented by numerous anniversary publications as well as other works. Examples are Jozef Pauco's *Sixty Years of the Slovak League of America* (1967); publications of the First Catholic Slovak Ladies Union and the First Catholic Slovak Union; souvenir journals of the First Slovak Wreath of the Free Eagle and the Ladies Pennsylvania Slovak Roman and Greek Catholic Union; the *Diamond Jubilee, 1893-1968* of the Pennsylvania Slovak Catholic Union; and souvenir and memorial books of the Slovak Catholic Sokol.

Historical works comprise both general histories and histories of Slovak Americans in particular areas. Also included are numerous works on the homeland. General works include *Panorama: A Historical Review of Czechs and Slovaks in the United States of America* (1971), Konstantin Culen's *Dejiny Slovakov v Amerike* (History of Slovaks in America, 1942), the Foreign Language Information Service's *Slovaks Under the Stars and Stripes* (1900), Sr. M. Martina Tybor's *Chronology: The Slovaks in America to the End of the Nineteenth Century* (1979), Howard F. Stein's *An Ethno-Historic Study of Slovak-American Identity* (1972), and *Slovaks in America: A Bicentennial Study* (1978). There are also histories and studies of Slovaks in New York, Ohio, California, Bridgeport, Chicago, Cleveland, Milwaukee, and Pittsburgh.

Slovak American political activity is reflected in works dealing with ties to the homeland and works pertaining to involvement in mainstream United States politics. M. Mark Stolarik's *The Role of American Slovaks in the Creation of Czecho-Slovakia, 1914-1918* (1968) is an example of the former.

Publications pertaining to the processes of migration and acculturation include Joseph Pauco's fictional *Flight to Wonderland* (1963); *Začiatky českej a slovenskej emigrácie do USA: Česká a Slovenská robotnicka emigrácia v USA v období I. internacionály* (The Beginnings of Czech and Slovak Emigration to the U.S.A.: Emigration of Czech and Slovak Workers to the USA in the Period of the First Internationale), edited by Josef Polišenský (1970); William P. Shriver's *Slovaci v Amerike* (Slovaks in America, 1935); M. Mark Stolarik's *Emigration, Education and Urbanization: A Comparison of the Actions, Ideas and Experiences of Slovaks in the Old World and the New, 1880-1918* (n.d.); Stolarik's *Immigration and Urbanization: The Slovak Experience, 1870-1918* (1974); and Greg M. Chaklo's *The Unmelting Ethnic: A Brief Profile of Early Slovak-American Immigration in the Metropolitan Pittsburgh Area* (1974).

Slovak American interests in and contributions to art, music, and especially literature are well documented in the collection. Musical works include religious music, folksongs, and choral works. Materials on art include biographies and exhibition catalogs such as *Slovak Art Exhibition in New York* (1938). The collection contains numerous works of poetry and fiction. Overviews are supplied by Ivan J. Kramoris's *Chronological Outline of Slovak Literature and History* (1946) and his *Anthology of Slovak Poetry* (1947), and by William E. Harkins's *Czech and Slovak Literature* (1950). Individual works include Thomas Bell's *Out of This Furnace* (1941), and Michael Simko's *Mila Nadaya* (Beloved Nadaya, 1968). Authors represented include Rudolf

Dilong, Jozef Ciger, Milos K. Mlynarovic, Pavol Orszagh, Josef Pauco, Mikulas Sprinc, and others.

Slovak American cultural activities are represented by travel books; humorous works; sports works, such as *Slet Manual; XI. Slet and Gymnastic Meet of the Slovak Gymnastic Union Sokol in U.S.A.*, compiled by Joe Skapik and Charles Bednar (1950); and depictions of folklore and customs, such as Jozef Duris's *Slovak Christmas, A Symposium of Songs, Customs, and Plays* (1960). The ethnic press is outlined in George Leo Yashur's *A Preliminary History of the Slovak Press in America* (1950). In addition, the collection includes several grammar books, citizenship manuals, and studies on philology such as Joseph M. Kirschbaum's *Contemporary Tendencies in Slovak Philology* (1960).

Newspapers

Amerikansko Slovenské Noviny (American-Slovak News), Pittsburgh, PA; New York, NY; and Connellsville, PA. Weekly. (Microfilm: 1893-1904).

Bratstvo (Brotherhood), Wilkes-Barre, PA. Frequency varies: 1963-date. Includes English.

Hlas (The Voice), Cleveland, OH. Weekly. (Microfilm: 1912-1913).

Horizont (Horizon), Munich, West Germany. Bi-monthly (monthly): 1972-1982.

Jednota (The Union), Middletown, PA. Weekly: 1965-date. (Microfilm: 1893-1940). Includes English.

Kanadsky Slovak (Canadian Slovak), Toronto, Ontario; Montreal, Quebec; and Winnipeg, Manitoba; Canada. Weekly: 1967-date. Includes English.

Katolícke Noviny (Catholic News), Nádas, Czechoslovakia. Semi-monthly. (Microfilm: 1896-1900, 1902-1906).

Katolícky Sokol (Catholic Sokol), Passaic, NJ. Weekly: 1969-1979. Includes English.

L'Udové Zvesti (People's News), Toronto, Ontario, Canada. Bi-weekly (weekly): 1971-date.

Ludové Noviny (People's News), Skalice, Czechoslovakia. Weekly. (Microfilm: 1906-1909).

Matičné Čítanie (Slovak Cultural Society's Readings), Martin, Czechoslovakia. Semi-monthly: 1968-1977.

Národni Hlásnik (The National Crier), Turčiansky Sv. Martin, Czechoslovakia. Weekly. (Microfilm: 1868-1881).

Národné Noviny (National News), Pittsburgh, PA. Semi-monthly (weekly): 1941-1948, 1950-1983. (Microfilm: 1901-1941). Includes English.

Národné Noviny (National News), Turčiansky Sv. Martin. Tri-weekly. (Microfilm: 1881-1914).

Náš Svet (Our World), Chicago, IL. Weekly: 1942.

New Yorský Dennik, New York, NY. Daily: 1956. Slovak.

Obzor (The Observer), Ružomberok, Czechoslovakia. Tri-monthly. (Microfilm: 1863-1904).

Priatel' Dietok (The Children's Friend), Passaic, NJ. Frequency varies: 1969-1972.

Slobodné Slovensko (Free Slovakia; previously titled **Černákov Oskaz**), Cologne, West Germany. Frequency varies: 1967-1974, 1976-date.

Slovák v Amerike (Slovak American), Middletown, PA. Weekly: 1951-1954, 1961-1964, 1966-date. (Microfilm: 1894-1938).

Slovenská Obrana (Slovak Defense; previously titled **Kritika; Kritika a Obrana; Obrana**), Middletown, PA. Weekly: 1914-1972.

Slovenské Ludové Noviny (News of the Slovak People), Bratislava, Czechoslovakia. Weekly. (Microfilm: 1910-1918).

Slovenský Orol (Slovak Eagle), Passaic, NJ. Quarterly: 1971. English.

Sokol Times, East Orange/Perth Amboy, NJ. Semi-monthly: 1971-date. English.

United Lutheran, (previously titled **Slovenský Hlásnik**), Allegheny, PA (previously published in Pittsburgh, PA). Weekly (semi-monthly, monthly). (Microfilm: 1908-1975). Includes English.

United Lutheran, Ligonier, PA. Monthly: 1975-1978. English.

Wisconsiňsky Slovak (Wisconsin Slovak), Milwaukee, WI. (Microfilm: 1936).

Serials

Americký Slovák (The American Slovak), Bratislava, Czechoslovakia. Monthly: 1920-1921.

Ave Maria (Hail Mary), Cleveland, OH. Monthly: 1920, 1924-1933, 1936-1950, 1952-1956, 1966-1968, 1970-1972, 1974-1975.

Besiedka; Listy Amerických Slovákov (Chat; Letters of American Slovaks), New York, NY. Monthly: 1936. Includes English.

Božské Srdce Ježiša (The Sacred Heart of Jesus), Bridgeport/Stratford, CT. Monthly: 1918-1933, 1935-1938, 1943-1948.

Božské Srdce Ježiša Kalendár (The Sacred Heart of Jesus Calendar), Bridgeport, CT. Annual: 1924.

Calvin, Pittsburgh, PA. Bi-monthly: 1964, 1969, 1971-date. English.

Children's Friend, Passaic, NJ. Ten issues per year: 1973-1977, 1979. English.

The Courier of the Slovak Luther League, Chicago, IL (previously published in Granite City, IL. Monthly: 1931, 1934-1944. English.

Dennica (Morning Star), Pittsburgh, PA. Frequency varies. (Microfilm: 1924-1930, 1932-1945).

Dobrý Pastier (Good Shepherd), Passaic, NJ. Annual: 1947-1950, 1957, 1962, 1965-1974, 1976-1977, 1980-1983. Includes English.

Dom a Škola (Home and School), Ružomberok, Czechoslovakia (previously published in Turčiansky Sv. Martin, Czechoslovakia). Monthly: 1885, 1887-1889. (Microfilm: 1886-1897).

Domobrana (Home Guard), Whiting, IN (Montreal, Quebec, and Toronto, Ontario, Canada). Monthly: 1954.

Ethnologia Slavica (Slovak Ethnology), Bratislava, Czechoslovakia. Monthly: 1971. Includes German, French, Russian or Ukrainian, and English.

Evanjelicko-Luteraňsky Kalendár (Evangelical-Lutheran Calendar; title varies: **Americký Kalendár pre Slovenských Evanjelikov Aug. V. Vz; Americký Kalendár pre Slovákov-**

Luteránov), Pittsburgh, PA (previously published in Streator, IL). Annual: 1914-1918, 1920-1921, 1923, 1930-1937, 1949, 1952-1954, 1960.

Fialky (Violets), Danville, PA. Annual: 1924-1970. Includes English.

First Catholic Slovak Ladies Union Ústava a Zákony (Constitution and Bylaws), Cleveland, OH. Irregular: 1915, 1922, 1928, 1937, 1952, 1964. Includes English.

First Catholic Slovak Union in the U.S.A. [Prvá Katolícka Slovenská Jednota] Directory; Adresár, Middletown, PA. Annual: 1944, 1946-1947, 1951-1952, 1956-1957, 1961, 1964, 1966, 1968-1969, 1972, 1980. Includes English.

First Catholic Slovak Union in the U.S.A. Ústava a Zákony (Constitution and Bylaws), Middletown, PA. Irregular: 1904, 1906, 1910, 1912, 1914, 1918, 1920, 1924, 1928, 1932-1962, 1971. Includes English.

First Catholic Slovak Union in the U.S.A. Zápisnica Konvencie (Convention Minutes), Middletown, PA. Irregular: 1912-1918, 1922-1926, 1931-1955, 1961-1970, 1976. Includes English.

First Catholic Slovak Union in the U.S.A. Zápisnica Ročnej Schôdze Hlavného Úradu (Minutes of the Annual Meeting of the Supreme Board), Middletown, PA. Annual: 1914, 1916-1921, 1923, 1926-1967, 1970, 1973-1974, 1980, 1983. Includes English.

First Catholic Slovak Union in the U.S.A. Zápisnica z Polročnej Schôdze Halvného Radu (Minutes of the Semiannual Meeting of the Supreme Board), Middletown, PA. Annual: 1944-1950, 1952-1957, 1963-1964, 1966-1967, 1969-1971, 1974, 1978. Includes English.

First Catholic Slovak Union in the U.S.A. Zpráva Hlavných Úradníkov (Report of the Supreme Officers), Middletown, PA. Irregular: 1920, 1922, 1926-1940, 1964, 1969-1970. Includes English.

First Catholic Slovak Union in the U.S.A. Junior and Sokol Branch By-laws, Middletown, PA. Irregular: 1912, 1914, 1916, 1920, 1924, 1928, 1931, 1934, 1937, 1940, 1943, 1946, 1949, 1952, 1955, 1958, 1965. Includes English.

Floridský Slovak (The Floridian Slovak), Maitland, FL. Quarterly: 1967, 1971, 1975-date. Includes English.

Fraternally Yours; Ženská Jednota (Ladies Union), Passaic, NJ. Monthly: 1960-1980. Includes English.

Furdek (Jednota Annual), Cleveland, OH. Annual: 1962-date. English.

Furdek (The Catholic Slovak Students Fraternity of America), Middletown, PA (previously published in Scranton, PA). Monthly: 1928-1933, 1935-1938. Includes English.

Glen Echos of Mount Trexler, Mt. Trexler/Limeport, PA. Monthly: 1968. English.

Hlas Mládeže (The Voice of Youth), New York, NY. Monthly: 1947, 1950, 1961.

Hlasy z Domová a z Misií (Voices from Homeland and Missions; previously titled Hlasy z Katolíckych Misií), Techny, IL (previously published in Ružomberok, Czechoslovakia). Monthly: 1930-1940, 1946-1948.

Hlasy z Ríma (Voices from Rome), Rome, Italy. Monthly: 1952-1963, 1969-1972.

Jednota; Katolícky Kalendár (The Union; Catholic Calendar), Middletown, PA. Annual: 1898, 1900-1920, 1923-date.

Kalendár Bratstvo pre Rimsko a Grećko Katoli'kov (Brotherhood Calendar for Roman and Greek Catholics), Wilkes-Barre, PA. Annual: 1914-1915, 1918, 1924-1925.

Kalendár Kanadskej Slovenskej Lígy (Canadian Slovak League Calendar), Toronto, Ontario, Canada. Annual: 1953-1958, 1960-1964, 1969-1971, 1977-1979, 1981, 1983-1984.

Kalendár Neodvislost' (Independence Calendar), New York, NY. Annual: 1928-1930.

Kalendár pre Slovenských Kalvínov (Calendar for Slovak Calvinists), Pittsburgh, PA. Annual: 1924, 1927.

Kalendár Slováka v Amerike (Slovak in America Calendar), New York, NY. Annual: 1920-1921, 1923, 1945.

Kalendár Živeny (Calendar Živeny), Pittsburgh, PA. Annual: 1924-1925, 1927.

Keeping in Touch, Middletown, PA. Frequency varies: undated issue. English.

Krajana; Vel'ki Obrazkovi Kalendár (Countrymen; Large Pictorial Calendar), New York, NY. Annual: 1921.

Krajanský Kalendár (Old-Country Calendar), Chicago, IL. Annual: 1958-1959.

Krestan (The Christian), Uniontown, PA. Monthly: 1929-1930.

Kruh Mládeže (Young Folks' Circle of the National Slovak Society; published as Section II of the newspaper **Narodne Noviny**, June 1934-December 1937), Pittsburgh, PA. Monthly: 1916-1924, 1926-1933. Includes English.

Kruh Mládeže (Young Folks Circle), Pittsburgh, PA. Semi-annual: 1983. English.

Leaflets of St. Francis, Pittsburgh, PA. Bi-monthly: 1969. English.

Listy Svätého Františka (Leaflets of St. Francis), Pittsburgh, PA (previously published in Lemont, IL). Monthly: 1925-1926, 1928, 1931-1932, 1943-1944, 1953, 1969-date.

Literárny Almanach Slováka v Amerike (Slovak in America Literary Almanac), Chicago, IL. Annual: 1953-1970, 1973-1975.

Logos, Cromwell, CT. Annual: 1970. English.

L'udový Kalendár (The People's Calendar), Pittsburgh, PA. Annual: 1950.

The Lutheran Beacon, Pittsburgh, PA (St. Louis, MO). Monthly: 1950-1955, 1957-1959. English.

Lutheran Haven Herald, Oviedo, FL. Quarterly: 1951. English.

Maria, Toronto, Ontario, Canada. Monthly: 1976-date. Includes English.

Matica Slovenská (Slovak Cultural Society), Turčiansky Sv. Martin, Czechoslovakia. Quarterly (early issues vary in frequency): 1922-1929, 1931-1932, 1934-1937.

Matičné Čítanie (Slovak Cultural Society's Readings), Turčiansky Sv. Martin, Czechoslovakia. Monthly: 1946-1949.

Medzi Nami (Between Us), Techny, IL. Monthly: 1955.

Misionársky Kalendár (Missionary Calendar), Techny, IL. Annual: 1927, 1932.

Mladost' (Youth), Buenos Aires, Argentina. Monthly: 1949-1952.

Mladý Katolík (Young Catholic), Panzerkaserne, West Germany. Quarterly: 1950.

Mladý Luterán (The Young Lutheran), Racine, WI/Pittsburgh, PA. Monthly: 1927-1930, 1933-1939. Includes English.

Most; A Quarterly for Slovak Culture (Bridge), Cleveland, OH. Quarterly: 1954-1962, 1965-1967, 1976-date.

Musical Advance, New York, NY. Monthly: 1939. English.

Muzeálna Slovenská Spoločnosť' Časopis (Slovak Museum Society Magazine), Turčiansky Sv. Martin, Czechoslovakia. Frequency varies: 1927, 1929-1930, 1934-1938, 1944, 1947-1949.

Muzeálna Slovenská Spoločnosť' Sporník (Slovak Museum Society Review), Turčiansky Sv. Martin, Czechoslovakia. Frequency varies: 1ᴖ26-1927, 1929-1930, 1932-1937. Includes some German.

Národniarsky Kalendár (Nationalist Calendar), Toronto, Ontario, Canada. Annual: 1963, 1965.

Národný Kalendár (The People's Calendar; title varies: Sborník Narodného Slovenského Spolku), Pittsburgh, PA. Annual: 1899-1901, 1903-1921, 1923-1949, 1951-1954, 1956-1973, 1975-1980, 1982-date. Includes English.

Náš Kalendár (Our Calendar), Békéscaba, Hungary. Annual: 1959-1962, 1964-1965.

Náš Život (Our Life), Toronto, Ontario, Canada. Monthly: 1951.

Naše Hlasy (Our Voice), Chicago, IL. Monthly: 1968, 1980-date. Includes English.

Naše Snahy (Our Trends), Elmhurst, NY. Bi-monthly: 1965-1966, 1970-1976, 1978-date. Includes Czech.

Nástup; Orgán Reprezentácie Slovenského Oslobodzovacieho Výboru vo Francúzsku (Assembly; Official Organ of the Slovak Liberation Commitee in France), Paris, France. Monthly: 1952.

National Slovak Society of the U.S.A. Finančná Správa (Financial Report), Pittsburgh, PA. Irregular: 1913, 1919, 1926-1930.

National Slovak Society of the U.S.A. Stanovy (Constitution and Bylaws), Pittsburgh, PA. Irregular: 1895, 1899, 1901, 1903, 1906, 1909, 1911, 1913, 1917, 1919, 1923, 1926, 1930, 1934, 1937, 1941, 1946, 1958, 1962, 1967, 1970. Includes English.

National Slovak Society of the U.S.A. Stanovy Kruhu Mládeže (Constitution and Bylaws of the Young Folks' Circle), Pittsburgh, PA. Irregular: 1913, 1919, 1923, 1926, 1930, 1934, 1937, 1941. Includes English.

National Slovak Society of the U.S.A. Zápisnica (Minutes), Pittsburgh, PA. Irregular: 1909, 1911, 1934.

National Slovak Society of the U.S.A. Zápisnica Pol-Ročnej Schôdze Hlavného Odboru (Minutes of the Semi-Annual Meeting of the Supreme Branch), Pittsburgh, PA. Irregular: 1936, 1955, 1959, 1963, 1969. Includes English.

National Slovak Society of the U.S.A. Zápisnice Riadnej Konvencie (Minutes of the Regular Convention), Pittsburgh, PA. Irregular: 1901, 1903, 1906, 1913, 1916, 1919, 1923, 1926, 1930, 1937, 1941, 1946, 1950, 1954, 1958, 1970. Includes English.

National Slovak Society of the U.S.A. Zápisnice Ročnej Schôdze Hlavného Odboru (Minutes of the Annual Meeting of the Supreme Branch), Pittsburgh, PA. Irregular: 1896, 1898-1900, 1904, 1905, 1907-1908, 1910, 1912, 1914-1915, 1917-1918, 1920-1922, 1924-1925, 1927-1929, 1931-1932, 1935-1937, 1939-1946, 1948-1951, 1953-1955, 1957-1958, 1962-1963, 1970-1971.

National Slovak Society of the U.S.A. Zprávy Úradníkov (Officers' Report), Pittsburgh, PA. Irregular: 1946, 1954, 1958, 1962, 1966. Includes English.

Nové Slovensko (New Slovakland), Pittsburgh, PA. Monthly: 1921-1922.

Obežník Slovenskeho Priekopnika (Circular of the Slovak Pioneer), Montreal, Quebec, Canada. 1943.

Obrana; Národný Kalendár (Defense; National Calendar), Scranton, PA. Annual: 1922.

Pennsylvania Slovak Catholic Union Zápisnica Konvencie (Convention Minutes), Wilkes-Barre, PA. Irregular: 1925, 1927, 1929, 1932, 1935, 1938, 1941, 1946, 1950, 1954, 1958, 1962, 1966. Includes English.

Pennsylvania Slovak Catholic Union Zprávy Hlavných Úradnikov (Report of the Supreme Officers), Wilkes-Barre, PA. Irregular: 1946, 1950, 1954, 1958, 1962, 1966, 1970. Includes English.

Pravda; Náboženský Evanj-Luteránskeho Smeru Mesačnik (The Truth; The Religious Evangelical-Lutheran Monthly Guide), Monthly: 1921.

Prehl'ad (General View), Middletown, PA. Semi-monthly: 1917-1918.

Rím; Slovenský Kultúry Časopis (Rome; Slovak Cultural Magazine), Rome, Italy. Monthly: 1949-1953.

Robotnícky Kalendár (Workers Calendar), Chicago, IL. Annual: 1921.

Rozhl'ady (Perspective; Independent Political Review; Slovak Study Center), New York, NY. Quarterly: 1956-1959.

Rozvoj (Development), Montreal, Quebec, Canada/Lauvain, Belgium. Semi-monthly: 1949-1950, 1952.

St. Procopius College Academy Announcements, Lisle, IL. Annual: 1937-1941. English.

Sborník Slovenského Katolíckeho Sokola (Slovak Catholic Sokol Almanac), Passaic, NJ. Annual: 1913, 1916, 1920, 1922, 1924-1934, 1936, 1940-1946, 1949-1950, 1957, 1960. Includes English.

Severov; Slovenský Kalendár a Domáci Lekár (North; Slovak Calendar and Domestic Doctor), Cedar Rapids, IA. Annual: 1926.

The Shepherd, Whiting, IN. Quarterly: 1934. Includes English.

Sion (Zion), Pittsburgh, PA. Monthly: 1971-1972. Includes English.

Sion Evanjelický Kalendár (Zion Evangelical Calendar), Cleveland, OH. Annual: 1911-1924, 1951.

Slobodné Slovensko (Free Slovakia), Ludwigsburg, West Germany. Weekly (monthly): 1947-1950.

Slováci v Zahraniči (Slovaks in Foreign Countries), Martin, Czechoslovakia. Frequency varies: 1971, 1974, 1980-1983. Includes English summaries.

Slovák; Časopis Slovákov V Cudzine (Slovak; Magazine for Slovaks in Foreign Lands), London, England. Monthly: 1952. Includes English.

Slovák a Svet; Vol'né Novinárske Listy (The Slovak and the World; Free Journalistic Letters), Chicago/Skokie, IL. Monthly: 1971-1972.

Slovak Catholic Sokol Supreme Assembly Zápisnica Ročnej Schôdze (Minutes of the Annual Meeting), Cleveland, OH. Annual: 1931-1934, 1937, 1945-1947, 1950-1951, 1956, 1959, 1967, 1973. Includes English

Slovak Digest, New York, NY. Semi-monthly: 1946. English.

Slovak Evangelical Lutheran Synod of the U.S.A. Zápisnica (Minutes), Pittsburgh PA (?). Irregular: 1933, 1935.

Slovak Heritage, Detroit, MI. Monthly: 1977-1979. Includes English.

Slovak Heritage Association, San Diego, CA. Monthly (?): 1984. English.

Slovak Information Service, Detroit, MI. Monthly: 1979-1980. English.

Slovak National Council Abroad Bulletin, Middletown, PA (previously published in New York, NY). Monthly (?): 1955-1958. English.

Slovak Newsletter, Middletown, PA. Monthly: 1949-1958. English.

Slovak Press Digest, New York, NY. Monthly: 1968-1972, 1974-1978, 1983. English.

Slovak Review, Scranton, PA. Quarterly: 1946-1947. English.

Slovak Studies, Cleveland, OH/Rome, Italy. Annual: 1961, 1963-1964, 1966-1981. English.

Slovak Studies Association Newsletter, Philadelphia, PA. Quarterly: 1978-1982, 1985. English.

Slovak World Congress Bulletin, New York, NY. 1971.

Slovakia, Middletown, PA. Annual (frequency varies before 1965): 1951-1984. English.

Slovakia, New York, NY. Monthly: 1938.

Slovakian, Ottawa, Ontario, Canada. Quarterly: 1949. English.

Slovenka (Slovak Woman), Chicago, IL. Monthly: 1940.

Slovenská Jednota; Orgán Strany Narodnej Jednoty (Slovak Unity; Organ of National Unity), Aurolzmünster, Austria. 1951.

Slovenská Mládež (Slovak Youth), Pittsburgh, PA. Monthly: 1917, 1919. Includes English.

Slovenská Národná Bibliografia (Slovak National Bibliography), Bratislava, Czechoslovakia. Monthly: 1975-date (?).

Slovenská Národná Bibliografia (Slovak National Bibliography), Martin, Czechoslovakia. Monthly: 1983-1984.

Slovenská Národná Bibliografia. Series B-J (Slovak National Bibliography), Martin, Czechoslovakia. Quarterly: 1983-1984.

Slovenská Ozvena z Venezuely (Slovak Echo from Venezuela), Caracas, Venezuela. Monthly: 1952-1953.

Slovenské Pohl'ady (Slovak Views), Bratislava, Czechoslovakia (previously published in Turčiansky Sv. Martin, Czechoslovakia). Monthly: 1881-1886, 1890-1901, 1903-1906, 1912, 1914, 1922-1940, 1947, 1964.

Slovenskí Jezuiti v Kanade Yearbook (Slovak Jesuits of Canada), Cambridge, Ontario, Canada. Annual: 1956-1972, 1974-1979, 1981.

Slovensko (Slovakia), Turčiansky Sv. Martin, Czechoslovakia. Monthly: 1934-1938.

Slovensko-Americký Vreckový Kalendár (Slovak-American Pocket Calendar), Scranton, PA (previously published in New York, NY). Annual: 1918, 1926.

Slovenský Evanjelický Kalendár (Slovak Evangelical [Lutheran] Calendar), Pittsburgh, PA. Annual: 1920, 1922, 1924-1927, 1929, 1935.

Slovenský Kalendár pre Južnu Ameriku (Slovak Calendar for South America), Buenos Aires, Argentina. Annual: 1935.

Slovenský Národ; Slovenský Literárny Časopis (Slovak Nation; Slovak Literary Magazine), Schenectady, NY. Monthly: 1925-1926.

Slovenský Národopis (Slovak Ethnography), Bratislava, Czechoslovakia. Quarterly: 1975. Includes German, Ukrainian or Russian.

Slovenský Sokol (Sokol Times; Official Publication of the Slovak Gymnastic Union Sokol), East Orange, NJ. Weekly. (Microfilm: 1907-1964). Includes English.

Slovenský Zpravodaj (Slovak Correspondent), Salzburg, Austria. Weekly: 1950-1951.

Slowakei (Slovakia), Munich/Cologne, West Germany. Annual: 1968-1969, 1975-1978, 1981, 1983-1985. German.

Slowakische Rundschau; Zeitschrift für Politik, Wirtschaft und Kultur (Slovakian Review; Newspaper for Politics, Economy, and Culture), Bratislava, Czechoslovakia. Monthly: 1941. German.

Sokolský Sborník (Sokol Almanac), Perth Amboy, NJ. Annual: 1921, 1926, 1928.

Štít (The Shield), Sydney, Australia. Monthly: 1952.

Stráž (Sentinel), Palmyra, PA. Semi-monthly: 1938.

Studia Historica Slovaca (Slovak Historical Studies; Slovak Academy of Sciences, History Institute), Bratislava, Czechoslovakia. Annual: 1964-1969. French, German, Ukrainian or Russian, and English.

Svätá Rodina; Časopis k Úcte Sv. Rodiny Nazaretskej a k Ochrane Rodín Krestanských (The Holy Family; Magazine for the Teaching of the Holy Nazareth Family and for the Protection of Christian Families), Arvanagyfalu, Hungary. Monthly: 1909, 1914-1915.

Svedok (The Witness), Pittsburgh, PA. Bi-monthly (monthly): 1910-1917, 1920-1931, 1935-1938, 1940-1956, 1958-1961, 1963, 1965-1966, 1968-date.

Tovaryštvo; Sborník Literárnych Prác (Merchandising; Literary Journal of Work), Ružomberok, Czechoslovakia. Bi-annual (?): 1893, 1895.

Tranovský Evanjelický Kalendár (Tranova Evangelical Calendar), Liptovský Mikuláš, Czechoslovakia. Annual: 1907, 1924, 1928.

Udalosti Sveta (World's Events), Hazelton, PA. Monthly: 1917-1918.

Vatra; Časopis pre Slovákov v Exile (Blaze; Magazine for Slovaks in Exile), London, England. Weekly: 1951.

Viestnik; Slovenský Týždennik (Guide; Slovak Weekly), Chicago, IL. Weekly: 1917.

Všenárodný Kalendár (National Calendar), New York, NY. Annual: 1942-1944.

Výber z Katolíckej Svetovej Tlače (Selection from Catholic World Presses), Buenos Aires, Argentina. Monthly: 1950-1951.

Za Pravdu Jánošika; Časopis Slovenskych Pacientov v Gautingu (For the Truth about Janošik; Slovak Magazine of Patients in Gauting), Gauting, West Germany. Monthly: 1953.

Zion Beacon, Chicago, IL. Monthly: 1933-1936. English.

Živena; Official Organ of the Živena Beneficial Society, Pittsburgh, PA/Chicago, IL. Monthly 1961, 1969-1971. Includes English.

Zora (The Aurora), Chicago, IL. Monthly: 1916-1917.

Zornička (Morning Star), Middleton, PA (previously published in Scranton, PA as a newspaper). Monthly (earlier issues vary in frequency): 1956, 1960-1971, 1978-date. Includes English.

1933 Chicago World's Fair parade float of Prvá Katolicka Slovenská Jednota (First Catholic Slovak Union).

Slovenian American Collection

Manuscript Collections

Alliance "Lily" of Wisconsin (Zveza "Lilija" Wisconsin) (Milwaukee, Wisconsin).
Records, 1935-1946. 10 linear in.

The Alliance was a mutual fraternal benefit organization created in late 1934 or early 1935. The organization was open to Slavs and non-Slavs, although most of its members were Slovenes. It was devoted to providing an economic service to its members, and it prohibited partisan political and religious activities. It apparently merged with the Slovene National Benefit Society in 1946.

Records are chiefly financial. Also included are records of the Juvenile Department, along with the constitution and bylaws. *Includes English. Inventory available. Related collection: Slovene National Benefit Society (Slovenska Narodna Podporna Jednota) (Chicago, IL).*

Ave Maria Printery (Lemont, Illinois).
Records, 1956-1967. 3.5 linear ft.

Records include correspondence of subscribers with the publishers of the monthly *Ave Maria* and the annual *Ave Maria Koledar.* Both the printery, which is associated with St. Mary's Seminary (Lemont, IL), and the magazine are still in existence. The magazine moved its offices to Lemont in the 1920s. *Inventory available. Collection closed until 1990.*

Berlisg, John (1882-1945).
Papers, 1920-1945. Ca. 2 linear in.

Born in Skala near Slovengradec, Berlisg came to the United States in 1908 and became a coal miner in Stone City, KS, where he also organized a singing club and tamburitza band and directed plays and operettas. He organized and directed musical groups and taught music, in Utah, Kansas, and Detroit, MI, and also became part owner in a coal mine.

Papers include a short biography, photographs of Berlisg and the singing group "Svoboda," translations of two operettas, and an obituary of him. *Inventory available.*

Glas Naroda **(The People's Voice) (New York, NY).**
Records, 1953-1963. Ca. 4 linear in.

The second Slovenian American newspaper in the United States (begun in 1893 in New York), *Glas Naroda* was founded, financed, and edited by Frank Sakser. The paper later became the official organ of the South Slavonic Catholic Union.

Records include correspondence, subscriber lists, and editorial material. Also included are correspondence pertaining to Anna P. Krasna's book selling business and letters to publishing houses in Slovenia. *Inventory available.*

Golobitsch, Mary.
Papers, 1945-1963.   Ca. 1 linear in.

Golobitsch was a Slovenian immigrant to Joliet, IL, whose husband, Anton, operated a grocery store. Papers consist of letters to and from her niece, Ana Sklander, in Yugoslavia. Many of the letters describe the life of Slovenian immigrants in America.

Grand Carniolian Slovenian Catholic Union (Kranjsko-Slovenska Katoliška Jednota) (Joliet, IL).
Records, 1894-1924.   Ca. 1 linear in.

The American Slovenian Catholic Union, a fraternal insurance organization, (formerly the Grand Carniolian Slovenian Catholic Union), was founded in 1894. It has about 44,000 members in 154 locals from twenty states and is headquartered in Joliet, IL. In addition to providing insurance benefits, it grants college and religious vocation scholarships and promotes cultural activities.

Records consist of board of directors' minutes (1894-95) and a 30th anniversary publication (1924).

Grebenc, Anthony.
Papers, ca. 1904-1920.   Ca. 1 linear in.

Papers of Grebenc consist of a manuscript which is an autobiographical sketch of immigrant life on Minnesota's Iron Range. The manuscript touches on Grebenc's parents' courtship and marriage, work in the mines, school experiences, and Slovenian village disputes continued in America. *In English.*

Ivan Cankar Dramatic Society (Cleveland, Ohio).
Records, 1926-1946.   Ca. 3 linear in.

The Society was named after a famous Slovenian writer. Primarily leftist, it was active in Cleveland until about 1946.

Records consist of minutes of the Society's meetings, playbills, souvenir booklets, and a souvenir album.

Jerich, John (1894-1973).
Papers, ca. 1908-1973.   Ca. 3.5 linear ft.

Jerich edited the Slovenian American newspapers *Novi Svet* (Chicago, IL), *Baragova Pratika*, and *Amerikanski Slovenec* (various locations, including Chicago and Joliet, IL). Papers consist of correspondence, photographs, publications, newspaper clippings, enlistment records, and certificates.

Jugoslav Socialist Federation (Jugoslovanska Socialistična Zveza) (Chicago, Illinois).
Records, ca. 1905-1952.   Ca. 20 linear ft. (91 ledgers).

The Federation was established in Chicago in 1905. The founders were Slovenian, Croatian, and Serbian representatives of several independent socialist and liberal organizations. Although not all Marxist, they were unified in opposition to industrial capitalism and the intrusion of organized religion into economic and political spheres. From 1905 until 1914, the Federation was the primary political organization among South Slav immigrants, dedicated to advancing socialist causes and to enriching the cultural life of its members. From 1912 to 1917, the Federation was affiliated with the Socialist Party of America; it favored entry of the United States into World War I. In 1919 it was expelled from the Socialist Party, and most of its Serbian and Croatian members joined the Communist movement. In 1922 the Federation reaffiliated with the Socialist Party and remained so until 1940. From 1940 until it ceased to exist in 1952, it functioned as an independent socialist and cultural organization, mostly composed of

Slovenes. It published two newspapers, *Proletarec* and *Radnička Straža*, as well as an annual, *Ameriški Družinski Koledar.*

Records of the Federation include correspondence, minutes, financial records, membership lists, and other material. Also included are records of the Federation's "Prosvetna Matica" and its publications. Branch records are included for Chicago, Cleveland (OH), Clinton (IN), Waukegan (IL), Piney Forks (OH), Sheboygan (WI), and places in Kansas. *Includes Serbian and/or Croatian. Inventory available.*

Klune, Frank.
Papers, ca. 1944-1964. Ca. 1 linear in.

Klune was president of the Slovenska Narodna Podporna Jednota, Lodge No. 110 (Chisholm, MN). Papers consist of related correspondence, minutes, and other records. *Includes English.*

Kotnik, Rev. Bertrand.
Papers, 1908-1965. Ca. 1.5 linear ft.

Papers of Kotnik, a Slovenian American priest at St. Mary's Seminary (Lemont, IL) consist of correspondence, parish jubilee books, programs, and sheet music. *Includes English. Inventory available.*

Molek, Ivan (1882-1962).
Papers, ca. 1880-1965. Ca. 3.5 linear ft.

An author, journalist, lecturer, and publisher, Molek was born in Slovenia near Metlika. He came to the United States in 1900 and worked briefly in Pennsylvania steel mills and in Calumet, MI, copper mines before taking up his life's work. From 1916 to 1944, Molek worked as an editor for *Prosveta*; he then resigned in protest of its pro-Tito policy. He organized the Committee for Democratic Action with John Langerholc, Sr., and Charles Pogorelec, Sr., and was active in the Jugoslav Socialist Federation, the Jugoslav Workmen's Publishing Co., and the Slovene National Benefit Society (Lodge Francisco Ferrer, No. 131).

Papers include newspaper clippings, copies of articles and editorials, correspondence, a calendar of correspondence compiled by his wife (Mary Molek), photographs, and a manuscript. Correspondents include George Hribljan. *Mainly in English and English translations of Slovenian.*

Mother of Sorrows Church (Cleveland, Ohio).
Records, 1906-1907. 1 microfilm reel.

Mother of Sorrows was founded in 1906 as the result of a schism within the St. Vitus Church Parish. The first pastor was Rev. Kazimir Zakrajšek, O.F.M. The new parish lasted only seven months; its parishioners were reunited with the St. Vitus Parish under the guidance of Rev. Bartholomew J. Ponikvar.

Records include baptism, marriage, and death registers. Also included is the baptism register (1893-1921) for St. Vitus Church (Cleveland, OH). *Related collection: St. Vitus Church (Cleveland, OH).*

Nemanich, Anton.
Papers, 1911-1963. Ca. 1 linear in.

Nemanich, an early Slovenian immigrant, was once president of the Grand Carniolian Slovenian Catholic Union (KSKJ). Papers include correspondence, minutes, and photographs. *Includes English.*

Pogorelc, Matija (1895-1957).
Papers, ca. 1920-1957. 8 linear ft.

Pogorelc was a vendor of Slovenian religious articles and jewelry who visited numerous Slovenian communities throughout the United States. Papers consist of correspondence with Slovenian Americans, Slovenian benefit societies, and the Slovenian Catholic Union; material pertaining to the museum honoring Msgr. J. F. Buh at the College of St. Scholastica (Duluth, MN); newspaper clippings, including articles Pogorelc wrote about his travels; and business ledgers. *Includes English. Partial inventory available.*

Prebilic, Michael Joseph
(ca. 1892-1958).
Papers, ca. 1933-1953. 4 linear in.

A Slovenian immigrant, Prebilic lived
in Eveleth, MN. His papers consist of
photocopies of newspaper articles he
wrote and his autobiography. *Inventory
available.*

Prushek, Harvey.
Papers, 1934-1935. 1 linear in.

Papers of Slovenian American artist
Harvey Prushek include correspondence
and prints.

St. Lawrence Church (Cleveland, Ohio).
Records, 1902-1959. 1 microfilm reel.

St. Lawrence Church was established
in 1901 to serve Slovenians in the
Newburgh area of Cleveland who had
been members of the St. Vitus Parish.
Rev. Francis Kerze, assistant to Rev.
Vitus Hribar of St. Vitus Church, was
appointed pastor.
Records comprise marriage and death
registers. *Includes English. Related
collection: St. Vitus Church (Cleveland,
OH).*

St. Vitus Church (Cleveland, Ohio).
Records, 1893-1957. 3 microfilm reels.

St. Vitus Church was organized in
1893 by the Rev. Vitus Hribar and had a
congregation of almost 1,000 Slovenes.
By 1930, it had become, and remains, the
largest Slovenian church in America.
Records comprise baptism,
confirmation, communion, marriage, and
death registers. *Includes English.
Related collection: Mother of Sorrows
Church (Cleveland, OH); St. Lawrence
Church (Cleveland, OH).*

Sholar, Wenceslau.
Papers, 1894-1937. 1.5 linear ft.

Sholar was a Slovenian immigrant
priest. Papers consist largely of letters
written to his brother in Slovenia,
describing the early years of Slovenian

settlement in Illinois and Minnesota,
where Sholar served.

Slavic Workers' Benefit Federation
(Slovanska Delavska Podporna
Zveza) (Conemaugh, Pennsylvania).
Records, 1908-1918. 3 linear in.

A fraternal insurance organization, the
Federation was founded in 1908 in
Conemaugh, PA. It was created to meet
the insurance needs of Slavic workers in
the coal fields and iron and steel
industries in Pennsylvania and
surrounding areas. The organization
attempted to serve political as well as
economic needs of its members. It
cooperated with other Slavic
organizations, especially Jugoslovanska
Socialistična Zveza and Slovenska
Narodna Podporna Jednota; it merged
with the latter in 1918.
Records consist of minutes of meetings
of the organizational leadership.
*Inventory available. Related collection:
Slovene National Benefit Society
(Slovenska Narodna Podporna Jednota)
(Chicago, IL).*

Slovene Benefit Society "St. Barbara"
(Slovensko Podporno Društvo "Sv.
Barbara") (Forest Hills,
Pennsylvania).
Records, 1904-1917. 1 ledger.

The Society was a small benefit
society organized by coal field workers in
western and central Pennsylvania. "St.
Barbara" locals were common among
Slovenian coal miners in the early 20th
century. The Society appears to have
merged with the Slovene National Benefit
Society after 1917.
Records consist of minutes. *Inventory
available.*

Slovene National Benefit Society
(Slovenska Narodna Podporna
Jednota) (Chicago, Illinois).
Records, 1904-1952. Ca. 16 linear ft.

A fraternal and insurance organization,
the SNPJ was established in Chicago, IL,
in 1904. The organization was secular
and progressive. Originally restricted to

Slovenian men, it was open by 1912 to Slovenian women and Croats and, eventually, to all Slavic Americans. In 1912, the SNPJ organized a loose federation of Slovenian benefit societies to coordinate the activities of various organizations. The SNPJ absorbed many other Slovenian fraternal organizations, most notably the Zveza "Lilija" Wisconsin and Slovenska Delavska Podporna Zveza. It published the newspaper *Prosveta* (formerly *Glasilo-SNPJ*).

Records of the Society contain supreme board minutes; convention minutes; membership records; financial records; records of lodges 1, 3, 7, 27, 131, 148, and 658; records of benefit payments; subscription records; athletic association records; records of book sales; and investment and bond records. Individuals prominent in the collection include Frank Bostič, Vincent Cainkar, Frank Klobučar, Frank Krže, Joseph Kuhelj, Jakob Mikačič, Filip Godina, Anton Goršek, John Hočevar, Frank Hren, Frank Mladič, Blas Novak, Frank Podlipec, Martin Potokar, Justina Rom, Joseph Siskovič, William Sitter, John Vogrich, Matija Turk, Frank Somrak, Anton Terlovec, Martin Konda, Ivan Molek, Frank Vider, Frank Verderbar, Martic Skubic, John Underwood, Frank Zaitz, and Jože Zavertnik. *Inventory available. Related collections: Slovene National Benefit Society, Lodge 5 (Slovenska Narodna Podporna Jednota, Lodge 5, "Naprej") (Cleveland, OH); and Slavic Workers' Benefit Federation (Slovanska Delavska Podporna Zveza) (Conemaugh, PA).*

Slovene National Benefit Society, Lodge 5 (Slovenska Narodna Podporna Jednota, Lodge 5 "Naprej") (Cleveland, Ohio).
Records, 1904-1923. 1 microfilm reel.

Lodge 5 is a branch of the national Slovenian American fraternal insurance and benefit society. Records consist of a minute book. *Originals held by John Krebel, Cleveland, OH. Related collections: Slovene National Benefit Society (Slovenska Narodna Podporna Jednota) (Chicago, IL); and Slavic Workers' Benefit Federation (Slovanska*

Delavska Podporna Zveza) (Conemaugh, PA).

Slovenian Library (Ely, Minnesota).
Records, 1915-1917. 1 linear in.

Photocopies of the Library records consist of board of directors' meeting minutes.

Slovenian Orphanage and Sanitarium (Slovenska Sirotišnica in Sanitarij) (Chicago, Illinois).
Records, 1912-1913. 1 ledger.

Records consist of minutes documenting the temporary alliance of many Slovenian American organizations to raise money to build an orphanage and/or hospital to serve Slovenian immigrants. *Inventory available.*

Slovenian Progressive Benefit Society (Slovenska Svobodomiselna Podporna Zveza) (Chicago, Illinois).
Records, 1909-1941. Ca. 11 linear ft.

A mutual benefit society, the SSPZ was founded in 1909 as successor to the Slovenska Narodna Podporna Zveza. It was primarily the creation of Martin Konda, a Slovenian editor and publisher of *Glas Svobode*. Konda also played an important role in creation of Slovenska Narodna Podporna Jednota (Slovene National Benefit Society, the SNPJ) and the Jugoslav Socialist Federation. Konda came into conflict with Slovenian socialists between 1905 and 1908, was expelled from the Socialist Party of the U.S.A., and founded the SSPZ to aid Slovenian immigrants. In 1941, the SSPZ merged with the SNPJ.

Records of the SSPZ consist of minutes, financial records, secretary's books, records of the Juvenile Department, records of the investment committee, and records of Lodge 47. Also included is material of or pertaining to Joseph Benko, Anton Duller, Dr. J. Dvorsky, Matthew Gaishek, Joseph Ivansek, John Kalan, Martin Konda, Joseph Matko, Joseph Wershay, Jacob Zajec, Ludwig Mayer, Anton Mladič, Louis Skubic, Carl Stover, *Glas Svobode*, the Northern Trust Company of Chicago (IL), the Second Ward Saving Bank of Milwaukee (WI), and Slovenska Narodna Podporna Jednota. *Includes some English. Inventory available.*

Šv. Lovrenc and Šmihel Churches (Dolenjsko, Slovenia).
Records, 1905-1950. 1 microfilm reel.

Church records consist of parish chronicles and a survey of emigrants from the Šmihel parish.

Yugoslav Republican Alliance (Jugoslovansko Republičansko Združenje) (Chicago, Illinois).
Records, 1922-1949. 3 linear in.

The Alliance, successor to Slovensko Republičansko Združenje (SRZ), was created in 1918 in Chicago, IL. The JRZ included Serbs and Croats in its membership. In the early years (1918-1922), the organization was dominated by Etbin Kristan and John and Frank Petrič. After 1922, Charles Pogorelec, Frank Zaitz (or Zajc) and Filip Godina played major roles in its policy formulation. The JRZ advocated the creation of a democratic, federated republic (Yugoslavia). Between the World Wars, the organization supported the social democratic opposition in Yugoslavia; during World War II and after, it supported the Partisan movement. As a result of the Yugoslav-Soviet split

of 1948 and anticommunist sentiment in the United States at that time, the JRZ ceased to function.

Records include correspondence, especially with Ljudska Tiskarna; financial records; and other internal records of the Alliance. *Inventory available.*

Yugoslav (Slovenian) Radio Hour (Milwaukee, Wisconsin).
Scripts, ca. 1942-1953. Ca. 7 linear in.

The Radio Hour collection consists of scripts used for the program. *Includes English.*

Zaplotnik, Rev. John L.
Papers, n.d. 5 linear ft.

A Catholic priest and missionary among Slovenian Americans, Rev. Zaplotnik came to the United States in 1902. He received a Doctor of Canon Law degree at Catholic University in Washington, DC. He wrote biographies of Slovenian priests in the United States and a biography of the missionary Janez Čebul, as well as a book on canon law. Rev. Zaplotnik was also founder, in 1917, of the SS. Peter and Paul Parish in Omaha, NE.

Papers comprise his personal library and maps, reflecting his missionary work among Slovenian Americans. Rev. Zaplotnik used the material in his own research and writings. *Includes English.*

Monographs

The Slovenian American experience on the whole is well represented in the ca. 450 books and pamphlets maintained by the IHRC. The strengths of this collection are revealed in the volume *Slovenes in the United States and Canada: A Bibliography* by Joseph Dwyer (1981), based largely on the holdings of this repository. Particularly abundant are works dealing with the history of regional settlements, religion, literature and arts, organizational activity, the Slovenian homeland, and Slovenian American individuals.

A comprehensive scholarly synthesis of Slovenian immigration to the United States has yet to be written. However, useful secondary works of a general nature do exist. The IHRC, for example, holds Marie Prisland's *From Slovenia--to America; Recollections and Collections* (1968), Giles Edward Gobetz's *Adjustment and Assimilation of Slovenian Refugees* (reprint 1962), Gobetz's *Slovenian Heritage, Volume I* (1981), and Joseph Zavertnik's *Ameriški Slovenci, pregled splošne zgodovine Združenih Držav, slovenskega naseljevanja in naselbin in Slovenske narodne podporne jednote* (American Slovenes,

Review of the General History of the United States, Slovenian Immigration and Settlements, and the Slovene National Benefit Society, 1925). Some of the most important writing on Slovenian American history is contained in studies on Yugoslavian or South Slavic immigration more broadly (see below). The collection's coverage of Slovenes in various regions largely coincides geographically with the general pattern of settlement of these immigrants. Areas best represented include Illinois (*Zgodovina slovenske naselbine Waukegan-North Chicago, Illinois, 1893-1952* [History of the Slovenian Settlement of Waukegan-North Chicago, Illinois], 1953), New York (John A. Arnez's *Slovenci v New Yorku* [Slovenes in New York], 1966), and Ohio (G. E. Gobetz's *Slovenian Americans in Greater Cleveland, Ohio; Their Settlement, Adjustment, Integration and Contributions*, 1972). Researchers can also find articles on Slovenes throughout the United States in periodicals such as *Ameriški Družinski Koledar* (Almanac of American Families) and *Slovenski Izseljenski Koledar* (Almanac of Slovenian Emigrants) and should consult the above-mentioned Dwyer bibliography for specific citations.

Publications dealing with religion are highlighted by several items chronicling the life and work of Bishop Frederik Baraga, the pioneer missionary of this immigrant group. Among these are Chrysostom Verwyst's *Life and Labors of Rt. Rev. Frederic Baraga, First Bishop of Marquette, Mich.; To Which Are Added Short Sketches of the Lives and Labors of Other Indian Missionaries of the Northwest* (1900), Franc Jaklič's *Misijonski škof Irenej Friderik Baraga* (Missionary Bishop Rev. Frederick Baraga, 1931), Maksimilijan Jezernik's *Frederick Baraga; A Portrait of the First Bishop of Marquette, Based on the Archives of the Congregatio de Propaganda Fide* (1968), and Leon Vončina's *Friderik Baraga, prvi slovenski apostolski misijonar in škof med Indijani v Ameriki* (Frederick Baraga, the First Slovenian Apostolic Missionary and Bishop among the Indians in America, 1896). Baraga's own writings are represented by *Slate jabelka* (1844) and two prayer books published posthumously. Also included are works relating to other early missionaries, including Joseph Buh and Francis X. Pierz (see Dwyer bibliography). Numerous prayer books, hymnals, and jubilee albums of individual churches in Cleveland, OH; Joliet, IL; Willard, WI; Johnstown, PA; Calumet, MI; and other locations are available as well.

The IHRC holds literary works of several Slovenian American authors. Most prominently represented is Louis Adamic, whose writings include *The Eagle and the Roots* (1952), *Cradle of Life; The Story of One Man's Beginnings* (1936), and *Grandsons; A Story of American Lives* (1935). Among the other authors, poets, and playwrights whose publications can be consulted are Janez Cigler, Joseph Grdina, Ivan Jontez, Etbin Kristan, Karel Mauser, Ivan Molek, Joseph Spillman, and Ivan Zorman. Gobetz's *Anthology of Slovenian American Literature*, published in 1977, furnishes a helpful, selective overview of the creative writing output of this ethnic group. Slovenian arts and music are described in works such as Gizella Hozian's *Spomini mladosti* (Memories of Youth, 1961), Albina Novak's *American and Slovenian Folk Songs* (1965), and the Lok Gallery's *Contemporary Slovenian Art Abroad* (1964).

The IHRC maintains a good collection of publications by and about Slovenian immigrant organizations, including fraternals, cultural institutions, cooperatives, political groups, Slovenian "homes," and publishing agencies. Some examples of these include anniversary albums, convention programs, and constitution and bylaws pamphlets of the Grand Carniolian Slovenian Catholic Union, the Slovene National Benefit Society, and the Slovenian Women's Union of America; jubilee/memorial publications of the Slovenian Co-operative Stores Company of Cleveland; *Socialistična knjižnica: zbirka poljudnih socialističnih spisov za slovenske delavce v Ameriki* (Socialist Library: A Collection of Popular Socialist Writings for Slovenian Workers in America, 1912) published by the Jugoslav Socialist Federation; souvenir books of the Slovenian National Home, Cleveland, and the Slovene Rest Home Association, Fontana, California; and a publication celebrating the fiftieth anniversary of the newspaper *Amerikanski Slovenec* (American Slovene, Cleveland, OH) as well as bibliographic works on Slovenian periodicals by Jože Bajec.

The recent publication of *Ameriški Slovenci in NOB v Jugoslaviji* (American Slovenes and the National Liberation War, 1987) by Matjaž Klemenčič constitutes a key addition to the large number of works dealing with Slovenian American relations with and perspectives on the Slovenian homeland. Several of these, such as Adamic's *Liberation, Death to Fascism! Liberty to the People! Picture Story of the Yugoslav People's Epic Struggle Against the Enemy--To Win Unity and a Decent Future, 1941-1945* (1945) and the United Committee of South Slavic Americans pamphlets, *The Yugoslav Peoples Fight to Live* (1944) and *Yugoslavia's New Constitution: A Study in 20th Century Democracy* (1946), are actually primary accounts rather than secondary studies (see IHRC's Yugoslav section). Other publications that fall in this category include *Shall Slovenia Be Sovietized? A Rebuttal to Louis Adamic; Gathered and Translated from the Pages of the Slovenian Daily, "Ameriška domovina"* (1944) and *The Slovenes and the Partisans; Slovenci in Partizani* (1944), both by the Union of Slovenian Parishes of America; and Niko Zupanič's *Slovenija vstani! Ameriškim Slovencem; govor ki ga ja imel Nikel Niko Zupanič pred Slovenci v Clevelandu 28, apr. 1916* (Slovenes Rebel! American Slovenes; Speech by Nikel Niko Zupanič before Slovenes in Cleveland, 1916).

Prominent Slovenian Americans (many of them mentioned above) are represented in materials written both by and about them. Some of Louis Adamic's works have already been identified. Others include *A Nation of Nations* (1945), *Laughing in the Jungle* (1932, reprint 1969), *From Many Lands* (1940), and *The Native's Return; An American Immigrant Visits Yugoslavia and Discovers His Old Country* (1934). Journalist Ivan Molek, among other publications, authored *Slovene Immigrant History, 1900-1950: Autobiographical Sketches* (translated, annotated, and published by his wife, Mary, 1979). In addition, autobiographical or biographical volumes are available on Ohio politician Frank Lausche and musicians Anton Schubel and Frank Yankovic. The book *Footsteps Through Time* by Irene M. Planinsek-Odorizzi, published in 1978, is a useful collection of memoirs of several less well-known Slovenian individuals.

Researchers interested in this ethnic group are encouraged to consult also the small collection of books (ca. eighty volumes) shelved and classified as "Yugoslav." Included here are works dealing with more than one of the South Slavic nationality groups. Predominant among these are secondary studies (many of them key publications) such as *Americans from Yugoslavia*, by Gerald G. Govorchin; *South Slavic Immigration in America*, by George Prpic; *Yugoslav Migrations to America*, by Branko Colakovic; *The Yugoslavs in America: 1880-1918*, by L. Blaisdell; and several studies by Adam Eterovich and others on Yugoslavs in particular states or regions. Also included in this section are books and pamphlets concerning the formation of the Yugoslavian nation, primarily written from the perspective of Yugoslav immigrants, and published in many cases by the United Committee of South Slavic Americans.

Newspapers

Amerikanski Slovenec (American Slovenian), Cleveland, OH. Weekly: 1963-date. Includes English.

Amerikanski Slovenec (American Slovenian; title varies: Amerikanski Slovenec-Edinost), Chicago, IL; Tower, MN; Joliet, IL; and Cleveland, OH. Frequency varies. (Microfilm: 1891-1946).

Ameriška Domovina (American Home; title varies: Nova Domovina; Clevelandska Amerika) Cleveland, OH. Frequency varies: 1963-date. (Microfilm: 1907-1962). Includes English.

Bodočnost (The Future), Milwaukee, WI. Weekly. (Microfilm: 1913).

Clevelandska Amerika (Cleveland's America), Cleveland, OH. Semi-weekly. (Microfilm: 1909, 1914).

Coloradske Novice (Colorado News), Pueblo, CO. Weekly. (Microfilm: 1905).

Coloradsko Solnce (Colorado Sun), Denver, CO. Weekly. (Microfilm: 1908).

Delavec (Worker), Detroit, MI (previously published in Chicago, IL, and Milwaukee, WI). Weekly. (Microfilm: 1926-1928).

Delavska Slovenija (Workingmen's Slovenia), Milwaukee, WI. Weekly. (Microfilm: 1922, 1925-1926).

Edinost (Unity; title changes to **Amerikanski Slovenec** in 1925), Chicago, IL. Frequency varies. (Microfilm: 1919-1925).

Edinost (Unity), Pittsburgh, PA. Weekly. (Microfilm: 1911).

Edinost (Unity), Toronto, Ontario, Canada. Semi-monthly. (Microfilm: 1942).

Enakopravnost (Equality), Cleveland, OH. Daily: 1922, 1948-1953. (Microfilm: 1919, 1940-1943, 1949, 1955-1956). Includes some English.

Glas Naroda (The People's Voice), New York, NY. Three times a week: 1933, 1948, 1950-1954. (Microfilm: 1893-1903, 1912, 1915-1917, 1919-1921, 1943, 1946, 1950).

Glas Svobode (The Voice of Liberty), Chicago, IL. Weekly. (Microfilm: 1907-1908, 1910-1911, 1918, 1922).

Glas Svobode (The Voice of Liberty), Pueblo, CO. Weekly. (Microfilm: 1902-1907).

Glasilo K.S.K. Jednote (The Voice of K.S.K. Union), Chicago, IL. Weekly. (Microfilm: 1915-1945).

Glasilo SNPJ (The Voice of SNPJ; organ of the Slovene National Benefit Society, superseded by **Prosveta**), Chicago, IL. Monthly, weekly. (Microfilm: 1908, 1910-1915).

Glasnik (The Herald; previously titled **Glasnik od Gorenjega Jezera**), Calumet, MI. Weekly. (Microfilm: 1901-1906, 1908, 1911, 1913-1915).

Gospodarstvo (Economy), Buenos Aires, Argentina. Monthly. (Microfilm: 1926).

Izseljenec (Emigrant), São Paulo, Brazil. (Microfilm: 1930).

Jugoslovenski Gospodar (Yugoslav Proprietor), Chicago, IL. Semi-monthly. (Microfilm: 1907).

Jugoslovenski Obzor (Jugoslav Observer), Milwaukee, WI. Weekly. (Microfilm: 1929, 1938).

Komar (Mosquito), New York, NY. Semi-monthly: 1906-1907.

Mir (Peace), Pueblo, CO. Weekly. (Microfilm: 1901-1903).

Moskito (Mosquito), Cleveland, OH. Weekly. (Microfilm: 1902).

Napredek (Progress), Cleveland, OH. Weekly. (Microfilm: 1936-1938, 1940-1941). Includes English.

Naprej (Forward), Pittsburgh, PA. Semi-monthly. (Microfilm: 1935, 1937-1941).

Narod (The People), Pittsburgh, PA. Weekly. (Microfilm: 1921).

Narodna Beseda (National Word), Cleveland, OH. Monthly. (Microfilm: 1899).

Narodni Vestnik (National Herald), Duluth, MN. Weekly. (Microfilm: 1911-1914, 1917).

Naš Dom (Our Home), New York, NY. Weekly. (Microfilm: 1924, 1927).

Two scenes from the funeral procession for the victims of the mine disaster at Cherry, IL, 1910.

Naš Glas (Our Voice), Montevideo, Uruguay. Monthly. (Microfilm: 1932).

New Era (previously Nova Doba), Cleveland, OH. Bi-weekly: 1936, 1938, 1944-1945, 1947-1953, 1963-1979. (Microfilm: 1938, 1940, 1945). Includes English.

Nova Domovina (New Homeland), Cleveland, OH. Weekly, semi-weekly, daily. (Microfilm: 1901-1902, 1906).

Novi List (New Gazette), Buenos Aires, Argentina. Weekly. (Microfilm: 1933).

Nuova Domovina (New Homeland), Buenos Aires, Argentina. Semi-monthly. (Microfilm: 1952).

Our Voice, Cleveland, OH. Semi-monthly: 1969-1983. Includes English.

Proletarec (The Proletarian), Chicago, IL. Weekly (monthly). (Microfilm: 1906-1918, 1929-1952). Includes English.

Prosveta (The Enlightenment), Chicago, IL. Daily (except Saturday, Sunday, and holidays): 1968-date. (Microfilm: 1916-1967). Includes English.

Pueblske Novice (Pueblo News), Pueblo, CO. Monthly. (Microfilm: 1916). Includes English.

Resnica (The Truth), Houghton, MI. Irregular. (Microfilm: 1914).

Ricinovo Olje (Medicinal Oil), Buenos Aires, Argentina. Bi-weekly. (Microfilm: 1930).

Šlebodni Orel (Free Eagle), New York, NY. Weekly: 1902.

Sloga (Unity), Cleveland, OH. Weekly. (Microfilm: 1915, 1919).

Slovan (The Slav), Pueblo, CO. Monthly. (Microfilm: 1915).

Slovenija (Slovenia), Milwaukee, WI. Weekly. (Microfilm: 1915-1916, 1919, 1921).

Slovenska Država (Slovenian State), Toronto, Ontario, Canada. Monthly: 1950-1964.

Slovenske Novice (Slovenian News; successor to Glasnik), Calumet, MI. Weekly. (Microfilm: 1916, 1919).

Slovenski Dom (Slovenian Home), Buenos Aires, Argentina. Weekly. (Microfilm: 1932).

Slovenski Glas (Slovenian Voice), Buenos Aires, Argentina. Bi-weekly. (Microfilm: 1946). Includes Spanish.

Slovenski List; Slovenska Krajina Priloga (Slovenian Gazette), Buenos Aires, Argentina. Weekly. (Microfilm: 1937).

Slovenski Narod (The Slovenian People; title varies: Slovenski Narod v Ameriki), New York, NY (previously published in Pueblo, CO). Daily (weekly, semi-weekly). (Microfilm: 1908-1909, 1912, 1915-1917).

Slovenski Svet (Slovenian World), Washington, DC. Weekly. (Microfilm: 1917).

Slovenski Tednik (Slovenian Weekly), Buenos Aires, Argentina. Weekly. (Microfilm: 1930).

Slovensko-Hrvatske Novine (Slovenian-Croatian News), Calumet, MI. Weekly. (Microfilm: 1930). Includes English.

Svoboda (Liberty), Chicago, IL. Weekly. (Microfilm: 1930, 1935). Includes English.

Svobodna Slovenija (Free Slovenia), Buenos Aires, Argentina. Weekly: 1964-date.

Vestnik (The Herald; title varies: **Vestnik in Naš Dom**), Milwaukee, WI. Weekly. (Microfilm: 1925, 1928).

Zarja (The Dawn), Ljubljana, Yugoslavia. Daily, semi-monthly. (Microfilm: 1912, 1914).

Zora (The Dawn), Chicago, IL. Weekly. (Microfilm: 1901).

Yugoslav

Jugoslavenski Glasnik (Yugoslav Herald), Chicago, IL/Calumet, MI/New York, NY. Weekly: 1938-1945. Serbian and/or Croatian.

Jugoslovenski Obzor (Yugoslav Observer), Milwaukee, WI. Semi-monthly: 1933-1945. Slovenian.

Serials

Akademik (Academic), St. Louis, MO. Frequency varies: 1952-1954; special supplement with no date.

American Fraternal Union Constitution and By-Laws (Ameriška Bratska Zveza; prior to 1940 called South Slavonic Catholic Union of America), Ely, MN. Irregular: 1924, 1936, 1941. Includes English.

Ameriški Družinski Koledar (American Family Calendar), Chicago, IL. Annual: 1915-1950.

Angelček (Little Angel), Chicago, IL. Monthly: 1921-1923. Includes English.

Ave Maria (Hail Mary), Lemont, IL (previously published in New York, NY). Monthly: 1910-date.

Ave Maria Koledar (Ave Maria Calendar), Lemont, IL (previously published in New York, NY, and Chicago, IL). Annual: 1913-1983.

Baragov Vestnik (Baraga's Herald), Buenos Aires, Argentina. Quarterly: 1963-1666 (?).

Baragova Pratika (Baraga's Practice), Berwyn, IL. Annual: 1942-1959.

Božja Beseda (The Word of God), Toronto, Ontario, Canada. Monthly: 1954-1962.

Bratstvo (Fraternity), Calumet, MI. Frequency varies. (Microfilm: 1926).

Brazda (Furrow), Chicago, IL. Monthly: 1954.

Cankarjev Glasnik (Cankar's Herald), Cleveland, OH. Monthly: 1937-1942.

Čas (Time; title changed to **Novi Čas** in 1928), Cleveland, OH. Monthly: 1915-1928.

Čuk na Pal'ci (Owlet on a Stick), Buenos Aires, Argentina. Bi-weekly. (Microfilm: 1930).

Delavski Koledar (Workers' Calendar), Milwaukee, WI. Annual: 1925-1926.

Dom in Svet (Home and World), Chicago, IL. Monthly. (Microfilm: 1929).

Domoljub; Vestnik Slovenske Ljudske Stranke (Patriot; The Herald of the Slovenian Popular Party), Washington, DC. Irregular: 1956-1957.

Domovina; Glasilo Slovenske Demokratske Stranke (Homeland; Organ of the Slovenian Democratic Party), Napa, CA. Quarterly (?): 1951-1952.

Družinski Koledar (Family Calendar), Ljubljana, Yugoslavia. Annual: 1913.

Glasilo Slovenske Narodne Podporne Jednote (Organ of the Slovene National Benefit Society), Chicago, IL. Monthly: 1908.

Glasnik Presvetega Srca Jezusovega (Herald of the Sacred Heart of Jesus), Chicago, IL. Monthly: 1920-1922.

Goriška Matica Koledar (Gorica Organization Calendar), Gorizia, Yugoslavia. Annual: 1924.

Grand Carniolian Slovenian Catholic Union of the United States of America, Amendments and Supplements to the Constitution and By-Laws, Joliet, IL. Every three-four years: 1942.

Grand Carniolian Slovenian Catholic Union of the United States of America Constitution and By-Laws, Cleveland, OH. Every four years (bi-annual): 1894, 1905, 1907, 1909, 1911, 1926, 1930, 1934, 1938. Includes English.

Grand Carniolian Slovenian Catholic Union of the United States of America Proceedings of the Regular Convention, Joliet, IL. Bi-annual: 1911, 1914, 1926, 1930, 1934, 1938.

Grand Carniolian Slovenian Catholic Union of the United States of America, Zapisnik Sej Glavnega Odbora K.S.K. Jednote (Minutes of the National Board Meeting of the Society), Joliet, IL. Every four years: 1924-1926.

Hail Mary, Joliet, IL. Monthly: 1950. English.

Iskra Buletin Slovenskih Delavcev (Spark Bulletin of the Slovenian Workers), Cleveland, OH. Monthly: 1935.

The Jugo-Slav Review (supersedes The Slovenian Review), Chicago, IL. Monthly: 1917-1919. Includes Croatian and English.

Jugoslovansko Republičansko Združenje (Yugoslav Republican Society), Chicago, IL. 1919.

Jugoslav Socialist Federation of America Constitution and By-Laws, Chicago, IL. Irregular: 1912, 1916, 1919, 1924, 1935. Includes English.

Klub Krog (Club Krog), Cleveland, OH. Quarterly (?): 1951.

Koledar Amerikanskega Sloveneca (Calendar of American Slovenian), Tower, MN. Annual: 1898-1900.

Koledar Družbe Sv. Cirila in Metoda (Calendar of the Society of SS. Cyril and Methodius), Ljubljana, Yugoslavia. Annual: 1913.

Koledar Družbe Sv. Mohorja (Calendar of the Society of St. Mohor), Celovec, Yugoslavia (previously published in Celje and Prevalje, Yugoslavia). Annual: 1896-1902, 1904-1917, 1919-1921, 1923-1941, 1947-1968.

Koledar Prešernove Knjižnice (Calendar of the Prešern Library), Ljubljana, Yugoslavia. Annual: 1951.

Konzument (The Consumer), Maribor, Yugoslavia. Monthly. (Microfilm: 1929).

Koprive (Nettles), Cleveland, OH. Monthly: 1950-1952.

Legija Imene Mariji v Fari Sv. Vida (The Legion of Mary's Name in Fara St. Vitus), Cleveland, OH. Frequency varies: 1962.

Letopis Matice Slovenske (The Annual of the Slovenian Matica), Ljubljana, Yugoslavia. Annual: 1872-1874, 1878, 1880-1881, 1884-1887, 1889-1907, 1910-1912.

Majski Glas (The May Herald), Chicago, IL. Annual: 1933-1945.

Mali Ave Maria (Little Ave Maria), New York, NY. Monthly: 1917.

Med Prijatelji (Among Friends), Cleveland, OH. Frequency varies: 1961.

Minnesotski Zvon (The Minnesota Chimes), Chicago, IL. Monthly: 1951-1954.

Misijonski Koledar (Missionary Calendar), Groblje, Yugoslavia. Annual: 1937.

Misijonski Zbornik (Missionary Register), Buenos Aires, Argentina. Annual: 1953.

Nada (Hope), Chicago, IL. Monthly. (Microfilm: 1905).

Naš Dom (Our Home), Buenos Aires, Argentina. Monthly: 1941.

Naš Gospodar (Our Proprietor), Chicago, IL. Monthly: 1912. (Microfilm: 1912-1913).

Naša Luč (Our Light; Society of St. Mohor), Celovec, Yugoslavia. Bi-monthly: 1952.

Naša Vez (Our Bond), Toronto, Ontario, Canada. Monthly: 1949-1950, 1952.

Niiwa, Buenos Aires, Argentina. Monthly (?). (Microfilm: 1937).

Nova Doba (New Era), Pittsburgh, PA. Monthly. (Microfilm: 1914).

Novi Amerikanec (New American), New York, NY. Monthly: 1949.

Novi Čas (New Time; previously titled Čas), Cleveland, OH. Monthly: 1915-1928.

Novi Svet (New World Herald), Chicago, IL. Monthly: 1938-1958, 1960-1965. Includes English.

Odmevi (Echoes; previously titled Odmevi z Osme and Odmevi Glasilo Društva Sava), New York, NY. Monthly: 1964-1965, 1968-1970, 1972-1974. Includes English.

Omnes Unum, Buenos Aires, Argentina. Bi-monthly: 1954-1960.

Our Lady of the Miraculous Medal Church Financial Report, Toronto, Ontario, Canada. 1962.

Ozare (Beautiful Fields), Cleveland, OH. Bi-monthly: 1957-1959.

Pomoč (Help), Pueblo, CO. Monthly. (Microfilm: 1929-1931).

Proletarec; Slovensko Glasilo Jugoslovenske Socialistčke Zveze (The Proletarian; The Slovenian Organ of the Yugoslav Socialist Alliance), Chicago, IL. Weekly: 1918-1929.

Prvi Majnik (May Day), Ljubljana, Yugoslavia. Annual (?): 1909.

Razgovori in Razgledi; List Študijskega Krožka za Slovensko Kulturo (Talks and Opinion; Newsletter of the Study Circle for Slovenian Culture), Willowdale, Ontario, Canada. Quarterly (?): 1955-1957.

Resnica (Truth; Slovenian Lodges of St. Mohor, Holy Cross, Danica, and Slovenian Men's Association), Chicago, IL. Monthly: 1949.

Rodna Gruda (Homeland), Ljubljana, Yugoslavia. Monthly: 1954-1972, 1983-date. Includes English.

St. Ciril's Slovenian Catholic Church Annual Report, New York, NY. Annual: 1963.

St. George's Slovenian Roman Catholic Church Annual Report, Chicago, IL (?). Annual: 1960. English.

St. John the Evangelist Parish Financial Statement, Milwaukee, WI. Annual: 1959. English.

St. Lawrence's Slovenian Catholic Church Annual Report, Cleveland, OH. Annual: 1938, 1940, 1945, 1949. Includes English.

St. Mary's Slovenian Catholic Church Annual Church, Cleveland, OH. Annual: 1948-1949. English.

St. Stephen's Chimes, Chicago, IL. Weekly: 1956-1958, 1965. English.

St. Stephen's Slovenian Catholic Church Annual Financial Report, Chicago, IL. Annual: 1938, 1951, 1953, 1959. Includes English.

St. Stephen's Slovenian Catholic Church Parish Roster, Chicago, IL. Annual: 1956, 1958. English.

St. Stephen's Slovenian Catholic School Alumni Bulletin, Chicago, IL. Frequency varies: 1964. English.

St. Thaddeus Slovenian Catholic Church, Joliet, IL. Weekly: 1964. English.

St. Therese's Slovenian Catholic Church Annual Report, Johnstown, PA. Annual: 1934. Includes English.

St. Vitus' Slovenian Catholic Church Financial Report And Envelope Account, Cleveland, OH. Frequency varies: 1944. Includes English.

St. Vitus' Slovenian Catholic Church Annual Report, Cleveland, OH. Annual: 1948. Includes English.

Sts. Cyril and Methodius' Slovenian Catholic Church Yearbook, Rock Springs, WY. Annual: 1931, 1934. English.

Sij Slovenske Svobode; Alba de la Libertad Eslovenia (The Glow of Slovenian Liberty), Buenos Aires, Argentina. Monthly: 1972, 1974-1976.

Sloga (Harmony; Sloga Fraternal Life Insurance Society; earlier issues titled Sloga; Official Lodge News, South Slavic Benevolent Union Sloga), Milwaukee, WI. Bi-monthly: 1942, 1951, 1963-1965, 1969-date. Includes English.

Slomškov List (Slomšk Gazette), Rome, Italy. Tri-annual: 1964-1966.

Slovene Diary (previously titled Dnevnik Diary), Toronto, Ontario, Canada. Monthly: 1976-1979.

Slovene National Benefit Society Constitution and By-Laws, Chicago, IL. Irregular: 1907(?), 1933, 1937, 1942, 1951, 1959-1962. Includes English.

Slovene National Benefit Society Proceedings of the Regular Convention, Chicago, IL. Every four years: 1925, 1929, 1933, 1937, 1941, 1946, 1950, 1954, 1958. Includes English.

Slovene National Benefit Society Reports of the Supreme Officers to the Regular Convention, Chicago, IL. Every four years (?): 1925, 1929, 1933, 1950. Includes English.

Slovene National Benefit Society Roster of Lodges, Federations, Juvenile Circles and Juvenile Directors, Chicago, IL. Annual: 1939-1941, 1943, 1949-1952. English.

Slovene Studies Journal (continuation of Papers in Slovene Studies and Society for Slovene Studies Newsletter), New York, NY. Semi-annual: 1979-1982. English.

Slovenian Research Center of America Newsletter, Wickliffe, OH. Quarterly: 1974-1975. English.

The Slovenian Review (Slovenian Republican Alliance), Chicago, IL. Monthly: 1917-1919. English.

Slovenian Women's Union of America Constitution, By-Laws and Regulations, Chicago, IL. 1939. Includes English.

Slovenska Narodna Zveza (Slovenian National Unity), Chicago, IL. Frequency varies: 1952-1954.

Slovenska Beseda (Slovenian Word), Buenos Aires, Argentina. Monthly: 1949-1958.

Slovenska Družina (The Slovenian Family), Cleveland, OH (previously published in Calumet, MI). Monthly: 1918-1919.

Slovenska Knjiga u Domovini in Tujini (Slovenian Book at Home and Abroad), Cleveland, OH. Frequency varies: 1952-1957.

Slovenska Pisarna (Slovenian Writing), Cleveland, OH. Frequency varies: 1956.

Slovenska Pot (Slovenian Path), Buenos Aires, Argentina. Frequency varies: 1954-1955.

Slovenska Pravica (The Slovenian Justice), Chicago, IL (previously published in Barberton, OH). Monthly: 1949-1950.

Slovenski Gladiator (Slovenian Gladiator), Milwaukee, WI. Monthly. (Microfilm: 1927-1928).

Slovenski Ilustrovani List (Slovenian Illustrated Gazette), New York, NY. Monthly. (Microfilm: 1913).

Slovenski Koledar (Slovenian Calendar; previously titled Slovenski Izseljenski Koledar), Ljubljana, Yugoslavia. Annual: 1954-1961, 1963-date.

Slovenski Visokošolski Zbornik (Slovenian High School Register), place of publication varies. Annual: 1956-1960.

Slovensko-Amerikanski Koledar (Slovenian-American Calendar; title varies: Amerikansko-Slovenski Koledar), New York, NY. Annual: 1895-1935, 1937-1941.

Smer v Slovensko Državo (The Direction into the Slovenian State), Buenos Aires, Argentina. Frequency varies: 1966. Includes Spanish.

Socialistična Zarja (Socialist Dawn), Cleveland, OH. Monthly. (Microfilm: 1922).

Society for Slovene Studies Letter, New York, NY. Irregular: 1979-1980. English.

Society for Slovene Studies Newsletter, New York, NY. Semi-annual: 1973-1978. English.

Stvarnost; Neodvisna Slovenska Revija (Reality; Independent Slovenian Review), Trieste, Italy. 1950-1951.

Svetovna Vojna (The World's War), New York, NY. Monthly (?). (Microfilm: 1914).

Svoboda (Liberty; Jugoslav Cultural Society), Berwyn, IL (previously published in Chicago, IL). Monthly: 1930, 1934.

Svoboda; Marksistični Mesečnik (Liberty; The Marxist Monthly), Ljubljana, Yugoslavia/Chicago, IL. Monthly: 1929-1935.

Svobodna Misel (The Free Thought), Prague-Vinograd, Czechoslovakia. Monthly: 1908-1912.

Tertiary Thoughts (Franciscan Fathers of the Commissariat of the Holy Cross), Lemont, IL. Monthly: 1953-1957. Includes English.

V Novo Bodočnost (Into the New Future; St. Mary's Seminary), Lemont, IL. Frequency varies: 1950. Includes English.

Vestnik (The Chronicle), New York, NY. Semi-monthly. (Microfilm: 1909).

Vestnik (The Herald), Pueblo, CO. Semi-monthly. (Microfilm: 1932). Includes English.

Vestnik "SAVE" (Herald, Slovenian Academic Society in America), Toronto, Ontario, Canada. Bi-monthly: 1959-1963.

Voice of Youth (previously titled **Mladinski List**; Slovene National Benefit Society Youth), Burr Ridge/Chicago, IL. Monthly: 1922, 1932, 1936-1944, 1946-1948, 1950, 1959-1961, 1967-1975. (Microfilm: 1924-1980). English.

Zarja (The Dawn), Chicago, IL. Monthly: 1929-date. Includes English.

Zbornik Občine Grosuplje (The Register of the Municipality of Grosuplje), Grosuplje, Yugoslavia. Annual: 1982, 1984, 1986.

Zbornik Svobodne Slovenije (The Register of Free Slovenia; title varies: **Koledar Svobodna Slovenija; Zbornik Koledar Svobodne Slovenije**) Buenos Aires, Argentina. Annual: 1950-1953, 1955-1969, 1971-1975.

Zgodnja Danica (Early Morning Star), Ljubljana, Yugoslavia. Weekly: 1849-1850, 1855-1857, 1860-1877, 1895-1898, 1901-1903.

Življenje in Svet (Life and World), Ljubljana, Yugoslavia. Monthly: 1928.

Zveze Bivših Slovenskih Protikomunističnih Borcev Vestnik (Alliances of the Former Anticommunist Fighters Newsletter), Buenos Aires, Argentina. Monthly: 1957-1960.

Yugoslav

Balkan and Eastern European American Genealogical and Historical Society, San Francisco, CA. Frequency varies: 1964-1966. English.

The Florida State University Center for Yugoslav-American Studies Proceedings and Reports (previously titled **The Florida State University Slavic Papers**), Tallahassee, FL. Annual: 1972-1977. English.

The Florida State University Joint Yugoslav-American Advisory Council Proceedings and Reports, Tallahassee, FL. Annual: 1978-1979. English.

Jugoslav Review, New York. Monthly. (Microfilm: 1923). Serbian and/or Croatian, Slovenian.

Jugoslaven (The Yugoslav), Västerås, Sweden. Quarterly: 1979. Croatian and English.

Jugoslavia Kalendar (Yugoslavia Calendar), Chicago, IL. Annual: 1939. Slovenian and English.

Kolo, New York, NY. Monthly: 1924. Slovenian.

Medunardoni Problemi (International Problems), Belgrade, Yugoslavia. Quarterly: 1982. Serbian and/or Croatian.

Naš Kalendar (Our Calendar), Toronto, Ontario, Canada. Annual: 1958. Slovenian.

Sokolski Vesnik (Sokol Herald), Milwaukee, WI. Quarterly: 1967-1975, 1980-1984. Serbian, Croatian, and Slovenian.

T & T (formerly **Today and Tomorrow**), Milford, NJ. Bi-monthly: 1945-1948, 1950. English.

The Tamburitzan, Pittsburgh, PA. Bi-monthly: 1959-1961, 1976. English.

That's Yugoslavia (supplement to **Hrvatska Domovina**), Hamburg, West Germany. Monthly: 1982. English.

United Committee of South-Slavic Americans Bulletin, New York, NY. Frequency varies: 1943-1946. English.

United Yugoslav Relief Fund of America News Bulletin (previously titled **Yugoslav News Bulletin**), New York, NY. Frequency varies: 1941-1945. English.

Yugoslav-American Academic Association of the Pacific Bulletin, Palo Alto, CA. Quarterly: 1977. English.

Yugoslav-American Society Newslettter, Minneapolis, MN. Bi-monthly: 1987-date. English.

Yugoslav Facts and Views, New York, NY. Monthly: 1975-1981. English.

Yugoslavia Ministarstvo Socijalne Politike Iseljenički Odsek Iseljenička Služba: Izveštaj Narodnoj Skupštini (Yugoslav Ministry of Social Policy Emigration Department Emigration Service: Report to National Assembly), Belgrade, Yugoslavia. Bi-annual: 1925-1927. Serbian and/or Croatian.

Ukrainian American Collection

Manuscript Collections

Anderson, Peter.
Papers, 1923-1958. 2 linear in.

Formerly Petro Andrushchak, Anderson was a prominent leader in the Minneapolis, MN, Ukrainian American community. He was a founder of St. Michael's Ukrainian Orthodox Church in Minneapolis.

Papers consist of correspondence and other material pertaining to the Ukrainian American Citizens' Club, the United Ukrainian Organization of the Twin Cities, and the Inter-Racial Service Council. *Includes English.*

Archimovych, Alexander (1892-1984).
Papers, 1962-1976. Ca. 1 linear in.

Archimovych was a botanist, born in what is now Briansk Oblast, RSFSR. At the end of World War II, he immigrated to Germany, then to Spain and finally, in 1953, to the United States. He was a member of the Shevchenko Scientific Society and the Ukrainian Academy of Arts and Sciences in the United States.

Papers consist of photocopies of his articles on production of sugar beets and other crops in Ukraine.

Association for the Liberation of Ukraine (New York, New York).
Records, 1966- . 4 linear in.

The Association (ALU) is a political organization with a conservative-right view and publishes the occasional journal *Misiia Ukraïny* (Mission of Ukraine). Founded in West Germany in 1952, since 1959 its headquarters has been in New York, with branches in other countries.

Records of the Association consist of materials pertaining to its activities in the United States. *Includes English.*

Association of Ukrainian Political Prisoners (Munich, West Germany).
Records, 1946-1949. Ca. 1.5 linear ft.

The Association was founded in 1947, in Munich, to care for its members and families of deceased prisoners and to collect, arrange, and publish works by or about Ukrainian political prisoners, living or deceased. Records include constitution and bylaws, minutes, correspondence, circulars, and two photo albums of the Ukrainian displaced persons camp in Mittenwald. Among the organizations represented in the collection are the Central Representation of Ukrainian Emigrants in Germany and the United

Ukrainian American Relief Committee. *Includes English. Inventory available.*

Avramenko, Vasyl' (1895-1981).
Papers, ca. 1939-1971. Ca. 1 linear in.

A ballet master and film producer, Vasyl' (Wasyl) Avramenko was born in Stebliv, Ukraine. He attended several dance and theater schools before serving in the Russian Army in World War I and the Ukrainian Army from 1918-1920. During his long career, Avramemko organized numerous dance schools and directed many performances in the United States and Canada, including events at the 1933 Century of Progress Exposition in Chicago and at the White House. He also produced Ukrainian language films and owned a dance studio in New York.

Papers comprise programs, flyers, and pictures of Avramenko's activities in the United States, Canada and Israel. *Includes English and Yiddish.*

Bachur, George.
Papers, 1968-1970. Ca. 1 linear in.

Papers of Bachur consist of photographs, program booklets pertaining to social events in the Detroit, MI, Ukrainian community, and miscellany. Included are his free translation of Ivan Franko's two essays on religious views and Bachur's essay on the Ukrainian poet Taras Shevchenko. *Includes English.*

Baczynskyj, Ivan.
Papers, 1917-1956. 1 linear in.

Papers of Baczynskyj consist of research material on the living conditions in Ukraine under the Soviet regime, interviews with survivors of the 1933 famine in Ukraine, information on the Federation of Ukrainian Students, Ukrainian currency, and programs of Ukrainian events in the United States. *Includes English.*

Bohdan, Andrii.
Papers, 1963-1969. Ca. 1 linear in.

Papers of Bohdan consist of flyers and programs pertaining to cultural events in the Philadelphia, PA, Ukrainian community. Included are a flyer of the Americans to Free Captive Nations, Inc., Ukrainian Division; and a program from the Ukrainian Bandurist Chorus 50th anniversary tour. *Includes English.*

Boiko, Maksym (1912-).
Papers, 1933-1957. Ca. 1 linear in.

Bibliographer, librarian, and co-founder of the Research Institute of Volyn in Winnipeg, Canada. Boiko (or Boyko) also founded the Volhynian Bibliographic Center (Bloomington, IN) in 1967 and published a number of bibliographies, articles, and monographs on Volhynia.

His papers consist of a personal letter from the Metropolitan Vasyl' Lepkiwsky, head of the Ukrainian Autocephalic Church in Kiev, Ukraine, 1918-1921, and a photograph of his Episcopacy. *Includes English.*

Bondarenko, Andreas (1890-1977).
Papers, ca. 1920-1977. 13 linear ft.

A professor of Ukrainian history, social studies, and linguistics, Bondarenko came to the United States via Buenos Aires in 1960 and lived in Minneapolis, MN. Papers include correspondence, class notes, documents, photographs, and miscellany. *Includes Russian. Partial inventory available.*

Bryzhun, Konstantyn.
Papers, ca. 1946- . 2.5 linear ft.

Bryzhun's papers include correspondence with the Ukrainian War Veterans League, Inc.; announcements and other records of Ukrainian social events in Toronto, Canada; and programs. *Includes English. Partial inventory available.*

Bunka, Alexander.
Papers, ca. 1916-1970. 4 linear in.

A railroad worker, Bunka was born in Fish Creek, Saskatchewan, of Ukrainian Canadian immigrants. He served as a Ukrainian-English interpreter for John G. Diefenbaker (later prime minister of Canada), until 1922. In 1928, he came to the United States; and in 1962, he retired to Tucson, AZ, where he served as president of the Tucson Ukrainian Society.

His papers consist of correspondence with editors and congressmen concerning Ukrainian political and social issues, a scrapbook pertaining to Ukrainians in Tucson, correspondence with congressmen and government officials, newspaper clippings pertaining to Ukrainian folk art and Ukrainian dissidents, photographs, and materials pertaining to churches and Ukrainians in Fish Creek. *Includes English.*

Bykovsky, Lev (1895-   ).
Papers, ca. 1945-1974.   Ca. 4.5 linear in.

A bibliographer and retired librarian, Bykovsky was born in the village of Vilkhivets, Kiev gubernia. He worked in libraries in Kiev, Kamianets-Podilskyi, and Warsaw. After coming to the United States, he became a member of the Ukrainian Academy of Arts and Sciences. He wrote many bibliographic studies and compiled numerous bibliographies.

Papers include correspondence, programs, and newspaper clippings pertaining to the Ukrainian Festival (Dauphin, Manitoba, Canada) and the Ukrainian Free University. Also included are two manuscripts and a typescript biography of Tekla and Hryhori Danys of San Francisco, CA. *Includes English, Russian, Slovak, and Polish.*

Central Representation of Ukrainian Emigrants in Germany.
Records, 1945-1960.   6 linear ft.

The Representation is a civic institution in the Federal Republic of Germany, elected at the first convention of Ukrainian immigrants in Germany and Austria in 1945. Its purpose then was to represent and intercede on behalf of Ukrainians with the occupying powers, and later with the German government, and to cooperate with foreign charitable organizations, both Ukrainian and non-Ukrainian. The organization represented all Ukrainians and until 1950 was based in Augsburg. In 1953 it moved to Munich and it presently unites

a series of cultural and community institutions with 91 branches throughout Germany.

Records include petitions requesting admittance to the United States. Organizations represented in the collection include the Central Ukrainian Relief Bureau (London, England), the International Refugee Organization, the United Ukrainian American Relief Committee, the United Nations Relief and Rehabilitation Administration, the Ukrainian Canadian Committee, the Ukrainian Free Academy of Arts and Sciences in the U.S.A., the International Committee of the Red Cross (Geneva, Switzerland), and the Ukrainian Orthodox Church of U.S.A. Also included is correspondence of officers of the organization, including M. Dorozhynsky, A. Melnyk, and Z. Pelensky. *Includes German, Russian, and English. Inventory available.*

Chabin, Dmytro.
Papers, ca. 1950-1964.   Ca. 1 linear in.

Papers consist of pamphlets, programs, and form letters sent to Chabin by Ukrainian social and church organizations such as T-vo Prykhyl'nykiv UNR, the Ukrainian Congress Committee of America, and others. *Includes English.*

Chegensky, John.
Papers, ca. 1950-1965.   1 linear in.

Papers of Chegensky include correspondence; materials pertaining to the Union of Ukrainian Community Centers in Winnipeg, Canada; the Ukrainian Canadian Committee; and the Ukrainian Self-Reliance League of Canada.

Chinchenko, John (1905-   ).
Papers, ca. 1934-1967.   2.5 linear ft.

John (Iwan Marian) Chinchenko was a botanist and plant physiologist. He was born in Ukraine, studied at Uman Agricultural Institute, and received his PhD from Laval University in 1959. He came to the United States following

World War II; after teaching and working at several universities, he went to Canada.

Chinchenko's papers include biographical material and articles and papers on various scientific topics. *Includes English. Inventory available.*

Chopek, Elias
Papers, ca. 1950-1959. Ca. 1 linear in.

Chopek's papers include a manuscript he read to a fifth grade class about his immigration to America in 1905. *In English.*

Chyz, Yaroslav (1894-1958).
Papers, ca. 1929-1958. Ca. 1.5 linear ft.

Chyz was an authority on American nationality groups, particularly Ukrainians. He was born in Dubliany, near Lvov, and became a civic and military leader. He immigrated to Prague and in 1922 graduated in philosophy from Prague University. In the United States, Chyz edited the paper *Narodna Volya*; in 1942, he became a member of the Common Council for American Unity. He acted as adviser to the United States government on ethnic affairs and was an organizer and executive of the Committee of the President's People-to-People program.

Papers consist of correspondence, newspaper clippings, reports, photographs, and miscellany. Included is a taped interview with Edward R. Murrow. *Includes English and Polish. Preliminary inventory available.*

Derbush, Mykola.
Papers, ca. 1950-1963. 1 linear in.

Papers consist of programs and jubilee booklets pertaining to Ukrainian Americans in Minneapolis-St. Paul, MN. *Includes English.*

Dziwak, Ivan.
Papers, ca. 1963-1966. Ca. 1 linear in.

Papers consist of programs and flyers on Ukrainian social activities in the United States and Canada. Also included is material on the Second Ideological

Congress of the Ukrainian Students of America. *Includes English.*

Feshchenko-Czopiwsky, Petro.
Papers, ca. 1925-1965. 4.5 linear in.

Papers contain correspondence and manuscript and published music scores of operas and operettas by Mykola M. Arkas (1853-1909) and other composers. *Partial inventory available.*

Fodchuk, Dmytro.
Papers, ca. 1968-1969. 3 linear ft.

Fodchuk is a prominent member of the Ukrainian community in Toronto, Canada. Papers include correspondence, clippings, leaflets, newspapers, programs, and published materials. Much of the collection pertains to Ukrainian social activities in the United States and Canada. *Includes English. Inventory available.*

Gerega, Barbara (Rudachek).
Papers, ca. 1903-1966. Ca. 1 linear in.

A Canadian Ukrainian, Gerega was born in the village of Svydiv, Western Ukraine. She came with her parents to a homestead near Hyas, Saskatchewan. After marriage, she moved to Flin Flon, Manitoba.

Papers consist of a photocopy of a manuscript relating the history of early Ukrainian settlers in Hyas, Saskatchewan. *Preliminary inventory available.*

Golash, Stephan (1919-).
Papers, ca. 1958-1972. 2 linear in.

An engineer and microbiologist, Golash was born in Ukraine. He became a U.S. citizen in 1957. Golash studied and taught at various technical institutes and colleges in Ukraine and the United States and was a member of numerous Ukrainian American cultural, educational, and professional organizations.

Papers include correspondence with the Society of Veterans of the Ukrainian Insurgent Army, Komitet Hromadskoï diï za Patriiarkhat UKTserkvy, Committee for the Defense of Soviet Political Prisoners, the Ukrainian Student Organization of

Michnovsky, and the Research Society for Ukrainian Terminology, as well as others. Also included are materials pertaining to Ukrainian community activities in the United States. *Includes some English.*

Granovsky, Alexander A. (1887-1976).
Papers, ca. 1900-1976. 80 linear ft.

A Ukrainian American entomologist, also an activist and poet, Granovsky was born in Berezhtsi, Ukraine, and came to the United States in 1913. He was educated at Colorado State Agricultural College and the University of Wisconsin, and taught entomology at the universities of Wisconsin and Minnesota. He became a leader in the Ukrainian American community locally and nationally and was president of the Organization for the Rebirth of Ukraine, Inc. (ODWU). In St. Paul, he was also an active member of St. Michael's Ukrainian Orthodox Church. Following World War II, he was active in resettlement of Ukrainian refugees.

Granovsky's papers include a genealogy, biographical materials, diaries, family correspondence, writings, and poetry. Also included are materials pertaining to Ukrainian American organizations and Easter eggs as well as information on Ukrainians in Minnesota, the Ukrainian Congress Committee (Minnesota branch), Ukrainian Folk Ballet and Chorus of the Twin Cities, St. Michael's Ukrainian Orthodox Church (Minneapolis, MN), the Minnesota Commission on Resettlement of Displaced Persons, the United Ukrainian American Relief Committee of America, Inc., and many other Ukrainian American organizations. In addition, there are materials pertaining to the Immigration History Research Center Ukrainian American collection and to the Organization for the Rebirth of Ukraine, Inc. *Includes English, German, and Russian. Inventory available. Section on ODWU closed for twenty-five years. Related collections: United Ukrainian American Relief Committee, John Panchuk, Ukrainian Congress Committee of America (Minnesota Branch).*

Grendzha-Dons'kyi, Vasyl (1897-1974).
Papers, ca. 1924-1973. Ca. 3 linear ft.

Grendzha-Dons'kyi was a writer and poet from Carpatho-Ukraine, the founder of modern literature of Carpatho-Ukraine. Papers include biographical material, poetry, prose, and correspondence with his daughter, Alice (Grendža-Donska) Danyluk of Minneapolis, MN. Also included are his translations of works by non-Ukrainian poets and writers into Ukrainian. *Inventory available.*

Halich, Wasyl (1896-).
Papers, 1921-1971. Ca. 4 linear ft.

A professor of Russian and European history, Halich was born in Strilbychi, on the northern slopes of the Carpathian Mountains. He came to the United States in 1912 and settled in Pittsburgh, PA, and attended Bloomfield College (Bloomfield, NJ), and then Dubuque College (Dubuque, IA), where he received a BA degree. In 1929, he received his MA and in 1934, his PhD from Iowa University. From then until his retirement, he taught at Wisconsin State University-Superior, pioneering the study of Ukrainians in America in his book *Ukrainians in the United States* (1933). He remained active in many professional and Ukrainian American organizations, including the Shevchenko Scientific Society in the United States, the Ukrainian American University Professors Association, and the Wisconsin State Historical Society.

Papers include biographical information, postcards, newspaper clippings, and correspondence. Also included is information pertaining but not limited to, agriculture in North Dakota, the Catholic Church-Oriental rites, mining industry finance and employees, Protestant churches and Protestants in Ukraine, the Surma Book and Music Company, Ukrainian history, art, music, business and agriculture, Ukrainian women, and organizations of Ukrainian Americans. Correspondents and subjects of correspondence include Alexander Archipenko, Yaroslaw Chyz, Andrew Dubovoy, Rev. Agapius Honcharenko, Rev. Basil Kusiw, Luke Myshuha, Rev. Alex Prystay, Taras Shevchenko, and Rev. Joseph Zelechivsky. Much of the material is related to Halich's book. *Includes English. Inventory available.*

Haydak, Mykola H. (1898-1971).
Papers, ca. 1945-1970. 10 linear ft.

Haydak came to the United States from Ukraine in 1930. He received his Ph.D. in entomology from the University of Wisconsin and then taught at the University of Minnesota. He published extensively in the entomology field and was a member of many professional societies. Prior to his arrival in America, Haydak had studied in Ukraine and Czechoslovakia and was a volunteer in World War I.

Papers include correspondence, materials pertaining to the Ukrainian Folk Ballet (Twin Cities, MN), a collection of Ukrainian Christmas and Easter cards, materials about Ukrainian immigrants, the *Slavonic Encyclopedia*, and Ukrainian-Jewish relations. Correspondents include: family members; Mykola Nebesenko; Simon M. Nechay; Petro Filipovich; Alexander Filipovich; Walter Galan, Executive Director of the United Ukrainian American Relief Committee; Ulas Samchuk; Evhen Onatsky; Dmytro Havrylenko; Andrii Kist; Ivan Kist; H. F. Wilson; Vily Peterča; Naukove Toverystvo im. Shevchenka (Shevchenko Scientific Society, Inc.); Ukraïns'kyi Tekhnichno-Hospodars'kyi Intstytut (Ukrainian Technical and Husbandry Institute); Ukrainian American Association of University Professors; and various World War II refugees. *Includes English and a few items in Czech. Preliminary inventory available.*

Hetmanite Association of Germany and Austria (Munich, West Germany).
Records, 1947-1967. 1 linear ft.

A Ukrainian political émigré organization of the former hetmanate government, the Association was founded in Munich in 1947. Records include constitution and bylaws, minutes, circulars, and correspondence. Among the organizations represented in the collection are Ukrainian Hetmanite Organization of America, International Relief Organization, and the Bulava

Publishing Company in New York. *Includes German and English. Inventory available.*

Hnizdovsky, Jacques (1915-1985).
Papers, ca. 1962-1976. Ca. 1 linear in.

A painter and printmaker, Hnizdovsky was born in Pylypcze, Galicia (Ukraine). He came to the United States in 1949 and became a citizen in 1954. Prior to emigrating, he had studied at the Academy of Fine Arts, Warsaw, and the Academy of Fine Arts, Zagreb. After coming to the United States, he won numerous prizes and awards for his art works and was a member of many professional and Ukrainian American organizations.

Papers consist of samples of woodcuts and book plates and include exhibit programs. *In English.*

Hordiienko, Havrylo.
Papers, ca. 1962-1971. 1 linear ft.

Papers of Hordiienko, a botanist, consist of newspapers in which his articles on botany and other topics appeared. Articles pertain mainly to the historical significance of plants in Ukraine and elsewhere and their use in Ukrainian and other literatures.

Horodysky, Orest Iwan (1918-).
Papers, ca. 1920- . 7 linear ft.

Horodysky, a draftsman, was born in Stanyslaviv, Ukraine. In 1939, he was arrested and convicted by Polish authorities for Ukrainian nationalist activities. He later served (1944-1945) with the Ukrainian National Army and was a prisoner of war in Rimini, Italy. In 1950, he received his MS from the Ukrainian Free University; he came to the United States in 1956. He was a founding member of the Brotherhood of Veterans of Ukrainian National Association, Ukrainian National Museum (Chicago, IL), and a member of Ukrainian War Veterans of America.

Papers include programs, brochures, and other materials pertaining to Ukrainian American and Ukrainian

Canadian social activities, Ukrainian Christmas cards, newspaper clippings from *Ameryka* and *Zorya*, and miscellany. Also included are correspondence, newspaper clippings from Polish and Ukrainian newspapers, biographical materials, materials pertaining to PLAST-Ukrainian Youth Organization, St. Joseph's Ukrainian Catholic Church (Chicago, IL), Immaculate Conception Ukrainian Catholic Church, and St. Nicholas Ukrainian Catholic Cathedral. Correspondents include Zenon Kuzelia and Jozef Cyhankiewicz. *Includes Polish and English. Inventory available.*

Humenna, Dokiia Kuzmiwna (1904-).
Papers, ca. 1928-1973. Ca. 1 linear in.

An author, Humenna was born in Zhashkiv, Kiev gubernia. She studied literature at the University of Kiev, graduating in 1926. She became a United States citizen in 1959. Humenna was active in Ukrainian American organizations and was a prolific writer.

Papers consist of two scrapbooks that include book reviews, publication announcements, epigrams, correspondence, and miscellany. *Inventory available.*

Kaniuka, Oleksander.
Papers, ca. 1950-1986. 1.5 linear in.

A painter and graphics artist, Kaniuka came to the Twin Cities in 1951. His papers consist of a notebook of original and sample versions of his graphic art works, exhibit catalogs, and newspaper clippings, as well as works used for flyers, newsletters, bulletins, and diplomas. Subjects include Ukrainian American community activities, Kaniuka's experiences in prison (1931-1933), and political cartoons on Ukraine during its occupation and struggle for independence.

Kanuik, Michael.
Papers, ca. 1920-1965. Ca. 1 linear in.

Papers of Kanuik include two life insurance certificate charts for him and his wife, Katherine, with the Ukrainian National Association; appeal letters for contributions; and several religious pictures. Kanuik was a member of the Minneapolis, MN, Ukrainian community. *Includes English.*

Kapschutschenko, Peter (1915-).
Papers, 1947-1966. 1 linear in.

A sculptor, Kapschutschenko (or Enko) was born in Ukraine. From 1947 to 1963, he lived in Buenos Aires, Argentina. He then came to the United States, settling in Philadelphia, PA. He has created numerous works in bronze, wood, and terra cotta, has exhibited internationally, and has received many awards.

Papers include photographs of his works, art exhibit programs, and miscellany. *Includes English and Spanish.*

Kikta, Stepan (1918-).
Papers, ca. 1973- . 1.5 linear in.

A philatelist and community activist, Kikta (or Oles Cherko) was born in Ukraine where, from 1936 to 1939, he was a correspondent for *Novyevei Chas* and *Batkivshchyna* and later was assistant director of the Union of Ukrainian Co-operatives. He came to the United States following World War II and has been active in numerous Ukrainian American organizations.

Papers consist of programs, flyers, and miscellany on Ukrainian community activities in Cleveland, OH, as well as reports of the Ukrainian Museum-Archives, Inc., and the financial reports of the Self-Reliance Credit Union, Inc. (Cleveland). *Includes English.*

Kist, Andrii (1891-1986).
Papers, ca. 1929-1962. Ca. 1 linear in.

Kist was an Orthodox priest active in the Minneapolis-St. Paul, MN, Ukrainian community and church life. He was pastor at St. Michael's Ukrainian Orthodox Church and St. George's Ukrainian Orthodox Church.

Papers consist mainly of photographs pertaining to the Ukrainian American church, social, and community events in the United States. *Includes English.*

Kizyma, Stefan (b. 1888).
Papers, ca. 1966-1968. Ca. 1 linear in.

An author and judge, Kizyma was born in Ukraine. He served in the Austrian army during World War I and with Ukrainian forces in 1919-1920. He received his JD from the University of Lvov in 1928 and worked as a judge in City Court for various Ukrainian cities. After coming to the United States, he settled in Los Angeles and became active in Ukrainian American organizations.

Papers consist of programs, form letters, announcements, and newspaper clippings pertaining to Ukrainian community activities in the United States.

Klepachivsky, Konstantyn Yosypovych (1887-1979).
Papers, ca. 1919-1956. 6 linear ft.

A lawyer and banker, Klepachivsky was born in Novo Ivanivka, Ukraine. He graduated from the University of Petersburg, Russia, in 1914, and worked in the Petersburg Court, the Government Bank in Petersburg, the Ukrainian Government Bank in Kiev, and the Bank of the Ukrainian National Republic. He transported and safeguarded the archives of the Ukrainian National Bank, which were later seized by the German army. Klepachivsky came to the United States following World War II.

Papers contain correspondence, materials pertaining to the State Bank of Ukraine, photographs, biographical materials, maps, periodicals, and miscellany. Also included are newspapers, correspondence, and miscellany of his wife Maria (Arkas) Klepachivsky. *Includes English. Inventory available.*

Klodnycky, Rev. Vladimir (1891-1973).
Papers, ca. 1917-1973. 11.5 linear ft.

A Ukrainian priest and former officer of the Ukrainian Galician Army, Rev. Klodnycky came to the United States in 1925 and was ordained an Eastern Orthodox priest in 1930. He served as pastor of churches in Pennsylvania and New Jersey, edited the monthly journal *Restoration,* and was active in Ukrainian American affairs and political life.

Papers of Klodnycky consist of correspondence, diaries, awards, copies of articles, newspaper clippings, and photographs. Correspondents and topics include the Ukrainian Orthodox Church of Holy Ascension (Newark, NJ), the Ukrainian-American Citizens League of New Jersey, Inc., the Ukrainian National Association, the Ukrainian Greek Orthodox Church of Canada, the Ukrainian Central Relief Association in Osterreich, the Ukrainian War Historical Institute (Toronto, Canada), the United Ukrainian American Organizations, the Anti-Defamation League of B'nai Brith, the Orthodox Eastern Church, Ukrainians in the United States and Germany, Senator H. Alexander Smith (NJ), Elizabeth Wherry, Luke Myshuha, W. Warren Barbours, Archbishop Theodorovych of the Ukrainian Autocephalic Orthodox Church in the United States, and Klodnycky's brother (Joseph Klodnycky), as well as other clergy and political figures. Topics include, in addition to the above, Ukrainian-Jewish and Ukrainian-Polish relations, and Ukrainians in New Jersey. *Includes English and German. Inventory available.*

Komichak, Michael (1919-).
Papers, 1938. 1 linear in.

A radio station engineer and manager, Komichak was born in McKees Rocks, PA. He worked as engineer and assistant manager for radio station WPIT AM & FM (Pittsburgh, PA), where he was director of Ukrainian radio programming. Komichak participated in several Ukrainian professional and cultural associations.

Papers consist of a manuscript of "Polkovnyk Konovalets', June 14, 1891 - May 23, 1938, Arnold, PA, 26 June 1938." *Includes English.*

Kostiuk, Oleksandra F. (1899-1985).
Papers, ca. 1948-1982. 2 linear ft.

An educator, author, and chemical engineer, Kostiuk was born and educated in Ukraine. She taught in a displaced persons camp in Germany and came to the United States following World War II. She settled in the Minneapolis-St. Paul, MN, region, where she was active professionally and in many Ukrainian American organizations, including the Ukrainian Orthodox Church. She was editor and co-editor of the musical quarterly *Visti* (The Herald, later *Muzychni Visti*).

Papers consist of personal and general correspondence, literary works, flyers, newspaper clippings, and other materials pertaining to the Ukrainian Literary Arts Club of Minnesota; the Ukrainian Congress Committee of America, Minnesota Branch; the Shevchenko Jubilee Committee; Ukrainian Gold Cross; Ukrainian Peasant Organization; Ukrainian Chorus Dnipro; and Ukrainian Saturday School of St. George's Ukrainian Orthodox Church (Minneapolis, MN). *Includes some English. Related collection: Visti (The Herald).*

Krascheninnikow, Serhij (1895-1987).
Papers, ca. 1950-1961. Ca. 1 linear in.

A scientist and zoologist, Krascheninnikow was born in Sluzk, Byelorussia. He taught veterinary medicine, and, after coming to the United States, worked for the U.S. Department of Agriculture. He received awards and grants for his work in zoology and parasitology, and published widely in those fields. He also wrote articles on Ukrainian culture, sometimes using the pseudonym "Suhak."

Papers consist of published articles on zoology and an article about Mykola Zerov, a Ukrainian poet and literary editor. *Includes English and German.*

Kuchar, Roman Volodomyr (1920-).
Papers, ca. 1950- . 3 linear in.

An educator and poet, Kuchar was born in Lvov, Ukraine. He studied at the University of Lvov, the Conservatory of Music (Vienna), the University of Heidelberg, the University of Colorado, the Pratt Institute, and the Ukrainian Free University. He came to the United States following World War II and became a citizen in 1958. He taught at various places and was active in many

educational, professional, and cultural organizations. He also was an author of poetry, novels, essays, plays, and works on art, literature, and languages.

Papers consist mainly of newspaper articles about Kuchar in the University of Denver (CO) paper and the *State College Leader* of Kansas State College, where he is a faculty member in the Language Department. *Includes English.*

Kuchlewsky, Stefan.
Papers, ca. 1950s. Ca. 1 linear in.

Papers include programs and announcements of Ukrainian American activities, newspaper clippings, postcards, and stamps.

Kudanowicz, Rev. Michael.
Papers, ca. 1949-1974. 4 linear in.

Kudanowicz served various parishes, including St. Mary Protectoress Church (Rochester, NY), SS. Volodymyr and Olga Ukrainian Orthodox Church (St. Paul, MN), St. Michael's Ukrainian Orthodox Church (Minneapolis, MN), and St. George's Ukrainian Orthodox Church (Minneapolis, MN). Papers consist of stamps, envelopes, and letterheads of various Ukrainian Plast (Scout) Youth organizations of the United States and Canada and their activities; material pertaining to the Ukrainian National Association Twenty-eighth Convention; commemorative buttons and ribbons of the Catholic and Orthodox Eastern Churches of America; and miscellaneous programs and flyers on activities of the Ukrainian community of Rochester, NY. *Includes English.*

Kukuruza, Pawlo (1896-1978).
Papers, 1946-1967. 1 linear ft.

A publisher, editor, and pedagogue, Kukuruza was born in Nova Ushchytsia, Podilia gubernia, Ukraine, and came to the United States in 1949 after living in Uzhgorod, where he organized the Pchilka Publishing House. Kukuruza also edited almanacs of the Prosvita society and various textbooks. From 1945 to 1949, he organized the publishing activities of

the Ukrainian Technical and Husbandry
Institute in Munich.

Papers include correspondence with the
United Ukrainian American Relief, Inc.,
the United Nations High Commission on
Refugees, Indemnification Fund, and
various Ukrainian Americans; newspaper
clippings; photocopies of journals
Kukuruza edited and published;
biographical materials; a bibliography of
sub-Carpathian literature; publications
about bee-keeping; and photographs.
*Includes English, German, and Czech.
Inventory available.*

Kulchycky, Bohdan.
Papers, ca. 1963-1972.   1 linear in.

Papers consist of letterheads, form
letters, and notebooks pertaining to the
Philadelphia, PA, Branch and Central
Executive of the Ukrainian Student
Organizations of Michnowsky (TUSM)
and to the World Federation of TUSM,
along with questionnaires, memoranda of
the Federation of Ukrainian Students
Organizations of America (SUSTA) and
programs. *Includes English.*

Kurdydyk, Anatol Julian (1905-).
Papers, ca. 1914-1975.   4 linear in.

An editor, author, and journalist,
Kurdydyk was born in Pidhajci, Galicia
(Ukraine). He was educated at the
University of Lvov and served with the
Polish Army, 1928-1929. He was
co-editor of *Ukraïnskyi Holos, Nedilia,*
and *Dilo* and was Vienna correspondent
for *Krakivski Visti.* After World War II,
he went to Canada, where he was
cofounder and editor of *Vilne Slovo*
(Toronto) and editor of *Novyi Shliakh* and
Postup. Kurdydyk wrote prolifically and
was active in numerous professional and
cultural organizations.

Papers consist of newspaper clippings
on Ukrainian community activities in
Canada and a document entitled "An Act
to Incorporate the Ruthenian Greek
Catholic Parishes and Missions in the
Province of Manitoba." *Includes English.*

Kurochka, Marian (1899-).
Papers, ca. 1900-1966.   Ca. 1 linear in.

Papers of Kurochka, an author, consist
of a manuscript copy of his work entitled
"Tsyhans'kymy dorohamy" (Gypsy
Roads). Also included are photographs
from his journey through various
countries before he arrived in the United
States.

Kuropas, Stephan (1900-).
Papers, ca. 1940- .   Ca. 1.5 linear ft.

A realtor and activist in Ukrainian
American affairs, Kuropas was born in
Pzemyszl, Galicia, and came to the
United States ca. 1929 after serving in
various military units during World War I
and after. He settled in Chicago, IL,
where he became involved in numerous
Ukrainian American organizations,
including the Ukrainian National
Association. He was a regular
contributor to *Svoboda,* editor of
"Samostiïna Ukraïna," and a contributor
to *Ukraïntsi u Vilnomu Sviti, J. C.*

Papers include correspondence and
programs for Ukrainian American cultural
events. Also included are materials
pertaining to Kuropas's travels in Poland
and Ukraine and to the Shevchenko
Freedom Award. *Includes English.
Inventory available.*

Kwitkowsky, Denys (1909-1979).
Papers, 1971.   1 linear in.

A prominent Ukrainian American
lawyer, Kwitkowsky was born in Sherivtsi
Dolishni, Bukovyna. He was educated at
the University of Chernivtsi, the
University of Berlin, and Wayne State
University (Detroit, MI). He practiced
law in Chernivtsi, in Bucharest, and in
Detroit. Kwitkowsky wrote many articles
for professional journals and the
Ukrainian press, and participated in
Ukrainian American and legal
organizations.

Papers consist of a typescript copy of
his work entitled *Human Rights: Theory
and Practice. Includes English and
Spanish.*

Lachowitch, Eugene (1900-).
Papers, ca. 1950-1956. Ca. 1 linear in.

A machine designer and journalist, Lachowitch was born in Ushnia, Ukraine. He served in the Ukrainian Army from 1918 to 1921, then studied in Danzig. After coming to the United States, he served as associate editor of *Svoboda*, as editor of *Visnyk* (New York), and as correspondent for several Ukrainian and Ukrainian American newspapers and publications.

Papers include material on the activities of the Ukrainian Congress Committee and some of its officials in the United States and Europe, an article on Ukrainian-Jewish relations, and miscellany. *Includes English.*

The Layman.
Records, ca. 1968-1969. Ca. 1 linear in.

Records of the *Layman* consist of material on the constitution of the Ukrainian Catholic Church, the Ukrainian Catholic Church of SS. Volodymyr and Ol'ha (Chicago, IL), and programs of Ukrainian social and religious activities in Chicago.

League of Americans of Ukrainian Descent, Inc. (Chicago, Illinois)
Records, ca. 1955. 2 linear in.

A civic, religious, and welfare organization, the League was founded in 1940. It has 8,000 members and fifty-two branches. The League coordinates the activities of similar organizations; its major emphasis is on helping Ukrainians in need. It also sponsors English language classes and conducts and participates in cultural activities.

Records consist of programs, announcements, and miscellany.

Leskiw, Myron (1909-).
Papers, ca. 1946-1958. 2 linear in.

A political activist and technical inspector, Leskiw was born in Pidtarkiv, Ukraine. He was an officer in the Ukrainian National Association and was active in political campaigns from 1948 to 1972. He was a chairman of the

Republican Heritage Groups Federation of the State of New Jersey and was also a founder and board member of the *Heritage Review* newspaper.

Papers include newspaper clippings, leaflets, brochures, and personal correspondence largely pertaining to the Ukrainian American community and its fight against communism. Also included are reports, newsletters, and other materials of the Ukrainian Congress Committee of America. Correspondents include United States senators and presidents. *Includes English.*

Levchuk, Dmytro (1900-1977).
Papers, 1957-1977. 10 linear in.

An educator and journalist, Levchuk contributed many articles to two Ukrainian American newspapers, *America* (Philadelphia, PA) and *Batkivshchyna* (Toronto, Canada). Papers consist of clippings of articles, compiled in four volumes. *Inventory available. Papers available as photocopies only.*

Lissiuk, Kalenik.
Papers, ca. 1918-1976. Ca. 1 linear in.

Lissiuk was a Ukrainian American philanthropist. Papers consist of copies of certificates he received from the Ukrainian Free Cossack Society, the American Christian College, and the Union of Ukrainian Veterans, along with newspaper clippings, letters from Pres. Gerald Ford and Dmytro Shtohryn, and biographical information on Petro Oleksiienko. *Includes some items in English.*

Lymarenko, P.
Papers, ca. 1951-1981. 1 linear in.

Papers of Lymarenko consist of typescripts, correspondence, brochures, and other information pertaining to the United Ukrainian American Relief Committee, Inc.; *Svoboda*; the American Ukrainian Resort Center, Inc.; St. Vladimir Ukrainian Orthodox Cathedral (Philadelphia, PA); the Ukrainian Bandurists Chorus; the International Institute of Philadelphia; the United

Ukrainian War Veterans of America, as well as a family photograph. *Includes some items in English.*

Malaniuk, Myron (1913-).
Papers, ca. 1939. Ca. 3 linear ft.

Malaniuk was born in Uhorci, Ukraine. He was taken into forced labor in Germany during World War II and later spent time in a displaced persons camp. In the camp, he was active in Ukrainian church life and with the Ukrainian branch of the YMCA and YWCA. He came to the United States in 1957, where he remained active in the Ukrainian community in Chicago, IL, especially with the Ukrainian National Museum. He also administered the literary journal *Dzvony* while it was published in Chicago.

Papers consist of correspondence, newspaper clippings, leaflets, brochures, form letters, and flyers relating to Ukrainian community life and activities in Chicago and elsewhere. *Inventory available.*

Malevich, Maria.
Papers, ca. 1950-1963. Ca. 1 linear in.

Papers include lists of addresses of Ukrainian National Association delegates meeting in Pennsylvania, photocopies of newspaper clippings about the Ukrainian Bandurist Chorus's United States concert tour, and miscellany. *Includes English.*

Manor Junior College (Jenkintown, Pennsylvania).
Records, 1972. Ca. 1 linear in.

The College, operated by the Sisters of St. Basil, is the only Ukrainian Rite college for women in the world. The sisters came to the United States in 1911, first operating an orphanage in Philadelphia, then a convent outside the city. The school was first a secondary school, begun in 1932. The college was founded in 1947. Many of the girls who attended were war orphans or children of political prisoners. The school affiliated with the Catholic University of America

(Washington, DC), and, after many difficulties, was granted accreditation in 1967.

Records consist of a typescript copy of "A History of Manor Junior College," and a Silver Jubilee edition, 1947-1972. *Includes English.*

Novak, Mykola A.
Papers, 1972. Ca. 1 linear in.

Novak was a founding member and past president of the Ukrainian Culture Center (Los Angeles, CA), and a member of the Mayor's Council for International Visitors. The Center (formerly the Ukrainian Social Center) was founded in 1944 to promote social and cultural life of its members and to provide sickness benefits.

Papers consist of information on the Center. Included are brochures, flyers, and leaflets. *Includes English.*

Novytski, Bishop Alexander (1905-1970).
Papers, ca. 1949-1969. 1 linear in.

Bishop Novystki lived in Chicago, IL. He was head of the Ukrainian Orthodox Church of the United States of America, Educational Council.

Papers consist of correspondence with his brother in Canada and with the Ukrainian Greek Orthodox Church of Canada and the Ukrainian Orthodox Church of the U.S.A. Also included is a paper on the All Canadian Conference of Priests of the Ukrainian Greek Orthodox Church in Canada (July 2-3, 1959, Edmonton, Alberta, Canada). *Includes English.*

Onatsky, Evhen (b. 1894).
Papers, 1918-ca. 1967. 37.5 linear ft.

An author and college professor active in the Ukrainian community, Onatsky was born in Hlukhiv, Ukraine. After completing his education he was elected to the Ukrainian Central Rada and was a member of the Ukrainian Presidium. In 1918, he became librarian of the Kiev Municipal Museum and continued his scientific research. In 1919, he was a Ukrainian delegate to the Paris Peace Conference and was with the Ukrainian diplomatic service in Italy; he later directed the Ukrainian-American Relief Committee in Rome. He compiled an encyclopedia of Ukrainian symbols, beliefs, customs, and traditions, as well as other publications. In March 1947, he emigrated to Argentina, where he continued his research in Ukrainian cultural heritage.

Papers consist of biographical material, diplomatic papers dating from his service in Italy, materials from his time teaching in Naples and Rome, papers of the Ukrainian-American Relief Committee in Rome following World War II, personal and professional correspondence from his editorship of *Nash Klych* in Buenos Aires, and materials pertaining to compilation of a Ukrainian encyclopedia. Correspondents include Dmytro Andrievs'kyi, Osyp Boidunyk, Ivan Buchko, Alexander A. Granovsky, Oleh Kandyba, Oleh Shtul, Andrii Melnyk, Ivan Ovechko, Ivan Tyktor, Eugene Wertyporoch, Mykola Chabatyi, Mykola Haydak, the Ukrainian American Relief Committee, and the Ukrainian Press Bureau (Rome). Also included are materials pertaining to Nikolai Vasilevich Gogol, Dokia Humenna, Oswald Burghardt, Dmytro Doroshenko, Ivan Franko, the Ukrainian National Republic, Ukrainian history, Ukrainians in South America, Galicia, the Pan-American Ukrainian Conference, and *Nash Klych*. *Includes French, German, Italian, English, and Portuguese. Inventory available.*

Pakulak, Wasyl (1912-1986).
Papers, ca. 1968-1985. 2 linear ft.

Pakulak was a Ukrainian American journalist. He lived in Minneapolis, MN, and wrote about the Twin Cities Ukrainian American community and Ukrainian topics in various Ukrainian newspapers.

Papers consist of newspaper clippings, scrapbooks of articles written by Pakulak, and other articles. *Includes some items in English.*

Panchuk, John (1904-1981).
Papers, ca. 1910-1981. 6.5 linear ft.

A lawyer, Panchuk was born in Gardenton, Manitoba, Canada. He was educated in Canada and the United States, receiving his LLB from the University of Michigan. After graduating, he was general counsel and secretary of Federal Life and Casualty Company (Battle Creek, MI). Panchuk was active in the Ukrainian American community as president of the Ukrainian War Relief, Inc., and of the United Ukrainian American Relief Committee. He also served as a representative of the State Department at the International Refugee Office Resettlement Conference (1948, Geneva, Switzerland) and was chair of the Michigan Commission on Displaced Persons. He had an active interest in Ukrainian folklore and traditions, which led him to the discovery of numerous ballads composed in the New World.

Papers of Panchuk consist of correspondence, newspaper clippings, and other materials about the American Slav Congress (Detroit, MI and Pittsburgh, PA), Ukrainian War Relief, Inc., United Ukrainian American Relief Committee, displaced persons, Matthew Stachiw, the Ukrainian Insurgent Army, and the Committee for Hungarian Refugee Relief in Michigan. Also included are materials on the Michigan Committee on Displaced Persons, the Ukrainian Youth League of North America, and the Bandurist Chorus, and correspondence and photographs on publications about Ukrainian settlers and settlements in Canada, including the Panchuk family. *Mainly in English. Inventory available. Related collection: United Ukrainian American Relief Committee.*

Patchowska, Neonilla (1890-1957).
Papers, ca. 1944-1957. Ca. 1 linear in.

Patchowska was born in Korytny, Ukraine. She settled in Long Island, NY, after coming to the United States.

Papers consist of an application to file for petition for naturalization, a photograph of her, newsletters of S.S. General Stuart Heintzelman, and commemorative stamps. *Includes English.*

Pechak, Lena.
Papers, ca. 1917-1967.   1 linear ft.

Pechak was active in the Ukrainian community of Rochester, NY.   Papers consist of currency of the Ukrainian National Republic, a certificate relating to the American Museum of Immigration, personal correspondence, newspaper clippings, programs, and announcements. Correspondents include Stefania Michalska, Maria Piatkovs'ka, Nadia Kushlyk, W. Sorokova, and P. V. Matkovs'ka. *Includes English and Polish. Inventory available.*

Perepeluk, William J. (1900-).
Papers, ca. 1960-1973.   1 linear ft.

A businessman, philanthropist, and community activist, William (or Wasyl) Perepeluk was born in Sifton, Manitoba, Canada.   He was active in numerous Ukrainian Canadian organizations, and was president of the national Ukrainian Festival (Dauphin, Manitoba).

Papers consist of programs, announcements, a film handbook, and other materials pertaining to Ukrainian community activities in Dauphin, Manitoba.   Included are materials pertaining to St. Vladimir Ukrainian Institute, Ukrainian Canadian Veterans' Association, Ukrainian Women's Association of Canada, and of the Ukrainian Festival. *Includes English. Inventory available.*

Plewako, Petro (b. 1888).
Papers, ca. 1920-1968.   8.5 linear ft.

Plewako was born in Kupiantsi, Ukraine, and emigrated to Paris.   He was founder and president of the Construction Committee of the Orthodox Ukrainian Church in Paris.

Papers consist of correspondence with Ukrainians in Canada and the United States, personal and business correspondence pertaining to the Construction Committee of the Orthodox Ukrainian Church in Paris and the Committee on the Guardianship of the Monument of Simon Petliura, and correspondence of Mrs. S. Petliura. Also included are correspondence,

photographs,and newspaper clippings pertaining to publication of a book on works of Plewako's brother, Mykola Plewako. *Inventory available.*

Powch, Myra.
Papers, ca. 1900-1957.   Ca. 1 linear in.

Powch's papers consist of a music book of the Ukrainian Eastern Orthodox liturgy composed by D. Bortniansky, Mat. Virbitsky, et al., a paper by Constantine Kostiw entitled "Metropolitan Dr. Ilarion As the Translator of the Bible," and newspaper clippings on Ukraine.

Proch, Wasyl (1900-1968).
Papers, ca. 1920-1925.   Ca. 1 linear in.

Proch was born in Ozirna, Galicia, and came to Minnesota ca. 1926.   He was active in St. Michael's Ukrainian Orthodox Church parish (Minneapolis, MN).

Papers include an affidavit for an American visa from the Merchants National Bank (St. Paul, MN), a Ukrainian passport, and photograph postcards. *Includes Czech and English.*

Pundyk, Youry (1918-1973).
Papers, ca. 1940-1973.   Ca. 6.5 linear ft.

A professor of economics at Hibbing Junior College (Hibbing, MN), Pundyk was active in the Ukrainian American community.

Papers include personal and professional correspondence, writings, newspaper clippings, newspapers, and photographs.   Correspondents include Oleh Shtul, Alexander A. Granovsky, Myron Kuropas, Denys Kwitkowsky, Andrii Melnyk, and others.   Materials pertain to Ukrainians in Minnesota and in South America, Ukrainian-Jewish and Ukrainian-Russian relations, Ukrainian literature and history, and organizations, including the Organization for the Rebirth of Ukraine, the Organization of Ukrainian Nationalists, the World Congress of Free Ukrainians, and the Ukrainian Youth Federation of America. *Includes English. Inventory available.*

Romanovs'kyi, Volodymyr.
Papers, ca. 1914-1965. Ca. 1 linear in.

Romanovs'kyi was active in the Ukrainian community of Minneapolis and St. Paul, MN. Papers consist of appeals of the Committee for Erection of the All-Ukrainian Church Monument in Paris, France; a mimeographed copy of *Chomu my povynni holosuvaty za demokrativ* (Why We Should Vote for Democrats); and financial reports of the Ukrainian Orthodox Parish of St. Michael's Church (Minneapolis, MN). *Includes Czech.*

Royick, George.
Papers, 1957-1966. 1 linear ft.

Papers of Royick consist of scrapbooks, newspaper clippings of articles by various Ukrainians, information on several Ukrainian American organizations, and miscellaneous correspondence. *Inventory available.*

Rudnyckyj, Jaroslav Bohdan (1910-).
Papers, 1970-1971. 3 linear in.

Rudnyckyj was born in Poland and came to Canada in 1949 after completing his education at Lvov, Prague, Heidelberg, and Munich. He organized the Department of Slavic Studies at the University of Manitoba and served as its head. He has published books and articles on linguistics and bilingualism and is a member of many professional and Ukrainian societies.
Papers consist of materials on the Manitoba Mosaic Congress and the Royal Commission on Bilingualism and Biculturism in Canada. Rudnyckyj contributed recommendations and reactions to the Commission's study of the status of ethnic languages in Canada. *Includes English and French.*

Salamacha, Peter.
Papers, 1964. Ca. 1 linear ft.

Papers of Salamacha consist mainly of programs and newspaper clippings pertaining to the unveiling of the Taras Shevchenko monument in Washington, DC. *Includes English.*

Seleshko, Michael (1901-).
Papers, 1960-1969. 6 linear in.

A journalist and engineer, Michael (or Mykhailo) Seleshko was born in Vytvysia, Ukraine. Following World War II, he settled in Canada, where he worked as a journalist and was active in Ukrainian Canadian professional and cultural organizations.
Papers consist of Ukrainian Christmas cards and illustrated Ukrainian wall calendars.

Shayda, Philip.
Papers, ca. 1957-1977. 2 linear ft.

Shayda is a long-time president of SS. Volodymyr and Olga Ukrainian Orthodox Church Choir and an active member of the Church Council (St. Paul, MN). Papers of Shayda consist of brochures, flyers, newsletters, and posters pertaining to Ukrainian social, political, and community activities in Minneapolis and St. Paul, MN. *Includes English.* *Inventory available.*

Shut, Wasyl (1899-1982).
Papers, 1951-1983. Ca. 1 linear in.

A composer and music teacher, Shut was born in Zolotonosha, Ukraine. After coming to the United States, he opened a music school in Chicago, IL, in 1951. He served as accompanist and choir director and composed prolifically.
Papers consist of a brief biography of Shut by his wife, Maria, along with programs and photographs.

Shyprykevich, Vladimir (1907-).
Papers, 1954-1966. 2 linear in.

An engineer, Shyprykevich was born in Ostrivcy, Ukraine. He was educated at the University of Warsaw and the Tech. Hochschule in Danzig (now Gdansk). He worked in Europe until the end of World War II, when he came to the United States and settled in Philadelphia, PA.
Papers consist of art catalogs and programs on art exhibits, a dedication booklet, and newspaper articles pertaining to the Taras Shevchenko Statue in Washington, DC. *Includes English.*

Sichynsky, Myroslav (1887-1979).
Papers, ca. 1912-1979. 1 linear ft.

A political and social activist, Sichynsky was born in Chernykhivtsi, Ukraine. In 1908, he assassinated the governor of Galicia, A. Pototski, in retaliation for the killing of Ukrainian peasants during the diet election of the same year. He was compelled to leave Ukraine and in 1914 arrived in America. In the 1930s, Sichynsky was the president of the Ukrainian Workingmen's Association (now the Ukrainian Fraternal Association). He died in Detroit, MI.

Papers consist of family and general correspondence, speeches, form letters, collection lists, flyers concerning Sichynsky's lecture tours, reports and appeals by the Ukrainian National Association and Ukrainian Fraternal Association, miscellaneous publications, newspaper clippings on Ukrainian and general world affairs, color slides, and a taped interview with Sichynsky. *Includes English.*

Slavutych, Yar (1918-).
Papers, 1965-1975. Ca. 1 linear in.

An author and educator, Slavutych was born in Blahodatne, Ukraine. He came to the United States following World War II and completed his education at the University of Pennsylvania. He then taught college, contributed to many publications, and was active in Ukrainian American and Ukrainian Canadian organizations.

Papers consist of programs and unpublished articles concerning Ukrainians in Canada. *Includes English.*

Sochocky, Julian.
Papers, ca. 1950-1970. 2.5 linear ft.

Papers of Sochocky include leaflets, programs, announcements, periodicals, and newspaper clippings pertaining to Ukraine, Ukrainian Americans, and Ukrainian Canadians, as well as to Cardinal Joseph Slipyj, Galicia, Polish-Galician affairs, Taras Shevchenko, and religious matters. *Inventory available.*

Solovey, Dmytro (1888-1966).
Papers, ca. 1940-1949. 8 linear in.

Papers of Ukrainian historian and economist Solovey consist of correspondence and typescript manuscripts of his works.

Solovey, Oksana (1919-).
Papers, ca. 1961-1972. 2 linear in.

An engineer and translator, Solovey was born in Poltava, Ukraine. She was educated at the University of Kharkiv and the University of Minnesota. Solovey worked as a translator and editor for companies and publications in the United States and Canada and has been active in Ukrainian American organizations.

Papers consist of announcements, correspondence, flyers, newspaper clippings, and other items pertaining to organizations such as the Ukrainian Writers' Association in Exile, "Slovo"; Ukrainian Socialist Party-Munich; Ukrainian National Republic in Exile; Ukrainian American Professional Club-Twin Cities (MN); and others. *Includes some English.*

Stachiw, Matthew (1895-1978).
Papers, ca. 1946-1957. Ca. 1 linear in.

A lawyer, educator, and editor, Stachiw was born in Nyshche, Ukraine. He received his LLD from the University of Prague after serving with the Ukrainian Army from 1918 to 1920; he then practiced law, taught at various universities, and served as editor and contributor for many publications.

Papers include announcements, flyers, and miscellany on Ukrainian American activities and a copy of *Overview of Battle Activities on Ukrainian Lands Occupied by Poland in 1922* (Ohliad boievoï diial'nosty na ukraïns'kykh zemliakh zaniatykh Pol'shcheiu za 1922-yi rik). *Includes English.*

Stangl, Vera Stetkevicz.
Papers, ca. 1910-1972. 1.5 linear ft.

Papers of Stangl, daughter of *Svoboda* editor Joseph Stetkevicz, include musical scores, two of which are hymns dedicated to Ukrainian Americans; music by Stanyslav Liudkevych (1879-1979); patterns of Ukrainian embroideries; and photographs, including those of opera singer Solomea Krushel'nyts'ka and Joseph Stetkevicz. *Includes English.*

Stefan, Augustin Cyril (1893-).
Papers, 1893-1984. Ca. 3.5 linear ft.

An educator, Stefan was born in Poroshkiv, Ukraine. He was educated in Uzhgorod and Budapest and taught at various academies and colleges in Germany and Ukraine before coming to the United States after World War II.

Papers include material for Stefan's memoirs, correspondence, family and other photographs, information on Carpatho-Ukraine, drafts for articles and books, newspaper clippings, maps, and several framed awards. *Includes English and Hungarian.*

Sydorenko, Petro.
Papers, ca. 1960-1967. Ca. 1 linear in.

Papers of Sydorenko, a Ukrainian American artist and director of the Children's Art Studio in Toronto, Canada, include art exhibit programs for Ukrainian Canadian artists and works of Ukrainian children, as well as informative booklets on various topics, including the Ukrainian community in Toronto. *Includes English.*

Teodorowycz, Jurij.
Papers, ca. 1960-1966. 2 linear in.

Papers include programs, souvenir booklets, and announcements of Ukrainian activities in the United States. *Includes English.*

Tyshovnytskyj, Omelan Mychajlo (1899-).
Papers, 1970-1982. 2 linear in.

A civil engineer, Tyshovnytskyj was born in Huta Bojaniwska, Poland. He served with the Austrian Army in 1917-1918, and in Ukraine, 1918-1920. He was educated in Cracow and worked in Ukraine, Poland, and Germany before coming to the United States after World War II. He then took an active interest in Ukrainian American cultural affairs in the Los Angeles, CA, area.

Papers consist of materials pertaining to the cultural activities of the Ukrainian community in Los Angeles. *Includes some English.*

Ukrainian Academy of Arts and Sciences in the United States, Inc. (New York, New York).
Records, ca. 1920-1967. 1 linear ft.

Founded in 1950, the Academy is the major Ukrainian scholarly organization in the United States. It promotes research and studies, scholarly conferences, and congresses. The organization also maintains a museum and archives. It publishes the *Annals of the Ukrainian Academy.*

Records include flyers, programs, newspaper clippings, photographs, and announcement of Ukrainian activities in the United States and Canada. Organizations represented include the Ukrainian Canadian Relief Fund, Women's Auxiliary; the Ukrainian Art Theatre; Ukrainian Democratic Club; and the ODWU (Orhanizatsiia Der'zhavnoho Vidrodzhennia Ukraïny). *Includes English.*

Ukrainian Artists Association in the United States America (New York, New York).
Collection, 1953-1966. 2 linear in.

The Association was founded in 1952 by Ukrainian painters and sculptors who had come to the United States following World War II. It stages art exhibits, and its members hold frequent individual showings. In addition to the New York group, there are local groups in Philadelphia, Chicago, Minneapolis, Detroit, and other cities.

Collection consists mainly of art exhibit programs and art catalogues. Artists represented include Roman Patchowsky, Kateryna Krychevsky, Serhiy Lytvynenko, Alexis Gritchenko, Vasyl H. Krychevsky, Boris Patchowsky, and others. *Includes English.*

(Top) Branch 38, St. Nicholas Brotherhood (founded in 1900), Ukrainian National Association, Auburn, NY; (bottom) Eleanor Roosevelt among Ukrainian women, New York City, NY, both ca. 1930s; from *Jubilee Book of the Ukrainian National Association in Commemoration of the Fortieth Anniversary of Its Existence*, Jersey City, NJ, 1936.

Ukrainian American Collection   361

Ukrainian Congress Committee of America, Baltimore Branch (Maryland).
Records, ca. 1965-1966. Ca. 1 linear in.

The Committee (UCCA) was founded in 1940 and serves as the major Ukrainian federation of organizations in the United States. It is a cultural, political, social, and educational organization which supports re-establishment of a free and independent Ukraine; serves as an information clearinghouse; publishes brochures, journals, and books on Ukraine; and organizes concerts and other cultural events. The Educational Council oversees seventy-five Ukrainian schools with an enrollment of 29,000 students. The UCCA also maintains a library and archives, and publishes the *Ukrainian Quarterly*.

Records of the Baltimore Branch consist of announcements, flyers, and miscellany pertaining to its activities.

Ukrainian Congress Committee of America, Minnesota Branch.
Records, ca. 1949-1986. 10 linear ft.

Records include correspondence, photographs, and other materials pertaining to the organization's activities. Records (1961-1964) of the Shevchenko Memorial Committee of Minnesota, which was organized by the UCCA, are also included. *Includes English. Related collection: Ukrainian Congress Committee of America, Baltimore Branch (MD).*

Ukrainian Jaroslaw Society (Cleveland, Ohio).
Records, ca. 1966- . 1 linear in.

A cultural organization, the Society was founded in Philadelphia, PA, in 1963 and reorganized in Chicago, IL, in 1965. The Society is composed of Ukrainians who emigrated following World War II from the region of Jaroslaw and the borderland west of the River Sian.

Records consist of information pertaining to the reunion gathering of Ukrainian emigrants from that region. *Includes English.*

Ukrainian Knowledge Society of New York City, Inc.
Records, 1908-1948. 8 linear in.

The Society was founded in 1908 and chartered in 1910. Its purpose was to unite the Ukrainian-Rusin nationality group residing in New York and surrounding areas and to provide financial aid in case of illness.

Records include the constitution, membership lists, minutes, and receipt books. Also included are thirty-one notebooks of Ukrainian plays produced by the Society along with two notebooks of songs and poetry by Konstantin Shynkar.

Ukrainians in North Dakota.
Collection, 1968-1971. Ca. 1 linear in.

Newspaper clippings pertain to Ukrainians in Belfield, Jamestown, Minot, and other areas of North Dakota. *Includes English.*

Ukrainian Students' Club, University of Minnesota (Minneapolis-St. Paul).
Records, ca. 1939-1977. Ca. 2.5 linear ft.

Founded in 1939 by A. A. Granovsky, the Club conducts lectures and discussions, provides scholarships for Ukrainian students, and acquaints students and faculty with Ukrainian culture and history.

Records consist of correspondence and minutes. *Includes English.*

Ukrainian Veterans Association (Munich, West Germany).
Records, 1945-1956. Ca. 1.5 linear ft.

The Association was established after the Second World War, in 1945, in Munich. Many of its members emigrated to North America, where they established new veterans' organizations.

Records include correspondence, briefs, minute reports, and circulars. Among the organizations represented in the collection is the Brotherhood of Former Soldiers of the First Ukrainian Division of the Ukrainian National Army (Mittenwald Branch). *Includes German. Inventory available.*

United Ukrainian American Relief Committee (Philadelphia, Pennsylvania).
Records, ca. 1945-1960. 260 linear ft.

Founded in 1944 by concerned Ukrainian American groups, the Committee sought to aid displaced Ukrainians, political refugees, and other war victims. The Committee was based in the United States and had representatives in various European countries. It was affiliated with the Ukrainian Congress Committee.

Records consist of correspondence, requests for assistance, applications, financial records, photographs, resettlement records, and other materials documenting the work of the Committee. Included are financial letters; nominal rolls (names of candidates for emigration); approved assurances; Ukrainian newspaper articles; individual assurances from Arkansas, Illinois, Indiana, Massachusetts, Michigan, New York, Ohio, Pennsylvania, and Rhode Island; and materials documenting work in various European countries. Additional records pertain to the Ukrainian Museum and the Ukrainian Congress Committee of America; the Department of Health, Education, and Welfare; CARE packages; and other relief organizations and activities. *Includes English. Inventory available. Related collections: John Panchuk, Alexander A. Granovsky.*

Visti **(The Herald).**
Records, ca. 1963-1972. Ca. 8 linear ft.

The musical quarterly *Visti* (The Herald) was founded in Minneapolis-St. Paul, MN, in 1962. Its main editor was Oleksandra F. Kostiuk. In 1972, the quarterly became known as *Muzychni Visti* and its publication headquarters was moved to Jersey City, NJ.

Records consist of correspondence, minutes, financial records, subscriptions, articles, and other materials. Major correspondents and contributors include Myroslav Antonovych, Vasyl Yemets, Jacques Hnizdovsky, Vasyl Vytvyts'kyi, Tetiana O. Koshets', Pavlo Matsenko, Roman Prydatkevych, Leonid Poltava, and others. *Includes English. Related collection: Oleksandra F. Kostiuk.*

Wakiriak, John (1921-1980).
Papers, ca. 1950-1978. Ca. 2.5 linear ft.

Papers of Wakiriak, an active member of the Minnesota Ukrainian community, consist of correspondence, programs, flyers, posters, and newspaper clippings. Materials pertain particularly to activities of Ukrainians in Minneapolis, MN, especially members of the St. Constantine Ukrainian Catholic Church community. *Includes English.*

Wasylowsky, Philip and Anna.
Papers, 1940- . Ca. 10 linear ft.

Papers of the Wasylowskys consist of correspondence and minutes of the American Ukrainian Republican Association and correspondence, publications, and newspaper clippings from the Ukrainian National Association. Materials pertain to Ukrainian Day (Chicago, IL), famine in Ukraine (1932-1933), and the Shevchenko Commemoration in Washington, DC. Also included are church anniversary booklets, and photographs and other papers of Dr. John E. Smuk. *Includes English.*

Willis, Judy Komar.
Papers, ca. 1970. Ca. 1 linear in.

Willis is from Lakeville, MN. Papers consist of a brief history of the Komar family. *In English.*

Wynnyk, George.
Papers, ca. 1960-1969. 1 linear in.

Wynnyk was active in the Massachusetts Ukrainian community. Papers include family photographs, newspaper clippings, a map of the Lemko region of Ukraine, and a letter from the Massachusetts governor's office. *Includes English.*

Yaremko, Alexander Wallace.
Papers, 1924-1929. Ca. 1.5 linear ft.

A journalist born in Pennsylvania, Yaremko was organizer, founder, and director of the Ukrainian Cultural Center, a youth organization. He also co-founded and edited the *Ukrainian Chronicle*, was involved with the Ukrainian Youth League of North America, and was active in many other Ukrainian American organizations.

Papers contain biographical information, personal correspondence, materials pertaining to Ukrainian American organizations and cultural activities, and historical material on Ukraine and Ukrainians in America. Included are papers, programs, clippings, and yearbooks pertaining to the Youth League; Ukrainian participation in the Chicago and New York World's Fairs; Ukrainian Catholics; art, ballet, music, and film in the United States and Canada; and poetry. *Mainly in English. Inventory available.*

Yermolenko, Serhij Syla (1905-1981).
Papers, 1943-1981. 6 linear ft.

An engineer, Yermolenko was born in Koliadivka, Ukraine. He was educated at the Mining Academy, Pribram, CSR, and at the University of Prague. He came to the United States in 1949 and settled in Minneapolis, MN. Yermolenko was active professionally and in the Twin Cities Ukrainian community. He held various offices in social, cultural, church, and political organizations.

Papers include correspondence, minutes, and financial records of the Ukrainian Cultural and Arts Club of Minnesota; records of the Commemorative Committee for the Famine in Ukraine; material pertaining to the Ukrainian Congress Committee of America, Minnesota Branch; and records, including photographs, of the Ukraïns'ke Zaporizhske Kozatstvo (Ukrainian Free Cossacks), whose headquarters were in Europe and Chicago, IL. *Includes German, Czech, and Russian.*

Zakharchuk, Dmytro (1894-1980).
Papers, ca. 1923-1987. 1 linear ft.

An artist and poet, Zakharchuk was born in Slowita, Ukraine. After coming to the United States, he studied at Carnegie Institute of Art. His works were commissioned by Ukrainian Orthodox and Catholic churches. His poems were published in Ukraine, the United States, and Canada.

Papers include manuscript and published poetry and an English translation of his experiences in Ukraine during World War I. *Includes English. Inventory available.*

Zelechivsky, Very Rev. Joseph (1890-).
Papers, ca. 1925-1961. 1.5 linear in.

Zelechivsky was born in Borynia, Ukraine. He was ordained as a Ukrainian Orthodox priest in Chicago, IL, in 1919 and served parishes in Kansas, North Dakota, New Jersey, Pennsylvania, New York, Rhode Island, and Massachusetts. During his long career, he was active in choirs and other cultural affairs.

Papers include programs and newspaper clippings on various Ukrainian social events in the United States, and a typescript about Ukrainian literature and Taras Shevchenko. *Includes English.*

Zozula, Yakiv Maksymovych (1893-).
Papers, ca. 1964. Ca. 1 linear in.

A lawyer, Zozula was born in Lebedyn, Ukraine. After serving in the Russian Army and in various government posts, he came to the United States following World War II. He taught at the Ukrainian Tech. Institute (New York), remained active in Ukrainian American and professional affairs, and wrote numerous articles.

Papers include stamps of the Fond Ukraïns'koï Politekhniky and a typescript of his paper entitled "Dr. Mykhaĭlo Briashchaĭko Na Soĭmi Karpats'koï Ukraïny." The typescript paper commemorates the 25th anniversary of Carpatho-Ukraine, especially remembering March 15, 1939, at the Soim (parliament) of Carpatho-Ukraine and Dr. Briashchaĭko's participation.

Monographs

The Ukrainian American monograph collection numbers nearly 4,400 volumes and is considered the largest and richest collection of published material on Ukrainian immigration in the United States. It touches upon virtually every aspect of the Ukrainian American experience. The majority of the collection relates to the period of Ukrainian migration to the United States from the end of World War I to the present.

The collection includes substantial reference works. Among these are *Ukraine: A Concise Encyclopedia*, two volumes (1963, 1971) and *Encyclopedia of Ukraine*, volumes I (A-F) and II (G-K) of five projected (1984-1992), both edited by Volodymyr Kubijovič; *Ukrainians in America: A Bibliographical Directory of Noteworthy Men and Women of Ukrainian Origin in the U.S.A. and Canada*, (1975), edited by D. M. Shtohryn; Alexander Sokolyszyn and Vladimir Wertsman's *Ukrainians in Canada and the United States* (1981); and *Guide to Ukrainian-American Institutions, Professionals, and Business* (1955), edited by Wasyl Weresh. Halyna Myroniuk and Christine Worobec's *Ukrainians in North America: A Select Bibliography* (1981) is based largely on the holdings of the IHRC.

The earliest secondary studies of Ukrainian social, political, and religious life in America were written by Ukrainians in the homeland, who traveled to the United States and Canada to conduct their research. Among the most significant works are Iuliian Bachyns'kyi's *Ukraïns'ka immigratsiia v Z'iedynenykh Derzhavakh Ameryky* (Ukrainian Immigration in the United States of America, 1914); Orest Kyrylenko's *Ukraïntsi v Amerytsi* (Ukrainians in America, 1916); and substantive memoirs, such as Lev Iasinchuk's *Za okeianom* (Over Seas, 1930) and Rev. O. Prystai's four-volume *Z truskavtsia u svit khmaroderiv; Spomyny z mynuloho i suchasnoho* (From Truskavets' into the World of Skyscrapers; Memoirs from the Past and the Present; 1933, 1935-1937).

Major efforts by Ukrainian Americans to chronicle their history began emerging in the 1930s. Among the three significant studies from that period are Wasyl Halich's *Ukrainians in the United States* (1937), M. Nastasivs'kyi's *Ukraïns'ka immigratsiia v Spoluchenykh Derzhavakh* (Ukrainian Immigration in the United States, 1934), and Yaroslav Chyz's *The Ukrainian Immigrants in the United States* (1939). Another significant early work is Stephen W. Mamchur's dissertation, *Nationalism, Religion, and the Problem of Assimilation among Ukrainians in the United States* (1942). More recent writing on Ukrainian American history includes a key study by Myron Kuropas, *The Making of the Ukrainian American, 1884-1939: A Study in Ethno-National Education* (1974), and his overview, *The Ukrainians in America* (1972). A new study is Oksana Grabowicz's *Persistence and Change in Values, Attitudes and Beliefs: A Study of the Ukrainian Community in the U.S. (1988).* Also available are Vladimir Wertsman's *The Ukrainians in America, 1608-1975: A Chronology & Fact Book* (1976), and *The Ukrainian Immigrant Experience in the United States: A Symposium*, edited by Paul R. Magocsi (1979). In addition, the collection includes two compilations of historical photographs: Donald P. Lokuta's *Ukrainian-Americans, An Ethnic Portrait* (1982), and Myron B. Kuropas's *To Preserve a Heritage: The Story of the Ukrainian Immigration in the United States* (1984).

The history of post-World War II Ukrainian refugees in dispaced persons' camps and their resettlement and the literature of that period (1945-1954) are well represented in the collection. A recent significant reference work is Yuri Boshyk and Boris Balan's *Political Refugees and "Displaced Persons," 1945-1954: A Selected Bibliography and Guide to Research with Special Reference to the Ukrainians* (1982). The resettlement effort is documented in Ostap Tarnavs'kyi's *Brat-Bratovi; Knyha pro ZUADK* (Brother's Helping Hand; Book about the United Ukrainian American Relief Committee, 1971). Memoirs of both the DP camp life and resettlement work are reflected in works such as Volodymyr Martynets's *Shliakhom taboriv D.P.: Rudolstadt, Coberg, Dachau, Karlsfeld; spohady iz Skytal'shchyny* (Through the D.P. Camps: Rudolstadt, Coburg, Dachau, Karlsfeld; Memoirs, 1950); Mariia Kuz'movych-Holovins'ka's *Chuzhynoiu: Spomyny* (On Foreign Soil: Memoirs, 197?); and Lubomyr Y. Luciuk's *Heroes of Their Day: The Reminiscences of Bohdan Panchuk* (1983).

Several regional and community studies complement the general histories described. Among these are Michael and Martha Wichorek's *Ukrainians in Detroit* (1968); *The Ukrainians of Maryland*, by Stephen Basarab, et al. (1977); *Ukrainians in Pennsylvania: A Contribution to the Growth of the Commonwealth*, edited by Alexander Lushnycky (1976); and Viktor Balaban's *Ukraïntsi v Teksasi: Materiialy do istoriï 200-richchia ZSA i 100-richchia ukraïnstiv v Amerytsi* (Ukrainians in Texas: Material for the Histories of the U.S.A. Bicentennial and Centennial of Ukrainians in America, 1976).

Ukrainian Canadian history is substantially represented in the monograph collection. The number of studies on the history of Ukrainians in Canada tend to overshadow those few titles on Ukrainian Americans. Major works include the five-volume *Studiï do istoriï ukraïntsiv Kanady* (Studies in the History of Ukrainians in Canada, 1964/65-1973/80), the two-volume *Istoriï ukraïntsiv Kanady* (History of Ukrainians in Canada, 1968-1974) and an English version, *The Ukrainian Canadians: A History* (1970), all by Mykhailo H. Marunchak; Vladimir J. Kaye's *Early Ukrainian Settlements in Canada, 1895-1900; Dr. Joseph Oleskow's Role in the Settlement of the Canadian Northwest* (1964); J. W. Stechishin's *Istoriia poselennia ukraïntsiv u Kanadi* (History of Ukrainian Settlements in Canada, 1975); and sociological studies such as Charles Hurlburt Young's *The Ukrainian Canadians, A Study in Assimilation* (ca. 1931) and *Changing Realities: Social Trends among Ukrainian Canadians*, edited by W. Roman Petryshyn (1980). The collection also includes Paul Yuzyk's *A Statistical Compendium on the Ukrainians in Canada, 1891-1976* (1980) and Bohdan S. Kordan's *Ukrainians and the 1981 Canada Census: A Data Handbook* (1985). Comparative studies of Ukrainians in both the United States and Canada include *Ukraïntsi v amerykans'komu ta kanads'komu suspil'stvakh: Sotsiolohichnyi zbirnyk* (Ukrainians in American and Canadian Society: Contributions to the Sociology of Ethnic Groups, 1976), edited by Wsevolod V. Isajiw. The collection's numerous volumes on Ukrainians in particular Canadian regions tend to focus on the western provinces.

Glimpses of individual Ukrainian American and Ukrainian Canadian immigrant experiences as well as their contributions are reflected in the numerous biographies, memoirs, and personal narrations. One of these traces back to the American Civil war, the biography of General John V. Turchin by Orest Horodys'kyi, *Heneral Ivan V. Turychyn: Osobystyi pryiatel' Prezydenta Linkol'na* (General Ivan V. Turchin: Personal Friend of President Lincoln, 1971). Among the more substantial works by or about Ukrainian Americans are Myron Surmach's *Istoriia moieï "Surmy"; Spohady knyharia* (History of My "Surma"; Memoirs of a Book Dealer, 1982); Ulas Samchuk's *Slidamy pioneriv: Epos ukraïns'koï Ameryky* (In the Footsteps of Pioneers: Epic of Ukrainian America, 1980); Ilarry Piniuta's *Land of Pain, Land of Promise: First Person Accounts by Ukrainian Pioneers, 1891-1914* (1978); Andrii Dubovyi's *Na bat'kivshyni: Z istoriï ukraïns'kykh pioneriv u Nort Dakoti* (In the Native Country: From the History of Ukrainian Pioneers in North Dakota, 1957); Theodore Luciw's *Father Agapius Honcharenko, First Ukrainian Priest in America* (1970); Wasyl and Theodore Luciw's *Agapius Honcharenko and the Alaska Herald: The Editor's Life and an Analysis of His Newspaper* (1963); Donald Lawrence Bern's *An American in the Making: The Biography of William Dzus, Inventor* (1961); Mykola P. Novak's *Na storozhi Ukraïny; Vlasni spohady, istorychni materialy, dokumenty, lystuvannia, arkhiv* (Guardians of Ukraine; Personal Memoirs, Historical Material, Documents, Correspondence, Archives, 1979) and its English component, *Guardians of Ukraine: Historical Documentary and Memoirs* (1978); Simon Demydchuk's *Pivstorichchia hromads'koï pratsi D-ra Semena Demydchuka, 1905-1955 (A Half Century of Ukrainian Community Work*, 1956); and Platon Stasiuk's *V Novomu Sviti; Spomyny i dumky byznesmena* (In the New World; Memoirs and Thoughts of a Businessman; 1958). Among the Ukrainian Canadian biographies is Michael Luchkovich's *A Ukrainian Canadian in Parliament; Memoirs of Michael Luchkovich* (1965).

The histories of Ukrainian American social organizations also constitute an important source of information on early Ukrainian immigrant life. Included among these are descriptions of the oldest Ukrainian American fraternal, the Ukrainian National Association, in *Iuvyleinyi al'manakh, 1894-1944: Vydani z nahody piat'desiatlitn'oho iuvyleiu Ukraïns'koho Narodnoho Soiuzu* (Jubilee Almanac: In Commemoration of the Fiftieth Anniversary of the Ukrainian National Association, 1944) and Anthony Dragan's *Ukrainian National Association: Its Past and Present* (1965). Other fraternals represented in the monograph collection are the Ukrainian Fraternal Association, the Providence Association of Ukrainian Catholics, and the Ukrainian National Aid Association. Histories of social organizations made up of women and youth, such as the Ukrainian Women's League of America, are contained in jubilee publications of their branches in various cities throughout the United States. Included, too, is the League's counterpart in Canada, Ukrainian Women's League of Canada, in Natalia L. Kohus'ka's *Chvert' stolittia na hromadskii nyvi: Istoriia Soiuzu Ukraïnok Kanady, 1926-1951* (Quarter of a Century of Community Work: History of the Ukrainian Women's Association of Canada, 1952). Concerns and activities of Ukrainian immigrant women are also documented in publications resulting from the World Congress of Ukrainian Women, held regularly, the first of which occurred November 12-13, 1948, in Philadelphia and is described in *Svitovyi Kongres Ukraïns'koho Zhinotstva* (World Congress of Ukrainian Women, 1948).

In the area of literature, the collection is dominated by works of nineteenth and twentieth century Ukrainian poets and writers, including Taras H. Shevchenko, Ivan Franko, Lesyia Ukrainka, and others. Early Ukrainian American writers wrote on "themes of longing for the homeland and hardships of immigrant life." This is reflected in the poetry of Dmytro Zakharchuk, *Z vesnianykh dniv: Poeziï* (From Spring Days: Poetry, 1923); Stephan Musiichuk, *Na krylakh v Ukraïnu: Virshi* (On Wings to Ukraine: Poems, 1946); and Alexander A. Granovsky, *Iskry viry; Poeziï* (Sparks of Faith; Poetry, 1953). An important English-language writer is Maria Bloch-Halun, well known in American literature and author of books for children dealing with problems of cultural adjustment and assimilation. Among them are *Aunt America* (1963) and, more recently, *Displaced Person* (ca. 1978).

The style and motifs of post-World War II émigrés are largely devoid of immigrant themes, with the exception of some novels and short stories, such as Dokia Hummena's *Sered khmaroderiv: Niu-Iors'ka mozaïka* (Amidst the Skyscrapers: New York Mosaic, 1962); Sofiia Parfanovych's *Karus' i My: avto-biohrafiia* (Carry and We: Autobiography, 1966) and *Na skhreshchenykh dorohakh* (On Crossroads, 1963); Mykola Ponedilok's *Smishni Sl'ozyny* (Funny Tears, 1966); and Ostap Tarnavsky's *Zhyttia: Vinok sonetiv* (Life: A Wreath of Sonnets, 1952). Also represented in the collection are poets and writers who began their careers in the United States after the 1950s, including Bohdan Boychuk and Bohdan Rubchak. Among the authors of children's literature who are represented by substantial holdings are Lesia Khraplyva and Roman Zavadovych.

An abundance of Ukrainian Canadian literature is available in the collection. Examples include Paul Crath's *Koly ziishlo sontse* (When the Sun Rose, 1918), Tedor Fedyk's *Pisni imigrantiv pro staryi i novyi krai* (Immigrant Songs about the Old and New Country, 1927), Iar Slavutych's *Trofeiï: 1938-1963* (Trophies, 1963), Ilia Kyriiak's *Syny zemli: Povist' z ukraïns'koho zhyttia v Kanadi* (Sons of the Land: Novel from Ukrainian Life in Canada, 1939-1945), and Gus Romaniuk's *Taking Root in Canada* (1954).

Religion, a major component of Ukrainian immigrant life, is represented by major studies on the history of the Ukrainian Orthodox, Catholic, and Protestant churches in North America and Ukraine. Among these are Ivan Vlasovs'kyi's four-volume work, *Narys istoriï ukraïns'koï pravoslavnoï tserkvy* (1955-1966) and English translation, *Outline History of the Ukrainian Orthodox Church*, volume I only (1956); Isydor Nahaievs'kyi's *Rym i Vyzantiia: Vselens'ka tserkva i patriiarkh Fotii* (Rome and Byzantium: The Universal Church and Patriarch Fotii (1956); Bohdan Procko's *Ukrainian Catholics in America: A History* (ca. 1982); Paul Yuzyk's thesis, *The Ukrainian Greek Orthodox Church of Canada, 1918-1951* (1958); and H. Domoshovets's *Narys istoriï Ukraïns'ko-baptysts'koï tserkvy* (An Outline of the History of the Ukrainian-Baptist Church, 1967).

The historical importance of education and language to Ukrainian ethnic communities is evident in the establishment of Ukrainian and parochial schools, publication of textbooks, and efforts to standardize curricula. This is reflected in the monograph collection through readers and language instruction books such as one by Ilarion (Metropolitan of Winnipeg and All Canada), *Ukraïns'kyi Literaturnyi Naholos: Movozanvcha monohrafiia* (Ukrainian Literary Accent: Linguistic Monograph, 1952); also Kost' Kysilevs'kyi's *Ukraïnoznavstvo v shkoli: Prohrama i dydaktyka* (Knowledge of Ukrainian Things in School: Program and Didactics, 1955); and Elias Shklanka's *Ukrainian Grammar* (1944).

Newspapers

Ameryka (America), Philadelphia, PA (previously published in New Britain, CT). Daily: 1925, 1939, 1943-date. Includes English.

Bat'kivshchyna (Our Country), Toronto, Ontario, Canada. Irregular: 1955-date.

Chas (Time), Nuremberg, Germany. Weekly: 1946-1949.

Detroïts'ki Visti (Detroit Ukrainian News; part of **Vil'ne Slovo**), Detroit, MI. Weekly: 1965-1967, 1969.

Dnipro (Dnieper; changes to magazine format after 1939), Philadelphia, PA. Monthly: 1931, 1934-1940. Includes some English.

Dzvin (The Bell), Allentown, PA. Monthly: 1929.

Dzvin (The Bell), Toronto, Ontario, Canada. Weekly: 1941-1942.

Federalist-Demokrat, Ottawa, Ontario, Canada. Semi-monthly: 1953-1954. Includes English.

Holos Lemkivshchyny (The Lemko Voice), Yonkers, NY. Monthly: 1963-1977.

Holos Molodi (Youth Speaks), Winnipeg, Manitoba, Canada. Monthly: 1949-1954. Includes English.

Homin Ukraïny (Echo of Ukraine), Toronto, Ontario, Canada. Weekly: 1950-1981.

Hromads'kyi Holos (Voice of the Commonwealth), New York, NY. Bi-monthly: 1941, 1943-1948, 1952-1953, 1956, 1958, 1960-1961, 1964-1965, 1968.

Ievanhel's'ka Pravda (The Truth of the Gospel), Toronto, Ontario, Canada. Monthly: 1951-1953, 1955-1956, 1958, 1962. Includes English.

Industriialist (Industrialist), New York, NY. 1919.

Kameniari (The Stonecutters), New Brunswick, NJ. Irregular: 1965.

Kanadiïskaia Zhyzn (Canadian Life), Winnipeg, Manitoba, Canada. Semi-monthly: 1923. Includes Russian.

Kanadiïs'kyi Farmer (Canadian Farmer), Winnipeg, Manitoba, Canada. Weekly: 1938, 1950, 1953-1956, 1959-1973.

Kanadiïs'kyi Ranok (Canadian Morning), Winnipeg, Manitoba/Toronto, Ontario, Canada. Monthly/bi-monthly: 1952-1953, 1955-1958, 1960. Includes English.

Kanads'ka Ukraïna (Canadian Ukraine), Edmonton, Alberta, Canada. 1976-1978.

Lemkivshchyna (Lemkovina), Toronto, Ontario, Canada. Bi-weekly (monthly): 1951.

Lemkivs'ki Visti (Lemko News), Toronto, Ontario, Canada/Camillus, NY. Monthly: 1958-1979.

Lemkivs'kyĭ Dzvin (The Lemko Bell), New York, NY (previously published in Passaic, NJ). Monthly: 1936-1940.

Literatura i Mystetstvo (Literature and Art), Toronto, Ontario, Canada. Monthly: 1958, 1962-1963, 1965-1966.

Literaturnyĭ Zoshyt (Literary Notebook), Neu-Ulm, Germany. Monthly: 1947.

Michigans'ka Ukraïns'ka Hazeta (Michigan Ukrainian Gazette; previously titled **Ukraïns'ka Gazeta**), Detroit, MI. Biweekly (weekly): 1936, 1959-1960, 1962-1963.

Na Chuzhyni (In a Foreign Country), Augsburg, Germany. 1946.

Na Zustrich (Toward a Meeting), Toronto, Ontario, Canada. Special issue: 1954.

Narodna Hazeta (People's Gazette), Winnipeg, Manitoba, Canada. Daily: 1939. Includes English.

Narodna Volya (People's Will), Scranton, PA. Weekly: 1917, 1927, 1929-date. (Microfilm: 1914-1973). Includes English.

Nash Chas (Our Time), Chicago, IL. Bi-weekly: 1968-1970.

Nash Stiah (Our Banner), Chicago, IL. Weekly: 1935, 1937-1942.

Nash Vik (Our Age), Toronto, Ontario, Canada/New York, NY. Weekly: 1949-1952.

Nasha Bat'kivshchnyna (Our Fatherland; format changes to magazine in 1972), New York, NY. Three times per month (semi-weekly): 1962-1972.

Nasha Derzhava (Our Country), Toronto, Ontario, Canada. Bi-weekly: 1953-1955.

Nasha Meta (Our Goal), Toronto, Ontario, Canada. Weekly: 1950-1960, 1964, 1968-1973, 1977-1981, 1983.

Nashe Zhyttia (Our Life), Augsburg, Germany. Weekly: 1946-1948.

Nashe Zhyttia (Our Life), Philadelphia, PA. Monthly: 1944-1945, 1947, 1949-1950. Includes English.

Natsionalist, New York, NY. Bi-weekly: 1935-1939. (Microfilm: 1935-1939). Includes English.

Natsionalist, Philadelphia, PA. Weekly: 1935.

Natsionalna Trybuna (The National Tribune), New York, NY. Weekly: 1950-1951, 1981-1984. Includes English.

Nedilia (Sunday), Schweinfurt, Aschaffenburg, and Augsburg, West Germany. Weekly: 1947-1950.

The New Canadians, Toronto, Ontario, Canada. Monthly (irregular): 1937-1938. English.

Nova Pora (New Era), Detroit, MI. Weekly: 1937, 1939. Includes English.

Nova Zoria (The New Star), Chicago, IL. Weekly: 1965-date. Includes English.

Novyĭ Shliakh (The New Way; organ of the Ukrainian National Federation), Toronto, Ontario, Canada. Weekly: 1935-1974, 1976-1980.

Novyĭ Svit (New World), Jersey City, NJ (previously published in New York, NY). Monthly: 1951-1954.

Novyĭ Svit (New World), Philadelphia, PA. Semi-monthly: 1950-1951.

Obrii (Horizons), New York, NY. Monthly: 1951.

Postup (Progress), Winnipeg, Manitoba, Canada. Weekly: 1960-1970, 1973-1974, 1976-1984.

Pravda (The Truth), Winnipeg, Manitoba, Canada. Bi-weekly (weekly): 1936.

Prometeĭ (Prometheus; previously titled **Ukraïnskyĭ Prometeĭ**), New York, NY/Detroit, MI. Weekly: 1951-1961.

Promin' (Sun Ray), Salzburg, Austria. Weekly: 1948-1949.

Robitnychyĭ Holos (Labor's Voice), Akron, OH. Monthly: 1925-1926.

Robitnyk (The Worker), New York, NY. Weekly: 1919.

Rozbudova (Expansion), Toronto, Ontario, Canada. Bi-weekly: 1957.

Shliakh (The Way), Philadelphia, PA. Weekly: 1940, 1942-1943, 1945-1946, 1950-1961, 1963-1966, 1968, 1971, 1974, 1979-1984. Includes English.

Sich, Chicago, IL. Weekly: 1933.

Sichovyĭ Klych (The Sitch Call), New York, NY. Monthly: 1936-1940. Includes English.

7 Mynulykh Dniv (Seven Passed Days), New York, NY. Weekly: 1951.

Skhidniak (Easterner), New York, NY. Semi-monthly: 1953.

Slovo (The Word), Regensburg, Germany. Weekly: 1945-1946.

Smoloskyp (The Torch), Ellicott City, MD. Quarterly: 1979-1982.

Sobornyk (Synodical), Cleveland, OH. Monthly (?): 1960-1961.

Sofiïs'ki Dzvony (Bells of Sophia), Grimsby, Ontario, Canada. 1971.

Sojuz (Union), Pittsburgh, PA. Weekly: 1911-1912, 1915.

Sport, Toronto, Ontario, Canada. Weekly: 1955-1956.

Sportovyĭ Reporter (Sports Reporter), New York, NY. Weekly: 1956.

Student, Edmonton, Alberta, Canada. Monthly: 1980. Mainly English.

Svitlo i Holos Pravdy (The Light and the Voice of Truth; changes to magazine format), Winnipeg, Manitoba, Canada. Monthly: 1953-1955.

Svoboda (Liberty), Jersey City, NJ. Daily: 1914, 1918-1919, 1921-1933, 1935-date. (Microfilm: 1893-1967).

Ukraïna (Ukraine), Chicago, IL. Weekly: 1931.

Ukraïna (Ukraine), New York, NY. Semi-monthly (weekly): 1939-1941. (Microfilm: 1939-1941). Includes English.

The Ukrainian-American, New York, NY. Monthly: 1975, 1977. English.

Ukrainian American News of Pennsylvania, Philadelphia, PA. Monthly: 1946-1948. Includes English.

The Ukrainian Record, Edmonton, Alberta, Canada. Monthly: 1960, 1963. English.

The Ukrainian Times, Winnipeg, Manitoba, Canada. Monthly: 1974-1975.

Ukraïns'ka Hazeta (Ukrainian Gazette), Detroit, MI. Bi-weekly: 1960.

Ukraïns'ka Hromads'ka Pora (Ukrainian Community Time), Detroit, MI. Weekly: 1945-1950.

Ukraïns'ke Narodne Slovo (The Ukrainian National Word; previously titled **Narodne Slovo**; official organ of the Ukrainian National Aid Association), Pittsburgh, PA. Bi-weekly: 1931-1934, 1938-1940, 1942-1980. Includes English.

Ukraïns'ke Slovo (Ukrainian Word), Blomberg, Germany. Weekly: 1948.

Ukraïns'ke Slovo (Ukrainian Word), Regensburg, Germany. Weekly: 1946.

Ukraïns'ke Slovo (Ukrainian Word), Winnipeg, Manitoba, Canada. Weekly: 1951.

Ukraïns'ke Zhyttia (Ukrainian Life), Chicago, IL. Monthly (bi-weekly): 1951, 1956-1981.

Ukraïns'ke Zhyttia (Ukrainian Life), Toronto, Ontario, Canada. Weekly.

Ukraïns'ki Novyny (Ukrainian News), Detroit, MI. Weekly: 1942. Includes English.

Ukraïns'ki Shchodenni Visti (Ukrainian Daily News), New York, NY. Daily: 1921, 1935, 1937-1940, 1943, 1949, 1951-1953, 1955.

Ukraïns'ki Visti (Ukrainian News), Detroit, MI (previously published in Neu-Ulm, West Germany). Weekly: 1946-date.

Ukraïns'ki Visti (Ukrainian News), Edmonton, Alberta, Canada. Weekly: 1949-1950, 1953-1954, 1959-1961, 1964-1983. Includes English.

Ukraïns'ki Visti (Ukrainian News), Neu-Ulm, Germany. Weekly: 1946, 1948.

Ukraïns'kyï Holos (Ukrainian Voice), Munich, Germany. Weekly: 1949.

Ukraïns'kyï Holos (Ukrainian Voice), Winnipeg, Manitoba, Canada. Weekly: 1910, 1925, 1927-1928, 1931, 1934-1935, 1937-date.

Ukraïnskyï Robitnyk (Ukrainian Toiler), Toronto, Ontario, Canada. Weekly: 1946, 1948, 1951-1956.

Ukraïns'kyï Selianyn (The Ukrainian Peasant), New York, NY. Monthly: 1953-1962.

Ukraïns'kyï Svit (Ukrainian World), Winnipeg, Manitoba, Canada. Monthly: 1967-1968.

Vidrodzhennia (Restoration), Scranton, PA. Monthly: 1930. Includes English.

Vil'ne Slovo (Free Word), Newark, NJ. Weekly: 1935.

Vil'ne Slovo (Free Word), Toronto, Ontario, Canada. Weekly: 1956-1981, 1983.

Vil'nyï Svit (Free World), Winnipeg, Manitoba, Canada. Weekly: 1966-1977, 1980-1981.

Visti z Ohaïo (News from Ohio), Cleveland, OH. Semi-monthly: 1936-1937.

Visti z "Provydinnia" (News from "Providence"), Philadelphia, PA. Monthly: 1958.

Visti z Ukraïny (News from Ukraine), New York, NY. 1941.

Vistnyk (The Herald), Winnipeg, Manitoba, Canada. Bi-weekly: 1935, 1940-1974, 1977, 1979, 1981, 1983-1984. Includes English.

Vpered (Forward), Toronto, Ontario, Canada. Bi-weekly: 1939-1940.

Za Povernennia na Bat'kivshchynu (For the Return to the Fatherland), West Berlin, West Germany. Weekly: 1956-1960.

Serials

Al'manakh Svitannia (The Daybreak Almanac; previously titled **Svitannia**), Toronto, Ontario, Canada. Quarterly: 1968-1972.

Al'manakh Ukraïns'koho Brats'koho Soiuzu (Almanac of the Ukrainian Fraternal Association; title varies: **Kaliendar Ukraïns'koho Robitnychoho Soiuza**), Scranton, PA. Annual: 1925-1928, 1931-1942, 1945-1951, 1979, 1988. Includes English.

Al'manakh Ukraïns'koho Narodnoho Soiuza (Almanac of the Ukrainian National Association; title varies: **The Little Russian Almanac, Kalendar Rus'koho Narodnoho Soiuza v Amerytsi, Kalendar Ukraïns'koho Narodnoho Souizu, Kalendar Al'manakh Ukraïns'koho Narodnoho Soiuza**), Jersey City, NJ. Annual: 1901-1903, 1905, 1907-1910, 1913-1915, 1917-1920, 1922-1933, 1949, 1951-1952, 1961-1962, 1964-1982, 1983, 1987. Golden Anniversary Edition 1917-1967.

American Friends of ABN Information Bulletin (Antibolshevist Block of Nations), New York, NY. Monthly: 1952. English.

The American-Ukrainian Youth, Cleveland, OH. Monthly: 1936-1937. English.

Americans for Human Rights in Ukraine, Newark, NJ. Annual: 1983. Includes English.

Amerykans'kyī Prosvitianyn (The American Member of the Organization "Enlightenment"), Lvov, Poland. Frequency varies: 1925-1926, 1932.

The Ark, Stamford, CT. Monthly: 1946-1947, 1949-1956, 1964.

Arka (The Ark), Munich, Germany. Monthly: 1947-1948.

Arkhyeparkhiial'ni Visti (Archdiocesan News), Philadelphia, PA. Monthly: 1971. Includes English.

Bahatstvo Dukhovne (The Spiritual Riches), Lakewood, OH. Monthly: two undated issues.

Basilian Torch, Fox Chase Manor, PA. Bi-monthly: 1955. English.

Bazar, New York, NY. Monthly: 1920-1921, 1923.

Beacon, Toronto, Ontario, Canada. Quarterly: 1972-date. English.

Bibliotechka Chornomortsia (Little Library of the Organization "The Black Sea"), Toronto, Ontario, Canada. Frequency varies: 1951.

Biblos, New York, NY. Quarterly: 1955-1968, 1970-1972, 1976, 1979.

Biuleten' (Bulletin of St. George's Ukrainian Orthodox Church), Grimsby, Ontario, Canada. Weekly: 1966.

Biuleten' Amerykans'koho Viddilu Naukovoho T-va im. Shevchenka (Bulletin of the American Branch of the Shevchenko Scientific Society), New York, NY. Quarterly: 1952-1964.

Biuleten' Bohoslovs'ko-Pedahohichnoï Akademiï (Bulletin of the Theological-Pedagogic Academy), Munich, Germany. Frequency varies: 1946-1947.

Biuleten' Bat'kivs'koho Komitetu pry Shkoli Ukraïnoznavstva (Bulletin of the Parents Committee of the Ukrainian Knowledge School), Chicago, IL. Quarterly: 1975-1977.

Biuleten' Federal'noï Kredytovoï Kooperatyvy Samopomich (Bulletin of the Federal Credit Union "Self-Reliance"), Chicago, IL. Quarterly: 1963-1965, 1967-1968.

Biuleten' Filiï UKKA (Bulletin of the Ukrainian Congress Committee of America Local Branch), St. Paul, MN. 1952.

Biuleten' Fondu Katedry Ukraïnoznavstva (Bulletin of the Ukrainian Studies Fund), New York, NY. Annual: 1959-1960.

Biuleten' Holovnoï Upravy Dobrus v SSHA (Bulletin of the National Council of the Democratic Association of Ukrainians Formerly Oppressed in the USSR in the USA), New York, NY. 1953.

Biuleten' Holovnoï Upravy Ob'iednannia Prykhyl'nykiv Ukraïns'koï Narodn'oï Respubliky v SSHA (Bulletin of the National Council of the Friends of the Ukrainian National Republic in the USA), New York, NY. 1960, 1962, 1964-1965, 1969-1970.

Biuleten' Kliubu Pryiateliv Ukraïns'koï Knyzhky (Bulletin of the Friends of the Ukrainian Book Club), Winnipeg, Manitoba, Canada. Frequency varies: 1951-1952.

Biuleten' Kolegiï Sv. Andreia (Bulletin of the College of St. Andrew), Winnipeg, Manitoba, Canada. Monthly: 1967. Includes English.

Biuleten' Komitetu Ukraïns'kykh Pravoslavnykh Myrian u ZDA (Bulletin of the Committee of Ukrainian Orthodox Laymen in the U.S.A.), New York, NY. 1961. English section. Includes English.

Biuleten' Komitetu Hromads'koï Iednosty (Bulletin of the Committee for a Unified Community), New York, NY. 1967.

Biuleten' Koordynatsiïnoï Rady Ideolohichno Sporidnenykh Natsionalistychnykh Orhanizatsiï (Bulletin of the Coordinating Council of Ideologically Related Nationalist Organizations), Toronto, Ontario, Canada. Monthly: 1966-1967.

Biuleten' Natsionalistychnoï Orhanizatsiï Ukraïns'kykh Studentiv Velykonimechychyny (Bulletin of the Nationalist Organization of Ukrainian Students in Germany (NOUS), Berlin, Germany. Monthly: 1944.

Biuleten' Natsional'no-Vyzvol'noho Ukraïns'koho Selians'koho Rukhu (Bulletin of the Ukrainian Peasant National Liberation Movement), New York, NY. Monthly: 1955.

Biuleten'. Naukove Tovarystvo Im. Shevchenka-Toronto (Bulletin of the Shevchenko Scientific Society-Toronto; previously titled **Kanadiis'kyi Viddil NTSH**, [Canadian Branch of SSS], Toronto, Ontario, Canada. 1953.

Biuleten' Naukovoho T-va Im. Shevchenka v Amerytsi (Bulletin of the Shevchenko Scientific Society in America), New York, NY. Quarterly: 1952, 1955-1956, 1974, 1979-1981.

Biuleten' Ob'iednannia Ukraïns'kykh Pedahohiv Kanady (Bulletin of the Association of Ukrainian Pedagogues of Canada), Toronto, Ontario, Canada. Monthly: 1963.

Biuleten' ODUM [Ob'iednannia Demokratychnoï Ukraïns'koï Molodi] (Bulletin of the Ukrainian Democratic Youth Association), New York, NY. Bi-monthly: 1951.

Biuleten ODVU [Orhanizatsiï Derzhavnoho Vidrodzhenia Ukraïny] (Bulletin of the Organization for the Rebirth of Ukraine), Detroit, MI. Frequency varies: 1974-1976.

Biuleten ODVU (Bulletin of the National Executive of the Organization for the Rebirth of Ukraine), New York, NY. Monthly: 1973-1975.

Biuleten' Okruzhnoï Rady SUA v Chikago (Bulletin of the Regional Council of the Ukrainian National Women's League of America in Chicago), Chicago, IL. 1969.

Biuleten' Okruzhnoï Rady SUA v Ditroïti (Bulletin of the Regional Council of the Ukrainian National Women's League in Detroit), Detroit, MI. Quarterly: 1966-1967.

Biuleten' Orhanizatsiï Ukraïns'koho Vyzvol'noho Frontu (Bulletin of the Organizations of the Ukrainian Liberation Front), Philadelphia, PA. 1963 (?).

Biuleten' Parafiï Sv. Andriïvs'koï Ukraïns'koï Pravoslavnoï Tserkvy v Los Andzheles (Bulletin of St. Andrew's Ukrainian Orthodox Church in Los Angeles), Los Angeles, CA. Monthly: 1973-1974, 1976-1982.

Biuleten' Parafiï Sv. Apostola Andriia Pervozvannoho u Vashingtoni (Bulletin of St. Andrew [the First-Called] Church in Washington), Washington, DC. Monthly (?): 1968.

Biuleten' Parafiial'noï Upravy Ukraïns'koï Pravoslavnoï Tserkvy Sv. Volodymyra i Sv. Ol'hy (Bulletin of the Parish Committee of SS Volodymyr and Olga Ukrainian Orthodox Church), St. Paul, MN. Monthly: 1968-1969.

Biuleten' Parokhiï Sv. Andreia (Bulletin of St. Andrew's Church), Winnipeg, Manitoba, Canada. Monthly: 1956-1963, 1974-1975.

Biuleten' Posviachennia Plastovoho Domu (Bulletin of the Dedication of the Plast Home; cover title **Biuleten' Komitetu Posviachennia Pershoho Plastovoho Domu v Ditroïti**), Detroit, MI. Monthly: 1951.

Biuleten'. Soiuz Ukraïns'koho Studentstva Kanady (Bulletin of the Association of Ukrainian Students of Canada), Toronto, Ontario, Canada. 1961.

Biuleten' Soiuzu Ukraïns'kykh Natsional'nykh Demokrativ u Zluchenykh Derzhavakh (Bulletin of the Association of Ukrainian National Democrats in the United States), Philadelphia, PA. 1950.

Biuleten' Soiuzu Ukr.-Kanad. Veteraniv i Ukr. Viddilu Kanad. Lehionu (Bulletin of the Association of Ukrainian-Canadian Veterans and Ukrainian Branch of the Canadian Legion), Toronto, Ontario, Canada. Monthly: 1954, 1961-1963.

Biuleten' Spilky Vyzvolennia Ukraïny, Kraïova Uprava v Kanadi (Bulletin of the Association for the Liberation of Ukraine), Toronto, Ontario, Canada. Monthly: 1966-1967.

Biuleten' Suspil'noï Sluzhby Ukraïntsiv Kanady-Viddil Toronto (Bulletin of Ukrainian Canadian Social Services-Toronto Branch), Toronto, Ontario, Canada. 1967.

Biuleten' SVU (Bulletin of the Association for the Liberation of Ukraine), [USA]. 1954, 1958.

Biuleten' Tovarystva Absol'ventiv UHA-UTHI (Bulletin of the Society of Graduates of the Ukrainian Husbandry Academy-Ukrainian Technical and Husbandry Institute; previously titled **Biuleten' Kontaktnoho Komitetu Absol'ventiv i Studentiv UHA-UTHI**), New York, NY. Monthly: 1956-1958, 1962, 1964-1973.

Biuleten' Tovarystva Prykhyl'nykiv Ukraïns'koï Narodn'oï Respubliky (Bulletin of the Alliance of Friends of the Ukrainian Democratic Republic in Minneapolis), Minneapolis/St. Paul, MN. Annual: 1957-1971, 1973-1974, 1977-1978.

Biuleten' T-va Prykhyl'nykiv Ukraïns'koï Narodnoï Respubliky v Detroïti (Bulletin of the Alliance of Friends of the Ukrainian Democratic Republic in Detroit), Detroit, MI. Bimonthly: 1966-1967.

Biuleten' Tovarystva Spryiannia Ukraïns'kiï Natsional'niï Radi (Bulletin of the Society for Supporting the Ukrainian National Council), Minneapolis/St. Paul, MN. Annual: 1951-1958, 1961-1964, 1966, 1969-1970, 1974-1975, 1979.

Biuleten' Tovarystva Ukraïns'kykh Inzheneriv Ameryky (Bulletin of the Ukrainian Engineers Society of America), New York, NY. Quarterly: 1969-1981.

Biuleten' Tovarystva Ukraïns'kykh Inzheneriv v Amerytsi (Bulletin of the Ukrainian Engineers Society of America), Detroit, MI. Monthly: 1953-1955, 1961.

Biuleten' Ukraïns'koho Ievanhel's'koho Obiednannia v Pivnichnii Amerytsi (Bulletin of the Ukrainian Evangelical Union in North America), Detroit, MI. 1960.

Biuleten' Ukraïns'koho Kongresovoho Komitetu Ameryky: Metropolital'nyĭ Viddil v Detroĭti (Bulletin of the Ukrainian Congress Committee of America: Metropolitan Branch of Detroit), Detroit, MI. 1967.

Biuleten' Ukraïns'koho Kongresovoho Komitetu Ameryky (Bulletin of the Ukrainian Congress Committee of America), Hamtramck, MI. 1960.

Biuleten' Ukraïns'koho Natsional'no-Derzhavnoho Soiuzu v SSHA (Bulletin of the Ukrainian National State Union in the USA), New York, NY. Bi-monthly: 1953-1959.

Biuleten' Ukraïns'koho Natsional'noho Ob'iednannia Kanady (Bulletin of the Ukrainian National Union of Canada), Toronto, Ontario, Canada. Monthly (?): 1956.

Biuleten' Ukraïns'koho Publitsystychno-Naukovoho Instytutu (Bulletin of the Ukrainian Information and Research Institute), Chicago, IL. Frequency varies: 1963, 1968-1970. Includes English.

Biuleten' Ukraïns'koho Zolotoho Khresta (Bulletin of the Ukrainian Gold Cross), Rochester, NY. Frequency varies: 1975-1981.

Biuleten' Ukraïns'koï Demokratychnoï Molodi (Bulletin of the Ukrainian Democratic Youth), Minneapolis/St. Paul, MN. 1955.

Biuleten' Ukraïns'koï Katolyts'koï Tserkvy v Los Angeles (Bulletin of the Ukrainian Catholic Church in Los Angeles), Los Angeles, CA. Monthly: 1962, 1968, 1970. Includes English.

Biuleten' Ukraïns'koï Vil'noï Akademiï Nauk. Canada (Bulletin of the Ukrainian Free Academy of Sciences), Winnipeg, Manitoba, Canada. 1968.

Biuleten' Ukraïns'koï Vil'noï Akademiï Nauk u SSHA (Bulletin of the Ukrainian Free Academy of Sciences in the U.S.A.), New York, NY. Bi-annual: 1951-1959.

Biuleten' Ukraïns'kykh Ievanhel's'ko-reformovanykh Tserkov v Toronti i Detroĭti (Bulletin of the Ukrainian Evangelical-Reformed Churches in Toronto and Detroit), East Detroit, MI. 1966.

Biuleten' Ukraïns'kykh Zluchenykh Orhanizatsiĭ (Bulletin of the United Ukrainian Organizations), Cleveland, OH. 1957. Includes some English.

Biuleten' Viddilu U.K.K.A. v Niu Heĭveni (Bulletin of the Ukrainian Congress Committee of America in New Haven), New Haven, CT. 1953.

Biuleten' Zbirkovoho Komitetu pry Ukraïns'kiĭ Pravoslavniĭ Tserkvi Sv. Sofiï v Montreali (Bulletin of the Collection Committee of the Ukrainian Orthodox Church of St. Sophia in Montreal), Montreal, Quebec, Canada. 1954.

Biuro Provid Ukraïns'kykh Natsionalistiv, Informatsiĭnyĭ Biuleten' (Bureau of the Leadership of Ukrainian Nationalists, Information Bulletin), [USA] Monthly: 1974-1975.

Bodiak (Thistle), New York, NY. Frequency varies: 1939.

Boh Ie Odyn (God Is One), Wilsonville, Ontario, Canada. Quarterly: 1979-1983.

Bohoslov (The Theologian), Munich, Germany. 1949.

Bohoslov (The Theologian), New York, NY. 1951.

Bohoslovs'kyĭ Visnyk (Theological Newsletter), Augsburg-Munich, Germany. Monthly: 1948.

Borot'ba za Voliu (The Struggle for Freedom), Winnipeg, Manitoba, Canada. Monthly: 1940.

Brats'kyĭ Lystok (Fraternal Newsletter), Chicago, IL. Quarterly: 1978, 1980-1984.

Brats'kyĭ Lystok (Fraternal Newsletter), Heidenau, Germany. Weekly: 1947-1949.

Brody-Lew, New York, NY. Annual: 1955-1957, 1959-1975.

The Bugler (Ukrainian American Veterans of Philadelphia), Philadelphia, PA. 1945.

Bukovyna (Bukovina), Toronto, Ontario, Canada. Quarterly: 1977-date.

Bulletin Immaculate Conception Ukr. Cath. Parish Basilian Fathers, Hamtramck, MI. Weekly: 1952-1953, 1956-1957, 1964, 1974. Includes English.

The Bulletin of Lemkovina, Yonkers, NY. Monthly: 1975.

Bulletin of Orthodox Christian Education, Nyack, NY. Semi-annual: 1958-1959. English.

Bulletin Ukrainian Congress Committee of America, New York, NY. Bi-monthly: 1981-1982. Includes English.

Bulletinette (Ukrainian Orthodox League of United States of America), Philadelphia, PA. Monthly: 1956, 1958-1961, 1968. English.

Canadian Institute of Ukrainian Studies Newsletter, Edmonton, Alberta, Canada. Frequency varies: 1976-date. Includes English.

Canadian Institute of Ukrainian Studies Register, Edmonton, Alberta, Canada. Annual: 1985-1986. English.

The Catholic Advocate, Washington, DC. 1948.

The Catholic Directory. Byzantine Rite, Archeparchy of Philadelphia, U.S.A (previously titled The Catholic Directory. Byzantine Rite Apostolic of Philadelphia), Philadelphia, PA. Annual: 1952, 1955-1956, 1958-1959, 1962-1965. English.

The Centre for Ukrainian Canadian Studies Courses and Programs, Winnipeg, Manitoba, Canada. Annual: 1982-1983. English.

Chikags'ki Visti (Chicago News), Chicago, IL. Frequency varies: 1963-1964.

Chornomorska Sitch Soccer Bulletin, Newark, NJ. 1966. English.

Christ the King Ukrainian Catholic Church Parish Bulletin, Nicetown, Philadelphia, PA. 1963. Ukrainian and/or English.

Chytaĭmo Vsi (Let's All Read), New York, NY. 1966.

Cleveland Selfreliance Credit Union Financial Report, Cleveland, OH. Annual: 1984. Includes English.

Consistory of the Ukrainian Orthodox Church of the USA Circular, South Bound Brook, NJ. Weekly: 1974-1975. English.

The Co-op Newsletter, Chicago, IL. Monthly: 1977. Includes English.

The Cossacks Life, Providence, RI. Monthly: 1953-1954, 1958, 1968.

De Nashi Dity (Where Are Our Children), Philadelphia, PA. Frequency varies: 1962.

Derzhavnyts'ka Dumka (Statesman's Thought), Philadelphia, PA. Quarterly: 1951-1952.

Derzhavnyts'kym Shliakhom (The Pathway to Statehood), Philadelphia, PA. Frequency varies: 1963.

Digest of the Soviet Ukrainian Press, Munich, West Germany (previously published in New York, NY). Monthly: 1957-1958, 1963-1967, 1970 (Annual Index), 1971. English.

Ditroïts'ki Novyny (Detroit News), Detroit, MI. Frequency varies: 1967-1969.

Diyaloh (Dialogue), Toronto, Ontario, Canada. Annual: 1971-1980, 1982-1983.

Dlia Ukraïny (For Ukraine), Detroit, MI. 1950.

Dnipro (Dnieper; newspaper prior to 1940), Philadelphia, PA. Monthly, Semi-monthly: 1940-1950, 1956, 1985. Includes English.

Do Vysot (To the Heights), Toronto, Ontario, Canada. 1959-1960, 1965.

Dobryĭ Pastyr' (Good Shepherd), New York, NY. Monthly: 1920-1921.

Dobryĭ Pastyr', Kalendar (Good Shepherd, Calendar), New York, NY. Annual: 1950, 1952.

Dobryĭ Pryiatel', Ievanhel's'kyĭ Kalendar (Good Friend, Evangelical Calendar), Winnipeg, Manitoba, Canada-Toronto, Ontario, Canada. Annual: 1956.

Dorohovkaz (The Guide; previously titled **Biuleten' Soiuzu Buvshykh Ukraïns'kykh Voiakiv u Kanadi**), Toronto, Ontario, Canada. Bi-monthly (quarterly): 1959-1970.

Dzvin (The Bell), Minneapolis/St. Paul, MN. Monthly: 1964-1965.

Dzvin (The Bell), Salzburg, Austria. Monthly: 1946.

Dzvinok (The Hand Bell), Minneapolis, MN. Annual: 1961-1964, 1975.

Dzvony (The Bells), Rome, Italy; Detroit, MI; and Chicago, IL. Monthly: 1978-1980.

Ekran; Illustrovanyi Dvo-Misiachnyk Ukraïnskoho Zhyttia (Screen; Illustrated Bimonthly of Ukrainian Life), Chicago, IL. Bi-monthly: 1961-1983. Includes English.

Emigrant, Lvov, Galicia. Five times per year: 1911. (Microfilm: 1910-1914).

Feniks, Zhurnal Molodykh (Phoenix, Journal of Social and Political Thought), Philadelphia, PA (previously published in Munich, West Germany). Frequency varies: 1951-1953, 1958-1959, 1961-1962, 1964-1966, 1970. Includes English.

Filiadel'fiïs'ki Visti (Philadelphia News; Ukrainian Congress Committee of America; Philadelphia Branch), Philadelphia, PA. 1954.

Filokaliia (Philocalia), Stamford, CT. Annual: 1974-1975.

For Your Information, McKees Rocks, PA. Monthly: 1978-1979. English.

Forum, Scranton, PA. Quarterly: 1966-date. English.

The Graduate Bulletin of the Ukrainian Graduates of Detroit and Windsor, Detroit, MI. Monthly: 1969-1979. English.

Harapnyk (The Whip). Edmonton, Alberta, Canada. Monthly: 1935.

The Harvard Ukrainian Research Institute, A Newsletter for the Friends of, Cambridge, MA. Quarterly: 1979-1982. English.

Harvard Ukrainian Studies Newsletter, Cambridge, MA. Monthly: 1970-1977. English.

The Herald (English supplement to **Visnyk**), Winnipeg, Manitoba, Canada. Bi-monthly: 1971. English.

Holos (The Voice), Los Angeles, CA. Bi-monthly (?): 1966.

Holos (The Voice), Meadowvale, Ontario, Canada. Quarterly: 1955.

Holos Bratstva (Voice of Brotherhood), New York, NY. Monthly: 1964-1966.

Holos Bratstva (Voice of Brotherhood), Trenton, NJ. Monthly: 1958-1959.

Holos Dazhbozhychiv (Voice of the Followers of Dazhboh), Atlantic City, NJ. Monthly: 1972, 1976.

Holos Derzhavnyka (Voice of a Statesman), Regensburg (?), Germany. Monthly (?): 1947.

Holos Instytutu (Mohyla Institute Newsletter), Saskatoon, Saskatchewan, Canada. Bi-monthly: 1968-1982.

Holos Kombatanta (Voice of the Combatant; first issues appeared as supplements to **Svoboda**), New York, NY. Quarterly: 1958-1961.

Holos Mazepynciv (Mazeppians' Voice), Chicago, IL. Monthly: 1932.

Holos Molodi (Youth Speaks), Winnipeg, Manitoba, Canada. Quarterly (monthly): 1949-1953. Includes English.

Holos Pravoslavnoho Bratstva (The Orthodox Fraternal Voice), Chicago, IL. Frequency varies: 1963-1968.

Holos Spasytelia (The Redeemer's Voice), Yorkton, Saskatchewan, Canada. Monthly: 1945, 1947-1957, 1960-1965, 1968, 1974-1976, 1978, 1983. Includes English.

Holos Spasytelia, Kaliendar (The Redeemer's Voice, Calendar), Yorkton, Saskatchewan, Canada. Annual: 1944, 1946, 1948, 1951-1955, 1957-1958. Includes English.

Holos Stanyslavivshchyny (Voice of the Stanyslaviv Region), Lorain, OH. 1965, 1968, 1970.

Holos Tserkvy (Voice of the Church), New York, NY. Frequency varies: 1953-1955.

Holovna Uprava Spilky Vyzvolennia Ukraïny (Headquarters of the Association for the Liberation of Ukraine), New York, NY. Monthly: 1964.

Holy Trinity Ukrainian Catholic Church Bulletin, Kerhonkson, NY. 1968.

Homin Ukraïny (Ukrainian Echo; title varies: **Al'manakh Kalendar "Homonu Ukraïny"**), Toronto, Ontario, Canada. Annual: 1956-1958, 1960, 1963, 1965-1966, 1982.

Horizons (Federation of Ukrainian Student Organizations of America), New York, NY. Frequency varies: 1956-1968. English.

Hospodars'ko-Kooperatyvne Zhyttia (Economic Cooperative Life), Augsburg-Munich, Germany. Monthly: 1947-1948.

Hotuïs' (Be Ready), Toronto, Ontario, Canada (previously published in New York). Monthly: 1955-1964, 1966-1971.

Hromadianka (Woman Citizen), Augsburg-Munich, West Germany. Monthly: 1948-1950.

Hromads'ke Zhyttia (Community Life), Detroit, MI. Monthly: 1944.

Hutsuliia, Chicago, IL. Quarterly: 1967-date.

Icon (Immaculate Conception Ukrainian Catholic High School), Hamtramck, MI. Annual: 1967-1969. Mainly English.

Ideia i Chyn (Idea and Action), Munich, Germany. Frequency varies: 1946.

Ievanhel's'ka Pravda (Evangelical Truth), Toronto, Ontario, Canada. Monthly: 1965-1967, 1969-1970. Includes English.

Ievanhel's'kyĭ Holos (Evangelical Voice), Toronto, Ontario, Canada. Quarterly: 1973.

Ievanhel's'kyĭ Palomnyk (Evangelical Pilgrim), New York, NY. Bi-monthly: 1953-1954, 1958, 1962, 1967, 1970-1971.

Ievanhel's'kyĭ Ranok (Evangelical Morning), Toronto, Ontario, Canada. Quarterly: 1961-date. Includes English supplement.

Iliustrovanyĭ Biuleten' (Illustrated Bulletin), Brooklyn, NY. 1966.

Iliustrovanyĭ Kalendar "Novyn" (Illustrated Calendar "News"), Edmonton, Alberta, Canada. Annual: 1915.

Iliustrovanyĭ Zahal'nyĭ Kalendar dlia Kozhdoho Viku i Stanu (Illustrated Universal Calendar for Every Age and Position), New York, NY. Annual: 1916.

Informator, (Informer); Brooklyn, NY. Frequency varies: 1964-1966.

Informator, (Informer; Radio Liberty Committee), New York, NY. Monthly: 1964-1969.

Informator Filiï ODUM-u (Informer for the Minnesota Branch of the Association of American Youth of Ukrainian Descent), Minneapolis/St. Paul, MN. Monthly: 1973-1979.

Informator Ob'iednannia Ukraïns'kykh Kanads'kykh Pidpryiemtsiv i Profesionalistiv (Informer of the Association of Ukrainian Canadian Businessmen and Professionals), Toronto, Ontario, Canada. Monthly: 1971.

Informatsiï Ukraïns'koï Pravoslavnoï Hromady Pokrovy Presviatoï Bohorodytsi (Information of the Ukrainian Orthodox Community of St. Mary the Protrectress), Montreal, Quebec, Canada. Monthly: 1966.

Informatsiĭna Sluzhba, UKR. Biuleten' (Informational Service for the Ukrainian Christian Movement. Bulletin), New York, NY. 1967.

Informatsiĭnyĭ Biuleten' (Informative Bulletin), Chicago, IL. Frequency varies: 1957, 1965-1971.

Informatsiĭnyĭ Biuleten' (Informative Bulletin), Heidenau, Germany. Three times weekly: 1946.

Informatsiĭnyĭ Biuleten' (Informative Bulletin; Association for the Liberation of Ukraine), New York, NY. Frequency varies: 1957, 1963-1967, 1969, 1973-1974.

Informatsiĭnyĭ Biuleten' (Informative Bulletin), Philadelphia, PA-Detroit, MI. Annual: 1963-1964.

Informatsiĭnyĭ Lyst (Newsletter), New York, NY. 1951.

Informatsiĭnyĭ Lystok (Newsletter of St. Volodymyr's Ukrainian Orthodox Cathedral), Chicago, IL. Quarterly: 1982-1983.

Informatyvno-Instruktyvni Lysty (Informational-Instructive Letters), New York, NY. Monthly: 1954-1956.

Informatyvnyĭ Lyst T-va Pryiateliv Kapeli Bandurystiv (Newsletter of the Friends of the Ukrainian Bandurist Chorus), Detroit, MI. Annual: 1964, 1966, 1968, 1970-1971, 1978.

Informatyvnyĭ Lystok OUVL (Journal of the Ukrainian Veterinary Medical Association), Chicago, IL. Quarterly, Semi-annual: 1950-1953, 1955, 1959-1976, 1978, 1980-1981.

Investytsiĭnyĭ Biuleten' (Investment Bulletin; Titanium Investment Clubs Association), Detroit, MI. Frequency varies: 1960-1961.

Iris, Philadelphia, PA. Quarterly: 1965. Includes English.

Iskra (Spark), Chicago, IL. Annual: 1981.

Iunak (Young Man), [Germany]. Monthly: 1946.

Iunats'ka Borot'ba (Young Man's Struggle), Augsburg-Munich, Germany. Frequency varies: 1947-1948.

Iuni Druzi (Young Friends), Munich, Germany. Three issues total: 1947.

Iunyĭ Natsionalist (Young Nationalist), [Germany]. Frequency varies: 1947-1948.

Iuvileinyĭ Biuleten' 15-ho Viddilu Ukraïns'koho Zolotoho Khresta (Jubilee Bulletin of the 15th Branch of the Ukrainian Gold Cross), Minneapolis/St. Paul, MN. Irregular: 1976.

Journal of Ukrainian Graduate Studies, Toronto, Ontario, Canada. Bi-annual: 1976-date. Includes English.

Kalendar-Al'manakh (Calendar-Almanac), Augsburg-Munich, Germany. Annual: 1948.

Kalendar Postup (Progress Almanac), Winnipeg, Manitoba, Canada. Annual: 1961, 1965, 1967.

Kalendarets' (Little Calendar), New York, NY. Annual: 1959.

Kalendarets' (Little Calendar), Regensburg, Germany. Annual: 1946.

Kameniari (Stone Cutters), Saskatoon, Saskatchewan, Canada. 1919.

Kanadiïs'kyĭ Farmer (Canadian Farmer; title varies: **Narodnyĭ Iliustrovanyĭ Kaliendar Kanadiïs'koho Farmera; Kaliendar Kanadiïs'koho Farmera; Kaliendar-Al'manakh Kanadiïs'koho Farmera**) Winnipeg, Manitoba, Canada. Annual: 1944, 1949, 1951-1954, 1957-1962, 1964-1966, 1968-1969.

Kanadiïs'kyĭ Ranok (Canadian Morning), Winnipeg, Manitoba, Canada. Monthly: 1958-1961. Includes English section.

Kanadyïs'kyĭ Rusyn (Canadian Rusin), Winnipeg, Manitoba, Canada. Annual: 1916-1917, 1920.

Karpats'ka Sich (Carpathian Sich), Toronto, Ontario, Canada. Frequency varies: 1950. (Microfilm: 1950, 1952, 1955-1956).

Karpatska Zoria (Carpathian Star), Jermyn, PA. Monthly: 1974-1975. Includes English.

Katedra Presviatoï Troïtsi; Tserkovnyĭ Biuleten' (Holy Trinity Cathedral; Church Bulletin), Winnipeg, Manitoba, Canada. 1965.

Katedral'ni Visti (Cathedral News), Chicago, IL. Weekly: 1963-1985. Includes English.

Katedral'nyĭ Lystok (Cathedral Newsletter), Edmonton, Alberta, Canada. Weekly: 1968-1970.

Kazachiĭ Istoricheskiĭ Kalendar' (Cossack Historical Calendar), Philadelphia, PA. Annual: 1953.

Kazak (Cossack), Astoria, NY. Monthly: 1966.

Keryx, Stamford, CT. Semi-annual: 1945, 1947-1949. English.

Khors (Ukrainian Magazine of Literature and Arts), Regensburg, Germany. Quarterly: 1946.

Khronika (Chronicle), Chicago, IL. Semi-annual: 1965-1967, 1969-1973, 1975-1982.

Khrystos Nasha Syla (Christ Is Our Strength), Munich-Mittenwald, Germany. Weekly: 1948.

Khrystos Nasha Syla (Christ Is Our Strength), Munich-Passing, Germany. Monthly: 1946.

Khrystyians'kyĭ Visnyk (Christian Herald), Winnipeg, Manitoba, Canada. Monthly: 1943, 1952-1954, 1959-1961, 1966-date.

Klych Natsiĭ (Call of the Nation), Philadelphia, PA. Bi-monthly: 1972-1975.

Kol'ka (Stinger), New York, NY. Frequency varies: 1937-1938.

Komar (Mosquito), Munich, Germany. Annual: 1948.

Komar (Mosquito), Winnipeg, Manitoba, Canada (previously published in Lvov, Ukraine). Semi-monthly: 1949-1950.

Komar-Ïzhak (Mosquito-Hedgehog), Munich, Germany. Bi-weekly: 1947-1948. Includes some English.

Komunikat (Communicate), Chicago, IL. Monthly: 1964-1968, 1970-1971.

Komunikat UTHI (News of the Ukrainian Technical and Husbandry Institute), New York, NY. Frequency varies: 1953.

Kongresovi Visti (Congressional News), New York, NY. Frequency varies: 1964-1966, 1969-1970, 1972. Includes English.

Konsystoriia Ukraïns'koĭ Pravoslavnoĭ Tserkvy v SSHA. Obizhnyk (Consistory of the Ukrainian Orthodox Church in the U.S.A.), South Bound Brook, NJ. Weekly: 1973-1975, 1977-1979.

Konventsiĭni Visti UNS (Convention News of the Ukrainian National Association), Chicago, IL. Frequency varies: 1966.

Konventsiĭnyĭ Biuleten' Naukovoho Zïzdu (Convention Bulletin of the Scientific Meeting), Cleveland, OH. Monthly: 1976.

Kooperatyvna Dumka (Credit Union Opinion), Rochester, NY. Quarterly: 1971-1973. Includes English.

Kooperatyvnyĭ Informator (Cooperative Informer), Chicago, IL. Quarterly: 1970-1973. Includes some English.

Kooperatyvnyĭ Lystok (Cooperative Newsletter), Chicago, IL. Quarterly: 1977-1984. Includes English.

Koordynator (Coordinator), Toronto, Ontario, Canada. Frequency varies: 1970, 1972-1973, 1975.

Kovcheh (The Arc), Stamford, CT. Monthly: 1946-1950, 1953-1956.

Kozak Harasym Chornokhlib (Cossack Harasym Black Bread); (Cover title: **Humorystychnyĭ Kaliendar Kozaka Harasyma Chornokhliba**; Humorous calendar of Cossack Harasym Black Bread), Winnipeg, Manitoba, Canada. Annual: 1921.

Krasa i Syla (Beauty and Strength), New York, NY. 1953.

Krylati (The Winged Ones; title varies: **Kryla**), New York, NY. Monthly: 1951-1954, 1963-date.

Kubans'kyĭ Kraĭ (Kuban Cossack Bulletin), Toronto, Ontario, Canada. Bi-monthly: 1953-1957, 1961.

Kul'tura i Osvita (Culture and Education), Winnipeg, Manitoba, Canada. Monthly: 1949-1950.

Title page from the Ukrainian American calendar *Robitnychyĭ Kalendar* (Workers' Calendar), published by the Ukrainian Federated American Socialist Party, New York, 1919.

Kul'turno-Mystets'kyï Kalendar-Al'manakh (Cultural-Artistic Calendar-Almanac), Regensburg, Germany. Annual: 1947.

Kyïv (Kiev), Philadelphia, PA. Bi-monthly: 1950-1964.

Kyshen'kovyï Kalendarets (Pocket Calendar), New York, NY. Annual: 1951.

Kyshen'kovyï Kalendarets' Dovidnyk (Pocket Calendar Guide; title varies: **Kyshen'kovyï Kaliendarets**, 1940), New York, NY/Winnipeg, Manitoba, Canada. Annual: 1940, 1951, 1967, 1969, 1973.

Lemkivschyna (The Lemko Land), New York, NY. Quarterly: 1979-1981.

Lemkivs'kyï Kalendar (Lemko Calendar), Toronto, Ontario, Canada.-Passaic, NJ. Annual: 1965-1969, 1970-1973.

Lemko Youth Journal, Yonkers, NY. Bi-monthly: 1960-1964. Mainly English.

Lemkovina (newspaper format until December 1972), Yonkers, NY. Monthly: 1971-1972, 1974-1978, 1980. Includes English.

Letiuchyï Lystok (Flying Newsletter), Chicago, IL. Weekly: 1970-1971.

Likars'kyï Visnyk (Medical Herald; Journal of the American Ukrainian Medical Association of North America, Inc.), New York, NY. Quarterly: 1954-1974, 1977-1979.

Lisova Shkola (Forestry School), New York, NY. Annual: 1970-1971.

Litavry (The Kettledrum), Salzburg, Austria. Monthly: 1947.

Literaturno-Mystets'kyï Ohliad. Biuleten' (Art and Literary Review), New York, NY. 1955.

Literaturno-Naukovyï Zbirnyk (Literary-Scientific Magazine), Korigen-Kiel, Germany (previously published in Hannover, Germany). Frequency varies: 1947.

Litopys Boykivshchyny (Journal Boykivshchyna), Philadelphia, PA. Semi-annual: 1969-1974, 1977, 1982-date.

Litopys U.M.A. (Chronicle of the Ukrainian Museum-Archives), Cleveland, OH. Frequency varies: 1984, 1987.

Litopys Ukraïns'koho Politviaznia (Chronicle of a Ukrainian Political Prisoner), Munich, Germany. Monthly: 1946-1947.

Litopys Volyni (Volhynian Chronicle), Winnipeg, Manitoba, Canada. Annual: 1953-1972, 1976.

Liubystok (Sweetheart), Toronto, Ontario, Canada. Annual: 1975-1980, 1983.

"Lodge" Herald, New York, NY. Weekly: 1939. English.

Lohos (Logos), Yorkton, Saskatchewan, Canada (previously published in Waterford, Ontario, Canada). Quarterly: 1950-1952, 1954-1956, 1965, 1982.

Luna, Cleveland, OH; Philadelphia, PA; and New York, NY. Monthly: 1958.

Lys Mykyta ((The Fox Mykyta) (title varies: **Lys** [The Fox] 1950-1951), Detroit, MI (previously published in Munich, Germany, and New York, NY). Bi-weekly, Monthly: 1948-date.

Lys Mykyta, Kalendar (The Fox, Calendar), Munich, Germany. Annual: 1949.

Lystok Druhoho Plastovoho Kongresu (Newsletter of the Second Plast Congress), New York, NY. Frequency varies: 1966.

Lystok Druzhby (Newsletter of Friendship), Philadelphia, PA (previously published in New York, NY). Bi-annual (?): 1959, 1964.

Lystok Plastpryiatu (Newsletter of the Friends of Plast), New York, NY. Monthly: 1967-1970.

Lysty (Letters; Ukrainian Missionary Committee), New York, NY. Monthly: 1952.

Lysty do Brativ Familiiantiv (Letters to Family Brothers), New York, NY. Monthly (?): 1974.

Lysty do Pryiateliv (Letters to Friends), New York, NY. Quarterly: 1953-1968.

Mali Druzi (Small Friends; title varies: **Molode Zhyttia**; Young Life), Augsburg, Germany. Frequency varies: 1947-1949.

Malyi Kaliendar Maryians'kyi (Marian Small Calendar; title varies: **Kaliendar Maryians'kyi**), Winterburg, Germany; Vienna, Austria; and New York, NY. Annual: 1913, 1914.

The Midwest Horizon, Chicago, IL. Bi-monthly (?): 1960-1961. Includes English, then English.

Mii Pryiatel' (My Friend), Winnipeg, Manitoba, Canada. Monthly: 1949-1963, 1965.

Minutes of the Seminar in Ukrainian Studies Held at Harvard University, Cambridge, MA. Annual: 1970-1977. English.

Misiia Ukraïny (Mission of Ukraine; Association for the Liberation of Ukraine), Toronto, Ontario, Canada. Semi-annual: 1957-1970, 1972-1975.

Misionar (The Missionary), Philadelphia, PA. Monthly: 1917, 1919-1922, 1925, 1928, 1935-1940, 1943-1955, 1961, 1966-1968, 1979-1980, 1983-1984. Includes English.

Mizhkraiova Plastova Zustrich (Interregional Plast Meeting), Montreal, Quebec; and Toronto, Ontario, Canada. Annual: 1967, 1971-1972.

Moloda Ukraïna (Young Ukraine; Ukrainian Democratic Youth Association of the U.S.A.), New York, NY. Monthly: 1953.

Moloda Ukraïna (Young Ukraine), Toronto, Ontario, Canada. Monthly: 1952-date.

Molode Zhyttia (Young Life; Ukrainian Youth Organization "Plast", Inc.) Detroit, MI; New York, NY; and Augsburg, West Germany. Bi-monthly: 1948-1950, 1952-1953, 1955-1956, 1958.

Molot (Hammer; bound with **Osa** [wasp] under title: **Dlia Rozrady: Zbirnyk Vuika "Lysa Mykyty"** [For amusement: Collections of Uncle "the Fox"]), New York, NY. Semi-monthly: 1920-1923.

Montreal's'kyi Informator (Montreal Informer), Montreal, Quebec, Canada. Monthly: 1966-1967.

MUN Beams (Dominion Executive of the Ukrainian National Youth Federation), Toronto, Ontario, Canada. 1957, 1963. Includes English.

MUN Moods, Chicago, IL. Monthly: 1960. English.

MUR (Mystets'ky̆i Ukraïns'ky̆i Rukh [Ukrainian Artistic Movement]), Munich, Germany. Frequency varies: 1946-1947.

MUR-Al'manakh (Ukrainian Artistic Movement-Almanac), Stuttgart, Germany. Annual: 1947.

Muzeïni Visti (Museum News; Ukrainian National Museum; previously titled **Na Slidakh**), Chicago, IL. Quarterly: 1957-1959.

Muzychni Visti (Music Herald; title varies: **Visti**), Jersey City, NJ (St. Paul, MN). Quarterly: 1962-1972. Includes some English.

My i Nashi Dity (We and Our Children), Toronto, Ontario, Canada-New York, NY. Monthly (?): 1959-1960, 1966-1967, 1970-1971, 1974, 1983.

My i Svit (We and the World), Toronto, Ontario, Canada. Monthly: 1950-1973, 1975, 1977.

Mykyta ("The Fox" Mykyta), New York, NY. Monthly: eight undated issues.

Myrianyn (The Layman), Chicago, IL. Monthly: 1967-1971, 1974, 1978.

Na Chuzhni (On Foreign Soil), Augsburg, Germany. Annual: 1947.

Na Chuzhni (On Foreign Soil), Korigen, Germany. Frequency varies: 1947.

Na Chuzhni (On Foreign Soil), Vilsbiburg, Germany. Weekly: 1946-1948.

Na Slidakh (On the Traces; title changes to **Muzeini Visti,** 1957), Ontario, CA. Bi-monthly: 1955-1956.

Na Storozhi (On Guard), [Germany]. Monthly: 1946-1948.

Na Varti (On the Watch), Toronto, Ontario, Canada. Monthly: 1949-1952.

Nadbuz'ka Zemlia (The Buh River Region), Jersey City, NJ. 1978.

Narid Maie Pravo Znaty (People Have the Right to Know), New York, NY. 1971.

Naperedodni (On the Eve), New York, NY. Bi-monthly: 1950-1952.

Nash Biuleten' (Our Bulletin), [Germany]. Monthly: 1945.

Nash Holos (Our Voice; title varies: **Biuleten Asotsiiatsii Ukraintsiv Ameryky**), Union, NJ (previously published in Trenton, NJ). Monthly: 1969, 1971-1984.

Nash Kontakt (Our Contact), Detroit, MI. 1954-1955, 1958.

Nash Pryiatel' (Our Friend), [Canada]. Frequency varies: 1946.

Nash Pryiatel' (Our Friend; title varies: **Ditochyi Pryiatel'**), Hartford, CT (Irvington, NJ). Monthly: 1959-1966.

Nash Shliakh (Our Road), [Germany]. Monthly: 1945-1946.

Nash Sport (Our Sport), Newark, NJ. Annual: 1962-1972 1975-1979, 1981-1982.

Nash Svit (Our World; **Novyi Svit** and **Nash Kontakt** merged in 1959 to form **Nash Svit**), New York, NY. Bi-monthly: 1959-1966, 1968-1982.

Nasha Batkiwschyna (Our Fatherland; previously published as a newspaper), Mountain Dale, NY. Monthly: 1972.

Nasha Borot'ba (Our Fight; URDP), Kornburg, Germany. Quarterly: 1946.

Nasha Borot'ba (Our Fight), Minneapolis, MN. Quarterly: 1986-1987.

Nasha Doroha (Our Road), Yorkton, Saskatchewan, Canada. Bi-monthly: 1970, 1973, 1981. Includes English.

Nasha Dumka (Our Opinion), Munich, Germany. Bi-weekly: 1947-1948.

Nasha Hromada (Our Society), Jersey City, NJ. Monthly: 1957, 1964, 1966-1968.

Nasha Kul'tura (Our Culture), Winnipeg, Manitoba, Canada (previously published in Warsaw, Poland). Monthly: 1935-1937, 1951-1953, 1955, 1957, 1961, 1963, 1967.

Nasha Mova (Our Language), Munich, Germany. Frequency varies: 1947.

Nasha Pratsia (Our Work), Minneapolis, MN. Monthly: 1953-1955.

Nasha Shkola (Our School), Chicago, IL. Annual: 1978-1980.

Nasha Shkola (Our School), Philadelphia, PA. Monthly: 1957, 1960.

Nasha Shkola (Our School), South Bound Brooks, NJ. Quarterly: 1965-1972.

Nasha Syla (Our Strength), Winnipeg, Manitoba, Canada. Monthly: 1913.

Nasha Tserkva (Our Church), Buffalo, NY. Monthly: 1953.

Nasha Vatra (Our Campfire), Toronto, Ontario, Canada. Annual: 1963-1964.

Nashe Slovo (Our Word), Detroit, MI. Monthly (?): 1953, 1957.

Nashe Slovo (Our Word), Los Angeles, CA. Frequency varies: 1968, 1975-1976.

Nashe Slovo (Our Word), Oshawa, Ontario, Canada. Monthly: 1933-1934.

Nashe Zhyttia (Our Life), New York, NY. Monthly: 1948-1986. Includes English.

Nashe Zhyttia (Our Life), Winnipeg, Manitoba, Canada. Monthly: 1941.

Nashi Visti (Our News), Munich, Germany. Monthly: 1946.

Nashym Ditiam (For Our Children), Munich, Germany. Frequency varies: 1947.

Nativity of the Blessed Virgin Mary. Bulletin, Hollywood, CA. Weekly: 1969, 1973-1975. Includes English.

Naukovyi Biuleten' Ukraïns'koho Tekhnichno-Hospodars'koho Instytutu, Scientific Reports (Scientific Bulletin of the Ukrainian Technical and Husbandry Institute), New York, NY. 1951.

Nazaret (Nazareth), Chicago, IL. Quarterly: 1971-1976, 1979-1980, 1983-1984.

Nestorian, New York, NY. Quarterly: 1931. English.

Nevydymoho Oka (The Unseen Eye), Rochester, NY. Monthly: 1938. Includes some English.

Newsletter of the Minnesota Ukrainian Bicentennial Committee, Minneapolis, MN. Quarterly: 1976. English.

Newsmonth, Edmonton, Alberta, Canada. Monthly: 1966-1967. English.

Notatnyk (Diary; title headed by Pryiatel' Iunaka), New York, NY. Annual (?): 1953.

Notatnyk (Diary), New York, NY. Monthly: 1963-1964, 1966-1967, 1970-1978.

Notatnyk z Mystetstva (Ukrainian Art Digest), Philadelphia, PA. Frequency varies: 1963-1966, 1968-1970, 1973, 1975-1981.

Nova Era (New Era), Canora, Saskatchewan, Canada. Monthly: 1933. Includes English.

Nove Lytsarstvo (New Knighthood), Augsburg, Germany. Monthly (?): 1946.

Nove Slovo (New Word), Winnipeg, Manitoba, Canada. 1955.

Nove Tochylo (The New Grindstone), New York, NY. Undated issue.

Novi Napriamy (New Directions), New York, NY. Quarterly: 1969-1973. Includes English.

Novi Poeziï (New Poetry), Rego Park, NY. Annual: 1959, 1961, 1964, 1966-1971.

Novi Skryzhali (New Tables of Commandments), Winnipeg, Manitoba, Canada. Quarterly: 1977-1984.

Novyĭ Litopys (The New Chronicle), Winnipeg, Manitoba, Canada. Quarterly: 1961-1965.

Novyĭ Shliakh, Kalendar Al'manakh (New Way, Calendar-Almanac), Winnipeg, Manitoba, Canada. Annual: 1936, 1941, 1944-1974, 1977-1983, 1986.

Novyĭ Svit (The New World), New York, NY (Jersey City, NJ). Bi-monthly: 1955-1959.

Novyĭ S'vit, Iliustrovanyĭ Kalendar (New World, Illustrated Calendar), Montreal, Quebec, Canada. Annual: 1917-1918.

Novyny; Informatsiĭnyĭ Biuleten' Taboru Im. Lysenka, (News; Informational Bulletin of the Lysenko Scout Scamp), Hannover, Germany. Daily: 1946-1947.

Novyny z Akademiï (News of the Academy), New York, NY. Semi-annual: 1981, 1984.

Nowi Dni (New Days), Toronto, Ontario, Canada. Monthly: 1946, 1950-date.

Nyva; Orhan Ukraïns'koho Dukhovenstva (The Sown Field; Organ of Ukrainian Clergy), Oshawa, Ontario, Canada. Tri-monthly: 1975-1979

Obizhnyĭ Lyst UKAP (Circulating Letter of the Association of the Ukrainian Catholic Press), Philadelphia, PA. 1968.

Obizhnyĭ Lystok U.V.F. (Circulating Letter of the Ukrainian Liberation Fund), New York, NY. Monthly: 1975-1976.

Objective, Roblin, Manitoba, Canada. Monthly: 1966. Includes English.

Obnova (Renewal), Munich, Germany. Bi-monthly: 1948-1949.

Obnov'ianyn (The Renewer), Winnipeg, Manitoba, Canada. Annual: 1955-1959. Includes English.

Oborona (Defense), Newark, NJ. Monthly: 1954-1957.

Obriï (Horizons), New York, NY. Monthly: 1951.

ODUM v Minnesoti (Ukrainian Democratic Youth Association in Minnesota), New London, MN. Annual: 1974-1975.

Odyn Rik v Tabori Elvangen, Iuvileĭnyĭ Al'manakh (One Year in the Camp at Ellwangen, Jubilee Almanac), Ellwangen, Germany. Annual: 1947.

Oko (The Eye), New York, NY. Semi-monthly: 1939.

Oko Svitu (Eye of the World), Montreal, Quebec, Canada. Bi-monthly: 1950.

Omiha (Omega), New York, NY. Monthly: 1974.

Opinion (Ukrainian Canadian Veterans' Association; previously titled **U.C.S.A. Newsletter, U.C.V.A. Newsletter**), Winnipeg, Manitoba, Canada. Monthly: 1945-1949. English.

Organizatsiia Oborony Chotyr'okh Svobid Ukraïny (Organization for the Defense of the Four Freedoms of Ukraine), New York, NY. 1946.

Orhanizatsiĭni Visty Oborony Ukraïny (Organizational News in Defense of Ukraine), Scranton, PA. Monthly: 1936-1941.

Orlyk (The Eaglet), Berchtesgaden, Germany. Monthly: 1946-1948.

Osa (The Wasp; bound with **Molot** under title **Dlia Rozrady; Zbirnyk Vuĭka "Lysa Mykyty"**), Chicago, IL. Semi-monthly: 1920.

Ostanni Novyny (Last News), Salzburg, Austria. Daily: 1945.

Our Viewpoint, Toronto, Ontario, Canada. Monthly: 1959. English.

Our Village Voice, Chicago, IL. Monthly: 1981-1985. English.

Ovyd (Horizon), Chicago, IL (previously published in Buenos Aires, Argentina). Quarterly (monthly): 1950-1951, 1953-1955, 1957-1975.

Oznaky Nashoho Chasu (Signs of Our Time), Mountain View, CA. Monthly: 1963-1968, 1977-1979.

Pace, Toronto, Ontario, Canada. Monthly: 1954-1956. English.

Parafiial'na Shkola (The Parochial School), South Bound Brook, NJ. Quarterly: 1960.

Parafiial'ne Slovo (The Parochial Word), Buffalo, NY. Weekly: 1969.

Parafiial'ne Zhyttia (Parish Life), Addison, IL. Annual: 1977, 1982-1983. Includes English.

Parafiial'ni Misiachni Novyny (Parish Monthly News), Miami, FL. Monthly: 1964-1965, 1967.

Parafiial'ni Visti (Parish News), Parma, OH. Quarterly: 1974-1975, 1977-1978, 1981-1982.

Parafiial'ni Visti (Parish News), Philadelphia, PA. Monthly: 1975-1976, 1981.

Parafiial'nyĭ Visnyk (Parish Herald), Newark, NJ. Monthly: 1961-1964.

Parafiial'nyĭ Visnyk Ukraïns'koï Pravoslavnoï Katedry Sv. Pokrovy v Detroïti (Parish Herald of the Ukrainian Orthodox Cathedral of St. Mary the Protectress in Detroit), Detroit, MI. Quarterly (?): 1963-1964.

Parokhiial'ni Visti (The Parochial News), Philadelphia, PA. 1978.

Parokhiial'nyĭ Visnyk Tserkvy Sv. O. Nykolaia (Parochial Herald Church of St. Nicholas), Toronto, Ontario, Canada. 1955.

Patriiarkhat (The Patriarchate; previously titled **Za Patriiarkhat**), New York, NY. Monthly: 1967-1983. Includes English.

Peredsoborovyĭ Biuleten' (Pre-Council Bulletin), New York, NY. Bi-monthly: 1950. Includes some English.

Pereselenets (The Emigrant), Munich, Germany. Monthly: 1947.

Peresliduvana Tserkva (Persecuted Church), Montebello, CA. Quarterly: 1975-date.

Persha Sproba (First Trial), Chicago, IL. Quarterly: 1964.

PIB (Pre-Collegiate Information Bulletin), Troy, NY. Quarterly: 1963. Includes English.

Pid Znam'iam Chornoho Kota (Under the Sign of the Black Cat), New York, NY. 1951.

Pislanets' Pravdy (Messenger of Truth), Chester, PA. Bi-monthly: 1948, 1950, 1954, 1959-1971, 1973-date.

Pivnichne Siaĭvo (Northern Lights), Edmonton, Alberta, Canada. Irregular: 1964-1965.

Plast, Los Angeles, CA. 1970.

Plastovyĭ Lystok (Plast Letter), Detroit, MI. Monthly: 1949-1951, 1973-1974, 1977.

Plastovyĭ Merkuriĭ (Plast Mercury), Detroit, MI. Annual (?): 1958-1959.

Plastovyĭ Shliakh (The Plast Way), Toronto, Ontario, Canada. Quarterly: 1950-1951, 1954, 1966-1974, 1984-1985.

Plastovyĭ Visnyk (The Plast Herald), Toronto, Ontario, Canada. Monthly: 1949-1950.

Pohliady (Opinions; title varies: **Biuleten' Tovarystva Ukraïns'koï Studiiuiuchoï Molodi im. M. Mikhnovs'koho**; Bulletin of the Mikhnovsky Ukrainian Student Association), Philadelphia, PA. Frequency varies: 1960-1962.

Pokhid (The March), Heidenau, Germany. Monthly: 1946.

Politv'iazen' (Political Prisoner), Munich, Germany. Monthly: 1946.

Poradnyk Pasichnykam (Handbook for Beekeepers), [Germany]. Frequency varies: 1949.

Poradnyk ta Informator (Adviser and Informer), Detroit, MI. Frequency varies: 1953.

Pravda (The Truth), Toronto, Ontario, Canada. Quarterly: 1969-1975.

Pravda i Volia (Truth and Liberty), Winnipeg, Manitoba, Canada. Monthly: 1932.

Pravnychyĭ Visnyk (Law Journal of the Ukrainian Lawyer's Association in the U.S.), New York, NY. Irregular: 1955.

Pravoslavnyĭ Kalendarets' (Orthodox Calendar), Landshut, Germany. Annual: 1947.

Pravoslavnyĭ Shliakh (Orthodox Pathway), Chicago, IL. Frequency varies: 1961. Includes English.

Pravoslavnyĭ Ukraïnets' (Orthodox Ukrainian; Ukrainian Autocephalous Orthodox Church of U.S.A.), Chicago, IL (Germany). Monthly: 1947, 1952-1976.

Pravoslavnyĭ Ukraïnets', Iuvileĭnyĭ Kalendar UAPTS (Orthodox Ukrainian, Jubilee Calendar of the Ukrainian Orthodox Church of the U.S.A.), Chicago, IL. Annual: 1956.

Premudrist' (Wisdom), South Bound Brook, NJ. Monthly: 1976. Includes English.

Presova Sluzhba (Press Service), New York, NY. 1953.

Presovi Visti (Press News), Winnipeg, Manitoba, Canada. 1956.

Pres'viata Rodyna (Holy Family), Winnipeg, Manitoba, Canada. Annual: 1914.

Prism; Visnyk Susta (Federation of Ukrainian Student Organizations of America, Inc.), New York, NY. Frequency varies: 1975-1976. Includes English.

Problemy (Problems), Munich, Germany. Monthly: 1947-1948.

Problysky (Flashes), [Canada]. One undated issue.

Profesors'ki Visti (Professors' News), Detroit, MI. Quarterly: 1971-1976.

Progress Credit Union Ltd. Postup, Winnipeg, Manitoba, Canada. Annual: 1974. Includes English.

Prolisky (Clearings among Trees), Cleveland, OH. 1957.

Prologue Quarterly, New York, NY. Quarterly: 1957-1958, 1960-1961. English.

Promin' (The Ray), Munich, Germany. 1948.

Promin' (The Ray), New York, NY. 1936.

Promin' (The Ray), Winnipeg, Manitoba, Canada. Annual: 1947-1951.

Promin' (The Ray), Winnipeg, Manitoba, Canada. Monthly: 1927.

Promin' (The Ray; Ukrainian Women's Association of Canada), Winnipeg, Manitoba, Canada. Monthly: 1961-1973, 1976, 1978, 1981. Includes English.

Prorochyĭ Holos (The Voice of Prophecy), Lakewood, OH. 1947.

Pros'vita (Enlightenment), Jersey City, NJ. Monthly: 1914-1916.

Pros'vita (Enlightenment; title varies: **Iliustrovanyĭ Narodnyĭ Kaliendar Tovarstva "Pros'vita"; Iliustrovanyĭ Kaliendar T-va "Pros'vita" z Literaturnym Zbirnykom**), Lvov, Poland. Annual: 1910, 1914, 1920, 1922-1926, 1932.

Prosvita. Kalendar (Enlightenment. Calendar), Toronto, Ontario, Canada. Annual: 1969.

Proty Shersty (Against the Grain), Landeck, Austria. 1947.

Providnyk. Kaliendar Kanadiĭs'kykh Ukraïntsiv (The Leader. Canadian Ukrainian Illustrated Calendar), Winnipeg, Manitoba, Canada. Annual: 1930, 1935.

Provydinnia, Al'manakh Kalendar (Providence, Almanac Calendar; title varies: **Kaliendar Provydinnia**) Philadelphia, PA. Annual: 1918, 1923(?), 1925-1930, 1932, 1943, 1945-1972, 1982. Includes English.

Pryiatel' Zhovnir, Iliustrovanyĭ Kaliendar (The Soldier's Friend, Illustrated Calendar), Winnipeg, Manitoba, Canada. Annual: 1916, 1924.

Pu-Hu, (Ukrainian National Magazine), Augsburg, Germany. Weekly: 1947-1949.

Radio-Visti (Radio-News), Munich, Germany. Daily: 1945, 1948.

Recenzija (Review of Soviet Ukrainian Literature), Cambridge, MA. Semi-annual: 1970-1972, 1974. English.

Reporter (title varies: **St. John's Institute Newsletter**), Edmonton, Alberta, Canada. Bi-monthly: 1964-date. Includes English.

Review (Ukrainian Canadian Professional and Business Federation), Edmonton, Alberta, Canada. Annual: 1974.

Revoliutsiĭnyĭ Demokrat (Revolutionary Democrat), Neu Ulm, Germany. Monthly: 1949.

Ridna Knyha na Chuzhyni (The Native Book on Foreign Soil), Munich, Germany. Monthly: 1949.

Ridna Nyva, Kalendar (The Native Field, Calendar; title varies: **Iliustrovanyĭ Kaliendar Ridna Nyva**), Winnipeg, Manitoba, Canada. Annual: 1948-1950, 1952-1963, 1965-1968, 1970.

Ridna Shkola (Native School), Cleveland, OH. 1960, 1963.

Ridna Shkola (Native School), Stamford, CT. Monthly: 1963-1964.

Ridna Shkola (Native School), Toronto, Ontario, Canada. Monthly (except July and August): 1958-1959.

Ridna Shkola Biuleten' (Native School Bulletin), New York, NY. Three times a year: 1967-1968, 1980-1983.

Ridna Tserkva (Native Church), Portland, OR. Quarterly: 1954-1955.

Ridna Tserkva; Biuleten' Bratstva Oborony Ridnoï Tserkvy (Native Church; Bulletin of the Brotherhood in Defense of the Native Church), Winnipeg, Manitoba, Canada. Monthly: 1935. Includes English.

Ridna Vira (Native Faith), New York, NY. Frequency varies: 1964-1967.

Ridne Slovo (Native Word), Munich, Germany. Monthly: 1945-1946.

Ridnoshkil'ni Visti (Native School News), Detroit, MI. 1957-1958.

The Rising Star, Detroit, MI. Monthly: 1937. English.

Robitnycha Hromada (Workers' Society), Newark, NJ. 1937.

Robitnychi Visty (Labor News), Toronto, Ontario, Canada. Bi-monthly: 1933-1935.

Robitnychyï Kalendar (Workers' Calendar), New York, NY. Annual: 1914, 1919.

Robitnychyï Vistnyk (The Workers' Herald), New York, NY. Monthly: 1919.

Rozbudova Derzhavy (Building of a Nation), Toronto, Ontario, Canada (previously published in Montreal, Quebec, Canada; Cleveland, OH; and Denver, CO). Bi-monthly (quarterly): 1951-1958.

Runvist (Native Ukrainian National Faith), Winnipeg, Manitoba, Canada. Monthly: 1969-1970.

Rus'ka Katolyts'ka Vydavnycha Spilka (Rusin Catholic Publishing Association Calendar), New Britain, CT. Annual: 1913-1914.

St. Andrew's College Calendar, Winnipeg, Manitoba, Canada. Annual: 1982-1983. English.

Saint Basil's Preparatory School, Le Chateau, Stamford, CT. Annual: 1974. English.

St. Constantine's Ukrainian Catholic Church Bulletin, Minneapolis, MN. Weekly: 1960-1962, 1966, 1969-1970. English.

St. George Ukrainian Greek Orthodox Church, Dauphin, Manitoba, Canada. Weekly: 1970. Includes English.

St. George Ukrainian Orthodox Church Bulletin, Minneapolis, MN. Monthly: 1955, 195?, 1973-1974, 1977. English.

St. John the Baptist Ukrainian Catholic Church Bulletin, Pittsburgh, PA. Weekly: 1955, 1957, 1967. Includes English.

St. John's Institute Yearbook, Edmonton, Alberta, Canada. Annual: 1950-1954, 1959, 1963-1964. English.

St. John's Ukrainian Catholic Church Yearbook, Detroit, MI. Annual: 1943. Includes English.

St. Joseph's Ukrainian Catholic Church, Chicago, IL. Weekly: 1970-1971, 1974-date. Includes English.

St. Joseph's Ukrainian Catholic Church, Parish Newsletter, Chicago, IL. Annual: 1974-1975, 1977. English.

St. Michael's Ukrainian Orthodox Church Weekly Newsletter, Minneapolis, MN. Weekly: 1954, 1966-1974, 1976, 1980-date. English.

St. Nicholas Church, Bulletin, Troy, NY. Bi-monthly (?): 1964. Includes English.

St. Nicholas Church, Bulletin, Winnipeg, Manitoba, Canada. Weekly: 1973-1978. Includes English.

St. Nicholas Gazette, Chicago, IL. Annual: 1981-1982. Includes English.

St. Nicholas Ukrainian Catholic Cathedral, Financial Report, Chicago, IL. Annual: 1968, 1971, 1982-1983. Includes English.

St. Nicholas Ukrainian Catholic Church Bulletin, Brooklyn, NY. 1955.

St. Peter & St. Paul Ukrainian Orthodox G.C. Church, Bulletin, Carnegie, PA. Weekly: 1970. English.

SS. Peter & Paul Ukrainian Orthodox Church, Weekly Bulletin, Chicago, IL. Weekly: 1958-1965. Includes English.

Samobutnia Ukraïna (Original Ukraine), Winnipeg, Manitoba, Canada. Monthly: 1969-1970, 1972, 1974-1982, 1984.

Samodopomoha (Self-Help; A Ukrainian Quarterly of Cooperation and Economy), Winnipeg, Manitoba, Canada. Quarterly: 1956-1962. Includes English.

Samostiïna Ukraïna (Independent Ukraine), Chicago, IL (Winnipeg, Manitoba, Canada; St. Paul, MN; New York, NY). Monthly: 1948-1969, 1971-1985.

Scope, Chicago, IL. Bi-monthly: 1959-1960. English.

Second Wreath, Edmonton, Alberta, Canada. Bi-monthly: 1985. English.

Seminariïni Visti (Seminary News), Hirschberg, Germany. Monthly: 1949.

Sen'iors'ka Vatra (Seniors' Campfire; scouting publication), Detroit, MI, New York, NY. Monthly: 1951, 1953.

Shashkevychiiana (Studies of Shashkevych), Winnipeg, Manitoba, Canada. Semi-annual: 1963-1964, 1977-1983.

Shchodenni Visti (Daily News), Augsburg, Germany. Daily: 1947.

Shliakh Molodi (The Way of Youth), Munich, Germany. Quarterly (?): 1947-1948.

Shliakh Pravoslavnoï Molodi (The Way of Orthodox Youth), New York, NY. Quarterly: 1964-1965.

Shtif Tabachniuk, Kaliendar (Calendar), Winnipeg, Manitoba, Canada. Annual: 1918.

Siiach (The Sower), Chicago, IL. Monthly: 1927.

Siiach; Besidy z Druziamy (The Sower; Conversations with Friends), Babylon, NY. Irregular: 1964.

Siiach Pravdy (Sower of the Truth), Hartford, CT. Bi-monthly: 1953-1954, 1956.

Skob (Scouts magazine), New York, NY, and Minneapolis/St. Paul, MN. 1967.

Slidy Rozban' (Footprints of Rozban'; scouting publication), Rochester, NY. Semi-annual: 1970-1972.

Slovo (The Word), New York, NY. 1961-1962.

Slovo (The Word), Scranton, PA. Monthly: 1904.

Slovo (The Word; Ukrainian Canadian Writers' Association), Toronto, Ontario, Canada (previously published in New York, NY, and Edmonton, Alberta, Canada. Irregular: 1962, 1964, 1968, 1970, 1978, 1980, 1981, 1987.

Slovo Istyny (The Word of the Truth), Philadelphia, PA. Monthly: 1962-1963, 1967.

Slovo Istyny (The Word of the Truth), Winnipeg, Manitoba, Canada. Monthly: 1947-1951.

Slovo I Dilo (Word and Deed; previously titled **Informatsíínyĭ Lystok NDTUT**), New York, NY. Frequency varies: 1973.

Slovo, Kalendar (The Word, Calendar), Toronto, Ontario, Canada. Annual: 1961-1962, 1964-1978.

Slovo na Storozhi (Word on Guard), Winnipeg, Manitoba, Canada. Annual: 1964-1980.

Slovo Pidhaiechan (Word of the Pidhaiechan), Detroit, MI. Semi-annual: 1970-date.

Slovo pro Zborivshchynu (Word about Zborivshchyna), Toronto, Ontario, Canada. Monthly: 1973.

Smikh i Pravda (Laughter and Truth), New York, NY. Semi-monthly: 1928.

Smoloskyp (The Torch), Toronto, Ontario, Canada; Paris, France; Baltimore, MD; and Montreal, Quebec, Canada. Bi-monthly: 1952-1957, 1960-1968.

Smoloskyp (The Torch; Helsinki Guarantees for Ukraine Committee and the Ukrainian Information Service), Washington, DC. Quarterly: 1979-date. Includes English.

Smoloskyp (The Torch), Winnipeg, Manitoba, Canada. 1970.

Smoloskyp Information Service, Press Release, Washington, DC (Ellicott City, MD). Monthly: 1974-1975. English.

Smoloskyp (The Torch), New York, NY. Semi-annual: 1971-1972. Includes English.

Sniatyn, Detroit, MI. Annual: 1968-1976.

Sobornyj Lystok (Cathedral Leaflet [of Ukrainian Orthodox Cathedral of St. Mary the Protectress]. Winnipeg, Manitoba, Canada. Weekly or Bi-weekly: 1976-1979. Includes English.

Sobornyk (Synodical), Hannover (?), Germany. 1949.

Society of Ukrainian Philatelists, Inc. Visnyk (Herald), Schenectady, NY. Frequency varies: 1971-1974, 1976-1979.

S'ohochasne i Minule (Current and Past), Munich, Germany-New York, NY. Quarterly: 1948-1949.

S'ohodni (Today), Augsburg, Germany. Monthly: 1947.

Soiuz Ukraïns'kykh Filatelistiv (Alliance of Ukrainian Philatelists), New York, NY. Monthly (?): 1952, 1954, 1961.

Soiuz Ukraïns'kykh Veteraniv Armiï UNR i Ukraïns'koho Rezystansu, Biuleten' (Association of Ukrainian Veterans of the Army of the Ukrainian National Republic and the Ukrainian Resistance, Bulletin), Minneapolis, MN. 1986.

Sonechko (The Little Sun), Württemberg-Baden, Germany. Monthly: 1947.

Soniashnyk (Sunflower), Toronto, Ontario, Canada. Monthly: 1956-1961.

Spilka Vyzvolennia Ukraïny (Association for the Liberation of Ukraine), Brooklyn, NY. 1965.

Sportovyĭ Biuleten' (Sports Bulletin), Detroit, MI. Monthly: 1966, 1969.

Sportovyĭ Biuleten' (Sports Bulletin), Philadelphia, PA. Frequency varies: 1961. Includes English.

Sportovyĭ Dovidnyk (Sports Guide), Regensburg, Germany. 1946-1947.

Sportovyĭ Klych (Sports Call), New York, NY. Quarterly (?): 1973. Includes English.

Stanychni Visti: (The Stanytsya News), Chicago (?), IL. 1968-1969.

Stezhi (Paths), Innsbruck, Austria-Munich, Germany. Frequency varies: 1946.

Strila (Arrow), New York, NY. Quarterly: 1959-1962.

Strilets'ki Visty (Veteran News), Winnipeg, Manitoba, Canada. Monthly: 1931.

Student, Heidenau-Göttingen, Germany. 1947.

Student, Munich, Germany. Monthly: 1945-1949.

Student, Philadelphia, PA. Frequency varies: 1963-1964.

Student, Toronto, Ontario, Canada. Monthly: 1970-1971.

Students'ke Zhyttia (Student Life), Munich, Germany. Monthly: 1949.

Students'ki Obriï (Student Horizon), Munich, Germany. Monthly: 1946-1947.

Students'ki Visti (Student News), Munich, Germany. Weekly: 1946.

Students'kyĭ Holos (Students' Voice), New York, NY. 1970. Includes English.

Students'kyĭ Klych (Students' Call), Graz, Austria. Monthly: 1947.

Students'kyĭ Prapor (Students' Flag), Graz, Austria. Quarterly: 1948.

Students'kyĭ Shliakh (Students' Way), Innsbruck, Austria-Munich, Germany. Frequency varies: 1945-1947.

Students'kyĭ Vistnyk (Students' Herald), Munich, Germany. Quarterly: 1947-1948.

Suchasnist' (Contemporary Times), Munich, West Germany. Monthly: 1961-1981.

Suchasnyk (The Contemporary), Neu Ulm, Germany. Quarterly: 1948.

Sumivets' (Member of the Ukrainian Youth Association of America), New York, NY. Tri-quarterly: 1960.

Sumkivets (Quarterly of the Canadian Ukrainian Youth Association of Canada), Saskatoon, Saskatchewan, Canada. Quarterly: 1970-1972, 1975. Includes English.

Surma; Iuvileĭnyĭ Kaliendar Al'manakh Knyharni Surma; (Bugle; Jubilee Calendar-Almanac of Surma Bookstore), New York, NY. Annual: 1945.

Sviata Sofiia (Saint Sofia), Philadelphia, PA. Monthly: 1980. Includes English.

S'vidoma Syla ([Swidoma Syla] Knowing Power), Toronto, Ontario, Canada. Monthly: 1915.

Svit Molodi (The Youth's World), Winnipeg, Manitoba, Canada. Monthly: 1927.

Svitannia (Dawn), Augsburg, Germany. Annual: 1946.

Svitanok (Daybreak), Minneapolis, MN. Bi-monthly (?), Quarterly (?): 1960-1961, 1963.

Svitlo (The Light), Toronto, Ontario, Canada. Monthly: 1950-1984, 1986. Includes English.

Svitlo, Kalendar (The Light, Calendar), Toronto, Ontario, Canada. Annual: 1953, 1955-1958, 1960-1970, 1972-1976, 1978-1980, 1982-1983.

Svitlo i Holos Pravdy (The Light and the Voice of Truth), Winnipeg, Manitoba, Canada. Annual (?): 1964, 1977.

Svoboda, Kalendar (Freedom, Calendar; title varies: **Iuvileĭnyĭ Al'manakh Svobody**), Jersey City, NJ. Annual: 1935, 1940, 1950, 1953, 1955-1960, 1963.

Syrits'kyĭ Dim, Kalendar (Orphan's Home, Calendar; title varies: **Iliustrovanyĭ Kaliendar Syrtis'koho Domu**), Philadelphia, PA. Annual: 1917, 1929, 1932, 1935-1943, 1952-1954. Includes some English.

Taborove Zhyttia (Camp Life), Carlos State Park, MN. Annual: 1959-1960.

Taborovi Visti (Camp News), Augsburg, Germany. Weekly: 1947.

Tam-Tam, South Orange, NJ. 1971.

Tekhnichnyĭ Kalendar (Technical Calendar), Augsburg, Germany. Annual: 1947.

Terem (Tower; Problems of Ukrainian Culture), Detroit, MI. Frequency varies: 1962, 1966, 1968, 1971, 1979.

Terenove Kerivnytstvo OUN v ZDA (Territorial Directorship of the Organization of Ukrainian Nationalists in the U.S.A.), Long Island City, NY. Monthly: 1974-1975.

Ternopil's'kyĭ Biuleten' (Ternopil Bulletin), Philadelphia, PA. Semi-annual: 1974-1977.

Tochylo (Grindstone), Winnipeg, Manitoba, Canada. Monthly: 1935. Includes English.

Tovarysh Imigranta, Kaliendar Ukraïns'koho Robitnychoho Soiuza (Comrade of the Immigrant, Calendar of the Ukrainian Workingmen's Association; title varies: **Tovarysh Imigranta Kaliendar Rus'koho Narodnoho Soiuza**), Scranton, PA. Annual: 1915-1920, 1922.

Tovarystvo Ukraïns'koho Robitnycho-Farmers'koho Domu v Kanadi i Bratnikh Organizatsiï (Society of the Ukrainian Labor-Farmer Temple Association's Home and Fraternal Organizations, Almanac), Winnipeg, Manitoba, Canada. Annual: 1929.

Tovarystvo Ukraïns'kykh Bibliotekariv Ameryky, Biuleten' (Society of Ukrainian Librarians of America, Bulletin), Boulder, CO. Frequency varies: 1962, 1965, 1971-1973. Includes some English.

T-vo Ukraïns'kykh Kuptsiv, Promyslovtsiv i Profesionalistiv v Chikago (Society of Ukrainian Businessmen, Tradesmen and Professionals in Chicago), Chicago, IL. Frequency varies: 1975.

Trendette, Rochester, NY. Monthly: 1952-1967. English.

Tri-denette, Bayside, NY. Monthly: 1957. English.

The Trident, Chicago, IL, then New York. Monthly: 1936-1941. English.

Trident, New York, NY. Bi-monthly: 1960, 1962, 1965. English.

The Trident, Pittsburgh, PA. Monthly: 1934. English.

Trident News, Chicago, IL. Monthly: 1935-1936. English.

The Trident Quarterly, Chicago, IL. Quarterly: 1960-1962. English.

Trident Visnyk (Herald), Springfield, VA. Bi-monthly: 1983-1984. Includes English.

Trybuna (Tribune), Detroit, MI. Quarterly: 1979-1986.

Tryzub (Trident), Minneapolis, MN. Quarterly: 1972-1987. Includes English.

Tryzub (Trident), New York, NY. Bi-monthly: 1960-1975.

Tserkovnyĭ Biuleten' (Church Bulletin), Minneapolis, MN. Weekly: 1972-1974, 1976, 1978.

Tserkovnyĭ Biuleten' (Church Bulletin), Winnipeg, Manitoba, Canada. Weekly: 1966.

Tserkovnyĭ Kalendar Al'manakh (Church Calendar Almanac), Chicago, IL. Annual: 1970-1977, 1982-1984.

Tserkovnyĭ Visnyk (Church Herald; title varies: **Visnyk Ukraïns'koï Parafiï Sviatykh Volodmyra i Ol'hy v Chicago**), Chicago, IL. Bi-weekly: 1968-date.

Tserkovnyĭ Visnyk (Church Herald), Munich, Germany. Bi-weekly: 1945-1946.

Tserkva i Narid (The Church and People), Winnipeg, Manitoba, Canada. Monthly: 1938, 1949-1951.

Tserkva i Zhyttia (Church and Life), Esslingen am Neckar, Germany. Monthly: 1946.

Tserkva ĭ Zhyttia (Church and Life), Los Angeles, CA (previously published in Chicago, IL). Bi-monthly: 1957-1977.

Tserkva Sv. Ivana Khrestytelia (Church of St. Ivana Khrestytelia), Hunter, NY. Annual: 1964.

Tsvitka (Floweret), Jersey City, NJ. Monthly: 1914-1915.

UALF News Digest (Ukrainian Anti-Libel Fund), South Orange, NJ. Bi-monthly: 1986. English.

U.N.Y.F. News (Ukrainian National Youth Federation), Toronto, Ontario, Canada. Monthly: 1946-1947. English.

U.O.L. Newsletter (Ukrainian Orthodox League), Minneapolis, MN. Weekly: 1972-1974.

U-Canteen News, Philadelphia, PA. Monthly: 1946. English.

Uchitesia! (Learn), Philadelphia, PA. Twice during school year: 1964.

Ukadet (Ukrainian Cadet), Minneapolis, MN. Monthly: 1941-1965, 1969-1973. Includes English.

Ukraïna (Ukraine), Chicago, IL. Monthly: 1947-1948.

Ukraïna (Ukraine), Winnipeg, Manitoba, Canada. Semi-annual: 1918.

Ukraine (The Ukrainian Alliance of America), New York, NY. Monthly: 1918. English.

Ukraine (Organization for the Rebirth of Ukraine), New York, NY. Monthly: 1941-1944.

Ukrainian Academy of Arts and Sciences in the United States, Annals, New York, NY. Frequency varies: 1951-1956, 1958-1972, 1978-1980. English.

Ukrainian Affairs Bulletin of Connecticut, Hartford, CT. Monthly: 1939-1946. English.

Ukrainian American Affairs Bulletin, New York, NY. Three times per year (?): 1944. English.

Ukrainian-American Archives Museum and Library, Detroit, MI. Annual: 1965-1967, 1970, 1974-1975, 1977, 1983, 1985, 1987-1988. Includes English.

Ukrainian-American Foundation in Memory of Roman W. Smook Inc., Chicago, IL. Irregular: 1977.

The Ukrainian-American Review, Philadelphia, PA. 1933. Includes English.

The Ukrainian-American Student News, Cleveland, OH. Quarterly: 1954, 1959. English.

Ukrainian Artists Association in America, New York Branch, New York, NY. Annual: 1964, 1966. Includes English.

Ukrainian Artist Association in U.S.A., Catalogue, New York, NY. Annual: 1953-1955, 1967. Includes English.

Ukrainian Baptist Youth Association, Bulletin, Chicago, IL. Quarterly: 1969-1970, 1973-1975. Mainly English.

The Ukrainian Bulletin (merged with the **Ukrainian Quarterly** in 1970), New York, NY. Semimonthly: 1948-1970. English.

Ukrainian Bureau, Washington, DC. Weekly: 1939-1940. English.

Ukrainian Canadian Committee, Biuleten', Winnipeg, Manitoba, Canada. Quarterly: 1946, 1953-1959, 1961-1962, 1967-1975, 1977-date.

Ukrainian Canadian Committee, Biuleten', Montreal, Quebec, Canada. Monthly: 1970.

Ukrainian Canadian Review, Winnipeg, Manitoba, Canada. Monthly: 1942-1944. English.

Ukrainian Chronicle, Philadelphia, PA. Monthly: 1936-1938. English.

Ukrainian Commentary, Winnipeg, Manitoba, Canada. Frequency varies: 1952-1958. English.

Ukrainian Cultural Institute, Newsletter, Dickinson, ND. Quarterly: 1980-date. English.

Ukrainian Digest, Winnipeg, Manitoba, Canada. Monthly: 1953, 1960. English.

Ukrainian Fraternal Society Library, Annual Bulletin, Vancouver, British Columbia, Canada. Annual: 1972-1973, 1978-1979. Includes English.

Ukrainian Graduates, Detroit, MI. Monthly: 1940. English.

Ukrainian Leader, New York, NY. Monthly: 1936-1937. English.

Ukrainian Life, Scranton, PA. Monthly: 1940-1942. English.

Ukrainian Muzyka, Montreal, Quebec, Canada. Quarterly: 1983. English.

Ukrainian National Committee of the United States, Bulletin, New York, NY. 1919. English.

Ukrainian Newsletter, New York, NY. Monthly: 1980-1983. English.

Ukrainian Orthodox Bulletin, New York, NY. Monthly: 1948-1949. English.

Ukrainian Orthodox League Bulletin, Ambridge, PA. Bi-monthly (quarterly): 1953, 1956, 1958-1972. English.

Ukrainian Orthodox Word (English edition of **Ukraïns'ke Pravoslavne Slovo**), South Bound Brook, NJ. Bi-monthly: 1967-1974, 1977-1983, 1985-date. English.

The Ukrainian Quarterly (Kvartal'nyk UKKA v Minnesoti), Minneapolis, MN. Quarterly: 1966.

The Ukrainian Quarterly, New York, NY. Quarterly: 1944-1984. (Cummulative index: 1948-1975). English.

The Ukrainian Review, New York, NY. Monthly: 1931. English.

Ukrainian Review, Winnipeg, Manitoba, Canada. Bi-monthly: 1937, 1941.

Ukrainian Technical Institute in New York, Bulletin, New York, NY. Annual: 1954-1955, 1959-1961. English.

The Ukrainian Trend, New York, NY (Newark, NJ). Quarterly: 1938-1942, 1947-1950, 1952-1969. English.

Ukrainian Tribune and Review, Edmonton, Alberta, Canada. Monthly: 1939. English.

Ukrainian Year Book, Winnipeg, Manitoba, Canada. Annual: 1946-1952. English.

Ukrainian Youth, Jersey City, NJ (Chicago, IL). Monthly: 1935-1938, 1942. Includes English.

Ukrainian Youth Bulletin, Detroit, MI. 1935. English.

Ukrainian Youth League, Chicago, IL. 1935. Mainly English.

Ukraïnka v Amerytsi (Ukrainian Woman in America), New York, NY. Monthly: 1941. Includes English.

Ukraïnka v Sviti (Ukrainian Woman in the World), Detroit, MI. Quarterly: 1963-1972, 1978, 1981-1986.

Ukraïns'ka Katolyts'ka Parafiia Sviatykh Volodymyra i Ol'hy, Finansovi Zvity (Ukrainian Catholic Parish of SS. Volodymyr and Olha, Financial Reports), Chicago, IL. Annual: 1978, 1980-1983.

Ukraïns'ka Katolyts'ka Tserkva Presviatoï Ievkharystiï (Ukrainian Catholic Church of the Most Holy Eucharist), Toronto, Ontario, Canada. Weekly: 1981. Includes English.

Ukraïns'ka Katolyts'ka Tserkva Sv. Iosafata, Biuleten' Komitetu Budovy Tserkyv (Ukrainian Catholic Church of St. Josaphat, Bulletin of the Church Building Committee), Parma, OH. Annual: 1982-1983. Includes English.

Ukraïns'ka Khata (Ukrainian Home), Kiev, Ukraine. Monthly. (Microfilm: 1909-1914).

Ukraïns'ka Knyha (Ukrainian Book), Philadelphia, PA. Quarterly: 1961, 1971-1974, 1981-1982.

Ukraïns'ka Knyharnia (Ukrainian Bookstore), Edmonton, Alberta, Canada. Bi-monthly: 1969-1971.

Ukraïns'ka Kredytova Spilka (Ukrainian Credit Union), Toronto, Ontario, Canada. Annual: 1954, 1965, 1969.

Ukraïns'ka Narodn'ia Pomich, Kalendar Al'manakh (Ukrainian National Aid, Calendar Almanac; title varies: Kaliendar Narodn'oï Pomochi Liubov; Kaliendar Ukraïns'koï Narod. Pomochi Liubov), Pittsburgh, PA. Annual: 1926-1932, 1938, 1954.

Ukraïns'ka Natsional'na Kredytova Spilka, Misiachnyï Biuleten' (Ukrainian National Credit Union, Monthly Bulletin), Montreal, Quebec, Canada. Monthly: 1966-1967.

Ukraïns'ka Nova Knyha; Zhurnal Bibliotekoznavstva ta Bibliohrafiï (Ukrainian New Home; Journal of Librarianship and Bibliography), State College, PA. Bi-monthly: 1968.

Ukraïns'ka Nyva (The Ukrainian Gospel Field), Saskatoon, Saskatchewan, Canada. Monthly: 1957, 1960-1964, 1966.

Ukraïns'ka Rodyna (The Ukrainian Family; A Journal of Popular Literature and History), Toronto, Ontario, Canada. Monthly: 1947-1949.

Ukraïns'ka Rodyna, Kalendar (Ukrainian Family, Calendar), Monder, Alberta, Canada. Annual: 1941-1942, 1945, 1947-1949, 1951-1952.

Ukraïns'ka Shkola (Ukrainian School), Augsburg, Germany. Monthly: 1947-1948.

Ukraïns'ka Spilka Obrazotvorchykh Mysttsiv v Kanadi (Ukrainian Association of Creative Artists in Canada), Toronto, Ontario, Canada. Annual: 1959-1961.

Ukraïns'ka Strilets'ka Hromada v Kanadi, Informator (Ukrainian Riflemen's Community of Canada, Informer), Toronto, Ontario, Canada. Monthly: 1955-1963.

Ukraïns'ka Strilets'ka Hromada, Informatsiĭnyĭ Lystok (Ukrainian Riflemen's Community, Informational Leaflet), Toronto, Ontario, Canada. Frequency varies: 1965.

Ukraïns'ka Zemlia (Ukrainian Land), New York, NY. Frequency varies: 1951, 1953, 1968, 1972, 1984, 1986.

Ukraïns'ke Henealohichne i Heral'dychne Tovarstvo, Biuleten' (Ukrainian Genealogical and Heraldic Society, Bulletin), Miami, FL. Bi-monthly: 1964-1971.

Ukraïns'ke Hromads'ke Slovo (Ukrainian Community Word), New York, NY. Monthly: 1953-1958.

Ukraïns'ke Istorychne Tovarystvo, Biuleten' dlia Chleniv (Ukrainian Historical Association Bulletin for Members), Miami, FL. Quarterly: 1967-1972.

Ukraïnske Kozatstovo (Ukrainian Cossackdom), Chicago, IL. Quarterly: 1968-1980, 1982-1983.

Ukraïns'ke Narodne Slovo (Ukrainian National Word), Chicago, IL. Quarterly: 1983.

Ukraïns'ke Natsional'ne Ob'iednannia Kanady, Kraĭova Ekzekutyva, Obizhnyk (Ukrainian National Alliance of Canada, Regional Executive, Circular), Toronto, Ontario, Canada. Frequency varies: 1955-1956, 1959-1962, 1964.

Ukraïns'ke Pravoslavne Slovo (Ukrainian Orthodox Word; absorbed **Dnipro** and **Ukraïns'kyĭ Visnyk**), South Bound Brook, NJ (previously published in New York, NY). Monthly: 1950-date.

Ukraïns'ke Vidrodzhennia (Ukrainian Rebirth), Hamilton, Ontario, Canada. Quarterly: 1983-1985.

Ukraïns'ki Kanadiĭs'ki Pidpryiemtsi i Profesionalisty, Kalendar-Al'manakh (Ukrainian Canadian Businessmen and Professionals, Calendar-Almanac), Toronto, Ontario, Canada. Annual: 1957.

Ukraïns'ki Pravoslavni Visti (Ukrainian Orthodox News), Minneapolis, MN. 1978.

Ukraïns'ki Shkil'ni Visti (Ukrainian School News), Newark, NJ. Monthly: 1929. Includes some English.

Ukraïns'ki Sichovi Stril'tsi (Ukrainian Sich Riflemen), Toronto, Ontario, Canada. Frequency varies: 1954, 1964.

Ukraïns'ki Visti, Kalendar (Ukrainian News, Calendar), Edmonton, Alberta, Canada. Annual: 1937-1938, 1962-1965, 1967.

Ukraïns'ko-Amerykans'ka Fundatsiia, Biuleten' (Ukrainian-American Foundation, Bulletin), Ontario, CA. Annual: 1959, 1961, 1977.

Ukraïns'ko Amerykans'ka Tsentralia v Niu Ĭorku, Biuleten' (Ukrainian American Central Organization in New York, Bulletin), New York, NY. 1945.

Ukraïns'kyĭ Bazar (Ukrainian Bazaar), Toronto, Ontario, Canada. Monthly: 1934. Includes English.

Ukraïns'kyĭ Biuleten' Informatsiĭ (Ukrainian Information Bulletin), Munich, Germany. Weekly: 1946-1948.

Ukraïns'kyĭ Filatelist (Ukrainian Philatelist), New York, NY/Cleveland, OH. Annual: 1951-1955, 1961-1975, 1977-1984. Includes English.

Ukraïns'kyĭ Holos, Kalendar-Al'manakh (Ukrainian Voice, Calendar-Almanac; title varies: Iliustrovanyĭ Narodnyĭ Kaliendar Ukr. Holosu; Iliustrovanyĭ Kaliendar Ukr. Holosu), Winnipeg, Manitoba, Canada. Annual: 1915, 1918, 1920, 1929, 1931-1932, 1934-1954, 1956-1972.

Ukraïns'kyĭ Hospodarnyk (The Ukrainian Economist), New York, NY-Irvington, NJ. Quarterly: 1954-1956, 1962-1963, 1969, 1971.

Ukraïns'kyĭ Ievanhel's'kyĭ Shliakh (Ukrainian Evangelical Way), Burnaby, British Columbia, Canada. Quarterly: 1971-1974.

Ukraïns'kyĭ Informator (Ukrainian Informer), Neustadt, Germany. Weekly: 1945.

Ukraïns'kyĭ Istoryk (The Ukrainian Historian), Kent, OH (previously published in New York, NY). Quarterly: 1963-1973, 1975-1976, 1983. (Cumulative index: 1963-1974). Includes English.

Ukraïns'kyĭ Kalendarets' (Ukrainian Calendar), Toronto, Ontario, Canada. Annual: 1958.

Ukraïns'kyĭ Kalendarets' (Ukrainian Calendar), Toronto, Ontario, Canada. Annual: 1953.

Ukraïns'kyĭ Katolys'kyĭ Vistnyk (Ukrainian Catholic Herald), Detroit, MI. Weekly: 1931. Includes English.

Ukraïns'kyĭ Khor "Dumka" v Niu Ĭorku, Biuleten' (Ukrainian Chorus "Dumka" in New York, Bulletin), New York, NY. 1963.

Ukraïns'kyĭ Kombatant (Ukrainian Combatant), Munich/Neu Ulm, Germany. Frequency varies: 1947-1963.

Ukraïns'kyĭ Kongresovyĭ Komitet Ameryky, Viddil v Chicago (Ukrainian Congress Committee of America, Chicago Branch), Chicago, IL. Semi-annual (?): 1983.

Ukraïns'kyĭ Litopys (Ukrainian Chronicle), Augsburg, Germany. Monthly: 1946-1948.

Ukraïns'kyĭ Medychnyĭ Arkhiv (Ukrainian Medical Archive), Chicago, IL. Annual: 1980-1984.

Ukraïns'kyĭ Ohliad (Ukrainian Digest), New York, NY. Bi-monthly: 1959-1961.

Ukraïns'kyĭ Politviazen', Kyshen'kovyĭ Kalendarets' (Ukrainian Political Prisoner, Pocket Calendar), Munich, Germany. Annual: 1948.

Ukraïns'kyĭ Praktychnyĭ Kalendar-Informator ta Providnyk po Shikago (Ukrainian Practical Informational Calendar and Guide around Chicago), Chicago, IL. Annual: 1952.

Ukraïns'kyĭ Pravoslavnyĭ Kalendar (Ukrainian Orthodox Calendar), South Bound Brook, NJ. Annual: 1951-1977, 1981, 1983, 1985-1986.

Ukraïns'kyĭ Pravoslavnyĭ Tserkovnyĭ Kalendar (Ukrainian Orthodox Church Calendar), Stuttgart, West Germany. Annual: 1947, 1949, 1950.

Ukraïns'kyĭ Pravoslavnyĭ Visnyk (Ukrainian Orthodox Herald), Jamaica, NY. Quarterly: 1971-1972, 1974-1978, 1982. Includes English.

Ukraïns'kyĭ Pravoslavnyĭ Visnyk (Ukrainian Orthodox Herald), New York, NY. Bi-monthly: 1949-1950. Includes English.

Ukraïns'kyĭ Samostĭnyk (Ukrainian Independent), Munich, Germany. 1947.

Ukraïns'kyĭ Svit (Ukrainian World), Lillooet, British Columbia, Canada (previously published in Winnipeg, Manitoba, Canada). Monthly: 1969.

Ukraïns'kyĭ Tantsiuryst (Ukrainian Dancer), Toronto, Ontario, Canada. 1951.

Ukraïns'kyĭ Terminolohichnyĭ Tsentr v Amerytsi, Bulletin (Center for Ukrainian Terminology in America, Bulletin), New York, NY. Irregular: 1966.

Ukraïns'kyĭ Vistnyk (Ukrainian Herald), New York, NY (Carteret, NJ). Quarterly (monthly): 1934, 1936-1945, 1947-1965.

Ukraïns'kyĭ Vistnyk (Ukrainian Herald), Winnipeg, Manitoba, Canada. Monthly, bi-monthly: 1934.

Ukraïns'kyĭ Zhurnalist (The Ukrainian Journalist), Newark, NJ. Frequency varies: 1967, 1969, 1976.

Ukrapres (Ukrainian Press Review), Greeley, CO. Monthly: 1982-1984.

Ukreklama (Ukrainian Advertising), Toronto, Ontario, Canada. Bi-monthly: 1969-1972.

United Ukrainian War Veterans of America, Bulletin, Philadelphia, PA. Annual: 1954, 1958.

V Dorohu z Iunatstvom (On the Road with Young Scouts), New York, NY. 1959.

Vartova Bashta (Watchtower), Brooklyn, NY. Monthly: 1956, 1959-1960, 1963, 1967, 1981.

Veselka (The Rainbow), Jersey City, NJ. Monthly: 1954-1978.

Vezhi (Towers), Munich, Germany. 1947-1948.

Vezhi (Towers), Philadelphia, PA. Bi-monthly: 1974, 1977.

Vidrodzhennia (Rebirth), Jefferson, OH. Quarterly: 1974.

Vil'na Ukraïna (Free Ukraine), New York, NY. Quarterly: 1954-1972.

Vil'ne Kozatstvo (Free Cossackdom), New York, NY. 1962-1964.

Vira (Faith), South Bound Brook, NJ. Monthly: 1976, 1978-1979, 1981-1983. Includes English.

Vira i Kul'tura (Faith and Culture), Winnipeg, Manitoba, Canada. Monthly: 1953-1967, 1982-1984.

Vira i Nauka (Faith and Science), Brookhaven, Chester, PA. Quarterly: 1962-1974, 1979.

Visnyk (Herald of the Association of the Ukrainian American Merchants, Manufacturers & Professionals in Chicago), Chicago, IL. 1975.

Visnyk (The Herald), Chicago, IL. Weekly (?): 1969.

Visnyk (The Herald), Los Angeles, CA. Quarterly: 1973-1980. Includes English.

Visnyk (The Herald of the Central Union of Ukrainian Students), Munich, Germany. 1945.

Visnyk (Herald of the Ukrainian Red Cross), Munich, Germany. 1945.

Visnyk (The Herald), New York, NY. 1967-1968, 1970.

Visnyk (Herald), New York, NY. Monthly: 1947-date.

Visnyk (The Herald), Toronto, Ontario, Canada. Semi-annual: 1974-1976, 1978, 1986-1987.

Visnyk (The Herald of the Ukrainian National Democratic Union, Trenton, NJ. 1972.

Visnyk (The Herald), Winnipeg, Manitoba, Canada. Semi-monthly: 1968, 1974.

Visnyk (The Herald of the Research Institute of Volyn), Winnipeg, Manitoba, Canada. Monthly: 1954, 1966, 1969.

Visnyk (The Herald of the Ukrainian Resistance Veterans Association in the U.S.A.), Yonkers, NY. 1977.

Visnyk Holovnoï Upravy Karpats'koho Soiuzu v ZSA (The Herald of the Executive Council of the Carpathian Alliance in the U.S.A.), New York, NY. Bi-monthly: 1970-1973.

Visnyk Pravdy (Herald of Truth), New York, NY. Semi-annual: 1966.

Visnyk Svitovoho Kongresu Vil'nykh Ukraïntsiv (Herald of the World Congress of Free Ukrainians), Toronto, Ontario, Canada. Annual: 1974-1982, 1986-1987.

Visnyk Ukraïns'koho Komitetu 200-Richchia ZSA v Minnesoti (Herald of the Ukrainian Committee for the U.S. Bicentennial Celebration in Minnesota), Minneapolis, MN. Quarterly: 1976.

Visnyk Ukraïns'kykh Revoliutsiïnykh Demokrativ (Herald of the Ukrainian Revolutionary Democrats), Toronto, Ontario, Canada. Monthly: 1951-1952.

Visti (News; Organization for the Rebirth of Ukraine), Cleveland, OH. 1952.

Visti (News; Bulletin of the Ukrainian Culture Center), Los Angeles, CA. Frequency varies: 1966-1968, 1970, 1972-1982.

Visti (News; Ukrainian Technical Institute in New York), New York, NY. Annual (?): 1955-1960.

Visti (News of Pokrova Ukrainian Catholic Parish and Community Center), Parma, OH. Quarterly: 1979-1980, 1982.

Visti (News), Toronto, Ontario, Canada. Monthly: 1966-1968.

Visti (News of Ukrainian Cultural and Educational Centre), Winnipeg, Manitoba, Canada. Quarterly: 1981. Includes English.

Visti Bratstva Sv. Volodymyra (News of the Brotherhood of St. Volodymyr), New York, NY. Semi-annual: 1965-1966.

Visti dlia Virnykh (News for the Faithful), Edmonton, Alberta, Canada. Weekly (?): 1979-1980.

Visti (Ukrainian Studies Chair Fund News), Lorain, OH. Frequency varies: 1971, 1973-1977. Includes English.

Visti Instytutu Sv. Volodymyra (St. Volodymyr Institute News), Toronto, Ontario, Canada. 1967, 1969.

Visti iz Stanytsi (News from the Scout Post), Detroit, MI. Monthly: 1959-1963, 1965.

Visti Kombatanta (Veteran's News), Toronto, Ontario, Canada. Bi-monthly: 1961-1978, 1983-1984.

Visti MUN (News of the Ukrainian National Youth Federation of America), Philadelphia, PA. 1972, 1974.

Visti-News (Ukrainian Congress Committee of Youngstown), Youngstown, OH. Monthly: 1974.

Visti Plast-Pryiatu (News of Plast [Scouts]-Friends), Toronto, Ontario, Canada. Frequency varies: 1963.

Visti T-va Pryiateliv Ukraïns'koï Kapeli Bandurystiv (News of the Society of Friends of the Ukrainian Bandurist Capella), Detroit, MI. Monthly: 1955.

Visti Tsentrali Ukraïns'kykh Kooperatyv Ameryky (Newsletter of the Ukrainian National Credit Union Association), Chicago, IL. 1979.

Visti U.Z.O. (Bulletin of the United Ukrainian Organizations of Greater Cleveland), Parma, OH. Quarterly 1978-1979, 1983-1984.

Visti Ukraïns'koho Kongresovoho Komitetu Ameryky (News of the Ukrainian Congress Committee of America), Chicago, IL. 1978.

Visti Ukraïns'koho Kongresovoho Komitetu Ameryky (News of the Ukrainian Congress Committee of America), New York, NY. Monthly: 1959-1960.

Visti Ukraïns'koho Natsional'noho Ob'iednannia (News of the Ukrainian National Alliance), Sudbury, Ontario, Canada. Bi-weekly: 1959.

Visti Ukraïns'kykh Inzheneriv (Ukrainian Engineering News; Ukrainian Engineers' Society of America and Ukrainian Technical Society in Canada), New York, NY. Quarterly: 1950-1982, 1985. Includes English.

Visti UKKA v Minnesoti (Minnesota UCCA Newsletter), Minneapolis, MN. Frequency varies: 1954, 1964-1965, 1967-1968, 1977. Includes English.

Visti UTHI (News of the Ukrainian Technical and Husbandry Institute), Regensburg-Munich, West Germany. 1947-1948, 1951-1953, 1957, 1958.

Visti UTHI v ZDA (News of the Ukrainian Technical and Husbandry Institute in the USA), New York, NY. Frequency varies: 1952-1953, 1955.

Visti UVAN (News of Ukrainian Academy of Arts and Sciences), New York, NY. Annual: 1970.

Visti z Ditochoï Vakatsiïnoï Oseli v Raundleïk (News from the Children's Vacation Resort in Roundlake), Chicago, IL. 1955.

Visti z Kolehiï (News of the College; St. Andrew's College), Winnipeg, Manitoba, Canada. Quarterly: 1972-1978.

Visti z Kredytivky (News of the Credit Union; Educational Committee of Self-Reliance), Detroit, MI. 1962. Includes some English.

Visti Zakhidn'oï Eparkhiï Ukraïns'koï Hreko-Pravoslavnoï Tserkvy v Kanadi (News of the Western Eparchy of the Ukrainian Greek-Orthodox Church in Canada), Edmonton, Alberta, Canada. Monthly: 1968. Includes English.

Visti Zluchenoho Ukraïns'koho Amerykans'koho Dopomohovoho Komitetu (News of the United Ukrainian American Relief Committee), Philadelphia, PA. Monthly (?): 1950.

Vistnyk Ob'iednannia Ukraïnskykh Lisnykiv i Derevnykiv (Bulletin of Ukrainian Foresters and Woodsmen), New York, NY. Frequency varies: 1962-1968.

Vistnyk Organizatsiï Derzhavnoho Vidrodzhennia Ukraïny (Newsletter of the Organization for the Rebirth of Ukraine), New York, NY. Monthly: 1933-1935. (Microfilm: 1932-1935). Includes some English.

Vistynk Carstva Bozoho [sic] (News of God's Kingdom), Cleveland, OH. One undated issue.

Vohon' Orlynoï Rady (Fire of the Eagles Council [Scouts]), New York, NY. (Connecticut). Quarterly: 1967-1968.

Volosozhar (Constellation of the Pleiades), Millville, NJ. Quarterly (?): 1958, 1967-1970.

Volyn' (Organ of the Society of Volyn' in New York), New York, NY. Quarterly: 1951.

Vovcheniata (Young Wolves), Munich, Germany. 1946.

Vpered (Forward), New York, NY. Annual: 1925, 1929.

Vsesvit (Universe), New York, NY. Semi-monthly: 1950.

Vydavnytstvo Tryzub, Kalendar Al'manakh (Trident Publishers, Calendar Almanac), Winnipeg, Manitoba, Canada. Annual: 1975.

Vyklyk (The Challenge; Canadian Ukrainian Youth Association), Edmonton, Alberta, Canada. Bi-monthly: 1965, 1967. Includes English.

Vyzvol'na Polityka (Liberation Politics), Munich, Germany. Monthly: 1946-1948.

World Lemkos' Federation, Camillus, NY. Annual: 1974-1975. Includes some English.

YAC Gazette (The Library of St. Vladimir's Ukrainian Greek Orthodox Church), Calgary, Alberta, Canada. 1965. Includes English.

Young Life, Nyack, NY. Monthly (except July and August): 1969-1971. English.

Youth, Edmonton, Alberta, Canada. Quarterly: 1947, 1968. English.

Yunak (The Youth), Toronto, Ontario, Canada. Monthly: 1963-1978, 1983.

Za Charom Sribnoï Zemli (For the Enchanting Silver Land), Detroit, MI. 1950.

Za Ridnu Tserkvu (For the Native Church), Toronto, Ontario, Canada. Bi-monthly: 1966-1967, 1969, 1971, 1973-1975. Includes some English and Spanish.

Za Synim Okeanom (Beyond the Blue Ocean), New York, NY. Monthly: 1959-1962.

Za Viru Pravoslavnu (For the Orthodox Faith), New York, NY. Bi-monthly: 1964.

Zakhar Berkut (Newsletter of the Ukrainian Youth Association of America, Minnesota Branch), Minneapolis, MN. 1966.

Zaporozhets' za Dunaiem (Cossack beyond the Danube), Winnipeg, Canada. Irregular: 1938.

Zapysky Ukraïns'koho Henealohichnoho i Heral'dychnoho Tovarystva (Proceedings of the Ukrainian Genealogical and Heraldic Society), Miami, FL. Bi-monthly: 1969-1971.

Zhinka (The Woman), Detroit, MI. Monthly: 1939-1940, one undated Christmas issue.

Zhinochyï Svit (Woman's World), Winnipeg, Manitoba, Canada. Monthly: 1933-1934, 1950-date.

Zhoda Bratstv, Kaliendar (Agreement of Brothers, Calendar), Olyphant, PA. Annual: 1921.

Zhyttia i Shkola (Life and School), New Haven, CT. Monthly: 1960-1968, 1970-1975, 1977-1982.

Zhyttia i Tserkva (Life and Church), New York, NY. Quarterly: 1956, 1961-1967.

Zirka (The Star), New Britain, CT. Quarterly: 1913.

Zorinnia Novoï Doby i Vistnyk Prysutnosty Khrysta (Dawn of New Era and News of God's Presence), Winnipeg, Manitoba, Canada. Monthly: 1960, 1977.

Zov Ordenu (The Order's Call; The Bulletin of the Knightly Order of the Sun God), Philadelphia, PA. 1954.

Zozul'ka (Young Cuckoo), Ottawa, Ontario, Canada. Quarterly: 1969-1970.

Blessing of St. Michael's Ukrainian Orthodox Church, Bishop Ioann Teodorovych, Revs. M. Zarparniuk and Iu. Zelechivsky, Minneapolis, MN, 1926.

Appendixes

IHRC Services and General Information

Location: 826 Berry Street, St. Paul, MN 55114, phone: (612) 627-4208 (map and local accommodations available upon request).

Hours of Operation: 8:30-4:30 M-F; Saturdays by appointment with curator; closed on University of Minnesota holidays.

Response to Inquiries: Along with assisting research visitors, IHRC staff will respond to mail and phone inquiries; written requests are preferred. Researchers should note that responses to these kinds of inquiries are seldom as comprehensive as the results of an actual research visit. For those who do intend to visit the IHRC, appointments or preliminary inquiries are not necessary but are appreciated and often advantageous to researchers.

Research Services:

Duplication. IHRC materials, unless restricted, may be either photocopied or photographically reproduced; procedures and regulations for each are delineated in the corresponding request forms for these services. Also, most microfilm reels for which the IHRC holds master negatives can be duplicated for purchase.

Computer Searching. IHRC manuscript collections are cataloged on microcomputer, facilitating subject searching of this material. Also, the University Libraries' on-line catalog, LUMINA, can be consulted at the IHRC. The curatorial staff will assist with use of these databases.

Microfilm Equipment. Five microfilm readers, including 2 reader-printers, are available for patron use. Written procedures for using this equipment are posted near the machines. In addition, curatorial staff will assist in orienting you to these procedures.

Interlibrary Loan (ILL). It is often possible for the IHRC to receive materials from other libraries via interlibrary loan. Please notify the curator if you wish to make such arrangements. (Note that this generally requires considerable time between the date of request and the actual receipt of materials.) The IHRC can also lend to participating ILL institutions many of its materials held on microfilm as well as inventories to manuscript collections.

Use of University Libraries. You are welcome to visit Wilson Library and Walter Library on the University's main campus. In addition, the IHRC can arrange borrowing privileges with these facilities for non-University affiliated researchers.

Service Costs: Prices are subject to change. Check for current costs.

Photocopying	15 cents/page (on-site visitor)
	25 cents/page + postage & handling (mail & telephone requests)
Microfilm Reader-Printer	20 cents/page (on-site visitor)
	30 cents/page + postage & handling (mail & phone requests)

Photographic Duplication $4.00 (2-1/4" x 2-3/4" negative strip); $4.50 (5" x 7" positive); $5.50 (8" x 10" positive)

Fee for Publication of Photo $7.50/image ($60.00 maximum)

Microfilm duplication $16.75/reel

Staff Research Services $10.00/hour
(beyond customary reference assistance)

Preferred Format for Citation/Credit:

Manuscript Collection example: "Anthony Capraro Papers, Immigration History Research Center, University of Minnesota"

Photograph Collection example: "Photograph Collection, Immigration History Research Center, University of Minnesota"

Should the IHRC prove to be a significant resource for a publication, please send a copy to the IHRC.

Access and Restrictions: The IHRC's collections are open to all who agree to comply with the institution's regulations for use of the material. Some of the manuscript collections and published items carry restrictions on access. Such restrictions are applied either in accord with the wishes of donors or for preservation, security, or legal purposes. In many cases, the terms of restriction allow for research use under certain conditions; researchers should consult with the curator whenever they encounter restricted material. As a general philosophy, the IHRC is committed to providing access whenever possible in order to further research pursuits. At the same time, the Center recognizes the need to limit access to certain materials, and it honors these limitations or restrictions completely.

Reference Collection: Located in the Reading Room, the Reference Collection consists of bibliographies, encyclopedias, dictionaries, guides, and other tools that facilitate access to the Center's holdings and the holdings of other repositories. Among the key titles in this collection are *Harvard Encyclopedia of American Ethnic Groups*, edited by Stephan Thernstrom (1980); *They Chose Minnesota*, edited by June Drenning Holmquist (1981); Wayne Charles Miller's *A Comprehensive Bibliography for the Study of American Minorities* (2 volumes, 1976); Lubomyr R. Wynar and Lois Buttlar's *Guide to Ethnic Museums, Libraries, and Archives in the United States* (1978); *The Immigrant Labor Press in North America, 1840's-1970's*, edited by Dirk Hoerder (3 volumes, 1987); Lubomyr R. Wynar and Anna T. Wynar's *Encyclopedic Directory of Ethnic Newspapers and Periodicals in the United States* (1976); *Ethnic Genealogy: A Research Guide*, edited by Jessie Carney Smith (1983); John D. Buenker and Nicholas C. Burckel's *Immigration and Ethnicity: A Guide to Information Sources* (1977); and August C. Bolino's *The Ellis Island Source Book* (1985). Also included are issues of frequently-consulted journals and newsletters in the field of immigration history, such as *Ethnic Forum, The Journal of American Ethnic History, The Journal of Ethnic Studies, The Immigration History Newsletter*, and the Center's own *Spectrum*.

Publications

The IHRC administers an active publication program, an important component of which is bibliographies, guides, and other descriptions of particular resources. The following are several of these works. (A complete publication catalog and order form are available upon request.) The IHRC is the publisher unless otherwise noted. The figures in parentheses are postage and handling charges. Contact the IHRC for information on large orders.

BIBLIOGRAPHY SERIES

No. 1 *Serbs in the United States and Canada: A Comprehensive Bibliography*, compiled by Robert Gakovich and Milan Radovich, edited by Joseph D. Dwyer; xii, 129 pages, photographs, 1976, **$6.00 ($2.00)**

No. 2 *Hungarians in the United States and Canada: A Bibliography*, compiled and edited by Joseph Szeplaki; viii, 113 pages, photographs, 1977, ISBN: 0-932833-00-4, **$6.00 ($2.00)**

No. 3 *Slovenes in the United States and Canada: A Bibliography*, compiled and edited by Joseph D. Dwyer; xiv, 196 pages, photographs, 1981, ISBN: 0-932833-02-0, **$7.00 ($2.00)**

OTHER BIBLIOGRAPHIES

Romanii Din America: Bibliografie Comentata, by Radu Toma, editate de Asociatia "Romania"; v, 234 pages, photographs, in Romanian, 1978, **No Charge ($2.00)**

Ukrainians in North America, A Select Bibliography, compiled by Halyna Myroniuk and Christine Worobec, co-published with the Multicultural History Society of Ontario; 236 pages + indexes, 1981, **$10.00 ($2.00)**

RECORD SURVEY GUIDES

Guide to the Minnesota Finnish American Family History Collection, compiled by Mary Koske; Suzanna Moody, editor; 42 pp., 1985, **$4.00 ($2.00)**

Guide to Polish American Newspapers and Periodicals in Microform, compiled by Frank Renkiewicz and Anne Bjorkquist Ng; 60 pp., 1988, **$5.00 ($2.00)**

Guide to the Records of the Order Sons of Italy in America, compiled by John Andreozzi, Project Coordinator; vii, 196 pp., photographs, 1989, ISBN: 0-932833-07-1, **$12.50 ($2.00)**

Guide to the Theodore Saloutos Collection, compiled by Louise Martin, 61 pp., 1989, ISBN: 0-932833-08X, **$8.00 ($2.00)**

The International Institute Movement: A Guide to Records of Immigrant Service Agencies in the United States, compiled by Nicholas V. Montalto; xvii, 74 pp., photographs, 1978, ISBN: 0-932833-01-2, **no cost ($2.00)**

Records of Ethnic Fraternal Benefit Associations in the United States: Essays and Inventories, vii, 169 pp., 1981, ISBN: 0-932833-03-9, **$7.50 ($2.00)**

Svoboda, A Select Index; Volume One: 1893-1899, compiled by Walter Anastas and Maria Woroby; xix, 406 pp., 1990, ISBN: 0-932833-10-1, **$25.00 ($2.00)**

PERIODICALS

Spectrum - periodic magazine, reports on publications based on research at the IHRC, new acquisitions, IHRC activities. Each issue's main article, on a specific theme, lists IHRC collections for research on the topic. Contact the IHRC for subscription information. Back issues are $2 each, listed below by theme of main article:

V1/#1 (Jan. '75) IHRC research will look at history of "white ethnics from the inside out"

V1/#2 (May '75) "From Farm to Factory: Immigrant Adjustment to American Industry" (Fin, It., Yugo)

V1/#3 (Sept. '75) "Immigrants and Religion: The Persistence of Ethnic Diversity" (Pol, Slovak, Ukr, S. Slavs, Fin, It, Hung)

V2/#1 (July '76) "'All the World's A Stage': Immigrants and the Performing Arts" (It, Pol, Fin, S. Slav, Hung)

V2/#2 (Sept. '76) "America and Europe's Refugees, 1933-1958" (agencies, Ukr, Pol, other E. Eur, Hung)

V2/#3 (Dec. '76) "'For Mutual Moral and Material Assistance': The Ethnic Fraternal in America" (Slovene, Slovak, Pol, Rom, Ukr, others)

V3/#1 (May '77) "International Institutes: Reaching Out to Immigrant Communities in America" (St. Louis, Boston, Minnesota)

V3/#2 (Mar. '80) "The Ethnic Press: Many Voices" (Czech, Slovak, Fin, It, Pol, S. Slav, Ukr)

V3/#3 (July '80)"Recapturing History: Immigrant Women and Their Daughters"

V4/#1 (Fall '82) "Louis Adamic (1898-1951): His Life, Work, and Legacy"

V4/#2 (Summer '83) "In Their Own Words: Immigrant Autobiographies (Czech, Slovak, Fin, It, Pol, S. Slav, others)

V4/#3 (Winter/Spring '84) "Philip K. Hitti"

V5/#1 (Winter '88) "Speak American!": The Linguistic Dilemma of Ethnic Americans (Fin, It, Ukr, others)

V5/#2 (Fall '88) "Balancing Two Cultures: The Lives of Immigrant Children"

IHRC News - quarterly newsletter reports on IHRC visitors, grants and projects, new acquisitions, publications. Incorporates the newsletter of the Friends of the IHRC, a nonprofit support organization with a nationwide membership. (For information about the organization, contact the IHRC.) *IHRC News* is sent free of charge upon request.

Index

The following index provides name, subject, and geographic access to the material in this guide, excluding only front matter, author-title information in the monograph essays, and individual listings in the newspaper and serial sections of each chapter. Titles of periodicals that appear in the descriptions of manuscript collections are indexed. Page numbers in italics indicate photographs.

A

Aamunkoitto Temperance Society (Brooklyn, NY), 69
Abbate, Paolo L. (1884-1973), 135
Abbate, P. S., 145
Abbruzzo-Molise, 158
Ablonczy, Pál, 117
ACEN. *See* Assembly of Captive European Nations (ACEN)
ACEP. *See* American Council for Emigres in the Professions (ACEP)
ACIM. *See* American Committee on Italian Migration (ACIM)
ACNS. *See* American Council for Nationalities Services (ACNS)
Actors and actresses: Finnish American, 83; Hungarian American, 121; Italian American, 145, 153, 158-59; Polish American, 247; unions, 153
Adamic, Louis, 6, 43, 45, 108, 331-32
Adler, Selig, 1
Adult education. *See* Education
Advance (newspaper), 151
Advance (serial), 248
Advisory Committee on Voluntary Foreign Aid, 246
AFL-CIO, 159
Afro-Americans, 6
Agnost, Frank P., 108
Agrarianism, 107
Agricultural extension work, Minnesota, 85
AHEPA. *See* American Hellenic Educational Progressive Association (AHEPA)
Ahlbeck, Karl (1881-1954), 69
Ahlbeck, Lila A. *See* Lindgren, Lila A. (Ahlbeck)
Ahlgren, Henry, 75
Ahmed, Frank, 237
Aho, John E., 69, 80
Ajami Family, 237
Ajami, Jocelyn, 237
Ajami, Selma (Bojolad), 237
Alabama: fraternal benefit societies, Italian American, 161
Al Akl, F. M. (1903-1971), 237
Alaska: missions and missionaries, Russian Orthodox, 294; Russian Americans, 294
Al-Balady family. *See* Najjar Family
Albania: emigration and immigration, 26; nationalism, 25; politics and government, 25
Albanian American Literary Society (Quincy, MA), 25
Albanian Americans, 14, 25-26; churches, 25; clubs and societies, 25; drama, 25-26; history, 25-26; Illinois, 4, 25; literature, 25-26; newspapers, 26; political activity, 25-26; priests, 25-26; religion and religious belief, 25-26; serials, 26
Albanian Orthodox Church in America, 25; clergy, 25-26
Albanian Orthodox Diocese of America, 25

Alba Nuova, 140
Alecks, Joseph, 245
Alexander Film Company (Colorado Springs, CO), 207
Alexeev, Wassilij, 293
Alfange, Dean, 108
Al-Hoda, 239
Aliens or Americans? (Howard B. Grose), *x*
Aliens, political activity, 12
All Canadian Conference of Priests of the Ukrainian Greek Orthodox Church in Canada, 354
Allegra, Pietro, 12, 140
Alliance Calendar, 254
Alliance College (Cambridge Springs, PA), 254, 258-59
Alliance "Lily" of Wisconsin (Zveza "Lilija" Wisconsin) (Milwaukee, WI), 325
Alliance of Poles in America (Cleveland, OH), 245
Alliance of Poles in the State of Ohio. *See* Alliance of Poles in America (Cleveland, OH)
Alliance of Transylvanian Saxons, 1
Alliance Publishing Company (Chicago, IL), 245-46
Alpha Phi Delta, 139
Amalgamated Clothing Workers of America, 137, 140, 151, 155, 173, 178-79
Amateur theater, 118
Ambassadors, Italian, 12
Ambrosino, Simone J., 135
America-Italy Society (New York, NY), 135-36
America Letters: Etelä-Pohjanmaa, Finland, 69
America Letters: Satakunta, Finland, 69
America Letters: Varsinais Suomi, Finland, 70
American Academy of Dramatic Arts, 151
American Action, 118
American Aid to Calabria, 171
American Arabic Association (Boston, MA), 237
American Association for the Education of Foreign-Born Soldiers in the United States, 260
American Christian College, 353
American Citizen, 173
American Civil Liberties Union, 6, 12-13, 112, 149, 176
American Committee for Armenian and Syrian Relief, 105
American Committee for Italian War Relief (St. Paul, MN), 136
American Committee for Refugee Scholars, Writers, and Artists. *See* American Council for Emigres in the Professions (ACEP)
American Committee for Resettlement of Polish Displaced Persons (Chicago, IL), 246, 253, 259
American Committee for the Protection of the Foreign Born, 14
American Committee for Yugoslav Relief, 43

American Committee on Italian Migration (ACIM), 155, 159, 181; Chicago Chapter (IL), 136

American Council for Emigres in the Professions (ACEP), 1-2

American Council for Nationalities Service (ACNS), 2, 7, 9, 11, 14

American Council of Polish Cultural Clubs (Falls Church, VA), 246

American Council of Voluntary Agencies, 4

American Council of Voluntary Agencies for Foreign Services, Inc., 246

American-Croatian Singers Federation (Američko-Hrvatski Pjerački Savez), 44

American Enterprise Institute (Washington, DC), 312

American Federation of International Institutes (AFII), 2, 7, 12-13. *See also* American Council for Nationalities Service (ACNS)

American Federation of Ramallah Palestine, 238

American Finnish Civic Club (Virginia, MN), 81

American Fund for Czechoslovak Refugees (New York, NY), 53-54

American Hellenic Educational Progressive Association (AHEPA), 106-9

American Hungarian Relief, Inc. Chapter 20 (Chicago, IL), 119-20

American Immigration and Citizenship Conference, 14

American Italian Historical Association (AIHA), 157, 182; Conference, 1972 (Boston, MA), 136; Stella del Nord Chapter (Upper Midwest), 136, 178

Americanization: Italian Americans, 173; Jews, 202

American Latvian Association (Washington, D.C.), 205, 207-209

American Museum of Immigration, 258, 356

American Polish Civil War Centennial Commission (New York, NY), 246

American Polish Club (Lake Worth, FL), 262

American Red Cross, 257

American Relief for Italy, Inc., 142

American Relief for Poland. District 33 (Chicago, IL), 246

American-Russian Chamber of Commerce, 5

American Service Institute of Allegheny County (PA), 8

American Slavic Congress (Detroit, MI and Pittsburgh, PA), 3

American Sokol Organization. Western District, 53

American-Soviet Friendship Society, 74

American Srbobran, 304, 305

American Star Congress (1949), 245

Americans to Free Captive Nations, Inc., 344; Ukrainian Division, 344

American Ukrainian Republican Association, 362

American Ukrainian Resort Center, Inc., 353

American University of Beirut. Alumni Association, 239

America (Philadelphia, PA), 353

Amerika-Hay Hanragitak Taregirk (American Armenian Encyclopedic Almanac) (Boston, MA), *30*

Amerikan Albumi (Brooklyn, NY), *93*

Amerikanski Slovenec (American Slovenian), 326, 331

Amerikan Uutiset (American News) (New York Mills, MN), 70

Ameriški Družinski Koledar, 327

Ameryka, 349

Ameryka-Echo, 247, 252

AMICO, 159

AMITA, 181

Anagnos, Michael, 109

Anarchism and anarchists, 6, 12; Italian American, 140

Ander, O. Fritiof, 108

Anderson, M. Margaret, 6

Anderson, Peter, 343

Anders, W., 259

Andic, Vojtech E., 311

Andreozzi, John, 136

Andrievs'kyi, Dmytro, 355

Andrushchak, Petro. *See* Anderson, Peter

Angeletti, Edward J., *136*

Annunzio, Frank, 136

Ansara, James M., 238

Antarctica, 207

Anthracite Relief Committee for Poland, 257

Anticommmunism: Italian Americans, 153; Ukrainian Americans, 353. *See also* Communism

Anti-Defamation League of B'nai Brith, 350

Antifascism and antifascists: Italian American, 137, 140-144, 153, 158-59, 171, 173-74, 177, 181-82. *See also* Fascism

Anti-fascist Alliance of North America, 143

Antonini, Luigi, 167

Antonovych, Myroslav, 362

Anytown, U.S.A., 5

Anzalone, Charles (1888-1959), 136-37

Apostolic Lutheran Church, 90

Arab Americans. *See* Near Eastern Americans *and individual ethnic groups*

Arab Cultural Center (San Francisco, CA), 238

Araldo (Cleveland, OH), 176

Aranicki, Pjoder, 45

Archacki, Henry (1907-), 246-47

Archimovych, Alexander (1892-1984), 343

Archipenko, Alexander, 347

Archives: Austrian, 2-3; Lithuanian, 223

Argoe, Kostis Tamias (191?-1982), 105, 107

Argus, M. K. *See* Eisenstadt-Jeleznov, Mikhail (1900-1970)

Arizona: fraternal benefit societies, Italian American, 157, 161, 164; Ukrainian Americans, 345

Arkas, Mykola M. (1853-1909), 346

Armenia: emigration and immigration, 27-28; history, 27

Armenian Americans, 27-*30*; authors, 27; autobiography, 28; California, 27; clubs and societies, 28; churches, 28; drama, 27; fraternal benefit societies, 28; history, 27-28; Massachusetts, 27-28; newspapers, 28-29; poetry, 27; serials, 29-*30*

Armenian Apostolic Church, 28

Armenian General Benevolent Union, 28

Armenian National Union of America, 28

Armenian Students' Association of America, 28

Armour & Co. Dried Beef Packing Department, 250

Chopek, Elias, 346
Choral societies: Croatian American, 44; Czech
American, 56; German American, 3; Illinois, 44;
Latvian American, 206, 209; Minnesota, 42, 357;
Pennsylvania, 44; Polish American, 250-52;
Slovenian American, 325; Ukrainian, 344;
Ukrainian American, 353-54, 357
Chór Warszawski, 251
Christ Child Community Center (St. Paul, MN), 179
Christian Democratic Union of Central Europe, 55
Christian Scientology and Movement of New
Thought (Church of Religious Science), 177-78
Christmas cards, Ukrainian, 348-49, 357
Christopher Columbus Society (Calumet, MI), 141
Christy, George, 108
Churches: Albanian American, 25; Armenian
American, 28; Bulgarian American, 31-32;
California, 109; Catholic, 136, 141-42, 261;
Connecticut, 261; Croatian American, 145; Greek
American, 105, 107, 109; Hungarian American,
121-23; Hungary, 118; Illinois, 25, 107, 353;
Indiana, 31-32; Latvian American, 209;
Massachusetts, 28; Minnesota, 141-42, 351, 404;
Nebraska, 330; New Jersey, 350; New York,
105, 305; Ohio, 327; Pennsylvania, 45, 107, 353;
Serbian American, 305; Slovenian American,
327, 330; Ukrainian American, 345, 349-51, 353
Church records and registers: Croatian American,
45; Finnish American, 70, 72, 74-75, 85, 90;
Illinois, 85, 148, 313; Italian American, 161, 169-
70; Massachusetts, 74; Michigan, 70, 72;
Minnesota, 72, 75, 81-82, 85, 87, 161, 170, 255,
259, 313; Missouri, 173; Ohio, 37, 119, 173,
313, 327-28; Pennsylvania, 45; Polish American,
255, 259; Slovak American, 313; Slovenia, 330;
Slovenian American, 327-28; Wisconsin, 72, 169
Chyz, Yaroslav (1894-1958), 346-47
Ciccotelli, Mario, 141
Cigler, Janez, 331
Circolo Culturale Italiano di Baltimora (Baltimore,
MD), 141
Circolo Libertario Pensiero ed Azione (NY), 143
Ciresi, Rose (1908-1988), 141-42
Ciszewski, Mrs. Barbara, 248
Citizens Committee and Recruiting Centre #20
(Minneapolis, MN), 248, 254
Citizens Committee on Displaced Persons (NY), 4
Citizenship, 146, 295-96; manuals, 14; Russian
Americans, 294-96; study and teaching, 9
City councilmen: Massachusetts, Italian American,
174
Civil engineers. *See* Engineers
Civilian Defense Volunteer Office, 149
Clarity, 84
Clark, Atty Gen. Tom, 43
Clemente, Egidio (b. 1899), 142, 154
Clergy: Albanian American, 25; Czech American, 54;
Florida, 88; Italian American, 154, 177-78;
Lithuanian American, 224. *See also under
names of denominations*
Clergy Club, 105
Cleveland Soccer League (OH), 3
Clothing. *See* Costume

Club Introdacquese (Youngstown, OH), 176
Clubs and societies. *See* Charitable organizations;
Choral societies; Drama societies; Fraternal
benefit societies; Political societies; Religious
societies; Sports societies; Women's
organizations; Youth organizations; *and under
names of ethnic groups*
Coalition of Italian American Associations, 160
Cole, Marie Chase, 4-5
Cole, Stewart G. (1892-), 4-5, 6
College of St. Scholastica (Duluth, MN), 327
College of St. Thomas (St. Paul, MN), 122
Colleges and universities: Finnish American, 77-78,
87-89; Minnesota, 88-89; Polish American, 254,
258-59; Ukrainian American, 354
College teachers: Croatian American, 45; Czech
American, 54-55; Finnish American, 76; Greek
American, 107-8; Indiana, 260; Italian American,
149, 158, 178; Minnesota, 108, 122, 356; Near
Eastern American, 238-39; New York, 248;
Polish American, 248, 260; Ukrainian American,
344, 347-48, 351, 354-55; Ukrainian Canadian,
357
Collins, John, 245
Colorado, 160; Latvian Americans, 207; legislators,
Italian American, 158; unions, mine workers, 158
Colorado Springs Latvian Society (CO), 207
Columbia Broadcasting System, 118
Columbian Federation, 158
Columbus Citizens Club (New York, NY), 159-60
Columbus Day, 139; celebrations, 138, 141-42, 145-
46, 162, 167, 172
Columbus Memorial Association of St. Paul, Inc.,
141-42, 170
Commemorative Committee for the Famine in
Ukraine, 363
Commemorative postage stamps, 355
Commission for Social Justice, Virginia Chapter, 138
Committee for Democratic Action, 327
Committee for Erection of the All-Ukrainian Church
Monument (Paris, France), 357
Committee for Hungarian Refugee Relief (MI), 355
Committee for the Defense of Soviet Political
Prisoners, 346
Committee for the League of Nations of Eastern
Europe, 260
Committee on the Guardianship of the Monument of
Simon Petliura, 356
Common Council for American Unity (CCAU), 2, 6,
346. *See also* American Council for Nationalities
Service
Commons, John R., 14
Communism and communists, 6, 12, 223;
cooperatives and, 77; Croatian American, 326;
Finnish American, 70, 73-75, 84, 91; Hungarian
American, 117, 121; Italian American, 140, 149,
157-58; Lithuanian American, 223; Polish
Ameican, 248; Serbian American, 326;
Wisconsin, 86. *See also* Anticommunism
Communist Party of America, 223
Community leadership, Greek Americans, California,
106
Community War Chests, 257

416   *Index*

Florida: clergy, 88; Finnish Americans, 77, 80, 88;
   Greek Americans, 110; fraternal benefit societies,
   Italian Americans, 163-64, 178; lawyers, 251;
   Polish Americans, 251, 262
Flour mills, Minnesota, 87
Flynn, Elizabeth Gurley (1890-1964), 6, 149, 154
Fodchuk, Dmytro, 346
Folk art. *See* Art
Folk Festival Council, 5
Folklore: Italian, 151; Lebanese American, 239;
   Polish American, 265; Romanian American, 288;
   Slovak American, 313, 315
Folk medicine, Carpatho-Rusin, 37
Folk music. *See* Music.
Folk songs. *See* Songs.
Folktales: Italian, 177; Italian American, 148; Latvian,
   209
Follia di New York, 174
Food, 5; Armenian, 28; Carpatho-Rusin, 37
Ford, President Gerald, 107, 353
Foreign Language Information Service (FLIS), 2, 5,
   11-12, 14. *See also* American Council for
   Nationalities Service
Foreign Students Night School (Lansing, MI), 13
Foresters, Hungarian, 121
Forestry schools and education. *See* Education
Fornari, Harry D., 149
Fort Bragg Toveri Club (CA), 73
Forte, Felix (1895-1975), 149
Fortunato, Rev. John B. (1880-1967), 149
Fortune Gallo Concern Company, 149
Fortune Gallo Enterprises, 149
Fortune Gallo Musical Company, 149
Forzley, Bashara Kalil, *244*
4-H Club, 55
Fourth Convention of Polonia Society, 261
Fox, Rev. Paul J. (1874-1963), 248
France: politics and government, 313; Ukrainians in,
   356
Franko, Ivan, 344, 355
Fra Noi, 157
Franzalia, Joseph, 164
Fraser, Donald M., 107
Fratellanza Italo-Americana. Abraham Lincoln (NY),
   141
Fraternal benefit societies: Armenian American, 28;
   California, 82, 85-86; Croatian American, 5, 43-
   47; Czech American, 54; Delaware, 135; Finnish
   American, 82, 85-86, 89, 92; German American,
   4; Greek American, 109; Hungarian American,
   117, 120; Illinois, 119, 254; Iowa, 43-44; Italian
   American. *See* Order Sons of Italy in America;
   Latvian American, 209; Minnesota, 82, 117, 254-
   55; Ohio, 1, 329; Pennsylvania, 43, 253, 328;
   Polish American, 245, 253-55, 257-58, 264;
   Romanian American, 287-88; Russian American,
   295; Slovak American, 311-12; Slovenian
   American, 326, 328-29; Texas, 255;
   Transylvanian Saxon, 1; Ukrainian American,
   365-66
Fraternities, Italian American, 139
Free Poland Society of Pittsburgh. Organizational
   Committee, 259

Friar, Kimon, 108
Friedel, Mieczyslaw, 248
Friends of Polish Culture (Boston, MA), 249
Fucilla, Joseph, 149
Funerals, Carpatho-Rusin, 37
Fuoco, 173
Furdek, 311
Fyffe, Letitia, 9

G

Gaishek, Matthew, 329
Galan, Walter, 348
Galicia (Poland and Ukraine), 253, 355, 358;
   emigration and immigration, 2-3; Uniate Church,
   3
Gallo, Fortune (1878-1970), 149
Garibaldi, Giuseppe, 163
Gąsiorowski, Wacław, 261
Gawrychowski, Bishop V., 262
Gay, Peter B. (1915-), 150
Gazeta Polonii, 249, 250
Gazzetta del Massachusetts, 147
Gemayel, Sheikh Pierre, 239
Genealogy: Croatian American, 44; Finnish
   American, 70, 81, 84; Lebanese American, 239.
   See also Family chronicles
General Casimir Pulaski Skyway (MA), 245
General collection, IHRC, 1-*24*
General Krzyżanowski Memorial Committee, 247
Geomagnetism, 207
Geophysicists, Latvian American, 207-8
Georgia: cooperative societies, Finnish American,
   80, 88; Greek Americans, 110
Gerega, Barbara (Rudachek), 346
German Americans: clubs and societies, 3-4, 13;
   Illinois, 4; Michigan, 13; Roman Catholic, 3-4
German Dramatic Club (Lansing, MI), 13
Germanotta, Rev. A., 154
Germany: displaced persons, camps, 343-44; foreign
   relations, 199, 261; refugees, 10; Ukrainians in,
   345, 348, 350
Geroulis, James A., 108
Giaccone, Francis X. (b. 1886), 150
Giles, H. H., 4
Gimino, Maria, 150
Giovannitti, Arturo, 140, 145, 150, 154, 173, 178-79,
   182
Giuffrida, Bruno S., 139, 150
Giuliani, Rev. August, 154
Glasilo-SNPJ, 329. See also *Prosveta*
Glas Naroda (The People's Voice) (New York, NY),
   325-26
Glas Svobode, 329
Glazer, Nathan, 14
Glen, Gen. Edwin F., 260
Glimpse (New Haven, CT), 144
Godina, Filip, 330
Gogol, Nikolai Vasilevich, 44, 355
Golash, Stephan (1919-), 346-47
Golaski, Walter M. (1913-), 249
Goldberg, Arthur, 171
Golobitsch, Anton, 326
Golobitsch, Mary, 326

Jerich, John (1894-1973), 326
Jewish Americans, 6, 14, 201-*4*; authors, 202; clubs and societies, 201; emigration and immigration, 202; history, 201-2; Illinois, 4; New York, *xxiv*, 202; Italian, 149, 179; journalists, 202; literature, 202; newspapers, 202-3; Ohio, 201; radicalism and, 202; Russian, *xxiv*; serials, *203-4*; theater, 202. *See also* Synagogues
Jobbágy, Domokos, 120
John Marshall College of Law (NY), 148
John R. Palandech Agency, 303
Johnson, President Lyndon B., 136
Joint Civic Committee of Italian Americans, 175
Jokinen, Walfrid J. (1915-1970), 76
Jokūbaitis, Antanas Juozas (1887-), 223
Jontez, Ivan, 331
Journalism and journalists, 82, ; Finnish American, 74; Greek American, 105-6; Hungarian American, 121; Hungarian Canadian, 121; Illinois, 105, 142, 247, 326; Italian American, 142, 147, 157, 160, 174-75, 178-79, 181; Jewish American, 202; Latvian American, 205; Lithuanian American, 223; Minnesota, 355; Polish American, 246-50, 260-61, 265; Russian American, 293; Slovak American, 312-13, 315; Slovenian American, 326-27; Ukrainian American, 353, 355-56, 362-63; Ukrainian Canadian, 352
Journals. *See* Serials
Jozef Pilsudski Institute of America, 251
Jubilee Book of the Ukrainian National Association in Commemoration of the Fortieth Anniversary of Its Existence, 360
Judges: Illinois, 171; Italian American, 149-50, 158, 171; Massachusetts, 150; New York, 158; Ukrainian American, 350
Jugoslav Socialist Federation (Jugoslovanska Socialistična Zveza) (Chicago, IL), 326-29, 331
Jugoslav Workmen's Publishing Company, 327
Juras, Rev. Msgr. Francis (1891-), 224
Justice for Cyprus Committee, 105
Justinian Society, 175

K

Kairanen, Paavo A., 70
Kajastus Finnish Laborers' Association (Milford, NH), 76-77
Kajencki, Lt. Col. Francis C., 255
Kajencki, Virginia, 255
Kalan, John, 329
Kalendár Jednota (yearbook), 311
Kalendarz Emigracyiny, *268*
Kalendarz Związkowy, 245
Kanadai Magyarsag, 121
Kandyba, Oleh, 355
Kaniuka, Oleksander, 349
Kansas: Czech Americans, 56; Slovenian Americans, 325; Ukrainian Americans, 351
Kansas State College, 351
Kantola, Matt, 70, 77
Kanuik, Katherine [Mrs. Michael], 349
Kanuik, Michael, 349
Kapschutschenko, Peter (1915-), 349
Karni, Ina (Laukala), 77

Karni, Michael G., 88
Karth, Joseph E., 107
Kassal, Msgr. Edward (1876-1975), 54
Katka, Terttu, 77
Kattainen, Adam, 77
Kauls Family, 206
Kauls, Gloria, 206
Kauls, Sara, 206
Kauls, Teodors, 206
Kazan, Elia, 110
Keller, Helen, 173
Kelley, Mary, 155
Kendall, Erick, 77
Kennedy, Edward M., 136, 250
Kennedy, Pres. John F., 147, 250
Kentucky, Polish Americans, 264
Kenyon, Mildred Adams, 10
Kepes Magyar Magazin, 117
Kerhin, Ana (Pepich) [Mrs. Zlatko Ivan], 44
Kerhin, Zlatko Ivan (1881-1968), 44
Kerhin, Zora, 44
Kerze, Rev. Francis, 328
Ketonen, John E., 77
Kherdian, David, 27
Khvikhpak River Mission (Yukon), 294
Kiełkowski, Victor (1896-), 250
Kierońska, Henia, 250
Kiev Municipal Museum (Ukraine), 354
Kikta, Stepan (1918-), 349
Kist, Andrii (1891-1986), 348-49
Kist, Ivan, 348
Kizyma, Stefan (b. 1888), 350
Klemi, Al. L. (1874-1924), 77
Klepachivsky, Konstantyn Yosypovych (1887-1979), 350
Klepachivsky, Maria (Arkas) [Mrs. Konstantyn Yosypovych], 350
Klimaszewski, Dr. Mieczyslaw, 259
Klobučar, Frank, 329
Klodnycky, Rev. Vladimir (1891-1973), 350
Klodnycky, Joseph, 350
Klub Leczan #1 (IL), 258
Klune, Frank, 327
Kniazeff, A. N., 293-94
Knights and Ladies of Kaleva, 78, 92; Nuoriso Chapter (Ely, MN), 77
Knipp, Mrs. George, 141
Koivisto, Arvid, 77
Koivisto, Edith (Laine) [Mrs. Arvid] (1888-1981), 77-78
Koivulehto, Lauri, 78
Kolko Polek Charitable Society, 247
Komar Family (MN), 362
Komichak, Michael (1919-), 350
Komitet Hromadskoï dïï za Patriiarkhat UKTserkvy, 346
Konda, Martin, 329
Konitza, Faik, 25
Kopan, Andrew T., 108
Kopernik Quincentennial Observance, 258
Korhonen, John P. (1874-1958), 78
Korolyi, Michael, 313
Kosciolowski, Sophie (ca. 1903-), 250

Murrow, Edward R., 346
Museums: Italian American, 156, 163; Minnesota,
327; Slovenian American, 327; Ukraine, 354;
Ukrainian American, 348, 354, 356, 362
Music: Estonian American, 66; Finnish American, 70,
86; folk, 259; Italian American, 153; Latvian
American, 209; Near Eastern American, 241;
Polish American, 249, 251, 259; sheet, 46, 153;
Slovak American, 313-14; Slovenian American,
331; Ukrainian American, 358-59, 362-63
Musicians, 120; Croatian American, 43; Finnish
American, 77; Illinois, 259; Polish American,
249-50, 262; Slovenian American, 325, 332. *See
also* Choral societies
Music teachers: Polish American, 249-50, 262;
Ukrainian American, 357
Muslims, 240
Mutual aid societies. *See* Mutual benefit societies
Mutual benefit societies: California, 120; Finnish
American, 72, 88; German American, 3-4; Greek
American, 109; Hungarian American, 120; Italian
American, 154, 183; Latvian American, 206;
Michigan, 154; New York, 88; Slovenian
American, 325, 329-30; Wisconsin, 325
Muzychni Visti, 351, 362
Myshuha, Luke, 347, 350

N

Naff, Alixa, 239
Naisten Viiri, 80
Najjar Family, 239
Narodna Volya, 346
Národný Kalendár, 312
Narod Polski, 257
Nash Klych, 355
Nashwauk Finnish Socialist Chapter and Related
Organizations (Nashwauk, MN), 82
Nashwauk Finnish Women's Cooperative Guild
(Nashwauk, MN), 82
Nashwauk Workers' Party Chapter (Nashwauk, MN),
82
National Armour Chain Bargaining Committee, 250
National Association for Armenian Studies and
Research, 28
National Association of Polish Americans, Inc., 261
National Association of Social Workers (Golden Gate
Chapter, CA), 13
National Association of Syrian-Lebanese American
Federations, 238
National Catholic Welfare Conference, 246; War
Relief Services, 246
National Committee for a Free Europe, 55
National Committee for Resettlement of Foreign
Physicians. *See* American Council for Emigres in
the Professions (ACEP)
National Committee on Immigration Policy, 4
National Conference of Christians and Jews, 5
National Consumers' League, 11
National Council for American-Italian Friendship, 169
National Council of Americans of Croatian Descent,
43
National Croatian Circle, 44

National Federation of Italian American
Organizations, 172
National Finnish Temperance Brotherhood in
America, 83
National Herald, 238
National Institute for Immigrant Welfare, 7
Nationalism: Albania, 25; Slavic, 2; Slovakia, 6, 119;
Yugoslavia, 43, 45-46
National Italian American Civic League, 168
National Italian American Coordinating Committee,
159
National Italian-American Day, 135
Nationalities Services Center (Cleveland, OH), 151
National Lawyers Guild, 171
National Liberal Immigration League, 14
National News (Národný Noviny), 312
National Organization of Russian Scouts, 294
National Publishing Company. *See* Idän Uutiset
(Eastern News) Publishing Company (Fitchburg,
MA)
National Renaissance, 105
National Sculptors' Council, 135
National Shrine of Our Lady of Częstochowa, 247
National Slovak Society (Pittsburgh, PA), 312;
Young Folks' Circle, 312
National War Chest Fund, 246
National War Fund. Italian-American Committee, 141
NATO, 248
Naturalization, 8, 146
Nazioni Unite, 153
Near Eastern Americans, 237-44; artists, 237;
authors, 240-41; autobiography, 241; biography,
241; California, 238; clubs and societies, 237-38,
240; college teachers, 238-39; historians, 238;
history, 240; literature, 240-41; Massachusetts,
244; Minnesota, 238; music, 241; newspapers,
239, 241-42; opera singers, 237; physicians and
surgeons, 237; political activity, 240; public
opinion, 241; publishers, 239; religion and
religious beliefs, 240; serials, 242-44
Nebesenko, Mykola, 348
Nebraska: churches, 330; Czech Americans, 53, 56;
fraternal benefit societies, 162, 165; Italian
Americans, 162, 165; Lithuanian Americans, 225;
Slovenian Americans, 330
Nechay, Simon M., 348
Nedilia, 352
Negovetti, John, 160
Nelson, Arvid (1890-1967), 82
Nemanich, Anton, 327
Nenni, Pietro, 140
New Bedford YWCA (MA), 8-9
New Hampshire: civilian relief, WWII, 81; clubs and
societies, 76-77; Finnish Americans, 76-77, 81;
legislators, 81; socialism and socialists, 76-77
New Haven Council of Social Agencies (CT), 9
New Horizon Handycraft Guild, 122
New Jersey: Byelorussians, 35; clubs and societies,
262; fraternal benefit societies, 156, 164-65;
Hungarian Americans, 119, 122; Italian
Americans, 137, 149, 156, 164-65, 170; labor
organizations, 122; newspapers, 137;
orphanages, 165; Polish Americans, 262; scouts

Transylvanian Saxons, 1; Ukrainian Americans, 349
Oleksiienko, Petro, 353
Onatsky, Evhen (b. 1894), 348, 354-55
On the Trail of the Immigrant (Edward A. Steiner), *xxiv*
Opera, 150, 346
Opera companies, 138, 149
Opera producers and directors, 149
Opera singers. *See* Singers
Optometrists, Polish American, 258
Oral history: Finnish American, 75; Italian American, 154
Orchard Lake Schools (IL), 258
Order of AHEPA. *See* American Hellenic Educational Progressive Association (AHEPA)
Order of Lafayette, 258
Order Sons of Italy in America, 146; Abruzzi No. 1376 (IL), 146; Alabama Grand Lodge, 161; Americo Vespucci Lodge No. 1722 (Kankakee, IL), 161; Anita Garibaldi Lodge No. 722 (OH), 139; Anti-Defamation Commission, 138, 147, 165; Arizona Grand Lodge, 161; Arturo Toscanini Lodge No. 2107 (East Northport, NY), 181; Ashtabula Lodge No. 1169 (OH), 157; Avanti Italiani No. 2381 (VA), 174; Benefit Insurance Commission, 173; Bessemer Lodge No. 1497 (AL), 161; Blue Island Lodge No. 1659 (Blue Island, IL), 161; Bylaws and Ritual Revision Committee, 169-70; Caesar Rodney Lodge No. 2359 (Wilmington, DE), 147; California Grand Lodge, 145, 150, 161-62, 175; Camelia-Colombo Lodge No. 1294 (Klamath Falls, OR), 161-62; Camelia Lodge No. 1802 (Klamath Falls, OR). *See* Camelia-Colombo Lodge No. 1294 (Klamath Falls, OR); Cassino Orphanage, 176; Cesare Battisti Lodge No. 622 (CT). *See* Fede e Amore No. 1505 (Southington, CT); Chicago Heights Lodge No. 1430 (IL), 141; Christopher Columbus Lodge No. 1199 (Charleston, WV), 162; Commission for Social Justice, 147, 159-60; Committee Against Bias, Bigotry, and Prejudice, 156; Connecticut Grand Lodge, 150, 160, 172, 176-77; Cooley's Anemia, 172; Cristoforo Colombo—Cesare Battisti Lodge No. 861 (MI), 162; Cristoforo Colombo Lodge No. 1033 (Hartford, CT), 162; Cristoforo Colombo Lodge (Wilmington, DE). *See* Lodge No. 1125 (DE); Cristoforo Colombo Lodge No. 1294 (Klamath Falls, OR). *See* Camelia—Colombo Lodge No. 1294 (Klamath Falls, OR); Cristoforo Colombo Lodge No. 1719 (NE), 162; Delaware Grand Lodge, 135, 142; 147, 156, 162; Deledda Lodge No. 1783 (MA), 169; Dorchester Lodge No. 1848 (Dorchester, MA), 169; Duluth Local Lodge Principe Ereditario Umberto II No. 992 (MN), 143; Elena di Savoia Regina D'Italia Lodge No. 1486 (NE), 162; Fede e Amore No. 1505 (Southington, CT), 162; Florida Grand Lodge, 163, 178; Fratellonza Lodge No. 333. *See* Hartford Lodge No. 333 (CT); Gabriele D'Annunzio Lodge No. 22 (Paterson, NJ), 156; Garibaldi-Meucci Museum, 156, 163, 165;

Garibaldi-Meucci Museum Commission, 159; George Washington Lodge No. 2038 (Vienna, VA), 170; Giuseppe Giusti Lodge No. 683 (Germantown, PA), 176; Glen Cove Lodge No. 1016 (NY), 163; Gloria Lodge No. 1117 (New London, CT), 172; G. Marconi Lodge No. 165 (PA), 144; Gorizia Lodge No. 704 (North Adams, MA), 163; Guglielmo Marconi Lodge No. 1140 (Clarksburg, WV), 163; Hartford Lodge No. 333 (CT), 163; Haverhill Mixed Lodge No. 1646 (Haverhill, MA), 168; Illinois Grand Lodge, 138, 141, 146, 160, 163-64, 175; Immigration and Naturalization Commission, 146, 147, 164-65, 175; Indiana Grand Lodge, 147, 155, 159-60; Italian—American Youth Lodge, 167; Joseph Franzalia Lodge No. 2422 (West Walton Beach, FL), 164; La Colomba Lodge No. 2439 (Glendale, AZ), 164; Lodge No. 1125 (DE), 172; Lodge No. 1974 (IL), 138; Loggia Nuova Camillo Benso Di Cavour No. 874 (Mt. Pleasant, PA), 41; Luce e Gloria Lodge No. 1430 (IL). *See* Chicago Heights Lodge No. 1430; Luigi Scialdone Lodge No. 2221 (Baltimore, MD), 138; Maggio 11, 1860 Lodge No. 10665 (East Chicago, IN), 160; Maria Cristina Di Savoia Lodge No. 1752 (Kankakee, IL), 164; Maryland Grand Lodge, 136, 138, 146, 164, 174; Massachusetts Grand Lodge, 139, 148-50, 156, 164, 173; Medford Lodge No. 1359 (MA), 173; Membership and Expansion Committee, 158; Michigan Grand Lodge, 168; Monmouth County-Mt. Carmel Lodge No. 1215 (NJ), 164; Monte Cassino Orphanage Fund, 165; National Foundation, 159, 165, 169-70, 173; National Historian, 158; National Home drive, 163; National Insurance program, 165; National Membership Committee, 169-70; National Office, 165; national officers, 139, 141-44, 146-50, 155-56, 159-60, 169-73, 175-77, 181; National Public Relations Comittee, 166; Nebraska Grand Lodge, 165; New Jersey Grand Lodge, 165; *News* Office, 166; New York Grand Lodge, 148, 150, 155-56, 158-60, 165-67, 181; North Adams Lodge No. 1417 (MA), 163; Northwest Bronx Lodge 2091 (NY), 158; Northwest Florida Lodge No. 2422. *See* Joseph Franzalia Lodge No. 2422 (West Walton Beach, FL); Northwest Grand Lodge, 153, 155, 172, 179; Ohio Grand Lodge, 139, 157, 166; Ontario Grand Lodge (Canada), 166; Organization and Education Commission, 173; *OSIA News*, 165-66; Peninsula Italian-American Lodge No. 2145 (Hampton, VA), 166; Pennsylvania District 12 (Fayette County, PA), 145; Pennsylvania Grand Lodge, 141, 145, 160, 176; Per Sempre Lodge No. 2344 (Rosedale, NY), 153; Piave Lodge, 167; Prima Italia Lodge No. 10 (New York, NY), 153; Prince of Piedmont Lodge (DE), 162; Pugliese Lodge No. 1375 (Los Angeles, CA), 145; Quebec Grand Lodge (Canada), 167; Renaissance-Alliance Lodge No. 1966 (RI), 167, 172; Rhode Island Grand Lodge, 167, 172; Riunite Lodge No. 889 (Lynn, MA), 139; Roma

T

About the Compilers-Editors

SUZANNA MOODY served as Guide Project Editor for the Immigration History Research Center during the production of this volume. She is currently working as a freelance indexer.

JOEL WURL has been Curator of the Immigration History Research Center since 1985.

THE TWO-HEADED READER

Books by Richard Condon

For Bill —

Richard Condon

The
TWO-HEADED
READER

by Richard Condon

*Being his two
most celebrated novels*

THE OLDEST CONFESSION

THE
MANCHURIAN CANDIDATE

COMPLETE AND UNABRIDGED

Random House　　New York

MANUFACTURED IN THE UNITED STATES OF AMERICA BY

THE HADDON CRAFTSMEN, SCRANTON, PA.

Design by Tere LoPrete

For

JEMMA

JUPP

THE
OLDEST
CONFESSION

Contents

I

Levantado

The bull is fresh and believes himself prepared for anything. He knows his strength, and has great confidence in his ability to conquer anything in the ring. He lunges at the cape with unbelievable speed.

THE SMALL HOTEL ON CALLE
de Marengo stood back-to-back with a German restaurant whose
cooks and kitchens had been flown from Berlin to Madrid by
the late Luftwaffe. Prior to that the hotel had been headquarters
for the Soviet General Staff in the river of blood of only twenty
years before. To those of a romantic turn, like James Bourne,
these conditions should have made the hotel seem endemically
sinister, but the warm press of spring helped to shoo away the
sachet of old death. It was still there, however, but like a touch
of insanity in a well-to-do family, it was never mentioned.

Off the main hall, in the American Bar, sat Dr. Victoriano
Muñoz, Marqués de Villalba; Representative and Mrs. Homer
Quarles Pickett (R., Ill.); a bullfighter named Cayetano Jiminez;
James Bourne, the American who leased and operated the hotel;
and the Duchess de Dos Cortes, whose full name and other titles
were Doña Blanca Conchita Hombria y Arias de Ochoa y Acebal,
Marquesa de Vidal, Condesa de Ocho Pinas, Vizcondesa Ferri.

Dr. Muñoz carried his cat, Montes, with him as he always did.
Muñoz was a tree to the cat. It climbed him continuously when

the climbing mood came upon it; it rested upon him, anywhere upon him, when resting suited it. The marqués had named this cat after the pasodoble El Gato Montes. Montes, a topaz cat, was the doctor's only real confidant.

The duchess was an intense, formidably prejudiced woman of memorable, sensual beauty and suspended youth, a tribal yo-yo on a string eight hundred years long, whose pale, blond hair was dark at the root. In seven years she had spent two years in prisons as the most reckless partisan of Spain's royal pretender. In his name she had breached the peace, resisted the law, inveighed against Franco, the Falange, and Communism. The Pretender is said to have written to her with considerable urgency from Portugal commanding that she cease and desist in her alarums against the Caudillo, and she is said to have replied by return mail that when he commanded her from Spanish soil she would obey, and not until. She had not seen her husband for three years, by his choice. The duchess was twenty-nine years old.

Cayetano Jiminez, whose father, grandfather, and great-grandfather had been bullfighters and whose great-great-grandfather had been a British rifleman who had entered Spain *sin pasaporte* with Wellington at Badajoz, had golden-red hair and milky skin. He was a tall man—not beside James Bourne, but certainly when next to Dr. Muñoz he seemed quite long. The illusion of even greater length came from his slimness, which was a good thing because when he fought bulls he went in close, without tricks, and that was no business for a plump man.

Tourists might be confused by the duchess's blondness and Cayetano's golden redness, but the Picketts at least looked typically Spanish. She was angularly thin and black with olive skin and large, dark passionate eyes which were at the moment sticky from the sound of her husband's voice and from four absinthe frappés. The bones of her shoulders and back seemed exhausted from having to hold up her large breasts. She was nearly twenty-five years younger than her husband.

Homer Pickett was a billowing man with a census of chins, very red lips and a highly pitched voice. He looked like a receiver of stolen goods or a jolly undertaker—that is, someone in a category at once sedentary and abnormal. His hands touched and fondled his person endlessly, from ear lobe to kneecap, as he talked. He was a prodigious talker. He spoke Castilian

Spanish, as did Mrs. Pickett. He could also speak Galician and Catalan, and if the Basque language could have been learned by an adult, Mr. Pickett would have learned Basque. He was between fifty and fifty-five years old.

Representative and Mrs. Pickett, prizes of Dr. Muñoz' who had read in that morning's paper of their presence in Madrid, had met these four new friends exactly fifty-five minutes before. Dr. Muñoz was an art lover, the duchess an art enthusiast, and Bourne an art student, in his way. Cayetano Jiminez was there because the duchess was there.

Representative Pickett was a world authority on the graphic art of Spain. When he spoke of Morales or Murillo or Valdés Leal with the frequently emotional and always interstitial information he could bring to these subjects, it made Dr. Muñoz narrow his eyes suddenly to keep back the mist which always filled them in the presence of Spain's beauty, and made Cayetano Jiminez, a person of clearly defined interests, seem to drink in the duchess's image and breathe more heavily. As Mr. Pickett spoke, the duchess stared at him with protuberant eyes and kept wetting her lower lip with the soft underside of her tongue.

It was not all reverential talk they exchanged. In fact, a great deal of the talk concerned contemporary Spanish painters and was pure gossip, much of it delicious. To this part of the feast it was Mr. Pickett who brought the appetite.

Victoriano Muñoz, behind thick lenses and under a third-rate mustache, wearing a tightly fitting suit over his small body which seemed martyred to the broad chocolate stripes over the blue material, and flashing that tiny tic at the corner of his mouth which, like the lock of a dam, released white moisture which he was continually wiping away, resembled a schoolmaster of an older time. His family had lost most of its enormous fortune, the basis of which had been twenty per cent of the Peruvian gold yield of Francisco Pizarro, by too public an alliance with Joseph Bonaparte. They had been that kind of Spaniard. Although the duchess, for example, would not recognize a title conferred by any Bonaparte, Dr. Muñoz still held a souvenir from the French in that he could, if he chose—which he most certainly did not, as he bitterly resented his family's past mistake in loyalties—call himself Comte de la Frontière. His consuming interest was the art of Spain. Representative Pickett was one of his heroes; James Bourne was the other. His warm devotion to

Bourne, an innkeeper and a foreigner, was one of the most discussed puzzles of fashionable Madrid. Because of Dr. Muñoz, Bourne was accepted by everyone in Spanish society. In return, Bourne discussed the Spanish masters with the marqués who was dismayed, awed, excited, fulfilled and engrossed by Bourne's knowledge.

Bourne spoke to the marqués in the form of a lecture or seminar. Otherwise, under any other condition of their meeting or association, Bourne rarely spoke to him directly. He could feel his laughter turn rancid when Muñoz joined in; he was uneasy over how long and how well he could continue to conceal his distaste for the doctor. Lack of talk itself was not indicative of aloofness with Bourne. It was a great effort, or he made it seem to be, for him to speak. The duchess and Cayetano Jiminez were perhaps the only exceptions to this rule of silence. He could be nearly garrulous with them.

Bourne either learned by listening or did not bother to listen at all, remembering instead all that he had been unable to understand throughout his life, remaining silent, chewing upon the statement of this fact, staring at the memory of that dream, awaiting some sign of recognition, some association of the words with reality. He was very tall, more than six feet four inches, a compactly muscular man whose elegant clothes and nervous grace made him seem slender. He had a huge head, though, and small features like cinders stuck in suet. Bourne always sat uncommonly still—uncommon at least for nearly everyone else of that decade—a monument to the strength of his nerves, which bayed like bloodhounds at the moon of his ambitions.

Bourne thought of himself as a criminal in the way others might think of themselves as lawyers or doctors. In countries where men are introduced as, for example, Engineer di Giorgio or Accountant Scheffler, Bourne to himself would have been simply Criminal Bourne. He had never been arrested. Excepting for his wife and his French associate, Jean Marie, Bourne was not known as a criminal to anyone else; most particularly was he unknown to the police or any other criminals. His account books, kept as meticulously as though he expected any day to have to justify his income tax returns to an examiner, showed that he had earned by criminal methods the equivalent of seven hundred and twelve thousand dollars over a period of sixteen years through efficiently executed crime in Pasadena, California;

London, England; Des Moines, Iowa; Paris, France; and in the Federal District of Mexico, among other places.

Bourne had had the hotel in Madrid under operating lease for three and one-half years, and had been so patient in the development of this Spanish criminal project—patience having been one of his strongest professional points—that he had been invited to play with the Danne String Quartet, a pool of gifted amateurs of great family, in charity concerts at the Royal Palace; had twice been invited to enjoy the festival of Our Lady of Rocio on the horses of Don Eduardo Miura; was considered to be the closest friend of the great Cayetano Jiminez; and was favored by the duchess, as were perhaps two dozen Spaniards, most of them of great age. This was all part of Bourne's exquisite sense of composition.

Michelangelo had said that the successful completion of a great mosaic must rest upon infinite design in the placement of a single tile. One could relate the developmental side of Bourne's crimes to that of the work of any fine artist. He assembled his tiles under demanding standards. He was willing to consume time and capital and to spend weeks at a time away from a new wife of only nine and three-quarter months while he considered the infinite design of his tasks. He did not assign himself to steal property merely because it was marked by vulgar display as worth stealing.

Bourne breathed the same air with his victims. He did not sentimentalize. His crimes were indigenous. In moving to Spain he had not known in advance what it was he had come to steal. He always waited for a worthy object to present itself to him. This was not difficult, for by prearrangement and somehow connected with his romanticism, Bourne had always arranged to move among riches.

His counters were in full play as he sat trying to listen to Representative Pickett talk ravenously of Ferrer Bassa, a Spanish primitive painter. Bourne fastened his concentration upon the duchess with the friendliest kind of detachment. It was only nine o'clock in the evening, maybe a little later. It was two hours to dinnertime, maybe a little longer.

Congressman Pickett could not remember where he had last seen Ferrer Bassa's work exhibited. The duchess merely said, "Jaime will know. Jaime?" Bourne heard his name and at once pulled the plastic covers off his expression.

"Yes, Blanca, darling?"

"Where are the Ferrer Bassas, sweet?"

"The altarpieces?"

"Yes, darling."

"Oh. At Pedralbes. You know—the convent near Barcelona."

"Thank you, darling. Do continue, Mr. Pickett."

Pickett shifted quite smoothly into the genius of Bernardo Martorell. It took rather a few words to do, but each one was spoken with such authority that everyone listened closely, or seemed to be listening.

Mrs. Pickett looked the most attentive, but she was the most experienced at listening to her husband. She focused her eyes on the bridge of his nose and leaned forward slightly in excited interest, her mouth the tiniest bit opened. With this tribute she freed herself. Her mind wandered out of the world of art and entered another to consider the gallantry of a man whom she admired beyond all others because after his wife had spent three weeks away from him in a Florida resort he had met her at the Newark Airport on her return with a private ambulance so that he could welcome her warmly and pleasure them both behind an ejaculating siren at seventy-three miles an hour across the Pulaski Skyway and the Jersey Flats. She mulled over it as one of the greatest compliments a woman had ever been paid.

"You would be *astonished*, my dear duchess," Congressman Pickett was saying, "how much Berenson knows about your own neoclassical school. It *is* astonishing, you know. I mean to say I can, of course, *converse* in his field. That is, I am familiar with *something* of Titian. I have, as a matter of pure fact, been trapped into lecturing for several hours on the Italians in a dreary *unconvincing* sort of way, haven't I, Marianne?" Mrs. Pickett nodded like The Hanging Judge. "But I mean to say, compared to Berenson in *my* field, I am as ignorant in *his* as— well, as some popular art critic, I suppose. *Spain is my field.* I mean, all of it. I mean I *do excel* with the Spanish quite a few *light* years beyond Berenson because, naturally, it is *my* field where it is *not* his. You see what I mean, Doctor?"

"I see what you mean. Yes. But I want to assure you with all the power at my command, Mr. Pickett, I am not interested in Italian painters or in such people who choose to be interested in them. I intend no rudeness by this, please. Mr. Pickett, please clear up one point for me. The Velázquez 'The Conde Duque of

Olivares on a White Horse' which is now in the Metropolitan in
New York—"

"Yes, Doctor?"

"It was acquired for over two hundred thousand dollars in
1952."

"Yes, Doctor."

"Who sold it to them?"

"Uh. Why—uh. Now that you mention it, I—was it—uh?—"

The duchess coughed slightly. The cat Montes leaped from
Muñoz' lap to his left shoulder but no one batted an eye except
Mrs. Pickett, who looked as if she'd like to swipe at the cat's
chops with the Ojen bottle. Cayetano pressed Bourne's thigh
with his knee. Bourne understood the gesture, if not the existence of any question. "Yes, Blanca? Am I missing something?"

"Sweet, who sold the Duque of Olivares on a white horse to
the New York museum?"

"You mean the name of the agent?"

"No, no, my dear Jaime," Dr. Muñoz said. "Who owned the
painting?"

"Well, it had been bought by the seventh Earl of Elgin in
Paris in 1806. Most people thought it was a copy with variations
of the Prado portrait. I saw it in '45 at the present Earl of Elgin's
place in Fifeshire. They found out it was no copy, all right, when
it was cleaned up for an Edinburgh Festival. Good heavens, any
of us could have told them that. The *pentimenti* around the hat
and the face gave the whole thing away. I rather think that
Olivares realized that the white horse caught the eye rather than
the rider, and had the color altered. Nor can one blame him."

"Whew! Man, what a talker. You just never stop, do you,
Jaimito?" Cayetano shook him by the nape of the neck, laughing. Bourne grinned back at him, but the vault of his lower face
had been resealed. His mind left them again. He began to go
through the steps of the problem again, leading away from his
objective to explore once more each contingency which might,
but which undoubtedly would not, arise.

The thought of Spanish masterpieces floating about in foreign
lands, being bought and sold with no hope of Spanish control,
launched the duchess on a virulent attack upon the efficiency,
aims, progress, permanent collections, influence or lack of it,
and general shortcomings of the Instituto de Cultura Hispanica,
a cultural arm of the Foreign Office and a source of abiding

pride to Generalissimo Franco. She chopped away in fine detail, as Dr. Muñoz and Congressman Pickett formed the other sides of the triangular argument.

As the duchess spoke with delicate eloquence and heated partisan fervor, Cayetano stared at her. His hands clenched his napkin, annoyed nut dishes, twisted his watch band or played with his necktie. They were long-fingered hands with wire-haired backs. The nails had been bitten so low that the ends of his fingers were stumpy and bald, each having the expression of blind men. He watched her, missing no move and hearing no word. His eyes addressed her with the intensity of demand which they were accustomed to employ only on the statues of the Virgin in the chapels of the bull rings in Madrid, Caracas, Seville, Mexico City or anywhere else like that near eternity. Before he knew what or why, Cayetano felt Bourne tap him, as the others stood up. The group left the hotel to move diagonally across the street through the gentling night to the *frontón*.

Victoriano Muñoz, carrying the topaz cat Montes like a baby, walked earnestly beside Mr. Pickett, nodding in continuing understanding as the Congressman fussed at the garments of the Spanish masters with unrelieved syntax. Bourne gave support to Mrs. Pickett who told him that she believed the bartender at the hotel was in love with her and had been serving her double absinthes. She smiled hazily up at Bourne and asked him if he knew just how much of an aphrodisiac absinthe was. He replied that he had had no experience with that sort of thing.

Cayetano walked slowly beside the duchess, twenty yards behind the others. They seemed to have nothing to say which was not being said by the gift of their presence to each other. Their fingertips, as they walked side-by-side, just touched, so that they might swing away from each other at any suspicion of vulgarity. They were walking slowly and without any interest in their destination to the *frontón* because Mrs. Pickett had begun to express her ideas and opinions about bullfights. The duchess had looked to Bourne as though she might become ill, so he had turned the conversation to *pelota* and Mrs. Pickett had insisted upon seeing it played.

Inside the *frontón* the noise was so abusive that the slumbrousness of the instant past seemed unreal. The sound of the crowd was that of a pet shop on fire. The smoke of cigars and cigarettes, some of it years old, settled in billows like damp organdy.

The party climbed to seats in the eleventh row and settled down to the sound of the ball hitting the walls with the tone of a nightstick hitting a shinbone, and to watch the small players make the giant gestures of throwing the ball from the long baskets as Van Gogh might have tried to throw off despair only to have it bound back at him from some crazy, new angle. Along the bottom aisle the *corredores* acted out the phrase in the prayer at the end of the Mass, seeming to roam through the world seeking the ruin of souls, flinging ruptured tennis balls into the mottled face of the crowd.

Bourne explained to Mrs. Pickett that *corredores* were betting commissioners. A bettor in the crowd would signal his sporting choice, gambling on the changes in lead between the blue or the white team on the court. The agent would stuff a blue and white slip containing the current odds quotation into a split tennis ball, fling it to the bettor who would return it crammed with the cash amount of his bet. Bourne yelled at a *corredore* who had a scar as red as an ambassador's decoration running diagonally across his face, and held up ten fingers. The agent yelled back like a dubbed version of Dizzy Dean and let fly at Bourne's head with the ball.

Bourne showed Mrs. Pickett the betting slip, but he concealed the other slip which said QUINN NUMERO 811. This he read and dropped on the floor.

Mrs. Pickett still didn't understand the game, and within a half hour they stood outside the *frontón*. The duchess decided for everyone that they would go to the garden at the Fenix for another drink.

Bourne turned her aside for a moment and excused himself. They agreed that he would rejoin them for dinner at the German restaurant at eleven o'clock, an hour and twenty-five minutes away. He helped Mrs. Pickett into the Bentley as Mr. Pickett complained that Byron's lines in *Don Juan* were unjust to the Spanish master, Ribera; Mr. Pickett quoted, "Spagnoletto tainted his brush with all the blood of all the sainted." As the Bentley drew away with Cayetano behind the wheel and the duchess close beside him, Bourne could still hear the marqués' answer from the tonneau. It promised to be a rather long anecdote concerning Ribera and the bastard half-brother of Philip IV.

Bourne crossed the street, walking slowly. He entered the lobby of the hotel and went to the desk to ask if the Paris plane had arrived at Barajas. The conserje looked up at the clock and told him that the flight had been on the ground for thirty-five minutes and that any passengers the hotel might expect should be arriving immediately. Bourne thanked him, then slipped around behind the desk and began a thoughtful examination of the room rack. He did not run his fingers down the cards, so that neither the conserje nor Gustavo Elek, the assistant manager, who had joined them silently, could discover which card Bourne was interested in reading.

WHEN one moves from airport to airport one can observe the restlessness which has come to the world since Hiroshima. Barajas Airport, which serves Madrid, had prospered in a few short years as the driven people, led by their Father William of a Foreign Secretary, had soared out across the world on a go-now-pay-later basis.

The girl was on the Iberia flight from Le Bourget. Her real name was Eve Lewis, or had been Lewis until she had married. She never questioned why she had changed it illegally four times on four sets of vital documents which had needed to be forged. She was a tall, young woman with dark hair, either gray-blue or green eyes and a straight nose. She was tastelessly dressed as if in a fruitless effort to discount her physical beauty which had brought her so much attention in the past that it had eventually led to the business of her changing her name. She walked across the apron of the field like a moving light, refreshing and refreshed. She carried a cardboard tube two and a half inches in diameter, three feet long.

Her clothes were tasteless in that they were frumpish and untidy, not loud or vulgar. There was a spot on her hat which could have come from greasy fingers holding a greasy sandwich on a tourist flight. Her skirt was longer on the right side than on the left. The lipstick on the corner of her full, soft, moist mouth was out of register with the line of her lip. She had the slightly tilted mouth of the secret self-pitier. Her eyes could not be said to pity anyone or anything, but the general lucky expression on her face and the way she carried her full body created excellent diversion from this—which, after all, not everyone would have regarded as a shortcoming.

In the *Aduanas* as she cleared Currency Control after a speechless ritual with the kelly-green passport, the baggage from the flight was just coming off the trucks, jarring the low customs counters. The *duanistas,* in field green with scarlet bursts, ignored the physical manifest of visitors until the last bag had been placed. Then they moved down the lines of cases, touching the cargoes softly, appealing with their eyes and waiting patiently until the baggage was opened for examination.

She had one large bag and a make-up kit besides the cardboard tube. She propped the tube against the counter carelessly and opened the big bag. The *duanista* patted the silken contents gingerly, then signaled for her to shut the bag and chalked it. He marked the make-up kit without asking her to open it and asked her, in English, what was in the cardboard tube. She answered, in Spanish, that it was the copy of a painting she had bought in Paris. He smiled briefly to acknowledge his appreciation of her courtesy in taking the trouble to learn his language, and held out his hand. She gave him the tube, then, losing interest, looked away over the heads of the departing crowd and called *"Portero! Portero!"*

A porter shouldered his way to her and she told him to put her bags in a taxi, not the bus. When she turned back to the *duanista* he was returning the rolled copy to the cardboard tube. He directed her to the chief of the *Aduanas* whose office adjoined the main room. There the chief entered a description of its contents in his charge book, explaining that this was done to convenience her as a tourist so that she could leave Spain with the same copy of a great painting without red tape and bother, also explaining how absolutely necessary it was that she be sure to leave Spain with the same article, as in the case of an oversight in this regard, the red tape would be bothersome indeed. She thanked him.

The chief smiled at her, appreciating her with great delicacy and staring at her breasts. He asked for her name and for her passport to complete the official forms. She told him her name was Carmen Quinn as she handed him the green book. He reminded her that Carmen was a very Spanish name and told her how very well she spoke Spanish. Again she thanked him. She had been born Mary Ellen Quinn, she said, as the words under the brutalized picture on her passport showed, but she adored Spain and the Spanish, and Carmen had been the only name she would answer to since the age of fourteen. She told him that she had saved for many years to come to Spain, and that at last her dreams of seeing with her own eyes the fabled cities of Madrid, Córdoba, Seville and Granada were about to come true. She told him she had always wished with all her heart that she could marry a Spaniard. She sighed. For an instant it seemed as though the chief could not look at her. "You are married?" she asked softly. He nodded. When he looked up he had finished staring at her breasts and looked into her eyes. He produced a pen and asked her to sign the form. His face seemed flushed. She signed carefully and he gave her the cardboard tube with a slight bow. He walked with her to the entrance of his office, signaled importantly to the pistoled guard at the outer door to allow her passage through, then smiled at her brilliantly. She wasted no more time on him and left hurriedly to find her cab.

THE elevator rose very slowly, Bourne almost filling it. He stared at the roof of the cage as he ascended, his head seeming to rest on his back. With his mouth open and his eyes staring fixedly upward into the gloom he had the look of a drowned man.

When the cage halted at the eighth floor Bourne fought the two doors open, then turned right in the corridor, fumbling in his trousers pocket to bring out a ring of master keys. He whistled softly, which made his heavy chin more prominent and gave his mouth the appearance of a boar's snout. As he walked, his fingers found the individual master key by feel. Everything in Bourne's physical plant was trained to move and act independently with maximum economy and without distracting his eyes from their constant vigil. He stopped at the door marked 811, opened it with the passkey, entered and closed it behind him. He carried a cardboard tube in his left hand.

She was in the chair by the window, still wearing the soiled hat. She was staring, without focusing, out the window, over the top of the Post Office, across the Plaza de los Cibeles and up toward the Gran Via, with that sentimental look many people get when they are daydreaming about impossible quantities of money. She didn't hear him until he closed the door.

"My God, what's *that* tube for?" she said. Hers was on the bed. Bourne propped his in the corner near the door and answered, "You'll have to take a tube along to Seville and so forth, and I'll need one for the project."

He walked to the bed, slipped the copy out of the tube Eve had brought from Paris and stared at it, nodding. He slid it back into the tube, then placed it across the marble top of the bureau.

"Jean Marie is a marvel," he said to no one but himself—to remind himself, perhaps, that he could not do without Jean Marie. Rubbing his hands with satisfaction, he went to the window sill and sat down between Eve and her view. He took an envelope printed in two colors from his pocket and dropped it gently in her lap. She held the envelope by the corners, staring down at it with that absent smile which marked her mouth with its stain of secret self-pity.

Bourne spoke more quietly than usual. It wasn't a whisper, but it wasn't a conversational tone either. "You'll have a wonderful time. Córdoba, Seville, Granada, then back to Madrid, all by luxury bus."

Her voice became just as subdued. "You're a smart man, Jim."

"If you say so, I believe it."

"I did everything you said at the airport. The clothes this way were a tremendous help. I said those outrageous things to the chief of customs, and everything happened as though it were all part of a play you had written. I don't even bother to worry any more. I just do it the way you rehearse me."

"You are my angel," he said, leaning over to lift her out of the chair by the waist as though she were a tiny slip of a thing instead of five feet ten and a half—as though she were a large stein of beer. He lifted her high enough to place her mouth on his, then to press her down on him. They clung to each other like human flies until she broke the fluid oneness of the still statue they had become by wrenching her heavy mouth away from his and dropping her head to rest on his shoulder, breathing heavily in the silence.

"What painting this time?"

He was breathing even more heavily. "Diego Rodríguez de

Silva y Velázquez," he said, "born on June 6th, 1599, of noble, if not aristocratic, parents. Court painter to Philip IV for thirty-seven years until his death in 1660. His work was proud, exquisitely refined and sensitive, gentle, serious and brilliantly intelligent. He was the painter of painters."

"How much will it bring?"

His hands seemed to grow into her back. His eyes, closed in pain or ecstasy, opened slowly. They became compassionate. The compassion congealed and their protoplasm was transmuted into green polystyrene flecked with gold. "Over a hundred thousand dollars," he whispered. Her mouth soared toward his again, and this time she gave up control of herself.

ALTHOUGH Bourne arrived ten minutes late at the German restaurant, he was twenty minutes ahead of his hosts. He sat at the table for six before an open window across from El Retiro, ordered white wine upon young strawberries, which is not as delicious as it sounds merely because it could not be, and went over his plans for the two hundredth time. His plans were sound because they remained general plans, going into minute and rigid detail only within the areas of possible contingencies. To remain elastic and yet to be able to move reflexively without the need to think at the moment of stress was a measure of Bourne's excellence in design. Years before he had planned his method of planning.

When the others arrived Mrs. Pickett, who was quite flushed, noticed in a loud voice that Bourne had changed his clothes, but the duchess glossed over this. Mr. Pickett was saying, ". . . perhaps it looked better above the altar than in the gallery alongside the other paintings. I must say I prefer the charming, serious-faced Blessed Henry Suso and Saint Louis Bertram which were designed to hang together. Or Saint Hugh of Grenoble Visiting the Refectory—he had the monks fasting, you know, refusing to eat the meat the cooks had served by mistake." Muñoz, the saffron, inky-eyed Montes still in the crook of his arm, insisted upon its being known that his Zurbarán favorite was the adorable Santa Marina in the black tricorne hat, black bodice and blue-green gown with red and olive-green bustle, holding a boat hook.

Their prattle caused Cayetano to shake his head violently like a muddled prizefighter. He held the silk scarf of the duchess loosely in his hands. He would stare at her, then force himself to look away for an equal period of time, then look back at her. The few drinks she had taken had brought gentle action to the capillaries beneath the duchess's fair skin so that she was sublimely rosy and white. Conscious of Cayetano's hungry stare, she was happy.

Mrs. Pickett caught the table captain's attention discreetly and told him she had heard about a French alcool called *framboise,* something she had been told had been distilled from raspberries, which she would very much like to taste. Equally discreetly, as privately as though they were planning an assignation, the table captain explained that while *framboise* was delicious indeed when served cold, it was an *after* dinner liqueur —which, by the way, madame should know, was the strongest of all liqueurs, running to one hundred and fifty-three proof. Mrs. Pickett thanked him for all that fascinating information and said that since she was only interested in smelling *framboise* to savor its delicate raspberry bouquet she would greatly appreciate his bringing some at once. While the table captain sent a man to fetch a bottle, Mrs. Pickett confided to Bourne that her husband was a gourmet who could order for everyone if they so wished.

A waiter brought the bottle of *framboise* in a mound of ice. While everyone was either talking or listening to talk about art Mrs. Pickett poured six tiny glasses full, then offered a glass to each one at the table, with gracious generosity. Everyone refused; Cayetano explained that he was allergic to fruit and the others were checking a point of information with Bourne about a painter named Ramón Casas. Mrs. Pickett said, as though propitiating a god, that, oh dear, now that they had been poured she certainly didn't want to see them wasted, and proceeded to empty every little glass into her own throat before settling down with the bottle and a little glass all her own.

They dined extremely well on venison stew, dumplings, apple sauce and other un-Spanish dishes. Bourne was beginning to feel that his pent-up tension would explode through the ends of

his fingers, hitting someone and mortally wounding them. Fortunately, years before he had conditioned the reflexes of his
friends to the realization that he spoke very little, usually only
when spoken to, so that he could sit very still and concentrate
upon controlling himself. He was a nervous man to be in such
work as high-stakes crime, but there was no doubt that his
sensitivity and imagination had made him a leader in that field.
He began a mental drill; the moves he had practiced again and
again and again in his locked room at the hotel. The clock in his
head stayed apace with the movements within his imagination,
and he was relieved to find that he had cut seconds from the
operation. This cheered him enormously. He began again from
the very beginning. It was true; he had shaved seven and one-
half seconds. Soon he would make the moves in reality, with the
reassurance which contact with material objects could bring.

Midway through the meal, Mrs. Pickett began to speak somewhat ramblingly about bullfighters, whom she adored. She asked
each one in grave turn, except her husband, if they had ever
met any. The duchess seemed most puzzled by the question, but
admitted that she had, turning to Cayetano with a questioning
shrug. Cayetano answered briskly. He had met several toreros,
he said, but he had seen so many newsreels about bullfighting,
that he felt as if he knew bullfighters very well. Bourne said he
didn't know many bullfighters but that he had met Ava Gardner.
Muñoz listened to her question with a blank expression, answered with a quick, yes of course, then turned to continue his
discussion with Mr. Pickett concerning Murillo's "Sagrada
Familia de Pararito" with the Christ Child holding the bird in
his hand in a perfectly charming manner, to say nothing of that
little dog, that precious little dog, looking up at it. Mrs. Pickett
explained that although she had never permitted herself to
attend a bullfight she absolutely adored bullfighters, then offered the thought that bullfighting was all tied up with the
national death wish of Spain—which of course proved how
morbid the Spanish actually were.

The duchess had no capacity to suffer such boredom. She
said, "Come, come, Mrs. Pickett, I have been Spanish for more
than nine centuries and I will thank you sincerely not to explain
Spaniards to me. We have a ninety-kilometer journey ahead of
us. Eat your food and stop parroting what the ignorant think

they think." Cayetano said, "It is rather morbid, you know. I'm a vegetarian myself." Bourne took exception to this, saying that plants were not only living things but that they made it possible for humans to live, supplying as they did the very oxygen in the air we breathe, and that for his part science damned well should come up with a chemical diet, an all-mineral chemical diet because there was nothing morbid about killing rocks. Mrs. Pickett retreated to her private world, pink as raspberries, where she always had a much better time anyway. She slowly undressed a tall, faceless film actor in her mind, then imagined him running to her pleading for her body. With delicacy and out of consideration of the others, she closed her eyes as she gave herself to him.

They left for Dos Cortes at one twenty A.M. to feast on the duchess's paintings. The duchess and Cayetano drove in a small, white Mercedes two-seater; the others traveled in the Bentley. Bourne drove. Mrs. Pickett fell asleep in the back seat beside her husband, looking rather pretty.

They waited for the duchess and Cayetano for nearly fifteen minutes in the great hall after they arrived. The waiting was a burden for Mrs. Pickett, who had become extremely sleepy and, through fatigue, slightly irritated. She kept asking her husband if he would for Christ's sake please stop talking about those goddam paintings, for Christ's sake? She inquired as to whether either his throat or Dr. Muñoz' throat ever got sore, that he had been talking steadily and saying nothing for nine goddam hours, for Christ's sake, and that she, for one, would be greatly cheered and gratified if he would kindly shut his goddam big expert mouth and go to bed, for Christ's sake. Her voice had hidden resources of volume, and so everyone agreed that the duchess and Cayetano must have had a flat tire, that the hour was late, and that they should indeed go up to bed. They made their way up the niagaran staircase with Dr. Muñoz pointing out, en route, a Goya here, a Zurbarán there, a Morales on the curve, a Murillo above it, an El Greco to the right, a Velázquez beyond that, all of them hanging high in the darkness and quite invisible.

The moment the group reached the top of the staircase the duchess and Cayetano entered the great hall below them and called out good night. The others waved back, then went their

separate ways, with Dr. Muñoz guiding the Picketts to their
apartment and with the sunshine-yellow cat Montes guiding Dr.
Muñoz.

Bourne was enormously relieved that his two friends had
arrived. The plan returned to normal. His internal timing mechanism began to function on its own again, constructing yet other
negative possibilities. When he was sure that the Picketts and
Dr. Muñoz were bedded down for the night, he relaxed as well
as he could in a niche in the stone wall while waiting for the
duchess and Cayetano to ascend the stairs and retire. He was
not impatient. He had many things to weigh and consider. He
amused himself thinking of the story he would have for Jean
Marie if he could get his work done before Mr. Pickett made his
talkative tour of all of the duchess's paintings in the morning.

An amateur might have felt that it would be taking a needless
risk, which was nonsense. First off, Mr. Pickett would be so
captured by the verisimilitude of the setting, by the legend of
the painter, by the monetary worth of the painting, by the
proximity of its illustrious companions that he would not be
able to judge it objectively or dispassionately. Bourne remembered the surge of elation he had felt when Muñoz had gabbled
about how he had succeeded in attracting the great Homer
Pickett to view Blanca's gallery, and how Bourne must come
and listen to such erudition concerning Spanish art as existed
nowhere else in the world. He remembered having realized instantly that if a world authority could be swept into pronouncing Jean Marie's copy as a masterwork of a great Spanish
painter, it would remain a masterwork throughout time as it
hung in concealment, high in the shadows above the staircase
at Dos Cortes. He knew that Mr. Pickett would never once doubt
that he was in the presence of an authentic Velázquez; he would
take it for granted because it was hanging in the castle of a
grandee of Spain. If through some miracle of fifth sight the man
did spot it as a forgery he would not, for fear of offending or
embarrassing his hostess, have one word to say concerning the
suspected fraud. Furthermore, if he was so totally lacking in
courtesy, sensitivity or gratitude as to expose such a painting as
being a copy, who could prove how long it had hung there? Who
knew but what some ancestor of the duke's, needing a large sum
of money, had not sold the whole lot of paintings, substituting
copies? That last thought gave Bourne pause for an instant, but

he dismissed it quickly as being impossible. To pass the time he began to think about business and what had brought him here, standing in a niche in stone and darkness.

One day three years before inside the great cathedral at El Escorial Bourne had noticed masterpieces of art hanging high in the darkness, beyond the sight of priest or communicant, and disclosed entirely accidentally by the huge lights of an American film company which had been producing a film about the Spanish War of Independence of 1810. As he watched the monks and the old priests stare up at the countless masterpieces, seeing them for the first time after a lifetime spent within the walls of the cathedral, some of them weeping as the theatrical lights illuminated all of this deathless beauty, Bourne forced himself to think through something which seemed to be just on the rim of his conscious thought.

When the movie maker's lights went out the paintings would disappear again, perhaps forever. Knowing this, it had been simple for Bourne to decide what his Spanish project would be. If one could succeed in substituting an excellent copy of a great master for the master's original work hanging on some darkened wall, no one would ever have any means of knowing whether the original had been taken—or if it had, no means of knowing exactly when it had been taken.

This consideration led to others, such as setting up a suitable Factory: production facilities to turn out excellent copies under blameless conditions by an utterly trustworthy person. He put that off to the side as being relatively simple compared to the problem of The Market: how to dispose of such paintings at prices close to their optimum extrinsic worth to a collector who would have to understand that they could never be shown or announced publicly as having been acquired.

Bourne pored over these problems for a number of months while he managed the hotel and continued his studies of Spanish art. He would muddle absent-mindedly through the days of a week nibbling away at his central problem, The Market. He knew that throughout the world there were any number of instantly lucky men who, wishing to propitiate something which disturbed them vaguely, would seek to endow their community with expensive beauty. In this manner rich museums had sprung up at country crossroads in the United States. Bourne felt, as time went by, that if he could bring a "safe" Sánchez

Coello, for example, to the trustees of such a museum through perfectly correct channels The Market could be created.

He turned the possibility over and over in his mind, together with the large tax advantages the donation of such a work could bring to stiffly correct channels of donation, and began to feel that this method could be made workable. If one of the twenty richest men in a country donated a "safe" Coello to earn a tax profit in a most unostentatious manner to a small provincial museum, who at the museum would want to investigate the starting point of the most authentic Sánchez Coello, and if they did who could say for sure on which dark, dark wall high beyond possible view this Coello had last been hung?

He lost eleven months following this turn before, characteristically, solving the problem of The Market quite differently.

BELOW, in the great hall, the duchess had walked briskly into an anteroom beyond a waiting room, across a common room too large to light, with Cayetano following her. They sat opposite each other on benches with high backs set at right angles to a fireplace which held a roaring fire.

Spain is a walled country where the eyes of the present continually record the manners of the past. The duchess and Cayetano exceeded the past by piling more tradition on tradition. Always, for what the duchess considered very good reasons, she and Cayetano comported themselves as though a large, round duenna sat, stifling belches, within the same room with them.

Their love for each other had left reason behind. They were monomaniacal. They could feel nothing else, think of little else than being together someday. They were tense and high-strung when they sat across from each other like this, with no one to watch them. They were waiting for something to happen. They expressed with every impulsive move they did not make, with every choked cry of joy they never uttered, that even though they might need to wait seven minutes this side of death before they were joined as one, body and soul, what they would share, when their moment did come, would be mountainous and holy. The clear fact that their pain and sense of suffocation could be

ended by one move on the part of the duchess had no meaning
to them, because they had accepted wholly and forever the
reason for their agony and had found it just. Cayetano could
almost understand what she had done and was doing to them.
The pressure of their emotion would cause implosion if one
were taken away before the other had been fulfilled.

They were two ecstatically happy, desperate people because
the duchess's seventy-two-year-old husband had chosen to journey through the world in his search for greater and more delec-
table sins. The duchess, to whom the Church was a living thing,
had sworn to cherish him until death did them part, while she
loved Cayetano operatically.

They sat in repose before the fire, finding survival in each
other's eyes.

"Where shall we go when he is dead?" asked Cayetano, looking through the cognac in his glass at the fire.

"To bed."

"Assuredly. Then where?"

"To London, I think. I have relatives there. We shall have tea
with the Queen."

"I don't speak English."

"That is fitting for a great matador of bulls."

"Luis Miguel speaks English."

"He pretends. You do understand, love, that absolutely no one
will mind if you don't speak English? Some of them speak
Spanish, after all, and we shan't go about much. We will go to
concerts and to the galleries and late at night before we go to
bed I will tell you everything everyone has said."

"Then we will go to bed."

"Oh, yes." They were silent for a little while until the duchess
decided it would be best to divert such thoughts. "I merely
thought it would be quite pleasant to meet the young Queen."

"Oh, yes."

"We are related, you know. Through the Scottish branch of
the family."

"I see."

"Where else would you like to go?" asked the duchess softly,
anxious to continue one of their favorite games.

"Mexico. Yucatan. There are beautiful little islands in the
Gulf of Mexico. I have seen them. Yes. After we go to London
and have tea with your relative and go to the concerts and the

galleries and drink some Scotch whiskey in commemoration of
your ancestors on the whiskey side of your family and make
love whenever we are alone, then we will go to an island near
Yucatan which I think by God I will buy tomorrow by cable. No
one can take anything away once we are there."

"No one can take away, wherever we go." The duchess's voice
was decisive, her policy, instantly formed, was firm, and that
was that. "Except death and then to be rejoined."

"I was thinking of politics, my sweetest, darling, little jail-
bird." He smiled at her deliciously, at all of her and then at just
a beautiful part of her, at the lobe of her left ear as it reflected
the moving color of the fire.

She purred at him. "You are jealous of Generalissimo
Franco?"

"No."

Cayetano thought of the Caudillo in the State Box draped with
flags, at the Plaza de Toros in Madrid or San Sebastián or
Sevilla, the crowds cheering him as affectionately as every
Spanish crowd has cheered their every chief of state in history,
even Ferdinand VII. Twice a year he and the Generalissimo
exchanged solemn bows across a hundred yards of air as
Cayetano *brindised* to the chief of the Spanish state and as the
chief of the Spanish state acknowledged the dedication with the
ineffable graciousness of a politician who does not have to depend on votes. During such afternoons each matador would go
to the state box, shake hands with the Generalissimo, who was a
virile and extremely pleasant man on those occasions, and receive a silver cigarette box suitably inscribed. Cayetano had
more of those silver cigarette boxes than he had cigarettes.
These exchanges were Cayetano's only brushes with politics
from one year to the next. He could not and would never be able
to comprehend the duchess's disapproval of the government. He
liked Mrs. Franco's taste in hats. He liked the Generalissimo's
darting movement, forward and across, to explain a fine point
of the faena of Antonio Ordonez, say, or the dentist-like precision and efficiency of the kill of Rafael Ortega, to a visiting
foreign dignitary.

The train of Cayetano's thought held for a moment on Ortega.
He was at least as emotional as a dentist as he worked the bulls,
and Cayetano had always felt he should carry an attaché case
in the paseo. But how the man could kill!

The people cheered Franco when he arrived and when he departed, particularly on the *sombra* side; Franco understood and liked bullfighting—after all the man *was* a Spaniard—and Mrs. Franco wore stunning hats. It was that simple to Cayetano, a simple artisan who earned thirty thousand dollars for an afternoon's work. However, if Blanca preferred to have a king in that box of state, then she should have a king. She had suffered greatly to have a king there.

"You are jealous of the King then?"

He stretched out a little on the bench and touched the tip of her shoe with the tip of his in a small, joshing gesture.

"Are there any bulls in the Gulf of Mexico?" she asked.

"I will not have you talking shop. It can only lead to maudlin praise of my work."

"What with my tendency to get arrested and your tendency to get gored, we—"

"Ah, no. I am adept. I have great art. Ask my manager."

"So they tell me."

"I am. I have some advertisements from the *Digame* which I paid for myself as a legitimate business expense which tend to prove this."

"Adept enough to have been gored twelve times, twice in the stomach and once in the throat."

"My foot slipped."

"That is a lot of slips."

"In a lifetime!"

"You are only twenty-seven years old now."

"It is a business of some risks. Not many to such an adept, but some. And it is a family business."

"Getting arrested is my family business."

"Yes. But you overdo it."

"For nine hundred years our family's business has been the monarchy. And we've drawn some dandies. What I do has to be done, and no one else seems to want to do it."

He leaned forward earnestly. His voice had the material texture of loving. "Tell me, my dearest," he said softly, "why it must be done? What will it change? The same sort of people will continue to be born and persist in dying. I don't have to understand what you know to be the truth, but I want to if I can."

She stared at him absently, savoring him, imagining him

inside her, knowing exactly what it would be like to be beside him, secure at his side throughout the eternity given to her by God if she protected God's love now by denying Cayetano's as long as He said she must deny. She talked to him softly, as though she were breathing an ecstatic exhaustion into his chest as he held her in his arms. "I am a desperate woman who will stay desperate until we know it is right that we be together. We wait and we wait. I think I cannot continue to live while I wait for such transcendence for my body and my soul and my heart which sings to you." She smiled at him, radiantly and suddenly, changing the mood. "When that day arrives I may not be able to assemble enough interest in the cause of the King to remember to mail a letter which could save his life."

They fell into silence and took to staring at the future beyond the fire.

BOURNE watched the duchess and Cayetano bow to each other at the top of the staircase and retire to rooms situated in opposite directions within the castle. He then allowed forty minutes to pass. At thirty-seven minutes before dawn, feeling that the preciseness of his calculations might be laughable to anyone not in his business, he left his room with Jean Marie's copy of the Velázquez, and made an efficient job of the highly technical work of transferring the copy of the painting to the bared frame of the original. Repeating precisely the various calesthenics and rigorous positionings he had practiced for over one hundred and fifty hours at his hotel, he succeeded in removing the original masterpiece and replacing it with the copy in twenty-eight minutes, seventeen seconds—eighty seconds less than his best previous time at the exercise.

Bourne was warmly dressed in a black sweat suit which tied at the wrists and ankles. He wore a black bandanna tied around his forehead at the hairline because it was extremely hot work and it would not have done to have sweat run into his eyes. He counted to himself throughout each section of the movements. His count accurately represented the passage of individual seconds, and the peril of his position in no way pressed him to hasten the cadence. He thought about what he was doing, as he had long ago trained himself.

It was extremely ticklish work, needing a good deal more than physical strength and coordination. Criminality implies a lack of herd discipline, yet in its more demanding strata it calls for infantile discipline of the kind utilized by a small boy or a salesman who will work to remember baseball batting averages back to Nap Lajoie. It is greed with a social sense removed because what is there to be taken must be commandeered in light of the criminal's inner resources, eliminating envy, a much smaller sin. Criminality is the grisly, freakish mutation of an artist's horror of keeping the hours other people keep, and enjoying the safety other people enjoy for the sake of safety, which is one of the reasons why there are so few women abstract expressionists, and why post-offices show so few women in the wanted posters. The non-organization man, the abjurer of gray flannel clothing, the comforting agony at rest behind the masochistic mask, all are compounded when practiced by the higher criminal orders. The most obedient physical discipline is required, and it must be as reflexively responsive as a submarine commander's, as each man's in an experimental rocket crew. It takes innate timing, and it must possess, at Bourne's level, a tactile virtuosity equal to, say, a second-year student surgeon.

The job Bourne undertook that morning called for an acrobat's sense of balance. Working against severe time limitations, Bourne had to lean half-body forward in complete darkness from a cold, stone niche fifteen feet above the great staircase and manage, in relative silence, to dislocate a frame which had been stiffened into position for several centuries, though even the Spanish must clean their paintings sometimes. Furthermore, his feet had to depend upon masonry of the middle ages; the castle had been constructed sometime in the reign of Alphonso VI by the same architect who had done the walls of Avila, which made the present stonework all too unreliable. However, as this occasion marked the third Spanish master Bourne had stolen from the Duchess de Dos Cortes, it was not as though he were utterly unfamiliar with the working area.

Whereas few honest people can understand, Bourne would explain to Eve, why a man would marshal such faculties and reactions for such an essentially juvenile feat, almost any criminal mind would warm to a description of Bourne's accomplishment in the execution of these three jobs over so wearying a course. His peers would have elaborated on Bourne's work in the way buffs refight the battles of the American Civil War by mail or in the way many honest folk are able to extrapolate the complex motivations of the entirely secret lives of their fellows from merely a few and, in most cases, even misleading pieces of gossip.

Bourne was in bed, and asleep, forty-two minutes after he had started when dawn put an eye over the edge of the world and, like many a bright business executive, began again the precise duplication of its own existence.

MR. PICKETT started the morning with the Goya quote, which meant he would make this his text for the day. It went: "I had three masters: Velázquez, Rembrandt and Nature." Dr. Muñoz began his textual counterpoint with an unrelievedly tedious description of his visit to Fuendetodos, Goya's birthplace.

Mr. Pickett discussed Goya with his accustomed brilliance. Dr. Muñoz listened, at first attentively, then with growing strain. His right hand, which had been patting Montes, a golden bunch on his lap, increased its tempo, stroking the cat faster and faster. The words trundled out of Mr. Pickett's throat with lumbering grace, every fourth or fifth word stabbed treacherously with the pointed end of an italic. "I most *certainly* would say that beginning with 1814 and the restoration of Ferdinand to the Spanish throne, Goya began to paint his most *thrilling*, most *brutal* and *most* exhilarating paintings."

Dr. Muñoz spat.

"Why did you *spit?*"

"For Goya!"

"You spit on *Goya?*" Mr. Pickett's hand rose to his breast as though to ward off an evil spirit.

Dr. Muñoz' dark face was flushed darker by a rush of blood. "Goya is why I am a poor man today. If there had been no Goya I would have had more than you, more than the duchess, more than most in this world."

Mr. Pickett gasped, "How is that?"

Dr. Muñoz poked an insistent finger into his own chest. "My

ancestors financed Pizarro. Francisco Pizarro. It brought us twenty per cent of all the Inca gold. I would have had whatever paintings in the world I wanted for my own. They would have been hanging on every wall of every house I chose to build, wherever I would build. You would have had to come to me to ingratiate yourself to learn from me about the Spanish masters. I could have journeyed anywhere to buy back the Spanish masters from the museums to return them to Spain where they belong, in my houses. I would have had more than anyone, more than you. I would have owned more than the Prado, more even than the Church, because everything I possessed would have gone to the paintings. What do you know of a love of Spanish art? What can you feel of the destiny of the Spanish masters? You read books and you write again what you have read! Can you love the history of our art as Cayetano loves Blanca de Dos Cortes? Can you turn yourself into a Spaniard whose ancient lines employed these masters as one employs a cook? Bah!" He leaned forward as though he were thinking of striking Representative Pickett. "Bah!"

Mr. Pickett was fascinated. True, he had recoiled at first, but this promised, really, to be too much to miss.

"*Well!* You must tell me about it!" he said softly, reeling with the gossip value of what must certainly come, appraising it as dinner conversation with a part of his mind knowing that he would be asked *everywhere* once he had patterned the exact responses effectively and polished the climaxes. "Good *heavens!* Goya! I never *dreamed!*"

"Pizarro, for one. In addition to that, my family took two merchantmen filled with gold bullion from the British at the time when the King was so indebted to us that he refused to take more than a tithe and protected us from losing too great a share to the Church as well. Did you know we controlled one third of the trade in Cuba for one hundred and six years? My family goes back to Pedro. We are over a thousand years old. Look about you. We are here at Dos Cortes. How old are they?" He laughed gratingly and bitterly. "Three hundred and two years!" He had to break off his baleful stare at Mr. Pickett to regain control of himself; he tried to speak in a less choked and more measured manner. "This duke is a degenerate. How old is the duchess's line? Only eight hundred and ninety-two years, although they have been a great family too. But Blanca is the

first—I say to you that Blanca is the *first*—to show any interest
in the art of Spain. She is interested because I have taught her.
Yet the walls of this small castle are rich with the masters, while
my walls are blessed to have paper copies fractions of their
size!"

Tentatively, as a naturalist might approach a bird in a garden
hoping desperately not to frighten it and see it fly away, Mr.
Pickett murmured, "But what of Goya? You spoke of Goya
actually costing you this fortune, or perhaps should I say this
opportunity in art."

Dr. Muñoz had regained control. He was embarrassed.
"Really, Pickett. You must forgive me, you know. Really. My
conduct is unsupportable. You see, I didn't sleep well last night
at all. I have been so stimulated by our talks and by the presence
of the masters on the other side of the very wall of my chamber,
and I do apologize. Please say you forgive me."

"Forgive you? Nonsense! There is nothing to forgive. My dear
man! I mean, well, you *know* how I would adore to catch such
an unknown and unexpected glimpse of Goya. Why, it sounds
positively melodramatic, in the best and most goyaesque sense
of that overused word I mean, of course. *Please* don't stop now
due to some impossible fancy that you have offended *me!* I am
dying to hear this entire *saga*. Imagine—Pizarro, pirates, a line
of over a thousand years. It is *all* really *too much*, you know."

Dr. Muñoz was distinctly flattered. He indulged in a brief
smile. "You see, in a word Goya was a police spy. He was the
lowest sort—really he was, Pickett. My family, for *excellent*
reasons, worked from within Spain to bring about the abdica-
tion of Charles IV." Dr. Muñoz spoke as though he, personally,
were as adjacent to that king as Harry Daugherty had been to
the late Warren Gamaliel Harding. "We elected to prepare our
country for Napoleon because he stood for a new era. We supported Joseph Bonaparte and progress. Our decision was taken
publicly and honorably. Goya's decision was taken craftily and
opportunistically. He had a genius for treachery, I can tell you.
He pretended to support Bonaparte—oh, yes indeed. He even
painted his portrait, as you know. He painted an endless succession of French generals. He was the chairman of the committee which selected the group of Spanish masterpieces for
Napoleon's collection in the Louvre! Oh, yes. Nothing was too
good for the Bonapartes. They were his idols, his rulers, his

liege lords! Bah!" Dr. Muñoz paused to spit. He shook his head as though he disapproved of himself for doing such a thing, but the disapproval must have been entirely for Francisco Goya, because he spat again.

"A turncoat, sir! A dog of a rotten turncoat! When Wellington entered Madrid in 1814, Goya's first move, after becoming a police spy and Wellington's fawning portraitist, was to impeach my family, to have us turned out by the British cutthroats, to have our estates and fortunes and world of paintings by the *greatest*"—he waved his arm in a wild sweeping gesture— "Spanish masters confiscated by Ferdinand VII. He was an informer, a cheap police informer. That is why I spit on Paco Goya!" Dr. Muñoz looked out over the parapet. His face was quite flushed and it appeared that only the greatest effort and grimacing were keeping him from weeping.

Representative Pickett reacted to this distress with soaring inner joy. It was simply priceless! That this absurd little man— and even though he *was* a marqués and a grandee of Spain he *was* an absurd little man—should reach the point of tears of *rage* over Francisco Goya, and have the absolute *gall* to call him Paco as though he were referring to the Spanish Diamond Jim Brady, was heaven on *toast!* But Mr. Pickett kept a solemn, long face and Dr. Muñoz succeeded in not weeping. He refilled their tiny cups with coffee and spoke in a low, shaking voice. "He was also, of course, one of the greatest masters of painting that the world has ever known, and his paintings will be forever treasured in an eternity of glory for Spain."

"You are quite right in *that* connection, my dear Doctor," Mr. Pickett said. He put a match to a large cigar and the two men fell to musing silently about art.

EACH group enjoyed four stimulating days in his own way. The first day began, immediately after breakfast, with a lecture tour of all of the paintings in Dos Cortes. Mr. Pickett was enthralled. He said he would have traveled twice round the world to see such Spanish paintings. He reserved special reverence for Jean Marie's copy of the Velázquez which Bourne had placed in the frame earlier in the day. Bourne watched and listened with outwardly grave composure. It had been a bad half hour as they had worked their way toward the Velázquez. Mr. Pickett's talk at each other painting had seemed interminable, and when he had finally drawn the group under the Velázquez by Jean Marie, Bourne suddenly discovered that he had been holding his breath. As he exhaled, his eyes darted to the group standing on both sides of him, but they were absorbed in what Mr. Pickett was feeling about this particular masterpiece, by what he assured them was the greatest painter Spain, or indeed perhaps all civilization, had ever produced. The humor of Mr. Pickett's extravagance, coming, as it did, in his opening remarks, cheered Bourne greatly and permitted him to relax and enjoy the rest of the Congressman's authoritative treatise.

After his sweepingly generous opening, Mr. Pickett continued with some of his famous technical observations, trenchant, omniscient and frequently witty. Reminding his listeners that Dostoevski had called Velázquez "a species of eternity within the space of a square foot," he proceeded to offer them more of the same.

"You see the back *only* of that long, lithe body, lissome as a hazel wand and stretching with Andalusian indolence. You'll notice that Velázquez was not the man to distract the beholder with two focuses. He is *simply* and *entirely* engrossed with the loveliness of flesh in light. Ah, *mercy!* Look at the *rhythm* and the *modeling* of that figure! Surely some *goddess* guided that hand which gave us this *utter, utter* beauty. See the transparent shadows that lurk where the lower curves of the back and leg slide into the drapes, glimmering with reflected lights? I am now going to say something to you quite *entirely* conscious of the *solemn* responsibility I hold unto the Spanish nation and the world of art. I will tell you that although I say it now for the *first* time I will say it *again and again* as long as the Lord preserves me, and I will write it and sign my name to it and cause it to be published wherever art is courted, that this Velázquez nude is lovelier than the hitherto *loveliest* of *all* nudes in the history of art. I speak of the Rokeby Venus by the same Diego Rodríguez de Silva y Velázquez, which before *this* day in my life, *this red letter day in my life,* I had thought, incomparable whenever I saw it in the National Gallery of London. My friends, before us here today, enriching us *forever* through the riot of memory, I say to you that this Dos Cortes Velázquez is the *greatest single nude* ever painted, across all of the pages of man's great art."

Dr. Muñoz shivered in ecstasy as he heard for the first time a new Mr. Pickett, the parliamentarian Pickett, Congressman Homer Pickett, (R., Ill.). The orator's face shone with the glory which would begin with the publication of the article already forming in his mind in *Art, Things and You*. He would cable ahead to the *New York Times;* he would change his plans and arrive by boat, not by plane, so that the reporters could have time with him and the many photographs he would bring back in his large and comfortable stateroom. What a buzz this would cause, and how absolutely just it would be! How could he have waited so many long years through a life devoted to the art of Spain to have finally seen this magnificent, incomparable, enchanting masterpiece? He had a great deal more to say, to which he himself, listening very carefully, taking notes as it were against the polishing days aboard the ship when he could begin to set the words down on paper. How very, very fulfilling art could be, he thought as he talked.

Cayetano grew bored after forty minutes of it and wandered off to the little bar to pour himself a cognac.

THE four days moved with much leisure, culture and comfort. Mrs. Pickett, to her surprise, stumbled on a selection of Spanish brandies which were excellent. She spent much of the four days dabbling and experimenting, then taking her siesta for five hours each afternoon so as never to be tardy for each evening's program of listening to the others. When she did have a chance to talk she discussed bullfighting with Cayetano and Bourne, conceding its exhilarating qualities but frankly stating that she could not abide pointless cruelty which did nothing but underscore, in a shameful way, the essential morbidity of the Spanish people. The men agreed with her gravely.

Cayetano and the duchess continued to express each other with gentle patience although they were seldom closer than four feet to each other, never further away than five. Bourne thought that if their hands should touch or their shoulders brush by accident or earthquake those in the room would be eternally blinded by the fire the contact would produce. But being a criminal, Bourne was a romantic—which is to say a faulty measure offering ten inches to the foot, or fourteen, but never the standard twelve.

Bourne still felt the pressure of having concealed his friend's property in his effects, and frequently sat up with a start to worry whether a servant might have blundered upon it before remembering that he had it under a stout lock. What might have seemed to have been sighs were not. He had to take deep breaths, then hold them, as part of the control he sought to maintain. No one was aware of the tension he felt. Or perhaps Cayetano was because he was sensitive to his friend Bourne, but if so it was in a most vague manner and therefore nothing he would attempt to correct.

Bourne used up the first afternoon by composing a telegram in code to Jean Marie in Paris. After that he disappeared into the library because, in his specialized way, he was as enthusiastic about books as the Congressman was about pictures. The Dos Cortes library was a rich one. On the third day he found exactly what he had hoped to find; a great volume containing virtual inventories of the art collections of small churches and large houses together with set upon set of precise floor plans. He made a mental note to ask Dr. Muñoz about the names of some of the people mentioned. He would surely know them and through him Bourne could easily wangle week-end invitations. It had been by this device that he had met the duchess. He borrowed the Congressman's camera and film without mentioning it and photographed many of the pages. The activity made him smile wryly as he remembered a summer, twenty-eight years before, when he had struggled and studied to win the Photography Merit Badge which had elevated him to the rank of Star Scout in the Boy Scouts of America.

That evening at dinner Mr. Pickett had come bursting in wildly excited with news about the Velázquez. Bourne felt the blood strike his head; he had to grasp both arms of the chair for a dizziness severe enough to topple him rushed to his brain. Mr. Pickett's words cured him. *"This* is absolutely *incredible!"* he cried as all eyes swung to his course when he dashed into the room. "I have been staring at that wonderful Velázquez trying to find out, as a scientist would try, what it was which gave the painting its transcendent glory. I peered. I studied. I *absorbed.*

Then all at once it came to me. I *knew*. I tell you I *knew*. And, because of your kindness in bringing me to the *presence* of this masterpiece, I am going to break a rule of long standing with relationship to my art scoops and share it all with *you*." He smiled at them like the bountiful father in the automobile advertisements. The duchess and Bourne, then the duchess and Cayetano, exchanged quick perplexed glances. Mrs. Pickett stared at the bridge of her husband's nose and thought of a certain shoe salesman who had fondled her foot in Minneapolis seven years before. Dr. Muñoz quivered. He quivered and blinked. He quivered and blinked and fluttered as he waited for Mr. Pickett to explode the bombshell.

"You will all recall," Mr. Pickett said, a substantial platform manner, "that stimulating event in the life of Velázquez, the visit of Rubens to Madrid in 1628 and 1629, on a diplomatic mission from the Stadtholder Isabella, which was quite possibly connected with negotiations for concluding peace between England and Spain."

Dr. Muñoz raised his hand. With the slightest show of irritation, Mr. Pickett recognized him and, for an instant, turned over the floor. "May I say in passing," asked Dr. Muñoz, "that a full account of the activities of Rubens in Spain is given by Pacheco in his book?"

"*Well!* I think everyone here knows *that*, Victoriano," Mr. Pickett stated acidly.

"Oh, yes. Of course. Please excuse me. Do go on."

Mr. Pickett sniffed. "It has been said that a change is to be observed in the style of Velázquez subsequent to the visit of Rubens, that brought about a new and all-pervading light and color to his paintings. Now—and *please* bear with me—this is to be a very, *very* thrilling moment for each of you and one which you may never forget. There is an entry in the Palace Archives for July 1629 in which Velázquez is credited with one hundred ducats—I quote—'on account of a picture of Troilus which he has made in my service.' The Troilus, as it was colloquially called, was painted under the very eyes of Rubens." Mr. Pickett shot his pointing finger onward and upward across the great hall to indicate the painting by Jean Marie whose official title was "Nude Spring." He peered at his listeners hypnotically and his flutelike voice went staccato. "Although Velázquez went on to become a far, far greater painter than Rubens, it is to be

doubly honored to sit beneath the very painting which contains
the divinity of both great men." He sank into a chair, too weak
by his discovery to support himself. His voice sounded hoarse.
"I am prepared to submit an affadavit which will swear that,
in my opinion, my *humble* opinion, both Velázquez *and* Rubens,
as a cosmic jest, rather in the manner of a tap dancing 'challenge
contest' of old-time vaudeville, painted that picture. Whatever
its value before this discovery, I can assure you, my dear duchess,
it has doubled now—which value I am prepared to assess in the
article I shall write upon the subject for *Art, Things and You.*"

Dr. Muñoz squeaked. The duchess said, "How enchanting!"
Bourne stood beside the Congressman and patted him gratefully
on the shoulder, murmuring that he owed it to the world of
art and artists to get that article into print at once.

Mr. Pickett was dazed by what he had wrought. He mopped
his forehead and whimpered, "What a day this has been for me!
I believe with all my heart that today is my apogee in adventures
with the Spanish masters." He stared up at Bourne with troubled,
gentle eyes. "Do you believe it would be amiss of me to cause
influential repetition of a reference to this painting as 'The
Pickett Troilus'?"

"I do not, sir," Bourne responded with hearty vigor. "You have
earned that right."

The bond of their glance was broken by what amounted to
an outcry from Dr. Muñoz. Words tumbled from him as though
the full consideration had just reached him. As he spoke he
advanced upon Mr. Pickett, his arms outstretched, as though
seeking some hidden pit. "Do you really have faith in that opinion, Pickett? No, no! I have offended you. Please take no offense.
I was utilizing rhetoric only. Think of it! Rubens and the blessed
Velázquez in united genius upon one canvas! Oh, what a fortunate thing that you could come here, Pickett! Oh, my blessed
saint, what a fortunate thing! We must tell the world of this!
The world! And we must celebrate. Come along, come along!
We must have some wine. This is so thrilling! I cannot remember when I have been so moved. Oh, we must have wine!"

Some of his words got through to Mrs. Pickett. She clambered
to her feet. "Yes. Wine. By all means we must have wine! Oh,
Homer, you have truly made a contribution today!"

. . .

DR. MUÑOZ prepared for bed, loosening his clothes, then stepping out of them as they fell at his feet. He did not remove his lumpy cotton socks or his old-fashioned camisole of tattletale pink, but dropped a large, muslin nightshirt over whatever did not respond to gravity. The nightshirt was striped, as his suits were striped—though not as hideously—in two shades of blue against one of green laid upon what had once been white. Tented, he sat at his dressing table and began the painstaking preparation of his Mustache Nourisher, a long, white piece of woolen cloth two inches wide at its center, then tapering out to strings at the ends which had cleverly patented slots for flat fastening. It resembled a money belt, but it held vaseline and a Secret Ingredient which had been developed by a Captain Hugh Fitz-Moncrieff, of London, England, formerly a guards officer, who had taken to sharing his secret with the readers of *News of the World* advertisements. Fitz-Moncrieff wore a magnificent mustache, thanks to the Nourisher, which resembled a busby laid crossways across the center of his nearly missing face. Dr. Muñoz, told not to expect overnight miracles from the device, had been applying it nightly to his pencil-line fringe for two months, but as yet no intimidating bushiness had shown itself. As he prepared this follicle feeding he spoke to the cat who had curled up on the dressing table, the better to ignore its master.

"What a world, Montes, what a stupid world," the marqués drawled in his fashionable style, "and what braying fools we have as neighbors wherever we go. I use my talents with them like a great actor in a very silly play, or like a pulsating, feeling, vibrant man of flesh and blood who has found himself wandering, without escape, through page after page of a child's repulsive storybook. Ugh! Aaah! Faugh, and other such expressions of distaste, disgust and disapproval. Thank heaven for you, my friend." He patted Montes, who purred in Spanish. Muñoz bowed gravely at the figure before him in the mirror which lifted the white Nourisher to its face. "And I thank heaven for you, my friend, and your exquisite mind, and your beautiful, magnanimous forbearance." He tied the strings at the back of his head in the prescribed, patented manner, thus avoiding cleverly any annoying bumps which could disturb a sleeper who preferred to rest on his back.

. . .

THE week-end visit was not all art discovery and crusading. There was sport. Among them they shot over thirty-two hundred pigeons, and the duchess and Cayetano rode a great deal. Before she had met Cayetano, the duchess had been an amateur *rejoneadora* much in demand at *tientas* throughout her own region and Andalusia. It is a talent which transmutes equitation into poetry. Afterwards, she abjured the bulls and everything but one to do with the ring. A Laplander would relate more closely to fighting bulls than the duchess after she met Cayetano.

Bourne was a prisoner of his own schedule. He knew when Eve had left Córdoba. He followed her in his mind through Seville; he pictured her as she left Granada in the large bus, with a book in her lap. Even though he had found in the library everything he had wanted to the completion of his task, Bourne stayed on in the large, dark comfortable room because Mrs. Pickett had become even more impossible and because a steady diet of Mr. Pickett and Dr. Muñoz was simply out of the question. So he stretched out on the leather couch, his feet higher than his head, and remained for hours on end in a semi-cataleptic state, thinking of Eve, thinking of the past, relating himself to the few things which were still important to him.

Bourne had tried to know himself, which is a witless phrase indeed since it implies a psychical status quo, a state which would be irresponsible to the community. He did try to examine the seams of the soul he took off every night and, before it was sent back to the cleaners of forgetfulness, he would check its size against the expanding waistband of his infamy. Bourne could use a word like infamous because he sat in the bleachers with the other people when he measured himself. But try as he might, self-search as he would, he never could retrace his motivational spoor to the fork in the forest where he had become trapped by money.

Bourne had gone to the right college after exactly the right preparatory school. He had a superior status because of his scholarship, and because of his strength and physical endurance he had been active in sports. After graduation with a degree in business administration *magna cum laude* he had entered his father's business, where he had become more effective than his father within seven years. He had resigned in his eighth year, a full partner, earning one hundred and three thousand dollars a year with handsome expense benefits and an enlightened pension system which he himself had instituted. He could not continue in business because he saw it only as a continual distortion of honesty and material morality. It was as though a grain of glass, one of the slivers of ice from the palace of Andersen's Snow Queen, had entered his eyes, then worked its way into his heart. He had pointed out instance upon instance upon instance of dishonest, immoral practices by his father's firm, by all of their competitors, by all of their friends in business and in the professions which was accepted by all as common practice, and his father was appalled that Bourne could so twist facts to reach such a shocking and unfair set of conclusions.

To Bourne there seemed to be nothing that they did or that was done in their world that was not dishonest, not decadent and immoral. To his father, Bourne was a sick man, a suddenly, rottenly, mentally sick man who had to be helped. Before he could help him, or organize a subterfuge to bring in doctors to help him, Bourne had vanished. He had taken substantial capital of his own with him and had left a childless wife, who had agreed with his father that he was ill, behind him. It had been easy to vanish, easy to assume a totally new life under a new name in a new country.

Bourne had chosen crime as his career because, in a manner entirely clear to him, he had known that the only way he could achieve a sense of honesty while doing what he had obviously been born to do, had been expensively trained to do, as had most all other men of his class—that is, to amass money—was to steal it. By the stated dishonesty of stealing money illegally, as opposed to the evaded dishonesty of acquiring it as he had among his father's friends, Bourne felt clean, honest and integrated. It was creative work, in its limited way, and it was diverting. He stole from anyone, not merely the rich. Robin Hood was not sentimental; criminals do not steal from the poor because the poor have nothing to steal. As for stealing from the rich to give to the poor, Bourne felt that everyone did this nearly every day of their existence. He was plagued by the thought of money, though he was grateful for the need for it because that need had made him an honest man in a world he saw as being owned by uncommitted thieves.

Bourne could remember a certain contempt for money when he had first married. Then he had matured to the point where he could read contempt for money as fear of it. He was always stopped there; he could not go beyond that point because he could not see what made him fear money. He had always had more than adequate amounts of it, but after he had recognized his fear he had fostered it by indulging himself in having large sums of money on deposit in several countries, in the event of war in one part of the world, or the possible interruption of communications in another. The fact remained that he could not think of one object he needed to buy requiring a large amount of money, except perhaps his first wife.

Money was at the root of all of his so-called self-study, so he never got very far with it. His present wife seemed to match his fear of money with her own, point for point at every point. As he knew her more and more he was horrified by the thought, when drunk, of witnessing his own genes in a feminine embodiment. The way she spoke about money, thought about money, dwelt upon money, was the way he did all of those things. When he was away from her on business, such as now, he would sit in the hotel apartment in Madrid with a whiskey bottle next to a tape recorder and play back all of the tapes he had recorded of their conversations without her knowledge. He thought he was analyzing her in this way; he did not realize that because most of his waking conversations with her had to do with money in one way or another, that because she loved him, her answers had to do with money. It was as though he could not hear his own voice, only hers, which was how he had come to believe that she was obsessed with the idea of money and that she was some mortal extension of himself.

BOURNE got through the four days in a mild shock of anticlimax after the effort of the first morning. On the last day he rode back to Madrid in the late afternoon in the white Mercedes with Cayetano. The duchess waved them off from the parapets in a manner resembling the ritual of fairy tales. Cayetano was depressed, an unusual state for him.

The Picketts were returned to Madrid in the Bentley with Dr. Muñoz driving. The jonquil cat Montes slept on his left shoulder. The car had not traveled sixty yards away from the walls of Dos

Cortes when Mrs. Pickett began to sing the lead role in The Woman's Opera, copyright Year One, by Lady Eve.

"Homer?"

"Yes, dear?"

"Isn't the duchess married? I mean is she a widow or—"

"Of course she's married. What kind of a question is that?"

"Then where is he?"

"Who?"

"The husband. The duke."

Dr. Muñoz cooperated, shrugging. "Paris, perhaps. Or Hollywood. Or in a sanitorium in Switzerland. He's a very old man."

"What about Cayetano?" Mrs. Pickett asked mildly.

"What about him?" answered her husband, who did not realize that much of the conversation he and his wife exchanged consisted almost entirely of questions on both sides.

"Isn't he awfully young?"

"Young for what?"

"Do you mean to sit here and say that you didn't notice that they were madly in love with each other?"

"Marianne, will you please stop this?"

"Are you going to tell me he isn't wildly attractive?"

"What has that got to do with anything?"

"Is he a gigolo?"

Dr. Muñoz hit the brakes involuntarily, jolting Montes into abrupt indignation, stared at Mrs. Pickett blankly, then recovered. As Mr. Pickett swung his massive façade full-rudder to starboard to face his wife, he seemed to rise like a gun turret. "A gigolo?" Mr. Pickett demanded. "He is the greatest bullfighter of his generation!"

Dr. Muñoz made a sharp, repetitious clicking sound of disapproval. "He is perhaps, I will say that he is judged by many experts to be, perhaps the greatest bullfighter who ever lived."

A copy of the Dos Cortes art catalogue reposed in Mrs. Pickett's lap. Her hand closed over it. Her face had drained white with humiliation. "A bullfighter? Cayetano is a bullfighter?" She took up the heavy catalogue like a truncheon and began to rain blows on her husband's head, cursing cubic oaths and weeping with rage.

. . .

THEY had left Ávila behind. Cayetano took the car too fast down out of the mountains but his coordination was so good that Bourne felt no nervousness. The painting was in his case behind them. He had forgotten Cayetano's earlier symptoms of depression because of the urgency of his own plans. Eve would be at the hotel when he returned to Madrid within the hour. She would leave tomorrow with the merchandise. Once through the Spanish customs, the rest was nothing. The French were not sufficiently interested in Spanish paintings to ransack baggage, and he would see to it that Eve wore extreme décolletage.

Neither he nor Cayetano had spoken since Segovia. The Spaniard stared at the road ahead. They left the mountains and the road flew straight ahead of them for miles across the plains of Castille.

Cayetano's smile, ready and willing at all hours of the day and night, was the desperate one of a man who pleads indiscriminately with everyone to like him. Unsuccessful actors frequently let themselves be seen this naked, but compared to matadors, actors are two-dimensional performers no matter how good their material. Matadors, good and bad, have every dimension there is in show business because flops make them bleed and sometimes die. Cayetano's great art as a torero made him particularly naked because with his exalted reputation the crowd insisted that he risk more. This made him increasingly aware that there might be very little time left to be liked and reassured, or disliked and ignored, and he had formed the habit of preferring the former. His profession had done for him what churches had failed to do for other men. A deep faith in the imminence of one's own death impels one to respect life more. Cayetano's obligation had been stated for him by his great-grandfather, his grandfather and his father. He could have continued on with a solid professional respect for death and an enlarged capacity for life until his turn came to be killed or to retire honorably. Unfortunately, he had met the duchess and they had each marked the other for their own. It was unfortunate because she was a victim of so many different varieties of honor.

Life had become too much of a familiar to Cayetano; his death had become too much of a familiar to the duchess. This had continued for six years. She had petitioned for an annulment of her marriage five years before. The matter had been taken by a French attorney as far as an ecclesiastical court in Munich, but several technical reasons had stood in the way. Four years before she had offered to ignore her marriage vows if he would leave the bulls. For the duchess this was an offer to sacrifice her soul throughout eternity to save his body. Since her soul had far more reality to him than his body, in that he knew it would be possible to avoid the horns but that if she gave in to him it would be impossible to avoid damnation, he refused by telling her that the bulls were the only way he knew how to live. Two years before Cayetano had decided to murder the duke, but Bourne had kept him drunk for four days and after that, in his weakness, he saw that it would have been the wrong solution.

When the emotion became unbearable for both of them, Blanca turned to her king for support and went to prison. This had happened twice in six years, and each time the sentence was one year. The six years gave the duchess a tendency to terrible headaches and a dread of continuing to live; it gave Cayetano a thirst for cognac and a desperate need for relief from the sudden fear of living.

Cayetano hit the brakes. The car screamed into a stop. He gripped the top of the steering wheel and yelled twice from deep in his belly like a *manso* bull, then put his head forward between his hands and did not move. Sweat glistened thickly on his neck.

Bourne waited for five minutes, not moving or speaking, then lit two cigarettes. When Cayetano pulled his head back Bourne passed one of the cigarettes to him and said, "There's a *fonda* a few kilometres along this road. Would you mind if we stopped for a while? I have a thirst."

Cayetano grunted. The car moved along, this time almost sedately. It was a cool, bracing spring evening.

BOURNE listened while the assistant manager chatted about the action in the hotel while Bourne had been away. The assistant manager was called Gonzalo Elek, and he was a very small, extraordinarily agreeable, perpetually smiling, pencil-line mustached man with limpid, large brown eyes and the whitest teeth. Years before he had inherited a wardrobe from a suicide in the old Ritz Hotel in New York, where he had been employed. The legacy consisted of fourteen suits of the finest weave and cut, comprising a model for every occasion. They had hardly been worn, but they had been made just before World War I and in style they ran to four-button jackets and peg-top trousers and whispered elegance. Fourteen suits permitted Señor Elek to wear each suit only twice each month; this brought him much joy because as he had explained to Bourne he would never wear the wardrobe out if he continued to live into his eighty-ninth year.

Bourne listened carefully to Elek's report. The principal problem was that the Castellana Hilton had stolen one of their best English-speaking telephone operators, so Bourne went with his assistant into their common office and called the manager of the Hilton.

"Walter—Jim Bourne." He listened with restrained politeness to the polite greeting. His hand would have been shaking if he did not have firm surfaces and objects to grasp. Twenty hours more and they would be in the clear. He must do everything at half speed, must welcome as much routine as possible, must be deliberate about every move for only twenty hours more. "Listen, Walter, this is the first and last time I'm going to discuss this with you. As a matter of fact, I'm surprised that I have to mention it at all." There was a pause while Walter made clear that he didn't know what Bourne was talking about. "Walter . . . Walter . . . listen to me. Either you stop stealing switchboard operators from me after we spend six weeks training them or I'll reply in kind." There was another pause. "What do I mean? I mean I own this hotel, I'm not an employee, and if I think it's necessary to embarrass you by hiring away your entire key desk crew and the reception men on a contract basis, I'll do it if it costs me ten thousand dollars. Can I make it any clearer than that, Walter?" He stared up at Señor Elek and shook his head. He kept trying to decide whether he should waste time giving Eve a cover story if the merchandise should be uncovered at the airport. Or, if they were discovered—if Eve were discovered, that is—perhaps he should work backward through the duchess to arrange clemency. No, it wouldn't do; Eve would have to—no. "Walter, if you say it was a mistake, it was a mistake because I know that you know that I mean what I say. Thank you, Walter."

He put the receiver into the cradle softly and spoke to Señor Elek. "How much does Walter pay his third conserje on day

duty? We have to make him understand." Señor Elek told him
at once, to the peseta. Bourne rubbed his chin and thought about
it. "That's a little more than I thought. Well, offer him the number two spot on the night desk here at no increase. He'll make
his own increase."

"What about Isidro?"

"His wife is French and her mother is sick, so I arranged
through a friend of mine to get Isidro the second day spot at the
Elysée Parc in Paris. If he needs any help with the exit permit
we'll want to help all we can. I meant to tell you about that."
He left the office, crossed the hall and entered the creaking cage
of the elevator.

Señor Elek followed him out. He spoke to the chief reception
clerk. "Isidro is going to be second man on the day shift at the
Elysée Parc in Paris. Hombre! He'll make his fortune!" The chief
clerk grinned happily at the news. Both men seemed as pleased
as though it had happened to them, but then Spain is two hundred years behind the rest of the West in everything.

EVE was in six twenty-seven, the two-room suite in the luxury annex of the building. Carrying the cardboard tube, Bourne
let himself in with a passkey.

Eve sat in a chair facing the door. "Did you get it?" she yelped
and threw herself at him. He caught her without effort, held her
high for an instant and kissed her with ardor. Then he put her
back into the chair and held the tube in his hands like an infantry sergeant demonstrating a rifle to a new recruit. "This is
the new tube," he said. "It looks exactly like the others, but it
will hold all three paintings—the Velázquez we just got, the
Zurbarán from the time before, and the El Greco from the first
time. The Zurbarán and the Greco surround the inside lining.
The Velázquez is inserted in the ordinary way. Since all three of
them leave the country together we cut the risks by two-thirds."

"And if I'm caught we lose them all at once."

"I didn't plan it for you to get caught. I planned it for you to
take all three paintings through."

"That's all right with me."

"Thank you, darling. Now the action tomorrow is simplicity

itself. You walk directly to the chief of customs, holding the tube out ahead of you, as though you were taking it for granted that he would want to take it from you. Smile as you walk toward him, and have the scarf slide off your shoulders just as you have rehearsed it. He won't take the tube. It is very important that he does not take the tube because it weighs more than four times as much as the first one weighed, and anyone can remember things they don't have to think about."

"What will I do if he does take it?"

"You mean if he *starts* to take it. You'll be holding it. Think of it as a baton in a relay race. If he reaches for it you drop it into your other hand and you undo the top. You slide the Velázquez out, just as though it were the copy he had seen you bring from Paris. You do this very slowly while you talk very rapidly about Spain and what this trip meant to you. If he still seems to want to look at the painting you tell him that you met a man in Sevilla. That you met a Spaniard. You have never experienced anything like it. That should do it."

"And if that doesn't do it shall I grab him by the pants and moan?"

"Only if you have to," Bourne said pretending that she had not made a joke. "I'm not afraid of his seeing the painting. Jean Marie's copy was fantastically accurate. He saw it and knew it was a good copy, and he probably doesn't know anything about art anyway, but I don't want him holding that tube. He knows every smuggler's dodge there is—except the ones I've developed for this, which are, after all, more psychological than physical—because that's his business. If he hefts that tube, you're sunk."

"We're sunk."

"That's not the way it works and you know it. If one of us gets the door locked behind him he'll need all the help on the outside he can get."

"I was only kidding."

"I know you were. Now, what the hell have you got that goddam dress on for?"

She seemed astonished by the question. "I thought you'd want to celebrate. I thought we'd go out to the Villa Rosa and live a little."

She was wearing a white evening dress, which is not a good color for a big woman, and the material was satin, which over-accents a lush woman. Bourne's eyes had become cold and un-

pleasant. He was sweating lightly, and his forehead shone.
"You did, hey?"

"Jim, we've been married for almost ten months and I see you
for two days at a time when I do see you!"

The words of recrimination released all the tension that
Bourne had been bottling inside himself, and he began to speak
in a flat, tight voice. After so much enforced silence it seemed
to spew out in spite of himself.

"If we are seen together, as sure as night follows day, one or
both of us will eventually be sentenced to live in a Spanish
prison. The customs chief will remember you. We designed it
that way. My people in the hotel will remember you, and they
most certainly know me. If and when the people who once
owned these paintings are made to realize that copies have been
substituted for them, a relentless search will be undertaken to
find the criminals responsible. Police are most thorough everywhere. Sooner or later they will talk to that chief of customs.
Sooner or later they will trace you to this hotel. If they fasten on
me as being the only one you've spent any time with in Madrid
—or in Spain for that matter—I'll be their man. Spaniards will
never give up as far as Diego Rodríguez de Silva y Velázquez
is concerned. He is a very important part of their national honor."

Bourne slammed his hand down on the top of the bureau. His
movements were spasmodic as he worked to release greater
tensions.

"What the hell is there to celebrate? We have three pieces
of Spanish national treasure in a hotel room. They're still in
Spain. When we get them out of the country the work just begins. Where can you sell national treasure? Where would you
sell the Liberty Bell if you could get it out of Philadelphia and
into Mexico? Where would you sell the British crown jewels
or the body of Lenin? Do you have an answer? Could you conceive of an answer to that if you thought for forty years? *I* have
the answer. *Only* I have the answer. You don't know and Jean
Marie doesn't know. He is the factory; you are the delivery girl.
I designed the project, I stole the paintings, I invested the capital,
I take the risks, and only I can dispose of the paintings! You are
a delivery girl, nothing else, nothing more! You are the least
important, most easily replaceable person in the entire silly,
childish business."

Although Bourne was allowing himself to get more and more

disturbed, his voice never rose above that same even tone below the sound of polite conversation. He glared and gestured, and once or twice he seemed to threaten violence, but his voice remained at the same low pitch.

Finally he stumbled backward into a chair and covered his face with his hands. She poured him a large shot of whiskey, but he did not look up at her when he took it. She put an ice cube in a towel and began to rub the back of his neck as he sipped the whiskey slowly. At last he grasped her free hand and began to kiss it softly. She leaned over and kissed his temple, his cheek and the top of his head while she whispered "my darling, my darling," over and over again.

THE night stumbled toward dawn. A single pair of heels, a block away, made sharp, clear, shaved noises. They lay in the darkness motionless, as though if they moved time might start again and pull them toward five illuminated minutes at Barajas at ten thirty-five in the morning when they might be separated forever. Bourne lay on his back, swallowing air hungrily, his stomach rising and falling like an exhausted prizefighter's. Eve lay on her side, touching him with her breasts and her stomach and the inside of her thigh, her breath coming just as hard as she stared into the darkness imagining the outline of the side of his face, feeling the wiry hairs of his chest on her soft underarm while her fingers held his far shoulder.

He tried to lift his arm to reach for a cigarette on the night table. Her hand blocked his, and she drew it away slowly, stopping for an instant to rest on his stomach, then, feeling him strain to breathe, dragging it inch by inch across his chest. He found the cigarettes, and slowly put two in his mouth. As he lighted them she saw that his face was like a marble mask. He passed one cigarette to her, exhaling smoke heavily.

She placed an ash tray on her bare stomach and they smoked the cigarettes in silence. When they put them out she slid the ash tray off her stomach and lowered it sightlessly to the floor. His mouth was soft and her lips opened to take the kiss as though they had never kissed and needed his touch to live. She felt his hands, his hips. She gathered him closer, then closer, then closer to her. Her hips cradled him. She surged. She stared into a sun and cried out.

A GIANT hand, so big it spanned the course of comets, rose up and plucked a star out of the sky, then another and another. Each night the hand returned and took more stars. The nights grew blacker and longer, but no one noticed for no one looked up any more.

THE duchess's eyes burned, but she continued to knit. When she was alone she knitted most of the night.

MRS. PICKETT slept soundly. She lay on top of the bedspread wearing a slip. Through some oversight she still had her shoes on. Mr. Pickett sat at the hotel desk writing with a four-color French ball-point pen on the thin sheets of hotel stationery. The writing was so small that it seemed as though thousands of letters covered the page in four different colors because Mr. Pickett wrote in italics by using contrasting colors to make the particular points of emphasis he deemed desirable. He put the pen down and began to read the letter through from the beginning. The Pickett Troilus was on its way to world fame.

DR. MUÑOZ slept on his back with his hands, lightly folded, reposing on his flat stomach. His upper lip was covered with the white, greased cloth tied at the back of his head which nourished his mustache. He seemed to smile slightly while he slept.

· · ·

CAYETANO rose from the bed and began to dress slowly. When the girl spoke to him he answered her politely. She pulled at his arm, but he disengaged himself, patted her cheek and continued dressing.

BOURNE was in a staff meeting with the chefs and the chief steward, projecting the bi-monthly supplies order when Victoriano Muñoz telephoned twenty minutes after Eve had left for the airport with the cardboard tube. Muñoz had found a new apartment on Calle Fortuny, and he wanted Bourne to come to tea the following week to see it, after he had had a chance to settle in, et cetera, et cetera, et cetera.

Bourne thanked him and told him he would be delighted to accept, though of course Victoriano would understand that they were beginning to move into the tourist season and that the pressure of hotel demands could force him to change his plans at the last moment. This threatened to lead into an interminable conversation with Bourne reduced to repeating the word yes and rolling his eyes pitiably at the chef and the chief steward while he thought about Eve's peril.

After he had hung up Bourne forced himself to write down the note of the appointment with Muñoz, then stood up impulsively, told the two men to complete the order without him and proceeded to break all of his own rules by driving to the airport.

EARLIER that morning Eve had dressed and packed, then had kissed Bourne with zest, and then with more zest because they had decided that once the paintings were safe in Paris, he would come to get her and bring her back to Madrid as his wife. They went through the tiresome but necessary business of making sure that the corridor outside the room was clear, and then Bourne kissed her again and departed. Everything was going to be all right, he said; she was not to worry about a thing. She smiled at him indulgently and patted his cheek as he slipped through the doorway.

Nor did she worry. Bourne had thought of everything, she was confident of that. It would be more intelligent to feel some kind of goose-pimples about the next hour or so, but thanks to the way he had briefed her she felt no more than if she were going through customs with an undeclared package of cigarettes.

She telephoned for a porter and a taxi. Two men came up for the luggage, which seemed odd because she had told the operator that she had only two pieces. Not only the two porters but the assistant manager, Señor Elek of the four high buttons, was there to serve.

Bourne managed to sail around the corner of the corridor with that comical self-confidence of a managing director in his own hotel, to bid Miss Quinn a polite good morning in Spanish through her opened door, and then surge on. The attendance of the three employees startled him as well, but for a different reason. Time and usage had convinced him that only he appreciated how excitingly beautiful she was. He suddenly realized, feeling both alarmed and thrilled, that perhaps she was beautiful enough to cause the chef, the barber, the doorman, and everyone else employed in the hotel to want to help her with her bags.

The two porters put Eve into a cab, but only one of them would take a tip. The other one just grinned, shook her hand, backed away and disappeared. Señor Elek handed her the cardboard tube, wished her a formidably pleasant journey and a quick return so that the hotel would not be too long without the endowment of her grace and beauty, instructed the driver to take her to the Barajas Airport and slammed the cab door.

Nine seconds later, as the cab turned into Alcalá and started toward the Plaza de la Independencia, the fear began to set in. It started in her stomach. First it was nausea; then it was like hardening concrete which rose in a column and jammed her throat. She felt feverish. She pushed the cardboard tube involuntarily and it fell to the floor with a rattle.

The cab turned off Alcalá into Calle Velázquez because of a detour caused by street construction. Each time they passed a cross street she would look up and read that threatening word:

Velázquez at Villaneuva, *Velázquez* at Jorge Juan. She leaned forward to ask the driver if he did not know a quicker way to Barajas. To humor her he turned right at the next intersection, at the corner of Velázquez and Goya. She closed her eyes and tried counting slowly to herself to blank her mind, then tried humming while she counted.

At Plaza de Manuel Becerra the driver took a short cut along Cartagena to Avenida de America, and then they were passing the city line. By that time she was wet with perspiration; on her light brown dress the stains of sweat were clear in dark, circular designs on the mild spring day. She began by thinking that such ugliness would repel the chief of customs when she was supposed to attract him, and ended by imagining that she would bleed in the same wet designs when they found her out and, as she ran away in panic, had to shoot her.

Her hands were shaking badly, but as the taxi rounded the traffic circle to turn off to the airport she fumbled with her purse, somehow separated a hundred peseta note from the others and dropped it on the seat beside her. When the cab pulled up at the porters' building she got out, managed to say "Air Iberia to Paris," then stood stock-still while the driver and porter took her two pieces of luggage. She realized that the silent driver was standing beside her waiting to be paid. "It is on the seat," she said. "What is on the seat, señora?" the driver asked, but she turned as abruptly as a drill master and walked off. The driver made a sound, understanding then, what she might have meant, looked into the cab and saw the note.

Eve walked directly past the Iberia desk where the porter was weighing her bags and handed the porter her ticket envelope without stopping. She walked past TWA and BEA, past the Information Desk, past the newsstand, past the Ladies' Room and into the bar, where she asked for a double gin. When it came she sipped it slowly and stared at the floor. As she drank her second double gin the porter found her and explained that the ticket agent would have to see her passport. She thanked him and gave him a ten peseta tip from the change on the bar. Her hand didn't shake.

At the Iberia counter she offered the clerk her passport and the baggage checks the porter had given her and asked, with a dazzling smile, for her large bag. He dragged it out for her at once and without a word she carried it to the Ladies' Room where she took off the dress which had been stained with fear and put on another. She returned to check her bag through again, and with a firm grip on the cardboard tube passed the *guardia* at the customs gate and moved across the room to the office of the chief of customs.

Bourne arrived too late to see her. He moved impatiently through the crowds, then through the restaurant to the terrace which overlooked the field. As he came up to the wire fence the Iberia Constellation was loading. He looked wildly about, fearing the worst, and when he finally saw her she was halfway up the steps to the plane, the cardboard tube in her hand, chatting pleasantly with an elderly nun who climbed the steep steps slowly ahead of her. She did not look back.

DURING his last criminal enterprise Bourne had lived in Paris for nearly three years. The task he had assigned himself involved an intricately designed and routinely executed insurance-company embarrassment which Bourne had decided never to repeat—not because there had not been enough risk, because he in no way appreciated risk, but because it had resembled far too closely the kind of dishonesty he had practiced in his father's firm. To Bourne, the insurance-company job had been dishonestly dishonest. The work had taken him four months less than three years and a certain amount of operating capital, but by ignoring taxes, as he could in his work, he was able to enhance his total outlay of twenty-one million francs, with a gross profit of ninety-six million francs, realized against a risk of twenty to thirty-five years in prison if he had been caught. He had reinvested two-fifths of his profit in annuities with the same insurance company because he was sure that they had learned an expensive lesson and would be extremely alert to any semblance of recurrence.

The project itself had no connection with the Spanish adventure, but the three years it had given Bourne in Paris had brought him friends and a wife. His friends and particularly his wife had turned out to have their own friends and connections within the pervasive art world of the city, and thus he had found Jean Marie.

EVE LEWIS was what many people might call a reject. While she was working for a fashion magazine in New York it was discovered that she had a tendency to weep without reason in inconvenient circumstances. She had wept once at a rather offhand description of a small boy being sent to camp from Grand Central Station, and once at the recollection of a method of fixing dog races with chewing gum. Even though it was discovered later that the tendency was due to her allergy to drugs and that a doctor had put her on dexadrine to enforce weight reduction, the peculiarity served to brand her as being essentially unstable. Also, she got the shakes regularly—which is to say that she overcompensated for a low resistance to alcohol.

Other indications which tend to prove that such people only get what they ask for—such as an abortion, a marriage and a divorce, in that order—by being sensitive, imaginative, creative, frightened and valuable, set her apart from those more completely adjusted women at the magazine who understood reflexively that there was no need for feeling rejected or disgraced by abortion or divorce. They knew, without getting morbid and overwrought about it, that there were pills for sleeping and pills for waking and pills for in between which erased all excuses for any kind of shakes. They were enlightened, modern women and she was one of those slobs who were just not able to cope, who were most certainly not able to compete, and if a person doesn't have the spirit or the interest to compete, how can they expect to survive?

Naturally, when one lived in a society which had the world's greatest standard of living one had to expect the world's highest cost of living. Wages might not exactly keep up with prices, but the Administration certainly saw to it that credit kept up with prices, and since the consequent way of life had evolved from painstaking world leadership, why keep calling the resulting personal condition debt? Or if one had to be old-fashioned and call it debt, why act as if there was any disgrace connected with it?

Everyone else lived the same way, but no one could pound that into Eve Lewis' head. She just didn't have it to survive. Consequently she did what a lot of other rejects had done: instead of killing herself or going into a convent, she escaped by moving to Europe to live year-in-year-out.

At first it had been exhilarating to live in Paris because it was like being invisible. She could travel anywhere there and not understand one word that people were saying if she stayed out of the Georges V, Le Calvados, and the Louvre. For weeks she envied people who had the good fortune to wear hearing aids which they could turn on or off and not be made old by gabble.

However, Eve was a natural linguist in the way that Darrow was a natural trial lawyer and Eisenhower was a natural golfer —which meant that the three of them had to study and work and devote almost all of their waking hours to the realization of their gifts. When she arrived in Paris she had no anticipation that she would one day speak six languages. After four weeks she met an improbably handsome Polish fashion photographer who spoke no English, and moved in with him on the third floor of a cold-water flat in the Place des Vosges. In four months she had polished her French to perfection, and in seven months she was equally adept in Polish, which is more difficult.

Working like this, with one teacher at a time, as good women do, she learned Italian in Rome while working as a feature writer with an American film company on location in Italy, and Spanish in Spain as the Madrid stringer and space-rate "columnist" for the Paris edition of an American paper. She learned German working as a publicity representative in Hannover, which is that part of Germany where the most perfect German is spoken, for a Chicago public relations firm's cosmetics account, a company owned by a former cartel which was now bigger than ever.

Fortunately, each man had been the most exciting thing in Eve's life while she was with him, which was the way it should be, and the Spanish language contributor was by far the most acceptable. She was twenty-six years old; in six years she had Parisian French and bad Polish—but then only Poles would or could ever acknowledge that there was such a thing as good Polish, because the only people she had a chance to speak it with were film people. She had Castilian Spanish, Roman Italian which would have been much better if the man she had fallen in love with had only been raised in Siena, and German which was high enough to threaten vertigo. Her English was only fair, having been acquired at Julia Richman High School in New York.

Eve was convinced she was a reject because dozens of friends in the States had taken a great deal of their valuable time to explain to her that she was a laughable anomaly, The Citizen Pelican Stuffed Into the System Ortolan. This understanding had in the past caused her to behave rather extravagantly at gatherings, but Bourne had changed all that by removing that freak feeling just as though it had been done by surgery, completely and forever.

Her names on passports and other documents had been Lewis, Cryder, Sment, Quinn and Sundeen—one of those being Bourne's real name and the others being used to transport the three copies of the Spanish masters across the frontier, each on a separate trip through a separate city of entry. Before the second name change, before she knew that he was a criminal and a thief, Bourne had transformed her into a healthy woman, needed and cherished, and by the time she had found out that he was a criminal he could do nothing wrong.

THE Avenue de la Motte-Picquet of Paris runs across the foot of the Champ de Mars to the Invalides and is as gloriously bourgeoise as anything either bank of the Seine has to offer. Eve went directly from Le Bourget to Jean Marie's studio at number eighteen. Holding the cardboard tube over her head because there was nowhere else to put it, she jammed herself and the two pieces of luggage into the tiny elevator and rose like a woman in vaudeville levitation to the top of the shaft, a millimeter at a time, at approximately the speed of a twelve-year-old child growing up. The *ascenseur* was extremely French, as was Jean Marie when she finally reached the top floor and rang the bell.

The door was flung open. He pulled her inside, leaving the baggage in the corridor outside, and bussed her wetly on the cheek. She made a half-sound to indicate that she had left her luggage outside, which he immediately understood and reopened the door, permitting her to carry the bulky luggage in while he watched sympathetically. To do so she had to prop the cardboard tube against the wall inside the door. Though he did not touch it at first, Jean Marie cried out, "Is this it? Are they in there? In the name of St. Joseph, Eve, tell me. Are they in there?"

She closed the door and grinned at him, nodding. He picked up the tube and ran toward the studio as Lalu rushed shouting through another door.

Lalu looked like a nursery doll, and her voice was higher than a dog whistle. Eve had to stoop over to kiss her. "Is it Eve! Was it a good trip? How was Jim? Will you move there soon? Did they like Jean Marie's painting?" The sounds she made were like a well filled with drunken canaries. She reached up and took Eve's hand and they trooped into the studio after Jean Marie.

It was an enormous room on the corner of the building with a half-roof of glass and two enormous windows. It was a studio befitting a man who within fourteen months had had two of the most successful shows that the art world of Paris could remember. The windows looked out over almost everything formidable south of the Seine. The Ecole Militaire had been placed in the right foreground, the Hôtel des Invalides was in the left foreground, the Eiffel Tower was in the right background, and there were more roofs in view than most North American pigeons had ever seen. Being March and close to spring, it was raining, but it is an inexplicable fact that conditions like rain and cold don't matter in Paris.

Eve tried to remember that Lalu was completely innocent of the purpose of the project, and wished that Jean Marie would too; he always seemed to be on the verge of giving the entire game away. He had decided to tease her by leaning against the piano indolently and staring at her. "Why don't you open it?" she asked.

"Why? They will be duplicates of the canvases I painted, nothing more, you may be sure."

"What do you mean, dear?" Lalu asked.

"He is teasing," Eve said. "You see, Jim wasn't able to sell Jean Marie's paintings. The man died."

"Oh, what a pity! For the man, I mean," Lalu said.

The explanation served to remind Jean Marie that he had pleaded that Lalu not be told what they were doing, and he smiled at Eve appreciatively. Eve smiled back at him, feeling happy about the paintings, happy for Bourne, happy for Jean Marie, and happier still to have been saved from a Spanish prison.

Jean Marie plumped himself down on a hassock and began to work the top of the tube open. It came off at once. He whistled and made exaggerated movements with his eyebrows, which made the two women laugh. It was a wonderful moment, and Eve wished deeply that Bourne could be there. Then she saw the puzzled expression on Jean Marie's face, saw him turn the tube upside down and pound at the bottom of it.

The tube was empty. There was nothing in it, no paintings, nothing. The tube was empty. It was truly empty because Eve took a pair of shears and opened it up. There was nothing there—no Velázquez, no Zurbarán, no Greek, nothing. She was never to forget the look on Jean Marie's face; he was never to forget the look on hers. There were no paintings, not one painting, in the tube.

DURING his second year in Madrid, Bourne had spent one four-day weekend each month in Paris, leaving from Barajas on Air France on the two-thirty plane and returning on the one o'clock Iberia from Le Bourget. The hotel ran smoothly in the hands of Señor Elek during these short periods of time. During the seventh of these visits, the month of his second date with Eve, he had met Jean Marie, husband of Eve's closest friend, Lalu.

Jean Marie was a gifted painter who claimed to prefer to copy because he said he had studied art as a business. In the tenth month, the second of their association, Bourne felt that he had prepared the painter sufficiently to reveal his proposal, and in twenty minutes an arrangement had been reached.

They sat on the tiny *terrasse* of the Café Benito Reyes on Boulevard Malesherbes. Jean Marie and Lalu lived on Rue Lavoisier at the time, behind an enormous Félix Potin supermarket. Jean Marie ate potato chips and drank chocolate, a filthy habit he had picked up by watching an American named

Charles Moses, a French-Italian scholar of the quarter who studied from opening to closing on the *terrasse*, eating and drinking the horrible mixture. Bourne watched Jean Marie as though fearful that the man would decide to dunk one of the salty slivers into the sugary, pinkish-brown mass.

Jean Marie was an exceedingly happy man by digestion, eugenics, metabolism and circumstances. He had been made even more sappy by meeting Lalu, and thereafter delirious once she had agreed to marry him. They had been married for eight years, and his joy had expanded rather than diminished. He was an average man in all but talent; that could have been genius, but his disposition was too good. His painting, in any style including his own, was incredibly good both technically and emotionally. He preferred to copy the masters because it impressed Lalu and because it brought in certain money. He freelanced, working in all museums, mostly at the Louvre, though he had just put in four straight months at the Delacroix Museum in the Place Furstenberg. He worked by commission, using six well-established dealers as agents and rendering precisely perfect copies, mostly of Rubens, Picasso, and Da Vinci, almost entirely for tourists from Germany and Sweden.

Bourne sipped Danish beer and outlined his project to Jean Marie. The painter listened without alarm, nodding frequently, sipping at the chocolate and staring at the traffic which moved about the Place Saint Augustin.

"That is excellent, my friend," he nodded when Bourne had finished. "For years I have been trying to think of some way of increasing the apparent values of my business, but of course one cannot play fast and loose in the Louvre—although I am sure, on the other hand, that one cannot merely walk into a great cathedral in Spain and have one's own way either." Jean Marie was a Parisian born and bred, and his French was like a beautiful song.

"You mustn't give that part of it a thought," answered Bourne. "All of that is my department and my problem."

"I just paint."

"Right."

"And we divide the profits fifty-fifty."

"I have a formula for that."

"Does the formula call for an equal division of the profits?"

"In effect, yes."

"Explain to me the effect, if you please."

"Do you wish to place an equal amount of capital with me as an investment?"

"I have no capital."

"I know that. So we will divide the net profit equally. Before we divide, I am to be reimbursed in full for all funds advanced by me."

Jean Marie was dubious. "I'm not sure I like that. Do you have a breakdown of the items which will require capital?"

"I have." Bourne took a sheet of accounting paper out of his pocket. Under a marching sequence of columns, neat, itemized figures had been set down. Jean Marie studied the sheet for some time while Bourne finished the bottle of Danish beer he was drinking and asked Henri, the waiter, to bring another.

In good time, Jean Marie looked up. "This is really first class, you know," he said.

"Thank you."

"But why do you have me down here for fifty thousand francs a week beginning next week?"

"Because beginning right now you will have to devote full time to research on Spanish masters and to planning and test painting and so forth."

Jean Marie grinned. "I don't work that way. I look and I paint. It all happens very fast. Incidentally, you must make every effort to get absolutely true, fabulously clear color transparencies of whatever we are going to copy."

"Consider it done," Bourne said. "But nonetheless you must stop this professional copying. We'll want everyone to forget you ever were a copyist."

"What will I do with my spare time?"

"Entertain Lalu."

"I do that now."

"I mean outside the apartment."

"She won't allow me to spend the money, but I see what you mean. I'll stop as soon as I finish this Delacroix I'm working on, which should be in about three days. He worked big, that one. A Goya derivative."

"Good. See if you can disappear as a copyist, Stay away from the museums and your six dealers. Move across the river— the Right Bank is no place for a painter anyway. There is nothing which says you can't work on your own paintings. After all, why shouldn't you?"

Jean Marie rubbed his jaw, then chewed on a quantity of potato chips. "Why shouldn't I?" He washed the potato chips down with a gulp of lukewarm, sweet chocolate and Bourne almost gagged.

They shook hands on the deal. Bourne's capital investment, repayable to him out of the first monies received, was not to exceed an amount equal to twelve and a half per cent of the projected total profit, which they agreed would be the appraised value when The Market and market price had been established. Jean Marie and Lalu and everyone they knew in the world of art were to tell everyone they knew that Jean Marie had seen a blinding light, that all copying was fraudulent and parasitical, that in the future he would only create his own seen images. He was to tell Lalu, who would be shocked at the idea of giving up such a regular income, that Bourne believed in him and would sponsor him at the rate of fifty thousand non-returnable francs a week, a cool fortune, until he was established. They shook hands on the understanding that Jean Marie would have a one-man show ready in six months, the exhibition of which Bourne would arrange and finance out of the aforementioned common fund, together with suitable publicity designed to erase forever the memory of Jean Marie as a copyist, and made possible by the quality of his original paintings establishing him as a serious painter.

It was at this point that Jean Marie made his suggestion. Bourne's immediate reaction demonstrated the reason for his pre-eminence as a criminal. His instant recognition of the main chance demonstrated a fluidity which allowed him to discard entirely The Marketing Plan he had built up so painstakingly over the past fourteen months. It took him not more than seven minutes to hear, digest and evaluate Jean Marie's information, which was proffered in a most casual manner that belied its possibilities, merely as a form of social acknowledgment of Bourne's reference to the eventual marketing of the merchandise.

A Swiss lawyer, known to be of high character and practice, a client of the most successful Parisian art dealer Jean Marie knew, had cultivated him over expensive lunches twice a month for three months now, just as Bourne had. The lawyer had convinced Jean Marie that the great dealer believed Jean Marie

to be the most gifted copyist who had ever lived. Seeing Jean
Marie's immediate appreciation of that observation, the lawyer
had proceeded to outline, in most general and entirely academic
terms, his point of view. He had a client. No matter how successfully these chats might proceed the client's name could
never be mentioned. The client was a man of exalted tastes
in art and of not inconsiderable means. He had recognized the
lawyer as a man of absolute integrity, as a man who would not
consent to discuss any matter which even seemed to take advantage of the law. He had told the lawyer of certain properties
which were his by right and which he desired to reacquire. He
would pay a fabulous amount for these, but to reclaim them
the client would need to have exact copies. This was the matter
which the lawyer would very much like to discuss with Jean
Marie at Jean Marie's convenience.

"Did you discuss it?" Bourne asked.

"No."

"Why?"

"He was a crook, that guy. I didn't like the way he put it
to me."

Bourne left Paris for Zurich that evening, after telephoning
ahead for an appointment on the following morning.

LAWYER CHERN was bald on top, and so yellow on the
sides of his head that he looked painted. He was yellow and pink
and blue and white, the last two colors being those of his clear
eyes and strong, square teeth. He was an excessively, even re-
pellently, healthy man whose handshake was too strong, voice
too loud, laugh too harsh, smile too broad, and whose every
move was so insincere that Bourne decided at once that if he
ever had the chance to recommend it, Lawyer Chern must
have a place on his father's payroll.

They concluded their arrangements the following day because
Lawyer Chern was duck soup. Bourne's father had taught him
how to screw chaps like Lawyer Chern before Bourne was out
of high school. The details of the agreement were clean.

The negotiations opened with Bourne relaxing and playing
into Lawyer Chern's greed, just as his father had taught him.
Bourne said, "It has come to my attention through a painter

friend of Margat and Sons that you represent a client who is interested in Spanish paintings."

"What painter friend of Margat and Sons is that?" Lawyer Chern asked.

"Jean Marie Calbert."

"Ah!"

"We are associated."

"Ah!"

Bourne stopped there. Chern being a lawyer and therefore doctrinaire fell back upon the law-school instruction of waiting silently while the world spilled out gratuitous information. Four silent minutes passed before Lawyer Chern volunteered that he had held discussions with a principal some time ago who had expressed an interest in reaching an arrangement with a special kind of art dealer who might be able to secure Spanish paintings, but that nothing had developed from the discussions, and that all this had been some time ago.

Bourne continued to stare at him. Exasperated, Lawyer Chern finally blurted, "Do you have a quantity of Spanish masters?"

"They are available."

"Are any of these available?" He opened the top drawer of his desk and slid two thin sheets of typewritten paper across the desk.

Bourne glanced at the lists without picking them up. "Some of them."

"Which ones?"

"Later."

"What do you mean later?"

"After I have a written agreement."

This secretly pleased the lawyer; agreements in writing have cabalistic meanings for lawyers, as has anything in writing. One's word wasn't worth spit with lawyers. Lawyer Chern began to chew absent-mindedly on his thumbnail. Minutes passed. Finally he said, "You understand that the name of my client may not appear in this agreement at any time?"

"My dear man," Bourne told him, "neither may mine."

"You are joking, of course."

Bourne did not bother to answer.

They concluded their arrangements that day. In the place of bona fides, Bourne agreed to post an amount of one hundred thousand Swiss francs in escrow against the delivery of the first of three Spanish master paintings, covered by lists known as Schedule A and B, within a period of not more than two hundred and eighty one days. At the time of the delivery of the first canvas the deposit money was to be returned in full to Bourne, plus a captive bonus of fifteen per cent of the good-faith amount held in escrow, plus the sum of one hundred and thirty thousand dollars if the painting delivered was on Schedule A or the sum of eighty-three thousand five hundred dollars if the painting delivered was on Schedule B. Information regarding the delivery of all paintings was to be sent to the premises of Traumer Frères, bankers doing business at 46 Rue Balzance, Paris, to one Wolfgang Gregory Mandel. In consideration of the good faith shown by Bourne in establishing the deposit under escrow, and realizing the necessity of advance expenses and charges made necessary by the gradual acquisition of the paintings in Spain, plus the costs of travel and maintenance to and in and from Spain, it was agreed that a sum equal to twenty per cent of the average valuation of the paintings listed in Schedules A and B, or a mean sum of twenty-one thousand three hundred dollars in nonreturnable and nonaccountable funds would be payable to Bourne, two-thirds upon signing and the remaining one-third upon delivery of the first painting.

At first there had been a good deal of haggling over Bourne's insistence that the client underwrite the expenses of the project, and later over Lawyer Chern's insistence that Bourne enter into the escrow agreement. Lawyer Chern said, "But it is eminently fair, my dear fellow. You insist upon being paid in advance for operating expenses, something which is unheard of in the art field. You are a specialist and I can see your argument, but what about your bona fides? You will not give me your name. I must take you, a stranger, on faith. How is my principal to know that you won't take this expense money—and you are talking about a very respectable amount of money, sir—and disappear. I mean, how are we to know you won't go to Spain and then come back saying you had no luck but that you unfortunately spent all the money? I mean, you are a specialist. If you had, let us say, acquired other paintings or, say, some jewels, for a principal in the past in this proposed manner—well, I could check on you. I would have bona fides even in your own unusual specialty. Oh, no. No, no. If you deliver the paintings, all right, we will pay the expenses, but

in the meantime it is only sound business to demand that you
agree to put a good-will deposit in escrow under an agreement
which will protect my principal."

"But the money may be tied up for eight months!"

"So?"

"Why should a bank enjoy the interest on my money because
you want to impress a client?"

"Are you asking if we will repay you for the idleness of your
money?"

"Yes.

"We will not. And that is final."

"Then we have finished." Bourne rose immediately and
started for the door.

"One moment . . . please."

Bourne kept walking. Lawyer Chern yelled, "All right!" Bourne
didn't smile or shrug as he returned to the chair and sat
down.

It was agreed that Bourne would sign the agreement under
the name of Werner Schrampft—agreed because he had given
no other name. Lawyer Chern, on behalf of his client, was to
sign as Wolfgang Gregory Mandel. Upon the signing of the
agreement each was to open a separate account with Traumer
Frères in Paris, London or Zurich in the amount required by
the bank for a number account—that is a nameless account
identified only by number and kept forever secret by the bank's
officers, in this case the Traumer Frères themselves. Upon delivery of the canvases to Lawyer Chern in Paris, identification
for contracted payments by the bank would be made by the
presentation of the numbers of each account as established by
the Schrampft and Mandel signatures used when opening
these accounts.

Bourne and Lawyer Chern concluded the transaction in the
bank's Zurich offices. Bourne deposited his check in escrow in
the amount of one hundred thousand Swiss francs, the equivalent of twenty-three thousand eight hundred and nine dollars
and fifty cents, and accepted a cashier's check from the bank,
issued upon receipt of a personal check from Lawyer Chern,
in the amount of fourteen thousand two hundred thirteen dollars
and thirty-two cents. They parted agreeing that when Bourne
was ready to deliver the paintings he would cable the word
TOLEDO to Lawyer Chern, who would proceed at once to the

Hôtel Rochambeau on the Rue la Boétie, Paris, for meetings on the day following the receipt of the cable.

When he left the bank with the signed agreement Bourne wired Jean Marie to tell Eve and Lalu to stand by for a celebration that evening. They had a wonderful time. He had returned to Madrid aching for another month to speed by so that he could see her, hear her and hold her again. They started the evening at the English Bar of the Plaza-Athénée because that would be an easy place to find a cab after they had made the complex decision about what to do with the evening. As they left number eighteen Avenue de la Motte-Picquet a private detective named Sacha Youngstein took their pictures with a camera equipped with a telescopic lens from an automobile across the street. Youngstein was one of those lucky men, a hypochondriac who was also interested in medicine, so there was no question of exhaustion on the job, no matter how late his prey stayed up. He arranged to have various night-club concessionaires take more pictures of them while he diagnosed his own twinges and speculated on the possible ailments of strangers around him. He followed Bourne to Eve's apartment on Rue du Boccador on a Vespa at three eighteen in the morning anticipating a bad cold. When he felt much better three days later he returned to the building and, using the photographs, bought information about Bourne from Eve's concierge. His client, Lawyer Chern, was a stickler for facts for the protection of his clients.

JEAN MARIE and Eve sat in numb silence in an indefectible restaurant called Lucien on Rue Surcouf. Somehow they had contained their consternation in the presence of Lalu. Until the moment of discovery everything had gone so effortlessly that neither of the amateur criminals could have foreseen their feelings, and now each one began to examine their fear. If someone knew enough to steal the paintings from Eve, that someone had been watching all of them for some time—which suggested peril, past and future. Then Jean Marie began to think of the amount of money his share of the sale would have represented, how much they were being cheated of, and became extremely indignant. He spoke bitterly about the kind of criminals who would be low enough to allow them to do all the work and undergo all the strain and then simply swoop down and carry the spoils away. It seemed to him that Eve looked at him somewhat sardonically as he spoke of all the strain, so he told her not to get her nose out of joint, that she knew bloody damned well what he meant. He was so incensed that he went as far as to order a Dubonnet.

"You must start from the absolute beginning," he told her. "Start from the instant you got up this morning," He stared at her expectantly; then his face blanked as though lightning had struck. "Aha!" he cried. "Are you sure the substitution was not made during the night?"

"Yes."

"How?"

"Jim was there. We didn't sleep much."

"Oh. Well, then, recall every move you made from the instant he left the room this morning."

"Send a wire to Jim. Tell him what has happened. Why are we sitting here? Send a wire to Jim!"

"Eve, we have to have something to tell him."

"I certainly think we meet the requirements there, my friend."

"I mean we must be able to say something more than that the paintings are missing. It sounds so childish. I mean—"

"Please, Jean Marie. Send Jim a wire. I don't know how to send it or I'd send it."

"It's time you knew. The brother of a friend of mine who runs a Basque restaurant on Rue de l'Université is a betting agent in the *jai alai frontón* across the street from Jim's hotel. His name is Jorge Mendoza-Diaz. Number twenty-three Calle de Marengo."

Jean Marie asked a waiter for paper and pencil. When it came he thought for some time, then wrote: DIEGO AND HIS BROTHERS DID NOT COME HOME SISTER IS HERE BUT MOTHER WORRIED CAN YOU HELP and signed it MIROIR. He showed it to Eve who told him it would be very clever when he translated it into Spanish instead of French, and he agreed. Jean Marie suggested that they send the wire right after lunch because the post office on Rue de Grenelle was on the way back to his studio, but she insisted that he go at once and send the message at the fastest rate.

When he returned Eve began the self-recriminations all over again.

"Jim will flip."

"Eve, stop it! There is no one to blame! Who could have fore-seen this? You brought the tube through. It isn't as though you had lost the tube."

"But the way he worked to get those paintings! He was sick, physically, actively sick, the night he got them back to the hotel. He's spent almost three years, and now—" She spread her empty hands out in front of her and looked as though she were going to cry.

"Please, Eve. Please don't be so upset. Look at me, sweet child. As of this minute I have lost sixty or seventy million francs. Am I crying?"

She smiled at him. "Frankly, darling, you look as though you're afraid to start to cry because you wouldn't be able to stop."

He grinned wanly. "In ten years I'll probably look back on today and shoot myself," he said. "But, look here, Jim is a professional. He thinks of everything, and he has undoubtedly thought of this, and I know we can be of help to him when he starts planning to get our paintings back. We must reconstruct every move you made from that hotel room to my studio. We must give him an intelligent, detailed accounting so that he may decide what must be done."

"But I can't think!"

"I don't want you to think. I want you to relax your mind utterly and *feel* what happened to you this morning." Eve shivered. "I wouldn't trust a person who could think at a mo-ment like this," he added.

Eve stared at the plate on the table in front of her, returned, in her mind, to the hotel in Madrid, and began to talk.

Jim left the room. He kissed her goodbye, then she looked up and down the hall to make sure that the coast was clear. He left. She put on lipstick, then called down for a porter. Where was the tube? Jean Marie asked. The tube was on the bed. Two porters had arrived. The assistant manager Señor Elek had come in. Jean Marie interrupted again to tell her not to remember with her mind, but to feel with her body and her senses. What had happened as she had moved and the other people had moved in relation to her? Did she feel anything about the two porters and the assistant manager?

Eve was concentrating so hard she might have been in a

trance. Yes. She felt that the two porters had arrived because they liked to look at her body. Good, good, Jean-Marie said; what about the assistant manager?

Lucien, the proprietor of the restaurant, stood discreetly at tableside, the *cartes* ready. Jean Marie shook his head imperceptibly, and lifted his glass to signal for a refill.

Eve said that though it had not registered on her mind at the time, the assistant manager, a man who, like the rest of the men in the hotel, had always indicated a silent but healthy interest in her body, had not had any interest in it while he was in the room that morning. He had been his usual friendly, agreeable self, but he'd had no interest in what she had always represented to him in the past. What did he do? Jean Marie wanted to know. He had bustled about supervising the ludicrous waste of manpower represented by two large men transporting a suitcase and a small make-up case.

Jean Marie held up his hand to stop her for a moment and paused to consider the significance of Señor Elek's uncharacteristically uncarnal attitude. He decided that it was very important and that her husband would see it as important. Feelings were much more to be trusted than logic, Jean Marie said, because no one could argue with feelings. Had anyone so much as touched the cardboard tube through all of this?

Eve explained that she had been drilled and rehearsed by her husband to treat the cardboard tube as casually as a rolled-up calendar. It was an inexpensive, unimportant souvenir; that was the attitude she was to follow. It had been on the bed. On the way out she had pretended to look around to see if she had forgotten anything, then had picked up the tube, almost as an afterthought, and had strolled toward the door where the porters had gotten into a Keystone Kop jam-up by both trying to take the baggage through at once. Everyone had laughed, and in the confusion someone had taken the tube from her hand.

Who had taken it?

She couldn't remember who had taken it.

"We will start again at the moment you felt the tube leave your hands," Jean Marie insisted. "You must *feel* this now, Eve—you must not think. You are at the door. Where are the porters?"

They were beside her. No, they were near here, near the door. How far away was the door? Could she reach out and touch the door? No, she had backed away to let them go through. She had backed three paces away. She could not touch the door. Where was the assistant manager? He was . . . he was standing beside her and talking to her. That was when she felt that he was totally disinterested in her body—at that precise moment. She had instinctively pushed her breasts out at him as she felt it, and had reached across him to the bureau top to pick up a package of cigarettes, but he had remained oblivious to her body. She could feel that now, very strongly. As she had reached for the cigarette package, he had taken the cardboard tube from her, saying something indistinctly about the cab in front of the hotel.

When they had reached the lift the two porters were out of sight. While riding down they had chatted about the shocking jewelry-store robbery on the Gran Via the day before. Then she had gone to the cashier and had checked out. Had he walked with her to the cashier? Jean Marie asked. No. How long was he away from her? Was he in sight? No. He was away as long as it took her to pay her small bill and walk to the cab. He had been standing beside the cab when she came out. The tube had been in his hand. One porter had taken a tip. Señor Elek had handed her the tube . . . no, he had propped it up against the far door inside the cab. When did she handle the tube again? At the airport. Did she feel it was the same tube? She could not feel anything. She was too frightened to feel anything but dread about the tube, but it had never been out of her sight or her hands from that instant until she was inside Jean Marie's studio. So there was only one possible answer. The assistant manager, Señor Elek, had substituted an empty tube for the real one. Jean Marie agreed. He felt she was absolutely right.

Having cracked the case they ordered lunch. Eve ate scrambled eggs with asparagus tips while Jean Marie explained that the one dish all competing chefs had to prepare for the judges in international cooking competitions was scrambled eggs; they were that difficult to make well. The scrambled eggs at Lucien's were so good that Eve ordered them again. Jean Marie had snails and a veal steak. The white wine was cold and supporting, and Lucien's grandfather's Armagnac was dark and lingering, with the slightest overtone of sweetness. They ate heartily because they felt they had been permitted to return to life again.

.   .   .

Bourne arrived early the next morning. He had come via Barcelona and Nice. He was steady and extremely considerate of their feelings.

The Duque Dos Cortes died in his sleep in a chair at Florian's in the Piazza San Marco in Venice, in the early morning of March 17th. It was not until late that night, as the chairs were being taken up after the concert, that the body had been discovered; his posture, even in death, was extremely good. The waiter was sure that the old man had died in the early morning because, when the duchess's lawyer and the police talked with him later, he remembered an American woman tourist pointing at the duke and saying to the waiter, "That old man looks dead," which the waiter remembered thinking extremely bad taste.

It had become very busy at the café almost immediately after that because a motion picture company headed by Miss Katherine Hepburn had photographed a scene on the terrace of the café in the duke's immediate foreground. He had been a man who would have invested any scene, real or cinematic, with enormous atmosphere, alive or dead. His friends all over the world who saw the movie two, three or four years later, depending on their nationality, were always surprised and delighted to see the dead old man rotting away in the background, easily dominating Miss Hepburn's clasping and unclasping nostrils as she registered that emotion she could turn on at will. Then the film company had moved to another location and the concert hour had arrived and, what with one thing and another, no one had noticed that the duke was dead until closing time.

With the help of the police, it took the duchess's attorneys no time to reconstruct what had happened. Their instructions had been explicit: things must be quick and quiet.

The cause of death was clear. The duke had overtaxed himself. He had died of simple exhaustion. Investigation revealed that he had rented a little boy in Hamburg. He had contemplated merely one week, but instead of going on to Montecatini for baths and rest and massage, he had suddenly decided that he would rather spend time with the child. This had meant leaving a large deposit with the boy's owner, and evidently there had been end-less haggling. The owner had cried that the boy was one of his best earners and that there was no precedent for the price to be charged for a lease. Then, when the price had seemed to be settled, the man had wailed that he had no way of knowing whether or not the duke ever intended to return the boy, and so on and on. Money had settled everything.

The child spoke only German and the duke's German was quite poor. The boy had been beautifully trained in his work, which talent, when extended over weeks against the pride and foolishness of a seventy-two-year-old man, no matter how strong, could only end in disaster for the lessee. No one had had time to instruct the boy differently, the duke having acted so im-pulsively.

It had killed the duke, of course. The police and the Milanese attorney had found the grave child on a straight-backed, wooden chair in the duke's rooms, staring at the Grand Canal and wearing dejected-looking, long winter underwear, efficient underwear for a northern port like Hamburg in the winter, but out of keeping for Venice in that season. They could not find his clothes at first. They had been left by the duke with the con-cierge so that the child would not be tempted to stray away with the duke's valuables, a policy which had not been directed against this particular boy but which had been formed by years of ex-perience in most of the great cities of the world.

They grouped about the boy, asking questions, the hotel manager interpreting. Suddenly, with an expression of disgust at the boy's answers, the manager lashed out with his open hand, knocking the lad to the floor. At once he realized the injustice of his action; the child spoke the way he had been trained to speak—to court and woo, or else go without his food. The manager picked the boy up, righted him on the chair, and apologized briefly.

The Milan representative charged his firm two hundred and fifty thousand lira for the disposition of the various problems relative to the sad death. He was a young, inexperienced man, so he made very little profit. The Milan firm charged the duke's representatives in Bilbao two million eight hundred thousand lira for having sent the young man to Venice and back. The Bilbao law firm, feeling sentimental because this was the last of many such commissions, submitted a bill which was the equivalent of twelve million lira in pesetas; after all, they had had to place a long-distance call from Bilbao to Milan.

No one objected. It was simply awesomely wonderful that the duke was dead. He was buried at Dos Cortes in the presence of his immediate family and many priests. All wore mourning, but no one wept. The family doctor had to give the duchess strong sedatives before the funeral and during the last rites at the grave to arrest her tendency to laugh whenever she looked at the casket.

BOURNE arrived at number eighteen Avenue de la Motte-Picquet just too late to see Lalu, who had been sent to her mother's so that Eve and Jean Marie could receive Bourne's open wrath. But Bourne seemed to have recovered well. He was almost tender in the way he spoke about the loss with Eve—so much so that she became afraid that for the second time in two days she was going to cry. He went over the routine, taking her back, in patient examination and cross-examination, from number eighteen to the airport and gradually all the way back to the hotel in Madrid. When he had finished they all regarded it as certain that Señor Elek was the only one who could have made the switch.

The conclusion amazed Bourne. "Gus has been with that one hotel for sixteen years," he said. "I don't mean just working with me. He was a part of that hotel. Besides, I just gave him a twenty per cent increase."

"And he was such a sweet, agreeable, childish, little man," Eve protested.

Jean Marie shrugged. "The period of naïveté is declared over," he said. "What do we do now?"

Bourne told him that he hadn't decided; he would try to have an answer by noon the next day. When he and Eve left the studio Jean Marie began to paint with philosophical detachment, almost cheerfully.

· · ·

BOURNE and Eve sat on two rented iron chairs in the Tuileries. A beautiful circular pond amused small boys in front of them; members of the league of the tranquil were all around them. On the left, through the toy arch of triumph, they could see the palace of the Louvre; on the right was the Place de la Concorde. Square miles of sky stretched directly overhead, vast because the buildings everywhere were so sensibly low.

They held hands. Bourne toyed absent-mindedly with the magnificent emerald ring on Eve's left hand which he had stolen many years before in Miami. "I've never been hijacked before," he murmured to himself.

"You'll think of something." Eve stroked the back of his hand.

"There is really only one thing to do."

"I know."

"I don't know where to begin."

"Think it through. You've got to think it through.

"I have to make Señor Elek talk. I hate it when things work out so there are no alternatives. He's very proud and he's tough, and I hate violence."

They watched a beautifully rigged ship sail across the pond. "What kind of violence?" Eve asked.

"I can assure you that a man like Elek will not volunteer information."

"I know," Eve said. "I realize that. But why must one thing lead to another? We're still in control of our own lives. We don't have to turn into gangsters just because someone has outsmarted us."

Bourne sighed. "It's my father in me. I hate it, but I can't take it this way. Just the same," he said, touching her cheek and then leaning over to kiss it, "don't you go worrying about barbarity and one thing leading to another. I'm no strongarm. I hate rough stuff. But this is too much. I mean, I worked a long time on this job, and to think of someone watching me plan and sweat and worry and then sending a messenger to walk away with everything—well, it's too much. I mean, under any circumstances no one could be expected to hold still for a mocking like that."

"I suppose not."

"Well, think about it."

"I have."

"All right. Okay, then."

"Jim, we're out of Spain. Why go back? We don't need money. I have a terrible feeling about our going back to Spain."

"We have to, honey."

"Balls."

"I have to anyway. I couldn't live with myself."

"Señor Elek is just a messenger?"

"Of course."

"Why?"

"You mean who. Who hired him? Well, that's what we have to find out. Personally, I think it was the same man who hired Chern. For all I know it may be Chern."

"We certainly don't have to go to Spain to talk to Chern."

"I know. I wired him. He'll be in Paris tomorrow and we'll talk it all over with him."

"Jim—what kind of violence?"

"What d'you mean?"

"On Señor Elek."

"Maybe violence was a poor choice of word. What comes to me is putting him in some pitch-black place for fifteen or twenty days with plenty of water but no food. That can't hurt him. *Then* I ask him. That's a very disturbing experience, and if he still doesn't want to talk maybe I threaten to repeat the whole thing —well, he should be ready to talk the second time around. And it can't really hurt him. In fact that kind of abstinence could be good for him in the long run. Gandhi thrived on that kind of a regime, you know."

"You sound miserable and frightened to me."

"Well, it figures. I'm new in the violence business."

"Please stay that way."

"This is my eleventh time at bat. Lucky eleven, and the first time in sixteen years that anything has missed. I'm supposed to anticipate these things. I could be slipping, letting myself be hijacked. I've been trained against that since boyhood."

"Was your father a bootlegger along with everything else?"

He laughed harshly. "Better than that. My father's principal business was raiding companies—legal hijacking—then milking their cash and throwing them away. I remember one time standing at the Men's Bar in the Waldorf and hearing a man five feet away telling his friend that Allied Mines and Metals had a book value of six hundred and five million dollars, and that the directors were in a fight over how much to expand, if at all. I never saw him again, and he never saw me at all. I finished my drink, and on the way back to the office I developed forty per cent of the plan my father used to take that company over. He completed the other sixty per cent in about three days, and then we called in the lawyers and the press agents who hyena those kinds of deals. In seventeen months we controlled Allied's cash surplus of a hundred and sixty-two million, and the Allied stockholders had paid every cent to get it for us. My father made me a partner the way Capone let Dion O'Banion have the North Side of Chicago in the days when people still stole outside the laws of etiquette. Oh, believe me, my father is a master thief, an absolute wonder, and I'm a piker with these silly little Spanish-master deals. Pop has stolen millions and they can't lay a finger on him."

He stood up and drew her to her feet. "It's getting chilly. Let's charge into La Florida and have an elegant lunch." He kissed her eyelids. "Your eyes are the color of Paris," he said, "sort of smoky, bluish-gray."

They strolled across the Rue de Rivoli and went along Castiglione toward Capucines and Rue de Sèze. They lunched elegantly at La Florida and drank quantities of Chambolle-Musigny '49. After lunch they stared soulfully at dachshund puppies in a pet store. Then Eve got to feeling amorous, and since Bourne always did, they flagged a cab and sped for the apartment on Rue du Boccador.

The concierge stopped them on their way in. She had a telegram for Bourne from the hotel in Madrid. It said that Señor Elek had been found murdered and inquired when Bourne could return.

THE universe which held the constellation containing the planet Earth was so small that it was not noticeable. This universe with its stars, planets, and suns was one of many which fitted into other, greater universes like wood atoms into a pipe bowl. All together, they were like grains of sand upon a beach which stretched into infinity.

II

Parado

After the banderillas have been planted the bull is not as sure of his prowess. He is only slightly winded, but has settled down and begins conserving his energy. He charges in quick, short spurts and pays close attention to his aim.

A GREAT DEAL OF RITUAL
went into the playacting which followed the funeral of the Duque
de Dos Cortes. There were acknowledgements of state expressions
of sorrow, of Falange expressions of sorrow, of relatives' expressions of sorrow, of the regrets which poured out of the dale of
monarchs at Estoril; there were the various lawsuits which had
been instituted from all over the world by young men and women
who claimed shares of the estate; there were endless masses
to be said in Rome, in Madrid, in Seville, in Escorial, at Santiago
de Compostela, and by the Archbishop Primate at Toledo—
masses which the soul of the duke must have sorely needed;
there was the narcotic of the linotyped fictions about the great
man which were to run serially in a daily paper, then appear in
book form; there was an exacting analysis of the estate, which
had been left to the duchess in its entirety and which required
four specialists at law to interpret and present to her, consisting
of the ownership of approximately eighteen per cent of the
population of Spain, including farms, mines, factories, breweries,
houses, forests, rocks, vineyards and holdings in eleven coun-

tries of the world, among which were shares in a major league baseball club in North America, an ice cream company in Mexico, quite a few diamonds in South Africa, a Chinese restaurant on Rue François Ier in Paris, a television-tube factory in Manila, and geisha houses in Nagasaki and Kobe.

With the estate in her control the duchess lost no time in increasing her nuisance value in the community. She had irritated the Spanish aristocracy for such a long time that she had to step up her program of annoyance each year to make sure that they got what they were looking for. She established four test cooperatives, two in industry and two in agriculture, which earned her the dread name of socialist. The resultant storm was far greater than the one of some years before when she had advocated compulsory education to the age of twelve years. In a letter to *Arriba,* the newspaper, the Marqués de Altomarches, stated that had the duchess been a man he would have demanded satisfaction by pistol for this "attempted sacking of Spanish ideals." As it was, he would "disdain her with silence" should they ever have occasion to meet again.

The duchess did not telephone Cayetano or allow herself to think about him very much until all the relatives had shuffled back to shuttered houses and all the priests had finished chanting.

CAYETANO fought in Madrid on the afternoon of the first Sunday in April, where some of the bulls of Don Carlos Nuñez had been assembled. The duchess was sitting in the barrera in Tendido Ten behind the matador's burladero, and he saw her from the center of the ring as he marched in the paseo. It was the first time he had ever seen her in a bull ring and it made the scene, familiar since his boyhood, thrillingly different.

As the bull for Vasquez came out of the toril, Cayetano slipped into the callejon and stood grinning up at her. She said, "I thought we might have a drink at El Meson later."

He blushed like a schoolboy and, knowing it, closed his eyes and shook his head at the wonder of what was happening. He was trying to think of too many things at once and it made his legs feel weak. He said, "I can have my mozo rush back to the apartment right now and bring my clothes here. They will be here before the second bull." He was wearing a traje of apple green and silver which contrasted with his golden-red hair and gold-flecked eyes.

"Oh, yes."

"If you could wait in the Patio de Caballos outside the chapel for five minutes after the last bull I might even drive you out to El Meson myself."

"I will. Oh, I will."

Cayetano moved in a daze back to the burladero.

He played the two bulls like a sleepwalker. He worked them mainly about fifteen yards in front of Tendido Ten. His templar moved like a wave of water: accumulatively, slowly and fluidly. His work had much art, but it was done with absent-mindedness, as though he were fighting with his grandfather's reflexes while his mind was employed with different glories. He made fourteen linked passes with the muleta, killed recibiendo and cut one ear on his first bull.

For the second bull his veronicas semed to be rooted into the earth, and the cape was leaden-slow. He handled his own sticks, his long body perfectly suited to project the greatest beauty in the instant he hung in the air, arms high, seeming to come out of the bull's morillo like a fountain as he shot the sticks. The crowd sang with an ecstatic voice.

For his faena, Cayetano gave them statuary and plastic friezes with the second bull. The illusion of extreme slowness plastered him and the bull together as one, no light between them; two friends who were spending Sunday afternoon together and who seemed to stop in mid-flight, so that the bull, whom the man had drawn slowly up to the level of his lips with a pase de la muerte, could cock an ear closely and hear the promise of death.

When Cayetano killed, going in, his elbow passed beyond the horns. He stretched out along the bull's back with casual grace, his right hand seemingly buried to the wrist in the bull's withers, his left hand soliciting the bull's attention as it held the crimson muleta beyond and below his right knee. They stayed together in this attitude for an eternity of truth. Then the still picture broke, and the bull fell at Cayetano's feet at he stepped back to honor it with a bow.

He cut two ears and a tail on the second bull. It was the third time a tail had been awarded in the history of the Madrid ring. The "*Olés!*" slapped at the sky the way a giant's hand might pound a bass drum as big around as the arena. Twenty thousand white handkerchiefs were agitated. The second bull had been so valorous that it was given three vueltas of the ring, by a team of union mules.

On his first bull Cayetano had been encouraged to take two vueltas, but after the second the vueltas were urged on him, one after another. He and his peons strode around the full turn of the arena with that slow-motion, long-stepping run of a triumphant matador, that gait used only in vueltas, and presumably designed for them, which resembled ballet masters pretending to be circus horses.

The crowd cried out for his immortality; it sang that he was numero uno of all of the matadors of the world. It cried "*Olé tu madre!*" and threw watches, flowers, cigars, shoes, brassières, hats and skins of wine into the ring, all of which the cuadrilla threw back after belting down the wine as they stood in the exact center of the world.

The duchess was standing as Cayetano came past Tendido Ten at the end of the fifth and last vuelta. Her eyes were shining with the glory of being a Spanish woman who had seen the most Spanish beauty and with the knowledge that she would soon be a part of this physical hymn. She was all he could see in a ring filled with twenty-two thousand people. Although he seemed to slow down as he passed, he did not stop. He saw her smile as she remembered Ibanez' gambit, and slip her wedding ring from her finger, run a tiny handkerchief through it and throw it into the piste. As he ran by he scooped it up, but against all custom he did not throw it back into the stands.

CAYETANO was dressed and standing in the Patio de Caballos outside the chapel before she could get there. The crowd was refusing to leave the scene of its triumph too quickly, but for some reason it did not molest him with its adoration. It parted respectfully and gave him free way, perhaps because it knew what it was seeing and, because of other miracles that afternoon, felt it was in the presence of a god and goddess.

El Meson is about four miles outside Madrid on the Burgos

road. It has outdoor tables, wine in pots, and a big view of the
Sierra de Guadarrama. They talked for a while, their heads
close together. He stared at her, suddenly popeyed at the realization of what was about to happen to them, unable to believe it.
She began to giggle at the look on him, reading it easily. He
kissed her then, the first time he had ever kissed her. They stood
together motionless, welded, their tears reflecting the sun in
the way that a statue, safe within a fountain, cloistered in a
green garden behind a high, cool wall, reflects the sun.

In Paris before that memorable Sunday, Bourne sat facing
Jean Marie and Eve in the salon of their apartment on Rue du
Boccador. It was on the ground floor, and it had a tiny garden
in the back and an ancient cellar for storing wine, or gold coins,
or for growing mushrooms. It had been rented furnished from
a French family in Kwangchowan, and though Bourne paid
ninety thousand francs a month for space which cost his landlords forty thousand a year, as rents went on furnished apartments off the Avenue Georges V they had a bargain.

Bourne explained his analysis of the situation and the conclusions he had reached about the recent business reverses they
had suffered.

"Now, understand me, I don't say that Chern knew that his
principal was going to hit us. On the other hand, for all we
know Chern may *be* the principal. We'll find that out this
evening—or at least we'll start to find that out this evening."

"What do you mean, start to find out?" Jean Marie who had
been in a filthy humor all the day suddenly asked.

"I mean it may take some time," Bourne answered lightly.
"He'll undoubtedly have to be persuaded to talk."

"Suppose he won't talk?"

"Oh, for heaven's sake, Jean Marie," Eve exploded, "stop
making faces like you were Jean Gabin in a *policier*. You know
you'd faint if Chern as much as yelled at you."

"Why should he yell at me? I won't be asking him the questions, Jim will. The more I think of this entire outrage, the
angrier I become. I feel like filing my teeth to sharp points and
biting this damned Swiss as he comes through the door."

"It's just terrible, that's what it is," Eve said, combing her hair with vicious swipes.

"And I repeat—suppose he won't talk?"

Bourne said, "In this meeting I am going to proceed as if we have already assumed that Chern will not tell us anything. I think we must plan as though he either will not or cannot tell us anything, because it is possible, after all, for him to get hit in the ass by a taxi on his way here, and we have to be ready for contingencies like that."

"How," Jean Marie demanded.

"That merchandise is worth a lot of money. We have to find out that it has been sold as soon as it has been sold—or, more importantly, we have to rig it so that we find out as soon as it's *offered* for sale. This isn't going to be flash and run; there'll be a lot of haggling over those pictures. If we connect everything right we can be there before they close any transfer."

"But how? Whom do we ask all these questions?"

"Crooks. Fences and thieves."

"But we don't know any crooks."

"Then we'll arrange to meet some. But first let's organize the legitimate side."

"Would you like some coffee, Jim?" Eve asked. "Jean Marie?" They both declined.

"The art business is like any other business," Bourne said. "Let an art dealer sneeze in Rome and a dealer in Amsterdam catches cold. If these three pieces are out and circulating, looking to attract some money, the news will be felt somewhere in the legitimate market. And that's your job, Jean Marie. You'll cover London, Amsterdam, Berlin, Geneva, Paris and Rome during the next week. You'll chat with the active dealers and you'll ask them to contact you if they hear of a Velázquez or a Zurbarán or a Greco becoming available. When they ask you which ones you're interested in you'll show them the pictures from the Dos Cortes catalogue which I'll cut out of the book and paste on stiff cards. These pictures haven't been seen out of Dos Cortes in two hundred years, so the dealers won't catch on that they're hot. They'll figure that you're a legitimate buyer or acting for a legitimate buyer. I doubt that even one of them will be sharp enough to spot them as Dos Cortes masters, but the pictures are so great that they'll remember them, and if they get a rumble on them it figures that they'll contact you, if only to get the bidding started."

"That won't do any good."

"I didn't ask you."

"But Jim, the maniac who took us is not a man who is going to sell the pictures. He's obviously some kind of an art nut. Why waste all that time and money traveling around Europe?"

"We don't know that. We don't know if the person who hijacked us is a man or a woman, a professional criminal or an art nut. I never told you, but I had figured out an entirely different kind of dodge as The Market for these paintings before you came in with the Chern wrinkle, and for all we know this one has figured out a wrinkle or two of his own. We know he can figure well because he certainly figured rings around us. Now please, Jean Marie, no arguments. There's just one boss on this job, and that's me."

"Then we are no longer a democratic group?" Jean Marie's feelings were hurt. "I have joined an army, is that it?"

Eve looked at him stonily. "This never was a democratic group, and you've probably thanked God for it every night in your prayers."

Bourne said, "Do you want to hear the rest, or do you want to go home and pack and start for London?"

"I will hear the rest," Jean Marie said loftily.

"All right. Thank you." Bourne turned to Eve. "We'll need a well-entrenched, well-organized criminal contact in Spain. That shouldn't be too hard to find."

"Shouldn't be too hard?" Jean Marie was incredulous.

"Aren't you glad this isn't a democratic little group?" Eve asked him.

"Call Frank Renaro, the publicity man over on Rue Stockholm," Bourne said to Eve. "You remember him. He handled both of Jean Marie's shows for us."

"Oh, I remember him all right," commented Eve in a sardonic tone, but made no other comment.

"Renaro knows Spanish criminals?" Jean Marie was shocked.

Bourne ignored him and concentrated on Eve and the problem at hand. "Ask him to call the editor of *The Populace* in London. It's a Sunday paper—national circulation and lots of dirt. If Renaro doesn't know somebody on the paper he'll know some

British newspaperman who does. Have him set up a meeting with the editor, Sam Gourlay, for you—tomorrow, if possible. *The Populace* has syndicated the memoirs of all the top hoodlums in England, and they have a man who knows every one of them like a brother."

"Would he know Spanish mobbies, too?" Eve asked.

"No, but it's like any other business. The English hoods have to do business outside the country from time to time. Perhaps a top British crook might not know a Spanish crook directly, but he'd know a French or a German one who could set up a Spanish boy."

"Why go all the way to England then?" Jean Marie shrugged patriotically. "If we have influential crooks in France why not make the arrangements here?"

"That makes sense," Eve said.

"I just think there is something much more reliable about a hoodlum who works year in year out to build his reputation up to a position where *The Populace* will be interested in his memoirs. A man like that is likely to be much more of a romantic than any of your grubby French hoods, and therefore much more likely to cooperate with our requests. I ask you, if you were a literary gangster and a beautiful, mysterious young woman came to you and asked for a Spanish contact, wouldn't you cooperate?"

"Yes, I suppose I would."

"Of course you would! A setup like that has all the makings for a really first-rate chapter in your memoirs. You'd have to cooperate!"

Eve asked, "Does that go for the editors of *The Populace* too? I mean, they've spent years conditioning these mugs to a literary frame of mind. Why should they just turn one over to me?"

"You're on the right track. One of the reasons I adore you is because you always ask exactly the right questions."

"As opposed to me," Jean Marie asked tartly.

"A few years ago, just after a film festival at Cannes, some people from Hollywood were staying at Cap Ferrat, and I got some shots of them. Not what you're thinking. It's just absolutely top stuff—intimate, informal pictures of two people who make it a point to be photographed as infrequently as possible, which makes it a layout of pure gold for Sam Gourlay of *The Populace*.

It will delight him to see that you are introduced to the elite of hoodlumry because that will be your stated fee for the pictures and he's a professional Scotsman."

"Shouldn't I have a reason for wanting to meet English muscle?"

"You are a lady novelist. A condition like that can explain any difficulty."

Eve stood up, said she'd get started by calling Renaro and asking him to lunch if she could find a pair of iron pants and walked into the bedroom and shut the door.

Bourne slapped Jean Marie on the back and went to the kitchen saying, "Let's have some coffee."

"Do you want me here for the meeting with Chern?" Jean Marie asked as he followed him.

"Solidarity is in order."

"Then you want me here?"

"It's up to you. Some pretty rough stuff may be necessary."

"That is exactly how I feel."

"Then you'll be here?" Bourne handed him a steaming cup of black coffee.

"Yes. Five o'clock?"

"Right." Bourne walked back to the salon with his own cup.

"I'll be here," Jean Marie said again. "Then I'm going to get an evening plane to Geneva. I'll swing through every city to Rome."

"Good."

"What happens after Rome?"

"Go straight to the hotel in Madrid. There we'll pool what we've been able to find out and see what we want to do next."

"All right."

"Let Lalu know where you'll be staying."

"Yes." Jean Marie walked away and stared out at the little garden in the back. "You know something, Jim?"

"What's that?"

"I wasn't so upset yesterday. I mean to me those copies were no different from a few hundred others I had made and, after all, from my end I couldn't feel bitter or outraged the way you do because I couldn't get the sense of having been directly violated. You know? Like if I had been there, I would have felt that way. You know what I mean?" Bourne nodded. Jean Marie's eyes were troubled. "What I mean is, they shouldn't have killed that fellow. That's what has me so upset today."

Eve had lunch with Renaro upstairs at Le Tangage and let him pinch her twice, then bore down heavily with a salad fork when he tried for her thigh under the table. Neither of them spoke of the other's tactic. Renaro made a sound like an ancient Chinese as the fork dug into him. It started with a sound something like *Aaaiiii,* then segued into the first-person pronoun beginning his next sentence. "Aaaiiiii certainly will be most happy to help, Mrs. Bourne. Your husband and I have had a wonderful association."

She left for London on the four o'clock plane to keep the seven o'clock appointment Renaro had made for her with Sam Gourlay, editor of *The Populace* at the Ivy in London. Renaro had walked with her, chattering away, from the restaurant to the Hôtel California on Rue de Berri, where he left her with Buchwald and Nolan, newspaper and airline peons respectively, who were sitting over a chessboard in the bar, while he went off to telephone a pal on *The Populace.* When the call had been completed he picked her up again and explained what he had arranged before putting her in a cab. After they had been gone five minutes Nolan asked Buchwald who the beautiful broad was with Renaro. Buchwald looked up at him from the chessboard as though Nolan had been chewing cocoa leaves. "What beautiful broad?" he demanded querulously.

Lawyer Chern was prompt. He arrived at Bourne's at one minute before five o'clock, beaming. Bourne showed him into the long living room where Jean Marie sat glowering. Chern crossed to shake hands with him briskly, not noticing the dourness.

"Well! I take it you were able to find some Spanish masters, hey?" He rubbed his hands and grinned some more.

"Sit down, Mr. Chern," Bourne suggested. Chern sat down

and crossed his legs precisely, arranging the crease of his trousers self-consciously.

"You have the paintings—or a painting?" Chern asked, directly this time.

"Yes."

"Good. Oh, that is good. On which list?"

"Schedule A."

"Oh, splendid. That is splendid."

He looked ingenuously from silent Jean Marie to silent Bourne. "May I see them?" They didn't answer immediately so he added, "Oh, would you prefer to wait until the formal transfer at the bank?"

Bourne cleared his throat nervously. "As a matter of fact, Mr. Chern, we *had* three of the paintings in our possession, but at the very last moment before we were to have left Spain, they were stolen from us."

"I don't understand."

"I say we *had* three paintings listed on Schedule A, but they were stolen from us just as we were leaving Spain."

"What is this?"

"Yes. They were."

"But how could that be? You mean you had the paintings but that you do not have them now?"

"Right."

"How could you wire me to rush to Paris then? I mean if there are no paintings to transfer how could you put me to this expense and inconvenience? I am a very busy man, Mr. Bourne. This is intolerable!"

"We were naturally chagrined at the loss of the paintings. In fact, we still feel quite ugly about the entire thing and we had hoped that you could help us," Bourne said politely.

"Help you? How could I help you?" Chern's eyes narrowed.

"It is clear when one studies the matter that you and your client were the only people who knew that we would have the paintings, Mr. Chern."

"Are you accusing me?"

"If I haven't, I will, Mr. Chern. Be sure of that. And bring the tone of your voice down, please."

"Yes," Jean Marie agreed, "please modify the tone of your voice. It is quite unpleasant."

"I shall do more than that," Mr. Chern stated flatly. "I shall

refuse to stay here and be insulted." He got up and strode across
the room. As he passed Bourne, Bourne hit him with a heavy
right hand. It was unexpected and Chern was unprepared for
it, so he fell heavily into the fireplace with a clatter of brass
andirons and lay there quite still. Bourne walked to the low table
in front of the sofa and saw to the tea, saying, "I hate this kind
of thing, but because of motion pictures it is one of the few
methods one can use, particularly in crime, to convince a man
that one is in dead earnest."

"Ah, he's such a stuffed shirt anyway," Jean Marie said.

Bourne filled a cup for Jean Marie and one for himself and
they sipped in silence until Chern stirred. He sat up, rubbed
his jaw, and stared at them with a kind of amazed fear. "You hit
me," he said.

"There can be no doubt about that," Jean Marie said.

"Will you have some tea?" asked Bourne.

Chern got slowly and ungracefully to his feet. "Yes, thank
you," he answered thickly. "I don't mind if I do." He sat down,
reached for a napkin which he spread on his knee and then
accepted the teacup from Bourne.

"What is your client's name?" Bourne asked conversationally.

"I have no idea and that is the truth, Mr. Bourne. The bank
contacted me on the client's behalf. I have never met the client
and I have never known his name."

"That's too bad."

"What do you mean?"

"Mr. Chern, either you or your client have very neatly swindled
us out of three hundred and thirty thousand dollars, which is
shocking. We were deliberately sought out to do all the painful
work and then we were fearfully duped. Only you and your
client knew we were working on the assignment. I must keep
repeating that. Furthermore, a professional criminal would not
have stolen the paintings from us while they were still in Spain
because of the peril involved in getting them out of Spain—if
indeed it was ever intended that they were to leave Spain. What
the hell, Mr. Chern, did you expect us to just forget the whole
thing? It's not only the three hundred and thirty thousand any
more. We have been grossly insulted, and a man has been
murdered."

Chern went white. "Murder? Who? Who was murdered?"

"The man who was employed to steal the paintings from us

was murdered the following night, the night before last, according to a cable I received yesterday."

"My God, this is terrible!"

"It certainly is," Jean Marie said with bitterness.

"You must see our point," Bourne told Chern. "First off, we have to determine that you yourself were not the client. That could be, you know."

"It could be, but it isn't."

"Don't act. You could have designed the entire undertaking yourself, you could have organized Mr. Calbert and myself—as you did in truth—while pretending there was an imaginary client. With the plane connections between Zurich and Madrid you could have done all the rest."

"The bank can establish the fallacy of that immediately, Mr. Bourne. They will tell you that I am not the client."

"I have never given you my present name, either. I gave you an entirely different name. The cable I sent to you yesterday was signed with the different name. Yet you call me by this name. And I was recognized in Madrid, as was my associate, Miss Lewis."

"I had to protect my client. I had you followed to Paris. I had your pictures taken as a matter of routine. It was my duty."

"You are now an accessory before and after the fact of murder, Mr. Chern."

"I am not, sir!"

"Will the bank reveal the name of your client?"

"I doubt that very much. In fact, we all know the answer is no. You know Swiss banks as well as I do."

"I agree that they would not reveal the name to me. But you are a lawyer practicing in Zurich. You must have done a good deal of work with the bank in the past if they chose you to represent this anonymous client so vitally interested in Spanish art."

"They know me, naturally."

"And I say that when you, a responsible Swiss attorney, go to a Swiss bank which has charged you with representing a principal who has turned out to be a thief and a murderer they will tell you the name. They have a responsibility to you, Mr. Chern. And you have a responsibility to us."

"I am sorry, I cannot agree. I could go to the bank and talk myself blue in the face. They will tell me that I cannot charge a man I do not know, cannot identify, and cannot prove exists, with a murder and a theft. They will tell me that a bank cannot be concerned with the personal, peripheral activities of anyone."

"Do you agree that you have a responsibilty to us?"

"I do not. As a legal agent I drew up an employment agreement between you and my client. At no time had I any responsibility to you."

"You agree that you have a responsibility to observe the letter of the agreement?"

"I do."

"When will my good-will deposit of one hundred thousand Swiss francs be returned to me?"

"When I have filed with the bank and the bank has advised my client that you wish to withdraw from the project."

"I should imagine he would give me permission to withdraw. After all, I was helpful to him."

"You read the agreement before you signed it."

"And do I get the remainder of the expense money?"

"I repeat, Mr. Bourne. You know the agreement. You have not delivered a painting. Therefore the remainder of the expense money will not be paid."

Bourne grinned sardonically. "That means your client has acquired a Velázquez, a Zurbarán and a Greco—peak works of each master—for fourteen thousand, two hundred and thirteen dollars and thirty-two cents."

"You have an excellent memory," Chern said sincerely.

"Yes." Bourne closed his eyes and rested for a moment.

"About forty-seven hundred dollars apiece," Jean Marie said. "Hah!"

"That is not my affair," Chern said stiffly.

"Then you must be persuaded to make it your affair," Bourne said.

Chern placed the teacup carefully on the low table. "How do you mean persuaded!" he asked anxiously.

"Exactly what you are thinking," Bourne answered gravely.

"But, Mr. Bourne, you *know* Swiss banks. The protection of the anonymity of their clients is their great hallmark."

"The protection of a murderer?"

"They have protected genocides! A Swiss bank is a building and vaults and locked books! Personalities do not exist for Swiss banks."

"How did you correspond with your client?"

"I wrote to the bank."

"To what name?"

"I wrote to Mr. Pierre Traumer referring to an account number. Return information would come through Mr. Traumer."

"What account number?" He stared at Chern until the lawyer took out a small book and read off the number. Bourne made a note of it.

"Have you been paid?"

"Yes. I was also to have received a certain bonus if the paintings were any of those appearing on Schedule A."

"So you were cheated too. Well, I can see that we could discuss this for many hours, even days, and not get anywhere," Bourne said, stolidly, getting up. Again Jean Marie noticed what a huge man he was. "Mr. Chern, I have decided to lock you up in the cellar of this house. There is a water tap down there, but—"

"No!" Chern made the word into a terrible sound. It was such an agonized no, such an hysterical objection that Bourne and Jean Marie exchanged quick glances, and then Bourne continued, "I am going to keep you down there for three weeks or so, and then we can—"

"Mr Bourne, please! I beg you! I fear rats greatly. And darkness. I had an experience during the war. I have not always been a Swiss. I was in the German army. Mr. Bourne, no! You cannot! I can do nothing to help you. I know nothing. You must see that!" The words jammed and crowded out of him. He could not back away any further because the wall was pressing him from behind as Bourne towered in front of him. He began to talk unevenly again, but the sound was cut off when Bourne's hand closed over his mouth, gripping cheeks, mouth and jaw in a huge vise, the other hand sinking into the material of his right trouser leg and lifting. He carried Chern like a sack out of the room, the lawyer's china-blue eyes staring at something an eternity away as he disappeared. Jean Marie, watching, shivered.

All Bourne said in reference to the incident when he returned from the cellar was, "I have never seen a man so afraid of the dark."

"I don't much like rats myself," Jean Marie told him.

. . .

MR. SAM GOURLAY, editor of *The Populace*, turned out to be a jolly man who had a lovely time living—in fact, a lovely time just breathing. He had khaki hair and purple cheeks through which the tracery of tiny crimson veins could be seen. Eve fell quite in love with him within the first fifty seconds at the Ivy, a carved mahogany restaurant, though he was some forty years older than she.

Mr. Gourlay liked the photographs Bourne had sent along, explaining how tired he got of the steady run of pornography which crossed his desk, pictures all right for English Sunday publication, but impossible to syndicate on the Continent or anywhere else in the world. He bubbled that the world rights to these photographs would bring a pretty packet, and that in three or four months she would indeed have a surprise on her hands when the first accounting from the sale of the pretty pictures came in. This was confusing until she remembered Bourne's description of the man as a professional Scotsman and realized that he was dancing this delightful waltz to discourage her from making a claim for immediate payment. It was merely his way of determining whether she was amateur or professional.

Eve thought he would petition for her beatification when she told him that she wanted no money at all for the pictures, then that she might be the death of him from sudden stroke when she said that she had an entirely different kind of a fee in mind. He recovered his joy at once, however, when she explained that she merely wanted to meet a distinguished British criminal through *The Populace* staff, and that this would be her fee.

He patted her hand and said that he could arrange everything. Merton, his crime editor, would grumble and carp at sharing his contacts with anyone, because criminals were Merton's profession, and a wonderful living it had been for him for twenty-six years, what with the tastes of the English reading public, but he was sure he could arrange everything for her.

Mr. Gourlay did not ask her why she wanted to meet a leading English criminal. He took it entirely for granted that all visiting young women would head directly for criminal leaders upon entry into any country. He did not ask whether she leaned more toward meeting a top murderer or a champion thief. She told him that her preference was the very top echelon of highly organized general crime, professional, diversified crime.

He understood at once. "I should think someone like Jack Tense would be what you'd need," he said thoughfully. "He's a leader. We've serialized him four times in all. We've done 'Race Course Gangs' with him, and a series on safe cracking, which was a specialty of his when he was first starting. Then we did six installments on 'King of British Crime Bar None' over his name, sort of an autobiography, and of course, he's published his recommendations on juvenile delinquency with us."

"He sounds exactly right!"

"Yes. I think he is."

"Would you say he had international connections?"

"Oh, definitely yes," said the jolly editor. "He was very, very big during the war. Spied for both sides and made a fortune. Would have been knighted, except for his record."

"My!"

"You know, that might not make a half-bad series. 'Crime Is An International Business,' I'd call it."

As it turned out, Mr. Merton did raise cain about being asked to share a contract as lucrative and as important as Jack Tense. First he claimed that Tense wouldn't talk to anyone but him, which Mr. Gourlay characterized as sheer nonsense. Then he offered someone named Albert Nickels, whom Mr. Gourlay said was nothing but a common slasher. Then he claimed that Tense was out of the country, an allegation which he didn't even bother to refute when he contradicted himself with the excuse that Tense was working on a book and that if he were to take time out to talk to every Tom, Dick, and Judy who came along he'd never get the work finished. When Merton felt he'd made his point he finally relented with the proviso that in the event Eve ever wrote anything concerning the encounter it could not be offered for sale without first being sent to Dorrance Merton of *The Populace* for first refusal, and with the further understanding that he had the full right to edit all copy and to pre-empt any or all of it for British publication without payment to Eve.

"Would that include fiction?" Eve asked innocently, "or only material which would be of interest to your newspaper?"

"Most definitely fiction!" Mr. Merton exploded. "Any kind of fiction, first and foremost. My dear Sam, if this young woman has it in mind to write fiction as a result of this proposed meeting with Tense I am afraid I will have to warn him of her intent."

"But it is not my intent. I merely asked. Besides, I won't be with Mr. Tense for more than half an hour. After all, I couldn't get very much of a novel out of him in half an hour, now could I?"

"I don't see why not," Mr. Merton answered hotly. "I did his 'King of British Crime Bar None' and his recommendations for juvenile delinquency without seeing him at all."

In the end it was all straightened out with Eve agreeing to every condition. Mr. Merton called Jack Tense and made an appointment at the Red Giant pub in Belgravia Mews for two o'clock the following afternoon.

The Red Giant is a simple workingman's pub run by a handsome Irish fellow who sings when feeling spirited. It is difficult to reach because of the Jaguars and Bentleys which sprawl all over the Mews, driven there by the Red Giant's simple workingmen customers. Eve sat behind a table in the pub with Jack Tense beside her. They both sipped ale. Tense was a slender, middle-aged man with fearfully hard dark eyes and a wrenched pale mouth. He wore a Tattersall vest which held a heavy gold chain to match many of his teeth. His hair might have been arranged with machine tools. He did not believe a word of Eve's story about being a lady novelist, and, most indirectly and enigmatically, cooperated in no way at all. At last, when it seemed as though he were going to leave in the next instant, Eve decided to be more explicit with him.

"All right, Mr. Tense. Here it is. We got away with three Spanish paintings in Madrid and we were hijacked the day the paintings were to leave the country."

He smiled for the first time. "That's more like it, ducks," he said, signaling for two more ales. "What kind of paintings?"

"Masters."

"Genuine?"

"Quite."

"Worth how much?"

"That depends on who bought them."

"I know."

"About fifty thousand quid," she lied.

"And now you need help."

"We're Americans. We don't know anybody in Spain who could run this down."

"Who's we?"

"My husband and I. Since we were hijacked in Spain they must be meant to stay in Spain, because why should anyone take the risk of getting them out of the country when they knew we were going to take them out anyhow?"

"You think they'll turn up in Spain then."

"If it was a professional job. Nobody would steal paintings worth this kind of money just to look at them. They have to sell them somewhere, and when they do move with them the Spanish underworld has to know about it."

"You're a smart girl figuring this out and getting to me like this."

"My husband has the brains."

"Why isn't he here?"

"He's running down some other leads."

"No duplication, I hope. One doesn't want two lads on the same errand."

"No duplication."

"I know the operation in Madrid and Barcelona. Very political-minded crooks, they are."

"I go to Paris tonight to meet my husband. I expect we'll be in Madrid by tomorrow night."

"I couldn't move that fast. One can't do these things by wire, you know."

"Of course you can."

"Well, maybe I can. But there'll be certain expenses involved."

"Of course."

"About a thousand pounds."

"Are you crazy? For sending one wire, then going back to sleep? Come off it!"

"Of course if you knew how to do it yourself you could get it done for nothing, couldn't you?"

"Look, Mr. Tense—"

"Call me Jack. Everybody calls me Jack."

"Look, Jack—I'll make you an even better deal. How would you like to get five per cent of the fifty thousand quid when we pick the paintings up again?"

He laughed with genuine enjoyment. It was a high-pitched, womanly laugh. He was so amused by her offer that he had to dab at his eyes with a handkerchief. He didn't bother to answer.

"We just don't have a thousand pounds," Eve said.

He sipped at his ale, still smiling warmly over that percentage offer.

"How much in cash?" she finally asked him. He grinned at her and patted the back of her hand. "I haven't laughed like that in years. How about dinner tonight?"

"I told you, I'm leaving for Paris."

"Change your plans. We can have dinner together at my place. Just the two of us. We'll have a fine time. Then, at breakfast tomorrow morning we can talk about a revised estimate of the fee."

"Of whose fee?"

"Why, bless your heart! My fee!" He smiled at her with delighted eyes as fondly as if she had been his own.

"That's good. I'm glad you didn't have my fee figured at any thousand pounds." She glared at him so indignantly that he began that shrill laugh, which was not unpleasant and which was even more boisterous this time. He pounded the mug on the table to emphasize his pleasure. When he calmed down at last he had to dab at his eyes again.

"What a chapter it would have made," he gasped, "if he'd only come along. Merton would split. Intrigue, sex, the Spanish underworld, great masterpieces, oh, he'd love it, Merton would, and I think we ought to write it anyway. Look here. When you get back to Paris will you send me your photograph with a passionate inscription in your own writing? Something like—'To Jack, my masterpiece—You gave me my castles in Spain.' Then sign it with your full name. Any name."

"Why?" she said, genuinely puzzled.

"*The Populace* will need illustrations when the chapter comes out. 'Crime Is My International Business'—how's that for a title?"

"My picture?"

"Well, I suppose not. Send me any pretty girl's picture you happen to come across. That's not asking much, is it?"

"Plus how much cash to find me some friends in Spain?"

"Ah—make it fifty quid."

.   .   .

JEAN MARIE's inquiries drew blank after blank with dealer after dealer in country after country, but each of them greatly admired the reproductions from the Dos Cortes catalogue. Out of the twenty-seven dealers he spoke to in seven countries, fourteen identified them as from the Dos Cortes collection, which would surprise Bourne, though none of them had ever seen the originals. They told Jean Marie that if the paintings showed up they would surely advise him, but that he would have to take his place in line with a few hundred others, and that he would have to have more money than a bank. Jean Marie was depressed.

Once the original topic was exhausted, which didn't take long, the dealers in Geneva, London and Rome persuaded Jean Marie to allow them to represent his work in their markets. Being a Parisian, he had not traveled at all, so he was gratified to learn how famous he had become in the art world. By the time he had left Ciampino for Madrid he had consigned all his leftover canvases to dealers in three cities and life once again began to take on that rosy glow which had been tarnished by the murder of Señor Elek. He reached Madrid two and a half days after Bourne and Eve, just in time for the party the duchess gave to celebrate the arrival of the newlyweds.

To establish the shy ambiance of newlyweddism, Bourne sent a cable to Cayetano in Barcelona which read: FEEL LIKE AWFUL SNEAK BUT MARRIED IN PARIS TODAY TO WONDERFUL GIRL RETURNING MADRID TOMORROW NOTICE YOUR SCHEDULE TAKES YOU VALENCIA THEN THREE DAYS PAUSE BEFORE JEREZ SO HOPE WE WILL SEE YOU AND BLANCA MADRID BEST BOURNE.

Chern had been a bit noisy what with his pounding for more than an hour in the early evening, but it was a thick, ancient door and only distant thuds, which gradually weakened and then stopped altogether, could be heard. Bourne had left a flashlight with him so that he could find his way to the water tap. He had decided that it would not be unhealthy not to give him any food, indeed that it might be very good for him to fast for sixteen to twenty days.

When Eve reached Paris the evening before the morning they left for Madrid, he decided not to mention Chern's presence in the cellar; since she never went near the cellar unless she was alone and looking for cognac, he decided not to disturb her about the matter. When she asked him how the meeting with Chern had gone he had told her that it had yielded nothing—which was the truth—and that Chern had been indignant about having been brought to Paris on a wild-goose chase—which was also strictly accurate.

Eve returned triumphantly. Two very elegant Frenchwomen had stopped her in the hall of the Savoy to ask her where she got her clothes; secondly she had accomplished her primary mission of establishing a crime cartel; and lastly and gloriously, she had succeeded in finding a copy of Robert Graves' *Antigua, Penny, Puce* on Charing Cross Road, which Penguin had let go out of print and which Bourne had been seeking for two years. She told Bourne that it was a great pity he had such a rigid policy about not fraternizing with other criminals because Jack Tense was a Warner Brothers hoodlum out of J. Arthur Rank. They had ended famous friends and he had driven her to the airport in a robin's-egg-blue Rolls almost as big as a Staten Island ferry-boat. He was already polling the London fences big enough to handle a deal like three Spanish masters, and he had assured her that he would jolly well know if there was any action and that she would be informed forthwith.

Bourne was apprehensive because he had not rehearsed her on a drop for receiving follow-up information, but she reassured him. Tense would get in touch with her through the Spanish contact, who was to reach her through the key desk of the Hotel Autentico on the Calle de la Cava Baja. She told him proudly that the Spanish crime executive whom Tense had found for her was actually the board chairman of the most effective operation in Northern Spain, meaning all but Andalusia. His drop name was to be Enrique López and he would appreciate it, Tense had said, if all exchanges could be made through innocuous notes left at the key desk at the Autentico. Tense had guaranteed that no one could dispose of the paintings in the Spanish underworld without Señor López knowing about it.

Bourne was as pleased with her as if she had won the women's singles at Wimbledon, but then there was very little she did which did not please him. If she had returned from London to report that it was not possible to arrange for a Spanish contact he would have accepted it and made other arrangements, because part of his love for her could be traced to the ever-growing conviction that her judgment was impeccable and that her loyalty to him and to their life together was eternally expanding and unmeasurable.

They spent the evening at home. Bourne read and smiled over the Graves book. Chern remained utterly silent. Bourne had taken the precaution of shutting the two doors leading to the pantry which held the cellar door, but twice during the evening he had gone to the kitchen on a pretense and not a sound could be heard. Eve packed their trunk and their suitcases, darned socks and puttered around in a breath-taking french-blue house coat as though it were a Mother Hubbard. She seemed entirely oblivious of the effect of her extraordinary figure in that slashed sheath until Bourne was forced to comment on it, to which she replied, "Why don't you do something about it?" He did, striking a decisive blow for togetherness.

Later, while he was back at his book and she was purring over her darning, he reminded her that she must remember that they had been married that afternoon and that they would be entering Madrid as bride and groom. She nodded. He said that he had known she wouldn't mind that he'd had a new marriage certificate made so that the servants at the hotel could find it and spread the verification. She told him that marrying him had given her three lives and four identities, had introduced her to an active, exciting community of people, which was something few women in the world had ever had, and that she was grateful and that she loved him and that she would always love him. He could not do any wrong; he was truth for her, which is what everyone seeks, she said.

For ten minutes or so he conjectured aloud as to whether or not Señor López could have been the man who had hijacked them. It was a thought which gave him comfort, if only because it gave their villain a shape and a place in space. Gradually he proved to his own satisfaction that this possibility was un-likely.

All at once Eve began to weep. Sitting on the edge of a hassock she tried to stifle the sound. He didn't ask why she was crying, knowing that she must have an excellent reason to weep. After a while it was over.

"I dread going back to Spain."

"Why?"

"I'm not sure why. I only know that there is something very wrong about this whole thing."

"It's the first time for you. There is always a strain the first time."

"We don't want those paintings if that man had to kill to get them."

"What man? We don't know it was a man."

"You know what I mean, Jim."

"Killing is a terrible thing," he said, "but people aren't to be feared just because they kill. Stupidity, not invincibility, makes a killer. He just didn't know what else to do. The murder of one man has no connection with the life or death of another."

Eve got up and went into the bathroom. He could hear the water running while she washed her eyes. Then she closed the door and he could hear the shower running. He went back to his book. After forty minutes she came out again wearing a pale blue nightgown and a pretty, filmy robe. She sat down opposite him and spoke in an even, friendly voice all the thoughts that she had been preparing and editing while bathing, and perhaps for some time before that.

"Jim, you know I'm not advocating a return to government by women's intuition, don't you?"

"You can if you want to; there's nothing wrong with that."

"It's just that—well, for one thing there's the duchess."

"Yes?"

"I have to say this sometime, so I'll say it now and get it out of the way. I can't accept the duchess's friendship. I don't like the feeling of hypocrisy. It makes me feel cheap and sick. We have exploited her and stolen from her."

He snorted. "It's about time you brought that up."

"Please, Jim, let me finish. There's Dr. Muñoz, too. I can't be natural with a man whose trust we have used so that we could steal with less risk from people who trusted us because Dr. Muñoz trusted us. And your friend, Cayetano Jiminez, your very dear friend, and you his—and yet we stole from the woman most important to him." She leaned back in her chair.

"Finished?"

"Yes."

"I am not reproaching you."

"I understand. I was not reproaching you. I only said I would rather not go to Spain and face those people."

"Eve, what business was your father in?"

"He was an insurance broker."

"You've carried different kinds of insurance, haven't you?"

"Yes, of course."

"For example, did you ever carry a floater policy?"

"Yes."

"Ever lose anything after you had the policy?"

"Oh, a camera once, I think."

"How much was it carried for on the policy?"

"I don't remember for sure. About two hundred dollars. Why?"

"You reported the loss right away?"

"Yes."

"When did the insurance company pay you?"

"Why—about five months later."

"How much did they pay you?"

"They wanted to replace the camera with another used camera, but I decided I'd take the cash. I think they paid me ninety-five dollars."

"Not two hundred dollars?"

"Well, you see, it was a used camera. It had depreciated."

"But when you bought the policy you thought the camera was insured for two hundred dollars? It said in the policy that the camera was insured for two hundred dollars?"

"Yes."

"Your father was able to face you, though?"

"I don't understand."

"What business was your grandfather in?"

"Jim, what are you trying to prove?"

He held up his hand for an instant. "In a minute. Tell me."

"Well, he's been in the restaurant business for nearly fifty years. He owns the Huxley chain."

Bourne exploded with a guffaw, then subsided into a grin. "You mean the chain that bought all that meat during rationing without any ration stamps while tens of thousands of hospital cases and old people needed it?"

She dropped her eyes and flushed.

"He was still able to face his family and friends and customers after the newspapers had finished disgracing him, wasn't he, honey? But he was exactly like everyone else in this world. There is an area for business, and there is an area for friends. They cannot overlap. If they were to overlap it would be like putting

Saint Francis d'Assisi in charge of the Roman games; it just couldn't work. It would be too moral, too Christian for our times."

He pulled his chair close to her and took both her hands. "Good heavens, there are thousands and thousands of examples to show that business must be separated from the social, fraternal world. There is hardly a business in existence today which does not practice cheating and dishonesty. If we are to accept these degrees of dishonesty, then we must make allowances for honest criminality like yours and mine. There is absolutely no doubt about our dishonesty, no shadings or degrees, so there may be no possible doubt about our complete honesty, either."

He pulled her head to his, kissed her roughly and then held her head to his with his enormous hands.

"Business is a form of hunting. It's shooting for the pot in modern terms, isn't it? If one's dearest friends walk across one's hunting grounds they can get shot, can't they? Furthermore, for all we know, the duchess or Cayetano or Victoriano Muñoz may have been our hijacker. They are far more likely candidates than Señor López or Lawyer Chern. The duchess has perfectly good copies hanging now in her ancestral halls. She, before anyone else, could offer the originals for sale because she is the ultimate authenticator. Victoriano Muñoz is art-crazy and on Spanish art is paranoically insane. Cayetano, for all I know, might be a big-time thief for the thrill of it; he does everything else dangerously. But forget all that. You have been trained to view crime as immoral. I have been forced to the conclusion that almost all business is immoral, and certainly all religion. I lived with that for a long time, and then I moved over into crime and lived with that for a long time, and I say that there is no right and there is no wrong and that there is no shape, nor beginning nor ending. Where does the definition for stealing illegally end and the definition for stealing legally begin? I am you and you are me and what can we do for the salvation of each other? That is all that matters. Stealing canvas and paint and wood from the stone wall of one of the nine houses of the Duchess of Dos Cortes is not an unkindness nor a sin, but to turn my back on her, to run and hide because of that canvas and paint, or for you, my wife, to say that you cannot face her and accept her friendship would be an unkindness and therefore a sin, because of all the things men give and take from one another there is only one sin which is punishable, and that is unkindness."

"How long will we stay in Spain?"

"I have not decided."

"Must we stay on until you find out who stole the paintings from us?"

"Those paintings represent an enormous amount of money."

"Must you always think first and last about money?"

"It is you who always thinks about money!" He flared up, his face reddening.

"If the money represented by the paintings leads us on and on into other things, perhaps into violent things, will you allow that it is possible there exists one more sin: the sin of the love of money, my learned Cardinal?"

"Sarcasm is not necessary," he said sullenly.

"Answer the question."

"Which part of the question?"

"Both parts."

"I have already been led to do a violent thing."

"What?"

"It is a sin, yes."

"How many sins will make you safe or get you enough money, then?"

"Eve, listen to me. The lease on the hotel has just under ninety days to run. We will go to Spain and I will try to find the paintings, and if I don't find them by the time the lease has expired we will leave Spain. Or we will stay in Spain, as you elect, but I will have finished with those paintings. Is that acceptable?"

"I'll accept it because I have to."

"All right, then."

"Jim, why did you accept this 'new' sin as a sin so readily? You contradicted yourself."

He was puzzled. "What new sin?"

"This new sin of violence," she said.

"New sin?" He snorted. "Violence is only childish unkindness." He got to his feet. "Come on. Get dressed. This is our last night in Paris for God knows how long. Let's walk up to Fouquet's and watch the world go by."

· · ·

THE town house of the Duquesa de Dos Cortes overlooked
the park of El Retiro, where God sat on a bench under the shade
trees fashioning houseflies and dreaming his terrible dreams.
The duchess insisted upon giving a gala party in honor of the
marriage three days before of her friends, Mr. and Mrs. James
Wallace Bourne. Seventeen servants polished glasses, roasted
birds, shined silver, skated on rags over waxen floors, chilled wine,
dampened cigars, sang horrendous flamenco, and were happier
than they had been for years and years because the duque was
dead, dead, dead, and the soul of their darling duchess had
soared.

The duchess and Cayetano had two days off from the bulls
and were en route from Valencia to Jerez de la Frontera where
he would fight in two days' time. They had drifted on a cloud
from Medinaceli to Zaragoza to Barcelona to Valencia, and now,
six bulls later, they were at the top of their form, dedicating,
commemorating and entertaining their dear friends en route to
more love and art in the south.

The duchess didn't talk to many people any more, and many
people didn't talk to the duchess as a result of her revolutionary
activities on behalf of the king, her establishment of the cooperatives, her contempt for widowhood, her flaunting of a
bullfighter and a variety of other reasons. As a result, the guests
who were assembled were very pleasant company indeed.

Among those present were Jean Marie Calbert, the brilliant
new French painter who had been discovered in residence at
Bourne's hotel; Cayetano's protégé, a dashing, young novillero
named Victoriano Roger who was a lawyer but who was too
sensible to stay with that trade, Cayetano said; and the other
Victoriano, Dr. Muñoz, Marqués de Villalba, who arrived early
wearing a black tweed dinner jacket with satin lapels and a
peony in his buttonhole. He explained the flower, which he'd
had bred for boutonniere use, to the bride by telling her that
he absolutely adored color and that she could be sure that he
was not one of those who would place the weighty color of a
fleshy peony against a background of mohair or silk, which was
why his jacket was made of tweed. He told her severely that a
fitness in some things prepares the way for a fitness in all
things, and then asked her how long Bourne had been her lover
before they had married—if indeed they were truly married.
She told him expressionlessly that they were really brother and

sister, which caused Muñoz to suck air sharply between his clenched, mouselike teeth, then to compliment her on her sense of the decadent. She yawned widely, looked down at him and turned away to find Jim. His face got very red.

Because Monsieur Calbert had accepted, Representative and Mrs. Pickett had been invited, for new, important painters of any nation made the Congressman happy, and Mrs. Pickett was sure to enjoy the cold wine. Sir Kenneth Danvers, the famous British photomicrographer of the insect world, danced through the evening with Miss Doris Spriggs, a beautiful insect cataloguer, singing two or three hundred songs of all nations. At one o'clock in the morning a troupe of gypsies swept in with guitars and firecracker shoes and iron palms and a flamenco was started from which the night never recovered.

THE population of the party swelled and shrank and swelled again from fourteen to sixty-four people, leveling off at about nineteen, counting Mrs. Pickett who really should have been counted out. All of them had Dublin thirsts, the glazed intensity of Glaswegians on New Year's Eve and enough party spirit to strike terror to the heart of Tamerlane. The fact that four-fifths of the guests were Spanish helped this effect; they drew energy from the music, from the gypsies who were acting as though they had just awakened from seven months of hibernation, and from a tonic called *sangría* composed of red wine, champagne, cognac and a little lemon for the teeth.

Neither Bourne nor Eve could ever remember such a perfect party where everyone—after Dr. Muñoz had taken the Picketts home—seemed endowed with love and joy, and everything that had happened to all of them was so worth celebrating.

Before the flamenquistas arrived, Dr. Muñoz took Bourne aside and told him that he had been put off for the last time, that he understood that matters like marriages and journeys to Paris had precedence over the mere requests of one's old friends, but that he could not condone one more postponement of Bourne's visit to his new flat. Surely Bourne would bring Mrs. Bourne, as delightful and beautiful a young woman as he had ever met. Bourne would. And perhaps he would bring the stimulating French painter, Monsieur Calbert, for the Picketts might drop by. Bourne would. Very well then, he would expect them on Saturday, three days away, at seven o'clock. Dr. Muñoz had many new things which made him very proud of Spanish art, and he wanted Bourne's forthright opinion, no hemming and hawing, about each one of them because, as Bourne well knew, he valued his opinion very highly.

When Bourne broke the news of the engagement to Eve the following day she kicked a hatbox clear across the room in a vile temper. He told her that these were the things one had to do, that was all, and that if they ever got back to the States she could get even with him by the invitations from some of her friends.

The duchess approved of Eve exceedingly, and Eve approved of the duchess even more so. She was a smashing hit with everyone there, but the duchess was particularly pleased with her because she had spent the five days since receipt of Bourne's cable in dread. To the duchess Bourne had been the most discriminating of men, so it would have been some kind of justice if he had selected someone bovine and shrill to marry. The duchess ended the evening as she had started it, hugging Jim and hugging Eve, and she told them that because they were all together, she and Cayetano, Bourne and Eve, at the moment of greatest happiness for each of them, they would be friends for the rest of their days, sharing all that there was to share. Very seriously she took Eve's hand, put Jim's great hand on top of that, then Cayetano's, and then her own at the summit. She looked from face to face in the soft light of dawn, her eyes shining and running over with tears. When she took her own hand off the top of the pyramid she kissed in turn those of the three other members of the pact with the humility of a great lady.

Time never cheats the great. Time is living, and life is only time in motion, fast or slow. The duchess simply did not bother with the unimportant moves, so that when she chose to move she endowed that space in time with greatness. Eve felt exalted and cleansed, Bourne felt stronger and more tender, and Cayetano, who was the truest receptacle of all that the duchess would ever feel, felt that he had been loosed among angels.

.   .   .

THAT night Mr. Pickett wrote a letter to Arthur Turkus Danielson, the hard-hitting editor of *Art, Things and You,* the dominating art weekly in the United States and one which even Mr. Pickett had only cracked twice in a long life given to art, and then over an eight-year interval. He wrote very slowly; every word would count with Danielson, and nothing got by him. What a man, Mr. Pickett thought with a sideways wag of his head. He had discovered Blore in a junkshop, ten years after the painter's sad death, and had found immortality for him beginning with that day. He had come out fearlessly against the shockingly dark backgrounds utilized by Titian, and by so doing had driven down the values of all Titians throughout the world by over three per cent, and the losses had stayed in that cellar for almost six months. Mr. Pickett could not be sure how much Danielson knew about the painters of Spain, past and present, because Danielson was not a man who would talk to contributors face-to-face, but from the notes they had exchanged Mr. Pickett knew the editor's comprehension of the subject to be more than sound—in fact in several instances almost echoing two of Mr. Pickett's books on the Iberian world. "Dear Mr. Danielson," he wrote. "In a setting suggesting the Middle Ages I have made a discovery which is destined to thrill the world. It is one which I humbly offer to *Art, Things and You* for final evaluation and stentorian announcement. If that sentence seems vainglorious to you, Mr. Danielson, then what I am about to set down will shatter and stun. In a canvas to be called, I hope, from this day forward, The Pickett Troilus, I have discovered the presence of two great brushes and two great palettes. I will frustrate you no longer. One canvas, two immortal masters; one painting, two great painters. You are saying, 'Who are these painters? What is this painting?' I am sure, sir. Upon my twenty-seven years of authority in the field of Iberian art, as author of three books which teach the art of Spain in the schools, colleges, universities and ateliers of the Western world, I pledge to you that the superb Troilus, the property of the Duchess de Dos Cortes, was painted by Diego Rodríguez de Silva y Velázquez *and* Peter Paul Rubens!"

Mr. Pickett paused, chewing on the end of his pen, baffled and annoyed over whether it was Peter Paul or Paul Peter. "One moment, sir!" he wrote on. "Within this communication you will have found a stout brown envelope containing three photo-

graphic slides. Project these slides, Mr. Danielson, and when you
have seen with your own eyes what I have claimed, then return to this letter and read my documentation which will make
the art story of the year."

Mr. Pickett took a fresh piece of paper and, setting down the
words THE PICKETT TROILUS, began to write his monograph.
Mrs. Pickett called out from the bed, "How long are you going
to sit there with the light on, you fat son-of-a-bitch? Are you
writing to some sailor? Why the hell couldn't I have stayed at
that party if all you were going to do was come home and write
all night with the light on, for Christ's sake!"

"In a minute, darling girl. In a minute."

"In a minute, my ass!"

"Have a drink, sweetheart. I'll be right there."

"A drink of what, you silly bastard?"

"There's a pint of bourbon in the night table drawer."

"Oh. Thank you, dearest."

THE message left by Señor López with the key man at the
Hotel Autentico read: NADA. VUELVA USTED DENTRO DE DOS SEM-
ANAS LOPEZ, in heavy black crayon on the back of a sheet from a
German desk calendar of 1943. Señor López had nothing to report. But Tense had chosen the right man; López was thorough,
and he would be in touch with her again in two weeks. When
she returned in two weeks, Eve decided, she would leave a note
asking to meet López just to satisfy herself on what he had
done and so Jack Tense could say he had earned the fifty pounds
and because she had promised a written report to Jack so that
Mr. Merton would have more material to fill out the serializa-
tion. Before she had left him, Tense had agreed that if "Crime
Is My International Business" were ever sold to films Glynis
Johns would play her part. "You'd make three of Glynis Johns,"
he said with deep admiration, but he'd agreed.

It was a beautiful day, so she decided to walk home. Thinking about what a sweet old thing Jack Tense was, she stopped
off at SEPU, Madrid's equivalent of a five and ten cent store
on the Avenida de José Antonio, and for five pesetas bought a
picture of a stereotypically beautiful, middle-European film ac-

tress with leaden eyelids and a mouth like a broken doughnut.
At the General Post Office she autographed the portrait for
Tense, writing *For Jack, who gave me Spain, with the memory
of fire, Marianne Pickett*, then mailed it care of *The Populace*,
London.

BOURNE had been mistaken about Dr. Muñoz' new apartment being on Calle Fortuny. It was on the extension of Fortuny,
Calle Amador de los Ríos, directly opposite The Jockey, a formidable restaurant.

Looking shorter than usual and altogether less attractive to
all of them, Dr. Muñoz was bubbling with good spirits when
he met them at the door of the apartment which took up the
entire top floor. Waving the houseman away, he shooed the
three guests ahead of him to a very small, very comfortably
furnished bar with enormously broad windows overlooking the
Paseo de la Castellana and out toward Las Ventas.

En route from the main floor to the bar he kept starting and
stopping them to look at a piece of carving here or a small
painting there. Everything was in breathtaking good taste,
which, probably because of personal revulsion for the doctor,
they found surprising.

"For a man who is always crying poverty you live pretty well,
old boy," Bourne said, attempting heavily the kind of false
camaraderie he loathed.

"My dear boy," Muñoz said, "when I refer to poverty, naturally
I speak of relative poverty. After all, if Goya hadn't cost my
family almost everything there would have been very few people
richer than me in all of Europe. What will you have, Mrs.
Bourne?"

"Sherry, please." Eve had perched herself on a high bar stool
near the window. The two men leaned their elbows on the bar
between Eve and the doorway under the immediate scrutiny of
the cat Montes who faced them from a place among the bottles,
while the host stood behind the bar, a corkscrew in his hand.

"Sherry? Come, come, come, Mrs. Bourne. That won't do at
all. I have put in a huge stock of whiskeys for you. Rare bottles

like bourbon which only Congressman Pickett could possibly hope to get into Spain. Impossible to get. Very American. Won't you have a glass of bourbon?"

"Sherry, please." The doctor seemed shot down in mid-air. He swallowed hard, then addressed Jean Marie as he poured a small glass of sherry for Eve.

"M'sieu Calbert? Quinquina? Amer Picon? St. Raphael?"

"Byrrh, I think."

"Oh." He looked distressed. "I find I don't have any Byrrh. What a pity! And I was being so very French when I prepared all this for you." He looked with hate at Jean Marie, his face a little fist, his pencil-line mustache like the seam in a dark, clenched glove.

"I'll take a Dubonnet then," Jean Marie said pleasantly.

"A Dubonnet?"

"Dubonnet is very French," Jean Marie said.

"Of course it is. But I haven't put it in."

"Then give me water. Your Madrid water is marvelous."

"Thank you. But you are sure you won't have a Quinquina, Amer Picon, or St. Raphael?"

"No, thank you. Water will be fine." As Dr. Muñoz poured the water his hand shook slightly.

"Jim!" he said briskly. "What will you have?"

"Anything, Victoriano. Anything at all."

"No, no, Jim! Please! I insist! You must have what you want. Perhaps some vodka. The Jockey gets me Iron-Curtain vodka from Poland. Marvelous stuff. Or Drambuie. Oh, my yes. There's something *really* smooth."

"You should do television commercials, Dr. Muñoz," Eve said.

"Pardon?"

"I said you have a wonderful voice for television."

"Ah. Well! Thank you, my dear. Now then, Jim, what will it be?"

"Vodka, I think. I'll try vodka with a little ice." Dr. Muñoz had it in front of him in a jiffy. When Eve asked him what he was going to have he explained that he didn't drink or smoke, then flashed his puerile smile.

They settled down to awkward talk.

"I've read a great deal about your work, M'sieu Calbert. Wonderful things."

"Thank you, sir."

"I don't paint myself, but I do pride myself that I am something of a judge of painting. I hope you concur, Jim?"

"Indeed you are, Victoriano."

"Are you interested in art, Mrs. Bourne?"

"Avidly."

"By the way," Bourne said, "you mentioned some new pieces you'd picked up. We're looking forward keenly to seeing them."

"Muchly," Eve said.

"Later. I shall certainly be honored to show them to you later. A friend is stopping by for just a moment to pick up a book. He won't stay but a minute; then we shan't be interrupted."

"What are your new pieces, doctor?" Jean Marie asked sleepily.

"Paintings. Spanish paintings. I'm really so anxious for Jim to see them before I show them to Mr. Pickett."

"Mr. Pickett?"

"Mr. Pickett is *the* authority on Spanish art," Bourne told Jean Marie. "He was at the party the other night."

Jean Marie turned to Eve. "Am I thinking of the same man?"

"Probably."

The Frenchman shrugged.

"Are you enjoying Madrid, Mrs. Bourne?" Dr. Muñoz darted away with the conversational ball.

"Very much."

"Is it your first trip?"

"No. No, I was a newspaperwoman here, Dr. Muñoz. I learned Spanish here."

"Well! You speak Spanish!" He said to the others, "We really should speak Spanish, you know." Dr. Muñoz spoke perfect English with a marked British accent. "Do you speak Spanish, M'sieu Calbert?"

"After a fashion. My French is much better."

Dr. Muñoz looked at him strangely. "Naturally," he said, then, brightening, exclaimed, "Well, why not?"

"Why not what?" asked Jean Marie.

"Why not speak French?" He spoke to Eve. "Do you speak French, Mrs. Bourne?"

"As you wish, doctor. Any language at all."

He bit his lower lip and blood rushed into his face again. Saved by the doorbell, he excused himself in French and hurried out of the room.

"I just may slug this cat," Eve said.

"He certainly is awful," Jean Marie acknowledged. "My God, Jim, how long do we have to stay here?"

"We leave after we admire his new pictures," Bourne said, sounding a little angry. "And I do mean admire. Get with it, Eve, for Christ's sake. It's a job. You've had worse jobs."

"I'm sorry, darling. I will. I can't get started, but I will."

They heard Muñoz approaching with his guest; he very nearly pushed the man into the bar. The guest, who was the chief of customs at Barajas Airport, took one look at Eve and then smiled as if he had invented false teeth. "Señorita Quinn!" he cried, pronouncing it Keen. "What a wonderful surprise!"

Dr. Muñoz was covered with happy confusion. "You know each other? That is marvelous!" They were all speaking Spanish now—that is, those who could speak.

"When did you return?" the chief asked Eve, and Dr. Muñoz said as if it were a witty joke, "Señora Bourne, may I present Colonel Gómez, chief of customs at our Barajas Airport?"

Bourne looked suddenly at Eve. She nodded slightly.

"Señora Bourne! Well! That was sudden, wasn't it?"

Eve moved in hurriedly but very smoothly. "You must have been my good luck token, Colonel. He isn't Spanish, but he lives in Spain." She hastened to explain almost everything to her husband. "The colonel and I have sort of a secret, darling. But I *can* tell you that we were discussing marriage and its blessings exactly ten days ago, the day before I met you."

"Secrets, hey?" Bourne, as square as a box, managed to boom that out.

The colonel laughed with delight. "Nothing serious, I can assure you, sir. But charming. Very, very charming."

Dr. Muñoz crowded Jean Marie up to the colonel, holding him firmly by the elbow, with Jean Marie unobtrusively fighting to get free. "Colonel, this is M'sieu Jean Marie Calbert, a very promising French painter." Jean Marie glared at the doctor.

The two men shook hands while Dr. Muñoz hastened behind the bar to fetch Colonel Gómez a sherry. The colonel beamed on the newlyweds. "So you met in Paris nine days ago. Oh, I like that very much. What a successful ending to a tour of Europe."

"To a tour of Spain," Eve corrected him gently. Then, holding her glass high, she said, "To Spain," as the colonel received his glass from Dr. Muñoz. Everyone but the marqués drank, and he stood at flag attention and looked very silly.

"How did you two happen to meet?" Dr. Muñoz asked. "After all, my Colonel, you are very much of a bridegroom yourself." They all had a nice, false, hollow laugh over that.

"Señora Bourne came to Spain with a very good copy of a Velázquez which I was permitted to register."

"Really a good copy?" Muñoz asked. Jean Marie glared at him.

"I don't mind telling you," said the colonel, "that it was so good we not only checked this young lady's routing in Spain, but we made it a point to call the owner of the original before Señora Bourne was allowed to leave the country." Jean Marie beamed. Bourne sat up a little straighter. "A mere formality, I assure you, señora. I like to do my job well. No offense meant."

"I forgive you," said Eve, smiling charmingly. Her forehead was moist all along her hairline. Beads of sweat, like the sweat in the taxi on the way to the airport when she had last seen the colonel, began to form around her ears. She could not look down at her dress; she was afraid that it would be marked with those enormous circular splotches again.

"That good a copy of Velázquez? That's marvelous. Where did you get it, Mrs. Bourne?" Muñoz asked.

"In Paris," she managed to say.

"They have some excellent copyists in the Rue de Seine," Bourne said quickly.

"As a matter of fact," Eve said, "that's just where I got it."

"Will you be staying in Madrid, Señora Bourne?" the colonel asked.

"I live here now," she answered. "My husband is in business in Madrid."

"I've been here for over three years," Bourne said.

As they chatted about housing and the climate, Eve's fear gradually subsided, although she could not have said what she feared. Then the colonel bid everyone farewell, telling them how pleasant the surprise had been and pleading with Eve that they must all arrange to meet soon. Eve took his wife's telephone number, and the colonel asked permission to tell his wife the secret. Eve managed to blush and nod virginally. The colonel left.

"A very good man," Dr. Muñoz said. "Regular tiger about the law, though. Relentless and all that." He had returned to English.

Bourne insisted harshly that they be allowed to see the doctor's new acquisitions, for they had promised Nicky Storich that they would stop by for cocktails and they were already late.

"Very well," the marqués said. "Though I'll wager you won't want to run right along after you've seen these beauties."

They followed him out of the room. In the corridor Dr. Muñoz fumbled with keys, then unlocked some tall, exquisitely carved double doors bracketed by dim lights at the end of the windowless hall. "This is a very thrilling moment for me," he said. As the doors opened they could see the brilliant sunlight streaming into the room through the large windows, but Dr. Muñoz leaned into the room and snapped on a light switch. Then he stood back and permitted the others to precede him.

They moved forward, shuffling in boredom, then pulled up short perhaps four paces within the large, long room. There were three brilliantly illuminated paintings on the walls. They were the Zurbarán, the Velázquez and the El Greco from the Dos Cortes collection. Eve made a sound far back in her throat and slipped limply to the floor.

Dr. Muñoz uttered an exclamation and scurried from the room. Bourne sat on the floor and held Eve's head in his lap, rubbing her wrists as a woodman would start a fire with two sticks. Jean Marie stood open-mouthed and motionless, staring at the pictures. The only sound was the rapid metallic tapping of the marqués' little shoes on the tiled floor of the corridor. He hastened back into the room carrying a bowl of tiny ice cubes which looked small enough to have been frozen in a honeycomb.

Bourne thanked the doctor formally, scooped up a handful of ice and pressed it to the back of Eve's neck. Her eyelids moved, then opened. She was staring directly at Dr. Muñoz.

"Did you have the paintings taken from us?" she asked.

"Yes."

"Did you kill Señor Elek too?"

"I had to," Dr. Muñoz answered. "You've no idea what a little adventurer that man turned out to be. He tried to blackmail me. It was all too fantastic and preposterous. Would you like a cognac?"

"Yes, please."

Dr. Muñoz darted out of the room again and rushed down the hall like Carroll's White Rabbit. Eve said, "You've come to a murderer, at last, Jim." He looked down at her, but did not answer.

"What do we do now?" Jean Marie asked. "This man is so bland he almost makes me feel as though I should thank him for showing us his beautiful paintings."

Bourne signaled Jean Marie to help Eve to her feet. He sat her in a chair as though she were a rag doll, then walked to the window to stare sullenly out at the Plaza de Colón and the National Library. She looked at his back anxiously, then to Jean Marie, who shrugged, then to Bourne's back again.

Muñoz nipped into the room carrying at shoulder height a silver tray on the tips of his fingers, like a comedy waiter in a revue sketch. The tray held four balloon glasses, and in the other hand he carried a bottle of French cognac. He set his burden down on a low table ringed by comfortable chairs, and began to pour the cognac as he said, "Please sit down. Be comfortable. We have a great deal to talk about."

Jean Marie sat down first, took up a glass and held it in both hands, inhaling the fumes. Bourne did not turn away from the window; the back of his neck was turkey-red. Eve sat with great care, the way a fragile old lady would sit, and her face was startlingly pale. She stared past Muñoz at her husband's back, knowing that he was fighting to hold his temper and that he could not trust himself to speak.

The large room was furnished in the Moorish style, with a lot of reds, a lot of leather, and a lot of cushions. The three paintings were magnificently displayed at exactly the proper eye-level, each one flooded with a bright, frame-contained light from the ceiling. Jean Marie seemed to find it difficult to stop staring at them, and the doctor seemed to gain much pleasure from watching him stare.

"There are paintings one can build a room around," he said blandly, wiping the spittle from the left corner of his mouth, "and there are paintings one can build a house around. These, one builds one's life around."

Jean Marie made an involuntary sound, not unlike a snort of contempt, but did not answer. No one spoke, but Muñoz accepted their sullenness and made himself merry.

"And so we meet again, M'sieu Calbert?" the doctor said to Jean Marie.

Bourne spun around. "Again?"

"We undertook several art transactions in Paris during the German occupation," the marqués explained.

Jean Marie said immediately, "I never knew his name until today. Or that he was Spanish. Who asks questions like that? He hired me to copy. I copied. He paid." Bourne turned away again and stared out of the window.

"Dear friends," Muñoz orated," "please listen to me. If you believe that I have brought you here to crow over you, you are wrong. Please try to remember that whereas you have planned your robbery for a mere year or two, I have been planning mine for my entire life. Please forgive me for causing you such disappointment. I really mean that. I have asked you here because I need your help."

"My God, what a man!" Jean Marie said. "He does us out of all the French francs in Spain, then wants a little favor!"

Bourne turned again. He tried to talk, but his voice sounded strange and choked. He coughed and started again. His voice wasn't normal, but he had control of himself. "I want a letter to go to Traumer Frères now, instructing them to release my escrow funds."

"I will," Muñoz answered. "At once."

"Now! Now, goddammit!" Bourne shouted. "We've been cheated out of a profit on this thing so far, but I'll be goddammed if we'll operate at a loss!"

"As you wish," the doctor said. He rose and moved out of the room, rapidly but with dignity. "I will write it now and you may mail it. You are entirely right."

"Are you going to bargain with him, Jim?" Eve's voice was strident. "He's a murderer. Let him haggle things out with the police."

"He's also crazy," Jean Marie said.

"Shut up, both of you! We've been cheated out of a lot of money and nearly three years of work. I cannot and I will not be made a chump by this foolish man. And don't talk to me about murder! We can't bring Elek back, and there'll be time enough for that after we dispose of these paintings."

"You heard him say he killed Señor Elek!"

"Eve. Please. This is no time for hysterical arguments about morals. We'll hear what he has to say and we'll move when I decide we know what we're doing."

"Jim, we've come to a murder. By our direct actions we have made a murder possible. We don't want to be dragged in any further. I'm not hysterical and you know it. That's what sin is, Jim. If we go any further doors will close all around us and we'll never get out."

Dr. Muñoz came back into the room carrying a sheet of letter paper and an envelope. He crossed the room and handed the note to Jim. "Having a family argument?" he asked. "Does not Mama love Papa?"

Eve looked at him as though he were a swarm of locusts seen through glass. "We were discussing my suggestion that you be turned over to the police to be tried for murder, you creep," she said conversationally.

The marqués, in his turn, snorted in contempt. "Is that letter satisfactory?" he asked Bourne. Bourne nodded, folded it, inserted it into the envelope and sealed it.

"What do you want, Victoriano?" he asked.

"I feel that with all this bold talk about giving me to the police perhaps it would be best if first I tell you what I have and then what I want. It will put an entirely different complexion on things. You must know that I have a case against each of you. For M'sieu Calbert's sake, I want to point out that I have a case against his wife."

"One moment, my friend. My wife has nothing to do with any of this."

"And I have, of course, an open-and-shut case against your wife, Jaime. Colonel Gómez is a dedicated civil servant who has befriended your wife, only to be cruelly deceived by her. Beyond that, she has violated many points of the Spanish law, and I am certain that I could arrange to keep her here, in prison, for thirty or more years."

Eve's face was bloodless, but her voice was steady. "I don't think you can operate that cool. You think you have this on us, but we have a murder on you."

"No, you have not, Mrs. Bourne. I can prove; you cannot. And as far as M'sieu Calbert is concerned, well! There is no doubt there. He will be greatly admired by the court and the press for the quality of his work, but if I choose he will die in prison in Spain." He grinned at Bourne foolishly. "And as for you. Ho-ho! Do you know that I have infrared photographs of you in the very act of stealing these paintings from Dos Cortes?

You'll need two lives to give to the Spanish government."

"I suppose you've considered the rather distressing thought that if you turn us in," Bourne said, "you'll have to give up these paintings and that we will most certainly implicate you."

"Of course I've considered that."

"And?"

"Jaime, I am a grandee of Spain, *in* Spain. You are foreigners, and I contend that when your and your wife's passports and other papers are placed under the scrutiny of your Federal Bureau of Investigation—with whom our government works on a daily basis—they will prove to be spurious. Oh, there is an entire chain of circumstances which would render you helpless to involve me," he crowed.

He poured more cognac into Eve's and Jean Marie's and his own glasses. Bourne had not touched his.

"Don't you see?" Muñoz continued. "I am not trying to bluff you. Look here. I am ready to go much further to convince you. I see it this way: No one likes me, so anyone would believe very nearly anything about me if I were charged by an unimpeachable source." He held up his finger. "I said *unimpeachable*. Also, everyone knows the lengths I would pursue to possess a certain masterpiece of Spanish painting, because I am considered crazy on the subject of my family and the wrongs which were done them. Well, perhaps they are right. I care about masterpieces of Spanish painting because they are one of the ancient rights and possessions of my ancient family which I myself have the power to restore. Therefore, and here at last I am getting to the point, if you force me to turn you over to the police and to the state—and I do not want that—I will do so in a manner which will reveal myself as the leader of this band of thieves, so that we may be tried together and so that I may testify against all of us to insure maximum sentences for each of us, including your wife, M'sieu Calbert, when our absolutely certain conviction is secured. That is how serious I am."

By the time he had finished, Bourne's and Jean Marie's faces were glistening with sweat, and the Frenchman's hand trembled as he leaned forward for the bottle again. Eve sat erect, looking like a classical ivory carving. Muñoz fumbled with his wristwatch band, which seemed to be a bit tight.

"Victoriano," Bourne said, leaning forward as though he were selling insurance, "let's start at the beginning. I'd like to get everything as clear as possible."

"By all means, Jaime. You must."

Bourne spoke deliberately, with some effort, thinking of each word before he chose to speak it. "You wanted these paintings for what you considered overpowering reasons. You have known Jean Marie for some time. It is possible that he told you of my plans for Spain."

"Think it through, my friend," Jean Marie said. "This one doesn't have much money. Your way I could have made more money than any of us have ever seen."

"In any event, I haven't seen or communicated with the man since nineteen forty-three," Dr. Muñoz said.

"All right," Bourne acknowledged. "At any rate you found out what I wanted to do just about eighteen months ago, because that was when you began to seek me out after the weekly concerts at the Royal Palace to discuss art."

"Yes. At about the time you began to meet Madrid society."

"And to discuss art with you."

"I am still astonished at what you know and feel about our art."

"Yes," Bourne answered. "And more so now than ever. Once you knew we had started—and I assume that you knew this in detail from Lawyer Chern—it was simple to keep a watch on Jean's studio and to know the dates of the transfer of the copies and by which frontier. Because you knew which copies had been executed, you knew which originals would be stolen and where they were hung. Each time I took an original from Dos Cortes you were among the guests."

"That is all quite true, as you say it," Dr. Muñoz told him. "However, I was rather proud of the way I wangled the great Homer Quarles Pickett to Dos Cortes to give his solemn judgment on all three copies, never realizing that he would exceed himself to the point of finding a bit of Rubens in the Velázquez."

"That was really droll," Jean Marie said. "My God. That was really comical."

"Killing Señor Elek—now that was *really* droll, if you appreciate the droll," Eve said.

The marqués pretended not to have heard her, but he flushed

and after a pause decided he had to answer her. "I killed him because he gave me reason to kill him. He tried to blackmail me."

"You would have killed him anyway," she said harshly.

He stared at her. His face softened. "That is true," he said.

"I don't want to discuss that now," Bourne said loftily. "You have the paintings. The dream of your life hangs in a locked room. The affair is finished. There are no loose ends. There are only blank walls for those of us whom you have cheated, while the others do not even know that their property has been stolen. The risk has been run, the deed is done. You not only have your paintings, but you are safe."

"And all done rather cleverly, I thought."

"Indeed, cleverly. Brilliantly."

"It is good of you to say that."

"Not at all. Then, not because of vanity, but as a part of the plan from its beginning, you telephoned me to come here for tea not forty minutes after my wife had left for the airport thinking that she had the three paintings in the tube. Why? That is incomprehensible to me."

"Entirely. I have never been so baffled," Jean Marie said. "Did you really think you could not be killed and the paintings taken from you?"

"You hear, Jim?" Eve asked. "A theoretical murderer is here with us. We are making progress just as I said we would. Theory and practice. Interest is the trigger. Cause and effect."

"I cannot agree with you less, M'sieu Calbert," Dr. Muñoz interrupted enthusiastically. "You people are not suited for kill-ing. You are all thought, no passion. You would have contempt for a man who would kill for anything he could just as well steal if he put his mind to it. Am I not right, Jaime?"

"I haven't thought about it."

"I think you are wrong," Jean Marie said slowly. "There is a lot of money involved here. I think I could kill you if I had a plan. And I may get a plan."

"No, no," the marqués rejoined good-naturedly. "Your wife is implicated here. You don't know whether or not I have given some lawyer or some banker the entire story, with the evidence in a sealed envelope and all that sort of thing, to be opened in the event of my unnatural death, et cetera, et cetera. Further-more, you will never see these paintings again. They will come down when you leave today and where they go no one but I will know, and it is not something anyone could make me reveal. No, I am master here, and Mrs. Bourne knew it long before you men knew it. There is nothing you can do but study hard what I am about to instruct you."

"What do you want us to do?" Bourne asked Muñoz.

"There is one more painting I must have."

"Ah."

"I do this for my family. Please see that—it is not for myself. I am content to live here within a mile of the greatest Spanish painters in the world, but the injustice done to my family is another matter entirely. We go back beyond Pedro of Aragon. We are a very old and extremely important line which has been cruelly and unnecessarily humiliated."

"What is the other painting?"

"I must tell you in my way." He paused to insure against interruptions. "If it may be said that my family fell from their high place on any particular date, that day must be the second of May in eighteen hundred and eight. On the second of May, the Spanish people decided to resist the forces of the Napoleonic commander, Marshal Murat, and under him Colonel Grouchy and Captain LaGrange. We—my family that is—had decided to cast our lot with Napoleon and his brother, which we did only, I most solemnly assure you, to help Spain. You know what Godoy was. Ferdinand was as stupid as his father and as vicious as his mother. We were rich and powerful, and we needed no privileges Napoleon could give. What we did was a deeply patriotic thing. I have been over every single document throwing any light on the motivations of my family at that time, again and again, until my head swims. What we did we did to bring Spain into Europe." He was pleading with them for understanding and for retroactive approval. "We did what we did to make Spain a modern country, abreast or ahead in the march of new commerce, of new expansion, of new bases of world power, and if that meant accelerating our country's dying, it would have accelerated her living far more."

Bourne seemed to have encountered an enormous immovable fact, a huge, melon-shaped, rank-smelling, pulpy fact which he could neither climb over nor walk around, yet a fact so dismaying that he could not believe it as it towered before him, not merely overwhelming him, but threatening him.

"Do you mean . . ." he asked Muñoz slowly, "are you telling us that . . . is this painting which you say you must have . . . could that painting be Goya's 'Dos de Mayo,' which is now in the Museo de Pinturas del Prado?" Bourne had taken each word out of his disbelief as deliberately as a housewife unpacks a grocery bag.

"Mon dieu! Get the handcuffs!" Jean Marie moaned.

Dr. Muñoz acknowledged neither the dazed question nor the outburst. He went on. "The painter Goya was the key factor in my family's humiliation. He had become a police informer for Ferdinand, he continued as an informer for Joseph Bonaparte, and when the French left he became an informer for Arthur Wellesley."

"Arthur Wellesley?" Jean Marie asked blankly.

"The English general. Later the Duke of Wellington. Crashing bore."

"Oh, yes." Jean Marie stared at Eve and shrugged.

"When Ferdinand returned to the Spanish throne, Goya had used up all trust," Muñoz said. He had informed on all sides for all sides. The king moved to prosecute him. He bargained to save himself with a dossier he claimed to have assembled on my family. A deal was made. They let him leave the country, he went to die in Bordeaux and my family was stripped."

"Victoriano?"

"Yes, Jaime?"

"Are you going to tell me that you want Goya's 'The Second of May'?"

"Yes." Muñoz nodded. He was calm, reasonable, even judicious in his manner.

"The painting is in the Prado."

"I know that.

"It is eight feet high and eleven feet wide."

"I certainly know the painting. Surely you aren't going to give me a short talk on Goya's painting, are you?"

"It can't be done. That's what I am giving you a short talk on. It is impossible to do. Do you understand me? Victoriano, it cannot be done."

"Jaime, please! You haven't even thought about it."

"I don't have to think about it!"

Eve put her hand on her husband's forearm. "Jim, don't bargain. He's crazy and he's a murderer, and there's nothing he can do to us."

"What do you mean, Eve?" Jean Marie said quickly.

"We'll tie him up and be out of the country before he can find a traffic cop. And when his servants untie him he'll think twice about throwing away these paintings."

"She's right, Jim," Jean Marie said to Bourne. Bourne looked calmly at Muñoz for the answer.

"She's right as far as she goes, M'sieu Calbert," Dr. Muñoz said patiently, "but to give you a convincing demonstration of my sincerity, I'll tell you what I'll do. I'll have your wife arrested tonight by the French police, which I had intended to do all along if any of you attempted to leave the country."

"I tell you to leave my wife out of this, Muñoz. If a minute of my wife's life is disturbed I will make you very sorry."

"But sir!" Dr. Muñoz protested. "That will be too late! Your wife will already be in prison. I am in a position to arrange with some of my very important friends in our Ministry of Security here to ask the Sureté in Paris to detain Madame Calbert for questioning by Spanish experts in connection with the mysterious disappearance of certain great pieces of French art twelve years ago."

Jean Marie sat quietly, everyone watching him. He gulped his cognac, poured more, and then turned toward Bourne, staring only at his chest, and said, "Tell your wife to stop her talking. Is she trying to hound Lalu? We must do what he says and stop all this talking and talking. It is *my* wife who is threatened."

Everyone seemed to stand at once. Dr. Muñoz said, "You run along now. I know that you are tired and that you have a great deal of thinking to do. Please call upon me for any help I can possibly give, and let's have lunch very soon to talk things over." He shepherded them along the corridor. "Don't do anything foolish, I implore you. Spanish law is inordinately severe on charges like these. I did not exaggerate when I outlined my frank interest and intentions. Who wants to die, I ask you that? Particularly in a dungeon."

He slipped ahead of them and opened the front door. Filing out of the apartment silently, they did not wait for the lift to come, but descended the stairs and passed quickly from the doctor's view.

. . .

THE duchess was splendidly naked in a square, sunny room in a graceful building overlooking the sea on the outskirts of Jerez de la Frontera. She had a red rose in her blondined hair, her feet were propped up on the bedstead and she was laughing like an alto saxophone. She was the incarnation of the great tart of all the world: generous, lewd, safe, irresistible and unresisting. Cayetano sprawled across her and the bed, also as naked as money, talking rapidly and interrupting his own words with grins, flashes of teeth, and bolts and bursts of laughter. He shifted his position, north by northeast, bracketing her beautiful head with his elbows and staring deep down into her eyes. She stopped laughing but she still smiled, for carnal is as carnal does. It was a different smile and it shot electrical jolts to his thighs and up into his belly. Her eyes closed to slits until only a glitter came from them. She stared up at him, and silently dared him to do again what he thought he had not had the strength to do. Her hands moved under him. Her breasts, which had waited so long for all of this and more of this and more than this, for the over and over and over and over of the lifetime of this, pushed up at him. Her hips rubbed his hips. He stopped grinning. She stopped smiling. Her mouth, loosened from its moorings of propriety, fell open, lush, wet and suggestively soft. Her long legs sought him. She made a glorious sound.

THE next evening Jean Marie walked the short distance from the hotel to the General Post Office and called Lalu in Paris from a booth because his experience with telephone operators in hotels had convinced him that it would be madness to expect privacy in a conversation from one's own room. He spoke his especially soft, musical French into the phone and told Lalu that Bourne's friend had liked his work very much, and that he had offered such a huge sum for a portrait of himself that Jean Marie had decided to stay on in Madrid to paint it. No, he would not say how much over the telephone. He would be in Madrid for at least a month. The weather was beautiful. It was not Paris, but it was an enchanting city; even she would love it. He liked it himself. He wanted her to come to Madrid. Never mind the expense! Lalu, darling! Stop fretting about the expense! Little cabbage, the fee for this one portrait would be the largest he had ever made. Little mouse, the tour of the European dealers had been an enormous success, as he had written to her. *Sacré bleu!* He wanted her to have a change. *Alors!* Would she visit her aunt in Bayonne if she would not come to Madrid? Would she please stop this constant resistance about expense? He should not have telephoned? A letter would have said what he had wanted to say much better and be much, much cheaper? All right! That was enough! He was no longer suggesting, he was commanding. She would get out of Paris before tomorrow evening and she would visit her aunt in Bayonne until he told her to return to Paris. No, nothing more! He hung up feeling very proud of her; he had a wife who looked after his substance. No frivolous waster, his Lalu, like others such as Eve Bourne with her two new dresses since arriving in Madrid, when she already had a trunk full of perfectly good dresses. Lalu knew the value of money.

Jean Marie squared his shoulders and made his way out of the building, then crossed to sit upon the *ramblas* to drink a coffee and watch the lively crowds—not as lively as in Paris, but very lively—and the pretty girls—not as pretty as the girls in Paris, but very pretty. They floated past like noisy flowers, talking harshly and incessantly from their rifled Spanish throats, some with happiness like a newly struck match in their faces, others deep in the study of their own pride. The Spanish women walked their backs, shoulders, throats, chins and eyebrows as the people of other nations might walk their dogs or children through a soft, warm and gentling evening which shuffled and dealt a packet of endless hours toward the next day. Their incessant and harsh voices, the rudeness of the trolley bells, the shrill repetition of the word *lotería* over and over, like identical designs upon invisible wallpaper, the boasting horns of the valorous cars, the rake and rapping of the men's high, hard heels upon the pavement, and the endless, multiple octaves of talk, talk, talk upon his ears soothed Jean Marie, who was very much a city man.

In this mood of calm it was easier for Jean Marie to shift the responsibility for the new problem presented by Dr. Muñoz to Bourne. Jean Marie thought of himself as only a student of what could be seen and felt. Bourne was the thinker; Bourne was the man in the present who coped with the future. But it was irritating to think about Muñoz again. It spoiled the evening.

At length, an amount of time made possible by a lifetime experience with sidewalk cafés, Jean Marie finished the tiny cup of coffee and crossed the Paseo de Calvo Sotelo to walk slowly up the hill of Calle Alcalá. When he reached the hotel he found Bourne far back in the corner of the room marked "American Bar," sitting at a table and sipping a whiskey. Jean Marie sat down beside him, motioning the waiter away.

"You are figuring everything out?" he asked.

"I was thinking how much I hate to be handled like an amateur, not to say a chump. The risks are so heavy in this business that it is an absolute law that the price has to be right."

"Can the painting be stolen?"

"I think so. I must think more about it."

"You think now he will pay us to get the Goya for him?"

"He wants that Goya more than salvation. As you saw he is not less than insane on this subject. No matter how much he threatens I'm not going to do this piece of work for nothing." He worked on the whiskey for a moment. "We'll wait a few days, then talk with Victoriano some more. We're not being unreasonable, you know. Right is right, and he's got to be made to see that."

"See what?"

"We are entitled to an equity in this transaction! He thinks we can get the Goya—and maybe we can. I won't say yes, I won't say no, but I will say absolutely yes to the man who will put his name on the dotted line and guarantee a fair fee for our labor and for the risk we will run."

"Sign? He'll never sign. What are you talking about?"

"He wants the Goya so much that he won't go through with any threats if I tell him we can get it. He'll listen to reason. And if we do get him that Goya I want those three paintings back, free and clear. That's what we came to Spain to get and that's what we're going to get."

"I think he'll agree," Jean Marie said. "I feel it the way you feel it."

"Yes."

"And you know what else I think? I think after we get those three paintings back that he should be killed. I know you're against that kind of thing, and, of course, for that matter, so am I. But he's unpredictable because he's crazy. We don't want to have to try to go through life expecting that one to drop police on us from every rooftop. Seriously, Jim, I think he should be killed."

"Yes," Bourne said. "I do too."

THE next morning Eve was awake and out of bed when Bourne opened his eyes in the calamine blue room with white carpets and lemon-chrome curtains which stood as frivolous, tall sentinels on either side of an enormous opera-pink bed. Months before, awaiting Eve's arrival, Bourne had had the room redecorated down to matchboxes. Jean Marie had composed the colors and Bourne had designed the space and placed the furniture. The over-all effect reduced Eve to the size she had cherished since childhood, to the daintiest, most feminine, and helpless illusion of the sometimes useful, often useless interpretation of woman. To the chambermaid the bed seemed as big as a badminton court, but when their large frames lay there it seemed normal size. Bourne was as big as a mausoleum, and he had always maintained that on Olympus the cupids would have played handball against Eve's fine behind.

Eve sat at a severe dove-white table containing just as much blue as the breath of frost, writing with a ball-point pen which was one end of the world's longest, most vulgar, white, furry feather, a wedding present from two nuns to whom she had once loaned five thousand lira at an airport in Milan after they had discovered they had left their purses in Torino.

Bourne felt himself being pulled out of the deep well of delayed sleep by a rope of light and sound which seemed to be fastened tightly around his forehead. "Whatta you doing?" he asked thickly.

"Writing to Jack Tense."

"Wha'?"

"It's only fair that I call him off. And I have a note for Señor López."

"You're right." He forced himself awake by swinging his legs out of the bed and his torso upright. His face looked like a used dumpling; it was squashed and bloated and seamed in all the wrong places. It wasn't so much that he looked old; he looked sick. "I couldn't sleep," he said, as though apologizing for this new face which he had not yet seen.

"I know," she said, and went on writing.

"Whatta you mean, you know? You slept like a snake inna warm pail."

She didn't answer. Suddenly he decided not to brook her silence. "Answer me! I asked you a question. What the hell is the matter with you?"

She spun out of her chair and moved at him crying, "What the hell is the matter with *you*, you foolish, doomed man?" She came so fast, like a good, rough fighter from a neutral corner, that he flinched at the physical ferocity rather than the words which he had hardly heard. Her anger contrasted markedly with the way, in spite of her near hysteria, she could keep her voice down. He too maintained the low level of his own voice when he answered. Their tones had the empty politeness of people who died more slowly than other people by living their lives in hotels.

Her voice clawed at him. "Don't tell me you can't sleep! You will not *dare* to tell me you can't sleep, you grotesque son-of-a-bitch, because you know why you can't sleep and you've become too spineless to change it." The words were bitter and her voice had a pain that was worse than pain because it contained the realization that she could not respect the man she must love, and that of the two, respect was the greater need.

"What's the matter, baby? I don't understand," he said. But he understood. He knew that contempt had displaced regard and that only he could change it back again.

"Let's talk some more about you with your dowdy clichés like 'honest dishonesty' and your father, the immoral money-changer. Does your father work with murderers?"

"Now just a minute, Eve. I've spent nearly three years on this project and I have a ri—"

"You invested a lot of money too, didn't you?"

"You're goddam right I invested money. A helluva lot of money and I have a ri—"

"You fool. Balls to you, you square!" She turned her back on him and went back to the desk. She put her face in her hands. "You know, Jim, I don't know what to do. I can't stay here. I can't go. I thought I understood you. I really believed that the only way you could find some kind of dignity for your starving, resentful soul was by stealing. I—I believed that, and I thought you believed it. And I thought I understood you when you talked about no right and no wrong and the unlikely possibilities of relative morality and all that jargon. But it turns out that you're just a cheap merchant with his hand in the till. You're your father's son grubbing for money and keeping a double set of books, and you'd even bargain with a murderer for an edge."

He forgot his hotel whisper. "What the hell do you think this is, Gilbert and Sullivan? *The Pirates of Penzance?* Would you enjoy thirty years in prison?" he shouted.

"Don't shout. You know better. Then use your head. You're a smart man, Jim. You're one of the smartest men anyone ever knew. Use your head. Get Lalu to Switzerland or to Greece. One cable will do that. Hire a ship or a rowboat at Málaga and we'll be in Tangier. Then we'll join Lalu wherever she is, or Jean Marie will join her, and we'll go anywhere we want in the world. This man can't touch us outside Spain, and he's afraid to touch us inside Spain. If I can think of all that, do you mean to tell me that you didn't think of it?"

"Yeah. I thought of it."

"Then who is singing the *Pirates of Penzance?* Who crumbles under the fear of thirty years in a Spanish prison?"

"Ahhhh, for Christ's sake, Eve," he said. "I'm entitled to get those three paintings back. I worked and I have to get paid, one way or another. I don't blame you for feeling queasy. You're a woman. I'll never blame you if you want to get out, and I'll get you out. And you're right, he can't touch you once you get out. And now that we have everything right out in the open, I want you to go. I couldn't bear it if anything happened to you."

"What do you think is happening to me now, my darling? You look at me and tell me that I'm upset and that you cannot understand why I am upset. You understand! But you understand money more! You need money more than you need me, and that is what is happening to me." She slammed her hand down on the desk. "Muñoz killed Elek. He killed! He threw a knife into the throat of Señor Elek and he stopped his life with it. But you are not intimidated; you are fearless. You cannot be pulled down and stained by this; you are aloof. You want your merchandise returned to you, and what does it matter if there is a little blood on it?" She stared at him piteously. "Jim, Jim, Jim!"

She went to him and clutched his upper arms, holding her

body away from him, the top of her head pressed into his chest. She did not weep, but keened tonelessly over the death of her joy.

CAYETANO JIMINEZ sat, drinking beer and recalling paradise, in the citron sunlight on the terrace of the outdoor café opposite the great mosque-synagogue-church in Córdoba. He was talking earnestly with the man who had guided his career from the beginning, a rumpled, bald, sad man who had managed his late uncle, killed at Santander the year before Cayetano had started.

"A lifetime is enough to give any profession," Cayetano said gravely. "You cannot tell me I have not spent all my life with the bulls."

"No."

"Also, you have my two brothers. Curro looks very good. Better than I did at nineteen."

"Yes."

"I want to get married. It is my right."

"Yes."

"This is no business for married men, especially happily married men."

"No."

"I took my *alternativa* in Madrid during San Isidro eleven years ago, so it is appropriate to finish in Madrid during San Isidro. Give me your blessing."

"You have my blessing wherever you go," the sad, small man answered, "but you belong with the bulls."

BOURNE paid the cab driver, then walked unhurriedly from the pavement of the Paseo del Prado to the columned entrance of the Museo de Pinturas. He nodded to the guard at the door on entering and walked directly forward to the staircase, ascending to a point opposite the entrance to the Sala Velázquez one floor above.

As he moved slowly along he remembered the pleasant shock

which had engulfed him on the day when he had seen the Prado for the first time. It had been like the discovery of a new world. It was the perfect hall of paintings; perhaps it was not as inclusive as the National Gallery in London or the Louvre in Paris, but in its own distinctive way, as a gallery of superb paintings brought together by a group of collectors with individual taste, it had no equal in the world. It had begun in the eighteenth century as a museum of natural history, but Maria Isabella of Braganza, queen to Ferdinand VII, had turned it into a gallery for royal pictures. Gradually the great paintings of Spain had been added from the Royal Palace in Madrid, from the Escorial and the Casita del Principe, then from La Granja, Aranjuez, and in legacies from the great families.

Bourne entered the Sala Goya, octagon in shape, well-lit from the ceiling and smelling of furniture polish and floor wax. He stopped in front of "The Second of May," but did not look at it until he had checked the stop watch in his hand and noted the time in a column of figures representing other time trials over the same course. Then he stared up at the enormous canvas eight feet high by eleven feet wide, its six dead showing and hundreds to come, with its desperate action—knives into French Mamelukes, split Zouave over white horse's rump, baggy red pants and turbans fighting peasants who needed haircuts badly, only two men's and one horse's blood focusing the composition of the picture. He turned about and walked away from it the way he had come, nodding in passing at two guards.

At the curb of the Paseo del Prado he consulted his stop watch again, set down the time on a sheet of paper in his small, clear hand and then hailed a taxi.

THERE was no more light in the room than in a womb. Bourne was talking in his sleep. Eve sat up in the great bed and, groping, took Bourne by the shoulders in her powerful hands and shook him. "Jim! Stop it! Stop it!" She took a clump of his hair and wrenched it, then shook his head with it.

"Aaaah!" He bolted up. "Eve! My God! What is it?" She snapped on the light and he stared around the room. She slapped him with full force across the mouth and knocked his head back

into the candy-pink linen of the headboard. "What did you do
to Chern?" she demanded. "Tell me, Jim! What did you do to
Chern?"

"I–I–I—" He let the words fall back into his throat. His right
hand pushed at the dirty stubble on his face as if he needed to
grip his cheeks to keep his face from falling apart. His eyes were
not nice to look at.

She hit him again. *"What did you do to Chern?"*

She had hit him very hard. He seemed dazed.

"Talk to me! Tell me!" Her voice was brutally harsh.

"I locked him in the cellar at Boccador."

"You locked—"

"You remember we were talking in the Tuileries? We were
talking about what we should do to make Elek talk?"

"When did you lock him in?"

"I don't know. I can't . . . the day you went to London. Yes.
I can't get him out. Muñoz. They'll take Lalu."

"We've got to get him out."

"I can't think any more. Jean Marie is a painter and he isn't
supposed to think, but he thinks. I'm the planner, but you think
of everything. If I could sleep, I could think."

"He's been locked in for nine days."

"Nine days."

"What are you going to do?"

"I can't figure. I'm in a fog. I can't figure it."

"We've got to get him out."

"I know. But I can't get him out. I can't call some casual
friend, I can't call the police. Lalu is absolutely no good for this."

"Why can't you call the police?"

"He has plenty of water. Nine days isn't much, only he didn't
do anything and he shouldn't be in there."

"We've got to get him out." She hit him on the thigh with
her balled fist with all her strength. He grunted sharply, and
then to increase his own sense of pain and her anxiety he said,
"He was terribly frightened when I put him in there. Something
happened to him in the war. Rats and the dark. I never saw a
man so scared as Chern. I got him down there and he—" Watching his wife's face, he could not allow himself to finish the
sentence.

"Call the Paris police," she snapped.

"Now just a minute, Eve—"

"Are you looking for murder? If you keep looking you'll find it."

"The police will trace the call. An international call is the easiest thing for them."

"Ah, Jim. You'll tell them that you're the managing director of this hotel. You'll say that you've just opened a letter which could not have been left by accident on your desk in your office at this hotel and which tells of a man being locked in the cellar at 97 Rue du Boccador in Apartment 3 for nine days without food. They'll ask you your name and you'll tell them your name and anything else they want to know except what you have to conceal."

"They'll have us by the throat with the apartment. My God, Eve, we live there."

"The apartment is in my name—my old true name. That girl has disappeared and no one living can find her, including herself."

"Do you think Chern is going to dust off his clothes, thank the police for their kindness and refuse to divulge how he happened to be shut up there? The Paris police know their business. They'll lean on him until he'll be happy to tell them how he got there."

"Like you, Chern lives for money."

"Eve, for Crissake—"

"Shut up. Chern won't tell them the time of day or press any charge or admit they found him there until he presses you to find out how much money you have for him to make up for the inconvenience."

"Eve, please don't say things like—"

"Don't touch me, you money-simple merchant. Call the French police!"

Bourne didn't move. Then, breathing heavily, he leaned across the huge bed and took up the telephone.

Teresita, the night operator, answered. He told her to call the Palais de Justice in Paris, office of the chief of detectives. The recurring lack of sleep, his wife's savage grief, the hollowness he felt inside himself and the indulgence of searching across a continent for an instrument of contrition all must have dulled him because he forgot the lesson contained in his betrayal by his trusted employee, Señor Elek. Teresita told him that she would call him as soon as she got the connection. He hung up to wait, to sit on the side of the bed, his back to Eve, his bearlike hulk hunched over in despair.

Teresita immediately dialed 34-78-92. Dr. Muñoz answered on the first ring and Teresita explained what Señor Bourne had told her to do. Dr. Muñoz thanked her sincerely for the service she had done and told her that when she awoke the following evening to go to work a handsome reward would be in her mother's hands. She suggested that if he preferred to leave the reward in her mother's hands would he please seal it in an envelope, or if it was all the same to him would he leave the envelope with the waiter, Jorge, at the Café Werba on the Calle de Bravo Murillo. He agreed with pleasure and she thanked him. Dr. Muñoz then suggested that she call him again in ten minutes, then ring her employer as though she had the Paris call ready and connect him with Señor Bourne. He reminded her to be sure to show the long-distance call in her log; in fact, later perhaps she should call Paris so that the charges would appear on the hotel's bill.

Teresita dutifully waited ten minutes, then called Dr. Muñoz, then rang Señor Bourne.

Bourne spoke into the phone in his belly voice, a timbre employed throughout the world by public relations experts and confidence men. " 'Allo?"

"I have your Paris call, Señor Bourne."

"Thank you."

" 'Allo?" Dr. Muñoz came on, using a high-pitched voice. "Le palais de justice ici."

" 'Allo?" Bourne answered. "Je veux vous faire savoir un crime, s'il vous plaît."

"Un moment, m'sieu," Dr. Muñoz replied. He put his hand over the telephone mouthpiece and sat very quietly in his over-stuffed chair wearing his cloth mustache cultivator. Montes tried to walk across the taut telephone wire but he fell, grabbing at the wire with his forepaws and swinging like a trapezist for a moment, then dropping to the floor. Muñoz counted to fifteen, lifted the telephone to his face, reconsidered, counted to forty-five, and then spoke into the mouthpiece in a deeper voice.

Bourne, with his good citizen's voice, dutifully reported the case to Detective Sergeant Orcel. Dr. Muñoz took down his full name and address with grave grunts, for authenticity's sake employing a real pencil, real paper, and real writing. He thanked Bourne. Bourne thanked him. He told Bourne, "Je serai sans doute forcé de vous déranger encore, mais alors peut-être pas," and hung up. Bourne hung up, greatly relieved. After a little while he slept for the first time in many nights. His wife held a small towel to her face as she lay on her side on the edge of the bed weeping silently. She was not going to allow Bourne to find a pillow stained with her tears.

EARLY the following afternoon, upon Dr. Muñoz' long, dark-wood Moorish table, Bourne unrolled the large sheets of architectural paper containing his precise diagrams of the Sala Goya, the Goya floor at the Prado, and the street floor leading to the Paseo. His jacket was off, his sleeves were rolled up and a pencil was stuck behind his ear. He seemed too large to be a grocery clerk and too immaculate to be a shipping-room boy; he most resembled an advertising-agency account executive ready to make his pitch. Dr. Muñoz helped the illusion with his air of stifled eagerness, resembling a prospective client whose packaged twenty-five-cent cancer inducer was about to be forced upon a nation. Montes, a taffy sculpture, sat erect and listened with the expression of a junior executive who will go far. Bourne sat on the corner of the table, swinging one leg boyishly and informally and facing Muñoz, friendly and relaxed. The marqués gave him his complete attention, pince-nez glittering.

"I've given your whole proposition a good deal of thought, Victoriano," Bourne said judiciously, "and I personally think it makes one helluva lot of sense to talk about the fee structure before we get down to the brass tacks of talking about the job." He spoke English because he felt much more solid and square in that language.

"The fee?" Muñoz was baffled. "The fee is your freedom."

"I know that you know that we have the necessary know-how, Victoriano," Bourne said. "And I tell you this flatly. We will not undertake the project without payment. I mean that."

Muñoz shrugged. "I could never pay your prices, Jaime. I'm not a poor man, but I'm not in your class either."

"That remains to be seen. And I'd like to point out that no matter how you look at it the risks on this kind of thing are very great."

"If you are saying that you might decide not to do this job because the fee isn't right, believe me, my friend, the alternatives are one bloody awful lot greater," the marqués said earnestly. "Prison must be a godawful thing for men of our age."

"Do you honestly believe we should undertake these risks after three years of time and money and danger without any fee whatsoever?"

"I haven't expressed myself either way."

"Do you think you are giving us incentive to solve this problem by refusing to discuss a fair fee?"

"Refuse? We are discussing it!"

"All right. Name the fee."

"I'm not a storekeeper. Tell me your fee!"

"I want the three Dos Cortes paintings. That's my fee."

The marqués shrugged. "Do you think you can get the Goya?"

"If certain peripheral problems are met. And in comparison with my central problem, these peripheral problems are nothing."

"Let me hear your plan to get the Goya. Then I will answer you regarding the fee."

"That wouldn't be good business. The plan is everything. Almost anyone could take the Goya if they had this plan."

Dr. Muñoz smiled his hopelessly banal smile. "I don't think so," he answered.

"Hombre, if I'm caught nobody will ever see me again. It would be safer trying to seal the British crown jewels."

"I should hope so."

"Well?"

"All right. I will pay you the three paintings if you get me the Goya." Muñoz pulled a chair away from the wall, carried it to the center of the room and sat down facing Bourne. "What is your plan?"

Again Bourne became as confidential and businesslike as an insurance salesman. "First we will need a permit from the Director of the Museo de Pinturas so that Jean Marie will be allowed to copy in the Prado."

Muñoz made a note with a gold pencil the size of a carpenter's nail on a small leather-bound pad. "Nothing difficult there," he said. "So you are going to have him copy 'The Second of May' in the Sala Goya and then switch paintings."

"No. He will copy 'The Second of May' at the hotel. It cannot be done at the Prado because no one is permitted to copy in actual size."

"But I don't understand. What do you want the permit for!"

"We will come to that. Get the permit in the name of Charles Smadja. He is a widely known copyist of the masters who is now on his annual fishing vacation off St. Raphael, Jean Marie tells me. The Prado people can check the name with the Louvre if they choose."

Muñoz wrote the name down, pausing to verify the spelling. "I was aware that copyists worked in the Prado all the time, but I did not know that they needed a license," he said.

"Be sure to point out that M'sieu Smadja has been commissioned by very dear friends of yours in Paris to copy three Spanish masterpieces."

"Three?" The marqués' eyebrows shot up. "Three? Mother of God, Jaime, do you propose to pick up two for yourself?"

Bourne laughed as though he were really enjoying himself for a moment, but it didn't last long. "No, nothing like that. But we must provide Jean Marie with time and the excuse to talk to the guards so that they will become quite accustomed to him sitting there day after day in the Sala Goya. He will paint a triptych; three paintings on one canvas in the manner of a *trompe l'oeil*, portraying in miniature 'The Second of May' exactly as it hangs against its background in the museum, flanked on the left by the 'Milkmaid of Bordeaux' and on the right by the Greek's self-portrait. One of those interior-decorator ideas."

"As I remember, the 'Milkmaid of Bordeaux' is on the right of our big canvas."

"No. To the left. It is as though your family were looking out of the big one. To *their* left."

"Ah, yes."

"The important thing is that the canvas on which Jean Marie will paint his clever triptych will be very nearly the size of the canvas holding 'The Second of May' "

"I'm not sure I follow. Why not exactly the same size?"

"For this reason. Jean Marie's master copy of our Goya will fit exactly inside the mother frame, which will be the triptych.

It will be virtually impossible to detect the second canvas packed inside the first unless one knows where to look. When we take the real Goya down from the wall and put the copy up, the real Goya will be housed, tightly locked, behind the *trompe l'oeil* which shields it in the mother frame."

"Oh, I say. That *is* amusing. Oh, I like that!"

"I should think so. It solves nearly everything."

"You said nearly everything?"

"As quickly as possible, tonight if you can get it from your friends at the Prado or from the Instituto de Cultura Hispánica, we must have the best color transparency in their files of 'The Second of May.' Try to get the largest size, which should be about ten inches by eight inches, Jean Marie tells me."

"I'll have it at your hotel tonight if it exists."

"If it doesn't exist you must arrange to have it photographed. But it will exist. It will be in the files." Bourne continued, noting the marqués' excitement, "Jean Marie works fast. He painted that Velázquez"—he gestured to The Pickett Troilus hanging on the Muñoz wall—"in four days. We'll use the rest of this week on our Goya. He's looking forward to it. He's spent the last two days at the Prado, and he's straining at the leash to start work."

"You wouldn't rather have him work with a photographically sensitive canvas?" the marqués asked cautiously.

"I would not. This isn't a coloring contest. It takes great art."

"It was only a suggestion. Please proceed. I am extremely pleased with what you have told me so far."

Bourne propped his charts against a makeshift pile of books on the table and assumed a lecturer's manner. "Follow me closely, if you will. Every morning, beginning next Monday morning, provided you have secured his permit—"

"He shall have his permit," Dr. Muñoz interrupted.

"—Jean Marie will enter the Prado through the gate on Calle Ruiz de Alarcón, trundling this huge canvas on which the *trompe l'oeil* will gradually be taking shape, upon a little double platform supported and propelled by roller skates. He will nod to the guards with whom he will make it a point to become more friendly each day. Occasionally he will do a portrait sketch of each of them in pencil as he takes cigarette breaks with them, away from the public halls. His copy of 'The Second of May' will be locked inside the outer, mother frame holding the canvas on which he paints, so that if a guard should help him to push the trundle cart he will be familiar with the exact weight."

Bourne adopted the unctuous self-confidence of a medicine-show pitchman as he traced Jean Marie's course in and out of the Prado day after day. "He will trundle in each morning behind his permit and trundle out each night for two full weeks, right up to the Feria of San Isidro when we will take the Goya for you."

"Ah, San Isidro. Much diversion. Very good, Jaime. Very good."

"Well, not quite, but I'm happy to see that you're right with it."

"What do you mean?"

"In a minute. We'll stay with the sequence for the moment. I propose that we take the Goya on the first Tuesday of San Isidro, which will be May 12th this year, at some time between four and five in the afternoon—after the bull fight has started and still close enough to closing time at the Prado so that Jean Marie can wheel the original Goya out in the mother frame before any remote, almost impossible off-chance that the copy will be discovered and the alarm raised."

"Of course. Any day you choose. Naturally!"

"And so comes my third and most important request, one which you have actually, in a way, anticipated."

"I did? What was that?"

"You must provide us with an extraordinary diversion. You must cause something to happen which will stand the entire city on its head for not less than twelve minutes and eighteen seconds."

Dr. Muñoz' interest was rapt. "What kind of a diversion?" he asked.

"Something completely grotesque. Something shocking. Something which will spread like wildfire across the city."

"But why do you need it? If you tell me why you need it, then I will understand it better."

"If you give me the kind of a diversion I must have, the news will reach the guards at the Prado as soon as it reaches the cafés, the vaults of the banks, the hospitals or the ear of Generalissimo Franco, because this is an excitable and very talkative city of gregarious, interdependent people. If it is the right diversion, the guards who hear it first will call all the other guards because everyone gets pleasure out of spreading such news, until little knots of Prado guards will be totally engaged— shocked, voluble, gesticulating, behaving like hysterical chickens for as long as it is possible to fully engage the attention of adult human beings. I need eleven minutes and eighteen seconds, and will gratefully accept the gift of sixty seconds leeway."

Dr. Muñoz rose from his chair in excitement and interest. He scooped up the yolk-colored Montes, cradled him to his bosom, releasing chorded purrs, and almost ran over to Bourne saying earnestly, "But what kind of a diversion? You have thought about this. You must have something vaguely appropriate in mind."

"Only vaguely appropriate. I leave this to you because really a Spaniard must design this thing. He must know to the last nuance what will explode like a shell in the midst of Madrileños. When it hits you you will know that this is exactly the right diversion for the job. You feel what I mean?"

"Yes. Oh, yes. Definitely. But perhaps you can give me an example. Perhaps one suggestion."

"Oh, something like turning a fire hose on a bishop while he is saying high mass—"

"*Madre de Dios!*"

"—or shooting a bull with a machine gun during a corrida. Something, as I said, grotesque or repellent, but definitely something completely shocking."

"Ah. Ah, yes. Of course. I see now. Hmm. Let me think about it. Put it entirely out of your mind. I will deliver to you a splendid diversion. Oh, yes, I'm sure of it now that I understand it."

"It is the most important single part of the plan. The rest is plain arithmetic. We begin our time and motion studies tomorrow morning. We'll go through the drill of taking one painting down and putting the other one up over and over again, so many times that it will ultimately become pure reflex." Bourne assumed again the huckster's flashing eye, his roguish smile, his braying voice and incipiently untrustworthy expression. "The rest is semi-automatic. Let's say that the diversion is timed for twenty-six minutes past four on that Tuesday afternoon. Jean Marie will be in the Sala Goya finishing the copying of the *trompe l'oeil*. I will stroll into the museum through the

Paseo entrance at five minutes past four. I will walk leisurely to the Sala Goya, arriving in front of 'The Second of May' at sixteen minutes after four o'clock. I ignore Jean Marie. He ignores me. At four thirty-one or four thirty-two, no later, I should hear the shout which means that your diversion has taken place and has spread across the city. If there is anyone in the gallery with me at that time I will shout the news at them, pointing away from the Sala Goya. Jean Marie will repeat this in another language, also pointing off. They will certainly leave. Then I will remove the Goya, with Jean Marie's help, and hang the copy. The original will snap into place behind the *trompe l'oeil* under the mother frame. I will saunter off to the other side of the Sala Goya. Jean Marie will continue his copying of the triptych. I will make my way out of the main exit at four fifty-two. At three minutes before five the guard will come to announce closing time to Jean Marie and to tell him the shocking news of your diversion. Jean Marie will trundle the huge mother canvas concealing the Goya out of the Sala Goya and past the guards who wave good night, just as he has been doing every day for three weeks. To tell the truth, Victoriano, the world may never discover that 'The Second of May' has been stolen."

"Then what do you do with the Goya?" Dr. Muñoz asked politely.

"I exchange it for the three paintings from Dos Cortes."

"Ah. Yes, I see," replied the marqués.

JEAN MARIE completed the copy of "The Second of May" in eight and a half days. Viewing it, Dr. Muñoz wept at its sweep, beauty and utter authenticity.

BOURNE had conducted two drills a day for nineteen days with Jean Marie. They began at seven thirty in the morning, after which they would breakfast. Then Jean Marie would stroll off with his cart to the Prado to begin his long day's work, which was dazzling the guards with its wizardry.

Now they were engaged in drill number thirty-nine. They worked in the salon of a large apartment on the top floor of the hotel. The furniture had been pushed to one side and covered with bed sheets. A large frame containing a blank canvas had been hung on a wall of the room, at the same height from the floor as Goya's "Dos de Mayo" in the Museo de Pinturas del Prado.

Jean Marie sat in a canvas-back chair in front of a large empty frame. He had lost nearly fifteen pounds and he was haggard and sick-looking. His hands in his lap, he stared disconsolately at Bourne, who stood gazing at the empty canvas hanging in the frame on the wall, talking in a low, even voice. Clearly he was calculating something else entirely.

"Jean Marie," he said distinctly but with preoccupation, "please continue to have confidence in me and in what I have to say to you. You can forget your nerves. What you think you are going through is the same condition encountered by film stars when they undertake to become stage actors. I mean it. They make themselves sick imagining what will happen when they make their first entrance from the wings and have to face that sea of faces. As the time grows shorter, as the rehearsals continue, just as our rehearsals are now continuing, their panic grows like a mushroom in a damp, dark cellar." Bourne's voice had taken on a cadence. It was soothing, insistent, and different from any other voice he ever used. "But they always do make their entrance on opening night, and, once they are on, they don't have time to be nervous because the director has given them so many things to do with their hands and bodies that they have neither the time nor the mental capacity to be nervous. The same goes for you." He walked to Jean Marie and put a hand on his shoulder. "Move over," he said.

"Move over?"

"Get out of the way. I want to start you counting this morning. I'll show you."

Jean Marie moved aside and Bourne sat down. "This is all you have to do," he said reassuringly, his voice massaging the Frenchman. "I nod to you. You stand up." Bourne stood up. "You move to your position at the far corner of the Goya frame. One, two, three, four, five, six, seven, eight." Bourne paced to the position, counting each of his steps as he went. He stood motionless at the far corner of the frame, looking serenely across the room at Jean Marie. He motioned to him to take that place. Jean Marie moved in and stood where Bourne was standing. Bourne moved to the directly opposite corner of the painting.

"Now, I will make my first moves. I take my bolt cutter. I snap the lower holding pins. One, two." He snipped at imaginary bolts. "I take out the folding stepladder. I set it against the wall. I climb the ladder. One, two and three. I snap the top holding pin. One. I step down the ladder. One, two and three."

Bourne looked over at Jean Marie expectantly. "Now we reverse positions. You walk across close to the frame. I walk outside of you. All right. Count as you go." Starting on Jean Marie's first count, they had changed places and were in position at the count of six. Jean Marie held firmly to his side of the frame as though supporting it, and Bourne repeated the identical moves he had made on the other side: bolt cutter, stepladder and counting. But this time he supported the canvas with his shoulder as he made the last snip, having cut from top to bottom on this side. "All right, the painting is free. We move it, walking backward, counting together. One, two, three, four, five, six, seven, eight." They had reached the empty mother frame with its imaginary painting. "In she goes," Bourne said, and each slid his end in, moving crab fashion, pushing it into place for the length of the frame, shoving air, rehearsing and pretending.

"Now all we have to do is to hang your copy in the place of the original and the job is done. Nothing to it. All you have to do is to be able to count to twenty-seven. There is absolutely nothing else you have to do but be able to count to twenty-seven. I merely have to be able to count to forty-six. It's that simple."

"I know," Jean Marie replied wearily. "It is simple. You have made it wonderfully simple. But I am an artist, not a thief. I am a highly imaginative man and I get nervous when I think about it and I can't stop thinking about it. I want to vomit when I think about it too long, and I live in fear that I will start to vomit while we are in the middle of the job. And I can't sleep. The more I don't sleep the more nervous I get. I was not born to be a thief. It is that simple."

"Perfectly natural. After all, I'm not a nerveless man, Jean Marie. In my own way I am a highly imaginative man too."

"I realize that, Jim. Please—there is no doubt about that."

"And I know as well as anyone that the part we call living is the internal life we have, the life of reflexive feeling, the poet's side of us, the ground on which all of our wars are fought." His voice stroked Jean Marie. "Because I understand this I seek to bring order to the external life, the less important part of life, because it is not life but rather the time-motion plasma which supports the internal life, where we truly live, as a river supports a cork as it bobs and moves along the endless stream from birth to death."

"Mmmm," Jean Marie hummed. "I can feel what we see and what you say."

Bourne made his voice a shade more monotonous and a beat slower. "Feel what I am saying to you. Absorb it into your innermost mind. When we finish the next drill, the second counting drill, number forty, you will go to your room and you will lie down and rest. While you rest you will think about what I have been saying and you will see the truth in it. You will see the strength you have been given to do this thing. By counting to twenty-seven, by reducing the entire action to twenty-seven simple movements you will have found complete external order. With the external in order, the internal life cannot be confused or troubled. Your imagination cannot carry you away and weaken you with insomnia and nausea. Twenty-seven simple moves outside your mind and body. Twenty-seven. Only twenty-seven. Feel it as we do it again. We will go through the real drill this time. We will actually take the frame down, move it into the mother frame, and hang your copy on the wall. Then it will all be over. Make yourself ready. Think only of the count. You are exhausted, but you will be refreshed if you think only of the count. Only twenty-seven numbers. We start now. When I nod to you we start." He nodded.

Jean Marie rose from the canvas chair and began his cross to the corner of the painting. "One, two, three, four, five, six, seven, eight." He was in position.

Bourne inserted the bolt cutter behind the frame and began his own first pattern. "One, two." The metallic clicks were sharp and clear as the cutter went through. Bourne removed the collapsible ladder from under his coat. "One, two and three," he said, his face serene, his manner relaxed and unhurried.

Jean Marie stared at him, impatient to begin his count again.

. . .

EACH pair had so looked forward to seeing the other again that their cars each slid into the parking slots in the Plaza de la República Argentina in front of the Commodore restaurant at exactly the appointed hour, two forty-five. This put them into an even more euphoric mood, though the manic state, while totally unexpected for the Bournes, was habitual with the duchess and Cayetano.

The ladies ascended in the tiny elevator, operated by a small boy with bright red hair, freckles and a scarlet suit with shining brass buttons, and the men climbed the short flight of stairs. They all sat at a large round table beside a wide-open window overlooking the courtyard, and ordered martinis con vodka as though it were part of a special ritual. The air shimmered. The duchess spoke Catalan with Señor Torte, the keeper of the keys, and three long-aproned waiters stood by warily lest ice cubes show signs of melting.

Cayetano observed that it seemed a sad thing that in a world so filled with facile lyricists no one had ever written a song to the first martini con vodka. Eve told him that she had once sung a dirge following the fifth martini con vodka.

"No dirges," the duchess admonished, "as I am thinking in terms of two hundred violins and estragon sauce, and because I have an announcement to make." She lifted her drink and told them that she and Cayetano would be married in Madrid on the concluding Saturday of the Feria of San Isidro, however banal that might sound. There was a storm of handshaking, kissing, backslapping and martini gulping, and an orthodox number of tears were contributed by Mrs. Bourne into a small handkerchief she always carried with her for just such occasions.

Bourne sent one waiter off for another round of martinis and another for a magnum of iced champagne. Eve wanted to know *where* they were to be married in Madrid, as if that mattered. She asked the question with that sense of desperate urgency that women can get about such things, and the duchess relieved her tension by stating that they would be married in her late husband's home on Alcalá and Lagasca because it would please the servants so. She told them that except for themselves she had decided to invite no one below the rank of bishop. Cayetano said that he had decided to invite no one below the rank of picadores over fifty because though none of the picadores would be likely to get any more religion, it would be a marvelous social opportunity for the bishops.

The actual ceremony would be at some church, the duchess supposed, so as not to shock the servants who, excepting the Bournes and Cayetano, would be the only real friends she would have left when the news was announced. But certainly the reception would be at her late husband's house, and she would ransack all of her houses for every known portrait of the late duque to be nailed on the walls of the reception room to increase everyone's sense of fun.

"I feel so good," the duchess said, "that I wish I could hire an entire regiment of Scottish bagpipers just to walk through this restaurant once, playing something awful. You look very thin to me, Jaime."

"That may be," Bourne answered, "but whatever you've been doing, you've never looked so wonderful." Then he heard what he said and started to blush.

"Stop that kind of talk, Jaime," the duchess said, "it embarrasses Cayetano."

"I haven't got the strength left to be embarrassed, and I'm only a boy," Cayetano told him.

"Just for that you get no more marzipan," said the duchess, finishing the drink before her. "Now that we're back here I can't tell you what a marvelous feeling it is to get away from Madrid —if only because one doesn't run into Picketts."

"One doesn't say one runs into a picket," Eve corrected, leaning forward so that the waiter could set down the second round of martinis. "One says one runs into a fence."

"Eve just made a joke in English, darling," the duchess told Cayetano.

"Have you seen the Picketts?" Bourne asked. "I thought he'd be back in Washington by now."

"Have we seen the Picketts?" Cayetano rolled his eyes. "To be perfectly frank, only one. The large one."

"You mustn't tease about him, Cayetano. He is so desperately earnest, the poor man," the duchess explained to all of them. "He is obsessed with his discovery of this . . . this Rubens trace in the Velázquez. It is all very sweet, really. He came to see me to ask whether I would have any objections to allowing the press to refer to the painting as 'The Pickett Troilus.' I don't know what he would do if anything ever happened to that painting.

He apologized for having hired a firm of propagandists in the United States and another one in London. Whatever for? I asked him. He told me this was the biggest single event of his life, that he must establish the authenticity of his theory everywhere, and that it would make him the great Spanish art authority in the world if it were handled with discretion and tact."

As the duchess spoke Eve held her martini con vodka in mid-air, then returned it to the table, careful not to take her eyes off the duchess. Bourne sat very still, but gave no other sign that the duchess's words had reached him.

The duchess continued. "Some American picture magazine is flying photographers here from Lausanne—or anyway one photographer—and Mr. Pickett pleads with me to simply throw open Dos Cortes to him. And while he was with me someone from the Duque de Luna's office at Turismo called and made the identical request for some German photographer who represents a magazine in Munich, and I decided then and there to tell them both that if they would take their pictures all at once, or at least all in one day, I would permit it. So I suppose the press of the world will shortly be publishing pictures of Mr. Pickett, Señor Velázquez and Herr Rubens shaking hands at the net. In the meantime, it's all for the great cause, so cheers for art and the Picketts and culture generally, and will one of you darling men please make discreet inquiries as to what the hell happened to that champagne?"

At that instant Señor Torte appeared, driving a magnum before him, and in no time at all thoughts of drinking brassy stuff like martinis con vodka were lost in memory. Señor Torte enquired at exactly the right moment whether they would like to order food, and Cayetano requested that he prepare whatever he chose for them in the style of S'Agaro, the meeting place of the great and near great on the Costa Brava. That was what he had been instructed to say, he told the duchess.

"Who instructed you, lamb?" the duchess asked.

"Jaime Arias."

"Oh, well. Then yes."

"Who's Jaime Arias?" asked Eve, looking slightly buzzed.

"He's a newspaperman from Barcelona who collects teacups which helps him to believe that he's an epicure, poor man."

"What kind of teacups?"

"The kind with printing on them. Ones which say 'Hotel

Dinkler-Plaza'—he actually has one which says that, you know —and 'The Negresco' in Nice. We had a few printed for him at Christmas last year because he's a darling man. They say 'The Kremlin, Moscow,' in red. They've become his most cherished pieces, though of course he keeps them out of sight."

Cayetano said, "This is a week of miracles, really. I ask everyone here. Who is the most improbable Spaniard you can think of who would announce that he was going to attend a bullfight?"

The duchess did not hesitate for an instant. "My cousin, el doctor, Victoriano Muñoz, el Marqués de Villalba." She drawled the name sounding precisely like Victoriano, and they all laughed uproariously.

"Your cousin?" Bourne blurted.

"Oh, now come, Jaime! He's not that bad. He just hates bull-fights and practically everything else that attractive people like."

"I couldn't tell you why I am so surprised," Bourne told her.

"Everyone is related to everyone, really, if you subscribe to that new Adam and Eve theory."

"It is a very decadent thing for the corrida, that Victoriano has decided to attend it," Cayetano said.

"Perhaps he is setting a precedent," Eve said.

"A precedent?" cried the duchess. "It is as though Winston Churchill took out Italian citizenship!" She turned to Cayetano, incredulous. "Did I hear you say that Muñoz was going to a corrida?"

"You grasp the general idea," Cayetano told her patting her hand, then kissing it. "He called me this morning and asked if I would kill in front of Tendido Two next week on my first bull because they were the only seats he could get. He has promised to take Mrs. Pickett and he is hoping that she won't last more than one bull, but he wants to make sure of that by making it as awful as possible, with the kill right under her nose, so that she will faint or get sick and they can leave immediately."

"He's certainly a clear thinker, my cousin. Who else do you know who could think his way out of a social trap like that?"

"There is no guarantee that Mrs. Pickett will faint, you know," Bourne said stoutly.

"Oh, she'll faint," Cayetano said confidently. "To help him out I might just botch things with the first sword."

"I feel buzzed," Eve said.

"It is the martinis and the champagne," the duchess said. "One is not to worry, my sweet."

"That is what I have decided," Eve replied. "Please cause the glasses to be filled again because we have not yet run out of announcements."

The duchess stared at her with joy. Her chin dropped and her eyes popped in woman's telepathy. "No!"

"No, what?" Bourne asked.

"Please cause the glasses to be filled," the duchess said, but Señor Torte had already signaled the waiters.

Eve lifted her glass. "I hope you will consider that I am engraving these words for you as I go along. Mr. and Mrs. James Bourne take great pleasure in inviting you to the christening of their first child in approximately five months, an announcement which it was possible to withhold until now because the child's mother is a tall woman who so far has carried it so well that it shows not more than a pocket watch would show in the evening clothes of Mr. Fred Astaire."

Bourne goggled at her. "What?" he exclaimed.

The duchess filled in smoothly. "You must call him Cayetano. We, in turn, to show our appreciation, will call our first-born Herbert Hoover Jiminez."

"Eve . . . My golly . . . Well, what wonderful news!" Bourne looked as if he had just finished a performance as the Sorcerer's Apprentice.

"Jaime!" Cayetano protested. "Enough of the little father faces! We have not yet drunk a toast!" He lifted his glass. "To the dear child of the dear Bournes," he said, and drank it down. The glasses were refilled.

"To the sweet, sweet baby's sweet, sweet mother!" cried the duchess, drinking it down. The glasses were refilled.

"To the wedding of my friends and the birthday of my child," Bourne boomed and drank it down. The glasses were refilled.

"To The Pickett Troilus and the swooning of Mrs. Pickett!" intoned Eve and drank it down. The glasses were refilled.

"To all of us, each and every one of us, may we love and live forever!" sang the duchess and drank it down. Something in the style of S'Agaro was served and the luncheon got under way.

. . .

TUESDAY was a lovely spring day. Bourne and Eve were sipping coffee in the living room of their apartment with the terrace doors swung wide, Eve fully dressed, Bourne in pajamas and robe, when there was a knock on their door. Bourne scurried into the bedroom and Eve answered the knock. Jean Marie came in.

"My God," she said, "you look terrible."

"I feel terrible. Believe me, chérie, I feel one hundred per cent lousy all the way through. It is something I didn't eat, no doubt. Big joke. Something I couldn't keep on my stomach. Do you mind if I try once again with your coffee? I will do my best not to vomit on your cushions. Coffee works sometimes. If I could get my hands and teeth on a good brioche I might survive at this time of day. Or a good anything at any time of day—Sweet Jesus, but the Spaniards are terrible cooks. Everyone is mystified why Americans continue to come to Paris when the prices are so high. I'll tell you why Americans keep coming to Paris. Eat some of this fantastically overcooked, underflavored Spanish food and you'll know why. Look at this weather. The Spaniards are very strong on beautiful weather. If Americans stayed in France for more than one week they'd see some of the lousiest weather ever manufactured, but Spanish weather is superb. One would think it didn't all come from the same place, there is such a difference. Well, today is the last day of this madness. The last day. The goddam, bloody very last day. I could not have gone on for one more day. I swear to God and Jesus and the Virgin that I could not have gone on. God alone knows whether I will be able to survive today. I don't think I have the strength in my hand to hold the brush to pretend to finish that bloody *trompe l'oeil*. Imagine me being forced to take three entire weeks to finish three lousy Goyas. I could have illuminated a Gutenberg Bible, hand-painted some neckties for the Pope and knocked off four large Breughels in the extra time. Of course Jim was right. Because I've been mopping and daubing for so long the guards are like my uncles now. That big one on the relief hitch must eat garlic rubbed with garlic. You cannot conceive of how that man smells. That's one more little pressure on me, the smell of garlic. Everything is crumbling under this pressure. My bowels, my joints, my sleep—everything, thank God, except my painting. I will never make a thief. That's the reason that the world is as honest as it is; the wear and tear of a life of crime is simply too excessive. I'll tell you one thing: if we can get that goddam *trompe l'oeil* out of the country I'm going to hang the goddam thing in my dining room. Jim said I could have it. Not that I need a souvenir—I'll never forget this goddam job, and that is for bloody, horrible goddam sure."

Bourne emerged from the bedroom, fully dressed. "Hi, kid. Where's Eve?"

"Eve?" He spun around comically, but there was no sign of her. The door to the corridor opened at that instant and Eve entered with a covered plate. "I went down myself instead of calling room service," she said. "Now you sit right down here and eat it."

"Eat what? I can't eat anything. I can't hold anything on my stomach."

"Two nice fresh brioches. And I happen to have some marvelous confiture—the same brand exactly that Lalu always has for you. And fresh butter. Come along now."

BOURNE's face was pinched with anxiety as he read the note from Dr. Muñoz on the heavy scented paper. He had not been able to reach Muñoz, or any of his servants for the past four days. The note, which had just arrived, had been delivered by hand to the concierge. It said that Muñoz had completed all arrangements for a magnificent diversion which would happen between four twenty and four twenty-nine and three-quarters, give or take a few seconds, and was written in a manner that suggested that the marqués was enjoying a joke against Bourne's precise timetable. The message assured Bourne that the diversion would do more than set Madrid on its head, and that it was the only possible choice of all possible diversions because it could not fail. It said that the doctor had decided not to reveal what the diversion would be, that surprises were the spice and all that, and it sincerely hoped that Bourne was in the best of health and spirits, and it closed with the assurance that Dr. Muñoz would be with him in spirit throughout the day.

Bourne picked up the telephone beside him and dialed Muñoz'

number impatiently once more. The phone rang and rang, but no one answered. Bourne slammed the phone into its cradle and looked up at the clock. It was three twenty-five, time to leave. He opened the top drawer of the desk, took out a small, green, glass vial, shook out two white pills upon the green desk blotter, recapped the vial and poured a half glass of water from the vacuum bottle on the telephone table. At a sound from the door, he looked up and found Eve standing there.

She closed the door behind her and stared him down. "How come the pills for the easiest job you've ever done?" she asked.

He swallowed the pills with some water. "Time to go," he said. He stood beside her, but she wouldn't look at him. He pinned her arms to her sides and kissed her. She didn't respond.

"I'll be back here at five ten," he said. "Please don't worry." He slid past her, opened the door and was gone.

She walked to his desk and sat down. The ticking of the clock sounded very loud. She sat and stared at the green desk pad. At four o'clock she opened the top drawer of Bourne's desk, took out the green, glass vial and swallowed two of the pills without any water.

In the Sala Goya, Jean Marie tried to give the impression of working steadily. He had come back from lunch at three thirty, but of course he had not been able to eat. The meal had started well enough; he had journeyed across the city to Calle Ternera because the restaurant called El Callejon was one of the few which cooked food even halfway appealing to him, but within ten minutes the nausea had returned and at last he had been forced to hasten deplorably to the facilities, where he had retched until his stomach felt scraped.

Back in the Sala Goya he daubed and wiped, but mostly stared at the great "Dos de Mayo." Sweet Christ, the size of it! He could not think of anything but its size and what it must weigh until he began to convince himself that his own expert eye detected a miscalculation in Bourne's design of the mother frame. Sweet Jesus, how could a monster like that bloody Goya ever fit into this mignon of a frame he was swatting away at? They would be tugging and pushing at the monster without a chance of ever jamming it into the goddam mother frame. Mother frame! Sweet Son of Mary, if a mother ever carried a child this size she'd split open right down the middle. What would they do? They would be tugging and pushing and the guards would walk right into the room and find them. He felt a humiliating flash of embarrassment as he imagined the expressions on the faces of his friends the guards when they discovered that he had betrayed their trust; he actually had to close his eyes when he thought of the scene. He forced himself to think less embarrassing thoughts. Was he ever to see Lalu again? He thought of the silent peace in the galleries of the Louvre and the Musée Delacroix and the twenty or so other galleries of Paris in which he had copied pictures. There was so much repose in that life, so much assurance. It was like living a life in a chair sled moving down a gentle slope of virgin snow, well bundled up, coasting toward a small cottage alight with warmth and Lalu. Tiny Lalu, sweet Lalu.

At that moment a guard almost caused Jean Marie's death by appearing out of nowhere and touching his shoulder. He thought he heard himself scream until he heard the guard apologize for jolting him while he was lost in a reverie of art. It is my fault, Jean Marie thought, I should have smelled the son-of-a-bitch. Sweet God, they've rubbed garlic into his hair today. The guard was anxious about Jean Marie because he was perspiring so; he must be running a body fever. The guard urged him to go home and purge himself, but Jean Marie explained that it was merely a mild stomach upset, that it would pass, and that at the moment he was so immersed in thinking through a most difficult problem that he could not possibly go home. This sent the guard away, awed and respectful.

THE white Mercedes moved along Lagasca slowly, the duchess seated quite alone in it. She turned right on Padilla, drove along until Silvela, then crossed into the Avenida de los Toreros, made the long curve above the Plaza de Toros, then came down to its level to the corner of the smaller parking lot directly opposite the gateway to the Patio de Caballos. A small, one-armed Civil War veteran with a patent-leather visor on his cap had held the space for her by sitting on it.

She had taken the only relatively clear route in the city. The feria was under way, the streets swarmed with traffic and police. The duchess gave the custodian of her private parking space five pesetas. As she walked away a fourteen-year-old gypsy girl carrying a four-month-old baby and dragging a three-year-old child, neither of them wearing shoes, came up out of the ground chanting the song which was the gypsies' vocation, if not profession, on fiesta days. The duchess was ready with a *duro* in her glove which she surrendered willingly.

As she walked on two small boys offered to sell her a brightly colored souvenir program which, they explained gravely as they walked beside her, also contained the history of the entire corrida. She thanked them solemnly but refused the opportunity. Three ticket scalpers, one after another, offered her excellent seats in *sombra,* in *sol* and in *sol y sombra.*

The excited crowds were everywhere, and the sunlight was so thick that the scene appeared as though through a bathysphere sunk in *goldwasser.* The noise was a splendid Spanish noise, a gay noise which packed the authority of *afición* and the preening self-esteem of many people jammed together who could afford to secure seats for the corrida during the Feria de San Isidro.

As she walked briskly toward the main entrance, gradually slowed by the thickening crowd, the duchess could see the four mounted police sitting like sleepy monuments caught in a flood. Great-busted, matronly women standing over capacious baskets offered single cigarettes for sale, single pieces of candy, single pieces of chewing gum. Impassive, gnarled men guarded stone jugs which had the nozzle velocity of water pistols and cried out with great joy that they were willing to sell a drink to absolutely anyone for fifty centavos. At the front entrance, the great gateway, the carteles for the day were emblazoned on either side of the arch. She was moving slowly now, part of the peanut-butter-thick crowd, and she read them as she moved forward. Printed in red, yellow, blue, brown and white, they carried a huge reproduction of a painting of Cayetano in a pase de pecho and proclaimed:

PLAZA DE TOROS   LAS VENTAS   MADRID
Grandiosos acontecimientos taurinos
para el Feria de San Isidro
el Martes 15 de Mayo de 1956

Las maximas
combinaciónes
Gran Corrida de Toros
Con superior permiso y si el tiempo
no lo impide se picarán, banderillearán
y seran muertos a estoque

6 Hermosos Toros 6
de la acreditada ganadería de Don Salvador Guardíola
Espadas

CAYETANO JIMINEZ

CÉSAR GIRÓN

GREGORIO SÁNCHEZ

The duchess saw Victoriano Muñoz five layers ahead of her in the crowd. She called out to him, but the noise swept the sound away and she couldn't get his attention. She craned her neck with no success to try to catch a glimpse of Mrs. Pickett, and when she looked again Victoriano had disappeared into the holiday bustle of arms, legs and faces, olive oil-crusted voices, dwarfs and children and beautiful women—the world's richest and the world's poorest pressed against photographers from Göteborg, distillers from Glasgow, secretaries from Winsted, Connecticut, and Arabs from the Riff. The duchess was swept along into Tendido Eight, where three ushers rushed to seat her, causing a bottleneck on the stairs in the chute leading to the stands. She was settled with many murmurs of *"mi duquesa"* in a barrera seat behind the matador's burladero.

BOURNE entered the Paseo del Prado entrance of the museum wondering how he could make his hands stay dry. His mind ticked off each movement and place which kept him abreast of his schedule. He had the look of a businessman about to go into a meeting in which he holds most of the power and knows how to maneuver the rest. He wasn't nervous, but his hands wouldn't stay dry, which was annoying. He wasn't aware that his jaws were chomped together, grinding his teeth into a vise and forming lumps at the corners of his face, nor that his sphincter muscles had tightened like a fist, nor that his throat was dry enough to strike a store match, nor that his back had a military-academy rigidity. He wiped his hands with a handkerchief for the third time in five minutes. His breathing was shallow as he entered the Sala Goya. An Arab in a burnoose and two in western clothes were standing in front of "The Second of May," silent and studious. Bourne moved to Jean Marie's extreme right to stand at the side of "The Maja Clothed" so that Jean Marie would notice him, which he did with a terrifying start.

THE brilliant sun divided the bull ring into halves, impartially but decisively. On the stroke of four o'clock the bugle sounded the notes summoning the two aguacils into the arena, riding schooled horses and dressed in the manner of sixteenth-century Spain. They galloped across the ring to doff their hats to the president, pretending to catch in their hats the keys to the toriles that traditionally were supposed to be thrown from the too-distant president's box. Then they reined away in opposite directions, one riding clockwise around the ring, the other counterclockwise to meet at the portal where the toreros had formed.

The aguacils led the paseo forward, the three matadors following behind them in a line abreast, with their cuadrillas filing after them. As senior matador, Cayetano marched on the extreme left. César Girón, cockier than any marcher who has ever strutted, was on the extreme right, his right elbow cocked almost as high as his shoulder as he advanced in his own distinctive style. Sánchez, heavily handsome, dedicatedly sullen and solid, marched in the middle.

Cayetano wore a suit of burnished silver, the masses of it crusted and heavy, over lavender silk, and he may even have looked as blithe, as brave and as beautiful as the duchess thought he looked. He would fight the first bull which Don Salvador would send out. Behind the three bravos came forty-two banderilleros, puntilleros, picadores, monosabios and mulillas, and as they completed the full cross each line acknowledged the presence of the president. Then the matadors moved left to their burladero, where Cayetano winked at the duchess but did not move into the callejon to speak to her because he had the first bull. His *mozo de espada* spread his cape before her just as he turned away. His peons took their positions behind the two other burladeros, the bugle sounded, the toril gate swung clear and the bull came crashing into the ring.

For the same reason that the carteles for this fight had to be reprinted eleven times within the next month to meet the tourist demand, no one can say whether it was a good fight, an indifferent fight, a dull fight, or a triumph of honor and skill. Naturally, the newspapers said it was the greatest single *lidia* that Jiminez had ever fought, and the people who were there said it was even greater, until eventually it became tauromaquia beyond the capabilities of any man who ever lived or will live. Still, what they said was the only possible judgment.

After the banderillas had been placed, Cayetano walked to the place in the ring beneath the president's box and, with his montera in his right hand, made the formal request to kill the bull. Then he strutted in that slow, self-assured way of his for twenty-five yards to stand directly in front of the duchess. He *brindised* to her with great solemnity, dedicating with the words "Va por ti," then breaking into his dazzling, boyish smile and looking deep into her eyes in that way which left her weak and stirred. He wheeled, tossed his montera over his shoulder into the stands for the duchess, then signaled to his peons to bring the bull from the far corner of *sol y sombra* to the section of the ring directly in front of Tendido Two, far to the left of the duchess, for the faena. While he waited, Cayetano caught Dr. Muñoz' eye and winked. The marqués grinned happily and winked back.

The magnificent Guardíola bull was an *asarajado*, meaning that his skin was as tawny as a lion's. It was an extremely brave bull which charged straight each time the lure called him. It followed the capotes of the peons obediently across the ring and was placed for the twists of Cayetano's muleta economically and well.

Afterwards the faena was a blur of movement and sound and pain; then it became blank, as though there was no room for it in any of the twenty-one thousand memories which had witnessed it. As Cayetano started his faena with a *derechazo*, which is a natural pass extremely moving in its simplicity, Dr. Muñoz left his seat in *contra barrera* and walked to the stairway immediately behind him, which led to the chute and thence to the street. Mrs. Pickett did not seem to be with him. Cayetano, passing the fine bull at the very peak of his art, took the waves of clear, separate "*Olés!*" which washed over his linked passes with blithe pleasure, grinning with sheer joy through the complete and absolute silence which the twenty-one thousand people presented to him between their thunder. Everyone was on the edge of his seat; the *guardias* at the steps at the mouth of the roofed chute were standing far forward, intent on the man and the bull. The *guardias* did not see Dr. Muñoz as he passed them, nor did they observe him as he stood on the deserted steps, the long knife in his hand at his side, looking out at Cayetano from behind them.

Cayetano squared the bull, profiled, then went in to kill, crossing his muleta and hitting the huge bull exactly true between the shoulder blades. As he was framed between the horns, Dr. Muñoz threw his knife. It rolled lazily through the air, end over end, traveling only fifteen yards to hit Cayetano directly between the shoulders. He sagged over the bull as the bull sagged under him, blood leaving both of them in gobbets.

They died together.

At four thirty-six Bourne left the Sala Goya and walked along the corridor. He was half the distance to the nearest guard on duty when he heard a great shout. As he stopped, he saw the guard stare straight ahead of him, saw him strain to listen, then saw him bolt and run out of sight. Bourne wheeled and proceeded rapidly into the Sala Goya, shouting in English and pointing over his shoulder. Jean Marie leaped to his feet and began to shout in French, pointing in the same direction. The three Arabs stared at them blankly, startled in a fixed frieze which broke as they ran out of the room in the opposite direction from which Bourne had pointed.

Neither man spoke. They walked to the mother frame, slipped the framed copy out of its hiding place and dragged it to the wall before the "Milkmaid of Bordeaux." There they propped it up, facing the wall. Jean Marie went stolidly to his corner of "The Second of May," counting under his breath as he moved. Bourne was waiting at his corner. He made the first three snips with his bolt cutter. He set up the stepladder. He climbed the three steps, unhurriedly. He made two snips. He stepped down daintily. He picked up the ladder and moved in the outside lane to Jean Marie's corner, while Jean Marie, counting as he went, moved to his. Bourne completed his work on the far side of the painting, moving exactly as he had moved through forty-nine drills and through the precise plans in his mind which he had sketched and studied on graphed paper.

THE crowd rioted at the bull ring as soon as it realized that what had happened before their eyes had really happened. Two children and one woman were trampled to death; twenty-six persons were injured, nine seriously. Two men, seated sixty yards apart in separate sections of the plaza, were identified as having thrown the knife but were miraculously saved from the mob by courageous police. Thousands of people looked up at the sky, seeking God, and wept. Hundreds in every section of the stands sat huddled and numb, staring at the spot on the sand where he had been murdered, tears streaming down their faces. They stayed there, thousands of them, long after darkness came. The Patio de Caballos overflowed with more thousands standing in silence outside the chapel where he would be laid. The streets were choked with mobs. Houses, cafés, stores and cars had emptied. People moved through the streets all during the night. Nine thousand of them set up a vigil outside the main police headquarters, and hundreds of others waited outside every neighborhood police station. Madrid had been canted; her people cascaded mindlessly down its arteries in a mass, agonized hopelessness of rage and loss.

Dr. Muñoz had told the strict truth in writing Bourne that it would be an extraordinarily successful diversion.

BOURNE and Jean Marie each held the great painting by a corner and by its side as they staggered backward with it to the mother frame. Just as they reached it, two elderly American tourists, a man and a woman, walked slowly past in the corridor outside the entrance to the room and stared directly at Jean Marie, registering absolutely nothing, not even seeing what was in front of them because they were looking for religious paintings by Bartolomé Esteban Murillo, and passed on.

But Jean Marie only knew that they stared at his guilt, had seen him while he stole, had documented his fear and had realized his nightmares. He did not slow his movement, he did not say anything, he merely dropped his corner of the painting and ran. He ran without thought, without hope of escape. He ran and left Bourne and the Goya and the mother frame and the *trompe l'oeil* and the huge identical copy which had so pleased Dr. Muñoz.

Bourne watched him go, but did not cry out after him because he was engulfed with despair. It was as if a chained man sat at the edge of a ferryboat while the wind blew all his life savings out of a hat at his feet and he could see the money, the green, paper money, float down the river toward the sea. But his mind reacted, the motor part of it, as it had been trained to; his instantaneous reflex was the fruit of the discipline he had subjected himself to over so many years. With his height and great strength, he managed to lift the bottom edge of the Goya into the mother frame, but it slipped and crashed to the floor. He lifted again, straining in agony, and placed it more solidly this time. He pushed one corner home, then slowly traversed the length of it, securing it to the mother frame; this time it held. He tapped it methodically all around its periphery to make sure that it was secure, then picked up his smart, dark blue homburg hat from the floor and strolled leisurely out of the room, using the exit opposite the one through which Jean Marie had fled, wiping his hands on his handkerchief as he went. En route to the gate on the Paseo, he paused, exactly on schedule, with some Swedish tourists to appreciate El Greco.

Bourne reached the door of his hotel room at ten minutes after five o'clock. There Eve told him that Cayetano had been murdered.

BY ten minutes after five the police and other security officers had sealed off the Sala Goya and its approaches from the rest of the Prado. The six guards of the wing were lined up against the far wall of the Sala, facing nine police officers of high rank. Six security officers were present, along with four representatives of the Instituto de Cultura Hispánica, including its young, stout director who held the assimilated rank of under-secretary of state. With him were the Director of the Museo del Prado with two Goya experts. They were grouped about Jean Marie's copy as it stood propped so incongruously against the wall under the great bare spot, looking as though the original had slipped from its moorings and had slid to the floor.

Each of the twenty-seven men in the room were whey-faced with shock and anxiety. As impossible as it sounded, the experts had just finished agreeing that because of the quality of pig-ment, the age of canvas, and the wood on the back of its frame, this representation before them which had to be "The Second of May" by Francisco Goya y Lucientes was not that painting, and while they did their best to cope with this obscene enigma they asked themselves, and then the police, where the original could have disappeared to.

Behind them at room center, as bulky as a battleship, stood the great false frame which seemed to hold only the triptych of the three Goyas on a single canvas. Guard after guard confirmed the story that for three weeks a man known as Charles Smadja had wheeled the great frame into this room to copy, by official museum permission, the three Goyas. Asked to test it, man after man insisted that the weight was exactly the same as it had always been.

With these points established, the police asked the Director of the Museo del Prado, who turned to ask his assistant, who

turned in his turn to ask *his* assistant, how the museum permit
had been granted. Eventually it was learned that it had been
issued to accommodate Dr. Victoriano Muñoz, the Marqués de
Villalba. The triptych was ordered impounded by the police, and
a police van carried it to a police warehouse, where it was
ticketed, crated and wrapped in strong brown paper. The Goya
painting called "The Second of May" was better concealed from
the eyes of its host, the Spanish state, than James Bourne could
have ever hoped.

III

Aplomado

❀

The bull is tired. His flanks are heaving and his breath is short. His speed is cut, but he is determined to use his horns on something solid. He is beginning to think there is something not quite right about the lure. He must be killed quickly now, respecting both his tiredness and his intelligence.

❀

THAT THE ART OF CAYETANO Jiminez was as impermanent as Nijinsky's or Booth's inasmuch as it could live on only as long as an individual physical performance lasted, or as long as the memory of its last living witness, made it no less great an art. Indeed, perhaps his art was more creative than those two interpreters, for it was not unlike Picasso's performance of drawing in the dark with electric lights —art only while you could see it, but undeniably great. That his courage had been confined by the ritual of the corrida, a choreography repeated since the beginning of man's practice of contempt for death in this form, made it no less gallant nor less formidable than any other human's exploration into any other unknown.

On the leading page of Spain's national newspaper on the day after Cayetano's death there appeared the following:

The shocking and senseless murder of Cayetano Jiminez in the full light of day within the arena of the Plaza of Bulls of Madrid yesterday closed a glorious cycle and presented the memory with an accumulation of feats, of ennobling passion, of art and wisdom, in all of which he played a leading role. Cayetano Jiminez was above all else the dominating figure, the axis of an epoch, the antenna around which revolved the turbulence of the fiesta. To trace his memory is both easy and complicated. It is easy because to some it would be enough to say that he was the greatest fighter of all time. It is complicated because to characterize him in every moment of the evolution of his art and in every trace of his style is a project more arduous. His outstanding quality was without a doubt his vocation for the profession, to which he gave himself without reservation from the time he was thirteen years old, as his illustrious ancestors had given on a like basis for the past one hundred and twenty-three years of the corrida. This was the killer of bulls who passed rapidly through the arenas, obtaining the highest consideration that any master could dream of, to die grotesquely at the age of twenty-seven in his full glory, without knowing the pain of failure, without showing the slightest symptom of decadence. It can thus be said that however heinous his passing and however exemplary his life, his death was transcendent in its completion of a cycle without a fault, with mythical perfection.

BOURNE could not seem to unclench his fists or to unknot his jaws when he was not speaking. Eve could not take her eyes off him. Her beauty had been paled by the news of Cayetano's death and by the raving, drunken, mumbling, guilt-ridden, immobile grief-ripped Bourne. The paleness she emanated contrasted with the gray-greenness of her large, dismayed eyes, her glistening, full, red mouth and her lush, shining body under the green Japanese kimono she held around herself loosely, partially open over her nakedness. She sat there trying to will Bourne to look at her body. She wanted to make him use it as an anodyne, to drive himself into it so that the pain and growing hopelessness could be driven out of him.

Bottles, ice buckets, glasses, pitchers, cigarette stubs, snarled used cigarette packages, thick smoke, broken fragments of food and wet heat pocked the room. Bourne had slumped forward in the unapproachable drunkenness of the enormous man, his hands dangling between his legs knotted into fists at the level of his ankles, his meaty shoulders low, his head sunk onto his chest, staring at the floor. Whenever he spoke brokenly about the duchess or Cayetano he had to shut his eyes. It was nine forty-five in the morning on the first day following Cayetano's murder. For the two hundredth time Bourne mumbled, "I didn't know. I didn't know."

Eve moved slowly across the room. The robe fell open as she stood directly in front of him, her rounded, opalescent stomach at the level of his bent head. When he looked up, she sat on the sofa beside him. Her breasts were full and high and had nipples like thumbs. She pulled him over to rest on her, holding him as he canted off his rump at an angle.

"It will all be settled today," she said, "you'll settle it all today."

"But I can't find him!"

"We'll find him. You'll see. We'll find him today." Bourne had telephoned Muñoz nearly forty times in fifteen hours but there had been no answer.

Eve turned his head with her right shoulder and with her right hand urged his face into her breasts, offering them as sanctuary.

"I was only trying to get what was mine," Bourne muttered. "I worked for three years for it. How could I know what he was going to do?"

"You were right, darling. You did right."

"That butler fills the door and keeps saying 'No, señor, the duchess is not here' when all the while she's writhing on a bed upstairs with the cords of her neck bursting from her throat while she says the word why over and over and over again."

"You'll see her today. And you'll see Muñoz today. You'll drag him to Blanca and you'll make him tell her what he did and make him tell her that you didn't know," she crooned.

"That's what I'll do. That's what I'll do today." He struggled to get up, but she held him close to her. "I'm going to get dressed now."

"Sleep first," she said. "Go to sleep, my dearest, go to sleep." He lay still, and she began to pray that they could both be turned to stone.

. . .

NOT only the Spanish press saw the truth in Cayetano from the perspective of his death. *Time* recorded in part his passing with these words:

North Americans would never be able to comprehend why men wept in the streets of Spain, or why holy candles burned in private houses in Peru, or why tens of thousands of Mexicans went into mourning, or why movie theatres in Venezuela were packed to show, again and again, newsreels of a man whose name most North Americans had never heard. Throughout that world plain people felt they had lost one who had given them, not delight, but a grim, transcendent excitement; a pageant of death, and of courage, death's enemy.

THE duchess sat in a straight-backed chair looking out into the darkness through the open window and across the Retiro near dawn on the third night after that afternoon. She had not slept; she had hardly stirred. To force her servants to leave her alone she would pretend to sip the broth and eat the food they brought. Her black eyes were protuberant in a bony, haggard face.

Many people had come to the house: from Madrid and Spain; from Rome, from London, from Cannes and Paris. Bourne, desperate with guilt and grief, had been turned away four times. The telephone had rung hundreds of times, but Pablo, the major-domo, had told the callers that his mistress was not there. The cooks wept. The chambermaids wept. The footmen were red-eyed. Josefina, Pablo's wife and the duchess's body servant, looked as though she were mirroring the face of the duchess's soul. All the while the duchess, having forgotten she had a mind or a body, sat staring out across the night.

As the false dawn of the third day appeared, the day before his funeral, the day before he would be taken far to the south to be buried forever, the duchess was at last able to leave the place and the time she was trapped in and the body in which she was contained with such pain. She became a fussy and finicky curator of memories, poking into display cases of sensation and old hurt, dusting statuesque desires from the far corners of the museum of her life with Cayetano. She had willed herself to become a satellite of her shining past, circling the planet of their world together, speeding with chilling loneliness through a vacuum, separated from all the substance she ached for. In her mind she became a learned scholar who studied her own dreams. She read and reread memory beginning on the afternoon in Sevilla when she had first met him; she devoured each nuance of their exchange, going over the minutes of her life with him as some other marooned scholar might read and reread the pages of the single book he had salvaged from a wrecked ship.

Just as she had clung so strongly to his life, now she struggled to lock it within herself after it had flown. Reason had no part in this; need was all and everything. She concentrated upon each instant she and Cayetano had shared, allowing one instant to cross her grateful memory at a time; each pearl part of a necklace, each instant brief and evanescent, immeasurable in time and, being timeless, eternal.

Time had no relationship in this new world, and what had happened and was then happening to all others beyond herself and Cayetano was totally unreal. Over and over she read her book whose first chapter was that afternoon in Sevilla, reading slowly, savoring each gesture and tactile sensation, finding wondrous new meanings each time, never tiring of the story any more than a child tires of a haunting fairy tale. Each time she read the book she always went through from start to finish, never doubling back when she reached a snag but making a note to investigate that moment or new memory or blank space the next time she started from the beginning to work her way to the ineradicable end.

On the morning of the third day something happened to these sequences. She grew more and more puzzled, then confused each time she reached the last few pages of the story. One puzzling inconsistency kept interrupting the even flow of her narrative to herself. She tried to push it away, but it would not leave.

It was that sunny, loving day when they had all met for luncheon at the Commodore. Now she excerpted the sequence, against all her rules, as one would start a home-movie projector at a favored place. She and Eve Bourne were riding up in the tiny elevator with the redhaired page boy. They swept into the dining room, and this time she noticed the golden-brown murals showing the horsemen and the hunters.

She relived the movement and sound of the luncheon with happiness. She loved the Bournes. Eve was a beautiful, warm and genuine girl; Jaime was good, solid and dependable, with a brilliant mind. They gave love to each other and to their friends. Cayetano had felt it and he had loved them too. As she watched Cayetano and heard him talk, the snag, now as big as a glacier, began to form again.

"This is a week of miracles, really. I ask everyone here. Who is the most improbable Spaniard you can think of who would announce that he was going to attend a bullfight?" She heard herself reply, *"My cousin, el doctor, Victoriano Muñoz, Marqués de Villalba."* She had imitated Victoriano's voice and everyone had laughed merrily.

She pulled herself forward through what was happening again. She saw Cayetano lean over and kiss her hand, and her left hand opened beseechingly as she relived the sensation. Then he said in a voice which had become louder each time she had relived it, *"He called me this morning and asked me if I would kill in front of Tendido Two next week on my first bull because they were the only seats he could get. He promised to take Mrs. Pickett and he is hoping that she won't last more than one bull, but he wants to make sure of that by making it as awful as possible."*

It had been as awful as possible.

A voice began to shout questions at her from a great distance within her head. Why had Victoriano agreed to go to any corrida? What could have persuaded him to overcome such a cherished prejudice? He had contempt for Mrs. Pickett; he had not spoken more than ten words to her on any given day since they had been thrown together. If she had caught fire before his eyes he would have rung for a servant to put the fire out, no more. Why would he take such a woman to the corrida when he detested the corrida even more than he felt contempt for the woman? The sound, disembodied and nonexistent then, which had come from a radio in an automobile passing under her open window during that first night came back to her now and entwined itself around Victoriano and Mrs. Pickett and herself. The sound was a radio voice which told with mournful

wonderment that at the instant of the death of the great Cayetano Jiminez, Francisco Goya's great masterpiece "The Second
of May" had been stolen from the Prado.

The duchess did not know, nor would she have cared, that
that was the only announcement ever made about the theft of
the Goya, that the story was killed forever eight seconds after
that announcement by highest authority, and that all inquiries
were blandly denied with the flat statement by the radio, the
press, the government and, most of all, by the Prado that the
announcement had never been made.

LOCKED in the suite where he had copied the Goya, Jean
Marie dreamed that one brutalized *agent de police* had him by
the hair, another by his right arm and that both of them were
striking him with large riot sticks, like the riot sticks the gendarmes had used on the Place de la Concorde during the Stavisky
riots when he had been a boy, as they dragged him through the
black gates of what could only be a prison.

AT eleven forty on the morning of the fourth day, which
was Saturday, the day of Cayetano's funeral and the day which
had been set for his wedding, the duchess's servants sat, silent
and expressionless, in the foyer of Dr. Muñoz' apartment. When
they heard his key scratching in the lock Pablo arose and opened
the door, surprising him.

"Eh!" Dr. Muñoz exclaimed, while from under his arm Montes
stared at the two servants. "Ah. Well. Pablo. Why are you here?
And Josefina. Did the duchess send you? Of course. Good heavens, has there been more bad news?"

Josefina stared at him malevolently. Pablo stood aside, clearing the entrance. "My duchess waits for you in the salon, marqués," Pablo said.

"The salon! Well! How long has she been waiting, for heaven's
sake?"

Pablo took out a large, gold pocket watch, snapped open the case and studied it carefully. "Eighteen hours and forty minutes, marqués," he said gravely.

"What? What the devil has happened?" Muñoz said sharply. He stared at Pablo, then at Josefina, but learned nothing. Moving rapidly across the foyer and down the corridor to the tall arch leading into the Moorish room, he hesitated at the closed doors, biting his lower lip nervously and pill-rolling his fingers on the balls of his thumbs. At last he turned the latch and entered.

The duchess sat facing the door, framed by the light from the large windows behind her, erect in one of the high-backed, heavy council chairs. Involuntarily, the marqués glanced up at the paintings illuminated on the wall. The brilliantly colored carpet beneath his feet seemed as soft as sand. He could not remember sensing that before. Everything of which he had ceased to be aware in that room seemed now to take on deeper dimensions. The lights flooding the paintings shone more brilliantly, and the atmosphere between himself and the duchess seemed pelagic. He knew that if he shouted no sound could be heard in that room.

The duchess watched him enter as one looks at a bellboy approaching with a message. She saw him as he was at that instant, not as she had always seen him: an extension of their childhood, a somewhat pitiable, resentful child held together by his pride and his forefathers' failings. All at once she was saddened to see that he was a comically effete man wearing not clothes, but some kind of flagrant plumage as he peered forward through his façade as though he were standing well behind himself. His greased hair shone like stars reflected in soup, his poor mustache resembled the vibrissae of a mouse, and his crenelated mouth moved without opening.

"Good day, Victoriano. Did you have a pleasant journey?"

"Journey? What do you mean?"

"You've been gone for four days, the porter said. I called that nice Castanos man at the Comisario de Policía, and in no time at all they were able to tell me that you were in Santiago de Compostela."

"Oh. Yes. Wonderful place for a rest, you know. Great peace. That sort of thing."

"Indeed, yes."

"I hope you have been comfortable here?"

"Thank you, Victoriano."

"If there is anything you need—"

"Nothing, thank you."

He took a deep breath and let it out slowly. "Blanca, I can explain the presence of these paintings."

"Sit down," she said. "Here." She touched the heavy council chair beside her. He thought about that for a moment, but then he walked to the chair uncertainly and sat down.

"Pablo!" the duchess called out in her strong, sweet voice. The servants appeared instantly in the doorway. The duchess turned to Dr. Muñoz and said, "You will think I have simply taken over your house."

"It is your house, my duchess," he answered gallantly as Pablo crossed behind him, flipped a loop of strong line over his head and bound him to the chair, across the chest, torso, legs and then one arm. The duchess watched with the simulated interest one assumes while watching someone else's child play a short piece on the piano. The marqués neither cried out nor spoke while he was being bound. Pablo did a rapid and thorough job and then stood silently, waiting for further instructions from his mistress. "Thank you, Pablo," she said and he left the room.

Muñoz tried to appear as natural as possible under these conditions, but he could not bring himself to look at the duchess. His right arm was free, and he lifted it slowly and regarded it as though it were a new, strangely shaped object, as though it were something he had read about but had never seen. Montes walked up his bound left arm, across his shoulders, then down his fragile chest on the right side, to settle down for a splendid sleep after a long journey in his lap.

The duchess, wearing black, sat with her hands reposed in her lap. Her hair looked like what is left on the ground after a fire in a cornfield, part yellow, part black. Her popping eyes, black and congenitally intense, watched him serenely. She wore many rubies against the black. At last her long white fingers moved, and she began to speak again quietly.

"I telephoned Mrs. Pickett. She told me that she had not been to the corrida with you."

"Blanca—"

"I was surprised to learn, as you will be, I know, that she had never been to a corrida. Yet it has always seemed to me that when she isn't hinting at what men would secretly like to do to her, she talks about nothing but bullfighting. It must still remain a romantic thing to her, like jousting or falconry."

"What I insist upon establishing here and now, Blanca, is the fact, the simple fact that—"

"I cannot explain to you why those particular words of Cayetano's about your attending last Tuesday's corrida stayed in my mind."

"Did he mention that?"

"He made it very amusing, as usual. He told us that you had called him and had urgently requested that he kill the first bull in front of Tendido Two, just to get the agony over for Mrs. Pickett that much more quickly."

She looked at him brightly. She had so much pain in her eyes that he moved as well as he could in his bonds to avoid them, knowing that if he looked at them again he would never be able to sleep. "Would you mind if I smoked?" he heard his cousin say.

"Blanca—" He started and stopped. "Nothing in this world is certain. That is to say, at the last moment Mrs. Pickett decided not to go to the corrida."

"Ah, that explains it."

"Yes. Yes, of course."

"But when I saw you outside the plaza you told me she was with you." This wasn't true, of course, but she wanted to hear his answer.

"I couldn't have."

"You did, though."

"Actually I didn't hear a word you said over the noise of that awful crowd. I just nodded, I suppose, or said something inane. She wasn't with me. She called at the very last moment and canceled everything."

"Then I must be mistaken."

"You most certainly are, Blanca dear. But no harm is done where none is meant."

"The old sayings are the best." The duchess struck the silver lighter in her hand and lit the long cigarette between her square white teeth. She assayed a smoke ring, and in the stillness of the air in that room it formed beautifully. "When I spoke with Mrs. Pickett this morning she told me that you had never in-

vited her to a corrida. She couldn't imagine that you would want
to invite her anywhere at any time. She told me that she hadn't
even spoken with you since you drove them back to Madrid
from my place, and that had been some time ago."

"That is outrageous!"

"My questioning her?"

"How could she dare to tell a lie like that?"

"Breeding, I suppose," the duchess said. " 'No manners, no
conscience' is another good old saying." She puffed at the cigarette and touched the ruby pendant hanging at her white throat.

"She must be mad. You will certainly admit that she behaves
like a madwoman."

"Do I behave like a madwoman?"

"Of course you don't." His constant movement under the ropes
in the chair had forced his left shoulder quite low and he
seemed unable to right himself again, but he was careful not to
call attention to it.

"Why did you go to the corrida last Tuesday, Victoriano?"

"Why did I go?"

"Come now, pet. Please don't tell me now that I didn't see you
outside the plaza."

"Of course I won't, but I'm not sure I understand the question."

"Forgive me. I asked you that because there is no Madrileño
more famous for his detestation of the bulls than you."

"Now, one moment, Blanca. Just one moment. I want this to
be clear now and forever—"

"Forever." She tipped her head back to stare at the ceiling. "If
someone could only tell me how long forever is."

"Pardon?"

She looked at him again, and he looked away quickly. "Nothing," she said. "Go on."

"You've been asking me some extraordinary questions. And
not only me, Blanca." His voice had the aggrieved indignation of
a pupil who has been unjustly told he must remain after school.
He looked piercingly at her right shoulder to indicate that he
would not tolerate this sort of thing, even from her.

"One question."

"Ask me anything. You *know* you can ask me anything," he
replied.

"Why have you not made any mention of the somewhat unusual, not to say eccentric, fact that my servant has entered this room and trussed you into your own chair?"

"I—what is there to say? It is all most embarrassing. I mean, if I were to acknowledge this condition you speak of, I said to myself, I should be required to become very angry with you, Blanca. We are old and dear friends. I mean, since childhood. I could not under any circumstances, that is to say, I thought that—" With his free right hand he brushed confusedly at the empty air.

"You thought that you deserved what would happen, whatever happened. You felt such guilt under my gaze that your guilt expected punishment."

"Blanca—I only knew that when you saw these three paintings you would reach the conclusion that I had stolen them from you. I decided at once that you had taken this unusual means to question me about them, and I could not fathom why you insisted upon dwelling upon the idiotically unimportant point of whether or not I had taken Mrs. Pickett to the corrida last week."

"Not last week. Last Tuesday."

He licked his lips, but his tongue was dry. "Stealing paintings such as these would be a most serious charge," he said, staring at the intense patches of light on the walls and trying to will her mind away from that afternoon. She turned with his glance slowly, seeming to move out of politeness rather than an appreciation of art.

"You stole these paintings from me?" She seemed utterly surprised. She rose from her chair and walked toward the Zurbarán to study it intently for a moment. "Why!" she exclaimed, "this is a painting from Dos Cortes!" She sidled along the wall to the Velázquez. "Upon my word, I believe this one is The Pickett Troilus!"

"The—what was that, Blanca?"

She wheeled to gape at him. "You stole these from me?"

"Is that not what you had decided?"

"To tell the truth, Victoriano, I have had so many things on my mind that I never looked at these paintings at all, and I have been sitting here for some time. Did you say you stole them from me?"

"I have nothing more to say."

The duchess walked to consider the Greco, her back to the marqués. "If I were to turn and look at you," she said, "I know that I would find your face set in that stupidly stubborn look you used when you were a boy and had been outwitted and bewildered, that hopeless look which means that you have decided that you will say nothing more, even if it were to mean your salvation."

"I am sorry, Blanca," he answered stiffly.

She walked to the fireplace and took up a poker from among the fire irons. "I know, for example, that even if I were to swing this iron back and crash it with all my force into the bone of your lower leg, then to swing it back again and bring it down with even more force to crush your kneecap—that even then you would not talk about this matter of the paintings because you have made up your mind and that is the way you are."

"That is the way I am," Dr. Muñoz answered simply.

"Then I am helpless."

"I do not know exactly what you wish to learn from me, but as regards those paintings I have closed my voice."

"I plead with you," she said languidly to the marqués ten feet behind her as she looked closely at the brushwork of the Greco.

"Forgive me. I cannot."

The duchess sighed and strolled to the long table standing against the far wall, its very joints redolent with Spanish history. She slid the drawer of the table open and removed a pair of long and heavy shears.

"Your resolve batters me," the duchess said. "I am helpless in the face of your will power." She turned with the shears in her hand.

"Thank you, Blanca," Dr. Muñoz said briskly, if not indulgently. "I am happy that you can see it as it is. Now cut these cords with those shears, my dear; my circulation is growing sluggish. We will speak of this no more. The incident will be our secret."

She walked across his gaze, which followed her, pulled a leather-backed chair from the wall and dragged it to a place directly in front of the Greco and in a direct line with the marqués' vision. She stepped daintily onto the chair as she said, "I have known of the iron nature of your character since you were a little boy, Victoriano. I know I cannot cope with it. I admit defeat."

"Why are you standing on that chair?"

She raised the points of the closed shears over her head, bringing them close to the face of the central saint in the painting. "I am going to destroy these paintings," she said with detachment.

"Blanca!" he screamed. "No! Stop! Blanca! That is the work of El Greco, the great and immortal El Greco!"

She lowered the shears. "Will you answer all my questions?" she asked.

"Yes. Please step down. Put the shears back in that table drawer, please. You cannot know what this does to me."

"Can you mean that your iron resolve has melted?"

"Yes. Step down, Blanca."

"How can I be sure? Perhaps I should destroy just one painting to demonstrate my sincerity." She made as if to turn toward the canvas again.

"Blanca, I have completely changed my mind! Please step down. Now. Step down, Blanca."

She stepped down, walked slowly to the great table, opened the drawer and returned the heavy shears to their place.

"Who would have dared to think that you would ever have relented?" she asked as she seated herself in the chair next to the marqués and crossed her legs. "You are really very, very chivalrous, you know, Victoriano, to have changed your steely resolve so quickly, a position from which I thought wild horses could not have dragged you."

He fought not to look at her; his free hand dragged at his collar. "I am always happy to advise you," he said. "Surely you know that. I value your friendship highly."

"Who stole the paintings for you? You have neither the intelligence nor the character to accomplish it." He flushed with fear because the charade was over. He had known her for such a long time, in so many circumstances, and in times when she had been parted from something she had honored, loved, or valued. He began to breathe heavily, but he still could not look into her eyes.

"That is true. I did not steal the paintings. Your friends obliged me—Mr. and Mrs. James Bourne." As he said the names he wished that he had not.

She struck heavily at the arm of his chair with the poker in her hand, splintering the wood as he drew his right hand away.

"Don't lie to me! Don't lie more than you already have to me!"

"It was not a lie. It is most difficult to believe, but it is true. He is a professional thief. She is his wife. She brought the copies to him from Paris where Calbert painted them. He never knew that I was interested. My own participation, quite unknown to him, was to bring Pickett along on the last foray to verify the copies."

She had grown very pale. She closed her eyes and did not seem to breathe. "I feel sick," she said. She was balancing herself on a thin, high wire above the crocodile mouth of catatonia. The wire seemed to be heated white-hot, sending shocking pain through her. She felt herself toppling as the crocodile grinned, then all at once was able to steady herself upon her hatred and her desire for what was right: an eye for an eye and a tooth for a tooth. The future became as clear to her as it had once been seen by an old gypsy woman who had told her own fortune with a pack of Tarot cards, had paused to peer through the light of a kerosene lamp in the woodshed of a farm house, confirmed what she had seen and cut her own throat.

While the duchess groped for support, Dr. Muñoz, who loved her on his own terms, spoke quietly. "It was an impersonal thing, Blanca," he said. "When Bourne met you he had no way of knowing how dear you are or that he would come so quickly to love you and respect you. Try to see him in a different light, because thief is a word which can trap you. He had worked everything out on scale drawings with time and motion studies and a thorough investigation of how he would market the paintings after he had acquired them. Why, he spent just over three years on this one project. Some time after he settled in Madrid he discovered the paintings of Dos Cortes in a book; afterward, he asked if he might meet you, if he might see the paintings. He played the role of an art lover most effectively, but he wanted to test his plans against the actual conditions at the castle. This man, I tell you this, Blanca, and I plead that you believe me, would never have been able to bring himself to hurt you. To him, they were paintings that hung too high in semi-darkness on a wall in a house which was seldom lived in, and it had nothing to do with you. Not in any way with any part of you. He stole those paintings from that house, and I had them stolen from him."

Muñoz felt freer for what he had said. He wished he could

be alone now and analyze what he had said, because something in those words or the way he had felt when he had said them had —well, not lifted his spirits, but had made him feel good enough again to be a friend of Blanca de Dos Cortes. He saw at once that he was entitled to have pride in himself, and it was an enormous discovery. He saw also that heretofore he had only had pride in his family, not the pride of self-respect. Supported by the cords around his small body, he literally let himself sink into this new, stunning sensation. What might he do for Blanca next? She was the key to pride in himself, the start of a new life. Pride was his word; it was Spain's word. After so many years this new revelation had been given him, and he must learn exactly what it meant. He wished he could be alone, that Blanca would go now, so that he could begin to work out the answers.

He thought that it must be some form of telepathy when she started to talk again. "I'm sure you're very proud of yourself for having said that. You have as much pride as any man I have ever known or read about, Victoriano. To me it is unnatural, But I do not pretend to have your view." She spoke slowly. She had just lost her last two friends whom she had loved; they were dead. She had mourned for them for a moment, but now she must return to her tasks and get them done. "Your pride is based entirely upon the past—which to me, and I say perhaps only to me—is an unpleasantness, like having a picnic in a cemetery."

He wanted to cry out that she was wrong. That might have been true in the past, but now she misunderstood the boundaries of his feelings. "Nonetheless," she went on, "no form of this protective pride—this touchy, face-losing-face-saving kind of pride —has any place between you and me. That has been acknowledged throughout our lives."

"I agree, Blanca. I have never feared that you would scorn me."

She burst out bitterly, "Then why didn't you say you wanted those paintings from me! Did you believe I would have refused you? You know that I know that Spanish painters are a great part of your most abnormal life, but if I had known that you had needed them like this!" She stared at him in despair, but he would not look into her eyes. "You could have had them for use in your lifetime. And you know that! Why did you want them stolen from me?"

"I needed them. I needed to use them to do something."

"What did you need that they could be traded for? What did you need which no one had the power to give you, but which you decided you would have to take, no matter what pain you caused? What was it?"

"The attack upon the Mamelukes in the Puerta del Sol." His voice was quiet but it was filled with pride. The first kind of pride, the pride in his family. If he could only regain for a moment that thrilling pride of self so that he could compare them just for a moment. Then later he could sit before the fire and think about it.

" 'The Second of May'? The Goya?"

"Yes."

"From the Prado?"

"Yes. For my family. I wanted to possess that symbol for the honor of my family, for what that man and that day did to my family." He composed his voice. "Blanca, we have spoken of those circumstances many times."

"I know." As she drew her hand across her eyes he looked up at her lovely face quickly, then looked away. She had been the good friend of his life. She had never ceased to protect him. No matter what, she had always defended him, and now—he could not grasp what made him want to cry—the light had gone out in her eyes. Her soul had died. He looked at her hands, reposed in her lap against the black of her mourning, as she spoke to him almost absent-mindedly.

"Two things were repeated over and over, until I had to do something about them. He was dead. There is that word 'forever,' which you used. He is dead forever. God gave me a way to return to him. I wanted to stay there, but two things, little things, stopped me."

"Forgive me, Blanca. Please forgive me."

"The Seine was eleven silver lakes to him, caught between the bridges. The air in London was wet, he said, and it washed the past away. Madrid was was the center of the universe and therefore not as important to lovers as Sevilla, where no one needed to be so self-conscious. He was dead. The first thing which pried at my memory was why you would take Mrs. Pickett anywhere—and, of all places, to a corrida. The other came to me from a car radio through my window on the Alcalá. I heard it because it said his name. Cayetano's name came to my ears, and the radio said that he had died at the very instant that the Goya had been stolen from the Prado. The Goya you have always said that someday you would possess." She looked at him with pity. "You didn't get it, did you, Victoriano?"

"No. I didn't get it. Or rather Bourne didn't get it. Almost. I almost had it, but I didn't get it."

"It must be a bitter disappointment to you."

"Well, nothing else really interests me very much."

"You'll never have another chance."

"No. I suppose not."

"You killed Cayetano to draw attention away from the activity at the Prado?"

"Yes. I'm sorry, Blanca. That was the way it was."

"Who else was with Bourne?"

"The French copyist."

"M'sieu Calbert?"

"Yes."

"I want you to telephone them now and tell them to come here. At once."

"What good will that do? What can a lot of talking accomplish?"

"Do as I say." She pushed the telephone across the low table, stopping it at his free hand. "Was Mrs. Bourne connected with the Prado operation?" the duchess asked.

"No. But if she had been, instead of that—"

"Call Bourne."

The marqués took up the receiver, put it on the table, dialed the hotel number, picked up the receiver again and held it to his head. "Señor Bourne, please," he said into the telephone. He waited. "Jim? Victoriano Muñoz here." He flinched as a gabble of furious voice escaped from the instrument. His face colored and hardened. "All right," he said sharply, "if you want to talk so much, come over here. Immediately. And bring Calbert with you." The crackling, furious, distant voice continued, but the marqués slammed the receiver into its cradle. "They botched everything, after I gave them everything they asked for, and now they are the ones who are angry," he said indignantly. "This is really too much, I must say."

The duchess stood up.

"Am I to remain trussed up like this while those men come over here to whatever pointless discussion you have in mind?"

"Thank you for calling, Victoriano," she said.

"Not at all," he replied, and unconsciously his eyes lifted and he looked directly into hers and he saw and understood what he had done for the first time.

"Goodbye. God have mercy on you." She struck him heavily across the crown of his skull with the heavy iron poker. There was a popping sound. She hit him twice more, swinging slowly, then dropped the poker from her gloved hand to the floor beside him. Montes did not awaken. She turned away from the man-into-corpse as formally as a movement in a folk dance and walked to the door onto the terrace. She opened the catch, went out upon the balcony and stared down impassively at the Calle Amador de los Ríos. In ten minutes Bourne's car turned into the street on two wheels from the Calle de Fernando el Santo and stopped directly in front of the entrance to Muñoz' building.

The duchess went back into the Moorish room, closing the door of the terrace carefully behind her, paying no attention whatsoever to the mess tied to the chair. She moved the telephone to the other side of the table and dialed.

"Police? Police, come quickly, come quickly," she said into the telephone. "Dr. Muñoz, the Marqués de Villalba, is being murdered! The men are still in there. Quickly! Number four Calle Amador de los Ríos. Dr. Muñoz."

She replaced the telephone and moved swiftly out of the room and along the corridor. As she crossed the foyer, Pablo held the door open for her. "It is done," she said. "The others will be here shortly."

She left the apartment, Pablo closing the door after her. She went down the stairway quietly just as Bourne and Jean Marie reached the top floor in the elevator. She had to pick her way with great care because the tears in her eyes were blinding her.

HOMER PICKETT burst into his suite at the Palace Hotel waving a copy of a different picture magazine in each hand and grinning rapturously at his wife who was rubbing a product called *Splendor* into her face.

"Both of them! Both of them!" he cried out. "And both in

color! 'The Pickett Troilus.' They both say it, just like that. I'm bigger than Berenson right now. All I need to do is follow up this advantage and I tell you, Marianne, I'll *stay* bigger than Berenson."

Mrs. Pickett walked to him rapidly, curlers in her hair over a smart, black Balmain sheath. "My God, Homer, did they run any of those pictures of me?"

"I'll say they did. Well, the German magazine did anyway."

"The German magazine!" She grabbed both magazines away from him and threw the American one on the sofa seven feet away. "Well, what the hell good is that? Who reads the German magazine except a lotta goddam Germans?" She flipped through the pages rapidly. "Where? Where is it?"

"Here." Mr. Pickett tried to wrest the periodical from her, but she swerved away. "Let me have it," he said. "Page seventy-eight. There. Look at that color reproduction."

"Where? Where am I?"

"Right there. Down in the corner."

"Aaaah!"

"Doesn't that Velázquez look marvelous?"

"Marvelous? What did that little son-of-a-bitch do to me? Why didn't you tell me my hat was practically over my chin? I look like a goddam drunk."

"Look here. Read this caption."

"Read the caption? I'll sue the goddam magazine."

"No, no. Here, look. The Pickett Troilus. A painting by Velázquez is called 'The Pickett Troilus' in the public prints."

"The public prints! A goddam German magazine."

"No, no. In both of them." He scampered to the sofa, scooped up the American picture magazine and opened it uncannily at the right page. "The title of the *entire goddam article* in this one is 'The Pickett Troilus.' Did you ever *dream* of such a gasper? Do you realize what this is going to mean to Arthur Turkus *Danielson*? I'll bet right now that he tries to sign me for a *minimum* of six pieces a year, plus a coast-to-coast lecture series. Oh, I tell you! Those public relations firms are worth every cent they cost."

"I suppose you're happy and proud about that picture of me?"

"Lecturing is like the best part of life in Washington, hon. It's one long cocktail party, day after day, with all kinds of people pressing up close and asking thousands of questions."

"Incidentally, what about Washington? How can you talk about a lecture tour? They'll hand you your head."

"Never mind, it'll all be handled. I take care of the Party and the Party takes care of me. I guess I'm entitled to a little sick leave. How would you feel about a lecture tour?"

Mrs. Pickett sat down in front of the large mirror and began to massage her face again, her neck protruding far forward, her nose almost touching the glass, as though she had terminal myopia from studying each pore in her face.

"*Look* at these layouts! I wonder if I shouldn't hop over and show them to the duchess."

"Uh-uh." Mrs. Pickett shook her head vigorously into the mirror.

"It might cheer her up," Mr. Pickett said speculatively. "After all, they *are* her paintings and I do feel I owe her something. If she's kinda down in the dumps because that fighter was killed maybe that's what I should do."

"I wouldn't, Homer," Mrs. Pickett said. "I talked to her on the telephone yesterday morning. Nothing in this life'll ever cheer up that woman."

Mr. Pickett sat down on the bed beside his wife's dressing table, his weight sinking him down into the mattress, until his eyes were below the level of Mrs. Pickett's. He cleared his throat. "I know this could sound actually *ghoulish* in a way, and I *certainly* wouldn't say it to anyone else but *you*, Marianne, but her connection with that bullfighter and the way he was killed just as they announced I had discovered The Pickett Troilus—you might say, you know it *could* be just the kind of thing that would absolutely *make* this lecture tour."

Mrs. Pickett thought this over for a moment or two as she stared at him soberly in the mirror. "I suppose you're right, hon," she said wrenching a metal curler from her hair. "In fact, now that I think about it, I know you're right. The art jazz is all right for snob appeal, but that under-a-bush-with-a-toreador stuff is what they really want to hear."

"I'll ask the press officer at the Embassy to get me some pictures of both of them," Mr. Pickett mused. "The newspapers here must have plenty of them."

. . .

In the four days between Cayetano's death and the equally abrupt passing of Dr. Muñoz, Bourne had tried to accomplish three things. He had searched unceasingly for Muñoz; he had sought, with desperation, to find the duchess; and he had done his best to cope with Jean Marie, who had fallen into a nervous collapse. When he was away from the hotel he had Eve telephone the Muñoz flat every half hour, and he had driven to the apartment every three hours to pound on the apartment door after ringing the bell and himself into a frenzy and eventually agitating the building porter to the extent that his nerves could be soothed, though not made whole again, by money. He had haunted the outside of the duchess's house on Calle Alcalá, pacing like a distraught animal, pleading with and futilely trying to bribe Pablo. He telephoned all her other houses twice a day.

Bourne's huge bulk absorbed alcohol like a sponge within a sponge. He talked to himself while he drove endlessly from the hotel, to Muñoz', to Alcalá. "What can I tell her? How can I prove it to her? Didn't know. Gotta see. What am I going to do? Muñoz. Find him and drag him to her. Where is he? Blanca, Blanca, Blanca."

He kept Jean Marie locked in the large suite on the top floor where they had conducted their drills. When he left him sitting on the edge of the bed with his face in his hands, whimpering, Bourne wanted to run and hide until it was all over and all of his friends were well and safe again, and then he would remember that Blanca could never be either well or whole again and the crazy circle would start all over again so that he could be saved from his guilt and so that he could begin to try to think how he could help again.

On the morning of the fourth day Bourne and Eve attended Cayetano's funeral. The body had been lying in state on a catafalque in the church of St. Rose de Lima since the morning of the second day. Twenty-one thousand people had moved past the bier in thirty-six hours.

After the requiem high mass the body was carried in its silver casket to the soot-black hearse which would lead the cortege from the church to the railroad station, where the coffin would be placed aboard a special train for burial in Sevilla. The bright, blue-domed day, the thousands on thousands of milling mourners, the overpowering, pervasive odor of the heavy flower pieces, the smiting music, and the desperate, fruitless search for the chief mourner who wasn't there were a nightmare for Bourne. He could not connect the long, silver box with the laughing, easy-going Cayetano. In the weary wrangle of his mind he kept seeing a huge cigarette box for the desk of a giant. He could not identify the collective grief of the crowd with his own feelings because they were celebrating a formal, respectable, solemn mass grief while his was a frantic horror like a live rat sewn into his stomach.

He moved through the church continuously before, during and after the ceremony, oblivious of the rite, searching for the duchess. At the moment that the silver box was being carried down the aisle of the church, she was seated in the Moorish room of the Muñoz apartment waiting for the marqués to arrive and enjoying a discussion about the *calamares* of Valencia with Cayetano in her memory.

As Bourne searched, Eve followed him, listening to the prayers around her and wishing that she knew the ritual so that she could repeat them. At the end he was standing next to the crew of the government No-Do newsreel, peering into the crowd as though he himself were the camera. Eve led him off to their car, and he sat, heavily and silently, in the front seat. She slipped behind the wheel, leaned forward to open the glove compartment, and took out a flask of brandy. Unscrewing the top, she passed it to Bourne.

"Thank you," he said thickly, and took it.

The crowds were thinning out. Soon it would be possible for a pedestrian to move in the direction of his choice rather than being taken wherever the crowd wished to move.

Eve held his left hand in hers, across her thigh. "Let's go home now, Jim," she said, and the pleading she was trying to hide seeped through the words. "Let's try to rest, sweetheart."

"I'd just like to stop at Muñoz' for a second."

"We'll call him the minute we get home. It's the same thing."

"No, baby. I have to stop by Muñoz'."

"You can't go on like this, Jim." She was near hysteria.

"I'd stop if I could," he replied dully. "I can't."

A white-helmeted traffic policeman appeared and asked them politely if they would please move the car along, that this was a difficult morning for traffic. Eve drove along the Paseo de Santa María de la Cabeza. Bourne looked out glassily at the buildings, exhausted. The car crossed the Plaza of Charles the Fifth and entered Retiro Park at its southwest corner.

Eve drove slowly. "Will we be out of this after you find both of them?" she asked.

"I don't know."

"Will you try to sleep when we get home?"

"All right."

"I am sick trying to think of how we'll handle Jean Marie."

Bourne said, "I thought maybe we could drive to Irún, then load him with sedatives. We could hire an ambulance and take him across the border to Hendaye as a mental case."

She swerved the car into a parking space and braked. "You've been thinking about getting out. Oh, Jim, oh, Jim, I love you!" She picked up his hand and pressed it to her lips.

His huge, dirty hand took the back of her head and brought it gently to his. He kissed her softly. "My love, my love," he whispered. "If I can show you just once how much I love you!"

"I know, darling. Really, I know."

"The grieving can smother us. Guilt can suffocate us. They can keep shoveling it on us, but what must be done has to be done, and I'm as proud of you that you understand this as I am ashamed of me that I ever let us come to it." He held her hand tightly. "They would have been married today." His eyes were feverish with this new opportunity to twist the knife in himself. There was a dirty stubble of beard on his face, and the hand which held her was bound at the wrist by a soiled white cuff closed by elegant gold cuff links. His fingernails had a high, glossy polish over thick lines of black. There was a sweet, sick smell of ruin about him. He closed his eyes. "I think maybe I'm going to be able to sleep," he said thickly. She backed the car out of the parking place and they moved off toward the hotel.

An hour and twenty minutes later, icily awake, Bourne unsnapped the lock of Jean Marie's suite and told him that Muñoz had called. An electrical change came over the painter. When Bourne entered he had been sitting in a torn bathrobe covering fish-white skin, apathetic and unshaven. The announcement that they were going to see Muñoz acted like a shock treatment. "We must kill the little pig," he suggested brightly. "Where is he? Come, come, let's go kill the little pig."

Bourne dragged him to the bathroom, pulled his robe off and

forced him under alternating hot and cold showers. Jean Marie did not seem to notice this treatment. "How can he have the brass to telephone you?" he kept saying, and, "What new kind of doom does he offer us this time?" When they left the hotel minutes later, they were both clean but they badly needed shaves. They were in front of the Muñoz building just twelve minutes after Bourne had taken Muñoz' call. Jean Marie seemed to be slipping into a relapse, and Bourne held his arm, fearing pneumonia and cursing himself for having given him the bath. They moved rapidly into the hallway and into the waiting elevator. Bourne punched the top-floor button savagely, and the lift doors slid closed. "I want you to sit quietly, Jean Marie," he told the painter. "You have nothing to think about. I'll handle everything that has to be done."

"Sure. Sure. What are you going to do?"

"First he's going to sign a paper confessing that he killed Cayetano; then I'll take him to the duchess."

Jean Marie started violently. "Cayetano? That young bullfighter? He killed Cayetano?" His conception of the trouble he was in began and ended when he had dropped the picture frame in the Sala Goya. Bourne looked at his companion as though he had stepped out of a time machine while Jean Marie pulled at his lapels and the car steadily ascended. "What has that killing got to do with us? Is it connected with the Goya? Jim! I'll never see my wife again. I'll never see Lalu." He began to cry helplessly. Bourne shook his head, took a deep breath, and rocked him with a slap across the face as the doors slid open at the top floor of the building. Bourne pushed Jean Marie ahead of him and looked for the bell. But Pablo opened the door instantly, not waiting for the ring. Bourne did not look at him, or recognize Josefina. "Dr. Muñoz expects us," he said. "Take us to him."

Pablo led them down the corridor to the high, double doors, opened one portal slightly and let Bourne push his way through, with Jean Marie behind him. When they were in the salon Pablo closed the door, locked it from his side and returned slowly along the corridor to take up his station again at the front door.

They stared at the sickeningly battered head and the slumped body. Jean Marie bent over and picked up the bloodstained poker from the floor.

"My God, my God," he moaned. "What a terrible mess. We've got to get out of here."

"Come on!" Bourne said, wheeling toward the door. They were bewildered to find that it would not open. "The door is stuck," Jean Marie said. "What a time for a door to be stuck."

"It's locked. We've been locked in. I don't know what the hell this is all about, but we're locked in," Bourne said dazedly.

Then there were many heavy voices beyond the door, at the end of the hall. The police station was two hundred and eighty feet away on the Calle de Fernando el Santo. They came down the corridor noisily, moving fast. Bourne could hear the key turn in the lock and the lock click. The police burst into the room, registered its contents in one professional, collective glance, then unhesitatingly beat Bourne and Jean Marie senseless with weighted leather billies. The time was five minutes after noon.

WHEN Eve was sure that Bourne had fallen into a deep sleep that morning she left the apartment on tiptoe for her regular Saturday morning appointment with the obstetrician. When she returned to the hotel at twelve twenty-five, Bourne was gone. She called the desk and inquired whether he had left a message, knowing with falling heart that he had taken up his compulsive search again. The desk told her that Señor Bourne had left the hotel in a great rush with Señor Calbert, and had left no message.

She let herself sink down on the edge of the bed while she conjectured. She had not seen Jean Marie since Tuesday, four days before, when he had been a reed-voiced, shaking stranger, but Bourne had told her that since then he had grown worse, if anything. Something must have happened, something electric enough to reactivate Jean Marie, something to do with money, his panacea and denominator. She had never known about the bloodthirsty side of Jean Marie because that was his fantast's side, seen by very few but Bourne and scattered astonished prostitutes.

Eve realized that the departure of the two men must be

connected with Dr. Muñoz. If the duchess had called, Bourne would not have taken Jean Marie with him, and nothing else but Dr. Muñoz would have persuaded both men to leave the hotel. By three o'clock she was concerned enough to think about telephoning the Muñoz apartment. But she didn't; she had her lunch sent up to the terrace, and occasionally when she thought she heard Bourne's car stop on the street below, she would stop trying to eat and would rise nervously to peer down through the treetops.

Out of necessity she began to concentrate on how the duchess's grief was going to affect herself. If her husband was to be so affected by the duchess's lot, she, Eve, must hold it at arm's length, never to be touched by it. For if she began to feel Blanca's grief for Blanca's life she would be trapped; she would need to offer up sacrifices to that grief. But her husband was the only sacrifice that grief would accept, and she would have to sacrifice herself if her husband were taken because she could not conceive of living without him. She railed at herself to reject the duchess. She was a housefly whose wings had been pulled off; she was insignificant except to herself; she did not exist where Eve and Bourne existed. She focused her concentration on the events in Blanca's life: the woman had a record of sadness the way a habitual felon had a record of crime. In twenty-nine years she had managed to find nine weeks of fulfillment; she was predisposed to tragedy. Eve told herself that she must deplore this in the way that women in fashionable restaurants, deploring starvation overseas, urge their escorts to put coins into collection cans pushed under their noses by other fashionable women. She had to find strength to protect herself and her husband from allowing themselves to propitiate that grief by giving themselves over to this stricken woman's terrible predilection.

She nearly ran toward the bathroom, stripping her clothes off, and stood under the shower and turned on the full force of cold water. She gasped as it hit her, but she stayed under the icy water for nearly five minutes until she was cold to the bone. As she dried herself she felt removed from the duchess's problems, and dispassionately objective about her husband. She decided that she would have to get him out of the country, cutting short his martyrdom, either by persuasion or threats— or, if need be, in that ambulance he had patronizingly planned for Jean Marie, heavily drugged to cross the border at Irún as a mental case.

At four twenty-five the telephone rang. Eve ran across the room and snatched it to her ear.

It was the duchess. "Eve? This is Blanca."

"Blanca! Darling, where have you been? We've been imagining the most terrible things." In spite of herself, she began again to feel the need for absolution from Blanca, as Bourne felt it.

"Forgive me, my dear."

"We were at the funeral. We looked for you everywhere. Oh, Blanca!"

"Yes. It is terrible."

"If there were only some way we could—"

"I would like to see you."

"We've been desperate to see you. Jim *must* see you."

"May I come round?"

"Yes. By all means. Or we'll come to you, whichever is best. Oh, Blanca. Forgive me for crying like this. It can't help you. It can't help Cayetano. Blanca, what are we going to do?"

"I'll be there at five-thirty, Eve, darling. Don't cry. Please don't cry for Cayetano any more."

THE Cárcel de Carabancheles, on the outskirts of southwestern Madrid, was the biggest jail in Spain and it accommodated transient boarders only. In the warden's office three four-men interrogation teams of police under Captain Isidro Galvan were assembled in an extraordinary session which included the Director of the Prado Museum, the Under-Secretary of the Foreign Office representing the Institute of Spanish Culture, the Superior Chief of Madrid Police, the Chief of the Police Commissariat and—seen for the first time in their lives by eleven of the policemen assembled in the squads present—the Minister of Government himself and the Director-General of Security. The seriousness of the occasion made large, cold lumps form in the stomachs of the men.

The Minister spoke. In his face and his voice a considerable amount of strain was evident, perhaps because for several days

the focus of government had been directed wholly upon him
and his ministry. His orders stressed that, under any conditions,
the painting known as "The Second of May" by Francisco Goya,
which was presently "missing" from the Prado, had to be recovered without fail and at the earliest instant.

The Minister spoke from notes which had been carefully
thought out. He understated the necessity of recovering the
painting because that needed no emphasis; every man in the
room was a Spaniard, after all. He gave details of the background of Victoriano Muñoz, and of his family fixation which
had been long forgotten by society. He advised his audience
that Victoriano Muñoz had secured a transparency photograph
in color of the Goya from the Institute of Spanish Culture itself
only two weeks before its disappearance. He told them that
through friends in the government—everyone in the room
understood this thoroughly and did not judge it, for in Spain
nothing can be accomplished unless it is done through friends
—Victoriano Muñoz had secured a license for his friend, pur-
portedly a painter named Charles Smadja who was a famous
French copyist and who, it had been discovered within the
past twenty-four hours, had never entered Spain at any time
of his life, to work as a copyist in the Sala Goya of the Prado.
All day-duty guards at the Prado had identified an equally well-
known French copyist named Jean Marie Calbert as the man
who had worked in the Sala Goya, entering and leaving the
premises by use of the permit issued to Charles Smadja. The
chief conserje at the hotel in which Jean Marie Calbert had
resided in Madrid attested to having used his passkeys to
examine the contents of an unused apartment on the top floor
during the absence of Jean Marie Calbert from the building,
and discovering a full-scale copy of the Goya painting in progress. This, along with projection equipment for viewing the
color transparency, was now missing. The hotel in which Jean
Marie Calbert resided was and had been under lease to James
Bourne for over three years. Two guards at the Prado had
identified Bourne as having spent considerable time in the
museum, particularly in the Sala Goya, both prior to the disappearance of the painting and on the day of its disappearance.
The Federal Bureau of Investigation of the Government of the
United States had identified Bourne's fingerprints as being those
of one Robert Evans Cryder, last known at the time of his death

in an automobile accident in London, England, at which time
he had been a captain in the U. S. Army assigned to the Cryp-
tography Section of Supreme Headquarters Allied Expeditionary
Forces. The Passport Division of the United States Government
stated that the passport in the name of James Bourne was a
forgery, inasmuch as neither the photograph nor the expiration
date matched the Cryder data. Both prisoners had consorted
with Victoriano Muñoz. All three were acquainted with and had
been the guests of the Duchess de Dos Cortes, owner of the
paintings by Velázquez, Zurbarán and El Greco found on the
premises occupied by the murdered man. The statement by
the duchess had identified the paintings as having been hers;
she said—here the Minister nodded at Captain Galvan, who
nodded at Augustin Termio, who took out his notebook, opened
it to a place held by a rubber band and, clearing his throat
carefully, began to read. He had never been in such exalted
company in his life and he was scared to death.

"Question: Can you identify these paintings, my duchess?
Answer: They are paintings which hung—which should now
be hanging—in the castillo at Dos Cortes. Question: Did not
the duchess notice that they had been taken? Answer: Somehow a substitution has been made. Paintings identical to these
are hanging at Dos Cortes at present. This is not like Dr. Muñoz.
I am mystified. Question: Can the duchess clarify her last statement? Answer: Yes. You see, Dr. Muñoz has always been intensely interested in all Spanish paintings, but he has said
so many times that the only painting he would ever wish to
possess for himself would be 'The Second of May' by Goya."

Augustin Termio snapped his notebook shut and stood at
attention. Everyone ignored him. The Minister asked for the
statement by the porter in the Muñoz building. Captain Galvan
nodded at Emilio de los Claros, a sergeant who had been in far
more distinguished company than this over a considerable
period of years. The embodiment of crisp coolness, disdaining
to address the Minister, he addressed himself directly to his
superior officer.

Claros flipped open his book, giving the impression in so
doing that he was a black belt in judo, and read in a harsh,
flat voice. "Statement by Ignacio Flan-Torres de Francisco,
building porter at number six Calle Amador de los Ríos: Oh,
yes. That's him all right. That is his picture all right." The

sergeant paused and stared hard at Captain Galvan. "He refers to a photograph of James Bourne, sir, known now as Roberto Eva Cryder." He returned to his reading. "I tell you I was frightened of that man. He came five or six times a day to the building. Sometimes he appeared late at night or early in the morning. He would shake the whole place with his fists as he beat on the marqués' door. He would curse in some foreign language and kick at the door, may his soul rest in peace. I have never seen such a violent type and I thought it was a lucky stroke that the marqués was away."

The Minister said that Dr. Muñoz had been at Santiago de Compostela for four nights and three days visiting his confessor and spending most of his time praying at the cathedral. He also told his audience that they were assigned to a case which called for the organization of evidence leading to the conviction of the person or persons who had murdered Dr. Victoriano Muñoz, the Marqués de Villalba; however, as was indicated by his presence at this meeting and by the statements made, a most vital concern was the recovery of the Goya, and there was no doubt that a clear connection had been established between the two cases. He did not wish to interfere with police routine, but evidence indicated that the prisoner Jean Marie Calbert would be the most vulnerable because reprisals against his wife, presently a resident of Paris, could be brought to bear by French justice, and he would appreciate it if they would begin the interrogation of Calbert as soon as he had recovered from the effects of the bludgeoning at the time of his arrest. The Minister added that there was sufficient evidence against Bourne's wife to arrest her, but for the present he considered that she could be more useful to them while at large since she might lead them to the Goya.

The Minister had become paler with inner tension as he talked. The Under-Secretary, whose brother was a doctor, diagnosed him as an incipient ulcer man or as a sphincter grinder. The eyes of the men staring at the Minister, as though they could see each word as it left his mouth, became larger and darker. They all understood what his speech meant in practical terms: that the man who found the Goya could jump four ranks, that he could be transferred to wherever he chose, within reason, that he would have the protection of the highest people in the government, and would be marked for the better things.

In short, the members of the teams were awed at having been called into the presence of a State Minister, the Director-General of Security, the Chief of the Commissariat of Police, the Superior Chief of all Madrid Police, an Under-Secretary of the Foreign Office and the Director of the Prado Museum, but they appreciated it very much and were eager to get on with their work.

To curb the more enthusiastic and patriotic spirits Captain Galvan raised the point for all of them. "There are many, many methods of questioning prisoners, your excellency," he said in a straightforward manner, "and I wish to assure your excellency on behalf of myself and my men that, as indicated by the information which you have so skillfully gathered and so generously shared with us, one or the other of the prisoners, if not both, will undoubtedly reveal where the Goya may be found."

"Bear two things in mind, Captain Galvan," the Minister said. "First, the prisoners must be in a condition, following your questioning, to stand public trial in approximately two weeks, if that can be arranged, and I am sure it can be. Second, they are foreign nationals who are principals in a case which will undoubtedly attract the attention of the foreign press."

"Yes, your excellency."

"Are there any more questions?"

"No, your excellency."

"That will be all," the Minister said, leaving the room and followed by his full entourage which included everyone but Captain Galvan and his teams.

BOTH prisoners were reported as having fully regained consciousness and having eaten at two fifty-three A.M., so Galvan and four of his young men decided to begin with Jean Marie in a squad room which had windows at the ten-foot level. They sat around him in a semicircle, except for Galvan who paced most of the time. A male stenographer worked in the corner of the room behind Jean Marie, who had been provided with an armchair.

The benzedrine in the coffee that the prisoner had been served with his meal made him seem even more French than ever.

He could not sit still and requested permission to pace about with Captain Galvan, just as important businessmen sometimes conduct important meetings while walking six miles around a golf course. Galvan said that he would be happy to have Jean Marie join him. Silently he hoped that the prisoner had not been drugged too much, because then they usually began bawling like babies for no accountable reason, and a benzedrine crying jag was almost impossible to stop.

Pacing with a high step, as though he were dictating to Marshal Ney, Jean Marie began to unwind by talking. He used the word gentlemen frequently, almost as punctuation.

"Let there be no mistake, gentlemen," he said. "Whatever we have done which could be considered illegal, I am absolutely ready and willing to admit to you. You will say that such an offer on my part, gentlemen, is most generous, but I reply that I have great respect for your organization, that I wish to conceal nothing, and that I wish to get all unpleasantness over with."

Jean Marie had no conception that he was being held for murder. He did not associate himself at all with the death of Dr. Muñoz. Somewhere in his disturbed, sensitive, shaken mind he believed that he was being questioned and held because he had dropped the corner of the painting by Goya in the Prado and had run—a misdemeanor.

"When the confession is typed I will read it, and if it is what I am about to tell you now I will sign it without delay," he continued after another full turn of the room with Captain Galvan while he allowed his audience to consider the magnanimity of his offer. "But one fact must stand absolutely clear and apart, gentlemen. I had absolutely nothing to do with the murder of Cayetano Jiminez or of that insane little insect Muñoz, or of that hotel fellow, what's-his-name, Señor Elek." As far as the listeners were concerned, cases were about to be cracked right and left, but they showed no expression. Captain Galvan stopped pacing in tandem with the prisoner and moved over to the stenographer as though to test the acoustics in that part of the room.

"Neither I nor my friend Señor Bourne had anything whatsoever to do with those murders. Is that quite clear? If so, we may proceed from there."

"That is entirely clear, Señor Calbert," Captain Galvan said

202 : 202 :

RICHARD CONDON

blandly and imperturbably. "Please proceed. Please tell us the entire experience with all of those masterful copies of those masterful paintings from beginning to end."

"Ah, you have seen the copies then?"

"Formidable, señor."

"Thank you, thank you."

"We would like to hear all about them."

Jean Marie sat down in his chair and pressed his hand to his forehead in order to help himself think better. "You see, gentlemen," he told them, "some time ago, well over a year ago, my colleague and partner, Señor Bourne, came to me in Paris and began to talk to me about various methods by which we could substitute copies of the paintings of masters for the original masterpieces." He turned to the stenographer behind him. "Do I speak too fast for you?" he asked.

"No, señor," answered the stenographer. "Please continue as you will." It was at this moment that Jean Marie went into shock. They pressed him, they even got rough with him, but the more they questioned him, the further he seemed to retreat into catatonia.

AT six o'clock in the morning, Captain Galvan joined the relief team of two men and a stenographer in the room with Bourne. He nodded pleasantly as he came in, but the prisoner looked back blankly, fatigue showing in every excruciated muscle of his body.

Bourne's face was bruised just under the hairline beside the left temple, and his right cheekbone was split and badly swollen. The stubble was longer and filthier, his eyes blearier, his hands dirtier, and the elegant tailoring of his jacket and shapeless, soiled trousers seemed comical on his hulk. The jail clock at which he kept staring said six ten but he didn't know whether it was evening or morning. Time has very little authority in jails.

"Anything new?" Captain Galvan asked his young men.

"Nothing, sir. He says he will talk after he has been able to see his lawyer."

"These American criminals come complete with lawyers. It is a result of the cinema."

"Yes, Captain."

"Who is his lawyer?"

"He has asked permission to see the Duchess de Dos Cortes, Captain, so that she may recommend a lawyer to him."

"He'll have a crowded cell if he keeps these requests up," the captain said.

"Yes, Captain."

"He's good and tired, isn't he, the poor fellow?"

"Yes, Captain."

"Good. Read this to him." He extended a typed copy of Jean Marie's statement. "That should wake him up." The young officer thanked his superior, settled down comfortably near Bourne's left ear and began to read in a clear voice just under a shout. The captain lighted a cigar and sat down with his chair tilted against the whitewashed wall. "Termio, please!" he remonstrated from his place sixteen feet away. "Not so loud!"

"Yes, Captain." Termio modulated his voice. Bourne seemed to be listening carefully.

"Would you care to initial that?" Galvin asked him when the reading was over.

"No. I mean, I cannot until I have been permitted to consult a lawyer."

"Where is the Goya?"

"Ask me later."

"When?"

"When you're ready to make a deal."

"No deals."

"No Goya."

Captain Galvan motioned the two policemen out of the room. "That's all. This man needs sleep."

"Yes, my Captain," Termio said and they vanished. Captain Galvan strode heavily to the nearest chair and pulled it toward Bourne while he talked easily. "What is this talk about deals, anyway? Perhaps I misunderstood your meaning, Señor Bourne." He grinned with vintage cynicism.

"I am very tired, Captain," Bourne said, "and I am not able to think clearly, but my feeling is that after our innocence has been established—after the trial, that is—all we will owe you will be a few relatively minor charges such as illegal entry, false papers and the theft of paintings which by now have already been returned to their owner, the duchess, and I doubt that you burn so much to see justice done that you wouldn't consider sending my wife and Calbert and me over the frontier in exchange for giving the Goya back to the people of Spain. That is what I had in mind when I used the word deal."

Bourne fought to focus. Each word he had managed to say had emerged from him as a unit, not as a part of a sentence. He fell asleep sitting up. The captain sighed, went out into the corridor and called Augustin Termio. The officer came running, but the captain's hand halted him. "You have fifteen minutes to get this man awake and keep him awake," he said.

"Yes, my Captain."

"Do you realize that you are the only man in the company who cries out yes, my Captain after every sentence I utter? No! Don't answer. I am going to have a bit of breakfast. I suggest that you get the surgeon to give this man some efficient restoratives. You will call me when he has been refreshed, which will not be later than fifteen minutes."

"Yes, my Captain."

Good God, the captain thought as he strolled down the hall in the opposite direction, the man must be in love with me. He walked toward his breakfast slowly, knowing that it would be at least forty-five minutes before he was summoned.

BOURNE was awake again. He felt packed in ice, and it seemed as though his head had come to a point. He had the illusion that his vision was fantastically keen, which couldn't be so because the same captain was sitting directly in front of him, obscuring most of what could be seen.

"You fell asleep," the captain said.

"No wonder," Bourne answered.

"Before you fell asleep you were saying that you felt we would be more inclined to make a deal with you after you had been acquitted of the charge of the murder of Victoriano Muñoz, because the remaining charges, not being what might be called capital charges, might be overlooked by us if you returned the Goya. I think that is substantially what you said."

"Yes. That's about it." He felt like a piece of heavy rubber being stretched for hundreds of miles by two airplanes pulling in opposite directions. He rather liked the feeling. His visual clarity was phenomenal.

"Well, I am afraid you will not be acquitted of that murder, and this is why. I work backward now. Victim killed with an iron poker. Only Calbert's finger prints on the poker. Next, you and Calbert in locked room with the victim at time of death fixed by the medical examiner." He held up his finger next to his nose. "A locked room. Your connection with the victim in two separate crimes—the Dos Cortes robberies *and* the theft of the Goya, *plus* the fact that the death of Jiminez, bless him, and the hotel employee Elek have been confessed to by your associate Señor Calbert. All this before a court to whom you have been unmasked as a passport forger and an ersatz identity. My dear chap, I don't know what you know about our prosecutors in Spain, but I can tell you that they are very keen fellows indeed and that they will wrap you like a small package and deliver you to the executioner."

Bourne smiled ruefully. "If they do, goodbye Goya."

"Irresistible force, your execution; immovable object, the Goya. I am merely suggesting that you might like to trade yours and Calbert's life for a painting you will never see again, no matter where it is now."

"Captain, you know your business. When I make a deal I'll make it with you."

"And I, Señor Bourne, when I make a deal I'll make it with you. How about now?"

"I want to talk to the Duchess de Dos Cortes."

"Why?"

"I have to—I want to ask her myself if she will be kind enough to find a lawyer for our defense. I wouldn't know how to find a lawyer I can trust, but I trust her to know a lawyer I can trust."

"You may be right. She has had more experience than most duchesses with lawyers and jails." He stood up and patted Bourne warmly on the back. "I'll see what I can do. I think you got the point." He walked to the door, Bourne's limitless eyes following him, but as he opened it he turned, almost as an afterthought. "You did get the point, didn't you, Señor Bourne?"

"The Goya," Bourne rasped.

"Very good, Señor Bourne. You'll get your lawyer." He closed the door just as both airplanes, on either side of the continent, simultaneously let go of the huge, stretched rubber strip which was Bourne. He slammed into himself from all sides and collapsed on the side of a mountain.

THE duchess was ten minutes late for her appointment, which brought her into Eve's crooning embrace at twenty minutes to six, while Bourne and Jean Marie were still unconscious at the Cárcel de Carabancheles. She wore black, but had removed the rubies and had added a tiny veil which covered whatever expression she might wear.

Both women wept for a time, truly each for the other as much as for self; then the duchess sat down abruptly and Eve sorted the tea things.

"The police called me this afternoon," the duchess said. "My cousin, Victoriano Muñoz, has been murdered."

Eve dropped an empty teacup and gave an anguished cry.

"Eve! Darling, what is it? I didn't mean to upset you. I had forgotten that you knew him."

"I—we met at your party," Eve said.

"It's all quite shattering. Violence upon violence. Both of them men of mine, you might say."

"It's shocking. Shocking."

"It is far more shocking than you think, Eve. I was summoned by the police to identify the paintings which were hung on his wall. They were my paintings. He had stolen them from Dos Cortes."

"Ah!"

"Is Jaime here? Pablo tells me that he has come to the house again and again."

"No. He isn't here." Eve picked up the cup again, her mind still, and set the cup on a saucer and filled it with hot tea. "I had thought he would be back by now. He will be at any moment, I'm

sure." It had happened. She had thought that she could pull
Bourne along with her, stumbling through the stench in the
cavern, running through the darkness ahead of doom, but
now it had happened; he had found the faceless wall he
sought, had found someone's death between his fingers as
she had known he would. She fell into a chair. All the life he
had poured into her was escaping as though through unstop-
pable holes in the ends of her fingers, escaping like gas when
she held her hands up and like water when she let them fall.
It was all over, and nothing could threaten her ever again or
seem important.

She sat and she stared and she remembered Bourne, as the
duchess sat remembering Cayetano, each justified, each depleted.
The tea grew cold.

The telephone rang. Eve, nearest to it, did not hear. The
duchess looked at her wrist watch, then rose to answer it as if
by appointment. She listened, spoke, and listened again, then
hung up.

"Eve. Eve, dearest."

Eve looked up at her.

"That—a friend who is quite powerful in government called to
say—to tell me—to ask me to tell you that Jaime has been
arrested with M'sieu Calbert for my cousin's murder."

Eve did not speak, only sat up straighter.

"Jaime wants to see me," the duchess said. "Why?"

"He will tell you, I am sure."

"I will call the Minister himself." She went to the telephone,
quickly dialed a number, spoke a name into the receiver and
waited. When she spoke again it was in a low, rapid voice which
became more insistent as the sentences became shorter. Finally
she repeated only one word, "No? No? No?" widely spaced, and
then hung up.

"No one may see him," she said. "I don't understand it. That
was the Minister. He has done far more difficult things for me
in the past."

Eve was at the mahogany bar at the corner of the room. As
she poured two drinks into large inhalers the duchess walked
slowly across the room to join her.

"He will have the best lawyer in Spain, of course," the duchess
said aggressively. "I will see to that this evening. The lawyer I'll
get for him will be able to go in and out of those cells at Cara-

bancheles like a turnkey." She sipped the brandy and openly appraised Eve's haggardness. She was not as exultant as she had thought she would be, but she felt stronger and less lonely.

THE government released the story for world-wide publication on Monday morning. There were pictures and general information about Bourne and Jean Marie, who was identified as a famous French painter. As edition after edition sold out, the Paris papers ran pictures of Lalu Calbert, who had been found in Bordeaux, who was tearfully mystified but sure it was all an enormous mistake, and who then suddenly disappeared. The French stringers and correspondents were alerted to look for her in Madrid, at the jail or at the trial.

Since the Associated Press sold color art and photos to about two hundred Japanese papers on a very lucrative contract, they needed a color angle fast, and so The Pickett Troilus became The Velázquez Curse. The story tacked on to the spread said that the great Spanish master, who had painted only for Spain, had hexed this particular painting on his deathbed, warning all foreigners to lay off. This was known as King Tut's Tomb copy in the trade, and it always sold well. But what started out to be a mere merchandising convenience for the Japanese market developed into a really worthwhile world-wide sale, particularly to the United States roto outlets and South American dailies. Not only was it an art story, which had class for the former, but it also had a Spanish angle for the Latin-American outlets.

Sam Gourlay of *The Populace,* London, squandered an overseas telephone call to talk to Eve from Fleet Street, insuring the bet by having the conversation monitored on his office tape recorder, but his questions were gentle, generous, general and innocuous. Mainly he seemed to want to know if there was any evidence indicating that this case was in any way linked with the alleged international art traffic which, it was stated in police circles, was controlled by Jack Tense, Britain's Master Criminal. Straightfaced, Eve went along. She said that if Spanish masterpieces had indeed been stolen from the castle at Dos Cortes and the Marqués de Villalba had been murdered as a result, it must be the work of some gang of international criminals because her husband, a respected businessman and pillar of society in Madrid whose reputation was impeccable, was innocent, and she, the wife of the accused, would be grateful for anything *The Populace* might do to prove her husband's innocence. Gourlay asked her if she would face Jack Tense if *The Populace* were to send him to Spain, and she replied that she would do anything which would serve the cause of her husband's vindication and freedom. Sam said that he felt he could get something juicy out of that, and he hoped it would help her because it would certainly build readership for Jack's next series.

Feature writers, magazine people, extra syndicate hands, and mail, wire and telephone stringers covering for the important American news magazines and for the Milan weeklies, which had abandoned active coverage in Spain, began to appear in Madrid. They looted every nook and cranny of the story, but none of them saw the prisoners. Eve and the duchess were also still barred from seeing Bourne. Paris *Match* fruitlessly submitted a petition signed by the entire French press corps in an effort to see the man the London and Glasgow papers called "Kithless Calbert," Jean Marie being without attendant kin. Some of the news people tried to camp in the lobby of the hotel to bushwhack Eve, or to push their way into the duchess's vestibule, but they were disposed of by silent *policía armada* within ten minutes after complaints had been received. This caused remarkably little outcry over the freedom of the press.

The No-Do government newsreel shots also serviced the National Broadcasting Company, the Columbia Broadcasting System, Movietone, British and French Gaumont and the French Pathé reels; this was more a matter of monopoly than salesmanship. The film was redistributed on a second-run basis to South America and Asia, providing work for planes, ticket takers and workers in film raw stock factories. The scenes photographed showed the outside of the Cárcel de Carabancheles on a sunny day, when it looked like a glove-manufacturing plant, the duchess alighting from her Pegaso and walking rapidly across the pavement behind a high muffler and dark glasses into her house, and close shots of copies of the Velázquez, the Zurbarán and the Greco, which footage was always accompanied by a vivid lecture, in several languages, by the beaming Representative Pickett of Illinois and his delightful young wife.

Mr. Pickett got more space out of the murder than the outside of the jail, than El Greco, than the murder weapon, than the building porter at the Calle Amador de los Ríos, or even than Mrs. Pickett—mainly because he was so articulate and available. He encountered one small squall when a Republican committeeman from Illinois placed an overseas phone call to ask him what the hell he thought he was doing when he knew goddam well that Congress was in session. Pickett fired right back that he was cementing U.S.-Spanish relations, and that he was proving that there was someone in politics who knew just a little something about how the great Spanish people felt about their great painters, for Christ's sake, and what the hell was this poison-pen talk like didn't he know Congress was in session? The boys knew goddam well how sick he was and how he was taking a lot of goddam chances with his health right now in order to make sure that this murdering renegade Bourne didn't bring the entire Spanish-American accord right down on their goddam heads. "Did you ever hold office, you silly son-of-a-bitch?" Mr. Pickett yelled. "Do you know the first goddam thing about practical politics? I tell you one goddam thing you'll know, you silly son-of-a-bitch, you've made one good, solid, lifetime enemy out of Homer Pickett!" He slammed the phone down from shoulder height, then crumbled into the chair beside it. Mewing at Marianne, he sounded perhaps forty years younger than the pol who had just belched smoking terror and reprisals into the phone.

"I *hate* to talk like a longshoreman," he wailed, "but it's the only language they seem to understand. That ridiculous Al Burgerfolz! I tell you, hon, if it takes my *last dollar* I'm going to have that one drummed out of the Party before he gets some idea that he's going to use *his* last dollar first. Oh, how I *hate* roaring like a lumberjack with all those operators listening in. How I absolutely *detest* and *despise* having to justify what is just about the best job of diplomatic front work being done today *throughout* Europe.

"Ah, the hell with him," Mrs. Pickett said. "No matter what he wants to do to you now he can't make it stick. Not any more he can't."

THE duchess's life was going through an unusual metamorphosis. Suddenly she began to cultivate the leading figures of the government, most of whom she had made tremble with anathema for most of her adult life. She held open house in Madrid. Invitations went out. She spent most of the mornings on the telephone, until two o'clock when she had to dress for lunch with the cabinet, their wives, their under-secretaries and their wives, the ambassadors and their wives, plus visiting prelates from Argentina. Beginning at eight every evening her salon was filled during the cocktail hour. She crackled and charmed and shocked and titillated nearly every guest, just as though she had always admired and envied each of them. By the dinner party following the fourth reception she had succeeded in having the rule that neither Bourne nor Jean Marie could have visitors reversed. She also had made a fast friend of the Acusador Fiscal, who would try the case for the state.

THE warden arranged for Eve to see Bourne in a large, square room which was empty except for two chairs. Two *guardias* brought Bourne in, then left them alone. They sat in the chairs and looked at each other. She offered him a cigarette, which he refused. She put them back in her purse without taking one for herself.

"It happened just about the way you said it would," he said.

"That doesn't matter."

All at once he felt the value of what she had given him, as a boy sees the value of the dead bird in his hand which he has just shot. In turn, he had bequeathed to her a desert of memories. He took her face between his hands and kissed her with longing and regret for what he had not given her. He pulled his chair directly beside hers, so that he was facing in one direction and she in the other, and spoke almost inaudibly into her ear in an effort to comfort her without comforting the microphones which he was sure had been sowed in the room.

"We're going to get out of this. I mean it. They are frantic about losing the Goya. They're going to make a deal." As he watched her she turned her head and stared at him, not understanding but trusting. "Don't answer," he said. "Wherever you can, just nod. Okay?" She nodded.

"Blanca. Here. Soon."

She nodded.

"We have to go high up. Only one we know they won't double-cross. Okay?" She nodded.

He stood up, moved his chair back to its original position, sat down again and held her hands. "No more of this kind of work afterwards. You can quote me that I have decided to retire. We'll open a bookstore in Sweden or a hotel in Switzerland. I've been damned near out of my mind I've been so scared, and that's no way to earn a living."

She leaned forward and entwined her arms around his neck. Resting in his arms, at peace, she puzzled over the dichotomy of being doomed and blessed for knowing where she belonged. Then the guards came in and announced regretfully that the visit was over.

JACK TENSE called Eve the following morning without mentioning his name, letting his voice identify him, and in professional fashion asked her if she expected to be at the airport for lunch that day. Before she could answer he told her that it was a very good restaurant and so crowded that "nobody is able to remember seeing nobody." He said that at two o'clock she might run into someone with news from home, then hung up abruptly as though the telephone booth was being surrounded by hostile police and troops.

She drove to the airport along the only perfect stretch of highway in Spain, called the Avenida de Americas before it reaches the city line, and the Barajas Road thereafter. It is the highway which takes the most exalted foreign visitors of state into Madrid, so it has to be perfect. Illogically, the half mile of pavement leading onto the perfect road from the airport has not been repaired in man's memory, and gives the appearance of having been shelled regularly every morning.

Tense looked right through her from his place at a table across the restaurant. He was wearing a popularization of an alpinist's hat with what appeared to be a whisk broom sticking out of the band. She sat down beside him. "You wore the right clothes," he said out of the side of his mouth. "Nobody will remember clothes like that. Good girl."

"If nobody remembers clothes like these I've been gulled out of four hundred dollars," Eve snapped, which made him shake with laughter until she realized he was back at his pleasure of teasing her again.

"Don't tell me if you don't trust me, and if you do trust me you must be crazy," Tense said, "but what happened with your husband's business affairs?"

She omitted nothing. She spoke with relief. She had to have someone to unburden to, and Tense had become one of her closest friends the day she had first met him. He liked the idea of Bourne holding out the Goya, deeming it to be an extremely professional calculation. She wanted reassurance on Bourne's estimate of the liberating power of the Goya, and exulted when Tense told her that there was no doubt but that a deal would be made and the entire matter written off once the trial was over. He asked her if she had considered everyone who might want to frame her husband for the Muñoz murder. She could think of no one, because there was no one, and her husband was just as baffled as she was.

Over paella, wine, flan and coffee Tense told her how sentimental Mr. Merton of *The Populace* had become about her since her husband's arrest and trial on so popular a charge. He arranged all his remarks so that she would make him laugh with comically affronted reactions throughout the meal. As they were sipping coffee and gazing at each other fondly, he asked her if she had discussed any of this with his friend Enrique López. The question baffled her; it would never occur to her to discuss anything like that with López, whom she had met only in writing, she said. When Jack explained that López could probably find out who was jobbing her husband her lovely mouth formed a perfect O. That was what a big organization was for, he said. If López couldn't find out what was happening in his line he wouldn't be able to stay in business very long, now would he? Eve was startled, confused and interested to think that there was any chance that she might help Bourne. Tense told her that he would talk to López because he had to pay his respects anyway while he was in the country, even if he was there as a gentleman journalist. He wanted her to understand that the whole inquiry might come to nothing, and that Bourne might not need to know, what with that Goya in hand for old-fashioned trading purposes; still, a man liked to know who was jobbing him, and nothing could be lost by trying. Eve told him that once again she just didn't know how to thank him, and he answered that if she really meant that they could go right back to her place and pop into bed because one thing was for sure, her husband wasn't likely to dart in on them. The outraged reaction she flashed at him gave him enormous pleasure.

He insisted that they leave separately. As she walked through the airport building she passed Colonel Gomez, the chief customs officer. He stared at her, flushed deeply and passed without speaking.

THE courtroom in the Palace of Justice in Madrid in which Bourne and Jean Marie were to be tried was one of the most elegant in Europe. Forty yards long and twenty yards wide, with a ceiling twenty feet high, it was richly furnished with panels of dark, polished wood to a height of six feet on all walls, above which a princely, rich maroon cloth continued to the ceiling.

On the wall behind the Magistrates' desk, which was made of solid mahogany and richly carved, the royal coat of arms had been fixed signifying that all called to the bar would be accorded the justice of the kingdom of Spain, so designated by its citizens in the public referendum of July 6th, 1947, which had voted eighty-two point two four per cent in favor of a pro-monarchic government. Between the royal coat of arms and the Magistrates' desk stood a large brass crucifix whose presence made the swearing of witnesses upon the Holy Bible unnecessary.

The Magistrates' desk faced the open end of a horseshoe-shaped dais on which had been placed the desks of the Public Prosecutor, Acusador Fiscal, and the Private Prosecutor, Acusador Privado; these were to the left of the direct vision of the Magistrates, and the desk of the Defense Attorney sat on the arm of the horseshoe to the Magistrates' right. The desks of the Magistrates and prosecution and defense were three feet higher than the level of the accused, who sat facing the Magistrates at a desk between the arms of the horseshoe.

According to custom, attorneys for both sides stayed in their seats, and even when addressing the President of the Court did not get to their feet. During important cases, attorneys and magistrates not directly connected with the procedure were allowed to enter the courtroom in their official robes and take such seats as were available at the desks of either the defense or prosecuting attorneys. When anyone crossed in front of the crucifix, they crossed themselves or genuflected.

The Magistrates, the president in the center, sat in severe, high-backed chairs lined with maroon satin. Along with the attorneys and the clerks of the court, they wore black gabardine robes. A separate black velvet yoke on each robe hung fore and aft, attached to the garment at the shoulders but not at the sides.

The determination of the press to find seats in the court somewhat defeated the hopes of the various sangrophiles and écouteurs among the public who had planned on attending, but as the red-faced man from United Press said, what the hell did they want to squeeze in there for and get pushed around when they could read all about it if they subscribed to a New York paper? This did not mean that the Spanish press suppressed any news of the Bourne-Calbert trial; they gave it, as a matter of policy on crime stories, about the same amount of space that the *New York Times* gives the Jersey City night court.

The trial was under the protection of a Magistrate President of the Court, sitting with two other Magistrates if no death penalty was requested by the Prosecution, and with four other Magistrates if there was. There was no jury.

Trials are broken into two daily sessions. Most murder trials in Spain require only three to seven sessions because both the prosecution and the defense are required to submit their entire cases in writing to the Magistrates beforehand. The briefs are read aloud to the court at the beginning of each trial session, together with the résumé of testimony recorded accumulatively at the trial. Both sides have full access to each other's complete cases in advance, including the right to examine witnesses, strategy and physical evidence in the manner in which civil cases are conducted in the federal courts of the United States. In addition, the attorneys for each side are required by law to advise their opponents, through the President of the Court, of any changes to be incorporated, so that the other party may adjust its own arguments to offset evidence or reasoning not anticipated. The trial itself is held to hear witnesses and to offer publicly all evidence, intent and motivations which have been placed before the court for judgment.

When the verdict has been reached by a Spanish court the sentence is not passed at the bar, but is delivered in writing to the accused in his cell, to his attorneys, to the prosecutors, and to the press.

EVE had walked the seven blocks from Calle de Marengo to the Palace of Justice on Calle de Bárbara de Braganza to stand helplessly before the building, unable to bring herself to enter. She walked aimlessly away from the building until, four blocks later, she found herself at the Calle Amador de los Ríos. She walked most of the day, seldom looking up to find where she was. At noon she called the duchess, but her friend had been invited to wait in an anteroom off the court until she would be called to testify—a deference to her rank as all other witnesses were required to wait in the corridor. At last Eve wandered into the tiny parklike plaza called the City of Paris at the side of the Palace of Justice and sat down. Then, all at once, worried that she might be summoned by some unknown urgency, she hastened back to the hotel to cast sidelong glances at the telephone as she paced endlessly back and forth.

THE trial of Robert Evans Cryder, known as James Bourne, and Jean Marie Calbert began on a Tuesday morning twenty-six days after the day of the murder of Dr. Victoriano Muñoz, the Marqués de Villalba. The President of the Court and four magistrates entered the courtroom from a door in the rear and seated themselves at the long desk. The president leaned forward to the clerk of the court and said, "*Audiencias pública!*" in a clear voice. Two attendants opened doors to the side corridor and the procession of attorneys and accused entered. The prisoners were not handcuffed or shackled, but they

walked between two armed police guards who carried carbines
and side arms. Eight people marched in the procession, each
to his assigned desk, the guards sitting directly behind the
prisoner to which they had been assigned. Finally the attendants opened the doors at the back of the room and the press,
with some battered members of the stronger public, boiled in.
All of this was done in a silence which would have been total
were it not for the muffled shuffling of feet. At the instruction
of the president, the clerk of the court stood and read the case
prepared by the prosecution; it demanded that the death sentence be passed upon the accused.

The prosecution's case was as long and tedious as extreme
thoroughness usually is. It said that it would prove that neither
of the defendants were morally competent; that Robert Evans
Cryder, known as James Bourne, was in Spain under forged
documents and identity; that he had devoted in excess of two
years to the planning and preparation of a robbery of certain
paintings and of substituting copies for these paintings which
had been painted by the co-defendant, Jean Marie Calbert, who
would be shown to have been an infamous trafficker in forged
paintings for criminal purposes over a number of years. The
prosecutor covered every point neatly set down in the confession
with which Jean Marie had provided Captain Galvan, plus
several other nuts and bolts. In passing, the prosecution mentioned Eve Bourne as the courier who had brought the copies
of Spanish masterpieces into Spain through three different
points of entry—which was not a crime per se—and stated
that the Customs Department would supply further testimony
in this regard.

No mention was made of the painting by Francisco Goya
called either "The Second of May" or "The Attack Upon the
Mamelukes in the Puerta del Sol." No mention was made of
the murder of Cayetano Jiminez. The Minister of Justice and
the Minister of Government had met with the President of the
Court and Acusador Fiscal and the Defense Attorney and had
exposed all of the government's knowledge of the crime linking
the theft of the Goya and the murder of Jiminez, with reasons
for bypassing these points at the present. Both sides had agreed
that justice would be served were the defendants tried for
murder without bringing in evidence of extraneous crimes. The
government's position was that the Goya was merely missing,

and they had faith that at the proper time someone would come
forward to assist them in recovering it. The prosecution was
willing to concede that this area of the case was irrelevant to
a successful trial leading to a conviction, and naturally the
defense readily agreed; one more murder and an attempted
crime as extraordinary as the theft of a Goya from the Prado
could not enhance his clients' chances.

However, the prisoners' lawyer did discuss the matter with
his clients before acceding to the request of the government.
Jean Marie gave it no consideration and left the decision entirely
in Bourne's hands. Bourne thought about little else. The government's tactics confirmed that they had not been able to
discover the Goya's hiding place, nor fathom why a freshly
painted duplicate had been found propped against the wall
where the original had hung. This fact permitted Bourne to
watch his trial for his own life with considerable detachment
and without morbidity, and it buoyed up Jean Marie's erratic
spirits because it meant that until the original could be found
his copy of the Goya would continue to hang in the Prado—
until, that is, as a popular song put it, the real thing came along.

As the voice of the reading clerk droned on, Bourne relaxed
in his chair, smiling slightly with a certain kindliness on the
proceedings. The brief emphasized that Robert Evans Cryder,
known as James Bourne, and Jean Marie Calbert had come to a
thieves' falling out with Victoriano Muñoz, and had murdered
him in consequence thereof. The prosecution's case displayed
considerable smugness; due to Jean Marie's confession, his
fingerprints on the murder weapon, and the testimony which
would be forthcoming from witnesses who had discovered the
defendants an instant after the murder, the boom could be
lowered by the court without any other needless consideration.

The statement by the prosecution took up the entire first
session, and the court was adjourned to meet again at three that
afternoon. The judges left the court, and then everyone else,
including the prisoners and their guards, made their way out
as best they could.

As the armed guard closed in, Bourne signaled to the defense
counsel, who nodded and moved on. The prisoners were taken
to separate cells in the basement of the building, where the
defense attorney, still in his robes, joined Bourne immediately.
Rafael Corruno-Baenz was a leading monarchist—that is, a

politician for monarchistic party activity—a friend of the
duchess's, and a self-consciously, impatiently brilliant man whose
quick manner disguised an ugly temper which had been born
of almost everyone else's inability to keep up with him. He was
still too young to slow down, and his political rise had been
retarded because his arrogance had insured resentment; now he
needed the duchess's great good will among the powers of the
Monarchist Party to have any hope for his future career.

Aside from a personality and vanity wholly unfit for the practice of politics, Corruno-Baenz was the most successful, expensive, and best-known trial lawyer in Spain, a country where youth
is so poorly served that his feat of pre-eminence was equal
roughly to the ascension of a Negro physician to the presidency
of the Mississippi Medical Association. Though accepting
Bourne's case meant turning down several other clients, he had
done so because the duchess had suggested that he take it. He
was efficient, if not compassionate. He admired Germans for
their science, orderliness and military skill; the British for their
literature and for their experience in law—though he was mystified by the jury system, which left justice to the emotions of
amateurs-at-law; and those Americans who had retained his
services in various capacities. He deplored the French, and for
the Italians he had a shrug and a sigh and a harsh noise made
at the back of his throat. The rest of the world was made up of
fantasts like the Communists or non-Catholics or Swedes or the
Chinese, people free to commit any horribly sexual act without
fear of sin. To them went more than disapproval; they received
his hatred.

Corruno-Baenz felt contempt for Jean Marie as a man and as
a Frenchman; here was a man who was admittedly guilty and
yet lacked that imperative sense of consequence which defined
manhood to Corruno. Bourne, whose physical strength, tailoring,
and political connections he envied and appreciated, represented
a human condition which he had not yet solved. There was
a preciseness about Bourne's presentation, and his prehensile
mind was to be admired, but he was not a serious man. He
showed no sense of the involvement, and he seemed unaware
of sin, legal or moral or spiritual; yet he was a man who demonstrated a nice feeling for the consequence of his acts.

The defense counsel had been looking forward to lunch, but
he knew his duty as well as the almost reflexive requirement of

all clients following the first session of their own trials; invariably they found it necessary to be reassured that the prosecution did not have a case promising to result in anything unpleasant. He told them all, naturally, that they were not to worry, and they, who had sat there while the Fiscal had woven around them a shroud of ineluctible reasoning and evidence, would believe him. Therefore he regarded Bourne patronizingly and, while waiting for the inevitable question, offered him a cigarette before sitting down languidly upon the stool in the corner of the cell. When he saw that Bourne intended to remain standing he rose quickly to his feet again, but then Bourne sat down on the edge of the bed, so Corruno re-seated himself upon the stool.

"I want to read your brief before you deliver it."

"You what?"

"Why wasn't I shown the prosecutor's brief? You're a legal technician. What the hell do you know about this case except what I tell you? Do you want to argue from the facts or do you want to do legal embroidery?"

Corruno sprang to his feet. "Who are you talking to?" he blazed. "I withdraw from the case, and I will so advise the president of the court immediately." He started to leave.

Bourne put his great hand on Corruno's chest and pushed him gently against the wall of the cell. "Think about it. You withdraw from this case and I will tell the duchess that you prepared this case entirely upon Jean Marie's confession to the police and that you have given me no opportunity of seeing either your brief or the prosecution's, even though his brief this morning contained statements which, if they have been sworn to, constitute perjury and which, if attacked and exploded, can mean acquittal. Is that the kind of a lawyer you are? You want to withdraw?"

Corruno stared down at the restraining hand, then looked levelly at Bourne until he took his hand away and stepped back. "I'm sorry," he said.

Corruno stared him down, then kept looking at him until his eyes gradually became expressionless again. "Sit down," he ordered. Bourne sat on the bed.

"All right. What testimony?"

"The servants, Pablo and Josefina Soltes, who have been the body servants of the duchess, our duchess, most of their lives, for some reason were working at Muñoz' apartment on the day of the murder. Nearly everything else they told the police is a lie. He says that Muñoz came out to greet us at the door to the salon after we arrived—a lie. He says that in fifteen minutes or so our violence and shouting were so frightening that his wife telephoned the police. A lie. The timing can be fixed by the medical examiner's report, the time that Muñoz' call came through the switchboard at my hotel, the time of the call recorded at the police station which is directly around the corner from the Muñoz apartment, and the time of the police arrival. Every one of those times must be a matter of record. The only guess will be the medical examiner's, but his time must fall in with those others because Muñoz died between the time he made the call to me and the time the call was made to the police."

"This is very, very significant evidence—if it all will hold together as you say." Corruno had become excited. "But why would the servants arrange such a thing? We must have a motive!"

"I've been thinking about it. A lot of things which change people's lives are done on the spur of the moment. They could have heard him summoning me to a meeting. He spoke with considerable anger. He was certainly in no danger of his life at that moment; I know enough about people to know that he couldn't have talked to me in that way if he realized he was about to be murdered. In that hard and arrogant way of his, not unlike your own, he had no intention of dying for many years, believe me."

"I regret my arrogance. It was unprofessional. Please go on."

"Let's say that the servants heard him make the call, and, in one of those flashes of amateur criminal inspiration, killed him, stole whatever they wanted to steal, called the police, and waited for us to walk in to be arrested for what they had done. I tell you, Pablo literally pushed us into that room with the corpse and locked the door after us. The police did the rest."

"This is all worth examining, and you may be sure that I will do so most thoroughly. However, I must point out that the motives presented by the Fiscal this morning as to why you and your colleague would have killed Muñoz were absolutely impeccable."

"Not if the police were to find any of the property of Muñoz in the effects of either of the servants."

"That is true. But it would not seem likely that such a condition would exist almost a month after the murder."

"We must insist that they be watched by the police. It would take time for amateurs to sell stuff like that. Don't you think that if the timing of the calls proves that my theory holds water, and if they were caught with stolen property, that there would be a very strong case against them?"

"Perhaps."

"And a substantially weakened case against us?"

"Perhaps."

Bourne thought of a faceless man named Enrique López. He watched López steal some dark object from the Muñoz apartment. He watched López put the dark object into the pocket of the heavy-set butler, Pablo. He watched the police pounce upon Pablo and his wife almost immediately. He shuddered and felt nauseous, and forced his mind to fill with the picture of "The Second of May" by Francisco Goya. He could not explain to himself why he had thought of Enrique López. He knew that he had been framed. He knew that he hadn't killed Muñoz and that those two servants were the only people who could have killed him, but it occurred to him that he was building fright inside this prison and that soon he would begin to agree to anything in order to get out, at whatever bloodying and eviscerating cost to any stranger. Vaguely he heard Corruno say that he would have to locate the Fiscal and the Magistrates at once, that changes in briefs must be made and an examination of those servants attended to. Then the voice stopped, and he was out of the cell and on his way before Bourne was fully aware that he had gone.

He sat on the bed, his back propped up against the wall, concentrating with all his strength upon something he remembered Eve telling him about what a psychiatrist had told her years and years before. The man had emphasized over and over again that it was perfectly permissible for Eve to think any thought she wished which came unexpectedly into her mind. Only when a thought found action and consequence by being carried out could a wrong be committed—which of course was in direct variance with almost all religious instruction, and therefore, Bourne reasoned hopefully, undoubtedly true.

He stared at the wooden stool, the bucket and the incongruous brightly-colored rug, and thought that if he could talk to Jean Marie he would not know what to say any more than he knew what to say to himself in explanation or apology for what had happened. If Eve had held tightly to that cardboard tube which had contained the three paintings by Velázquez, Zurbarán and the Greek while Elek and the porters had been in her room at the hotel, he wondered if any of this could have happened. Would Cayetano still be alive? Or Elek and Muñoz? Or when she had reached the airport would Muñoz have telephoned the police that she had stolen national treasure and was trying to take the paintings through? Then Eve would have been in jail. He could not conceive of her in jail. All at once he remembered her three passports and three false names and the Colonel Gómez who had remembered her so well that afternoon when he had stopped by to see Muñoz. He knew that she was free because they thought she might somehow lead them to that Goya. It was then that Bourne saw where the slip had been made, where the crime had become something less than his sixteen-year standard of perfection. The fault had been with Francisco Goya betraying the Muñoz family in 1810. If that hadn't happened Victoriano would have had no interest in Bourne's work, and they would all be free and richer than ever. The trouble with an irrefutable cause like that was that one could not plan around it; a cause had to have an effect.

Regret was only worry about the past, but still he regretted his sense of pride and propriety which had insisted that they regain the loot from Muñoz, which in turn had resulted in Jean Marie going mentally askew. For sixteen years, from the autumn of 1941 when he had begun to plan his first criminal project, which had been interrupted by the war, Bourne had considered prison as a concrete possibility, as a sort of fine for being caught offside. Prison was the inevitable consequence of incompetence at his work. It was a part of his professional thinking because it was a natural component of each crime he would commit, and a larger component within the complex of his accumulated criminal accomplishments.

Now he was in prison, and he could find no incompetence which had brought about this clear consequence. He had acquired the paintings from Dos Cortes with considerable skill; it had been a business matter well executed. The murder of Gustavo

Elek marked where business had ended and true crime had begun. If only he had understood the meaning of murder the way Eve had understood it. Because he had not committed the murder he could not see its connection to himself, and since he had bargained with Muñoz he could accept the thought of prison abstractly. He had taught himself that if and when he had made a mistake prison was the inevitable consequence, and he had delivered that pre-judgment wholly unaware of his hopeless inability to understand the threat of true sin, of murder and of the condonement of murder. The essence of his joy in realizing that the Goya would allow him to escape the punishment he had earned was that he knew that none of it could ever happen again, that he must abandon his profession, because if his moral judgment was so faulty he would pay for it in the only way one can pay for lack of criminal judgment—by dying in prison or by a noose.

Bourne realized that he had thought so deeply and with such concentration about himself and his predicament that he did not remember to feel sorrow for Cayetano's silence in a silver box under the ground, or for the duchess's horror of awakening every morning, of driving herself to live throughout the day and of trying to sleep when night came. The disadvantage, when he examined it closely, his mind turning upon his guilt, was that prison, a factor which he had treated with scientific considera- tion for so many years, had somehow overtaken him, and that his misunderstood insensitivity to danger, in this case a murder, had brought him there. So do all stumble when they examine history.

A few minutes later Bourne was notified that the afternoon session of the court had been postponed to the following day at three o'clock, by order of the President of the Court and at the request of the attorney for the defense. At ten twenty that night he was told by a jailer that word had been received from the Office of the Minister of Government that an appointment had been granted to the Duchess of Dos Cortes to see him at seven o'clock the following evening. His analytical, professorial manner with himself dissolved; he was to see her at last, to have a chance to beg her to believe that he had not known what Victoriano was going to do. She would comfort him and tell him that she under- stood and that she forgave him for any part he might have had in the terrible affair. She would tell him that he did not need to produce Victoriano to swear that he had murdered Cayetano without ever telling Bourne. She would look into his eyes and smile at him and forgive him, and then she would listen attentively and carefully about what she needed to say to the highest officials of government about the Goya so that he could be freed immediately and they could all go away from this terrible place of trouble and shame and horror and pain and live happily in kindness to each other.

At three seventeen the following afternoon when the court convened, the President of the Court instructed the clerk to read the argument for the defense. Jean Marie had obtained a sketch pad from a jailer and, holding it in his lap, drew with concentration and complete disregard for the developments of the trial. Bourne, having rested better than he had in weeks, regarded the scene with vast calm, listening politely to Corruno's brief which he had read at noon. The defense brief was shorter than that presented by the Fiscal, but it was excellently reasoned, a fact which reflected credit upon Corruno, who had not slept at all the night before as he assembled its new contents and wording.

The defense would prove the improbability—and perhaps the impossibility—of the defendants' being able to have caused the death of Victoriano Muñoz, and in so doing might assist the police in apprehending the actual person or persons who had committed the murder, an opening which was received gratefully by the press in the courtroom.

Corruno then quoted from the brief of the Fiscal that the time of the death of the deceased would be established through the testimony of an expert witness, the medical examiner, who was to be heard in court. The time of the death as so established would be contrasted with the time Dr. Muñoz had made his telephone call to Bourne through the hotel switchboard, with the official police records which would show the time of the call summoning them to the scene and their time of arrival at the apartment. In short, the defense, supported by the record, would reveal that the time disparities were so great that the murder must have occurred between fourteen and sixteen minutes before the defendants could possibly have arrived at the Muñoz residence.

It would also be shown that only Pablo Soltes and his wife Josefina were on the murder premises at the time of the death of Victoriano Muñoz by violence, which offered the possibility that Pablo and Josefina Soltes had perjured themselves, and the defense would demand that they be produced to confirm or deny their original statements under oath.

"Reasonable doubt. At last an about-face for tomorrow's editions," *France-Soir* said to the London *Daily Sketch*.

"Reasonable doubt won't help us sell papers," said *Daily Sketch*. "Conviction of a couple of servants isn't what the public wants to read. That's a classic anticlimax."

"Not in France."

"Well, after all, your man is French. You have tomorrow's story all written for you."

The clerk of the court announced that under other circumstances the defense brief would have begun with a description of the exemplary character of the defendant Robert Evans Cryder, called James Bourne, which would be supported by laudatory character references from officers under whom he had served in the United States Army. It was known that the defendant had been a respected businessman in Madrid, active in charitable enterprises, a valued member of the most distinguished Madrid society, a musician of talent, a respected scholar in the field of Spanish art, and an excellent horseman. Each of these attributes would be attested to by character witnesses of high station in Spanish life who would testify voluntarily on the defendant's behalf. The defense would show that there was nothing sinister about the false passport and identity carried by the defendant at the time of his arrest, as claimed by the Fiscal. According to the sworn records and statements of the United States Army and of affidavits submitted by agents of the Federal Bureau of Investigation of the United States Government, the defendant, Robert Evans Cryder, called James Bourne, at the conclusion of World War II in England had been struck upon the head in such a manner as to cause severe injury and amnesia in an omnibus accident from which he had been the sole survivor, and, in the confusion of the rescue, the passport of an accident victim named James Bourne had been retrieved by the prisoner from the wreck. This would be supported entirely by the record which would also show that since 1945 Robert Evans Cryder, believing himself to be James Bourne, had been a resident of London, Paris and Madrid.

As the clerk of the court read on Bourne looked across at Rafael Corruno-Baenz with freshened respect; in fact, he goggled at the defense attorney who happened to look his way and nod in boredom at that moment. Bourne had stolen the passport from the bus wreck and had planted his own on the nearest corpse. He could not imagine what Eve had told Corruno, but it must have taken a magnificent performance to impel the young lawyer to run down every official agency source on the accident and insert it into the record. He felt a little giddy that two such artists' hands had been at work on his behalf.

The *Time* man told the footless Magnum photographer next to him that they just might see the two defendants sprung. The Magnum man, feeling emasculated without his camera, could not care less; he was trying to decide whether he should attempt to get some shots with a Minox, whether he could get away with it if he did, and how much money the shots would bring if he could pull it off. It was a deadly dull nothing of a trial, but that Frenchman was going crazy quietly right before their eyes and some studies of him would sell if he worked fast, and if nothing big happened by the last day he would risk it.

The droning seemed to go on without pause until after a while the clerk sat down. Everyone suddenly felt wide-awake again, and the president adjourned the court until ten o'clock the following morning.

THE duchess came to Bourne's cell, led by the old jailer who had been greatly pleased and greatly honored by her beauty and presence a few years before when she had been remanded to a cell in the building during her trial. They chatted like old friends as they walked along, he skittering almost sideways just half a step ahead of her so that he could look up at her as they went. Her hair was coming in very dark because there was no Cayetano to enjoy its blondness, she wore mourning and her eyes were dull black.

The old man opened the door of Bourne's cell, then scurried away into darkness. The duchess entered, holding out her hand which Bourne took in both of his and kissed. He looked into her eyes and knew what he saw there, the way a patient sometimes can read the eyes of a doctor. He felt himself shiver as he asked her to sit down. She had not spoken or smiled, but when she was seated on the edge of the bed, her long, white hands in graceful repose in her lap, she said, "Eve told me you wanted to see me."

"Thank you for coming here, Blanca."

She nodded.

"How is Eve?"

"In good health, I think."

"I have nearly been out of my mind since Cayetano—"

"I too."

"I want to thank you for finding Rafael Corruno-Baenz and persuading him to take this case."

"I could do no less for you."

"After what happened that Tuesday I went to your house every three hours like clockwork. I telephoned to Dos Cortes and to the south. I couldn't find you. I had to speak to you."

"And now I am here. Or, more to the point, you are here. Speak, Jaime."

"When Victoriano was alive I tried to find him to bring him to you. I wanted to drag him before you to make him tell you."

"Victoriano is dead. Whatever you wanted to have him tell me you will have to tell me yourself."

He had tried not to look at her, but now his eyes returned to hers. As he looked at his friend, he exploded with talk which healed him as it fell upon both of them. As he talked she offered no comment, and her facial expression did not change in any way. He sat beside her and held her left forearm, one great hand gripping her wrist, the other clenching below the elbow as he tried to give her his anguish. But like a child's ball thrown against a wall, it kept coming back to him.

"I knew nothing about it. I was involved in a certain remote way, Blanca, but I never knew what was going to happen. It could not have happened if I had known. Never. I loved Cayetano as I love you. I had no truer friends than you, and I have needed so terribly to tell you *how* I am a part of the cause of your loss, but an unknowing part. Not an innocent part, but I did not know what was going to happen, or that Cayetano was in any way involved, or that what was going to happen could even touch you or Cayetano. Everything moved in such a way that sometimes I don't know where it started or where it could have been stopped. I stole those paintings from Dos Cortes, Blanca, but I wasn't taking anything from you. I know they aren't important to you and never were. I took some colored canvas down from dark walls, canvases no one ever looked at, and when Victoriano stole them from me I considered that it was my property he had taken. The thief divested, the thief gulled, the thief self-righteously indignant, the thief at once willing to fall in with the plans of this man he sees as a fool. Mind you, Blanca, he still sees the man who has gulled him as a fool; the man who has murdered to get these paintings is still seen as a fool. And then the fool suddenly becomes his master. Eve told me over and over that I had lost, and that if I went along with Victoriano I would be even worse off, but I wanted my property —the property I had stolen from you."

He stared at her in pleading, and she turned her head slowly to regard him with an expressionless stare, waiting for him to complete his confession.

"All I could see were the three paintings I had worked three years to acquire. I could get him the Goya. In theory there was nothing particularly difficult about stealing the Goya; the human element is another thing, of course. But to get the Goya I told Victoriano that I needed some public diversion. I couldn't handle both the diversion and the Goya part of it, and so Victoriano undertook the diversion. Blanca, I knew he was already a murderer. I knew he was a disturbed man, even an unbalanced man, but who—how—was there any way to—was there any way to anticipate how insane he was, to foresee what he would do? Do you understand what I am saying, Blanca? I tried to find out. For three days before we were to take the Goya I tried to discover what he was planning, but he had disappeared. The last time I saw him, six days before everything happened, I demanded to know what the diversion would be and he told me that he was investigating four alternate schemes and that they would prove or eliminate themselves by Saturday, three days before it happened. When I tried to find out more, he said that what he had was too inconclusive, that I had enough on my mind and that he would tell me Saturday. But he wasn't there on Saturday. We tried to reach him on Sunday and Monday, and on Tuesday, I went to his house three times and beat on the doors. I telephoned every hour on the hour that day, but at three thirty in the afternoon I had to go to the Prado. The point is that if I could have found out what he intended to do, it never would have happened. But I didn't know, Blanca!

"We went through all the motions with the Goya, and then Jean Marie funked out. It wasn't his fault; it was my fault. He was never meant for that kind of work. When I left the Prado the streets were a nightmare, in a state of siege from horror. No one walked, everyone ran. In *Spain* people were running and weeping—it was like the tenth day of a plague. When I got home Eve told me. Then I knew what the diversion was, and I had to find you to make you understand that I never knew what was going to happen. I didn't know what Victoriano was going to do. I couldn't have known because you know I would have stopped him. But he's dead now, and he can't tell you that I didn't know; he can't stand here before you to clear me so that I can be sure that you believe me."

"But I do believe you, Jaime."

"God bless you."

"I have known for some time. Not as directly as this, of course. But Victoriano did tell me almost everything before I killed him, and I could see that he had used you." She was so composed that she gave the impression of a cooperative friend helping to clear up a misunderstanding. Disengaging her forearm from his hands which had suddenly gone limp, she stood up and patted him on the shoulder.

"I must go now. You have said everything you wanted to say to me? That was all, wasn't it, Jaime?"

His mind filled again with the liberating vision of the great canvas called "The Second of May" which only he and Eve could ever find, and the meaning of the salvation it would bring braced him somehow to sit erect and look up at her to say, "That is all. Thank you, Blanca." With a pure mind which had created a pure sin he saw his hope for the purest kind of punishment, but he sent it back into the darkness of his mind identified only as a hope. He wanted to lose that hope until he could stand freedom no longer and it had to be found. Until then he wanted to defer the pure punishment, to suffer the memory of her eyes and the sound of her voice. But that hope remained in merciful limbo for only two dimensional seconds, for as she passed out of the cell the duchess said casually, "Eve told me where we can find the Goya, Jaime. I think they must have it by now. It will be back in its place in the Prado in the morning."

She walked down the long, dimly lighted corridor the way she had come, and her friend, the old man, gamboled along the passageway to meet her. They chatted like old friends as they walked together, he greatly pleased by the beauty and the presence he had known from years before when she could not bear to remain at large and in freedom without being in her lover's arms.

IT was a warm, sunny day, and the terrace doors of the Bourne apartment were open. A lazy breeze sauntered through the delicious air to the hassock near the center of the room where Eve sat. She started violently when the telephone rang, and when she could make herself move, she answered it. Her right knee struck a small tabouret in passing and knocked it over. She almost lost her balance, but she managed to weave through the bright sunlight and pick up the telephone on its sixth ring.

"Hello?" Her voice was as bright as a child movie star's.

"Eve? This is Blanca." The voice had urgency and will.

"Hello, Blanca."

"Are you all right?"

"Yes."

"You must listen to me carefully, Eve."

"Blanca?"

"They are going to order your arrest this afternoon. If you stay where you are they will arrest you."

"Arrest me."

"I would if I could come to help, but I am lunching with the people of the prosecution. You must leave the hotel now."

"I'm drunk."

"No matter. Do you understand me?"

"Yes. Blanca?"

"Don't pack anything. Take whatever jewels or small things you feel you have to take, then walk slowly to my house. They will expect you. Do you understand me, Eve?"

"Yes. Blanca. Blanca?"

"Yes."

"Did you see Jim?"

"Yes."

"Are you making a deal with them for the Goya? Is he going to be all right?"

"We can't talk now, dear. There is no time. You can't help Jaime if both of you are in prison. Go now, Eve. Start at once. We will talk as soon as I testify this afternoon, and you will be safe at my house whether I am there or not. Now, go!" She hung up.

Eve began to move about the room in several directions, bumping into furniture, falling once. She rose to her feet uncertainly and pawed about on a closet shelf until she found a large purse. Clutching it, she tacked to the bathroom where she held onto the towel rack and let her clothes drop, piece by piece, in a heap at her feet. She moved gingerly across the tiled floor to the shower, the purse hooked over her left forearm, and was standing under the cold spray before she remembered it. Trying to bend over to put it on the floor beside the tub, she almost toppled forward and had to let it drop heavily.

Her reflexes seemed better when she got out of the shower. She rubbed herself violently with the rough bath towel, bringing a high glow to her firm flesh and perhaps moving the alcohol faster through her bloodstream. She bound her hair under a kerchief hanging behind the bathroom door and pulled her clothes on, picking each piece up slowly and squatting, not bending, to get it. Then she took the purse to another room to fill it with items of instinctive value. Working like a computer, she packed six of Bourne's handkerchiefs, three pairs of cuff links, four pairs of nylon stockings, two nylon panties, a brassière, Bourne's letters to her, a well-marked road map, her diaphragm and a strangled tube of vaginal jelly, nine small snapshots, two compacts, three lipsticks, two pairs of Bourne's socks and a cigarette lighter. She put four jeweled rings on her fingers, snapped two flashing bracelets on either wrist and started to put on a second necklace before dropping it into her purse. She took all the money in the apartment: three hundred and twenty dollars' worth of traveler's checks, six thousand pesetas, seventy-three thousand French francs, a Swiss bankbook, a Tangier bankbook, a New York bankbook, the keys to eight safe deposit vaults and Bourne's lucky Mexican peso which he always forgot to carry. She put her several passports into the great purse. They were made out variously to Eve Lewis, her own name, together with such others, borrowed or invented, as Evangeline Lewis, as dopey a name as she could remember reading anywhere.

All at once she felt bleary again. She tottered to the bed, lay face down and concentrated upon remembering Bourne with her body until she believed that she could smell him. Her eyes were as dry as a turtle's.

The telephone rang again, directly beside her. She answered it brightly again, not as brightly as before because she wasn't as drunk. The unidentified voice was a London one, and she said, "Hello, Jack," realizing too late that she had violated his rules. But Tense was too absorbed in thinking how he was going to say what he had to say to notice.

"Ducks?"

"Yes, this is Ducks."

"I want you to meet me. Straight off."

"All right."

"You know where Velázquez Street is?"

"Yes."

"You know the cafés on the walks in the middle?"

"Yes."

"The one nearest the end toward the Park? The one done in bamboo? Sort of south-seaish? All right?"

"Yes."

"In ten minutes then. I've talked to our friend."

"Who?"

"My friend. You know, my Spanish business contact."

"Who?"

"Are you drunk?"

"Yes."

"Eve, go downstairs now and stand in front of the hotel. I'm directly around the corner at the post office. I'll be by the hotel with a taxi straight off. All right, love?"

"All right. Jack?"

"Yes, ducks?"

"Have you seen Señor López? You know—your friend?"

"Yes, ducks. Now you go straight down and stand on the pavement in front of that hotel and I'll tell you all about it. All right, love?"

"Yes, Jack." She disconnected and climbed blearily to her feet, balancing unsteadily. Carrying the purse she crossed to the table which held the gin and ice and pitcher of water. She held the gin bottle up. There were about two fingers left, and she made herself a gin on the rocks. She stared out toward nothing as she sipped it, and when it was gone she turned to the door and left the apartment for the last time in her life, testing the latch carefully just as though she were a sober and careful guest in the hotel.

Jack's taxi rolled up as she came out the front door of the hotel, and he was pleased that no doorman was there to remember whom the boss's wife had gone riding off with. The cab drove to Alcalá, then turned right up the short hill to the plaza at Puerta Alcalá and swung halfway around the arch to stop at the Calle de Serrano. Tense dismissed the cab there and took Eve's arm as they walked up the gentle hill toward Velázquez, across from the Retiro, passing the house of the Duchess de Dos Cortes on the way.

When they were seated in the café on the Ramblas Tense ordered three hot, black coffees. What Spanish he had conflicted with the waiter's conception of the language, and Eve had to straighten them out. Tense made her drink two cups while he toyed with his own. When she had finished he gave her his full cup and ordered two more as she sipped. Occasionally a trolley car would clang, or the brakes of a bus would hiss, but otherwise it was a serenely quiet day, warm and wondrously clear, its soft sounds embellished by the soughing of the light wind combing the trees. Tense sat enjoying her, apprehensive of her reactions to what he had to say, but mainly astonished at what this very nearly unknown girl had done to change his hard-eyed objectivity.

"What did Señor López say?" she asked suddenly.

"Oh, yes. Well, I saw him two nights ago and I mentioned what we had talked about, and he seemed to know what I wanted. He didn't say much, but that's his way. Then a small boy comes to my hotel this morning as I was leaving to cover the trial. The boy had a note for me which says our friend wants to see me. You follow? So I saw our friend." To punctuate, Tense leaned over and touched Eve's bare forearm with the tips of his fingers. He had the shaped fingers of the storybook safecracker, long, slim, sensitive and very clean. "I have been trying to tell

myself how to say this to you, ducks. I like you pretty well, you
see. López had bad news, ducks. Very bad news indeed."

She implored him with her gin-flawed eyes. They pleaded with
him to be mistaken, that all her weariness of endless trouble be
mistaken.

"The government has the Goya painting," Tense said, dropping his eyes. "They won't need to make a deal any more."

She made a sound which caught in her throat like a bubble,
then looked away from him quickly as though expecting to see
hope and deliverance standing across the street.

He took her limp, damp hand in his and held it with love.
"They had to find it, you know, ducks, what with every policeman in the country looking for it," he said lamely.

"How did they find it, Jack?" she asked.

He inhaled heavily, then breathed out slowly with a sigh that
seemed to stop life for a fraction of an eternity. "I don't know
what's come over me," he answered. "I wasn't going to tell you,
as though you shouldn't know who your enemies are. But you
have to know, the same way I would have to know if it was me
in your place." He paused in sadness. "It was your friend who
told them where it was," he said. "Your friend, the duchess. I
don't know how she found out, but it was she who told them."

Eve sat motionless, absorbing the meaning of what he had
said, then stood up slowly. "I told her," she said. She leaned over
and kissed Tense as he sat in the dappling sunshine. "That's
how she found out." She walked slowly away, along the Ramblas
toward the park, clutching the large purse. "I told her."

THE clerk of the court called the next witness, Colonel
Gonzalo Gómez, chief of the Customs Service at Barajas.

The prosecutor launched his line of questioning and the
colonel testified, somewhat sullenly, that a superb copy of the
Velázquez on exhibition in the court had been brought into
Spain by Eve Bourne, wife of the accused known as James
Bourne. He supplied the date of Mrs. Bourne's entry and handed
over to the court a certified copy of customs records establishing
the temporary importation of the copy of the painting by one
Mary Ellen Quinn. When he was asked whether the Customs

Service could produce records showing the temporary importation of copies of other paintings, such as the Zurbarán and
Greco on exhibition in the court, Colonel Gómez produced copies
of certificates attesting to such importation at Irún and La Junquera, respectively, by American citizens named Alicia Sundeen
and Thelma Cryder, respectively.

The prosecutor asked Colonel Gómez to read the spelling of
the name Cryder from the customs department record, then
asked the clerk of the court to read the spelling of the name of
the accused Robert Evans Cryder to the court.

"Thank you. Colonel Gómez, under what name did the wife
of the defendant enter Spain at Barajas when she imported the
copy of the Velázquez painting?"

"Under the name of Mary Ellen Quinn."

"That was the name on the passport which she submitted. Her
photograph, of course, was in that passport."

"Yes sir. I have the records and numbers here, sir." The
colonel sounded bitter.

"Colonel, please tell the court how you became certain that
Mary Ellen Quinn, who had presented this passport for entry
into Spain, was in truth the wife of the defendant called James
Bourne?"

"I was introduced to Mr. and Mrs. Bourne by Dr. Muñoz."

"Where?"

"At his apartment. I was told that they had just been
married."

"How long ago was that?"

The colonel told him.

"To your knowledge were the customs officers at Irún and La
Junquera, respectively, shown photographs of the women who
had identified themselves as Alicia Sundeen and Thelma
Cryder?"

"Yes sir."

"Did they identify the photographs?"

"Yes sir."

"Will you tell us who these officers identified?"

"Mrs. James Bourne."

"I believe depositions were taken to that effect?"

"Yes sir."

The clerk of the court collected the depositions and the Fiscal
nodded benignly to the witness. "Thank you, colonel."

"No questions," Rafael Corruno said. He was not there to defend a woman for illegal entry, and since there could be no doubt that the copies were in the country it was obvious that someone had brought them there.

The President of the Court spoke slowly and clearly. "This court orders the arrest of Mrs. James Bourne, wife of the co-defendant, on the charges of illegal entry, possession of forged papers, and conspiracy."

Bourne stared at the floor, breathing heavily, biting his tongue.

"Proceed," the president ordered.

The clerk of the court rose and called Doña Blanca Conchita Hombria y Arias de Ochoa y Acebal, Marquesa de Vidal, Condesa de Ocho Pinas, Vizcondesa Ferri, Duquesa de Dos Cortes. Within a moment the duchess had made her way into the courtroom.

"Your name?"

"Blanca de Dos Cortes, excellency."

"What is your age?" The president coughed.

"Twenty-nine years, my President."

"Do you live in Madrid?"

"Yes, excellency."

"Do you know the accused?"

"Yes, excellency."

"Do you swear to tell the truth?"

"Yes, my President."

"Please answer the questions which will be put to you by the Acusador Fiscal."

The Fiscal cleared his throat delicately. His fingers, seemingly ropes with separate consciousness, began to worry a ruler while he conveyed his extreme esteem for the distinguished witness by clearing his throat twice more and by moving the black, poly-angular hat from one side of his desk to the other. The extra seats at the Fiscal's desk, at the desk of the nonexistent Acusa-dor Privado, and at Corruno's desk suddenly had filled with interested, robed men.

Jean Marie stopped his sketching and stared at the duchess with naked fear. Earlier that morning, for the first time since he had been questioned by the police, he seemed to be aware of what was happening to him. His right hand clutched a blue letter which he had discussed emptily with Bourne as they had been marched from the cells to the courtroom. Lalu had written to tell him that she loved him, but that she had been forced to leave Paris because of what had happened and that she knew he would understand that she had to take care of herself. The letter had been mailed from Paris, and he understood without reservation. Now he watched the duchess, fascinated with the doom which had appeared at last, so far from where he had expected to meet it.

Bourne stared at the floor and concentrated on counting by sevens.

"My duchess," the Fiscal asked, "are the paintings on exhibit to your left, painted by Zurbarán, El Greco and Velázquez respectively, your property?"

The duchess blinked her eyes rapidly as though not quite comprehending. "Which part of that question would you like me to answer first?"

"I am not sure that I understand your request, my duchess. Shall I repeat the question?"

"No, no. I will try to answer. I believe the paintings are my property, but if they are truly my property they were not painted by Zurbarán, El Greco or Velázquez."

There was a hum in the courtroom as though a large generator had been turned on.

It was the Fiscal's turn to blink rapidly. "Pardon, duchess," he said, "but is not the Velázquez the famous Pickett Troilus?"

The duchess looked away, baffled, as though she would be willing to change the subject if the Fiscal would. Mrs. Pickett sat up straight. The newspapermen in the rear of the courtroom became very quiet and glanced at one another expectantly.

The president said, "The witness will explain herself for the record."

"My President, the first and last time Mr. Homer Pickett was a guest at Dos Cortes he positively identified these paintings as having been painted by Zurbarán, El Greco, and Velázquez. He even purported to have discovered the hand of the Dutch painter Rubens in the second copy of the Velázquez. Foreign picture magazines have been filled with the nonsense."

A stringer representing thirty-one middle western American dailies, including one Democratic and one independent paper in Chicago, decided that he could not wait to hear any more and left the courtroom in a rush. Mrs. Pickett watched him go, knowing exactly what outlets he represented because he had interviewed her husband twice at the hotel. She rose and made her way slowly across the legs and feet of the row to the aisle. When she got into the open she began to walk more quickly, and when the courtroom door closed behind her she ran through the clumps of waiting witnesses in the corridor to reach her husband before anyone else could get to him—to convince him, to bully him if she had to, that his back had not been broken politically, artistically and, above all, as the lecturer-critic who would rival Mr. Berenson.

The representatives of the principal competitors of both foreign magazines which had published the nonsense in full color sent assistants to telegraph offices with messages suggesting top priority standby. The competitor of the American magazine which had proclaimed The Pickett Troilus even went so far as to add the words "practice smiling" at the end of his message, confident that he would never be asked to pay for the extra words.

"Did the witness mention a second copy?" the court asked.

"Yes, excellency. Mr. Bourne stole the first copies and replaced them with second copies."

A stout magistrate to the left of the president scribbled a note and passed it along for consideration. The president read it. "Where are the originals?" he asked, clearly shocked, for Spanish law and custom on its art treasures was most definite and clear.

"My late husband, the duke," the duchess explained, "had the original paintings removed from the walls in 1944 and replaced by the first copies."

"Where are the original paintings?"

"In Japan, excellency." The duchess was being sincerely co-operative. "They hang in a geisha house in Kobe which was one of my husband's many business interests." The AP man reeled at the bonus he would nerve himself up to ask for, then cut it in half, over the art and features this would move in Japan.

"This was done in 1944? During a war?"

"Oh yes, excellency, if it had not been for the war none of this could have happened. You see, it was through the war that my husband, himself an extremely highly regarded figure in our government, happened to find M'sieu Calbert, the defendant there, who is the supreme artist who has done both copies of all of these paintings and many more." The duchess, sweet and patient in the confusion, treated all inquiries with the unruffled kindness of a teacher in a nursery school.

"You are saying then, my duchess," the Fiscal said slowly, hoping perhaps to be contradicted, "that the paintings on exhibit in the court were not painted by Zurbarán, El Greco, or Veláz-quez, but are instead forgeries executed by the co-defendant, Jean Marie Calbert?"

"Yes sir." The Fiscal, as well as everyone else in the courtroom, turned to look at Jean Marie who sat in a sick nimbus, staring at the duchess. While all stared at him, the duchess looked into his sunken eyes with her dead ones and smiled a twisted, venge-ful smile which lived for a moment only on one side of her face. So casually was it done that only Jean Marie, Bourne and the duchess were aware that the duchess had struck up the overture to Jean Marie's doom. Feeling an instant of panic, Bourne darted his glance to Jean Marie's pale profile. His eyes were closed, and his lips were moving silently and just perceptibly. Bourne felt the cold begin in his middle, then spread toward his heart and his head, his loins and his feet. He sat up as straight as a West Point plebe while the President of the Court continued his questioning of the duchess.

"The exportation of these paintings to Japan by your late husband, if indeed this be so, is a serious and grave matter. You will please give the court the full background of this occur-rence, to the best of your memory."

"I will try to remember everything which pertains to this matter, your excellency," the duchess said. She dropped her head for a moment and swallowed hard, and when she spoke again her eyes were looking far, far beyond the president, toward her duty which seemed to hang on the horizon of her days, where she could not avoid seeing it. "In 1942, excellency," she began, "my late husband became a close friend of Reichs-marschall Goering while he was in Paris as a member of the government commission which was so successful in regaining some of the many great Spanish paintings from the Louvre which Napoleon had looted from us in 1810 to 1812. I might say that painting was not the least of the interests which Reichsmar-schall Goering shared with my late husband. In any event, my husband elected to remain in France throughout almost the whole period of the Nazi occupation. Because he was a known art authority who was greatly admired by the most influential

Germans from Herr Hitler down, the then Political Commissar
of Paris, a gentleman named Herr Abetz, who wished to further
the interests of his young mistress, introduced a plan which had
been developed by his mistress's husband, who was the defendant Jean Marie Calbert, to my husband."

Jean Marie's lips were moving silently. The nine journalists
representing French news outlets were half out of their seats.
Exchanging silent glances, they effected a truce that one would
not leave the courtroom without the others.

"This plan so delighted my husband, who had an extraordinary
contempt for all of mankind and mankind's works—which perhaps was what had attracted Marshal Goering to him in the first
place—that he brought it to the attention of the Reichsmarschall,
who ordered it put into execution immediately. It was a simple
plan. M'sieu Calbert, the defendant, was to have single access
to the Louvre and to ostensibly unknown repositories of French
art, and was to be permitted to copy what great paintings still
remained from the alleged allotment which the French had
claimed to have shipped to safety. Thus, those paintings which
eventually were exhibited in the Louvre and other French museums were copies by M'sieu Calbert, while the originals were
shipped back to Germany as culture bonuses for the German
High Command, where they are today. It was the sort of plan
which delighted my husband, who had been bred to this kind
of depravity. I do not know how or where M'sieu Calbert or his
wife came by it.

"M'sieu and Madame Calbert made a considerable amount
of money in this way, my late husband told me. I know that
my husband paid him exceedingly well for copying three Italian
masterpieces in the Reichsmarschall's collection, pieces which
were Herr Goering's deep pride and which my husband, as a
further joke, undertook to substitute because it pleased him to
think of the Germans, or anyone else for that matter, worship-
ping junk. These paintings hang in a geisha house now, which
of course pleased the duke because mostly seamen patronize the
establishments he owns and they think the paintings are cheap
copies. No one ever really looks at them, he told me delightedly.
M'sieu Calbert's work was so remarkably faithful to the work of
the original masters that it was then that my husband conceived
of his geisha plan. When the Germans were forced to withdraw
from Paris and the Calberts might have been in severe personal

trouble, my husband gave them a haven at Dos Cortes, where M'sieu Calbert copied every painting we owned. Every painting on every wall in every house my husband owned now exhibits M'sieu Calbert's work."

The French press could not wait any longer because the Italian and the British newsmen were leaving at top speed. Those at the rear of the courtroom seemed to rise as one man and fight toward the two small doors to the corridor and the street.

"This court is adjourned until ten o'clock tomorrow morning," the President of the Court said suddenly, standing up. No one knew whether the duchess had completed her testimony for the prosecution, but it no longer seemed important.

If the government could have stopped the news stories they would have done so, but it was all on the public record and publication could be delayed only as long as the foreign journalists were detained within the country. The duchess was proscribed by her nation, her society and her community. The Fiscal hurried past her, glancing sideways at her as he went, his eyes filled with horror. Even Rafael Corruno-Baenz went out of his way to avoid her. She had held the sacred memory of one of Spain's greatest aristocrats, a proprietor of the nation, up to public ridicule with the irrefutable authority which she alone possessed. The commoners and the soldiers and the teachers and the bankers who had taken over the government, as well as the minuscule number of persons who actually owned the country, were never to forgive her.

The prisoners were returned to their cells. The duchess sat alone in the box until the courtroom had entirely cleared, then rose and walked absent-mindedly out of the Palace of Justice and into the street to look for her car and driver, thinking only that she now must face Eve Bourne who had held the matching half of the only truth which would ever be left to either of them.

AT that precise moment Jean Marie succeeded in hanging himself, because the jailer was not there to interfere. He managed it with a bed sheet looped around the bars of the cell's high window. Standing on the bed with the sheet knotted around his neck, he jumped as high in the air as he could go, so that the force of his descent would provide the maximum snap. No one but Jean Marie ever knew whether he died quickly or slowly. The old jailer had been so wearied by the emotion of seeing the duchess again that he rested, then dozed, then slept, and Jean Marie's suicide was not discovered until the evening meal was served to the cells at ten o'clock that night. Since Spain is a Catholic country, the death was greatly deplored.

THE duchess found Eve waiting in the enormous sitting room-bedroom facing the Retiro on the third floor of the house, the room in which she had explored her own grief so assiduously. The room was reached by an individual elevator, which opened through a wall panel invisible when not in use. When the duke had been alive she had never entered the room in any other way, always keeping the main door to the room bolted because he had been a man who could become ravening, not to say bestial, from reading the financial page of a newspaper or from eating a piece of milk toast, and she had learned in the first year of her marriage, at the age of sixteen, that syphilis was a worrisome, persistent disease and, at that time, very nearly endless in its treatment and cure. Apart from the humiliation, it had settled the matter of her having children once and for all.

Although she used the elevator, the duchess had Pablo send a floor maid ahead to tell Eve that she was on her way up, for the sight of death emerging from a secret panel is not calculated to be a pleasant surprise for anyone. The duchess had always seen herself as death holding court—many kinds of death, not all of them as direct as Cayetano's or her cousin's. She was Spain's own vector of catastrophe, she had told herself while growing up. By loving she could maim; by giving she took life. These insights had been gleaned when she was very young and her capacity for anguish had seemed romantic.

When the duchess was a schoolgirl, walled up within the tragedy which had been her family—a father who was a suicide, a mother who had become a mumbling nun with skin like a baked apple—she had learned to live with the perpetual affliction of her life. If the thought of suicide had not disgusted her, if suicide for everyone had not been regarded with such cheerful approval by her late husband, and if her own death, in any form, did not seem so horrendously passive, she would have undertaken her own destruction years ago when she had been a schoolgirl with the unschoolgirlish thought which implacably demanded that pain accompany decay. She had sensed long ago that the source of her trouble was that she was too ancient. Victoriano had worn his hoariness as a belled leper goes forth, and with an ineffable sense of design had managed to die of what had made him live. She, on the contrary, had always fought to conceal the weight of her nine hundred years. She was a grandee of Spain, a cousin of the king, forced in part to live inside the mists of her history, where the past was always now, where she was one with the men who had ridden with El Cid and with the hard-mouthed women who had ruled the men. The last of the long line, she was an adept at tragedy; she had been toughened to the point where she lived by it.

But that was not the case, the duchess knew, with the beautiful and pregnant newcomer to disaster who was waiting for her. When the elevator reached the third floor she knocked softly to announce herself.

Eve sat facing her. Her face was bleak. She was sober. She didn't speak. The duchess crossed the room and kissed her in sisterly fashion on the cheek, removed her hat, and sat in a chair within two feet of Eve.

"Would you like some hot tea, my dear?" the duchess asked.

"Yes. Thank you."

The duchess rang. "I suppose Rafael Corruno, Jaime's lawyer, will cross-examine me tomorrow, but I can say with a sense of finality that I have finished my work today. We can leave Spain."

"We?"

"You must leave tonight. As the Fiscal told me they would, the court ordered your arrest today. Do you have an unused passport—that is, a perfectly usable passport?"

"Yes. My own. My real passport."

"Fine. You must take the Daimler which carries a royal crest on its radiator—I bought the thing years ago because it eased traffic at the feria in Sevilla—and a chauffeur *and* a footman. They will take your passport into the *aduanas* at Irún, and then you will simply roll across the bridge. No one would dream of stopping that Daimler."

She suddenly peered more intently at Eve. "Have you discovered somehow that I told the government where to find the Goya which would have freed Jaime?"

"Yes."

"You would have done the same, would you not?"

Eve ran her hand through her hair, then across her closed eyes. When she finally opened them, she said, "I suppose I would have."

"Yes. I know you. You would have. It was a thing which faithful women have to do, my dear."

"Will they kill Jim?"

"No."

"What will happen to him?"

"The timing of the murder, which Rafael will support with the records when the defense presents its case beginning tomorrow afternoon, will show reasonable doubt, the Fiscal thinks, so Jaime will probably be sentenced to thirty years and a day."

"There is nothing to be done?"

"No, dear."

"Months ago," Eve said slowly, "when we discovered in Paris that the paintings we had stolen from you had been stolen from us, we made contact with an organized group of Spanish criminals in case we needed to trace the paintings here. As though it had been an ordinary, simple hijacking operation."

Two servants came in with a tea service on a great cart. Though Eve had been speaking English, which the servants did not understand, she fell silent. The duchess directed operations crisply, and after dismissing the staff poured tea and arranged small pieces of the beautiful food on a plate for her companion.

After awhile Eve began to talk again. "The man told me today that you had told the government where to find the Goya. He said that he had not intended to tell me, just that the government had the Goya, killing any chance for a deal, but at last he had decided that I must know who my enemies were. I walked away from him believing that. Then all at once I knew you had killed Victoriano Muñoz, and just now when you inquired whether or not I would have given the government the Goya had it been Jim who had been so senselessly murdered and Cayetano who was on trial, I could understand that it would only make everything more hopeless if I saw you as my enemy, because I feel with every sense I have that Jim knows what has happened to all of us and that he understands what has been done and why it was done, and that he must love you more now because he helped to make you suffer so much. I love you more now because I was part of the cause of your suffering, and because now I stand beside you with one-half of what I have left. Since we cannot snap our fingers and stop living, I must somehow find peace for you, and you must struggle to find peace for me, because alone we will never be able to find it for ourselves. Our eyes have gone for that. I believe our eyes were always blinded, as every living being must be blinded in that way of finding hope for themselves, because peace must be bound up in loving, and no one is allowed to love himself so prodigiously. If we had all begun where we are now, knowing that we can only help each other and that we can have no reason to hope in any other way, Cayetano would be alive and Jim would be free. But that can't be, and we are the only two who are left— truly the only two who know the secret. When I walked toward your house this afternoon, I knew that you knew something that I didn't understand, because you have known all these terrible things much longer than me. I knew you had something which you felt compelled to offer to me, the way religion must have been offered when it first began. You didn't know whether I had been prepared enough to be able to accept it, and you had no reason to foresee that I would know what it was before you brought it to me. We are in one form, body and soul—that everyone must see and agree—but more than that, I am you and you are me and what have we done to each other?"

The dam broke within the duchess. The tears she had sought since the terrible days when she was very young, the tears which had been denied to her through all of the battering, came to her now. She wept helplessly but joyously, released and purified, as Eve sipped at her tea and retreated into her bleakness.

EVE left in the Daimler at two o'clock the following morning. They arrived at Irún at ten minutes after eight, and as the duchess had predicted, her passport was stamped with deference and they rolled across the bridge into France.

She had breakfast in Bayonne. While she ate a croissant and

drank a café au lait she read that Jean Marie had hanged himself
in his cell. She could only remember the words to the Lord's
Prayer, and since she knew no other she sat with her head in
her hands and said it three times.

She spent the night in Vendôme and reached Paris early the
next morning. She had been drinking steadily all the way, but
she was not drunk.

The apartment she and Bourne had lived in seemed alien. She
needed a brandy, but the decanter was empty. She went into the
kitchen and opened the cellar door. A stench assailed her, and she
looked down. Chern's dead hand reached; his ruined face stared.
She screamed and screamed again. She could not stop screaming.

THE
MANCHURIAN
CANDIDATE

I IT WAS SUNNY IN SAN
Francisco; a fabulous condition. Raymond Shaw was not unaware of the beauty outside the hotel window, across from a
mansion on the top of a hill, but he clutched the telephone like
an *osculatorium* and did not allow himself to think about what
lay beyond that instant: in a saloon someplace, in a different
bed, or anywhere.

His lumpy sergeant's uniform was heaped on a chair. He
stretched out on the rented bed, wearing a new one-hundred-and-
twenty-dollar dark blue dressing gown, and waited for the telephone operator to complete the chain of calls to locate Ed
Mavole's father, somewhere in St. Louis.

He knew he was doing the wrong thing. Two years of Korean
duty were three days behind him and, at the very least, he
should be spending his money on a taxicab to go up and down
those hills in the sunshine, but he decided his mind must be bent
or that he was drunk with compassion, or something else improbable like that. Of all of the fathers of all of the fallen whom

he had to call, owing to his endemic mopery, this one had to work nights, because, by now, it must be dark in St. Louis.

He listened to the operator get through to the switchboard at the *Post-Dispatch*. He heard the switchboard tell her that Mavole's father worked in the composing room. A man talked to a woman; there was silence. Raymond stared at his own large toe.

"Hello?" A very high voice.

"Mr. Arthur Mavole, please. Long distance calling." The steady rumble of working presses filled the background.

"This is him."

"Mr. Arthur Mavole?"

"Yeah, yeah."

"Go ahead, please."

"Uh—hello? Mr. Mavole? This is Sergeant Shaw. I'm calling from San Francisco. I—uh—I was in Eddie's outfit, Mr. Mavole."

"My Ed's outfit?"

"Yes, sir."

"Ray Shaw?"

"Yes, sir."

"The Ray Shaw? Who won the Medal of—"

"Yes, sir." Raymond cut him off in a louder voice. He felt like dropping the phone, the call, and the whole soggy, masochistic, suicidal thing in the wastebasket. Better yet, he should whack himself over the head with the goddam phone. "You see, uh, Mr. Mavole, I have to, uh, go to Washington, and I—"

"We know. We read all about it and let me say with all my heart I got left that I am as proud of you, even though I never met you, as if it were Eddie, my own kid. My son."

"Mr. Mavole," Raymond said rapidly, "I thought that if it was O.K. with you maybe I could stop over in St. Louis on my way to Washington, you know? I thought, I mean it occurred to me that you and Mrs. Mavole might get some kind of peace out of it, some kind of relief, if we talked a little bit. About Eddie. You know? I mean I thought that was the least I could do."

There was a silence. Then Mr. Mavole began to make a lot of slobbering sounds so Raymond said roughly that he would wire when he knew what flight he would be on and he hung up the phone and felt like an idiot. Like an angry man with a cane who pokes a hole through the floor of heaven and is scalded by the joy that pours down upon him, Raymond had a capacity for using satisfactions against himself.

When he got off the plane at St. Louis airport he felt like running. He decided Mavole's father must be that midget with the eyeglasses like milk-bottle bottoms who was enjoying sweating so much. The man would be all over him like a charging elk in a minute. "Hold it! Hold it!" the pimply press photographer said loudly.

"Put it down," Raymond snarled in a voice which was even more unpleasant than his normal voice. All at once the photographer was less sure of himself. "Whassa matter?" he asked in bewilderment—because he lived at a time when only sex criminals and dope peddlers tried to refuse to have their pictures taken by the press.

"I flew all the way in here to see Ed Mavole's father," Raymond said, despising himself for throwing up such corn. "You want a picture, go find him, because you ain't gonna take one of me without he's in it."

Listen to that genuine, bluff sergeant version of *pollice verso,* Raymond cried out to himself. I am playing the authentic war buddy so deeply that I will have to mail in a royalty check for the stock rights. Look at that clown of a photographer trying to cope with phenomena. Any minute now he will realize that he is standing right beside Mavole's father.

"Oh, Sergeant!" the girl said, so then he knew who *she* was. She wasn't red-eyed and runny-nosed with grief for the dead hero, so she had to be the cub reporter who had been assigned to write the big local angle on the White House and the Hero, and he had probably written the lead for her with that sappy grandstand play.

"I'm Ed's father," the sweat manufacturer said. It was December, fuh gossake, what's with all the dew? "I'm Frank Mavole. I'm sorry about this. I just happened to mention at the paper that you had called all the way from San Francisco and that you had offered to stop over and see Eddie's mother on the way to the White House, and the word somehow got upstairs to the city desk and well—that's the newspaper business, I guess."

Raymond took three steps forward, grasped Mr. Mavole's hand, gripped his right forearm with his own left hand, transmitted the steely glance and the iron stare and the frozen fix. He felt

like Captain Idiot in one of those space comic books, and the
photographer got the picture and lost all interest in them.

"May I ask how old you are, Sergeant Shaw?" the young chick
said, notebook ready, pencil poised as though she and Mavole
were about to give him a fitting, and he figured reflexively that
this could be the first assignment she had ever gotten after years
of journalism school and months of social notes from all over.
He remembered his first assignment and how he had feared the
waffle-faced movie actor who had opened the door of the hotel
suite wearing only pajama bottoms, with corny tattoos like So
Long, Mabel on each shoulder. Inside the suite Raymond had
managed to convey that he would just as soon have hit the man
as talk to him and he had said, "Gimme the handout and we can
save some time." The traveling press agent with the actor, a
plump, bloodshot type whose glasses kept sliding down his nose,
had said, "What handout?" He had snarled that maybe they
would prefer it if he started out by asking what was the great
man's hobby and what astrology sign he had been born under. It
was hard to believe but that man's face had been as pocked and
welted as a waffle, yet he was one of the biggest names in the
business, which gives an idea what those swine will do to kid the
jerky public. The actor had said, "Are you scared, kid?" Then,
after that, everything seemed to go O.K. They got along like a
bucket of chums. The point was, everybody had to start someplace.

Although he felt like a slob himself for doing it, he asked Mr.
Mavole and the girl if they would have time to have a cup of
coffee at the airport restaurant because he was a newspaperman
himself and he knew that the little lady had a story to get. The
little lady? That was overdoing it. He'd have to find a mirror
and see if he had a wing collar on.

"You were?" the girl said. "Oh, Sergeant!" Mr. Mavole said a
cup of coffee would be fine with him, so they went inside.

They sat down at a table in the coffee shop. The windows
were steamy. Business was very quiet and unfortunately the
waitress seemed to have nothing but time. They all ordered
coffee and Raymond thought he'd like to have a piece of pie but
he could not bring himself to decide what kind of pie. Did
everybody have to look at him as though he were sick because he
couldn't set his taste buds in advance to be able to figure which
flavor he would favor before he tasted it? Did the waitress just

have to start out to recite "We have peach pie, and pumpk—"
and they'd just yell out Peach, peach, peach? What was the
sense of eating in a place where they gabbled the menu at you,
anyway? If a man were intelligent and he sorted through the
memories of past tastes he not only could get exactly what he
wanted sensually and with a flavor sensation, but he would
probably be choosing something so chemically exact that it
would benefit his entire body. But how could anyone achieve
such a considerate deliberate result as that unless one were
permitted to pore over a written menu?

"The prune pie is very good, sir," the waitress said. He told her
he'd take the prune pie and he hated her in a hot, resentful flash
because he did not want prune pie. He hated prune pie and he
had been maneuvered into ordering prune pie by a rube waitress
who would probably slobber all over his shoes for a quarter
tip.

"I wanted to tell you how we felt about Ed, Mr. Mavole,"
Raymond said. "I want to tell you that of all the guys I ever met,
there was never a happier, sweeter, or more solid guy than your
son Ed."

The little man's eyes filled. He suddenly choked on a sob so
loud that people at the counter, which was quite a distance
away, turned around. Raymond spoke to the girl quickly to cover
up. "I'm twenty-four years old. My astrological sign is Pisces. A
very fine lady reporter on a Detroit paper once told me always to
ask for their astrology sign because people love to read about
astrology if they don't have to ask for it directly."

"I'm Taurus," the girl said.

"We'd be very good," Raymond said. She let him see just a
little bit behind her expression. "I know," she said.

Mr. Mavole spoke in a soft voice. "Sergeant—you see—well,
when Eddie got killed his mother had a heart attack and I wonder if you could spare maybe a half an hour out and back. We
don't live all the way into the city, and—"

O Jesus! Raymond saw himself donning the bedside manner. A
bloody cardiac. The slightest touchy thing he said to her could
knock the old cat over sideways with an off-key moan. But what
could he do? He had elected himself Head Chump when he had
stepped down from Valhalla and telephoned this sweaty little
advantage-taker.

"Mr. Mavole," he said, slowly and softly, "I don't have to be in

Washington until the day after tomorrow, but I figured I would allow a day and a half in case of bad weather, you know? On account of the White House? I can even get to Washington by train from here overnight, the Spirit of St. Louis, the same name as that plane with that fella, so please don't think I would even think of leaving town without talking to Mrs. Mavole—Eddie's mother." He looked up and he saw how the girl was looking at him. She was a very pretty girl; a sweet-looking, nice, blond girl. "What's your name?" he asked.

"Mardell," she said.

"Do you think I'll be able to get a hotel here tonight?"

"I'm absolutely sure of it."

"I'll take care of that, Sergeant," Mr. Mavole said hurriedly. "In fact, the paper will take care of everything. You would certainly be welcome to stay at our place, but we just had the painters. Smells so sharp your eyes water."

Raymond called for the check. They drove to the Mavoles'. Mardell said she'd wait in the car and just to forget about her. Raymond told her to get on in to the paper and file her story, then drive back out to pick him up. She stared at him as if he had invented balk-line billiards. He patted her cheek, then went into the house. She put her hand on her stomach and took three or four very deep breaths. Then she started the car and went into town.

The session with Mrs. Mavole was awful and Raymond vowed that he would never take an intelligence test because they might lock him up as a result of what would be shown. Any cretin could have looked ahead and seen what a mess this was going to be. They all cried. People can certainly carry on, he thought, holding her fat hand because she had asked him to, and feeling sure she was going to drop dead any minute. These were the people who let a war start, then they act surprised when their own son is killed. Mavole was a good enough kid. He certainly was a funny kid and with a sensational disposition but, what the hell, twenty thousand were dead out there so far on the American panel, plus the U.N. guys, and maybe sixty, eighty thousand more all shot up, and this fat broad seemed to think that Mavole was the only one who got it.

Could my mother take it this big if I got it? Would anyone living or anyone running a legitimate séance which picked up guaranteed answers from Out Yonder ever be able to find out whether she could feel anything at all about anything or any-body? Let her liddul Raymond pull up dead and he knew the answer from his liddul mommy. If the folks would pay one or more votes for a sandwich she would be happy to send for her liddul boy's body and barbecue him.

"I can tell you that it was a very clear action for a night action, Mrs. Mavole," Raymond said. Mr. Mavole sat on the other side of the bed and stared at the floor, his eyes feverish captives in black circles, his lower lip caught between his teeth, his hands clasped in prayer as he hoped he would not begin to cry again and start her crying. "You see, Captain Marco had sent up some low flares because we had to know where the enemy was. They knew where we were. Eddie, well—" He paused, only infinitesi-mally, to try not to weep at the thought of how bitter, bitter, bitter it was to have to lie at a time like this, but she had sold the boy to the recruiters for this moment, so he would have to throw the truth away and pay her off. They never told The Folks Back Home about the filthy deaths—the grotesque, debasing deaths which were almost all the deaths in war. Dirty deaths were the commonplace clowns smoking idle cigarettes backstage at a cir-cus filled with clowns. Ah, no. No, no, no, no, no, no, no. Only a clutch of martial airs played on an electric guitar and sung through the gaudy juke box called Our Nation's History. He didn't know exactly how Mavole caught it, but he could figure it close. He'd probably gotten about sixteen inches of bayonet in the rectum as he turned to get away and his screaming had scared the other man so much that he had fought to get his weapon out and run away, twisting Mavole on it until the point came out under Mavole's ribs where the diaphragm was and the man had had to put his foot on the back of Mavole's neck, breaking his nose and cheekbone, to get the sticker out, while he whimpered in Chinese and wanted to lie down somewhere, where it was quiet. All the other people knew about how undig-nified it was to lose a head or some legs or a body in a mass attack, except his people: the innocents hiding in the jam jar. Women like this one might have had that li'l cardiac murmur stilled if her city had been bombed and she had seen her Eddie with no lower face and she had to protect and cherish the rest, the ones who were left. "—well, there was this very young lad in our outfit, Mrs. Mavole. He was maybe seventeen years old, but I doubt it. I think sixteen. Eddie had decided a long time ago to

help the kid and look out for him because that was kind of man
you son was." Mr. Mavole was sobbing very softly on the other
side of the bed. "Well, the boy, little Bobby Lembeck, got separated from the rest of us. Not by far; Ed went out to cover him.
The boy was hit just before Eddie could make it to him and, well,
he just couldn't leave him there. You know? That's the kind
of a man, I mean; that was Ed. You know? He couldn't. He tried
to bring the youngster back and by that time the enemy had a fix
on them and they dropped a mortar shell on them from away up
high and it was all over and all done, Mrs. Mavole, before those
two boys felt a single thing. That's how quick it was, Mrs.
Mavole. Yes, ma'am. That quick."

"I'm glad," Mrs. Mavole said. Then suddenly and loudly she
said, "O my God, how can I say I'm glad? I'm not. I'm not. We're
all a long time dead. He was such a happy little boy and he'll be
a long time dead." She was propped up among the pillows of the
bed and her body moved back and forth with her keening.

What the hell did he expect? He came here of his own free
will. What did he expect? Two choruses of something mellow,
progressive, and fine? O man, O man, O man! A fat old broad in
a nine-by-nine box with a sweat-maker who can't get with it.
How can I continue to live, he shouted at high scream under the
nave of his encompassing skull, if people are going to continue to
carry bundles of pain on top of their heads like Haitian laun-
dresses, then fling the bundles at random into the face of any
bright stroller who happened to be passing by? All right. He had
helped this fat broad to find herself some ghoulish kicks. What
else did they want from him?

"The wrong man died, Mrs. Mavole," Raymond sobbed. "How
I wish it could have been me. Not Eddie. Me. Me." He hid his
face in her large, motherly breasts as she lay back on the pillows
of the bed.

THROUGH arrangements beyond his control, Raymond
had developed into a man who sagged fearfully within a suit of
stifling armor, imprisoned for the length of his life from casque
to solleret. It was heavy, immovable armor, this thick defense,
which had been constructed mainly at his mother's forge, ham-

mered under his stepfather's noise, tempered by the bitter tears
of his father's betrayal. Raymond also distrusted all other living
people because they had not warned his father of his mother.

Raymond had been shown too early that if he smiled his stepfather was encouraged to bray laughter; if he spoke, his mother
felt compelled to reply in the only way she knew how to reply,
which was to urge him to seek popularity and power with all life-
force. So he had deliberately developed the ability to be shunned
instantly no matter where he went and notwithstanding extraneous conditions. He had achieved this state consciously after year
upon year of unconscious rehearsal of the manifest parapher-
nalia of arrogance and contempt, then exceeded it. The shell of
armor that encased Raymond, by the horrid tracery of its design,
presented him as one of the least likeable men of his century. He
knew that to be a fact, and yet he did not know it because he
thought the armor was all one with himself, as is a turtle's shell.

He had been told who he was only by his whimpering unconscious mind: a motherless (by choice), fatherless (by treachery), friendless (by circumstance), and joyless (by consequence) man who would continue to refuse emphatically to live
and who, autocratically and unequivocally, did not intend to die.
He was a marooned balloonist, supported by nothing visible,
looking down on everybody and everything, but yearning to be
seen so that, at least, he could be given some credit for an
otherwise profitless ascension.

That was what Raymond's ambivalence was like. He was held
in a paradox of callousness and feeling: the armor, which he told
the world he was, and the feeling, which was what he did not
know he was, and blind to both in a darkness of despair which
could neither be seen nor see itself.

He had been able to weep with Mr. and Mrs. Mavole because
the door had been closed and because he knew he would be
careful never to be seen by those two slobs again.

At seven-twenty on the morning after he had reached
St. Louis, there was a discreet but firm knocking at Raymond's
hotel room door. These peremptory sounds just happened to come
at a moment when Raymond was exchanging intense joy with

the young newspaperwoman he had met the day before. When the knocking had first hit the door, Raymond had heard it clearly enough but he was just busy enough to be determined to ignore it, but the young woman had gone rigid, not in any attitude of idiosyncratic orgasm, but as any healthy, respectable young woman would have done under similar circumstances in a hotel room in any city smaller than Tokyo.

Lights of rage and resentment exploded in Raymond's head. He stared down at the sweet, frightened face under him as though he hated her for not being as defiant as a drunken whore in a night court, then he threw himself off her, nearly falling out of bed. He regained his balance, slowly pulled on the dark blue dressing gown, and walking very close to the door of the room, said into the crack, "Who is it?"

"Sergeant Shaw?"

"Yes."

"Federal Bureau of Investigation." It was a calm, sane, tenor voice.

"What?" Raymond said. "Come on!" His voice was low and angry.

"Open up."

Raymond looked over his shoulder, registering amazement, either to see whether Mardell had heard what he had heard or to find out if she looked like a fugitive. She was chalk-white and solemn.

"What do you want?" Raymond asked.

"We want Sergeant Raymond Shaw." Raymond stared at the door. His face began to fill with a claret flush that clashed unpleasantly with the Nile-green wallpaper directly beside him. "Open up!" the voice said.

"I will like hell open up," Raymond said. "How dare you pound on this door at this time of the morning and issue your country constable's orders? There are telephones in the lobby if you needed to make some kind of urgent inquiry. I said, how dare you?" The hauteur in Raymond's voice held no bluster and its threat of implicit punishment startled the girl on the bed even more than the FBI's arrival. "What the hell do you want from Sergeant Raymond Shaw?" he snarled.

"Well—uh—we have been asked—"

"Asked? *Asked?*"

"—we have been asked to see that you meet the Army plane

which is being sent to pick you up at the Lambert Airport in an hour and fifteen minutes. At eight forty-five."

"You couldn't have called me from your home, or some law-school telephone booth?"

There was a strained silence, then: "We will not continue to discuss this with you from behind a door." Raymond walked quickly to the telephone. He was stiff with anger, as though it had rusted his joints. He picked up the receiver and rattled the bar. He told the operator to please get him the Mayflower Hotel in Washington, D.C.

"Sergeant," the voice said distinctly through the door, "we have orders to put you on that plane. Our orders are just as mandatory as any you ever got in the Army."

"Listen to what I'm going to say on this phone, then we'll talk about orders," Raymond said nastily. "I don't take any orders from the FBI or the Bureau of Printing and Engraving or the Division of Conservation and Wild Life, and if you have any written orders for me from the United States Army, slide them under the door. Then you can wait for me in the lobby, if you still think you have to, and the Air Force can wait for me at the airport until I make my mind up."

"Now, just one minute here, son—" The voice had turned ominous.

"Did they tell you I am being flown to Washington to get a Medal of Honor at the White House?" Maybe that silly hunk of iron he had never asked for would be useful for something just once. This kind of a square bought that stuff. A Medal of Honor was like a lot of money; it was very hard to get, so it took on a lot of magic powers.

"Are you that Sergeant Shaw?"

"That's me." He spoke to the phone. "Right. I'll hold on."

"I'll wait in the lobby," the FBI man said. "I'll be standing near the desk when you come down. Sorry."

Holding the telephone and waiting for the call, Raymond sat down on the edge of the bed, then leaned over and kissed the girl very softly at a soft place right under her rigid right nipple, but he didn't smile at her because he was preoccupied with the call. "Hello, Mayflower? This is St. Louis, Missouri, calling Senator John Iselin. Sergeant Raymond Shaw." There was a short wait. "Hello, Mother. Put your husband on. It's Raymond. *I said put your husband on!*" He waited.

"Johnny? Raymond. There's an FBI man outside my hotel room door in St. Louis to say that they are holding an Army plane for me. Did you tell the Army to request FBI cooperation, and did you have that plane sent here?" He listened. "You did. Well, I knew damn well you did. But why? What the hell did you decide to do a thing like that for?" He listened. "How could I be late? It's Wednesday morning and I don't have to be at the White House until Friday afternoon." He listened. He went totally pale. "A parade? A *par—ade?*" He stared at the details offered by his imagination. "Why—you cheap, flag-rubbing bastard!"

Mardell had slipped out of bed and was starting to get dressed, but she didn't seem to be able to find anything and she looked frightened. He signaled her with his free hand, caught her attention, and smiled at her so warmingly and so reassuringly that she sat down on the edge of the bed. Then she leaned back slowly and stretched out. He reached over and took her hand, kissed it softly, then placed it on top of her flat smooth stomach, while the telephone squawked in his ear. She reached up and just barely allowed her hand to caress the length of his right cheek, unshaven. Suddenly his face went hard again and he barked into the telephone. "No, don't put my mother on again! I know I haven't spoken to her in two years! I'll talk to her when I'm good and ready to talk to her. Aaah, for Christ's sake!" He gritted his teeth and stared at the ceiling.

"Hello, Mother." His voice was flat.

"Raymond, what the hell is this?" his mother asked solicitiously. "What's the matter with you? If we were in the mining business and you struck gold you'd call us, wouldn't you?"

"No."

"Well, it just so happens that you're a Medal of Honor winner —incidentally, congratulations—I meant to write but we've been jammed up. Johnny is a public figure, Raymond. He represents the people of your state just the same as the President represents the people of the United States, and I notice you aren't making any fuss about going to the White House. Is there something so slimy and so terrible about having your picture taken with your father—"

"He is *not my father!*"

"—who represents the pride the people of this nation feel for what you have sacrificed for them on the field of battle?"

"Aaah, fuh crissakes, Mother, will you please—"

"You didn't mind having your picture taken with that stranger in St. Louis yesterday. Incidentally, what happened? Did the Army PRO send you in there to slobber over the Gold Star Mother?"

"It was my own idea."

"Don't tell me that, Raymond darling. I just happen to know you."

"It was my own idea."

"Well, wonderful. It was a wonderful idea. All the papers carried it here yesterday and, of course, everywhere this morning. Marty Webber called in time so we were able to work in a little expression from Johnny about how he'd do anything to help that dead boy's folks and so forth, so we tied everything up from this end. It was great, so you certainly can't stand there and tell me that you won't have your picture taken with the man who is not only your own family but who happens to have been the governor and is now the senator from your own state."

"Since when do you have to get the Army to ask the FBI to set up a picture for Johnny? And that's not what we're arguing about, anyway. He just told me about a filthy idea for a parade to commemorate a medal on which you and I might not place any particular value but which the rest of this country thinks is a nice little thing—for a few lousy votes for him, and I am not going to hold still for any cheap, goddam parade!"

"A parade? That's ridiculous!"

"Ask your flag-simple husband."

Raymond's mother seemed to be talking across the mouthpiece in an aside to Johnny, but Johnny had left the apartment some four minutes before to get a haircut. "Johnny," she said to nobody at all, "where did you get the idea that they could embarrass Raymond with a parade? No wonder he's so sore." Into the telephone she said, "It's not a parade! A few cars were going out to the airport to meet you. No marching men. No color guard. No big bands. You know you are a very peculiar boy, Raymond. I haven't seen you for almost two years—your mother —but you go right on mewing about some parade and Johnny and the FBI and some Army plane, but when it comes to—"

"What else is going to happen in Washington?"

"I had planned a little luncheon."

"With whom?"

"With some very important key press and television people."

"And Johnny?"

"Of course."

"No."

"What?"

"I won't do it."

There was a long pause. Waiting, staring down at the girl, he became aware that she had violet eyes. His mind began to spin off the fine silk thread of his resentment in furious *moulinage*. For almost two years he had been free of his obsessed mother, this brassy bugler, this puss-in-boots to her boorish Marquis de Carrabas, the woman who could think but who could not feel. He had had three letters from her in two years. (1) She had arranged for a life-sized cut-out of Johnny to be forwarded to Seoul. General MacArthur was in the area. Could Johnny arrange for a picture of the two of them with arms around the photographic cut-out of Johnny, as she could guarantee that this would get the widest kind of coverage? (2) Would he arrange for a canvass of fighting men from their state to sign a scroll of Christmas greetings, on behalf of all Johnny's fighting buddies everywhere, to Johnny and the people of his great state? And (3) she was deeply disappointed and not a little bit shocked to find out that he would not lift one little finger to carry out a few simple requests for his mother who worked day and night for both of her men so that there might be a better and more secure place for each of them.

He had been two years away from her but he could feel his defiance of her buckling under the weight of her silence. He had never been able to cope with her silence. At last her voice came through the telephone again. It was changed. It was rough and sinister. It was murderous and frightening and threatening. "If you don't do this, Raymond," she said, "I will promise you on my father's grave right now that you will be very, very sorry."

"All right, Mother," he said. "I'll do it." He shuddered. He hung up the telephone from a foot and a half above the receiver. It fell off, but he must have felt he had made his point because he picked it up from the bed where it had bounced and put it gently into its cradle.

"That was my mother," he explained to Mardell. "I wish I knew what else I could say to describe her in front of a nice girl like you."

He walked to the locked door. He leaned against the crack in despair and said, "I'll be in the lobby in about an hour." There was no answer. He turned toward the bed, untying the belt of his new blue robe, as a massive column of smoke began to spiral upward inside his head, filling the eyes of his memory and opaquing his expression from behind his eyes. Mardell was spilled out softly across the bed. The sheets were blue. She was blond-and-ivory, tipped with pink; lined with pink. It came to him that he had never seen another girl, named Jocie, this way. The thought of Jocie lying before him like this lovely moaning girl excited him as though a chemical abrasive had been poured into his urethra and she was assaulted by him in the most attritive manner, to her greater glory and with her effulgent consent, and though she lived to be an old, old woman she never forgot that morning and could summon it back to her in its richest violence whenever she was frightened and alone, never knowing that she was not only the first woman Raymond had ever possessed, but the first he had ever kissed in passion, or that he had been given his start toward relaxing his inhibitions against the uses of sex not quite one year before, in Manchuria.

II A CHINESE ARMY construction battalion arrived at Tunghwa, forty-three miles inside the Korean frontier, on July 4, 1951, to set underway the housing for events, planned in 1936, that were to reach their conclusion in the United States of America in 1960. The major in charge of the detail, a Ssu Ma Sung, is now a civilian lawyer in Kunming.

Manchuria is in the subarctic zone, but the summers are hot and humid. Tunghwa handles industry, such as sawmilling and food processing with hydroelectric power. It is a city of approximately ninety thousand, about the size of Terre Haute, Indiana, but lacking a public health appropriation.

The Chinese construction battalion set up the job near a military airfield nearly three miles out of town. Everything they put up was prefabricated, the sections keyed by different colors; this, when the pieces were scattered around the terrain, made the men seem like toy figures walking among the pieces of a giant jigsaw puzzle. When these were assembled into a building, they were sprayed with barn-red lead paint to banish the quilted effect. By July 6, at seventeen-nineteen, the battalion had completed a two-story, twenty-two-room structure with a small auditorium. The building was called the Research Pavilion and had some one-way transparent glass walls. It also had a few comfortably furnished guest rooms without glass walls on the first floor; these had been reserved for the brass from Moscow and Peiping.

Each floor held different-colored, varipatterned asphalt tile as a guide for furniture and equipment placement. Each wall, as it was erected, had decorations riveted into it. The windows, cut through each outer wall, had curtains and drapes fastened to them. The thousand pieces of that house gave the impression that it was a traveling billet for political representatives of the allied People's Governments: a structure forever being built, struck, then sent on ahead to be built again for the next series of meetings and discussions. All of the furniture was made of blond wood in mutated, modern Scandinavian design. All of the interior coloring, except the bright yellow rattan carpeting on the second floor, was the same green and apricot utilized by new brides during their first three years of marriage.

The second floor of the building held one large corner suite of rooms and ten other compact cubicles that had three solid walls each and one building-long common wall of one-way transparent glass facing a catwalk that was patrolled day and night by two Soviet Army riflemen. Each cubicle contained a cot, a chair, a closet, and a mirror for reassurance that the soul had not fled. The large apartment had similar fittings, plus a bathroom, a large living room, and an additional bedroom. All of the walls here were opaque. The invigorating scent of pine-tree incense pervaded the upper floors, subtly and pleasantly.

THE marvelous part of what they were doing several hundred miles to the south of Tunghwa was that every time Mavole moved, the girl moved, and every time Mavole bleated, the girl bleated. It was really a money's worth and after Mavole came downstairs he told the guys that the classy part about the joint was that when he took the broad upstairs in the first place, there had been no jeers or catcalls. Mavole's co-mover and bleater was a young Korean girl who had adapted to prostitution a variation of the Rochdale principle on which had been based the first cooperative store in 1844, in that she extended absolutely no credit but distributed part of the profits in the form of free beer. Her name was Gertrude.

Freeman had left to check gear, but Mavole and Bobby Lembeck sat around and drank a few more beers while they waited for the corporal to get finished upstairs. They tried to explain to the two little broads that it was not necessary to smile so hard but they couldn't speak Korean, except for a few words, and the girls couldn't speak American, so Bobby Lembeck put his two forefingers at the corners of his mouth and pulled an inane prop smile down. The girls caught on but it looked so funny the way he did it that Bobby and Mavole started laughing like crazy, which started the girls laughing again so that when they stopped laughing they were still smiling.

To the extent that wartime zymurgists imperil the norm, the Korean beer was about as good as local Mississippi beer or Nebraska beer, which is pretty lousy, but it was hot. That was one thing you could say about it, Mavole pointed out.

"Eddie, why do we have to spend all of our time off in a whorehouse?" Bobby asked.

"Yeah. Rough, ain't it?"

"I don't mean it's hard to take, but my hobby is birds. There are a lot of new birds around this part of the world."

"We spend our time off here because it's the only place on the entire Korean peninsula that Sergeant Raymond Shaw doesn't walk into."

"You think he's a fairy, or very religious?"

"What?"

"Or both?"

"Sergeant Shaw? Our Raymond?"

"Yeah."

"What are you? Out of your mind? It's just that Raymond doesn't give to anybody. And it's a common vulgar thing—sex—to Raymond."

"He happens to be right," Bobby Lembeck said. "It sure is. I'm only a beginner but that's one of the things I like about it."

Mavole looked at him, nodding his head in a kind of awe. "It's a very funny thing," he said slowly, "but every now and then I think about you coming all the way to Korea from New Jersey to get your first piece of poontang and it makes me feel like I'm sort of a monument—part of your life. You know? And Marie Louise too. Of course." He nodded equably to indicate the small Japanese girl who was sitting beside Bobby Lembeck, holding his right wrist like a falcon.

"She certainly is," Bobby agreed. "What a monument."

"It's kind of a very touching thing to me that you have never had a fat broad or a tall broad, say."

"It's different?"

"Well—yes and no. It's hard to explain. These little broads, while very nice and with lovely dispositions and with beer included, which is very unusual, they *are* very little—spinners, we used to call them—and although I hate to say this even though I know they can't understand me, they are very, very skinny."

"Just the same," Bobby said.

"Yeah. You're right."

Melvin, the corporal, came rushing down the stairs. He was combing his hair rapidly, head tilted to one side, like a commuter who had overslept. "Great!" he said briskly. "Great, great, great!" he repeated, running the words together. "The greatest."

"You're telling me?" asked Bobby Lembeck.

"Look at him," Mavole said proudly. "Already he's an expert on getting laid."

"All right, you guys," Melvin said in a corporal's voice. "We move up north in a half an hour. Let's go."

Bobby Lembeck kissed Marie Louise's hand. "*Mansei!*" he said, using the only Korean word he knew; he voiced a gallant hope, for it meant "May our country live ten thousand years."

SERGEANT SHAW was capable of weeping objective, simulated tears at several points in the story of his life, which Captain Marco always encouraged him to tell to pass the time during quiet hours on patrol. The sergeant's rage-daubed face would shine like a ripped-out heart flung onto stones in moonlight, and the captain liked to hear the story because, in a way, it was like hearing Orestes gripe about Clytemnestra. Captain Marco treasured poetic, literary, informational, and cross-referenced allusions, military and nonmilitary. He was a reader. His point of motive was that on many Army posts one's off-time could only be spent drinking, bridge-playing, or reading. Marco enjoyed beer, abjured spirits. He had no head for cards; he always seemed to win from his superior officers. His fellow officers were used up on conversations of a nonprofessional nature, so he transhipped boxes of books about anything at all, back and forth between San Francisco and wherever he was stationed at the time, because he was deeply interested in the problems of Bilbao bankers, the history of piracy, the paintings of Orozco, the modern French theater, the jurisprudential factors in Mafia administration, the diseases of cattle, the works of Yeats, the ramblings of the Bible, the novels of Joyce Cary, the lordliness of doctors, the psychology of bullfighters, the ethnic choices of Arabs, the origin of trade winds, and very nearly anything else contained in any of the books which he paid to have selected at random by a stranger in a bookstore on Market Street and shipped to him wherever he happened to be.

The sergeant's account of his past was ancient in its form and confusingly dramatic, as perhaps would have been a game of three-level chess between Richard Burbage and Sacha Guitry. It all seemed to revolve around his mother, a woman as ambitious as Daedalus. The sergeant was twenty-two years old. He was as ambivalent as a candle burning at both ends. Awake, his resentment was almost always at full boil. Asleep, Captain Marco could understand, it simmered and bubbled in the blackened iron pot of his memory.

Raymond had made tech sergeant because he was a bleakly good soldier and because he was the greatest natural marksman in the division. Any weapon he could lift, he could kill with. He pointed it languidly, pulled the trigger, and something always fell. Some of the men appreciated this quality very much and liked to be with or near Raymond when any action occurred, but otherwise he was scrupulously shunned by all of them.

Raymond was a left-handed man of considerable height—to which he soared from wide hips, narrower shoulders—with a triangular face which suspended a pointed chin that was narrow and not very firm. The vertical halves of his face pouted together sullenly, projecting the effluvia of self-pity. His skin was immoderately white, which made the prominent veins of his arms and legs seem like blue neon tubing. His cropped hair was light blond and it grew down low and in a round shape over his forehead in a style affected by many American businessmen of a juvenile or eunuchoid turn.

Despite that specific inventory of his countenance, Raymond was a very handsome man, very nearly a pretty man, who had heavy bones, great physical strength, and large glaucous eyes with very large whites, like those of a carousel horse pursued by the Erinyes, those female avengers of antiquity.

When the flautist Boehm engineered the new design and the new note value system for the clarinet, his system took a half note away from the thumb and a half note away from the third finger on each hand, as it would have been played on the standard Albert clarinet. By so doing he created an aural schism and brought a most refined essence of prejudice to a world of music. He created two clarinetists with two subtly different qualities of sound, where there had been one before, and provided, amid this decadence, many bitter misunderstandings. It was as if Raymond had been built by Herr Boehm to have had his full notes dropped to half notes, then to quarter notes, then to eighth notes, for his was an almost silent music, if music Raymond contained at all.

In spite of himself the captain liked Shaw, and the captain was a matured and thoughtful man. He liked Raymond, he had decided after much consideration of the phenomenon, because, in one way or another, Shaw was continuously demonstrating that he liked the captain and the captain was too wise a man to believe he could resist a plea like that.

Nobody else in Company C liked Raymond, and perhaps no one else in the U.S. Army did. His comrades skirted him charily or they pretended he was not there, as the fathers of daughters might regard an extremely high incidence of rape in their neighborhood.

It was not that Raymond was hard to like. He was impossible to like. The captain, a thoughtful man, understood that Shaw's attention to him was merely the result of the pressure of a lifetime of having his nose rubbed in various symbols of authority, and as the sergeant's life story droned on and on the captain came to realize that Raymond was pouring out a cherished monologue upon the beloved memory of his long-dead, betrayed father, who had been cast off by that bitch before Raymond could begin to love him. Amateur psychiatric prognosis can be fascinating when there is absolutely nothing else to do. Also fascinating was the captain's unending search for one small, even isolated address of Raymond's that was warm or, in any human way, attractive.

Raymond's crushing contemptuousness aside, examining such a minute thing as the use of his hands while talking could be distressing, and the captain could see how little fragments of Raymond's personality had formed one great, cold lump. Raymond could not stop using one horrid gesture: a go-way-you-bother-me, flicking sort of gesture that he managed by having his long, fish-belly white fingers do small, backhand, brushing gestures to point up anything he said. Anything. He made the brush if he said good morning. If. He flicked air away from himself when he talked about the weather, politics (his field), food, or gear: anything. This *digitorum gesticulatione* was about the most irritating single bit of movement that the captain could ever remember seeing, and the captain was a thoughtful man. He had burst out against it early one morning while the sky was flinging light all around them, and Raymond had responded with a look of confusion, unaware of his fault, and disturbed. He had said to the captain that he, flick-flick, did not understand what the captain meant, brush-brush, and at last the captain had chosen to overlook it, as it was a relatively minor thing to a man who planned to be a wartime or a peacetime general of four stars someday and who had permitted himself to decide that he would be crazy to refuse to understand a hero-worshiping sergeant whose relative might someday be chairman, or have direct influence on the chairman, of the Armed Services Committee of the Congress.

It took that kind of objectivity to begin to tolerate Raymond, who was over full of haughtiness. Raymond stood as though someone might have just opened a beach umbrella in his bowels. His very glance drawled when he deigned to look, seldom deigning to speak. There were wags in the company who said he put his lips up in curl papers each night, and all of these things are sure ingredients for arousing and sustaining the hostility of others. In theory, Shaw possessed a manner that should become a sergeant, and perhaps would become a drill sergeant or a Marine Corps public-relations sergeant, but not a combat noncom because under heightened realism any attitude of power must always be accompanied by something that makes the privilege of power pardonable, and Shaw possessed no such rescuing qualifiers. His resentment of people, places, and things was a stifling, sensual thing.

The captain's name was Ben Marco. He was a professional officer. He had been sixth in his class at the Academy. His family had claimed the Army as a trade ever since a gunnery lieutenant who had grown up with Hernando de Soto at Barcarrota, Spain, had left Pizarro for a look at the upper Mississippi River. Marco followed his father's vocation because it was the last preserve of intimate feudalism: terraced ranks of fief and lord, where a major can always remain a peasant to a general and a lieutenant a peon to a major.

Marco was an intelligent intelligence officer. He looked like an Aztec crossed with an Eskimo, which was a fairly common western American type because the Aztec troops had drifted down from Siberia quite a long time before the Spaniards of Pizarro and Cortez had drifted north out of the Andes and Vera Cruz. He had metallic (copper-colored) skin and strong (very white) teeth but, aside from pigmentation, the straight (black) hair, the aboriginal look, and the eyes colored like Pôtage St. Germaine, the potage's potage (green); he had had the contrasting fortune of being born in New Hampshire, where his father had been stationed at the time, just prior to duty in the Canal Zone. He stood five feet eleven and three-quarter inches and looked small when standing beside Raymond. He had a powerful frame and the meat on it was proportioned like the stone meat on an Epstein statue. He had the superior digestive system which affords almost every man blessed with it the respose to become thoughtful.

They were an odd combination: the civilian who tried to talk like a soldier and the soldier who had been ordered by the Joint Chiefs in this new and polite Army to damn well learn how to talk like a civilian; the frosty Bramin with the earthy, ambitious man; the pseudomystagogue with the counter-puncher; the inhibitory with the excitatory, the latter being a designation used by the physiologist Ivan Petrovich Pavlov.

. . .

MARCO led the Intelligence and Reconnaissance patrol of nine men and his sergeant, Ray Shaw, on their fourteenth reconnaissance that night. Chunjin, Marco's orderly, appeared suddenly at his elbow, out of the almost total darkness and persistent silence. Chunjin was the captain's interpreter, the general guide over terrain, who, no matter where they were sent in Korea always insisted gravely that he had been born within two miles of the spot. Chunjin was a very good man with a frying pan, a shoe brush, a broom, a shaving kit, and at crating and transhipping books to San Francisco. He was small and wiry. He was a very, very tough-looking fellow against any comparison. He had the look of a man who maybe had been pushed around a lot and then had taken his life into his hands by deciding not to take any more of that kind of stuff. He always looked them right in the eyes, from private to colonel, and he did not smile at any time.

"What?" Marco said.

"Bad here."

"Why?"

"Tricky."

"How?"

"Swamp all around thirty yards up. May be quicksand."

"Nobody told me about any quicksand."

"How they know?"

"All right! All right! What do you want?"

"All walk in single line next two hundred yards."

"No."

"Patrol sink."

"It is tactically unsound to go forward in a single file."

"Then patrol sink in thirty yards."

"Only for two hundred yards ahead?"

"Yes, sir."

"We can't go around it?"

"No, sir."

"All right. Pass the word."

Raymond was at the head of the line, right behind Chunjin, in guide position. Marco finished the twelve-man line. I&R patrols go out at night, unarmed except for knives. They are unarmed because rifle fire draws other fire and I&R patrols do what they do by staying out of trouble. There was very little light from a pallid crescent of moon. There was about twenty feet of distance between each man. The line was about seventy yards long. When it had moved forward about sixty yards, two human forms rose up in front of and behind each man on the line. The forward form hit its man at the pit of the stomach with a rifle butt, while the back man brought the stock down hard at the back of each man's head when the bodies doubled forward. Excepting Chunjin, they all seemed to go down at the same time. It was an extremely silent action, a model action of its kind. Without pause each two-man team of attackers built a litter out of the two rifles and rolled their charges aboard. Two noncoms checked each team out, talking quietly and occasionally slapping a man on the shoulder with approval and self-pleasure.

Chunjin led the litter teams on a route that was at right angles to the direction taken by the patrol, across the dark, firm terrain. Twenty-two men carried eleven bodies in the improvised stretchers at a rapid dogtrot while the noncoms sang the cadence in soft Russian. The patrol had been taken by Three Company of the 35th Regiment of the 66th Airborne Division of the Soviet Army, a crack outfit that handled most of the flashy assignments in the sector, and dined out between these jobs with available North Korean broads and the young ladies of the Northeast Administrative Area, on the stories emanating therefrom.

The patrol was taken to two trucks waiting a quarter mile away. The trucks rode them twelve miles over bad terrain to a temporary airfield. A helicopter took them north at about twelve hundred feet. They had cleared the Yalu before the first man began to climb back into sluggish consciousness to see a uniformed country boy from Ukhta holding a machine rifle at ready and grinning down at him.

DR. YEN LO and his staff of thirty technicians (all of whom were Chinese except two overawed Uzbek neuropsychiatrists who had jointly won an Amahlkin award; as a reward, their section had arranged for them to spend a thirty-day tour with this man whom they had always thought of as a shelf of books or the voice behind the many professors in their short lives—the living monument to, and the continental expander of, the work of Pavlov) installed their peculiar establishment during the night

of July 6 and worked at the fixtures necessary until mid-morning
of July 7. Their pharmacy was an elaborate affair, for one thing.
For another, they had brought in four compact electronic
computers. Included in the effects was an electrical switchboard
that seemed large enough to have handled the lighting for the
State Opera in Vienna, where, quite possibly, it originated.

Old Yen was in fine spirits. He chatted freely about Pavlov
and Salter, Krasnogorski and Meignant, Petrova and Bechtervov,
Forlov and Rowland, as though he had not made his departure
from the main stream of their doctrine some nine years before
when he had come upon his own radical technology for descent
into the unconscious mind with the speed of a mine-shaft elevator. He made jokes with his staff. He taunted the two Uzbeks
just as though he were not a god, about Herr Freud, whom he
called "that Austrian gypsy fortuneteller" or "the Teuton fantast"
or "that licensed gossip," and he permitted his chief of staff to
visit General Kostroma's chief to arrange for the mess and the
billeting of his people.

During the pleasantly cool evening before the morning when
the American I&R patrol was brought in for him, Yen Lo and his
staff of thirty men and women sat in a large circle on a broad,
grassy space, and as the moon went higher and the hour got
later, and all of the voices seemed to fall into lower pitch preparing for sleepiness, Yen Lo told them a fairy story, which was set
thirty-nine centuries before they had been born, about a young
fisherman and a beautiful princess who had journeyed through
the province of Chengtu.

THE AMERICAN patrol was brought to the Research Pavilion at six-nine the following morning, July 8. Yen Lo had them
bathed, then inoculated each of them personally. They were
dressed again while they slept and set down, excepting for Raymond Shaw, one man to a cot to a cubicle, where Yen Lo got
three implantation teams started on them, staying with each
team through the originating processes until he had assured himself that all had been routined with smoothness. When he had
assured himself to the point of downright fussiness, he brought
his assistant and two nurses with him into the corner apartment

where Raymond slept and began the complex work on the reconstruction of the sergeant's personality.

The principles of excitation, as outlined by Pavlov in 1894, are
immutable and apply to every psychological problem no matter
how remote it may appear at first. Conditioned reflexes do not
involve volitional thinking. Words produce associative reflexes.
"Splendid," "marvelous," and "magnificent" give us an unconscious lift because we have been conditioned to that feeling in
them. The words "hot," "boiling," and "steam" have a warm
quality because of their associativity. Inflection and gesture have
been conditioned as intensifiers of word conditionings, as
Andrew Salter, the Pavlovian disciple, writes.

Salter shows that when one sees the essence of the unconscious mind to be conditioning, one is in a strategic position to
develop a sound understanding of the deepest wellsprings of human behavior. Conditioning is based upon associative reflexes
that use words or symbols as triggers of installed automatic reactions. Conditioning, called brainwashing by the news agencies, is the production of reactions in the human organism
through the use of associative reflexes.

Yen Lo approached human behavior in terms of fundamental
components instead of metaphysical labels. His meaningful goal
was to implant in the subject's mind the predominant motive,
which was that of submitting to the operator's commands; to
construct behavior which would at all times strive to put the
operator's exact intentions into execution as if the subject were
playing a game or acting a part; and to cause a redirection of his
movements by remote control through second parties, or third or
fiftieth parties, twelve thousand miles removed from the original
commands if necessary. The first thing a human being is loyal to,
Yen Lo observed, is his own conditioned nervous system.

On the morning of July 9, the members of the American
patrol, excepting Shaw, Marco, and Chunjin, the Korean interpreter, were allowed to walk in and out of each other's rooms
and to lounge around in a comfortable common room where
there were magazines only two or three years old, printed in
Chinese and Russian, and an Australian seed catalogue dated
Spring 1944, with attractive color pictures. Yen Lo had conditioned the men to enjoy all the Coca-Cola they could drink,
which was, in actuality, Chinese Army issue tea served in tin
cups. There were playing cards, card tables, and some dice. Each

man had been given twenty strips of brown paper and told that these were one-, five-, ten- and twenty-dollar bills of U.S. currency, depending on how they had been marked in pencil on the corners.

The yellow rattan carpet, the simulated sunlight from the fluorescent tubing, and the happy, blond furniture in the windowless room were quite cheery and bright and the men had been instructed to enjoy their surroundings. About thirty pin-up pictures of Chinese and Indian movie stars were clustered thickly on one wall around a calendar that advertised Tiger Beer of Singapore (fourteen per cent by volume) and offered a deminude Caucasian cutie dressed for Coney Island in the mode of the summer of 1931. There were cigarettes and cigars for everyone, and Yen Lo had allowed his boys to have a little fun in the selection of out-landish tobacco substitutes because he knew that word of it would pass through the armies, based upon the sure knowledge of what made armies laugh, rubbing more sheen into the legend of the Yen Lo unit. They would be talking about how much those Americans had savored those cigars and cigarettes from Lvov to Cape Bezhneva inside of one week, as yak dung tastes good like a cigarette should.

The nine men had been conditioned to believe that they were leveling off on a Sunday night after a terrific three-day pass from a post forty minutes outside of New Orleans. They were all convinced that each had won a lot of money and that in spending most of it they had reached exhaustion with warm edges and an expensive calm feeling.

Ed Mavole had received the spirit of Yen Lo's suggestion so strongly that he confided to Silvers that he was slightly worried and wondered if maybe he wouldn't be doing the right thing if he stepped out for a minute to a prophylactic station.

They were worn down from all that whisky and those broads, but they were relaxed and euphoric. Three times a day Yen's staff men gave each man his deep mental massage, stacking up the layers of light and shadow neatly within each unconscious mind, as ordered. The men spent two days in and out of the common room, sleeping and eating when they felt like it, believing it was always the same time on the same Sunday night, remembering that clutch of sensational broads as if they had just rolled off them.

. . .

THE DISTINGUISHED commission of distinguished men, including one who was a member of the Central Committee, and another who was a security officer wearing the uniform of a lieutenant general of the Soviet Army inasmuch as he was traveling through a military zone and because he happened to like to wear uniforms, arrived with their staffs at the Tunghwa military airport, accompanied by two round Chinese dignitaries, at five minutes to noon on the morning of July 12, 1951. There were fourteen in the group. Gomel, the Politburo man, in mufti, had a staff of five men who were in uniform. Berezovo, the security officer, in uniform, had a staff of four men and a young woman, in mufti. The two Russian groups seemed remote from each other and from the two young Chinese who may only have seemed young because of an eighty-three per cent vegetable diet.

They all ate at General Kostroma's mess. He was the army corps commander who had been transferred too suddenly from work that had suited him so well at the Army War College to be pressed into supervising Chinese who seemed to have no understanding of military mission and who were fearfully spendthrift with troops.

There appeared to be four entirely separate groups dining at the same large table.

First, Kostroma and his staff: bravely silent men who realized now that they had made a chafing mistake when they had wangled places with this general; they were continuously wondering where they had gone wrong in their judgment, trying to analyze retrospectively whether anyone along the line had encouraged them to think that a berth with Kostroma would be a shrewd move. General Kostroma himself remained mute because a Central Committee member was present, and as Kostroma had evidently made mistakes in the past which he had not known he had been making, he did not want to make another.

The second group, Gomel's, was made up of men whose average length of service among the trench-mortar subtleties of party practice and ascent through the ranks had been a total of eighteen years and four months each. They were professional politicians, wholly independent of the whims of popular vote. They saw their community duty as that of appearing wise and stern, hence they observed silence.

The Berezovo group was silent because they were security

people. Berezovo is dead now. For that matter, so is General Kostroma.

Those three groups, however silent, were well aware of the fourth, chaired by Yen Lo (D.M.S., D.Ph., D.Sc., B.S.P., R.H.S.) who kept his own executive staff and the two young (one should call them young-looking rather than young) Chinese dignitaries in high-pitched, continual laughter until the meal had spent itself. All jokes were in Chinese. Even without pointed gestures, Yen managed to convey the feeling that all of the gusty sallies were at their gallant Russian ally's expense. Gomel glared and sweated a form of chicken fat. Berezovo picked at his food expressionlessly, and pared an apple with a bayonet.

Gomel, who established himself as being hircine before anything else, was as stocky as an opera hat, with a bullet head and stainless-steel false teeth. It would be difficult to be more proletarian-seeming than Gomel. The teeth had made him carniverously unphotogenic and therefore unknown to the newspaper readers of the West. He dressed in the chic moujik style affected by his leader; loose silk everythings rushing downward into the tops of soft black boots. His smell tended to worry his personal staff lest their expressions make it seem as though they were personally disloyal to him. He was a specialist in heavy industrial management.

Berezovo, who was younger than Gomel, represented the new Soviet executive and resembled a fire hydrant in a run-down neighborhood: short, squat, stained, and seamed, his head seeming to come to a point and his fibrous hair parted in several impossible places, like a coconut's. Berezovo was all brass; a very important person. Gomel was important, no doubt about that. He had *dachi* in both Moscow and the Crimea, but there were only two men higher than Berezovo in the entire, exhaustingly delicate business of Soviet security.

Each man had successfully concealed from the other that he was present at the seminar as the personal and confidential representative of Josef Stalin, proprietor.

YEN LO's lectures began at 4 P.M. on July 11. General Kostroma was not invited to attend. The group strolled in pairs, not unlike dons moving across a campus, toward the lovely copse which framed that little red schoolhouse wherein Yen Lo had inserted so many new values and perspectives into the minds of the eleven Americans. It was a glorious summer afternoon: not too hot, not too cold. The excessive humidity of the morning had disappeared. The food had been excellent.

The single extraordinary sight in the informal but stately procession led by Yen Lo and Pa Cha, the senior Chinese statesman present, was that of Chunjin, the Korean interpreter hitherto attached to the U.S. Army as orderly and guide for Captain Marco, walking at Berezovo's side, chewing on and smoking a large cigar which was held in his small teeth at a jaunty angle. Had any member of the American patrol still retained any semblance of normal perspective he would have been startled at seeing Chunjin there, for when natives were captured by a military party of either side their throats were always cut.

Yen Lo had telephoned ahead from the mess so that when the commission entered the auditorium of the Research Pavilion the American patrol had been seated in a long line across the raised stage, behind a centered lectern. They watched the Sino-Soviet group enter with expressions of amused tolerance and boredom. Yen Lo moved directly to the platform, rummaging in his attaché case while the others found seats, by echelon, in upright wooden chairs.

Large, repeated, seven-color lithographs of Stalin and Mao were interspersed on three walls between muscularly typographed yellow-on-black posters that read: LET US STOP IMITATING!!! as a headline, and as text: *Piracy and imitations of designs hamper the development and expansion of export trade. It is regrettable that there are quite a few cases of piracy in the People's Republic. Piracy injures the Chinese people's international prestige, causes the boycott of Chinese goods, and makes Chinese designers lose interest in making creative efforts.* The smell of new paint and shellac and the delicious clean odor of wood shavings floated everywhere in the air of the room, offering the deep, deep luxury of absolute simplicity.

On stage, Ben Marco sat on the end of the line at stage right, in the Mr. Bones position. Sergeant Shaw sat on the other end of the line, stage left. Between them, left to right, were Hiken, Gosfield, Little, Silvers, Mavole, Melvin, Freeman, Lembeck.

Mavole was at stage center. All of the men were alert and serene.

The audience was divided, physically and by prejudice. Gomel did not approve of Yen Lo or his work. Berezovo happened to see in Yen Lo's methods possibilities that would hasten revolutionary causes by fifty years. Five staff members sat behind each of these men who sat on opposite sides of the room, re-creating an impression of two Alphonse Capones (1899-1947) attending the Chicago opera of 1927. The two Chinese representatives sat off to the left, closer to the platform than the others, as bland as two jars of yoghurt. Yen Lo winked at them now and again as he made his address with asides in various Chinese dialects to annoy Gomel.

The stage was raised about thirty inches from the floor and was draped with bunting of the U.S.S.R. and the People's Republic of China. Yen Lo stood behind the centered lectern. He was wearing an ankle-length dress of French blue that buttoned at the side of his throat and fell in straight, comfortable lines. The skin of his face was lapstreaked, or clinker-built, into overlapping horizontal folds like the sides of some small boats, and it was the color of raw sulphur. His eyes were hooded and dark, which made him seem even older than did the wrinkles. His entire expression was theatrically sardonic as though he had been advised by prepaid cable that the late Dr. Fu Manchu had been his uncle.

Yen Lo instructed the Russians with bright contempt, with the slightly nauseated fixity of a vegetarian who must remain in a closed room with carnivores. He used a pointer to indicate the various U.S. Army personnel behind him. He introduced each man courteously and by name. He explained their somewhat lackadaisical manners by saying that each American was under the impression that he had been forced by a storm to wait in a small hotel in New Jersey where space restrictions made it necessary for him to watch and listen to a meeting of a ladies' garden club.

Yen motioned to Raymond Shaw. "Pull your chair over here, Raymond, if you please," he said in English. Raymond sat beside Yen Lo, who placed his hand lightly on the young man's shoulder as he spoke to the group. Raymond's bearing was superciliously haughty. His pose, had it been executed in oils, might have been called "The Young Duke among the Fishmongers." His legs were crossed and his head was cocked with his chin outstretched.

The male stenographer on Gomel's team and the female stenographer on Berezovo's squad flipped their notebooks open on their laps at the same instant, preparing to record Yen's remarks. The shorter Chinese emissary, a chap named Wen Ch'ang, got his hand under his dress and scratched his crotch.

"This, comrades, is the famous Raymond Shaw, the young man you have flown nearly eight thousand miles to see," Yen Lo said in Russian. "Your chief, Lavrenti Pavlovich Beria, saw this young man in his mind's eye, only as a disembodied ideal, as long as two years before he was appointed to head the Ministry of Internal Affairs and Security in 1938, and that was thirteen eventful years ago. I feel I must add at this point my humble personal gratitude for his warm encouragement and fulfilling inspiration. It is to Lavrenti Pavlovich that this little demonstration will do homage today."

Berezovo nodded his head graciously in silent acknowledgement of the tribute, then the five staff people behind him just as graciously nodded their heads.

Yen Lo told the group that Raymond Shaw was a unique combination of the exceptional: both internally and externally. With oratorical roundness he presented Raymond's external values first. He told them about Raymond's step-father, the governor; of Raymond's mother, a woman of wealth and celebrity; of Raymond's uncle, a distinguished member of the U.S. diplomatic service. Raymond himself was a journalist and when this little war was over might even rise to become a distinguished journalist. All of these attributes, he said, made Raymond welcome everywhere within the political hierarchy of the United States, within both parties.

The line of American soldiers listened to the lecture politely, as though they had to make the best of listening to club women discuss fun with hydrangeas. Bobby Lembeck's attention had strayed. Ed Mavole, who was still firmly convinced that he had just finished the most active three-day pass of his Army career, had to stuff a fist into his mouth to conceal a yawn. Captain Marco looked from Shaw to Yen Lo to Gomel to Berezovo's recording assistant, a fine-looking piece with a passionate nose who was wearing no lipstick and no brassière. Marco mentally fitted her with a B cup, enjoyed the diversion, then turned back

to try to pay attention to Yen Lo, who was saying that as formidable as were Raymond's external attributes, he possessed internal weaknesses that Yen would show as being incredible
strengths for an assassin.

"I am sure that all of you have heard that old wives' tale," Yen
stated, "which is concerned with the belief that no hypnotized
subject may be forced to do that which is repellent to his moral
nature, whatever that is, or to his own best interests. That is
nonsense, of course. You note-takers might set down a reminder
to consult Brenmen's paper, 'Experiments in the Hypnotic Production of Antisocial and Self-injurious Behavior,' or Wells' 1941
paper which was titled, I believe, 'Experiments in the Hypnotic
Production of Crime,' or Andrew Salter's remarkable book, *Conditioned Reflex Therapy*, to name only three. Or, if it offends you
to think that only the West is studying how to manufacture more
crime and better criminals against modern shortages, I suggest
Krasnogorski's *Primary Violence Motivation* or Serov's *The Uni-
lateral Suggestion to Self-Destruction*. For any of you who are
interested in massive negative conditioning there is Frederic
Wertham's *The Seduction of the Innocent*, which demonstrates
how thousands have been brought to antisocial actions through
children's cartoon books. However, enough of that. You won't
read them anyway. The point I am making is that those who
speak of the need for hypnotic suggestion to fit a subject's moral
code should revise their concepts. The conception of people acting against their own best interests should not startle us. We see
it occasionally in sleepwalking and in politics, every day."

Raymond sighed. The youngest man on Gomel's staff, seated
farthest back in the rows of irregularly placed chairs, picked his
nose surreptitiously through the ensuing silence. Berezovo's recording assistant, her breasts pointing straight out through the
cotton blouse without benefit of B cup, stared at Marco just
below the belt buckle. The Chinese had become aware of how
much Conrade Gomel smelled like a goat. Bobby Lembeck was
thinking about Marie Louise.

Most of the Russians understood clearly that what Yen Lo had
done was to concentrate the purpose of all propaganda upon the
mind of one man. They knew that reflexes could be conditioned
to the finest point so that if the right person leveled his finger
from the right place at the right time and cried "Deviationist!" or
"Trotskyite" that any man's character could be assassinated or a

man could be liquidated. Conditioning was intensified repetition.

Ed Mavole had to go to the john. He looked furtively to the right and left, then he caught Marco's eyes and made a desperate series of lifts with his eyebrows combined with some compulsive face tics. Marco coughed. Yen Lo looked over at him serenely, then nodded. Marco went to Yen's side and whispered a message. Yen shouted a command in Chinese and a man appeared in the open doorway at the back of the auditorium. Yen suggested that Mavole follow that man and he told Mavole not to be embarrassed, because the ladies did not understand Chinese. Mavole thanked him, then he turned to the line of sitting soldiers and said, "Anybody else?" Bobby Lembeck joined him and they left the room. Marco returned to his chair. Gomel demanded to know what the hell was going on anyway. Yen Lo explained, deadpan, in Russian, and Gomel made an impatient, exasperated face.

Yen Lo carried his thesis forward. Neurotics and psychotics, he told the group, are too easily canted into unpredictable patterns and the constitutional psychopaths, those total waste products of all breeding, were too frivolously based. Of course, he explained, the psychotic group known as paranoiacs had always provided us with the great leaders of the world and always would. That was a clinical, historical fact. With their dedicated sense of personal mission (a condition that has been allowed to become tainted semantically, he pointed out, with the psychiatric label of megalomania), with their innate ability to falsify hampering conditions of the past to prevent unwanted distortion of the future, with that relentless, protective cunning that places the whole world, in revolving turn, into position as their enemies, paranoiacs simply had to be placed in the elite stock of any leader pool.

Mavole and Lembeck came back, picking their way carefully through the chairs and moving very properly, Mavole leading. They climbed back upon the platform almost daintily while the speaker and the audience waited politely. Mavole inadvertently broke wind as he sat down. He excused himself with a startled exclamation and flushed with embarrassment before all those garden ladies. His consternation sent Gomel into barking laughter. Yen Lo waited icily until the commissar had finished his pleasure, whacking his packed thighs and wheezing, then pointing his stunted finger up at Mavole on the platform while he guffawed helplessly. When the laughter finally subsided, Yen threw an aside at his countrymen in Chinese. They tittered like *thlibii,* which shut Gomel up. Yen Lo continued blandly.

"Although the paranoiacs make the great leaders, it is the resenters who make their best instruments because the resenters, those men with cancer of the psyche, make the great assassins." His audience was listening intently again.

"It is difficult to define true resentment for you. The Spanish medical philosopher Dr. Gregorio Marañon described it as a passion of the mind. Some blow of life which produces a sharp moan of protest, when it is not transformed by the normal mental mechanism into ordinary resignation, ends by becoming the director of our slightest reactions. Raymond's mother helped to bring about his condition to the largest and most significant extent for, in Andrew Salter's words, 'the human fish swim about at the bottom of the great ocean of atmosphere and they develop psychic injuries as they collide with one another. Most mortal of all are the wounds gotten from the parent fish.'

"It has been said," the Chinese doctor continued, "that only the man who is capable of loving everything is capable of understanding everything. The resentful man is a human with the capacity for affection so poorly developed that his understanding for the motives of others very nearly does not exist." Yen Lo patted Raymond's shoulder sympathetically and smiled down at him regretfully. "Raymond is a man of melancholic and reserved psychology. He is afflicted with total resentment. It is slowly fomenting within him before your eyes. Raymond's heart is arid. At the core of his defects is his concealed tendency to timidity, sexual and social, both of which are closely linked, which he hides behind that formidably severe and haughty cast of countenance. This weakness of will is compounded by his constant need to lean upon someone else's will, and now, at last, that has been taken care of for the rest of Raymond's life."

"Has the man ever killed anyone?" Berezovo asked loudly.

"Have you ever murdered anyone, Raymond?" Yen Lo asked the young man solicitously.

"No, sir."

"Have you ever killed anyone?"

"No, sir."

"Not even in combat?"

"In combat, yes, sir. I think so, sir."

"Thank you, Raymond. Dr. Marañon tells us that resentment is entirely impersonal, as opposed to hatred, which has a strictly individual cast and presupposes a duel between the hater and the hated. The reaction of the resenter is directed against destiny." The pace of Yen Lo's voice slowed and it had softened when he spoke again. "Pity Raymond, if you can. Beneath his sad and stony mask, wary and hypocritical, you must remember that his every act, every thought, and all of his ends, are permeated with an indefinable bitterness. An infinite anguish must mark his life. He flees the world to find himself in solitude and solitude terrifies him because it is too close to his despair. His soul has been rubbed to shreds between the ambivalence of wanting and not wanting; of being able and unable; of loving and hating; and, as Dr. Marañon has demonstrated, his feeling lives like two brothers, at one and the same time Siamese twins and deadly enemies."

The commission stared at this dream by Lavrenti Beria: the perfectly prefabricated assassin, this bored, too handsome, blond young man with the pointed chin and the pointed ears, whose mustard-colored eyes looked through them as a cat's would, and who would not be able to stop destroying once the instructions had been fed into him. All but four of them had had experience in one soviet or another with the old-fashioned, wild-eyed, cause-torn name-killers of the domestic politics of the past twenty-five years, and every one of those had been a shaky, thousand-to-one shot as far as being able to guarantee success, but here was Caesar's son to be sent into Caesar's chamber to kill Caesar. Steady, responsible, shock-proof assassins were needed at home because assassination was a stratagem requiring secrecy and control, and if an assassination were not to be committed secretly then it had to be arranged discreetly and smoothly so that the ruling cliques realized that it was an occasion not to be advertised. If the assassin were to be used in the West, as this one would be, where sensationalism is not only desirable but politically essential, the blow needed to be struck at exactly the right time and place, at a national emotional apogee, as it were, so that the selected messiah who would suceed the slain ruler could then defend all of his people from the threatening and monstrous elements at whose doorstep the assassination of an authentic national hero could swiftly and effectively be laid.

Berezovo was thinking of Yen Lo's proud claim of prolonging posthypnotic amnesia into eternity. Berezovo had been life-trained in security work, particularly that having to do with Soviet security problems in North America, where this killer would operate. If a normally conditioned Anglo-Saxon could be taught to kill and kill, then to have no memory of having killed, or even of having had the thought of killing, he could feel no guilt. If he could feel no guilt he could not fall into the trap of betraying fear of being caught. If he could not feel guilt or the fear of being caught he would remain an outwardly normal, productive, sober, and respectful member of his community so that, as Berezovo saw it, this killer was very close to being police-proof and the method by which he was created must be very, very carefully controlled in its application to other men within the Soviet Union. Specifically, within Moscow. More specifically within the Kremlin.

Gomel was multiplying Raymond. If Yen Lo could manufacture one of these he could manufacture an elite corps of what could be the most extraordinary personal troops a leader could have. By having immutable loyalty built into a cadre of perhaps one hundred men a leader could not only take power but he would become unseatable because after the flawless, sefless guardians had removed the others they could be conditioned to take portfolios under the new leader from which they would never, never plot against the new leader and would reflexively choose to die themselves rather than see any harm come to him. Gomel felt himself grow taller but, all at once, he thought of the power of Yen Lo and it spoiled his vision. Yen Lo would have to manufacture these assistants. Who would ever know what else he had built into their minds, such as acting to kill within an area where they were supposed to be utterly immobile? He had disliked Yen Lo before this but now he began to feel a bitter hatred toward him. But what could be done to such a man? How could fear be put into him to control him? Who knew but that he had conditioned other unknown men to strike at all authority if they were to hear of Yen Lo's arrest or death by violence, or for that matter, death under any circumstances whatsoever?

Marco knew he was sick but he did not know, nor did he seem to be able to make himself learn how to know why he thought he was sick. He could see Raymond sitting in calmness. He knew they were waiting out a storm in the Spring Valley Hotel, twenty-

three miles from Fort Monmouth in New Jersey, and that they
had been lucky indeed to have been offered the hospitality of the
lobby, which, as everyone knew, in the off season was reserved
almost exclusively on Wednesday afternoons for the Spring Valley Garden Club. He was conscious of boredom because he had
little interest in flowers except as a dodge to jolly a girl into bed,
and although these ladies had been very kind and very pleasant
they were advanced in terms of years beyond his interest in
women. That was it. There it was. Yet he sat among them distorted by the illusion that he was facing a lieutenant general of
the Soviet Army, three Chinese, five staff officers, and six civil-
ians who were undoubtedly Russian because the bottoms of their
trousers were two feet wide and the beige jackets seemed to
have been cut by a drunken chimpanzee, plus one randy broad
who never took her eyes off his pants. He knew it was some kind
of psychiatric hallucination. He knew he was sick, but he could
not, on the other hand, figure out why he thought he was sick.
Spring Valley was a beautiful, lazy place. A lovely, lovely, lazy,
lazy place. Spring Valley.

Yen Lo was explaining his methods of procedure. The first
descent into the deep unconscious, he explained, was drug-
induced. Then, after the insistence of various ideas and instructions which were far too tenuous to take up time with, the subject was pulled out for the first time and four tests were made to
determine the firmness of the deep control plant. The total immersion time into the unconscious mind of the subject during the
first contact had been eleven hours. The second descent was light-
induced. The subject, after further extensive suggestion which
took up seven and three-quarter hours and required far less
technique than the first immersion, was then pulled out again. A
simple interrogation test based upon the subject's psychiatric
dossier, which the security force had so skillfully assembled over
the years, and a series of physical reflexive tests, were followed
by conditioning for control of the subject by hand and symbol
signal, and by voice command. The critical application of deep
suggestion was observed during the first eleven hours of immersion when the primary link to all future control was set in. To
this unbreakable link would be hooked future links that would
represent individual assignments which would motivate the subject and which would then be smashed by the subject's own
memory, or mnemonic apparatus, on a presignaled system

emanating from the first permanent link. At the instant he killed, Raymond would forget forever that he had killed.

Yen Lo looked smug for an instant, but he wiped the expression off before anyone but Berezovo had an opportunity to register it. So far, so good, he said. The subject could not ever remember what he had done under suggestion, or what he had been told to do, or who had instructed him to do it. This eliminated altogether the danger of internal psychological friction resulting from feelings of guilt or from the fear of capture by authorities, and the external danger existent in any police interrogation, no matter how severe.

"With all of that precision in psychological design," Yen said, the most admirable, the most far-reaching characteristic of this extraordinary technology of mine is the manner in which it provides for the refueling of the conditioning, and this factor will operate wherever the subject may be—two feet or five thousand miles away from Yen Lo—and utterly independently of my voice or any assumed reality of my personal control. Incidentally, while we're on that subject, we presented one of these refueling devices to the chairman of your subrural electrification program who faced a somewhat lonely and uncomfortably cold winter on the Gydan Peninsula. Our subject was a thoroughly conditioned young ballet dancer whom the commissar had long admired, but she was most painfully, from his view, married to a young man whom she loved not only outrageously but to the exclusion of all others. Comrade Stalin took pity on him and called me. By using our manual of operating instructions he found himself with the beautiful, very young, very supple dancer who never wore clothes because they made her freezing cold and who undertook conditioned sexual conceptions which were so advanced that the commissar's winter passed almost before he knew it had started."

They roared with laughter. Gomel slapped welts on his thighs with his horny hand. The recording assistant beside Berezovo couldn't stop giggling: a treble one-note giggle which was so comical that soon everyone was laughing at her giggle as well as Yen Lo's story. Berezovo finally rapped on the wooden back of the chair in front of him with the naked bayonet he was carrying. Everyone but Gomel stopped laughing in mid-note, but Gomel had just about laughed himself out and was wiping his eyes and shaking his head, thinking of what could be done with a beautiful, nubile young woman who had also been conditioned to kill efficiently.

"Now," Yen Lo said, "to operate Raymond it amused me to choose as his remote control any ordinary deck of playing cards. They offer clear, colorful symbols that, in ancient, monarchial terms, contain the suggestion of supreme authority. They are easily obtainable by Raymond anywhere in his country and, after a time, he will probably take to carrying a deck of cards with him. Very good. I will demonstrate." He turned to the sergeant. "Raymond, why don't you pass the time by playing a little solitaire?" Raymond sat erect and looked alertly at Yen Lo. "Pull that table over, Raymond," the old Chinese said. Raymond walked to stage right and carried back with him a small table on whose top had been placed a pack of cards. He sat down.

"The first refueling key was the sentence suggesting solitaire in those exact words, which unlocks his basic conditioning. Then the queen of diamonds, in so many ways reminiscent of Raymond's dearly loved and hated mother, is the second key that will clear his mechanism for any assignments." As Yen spoke, Raymond had been shuffling the cards and was laying out the seven-card spread that is variously called solitaire, Klondike, or patience.

"He will play the game until the queen of diamonds enters the play, which will be soon because we arranged it that way to save your time. Ah, here it is." Raymond's play had turned up the queen. He scooped all the other cards together neatly. He squared them, placed them face down on the table, and put the queen of diamonds face up on top of the pack, then sat back to watch the card with offhand interest, his manner entirely normal.

"May I have that bayonet, please?" Yen Lo asked General Berezovo.

"Not with the knife," Gomel barked. "With the hands."

"His hands?" Yen responded distastefully.

"Here," Berezovo said. "Have him use this." He handed a white silk scarf to an assistant who carried it to Yen Lo. Yen knotted the scarf tightly in three close places, speaking to Raymond as he did so.

"Raymond, whom do you dislike the least in your group who are here today?"

"The least?"

"That's right."

"Well—I guess Captain Marco, sir."

"Notice how he is drawn always to authority?" Yen asked the group. Then he said to Raymond. "That won't do. We will need the captain to get you your medal. Whom else?" Both Gomel's and Berezovo's translators were right at their masters' ears, keeping up with the conversation in English on the stage.

"Well—" It was a difficult question. Raymond disliked the rest of them in the same detached and distant way. "Well, I guess Ed Mavole, sir."

"Why?"

"He is a funny fellow, sir. I mean very humorous. And he never seems to complain. Not while I'm around, anyway."

"Very good, Raymond. Now. Take this scarf and strangle Ed Mavole to death."

"Yes, sir."

Raymond got up from the table and took the scarf from Yen. He walked to the end of the line of seated men at stage left, then moved along behind the row to a position directly behind Mavole, fifth man from the end. Mavole was chewing gum rapidly and trying to watch both Yen and Raymond at the same time. Raymond looped the scarf around Mavole's throat.

"Hey, Sarge. Cut it out. What is this?" Mavole said irritably, only because it was Raymond.

"Quiet, please, Ed," Yen said with affectionate sternness. "You just sit there quietly and cooperate."

"Yes, sir," Mavole said.

Yen nodded to Raymond, who pulled at either end of the white scarf with all of the considerable strength of his long arms and deep torso and strangled Ed Mavole to death among his friends and his enemies in the twenty-first year of his life, producing a terrible sight and terrible sounds. Berezovo dictated steadily to his recording assistant who made notes and watched Mavole at the same time, showing horror only far back behind the expression in her eyes. As she set down the last Berezovo observation she excused herself, turned aside, and vomited. Leaning over almost double, she walked rapidly from the room, pressing a handkerchief to her face and retching.

Gomel watched the strangling with his lips pursed studiously and primly. He belched. "Pardon me," he said to no one at all.

Raymond let the body drop, then walked along the line of

men to the end of the row, rounded it, and returned to his chair. There was a rustle of light applause which Yen Lo ignored, so it stopped almost instantly, as when inadvertent applause breaks out during an orchestral rest in the performance of a symphony.

"Very good, Raymond," Yen said.

"Yes, sir."

"Raymond, who is that little fellow sitting next to the captain?"

The sergeant looked to his right. "That's Bobby Lembeck, sir. Our mascot, I guess you could call him."

"He doesn't look old enough to be in your Army."

"Frankly, sir, he isn't old enough but there he is."

Yen opened the only drawer in the table in front of Raymond and took out an automatic pistol. "Shoot Bobby, Raymond," he ordered. "Through the forehead." He handed the pistol to Raymond who then walked along the front of the stage to his right.

"Hi, Ben," he said to the captain.

"Hiya, kid."

Apologizing for presenting his back to the audience, Raymond then shot Bobby Lembeck through the forehead at point-blank range. He returned to his place at the table, offering the pistol butt to Yen Lo who motioned that it should be put in the drawer. "That was very good, Raymond," he said warmly and with evident appreciation. "Sit down." Then Yen turned to face his audience and made a deep, mock-ceremonial bow, smiling with much self-satisfaction.

"Oh, marvelous!" the shorter Chinese Wen Ch'ang, cried out in elation.

"You are to be congratulated on a most marvelous demonstration, Yen Lo," said the other Chinese, Pa Cha, loudly and proudly, right on top of his colleague's exclamation. The Russians broke out into sustained applause and were tasteful enough not to yell "Encore!" or "Bis!" in the bourgeois French manner. The young lieutenant who had been picking his nose shouted "Bravo!" then immediately felt very silly. Gomel, who was applauding as heavily and as rapidly as the others, yelled hoarsely, "Excellent! Really, Yen, really, really, excellent!" Yen Lo put one long forefinger to his lips in an elaborate gesture. The line of soldiers watched the demonstration from the stage with tolerance, even amusement. Yen turned to them. The force of the bullet velocity at such close range had knocked little Bobby Lembeck over backward in his chair. His corpse without a forehead, never having known a fat lady or a tall one, sprawled backward with its feet still hooked into the front legs of the overturned chair, as though it were a saddle which had slipped off a running colt.

Mavole's body had fallen forward. The color of the face was magenta into purple and the eyes seemed to pop out toward Yen in a diligent effort to pay him the utmost attention.

The other men of the patrol sat relaxed, with the pleasant look of fathers with hang-overs who are enjoying watching a little girls' skating party in the moist, cool air of an indoor rink on a Saturday morning.

"Captain Marco?" Yen said briskly.

"Yes, sir."

"To your feet, Captain, please."

"Yes, sir."

"Captain, when you return with your patrol to your command headquarters what will be among the first duties you will undertake?"

"I will submit my report on the patrol, sir."

"What will you report?"

"I will recommend urgently that Sergeant Shaw be posted for the Medal of Honor, sir. He saved our lives and he took out a full company of enemy infantry."

"A full company!" Gomel said indignantly when this sentence was translated to him. "What the hell is this?"

"We can spare an imaginary company of infantry for this particular plan, Mikhail," Berezovo said irritably.

"All right! If we are out to humiliate our brave Chinese ally in the newspapers of the world we might as well go ahead and make it a full battalion," Gomel retorted, watching the Chinese representatives carefully as he spoke.

"We don't object, Comrade," the older Chinese said. "I can assure you of that."

"Not at all," said the younger Chinese official.

"However, thank you for thinking of the matter in that light, just the same," said the first Chinese.

"Not at all," Gomel told him.

"Thank you, Captain Marco," Yen Lo told the officer. "Thank you, everyone," he told the audience. "That will be all for this session. If you will assemble your questions, we will review here

in one hour, and in the meantime I believe General Kostroma
has opened a most pleasant little bar for all of us." Yen motioned
Raymond to his feet. Then, putting an arm around his shoulders,
he walked him out of the auditorium saying, "We will have some
hot tea and a chat, you and I, and to show my appreciation for
the way you have worked today, I am going to dip into your
unconscious and remove your sexual timidity once and for all."
He smiled broadly at the young man. "More than that no man
can do for you, Raymond," he said, and they passed from the
room, out of the view of the patient, seated patrol.

THERE was a final review for the patrol that evening, conducted by Yen Lo's staff as a last brush-up to recall the details of
the imaginary engagement against the enemy that, in fantasy,
Raymond had destroyed. In all, Yen Lo's research staff provided
four separate versions of the over-all feat of arms, as those versions might have been witnessed from four separate vantage
points in the action and then later exchanged between members
of the patrol. Each patrol member had been drilled in individual
small details of what Raymond had done to save their lives. They
had been taught to mourn Mavole and Bobby Lembeck who had
been cut off before Raymond could save them. They had absorbed their lessons well and now admired, loved, and respected
Raymond more than any other man they had ever known. Their
brains had not merely been washed, they had been dry-cleaned.
　The captain was taught more facets of the lie than the others
because he would have observed the action with a schooled eye
and also would have assembled everyone else's report. Raymond
did not attend the final group drill. Yen had locked in his feat of
valor personally, utilizing a pioneer development of induced
autoscopic halluncination which allowed Raymond to believe he
had seen his own body image projected in visual space, and he
had given the action a sort of fairy-tale fuzziness within Raymond's mind so that it would never seem as real to him as it
always would remain to most of the other members of the patrol.
By seeming somewhat unreal it permitted Raymond to project a
sense of what would seem like admirable modesty to those who
would question Raymond about it.

The patrol, less Ed Mavole and Bobby Lembeck, was loaded aboard a helicopter that night and flown into central Korea near the west coast, not too far from where they had been captured. The Soviet pilot set the plane down on a sixteen-foot square area that had been marked by flares. After that, no more than seventy minutes after they had been pointed on their way, the patrol came up to a U.S. Marine Corps outfit near Haeju, and they were passed back through the lines until they reached their own outfit the next afternoon. They had been missing in action for just less than four days, from the night of July 8 to the mid-afternoon of July 12. The year was 1951.

In the deepening twilight hours after the Americans had been sent back to their countrymen and his own work in the sector had been completed, Yen Lo sat with the thirty boys and girls of his staff in the evening circle on the lovely lawn behind the pavilion. He would tell them the beautiful old stories later when the darkness had come. While they had light he made his dry jokes about the Russians and amused them or startled them or flabbergasted them with the extent of his skill at *origami*, the ancient Japanese art of paperfolding. Working with squares of colored papers, Yen Lo astonished them with a crane that flapped its wings when he pulled its tail, or a puffed-up frog that jumped at a stroke along its back, or a bird that picked up paper pellets, or a praying Moor, a talking fish, or a nun in black and gray. He would hold up a sheet of paper, move his hands swiftly as he paid out the gentle and delicious jokes, and lo!—wonderment dropped from his fingers, the paper had come to life and magic was everywhere in the gentling evening air.

III

THE NATION GUARDS its highest tribute for valor jealously. In the Korean War only seventy-seven Medals of Honor were awarded, with 5,720,000

personnel engaged. Of the 16,112,566 U.S. armed forces
mobilized in World War II, only two hundred and ninety-two
Medals of Honor were awarded. The Army reveres its Medal of
Honor men, living and dead, above all others. A theater commander who later became President and a President who had
formerly been an artillery captain both said that they would
rather have the right to wear the Medal of Honor than be
President of the United States.

After Abraham Lincoln signed the Medal of Honor bill on July
12, 1862, the decoration was bestowed in multitude; on one occasion to every member of a regiment. The first Medal of Honor
was awarded by Secretary of War Stanton on March 15, 1863, to
a soldier named Parrott who had been doing a bit of work in
mufti behind enemy lines. Counting medals that were later re-
voked, about twenty-three hundred of them were awarded in the
Civil War era, up to 1892. Hundreds were poured out upon
veterans of the Indian campaigns, specifying neither locales nor
details of bravery beyond "bravery in scouts and actions against
the Indians."

In 1897, for the first time, eyewitness accounts were made
mandatory and applications could not be made by the candidate
for the honor but had to be made by his commanding officer or
some other individual who had personally witnessed his gallantry in action. The recommendation had to be made within
one year of the feat of arms. Since 1897, when modern basic
requirements were set down, only five hundred and seventy-
seven Medals of Honor have been awarded to a total of 25,000,-
000 Americans in arms, which is why the presence of a medal
winner can bring full generals to their feet, saluting, and has
been known to move them to tears.

In 1904 the medal was protected from imitators and jewelry
manufacturers when it was patented in its present form by its
designer, Brigadier General George L. Gillespie. On December
19, 1904, he transferred the patent to "W. H. Taft and his successor or successors as Secretary of War of the United States of
America." In 1916, the Congress awarded to Medal of Honor
winners a special status, providing the medal had been won by
an action involving actual conflict with the enemy, distinguished
by conspicuous gallantry or intrepidity at the risk of life above
and beyond the call of duty. The special status provided that the
Medal of Honor winner may travel free of charge in military

aircraft; his son may get Presidential assistance in an appointment to West Point or Annapolis; if he is an enlisted man two dollars extra per month is added to his pay, and when he reaches the age of sixty-five he becomes eligible to receive a pension of $120 per year from which, if he smokes one package of cigarettes a day, he would have $11.85 left over for rent, food, hospitalization, entertainment, education, recreation, philanthropies, and clothing.

An Army board was convened in 1916 to review all instances of the award of the Medal of Honor since 1863 to determine whether or not any Medal of Honor had been awarded or issued "for any cause other than distinguished conduct involving actual conflict with the enemy." Nine hundred and eleven names were stricken from the list, and lesser decorations were forthwith created so that, as Congress had demanded, "the Medal of Honor would be more jealously guarded."

There was every reason for the awe in which Medal of Honor men were held. Some of their exploits included such actions as; had taken eight prisoners, killing four of the enemy in the process, while one leg and one arm were shattered and he could only crawl because the other leg had been blown off (Edwards); had captured a hundred and ten men, four machine guns, and four howitzers (Mallon and Gumpertz); wounded five times, dragged himself across the direct fire of three enemy machine guns to pull two of his wounded men to safety amid sixty-nine dead and two hundred and three casualties (Holderman); singly destroyed a fourteen-man enemy ambush of his battalion and, in subsequent actions, with his legs mangled by enemy grenade and shot through the chest died taking a charge of eight enemy riflemen, killing them (Baker); held his battalion's flank against advancing enemy platoons, used up two hundred rounds of ammunition, crawled twenty yards under direct fire to get more, only to be assailed by another platoon of the enemy, ultimately firing six hundred rounds, killing sixty and holding off all others to be one of twenty-three out of two hundred and forty of his comrades to survive the action (Knappenburger); a defective phosphorus bomb exploding inside his plane, blinding and severely burning him, the radio operator scooped up the blazing bomb in his arms and, with incalculable difficulty, hurled it through the window (Erwin).

. . .

RAYMOND waited in the Rose Garden of the White House while an assistant press secretary tried to talk to him. It was a bonny sunny day. Raymond was stirred by the building near him; moved by the color of the green, green grass. Raymond was torn and shamed and he felt soiled everywhere his spirit could feel. Raymond felt exalted, too. He felt proud of the building near him and proud of the man he was about to meet.

Raymond's mother was across the garden with the press people, pulling her husband along behind her, explaining with brilliant smiles and leers when necessary that he was the new senator and Raymond's father. Raymond, fortunately, could not hear her but he could watch her hand out cigars. They both handed out cigars whether the press people wanted cigars or not. Raymond's mother was dressed up to about eight hundred dollars' worth of the best taste on the market. The only jarring note was the enormous black purse she carried. It looked like a purse. It was a portable cigar humidor. She would have given the press people money, Raymond knew, but she had sensed somehow that it would be misunderstood.

All the cameras were strewn about in the grass while everybody waited for the President to arrive. Raymond wondered what would they do if he could find a sidearm some place and shoot her through the face—through that big, toothy, flapping mouth? Look how she held Johnny down. Look how she could make him seem docile and harmless. Look how she had kept him sober and had made him seem quiet and respectable as he shook hands so tentatively and murmured. *Johnny Iselin was murmuring!* He was crinkling his thick lips and making them prissy as he smirked under that great fist of a nose and two of the photographers (they must be his mother's tame photographers) were listening to him as though he were harmless.

The airport. O Jesus, Jesus, Jesus. She got the AP photographer by the fleshy part of his upper right arm and she had got Johnny by the fleshy part of his upper left arm and she had charged them forward across that concrete apron at the National Airport yelling at the ramp men, "Get Shaw off first! Get that sergeant down here!" and the action and the noises she made had pulled all thirty news photographers and reporters along behind her at a full run while the television newsreel truck had rolled along sedately abreast of her, filming everything for the

world to see that night, and thank God they were not shooting
with sound.

The lieutenant had pushed him out of the plane and his
mother had pushed Johnny at him and Johnny had pulled him
down the ramp so he wouldn't look too much taller in the shot.
Then to make sure, Raymond's mother had yelled, "Get on that
ramp, Johnny, and hang onto him." Johnny gripped his right
hand held his right elbow, and towered over him. Raymond's
mother didn't say hello. She hadn't seen him for over two years
but she didn't say hello and neither did Johnny. Thank God they
were a family who didn't waste a lot of time on talking, Raymond thought.

Johnny kept grinning at him insanely and the pupils of his
eyes were open at about f.09 with the sedation she had loaded
into him. The pressmen were trying to keep their places in a
tight semicircle and, as always at one of those public riots where
every man had been told to get the best shot, the harshest, most
dominating shouter finally solved it for all the others: one big
Italian-looking photographer yelled at nobody at all, "Get the
mother in there, fuh crissake! Senator! Get your wife in there,
fuh crissake!" Then Raymond's mother caught on that she had
goofed but good and she hurled herself in on Raymond's offside
and hung off his neck, kissing him again and again until his
cheek glistened with spit, cheating to the cameras about thirty
degrees, and snarling at Johnny between the kisses, "Pump his
hand, you jerk. Grin at the cameras and pump his hand. A TV
newsreel is working out there. Can't you remember anything?"
And Johnny got with it.

It had taken about seven minutes of posing, reposing, standing, walking toward the cameras, then the photographers broke
ranks and Raymond's mother grabbed Johnny's wrist and took
off after them.

The assistant press secretary from the White House steered
Raymond to a car, and the next time Raymond saw his mother
she was handing out cigars in the Rose Garden and paying out
spurts of false laughter.

Everybody got quiet all of a sudden. Even his mother. They
all looked alert as the President came out. He looked magnificent. He was ruddy and tall and he looked so entirely sane that
Raymond wanted to put his head on the President's chest and

cry because he hadn't seen very many sane people since he had left Ben Marco.

He stood at attention, eyes forward.

The President said, "At ease, soldier." The President leaned forward to pick up Raymond's right hand from where it dangled at his side and as he shook it warmly he said, "You're a brave man Sergeant. I envy you in the best sense of that word because there is no higher honor your country has to give than this medal you will receive today." Raymond watched his mother edge over. With horror, he saw the jackal look in her eyes and in Johnny's. The President's press secretary introduced Senator Iselin and Mrs. Iselin, the sergeant's mother. The President congratulated them. Raymond heard his mother ask for the honor of a photograph with the President, then moved her two tame photographers in with a quick low move of her left hand. The others followed setting up.

The shot was lined up. Raymond's mother was on the President's left. Raymond was on the President's right. Johnny was on Raymond's right. Just before the bank of press cameras took the picture, Mrs. Iselin took out a gay little black-on-yellow banner on a brave little gilded stick and held it over Raymond's head. At least it seemed that she must have meant it to be held only over Raymond's head, but when the pictures came out in the newspapers the next day, then in thousands of newspapers all over the world beginning three and a half years hence, and with shameful frequency in many newspapers after that, it was seen that the gay little banner had been held directly over the President's head and that the lettering on it read: JOHNNY ISELIN'S BOY.

IV

IN 1940, RAYMOND'S mother had divorced his father, a somewhat older man, while she was six months pregnant with a second child, to marry Raymond's father's law partner, John Yerkes Iselin, who had a raucous laugh and a fleshy nose. There was more than the usual talk in their community that loud, lewd Johnny Iselin was the father of the unborn child.

Raymond had been twelve years old at the time of his mother's remarriage. He hadn't particularly liked his father but he disliked his mother so much more that he felt the loss keenly. In later years the second son, Raymond's brother, could have been said to have favored noisy Johnny more than did the dour and silent Raymond, as he had many of the identical interests in making sounds for the sake of making sounds, and also the early suggestion of a nose that promised to be equally fleshy—but Raymond's brother died in 1948, greatly helping John Iselin's bid for the governorship by interjecting that element of human sympathy into the campaign.

The unquestionable fact was that Eleanor Shaw's marriage to John Iselin was a scandal and the questions that aroused curiosity must have been an insufferable torment in the mind of young Raymond as his awakening consciousness absorbed the details which kept filtering fresh drops of bitterness into his memory.

Raymond's father had paused with his grief for six years before killing himself. At this disposition, Raymond, if no one else, was inconsolable. In the driving rain, in the presence of so few witnesses, most of whom having been rented through the funeral director, he made a graveside oration. As he spoke he looked only at his mother. He told, in a highpitched, tight voice, of what an incomparably noble man his father had been and other boyish balderdash like that. To Raymond, from that day in 1940 when he had seen his father's tears, his mother would always be a morally adulterous woman who had deserted her home and had brought sadness upon her husband's venerable head.

Iselin, the stepfather, was doubly hateful because he had offended, humiliated, and betrayed a noble man by robbing him of his wife, and because he seemed to make noises with every movement and every part of his body, forsaking silence awake and asleep; belching, bawling, braying, blaspheming; snoring or shouting; talking, always, always, never stopping talking.

Raymond's father and Johnny Iselin had been law partners until 1935 when Johnny had switched his party affiliations to run for judge of the three-county Thirteenth Judicial District. The announcement of his candidacy had come as a staggering blow to his partner and benefactor who had had his heart set for some time on running for the circuit judgeship in that district, so words were exchanged and the partnership was dissolved.

Johnny had noise and muscle on his side in anything he ever decided to do. He won the election. He served for four years before the State Supreme Court rebuked him for improper conduct on the bench. Judge Iselin had found it necessary to order the destruction of a portion of the record and had, in general, created "a highly improper and regrettable state of affairs," but, simultaneously, he had earned himself a nice thirty-five hundred dollar off-bench fee.

Johnny always kept his gift for merchandising justice. Just about ten months after the exhibitionistic politicking by the State Supreme Court against him, he began to grant quickie divorces to couples not resident in his judicial district. Later, records indicated that in several of these cases, one of the principals, or their attorneys, or both, were active in supporting Johnny's political pretensions, sometimes with cash. His practice of favoring the generous gave at least one editorial writer his morning angle when the *Journal,* the state's largest daily, wrote: "Is state justice to be used to accommodate the political supporters of the presiding judge? Are our courts to become the place in which to settle political debts?" By this time Raymond's mother had seen her duty and had taken to lolling around on a bed with Johnny in a rented-by-the-hour-or-afternoon summer home near a gas station off a secondary highway. When she finished reading that editorial aloud to Johnny she snorted and described the editorial writer, whom she had never met, as a jerk.

"You are so right, baby," Johnny answered.

The most famous case Judge Iselin ever disposed of on the circuit bench was reflected in the consequences of his granting a divorce in the case of Raymond's mother versus Raymond's father. The newspapers paid out the juicy facts that Mr. Shaw had been Judge Iselin's law partner. Second, they announced that Mrs. Shaw was six months pregnant and ran a front-page picture that make her look as though she had strapped a twenty-one-inch television set to her middle. Thirdly, the readers were told that Mrs. Shaw and Judge Iselin would become man and wife as soon as the divorce became final. Raymond's mother had been twenty-nine years old at the time. Judge Iselin was thirty-two. Raymond's father was forty-eight.

Mr. Shaw had married Raymond's mother when she was sixteen years old, after two ecstatic frictions on an automobile seat. Raymond had been born when she had just reached seventeen.

During the thirteen years of her marriage to Raymond's father she had been a member or officer or founder or affiliate of organizations including: the St. Agnes Music Club, the Parent-Teachers' Association, the Association of Inner Wheel Clubs, the Honest Ballot Association, the International Committee for Silent Games, the Auxiliary Society of the Professional Men's League, the Third Way Movement, the Society for the Prevention of Cruelty to Animals, the Permanent International Committee of Underground Town Planning, the Good Citizen's Shield, the Joint Distribution Committee for Anti-Fascist Spain, the Scrap Metal User's Joint Bureau, the International Symposium on Passivity, the American Friends of the Soviet Union, the Ladies' Auxiliary of the American Legion, the Independent Order, the English-Speaking Union, the International Congress for Surface Activity, the Daughters of the American Revolution, the International Union for the Protection of Public Morality, the Society for the Abolition of Blasphemy Laws, the Community Chest, the Audubon League, the League of Professional Women, the American-Scandinavian Association, the Dame Maria Van Slyke Association for the Abolition of Canonization, the Eastern Star, the Abraham Lincoln Brigade Memorial Fund, and others. Raymond's mother had, quite early in life, achieved an almost abnormal concentration upon an interest in local, state, and national politics. She used all organizations to claw out recognition for herself within her chosen community. Her ambition was an extremely distressing condition. She sought power the way a superstitious man might look for a four-leaf clover. She didn't care where she found it. It would make no difference if it were growing out of a manure pile.

The newspapers knew the three sets of facts about Raymond's mother's divorce because Raymond's mother, always keeping an eye upon a public future, had made sure they were told about it in a series of letters which she had typed without signature and mailed herself the day before the divorce action had reached Judge Iselin's court. She had explained to Johnny why she was going to do it before she did it. She made it clear that the entire thing would serve to humanize him like nothing else could, later on. "Every one of the jerks lives in the middle of one continuous jam," she had explained sympathetically, the jerks being the great American people in this instance. "Isn't it better if they think you got me this way than if they get the idea the baby is

his and I walked out on him for you? You see what I mean,
Johnny? We'd be taking his own child away from him, which is a
very precious possession—as the jerks pretend about kids while
they knock them out like hot cross buns, then abandon them or
ignore them. And we'll get married right away. At the split second that it becomes legal under the great American flag, see,
lover? We'll be as respectable as anybody else right at that instant, except just like everybody else, underneath. You know
what I mean, lover? They're all tramps in their hearts and we'll
want them to identify with us when the time comes to line up at
the polls. Right, sweetheart?"

Raymond's mother had not been unfaithful to his father until
he had forced her into it. She had used exactly the same political
blandishments on him first that she had had to use on Johnny
later, and long before she had exposed either them or her body
to John Iselin, which is to say that Raymond's father could have
become just as big a man in the United States and the
world as she eventually made Johnny, a fact that Raymond never
realized in his harsh evaluation of his mother. After she had
finished detailing her political plan to Raymond's father, instead
of striking her, the man had actually tried to instill into her a
devotion to the ancient ideals of justice, liberty, fair play, and
the Republic until she had at last needed to cuckold him to be
rid of him. Later on she had explained the whole thing to Johnny
as though the entire sordid mess had come about as the result of
her shrewd design.

The most sordid part of the sordid, rationalized mess was what
it did to Raymond, but even if she had acknowledged that to
herself as a mother, she knew it was worth it because for more
than five years Johnny Iselin was a very big man in the United
States of America and Raymond's mother ruled Johnny Iselin.
So, it can be seen that Raymond's mother had been assiduously
fair with her first husband. She told him how she had worked
and worked behind the scenes in politics to have him run for the
Senate and she laid out her sure-fire platform for him. When he
heard what she proposed to have him do, her husband gave her
a tongue lashing that finally made her plead for relief, so long
and so hostile was its address. After that she was silent. Not for
the rest of the day nor the rest of the week; she did not speak to
him again until the day she left him, six months later, after
deliberately seeking insemination from Judge Iselin, then leaving

Raymond's father forever, holding one son by the hand and the other by the umbilicus.

John Iselin had been the marital candidate in reserve for some years. They had all been close friends during the time the judge and Raymond's father had been partners. As she had anticipated he would, Johnny Iselin had agreed with everything she said, which, when boiled down, expressed the conviction that the Republic was a humbug, the electorate rabble, and anyone strong who knew how to maneuver could have all the power and glory that the richest and most naïve democracy in the world could bestow. Boiled down, Judge Iselin's response expressed his lifelong faith in her and in her proposition: "Just you tell me what to do, hon, and I'll get it done." Falling in love had been as simple as that because she had set out, from that moment on, to bring his appreciation of her and dependence on her to a help-less maximum, and when she had finished her work he was never again to be able to recall his full sanity.

Raymond's father, having been told by his beautiful, young wife that she was with child and that he was not the father and that she would die before she would have another child by him, a coward, took it all like the booby that he was, a willingness aided and abetted by the fact that there can be no doubt that he was a registered masochist. He marched like a little soldier to the man who had double-crossed him once before, mumbling some-thing ludicrous, such as: If you love this woman and will marry her honorably, take her; only let the decencies be observed.

The lout Iselin made a loud, garbled fuss (the whole thing took place on the porch of the country club in August), swearing and sweating that he would marry Raymond's mother just as soon as he could confer a divorce upon her, presumably even if he had to open his court on a Sunday, then marry her immedi-ately, and never, never, never, ever, ever cast her off. He bound himself, in the presence of nine per cent of the membership, by the most frightful, if meaningless, oaths.

Secretly, Raymond's father, loving Raymond's mother as deeply as he did, regarded this infatuation of hers as a form of divine punishment on himself, having a capacity exceeded only by other humans for taking himself so seriously as to know he had been under continuous divine scrutiny, because over the period of sixteen years past as the sole executor of two large estates he had been looting, systematically, the substance of two

maiden ladies and an institution-committed schizophrenic. He
was so affected by these secret sins that, while he never stopped
looting the two estates and it was never revealed that he had
done so, it was quite clear that it would have been a matter of
only slight effort to have persuaded him to give the bride away
at the Iselin wedding as part of due punishment.

The result of this attitude was, naturally, that Raymond's
mother felt angry and ashamed; humiliated, as it were, in the
eyes of their common community, that he seemed to take the
matter so calmly, giving her up so tamely as though she were a
thing of little worth. She had a not inconsiderable fortune, by
inheritance, as did Raymond, all from her father's estate, then
her mother's estate, and she spent a fraction of it on private
detectives from Chicago, trying to uncover other women in his
life. She told Johnny that she would take the old bastard's skin
off if he had been setting her up all this time just to get rid of
her, but, of course, nothing came of the investigations, and she
had to wait six years for the afternoon when he killed himself out
of yearning and loneliness, by administering a large dose of
barbiturate Thiopentone by intercardiac injection, causing permanent cessation of respiration within two seconds, which was
little enough punctuation to fifty-four years of living. Raymond's
mother admired him, technically, for the method used, and also
emotionally for the act itself because, in a way, it made her look
good to those who still remembered what effect he had achieved
with his public dignity and cool indifference at the time she had
left him. On many counts beyond his thoughtful suicide, however, she had been very, very fond of him.

RAYMOND's mother's brother, the clot, had become a non-
political federal commissioner of such exalted station that it
often brought her to the point of retching nausea when she
encountered its passing mention in a news story. She had despised this son-of-a-bitch of a sibling ever since the faroff summer afternoon when her beloved, wonderful, magnetic, pleasing,
exciting, generous, kind, loving, and gifted father had died sitting upright in the wooden glider-swing with a history of Scan-

dinavia in his lap and this fool they said was her brother had announced that he was head of the family. This foolish, insensitive, ignorant, beastly nothing of a boy who had felt that he could in any way, in any shocking, fractional way, take the place of a magnificent man of men. Then he had beaten her with a hockey stick because he had objected to her nailing the paw of a beige cocker spaniel to the floor because the dog was stubborn and refused to understand the most elemental instructions to remain still when she had called out the command to do so. Could she have called out and made her wondrous father stay with her when he was dying?

She had loved her father with a bond so secret, so deep, and so thrilling that it surpassed into eternity the drab feelings of the other people, all other people, particularly the feelings of her brother and her clot of a mother. She had had woman's breasts from the time she had been ten years old, and she had felt a woman's yearnings as she had lain in the high, dark attic of her father's great house, only on rainy nights, only when the other slept. She would lie in the darkness and hear the rain, then hear her father's soft, soft step rising on the stairs after he had slipped the bolt into the lock of the attic door, and she would slip out of her long woolen night dress and wait for the warmth of him and the wonder of him.

Then he had died. Then he had died.

Every compulsively brutal blow from that hockey stick in the hands of that young man who wanted so badly to be understood by his sister but who could not begin to reach her understanding or her feeling had beaten a deep distaste and comtempt for all men since her father into her projective mind, and right then, when she was fourteen years old, she entered her driving, never-to-be-acknowledged life competition with her only brother to show him which of them was the heir of that father and which of them had the right to say that he should stand in that father's shoes and place and memory. She vowed and resolved, dedicated and consecrated, that she would beat him into humiliation at whatsoever he chose to undertake, and it was to the eternal shame of their country that he chose politics and government and that she needed therefore to plunge in after him.

Her clot of a brother had absorbed the native clottishness of her mother, a clot's clot. How could her father have loved this woman? How could such a shining and thrilling and valiant knight have lain down with this great cow? Everyone who knew them said that Raymond's mother was the image of her mother.

After her beating with the hockey stick she had given her family no rest until she had been sent away to a girls' boarding school of her own choice in the Middle West. It was chosen as her natural base of operations in politics because it was in the heart of the Scandinavian immigrant country; at the chosen time the outstanding Norse nature of her father's name and his heroic origins could be turned into blocs of votes.

At sixteen, because she had taught herself to believe that she knew exactly what she wanted, no matter what she got, she escaped from the school every weekend, dressed herself to look older, and arranged to place herself in locations where she could use herself as bait. She seduced four men between the ages of thirty and forty-six, got no pleasure from it nor expected any, had definitely lost two of the contests after a gluttonous testing period, could have turned either of the remaining two in any direction she chose, decided on Raymond's father because the man had a good, open face for politics and hair that was already gray although he was only thirty-six years old. She married him and bore him Raymond as soon as the gestation cycle allowed.

Generalities, specifics, domestic manifestations, or her youth never made Raymond's mother's thinking fuzzy or got in the way of her plan. She knew, like a mousetrap knows the back of a mousie's neck, that she was far too immature to be accepted publicly as the bride of a man seeking public office. She knew that it was possible that her husband might even get slightly tarred because of her age, so she had set her own late twenties as the time when she would have Raymond's father make his move. Her reasoning was sound: by that time, when it was reported during a campaign that Raymond's father had taken a child bride of sixteen some twelve faithful, productive years before, it would have become a romantic asset and Raymond's father would be seen by women voters as a suggestively virile candidate. Meanwhile, she had accomplished her primary objective of escaping the authority of her mother, her brother, and the school. She had her share of her father's substantial estate. She had started a family unit that, with few modern exceptions, was essential to success in American politics.

Raymond's mother was an exceptionally handsome woman

who was dressed in France. This was quite shrewd, because money displaces one's own taste when one chooses to be dressed in France. She was coiffed in New York and her very laundry seemed to have been washed in Joy de Patou. Her hair was straw blond, in the Viking tradition, and it was kept that way, no matter the inconvenience. Her sense of significant birth, her grinding virtue, and her carriage completed her pre-eminence in any group of women, and she assiduously recultivated all three attributes as a fleshy-plant fancier might exalt and extend orchid graftings. What was especially striking in the earlier photographs of Raymond's mother was the suggestion of a smile on her full lips as they counterfeited sensuality, and in her large ecstatic eyes, which were like those of a sexually ambitious girl. In later likenesses, such as the *Time* cover in 1959 (and she being of the same political party as *Time*'s persuasion, its editors therefore made an effort to supervise a most honest likeness) where she was clad as a matron, the supple grace was gone but the perfect features and the whole figure were stamped with the adaptable and inflexible energy that marked her maturity.

ONE of Big John Iselin's favorite perorations in campaign oratory after the war, or rather, after Johnny's interrupted service in the war, was the recollection of what he had seen and done in battle and what he would never be able to forget "up there at the top of the world, alone with God in a great cathedral of ice and snow in the stark loneliness of arctic night where the enemy struck out of nowhere and my boys fell and I cried out piteously, 'O Lord, they are young, why must they die?' as I raced forward over ice which was thirty miles deep, pumping my machine rifle, to even the score with those Nazi devils who, in the end, came to have a superstitious fear of me."

The point Johnny seemed to want to make in this section of this speech, his favorite speech, was never quite clear, but the story carried a powerful emotional impact to those whose lives had been touched by the tragedy of war. "At night while my spent, exhausted buddies slept," he would croon into the platform microphone, "I would prop my eyes open with matchsticks and write home—to you—to the wives and the sweethearts and the blessed mothers of our gallant dead—night after night as the casualties mounted—to try to do just a little more than my part to ease the heartbreak which Mr. Roosevelt's war had caused."

The official records of the Signal Corps of the U.S. Army show that Johnny's outfit (SCB-52310) had lost all together, during the entire tour outside the continental United States, one chaplain and one enlisted man, the former from a nervous breakdown and the latter from delirium tremens (a vitamin deficiency). The outfit, whose complement was a half-company of men, had been posted in northern Greenland as defenses for the comprehensive meteorological installations that predicted the weather for the military brass lower down on the globe, operating in mobile force far up on the ice cap, mostly between Prudhoe Land and the Lincoln Sea.

The enemy's weather forecasting installations were mostly based somewhere above King Frederick VIII Land, on the other side of the subcontinent, below Independence Sea. Greenland is the largest island in the world. Both sides, although continually aware of each other, remained strictly aloof and upon those occasions where they found that they were working in sight of each other they would both move out of sight without acknowledgment, as people will act following a painful social misunderstanding. There was no question of shooting. Their work was far too important. It was essential that both sides maintain an unbroken flow of vital weather data, which was an extremely special contribution when compared to the basically uncomplicated work of fighting troops.

It just did not seem likely that even Johnny would send the families of those two casualties a different letter every night, harping on a nervous breakdown and the D.T.'s, and besides the mail pickup happened only once a month when the mail plane was lucky enough to be able to swoop low enough and at the right ground angle to be able to bring up the gibbeted mail sack on a lowered hook. If they missed after three passes they let it go until the next month, but they did bring the mail in, which was far more important, and did maintain a reasonably high average on getting it out, considering the conditions.

No CITIZEN of the United States, including General Mac-
Arthur and those who enlisted from the film community of Los
Angeles, California, entered World War II with more fanfare
from the local press and radio than John Yerkes Iselin. When the
jolly judge arrived at the State Capitol on June 6, 1942, and
announced to the massive communications complex that Raymond's mother had assembled over a two-day period from all
papers throughout the state, from Chicago, and three from
Washington, at an incalculable cost in whisky and food, that he
had seen his duty to join up as "a private, an officer, or anything
else in the United States Marine Corps," the newspapers and
radio foamed with the news and the UP put the story on the
main wire as a suggested boxed news feature because of Raymond's mother's angle, which had Johnny saying: "They need a
judge in the Marines to judge whether they are the finest fighting
men in the world, or in the universe." The Marines naturally had
gotten Raymond's mother's business because, she told Johnny,
they had the biggest and fastest mimeographing machines and
earmarked one combat correspondent for every two fighting
men.

She started to run her husband for governor as of that day,
and the first five or six publicity releases emphasized strongly
how this man, whose position as a public servant demanded that
he *not* march off to war but remain home as part of the civilian
task force to safeguard Our Liberties, had chosen instead, had
volunteered even, to make the same sacrifices which were the
privileged lot of his fellow Americans and had therefore enlisted
as a buck-private marine. She had only two objectives. One was
to make sure Johnny got overseas somewhere near, but not too
near, the combat zones. The second was that he be assigned to a
safe, healthy, pleasant job.

It was at that point that something got screwed up. It was
extremely embarrassing, but fortunately she was able to patch it
up so that it looked as if Johnny was even more of a patriotic
masochist, but it brought her anger she was careful never to lose,
and because of what happened to outrage her, it spelled out her
brother's eventual ruin.

This is what happened. Through her brother, whom she had
never hesitated to use, Raymond's mother had decided to negoti-
ate for a Marine Corps commission for Johnny. She would have

preferred it if Johnny had enlisted as a private so that she could arrange for a field commission for him, following some well-publicized action, but Johnny got stubborn at the last minute and said he had agreed to go through all this rigmarole to please her but he wasn't going to sit out any war as a goddam private when whisky was known to cost only ten cents a shot at all officers' clubs.

Her brother was sitting on one of the most influential wartime government commissions that spring of 1942, and the son-of-a-bitch looked her right in the eye in his own office in the Pentagon in Washington and told her that Johnny could take his chances just like anybody else and that *he didn't believe in wirepulling in wartime!* That was that. Furthermore, she found out immediately that he wasn't kidding. She had had to move fast and think up some other angle very quickly but she hung around her brother's office long enough to explain to him that her turn would come someday and that when it came she was going to break him in two.

She rode back to the Carlton, shocked. She blamed herself. She had underestimated that mealy-mouthed bastard. She should have seen that he had been waiting for years to turn her out like a peasant. She concentrated upon preserving her anger.

Johnny was pretty drunk when she got back to the hotel, but not too bad. She was sweet and amiable, as usual. "What am I, hon?" he asked thickly, "A cappen?" She threw her hat away from her and walked to the small Directoire desk. "A cappency is good enough for me," he said. She pulled a telephone book out of the desk drawer and began to flip through the pages. "Am I a cappen or ain't I a cappen?" he asked.

"You ain't a cappen." She picked up the phone and gave the operator the number of the Senate Office Building.

"What am I, a major?"

"You're gonna be a lousy draftee if something doesn't give," she said. "He turned us down."

"He never liked me, honey."

"What the hell has that got to do with anything. He's my brother. He won't lift a finger to help with the Marines and if we don't get an understanding set in about forty-eight hours you're going to be a draftee just like any other jerk."

"Don't worry, hon. You'll straighten it out."

"Shaddup! You hear? Shadd*up!*" She was pale with sickening

bad temper. She spoke into the phone and asked for Senator Banstoffsen's office, and when she got the office she asked to speak to the senator. "Tell him it's Ellie Iselin. He'll know."

Johnny poured another drink, threw some ice into the glass, put some ginger ale on top of it, then shambled off toward the john, undoing his suspenders as he walked.

Raymond's mother's voice had suddenly gotten hot and sweet, although her eyes were bleak. "Ole, honey?" She paused to let those words make her point. "I mean—is this Senator Banstoffsen? Oh, Senator. Please forgive me. It was a slip. I mean, the only way I can explain is to say—is—I guess that's the way I think of you all the time, I guess." She rolled her eyes toward the ceiling in disgust and sighed silently. Her voice was all breath and lust. "I'd sure like to see you. Yes. Yes." She rapped impatiently with the end of a pencil on the top of the desk. "Now. Yes. Now. Do you have a lock on that office door, lover? Yes. Ole. Yes. I'll be right there."

Johnny Iselin was sworn in as a captain in the Signal Corps of the Army of the United States on July 20, 1942. Raymond's mother had made a powerful and interested political ally in her home state, and although he didn't know it, that was not to be the last favor he would be asked to deliver for her, and sometimes he came to be bewildered by how one simple little sprawl on an office desk could get to be so endlessly, intricately complicated.

DURING the intensive training in Virginia necessary for the absorption of vital technical and military information, Johnny and Raymond's mother lived in a darling little cottage just outside Wellville in Nottoway County, where she had found a solid connection for black-market booze and gasoline and a contact for counterfeit red points to keep those old steaks coming in. Johnny moved out of the staging area and sailed with his outfit for Greenland in December, 1942, and Raymond's mother went back home to handle the PR work for her man. The recurring theme she chose for the first year of propaganda was hammered out along the basic lines of "Blessed is he who serves who is not called: blessed is he who sacrifices self to bring about

the downfall of tyrants that others may prosper in Liberty."
It was solid stuff.

She got herself a women's radio show and a women's-interest
newspaper column in the *Journal,* the biggest paper in the state
and one of the best in the country. There were a lot of specialized jobs going for the asking. Mainly she read or reprinted all of
Johnny's letters on every conceivable variety of subject, whether
he sent her any letters or not.

The official records show that Johnny was an intelligence officer in the Army, but his campaign literature, when Raymond's
mother ran him for governor, revealed that he had been "a
northern Greenland combat commander." About ten years after
the war was over, well after Johnny's second term as governor,
the *Journal* did a surprising amount of careful research on
Johnny's record, at considerable expense. They dug up documents, and men who had served with Johnny, and they virtually
reconstructed a most careful, pertinent, and accurate history of
his somewhat distorted past. A public relations officer who had
been attached to Iselin's unit, a Lieutenant Jack Ramen, now of
San Mateo, Caifornia, told the *Journal* in 1955 on a transcribed,
long-distance-telephone tape recording, which was monitored by
the *Journal's* city editor, Fred Goldberg, and witnessed by a
principal clergyman and a leading physician of the state, of the
lonely incident that had lent credence to the popular belief that
Johnny had seen combat while in service.

"Yeah," Ramen said. "I remember the day we were both at a
tiny Eskimo settlement above Etah there on Smith Sound and
Johnny was looking to make some kind of good trades on furs
with the natives when a supply ship the name of *Midshipman
Bennet Reyes* came in, covered all over with ice. They were
having propeller trouble and they were due in at Etah to unload
groceries and while they were standing by for repairs the skipper
told them to test the guns, all the guns, everything. We find out
about it when Johnny and I go aboard; we were off duty, and
Johnny always operates under orders from his wife to make
friends no matter where. He actually brought the skipper of that
ship the stiffest piece of sealskin you ever saw and made such a
big thing out of it that the guy probably even kept it. He give
Johnny a half gallon of pure grain alcohol to show his appreciation, and we needed it. Man, was it cold. I can never ever explain to anybody how cold it was all the time I was in the Army

and, for what reason please don't ask me, the cold absolutely does not ever seem to bother Johnny. He used to say it was because his nose was radioactive. Actually, he was always so full of antifreeze that he couldn't feel much of anything. Anyway, Johnny hears these Navy guys cursing about having to test all the guns and he asks them if they will mind if he fires a few rounds because he has always wanted to shoot a gun of some kind, any kind. They look at each other quick, then say sure, he can fire every single gun on the ship if he likes. So he did. And he took some pretty rugged chances because if the Martians had attacked or he had slipped on the deck he could have hurt himself. Anyway, I had a job to do which was called public relations, so I wrote a little routine story about the 'one-man battleship' which in a certain way was strictly true. It had a certain Army flavor, and after all they weren't paying me to do public relations for the Navy, you know what I mean? I slugged it 'From an arctic outpost of the U.S. Army,' and I wrote how one lone Army officer had fired all the guns of a fighting ship on top of the world where all the forgotten battles are fought and where the Navy fighting men had been put out of action by the cruelest enemy of all, the desperate, bitter cold of the arctic night, and how when the last gun had been stilled not an enemy form or an enemy plane could be seen moving on the ancient ice cap, tomb of thousands of unknown fallen. You know. It was filler copy. Not strictly a lie, you understand. Every fact was strictly factual all by itself but—well, it was what they always said was very, very good for morale on the home front, you know what I mean? Anyway, I forgot about the whole thing until Johnny came around with a fistful of clippings and a letter from his wife which said my story was worth fifty thousand votes and he was supposed to buy me all the gin I could hold. I liked gin at the time," Ramen concluded.

With characteristic candor, in his autobiographical sketch in the Congressional Directory of 1955, Johnny claimed "seventeen arctic combat missions," but when testifying in 1957 in a legal proceeding that was attempting to investigate various amounts of unusual income he had received, both as to amount and source, Johnny said (of himself): "Iselin was on thirty-one combat missions in the arctic, plus liaison missions" and added inexplicably that the nights in the arctic region were six months long. "Iselin saw enough battle action to keep him peaceful and quiet for the rest of his days." Raymond's mother had taught Johnny to call himself Iselin whenever testifying or being interviewed, on the principle that it constituted a continuing plug for the name at a time when Johnny was being quoted on land, sea, and in the air, as often and as much as the New York Stock Exchange.

The question of combat would not permit any settlement. When Raymond's mother had Johnny make formal application for the Silver Star, presumably because no one else had made application for him, in a claim supported by "certain certified copies from my personal military records," it attracted an apoplectically outraged letter of complaint from a constituent, bitter about the violation of propriety in which Johnny had received a medal at his own request. Raymond's mother dictated, and Johnny signed, a return letter that contained this brave turn of phrase: "I am bound by the rules which provide how such awards shall be made and as much as I felt distaste there just wasn't any other way to do it."

However, as the years carried Big John and Raymond's mother forward through their national and international duels on behalf of a more perfect America, the most disputed part of Johnny's record continued to be the "wound" he most blandly claimed to have suffered in military combat. Although he did not receive the Purple Heart and although the former Secretary of the Army who reviewed his personnel file disclaimed any Iselin wound in action, when Big John was asked at a veterans' rally why he wore built-up shoes (how else the big in Big John?) Governor Iselin said he was wearing the shoes because he had lost most of his heel in arctic combat. There is disagreement among those who heard him at that time as to whether he said "lost most of my foot" or a lesser amount of tissue.

The relentless *Journal*, in the year of its gallant but futile attempt to discredit Johnny in a meaningful sense, uncovered the personal journal of an officer who had served with Johnny all during the tour, a Francis Winikus, who subsequently made a reputation as an authority on migratory elements of population in Britain and Europe. Under the date of June 22, 1944, the Winikus diary threw a white and revealing light on the circumstances leading to Johnny's wound by recording: "Johnny Iselin has become possessed by the idea of sex. To get that interested in sex on the top of this ice cap is either suicidal or homosexual, on its surface, but Johnny isn't either. He is a persistent and determined zealot. There is a new Eskimo camp about three miles across that primordial field of ice under that gale of wind which carries those flying razor blades to cut into the face from the direction of the village. There are women there. Everybody knows that and everybody agreed it was a very good thing until we walked, secretly and one at a time, with ice grippers tied to our shoes, across that shocking three-mile course in cold worse than the icy hell the old German religions called Nifelheim and came up to the igloos down wind and lost all interest in sex for the rest of the war. I was exhausted when I made the run, but I came back faster than I went over, to get away from that smell. It is the special smell of the Eskimo women and there is no smell like it because they wash their hair in stored urine, they live sewed up in those musty skins, and they eat an endless diet of putrescent food like fish heads and whale fat.

"Johnny said he was going to get around these 'surface disadvantages' because he had to have a woman or the top of his head would come off. He has been practicing eleven days, making that run over and back every single day. The cold and the wind simply do not seem to exist for him. All he can think of is the women. He comes back here and rests and moans and bleats with this longing, and he says proudly that *he is getting used to the stink of the women.* He says that if Eskimo men went to Chicago and smelled our women wearing those expensive French perfumes that it would sicken them, too, and that all these things are just a matter of getting used to them.

"Yesterday he decided he was ready. He crossed the ice cap again in that blackness, following a compass and watching for the lights, if any. He filled me in on the whole story this morning before they took him out in the sled to Etah, where they will hold him for pickup by relief plane to Godthaab. He was welcomed hospitably, he said, about thirty yards outside a lot of ice mounds which turned out to be igloos. Johnny doesn't speak their language and they don't speak Johnny's but he used his hands so suggestively—well, what he did with his hands when he was telling me how he showed them what he wanted makes me wonder how I will be able to get through the winter. He says they were completely sympathetic and immediately understanding and motioned him to crawl behind them into one of the blocks of ice. Before he entered, he distributed some K-ration and he told me he remembered thinking how easy this was going to be as soon as he could figure out which were the women and which were the men, because they were all wrapped in furs and their faces were as round and flat and shiny as a silver dollar. He made it into the igloo on his hands and knees, then almost fainted from the smell. He had gotten used to the smell of the women *in a high arctic wind OUTSIDE* the snow houses. The heat was tremendous for one thing: hot bricks, body heat, burning blubber, and smoking dried moss and lichens. Artfully placed around the perimeter were leather buckets of straight aged urine. Johnny said he must have stumbled into the local beauty parlor. His other quick impression was that a considerable amount of last season's fish had rotted, and, too, there was the smoky, blinding smell of long imprisoned feet. This morning as the infection turned toward fever, every now and then Johnny would say, 'O my God, those feet!' There were about fourteen people in the igloo, although he feels that they could have been sitting on a few old ladies. They had slipped out of their clothing and the ripeness of all of them hit him like a stone ax and he says he keeled over although he didn't pass out. He said they immediately offered him three different people whom he decided must have been women, and some of the fellows there even seemed ready to lift him on. Although he discovered that it was impossible to get used to the congress of smells he was able to concentrate on them just being *women* and all other considerations in that tiny space actually left his mind. He said it was no question of poontang next year with a girl who smelled like flowers, it was a case of poontang now and he began to get out of his clothes. He was actually getting undressed in front of all of those people and he said he would pause every now and then to give the nearest shape that he assumed was a girl a little pinch or a tiny tickle when all of a sudden one of the Eskimos started to yell at him in *German.*

"Johnny said he doesn't speak German but he knows it when he hears it because they speak a lot of it in his home state. Then this Eskimo began to take off his furs in that way a man takes off his coat when he wants to start a fight, yelling all the time in German and pointing at the Eskimo woman Johnny had been diddling and who was now giggling up at Johnny, when Johnny sees that this man is wearing a *German officer's uniform* under the skins. As this was the first time Johnny had ever believed that there was any enemy, he said he was absolutely flabbergasted. The Eskimos in the igloo began to yell at the German to shut up, or maybe they felt that he had impugned their hospitality by interrupting Johnny, or maybe they were sore because they liked to watch, and by now the woman had reached up and she had Johnny firmly by the privates and she wasn't letting go because for whatever crazy reason she *liked* Johnny. The noise bounced back and forth from ice wall to ice wall, dogs started barking, kids started crying, the German was yelling and weeping through what was obviously a broken heart, and Johnny said he felt very embarrassed. He realized he had been making a pass at this guy's girl right in front of the guy himself which must have hurt him terribly, and it wasn't right even if he *was* the enemy, Johnny felt. He didn't know what to do so he hit the man and as the man fell he knocked four of the small Eskimos over with him. This turned the tables. The other Eskimos now got sore at Johnny and three of them rushed him waving what Johnny calls 'Stone Age power tools.' He swept his arms out in front of him and sent the attackers over backward into the mob, all of this happening, he said, inside an area about as big as Orson Welles's head, with everybody howling for blood. He decided then that he wasn't going to score after all and that he'd better get the hell out of there, so he tried to dive through the tunnel which led to the full force arctic hurricane outside, forgetting entirely that the Eskimo woman had him by the family jewels and she had decided to keep those jewels for her very own. Johnny says he never felt anything quite like what he felt then and that he thought he had actually lost his reason for living. Rejecting her both physically and psychologically, he let fly with his left foot, catching her smartly in the face. She sank her overdeveloped teeth into his foot, then she crunched down again, then settled down to a steady munching, and he says if it hadn't been for her getting hit by someone in that yelling, milling throng behind her in the igloo she might have chewed his foot off. How he got back here in that weather with that foot I will never know. The wound had festered badly by this morning. They took him out of here for Etah about an hour ago. I guess that's the end of the war for old Johnny."

. . .

IN AUGUST, 1944, Johnny came limping home to take up
his part in the red-hot campaign that "friends" (meaning Raymond's mother and, to a conclusive extent, even though it seems
absolutely impossible in retrospect, the Communist party) had
been carrying forward since the day he had gone off to war. All
Johnny had to do was to wear his uniform, his crutches, and his
bandaged foot and shout out a few hundred topical exaggera-
tions that Raymond's mother had written up and catalogued over
the years to evade any conceivable demand. Because of the clear
call from the people of his state, Johnny was permitted to resign
from the armed forces on August 11, 1944.

He was elected governor of his state in the elections of 1944
and re-elected in 1948. As he entered his second term he was
forty-one years old; Raymond's mother was thirty-eight. Raymond was twenty-one and was working as a district man for the
Journal, having graduated from the state university at the head
of his class.

At forty-one, Governor Iselin was a plain, aggressively humble
man, five feet eight inches tall in specially shod elevator shoes.
There was a fleshiness of the nose to mark him for the memory.
His hair was thin and, under certain lighting, appeared to have
been painted in fine, single lines across his scalp over rosettes
and cabbages of two-dimensional liver spots. His clothes, from a
time shortly after his marriage to Raymond's mother, were of
homespun material but they had been run up by the hands of a
terribly good and quite wealthy tailor in New York. Raymond's
mother had Johnny's valet shine only the lower half of his high
black shoes so that it would seem, to people who thought about
those things, that he managed to shine his own shoes between
visits of the Strawberry Lobby and the refusal of pardons to the
condemned. An abiding mark of the degree of Johnny's elemental friendliness shone from the fact that he could look no one
in the eye and that when he talked he would switch syntax in
seeming horror of what he had almost said to his listener. The
governor never shaved from Friday night to Monday morning,
no matter what function might be scheduled, as though he were
a part-time Sikh. He would explain that this gave his skin a rest.
Raymond's mother had invented that one, as she had invented
very nearly everything else about him excepting his digestive
system (and if she had invented that it would have functioned a

great deal better), because not shaving "made him like some slob, like a farm hand or some Hunky factory worker." It is certain that over a weekend, when Big John was generating noise out of every body orifice, switching syntax, darting his eyes about, and flashing that meaty nose in his unshaven face, he was the commonest kind of common man forty ways to the ace. However, he had been custom-made by Raymond's mother. She had developed Johnny (as José Raoul Capablanca had developed his chess play; as Marie Antoine Carême had folded herbs into a sauce for Talleyrand) into the model governor, on paper that is, of all the states of the United States, and in some of those other states the constituents read more about Jolly Johnny than about their own men. She had riveted into the public memory these immutable facts: John Yerkes Iselin was a formidable administrator; a conserver who could dare; an honest, courageous, conscience-thrilled, God-fearing public servant; a jolly, jovial, generous, gentling, humorous, amiable, good-natured, witty big brother; a wow of a husband and a true-blue pal of a father; a fussin', fumin', fightin', soldier boy, all heart; a simple country judge with the savvy of Solomon; and an American, which was the most fortuitous circumstance of all.

Raymond's mother hardly showed one flicker of chagrin when General Eisenhower was persuaded to make the stroll for the nomination in 1952, the one unexpected accident that could have blocked her John from the White House. She broke a few little things at the Mansion when she heard the news: mirrors, lamps, vases, and other replaceable bric-a-brac. She was entitled to a flash of violence, one little demonstration that she could feel passion, and it harmed no one because Johnny was dead drunk and Raymond had marched off to the Korean War.

In the Autumn of 1952, two weeks before Raymond's return from Korea to receive the Congressional Medal of Honor, almost two months before the end of Big John's statutory final term as governor, U.S. Senator Ole Banstoffsen, the grand old man who had represented his state in Washington for six consecutive terms, succumbed to a heart attack almost immediately after a small dinner with his oldest and dearest friends, Governor and Mrs. John Iselin, and died in the governor's arms in the manner of a dinner guest of the Empress Livia's some time before in ancient Rome. The exchange of last words made their bid to become part of American history, for through them Big John found his life's mission, and the words are set down herewith to complete the record.

SENATOR BANSTOFFSEN

John—Johnny, boy—are you there?

GOVERNOR ISELIN

Ole! Ole, old friend. Don't try to speak! Eleanor! *Where is that doctor!*

SENATOR BANSTOFFSEN
(*his last words*)

Johnny—you must—carry on. Please, please, Johnny swear to me as I lay dying that you will fight to save Our Country—from the Communist peril.

GOVERNOR ISELIN
(*greatly moved*)

I pledge to you, with my soul, that I will fight to keep Communists from dominating our institutions to the last breath of my life, dear friend.

(*Senator Banstoffsen slumps into death, made happy.*)

GOVERNOR ISELIN

He's gone! Oh, Eleanor, he's gone. A great fighter has gone on to his rest.

THE verbatim record must have been set down by Raymond's mother, as she was the only other person present at the senator's death, and she undoubtedly found time to make notes while they waited for the doctor and while the words were still so fresh in her mind, but Johnny did not use them for almost three years, during which time they had undoubtedly been carefully filed for their value as Americana and as a source of inspiration to others.

Governor Iselin appointed himself to succeed Senator Banstoffsen, to fight the good fight, and his re-election followed. He was sworn in on March 18, 1953, by Justice Krushen, after his wife had insisted that he take The Cure for two and a half months at a reliable, discreet, and medically sound ranch for alcoholics and drug addicts in sun-drenched New Mexico, following the booze-drenched Christmas holidays of 1952.

V WHAT IS THE CON-
sciousness of guilt but the arena floor rushing up to meet the
falling trapeze artist? Without it, a bullet becomes a tourist flying without responsibility through the air. The consciousness of
guilt gives a scent to humanity, a threat of putrefaction, the
ultimate cosmetic. Without the consciousness of guilt, existence
had become so bland in Paradise that Eve welcomed the
pungency of Original Sin. Raymond's consciousness of guilt,
that rouged lip print of original sin, had been wiped off. He
had been made unique. He had been shriven into eternity,
exculpated of the consciousness of guilt.

Out of his saddened childhood, Raymond had grown to the
age for love. Because he was mired down within an aloof, timid,
and skeptical temperament he was a man who, if he was to be
permitted to love at all, was suited to find the solution of his
needs only in reassuring monogamy. He had no ability to make
friends. As he had grown up he was dependent upon the children of friends of the people who were his mother's garden:
mostly politicians and their lackeys, and other people who could
be used by politicians: newspaper types, press agents, labor
types, commerce and industry edges, hustlers of veterans and
hustlers of minorities, patriots and suborners, confused women
and the self-seeking clergy.

By an accident, when he was just past twenty-one years old,
Raymond met the daughter of a man whom his mother would
not, under any condition, have entertained. Her name was
Jocelyn Jordan. Her father was a United States senator and a
dangerously unhealthy liberal in every sense of that word,
though a member of Johnny Iselin's party. They lived in the
East. They happened to be in Raymond's mother's state because
it was summertime, when schoolteachers and senators not up for
re-election are allowed time off to spend their large, accumulated
salaries, and they had been invited by Jocie's roommate to use
her family's summer camp while the family toured in Europe. It
is certain that they had no knowledge that they would be keeping calm and cool beside the same blue lake, with its talking bass
and balsam collar, as Governor Iselin and his wife or else they

would have politely refused the invitation. When they did find out, they were established in the summer camp and had not been shot at so it was too late to do anything about it.

Jocie was nineteen that summer when she came around a turning of the dusty road at the moment the snake had bitten Raymond, as he lay in his wine-colored swimming trunks where he had tripped and fallen in the road, staring from the green snake as it moved slowly through the golden dust toward the other side of the road, to the neat, new wound on his bare leg. She did not speak to him but she saw what he saw and, stopping, stared wordlessly at the two dark red spots against his healthy flesh, then moved quickly to the small plastic kit attached to the back of her bicycle seat, removed a naked razor blade and a bottle of purple fluid, and knelt beside him. She beamed expert reassurance into his eyes from the sweet brownness of her own and cut crosses with the razor blade in each dark, red spot, traversed both of them with a straight cut, then put her mouth to his leg and drew two mouthfuls of blood out of it. Each time after she spit the blood out she wiped her mouth with the back of her hand like a laborer who had just finished a hero sandwich and a bottle of beer. She poured the purple fluid on the cuts, bound Raymond's leg with two strips of a handkerchief she had ripped in half, then saturated the improvised bandage with more purple liquid, over the wounds.

"I hope I know what I'm doing," she said in a tremulous voice. "My father is scared tiddly about snakes in this part of the country, which is how I happen to ride around with a razor blade and potassium permanganate solution. Now don't move. It is very, very important that you don't move and start anything that might be left from that snake circulating through your system." She walked to her bicycle as she talked. "I'll be right back with a car. I won't be ten minutes. You just stay still, now. You hear?" She pedaled off rapidly around the same turning of the road that had magically produced her. She had vanished many seconds before he realized that he had not spoken to her and that, although he had expected to die when the snake had bitten him, he had not thought about the snake, the snake's bite, nor his impending death from the instant she had appeared. He looked bemusedly at his crudely bandaged leg below the swimming trunks. Purple ink and red blood trickled idly along his leg in parallel courses and it occurred to him that, if this had been happening to his mother's leg, she would have claimed the purple mixture as being her blood.

A car returned, it seemed to him almost at once, and Jocie had fetched her father along because it would give him such a good feeling to know that all of those warnings about the snakes in those woods had been just. A man has few enough opportunities like that when he assists in the raising of children, who must be hoisted on the pulley of one's experience every morning to the top of the pole for a view of life as extensive as that day's emotional climate would bear, then lowered again at sundown to be folded up and made to rest, and carried into their dreams with reverence.

They brought Raymond back to the summer camp, believing him to be in a state of shock because he did not speak. Raymond sat beside Jocie in the back seat with his fanged leg propped up on the back of the front seat. The senator drove and told horrendous snake stories wherein no one bitten ever recovered. The way Raymond looked at Jocie in that back seat told her well that he was in a state of shock but she was, at nineteen, sufficiently versed to be able to differentiate between the mundane and the glorious kinds of shock.

At the camp the senator made his examination of the wound and was thrown into high glee when there seemed to be no swelling on, above, or below the poisoned area. He took Raymond's temperature and found it normal. He cauterized the wounds with a carbolic acid solution while Raymond continued to stare respectfully at his daughter. When he had finished, the senator asked the only possible, sensible question.

"Are you a mute?" he said.

"No, sir."

"Ah."

"Thank you very much," Raymond said, "Miss— Miss—"

"Miss Jocelyn Jordan," the senator said. "And considering that you two are practically related by blood, it is probably time you met."

"How do you do?" Raymond said.

"And now, under the quaint local custom, it is your turn to tell your name," the senator explained gravely.

"I am Raymond Shaw, sir."

"How do you do, Raymond?" the senator said, and shook hands with him.

"I have saved your life," Jocie said with a heavy vaudeville Hungarian accent, "and now I may do with it what I will."

"I would like to ask your permission to marry Jocelyn, sir." Raymond was deadly serious, as always. The Jordans exploded with laughter, believing Raymond was working to amuse them, but when they looked back to him to acknowledge his sally, and saw the confused and nearly hurt expression on his face, they became embarrassed. Senator Jordan coughed violently. Jocelyn murmured something about gallantry not being dead after all, that it was time she made some coffee, and went off hastily toward what must have been the kitchen. Raymond stared after her. To cover up, although for the life of him he could not have explained or understood what he was covering up, the Senator sat down on a wicker chair beside Raymond. "Is your place near here?" he asked.

"Yes, sir. It's that red house directly across the lake."

"The Iselin house?" Jordan was startled. His expression became less friendly.

"My house," Raymond said succinctly. "It was my father's house but my father is dead and he left it to me."

"Forgive me, I had been told that it was the summer camp of Johnny Iselin, and of all places in this world for me to spend a summer this—"

"Johnny stays there sometimes, sir, when he gets too drunk for my mother to allow him to stay around the Capitol."

"Your mother is—uh—Mrs. Iselin?"

"That's right, sir."

"I once found it necessary to sue your mother for defamation of character and slander. My name is Thomas Jordan."

"How do you do, sir?"

"It cost her sixty-five thousand dollars and costs. What hurt her much more than the payment of that money was that I donated all of it to the organization called the American Civil Liberties Union."

"Oh." Raymond remembered the color of his mother's words, the objects she had broken, the noises she had made, and the picture she had painted of this man.

Jordan smiled at him grimly. "Your mother and I are, have been, and will always be divergent in our views, not to say inimical of one another's interests, and I tell you that after long study of the matter and of the uses of expediences by all of us in politics."

Raymond smiled back at him, but not grimly, and he looked amazingly handsome and vitally attractive, Jocie thought from far across the room as she entered, carrying a tray. He had such even white teeth against such a long, tanned face, and he offered them the yellow-green eyes of a lion. "If you weren't sure of that, sir," Raymond said, "you couldn't be sure of anything, because that is the absolute truth." They both laughed, unexpectedly and heartily, and were friends of a sort. Jocie came up to them with the cups and the coffee and a bottle of rye whisky, and Raymond began to feel the beginnings of what was to be a constant, summer-long nausea as he tried to equate the daughter of Senator Jordan with the ancient, carbonized prejudice of his mother.

That summer was the only happy time, excepting one, the only fully joyous, concentrically transforming time in Raymond's life. Two pure and cooling fountains were all Raymond ever found in all that aridness of time allotted to him. Two brief episodes in his entire life in which he awoke each morning looking forward in joy to more joy and found it. Only twice was there a time when he did not maintain the full and automatic three-hundred-and-sixty-degree horizon of raw sensibilities over which swept the three searing beams of suspicion, fear, and resentment flashing from the loneliness of the tall lighthouse of his soul.

Jocie showed him how she felt. She told him how she felt. She presented him, with the pomp of new love, a thousand small and radiant gifts each day. She behaved as though she had been waiting an eternity for him to catch up with her in the time continuum, and now that he had arrived with his body to occupy a predestined place in space beside her, she knew she must wait still longer while he tried desperately to mature, all at once, out of infancy until he could understand that she only wanted to give to him, asking nothing but his awareness in return. She behaved as though she loved him, a condition that could swing in suspension to fix his concentration but which, when he could understand, would need to blend with his love, matching it exactly.

He walked beside her. Once or twice he touched her, but he did not know how to touch her or where to touch her. However she saw right on the surface of him how greatly he was trying to learn, how he was struggling to lose the past so he could tell her of the glories she made him feel and of how enormously he needed her.

Every morning he waited outside her house, staring as though he could see through the walls, until she came running out to him. They spent all of every day together. They separated late, in the late darkness. They did not speak much but each day she moved him closer to breaking through his barriers and willed him with her love to say more each day, and she was filled with the ambition to make him safe with her love.

The summer was the second-best time in his merely twice-blest living span. The first time was not the equal of the second time because of his fear; the conviction that it would be taken from him the instant he voiced his need for it. Whatever they did together he held himself rigid, awaiting the scream of his mother's rage, and it cost him thirty pounds of his flesh because he could not keep food down as he battled to hold the thoughts of his mother and Jocie apart. His mother found out about Jocie in time, and who Jocie's father was, of course, and it was all over.

JOHNNY said he didn't want to be around when she told Raymond what had to be. He went back to the capital where he had a lot of work to do anyway. Raymond got home late that night. His mother was waiting for him. She was wearing a fantastically beautiful Chinese house coat. It was orange-red. It had a deep black Elizabethan collar that stood up straight behind and around her shining blond head, in the mode of wicked witches, but it made her look very lovely and very kind and she smelled very beautiful and enlightened as Raymond dragged his dread behind him into the room, sickened to find her awake so late.

There she sits like a mail-order goddess, serene as the star on a Christmas tree, as calm as a jury, preening the teeth of her power with the floss of my joy, soiling it, shredding it, and just about ready to throw it away, and she is getting to look more and more like those two-dimensional women who pose for nail polish advertisements, and I have wanted to kill her for all of these years and now it is too late.

"What the hell do you want, Mother?"

"What the hell kind of a greeting is that at three-thirty in the morning."

"It's a quarter to three. What do you want?"

"What's the matter with you?"

"I'm shocked to be in a room alone with you after all these years, I guess."

"All right, Raymond. So I'm a busy woman. Do you think I work and work and ruin my health for myself? I do it for you. I'm making a place for you."

"Please don't do it for me, Mother. Do it for Johnny. Worse I couldn't wish him."

"What you're doing to Johnny is the worst you could wish him."

"What is it? I'll double it."

"I speak of that little Communist tart."

"Shut up, Mother! Shut up with that!" His voice rose to a squeak.

"Do you know what Jordan is? Are you out to crucify Johnny?"

"I can't answer you. I don't know what you're talking about. I'm going to bed."

"Sit down!" He stopped where he was. He was near a chair. He sat down.

"Raymond, they live in New York. How would you see her?"

"I thought of getting a job in New York."

"You have to do your Army service."

"Next spring."

"Well?"

"I might be dead next spring."

"Oh, Raymond, for Christ's *sake!*"

"No one has given me a written, printed, bonded guarantee that I will live another week. This girl is now. What the hell do I care about her father's politics any more than I care about your politics? Jocie—Jocie is *all* I care about."

"Raymond, if we were at war now—"

"Oh, Mother, for Christ's *sake!*"

"—and you were suddenly to become infatuated with the daughter of a Russian agent—wouldn't you expect me to come to you and object, to beg you to stop the entire thing before it was too late? Well, we *are* at war. It's a cold war but it will get worse and worse until every man and woman and child in this country

will have to stand up and be counted to say whether or not he or
she is on the side of right and freedom, or on the side of the
Thomas Jordans' of this country. I will go with you to Washington tomorrow, if you like, and I will show you documented proof
that this man stands for evil and that he will do anything to win
that evil—"

That was the gist of it. Raymond's mother began her filibuster
at approximately three o'clock in the morning and she kept at
him, walking beside him wherever he went in the house, standing next to him talking shrilly of the American Dream and its
meaning in the present, pulling stops out bearing the invisible
labels left over from Fourth of July speeches and old Hearst
editorials such as "The Red Menace," "Liberty, Freedom, and
America as We know It," "Thought Police and The American
Way," until ten minutes to eleven o'clock the following morning,
when Raymond, who had lost so much weight that summer and
who had been running a subnormal fever for three weeks, collapsed. She had talked through each weakening manifestation of
defiance he had made—through his shouts and screams, through
his tears and pleadings and whimperings and sobs—and the sure
power of her limitless strength slowly and surely over-came his
double weakness: both the physical and the psychological, until
he was convinced that he would be well rid of Jocie if he could
trade her for some silence and some sleep. She made him take
four sleeping pills, tucked him into his trundle bed, and he slept
until the following afternoon at five forty-five, but was even then
too weak to get up. His mother, having put her little boy to
beddy-by, took a hot shower followed by a cold shower, ran a
comforting amount of morphine into the large vein in her left
forearm (which was always covered with those smart, long
sleeves) and sat down at the typewriter to compose a little note
from Raymond to Jocie. She rewrote it three times to be sure,
but when it was done it was done right, and she signed his name
and sealed the envelope. She got dressed, popped into the pickup truck, and drove directly to the Jordan camp. Jocie had gone
to the post office on an errand for her father, but the senator was
there. Raymond's mother said it would be necessary for them to
have a talk so he invited her inside the house. The Jordans
packed and left the lake by six o'clock that evening.

Jocie, who had fallen as deeply in love with Raymond as he
with her, and more than that because she was healthy and

normal, never really understood quite why it was all over. Her father told her that Raymond had enlisted in the Army that morning, had telephoned only to say that he could not see Jocie again and good-by. Her father, having read the terrible letter, had shuddered with nausea and burned it. Raymond's mother had explained to him that despite their own personal differences she had come to say to him that his daughter was far too fine a girl to be hurt or twisted by her son, that Raymond was a homosexual and in other ways degenerate, and that he would be far, far better forgotten by this sweet, fine child.

VI

IN FEBRUARY, 1953, just a little more than two months after his discharge from the Army, Raymond got a job as a researcher-legman-confidant for, and as janitor of the ivory tower of, Holborn Gaines, the distinguished international political columnist of *The Daily Press*, in New York; this on the strength of (1) a telephone call from the managing editor of the *Journal* to Joe Downey, managing editor of *The Daily Press*, (2) his relationship to Mrs. John Yerkes Iselin, whom Mr. Gaines admired and loathed as one of the best political minds in the country, and (3) the Medal of Honor.

Mr. Gaines was a man of sixty-eight or seventy years who wore a silk handkerchief inside his shirt collar whenever he was indoors, no matter what the season of the year, and drank steady quantities of Holland beer but never seemed to grow either plump or drowsy from it, and found very nearly everything that had ever happened in politics from Caesar's ascension to Sherman Adams' downfall to be among the most amusing manifestations of his civilization. Mr. Gaines would pore over those detailed never-to-be-published-in-that-form reports from one or another of the paper's bureau chiefs around the world, which provided the intimate background data of all real or imagined political maneuvering, and sip at the lip of a beer bottle, chuckling as though the entire profile of that day's world disaster had been written by Mark Twain. He was a kind man who took the trouble to explain to Raymond on the first day of his employment that he did not much enjoy talking and fulsomely underscored how happy they would be, both of them, if they could train each other into one another's jobs so that conversation would become unnecessary. This suited Raymond so well that he could not believe his own luck, and when he had worked even faster and better than usual and needed to sit and wait until Mr. Gaines would indicate, with a grunt and a push at a pile of papers, what the next job would be, he would sit turned halfway in upon himself, wishing he could turn all the way in and shut everything out and away from himself, but he was afraid Mr. Gaines would decide to talk and he would have to climb and pull himself out of the pit, so he waited and watched and at last came to see that he and Mr. Gaines could not have been more ecstatically suited to one another had one worked days and the other worked nights.

The promotion manager of *The Daily Press* was a young man named O'Neil. He arranged that the members of the editorial staff give Raymond a testimonial dinner (from which Mr. Gaines was automatically excused for, after all, he had actually met Raymond), welcoming a hero to their ranks. When O'Neil first told Raymond about the dinner plan they were standing, just the two of them, in Mr. Gaines's office, one of the many glass-enclosed cubicles that lined the back wall of the city room, and Raymond hit O'Neil, knocking him across the desk and, as he lay there for an instant, spat on him. O'Neil didn't ask for an explanation. He got up, a tiny thread of blood hanging from the left corner of his mouth, and beat Raymond systematically and quietly. They were both about the same age and weight, but O'Neil had interest, which is the key to life, on his side. The beating was done well and quickly but it must be seen that Raymond had, if even in the most negative way, made his point. No one else ever knew what had happened and because the dinner was only a week away and O'Neil knew he would need pictures of Raymond posed beside various executives of the paper, he was careful not to hit Raymond in the face where subsequent discolorations might show. When it was over, Raymond agreed that he would not concede the dinner, at any time, to be a good idea, holding it to be "a commonness which merchandised the flag," but he did agree to attend. O'Neil, in his turn, inquired that if there was anything more a part of our folklore than hustling the flag for an edge, that he would appreciate it if Raymond would point it out to him, and agreed to limit the occasion to one speech which he would make himself and keep it short, and that Raymond would need only to rise in acknowledgment, bow slightly, and speak not at all.

In December, 1953, Raymond was guest of honor at a dinner given by the Overseas Press Club at which an iron-lunged general of the Armies was the principal speaker, and Raymond could not fight his way out of this invitation to attend and to speak because his boss, Mr. Gaines, was chairman of the dinner committee. What Raymond did say when he spoke was "Thank you, one and all." The way the matter had been handled differed sharply from the O'Neil incident. Mr. Gaines had come in one morning, had handed Raymond a printed invitation with his name on it, had patted him understandingly on the back, had opened a bottle of beer, sat down at his desk, and that was that.

VII

THE WAR WAS OVER in Korea. That camera which caught every movement of everyone's life was adjusted to run backward so that they were all returned to the point from which they had started out to war. Not all. Some, like Mavole and Lembeck, remained where they had been dropped. The other members of Marco's I&R patrol whose minds believed in so many things that had never happened, although in that instance they were hardly unique, returned to their homes, left them, found jobs and left them until, at last, they achieved an understanding of their essential desperation and made peace with it, to settle down into making and acknowledging the need for the automatic motions that were called living.

Marco didn't get back to the States until the spring of 1954, on the very first day of that spring. His temporary orders placed him with the First Army on Governor's Island in the New York harbor, so he blandly took it for granted that he would be more than welcome to spend his stateside leave as Raymond's guest in

Raymond's apartment. As far as Raymond was concerned, and this feeling mystified Raymond, Marco was more than welcome.

Raymond lived in a large building on Riverside Drive, facing the commercially broad Hudson at a point approximately opposite an electric spectacular on the New Jersey shore which said SPRY (some experiment in suggestive geriatrics, Raymond thought) to the *démodé* side of Manhattan Island.

The apartment was on the sixteenth floor. It was old-fashioned, which meant that the rooms were large and light-filled, the ceilings high enough to permit a constant circulation of air, and the walls thick enough for a man and his loving wife to have a stimulating argument at the top of their lungs without invading the nervous systems of surrounding neighbors. Raymond had rented the apartment furnished and nothing in the place beyond the books, the records, and the phonograph was his.

The bank issued rent checks for the apartment's use, as they paid all the bills for food, pressing, laundry, and liquor. These the local merchants sent directly to Raymond's very own bank officer, a Mr. Jack Rothenberg, a formidably bankerish sort of a man excepting for the somewhat disturbing habit of wearing leather tassels on his shoes. Raymond believed that the exchange of money was one of the few surviving methods people had for communicating with each other, and he wanted no part of it. The act of loving, not so much of the people themselves but of the cherishment contained in the warm money passed from hand to hand was, to Raymond, intimate to the point of being obscene so that as much as possible he insisted that the bank take over that function, for which he paid them well.

Each Monday morning at fifteen minutes past ten, a bank messenger came to Raymond's office with a sealed Manila envelope containing four twenty-dollar bills, four ten-dollar bills, five five-dollar bills and thirty singles—a total of one hundred and seventy-five dollars—for which Raymond would sign. This was his walking-around money. He spent it, if he spent it, on books and off-beat restaurants for he was a gourmet—as much as a man can be who eats behind a newspaper. His salary from *The Daily Press* of one hundred and thirty-five dollars and eighty-one cents, after deductions, he mailed personally to the bank each Friday and considered himself to be both lucky and shrewd to be living in the biggest city on the Western continent for what he regarded as a net of forty dollars per week, cash. The living expenses, rent, and such, were the bank's problem.

As much as possible, he ate every meal alone, excepting perhaps once a month when he would be forced into accepting an invitation from O'Neil, with some girls. All the men Raymond ever knew seemed to be able to summon up girls the way he might summon up a tomato juice from a waiter. Raymond was a theatrically handsome man, a well-informed man and an intelligent one. He had never had a girl inside his large, comfortable apartment. He bought the sex he needed for twenty-five dollars an hour and he had never found it necessary to exceed that time period, although he filled it amply every time. Out of distaste, because she had suggested it herself the first time he had been there, and most certainly not out of any unconscious desire to be liked, he would give the maid who ran the towels a dollar-and-a-quarter tip, because she had asked for a dollar, then would stare her down coldly when she thanked him. Raymond had found the retail outlet with efficiency. He had told the Broadway columnist on the paper that he would appreciate it greatly if one of the press agents with whom the columnist did business would secure him maximum-for-minimum accommodations atop some well-disposed, handsome professional woman. Had he known that this ritual and the attendant expense were the direct result of the release conferred on him by Yen Lo in Tunghwa, he would have resented it, because although the money meant little to him and although he enjoyed the well-disposed, handsome professional woman very much, he would just as well have preferred to have remained in the psychological position of ignoring it, because it meant getting to bed on the evenings he was with her much later than he preferred to retire and it most certainly had cut into his reading.

Marco gave him no warning. He called Raymond at the paper and told him he would be in town for a while, that he would move in with Raymond, and they met at Hungarian Charlie's fifteen minutes later, and that had been that. When Marco moved in, every one of Raymond's time-and-motion study habits was tossed high in the air to land on their heads. For ten days or so everything was turned upside down.

Marco didn't believe in buying sex because he said it was so much more expensive the other way, and he was loaded with loot. Drunk or sober, Marco found matched sets of pretty girls, bright and entertaining girls, rich girls, poor girls, and even one very religious set of sisters who insisted on getting up for church in the mornings, whether it was Sunday or not, then raced back to Marco's bed again. Marco had girls stashed in most of the rooms of Raymond's apartment whenever he thought it was a good idea (day and night, night and day), severely disturbing the natural rhythm of Raymond's life. There were too many cans of beer in the icebox and too few cans of V-8. Men kept ringing the back door bell, bringing boxes or paper bags filled with liquor or heavy paper sacks of ice cubes. Everybody seemed to be an expert on cooking spaghetti and there was a film of red sauce on every white surface in the kitchen. In the foyer, in the living room, in the dining room (which Raymond had converted into an office), brassières were strewn, and slips, and amazingly small units of transparent panties. Marco made everyone wear shoes as a precaution against athlete's foot. He did not believe in hanging up his clothes when he was not in Army service because he said the agonizing reappraisal of the piles of clothing every morning in each room made him appreciate the neatness of Army life all the more. The positive thing to be said for Marco was that although he crowded the apartment with girls and loud music and spaghetti and booze, he never invited any other guys, so what was there was fifty per cent Raymond's. The women were all size and colors, sharing with each other only Marco's requisite of a good disposition, and he rarely hesitated to hand out a black eye if this rule were violated.

Raymond found it enjoyable. He could not have stood it as a constant diet (and he believed that there were people who could stand it as a constant diet) and it was all extremely confusing to him at first, from his doctrinaire perspective, because the properly dressed, immaculately spoken women seemed to him to be the wantons, and the naked or near-naked babes who talked like long-shoremen seemed to be there as professional comics or entertainers on the piano or on the long-distance telephone. They were talking, talking, always talking, but never with the unpleasant garrulity of Johnny Iselin.

At first when Raymond allowed himself to get around to feeling like having a little action for himself he would grow flustered, be at a loss as to how to proceed, and he would close the door behind him in the converted dining room he called an office and try to forget about the whole thing, but that simply was not satisfactory. He did that the very first night Marco had guests and he sat there, nearly huddled up with misery, fearing that no one would ever come in to make him come out, but finally the door was flung open and a small but strapping redheaded girl with a figure that made him moan to himself, stood in the doorway and stared at him accusingly. "What the hell is the matter with you, honey?" she asked solicitously. "Are you queer?"

"Queer? Me?" Strapping was definitely the word for this girl. Everything she had was big in miniature and in aching proportion.

"There are four broads out there, honey," she said, "and one man. Marco took me aside and told me that there was one more in here and although I ran right in here I've been worrying all the way because what the hell are you *doing* in here with very very ready broads out there?"

"Well—you see—" Raymond got up and took a slight step forward. "I'd like to introduce myself." The excitement was rising and he forgot to think about himself. He was aware vaguely that this was the first time he had ever been courted and if she could keep the thing within bounds everything was going to be all right. "I'm Raymond Shaw."

"So? I'm Winona Meighan. What has names got to do with what Marco promised I would be doing if I came here, but now I find out I may have to stand in line like at Radio City on a Sunday night?"

"I—I guess I simply didn't know what else to say. I'm just as avidly interested as you are," Raymond said, "but, I guess—well, I suppose you could say I am shy. Or new at all this. Shy, anyway."

She waved her hand reassuringly. "All the men are shy today. Everything is changing right in front of our eyes. It's become such a wonderful thing to find a man who actually is willing to go to bed with a woman that the women get all charged up and they press too much. I know it but I can't change it." As she talked she closed the door behind her. She couldn't find any way to lock it so she pulled a heavy chair in front of it. "So if you're shy we'll put out the lights, sweetheart. Winona understands, baby. Just get out of those bulgy pants and come over here." She unzipped the side of her dress and began to struggle out of it impatiently. "I have to get back downtown for an eleven o'clock show tonight, lover, so don't let's waste any more time."

By the third night Raymond felt that he was fully adjusted to the new way of life. Winona had been extremely grateful for the extreme care he had put into his work with her and that squealing, activated gratitude, which had been coupled with an absolute insistence that he take her name and permanent address and that she write down his name and permanent address because her company was leaving in the morning for eight weeks in Las Vegas, had given him considerable confidence. After she had had to leave, both of them feeling exhausted but *triste* after the parting, he had moved quietly and weightlessly into the living room where Marco was playing at séance, explaining to the four girls that he understood, academically, exactly how a séance should operate because he had researched every necessary move and that if they would all cooperate by believing perhaps he could make something interesting happen the way things had happened in a fascinating textbook he had pored over all the way from San Francisco. It hadn't worked, but everybody enjoyed themselves and when bedtime came two of the girls joined up with Raymond as though they had all been assigned to each other by a lewd housemother and, after loads of fun, they had all dropped off to sleep and had slept like lambs.

Raymond awoke twice during the night for a few languorous moments of trying to puzzle out how come he did not feel invaded by all these bodies that were hurling themselves at him or dotting the landscape of his privacy, but he could not reach the answer before he fell asleep and, in the morning, with the girls getting ready to go off to offices or studios or dress houses or stores, no one had much more time than to wait patiently for a turn to put on lipstick hurriedly in the bathroom and rush out without any breakfast.

The extraordinary thing to Raymond was that none of them ever returned.

Marco would spend all of his day in the reading room of the Forty-second Street library, then, in the late afternoon, devote two hours to fruitful bird-dogging that was, mysteriously to Raymond, always successful, and when Raymond got back to the apartment at six twenty-two every day there would never be less than three interested and interesting girls there, making spaghetti or using the telephone.

Marco explained, on the first Saturday morning, that women were much more like men, in many almost invisible ways, than men were. Particularly in the noninvolvement area in which they were many, many more times like men simply because their natural instinct to capture and hold could be suspended. Marco said that there was not a healthy woman alive who would not gladly agree to rush into bed if that action displaced only the present and did not connect with the past nor had any possibility of any shape in the future. Good health could be served in this way, he said. No fears of reputation-tarnish could threaten. It meant sex without sin, in the sense that, in the middle of the twentieth century, when sexual activity is credited to a woman by several men, creating what was termed a past could also penalize her for any sexual activity in the future. Since good health demands good sex, he assured Raymond that very nearly the entire female population of the city of New York would happily cooperate with them if approached in the proper, understanding manner.

"But how?" Raymond asked him in awe and bewilderment.

"How what?"

"How do you approach them?"

"Well, I do have the edge on others by being patently an officer and a gentleman by act of Congress, and I *am* graced with a certain courtliness of manner."

"Yes. I agree. But so am I."

"I approach them smiling. I tell them I am an officer passing through New York, leaving in the morning for my new station in Hawaii, and that merely by looking at them I find them enormously attractive sexually."

"But—what do they say?"

"First, of course, they thank me. They are with it, Raymond. Believe me, they are even away ahead of me and depending on whether they need to be at home that evening to greet a loyal breadwinner, or under the clock at the Biltmore to persuade a courtier, or are committed to one or another irrevocable obligations which mar metropolitan life, they are keenly aware that one night is such a short, short burst of time in such a packed and crowded concealing city as New York."

"But when do they say—"

"Actually," Marco told him pedantically, "I don't actually know until I get back here, and the door bell begins to ring, who will arrive and who won't. I always invite six. Every afternoon. So far we have not had to make do with less than three and—"

"But how do you—"

"How do I get them here?"

"Yes."

"I explain I am using a friend's apartment. I write down the address, tear out the slip and press it into their hands, always smiling in a pleasant, lustful way, and I murmur about cold champagne and some great records. Then I pat them on the rear and walk on. I assure you, Raymond, that is all there is to it and everyone is richer all around."

"Yes. I see. But—"

"But what?"

"Don't you ever have any *permanent* alliances?" Raymond asked earnestly.

"Of course," Marco said stoutly. "What do you think I am—a zombie? In London, before this last post where I met you, I was head over heels in love with my colonel's wife and she with me. And we stayed that way for almost two years."

One night Marco took two young things by the wrists and headed off for rest. One was a Miss Ernestine Dover who worked at an exceptionally fine department store on Fifth Avenue and the other a Mrs. Diamentez who was married to one of the best professional third basemen in the nation. After a while they all fell asleep.

Raymond was enjoying tremendous pleasure on a large bed in an adjoining room with a recording and variety artist, then unemployed, who was of Hawaiian, Negro, and Irish extraction and whom Marco had met that afternoon in the vestibule of a church, where he had gone to light a cigar out of the wind.

They all sat bolt upright, as one person—Raymond and June, Miss Dover and Mrs. Diamentez—because Marco was yelling "Stop him! Stop him!" in a wild, hoarse voice and trying to get out of the bed at something, his legs hopelessly entangled in the bedclothes. Mrs. Diamentez recovered first—after all, she was married—and she took Marco by the shoulders and threw him over backward on the bed, pinning his torso down with her own body while Miss Dover held down his thrashing legs with hers.

"Ben! Ben!" Mrs. Diamentez yelled.

"It's O.K., lover, it's O.K. You ain't over there, you're over here," Miss Dover shrilled.

Raymond and June stood naked in the doorway. "Whassamatter?" Raymond said.

Ben was rolling and pitching, his eyes wide open, as feral as a trapped animal who is willing to leave a paw behind if it can only get away from the teeth. June swooped an old highball up from the bureau and, rushing across the room, poured it on Marco. It brought him out. The girls climbed off him. He didn't speak to anyone but he stared at Raymond apprehensively. He shuffled dazedly out of the room and into the bathroom. He shook his head slowly from side to side as he walked, in tiny arcs, like a punch-drunk fighter, and his left cheek flinched with a tic. He closed the bathroom door behind him and they heard the lock snap and the light go on. Miss Dover went to the bathroom door and listened and suddenly the tub taps were turned on with full force. "Are you all right, honey?" Miss Dover said, but there was no answer. After a while, although Marco wouldn't get out of the bathtub or speak, they all went back to sleep and Mrs. Diamentez went in with Raymond and June.

MARCO's ninth day was a Sunday. Without any warning, they were suddenly alone. All the chicks had gone to other roosts. Marco brooded over such a hang-over as had not happened to him in fourteen years, since he had mixed Beaujolais wine with something called Wilkins' Family Rye Whisky. They ate steak for breakfast. Raymond opened the French windows and sat idly watching the river traffic and the multicolored metal band that never stopped moving along the West Side Highway. After a while, with Marco sunk into the silence of his perfect hang-over, Raymond began to talk about Jocie. She had gotten married two months before. She was living in the Argentine. Her husband was an agronomist. It had run on the society page of his own newspaper and he said it as though if they had not run the item the marriage would not have been solemnized and she would be free to go to him.

Marco was ordered to Washington the following Thursday and he left without ever having seen the inside of a building at Governor's Island. He was ordered to the Pentagon, where he was assigned to active duty in Army Intelligence and promoted to major.

Of the nine men left from the patrol that had won Raymond

the Medal of Honor only two had nightmares with the same awful context. They were separated by many thousands of miles and neither knew the other was suffering through the same nightmares, scene for scene, face for face, and shock for shock. The details of the nightmares and the rhythm of their recurrence were harrowing. Each man dreamed he was seated in a long line with the other men of the patrol on a stage behind Sergeant Shaw and an old Chinese, facing an audience of Soviet and Chinese officials and officers, and that they smiled and enjoyed themselves in a composed and gentling way, while Shaw strangled Ed Mavole then shot Bobby Lembeck through the head. A variation of that dream was the drill-session dream where they faced a blackboard while drillmasters took them through an imaginary battle action until they had memorized all details assigned to them. The incomprehensible part of the nightmare was that the details of the battle action they were taught exactly matched the battle action that had won Shaw the Medal of Honor. There was more.

One of these men had no course but to try to forget the nightmares as soon as they happened. The other man had no course but to try to remember the dreams while he was awake, because that was the kind of work he did, no other reason. Marco had been trained into wasteless usage of his highly developed memory. The first nightmare had come to him in bed with Miss Dover and Mrs. Diamentez. It had frightened him as he had never been frightened before. He had sat in that bathtub filled with cold water until daybreak and if the humorous, noisy women had not been there he would not have been able to face Raymond that morning. The dreams started again with regularity after he got to Washington. When he dreamed the same terrifying dream every night for nine nights, and began to develop hand tremors at his work, it grew into an obsession with him which he could not share with anyone else. The Soviet uniforms haunted him. Watching his friend kill two of his men in front of all of them every night, causing himself to become part of the Technicolor print of the action, complete and edited, was like an attack upon his sanity. He could not tell anyone else about it until he felt he might understand any part of it, so that people would have some reason to listen to him. Marco began to live with the incubus, inside of it when he was awake; it appeared inside of him when he was asleep. He would fight his way out, knowing he would be returned to it later because he could not stay out of sleep; and he made detailed written records of the section of the nightmare he had just left behind, and which waited to threaten him again. He gave up women because what happened to him while he slept frightened them, and he was fearful that he would talk or shout and that the word would go out that he was slightly shock simple. He must have been getting a little strange to give up women. Women were food to Marco, and drink and exciting music. The written notes grew voluminous and after a while he transferred them all to a large loose-leaf notebook. They said things such as: Where did the interpreter, Chunjin, get a cigar? Why was he allowed to sit as an equal in a chair beside a Soviet general? Marco began to keep careful score as to how many times such things appeared in the dreams. What is that blackboard? he would note. Three different colors of chalk. Why do the Chinese know in advance and in such detail about an action which will wipe out one full Chinese infantry company? Why are the men of the patrol being worked so hard to remember so many details and different sets of details? His conflict between the love and admiration and respect for Raymond, which Yen Lo had planted in his mind, and his detailed, precise notes on exactly how Raymond had strangled Mavole and shot Lembeck had him beginning to live in dread and horror that everything which he still believed was happening in his imagination might somehow, someday, be proved to have happened in life. Marco had no thought that these things had ever happened. The notes were to keep him from unhinging, to provide the tools of his daily work to hold down his sanity. The dreams settled down to an occurrence of about three times a week in 1955, then began to step up inexorably in their appearances in 1956 until Marco was stumbling through his days on just about three hours' sleep each night. He never knew, all during that time, that he had remained sane.

IN JULY, 1956, at about nine-twenty on a hot night for most New Yorkers, Raymond was reasonably cool as he sat before his opened French windows just inside the small balcony that was cleared by a strong breeze which had bowled down the

Hudson River Valley. He was reading Le Compte and Sundeen's *Unified French Course,* because he had decided he would like to work directly from the notes of Brillat-Savarin and Escoffier during his recreational cooking periods, a new interest that had come to him since the many pleasant evenings when he had assisted so many expert young women in making so many different kinds of spaghetti sauce.

The telephone, on the desk beside his chair, rang. He picked it up.

"Raymond Shaw, please." It was a pleasant male voice with an indefinite accent.

"This is he."

"Why don't you pass the time by playing a little solitaire?"

"Yes, sir." Raymond disconnected. He burrowed through the desk drawers until he found playing cards. He shuffled the cards carefully and began to play. The queen of diamonds did not show up until the third layout. The telephone rang again forty minutes later as Raymond was smoking and watching the queen on top of the squared deck.

"Raymond?"

"Yes, sir?"

"Can you see the red queen?"

"Yes, sir."

"Do you carry an accident insurance policy?"

"No, sir."

"Then tomorrow you will apply through the insurance department of your newspaper. Take all the standard benefits on a replacement income of two hundred dollars per week for total disability for as long as you have to be away from your job. Also take hospital insurance."

"The paper carries that for me, sir."

"Good. One week from next Saturday, on the fourteenth of July, you will report at eleven-ten A.M. to the Timothy Swardon Sanitarium at 84 East Sixty-first Street. We want you here for a check-up. Is it clear?"

"Yes, sir."

"Very good. Good night, Raymond."

"Good night, sir." The connection was discontinued. Raymond went back to Le Compte and Sundeen. He drank a bottle of Coca-Cola. He went to bed at eleven o'clock after a sensible shower, and slept dreamlessly. He breakfasted on figs and coffee, arrived at his desk at nine-forty-five, and called the personnel department immediately and made the arrangements for the insurance, naming in the life clause, his only friend, Ben Marco, as beneficiary of fifty thousand dollars if his death occurred by accident or by violence.

SENATOR Iselin's office forwarded a personal letter addressed to Raymond, care of the senator, to the newspaper office in New York. It was postmarked Wainwright, Alaska. Raymond opened it warily and read:

Dear Sarge:

I had to say this or write this to somebody because I think I am going nuts. I mean I have to say it or write it to somebody who knows what I'm talking about not just anybody and you was my best friend in the army so here goes. Sarge I am in trouble. I'm afraid to go to sleep because I have terrible dreams. I don't know about you but with me dreams sometimes have sounds and colors and these dreams have a way everything gets all speeded up and it can scare you. I guess you must be wondering about me going chicken like this. The dream keeps coming back to me every time I try to get to sleep. I dream about all the guys on the patrol where you won the Medal for saving us and the dream has a lot of Chinese people in it and a lot of big brass from the Russian army. Well, it is pretty rough. You have to take my word for that. There is a lot of all kind of things goes on in that dream and I need to tell about it. If you should hear from anybody else on the Patrol who writes you that they are having this kind of a dream I will appreciate if you put them in touch with me. I live in Alaska now and the address is on the envelope. I have a good plumbing business going for me here and I'll be in good shape if these dreams don't take too much of the old zing out of me. Well, sarge, I hope everything goes good with you and that if you're ever around Wainwright, Alaska, you'll give me a holler. Good luck, kid.

Your old corporal,
Alan Melvin

Raymond had himself reread one part of the letter and he stared at that with distaste and disbelief. It offended him so that he read it and read it again: "you was my best friend in the army." He tore the letter across, then in quarters, then again. When he could no longer tear it smaller, he dropped the pieces into the wastebasket beside his desk.

VIII

FOR THREE YEARS after taking the oath of office as United States Senator in March, 1953, Johnny had been moved slowly by Raymond's mother to insure acceptance within the Senate and in official Washington, to learn to know all of the press gentlemen well, to arrange the effective timing for the start of his run for re-election; in short, to master the terrain. It seems almost impossible now to credit the fact that, halfway through his first time in office, Johnny Iselin was still one of the least-known members of the Senate. It was not until April, 1956, that Raymond's mother decided to try out the first substantial issue.

On the morning of April 9, Johnny showed up at the press briefing room at the Pentagon to attend a regularly scheduled press conference of the Secretary of Defense. He walked into the conference with two friends who represented Chicago and Atlanta papers respectively. They had had coffee first. Johnny had asked them elaborately what they were up to that morning. They told him they were due at the Secretary's regular weekly press conference at eleven o'clock. Johnny said wistfully that he had never seen a really big press conference in action. He was such an obscure, diffident, pleasant, whisky-tinted little senator that one of them good-naturedly invited him to come along and thereby unwittingly won himself a $250 prize bonus, three weeks later, from his newspaper.

Johnny was so lightly regarded at that time, although extremely well known to all the regulars covering the Washington beat, that if he was noticed at all, no one seemed to think it a bit unusual that he should be there. However, immediately after the press conference writers who had not been within five hundred miles of Washington that morning claimed to have been standing beside Johnny when he made his famous accusation. Editorialists, quarterly-magazine contributors, correspondents for foreign dailies, and all other trend tenders used up a lot of time and wood pulp and, collectively, earned a lot of money writing about that extraordinary morning when a senator chose to cry out his anguish and protest at a press conference held by the Secretary of Defense.

The meeting, held in an intimate amphitheater that had strong lights for the newsreel and television cameras, and many seats for correspondents, opened in the expected manner as the Secretary, a white-haired, florid, terrible-tempered man, strode on stage to the lectern flanked by his press secretaries and read his prepared statement concerned with that week's official view of integration of the nation's military and naval and air forces into one loyal unit. When he had finished he inquired into the microphones with sullen suspicion whether there were any questions. There were the usual number of responses from those outlets instructed to bait the Secretary, as was done in solemn rotation, to see if he could be goaded into one of his outrageous quotes that were so contemptuous of the people as to not only sell many more newspapers but to give all of the arid columnists of think pieces something significant to write about. The Secretary did not rise to the bait. As the questions came in more slowly he began to shuffle his feet and shift his weight. He coughed and was making ready to escape when a loud voice, tremulous with moral indignation but brave with its recognition of duty, rang out from the center of the briefing room.

"I have a question, Mr. Secretary."

The Secretary peered forward with some irritation at this stranger who had seen fit to take his own slow time about getting to his stupid question. "Who are you, sir?" he said sharply, for he had been trained into politeness to the press by a patient team of wild horses and by many past dislocations, which had been extremely painful, resulting from getting his foot caught in his mouth.

"I am United States Senator John Yerkes Iselin, sir!" the voice rang out, "and I have a question so serious that the safety of our nation may depend upon your answer." Johnny made sure to shout very slowly so that, before he had finished, every newspaperman in the room had located him and was staring at him with that expectant lust for sensation which was their common emotion.

"Who?" the Secretary asked incredulously, his voice electronically amplified, making it sound like the mating call of a giant owl.

"No evasions, Mr. Secretary," Johnny yelled. "No evasions, if you please."

The Secretary owned a tyrant's temper and he had been one of the most royal of big business dynasts before he had become a statesman. "Evasions?" he roared. "What the hell are you talking about? What kind of foolishness is this?" That sentence alone, those few words all by themselves, served to alienate the establishment called the United States Senate from sympathy with his cause for the rest of his tenure in office for, no matter what the provocation, it is the first unwritten law of the United States of America that one must never, never, never speak to a senator, regardless of his committee status, in such a manner before the press.

The members of the press present, who now recognized Johnny in his official status, grew lightheaded over the implications of this head-on encounter of two potentially great sellers of newspapers, magazines, and radio and television time. It was one of those pulsing moments auguring an enormous upward surge in profits, when one-half of the jaded-turned-thrilled stamped out their cigarettes and the other half lighted up theirs; all staring greedily.

"I said I am United States Senator John Yerkes Iselin and I hold here in my hand a list of two hundred and seven persons who are known to the Secretary of Defense as being members of the Communist party and who, nevertheless, are still working and shaping the policy of the Defense Department."

"Whaaaaat?" The Secretary had to shout out his astonishment into the microphones to be heard over the excited keening and rumbling of the voices in the room.

"I demand an answer, Mr. Secretary!" Johnny cried, waving a clutch of papers high over his head, his voice a silver trumpet of righteousness.

The Secretary had turned from beet-red to magenta. He was breathing with difficulty. He gripped the lectern before him as though he might decide to throw it at Johnny. "If you have such a list, Senator, goddamit," he bellowed, "bring it up here. Give me that list!"

"There will be no covering up, Mr. Secretary. You will not put your hands on this list. I regret deeply to say in front of all of these men and women that you no longer have my confidence."

"Whaaaaat?"

"This is no longer a matter for investigation by the Department of Defense. I am afraid you have had your chance, sir. It has become the responsibility of the United States Senate." Johnny turned and strode from the room, leaving chaos behind him.

On the following day, consistent with a booking made weeks previously and involving a token "expenses" payment of $250, Johnny was to appear on Defenders of Our Liberty, a television program that was a showcase for the more conservative members of the government; an interview show on which questions of a nonstraightforward nature were asked before a national audience representing one of the lowest ratings of any program in the history of the medium, the program remaining on the air only because the sponsoring company found it generally useful and, of course, pleasant to be able to dine with the important weekly guests, following each show, when a special vice-president would make firm friends with them to continue the discussions of government problems and problems with government of a more or less specific nature over the years to come.

Johnny had been invited to appear on the show because he was one of the two senators remaining in office whom the company's special vice-president had never had to dinner, and the special vice-president was not one to underestimate.

However, on the day of his scheduled appearance, Johnny was the hottest statesman in the country as a result of thirty hours of continuous coverage and he had become an object of great importance to the television show and to its network. Wherever they could, in the extremely short time they had in which to turn around, they bought half-page advertisements in big city newspapers to herald Johnny's live appearance on the show.

Raymond's mother let everything develop in a normal manner, up to a point. Johnny was due to go on the air at seven-thirty P.M. At one P.M. she told them regretfully that he would not be available, that he was too busy preparing what would be the most important investigation the Senate had ever held. The network reeled at this news. The sponsor reeled. The press prepared to reel. After only the least perceptible stagger the special vice-president asked that a meeting between Raymond's mother and himself be quickly and quietly arranged. Raymond's mother preferred to hold this kind of a meeting in a moving car, far away from recording devices. She drove herself, and the two of them rode around the city of Washington and hammered out an agreement that guaranteed Johnny "not less than six nor more than twelve" appearances on Defenders of Our Liberty each year for two years at the rate of $7500 worth of common stock of the sponsoring company per appearance, and for which Johnny would supply the additional consideration of "staying in the news" in such a manner as could be reviewed after every three shows by the special vice-president and Raymond's mother jointly, to the point where the contract could be canceled or extended, by mutual consent.

Therefore, Johnny was most certainly on hand to face the fearless panel of five newspapermen before the television cameras at seven-thirty that evening. The developments and charges of the previous day were laid on all over again, with one substantial difference concerning the actual number of Communists in the Defense Department. What follows is an excerpt from the record of the telecast:

SEN. ISELIN: Yesterday morning I—uh—discussed the—uh —Communists high up in the—uh—Defense Department. I stated that I had names of— uh—fifty-eight card-carrying members of the Communist party. Now—uh—I say this. They must be driven out! They must be dragged out into the open from under the protection of the Defense Department!

JAMES F. RYAN   But you do have the names of fifty-eight actual (*Stamford Bee*)   card-carrying members—absolute Communists —who direct the policy of the Department of Defense—actual card-carrying Communists?

SEN. ISELIN: I do—uh—Jim. Yes.

JAMES F. RYAN   Well, I am just a common man who's got a family and daughters and a job. You mean to say there are fifty-eight actual card-carrying

	Communists in our Defense Department that direct or control our Department of Defense policy or help direct it?
SEN. ISELIN:	Well—uh—Jim, I don't want to give you or—uh—the rest of the American people the reassurance that there are only fifty-eight Communists high—uh—in the Defense Department. I say I have the names of only fifty-eight.
JAMES F. RYAN	It is my duty to ask this question and face the consequences of asking it later. Is the Secretary of Defense one of the names on that list?
SEN. ISELIN:	I refuse to answer that question at this time—uh—Jim. And I am sure you know what I mean.

THE PROGRAM was interrupted for the closing commercial right at that point, and it was an enormous success. As Raymond's mother told Johnny from the very beginning, it wasn't the issue itself so much as the way he could sell it. "Lover, you are marvelous, that's all. Just absolutely goddam marvelous," she told him after the television show. "The way you punched up that stale old material, why, I swear to God, I was beginning to feel real deep indignation myself." She did not bother him with the confusion that had immediately arisen over the differences in figures she had given him on the two days. She was more than satisfied that the ruse had had people arguing all over the country about how many Communists there were in the Defense Department rather than whether there were any there at all, and it didn't interest Johnny anyway whether the true figure was two hundred and seven or fifty-eight, until the day she handed him the speech he was to read on the floor of the Senate on April 18. In that speech Johnny said there were eighty-two employees of the Defense Department who ranged from "persons whom I consider to be Communists" down to individuals who were "bad risks." On April 25, Raymond's mother reduced this figure at a press conference that had been called by the press of the nation itself, and not by Johnny's team, at which Johnny announced that he would "stand or fall" on his ability to prove that there was not just *one* Communist in the Department of Defense but one who was "the top espionage agent of an inimical foreign power within the borders of the United States of America."

Johnny had taken a riding in the Senate cloak room after he had changed the figures for the second time, in the Senate speech, and he was as sore as a pup at having been made to look silly in front of his pals. When Raymond's mother told him he was to drop the figure to one Communist, to one Communist from two hundred and seven in less than a month, he rebelled bitterly.

"What the hell do you keep changing the Communist figures for, all the time?" he asked hotly just before the press conference was to open. "It makes me look like a goddam fool."

"You'll be a goddam fool if you don't go in there and do as you're told. Who the hell are they writing about all over this goddam country, for crissake?" Raymond's mother asked. "Are you going to come on like a goddam expert, all of a sudden, like you knew what the hell you were talking about, all of a sudden?"

"Now, come on, hon. I was only—"

"Shuddup! You hear? Now get the hell out there!" she snapped at him—so Senator Iselin had to face a battery of microphones, cameras, and questions, as big as ever had been assembled for any President of the United States, to say: "I am willing to stand or fall on this one. If I am wrong on this one I think the subcommittee would be justified in not taking any other cases I ever brought up too seriously."

If the scorecard of working Communists in the Defense Department seems either tricky or confusing, it is because Raymond's mother chose to make the numbers difficult to follow from day to day, week to week, and month to month, during that launching period when his sensational allegations were winning Johnny headlines throughout the world for two reasons. First, it was consistent with one of Raymond's mother's basic verities, that thinking made Americans' heads hurt and therefore was to be avoided. Second, the figures were based upon a document that a Secretary of Defense had written some six years before to the Chairman of a House committee, pointing out that, at the end of World War II, 12,798 government employees who had worked for emergency war agencies had been temporarily transferred to the Defense Department, then that group had been reduced to 4,000 and "a recommendation against permanent em-

ployment had been made in 286 cases. Of these, 79 had actually
been removed from the service." Raymond's mother's subtraction
of 79 cases from 286 cases left 207 cases, the number with which
she had had Johnny kick off. She had made one other small
change. The Secretary's actual language had been "recommendation against permanent employment," which she had changed to
read: "members of the Communist party," which Johnny had
adjusted to read: "card-carrying Communists."

Sometimes it tended to get a little too confusing until Johnny
came at last to refer to it as "the numbers game." On one edgy
day when Johnny had been drinking a little before he went on
the Senate floor to speak, things got rather out of hand when he
began to switch the figures around within the one speech, reported in the *Congressional Record* for April 10, in which he
spoke of such varying estimates as: "a very sizable group of
active Communists in the Defense Department," then referred to
"vast numbers of Communists in the Defense Department." He
recalled the figure of two hundred and seven, then went on to
say, almost immediately following: "I do not believe I mentioned
the figure two hundred and seven at the Secretary's press conference; I believe I announced it was over two hundred." He there-
upon hastened to claim that "I have in my possession the names
of fifty-seven Communists who are in the Defense Department
at present," then changed that count at once by saying, "I know
absolutely of one group of approximately three hundred Communists certified to the Secretary of Defense in a private communication who have since been discharged because of communism," and then at last, sweating like a badly conditioned wres-
tler, he sat down, having thoroughly confused himself.

He knew he was going to catch hell when he got home that
night, and he did. She turned on him so savagely that in an effort
to defend himself and to keep her from striking him with a blunt
object he demanded that they agree to stay with one goddam
figure he could remember. Raymond's mother realized then that
she had been taxing him and making his head hurt so she settled
on fifty-seven, not only because Johnny would be able to remember it but because all of the jerks could remember it, too, as
it could be linked so easily with the fifty-seven varieties of
canned food that had been advertised so well and so steadily for
so many years.

Within three months Johnny bought Raymond's mother a case

of gin for making him the "most famous man in the United States," and he was doing just as well all over the world. The whole thing was so successful that within five months after his first charges a Senate committee undertook a special investigation of Johnny, a public investigation that produced over three million words of testimony, of which Johnny claimed, later on, to have produced a million of those words himself.

Some important individuals refused to tolerate Johnny and said so publicly, and other bodies of elected public servants seemed to disagree with him, but when they came up to it, in the end, they equivocated because by that time Johnny had generated an extraordinary amount of fear, which he beamed directly into the eyes of all who came close to him.

IX

A SHORT MAN WITH dark hair and skin, blue eyes, and blond eyebrows called for Raymond at his apartment at ten-seventeen the morning of July fourteenth, 1956, the day after the investigating committee had published their report on Johnny, and a hot Saturday morning it was. The man's name was Zilkov. He was Director of the KGB, or Committee of State Security, for the region of the United States of America east of the Mississippi River. The MVD, or Ministry of Internal Affairs, is much larger. The MVD had very wide powers and functions but they hold to a jurisdiction of a somewhat more public nature *inside* the Soviet Union. The KGB, however, is the *secret* police. Its director has ministerial rank today and is a much more feared personality than Gomel, the present MVD head. Zilkov was proud of the power he represented.

Raymond opened in response to the door bell, and stared coldly at the strange man. They disliked each other instantly, which was nothing against Zilkov because Raymond disliked almost everyone instantly.

"Yes?" Raymond drawled obnoxiously.

"My name is Zilkov, Mr. Shaw. As you were advised by telephone this morning, I have come to drive you to the Swardon Sanitarium."

"You are late," Raymond told him and turned his back to walk toward his baggage, leaving the man to decide whether he would enter or wait in the corridor.

"I am exactly two minutes late," the short man snapped.

"That *is* late, isn't it? An appointment is an oral contract. If we should happen to have any other business in the future, try to remember that."

"Why do you have three bags? How many bags do you think you will need in the hospital?"

"Have I asked you to help me with the bags?"

"That is not the point. An accident case is not admitted to a hospital with three pieces of baggage. At the most you may bring some necessaries in an attaché case."

"An attaché case."

"You do know what that is?"

"Of course I know what that is."

"Do you have one?"

"One? I have three!"

"Please to place your necessaries into one of your three attaché cases and we will go."

"No."

"No?"

"I will get there myself. I was told absolutely nothing about having to pack only the bare necessities into a leather envelope. I was told absolutely nothing about having to have to cope with a minor functionary of an obscure little hospital. That will be all. Return to your work. I will handle this myself." Raymond began to close the door in Zilkov's face.

"Wait!"

"Wait nothing. Get your foot out of the door, you boor. Out! Out!"

"You cannot!" The short man threw his weight against the door, but Raymond's greater weight and superior strength gradually slid the security chieftain backward. "Stop! Stop!" Zilkov cried.

"Out!" said Raymond inexorably.

"No! Please! Shaw, listen to me! Why don't you pass the time by playing a little solitaire?"

Raymond stopped pushing. Zilkov slipped into the apartment and shut the door behind him.

THE TIMOTHY Swardon Sanitarium had been a monument to personal philanthropy. Mr. Swardon, dead for eleven years, had been a wealthy alcoholic whose two daughters had been caught up in the narcotics habit. He had founded the superb private hospital mostly for himself and his family, but also for the benefit of other drunks and junkies who were friends of the family, or friends of friends. Through the spontaneity of this ever widening circle, the establishment had come to the attention of Giorgi Berezovo's organization men who protected Soviet security on the eastern seaboard of the United States, and eventually two full floors of the seven-floor hospital were taken over entirely for security use; the entire establishment having been bought at a real bargain from the youngest daughter who had still not been able to kick the cocaine habit, regardless of the advantages her father had showered on her medically. Under the new management, the little haven was in its second successful year of operation as one of the few money-making operations maintained by the Soviets, thanks to the many patients still loyal to the Swardon family.

Raymond had not actually been hit by a hit-and-run driver, but the many hospital and insurance and police forms served to legitimatize his stay, or the visits of others who, from time to time, found it necessary to go to Swardon for check-ups. Raymond had taken a taxi to the hospital and had checked in as he would have into a hotel, and within a half-hour two Soviet nurses had him in bed on the sealed fifth floor. His right leg was put into a plaster cast, then in traction, and his head was bandaged. He had been put into unconsciousness by voice signal while this was being done and the memory of the morning's events was erased. The office staff at the hospital had notified the police and a squad car came by immediately to interview the cab driver who had brought Raymond in after seeing him hit by a green station wagon with Connecticut plates. Fortunately, three other witnesses corroborated the account: two women who lived in the neighborhood and a young lawyer from Bayshore, Long

Island. The personnel manager at *The Daily Press* was notified to activate both the hospital and accident policies indicated by the identification cards found in Raymond's wallet. The technicians assembled the X-rays which proved Raymond to have suffered a brain concussion and ripped calf muscles. *The Daily Press* published a short account of the accident on its back page. This was how Major Marco learned about it, and how Raymond's mother and Johnny got the news.

Raymond's boss, Holborn Gaines, dropped everything (a beer bottle and a report from the Manila office) and rushed to the hospital to see if there was anything he could do to help. The desk attendant, a Soviet Army lieutenant, upon studying his credentials and checking them against a list of Raymond's probable and therefore accredited visitors, sent him to the fifth floor just as though it were not a sealed floor. He was met at the elevator by a rugged army nurse who was wearing the traditional cap worn by graduates of the Mother Cabrini Hospital of Winsted, Connecticut, where she had never studied but which gave the establishment a certain amount of professional verisimilitude. Mr. Gaines was permitted to look in on Raymond, unconscious though he was, in traction and in presumed travail, and was told the running wheeze of the profession everywhere, that Raymond was doing as well as could be expected. Gaines left a bottle of Scotch for Raymond with the pretty young nurse (five feet tall, 173 pounds, mustache, warts). He also passed the word along that Raymond was to take it easy and not worry about anything, which the nurse was careful not to tell Raymond, in the event of possible prearranged code use. Technicians who worked directly under Yen Lo, albeit also possessing a political rating or classification, were flown in on embassy quota from the Pavlov Institute in the Ukraine. They went to work on Raymond between visiting hours, checking his conditioned apparatus from top to bottom. Five years had elapsed from the time the controls had first been installed at Tunghwa. All linkages were found perfect.

A courier took the detailed lab reports to the embassy in Washington; from there they were transmitted by diplomatic pouch to the project supervisors, who were ostensibly Gomel, Berezovo, and Yen Lo, but Berezovo had been deemed insufficiently worthy, following the disappointment that Lavrenti Beria had been to the Kremlin, and he was dead, and Yen Lo refused to look at the reports, saying with a mild smile that they could

not do otherwise than certify the excellence of Raymond's conditioned reflexive mechanism, so only Gomel pored over the reports. He was mightily pleased.

Following the transmittal of the reports overseas, Raymond
met his American operator who was to become his sole manager
from that moment on, and whom he would never remember as
having seen and whom he would never be able to recognize as
his operator no matter where or when they met, because it had
been designed that way. They were introduced, as it were, then
the American asked to be alone in the room with Raymond.
They conferred together for nearly two hours before Zilkov interrupted them. The two visitors in Raymond's room got into a
heated argument, with Raymond watching them like a tennis
spectator. Zilkov was a militant, bright young man. He maintained emphatically that Raymond must carry out a test assassination in order to complete the reflex check-out in a conclusive
manner. The American operator opposed the suggestion violently and pointed out that it was both surprising and shocking
that a security officer, with responsibility such as he held, would
seek to risk a mechanism as valuable as Raymond.

Raymond listened gravely, then turned his eyes to hear
Zilkov's rebuttal, which, of course, pointed out that the mechanism had been designed for assassination, that it had been five
years since it had been tested, that conditions offering minimum
risk for police reprisal could be designed, and that as far as he
was concerned the test must be made before he would sign any
certification that the mechanism was in perfect working order.
The American operator said, very well, if that was how Zilkov
felt about it then Raymond should be instructed to kill an employee of the hospital on one of the sealed floors. Zilkov said he
would order nothing of the sort, that the table of organization in
the area was under acceptable strength as it was, as far as he was
concerned, and that Raymond could damned well kill some non-
productive woman or child on the outside. The American operator said there was no reason for Raymond to kill anyone unpro-
ductive—that there might as well be some feeling of gain out of
this since Zilkov was insisting on the risk—and recommended
that Raymond's position at the newspaper and therefore his general value to the party might be considerably strengthened if he
were to kill his immediate superior, Holborn Gaines, as it was
possible that, after five years as Gaines's assistant, Raymond

would be given his job, which, in turn, would bring him wider influence within the inner chambers of the American government. Zilkov said he had no interest in whom Raymond assassinated so long as he worked efficiently and obediently. It was decided that Mr. Gaines should die two nights hence. Subsequently, the American operator complained bitterly through channels that Zilkov had been reckless and foolhardy with one of the Party's most valuable pieces of apparatus in the United States, and most entirely needlessly because Raymond had been checked out by Pavlov technicians. Unfortunately the complaint was not made in time to save Mr. Gaines, but within two weeks Zilkov was recalled and severely reprimanded. On his return to the United States, he could not have been more careful, both with Raymond and Raymond's operator, than if they had been his own department heads.

ON THE morning of the ninth day at Swardon, less than two days before he murdered Mr. Gaines, Raymond awoke as from a deep sleep, surprised to find himself in a strange bed and in traction, but even more shocked to find himself staring directly into, and on a level with, the grief-ravaged face of his mother. Raymond had never seen his mother's face as being anything but smoothly held, enforced, carefully supported, arranged, and used to help her get what she wanted as a Cadillac was used to get her where she wanted to go. The skin on his mother's face had always been flawless; the eyes were exquisitely placed and entirely clear, the whites unflecked by tiny blood vessels, merely *suggesting* malevolence and insane impatience. Her mouth had always been held well, in, as the mouths of city saddle horses, and the perfect blond hair had always framed all of this and had always softened it.

To open his eyes and find himself looking into a wracked caricature of that other vision made Raymond cry out, and made his mother aware that he was conscious. Her hair was ragged and awry. Her eyes were rabbit-red from weeping. Her cheeks shone with wet, washing away the cosmetic that always masked the wrinkles. Her mouth was twisted in ugly self-pity, while she sobbed noisily and blew her nose into too small a handkerchief.

She drew back instantly at his sound and attempted to compose her face, but it could not be done convincingly on such short order, and unconsciously she wanted to gain a credit for the feat she knew would be unbelievable to him: her tears because of him.

"Raymond, oh, my Raymond."

"Whassa matter?"

"Oh—"

"Is Johnny dead?"

"What?"

"What the hell is the matter with you?"

"I came here as soon as I could. I flew here the instant I was able to leave."

"Where? Pardon the cliché, but where am I?"

"The Swardon Sanitarium."

"The Swardon Sanitarium where?"

"New York. You were hit by a hit-and-run driver. Oh, I was so frightened. I came as soon as I could."

"When? How long have I been here?"

"Eight days. Nine days. I don't know."

"And you just got here?"

"Do you hate me, Raymond?"

"No, Mother."

"Do you love me?"

"Yes, Mother." He looked at her with genuine anxiety. Had she run out of arm sauce? Had she broken the armbanging machine? Or was she just a very clever impersonator sent over to play the mother while my true mummy tries to sober up the Great Statesman?

"My little boy. My darling, little boy." She went into a paroxysm of silent weeping, working her shoulders up and down in a horrible manner and shaking the chair she sat in. There was nothing faked about this, he knew. She must have hit some real trouble along the line. It simply could not possibly be that she was weeping over him being stretched out in a hospital. Mucus slid from the tiny handkerchief and rested on her left cheekbone. Raymond closed his eyes for a moment, but he would not tell her what had happened and felt a deep satisfaction that ultimately she would look in some mirror after she had left him and see this mess on her face.

"You are such a fraud, Mother. My God, I feel as well as I

have ever felt and I know that you have been all over this with whatever doctors there are out there on the telephone days ago, and now you're at the hospital because there is probably a sale at Bloomingdale's or you're having a few radio actors blacklisted and you make a production out of it like I was involved some-how in your life." His voice was bitter. His eyes were hard and dry.

"I have to be a fraud," she said, straightening her back and slipping several lengths of steel into her voice like whalebone into a corset. "And I have to be the truth, too. And a shield and the courage for all the men I have ever known, yourself in-cluded, excepting my father. There is so much fraud in this world and it needs to be turned away with fraud, the way steel is turned with steel and the way a soft answer does not turneth away wrath." She had emerged, dripping with acid, from her grief. Her face was a mass of ravaged colors and textures, her hair was like an old lamp shade fringe and that glob of mucus still rested on her left cheekbone disgustingly, but she was her-self again, and Raymond felt greatly relieved.

"How's Johnny?"

"Fine. He'd be here, but that committee just finished working him over—ah, wait until that one is up for re-election." She sniffed noisily. "So I told him he must stay there and stare them down. You have no use for him anyway so I don't know why you bother to ask for him unless you feel guilt about something."

"I do feel guilt about something."

"About what?" She leaned forward slightly because informa-tion is the prime increment of power.

"About Jocie."

"Who's Jocie?"

"Jocie Jordan. The senator's daughter."

"Oh. Yes. Why do you feel guilt?" his mother asked.

"Why? Because she thinks I deserted her."

"Raymond! Why do you dramatize everything so? You were babies!"

"I thought that since we're having our first meeting since I got the medal, since I got back from Korea, and I was in Korea for two years, I thought since you've been pretending to be two other people—you know, honest and maternal and wistfully remorseful about how we had let our lives go along—coldly and separately—and I thought that before we got any more honest and hated ourselves in the morning, that we might just pay Jocie the respect of asking for her—you know, mentioning her name in passing the way they do about the dead?" His voice was choked. His eyes were not dry.

As though he had reminded her of what had triggered her in the first place, she began unexpectedly to weep. The lemon sunlight was reflected from the bright white blank wall outside the window at her back and it lingered like St. Elmo's fire around the ridiculously small green hat she was wearing, a suspicion of a hat that had been assembled for seventy dollars by an aesthetic leader for whom millinery signified the foundation stone of culture.

"What is the *matter* with you, Mother?"

She sobbed.

"You aren't crying about *me*?"

She sobbed and nodded.

"But, I'm all *right*. I don't have a pain or an *ache*. I am absolutely *fine*."

"Oh, Raymond, what can I say to you? There has been so much to get done. We have so far to go. Johnny is going to lead the people of our country to the heights of their history. But I have to lead Johnny. Raymond. You know that. I know you know that. I have given my life and many, many significant things for all of this. My life. Simply that and I can see that if I were to ransack my strength—remembered strength or future strength—I could not give more to this holy crusade than I have given. Now I have come face to face with my life where it has failed to cross your own. I can't tell you how a mother feels about that, because you wouldn't understand. It made me weep for a little bit. That's all. What's that? Anybody and everybody recovers from tears, but I'm not sad and I don't have regrets because I know that what I did and what I do is for the greatest possible good for all of us." Raymond watched her, then made the small despising gesture with his right hand, brushing her world out of his way as it came too close to him.

"I don't understand one word of what you are saying," he told her.

"I am saying this. Some terrible, terrible changes are going to come to this country."

He flicked at the air with his hand violently, unaware of the movement, and he closed his eyes.

"This country is going to go through a fire like it has never seen," she said in a low and earnest voice. "And I know what I am saying because the signs are there to read and I understand politics, which is the art of reading them. Time is going to roar and flash lightning in the streets, Raymond. Blood will gush behind the noise and stones will fall and fools and mockers will be brought down. The smugness and complacency of this country will be dragged through the blood and the noise in the streets until it becomes a country purged and purified back to original purity, which it once possessed so long ago when the founding fathers of this republic—the blessed, blessed fathers—brought it into life. And when that day comes—and we have been cleansed of the slime of oblivion and saved from the wasteful, wrong, sinful, criminal, selfish, rottenness which Johnny, and only Johnny is going to save us from, you will kneel beside me and thank me and kiss my hands and my skirt and give only me your love as will the rest of the great people of this confused and blinded land."

He put his hand over hers on the bed, then lifted it to his lips. Suddenly, he felt himself being made soft with pity for both of them. He could not comprehend that his mother had any feelings, and it shocked him deeply.

Two days later, immediately after Raymond ate dinner in the room at Sardon with his leg still in a cast, Zilkov and the American operator came to the room with a package of playing cards and subsequently gave him detailed instructions as to how he was to kill Holborn Gaines. The time they set was three forty-five the following morning. Gaines lived in an apartment house, alone. The house maintained a self-service elevator after one A.M. when the night man went off duty. There was no doorman. Zilkov had had a key made to fit the front door of the building and to Mr. Gaines's apartment, which was one of four on the ninth floor. The security man went over the pencil-sketched, then photostatted floor plan of Gaines's small unit of three rooms and a bath, indicating where the bedroom was and suggesting that Raymond strangle him, as it was the quietest and least complicated method and, considering the close quarters in which he would have to work, the neatest. He added that Raymond must accept it as a rule, then and forever, that in the event that anyone, repeat anyone, ever discovered him on the scene of the assignment, this other person or persons must be killed. Was that clear? Zilkov may have reconsidered the risk he had decided to have Raymond run, for, to make sure this condition was understood, he asked the American operator to repeat the admonition.

As it worked out, Mr. Gaines was alone but he was not asleep as he should have been to save Raymond considerable embarrassment. He was reading in bed, a four-poster feather bed, with nine soft pillows all around behind him and a shocking-pink maribou bed jacket around his shoulders; chuckling over a few pounds of confidential reports from bureau chiefs in Washington, Rome, London, Madrid, and Moscow. The windows were closed tight and, as in the office at all times, an electric heater was beaming up at him from the floor nearby: in July.

As Raymond opened the door to the apartment he knocked over the tall paper screen that Mr. Gaines kept in front of the opened door in the summer time. As it fell it dislodged a picture hanging on the wall; it hit the floor with a crash. There could be no doubt that someone had come to call, and Raymond cursed himself as a blunderer because he knew well that Mr. Gaines would be tart about the visit, in any event.

"What the hell is that?" Mr. Gaines yelled shrilly.

Raymond flushed with embarrassment. It was an entirely new feeling for him and Mr. Gaines was the only living person who could have made him feel that way, because Mr. Gaines made him feel helpless, gawky, and grateful all at the same time. "It's me, Mr. Gaines," he said. "Raymond."

"Raymond? Raymond?" Mr. Gaines was bewildered. "My assistant? Raymond Shaw?"

Raymond appeared in the bedroom doorway at that moment. He was wearing a neat black suit, a dark gray shirt, a black tie, and black gloves. "Yes, sir," he said. "I—I'm sorry to disturb you, Mr. Gaines."

Mr. Gaines fingered the maribou bed jacket. "Don't get any ideas about this silly-looking bed jacket," he said irritably. "It was my wife's. It's the warmest thing I have. Perfect for reading in bed at night."

"I didn't know you were married, Mr. Gaines."

"She died nearly six years ago," Mr. Gaines said gruffly, then he remembered. "But—but, what the hell are you doing here at—" Mr. Gaines looked over at the alarm clock on the night table. "At ten minutes to four in the morning."

"Well—I—uh—"

"My God, Raymond, don't tell me you've come here to talk something over? I mean, surely you aren't going to pour out your heart with the details of some sordid love affair or anything like that?"

"No, sir, you see—"

"Raymond, if you feel you must resign for any reason—a circumstance which I would regret, of course—surely you could leave a little note on my desk in the morning. I hate chattering like this! I thought I had explained to you that I loathe having to talk to people, Raymond."

"Yes, sir. I'm sorry, Mr. Gaines."

Mr. Gaines suddenly seemed to remember something significant. He lifted his left hand and pointed vaguely toward the door, looking, because of the fluffy feathers all around his white hair, something like the ancient Mrs. Santa R. Claus. "How did you get in here? When I close that door, it locks."

"They gave me a key."

"Who did?"

"The people at the hospital."

"What hospital? But—why? Why did they give you a key?"

Raymond had been moving slowly around the bed. At last he stood at Mr. Gaines's side, looking down at him sunk into the feather bed. He felt sheepish.

"Raymond! Answer me, my boy! Why are you here?"

It was a relatively effortless job because Mr. Gaines, being such an old man, did not have much strength and Raymond, because of feelings of affection and gratitude for Mr. Gaines did everything he could, with his great strength, to terminate his friend's life as quickly as possible. He thought of extinguishing the bed light as he left, but turned it on again, remembering that he wouldn't be able to find his way out to the front door if he left the room in darkness.

He walked four blocks west before taking a cab north on Lexington Avenue; he left it three blocks away from Swardon. He entered the sanitarium through the basement door, off the back areaway, showing his pass to the Soviet Army corporal in

overalls who had taken him under the throat with the left forearm without speaking and held until Raymond tapped his third
finger twice, then showed the pass. When Raymond got to his
room the American operator was waiting for him.

"Still up?" Raymond said conversationally. "It's almost four-
thirty."

"I wanted to make sure you were all right," the operator said.
"Good night, Raymond. I'll send the nurses in to rig you up
again."

"Do I have to have those casts put on again?"

"Those casts must stay on until you are discharged. How do
you know who'll show up here as a visitor now that Mr. Gaines is
dead?" The operator left the room. The nurses had Raymond
undressed and bandaged in no time at all.

RAYMOND, as it turned out, did have two more visitors
before he left the hospital. Joe Downey, the managing editor of
The Daily Press, stopped by after Mr. Gaines's funeral and
offered Raymond the job of writing the column, which meant a
two-hundred-dollar-a-week raise in pay and a net saving of three
hundred dollars a week to the paper because, naturally, they
didn't figure to start Raymond at the figure Mr. Gaines had
finished at, and Mr. Gaines had been political columnist for the
paper for twenty-six years. They also offered Raymond fifty per
cent of the syndication money, a net increase of one hundred per
cent to the paper because under the prior arrangement Mr.
Gaines had kept it all, excepting the sales and distribution and
promotion percentage. To the paper's owners, Mr. Downey allowed that Raymond was new and had such an unpleasant personality that it was better than five to one that no one would
ever get around to telling him that he rated all the syndication
money. It was fair. The reports from the bureau chiefs made up
most of the columns and the paper, not Raymond, had to pay the
bureau chiefs. Besides, one half of the syndication money came
to five hundred and six dollars per week, which lifted Raymond's
take-home pay by seven hundred and six dollars per week; Mr.
Downey estimated this as being a bargain because the paper
would have the only Medal of Honor columnist in the business,

which certainly should open the doors to information at the Pentagon, and he had that crazy stepfather who could scare people into talking to Raymond, and that mother who could get him in anywhere, even to share a double bed with the President if he felt like it, and he had had five solid years of learning his job from Holborn Gaines. Seven hundred and six dollars a week is a nice raise for a young fellow, particularly if he likes money.

Actually, the increased income took the edge off the promotion for Raymond but, the way he would handle it, he figured the money would be the bank's problem, not his.

Raymond was distraught over the murder. He had had great regard for the old man and a fondness that was unusual inasmuch as he felt fondness for only two other people in the world, Marco and Jocie, and Jocie should not be included in the category because the feeling for her was vastly different again. He just could not get it through his head that anyone would want to murder Mr. Gaines. He had been a kind and gentle and helpless old man, and how could anyone do such a thing? Mr. Downey expressed the police opinion that it must have been some mentally unstable political crank. "Holly was one of the oldest friends I had left," Mr. Downey said sadly, mourning for himself.

"Is the paper going to post a reward?"

Mr. Downey rubbed his chin. "Hm. I guess we should, at that. We certainly should. Can charge it to promotion if we ever have to pay it."

"I want to pledge five thousand dollars of that reward," Raymond said hotly.

"You don't need to do that, Raymond."

"Well, I want to, goddamit."

"Well, O.K. You pledge five and we'll pledge ten, although the board'll have to O.K. it of course, and I'll call Centre Street soon as I get back to the office so they can send out paper on it. By God, we'll pay for a general alarm, too. The dirty bastard." Downey was doubly upset because he hated to spend the paper's money and he knew damned well that Holly Gaines, wherever he was, wouldn't approve of a goddam, boy-scout, grandstand play like that, but, what the hell, there were certain things you pretended you had to do.

. . .

MARCO came in to see Raymond the same afternoon. "Jesus, you look like hell," Raymond said from under his head bandage and traction equipment. "What happened?"

Marco looked worse than that. The old sayings are the best, and Marco looked like death warmed over. "What do you mean, what happened?" he said. "I'm not in a hospital bed, am I?"

"I just mean I never saw you look so lousy."

"Well, thanks."

"What happened?"

Marco ran his hand across his face. "I can't sleep."

"Can't you get some pills?" Raymond said tentatively—having a narcotics addict for a mother, he had developed an aversion to drugs. Also, it was difficult for him to understand any kind of a sleeping problem, since he himself could have fallen asleep hanging by one ankle in a high wind.

"It's not so much that I can't sleep. It's more that I'd rather not sleep. I'm walking around punchy because I'm scared. I keep having the same nightmare." Raymond, lying flat on his back, made the flicking gesture with his right hand.

"Is it a nightmare about a Soviet general and a lot of Chinese and me and the guys who were on the patrol?" Marco came out of the chair like a tiger. He stood over Raymond, gripping the cloth of his pajama jacket in both fists, staring down at him with wild eyes. "How did you know that? How did you know that?" His voice went up and up like eccentric stairs in front of a hilltop summer beach house.

"*Take—your—hands—off—me.*" With that sentence Raymond's voice fell back into his horrid drawling manner; into his repulsive, inciting, objectionable voice that he used to keep the rest of the world on the other side of the moat surrounding the castle where he had always lain under the spell of the wicked witch. It was curdingly unfriendly, and so actively repellent that it drove Marco backward into the chair, which was a good thing because Marco had gone into a sick yellow-ivory color, his breathing was shallow, and his eyes shone with an ever so slight sheen of insanity as he had reached out to take the shape of his oppression into the muscles of his fingers and hands and punish it for what it had been doing to his dignity, which is man's own inner image of himself.

"I'm sorry, Raymond."

Raymond became Marco's friend again instantly, as though there had been no lapse.

"Please tell me how you knew about my nightmare, Raymond."

"Well, you see, I didn't really, I mean, it's just that Melvin—you know: Al Melvin, the corporal on the patrol—he wrote me a long letter about a week ago. I was naturally surprised to hear from him because—well—as you know, I was never much one for fraternizing, but he said in the letter that I was the only one he knew how to reach—he sent the letter to Johnny because everybody certainly knows how to reach him—because he had to tell somebody in the patrol about this nightmare or he was afraid he would lose his mind and—"

"Please tell me about the nightmare, Raymond."

"Well, he dreams that the patrol is all sitting together. He says he dreams about a lot of Soviet officers and some Chinese brass and us being on the patrol. What is such a nightmare about that?"

"Where's the letter? Do you have the letter?"

"Well, no. I mean, I never keep letters."

"Is that all he wrote? Is that all about the nightmare?"

"Yeah."

"It just stops right there?"

"I guess so."

"Man!"

"Is it like your nightmare?"

"Yeah. As a matter of fact, mine is a lot like that."

"You guys ought to get together."

"Right away. You don't know what this means to me. I just can't explain to you what this means to me, Raymond."

"Well, you can't see him right away, though, Ben. He lives in Wainwright, Alaska."

"Alaska? Alaska?"

"Yes."

"Jesus. Wainwright, Alaska. You have to be kidding!"

"No. I wish I was, Ben. I'm not. But, so what? What's the difference?"

"What's the difference? I told you I can't sleep. You told me I look like hell. Well, I feel like hell and I'm shaking all to pieces and I think sometimes I should kill myself because I'm afraid of

going insane, and then you tell me like you were talking about
the weather that another man who was on the patrol is having
the same delusions that I was afraid were driving me crazy, and
you tell me he lives in some place called Wainwright, Alaska,
where I can't sit down and talk to him and find out if he's
cracking up like I am and how we can help each other, and you
say what's the difference."

Marco began to laugh hysterically, then he put his face forward into his large hands and wept into them, squeezing tightly
at his cheekbones, his heavy shoulders moving grotesquely and
causing the four rows of his decorations to jump up and down.
He made such tearing sounds that the two Soviet Army nurses
on the floor came running in. After six or seven minutes of
Marco's reckless, unrelieved, and shocking sobbing, at which
Raymond stared helplessly, they hit him with a hypo to calm him
down and get him the hell out of there.

All in all, Raymond had had a most ironic hospital stay, what
with a visit from the wife of America's most gallant and noisy
anti-Communist to a hospital operated by the Soviet secret
police, what with a U.S. Army Intelligence officer breaking down
and embarrassing the staff of the same place, what with contributing five thousand dollars to a reward for his own capture, and
what with learning that two grown men were capable of behaving like children over a perfectly harmless, if repetitious,
dream.

X

JOHNNY HAD BECOME
chairman of the Committee on Federal Operations and chairman of its Permanent Subcommittee on Investigations, with
a budget of two hundred thousand dollars a year and an
inculcating staff of investigators. He grew sly, in the way
he worked that staff. He would sidle up to a fellow senator
or another member of the government placed as high and mention the name and habits of some young lady for whom the
senator might be paying the necessities, or perhaps an abortion
here, or a folly-of-youth police record there. It worked wonders.

He had only to drop this kind of talk upon five or six of them and at once they became his missionaries to intimidate others who might seek to block his ways in government.

There were a few groups and individuals who were able to find the courage to assail him. One of the most astute political analysts of the national scene wrote: "Iselinism has developed a process for compounding a lie, then squaring it, which is a modern miracle of dishonesty far exceeding the claims of filter cigarettes. Iselin's lies seem to have atomic motors within them, tiny reactors of such power and such complexity as to confound and baffle all with direct, and even slightly honest, turns of mind. He has bellowed out so many accusations about so many different people (and for all the public knows these names he brandishes may have been attached to people of entirely questionable existence) that no one can keep the records of these horrendous charges straight. Iselin is a man who shall forever stand guard at the door of the mind to protect the people of this great nation from facts."

The American Association of Scientists asked that this statement be published: "Senator Iselin puts the finishing touches on his sabotage of the morale of American scientists to the enormous net gain of those who work against the interests of the United States."

Johnny was doing great. From a semi-hangdog country governor, Raymond's mother said, utterly unknown outside domestic politics on a state level in 1956, he had transformed himself into a global figure in 1957. He had a lot going for him beyond Raymond's mother. His very looks: that meaty nose, the nearly total absence of forehead, the perpetual unshavenness, the piggish eyes, red from being dipped in bourbon, the sickeningly monotonous voice, whining and grating,—all of it together made Johnny one of the greatest demagogues in American history, even if, as Raymond's mother often said to friends, he was essentially a lighthearted and unserious one. Nonetheless, her Johnny had become the only American in the country's history of political villains, studding folk song and story, to inspire concomitant fear and hatred in foreigners, resident in their native countries. He blew his nose in the Constitution, he thumbed his nose at the party system or any other version of governmental chain of command. He personally charted the zigs and zags of American foreign policy at a time when the American policy was a monstrously heavy weight upon world history. To the people of Iceland, Peru, France, and Pitcairn Island the label of Iselinism stood for anything and everything that was dirty, backward, ignorant, repressive, offensive, anti-progressive, or rotten, and all of those adjectives must ultimately be seen as sincere tributes to any demagogue of any country on any planet.

After Raymond's mother had written the scriptures and set the tone of the sermons Johnny was to make along the line to glory, she left him bellowing and pointing his finger while she organized, for nearly fifteen months, the cells of the Iselin national organization she called the Loyal American Underground. This organization enrolled, during that first period of her work, two million three-hundred thousand members, all militantly for Johnny and what he stood for, and most deeply grateful for his wanting to "give our friends a place from which they may partake of a sense of history through adventure and real participation in the cause of fanatic good government, cleansed of the stain of communism."

Raymond's mother and her husband held their mighty political analysis and strategy-planning sessions at their place, which was out toward Georgetown. They would talk and drink bourbon and ginger ale and Johnny would fool around with his scrapbook. He always had it in his mind that cold winter nights would be the best time to paste up the bundles of clippings about his work into individual books, with the intent of someday providing the vast resources for a John Yerkes Iselin Memorial Library. The analyses of the day's or the week's battles were always informal and usually productive of really constructive action for the immediate future.

"Hon," Raymond's mother said, "aren't there times when you're up there at the committee table when you have to go to the john?"

"Of course. Whatta you think I'm made of—blotting paper or something?"

"Well, what do you do about it?"

"Do? I get up and I go."

"See? That's exactly what I mean. Now tomorrow when you have to go I want you to try it my way and see what happens. Will you?"

He grinned horribly. "Right up there in front of all those TV cameras?"

"Never mind. Tomorrow when you have to go I want you to throw yourself into a rage—making sure you are on camera—wait for a tight shot if you can—and bang on the desk and scream for the chairman and yell 'Point of order! Point of order!' Then stand up and say you will not put up with this farce and that you will not dignify it with your presence for one moment longer."

"Why do I do that?"

"You have to start making the right kind of exits for yourself, Johnny, so that the American people will know that you have left so they can sit nervously and wait for you to come back."

"Gee, hon. That's a hell of an idea. Oh, say, I like that idea!"

She threw him a kiss. "What an innocent you are," she said, smiling at him dotingly. "Sometimes I don't think you give a damn what you're talking about or who you're talking about."

"Well, why the hell should I?"

"You're right. Of course."

"You're damn right, I'm right. What the hell, hon, this is a business with me. Suppose we were lawyers, I often say to myself. I mean actual practicing lawyers. I'd be the trial lawyer working out in front, rigging the juries and feeding the stuff to the newspaper boys, and you'd be the brief man back in the law library who has the research job of writing up the case." He finished the highball in his hand and gave the empty glass to his wife. She got up to make him another drink and said, "Oh, I agree with that, honey, but just the same I wish you would try a little bit more to feel the sacredness of your own mission."

"The hell with that. What's with you tonight, baby? I'm like a doctor, in a way. Am I supposed to die with every patient I lose? Life's too short." He accepted the highball. "Thank you, honey."

"You're welcome, sweetheart."

"What is this stuff? Applejack?"

"Applejack? It's twelve-year-old bourbon."

"That's funny. It tastes like applejack."

"Maybe it's the ginger ale."

"The ginger ale? I always drink my bourbon with ginger ale. How could it taste like applejack because of the ginger ale. It never tasted like applejack before."

"I can't understand it," she said.

"Ah, what's the difference? I happen to like applejack."

"You're so sweet it isn't even funny."

"Not so sweet as you."

"Johnny, have you noticed that some of the newspaper idiots are getting a little nasty with their typewriters?"

"Don't pay any attention." He waved a careless hand. "It's a business with them just like our business. You start getting sensitive and you just confuse everybody. The boys who are assigned to cover me may call themselves the Goon Squad but I don't notice that any of them have ever asked to be transferred. It's a game with them. They spend their time trying to catch me in lies, then printing that I said a lie. They like me. They try to knife me but they like me. I try to knife them but we drink together and we're friends. What the hell, hon. All we're all trying to do is to get a day's work done. Take it from me, never get sensitive."

"Johnny, baby?"

"Yes, hon?"

"Do me a favor and tomorrow at the lunch break please make it a point to go into that Senate barbershop for a shave. You can stand two shaves a day. I swear to God sometimes I think you can grow a beard in twenty minutes. You look like a badger in a Disney cartoon on that TV screen."

"Don't worry about it, hon. I have my own ways and I look my own way, but I'm very goddam American and they all know it out there."

"Just the same, hon, will you promise to get a shave tomorrow at the lunch break?"

"Certainly. Why not? Gimme another drink. I got a big day coming up tomorrow."

JOHN Yerkes Iselin was re-elected to his second six-year term on November 4, 1958, by the biggest plurality in the history of elections in his state. Two hundred and thirty-six fist fights went unreported the following evening in the pubs, cafés, bodegas, cantinas, trattorias, and sundry brasseries of western Europe between the glum American residents and the outraged, consternated natives of the larger cities.

· · ·

EARLY one Monday morning in his office at *The Daily Press* (for he had taken to arriving at work at seven-thirty rather than at ten o'clock now that he was the department head, just as had Mr. Gaines before him) Raymond looked up and saw, with no little irritation at the interruption, the figure of Chunjin standing in the doorway. Raymond did not remember ever having seen him before. The man was slight and dark with alert, liquid eyes and a most intelligent expression; he stared with wistful hopefulness mixed with ascending regard, but these subtleties did not transport Raymond to remembering the man.

"Yes?" he drawled in his calculatedly horrid way.

"I am Chunjin, Mr. Shaw, sir. I was interpreter attached to Cholly Company, Fifty-second Regiment—"

Raymond pointed his outstretched finger right at Chunjin's nose. "You were interpreter for the patrol," he said.

"Yes, sir, Mr. Shaw."

Other men might have allowed their camaraderie to foam over in the warming glow of the good old days, but Raymond said, "What do you want?" Chunjin blinked.

"I mean to say, what are you doing here?" Raymond said, not backing away from his bluntness but attempting to cope with this apparent stupidity through clearer syntax.

"Your father did not say to you?"

"My *father*?"

"Senator Iselin? I write to—"

"Senator Iselin is *not* my father. Repeat. He is *not* my father. If you learn nothing else on your visit to this country memorize that fact."

"I write to Senator Iselin. I tell him how I interpret your outfit. I tell him I want to come to America. He get me visa. Now I need job."

"A job?"

"Yes, sir, Mr. Shaw."

"My dear fellow, we don't use interpreters here. We all speak the same language."

"I am tailor and mender. I am cook. I am driver of car. I am cleaner and scrubber. I fix anything. I take message. I sleep at house of my cousin and not eat much food. I ask for job with you because you are great man who save my life. I need for pay only ten dollars a week."

"Ten dollars? For all that?"

"Yes, sir, Mr. Shaw."

"Well, look here, Chunjin. I couldn't pay you only ten dollars a week."

"Yes, sir. Only ten dollars a week."

"I can use a valet. I would like having a cook, I think. A good cook, I mean. And I dislike washing dishes. I had been thinking about getting a car, but the parking thing sort of has me stopped. I go to Washington twice a week and there is no reason why I shouldn't have the money the airlines are getting from this newspaper for those trips and I'd rather not fly that crowded corridor anyway. I would prefer it if you didn't sleep in, as a matter of fact, but I'm sorry, ten dollars a week just isn't enough money." Raymond said that flatly, as though it were he who had applied for the job and was turning it down for good and sufficient reasons.

"I work for fifteen, sir."

"How can you live on fifteen dollars a week in New York?"

"I live with the cousins, sir."

"How much do the cousins earn?"

"I do not know, sir."

"Well, I'm sorry, Chunjin, but it is out of the question." Raymond who had still not greeted his old wartime buddy, turned away to return to his work. From his expression he had dismissed the conversation, and he was anxious to return to the bureau reports and to some very helpful information his mother had managed to send along to him.

"Is not good for you to pay less, Mr. Shaw?"

Raymond turned slowly, forcing his attention back to the Korean and realizing impatiently that he had not made it clear that the meeting was over. "Perhaps I should have clarified my position in the matter, as follows," Raymond said frostily. "It strikes me that there is something basically dishonest about an arrangement by which a man insists upon working for less money than he can possibly live on."

"You think I steal, Mr. Shaw?"

Raymond flushed. "I had not considered any specific category of such theoretical dishonesty."

"I live on two dollars a week in Mokpo. I think ten dollars many times better."

"How long have you been here?"

Chunjin looked at his watch. "Two hours."

"I mean, in New York."

"Two hours."

"All right. I will instruct the bank to pay you a salary of twenty-five dollars a week."

"Thank you, Mr. Shaw, sir."

"I will supply the uniforms."

"Yes, sir."

Raymond leaned over the desk and wrote the bank's address on a slip of paper, adding Mr. Rothenberg's name. "Go to this address. My bank. Ask for this man. I'll call him. He'll give you the key to my place and some instructions for stocking food. He'll tell you where to buy it. We don't use money. Please have dinner ready to serve at seven-fifteen next Monday. I'll be in Washington for the weekend, where I may be reached at the Willard Hotel. I am thinking in terms of roast veal—a boned rump of veal—with green beans, no potato—please, Chunjin, never serve me a potato—"

"No, sir, Mr. Shaw."

"—some canned, not fresh, spinach; pan gravy, I think some stewed fruit, and two cups of hot black coffee."

"Yes, sir, Mr. Shaw. Just like in United States Army."

"Jesus, I hope not," Raymond said.

XI

ON APRIL 15, 1959, the very same day on which Chunjin got his job with Raymond on transfer from the Soviet Army, another military transfer occurred. Major Marco was placed on indefinite sick leave and detached from duty.

Marco had undergone two series of psychiatric treatments at Army hospitals. As the recurring nightmare had grown more vivid, the pathological fatigue had gotten more severe. No therapy had been successful. Marco had weighed two hundred and eight pounds when he had come into New York from Korea. At the time he went on indefinite sick leave he weighed in at one hundred and sixty-three and he looked a little nuts. Every nerve end in his body had grown a small ticklish mustache, and they sidled along under his skin like eager touts, screaming on tiptoe. He had the illusion that he could see and hear everything at once and had lost all of his ability to edit either sight or sound. Sound particularly detonated his reflexes. He tried desperately not to listen when people talked because an open *A* sound repeated several times within a sentence could make him weep uncontrollably. He didn't know why, so he concentrated on remembering the cause, when he could, so that he would not listen so attentively, but it didn't work. It was an *A* sound that must have been somewhat like a sound he had heard many, many years before, in utter peace and safety, which through its loss or through his indifference to it over the years could now cause him to weep bitterly. If he heard the sound occur once, he quickly hummed "*La Seine,*" to push the *A* sound off to the side. His hand tremors were pronounced when his arm was extended unsupported. Sometimes his teeth would chatter as though he had entered a chill. Once in a while, after four or five unrelieved nights of nightmare, he developed a bad facial tic, and it wasn't pretty. Marco was being rubbed into sand by the grinding stones of two fealties. He was being slowly rubbed away by two faiths he lived by, far beyond his control; the first was his degree of holy reverence for the Medal of Honor, one of the most positive prejudices of his life because his life, principally, was the Army; and the second was the abnormal degree of his friendship for Raymond Shaw, which has been placed upon his mind, as coffee will leave a stain upon a fresh, snowy tablecloth, by the deepest psychological conditioning.

When Marco completed, for the want of any other word, the second course of treatment and was ordered to rest, they knew he was through and he knew they knew it. He headed for New York to talk to Raymond. He had never been able to tell the doctors the part of the dream where Raymond killed Mavole and Lembeck, on a continuous-performance basis, and he had not allowed himself to mention every phase of the four variations on the drill that had been used to win Raymond the Medal of Honor. He had written to Al Melvin and, between them, he and Melvin had spent over three hundred dollars talking to each other on the long-distance telephone, and it had brought considerable relief to each to know that the other was suffering as deeply from the same malady, but it did not stop the nightmares. Marco knew that he must talk to Raymond. He must, absolutely must. He knew that if he did not talk to Raymond about most of the details in his dreams he would die from them. Ironically, as Marco was riding one train to New York, Raymond was riding another to Washington.

Marco sat like a stone in the train chair, riding sideways in the club car. The car was about half filled. Almost all of the seats were occupied at one end, Marco's end, by businessmen, or what seemed to be businessmen but were actually an abortionist, an orchestra leader, a low-church clergyman, an astrologer, a Boy Scout executive, a horticulturist, and a cinematographer, because, no matter how much they would like the world to think so, the planet is not populated entirely by businessmen no matter how banal the quality of conversation everywhere has become. Some women were present; their dresses gave the car the only embarrassing touch of color, excepting the garish decorations on the upper left side of Marco's blouse.

Marco had a rye old-fashioned placed on the round, metal stand in front of him, but he hadn't tasted it. He kept wishing he had ordered beer not to taste and he was careful not to look at anybody, because he had stopped doing that several weeks before. He sweated continuously. His face had very little color. His palms drenched his trousers at the tops of his knees. He was battling to make a decision as to whether he wanted to smoke a cigar or not. His eyes burned. He felt an agony of weariness. His stomach hurt. He concentrated for an instant on not clenching his teeth but he could not retain the thought. His jaws were tired and some doctor had told him that he would grind the dentine off his molars if he didn't concentrate on not clenching his jaws. He turned his body slightly, but not his head, toward the person sitting beside him, a woman.

"Do you mind cigar smoke," he mumbled.

"Not at all," she murmured. He turned away from her but made no move to find a cigar.

"Go ahead," she said. "As a matter of fact, I wish you'd smoke two cigars at the same time."

"You must really like cigar smoke."

"Not especially, but I think two cigars going at the same time would *look* awfully amusing."

He turned his body again toward the woman sitting beside him. He lifted his eyes slowly, hesitantly, beyond the long, scarlet-tipped fingers at repose in her lap, past a shining silver belt buckle shaped as Quetzalcoatl, an urbane feathered serpent; past uptilted, high-setting, pronounced breasts that stared back at him eyelessly through dark blue wool; past the high neckline and the discreet seed pearls around a long throat of white Carrara marble, to a mouth whose shape he had yearned to see in living flesh since he had seen its counterpart within a photograph he had found in a German magazine twenty-three years before, rolled up in his father's effects in the trunk of a command car. In abstract, it was a sexual object. It was a witty mouth. It looked insatiable. It told him about lust which had been lost far back in mythology, lust which could endow its tasters with eternal serenity, and it was the mouth of many varieties of varying kinds of woman. He regretted having to leave off his concentration on the sight of it; with difficulty he moved his eyes upward to the questing horn of a most passionate nose; a large, formed, aquiline, and Semitic nose, the nose of a seeker and a finder of glories, and it made him remember that every Moslem who attains heaven is allotted seventy-two women who must look exactly like this between the eyes and the mouth, and he thought across the vast, vast distance of the *huanacauri* rock of Incan puberty to the words of the black, black, black song that keened: "If she on earth no more I see, my life will quickly fade away." Then at last his eyes came to the level of the eyes of a Tuareg woman and he rushed past a random questioning as to whether the Berlitz Schools taught Temajegh, and he thought of the god of love who was called bodiless by the Hindus because he was consumed by the fire of Siva's eyes, then he closed his own eyes and tried to help himself, to stop himself, to—SWEET GOD IN HEAVEN!—he could not. He began to weep. He stumbled to his feet. The passengers across the aisle stared at him hostilely. He knocked his drink over, and the metal stand over. He turned blindly and noisily to the left, unable to stop weeping, and made it, from behind the wet opaqueness, to the train door and the vestibule. He stood alone in the vestibule and put his head against the window and waited for time to pass, feeling confident that it would pass, when his motor would run down and this sobbing would slowly subside. Trying to analyze what had happened, as though to fill his mind, he was forced into the conclusion that the woman must have looked the way that open *A* sounded to him: an open, effortless, problemless, safe, and blessed look. What color had her hair been? he wondered as he wept. He concentrated upon the words by which angels had been known: yaztas, fravashi, and Amesha Spentas; seraphim and cherubim; hayyot, ofanim, arelim, and Harut and Marut who had said: "We are only a temptation. Be not then an unbeliever." He decided that the woman could only be one of the fravashi, that army of angels that has existed in heaven before the birth of man, that protects him during his life, and is united to his soul at death. He sobbed while he conjectured about the color of her hair. At last, he was permitted to stop weeping. He leaned against the train wall in exhaustion, riding backward. He took a handkerchief slowly from his trousers pocket and, with an effort of strength which he could not replenish with sleep, slowly dried his face, then blew his nose. He thought, only fleetingly, that he could not go back into that club car again, but that there would be plenty of other seats in the other direction, toward the rear of the train. When he got to New York, he decided, he would pull on a pair of gray slacks and a red woolen shirt and he'd sit all day on the rim of the map of the United States behind Raymond's big window, looking out at the Hudson River and that state, whatever its name was, on the other shore and think about the states beyond that state and drink beer.

When he turned to find another seat in another car, she was standing there. Her hair was the color of birch bark, prematurely white, and he stared at her as though her thyroid were showing its excessive activity and her hypereroticism. She stood smoking a new cigarette, leaning back, riding forward, and looking out of the window.

"Maryland is a beautiful state," she said.

"This is Delaware."

"I know. I was one of the original Chinese workmen who laid track on this stretch, but nonetheless Maryland is a beautiful state. So is Ohio, for that matter."

"I guess so. Columbus is a tremendous football town. You in the railroad business?" He felt dizzy. He wanted to keep talking.

"Not any more," she told him. "However, if you will permit me to point it out, when you ask someone that, you really should say: 'Are you in the railroad line?' Where is your home?"

"I've been in the Army all my life," Marco said. "We keep moving. I was born in New Hampshire."

"I went to a girls' camp once on Lake Francis."

"Well. That's away north. What's your name?"

"Eugénie."

"Pardon?"

"No kidding. I really mean it. And with that crazy French pronunciation."

"It's pretty."

"Thank you."

"Your friends call you Jenny?"

"Not yet they haven't."

"I think it's a nice name."

"You may call me Jenny."

"But what do your friends call you?"

"Rosie."

"Why?"

"My full name—the first name—is Eugénie Rose. I have always favored Rosie, of the two names, because it smells like brown soap and beer. It's the kind of a name that is always worn by the barmaid who always gets whacked across the behind by draymen. My father used to say it was a portly kind of a name, and with me being five feet nine he always figured I had a better chance of turning out portly than fragile, which is really and truly the way a girl using the name Eugénie would have to be."

"Still, when I asked you your name, you said Eugénie."

"It is quite possible that I was feeling more or less fragile at that instant."

"I never could figure out what more or less meant."

"Nobody can."

"Are you Arabic?"

"No."

He held out his hand to be taken in formal greeting. "My name is Ben. It's really Bennet. I was named after Arnold Bennet."

"The writer?"

"No. A lieutenant colonel. He was my father's commanding officer at the time."

"What's your last name?"

"Marco."

"Major Marco. Are you Arabic?"

"No, but no kidding, I was sure you were Arabic. I would have placed your daddy's tents within twelve miles of the Hoggar range in the central Sahara. There's a town called Janet in there and a tiny little place with a very rude name that I couldn't possibly repeat even if you had a doctorate in geography. When the sun goes down and the rocks, which have been heated so tremendously all day, are chilled suddenly by the night, which comes across the desert like flung, cold, black stout, it makes a salvo like a hundred rifles going off in rapid fire. The wind is called the khamseen, and after a flood throws a lot of power down a mountainside the desert is reborn and millions and millions of white and yellow flowers come to bloom all across the empty desolation. The trees, when there are trees, have roots a hundred feet long. There are catfish in the waterholes. Think of that. Did you know that? Sure. Some of them run ten, twelve inches. Everywhere else in the Arab world the woman is a beast of burden. Among the Tuareg, the woman is queen, and the Hoggar are the purest of the Tuareg. They have a ceremony called *ahal,* a sort of court of love where the woman reigns with her beauty, her wit, or the quality of her blood. They have enormous chivalry, the Tuareg. If a man wants to say 'I love!' he will say 'I am dying of love.' I have dreamed many times of a woman I have never seen and will never see because she died in 1935, and to this day the Tuareg recall her in their poetry, in their *ahals,* telling of her beauty, intelligence, and her wit. Her name was Dassine oult Yemma, and her great life was deeply punctuated by widely known love affairs with the great warriors of her time. I thought you were she. For just an instant, back there in that car a little while ago, I thought you were she."

His voice had gotten more and more rapid and his eyes were feverish. She had held his hand tightly in both of hers as he had spoken, ever since he had introduced himself. They stared at each other.

"Thank you," she said.

"You became one of my best and bravest thoughts," he told her. "I thank you." The taut, taut band around his head had loosened. "Are you married?"

"No. You?"

"No. What's your last name?"

"Cheyney. I am a production assistant for a man named Justin who had two hits last season. I live on Fifty-fourth Street, a few doors from the Museum of Modern Art, of which I am a tea-privileges member, no cream. I live at Fifty-three West Fifty-fourth Street, Three B. Can you remember that?"

"Yes."

"Eldorado nine, two six three two. Can you remember that?"
"Yes."

"You look so tired. Apartment Three B. Are you stationed in New York? Is stationed the right word? Fifty-three West Fifty-fourth Street."

"I'm not exactly stationed in New York. I have been stationed in Washington but I got sick and I have a long leave now and I'm going to spend it in New York."

"Eldorado nine, two six three two."

"I stay with a friend of mine, a newspaperman. We were in Korea together." Marco ran a wet hand over his face and began to hum "*La Seine*." He had found the source of the sound of the open *A*. It was far inside this girl and it was in the sound of the name Dassine oult Yemma. He couldn't get the back of his hand away from his mouth. He had had to shut his eyes. He was so tired. He was so tired. She took his hand gently away from his mouth. "Let's sit down," she said. "I want you to put your head on my shoulder." The train lurched and he almost fell, but she caught and held him, then she led the way into the other car where there were plenty of seats.

RAYMOND's apartment was on the extreme west coast of the island where firemen had heavy bags under their eyes from piling out four and five times a night to push sirens to brownstone houses where nobody had any time to do anything about too many bone-weary Puerto Ricans living in one room. It was a strip of city too dishonest to admit it was a slum, or rather, in all of the vastness of the five boroughs of metropolis there was a strip of city, very tiny, which was not a slum, and this was the thin strip that was photographed and its pictures sent out across the world until all the world and the minuscule few who lived in that sliver of city thought that was New York, and neither knew or cared about the remainder of the six hundred square miles of flesh and brick. Here was the ripe slum of the West Side where the city had turned so bad that at last thirteen square blocks of it had had to be torn down before the rats carried off the babies. New York, New York! It's a wonderful town! The west side of the island was rich in façades not unlike the possibilities of a fairy princess with syphilis. Central Park West was all front and faced a glorious park betrayed only now and then by bands of chattering faggots auctioning bodies and by an excessive population of emotion-caparisoned people in the somewhat temporary-looking sanitariums on so many of its side streets. Columbus and Amsterdam avenues were the streets of the drunks, where the murders were done in the darkest morning hours, where there were an excessive number of saloons and hardware stores. They were connected by trains of brownstone houses whose fronts were riotously colored morning and evening and all day on Sunday by bursts and bouquets of Puerto Ricans, and beyond Amsterdam was Broadway, the bawling, flash street, the fleshy, pig-eyed part of the city that wore lesions of neon and incandescent scabs, pustules of lights and color in suggestively luetic lycopods, illuminating littered streets, filth-clogged streets that could never be cleansed because when one thousand hands cleaned, one million hands threw dirt upon the streets again. Broadway was patrolled by strange-looking pedestrians, people who had grabbed the wrong face in the dark when someone had shouted "Fire!" and were now out roaming the streets, desperate to find their own. For city block after city block on Broadway it seemed that only food was sold. Beyond that was West End Avenue, a misplaced street bitter on its own memories, lost and bewildered, seeking some Shaker Heights, desperately genteel behind an apron of shabby bricks. Here was the limbo of the lower middle class where God the Father, in the form of sunlight, never showed His face. Raymond lived beyond that, on Riverside Drive, another front street of large, grand apartments that had become cabbage-sour furnished rooms which faced the river and an excessive amount of squalor on the Jersey shore. All together, the avenues and streets proved by their decay that the time of the city was long past, if it had ever existed, and the tall buildings, end upon end upon end, were so many extended fingers beckoning the Bomb.

MARCO paid the cab off in front of Raymond's building. On an April day the city was colder than Labrador, and the wind had found teeth which tore at his face.

Marco felt like a giant. He had slept three hours on the train without dreaming and he had awakened in Rosie Cheyney's arms. He would have a very delicious therapy to tell those pate doctors about when this was all over. When it was all over but the sobbing. Big joke. All over but the sobbing, he thought, giving the driver a quarter tip. He got into the elevator feeling confident that behind Raymond's mustard-colored eyes there was an almost human understanding, not that Raymond was any monotreme but he seemed pretty much like a Martian some- times. Fifty-three West Fifty-fourth, apartment Three B. He just wanted to hear Raymond tell how he had gotten the Medal of Honor. He just wanted to talk about blackboards and pointers and Chinese and that crude animated cartoon with the blue spot. Eldorado nine, two six three two. He wouldn't talk to Raymond about the murders in the nightmares. Rosie. Eugénie Rose. My Wild Arab Nose. Oh, What a Gorgeous Nose! *Cyrano:* Act I, Scene 1: Pedantic: Does not Aristophanes mention a mythologic monster called Hippocampelephantocamelos? That projection room and the American voice on the sound track and the flat, empty, half film cans like pie plates used as ash trays. Suddenly, he could taste the yak-dung cigarettes again and it was mar- velous. If he could only remember the name of that brand, he thought, but somehow he never could. He thought about the movement of the many red dots on the screen, then of Raymond, symbolized by the blue dot, and the canned voice telling them that they were seeing the battle action in which Raymond had been willing to sacrifice his life, again and again, to save them all.

The elevator operator indicated the doorway directly across the hall. Marco rang the door bell while the operator waited. Chunjin answered the door. He stood clearly under good light wearing black trousers, a white shirt, a black bow tie, and a white jacket, looking blankly at Marco, waiting for an inquiry, not having time to recognize the major, and most certainly not expecting him. To Marco he was a *djinn* who had stepped into flesh out of that torment which was giving him lyssophobia. Not more than four-fifths of a second passed before Marco hit Chunjin high in the chest, having thrown the desperate punch for the center of the man's face, but the Korean had stepped backward reflexively and had saved himself, partially, from the unexpectedness of Marco's assault. Because he had not thought of himself as being on duty while Raymond was out of the city, Chunjin was unarmed. However, he was a trained agent and a good one. He held the rank of lieutenant colonel in the Soviet security forces and he had been assigned to Raymond on a crash basis. He had recognized Marco too late. He was entirely current on Marco's dossier because the major was Raymond's only friend.

The elevator operator, a sturdy twenty-eight-year-old, watched the Korean carried backward and the door flung inward to bang against the pink plaster wall. He rushed in fast behind Marco and tried to pull him back. Marco held Chunjin off with his left hand and cooled the elevator man with his right. Chunjin took that left arm and drew Marco into a prime judo catch and threw him high across the room so he could get at Marco's neck, coming down on it hard enough to break it in the follow-up, but Marco rolled and kept rolling when he hit the floor and slipped locks on hard when Chunjin came down, missing him.

They were both Black Belts, which is the highest judo rank there is, this side of a Dan. Marco had weight on his man, but Marco was in a run-down condition. However, he had been lifted into a murderous exhilaration and was filled to his hairline with adrenalin because he had at last been permitted to take those nightmares and one of the people in them into the fingers of his hands to beat and to torture until he found out why they had happened and where they had happened and how they could be made to stop. What worked the best was the twenty-nine extra pounds of weight and, as four neighbors watched with studious curiosity from the safer side of the doorsill, he broke Chunjin's forearm. The Korean almost took the side of his face and his neck off, not losing a beat of his rhythm during the fracture and appalling Marco that such a slight man could be so tough. Then Marco dislocated the man's hip joint as he leaped to jab his foot into Marco's larynx, and it was that second catch which brought out the great scream of agony.

He was pounding the back of Chunjin's head into the floor and asking him a series of what he thought were deliberative questions when the youngest squad-car cop came into the room first and fast, hitting him behind the head with a sap, and the entire, wonderful opportunity passed.

. . .

At St. Luke's Hospital, Chunjin was adamant about two things: (1) he was emphatic in his refusal to press charges against his former commanding officer whom he had served long and intimately as orderly and interpreter, and who had most obviously mistaken him for an intruder in Mr. Shaw's apartment, knowing that Mr. Shaw had never employed a servant before, and (2) it would be most necessary for the hospital staff to get him out of the place not later than noon on Monday so he could shop for food, then cook the first meal on his job for Mr. Shaw, because if they did not get him out he could lose his job and it was the only job he wanted in the United States of America. He could not, of course, explain that he would be shot if he lost it.

At the Twenty-fourth Precinct House at 100th Street and Central Park West, after riding the uniformed, half-conscious Marco from Raymond's apartment in the squad car, they went through his effects, found his AGO card, made his branch, and called the Military Service Bureau downtown at the Police Academy, which maintained liaison between the New York police and branches of the armed forces. The bureau reached the duty officer at Army Intelligence, Washington, early in the evening. Marco was identified. The police were told with a very special sort of a voice, effactually a pleader's voice, that Marco was one of the best men they had and that he had been having a very hard time. The voice explained, with great attention to their credulity, that Marco had picked up a sort of infection in his imagination while in the forward area in Korea, that he had run two hospital courses which had proved that he was as sane as anybody else but, well, Marco had had a hard time and anything the New York police could do that would tend to pull him together and send him on his way would be greatly appreciated by the U.S. Army.

Under proper conditions, there is no more cooperative institution than the New York Police Department, but they had had so much experience with top-blowers they insisted that Marco leave the station house in some custody which could be certified as being equable. Marco's head still wasn't very clear. He had been slugged. He had been in a rough fight and the adrenalin had turned to curds and whey in his veins. He was exhausted and he hadn't been eating very much, but he knew enough to ask them to call Eldorado nine, two six three two and ask for Miss Eugénie Rose Cheyney.

They left him in a cell while they made the call and before the cell door had closed he was asleep. Rosie got to the station house in thirty-seven minutes. Unfortunately, just as she and the two detectives came along the cell-block corridor, he had been sleeping just long enough to have reached the auditorium at Tunghwa where Raymond was strangling Mavole with a silk scarf. As they stared into his cell, motionless for an instant, even the two cops were stricken with fright at the piteousness of his sounds and the imploring motions he succeeded in shaping with his hands. One detective got the door open. Eugénie Rose had gone chalk-white and was gripping her whole lower lip in her teeth to keep from yelling. She slid into the cell ahead of the second cop and got on her knees beside Marco's bunk and shook him by the shoulders, talking steadily; then, desperate to get him out of the trap he was in, she whacked him with the full strength of her splendid arm across the left cheek and he came out of it, shaking. She held him in her arms. "It's O.K., sweetheart," she said. "It's Rosie. It's all right now. The dream is over. It's Jennie." And stuff like that.

She signed out for him at the desk as though he was a ripped purse some cannon had torn off her arm. He swayed slightly as he waited for her. She shook hands like a fight manager with the desk lieutenant, the two detectives, and a patrolman who happened to be passing through, and she told them if she could ever line up any hard-to-get theater seats for them they were to call her at Job Justin's office and she would handle it with joy. She took Marco out into the air of that freak night; a cold, cold night in mid-April that was just one of the vagaries that made New York such an interesting place to die in.

He was wearing a uniform overcoat and an overseas cap. He did not look so bad in the half light. Everything was pressed. There was just a little blood on his right sleeve from Chunjin's face from when he had overshot with the second right-hand punch. Eugénie Rose called a taxi as if it were her own hound dog: it came to heel with a hand signal. She put Marco in first, then she got in and closed the door. "Just drive through the park," she said to the driver, "and discard the conversation you've been hoarding up since the last fare."

"I don't talk to passengers, lady," the driver said. "I hate people until they tip me and then it's too late."

"I think you should eat something," she said to Marco.

"I love food," he answered. "I always have but I can't swallow very well any more."

"We'll try, anyway," she told him and leaned forward to tell the driver to take them to the Absinthe House, a calorie and beverage bourse catering to some of the craftiest minds this side of the owl and the pussycat, on West Forty-eighth. She leaned back on the seat and looped her arm through his. She was wearing a dark blue polo coat, some firm, dark skin, some white, white teeth, egg-sized dark eyes, and white hair.

"It was very original of you to have the Police Department call so shyly and ask for our first date," she said softly.

"They asked me who I would—who would be willing, and I just—I—"

"Thank you. Very much." She decided they needed more air and started to open all windows, telling the driver, "Sorry about all this air, but it's very important. Take my word."

"Lissen, lady, while the meter is going it's your cab arreddy. Go ahead take the doors off it gets stuffy." Marco's teeth began to chatter. He tried to hold them clamped shut because he wanted her to feel efficient about opening the windows, but he sounded like a stage full of castanets. She closed the windows.

"Let's pick up a can of soup and go to your place."

"Sure." She gave the driver the changed destination.

"You think they'll let me visit that fellow at St. Luke's tonight?"

"Maybe first thing in the morning."

"Would you come with me? It would keep me calm. I wouldn't want to hit him lying down like that."

"Sure."

"I have to find out where Raymond is."

"The newspaperman you told me about? Why not call his newspaper?"

"Yeah. You're right. Well, sure. So let's go to the Absinthe House if you'd rather do that. I feel better."

"You know what I was doing when you had the police call me?"

"I could guess, if I wasn't so tired. I give up."

"Well, after you dropped me off and I got upstairs, and before I took my coat off, I telephoned Lou Amjac, my fiancé—" Marco came forward, alert and alarmed. "—and he came over as soon as he could, which was instantly, and I told him I had just met you and I gave him his ring back." She held up her naked, long fingers of the left hand, and wriggled them. "I tried to convey my regrets for whatever pain I might be causing him. Then, just then, you had the police call me with the invitation to go into the tank at the Twenty-fourth Precinct. I grabbed this coat. I kissed Lou on the cheek for the last time in our lives that I would ever kiss him and I ran. At the station house they told me you had beaten up a very skinny little man but that you were a solid type yourself, according to Washington, so I figured that if they were willing to go to the trouble to get a comment on you out of George Washington, you all must have had a really successful sé- ance while you were in the poky, and I must say it was real sweet of General Washington with you only a major, and I hadn't even known you two had met, but if those policemen were the tiniest bit puzzled about you, they could have asked me. Oh, indeed yes, my darling Ben—I would have told them."

He glared at her fiercely and possessively, clapped an arm about her shoulders, and pulled her evocative mouth into his while the driver, intent upon estimating within two per cent the amout of the tip he would be paid, cleared one more stop light just as it changed, heading east on Fifty-fourth Street.

XII

AFTER DAYS OF WON- derful, dreamless sleep upon the bed and breast of Miss Cheyney, Marco called *The Daily Press* early Monday morn- ing and learned that Raymond was in Washington. He reached Raymond at the *Press* office in Washington a few minutes later. When he told Raymond he wanted very much to see him, Raymond invited him to dinner in New York that eve- ning to help him rate a new cook, then, remembering, babbled the news. "I just remembered. Your own orderly. Yeah. Re- member your orderly in Korea, the little guy who was interpreter on the patrol—Chunjin? That's my new cook! Hah! I mean, would you ever have been able to anticipate that?" Marco stated that he would not have been able to so anticipate; and inquired as to what time Raymond would arrive from Washington for the tasting.

"Estimating the traveling time from Penn Station—and I believe you'll find I won't be more than five minutes off either way —I should arrive at the apartment at—say—six twenty-two."

"Even if you have to wait out on the corner to do it."

"I wonder if you'd mind calling Chunjin and telling him there'll be an extra place for dinner? You're probably dying to talk to him anyway. I know you old Army guys."

"I'll take care of everything, Raymond," Marco said, and they both hung up.

RAYMOND opened the door.

"Chunjin isn't here," he said. "There's no dinner to offer you."

"Or you."

"But I did find a note. It's from him and it says you beat him up and that he's now in St. Luke's Hospital."

"One thing is for sure," Marco said. "There are plenty of sensational delicatessens in this neighborhood."

"Why, that's a marvelous idea!" Raymond said. He walked away from the door, allowing Marco to close it or not close it as he chose, and flipped open a telephone book across the square foyer. "I never seem to be able to think of it myself. And I love it. Pastrami and those pickles and that crazy rye bread with the aphrodisiacal seeds and maybe a little marinated herring and some pot cheese with a little smoked salmon and some of that indigestible sauerkraut they make out of electric bulb filaments and some boiled beef." He began to dial. "On account of this I am absolutely grateful to you for getting Chunjin out of the way."

"Ah, that's all right," Marco said. "Glad to do it."

"The elevator man was singing the blues so I gave him five."

"He sure can keep a secret. He just sang a second chorus for me and I gave him five."

"What did you hit *him* for?"

"He was determined to play peacemaker."

"What did you whack Chunjin for?"

"That's all part of what I came to tell you about."

"Hello—Gitlitz? This is Shaw. Right. Now hear this." Raymond ordered food for ten, as one does when one calls a delicatessen situated anywhere on Broadway in New York between Thirty-fourth and Ninety-sixth streets, and told them where to send it.

"I've been in the hospital off and on quite a bit over the past two years."

"Hospital? What was the matter with you?" Raymond opened a can of beer. The room was fragrant with the smell of furniture polish from Chunjin's working weekend. Marco looked very thin, but no longer drawn. The Cheyney method of soul massage had elements of greatness. He was dressed in civilian clothes, and his face had a distant, inactive look such as a man about to practice a banquet speech alone in a hotel room might have. Eugénie Rose had him coked to the gills on tranquilizers.

The authority which had come with writing a successful column on national affairs had settled Raymond considerably, Marco thought, and had made him seem taller and broader. Raymond was thirty years old. He could not have moved up the scale to a better tailor because he had always used the best. He could not have worn whiter linen. His fingernails gleamed. His shoe tips glowed. His color shone. His teeth sparkled. The only fault with the lighting circuit was behind his eyes. Raymond may have believed that his eyes did light up, but unfortunately they could shine only within the extent of his art as a counterfeiter of emotions. Raymond did not feel emotion, and that could not be changed. When he was content he would try to remember how other people had looked when they had manifested happiness or pleasure or satisfaction, and he would attempt to counterfeit the appearance. It was not effective. Raymond's ability to feel anything resembling either sympathy or empathy was minimal and that was that.

As Raymond listened to Marco's story with all of his attention he could only understand that an all-out attack had been mounted against his friend and that it had almost destroyed him. He supposed he would be expected to be upset as they went on to talk about that lousy medal which had always been a lot of gas to him—tin-soldier-boy stuff: he had never asked for it, had never wanted it, and if there was some strange way that medal could keep his friend in the Army and get him his health back, then they had to make sure that he found out exactly what that was, and, if necessary to straighten this out and keep Ben safe, why, for crissake, he'd even call in Johnny Iselin. He did not say any of this to Marco. He concentrated on trying to counterfeit some of the reactions he felt Marco must expect.

"If what you've been dreaming actually happened, Ben," he said slowly, "then it happened to me and it happened to everyone else on the patrol."

"Such as Chunjin," Marco replied.

"How about an investigation?" Raymond said. "That ought to do it."

"Ought to do what?"

"Uncover what happened that made you dream all that."

"What kind of an investigation?"

"Well, my mother can always get Johnny Iselin's committee in the Senate to—"

"Johnny Iselin?" Marco was utterly horrified. "This is *Army!*"

"What has that got to do with—"

"All right, Raymond. I won't explain that part. But what happened is inside my head and Melvin's head and the best head doctors in this country haven't been able to shake it out and don't have even the first suspicion of what could be causing it. What could a Senate committee do? And *Iselin!* Jesus, Raymond, let's make an agreement never to mention that son-of-a-bitch ever again."

"It was just an idea. To get started. I know Johnny is a swine better than you do."

"Then why bring it up?"

"Because we have to dump a thing like this on the specialists. What the hell, Ben, you said so yourself—the Army can't cope with this. What there has to be, if we're going to get anywhere with it, is a big, full-scale investigation. You know—somebody has to make people talk."

"Make who talk?"

"Well—us—I—"

"Yeah."

"Well, the patrol. If my Medal of Honor is a fake, and believe me I don't see how it could be anything else because it doesn't figure that I'm going to stand up in front of a lot of bullets and be a big hero for that passel of slobs, then somebody has to remember and somebody else has to make the rest of those guys remember that we've all been had. That's all. We've been had. If you can't stand the idea of Johnny Iselin, and I don't blame you, then I guess you'll just have to demand your own court-martial."

"How? What do you mean? What are you talking about?" Marco looked as though he was just beginning to understand what Raymond was talking about, almost but not quite.

"You have to charge yourself with falsifying your report that led to me getting the Medal of Honor and you'll have to demand that the Army investigate whether or not that was done in collusion with the men of the patrol. That's all there is to it."

"They wouldn't be able to comprehend such a thing. A Medal of Honor—why, a Medal of Honor is a sacred thing to the Army, Raymond. I mean—I—Jesus, the roof would come off the Pentagon."

"Sure! That's what I'm saying! Throw it wide open! If the Army can't understand, then, what the hell, believe me, Iselin'll understand. He'll get you off the hook."

"No. No, never."

"It's got to be done the sensational way just to make sure it's done and that the Army doesn't get to sit on another ridiculous mistake and let you stay sick like this. What would they care? You're expendable. But they made a hero out of me so I'm not expendable. They couldn't take back a mistake as big as this one."

"Raymond, listen. If it wasn't for those Soviet generals and those Chinese in that dream, I'd be willing to be expendable."

"All right. That's your problem."

"But with the chance, just the sick chance that there may be such an enormous security risk involved I have to make them dig into this thing. You're right, Raymond. I have to. I have to."

"Why should I have gotten a Medal of Honor? I can't even remember being in the action. I remember the *facts* about the action, sure. But I don't remember the *action*."

"Talk about it. Keep talking about it. Please."

"Well, look. Let's reconstruct. We're on the patrol. You'll be at the center of that line and I'll be off on their right flank. You know? It will be dark. I'll yell out to you, 'Captain! Captain Marco! Get me some light twenty yards ahead at two o'clock!' And you'll yell back, 'You got it, kid,' and very soon a flare will break open and I'll pour on some enfilade fire on their column and, as everyone who reads comic books knows, I am a very good shooter. I'll start to move in on them and I'll take up one of their own heavy machine guns as I go and I'll move eight of their own grenades up ahead of me as I move along."

"Yeah, yeah," Marco said. "But you don't remember *doing* all those things."

"That's what I'm trying to tell you," Raymond answered irritably and impatiently. "Every time I'm directed to think about the action I always know what *will* happen exactly, but I never get to the place where it actually happens."

"Do you remember anything about a blackboard? Chinese instructors?"

"No."

"Memory drills? Anything about a movie projection room and animated cartoons with a sound track in English and a lot of Chinese guys standing around?"

"No."

"You must have gotten a better brainwashing than I did. Or Melvin."

"Brainwashing?" Raymond did not like that note. He could not abide the thought of anybody tampering with his person so he rejected the entire business then and there. Others, told the same set of conjectures, might have been fired into action or challenged, but not Raymond. The disgust it made Raymond feel acted like a boathook that pushed the solid shore away from him to allow him to drift away from it on the strong-flowing current of self. It did not mean that he had instantly closed his mind to Marco's problem. He most earnestly wanted to be able to help Ben find relief, to help to change his friend's broken mechanism, to find him sleep and rest and health, but his own participation in what he had started out to make a flaming patriotic crusade when he had first started to speak had been muted by his fastidiousness: he shrank from what he could only consider the rancid vulgarity of brainwashing.

"It has to be a brainwash," Marco said intensely. "In my case it slipped. In Melvin's case it slipped. It's the only possible explanation, Raymond. The only, only explanation."

"Why?" Raymond answered coldly. "Why would the Communists want me to get a Medal of Honor?"

"I don't know. But we have to find out." Marco stood up. "Before I take this first step, before I leave here, I'd like to hear you say that you understand that I'm going to explode this whole thing with a court-martial, not because—not to save myself from those dreams—"

"Ah, fuh crissake, Ben! Whose idea was it! Who gives a goddam about that?"

"Let me finish. This is an official statement because, believe me, pal, I know. Once I get that court-martial started—my own court-martial—it can get pretty rough on both of us." He rolled his eyes toward the ceiling. "My father—well, it's a good thing my father is dead—with me starting out to make a public bum out of a Medal of Honor man. Shuddup! But I have to do it. Security. What a lousy word. I look right into the horrible face of something that might kill my country and the only word for the danger is a word that means the absolute opposite. Security. Well, as you said—with stakes like that I'm expendable. And so are you, Raymond pal. So are you."

"Will you stop? Who thought it up? Me. Who practically made you agree to do it? Me. And you can shove that patriotic jive about saving our great country. I want to know why a bunch of filthy Soviet peasants and degraded Chinese coolies would dare to confer the Medal of Honor on me."

"Raymond. Do me a favor? Tell me about the action again. Please."

"What action?"

"Come on! Come on!"

"You mean go on from where I was?"

"Yeah, yeah."

"Well—you will throw up another flare but you'll throw it about twenty yards ahead of me at maybe twelve o'clock, at maybe dead center of the line, because you will figure I'll be moving across the terrain up that ridge so—"

"Man, oh man, this is something."

"What?"

"Each time you talk about the action you even tell it as though it hadn't happened yet."

"That's what I'm saying! That's the way I always think about it! I mean, when some horrible square comes out of nowhere at a banquet, the paper makes me go too, and he starts asking me about it. Come on, Ben. You made your point. Let's go meet your girl."

Marco ran his fingers through his thick hair on both sides of his head. He put his elbows on his knees and covered his face with his hands. Raymond stared down at him, almost tenderly. "Don't be embarrassed if you feel like you're going to cry, Ben," Raymond said gently.

Marco shook his head. Raymond opened another can of beer.

"I swear to sweet, sweet God I think I am going to be able to sleep," Marco said. "I can feel it. There isn't anything about those crazy voices and those fast, blurring colors and the eyes of that terrible audience that frightens me any more." He took his hands away from his face and reflexively reached over to take Raymond's can of beer out of his hand. Raymond reached down and opened another. Marco fell asleep, sitting up. Raymond stretched him out on the sofa, brought him a blanket, put out the lights, and went into his office to listen to the river wind and to read a slim book with the highly improbable title of *Liquor, the Servant of Man.*

MARCO was still asleep when Raymond left the apartment the next morning. Eugénie Rose Cheyney called him soon after he reached his office. She asked if Marco had been sleeping quietly. Raymond said he had. She said, "Oh, Mr. Shaw, that's just wonderful!" and hung up.

XIII

RAYMOND'S MOTHER called him from the Idlewild Airport. She wanted him to have lunch with her. He tried to think quickly of somebody whom he could say he had to have lunch with but she said he was not to stall her, that she was well aware that he disliked people too much to be stuck for an hour or more at a luncheon table with one, so he could damn well show up wherever they let ladies eat luncheon at the Plaza Hotel at one o'clock. He said he would be there. Beyond having acknowledged that his name was

Raymond when she had first spoken, it was all he said to his
mother.

She was hard at work making a scene by bossing the *maitre
d'hotel,* a table captain, and two waiters at a table that faced the
park in the big corner room when he arrived at the Plaza at ten
seconds before one o'clock. She motioned him to stand beside
her chair until she finished her oration about exactly how they
were to stuff the oysters into a carpetbag steak and that she
would not tolerate more than eleven minutes of broiling on each
side, in a preheated grill, at four hundred degrees. The waiters
bowed and left. Raymond's mother gave the *maitre d'* the full
glare of her contempt for an instant, then spoke to Raymond. "I
ask you to imagine a restaurant," she said, "which does not list
Clos de Lambrays or a Cuvée Docteur Peste!" She waved the
man away, with bitterness. She permitted Raymond to kiss her
on the right cheek, ever so lightly, then motioned him to his chair
at the table for four, not at her right or directly across from her,
but at her left, which made it impossible for either of them to
look out of the window at the park.

"How have you been?" she asked.

"Fine."

"As am I. Not that you asked."

"When I heard you ordering a steak stuffed with oysters I had
a clue."

"The steak will be mainly for you."

"Sure."

"Johnny is fine."

"You mean his physical health, I presume?"

"I do. And everything else."

"Is he in a jam?"

"Of course not."

"Then why are we here?"

"Why are we here?"

"Why are we having our annual meeting?"

"I am your mother, which is a sufficient reason. Why did you
ask if Johnny is in a jam?"

"It occurred to me that you might have decided that you
would have use for my column, which has so carefully disquali-
fied itself from ever printing Johnny's name despite the fact that
he is an assassin, pure and simple. An assassin of character and
the soul. He reeks of death, you know?" Raymond exceeded his

own gifts for being obnoxious and impossible when he was with his mother. His brushing gesture worked for him almost all the time, punctuating his haughtiness and scorn. His posture was as attenuated as liquid being drawn up through a drinking straw.

His mother closed her eyes tightly as she answered him. "My dear boy, one more column of type in this weltered world spelling our Johnny's name would not be much noticed."

"I'll remember that."

She opened her eyes. "What for?"

Raymond, when he was with his mother, always felt a nagging fear that he was gaping at her beauty. As they spoke, whenever they met, his eyes searched each millimeter of her skin for a flaw and weighed each of her gestures, anxious that he might discover some loss of grace, but to no avail. He was dismayed and gratified to fall back upon the mockery of her pretense at disappointment because there had been no Clos de Lambrays or Cuvée Docteur Peste, which so failed to find harmony with the fact that Johnny Iselin drank bourbon with his meals.

"Mother, in God's name, where did you ever hear of a thing like a carpetbag steak? Johnny found it, didn't he? Johnny had to find it, because in the world's literature of food there couldn't be a dish which expresses his vulgarity better than a thick, contemptuously expensive piece of meat pregnant with viscous, slippery, sensual oysters."

"Raymond, please! Watch your language." She leered at him.

"It's disgusting and he's disgusting."

"The reason I asked you to lunch today, Raymond," his mother said smoothly, "is that I have not, actually, been entirely well and my doctor has suggested a trip to Europe this summer."

"What's the matter with you?" He stretched out the diphthongs of the drawl until its sounds reverberated nasally into his soft palate, thinking: Has there ever on God's earth been a liar like this woman? Does she at any square inch of her mountainous vanity, conceive that I can be had through the delicate health appeal? Will she produce a forged electrocardiogram? Will a malpracticing doctor with an even gaze suddenly happen to discover that we are lunching here? She would never pull anything as crude as a faint, but she could play a great scene with any given kindly old physician who had been coached in his lines.

"The doctor was a fool, of course," his mother said. "I went to the Leahy Clinic and to the Mayos for two separate checkups. I am as sound as a Swiss franc."

Raymond's resentment of her made him feel as though steel burrs were forming everywhere under his skin. I am going to lose this, he thought, just as I lose them all with her. I am being blindfolded as I sit here and she will win if I cannot anticipate where she is leading me. Oh, what a woman! What a beauty she is and what a dirty fighter. She is where the world should spit when they seek to spit upon Johnny Iselin. How can I forget that? How can I look into those serenely lovely eyes, how can I be so deeply thrilled by the carriage of her exquisitely wholesome body and grow so faint at the set, the royal set of that beautiful head and not remember, not always and always and always remember that it encases a cesspool of betrayal, a poisoned well of love, and a city of deadly snakes? Why am I here? Why did I come here?

"I am glad to hear it," he said. "But I distinctly remember you telling me that you had not, actually, been entirely well. Just a few seconds ago. In fact, that was exactly the way you phrased it."

She smiled at him with forbearance, showing rows of perfect white teeth. "I said—oh, Raymond! For heaven's sake, what does it matter what I said?"

"I'd like a drink."

"At lunch?"

"Yes."

"You generally sulk if people drink at lunch."

She tilted her head back and made a repulsive kissing sound with her pursed lips. A waiter sprinted toward her so rapidly that Raymond thought the man had decided to kill her, but that was not the case. He came to a point beside her and stared at her abjectly as though pleading for the knout. Raymond's mother had that effect upon many people.

"Speak up, Raymond."

"I would like to have some beer. Served in the can."

"Served in the can, sir?" the waiter asked softly. Raymond's mother snarled and the man shrilled "Yes, sir!" and was off.

"And who is the more vulgar now?" she asked in a kindly tone. "How about a can of beans, opened with a hatchet, with the can of beer?"

"Mother, for crissake, will you please tell me how come we are having lunch today?"

"Oh. Well, this fool of a doctor whom I shall expose as an alarmist, I assure you, told me that I should go to Europe for a change and whether it was from the wrong reason or not, it did plant the idea. So, since I can't go alone and since it would present too many security difficulties for Johnny to go with me, I wondered . . . and I most certainly expect you to accept for professional reasons as I will be traveling as a full, accredited representative of the Appropriations, Foreign Relations, and Finance Committees—I will be representing the Senate, you might say—and I will be there to remind the forgetful rulers of Europe and England that the United States was established not as a democracy but as a Federal Union and Republic that is controlled by the United States Senate, at this moment in our history, through a state-equality composition designed to maintain this establishment and that it exists, in the present moment of our history, to protect minorities from the precipitate and emotional tyranny of majorities. That means, of course, that I will be able to get you into places and cause you to be adjacent to people which neither your newspaper nor your column could reach in a decade of Sundays. I assure you, before you answer as to whether or not you will consent to accompany me, your own mother, on a tour of Europe at no cost whatever to you, that there is no one in the British Isles or on that entire subcontinent of Europe whom you might decide that you would like to meet —and for reasons of publication should you so choose—that I cannot deliver to you. Should you also decide that you would enjoy extending the already influential syndication of your daily writings to other languages and to foreign newspapers and opinion-molding periodicals, I should think that could be arranged. Furthermore—" Raymond's mother was wooing him as she had wooed Johnny Iselin. Raymond's own father must have been a dreamer, indeed, to have lost her point so far back in the thickening fullness of her youth.

"I would love to go to Europe with you this summer, Mother."

"Good. We will sail from West Forty-sixth Street on June 15, at noon, on the *United States*. My office will mail you the itinerary and hotels and indicate the shape of appointments and meetings, business and social. Would you like to see the Pope?"

"No."

"I'll do that alone then."

"What else?"

"Isn't this carpetbag steak absolutely delicious? Eating it is an absolute sexual experience! What a marvelous conception—steak and oysters, I mean. Johnny eats it all the time, you know."

"It figures."

"Is there anything I can get done for you in Washington, dear heart?"

"No. Thank you. Yes. Yes, there is something. I have a friend—"

"A friend? You have a friend?" She stopped chewing for a moment and put her fork down.

"Sarcasm is the cheapest kind of a crutch to humor, Mother."

"Please forgive me, Raymond. I was not attempting sarcasm. You must believe that. I was startled. I had never heard you mention a friend in your entire life before. I am very, very happy that you do have a friend and you may be sure, darling, that if I may help your friend I most certainly will be overjoyed to do so. Who is he?"

"He's a major in Army Intelligence in Washington." Raymond's mother had whipped out an efficient-looking looseleaf notebook.

"His name?"

He told her.

"Academy?" He said yes.

"Would full colonel be what you had in mind?"

"That would be fine, I guess. I hope there is some way it can be done without PI being stamped all over his personnel file."

"What is PI?"

"Political influence."

"Of course they'll stamp PI all over his personnel file! Are you out of your mind? What's wrong with letting the Board know that he happens to have a little muscle in the right places? Sweet Jesus, Raymond, if it weren't for PI some of the brass we call our leaders would be the oldest crop of second lieutenants in military history. I swear to God, Raymond," his mother said in extreme exasperation, chopping savagely at a large gooseberry tart that glistened with custard filling, "sometimes I think you are the most naïve of young men, and when I read your column, I am sure."

"What's wrong with my column?"

She held up her hand. "Not now. We will reorganize your column aboard ship in June. Right now let's make your friend a chicken colonel." She looked at her notes. "Now, is there any-thing—well, anything negative I should know about this one?"

"No. He's a great officer. His father and grandfather and great-grandfather were great officers."

"You know him from Korea?"

"Yes. He—he led the patrol." Raymond hesitated because mentioning the patrol made him think of that filthy medal again and of how much his mother had made that medal mean to Johnny Iselin and what a fool she had made of herself at the White House and later what a fool Johnny had made of himself in front of the TV cameras and press cameras at that goddam, cheap, rotten, contemptuous luncheon where he had been humiliated, and all of a sudden he saw that it would be possible, too, for him to take a little bit of her skin off painfully and to kick Johnny right between the eyes with the medal nailed to the toe of his boot so that he, Raymond, would finally have a little pleasure out of that goddam medal himself, finally and at last. He was patiently quiet until she sensed the meaning of his hesi-tation and took it up.

"What's the matter?" she asked.

"Well, there is one thing which the Army might figure as nega-tive. In the past. I think it's all right now."

"He's a fairy?"

"Hah!"

"This little negative thing. You say you *think* it's all right now?"

"Yes."

"You don't think you should tell me what it is?"

"Mother, are you going to put Johnny up for the Presidency at the convention next year?"

"Raymond, shall we make your friend a colonel or not? I don't think Johnny can make it for the Presidency. I may go after the number-two spot."

"Will you enter him in the primaries next spring?"

"I don't think so. He has too much strength for that. I don't think I need any popularity contests for Johnny. Now—about the negative side of the major." Raymond folded his hands neatly before him on the table. "He's been in Army psychiatric hospitals twice in the past year."

"Oh, that's all," she drawled sarcastically and shrugged. "And all the time I thought it might have been something which could present a problem. My God, Raymond! A psycho! Have you ever seen what that looks like when it's stamped across a personnel file?"

"It's not what you might think, Mother. You see, due to an experience in Korea, a very vivid experience, he has been suffering from recurring nightmares."

"Is that right?"

"What happened to him could give anyone nightmares. In fact, it might even give you a nightmare or two after you hear it."

"Why?"

"Because it's quite a story and I'm involved in it up to my ears."

Her voice picked up a cutting edge. "How are you involved?"

He told her. When he had finished explaining that Marco had decided to demand his own court-martial to prove falsification and collusion in conjunction with the conferment of that Medal of Honor, savoring each word and each shocked look on his mother's face with great and deep satisfaction, she was the color of milk and her hand trembled.

"How dare he?"

"Why, Mother, it is his duty. Surely you can see that?"

"How dare the contemptible, psychoneurotic, useless, filthy little military servant of a—?" She choked on it.

Raymond was startled at the intensity of her attack. She brought her fist down on the table top with full force from two feet above it, in full tantrum, and the glasses, plates, and silver jumped and a full water pitcher leaped into the air to crash to the floor. Everyone in the dining room turned to stare and some stood up to look. A waiter dashed toward the table and went to his hands and knees, fussing with the sopping carpet and the fragments of heavy glass. She kicked him in the thigh as she sat, with vicious vigor. "Get out of here, you miserable flunky," she said. The waiter stood up slowly, staring at her, breathing shallowly. Then he left abruptly. She stood up, breathing heavily, with sweat shining on her upper lip. "I'll help your friend, Raymond," she said with violence in her voice. "I'll help him to defame and destroy an American hero. I'll cheer him as he spits upon our flag." She left him there, striding rapidly through knots of people and attendants, shouldering some. Raymond stared after her, knowing he had lost again but not knowing what he had lost. But he was not dismayed, because losing was Raymond's most constant feeling.

She went to the manager's office in the hotel. She brushed past his secretary and slammed the door behind her. She said she was the wife of Senator John Yerkes Iselin and that the two people then meeting with the manager, two barber-pinked businessmen each wearing a florid carnation, would oblige her by leaving the room. They excused themselves and left immediately, vaguely fearful of being proved Communists. She told the manager that it would be necessary to use his office and his telephone and that it would be necessary for her to have utter privacy as she would be talking about an emergency matter with the Secretary of Defense at the Pentagon, and that she would greatly appreciate it, in fact she would regard it as a patriotic service, as would indeed her husband, Senator Iselin, if he were to go to the telephone switchboard in person and direct the placement of the call to the Secretary, reversing the charges, and standing by at the operator's shoulder to make sure there was no eavesdropping on the call, a natural and human tendency under the circumstances.

Raymond paid the check and wandered about the lobby looking for his mother. He concluded that she had left so he went out of the hotel on the Fifth Avenue side, deciding to walk back to his office. When he reached the office he found a message to call Army Intelligence in New York. He called. They asked if he could help them locate Major Bennett Marco. Raymond said he believed Major Marco was presently at his apartment, as he was visiting him in New York. They asked for the telephone number. He gave it to them, explaining that they were not to give it to anyone else, then felt silly having said such a thing to professional investigators. He got busy after that on a call from the governor's press secretary and the three check-up calls that were made necessary by that call. When he called Ben at the apartment there was no answer. He forgot about it. That night, when he got home at six twenty-two, he found a note from Ben thanking him and saying that his indefinite sick leave had been canceled and that he had been recalled to Washington. The note also urged Raymond not to question Chunjin in any way after he came out of the hospital.

In Naples, in the summer of 1958, in discussing the most pow-

erful men in the world with Leonard Lyons, the expatriate
Charles Luciano had said: "A U.S. Senator can make more trouble, day in and day out, than anyone else." The condition as
stated then had not changed perceptibly a year later.

XIV

WHEN LIEUTENANT
General Nils Jorgenson had awakened that morning, a celebrant
of his fortieth anniversary in the United States Army, he had
been euphoric. When he left the office of the Secretary and the
further presence of the Army's Congressional liaison officer, he
was dismayed, cholerically angry, but mostly horrified. The
general was a good man and a brave man. He locked the doors
when he and Marco were alone in his office, then demanded
that Marco confirm or deny that Marco had planned to request
a court-martial of himself to enforce a public investigation of
circumstances involving a Medal of Honor man. Marco confirmed it. The general felt it necessary to tell Marco that he had
known Marco's father and grandfather. He asked Marco what
he had to say.

"Sir, there is only one person in the world with whom I have
discussed this course and that was Raymond Shaw himself, at his
apartment last night, and it was Shaw, sir, who urged the course
and originated the conception. May I ask who has made this
accusation to the Secretary, sir? I cannot understand how—"

"Senator John Yerkes Iselin made the accusation, Major.
Now—I offer you this because of your record and the record of
your family. I offer you the opportunity to resign from the
Army."

"I cannot resign, sir. It is my belief, sir, that the Medal of
Honor is being used as an enemy weapon. I—if the general will
understand—I see this as my duty, sir."

The general walked to the window. He looked out at the river
for a long time. He went to a casual chair and sat down and he
leaned far, far forward, almost bent double, staring at the floor
for a long time. He went to his desk and took a chewed and
battered-looking pipe from its top drawer, plugged tobacco into

it, lighted it, and smoked furiously, staring out of the window again. Then he went back to the desk and sat down to stare across at Marco.

"You not only will not get the court-martial but I am advising you that you will have no rights of any kind." He snorted with disgust. "On my fortieth anniversary in the Army I find myself telling an American officer that he will have no rights of any kind."

"Sir?"

"Senator Iselin is the kind of a man who would work day and night to block the entire defense appropriation if he were crossed on a matter as close to him as this. Senator Iselin is capable of wrecking the entire military establishment if an investigation of his stepson's glorious heroism were permitted to go through. He would undertake a war upon the United States Army which would be far more punishing and ruinous than any ever inflicted by any enemy force of arms in our history. To convey to you the enormity of the responsibility you carry, I have been ordered to tell you this, and it violates everything I stand for. Under orders, I will now threaten you." His voice trembled. "If you persist in urging your own court-martial for the purpose of examining Raymond Shaw's right to wear the Medal of Honor, you will be placed in solitary confinement."

Marco stared at the general.

"Have you ever had to threaten a private to force him to police a yard, Major? The Army, as we have known it, has heretofore functioned under a system utilizing orders. Do you remember? I must now tell you that I have not been permitted to consider this conversation a travesty on both our lives. I have been ordered not to halt at merely threatening you. Senator Iselin has decided that I was to be ordered to bribe you. If you will agree to ignore your honor as an officer and will sign a paper which has been prepared by Senator Iselin's legal counsel which guarantees that you will not press for the investigation of this matter, I am to advise you that you will be advanced in rank to lieutenant colonel, then effective instantly, to the rank of full colonel."

The nausea rose in Marco like the foam in a narrow beer glass. He could not speak even to acknowledge that he had heard. The general took a paper from his blouse and placed it on the desk, on the far side of it, in front of Marco. "So much for Iselin," he

said. "I order you to sign it." Marco took up the desk pen and
signed the paper.

"Thank you, Major. Dismiss," the general said. Marco left the
office at four twenty-one in the afternoon. General Jorgenson
shot himself to death at four fifty-five.

XV

THERE IS AN IMMU-
table phrase at large in the languages of the world that places
fabulous ransom on every word in it: The love of a good
woman. It means what it says and no matter what the perspective or stains of the person who speaks it, the phrase de-
fies devaluing. The bitter and the kind can chase each other
around it, this mulberry bush of truth and consequence, and the
kind may convert the bitter and the bitter may emasculate the
kind but neither can change its meaning because the love of a
good woman does not give way to arbitrage. The phrase may be
used in sarcasm or irony to underscore the ludicrous result of
the lack of such love, as in the wrecks left behind by bad women
or silly women, but such usage serves to mark the changeless
value. The six words shine neither with sentiment nor senti-
mentality. They are truth; a light of its own; unchanging.

Eugénie Rose Cheyney was a good woman and she loved
Marco. That fact gave Marco a large edge, tantamount to wiping
out the house percentage in banker's craps. No matter what the
action, that is a lot of vigorish to have going for anybody.

Eugénie Rose had had her office route all business to her home
that day, because she knew Marco would call whenever he woke
up at Raymond Shaw's apartment. Her boss, Justin, was overdrawn at the bank, and it irritated her that they would seek to
bother him about such a thing. He was overdrawn for a tiny
period every sixty days or so, at which time he always managed
to make an apple-cheeked deposit that kept the bank not only
honest but richer. The set construction company had called at
about eleven o'clock about some bills that the general manager
had questioned. She had all of his questions ready and a set of

the only answers in Christendom so she was able to cut four hundred and eleven dollars and sixty-three cents from the construction of a fireplace for the main room of the castle. After that call sixteen persons of every stripe, meaning from quarter-unit investors in the next show down to press agents for health food restaurants, called to try to get house seats for specific performances, and she had to invent a new theatrical superstition to fit the problem, which was how the others had come into being, by saying that surely they knew it was bad luck to distribute seat locations for the New York run until the out-of-town notices were in. And so chaos was postponed again. When she hadn't heard from Marco by seven-ten that evening she decided that he must have tried and tried to call her while all those other calls had been coming through, so she called Raymond at home, reading Marco's handwriting as he had written the number down as though it had the relative value of the sound of his voice at her very ear. Before Raymond answered, as the instrument purred the signal, she heard the elevator door open, pause, then close in the hallway just outside her door. She decided she knew it must be Marco. She slammed the phone down and rushed to the door worrying about her hair, so that she could hold it open in welcome before he could have a chance to ring the bell.

He looked terrible.

He said, "Let's get married, Rosie." He stepped over the threshold and grabbed her as though she were the rock of the ages. He kissed her. She kicked the door shut. She started to kiss him in return and it turned his knees to water.

"When?" she inquired.

"How long does it take in this state? That's how long." She kissed him again and massaged his middle with her pelvis. "I want to marry you, Ben, more than I want to go on eating Italian food, which will give you a slight idea, but we can't get married so quickly," she breathed on him.

"Why?"

"Ben, you're thirty-nine years old. We met three days ago and that's not enough time to get a bird's-eye view or a microscopic view of anyone. When we get married, Ben, and please notice how I said when *we* get married, not when *I* get married, we have to stay married because I might turn into a drunk or a *religieuse* or a crypto-Republican if we ever failed, so let's wait a week."

"A week."

"Please."

"Well, all right. There is such a thing as being overmature about decisions like this but we won't get married for a week. But we'll get the papers and take the blood tests and post the banns and plan the children's names and buy the ring and rent the rice and call the folks—"

"Folks?"

He stared at her for a moment. "You neither?"

"No."

"An orphan?"

"I used to be convinced that, as a baby, I had been the only survivor of a space ship which had overshot Mars."

"Very sexy stuff."

"You look a different kind of awful from yesterday. Mr. Shaw told me you slept all night. Quietly."

"Ah. You talked to Raymond."

"This morning. He is very formal about you."

"Poor Raymond. I'm the only one he has. Not that he needs anybody. Old Raymond has only enough soul to be able to tolerate two or three people in his life. I'm one of them. There's a girl I think he weeps over after he locks the doors. There's room for just about one more and he'll be full up. I hope it's you because having Raymond on your side is not unlike being backed up by the First Army."

"Did you have a bad time today?"

"Yeah. Well, yes and no."

He sat down as suddenly as though his legs had broken. She descended like a great dancer to rest on the floor beside his chair. He rubbed the back of her neck with his right hand, absent-mindedly, but with sensual facility.

"You are the holiest object I have in the world," he said slowly and with a thick voice, "so I swear upon you that I am going to get even with Senator John Iselin for what happened today. I don't know how yet. But how I will do it will always be somewhere in my mind from today on. From today on I'll always be thinking about how I, Marco, am going to make him pay for what he did today. I probably won't kill him. I found out today that I will probably never make a murderer."

She stared up at him. His face glistened with sweat and his eyes were sad instead of being vengeful. Her own eyes, the

Tuareg eyes, were black almonds with blue centers; a changing blue, like mist over far snow. They were the eyes of a lady left over from an army of crusaders who had taken the wrong turning, moving left toward Jarabub in Africa, instead of right, toward London, after Walter the Penniless had sent them to loot the Holy Land in 1096, to settle forever in the deep Sahara, to continue the customs of the lists, knight errantry, and the wooing of ladies fair for whose warm glances the warriors sang their songs. She stared at him steadily, then rested her head on the side of his leg and sat quietly.

"Iselin is Raymond's stepfather," Marco told her. "He sits right there in his office on the Hill. He's the most accessible, available senator we have, you know, because most of our newspapers are published right in his office nowadays. Senator Iselin is really fond of Raymond because Johnny is a terrific salesman. Raymond has no use for him, and a lack of buyer feeling about the product has always been a tremendous challenge to a salesman. All I needed to do was to call Johnny, tell him Raymond sent me, be shown right into his office, lock the door, and shoot him through the head. Or maybe beat him to death with a steel chair." Marco was talking quietly, through his teeth. He thought about his lost opportunity for a moment.

"Did you know Raymond was a Medal of Honor man, Rosie?" he asked almost rhetorically. She shook her gray-white head without answering. "I wish I could explain to you what that means. But I'd have to find a way to send you back to grow up on Army posts and put you through the Academy and find you a couple of wars and a taste for Georgie Patton and Caesar's *Commentaries* and Blucher and Ney and Moltke, but thank God we can't do any of that. Just believe it because I say it, that a Medal of Honor man is the best man any soldier can think of because he has achieved the most of what every soldier was meant to do. Anyway, after Raymond got the medal, I began to have nightmares. They were pretty bad. I had come to the worst of them when I found you, thank God. The nightmares were always the same for five years and they took a lot of trouble to suggest that Raymond had not won the medal rightfully after I had swore he had won it and the men of my patrol had sworn to it. In the end, the dreams have convinced me that we were wrong. I am sure now that the Russians wanted Raymond to have the medal so he got it. I don't know why. Maybe, if I'm lucky, I never will know why. But I'm an officer trained in intelligence work. I filled a notebook with details about furniture and clothing and complexions and speech defects and floor coverings. I talked everything over with Raymond. He got the idea that I should request my own court-martial for falsifying the report and explode a public investigation so that the enemy, at the very least, would think we knew more than we knew. That idea ended this afternoon with a lieutenant general putting a bullet into his head because it was the only possible thing he could have done to make Iselin hear the Army's protest against what Iselin had done to us. I knew that general. He liked living and he had a big time at it but he saw that protest as being an important Army job and he had been trained to accept responsibility." Marco's voice got bleak. "So I swear on you, on my Eugénie Rose, that the day will come that I, Marco, will make Senator John Iselin pay for that, and if he has to be killed, and I can't kill him, I'll have someone kill him for me." He closed his eyes for a few beats. "We got any beer in the house?" he asked her.

She got some. She drank plain warm gin.

Marco drank a can of the beer before he spoke again. "Anyway I was stopped," he said at last. "Before he shot himself the general ordered me to forget the court-martial, so that is that. I'm frozen with my terrible dreams inside of a big cake of ice and I'll never get out."

"You'll get out."

"No."

"Yes you will."

"How?"

"Do you remember that thing I told you which no girl in her right mind would ever tell a man she had gone limp over, about how I called up the man I was engaged to and resigned from the whole idea because you happened to smell so crazy?"

"I thought you just said that to get me to kiss you."

"His name was Lou Amjac and you happen to be right."

"You know, you weren't attracted to me irrevocably only because I smell this way. Don't forget I cried like a little, lost tyke the instant I first looked at you. Stuff like that is a steam roller for a potential mother."

"Have you ever done that with another woman? The smell you can't help, but I don't think I could stand sharing your sniveling with another woman."

"Never mind. That's the kind of stuff that'll come out after we're married. What about Lou Amjac?"

"He's an FBI agent. They are good at their work. I have a whole intuitive thing about how they can help you with that notebook—The Gallant Major's Gypsy Dream Book."

"I'm Army Intelligence, baby. We don't take our laundry to the FBI. Macy's definitely does not tell Gimbel's."

"The way you told it to me, you *were* Army Intelligence. If the FBI can prove you have something worth going on with, then your side will take you back and you can run the whole thing down yourself."

"Jesus."

"Isn't it worth trying?"

"Well, yeah, but still, I don't see Lou Amjac going out of his way to help me. After all, you were his girl."

"He might not be pleasant about it, that's true, but he's an agent of the Federal Bureau of Investigation and if you've got something in his line, you're not going to be able to shake him."

AMJAC *wasn't* entirely pleasant about Marco. In fact, he was particularly surly. Amjac was a skinny man with watery eyes and when Marco saw them for the first time he had a hot flash of jealousy go through him, feeling that maybe Eugénie Rose was nearsighted and that perhaps when she had first seen this guy she had thought he was crying. Amjac was tall. He had florid skin and sandy hair, freckles all over the backs of his hands, and looked as though he had a tendency to boils on the back of his neck. His hair was fine lanugo and he couldn't have grown a mustache if he had stayed in bed for a year. He had a jaw like a crocodile and as he sat in Rosie's small, warm, golden-draped room, which had horrible, large cabbage roses woven into the carpets and ancient northern European brewery posters on all walls, separated by mountain goat heads mounted on stained ash, he looked as though he would be happy to be invited to bite Marco's right arm off.

When he entered the apartment and had stood staring down, repelled, at Marco, Eugénie Rose had said serenely, "This is

Bonny Benny Marco, the chap I was telling you about, Lou. Benny boy, this here is a typical, old-time shamus right out of *Black Mask Magazine* name of Lou Amjac."

"Did you bring me all the way over here in the rain just to meet this?" Amjac inquired.

"Is it raining? Yes, I did."

"What am I supposed to do? Arrest him for impersonating an officer?"

Marco figured it would be better just to let the two old friends chat together.

"Would you like a nice plebeian rye highball, Lou?"

"Plebeian? Your friend is drinking beer right out of the can."

"Wow, you FBI guys don't miss a trick, do you?" Eugénie Rose said. "Do you want a rye highball or don't you?"

"Yeah."

"Yeah, what?"

"Yeah, yeah."

"That's better. Give me your coat. How is your elbow with the weather changing like this? Now sit down. No. Walk with me to the kitchen whilst I decant. Did your mother get back from Montreal?"

Amjac took off his coat.

"You know, I think if I was right-handed I would have had to quit the Bureau, Rose. I could hardly bend my elbow this afternoon, believe it or not. This Dr. Weiler—you met Abe Weiler, the specialist, didn't you, Rose?—he may be a good man at certain things—you know what I mean—but I don't think he even knows where to grope when it comes to arthritis." He followed her into the tiny kitchen and Marco watched them go, goggle-eyed. "My mother decided to stay over another week," he could hear Amjac say. "They sell very strong ale up there and since my sister's husband won't be home from the road until Monday, why not?"

"Of course, why not?" Rosie's voice said. "Just make sure she's out before he's home, is all. He'd love to punch her right on her sweet little old-lady nose, he told me."

"Aaaah, that's a lot of talk," Amjac said petulantly. "Thanks." He accepted the stiff highball.

"Are your lads still interested in this and that about the Soviet lads? Spy stuff?"

Amjac jerked his head back toward Marco. "Him?"

"He knows a couple," she said. They walked back into the living room with Rosie carrying four beer cans at stomach level.

"Can he talk?" Amjac asked.

"He talks beautifully. And, oh Lou, I wish you could *smell* him!" Amjac grunted and stared hard at Marco who seemed considerably embarrassed. "Just the same I'd like to tell you the story," Rosie said, "because you are gradually making Major Marco believe that after eleven years of rooming with you at the Academy he has stolen your wife, and as you know the very best in the world that just isn't the case."

"So tell!" Amjac snarled.

She told it. From the patrol forward. She went from the Medal of Honor to the nightmares, to Melvin in Wainright, to the Army hospitals, to Chunjin and Raymond, to Raymond's mother and Senator Iselin, to Marco's court-martial project and General Jorgenson's suicide. They were all quiet after she had finished. Amjac finished his highball in slow sips. "Where's the notebook?" he asked harshly.

Marco spoke for the first time. "It's with my gear. At Raymond's."

"You think you can remember any of the faces of the men in your dreams?"

"Every man, every face. One woman."

"And one lieutenant general?"

"With Security service markings."

"And this Melvin dreamed the same thing?"

"He did. And that man who was sitting beside the lieutenant general is now Raymond Shaw's house man."

Amjac stood up. He put his coat on with deliberate movement. "I'll talk it over with the special agent in charge," he said. "Where can I reach you?" Marco started to answer but Eugénie Rose interrupted him. "Right here, Louis," she said brightly. "Any time at all."

"I live at Raymond Shaw's," Marco said quickly, coloring deeply. "Trafalgar eight, eight-eight-eight-one."

"I cannot believe it," Amjac said to Rosie. "I simply cannot believe that you could ever turn out to be this kind of hard, cruel girl." He turned to go. "You never gave a damn about me."

"Lou!"

He got to the door but he had to turn around. She was staring at him levelly, without much expression.

"You know I cared," she said. "I know that you know exactly how much I cared."

He couldn't hold her stare. He looked away, then looked at the floor.

"With all the girls there are in the world," she asked, "do you think a thirty-nine-year-old bachelor who has been batting around the world most of his life wants to get married? Well, he does, Lou. And so do I. Maybe if you had been able to make up your mind between me and your elbow and your mother, you and I would have been married by now. We've been together four years, Lou. Four years. And you can say that I never cared about you and I can only answer that the cold-turkey cure is the only way for you because I have to make sure that you understand that there is only Ben; that it is as clear as daylight that Ben is the only man for me. Someday, if you keep playing the delaying game, and I guess you will, some girl may pay you out on a slow rope, then cast you adrift miles and miles away from shore and you'll know that my way—this hard, cruel way you called it—is the way that leaves the fewest scars. Now stop sulking and tell me. Are you going to help us or not?"

"I want to help him, Rosie," Amjac said slowly, "but somebody else has to decide that, so I'll let you know tomorrow. Good night and good luck."

"Night, Lou. My best to your mother when she calls later."

Amjac closed the door behind him.

"You don't just fool around, do you, Eugénie Rose?" Marco asked reverently.

AMJAC was one of the four men in the large room in the New York office of the Federal Bureau of Investigation toward noon the next morning. Another man was the special agent in charge. Another man was a courier who had just come in from Washington. The fourth man was Marco.

The courier had brought one hundred and sixty-eight close-up photographs from one of the Bureau's special files. The close-ups included shots of male models, Mexican circus performers, Czech research chemists, Indiana oil men, Canadian athletes, Australian outdoor showmen, Japanese criminals, Asturian miners,

French head waiters, Turkish wrestlers, pastoral psychiatrists, marine lawyers, English publishers, and various officials of the U.S.S.R., the People's Republic of China, and the Soviet Army. Some shots were sharp, some were murky, Marco made Mikhail Gomel and Giorgi Berezovo the first time through. No one spoke. The second time through he made Pa Cha, the older Chinese dignitary. He pulled no stiffs, such as North Carolinian literary agents or Basque sheep brokers, because he had done so much studying so well through five years of night.

The courier and the special agent took the three photographs which Marco had chosen and left the room with them to check their classifications against information on file. Marco and Amjac were left in the room.

"You go ahead," Marco said to Amjac. "You must have plenty to do. I'll wait."

"Ah, shut up," Amjac suggested.

Marco sat down at the long polished table, unfolded *The New York Times* and was able to complete two-thirds of the cross-word puzzle before the special agent and the courier returned.

"What else do you remember about these men?" the special agent asked right off, before sitting down, which caused Amjac to sit up much straighter and appear as though a dull plastic film had been peeled off his eyes. The courier slid the three photographs, face up, across the table to Marco. "Take your time," the special agent said.

Marco didn't need extra time. He picked up the top photograph, which was Gomel's. "This one wears stainless-steel false teeth and he smells like a goat. His voice is loud and it grates. He's about five feet six, I'd figure. Heavy. He wears civilian clothes but his staff is uniformed, ranging from a full colonel to a first lieutenant. They wear political markings." Marco picked up the shot of the Chinese civilian, Pa Cha. "This one has a comical, high-pitched giggle and killer's eyes. He had the authority. Made no attempt to conceal his distaste and contempt for the Russians. They deferred to him." He picked up Berezovo's picture, a shot that had been taken while the man was in silk pajamas with a glass in his hand and a big, silly grin across his face. "This is the lieutenant general. The staff he carried was in civilian clothes and one of the staff was a woman." Marco grinned. "They looked like FBI men. He speaks with a bilateral emission lisp and has a very high color like—uh—like Mr. Amjac here."

A new man came into the room with a note for the special agent who read it and said, "Your friend Mr. Melvin has been cooperating with us in Wainwright, Alaska. He's made one of these men, Mikhail Gomel, who is a member of the Central Committee." Marco beamed at Amjac over this development, but Amjac wouldn't look at him.

"Can you return to Washington today, Colonel? We'll have a crew of specialists waiting for you."

"Any time you say, sir. I'm on indefinite leave. But the rank is major."

"You have been a full colonel since sunrise this morning. They just told me on the phone from Washington."

"No!" Marco yelled. He leaped to his feet and gripped the table and kept shouting, "No, no, no!" He pounded and pounded on the shining table with rage and frustration. "That filthy, filthy, filthy son-of-a-bitch. He'll pay us for this! He'll pay us someday for this! No, no, no!"

Potentially, Marco might have been a hysteroid personality.

COLONEL Marco worked with the Federal Bureau of Investigation and his own unit of Army Intelligence (into which he had been honorably and instantly reinstated upon the recommendation of the FBI's director and the Plans Board of the Central Intelligence Agency). There was no longer any question of a need for a court-martial to institute a full investigation. A full unit was set up, with headquarters in New York and conference space at the Pentagon, and unaccountable funds from the White House were provided to maintain housing, laboratories, and personnel, including three psychiatrists, the country's leading Pavlovian practitioner, six espionage technicians (including three librarians), a mnemonicist, an Orientalist, and an expert on Soviet internal affairs. The rest were cops and assistant cops.

Marco was in charge. His aide, assistant, and constant companion was Louis Amjac. The other side-kick was a round type, with the nerves of a Chicago bellhop, named Jim Lehner. He was there representing the CIA. They worked out of a capacious, many chambered house in the Turtle Bay district of New York, right through the summer of 1959 but they did not get one step further than the alarming conclusions which had been reached originally by Marco. It is questionable whether any definitive conclusions beyond those reached could have been attained if Marco had been able to allow himself to tell the part of his dreams having to do with Raymond's murders, but he could see no connection, he didn't think the time had come, he couldn't keep the thought in his mind, and so on and on into many splinters of reasons why he did not divulge the information. Thousands of manhours were put in on the project and as time went on the pressure from exalted sources grew and grew. A three-platoon system of surveillance was put around Raymond. The total cost of the project which the doctrinaire romantics in the service classified as Operation Enigma has been estimated at, or in excess of, $634,217 and some change, for travel, salaries, equipment, lease, and leasehold improvements, maintenance and miscellaneous expense—and not a quarter of it was stolen beyond a few hundred rolls of Tri-X and Hydropan film, but even accountants don't recognize such losses because all photographers everywhere are helpless about film stocks to the point where it is not even considered stealing but is called testing.

The Army flew Alan Melvin, the former corporal turned civilian plumber, from Alaska to the Walter Reed Hospital in Washington, then to the house in Turtle Bay in New York, but the interviews with him revealed no more than what had been gleaned from Marco. However, the call to Operation Enigma seemed to have come in time to have saved Melvin's sanity— even his life. The nightmares had caused a weight loss of seventy-one pounds. He weighed one hundred and three pounds when picked up at Wainwright. He could not be moved for seventeen days, while he received high-caloric feeding, but by that time he had talked to Marco. When he learned that what he had dreamed had reached such a point of credibility that it had become one more terrible anxiety for the President of the United States, it seemed as though all dread was removed instantly, enabling Melvin to sleep and eat, dissolving the concretion of his fears.

Upon his restoration to active duty Colonel Marco requested, and was granted, an informal meeting with representative officers of the Board. They explained that it would not be possible for Colonel Marco to refuse advancement to the rank he held but that it was to his great credit that he felt so strongly about the matter. They explained that such an action could disturb legislative relationships in the present climate, so extraordinary that it had to be considered the far, far better part of valor for government establishments to run with the tide. Colonel Marco asked that he be permitted to register his vociferous distaste for Senator Iselin and be allowed to demonstrate that he rejected any and all implied sponsorship of himself by such an infamous source; he wished the condition to be viewed by the Board as being and having been untenable to him as well as having been unsolicited by him and undesirable in every and any way. He added other stern officialese. He asked that he be allowed to express, in an official manner, his innermost fears that this promotion to the rank of full colonel would inconsiderately prejudice the future against his favor for an optimum Army career.

The Board explained to him, informally and in a most friendly manner, that whereas it was true that it would be necessary that his personnel file forever retain Senator Iselin's stain to explain Colonel Marco's—uh—unusual—uh—advancement, the Chairman of the Joint Chiefs, with his own hand, had appended an explanation of the attendant circumstances, absolving the colonel of any threat of shadow.

All in all, because he was human to extreme dimension, Marco secretly felt he had done pretty well out of the Iselin brush, which in no way forgave Iselin or diminished Colonel Marco's prayers for vengeance. The single negative factor connected with the mess had been the death of General Jorgenson, but that was another matter entirely and one not pertinent to his promotion. Someday, he thought fervently, he would like to see the notation made by the Chairman of the Joint Chiefs upon the personnel file of General Jorgenson before it was permitted to pass into Army history. As a soldier, Colonel Marco knew that the general's death had been a hero's death, in the sense that a Hindu priest would believe deeply in the right of a widow to burn herself upon her husband's funeral pyre, becoming a saint and joining Sati. So saved are all those who enable themselves to believe, and therefore was the military mind called a juvenile mind. It was constant; it observed a code of honor in a world where any element of devotion to a rationale summoned scorn; but the world itself knew itself was sick.

Colonel Marco puzzled his past nightmares and decided they could make him a full general yet.

While Raymond toured Europe with his mother, Marco toured the United States with Amjac and Lehner and completed a formal canvass of the survivors of the patrol. This yielded nothing. Nightly, in the manner of a lonely drummer distracted by the boredom of the road, Marco telephoned his girl whom he had not yet had either the time or the opportunity to marry. She comforted him. The three men moved through seven cities from La Jolla, California, to Bayshore, Long Island. Marco and Melvin had been the only two men on the patrol who had ever dreamed of it.

XVI

MRS. JOHN ISELIN'S tour of Europe in the summer of 1959 with her son developed into the most shocking string of occasions, as redolent of that decade as a string of garlic pearls. Mrs. Iselin achieved more for sustained anti-Americanism and drove infected wedges more deeply between America and her allies than any other action by any individual or agency, excepting her husband, of the twentieth century.

It would seem that wherever Mrs. Iselin set down with her personable, strangely expressed son, she gave a different account of why she was traveling. In Paris, she was looking for inefficiency in United States Government offices overseas. In Bonn, she said she was looking for subversives in United States Government offices overseas. In Munich, she said she was looking, actually, for both, because "any concept of efficiency in government must include complete political responsibility. If anyone should favor the Communists, then he cannot be efficient," Mrs. Iselin explained to the German (and world) press.

Mrs. Iselin's only brother was, at the time of her visit to Rome in late July, the American ambassador to Italy. He extended an invitation to his sister and his nephew to stay with him and his family, which Mrs. Iselin accepted via the Associated Press. "My brother is so dear to me," she said for publication in many languages, "and I do so ache to see him again after a long separation, listen to his wisdom, and rejoice in his embrace. Pressure of work for our country has kept us apart too long. We are out of touch." It was not told that what had put them in direct touch again was a specific coded order from the Secretary of State ordering his ambassador to invite his sister to be his house guest.

Mrs. Iselin moved out of the ambassador's residence to the Grand Hotel on the afternoon of the second day she had been her brother's guest and immediately called a press conference to explain her action, saying, according to the transcript which was printed in full in *The New York Times* for July 29, 1959, "In every sense of that melodramatic word I am standing before you as a torn woman. I love my brother but I must love my country more. My loyalty as a sister of a beloved brother must be moved to serve a greater loyalty to the unborn of the West. My brother's embassy is wholly directed by American Communists under direct manipulation by the Kremlin, and I pray before you today that this is a result of my brother's ineptness and ignorance and not of his villainy."

After the press had left, Raymond languidly asked his mother what in the world had ever possessed her to do such an unbelievably malicious thing. "Raymond, dear," his mother said, "in this life one can turn the other cheek in a Christian manner only so many times. A long, long time ago I told that brother of mine that I would see him nailed to the floor and today he knows that I kidded him not. I kidded him not, Raymond, dear."

MRS. ISELIN's brother resigned at once as ambassador to Italy and his resignation was at once accepted by the State Department and refused by the White House because Foster had not cleared through Jim or Jim had not cleared through Foster. For thirty-six hours thereafter the matter remained in this exquisite state of balance until, on return from the greenest kind of rolling countryside in Georgia, the President's will prevailed and the ambassadorship of Raymond's mother's brother was restored, the wisdom of the President's decision being based upon the choleric rages into which the mention of Johnny Iselin's name could throw him.

As his wife succeeded with such consistency in gaining so

much space in the press of the world, Senator Iselin found it necessary to issue his own directive as to his wife's mission in Europe, from Washington. In close-up on television during his formal investigation of atheism in the Department of Agriculture he said to the millions of devoted viewers throughout the country, "My wife, a brilliant woman, an American who has suffered deeply before this, long before this, in the name of her great and abiding patriotism, was sent abroad as unofficial emissary of the United States Senate to bring back a report on the amount of money that this Administration has spent to further the cause of communism in the Western World. It is my holy hope that this will answer the question of certain elements in this country for once and for all with regard to this matter."

Alas, the statement did not settle the matter for once and for all, as the President insisted that his Minority Leader in the Senate make a policy answer to settle Senator Iselin's statement for once and for all. The President, being of the Executive Branch, overlooked the fact that the Minority Leader was first a member of the Senate, an establishment which has always taken a dim view of any directives from the Executive.

The Minority Leader's text was a model of political compromise. As Senate spokesman the leader denied, in a sense, that Mrs. Iselin was an "official" emissary of the United States Senate although he conceded that the Senate would indeed feel honored to think of her as its "unofficial" emissary at any time. "Mrs. Iselin is a beautiful and gracious lady," this courtly gentleman said, deeply pleased that the White House was so discomfited, "a delightful woman whose charm and grace are only exceeded by her outstanding intelligence, but I do not feel that either she or her distinguished husband would want it said that anyone not actually elected by the great people of the states of the United States to the sacred trust of the United States Senate could be said to represent that body. Say, rather, that Mrs. Iselin represents America wherever she may be." (Applause.) The gentleman received a written citation from the Daughters of the American Struggles for Liberty for his gallantry to American womanhood.

Citations from the presses of Europe, mainly those of a conservative stripe, took a different tack. In Stockholm, *Dagens Nyheter*, Sweden's largest and most influential daily, wrote: "What the wife of Senator John Iselin possibly might have discovered, she has already spoiled by foolishness and arrogance. She has introduced anti-American feeling far more effective than any that could possibly have been initiated by the Committee and their paid agents. The unanimous opinion of Europe is that Iselin symbolizes exactly the reverse of what America stands for and what we have learned to appreciate. Iselinism is the arch-enemy of liberty and a disgrace to the name of America."

Throughout the tour, until its closing days in England, Raymond had not so much as acknowledged the existence of his mother or his stepfather in the newspaper column that he wrote daily and transmitted by cable as he covered, with considerable cogency, a startlingly intimate view of the European political scene. *The Daily Press*, his employer in New York, was said to have had to resort to threats to force Raymond into writing and publishing a statement regarding his own position. This was the sheerest nonsense: the kind stimulated by the need of metropolitan people who feel that they simply must be seen as having inside information on everything. The fact of the matter was that Raymond's publisher, Charles O'Neil, was a more than ordinarily perceptive man. He telephoned Raymond at the Savoy Hotel in London and, after an exchange of information on the prevailing weather conditions in each country, a report of past weather phenomena, and a foretelling of what might be expected from the weather on either side of the Atlantic, O'Neil, who was paying for the call, broke in saying that he felt Raymond could have no conception of the extent of the publicity his mother's European tour had been producing all over the country, nor could he have any way of realizing how closely he, Raymond Shaw, had been allied with Iselin's actions and purposes. He read from a few articles, shuddering at the cost of the telephone tolls. Raymond was aghast. He asked what O'Neil thought he should do. The publisher said he saw no reason why the cost of the entire call could not be charged to the syndicate—uh—he meant, rather, that he felt both the paper and Raymond should relent from their fixed position on the matter of Raymond's family being mentioned in his writings, and that Raymond should at once file at least one column of opinion on Iselinism and the present tour.

Raymond complied that day and the column was reprinted more than any other single piece the paper had ever caused to be syndicated and the toll charges for the call to London were

absorbed by the syndicate without the slightest demurral. The
column read, in part: "I have known John Yerkes Iselin to be an
assassin and a blackguard since my boyhood. He lives by attack-
ing. He is the cowardly assassin in politics who strikes from the
dark and evil alley of his opportunism. With no exceptions, the
justifications for these attacks have been so flimsy as to have no
standing either in courts of law or in the minds of individuals
capable of differentiating repeated accusation from even a reasonable presumption of guilt. The ultimate result is a threat to
national security. Iselin is laying a foundation for the agencies of
American government to serve totalitarian ends rather than the
Government of the United States as we have hitherto known
it."

Raymond insisted upon reading the dispatch to his mother
before he sent if off. He read it in a monotone with a stony face,
fearful of the response it would bring. "Oh, for crissake, Raymond," his mother said, "what do you suppose I'm going to
do—sue you? I know you aren't asking me, but send the silly
thing. Who the hell reads beyond the headlines anyway?" She
waved him away contemptuously. "Please! Go cable your copy.
I'm busy."

RAYMOND was unaware of being in an anomalous position in London after his column on Johnny and his mother appeared in the States. It was reprinted in the English newspapers
at once. Writing of his mother's part in what he termed their
"conspiracy of contempt for man," Raymond had described her
as "a caricature of the valiant pioneer women of America who
loaded the guns while their husbands fought off the encircling
savages" in that he saw his mother and Johnny as the savages
and "if a nation's blood is its honor and its dignity before the
world, then that blood covered their hands." This appeared to
be in direct opposition to basic policies of some British newspapers that had made a pretty pound indeed out of that steely
treacle of Home and Mother, so that at least a portion of the
press that attended Raymond's mother's farewell conference at
the Savoy Hotel viewed Raymond not at all enthusiastically. Had

they been able to measure how Raymond viewed them, as he viewed all the world, the shooting would have started, straight off. On the other hand, another section of the British press so detested Senator and Mrs. Iselin that it quite approved of Raymond's attack upon his mother, although it would not, of course, ever permit itself to print that view.

Both sides had the opportunity to air their views, however indirectly. Before she left London Mrs. Iselin told the reporters who had assembled in a large room named after a production of Richard D'Oyly Carte that she would urge her husband's Senate committee to investigate the Labour Party of Great Britain, as she had assembled documentary proof that it was a nest of Socialists and crypto-Communists and that this political party could, if returned to power, "smash the alliance upon which the friendship of our two great nations has been based and, under the guise of honest difference of opinion, sabotage the great American purpose before the world." It was as though the great glacier had slid down from the top of the world and enveloped the hotel. Sixty men and women stood staring at her, their chins resting comfortably on their chests, mouths wide open, eyes glazed. One gentleman of Fleet Street threw his full glass of whisky and water backward over his head in a high arc to crash in the corner of the large room rather than drink it, which is criticism indeed from a newspaperman of any country. He said, "Madame, my name is Joseph Pole of the *Daily Advocate-Journal.* I repudiate you, your husband, and your most peculiar son." He turned to a lady journalist on his left and took the highball from her hand. "May I?" he asked. Then he threw the contents of the drink into Mrs. Iselin's ankles.

Raymond knocked him right through the throng. At this juncture, that portion of the journalistic group which had objected to Raymond in the first place for having attacked the profitable institution of Motherhood in his column, took this chance to strike out at him, while the group which had secretly approved Raymond's utter public rejection of his mother now saw their chance to have at her themselves, and were led forward by female colleagues brandishing raised umbrellas. The result was a melee. Mrs. Iselin swung chairs, water carafes, and broken whisky bottles, doing most painful damage but emerging physically unharmed. Raymond lay about him with his extraordinary strength and his natural antipathy. The news photographers present very nearly swooned with ecstasy over the turn taken, for, from every British newspaper-reader's point of view, here was Iselinism in action with British righteousness whacking it over the head.

Beginning with the very next editions, the British press indulged in its own sort of good-natured London journalists' fun, which could be described by the subject of their reporting as being an experience not unlike falling nude into a morass of itching powder while two sadistic dentists drilled into one's teeth at the instant of apogee of alcoholic history's most profligate hang-over. The ultimate end of all of these combative news stories was that when Mrs. Iselin and her son needed to journey to Southampton to embark for home, some one hundred and fifteen London policemen, whom the world knows affectionately as "bobbies" after their founder, Sir Robert Peel, needed to bludgeon a path through the howling mass of outraged citizenry to get them out of their hotel, following which a semimilitary motorcade was formed to race them to the ship. The entire incident was a stiff test of Anglo-American relations, beyond a doubt, and somewhat scored John Iselin's own lack of popular favor in the British Isles.

WHILE Raymond had been in Paris, in late June, a member of the French Chamber of Deputies who was co-leader of the political party having the record of greatest resistance to the government then in power, was assassinated in his *hôtel particulier* on Rue Louis David in the sixteenth *arrondissement,* baffling police and security agencies.

While Raymond was in London, on the evening before his mother's famous debate with the British press, a peer who was greatly admired for having articulated a liberal, humanistic, and forward-looking life as publisher of a chain of national newspapers and periodicals, Lord Morris Croftnal, was murdered while he slept. There was not a clue as to the identity or motivation of his killer.

XVII

RAYMOND'S SHIP docked in New York on a Wednesday in late August, 1959. He reported for work at *The Daily Press* early Thursday morning. Marco called him and made a date to meet him at four o'clock in Hungarian Charlie's, the saloon across the street from the paper, saying he would be bringing two of his side-kicks with him if Raymond wouldn't mind. Raymond didn't mind.

The four men sat at a table far in the rear of the saloon, which was a solid, practical saloon set up to sell a maximum amount of booze and, with careful attention to unsanitary-seeming *décor*—a little dirt here, a little grease there—a minimum amount of food, which, after all, has a tendency to spoil after a week or so and can be a loss. The air was nearly gelid from the huge air-conditioning unit that looked big enough to chill an automobile assembly plant. A giant juke box, manufactured by The Giant Juke Box Company of Arcana, Illinois, was belting everything living right over the head with a loudly lovable old standard out of Memphis, Tennessee, in which the rhyme of the proper name Betty Lou and the plural noun *shoes* were repeated, in a Kallikakian couplet, over and over again. A giant juke box is constructed to make a sound like two full-sized, decibel-pregnant juke boxes going at top volume at the same time, but two separate juke boxes each playing a different tune, each in a different tempo, and, if possible, in a different language. The joint was noisy from opening to closing because Hungarian Charlie liked noise and was, in every vocal manner, very much like a giant juke box himself.

After minimum hand-shaking and ordering a highball for Amjac and Lehner and beers for Raymond and himself, Marco went right to business by asking Raymond to tell his version of the battle action, which Raymond did forthwith and in detail, utilizing only the future tense in verb forms. Lehner carried the tape recorder in a shoulder sling.

"You sound as though you got those nightmares straightened out. In fact, you look it," Raymond said warily, not sure whether it was proper to talk about such things in front of these house-detective types. Marco looked great. He had gained the weight back.

"All over."

"Did you—was it—did that thing we were talking about help any?"

"The court-martial?"

"Yeah."

"The way it worked out, it wasn't necessary but I still have you and only you to thank for losing those nightmares. We got a different kind of an investigation started, just the way you said it had to be, and the nightmares were gone. Forever. I hope."

"Didn't you investigate the medal?"

"Sure. What else?"

"Any progress?"

"Slow, but good."

"Is it working out the way we thought?"

"Yeah. Right down the line."

"The medal is a phony?"

"It certainly looks that way."

"I knew it. I *knew* it." Raymond looked from Amjac to Lehner, shaking his head in awed disbelief. "How about that?" he asked with mystification. "Will you tell me why a lot of Communist brass would want to steal a Medal of Honor for a complete stranger?"

Amjac didn't answer. He seemed embarrassed about something. Raymond became aware of his silence and stared at him coldly. "It was a rhetorical question," he said haughtily.

Amjac coughed. He said, "It scares hell out of us, if you want the truth, Mr. Shaw. We have run out of ideas and we don't know where else to look, if that gives you some idea." Raymond swung his gaze to Lehner, who had a head like a gourd, a small mustache, and eyes like watermelon seeds, and Lehner stared him down.

"Have you talked to Al Melvin?" Raymond said. The voice of a sick child whined out of the giant juke box behind them as though trying to escape the hateful noises behind it. "You know, Ben, Al. In Alaska."

"Yes, sir. We have," Amjac said grimly.

Marco said, "Raymond, there is no known area of this case which we haven't covered in many ways. We've talked to every member of the patrol. We've traveled maybe ninety-two hundred miles around the country. We're sure Chunjin is here as an enemy agent, assigned to you as a body guard and assassin, if necessary. I have a unit in New York and Washington which does nothing but concentrate on this problem. There are seventeen of us, all told. Mr. Amjac is on loan from the FBI and Mr. Lehner is with us as an expert from Central Intelligence. Working on that riddle of why the enemy should go to enormous trouble to secure the Medal of Honor for you is all I do, day and night. It's all Amjac and Lehner do. It's all the seventeen of us do, and the White House wants to know what happened in a report every week and a copy of that report goes to the Joint Chiefs. And you want to hear something off-beat, Raymond? I mean something that will throw this out of context for a moment to let you see what a unique person you have become? A copy of the report goes to the Prime Ministers of Britain and Canada and to the President of Mexico."

"But what the hell for?" Raymond seemed outraged at this invasion, as though he were being shared by four heads of government. "What the hell do the Mexicans and the bloody British, who tried to kill my mother, incidentally, have to do with that lousy medal?"

Lehner tapped Raymond on the forearm. Raymond looked at him, drawing his arm away. "Why don't you listen?" Lehner said. "If you talk you can't learn anything."

"Don't touch me again," Raymond said. "If you want to remain here with us, doing your clerk's tasks and waiting for your pension, do not touch me again." He looked at Marco. "Continue, Ben," he said equably.

"It is our considered opinion," Marco said, "that we are moving into the area of action which will reveal why they wanted you to have the Medal of Honor. The patrol happened in 1951. Chunjin didn't arrive to take up his duties until '59. Eight years' lapse. Whatever is going to happen is going to happen soon. You're a marked man, Raymond. They've marked you and they guard you. We've marked you. Am I frightening you, Raymond?"

"*Me?*" Nothing frightened Raymond. A man needs to have something to lose to become frightened. Even only one thing that is his and that he values will make it possible for threat to scare a man, but Raymond had nothing.

"That's what I explained to our unit. And that's what our

psychiatrists had projected on you, that attitude, that—that fear-lessness, you know?—but I have to frighten you, Raymond, be-cause we need you to think of yourself as some kind of time bomb with a fuse eight years long. You walk barefooted on the edge of a razor. Only you will know when the change comes, when the mission is divulged, when your move is to be made, and it can only end one way. Your country, my country, this country will have to be in danger from you and you will be expected to do exactly as you have been told or will be told. They got inside your mind. They did. I swear before God."

"Aaaah!" Raymond disliked this kind of talk. It sickened him. What kind of a world of fondlers had this become? Why did Marco have to say that those thick-necked pigs were *inside* his mind?

"I told you that we talked to every member of the patrol this summer. You know what they said about you, every one of them? That you were the greatest, warmest, most wonderful single guy they had ever met. They remembered you with love and affection, Raymond. Isn't that funny?"

"Funny? It's ludicrous."

"How do you account for it?"

Raymond shrugged and grimaced. "I saved their lives. I mean, they thought I had saved their lives. I suppose the poor slobs were grateful."

"I don't think so. I've had to work all this out with our psychia-trists because I don't have a very objective view, either, but my actual memory is that there was a broad chasm between you and those men before the patrol. They didn't hate you, they seemed rather to fear your scorn, you know? You had a way of freezing their dislike and keeping them uneasy and off balance. The psychiatrists will tell you that an attitude, a group attitude as well as individual attitudes like that, can't be changed into warm and eager interest, into such admiration, and deep respect merely because of gratitude. No, no, no."

"Life isn't a popularity contest," Raymond said. "I didn't ask them to like me."

"I'm going to start to prove right now that they have gotten inside your mind, Raymond, because you once told me, in a joking way, that you had come out of the Army with much more of an active interest in women than when you went in—and because I have to frighten you, I will have to embarrass you, too.

We checked. We are experts. Experts' experts, even. We went back over the seams of your life, looking for lint. You were twenty-two, going on twenty-three years old, when you left the Army, and you had never been laid. More than that. You had never even kissed a girl, had you, Raymond?" Marco leaned across the table, his eyes lambent with affection, and he said softly, "You never even kissed Jocie, did you, Raymond?"

"You had men talk to Jocie? In Argentina?" Raymond wasn't outraged. Long before, he had set all his dials so that Marco could do no wrong with him, but he was extremely impressed and for the first time. He felt elated to be in connection with anyone who had looked at Jocie, had sat beside her and had spoken to her about anything at all, and to have spoken to her about him, about that wondrous summer together and about— about kissing. He felt as though his eyes had climbed into the upper space above the earth and that he could see himself as he sat in Hungarian Charlie's and at the same time watch sweet, sweet Jocie as she sat in a bower, under pink roses, knitting something soft and warm, in the Argentine.

"I had to know. And I had to make you understand that going ten thousand miles and back for the answer to one question is very little to do in the face of the pressure and the threat that is implied."

"But, Ben—Jocie—well, after all, Jocie—"

"That's why I brought these two strangers. The only reason. Do you think I would talk about such things—things which I know are sacred to you when I also know that nothing else in this whole world is sacred to you—in front of two strangers if I wasn't desperate to get through to you?" Raymond did not answer; he was thinking about Jocie, the Jocie he had lost and would never find again.

"They are inside your mind. Deep. Now. For eight years. One of their guys with a big sense of humor thought it would be a great gag to throw you a bone for all of the trouble they were going to put you to, and fix it up inside your head so that, all of a sudden, you'd get interested in girls, see? It meant nothing to them. It was only a gratuitous gesture, a quarter tip to the men's-room attendant, considering all the other things they were going to do inside your head and have already done from inside your head."

"Stop it! Stop it, goddamit, Ben. I will not listen to this. You

nauseate me. Stop saying that people and things and a lot of
outside filth are inside my head. Just say it some other way if you
have to talk to me. Just say it some other way, and what the hell
are you talking about—what they have already done from inside
my head?"

"Don't shout," Lehner said. "Take it easy." However, he did
not touch Raymond this time.

The giant juke box had found a giant guitar. It was being
strummed insanely, alternating between two of the most simply
constructed chords while a farmer's voice bellowed cretinous
rhymes above it.

Marco stared at Raymond compassionately and held his gaze
for a long moment before he said, "You murdered Mavole and
Bobby Lembeck, kid."

"What? Whaaaat?" Raymond pushed at the table but his back
was against the wall, literally as well as figuratively, so that he
could not move backward to escape the words. His glaucous eyes
in the long, bony face held some of the terror seen in the eyes of
a horse falling on ice. He was incredulous but Marco and Amjac
and Lehner knew that Marco was getting through because they
knew Raymond the way a marine knows his own rifle, because
they had been drilled on Raymond, his reactions and inhibitions,
for hours of day and hours of night.

"You killed them. Not your fault. They just used your body the
way they would use any other machine. You strangled Mavole
and you shot Bobby."

"In the dream?"

"Yes."

Raymond was unutterably relieved. He had been greatly startled but at last things had been returned to reality. These men
with Marco were captives of their belief in that unfortunate
man's delusion which had almost cost him his sanity late the year
before. Everything fell into place for Raymond as he understood
the motivation of all of this fantasy. Ben was his friend and
Raymond would not let him down. He would go right along as
he was supposed to, becoming agitated now and then if necessary, because Ben looked as though he had regained his health
and his ability to sleep and Raymond would have fought off an
army to preserve that.

"The dream happened again and again in my sleep because it
had happened so indelibly in my life. I have to frighten you,

Raymond. If you can live in continuous fear perhaps we can force you to see what we aren't able to discover. Whenever it happens—this thing that has been set to happen—we have to find some way to reach you, to give you new reflexes so that you will do whatever we will tell you to do—even kill yourself if that has to be—the instant that you know what it is they have built you to do. They made you into a killer. They are inside your mind now, Raymond, and you are helpless. You are a host body and they are feeding on you, but because of the way we live we can't execute you or lock you up to stop you."

Raymond did not need to simulate alarm. Every time Marco told him of the invasion of his person by those people it made him wince, and to think of himself as a host body on which they were feeding almost made him cry out or stand up and run out of the saloon. His voice became different. It was not the flat, undeigning drawl. It was a voice he might have borrowed from an Errol Flynn movie in which the actor faced immolation with hopeless resigned gallantry. It was a new voice for him, one he created specifically to help his friend through the maze of his fantasy, and it was most convincing. "What do you want?" the hoarsened new voice said.

Marco's voice attacked. It moved like a starving rodent which gnaws at flaws behind the doors, mad to get through to an unknown trove of crazing scent on the other side.

"Will you submit voluntarily to a brainwashing?" that voice asked.

"Yes," Raymond answered.

The giant juke box spat the sounds out as though trying to break the rows upon rows of shining bottles behind the bar.

FRIDAY morning, just before noon, a psychiatric and bio-chemical task force began to work Raymond over on the fourth floor of the large house in the Turtle Bay district. The total effort exhausted and frustrated both the scientists and the policemen. The effect of the narcotics, techniques, and suggestions, which resulted in deep hypnosis for Raymond, achieved a result that approximated the impact an entire twenty-five-cent jar of F. W. Woolworth vanishing cream might have on vanishing an aircraft carrier of the *Forrestal* class when rubbed into the armor plate. They were unable to dredge up one mote of information. Under the deep hypnosis, loaded to the eyes with a cocktail of truth serums, Raymond demonstrated that he could not remember his name, his color, his sex, his age, or his existence. Before he had been put under he had been willing to divulge anything within his power. In catalepsy, his mind seemed to have been sealed off as an atomic reactor is separated from the rest of a submarine. It all served to confirm what they already knew. Raymond had been brainwashed by a master of exalted skill. The valiant, long-cherished hope that they would be able to counterplant suggestion within Raymond's already dominated unconscious mind never had a chance of being put into work.

When it was over, the medical staff wanted to tell Raymond that the explorations had been entirely successful, on the grounds that he was able to accept suggestion with his conscious mind, but Marco overruled that. He said he would tell Raymond that he was beyond their reach, that he was going to be directed entirely by the enemy, that they could not help him but that they had to stop him and that they would stop him. Marco wanted Raymond to stay scared, as much as he disbelieved that Raymond could sustain any feeling.

After that first afternoon when Marco had poured it on him in Hungarian Charlie's, Raymond had dug in to what he was determined to maintain as a fixed position. He was a lucid man. He knew he was in excellent health, mental and physical. He knew Marco's health was a long way from what it had once been. He knew it was Marco who had been having the nightmares and breakdowns and that for unknown reasons, probably relative to the phrase "the Army takes care of its own," his commanders had decided to humor Marco. Well, Raymond decided, I will out-humor and outbless them. Marco is closer to me than any one or all of those uniformed clots. Raymond accordingly formed his policy. It deployed his imagination like the feelers of an insect, advancing it ahead of him wherever his mind, which moved on thousands of tiny feelers of prejudice, took him in its circuitous detour that would allow him to avoid exposing himself to himself as a murderer, a sexual neutral, and a man despised and scorned by his comrades. He put his back into the performance. He used all the tricks of the counterfeiter's art he could summon to project all of the surface emotions which their little playlets seemed to require of him. He bent, or seemed to bend, into their intentions to halt what he saw as a comic-book plot in which a sinister foreign power, out to destroy America, would achieve its ends by using him as an instrument. They wanted him to be scared. He would seem, when under observation, to be scared, and he worked hard for an effect of seeming as distressed and as aware as game running ahead of guns.

Fortunately, he remembered that the vegetable substitute for benzedrine, which he had taken at one time to lose weight, always gave him hand tremors, so that helped. He knew that a double dose or more of it could produce an authentic crying jag in him, with uncontrollable tears and generally distraught conduct, so that helped.

Marco's surveillance teams duly reported his purchases of this drug and the unit's psychological specialists confirmed the side-effects they would produce, so Marco was not deceived by Raymond's somewhat piteous conduct from time to time. He was very proud of Raymond, however, because he could see that Raymond was going to intolerable trouble, for Raymond, to meet Marco's urgent requirements, but the discouraging and depressing fact remained that all of them were armless in their attempt to stave off shapeless disaster.

However, there was one relentless, inexorable strength on Marco's side: in combination or singly, the Federal Bureau of Investigation, Army Intelligence, and the Central Intelligence Agency represented maximum police efficiency. Such efficiency suspends the law of averages and flattens defeat with patience.

XVIII

EUGÉNIE ROSE was in Boston with Justin's new musical show, which, secretly, had been based upon a map of the heavens issued by the National Geographic Society two years before. Marco planned to join her the next day. She and Marco talked on the telephone at odd hours. They were still dedicated to an early marriage and seemed more than ever convinced that, in a world apparently so populated, no one else existed.

It was Christmas Eve. Raymond had invited Marco for dinner, telephoning him from the office to say that he had given Chunjin the night off and that Chunjin had resisted. Marco said that was because Chunjin was undoubtedly a Buddhist and not a celebrant at Christmas. Raymond said he was sure Chunjin was not a Buddhist because he left books by Mary Baker Eddy around the pantry and kitchen and was forever smiling. Marco said he felt a sense of disappointment at that news because he had figured that if he sent Chunjin a Christmas card, Chunjin would then be obligated to send him a card on Buddha's birthday, or lose face.

Marco arrived at Raymond's apartment at seven o'clock and brought two bottles of cold champagne with him. Unfortunately for the hang-overs the following day, Raymond had also put two quarts of champagne in the refrigerator. They decided they would sidle toward food a little later and settled down in Raymond's office behind the big window, and with commendable seasonal cooperation it began to snow large goose feathers, a present from the Birthday Boy himself, in lieu of peace on earth.

After two goblets of the golden bubbles, Raymond reached under his chair and, stiffly, handed Marco a large, gift-wrapped package.

"Merry Christmas," he said. "It has been good to know you." Raymond, saying those words, sounded more touching than anyone else who could have said them because, while Raymond had been marooned in time and on earth and in all the pit-black darkness of interstellar space, Marco was the only other being, except Jocie, who had acknowledged he was there.

Marco ripped away the elegant gold and blue paper, revealing the three volumes of Fuller's *A Military History of the Western World* re-bound in limp morocco leather. Marco held onto the books with one hand and pounded the embarrassed, grinning Raymond with the other. Then he put the books upon the desk and reached into his pocket. "And a merry, merry Christmas to you, too, young man," he sang out, handing Raymond a long flat envelope. Raymond started to open the envelope, slowly and with wonderment.

"Wait, wait!" Marco said. He hurried to the record-player, shuffled through some albums, and slid out a twelve-inch record of Christmas carols. The machine conferred silvered voices upon them singing "We Three Kings of Orient Are."

"O.K., proceed," Marco said.

Raymond opened the envelope and found a gift certificate in the amount of fifty dollars to be drawn on *Les Pyramides* of middle Broadway, the Gitlitz Delicatessen. The frosty carol swelled around them as Raymond smiled his always touching smile at the gift in his hands.

> *"We three kings of Orient are,*
> *Bearing gifts we traverse afar,*
> *Field and fountain, moor and mountain,*
> *Following yonder star.*
> *O, Star of wonder, star of night,*
> *Star with royal beauty bright,*
> *Westward leading, still proceeding,*
> *Guide us to the perfect light."*

Marco thought of their own three kings of Orient: Gomel, Berezovo and that old, old Chinese who had handed Raymond the gun to kill Bobby Lembeck. Raymond said, "What a wonderful present. I mean, who else in the world but you could even think of such a wonderful present? This—well—well, it's simply great, that's what it is." They sat down again, fulfilled by giving. They watched the snow, listened to the *Mannergesangsverein*, finished the first bottle of wine, and overflowed with Christmas spirit. Raymond was opening the second bottle when he said, steadily, "Jocie's husband died."

"Yeah?" Marco sat straight up. "When?"

"Last week."

"How'd you find out?"

"Mother told me. She had told the embassy to keep an eye on Jocie. They told her."

"What are you going to do?"

"I saw Senator Jordan. We're pretty good friends. At first it was hard because Mother had told him I was a pervert and that they would have to save Jocie from me, but, in a way, he had to see me because he's in politics and I'm a newspaperman. After a while, when we reached an understanding about what a monster my mother is, we were able to get to be pretty good friends. I asked him if I could help in any way. The paper has an office there. He said no. He said the best thing I could do would be to wait and give Jocie a chance to recover; then, if she doesn't start for home in six months, say, he thinks maybe I should go down there and get her. At least go down there and ask her. You know."

"I take it your mother isn't against Jocie any more."

"No."

"Some switch."

"Try not to laugh and so will I, but that is exactly the case. Some switch. Jocie's father has become very big in his party, particularly in the Senate. Mother saw it coming before anyone else and she's done everything she can to be fast friends with him, but he isn't having any, so I guess she decided if she couldn't get him on their side positively she could cancel him out by marrying me off to his daughter, little knowing that I incite Senator Jordan against her and Johnny more than any other one agency excepting their own lovable personalities."

"What a doll. If she were my wife, I'd probably be Generalissimo Trujillo by now. At least."

"At least."

"So she thinks it might be a good idea for you and Jocie to get married?"

"That is the general feeling I am allowed to get."

"How did Jocie's husband die?"

"That is a good morbid question. It just so happens he was struck down by an unknown hand in a flash riot in a town called Tucumán. He was an agronomist."

"What has that got to do with it?"

"Well, I guess that's how he happened not to be in Buenos Aires with Jocie."

"Have you written to her?"

Raymond looked out of the window, at the snow and the night, and shook his head.

"If you think I can, I'd like to help you with the letter."

"You'll have to help me," Raymond said, simply. "I can't do it. I can't even get started. I want to write her and tell her things but I have those eight years choking me."

"It's all a matter of tone, not so much words," Marco explained, not having the faintest idea of what he was talking about but knowing he was light-years ahead of Raymond in knowledge of human communication. "Sure, wait. If that feels right. But no six months. I think we should get a letter off fairly

soon. You know, a letter of condolence. That would be a natural
ice-breaker, then after that we'll slide into the big letter. But
don't wait too long. You'll have to get it over with so you'll both
know for once and for all."

"Know what?"

"Whether—well, she should know that you want her and—you
have to know whether she wants you."

"She has to. What would I do if she didn't?"

"You've been managing to get along."

"No. No, it won't do, Ben. That is not enough. I may not have
much coming to me but I have more coming to me than I'm
getting."

"Listen, kid. If that's the way it's going to be, then that's the
way. Now take it easy and, please, figure on one step at a
time."

"Sure. I'm willing."

"You've got to give the thing time."

"Sure. That's what Senator Jordan said."

MAJOR General Francis "Fightin' Frank" Bollinger, a
long-time admirer of John "Big John" Iselin, consented, with a
great deal of pleasure, to Raymond's mother's suggestion that he
head a committee of patriots called Ten Million Americans
Mobilizing for Tomorrow. This was at a small dinner, so small
that it fed only Johnny, the general, and Mrs. Iselin, at the Iselin
residence in Washington in January, 1960. Bollinger pledged,
with all of his big heart, that on the morning of the opening of
his party's Presidential nominating convention, to be held at
Madison Square Garden in July, he would deliver one million
signatures of one million patriots petitioning that John Yerkes
Iselin be named the party's candidate for the Presidency.

General Bollinger had retired from active duty to take up the
helm of the largest dog-food company the world had ever
known. He had often said, in one of the infrequent jokes he
made (it does not matter what the other joke was), which, by
reason of the favoritism he felt for it, he repeated not infrequently: "I'd sure as hell like to see the Commies try to match

Musclepal, but if they ever did try it they'd probably call it Moscowpal. Get it?" (Laughter.) He had been a patriot, himself, for many years.

MARCO's unit waited out the winter and the spring without any action or any leads. In March the FBI learned that Raymond's name appeared on the final list of possible suspects in connection with the murder of the anti-Communist deputy, François Orcel, the previous June. Later that month they also learned that Raymond's name appeared on a similar listing prepared by Scotland Yard in conjunction with the murder of Lord Croftnal. The French listing included eight names of Americans or foreigners then in the United States who could be placed anywhere near the scene of the crime. The Scotland Yard list contained three such names. Both agencies asked for routine FBI check and comment. Raymond's name was the only name to appear on both listings.

In late May Senator and Mrs. Iselin took a house on Long Island, anticipating the social demands of the political convention and so that, Mrs. Iselin explained, she could lend a woman's touch in preparing for the imminent homecoming of Senator Jordan's widowed daughter, Jocie, she and her father being old, old friends. She confided all of this to the society editor of *The Daily Press*, after asking Raymond to ask the society editor to call her. It remained for Raymond to read the news about Jocie's homecoming as any other reader of the newspaper might and he became savage in the fury of his resentment when he reached her on the telephone. Raymond's mother allowed him to curse and cry out at her until she was sure he had finished. He spoke for nearly four minutes without stopping, the sound of the words like a stream of bullets, his phrasing erratic and his breathing heavy. When she was sure of his pause, she invited him to a costume ball she was staging on the very day of Jocie's return from Buenos Aires. She said she was sure that he would accept because Jocie had already accepted and that it *had* been a dog's age since he and Jocie had met. She maintained her control all during Raymond's shouted obscenities and screamed vituperation; then she hung up the instrument with such vigor that she knocked it off her desk. She was drawn forward into an even blacker rage. She picked the telephone up and ripped it out of the wall and crashed it through a glass-topped table four feet away. She picked up the shattered table and flung it through the short corridor that led to the open bathroom door, disclosing warm pink tile behind the glass shower curtain. The table splintered the glass, crashed through to the tile wall, and fell noisily in the tub.

AFTER a sleepless, tortured night, Raymond, who had decided he must get to the office at seven o'clock the following morning to do what he had to do, finally fell asleep near dawn and slept through until eleven. He nearly knocked Chunjin down, when the man said good morning, because he had not troubled to call him when he knew that Raymond never, never, never slept later than eight o'clock in the morning.

When Raymond got to the office he locked the door behind him. Utilizing the nastiest voice tone in his ample store, he told the telephone switchboard that they were not to ring his telephone no matter who called.

"Including Mr. Downey, sir?"

"Yes."

"And Mr. O'Neil, sir?"

"Everyone! Anyone! Can you get that through your heads?"

"Heads, sir? I have one head, sir."

"I'm sure," Raymond snapped. "Then are you able to get it through your head? No calls. Do you understand?"

"Bet on it, sir. Everything. Bet your house, your clothes."

"Bet? Oh. One moment, there. I will revise my orders. I *will* take any calls from Buenos Aires. You probably pronounce that Bewnose Airs. I will accept calls from there."

"Which, sir?"

"Which what?"

"Which city?"

"I don't understand."

"Buenos Aires or Bewnose Airs, sir?"

"It's the same place!"

"Very good, sir. You will accept calls from either or both. Now, would you like to revise those orders, sir?" Raymond hung up his phone as she was speaking.

"Oh boy, oh boy, oh boy," the operator said to the girls working on either side of her. "Am I gonna get that one someday. I wouldn't care if I was offered four times the money on some other job which had half the hours. I would never leave this here job as long as he works here. Someday, I may be a liddul old lady sittin' at this switchboard, but someday—the day will come —an' oh, boy, oh boy, oh boy!" She was grinding her teeth as she talked.

"Who? Shaw?" the girl on her left asked.

"What's the use?" the girl on her right said. "If you get that offer for four times the money you take it. Nobody is ever gonna be able to do anything about Shaw."

DEAR JOCIE:
This is a difficult letter to get written. It is nearly an impossible letter for a weak and frightened man to write, and I have surprised myself with that sentence because I have never thought that of myself and I have never said anything less than a sufficiency about myself. I will set down at the outset that I am going to open myself up to you and that it will probably be a long, long letter so that, should it hurt you to read any such things any further, you may stop now and it will all be over. To have to love you as much as I do (as I *did* was what I had started to write, so that I could plot its progression and its growth over the nine empty and useless years without you) and to feel my love for you grow and grow and grow and to have no place to store this enormous harvest within the emptiness, I have found that I must carry it ahead of me wherever I go, bundled in my arms like old clothes which no one else can use and no one wants but which have warmth in them still if someone, as bleakly cold as I have been, can be found to wear them. You will return to New York next month. I have started this letter almost thirty times but I cannot postpone writing it and mailing it for another day because if I do it may not reach you. I cannot write this letter but I must write this letter because I know that I have not got the character nor the courage, the habit of hope nor the assurance

that comes from having a place in a crowded world, and I could never be able to speak to you about this long pain and bitterness which—

He stopped writing. He had smudged the paper with several genuine tears.

XIX

THE FIRST BREAK in the long, long wait through dread, even though it was a totally incomprehensible break, came in May, 1960. It happened when Marco was late for a two o'clock date with Raymond at Hungarian Charlie's booze outlet, across the street from the flash shop.

It was a fairly well-known fact to practically anyone who did not lack batteries for his hearing aid that Hungarian Charlie was one of the more stridently loquacious publicans in that not unsilent business. Only one other boniface, who operated farther north on Fifty-first Street, had a bigger mouth. Charlie talked as though Sigmund Freud himself had given permission, nay, had urged him, to tell everyone everything that came into his head, and in bad grammar, yet. Ten minutes before Marco got to the saloon, with Raymond seated at bar center staring at a glass of beer on a slow afternoon, Charlie had pinned a bookmaker at the entrance end of the bar, a man who would much rather have talked to his new friend, a young, dumpy blonde with a face like a bat's and the thirst of a burning oil field. Charlie was telling them, loud and strong, hearty and healthy, about his wife's repulsive older brother who lived with them and about how he had followed Charlie all over the apartment all day Sunday telling him what to do with his life, which was a new development brought on by the fact that he had just inherited twenty-three hundred dollars from a deceased friend whom he had been engaged to marry for fourteen years, which was a generous thing for her to have done when it was seen from the perspective, Charlie said, that this bum had never given the broad so much as a box of talcum powder for Christmas, it having been his policy always to pick a fight with her immediately preceding gift-exchanging occasions.

"Lissen," Charlie yelled, "you inherit that kinda money and you naturally feel like you know alla answers and also it puts me in a position where I can't exactly kick him inna ankle, you know what I mean? So, wit' the new pernna view, I say tuh him, very patient, 'Why don't you pass the time by playing a liddul solitaire?' "

Raymond was on a bar stool twelve feet away from Charlie and had in no way been eavesdropping on the conversation, as that could have been judged suicidal. He rapped on the bar peremptorily with a half dollar. Charlie looked up, irritated. One lousy customer in the whole lousy joint and he had to be a point killer.

"What arreddy?" Charlie inquired.

"Give me a deck of cards," Raymond said. Charlie looked at the bookmaker, then rolled his eyes heavenward. He shrugged his shoulders like the tenor in *Tosca,* opened a drawer behind him, took out a blue bicycle deck, and slid it along the polished surface to Raymond.

Raymond took the deck from its box and began to shuffle smoothly and absent-mindedly, and Charlie went back to barbering the bookmaker and the young, dumpy blonde. Raymond was laying down the second solitaire spread when Marco came in, ten minutes later. He greeted Charlie as he passed him, ordering a beer, then stood at the bar at Raymond's elbow. "I got held up in traffic," he said ritualistically. "And so forth." Raymond didn't answer.

"Are you clear for dinner, Raymond?" Marco wasn't aware that Raymond was ignoring him. "My girl insists that the time has come to meet you, and no matter how I try to get out of it, that's the way it's got to be. Besides, I am about to marry the little thing, ringside one hundred and thirty-nine pounds, and we would like you to be the best man."

The queen of diamonds showed at the twenty-third card turn. Raymond scooped the cards together, ignoring Marco. Become aware of the silence, Marco was studying Raymond. Raymond squared the deck, put it face down on top of the bar, placed the queen of diamonds face up on top of the stack, and stared at it in a detached and preoccupied manner, unaware that Marco was there. Charlie put the glass of beer in front of Marco at the rate of one hundred and thirty-seven words a minute, decibel count well above the middle register, then turned, walking back to the bookmaker and the broad to punctuate his narrative by recalling the height of the repartee with his brother-in-law: "Why don't you take a cab quick to Central Park and jump inna lake, I says," and his voice belted it loud and strong as though a sound engineer were riding gain on it. Raymond brushed past Marco, walked rapidly past the bookmaker and the girl, and out of the saloon.

"Hey! Hey, Raymond!" Marco yelled. "Where you going?" Raymond was gone. By the time Marco got to the street he saw Raymond slamming the door of a cab. The taxi took off fast, disappearing around the corner, going uptown.

Marco returned to the saloon. He sipped at his beer with growing anxiety. The action of the game of solitaire nagged at him until he placed it in the dreams. It was one of the factors in the dreams that he had placed no meaning upon because he had come to regard the game as aberration that had wriggled into the fantasy. He had discussed it because it had been there, but after one particularly bright young doctor said that Raymond had undoubtedly been doing something with his hands which had *looked* as though he were playing solitaire, Marco had gradually allowed the presence of the game in the dream to dim and fade. He now felt the conviction that something momentous had just happened before his eyes but he did not know what it was.

"Hey, Charlie."

Business of rolling eyes heavenward, business of slow turn, exaggerating the forbearance of an extremely patient man.

"Yeah, arreddy."

"Does Mr. Shaw play solitaire in here much?"

"Whatta you mean—much?"

"Did he ever play solitaire in here before?"

"No."

"Give me another beer." Marco went to the telephone booth, digging for change. He called Lou Amjac.

Amjac sounded sourer than ever. "What the hell happened to you?"

"Come on, save time. What happened?"

"Raymond is at the Twenty-second Precinct in the middle of the park on the Eighty-sixth Street transverse."

"What did he do? What the hell is the matter with you?"

"He rented a rowboat and he jumped in the lake."

"If you're kidding me, Lou—"

"I'm not kidding you!"

"I'll meet you there in ten minutes."

"Colonel Marco!"

"What?"

"Did it finally break?"

"I think so. I—yeah, I think so."

AT FIRST, Raymond flatly denied he had done such a thing but when the shock and embarrassment had worn off and he was forced to agree that his clothes were sopping wet, he was more nearly ready to admit that something which tended toward the unusual had happened. He, Amjac, and Marco sat in a squad room, at Marco's request. When Raymond seemed to have done with sputtering and expostulating, Marco spoke to him in a low, earnest voice, like a dog trainer, in a manner too direct to be evaded.

"We've been kidding each other for a long time, Raymond, and I put up with it because I had no other choice. You didn't believe me. You decided I was sick and that you had to go along with the gag to help me. Didn't you, Raymond?" Raymond stared at his sodden shoes. "Raymond! Am I right?"

"Yes."

"Now hear this. You stood beside me at Hungarian Charlie's and you didn't know I was there. You played a game of solitaire. Do you remember that?"

Raymond shook his head. Marco and Amjac exchanged glances.

"You took a cab to Central Park. You rented a rowboat. You rowed to the middle of the lake, then you jumped overboard. You have always been as stubborn as a dachshund, Raymond, but we can produce maybe thirty eye-witnesses who saw you go over the side, then walk to shore, so don't tell me again that you never did such a thing—and stop kidding yourself that they are not inside your head. We can't help you if you won't help us."

"But I don't *remember*," Raymond said. Something had happened to permit him to feel fear. Jocie was coming home. He might have something to lose. The creeping paralysis of fright was so new to him that his joints seemed to have rusted.

THE CAPACIOUS house in the Turtle Bay district jumped with activity that evening and it went on all through the night. A board review agreed to accept the game of solitaire as Raymond's trigger; and once they had made the connection they were filled with admiration for the technician who had conceived of it. Three separate teams worked with Hungarian Charlie, the talker's talker, the bookmaker, and the young, dumpy blonde.

At first, the blonde refused to talk, as she had every reason to believe that she had been picked up on an utterly non-political charge. She said, "I refuse to answer on the grounds. It might intend to incriminate." They had to bring Marco in to bail her attitude out of that stubborn durance. She knew Marco from around Charlie's place and she liked the way he smelled so much that she was dizzy with the hope of cooperating with him. He held her hand for a short time and explained in a feeling voice that she had not been arrested and that she was cooperating mainly as a big favor to him, and who knew? the whole thing could turn out to be pretty exciting. "I dig," she said, and everything was straightened out although she seemed purposely to misunderstand his solicitude by trying to climb into his lap as they discussed the various areas, but everybody was too busy to notice, and he was gone about two seconds after she had said, listen, she'd love to cooperate but why did they have to cooperate in different rooms?

The bookmaker was even more wary. He was a veritable model of shiftiness, which was heightened by the fact that he was carrying over twenty-nine thousand dollars worth of action on the sixth race at Jamaica, so he couldn't possibly keep his mind on what these young men were talking to him about. They persuaded him to take a mild sedative, then a particularly sympathetic young fellow walked with him along the main corridor and, in a highly confidential manner, asked him to feel free to

discuss what had him so disturbed. The bookmaker knew (1)
that these were not the type police which booked gamblers, and
(2) he had always responded to highly confidential, whispering
treatment. He explained about his business worries, stating, for
insurance, that a friend of his—not he himself—was carrying all
that action. Amjac made a call and got the race result. It was
Pepper Dog, Wendy's Own, and Italian Mae, in that order. Not
one client had run in the money. The bookmaker was opened up
like a hydrant.

Hungarian Charlie, natch, was with it from the word go.

MARCO played through one hundred and twenty-five solitaire layouts until the technicians were sure, time after time and
averaging off, where Raymond had stopped his play in Hungarian Charlie's saloon. They tested number systems as possible
triggers, then they settled down to a symbol system and began to
work with face cards because of the colors and their identification with human beings. They threw out the male face cards,
kings and knaves, based on Raymond's psychiatric pattern. They
started Marco working with the four queens. He discarded the
queens of spades and clubs, right off. They stacked decks with
different red queens at the twenty-third position, which fell as
the fifth card on the fifth stack, and Marco dealt out solitaire
strips. He made it the queen of diamonds, for sure. They kept
him at it, but he connected the queen of diamonds with the face-
up card on the squared deck on the bar, then all at once, as it is
said to happen to saints and alcoholics, a voice he had heard in
nightmares perhaps seven hundred times came to him. It was
Yen Lo's voice saying: "The queen of diamonds, in so many ways
reminiscent of Raymond's dearly loved and hated mother, is the
second key that will clear his mechanism for any assignments."
They had it made. Marco knew they had it made. Hungarian
Charlie, the bookmaker and the young, dumpy blonde filled in
the background of minor confirmations.

The FBI called Cincinnati and arranged to have one dozen
factory-sealed force-packs flown to New York by Army plane.
The cards reached the Turtle Bay house at 9:40 A.M. A force
pack is an item usually made up for magic shops and novelty

stores for party types who fan out cards before their helpless quarries saying, "Take a card, any card." Force packs contain fifty-two copies of the same card to make it easier for the forcer to guess which card has been picked; the dozen packs from Cincinnati were made up exclusively of queens of diamonds. Marco figured the time would come to try Raymond out as player of the ancient game of solitaire that very morning, and he didn't want to have to waste any time waiting for the queen of diamonds to show up in the play.

AN HOUR after Chunjin had made his report to the Soviet security drop from the red telephone booth at the Fifty-ninth Street exit from Central Park, a meeting was called between Raymond's American operator and a District of Columbia taxi driver who also served as chief of Soviet security for the region. As they drove around downtown Washington, with Raymond's operator as passenger, the conversation seemed disputatious.

Raymond's operator told the hackman emphatically that they would be foolish to panic because of what was obviously a ten thousand to one happenstance by which some idiot had unknowingly stumbled upon the right combination of words in Raymond's presence.

"If you please."

"What?"

"This is a professional thing on which I cannot be fooled. Cannot. They have been working over him. He has broken. They have chosen this contemptuous and insulting way of telling us that he has cracked and is useless to us."

"You people are really insecure. God knows I have always felt that the British overdo that paternal talk about this being a young country but, my God, you really *are* a young country. You just haven't been at it long enough. Please understand that if our security people knew what Raymond had been designed to do they would not let you know they knew. Once they find out what Raymond is up to, which is virtually impossible, they'll want to nail whoever is moving him. Me. Then, through me, you. Certainly you people do enough of this kind of thing in your own country, so why can't you understand it here?"

"But why should such a conservative man jump in a lake?"

"Because the phrase 'go jump in the lake' is an ancient slang wheeze in this country and some boob happened on the trigger accidentally, that's how."

"I am actually sick with anxiety."

"So are they," Raymond's operator said blandly, enjoying the bustle of traffic all around them and thinking what a hick town this so-called world capital was.

"But how can you be so calm?"

"I took a tranquilizer."

"A what?"

"A pill."

"Oh. But can you be so sure that is what happened?"

"Because I'm smart. I'm not a stupid Russian. Because Raymond is at large. They allow him to move about. Marco is tense and frightened. Read the Korean's reports, for Christ's sake, and get a hold of yourself."

"We have so little time and this is wholly my responsibility as far as my people are concerned."

"Heller," Raymond's operator said, reading the name from the identification card which said that the driver's name was Frank Heller, "suppose I prove to you that Raymond is ours, not theirs."

"How?" The Soviet policeman had to swerve the cab to avoid a small foreign car that hurtled across from a side street at his left; he screamed out the window in richly accented, Ukrainian-kissed English. "Why dawn't you loo quare you are gung, gew tsilly tson-of-a-bitch?"

"We certainly have a severe case of nerves today, don't we?" Raymond's operator murmured.

"Never mind my nerves. To be on the right of an approaching vehicle is to have the right of way! He broke the law! How can you prove Raymond is not theirs?"

"I'll have him kill Marco."

"Aaaaah." It was a long, soft, satisfaction-stuffed expletive having a zibeline texture. It suggested the end of a perfect day, a cause well served, a race well run.

"Marco is in charge of this particular element of counter-espionage," Raymond's operator said. "Marco is Raymond's only friend. So? Proof?"

"Yes."

"Good."

"When?"

"Tonight, I think. Let me off here."

The cab stopped at the corner of Nineteenth and Y. Raymond's operator got out and slammed the door—too quickly. It closed on flesh. The operator screamed like a lunch whistle. Zilkov stopped the cab. He leaped out, ran around behind it, and stood, wincing with sympathetic pains, while the operator held the mashed hand in the other hand and bent over double. "It's terrible," Zilkov said. "Terrible. Oh, my God! Get into the cab and I'll get you to a hospital. Will you lose the nails? Oh, my God, what pain you must feel."

XX

WHEN RAYMOND RE-turned home from the Twenty-second Precinct House, wearing damp clothes and soggy shoes, it was late afternoon. He had to order Chunjin to the kitchen because the man persisted in asking ridiculous questions. They had a brisk exchange of shouts and sulks, then Raymond showered and took a two-hour dreamless nap.

He awoke thinking about Jocie. He decided that she should be clearing customs just about then. He could not think about his letter, whether she had read it or torn it up in distaste; he could not imagine what she felt or would feel. He dressed slowly and began to pack for the weekend. He removed the gaucho costume from its cardboard box and packed it carefully. He felt a flood of panic as he folded it in. Maybe this silly monkey suit would remind Jocie of her husband. Why in the name of sweet Jesus had he ordered such a costume? It couldn't possibly resemble anything in real life, he decided. Cattle people didn't wear silk bloomers. They were for Yul Brynner or somebody who was kidding. It was probably the kind of a suit they wore to dances or fiestas a couple of times a year. Surely neither Jocie nor her husband would have attended such dances. But what the hell was he being so literal for? You didn't have to see a lot of people walking around in suits like these to know that they were symbolic of the Argentine. What would she think? Would she think he was being cruel or unkind or rude or insensitive? He fussed and pottered and grumbled to himself, conjecturing about the reactions of a woman he hadn't seen since she had been a girl, but did not give a thought to having jumped out of a rowboat into a shallow lake in broad daylight in the center of the city because it embarrassed him to have to think of himself as having so lacked grace in front of all those strangers and those goddam policemen who had treated him as if he was Bellevue Hospital's problem and not theirs. He also would not think of it because he could not afford to get angry with Joe Downey, his boss, who could have at least had the consideration to keep the story out of all the newspapers, and if not all the newspapers, surely out of his own front page.

He snapped the suitcase shut. He carried it to the bedroom door, worrying about what the hell Jocie would think of him when she saw those idiot newspapers at the airport. He flung open the door then began a tug of war over the suitcase with Chunjin as he dragged both of them toward the square, tile foyer.

"For cris*sake*, Chunjin!" It made him even angrier for having spoken to this pushy little type at all and a loud discussion started.

Chunjin did not want him to take the Long Island Railroad to his mother's house. Opposing it bitterly, he maintained that it was not sound for a rich man to wrestle with a large bag in a crowded railroad car. Raymond said he certainly was not going to put up with this kind of insubordination and if it continued for just about two more sentences Chunjin could go in and pack his own cardboard suitcase and get the hell out for good. He felt foolish as soon as he had said it because he remembered suddenly that Chunjin did not sleep in and, of course, had no suitcase on the premises.

Chunjin said loudly that he had taken the liberty of renting an automobile and the correct, dark uniform of a proper chauffeur, the jacket of which Mr. Shaw could look upon as he was even now wearing it. Chunjin said he would drive Mr. Shaw to his mother's house in comfort and at a level with Mr. Shaw's dignity and position in the world.

To Raymond, all of this was an utterly new conception, perhaps as television would have been to the inventor of the wheel.
Raymond had loved automobiles all his life, although he could
not drive one, but he had never thought of renting one. He was
transformed, enchanted.

"You *rented* a car?"

"Yes, sir, Mr. Shaw."

"What kind?"

"Cadillac."

"Well! Marvelous! What color?"

"West Point gray. French blue seats. Leather. Genuine. Rear
seat radio."

"Wonderful!"

"Tax deductible also."

"Is that so? How?"

"You will read the booklet in the car, Mr. Shaw." Chunjin put
on his dark chauffeur's cap. He took the suitcase away from
Raymond without a struggle. "We go now, Mr. Shaw? Seven
o'clock. Two hours to drive."

"I don't know this house, you know. It's a rented house. I don't
know about a place for you to stay."

"My job find place. You not think. Ride and read reports
from newspaper. Think about condition of world."

DRESSED as a costumer's conception of a gaucho, Raymond came down his mother's rented, winding stairs, railed in
English copper, stainless steel, and lucite, and into an entrance
hall that might have been hewn by a cast of Grimm Brothers'
gnomes out of a marble mountain. It was studded with bronze
zodiacal designs and purred with concealed neon light in an
arrangement that pulled Raymond toward the great drawing
room on the threshold of which Senator and Mrs. Iselin were
receiving their guests. The older guests who shook hands with
the Iselins that night had been followers of Father Coughlin; the
group just younger than them had rallied around Gerald L. K.
Smith; and the rest, still younger, were fringe lice who saw
Johnny's significance in a clear, white light. The clan had turned
out from ten thousand yesterdays in the Middle West and

neolithic Texas, and patriotism was far from being their last refuge. It was a group for anthropologists, and it seemed like very bad manners or very bad judgment on Raymond's mother's part to have invited Senator Jordan to walk among the likes of these.

Johnny and Ellie (as Raymond's mother was called by most of the guests) were costumed as honest dairy-farm folk would look if honest dairy farmers had had their work clothes built by Balenciaga. Raymond's mother had figured that the press photographs of these costumes would be viewed with great favor in the Iselin home state, where building foundations were made of butter; voters would be told that Big John never forgot where he came from. As she embraced Raymond in their mutually distasteful greeting, she whispered that Jocie's plane had run late out of San Juan but that she was now in the house next door and she had telephoned to say that she would be over no later than midnight and had asked anxiously if Raymond would be there. He felt, for an instant, that he might faint.

"Anxiously? Why anxiously? Did she sound as though she were fearful that I might be here?"

"Oh, don't be such a jerk, Raymond! If you weren't here do you think for a moment that the Jordans would come here?"

"Don't call me a jerk, Mother."

"Go have a drink or a tranquilizer or something." She turned to her husband. "Raymond can certainly be a pain in the ass," she said with asperity.

"She's kiddin' yuh," Johnny said. "You sure look great, kid. What are you supposed to be, one of those Dutch skaters?"

"What else?" Raymond answered. He walked through the crowds acknowledging greetings forbiddingly and feeling his heart beating as though it were trying to splinter a way out through his ribs. He walked among, but shunned contact with, the crowds on the broad lawns behind the house, all of which, excepting one section, were brilliantly illuminated with non-Communist Japanese lanterns and filled with striped tents. The dark section pulled Raymond to it. It faced the Jordan house. It was a walled-off piece of ground, as isolated as a private deck on an ocean liner. He stood there beside the wall staring across at the Jordan house without the reward of being able to observe any movement there. Frustrated, and more than usually resent-

ful, he wandered back to the Iselin house through crowds of
stout, blond Carmens and Kansas Borgias, unhorsed Godivas,
unfrocked Richelieus, and many businessmen dressed as pirates.
Many of the costumes were quaint American Legion uniforms so
like those of the *squadristi* of former days in Italy, encasing
various sizes of fleshy prejudice which exchanged opinions they
rented that week from Mr. Sokolsky, Mr. Lawrence, Mr. Pegler,
and that fascinating younger fellow who had written about men
and God at Yale. The three orchestras tried to avoid playing at
the same time. The Iselins had provided very nearly everything
but balalaikas in the way of music. There was a "society" orchestra, a three cha combo, and an inundation of gallant White
Russian fiddlers who migrated across the grounds and in and out
of the house en masse, sawing like locusts, and not only did they
accept tips but they very nearly frisked the guests to get them.
Raymond stopped at one of the four bars and drank a half glass
of champagne. He refused offers to dance with three young
women of different sizes. His mother found him later, far in a
corner of the large salon, behind a pastel sofa, under two threats
of Salvador Dali, a Catalan.

"My God, you look as though your head will come to a point
any minute," she told him. "Raymond, will you *please* take a
tranquilizer?"

"No."

"Why?"

"I have a revulsion for drugs."

"You look absolutely miserable. Never mind. A half-hour more
and she'll be here. My feet hurt. Why don't we just sneak away
for a few minutes until Jocie and her father arrive. We can sit in
the library and sip cold wine."

Raymond looked right at her and, for the first time in many,
many years, actually smiled at her, and she thought he looked
positively beautiful. Why—why he looks like Poppa! Raymond,
her own Raymond, looked exactly like her darling, darling
Poppa! She clutched his hand as she led him out of the salon and
along the two corridors to the library, causing one woman guest
to tell another woman guest that they looked as though they
were rushing off to get a little of you-know-what, Mrs. Iselin
trailing a delicious scent of Jolie Madame because she had read
that Lollobrigida wore it and she had always wished she could

be short like that, and stopping only to get a bottle of wine and to tell the butler where they would be.

The library was a small, pleasant room and the books were real. The fourth wall was transparent glass and faced that walled deck of land and Jocie's house. Raymond stood rubbing his hands together, so very tall and so preposterously handsome in the short, shining boots, the ballooning trousers, and the wide expanse of white silk shirt. "Do you *know* they got in from the airport?" he asked as he poured the lemon-yellow wine into two sherbet glasses.

"I *told* you," his mother said. "She telephoned me. From that house."

"How did she sound?"

"Like a girl."

"Thanks."

She leaned forward tensely in the raspberry-colored chair, splendid in pink chiffon. "Raymond?"

"What?" He handed her one of the filled glasses. She took it with her bandaged left hand. "What did you do to your hand?" he asked, seeing the bandage for the first time.

"I got careless in Washington this afternoon and got it caught in the door of a taxi." He grunted involuntarily. "Raymond," she said, transferring the wine to her right hand and lifting it shakily. "Why don't you pass the time by playing a little solitaire?"

XXI

MARCO SQEEZED THE inside of Eugénie Rose's splendid thigh, not at all sexually —well, perhaps just a little bit sexually—but mostly out of the greatest of good spirits because, after all, this time of sick fear, the work seemed to be leading to the conclusion which they had dreaded they would never be able to find.

"Hey!" Eugénie Rose said.

"What?"

"Don't stop."

It was after midnight and it was Marco's dinner break from

the unending games of solitaire, from the examinations of Hungarian Charlie, the bookmaker, and the young, dumpy blonde, from the number systems and symbol systems, and Marco knew the end was in sight.

"This time tomorrow night, oh boy! I'll have lunch with Raymond tomorrow, then a little solitaire, then a nice long chat about the good old days in Korea and a few Russian and Chinese friends of ours, then a few suggestions made to crumble up their systems and mechanisms forever—sort of removing the controls, ripping out the wiring—and, lady, it's all over. All over. All done with. Done."

"Finished."

"Completed."

"Through."

"Mission accomplished."

"Check."

They were in an all-night restaurant on Fifty-eighth Street, and when he wasn't clutching her hands, Rosie nibbled on cinnamon toast as daintily as a cartoon mouse. Marco was shoveling in large wedges of gooey creamed chipped beef and humming chorus after chorus of "Here Comes the Bride."

"That's a pretty tune you're humming. What is it?" she asked.

"Our song."

"Oh, Benny boy. Oh, my dear colonel!"

XXII

RAYMOND FOUND the cards in the desk. They were elegant rented cards that had come with the house. They had gold edges and were imprinted with the name and the grotesque crest of a hotel maintained for the expense-account set on the North Side of Chicago. He dealt out the play. The queen of diamonds did not show in the first game. As he placed the cards precisely his mother sat on the edge of her chair with her face buried in her hands. When she heard him squaring up the pack she sat up straight and her face was twisted bitterly. Raymond placed the red queen face up on top of the deck and studied it noncommittally.

"Raymond, I must talk to you about a problem with Colonel Marco, and I must talk to you, as well, about many other things but there will be no time tonight. It seems that there is never time." There was a brisk knocking at the door, which she had locked. "Damn!" she said and walked to the door. "Who is it?"

"It's me, hon. Johnny. Tom Jordan is here. I need you."

"All right, lover. I'll be right out."

"Who the hell are you in there with anyway?"

"Raymond."

"Oh. Well, hurry it up whatever it is, hon. We have work out here."

She walked back and stood behind Raymond with her hands on his shoulders. As he watched the red queen she repaired her face as best she could. Then she leaned over him and took the card. "I'll take this with me, dear," she said. "It might bring mischief if I leave it here."

"Yes, Mother."

"I'll be back as soon as I can."

"Yes, Mother."

She left the library, locking the door behind her. As soon as she was gone something rattled at the terrace door. Raymond looked up just as the smiling, beautiful young woman closed the door behind her. She was dressed for the masquerade party, costumed as a playing card. The rich gold and scarlet cowl fell from her crown to her shoulders. Gold incrusted jewels banded the lush black and white ruff at her throat. The kaleidoscopic complex of inlays of metallic oranges, yellows, purples, scarlets, blacks, and whites fell to her bodice and below. From the top of her head, stiffly parallel to her shoulders, then falling at right angles full down the sides of her body, was a white papier-mâché board on which was printed a regal Q, a red diamond standard directly below it at the left corner, while at the right there stared a large red diamond against the shining white background. It was the queen of diamonds, his patron and his destiny. She spoke to him.

"I saw you through my window just before we left the house," she said huskily. "My heart almost shot out of my body. I had to see you alone. Daddy went around the front way and I slipped through that old iron door in the stone wall."

"Jocie." She was Jocie and she was his queen of diamonds. She was the queen of diamonds, his special lady from the stars, and she was Jocie.

"Your letter—oh, my darling."

He moved across the room and held her by the shoulders, swaying. He looked down at her with such a force of pure love that she shivered and they were together in love forever. He kissed her. It was the first time he had ever kissed her after having possessed her completely in imaginations through nine risings of April and the deaths of eight Decembers. He pulled her down on the couch and his hands fumbled with her royal clothes and royal person while his mouth and his body sought his salvation with the only woman he would ever love, with the only woman who had ever allowed him to love her; the cardboard queen he served, and the lovely girl he had adored from the moment he had come to life beside her near a lake, near a snake, within an expanding dream.

SENATOR Jordan's costume was the toga and sandals of a Roman legislator, combined with a blanked expression. He stood next to Senator Iselin, equidistant from the marble walls at the center of the foyer. The three cha combo scattered sounds over them from the bottomless fountain of its noises. When the two men spoke they spoke guardedly, like convicts in a chow line.

"I am here," Senator Jordan said to Johnny, "because my daughter asked me to come, saying that it was extremely important to her, that is to say, important to her happiness, that I come. There is no other reason and my presence here is not to be misunderstood nor is it to be exploited by that industry of gossip which you control. I feel loathing toward you and for what you have done to weaken our country and very nearly destroy our party. Is that clear?"

"That's all right, Tom. Glad to have you," Johnny said. "I was tickled when Ellie told me that we were going to be next-door neighbors."

"And I am wearing this ridiculous costume because my daughter cabled ahead for it from Puerto Rico and because she asked me to wear it, assuring me that I would be less conspicuous at this Fascist party rally if I did."

"It looks great on you, Tom. Great. What are you supposed to be, some kind of an athlete or something?"

"An interne. Furthermore, I hope none of this lunatic fringe who are your guests tonight, and who are ringing us like hyenas to watch us chat so amiably, are getting the wrong idea about me. If they link you with me I'll take ads to repudiate you and them."

"Don't give it a thought, Tom. If anything, old buddy, they're probably getting the wrong idea about me. They are very possessive about their politics. They're a great bunch, actually. You'd like them."

The restless guests moved all around them. The scent of masked ambergris mixed with abstractions of carnations and musk glands, lemon rinds, and the essences of gunpowder and tobacco. Raymond's mother came like a flung harpoon through the crowds to greet her honored guest. She shook his hand vigorously, she said again and again and again how honored they were to have him in their house, and she forgot to ask where Jocie was. She asked Johnny to represent them among their other guests because she just had to have a good old-fashioned visit with Senator Tom. Before Johnny slunk away gratefully he mumbled amenities and moved to shake hands, which Senator Jordan tactfully overlooked.

Raymond's mother stopped a waiter and took his tray of four filled champagne glasses. She carried it off in the opposite direction from the library, followed stiffly by the senator, to the small room which was known to the domestic staff as "the Senator's den" because Johnny liked to drink in there, unshaven.

It was a vivid room, vivid enough to make a narcoleptic sit up popeyed, with bright, white carpet, black walls, and shining brass furniture with zebrine upholstery. Raymond's mother set the tray down upon the black desk with the shining brass drawer handles, then asked her neighbor to sit down as she closed the door.

"It was good of you to come over, Tom."

He shrugged.

"I suppose you were surprised to learn that we had taken this house."

"Surprised and appalled."

"You won't have to see much of us."

"I am sure of that."

"I would like to ask a question."

"You may."

"Will you carry this personal feeling you have for me and for Johnny over into other fields of practical politics?"

"What other fields?"

"Well—the convention, for example."

His eyebrows shot up. "In what area of the convention?"

"Would you try to block Johnny if his name is brought forward?"

"You're joking."

"My dear Tom!"

"You are going to go after the nomination for Johnny?"

"We may be forced into that position. Your answer will help me to form the decision. A lot of Americans, you know, look upon Johnny as one of the few men willing to fight to the death for the preservation of our liberties."

"Aaaaaah!"

"And I mean a *lot* of people. Votes. The Loyal American Underground is five million voting Americans. To say nothing of the wonderful work Frank Bollinger is doing, and with no urging from us. He says flatly that he will walk into that convention with a petition of not less than one million votes pledged for Johnny as a down payment on ten million."

"You haven't answered me. Are you going after the nomination for Johnny?"

"No," she answered calmly. "We couldn't make it. But we can make the vice-presidency."

"The vice-presidency?" Jordan was incredulous. "Why would Johnny want the vice-presidency?"

"Why wouldn't he?"

"Because he wants power and a big stage to dance on. There's no power in the vice-presidency and the only place where there is more power than where Johnny is right now is in the White House. Why would he want the vice-presidency?"

"I answered your question, Tom, but you haven't answered mine."

"What question?"

"Will you block us?"

"Block you? I would spend every cent I own or could borrow

to block you. I have contempt for you and fear for you, but mostly I fear for this country when I think of you. Johnny is just a low clown but you are the smiler who wraps a dagger in the flag and waits for your chance, which I pray may never come. I tell you this: if at that convention one month from now you begin to deal with the delegations to cause Johnny's name to be put on that ticket, or if in my canvass of all delegations which will begin on my telephone tomorrow I learn that you are so acting, I am going to bring impeachment proceedings against your husband on the floor of the Senate and I will hit him with everything in my carefully documented book."

Raymond's mother came out of her chair, spitting langrel.

XXIII

JOCIE LEFT A long letter for her father after she had changed and packed, before she and Raymond drove her car into New York. The letter told him that they were going to be married immediately and that they had decided to have it done quietly, even invisibly, for the entirely apparent political considerations. The letter also told him of how sublimely, utterly happy she was; it said they would return as soon as possible and beseeched her father to tell no one of the marriage because Raymond's conviction was that his mother would use it at once to political advantage, and that he felt his mother's political advantages were profitless, even detrimental, to anyone concerned.

Jocie and Raymond reached his apartment at three in the morning after driving into the city in Jocie's car. They undressed instantly and reflexively and found each other hungrily. Jocie wept and she laughed with joy and disbelief that her true life, the only life she had ever touched because it had touched her simultaneously, had been given back to her. Such an instant ago he had paddled their wide canoe across that lake of purple wine toward a pin of light high in the sky which would widen and widen and widen while she slept until it had blanched the blackness. Another day would have lighted his face as he stood there before her. She had been dreaming. She had not been waiting so long for him, she had been dreaming. She had gone to sleep beside a mountain lake and she had dreamed that he had gone away from her and that they had waited, across the world from each other, until the dream had finished. He loved her! He loved her!

RAYMOND mailed a concise letter to Joe Downey of *The Daily Press* concerning his first vacation in four years, explained that his column had been written ahead for five days, and announced that he would return, without saying where he was going, in time to cover the conventions.

They drove her car to Washington and parked it in the Senate garage. They took the first flight out of Washington to Miami, using the names John Starr and Marilyn Ridgeway for the manifest, then an afternoon plane from Miami to San Juan, Puerto Rico.

They were married in San Juan at 5:37 P.M., using their passports for identification in lieu of birth certificates; a condition which helped the justice to remember them two days later when the FBI office in San Juan responded to the Bureau's general alarm for Raymond. They left San Juan via PAA at 7:05 P.M. and arrived soon after in Antigua, where the presentation of one of the many mysterious cards in Raymond's wallet secured him credit and lodgings for their wedding night at the Mill Reef Club.

The following afternoon they set sail as the only passengers aboard a chartered schooner with a professionally aloof crew, on a honeymoon voyage through the islands of Guadeloupe, Dominica, Martinique, St. Lucia, Barbados, Grenada, Tobago, and Trinidad.

WHEN Raymond's mother returned to the library and found him gone, she panicked for the first time in her memory. She had to force herself to sit very, very still for nearly twenty minutes to regain control of herself. By then she needed a fix so badly that she nearly scrambled up the back stairs to get heroin and an arm banger. She changed from the costume of the dainty milkmaid, coked to the very retinas, and calmly slipped into something she could wear to the airport, thence to Washington. She leaned back and closed her eyes, her body allowing the serenity to wash over it, and she considered quite objectively what must be done to move through this catastrophe. Although she had the servants seek Raymond throughout the house and grounds and she checked his room herself, she understood best the intuition which told her that he must have fled from her, and that his mechanism had broken down. She knew as well as she could tell the time that, having been triggered by the red queen, when the red queen had been removed from his sight he would have remained in the locked room for the rest of his days in complete suspension of faculties if the mechanism had been operating as constructed. She had elaborate cause to panic.

Chunjin missed Raymond approximately two hours later than his mother did, but his alarm was relayed into the Soviet apparatus via a telephone tape recorder in Arlington, Virginia, immediately so that they knew about Raymond's disappearance before his mother could reach Washington to tell them. They had panicked, too. A general order was issued to trace the fugitive through their own organizations, but as they confined their search within the borders of the continental United States they got nowhere as the days went on and on.

The FBI resumed its interrupted surveillance of Raymond at Martinique. They were able, through some fine cooperation, to persuade two crew members to jump ship, whereupon two agents of the Bureau were signed on the schooner as working hands.

The Bureau had found Jocie's car in the Senate garage, and she and Raymond were immediately identified as connections of senators and he as the well-known newspaperman. The Bureau was about to discuss the matter with Senator Jordan when the San Juan office reported the marriage. After that the names of Mr. and Mrs. Raymond Shaw showed up on the PAA manifest for the skim to Antigua, then quickly after that, like gypsy finger-snapping, at the Mill Reef Club, on the right wharf, on the voyage plot filed at the company's office, then at Martinique, where the two agents boarded to protect the blissfully ignorant couple from they knew not what.

If Marco had not been the Little Gentleman about the whole thing,—if he had not been so hipped on the sanctity of the honeymoon in an entirely subjective manner—he would have been one of those two agents who boarded as crew and he would have had a force deck of fifty-two queens of diamonds in his duffel, those with keen hindsight said later. However, he could see no harm coming to them while they were that far out at sea so he planned to visit Raymond at the earliest possible moment upon the honeymooners' return.

JOCIE and Raymond returned to New York on the Friday evening before the Monday morning when the convention was scheduled to open at Madison Square Garden. They had been away for twenty-nine days. They moved into Raymond's apartment with golden tans and foaming joys. It took two calls to locate Jocie's father because he had closed the summer house on Long Island and had moved back to the house on Sixty-third Street. He insisted that they have a wedding celebration that evening because of the wonderful sounds and the sounds within those sounds far within his daughter's happy voice. They celebrated at an Italian restaurant on East Fifty-fifth Street. The city was rapidly tilting with the arrival of politician-statesmen and statesmen-politicians and just routine hustlers for the convention so it was no trick at all for the newspaper in opposition to *The Daily Press* to learn of the celebrating party of three, and in no time a photographer had appeared on the scene, taken a picture, and confirmed the story of the marriage. That being the case, Raymond explained earnestly to Jocie, he had no choice but to alert his own paper because it would be a bitter occasion indeed if they were beat to the street with his own picture, so a *Press* photographer and reporter were rushed to the restaurant, which heretofore had been famous only for the manufacture of the most formidable Martinis on the planet. A journalistic coincidence was duly observed in The Wayward Press department of *The New Yorker* in a subsequent examination of the national press reports published during the national political conventions. The survey noted that both newspapers reporting the Jordan-Shaw marriage at the same instant employed lead paragraphs

that were almost identical. Each newspaper made a comparison
with the plot of *Romeo and Juliet*, a successful play by an English writer which had been taken from the Italian of Massucio
di Salerno. Both paragraphs referred to the groom as being of
the House of Montague (Iselin) and to the bride as being of the
House of Capulet (Jordan), then went on into divergent reviews
of the murderous bitterness between the two senators, recalling
Senator Iselin's startling press conference of one week previous
at which he had charged Senator Jordan with high treason,
brandishing papers held high as "absolute proof" that Jordan had
sold his country out to the Soviets and stating that, at the instant
the Senate reconvened he would move for (1) Senator Jordan's
impeachment and (2) for a civil trial at the end of which, the
senator demanded passionately, the only possible verdict would
be that "this traitor to liberty and to the only perfect way of life
must be hanged by the neck until dead." Senator Jordan's only
response had been made upon a single mimeographed sheet
holding a single sentence. Distributed to all press agencies, it
said: "How long will you let this man use you and trick you?"

Senator Jordan did not mention the Iselin attack to the bride
and groom while they were in the restaurant. He knew they
would hear about it all too shortly.

Before the stories and pictures announcing Raymond's return
and their wedding could appear in the morning editions, friends,
agents, and sympathizers had passed the word along through
channels to the Soviet security command. The command issued
its wishes to Mrs. Iselin, in Washington, and she reached Raymond by telephone the next morning. She chided him gently for
not having told her of his great happiness and was so gently
convincing in her most gentle hurt that Raymond was surprised
to realize that he felt he had behaved somewhat badly toward
her.

She told him that the Vice-President and the Speaker of the
House were coming to the Iselin residence at three o'clock that
afternoon for an unusual policy meeting relative to civil rights
and that since they had decided it would be advantageous to
allow the story to "leak" to the public, she had immediately put
in a bid for her syndicated son and everyone had concurred on
the choice. Therefore he would need to catch a plane immediately for Washington so that they could lunch together and she

could fill him in on the entire background of the meeting and the plans. Raymond readily agreed.

Jocie was a girl who had mastered every *expertise* on sleeping. He didn't waken her. He left a note explaining why he had to leave and saying he would write the piece itself in Washington that night and would be back at her doorstep before she woke up the next morning.

Raymond learned about Johnny's fantastic attack on his father-in-law from a newspaper during the flight to Washington, and he began to feel the numbness of great rage and the purest kind of joy: the substance of the attack released in him something he had always wanted to do but had always inhibited to the point where he had never recognized it before. He would go to the Iselin house and he would lock Johnny in a room and he would beat him and beat him and beat him. Another great light broke over his head. He would shave his mother bald.

Jocie learned about the attack at breakfast from the same morning newspaper, in the story under the front-page, three column picture of herself, her husband, and her father. The references to the Iselin charges were bewildering to her; she had lived so long in the Argentine that she had not developed a native callousness to any allegation made by Johnny. She dressed at once, telephoned her father, told him she would be right there, and hurried out of the house taking an overnight bag with her and leaving a note for Raymond explaining briefly and asking him to come to her father's house as soon as he could the following morning. She signed the note "with all my love forever" and propped it up for his attention on the foyer telephone.

Colonel Marco, that constant brooder over the marriage state, deferred too long in his plan to awaken/disturb the newlyweds. When he went to Raymond's apartment with his force cards to sweep the destructions out of Raymond's mind, Raymond and Jocie had both gone. No one answered the door bell to give him information as to where they had gone. Chunjin could see the caller by opening the service door just a crack, fifteen yards along the hall to Marco's right.

· · ·

RAYMOND's mother gave Raymond no chance to put his vengeance into effect when he reached her house in Washington. As he charged wildly into her office on the second floor—the office was decorated like the inside of a coffin—she suggested that he pass the time by playing a little solitaire, which cut him off in mid-curse. She locked the door.

The queen of diamonds showed as the fourteenth card in the first layout. Raymond listened with absorption to what his mother had to say. She questioned him and he gave her a detailed report on how and why and when he had disappeared from the house on Long Island, and she was so relieved that she laughed hysterically as he told her about Jocie's costume and his total, eternal obedience to the queen of diamonds. When she had dried the tears of nervous joy from her eyes and had fired four more short bursts of hysterical laughter she got down to business and laid out his job of work.

She had been ordered to make a full test of his reflex mechanism and, because Senator Jordan was potentially so dangerous to Johnny and her terminal plans, she had selected him for execution. She set down her orders to Raymond with clarity and economy. It was now 11:22 A.M. Raymond was to go to the Washington bureau of *The Daily Press* and talk about convention coverage problems with the bureau chief so that his presence in the city would be established. He would then have lunch at the Press Club and talk to as many acquaintances at the bar as possible. Raymond reported stolidly that he did not have acquaintances. His mother said he knew Washington newspapermen, didn't he? He said he did. She said, "Well, you can just stand next to them and talk to them and it will be such a shock that they'll place you in Washington this weekend for many years to come." After lunch he would appear on the Hill and find an excuse to visit with the Speaker. At five o'clock he would stop by at the press room at the White House and annoy Hagerty by pushing for a breakfast date the following morning at seven o'clock. Hagerty would not be able to accept, even if he could stand the idea of breakfasting with Raymond, because of the convention opening in New York Monday morning, but Raymond's insistence would be sure to rile Hagerty and he would remember Raymond as having been in Washington on Saturday and on Sunday. At six-fifteen he would return to the Press Club bar for forty-five minutes of startling conviviality, then he would return to the Iselin house to have dinner with friends. It would be an entirely informal dinner but with quite good people like Mr. Justice Calder and the Treasury Undersecretary and that young what's-his-name criminal lawyer and his darling wife. At eleven forty-five a television repair truck would be at the back entrance to the house with his own man, Chunjin, driving. Raymond would get into the back of the panel truck, where there would be a mattress. He was to sleep all the way to New York. Did he understand that? Yes, Mother. Chunjin would give him a revolver with a silencer when they got into the city and would let him out of the truck in front of the Jordan house on East Sixty-third Street at approximately 3:45 A.M. Chunjin would give him the keys to the front door and the inside door. Raymond went over a diagram of the inside of the house while his mother explained precisely how he was to find the senator's sleeping room on the second floor, after having first checked the library downstairs in the event the senator had been bothered with one of his intermittent spells of insomnia. It would all be quite as easy as the liquidation of Mr. Gaines had been, but he was to take no chances and it was essential that he take every precaution against being identified, and she did not need to specify the precautions, she was sure, beyond that. After the assignment had been completed he was to return to the back of the truck and go to sleep at once. He would awaken at Chunjin's touch when they had reached the back door of this house again. He was to go to his room, undress, put on pajamas, and immediately go to sleep until he was called and, of course, he was to remember nothing, not that he would ever be able to, in any event.

XXIV

MARCO DIS-
covered that Raymond was in Washington very quickly. However, by appearing at the Press Club (where he had found himself, to his chagrin and resentment, exactly once before in the years of his political reporting) Raymond unwittingly eluded the men of Marco's unit. The unit was out in force and in desperate earnest. They knew how to unlock the mystery,

that is, they held the key in their hands, but now they could not find the lock. As each day had passed since the afternoon Raymond had rented the rowboat in Central Park, and Raymond had been beyond their reach, every element of responsibility in the unit, and in the direction of the nation, had watched and waited tensely, fearing that they might have arrived at the solution too late. By going to the Hill and to the White House on a Saturday afternoon in summer, Raymond kept showing up exactly where they did not expect him to appear, so they missed him again. Fifty minutes after he had left the Washington bureau of *The Daily Press*, and after the bureau chief had taken off for the weekend in an automobile with his wife and their parrot and the information as to where and how Raymond would spend the day, two men from Marco's unit arrived to take up permanent posts waiting for Raymond to return to the office. At the White House Raymond duly registered the fact that he would be in Washington for the weekend but Hagerty said how the hell could he have time to have breakfast when there was a national convention opening Monday?

Because Raymond was known to detest his mother and step-father under any normal circumstances and because Marco's unit calculated that he would never speak to the Iselins again after the viciousness of Johnny's smear of Raymond's father-in-law, they missed Raymond again by ignoring the Iselin house. Marco's unit ate, drank, and slept very little. They had to find Raymond so that he could play a little solitaire to pass the time and tell them what they had to know because something was about to cut the thread that held the blazing sword which was suspended directly overhead from the blazing sun.

Just before midnight, Raymond crawled into the back of the panel truck, stretched out, and went to sleep. It had started to rain. As the truck came out of the Lincoln Tunnel into New York, thunder was added and lightning flashed, but Raymond was asleep and could not heed it.

Raymond's mother had been merciful. She had understood completely the operation of the Yen Lo mechanism. She knew Raymond had to do what he was told to do, that he could have no sense of right or wrong about it, nor suspect any possibility of the consciousness of guilt, but she must have sensed that he had to retain a sense of gain/loss, that he would know when the time came, that by having to kill Senator Jordan he would be losing something, and that his wife, too (and so very much more dimensionally), would suffer an infinity of loss. So, out of mercy, she instructed Chunjin to let Raymond sleep until he arrived within a block of the Jordan house.

Chunjin stopped the truck on the far side of the street, opposite the house. It was raining heavily and they alone seemed to be alive in the city. Three other cars were parked in the block, an impossibly low number. Chunjin leaned over the seat and shook Raymond by the shoulder.

"Time to do the work, Mr. Shaw," he said. Raymond came awake instantly. He sat up. He clambered to sit beside Chunjin in the front seat.

Chunjin gave him the gun, to which a silencer had been affixed, making it cumbersome and very nearly impossible to pocket. "You know this kind of gun?" he asked efficiently.

"Yes," Raymond answered dully.

"I suggest you keep it under your coat."

"I will," Raymond said. "I have never felt so sad."

"That is proper," Chunjin said. "However, sir, if you do the work quickly it will be over for you, and for him, although in different ways. When the work is done you will forget."

The rain was like movie rain. It streamed heavily against the windows and made a tympanous racket as it hit the roof of the truck. Chunjin said, "I circle block with car, Mr. Shaw. If not there when you come out you walk slowly toward next street, Third Avenue. Bring gun with you."

Raymond opened the car door.

"Mr. Shaw?"

"What?"

"Shoot through the head. After first shot, walk close, place second shot."

"I know. She told me." He opened the door quickly, got out quickly, and slammed it shut. He crossed the street as the panel truck pulled away, the pistol held at his waist under his light raincoat, the rain striking his face.

He felt the sadness of Lucifer. He moved in the flat, relentless rhythm of the oboe passages in "Bald Mountain." Colors of anguish moved behind his eyes in vangoghian swirls, having lifted edges to give an elevation to the despair. His nameless grief had handles, which he lifted, carrying himself forward toward the center of the pain.

The doors of the house, outer and inner, opened with the master keys. There were no lights in the rooms on the main floor, only the night light over the foot of the stairs. Raymond moved toward the staircase, the pistol hanging at his side, gripped in his left hand. As his foot touched the first riser he heard a sound in the back of the house. He froze where he was until he could identify it.

Senator Jordan appeared in pajamas, slippers, and robe. His silver hair was ruffled into a halo of duck feathers. He saw Raymond as he stood under the light leaning against the wall, but showed no surprise.

"Ah, Raymond. I didn't hear you come in. Didn't expect to see you until around breakfast time tomorrow morning. I got hungry. If I were only as hungry in a restaurant as I am after I've been asleep in a nice, warm bed for a few hours, I could be rounder and wider than the fat lady in the circus. Are you hungry, Raymond?"

"No, sir."

"Let's go upstairs. I'll force some good whisky on you. Combat the rain. Soothe you after traveling and any number of other good reasons." He swept past Raymond and went up the stairs ahead of him. Raymond followed, the pistol heavy in his hand.

"Jocie said you had to go down to see your mother and the Speaker."

"Yes, sir."

"How was the Speaker?"

"I—I didn't see him, sir."

"I hope you didn't get yourself all upset over those charges of Iselin's."

"Sir, when I read that story on the plane going to Washington I decided what I should have decided long ago. I decided that I owed him a beating."

"I hope you didn't—"

"No, sir."

"Matter of fact, an attack from John Iselin can help a good deal. I'll show you some of the mail. Never got so much supporting mail in twenty-two years in the Senate."

"I'm happy to hear it, sir." They passed into the Senator's bedroom.

"Bottle of whisky right on top of that desk," the Senator said as he climbed into bed and pulled up the covers. "Help yourself. What the hell is that in your hand?"

Raymond lifted the pistol and stared at it as though he weren't sure himself. "It's a pistol, sir."

The Senator stared, dumbfounded, at the pistol and at Raymond. "Is that a silencer?" he managed to say. "Yes, sir."

"Why are you carrying a pistol?"

Raymond seemed to try to answer, but he was unable to. He opened his mouth, closed it again. He opened it again, but he could not make himself talk. He was lifting the pistol slowly.

"Raymond! No!" the Senator shouted in a great voice. "What are you doing?"

The door on the far side of the room burst open. Jocie came into the room saying, "Daddy, what is it? What is it?" just as Raymond shot him. A hole appeared magically in the Senator's forehead.

"Raymond! Raymond, darling! Raymond!" Jocie cried out in full scream. He ignored her. He crossed quickly to the Senator's side and shot again, into the right ear. Jocie could not stop screaming. She came running across the room at him, her arms outstretched imploringly, her face punished with horror. He shot her without moving, from the left hand. The bullet went through her right eye at a range of seven feet. Head going backward in a punched snap, knee going forward, she fell at his feet. His second shot went directly downward, through her left eye.

He put out the bed light and fumbled his way to the stairs. He could not control his grief any longer but he could not understand why he wept. He could not see. Loss, loss, loss, loss, loss, loss, loss.

When he climbed to the mattress in the back of the panel truck the sounds he was making were so piteous that Chunjin, although expressionless, seemed to be deeply moved by them because he took the pistol from Raymond's hand and struck him on the back of the head, bringing forgetfulness to save him.

THE BODIES were discovered in the morning by the Jordan housekeeper, Nora Lemmon. Radio and TV news shows had the story at eleven-eighteen, having interrupted all regular programs with the flash. In Washington, via consecutive telephone calls to the news agencies, Senator Iselin offered the explanation that the murders bore out his charges of treason against Jordan who had undoubtedly been murdered by Soviet agents to silence him forever. The Monday morning editions of all newspapers were on the streets of principal cities on Sunday afternoon, five hours before the normal bulldog edition hit the street.

Raymond's mother did not awaken him when the FBI called to ask if she could assist them in establishing her son's present whereabouts. Colonel Marco called from New York as Raymond's closest friend, saying he feared that Raymond might have harmed himself in his grief over his wife's tragic death, almost begging Mrs. Iselin to tell him where her son was so that he might comfort him. Raymond's mother hit herself with a heavy fix late Sunday afternoon because she could not rid her mind of the picture of that lovely, lovely, lovely dead girl which looked out at her from every newspaper. She went into a deep sleep. Johnny called all the papers and news agencies and announced that his wife was prostrate over the loss of a dear and wonderful girl whom she had loved as a daughter. He told the papers that he would not attend the opening day of the convention "even if it costs me the White House" because of this terrible, terrible loss and their affliction of grief. Asked where his stepson was, the Senator replied that Raymond was "undoubtedly in retreat, praying to God for understanding to carry on somehow."

XXV

SUNDAY NIGHT

Marco drank gin with his head resting across Eugénie Rose's ample lap and listened to the *Zeitgeist* of zither music until the gin had softened the rims of his memory. He looked straight up, right through the ceiling, his face an Aztec mask. Rosie had not spoken because she had too much to ask him and he did not speak for a long time because he had too much to tell her. He pulled some sheets of white paper from the breast pocket of his jacket, which had been hung across the back of the chair beside them.

"I grabbed this from the files this afternoon," he said. "It's a verbatim report. Fella took it down on tape in the Argentine. Read it to me, hah?"

Rosie took the paper and read aloud. "What follows is a transcribed conversation between Mrs. Seward Arnold and Agent Graham Dundee as transcribed by Carmelita Barajas and witnessed by Dolores Freg on February 16, 1959." Rosie looked for a moment as though she would ask a question, then seemed to think better of it. She continued to read from the paper while Marco stared from her lap at far away. She read slowly and softly.

DUNDEE:	Mrs. Arnold, if I may say so, this is the most unusual assignment of my career. I have been awake half the night studying how I could try to explain what I have been sent here to ask you.
MRS. ARNOLD:	Sent by whom, Mr. Dundee?
DUNDEE:	I don't know. If I did know I should probably have been instructed not to reveal that. I am a physician. A psychiatrist. I am attached to the Federal Bureau of Investigation of the Department of Justice of the government of the United States in that capacity. Here are my credentials.
MRS. ARNOLD:	I see. Thank you, but—
DUNDEE:	I have been flown from New York for this chat with you and when we have finished I shall take the first plane back to New York. It is a terrible journey when one makes it that way. Some thirteen thousand miles of catered food and the wrong people in the seat beside one. Talkers, mostly.
MRS. ARNOLD:	It sounds terribly important.
DUNDEE:	You may be sure of that.
MRS. ARNOLD:	But how can I help you? I'm not important, thank heaven. Does this involve my father?
DUNDEE:	No, Mrs. Arnold. It involves a man named Raymond Shaw.

(TRANSCRIBER AND WITNESS TIMED INTERVAL SILENCE OF ELEVEN SECONDS HERE.)

DUNDEE: Do you remember Raymond Shaw?

MRS. ARNOLD: Yes.

DUNDEE: Will you tell me what you remember about him, Mrs. Arnold?

MRS. ARNOLD: But—why?

DUNDEE: I don't know. There is so much we must do on faith alone. I only know that I must ask you these questions and pray that you will decide to answer. As a psychiatrist I have been assigned to work on and collect data concerning the character and personality and habits and reactions and inhibitions and repressions and idiosyncrasies and compulsions of Raymond Shaw for fourteen months, Mrs. Arnold. I have not been told why. I know only that it is desperately important work.

MRS. ARNOLD: It has been seven years since I have seen or spoken to Raymond Shaw, Mr.—rather, Dr. Dundee.

DUNDEE: Thank you.

MRS. ARNOLD: I was only a girl. I mean to say I did not consciously store up information about him. I mean, to get me started perhaps you would tell me what you know about Raymond Shaw.

DUNDEE: What I know? Mrs. Arnold, I know more about him than he knows about himself but I would not be permitted to tell *him*, much less you, because Raymond Shaw is classified information; his recreations and habits are top secret and his thoughts and dreams are top, *top* secret. Will you tell me about him?

MRS. ARNOLD: Raymond was twenty-one or twenty-two years old when I first saw him. I thought, and I still think, he was the handsomest man I have ever seen in life, or in a photograph or in a painting. His eyes had such regret for the world. They seemed to deplore that the world had taken him upon it and had then made him invisible.

DUNDEE: Did you say invisible, Mrs. Arnold?

MRS. ARNOLD: That was his own description of himself, but I never knew anyone who ever saw Raymond. My own father, who is a sensitive, interested man, was not able to see him. My father saw a neurotic slender giant of a child who seemed to pout and who stared rudely at every movement, the way cats do. Surely, Raymond's mother never saw him. I am not even sure that his mother ever looked at him.

DUNDEE: Still, his mother manufactured Raymond.

MRS. ARNOLD: The cold, unfriendliness of him. The resentful retreater. The hurt and defiant retreater who wept stone tears behind a shield of arrogance.

DUNDEE: But he was not invisible to you.

MRS. ARNOLD: No. He allowed me to see him. He was very shy. He had so much tenderness. He was nearly pathetic with his need to please, once he had been allowed to understand that it was wanted for him to be pleasing. He was so sparing with his warm thoughts, except with me. His loving and unresentful thoughts. He doled them out through that eye dropper which was his fear and shyness, then he grew until he could give spoonfuls of it until, at last, when he knew that I loved him he could have learned to give and partake of feeling and warmth and love the way the gods do.

DUNDEE: Mrs. Arnold, I won't pretend to try to be casual about this. What I must ask you is tremendously important and has a direct bearing upon essential psychiatric evidence, you must be sure of that, or I would never, never, never presume to ask you such an extraordinary question, but you see we—I—

MRS. ARNOLD: Did Raymond ever possess me? Did we ever sleep together? Is that the question, Doctor?

DUNDEE: Yes. Thank you. That is it, Mrs. Arnold. If you please.

MRS. ARNOLD: I wish he had—that we had. I wish he had and

if he had I could not have told you. But he
did not, so I can. Raymond never—we never—
Raymond and I never so much as kissed, Dr.
Dundee.

MARCO reached up and took the transcript gently out of
Rosie's hands. He folded it and slid it back into the pocket of his
jacket.

"Who was Mrs. Arnold?" Rosie asked.

"That was Jocie. Raymond's girl."

"His wife."

"Yeah."

He got to his feet laboriously. He could not have made it
straight up into an erect position. He had to roll off her lap and
the sofa to his hands and knees, then get to his feet holding onto
a chair. He took the empty gin bottle to the kitchen, lurching
slightly, and stored it neatly in a wastebasket. He got another
bottle. On the way back to Rosie he picked up the newspaper he
had brought in with him at six o'clock and which had lain, rolled
up, on a table near the door. He dropped the newspaper into her
lap, then sat down beside her. "Raymond shot and killed his wife
this morning," he said.

She tried to read the paper and watch Marco at the same time.
She drew astonishment from the paper and horror from the sight
of Marco because he looked so ravaged. He drank a few fingers
of warm gin while she read the story. When she had finished it
she said, "The paper doesn't say that Raymond killed his wife."
Marco didn't answer. He drank and thought and listened
through one more side of zither music, then he fell forward on
his face to the horrendous pink cabbage roses in the French blue
rug. She held him and kissed him, then she dragged him by his
feet into the bedroom, undressed him, and rolled him up across
the bed in several stages.

XXVI

RAYMOND watched the queen of diamonds on top of the squared deck while his mother spoke to him.

". . . and Chunjin will give you a two-piece Soviet Army sniper's rifle with all of its native ballistic markings. It sets nicely into a special bag which you can carry just as though it were a visiting doctor's bag. You'll take it with you to the hotel at Newark. We have come to the end of this terrible road at last, Raymond darling. After years and years and so much pain it will all be over so soon now. We have won the power, and now that they have given it to us they can just begin to fear. We may reply now, my dearest, for what they have done to you, to me, and to your lovely Jocie."

Raymond's mother had banged a charge into her arm just before this session of briefing Raymond and it most certainly agreed with her. Her magnetic, perfectly spaced blue eyes seemed to sparkle as she talked. Her lithe, solid figure seemed even more superb because of her flawless carriage. She wore a Chinese dressing gown of a shade so light that it complemented the contrasting color of her eyes. Her long and extremely beautiful legs were stretched out before her on the chaise longue, and any man but her son or her husband, seeing what she had and yet knowing that this magnificent forty-nine-year-old body was only a wasted uniform covering blunted neutral energy, might have wept over such a waste. Her voice, usually that of a hard woman on the make for big stakes, had softened perceptibly as she spoke because she was pleading and her voice had new overtones of self-deception. In the years since Raymond had been returned from the Army and shock had been piled upon shock, the sanity-preserving part of her mind, which labored to teach her how to forgive herself, and thus save herself, had been working and scheming against the day when she must explain everything to Raymond and expect to receive his forgiveness.

"I am sure you will never entirely comprehend this, darling, and I know, the way you are right now, this is like trying to have a whispered conversation with someone on a distant star, but for my own peace of mind, such as that is, it must be said. Raymond, you have to believe that I did not know that they would do what they did to you. I served them. I thought for them. I got them the greatest foothold they will ever have in this country and they paid me back by taking your soul away from you. I told them to build me an assassin. I wanted a killer who would obey orders from a stock in a world filled with killers, and they did this to you because they thought it would bind me closer to them. When I walked into that room in that Swardon Sanitarium in New York to meet this perfect assassin and I found that he was my son—my son with a changed and twisted mind and all the bridges burned behind us . . . But we have come to the end now, and it is our turn to twist tomorrow for them, because just as I am a mother before everything else I am an American second to that, and when I take power they will be pulled down and ground into dirt for what they did to you and for what they did in so contemptuously underestimating me." She took his hand and kissed it with burning devotion, then she held his face in her hands and stared into it tenderly. "How much you look like Poppa! You have his beautiful hands and you hold your beautiful head in that same proud, proud way. And when you smile! Smile, my darling."

Raymond smiled, naturally and beautifully, under orders. She caught her breath in a gasp. "When you smile, Raymond dearest, for that instant I am a little girl again and the miracle of love begins all over again. How right that seems to me. Smile for me again, sweetheart. Yes. Yes. Now kiss me. Really, really kiss me." Her long fingers dug into his shoulders and pulled him to her on the chaise, and as her left hand opened the Chinese robe she remembered Poppa and the sound of rain high in the attic when she had been a little girl, and she found again the ecstatic peace she had lost so long, long before.

XXVII

THEODORE Roosevelt said that the right of popular government is incomplete unless it includes the right of voters not merely to choose between candidates when they have been nominated, but also the right to determine who these candidates shall be.

Three major methods have been used by the parties, in American political history, to name candidates: the caucus, the convention, and the direct primary. The caucus was discarded early because it gave the legislature undue influence over the executive. The convention method for choosing Presidential candidates was first used in 1831 by the Anti-Masonic party, but the basic flaw in any convention system is the method of choice of delegates to the convention. The origin of the direct primary is somewhat obscure but it is generally considered as having been adopted by the Democratic party in Crawford County, Pennsylvania, in 1842; however, not until Robert M. La Follette became governor of Wisconsin, early in 1900, was a political leader successful in pushing through a mandatory, statewide, direct primary system.

Because no public regulation exists to control it, the national convention has developed into one of the most remarkable political institutions in the world. In no other nation on this planet is the selection of national leaders, whose influence is to be felt profoundly throughout the world, and the formulation of ostensibly serious policies placed in the hands of a convention of about three thousand howling, only cursorily consulted delegates and alternates. M. Ostrogorski, a French observer of the American political scene, wrote in 1902 of the convention system: "You realize what a colossal travesty of popular institutions you have just been witnessing. A greedy crowd of officeholders, or of office seekers, disguised as delegates of the people on the pretense of holding the grand council of the party, indulged in, or were victims of, intrigues and maneuvers, the object of which was the chief magistracy of the greatest republic of two hemispheres— the succession to the Washingtons and the Jeffersons. Yet when you carry your thoughts back from the scene which you have just witnessed and review the line of presidents you find that if they have not all been great men—far from it—they were all honorable men; and you cannot help repeating the American saying: 'God takes care of drunkards, little children, and of the United States.'"

The climate of welcome in which the convention of 1960 opened was like many of those that had preceded it. Hotels were festooned with bunting. Distillers had provided all saloons with printed partisan displays, the backs of which carried the same message in the name of the other party, whose convention would follow in three weeks. The mid-town streets were choked with big-hipped broads wearing paper cowboy hats. Witty Legionnaires rode horses into hotel lobbies. Witty Legionnaires squirted friendly streams from water pistols at the more defenseless-looking passers-by. Gay delegates hung twenty-dollar call girls by their heels out of high hotel windows. Ward heelers issued statements on party unity. Elder statesmen were ignored or used depending on the need. The Pickpocket Squad worked like contestants in a newsreel husking bee. One hundred and four men's suits were misplaced by the dry-cleaning services of thirty-eight hotels. Petitions and documentations were submitted to the Resolutions Committee by farm lobbies, labor unions, women's organizations, temperance groups, veterans' blocs, antivivisection societies, and national manufacturers' Turnvereins. Two thousand one hundred and four hand towels over the minimal daily quota would be used, on an average, for each night the convention sat in the city. A delegate was arrested, but not prosecuted, for wrestling with a live crocodile in Duffy Square to call attention to the courage of a Florida candidate for the vice-presidency. The world's largest campaign button was worn by a bevy of lovely young "apple farmers" from the Pacific Northwest although their candidate came from Missouri (he happened to be in the apple business). At 8 A.M., two hours before the convention opened on Monday morning, Marco conducted a drill of two hundred FBI and Army Intelligence agents and three hundred and ten plain-clothes men and women of the New York Police Department, assembled in the backstage area of the Garden where they were briefed on the over-all assignment. Marco was so frantic with worry and fear that his hand shook as he used the chalk on the large blackboard, on a high platform. After Marco's briefing, more and more detailed briefings were conducted down through the units of command to squad level, until Marco, Amjac, Lehner, and the chief inspector of the New York police were sure that each man knew what he was to do.

The twenty-seventh national convention of the party was opened by Miss Viola Narvilly of the great Indianapolis Opera Company singing the National Anthem. This one, as her manager explained, was a bitch of a song to sing, as any singer, professional or otherwise, would tell you, and, he said hotly, it like to have lifted Miss Narvilly out of her own body by her vocal cords to get up to those unnatural notes which some idiot thought he was doing great when he wrote it. Miss Narvilly's manager tried to throw a punch at the National Chairman—he had practically begged them to open the convention singing the lousy song, then not one single television shot had been taken of Miss Narvilly from beginning to end, before or after, and they had spent their own loot to come all the way in from a concert in Chicago.

After the National Chairman got some help from two sergeants at arms in shaking Miss Narvilly's manager loose he called the first session to order. Nearly six hundred of the three thousand delegates settled down to listen to the welcoming speech by the party's senator from New York. The Chairman made his formal address following this token welcome and the hall filled up just a little more, and the business of permanent organization, credentials, rules and order of business, platform and resolutions got under way and filled the time nicely until the keynote speaker took over in the TV slot that had been bought on all networks for nine to nine-thirty that evening.

Although Senator Iselin and his wife did not attend the first day's session, an Iselin headquarters had been established on a full floor of the largest West Side hotel near the Garden. Also, the Loyal American Underground had established recruiting booths for Johnny in the lobbies of every "official" convention hotel and had rented a store opposite the Eighth Avenue entrance to the Garden; the store had been an upholstery store before the convention and would be an upholstery store again. One enthusiastic newspaper reported that these recruitment booths had registered four thousand two hundred members (Mrs. Iselin had thought it prudent to register the same one hundred people again and again throughout the days to insure the excitement of action at all booths), but the exact number of new recruits could not be determined accurately.

On the opening Monday, true to his word as an officer and a gentleman, General Francis "Fightin' Frank" Bollinger headed a parade made up of state and county chairmen of Ten Million Americans Mobilizing for Tomorrow, down Eighth Avenue from Columbus Circle to the Garden. They were two hundred and forty-six strong from the forty-nine states, plus an irregular battalion made up of loyal wives and daughters, various uncommitted New Yorkers who enjoyed parading, and a police squad car. They marched the nine short blocks with Fightin' Frank holding in one gloved hand the front end of a continuous paper petition that stretched out behind him for eight and a half blocks and contained at least four thousand signatures, many of which had been written by the general's own family to fill out the spaces and add to the fun. Many of the newspaper reports got the figure wrong, reporting as many as 1,064,219 signatures, although at no time did any representative of any newspaper attempt to make a count. The petition urged the nomination of John Yerkes Iselin to the Presidency of the United States candidacy under the general indivisive slogan of "The Man Who Saves America."

Mrs. Iselin arrived at Johnny's campaign headquarters at eight o'clock Monday night. For the next several hours she received the prospective candidates for the Presidency, together with their managers, in separate relays in her suite. At 1:10 A.M. she made the deal she wanted and committed Senator Iselin's entire delegate support to the candidate of her choice, accepting, on behalf of Senator Iselin, the assurance of nomination for the office of vice-presidency and losing for Fightin' Frank Bollinger the assurance of portfolio as Secretary of State.

The party's platform was presented to the convention on Tuesday morning and afternoon, together with many statesmanlike speeches. Professor Hugh Bone, when writing of party platforms as delivered at conventions said: "If the voter expects to find specific issues and clearly defined party policy in the platform he will be sorely disappointed. As a guide to the program to be carried out by the victorious party the platform is also of little value." The British political scholar Lord Byrce observed that the purpose of the American party platform appears to be "neither to define nor to convince, but rather to attract and confuse." The 1960 platform of the party committed itself as follows: for free enterprise, farm prosperity, preservation of small business, reduction in taxes, and rigid economy in government. The latter plank had been axiomatic for both major parties since 1840. Due to the insistence of Senator Iselin the platform also demanded "the eradication of Communists and Communist thought without mercy wherever and whenever Our Flag flies."

The roll call for the nomination got under way on Tuesday afternoon, July 12. Alabama yielded. The nominating speech, the demonstration following that, the seconding speech, and the

demonstration following that, gave the convention the first aspir-
ant in nomination at six twenty-one. The identical ritual for the
second favorite son took up the attention of the convention to
ten thirty-five. The third candidate proposed was nominated on
the first ballot by unanimous vote of the convention, as had been
ten candidates of the party since 1900, at twelve forty-one on
July 12, 1960, when the convention was adjourned until noon the
following day when it would meet to deliberate over its choice of
candidate for the office of vice-president, then await the historic
acceptance speeches by both leaders the following night.

XXVIII RAYMOND

left the hotel in Newark, where he had been told to rest, at
4 P.M. Wednesday. He carried a nondescript black satchel.
He took the tubes under the river, then the subway to Times
Square. For a while he wandered aimlessly along West Forty-
second Street. After a while he found himself at Forty-fourth
and Broadway. He went into a large drugstore. He got change
for a quarter at the cigarette counter and shuffled to one of
the empty telephone booths in the rear. He dialed Marco's
office number. The agent on duty answered. He was alone in
the large house in Turtle Bay.

"Colonel Marco, please."

"Who is calling, please?"

"Raymond Shaw. It's a personal call."

The agent inhaled very slowly. Then he exhaled slowly.
"Hello? Hello?" Raymond said, thinking the connection had
been broken.

"Right here, Mr. Shaw," the agent said briskly. "It looks as
though Colonel Marco has stepped away from his desk for a
moment, but he'll be back practically instantly, Mr. Shaw, and
he left word that if you called he wanted to be sure that he could
call you right back, wherever you were. If you'll give me your
telephone number, Mr. Shaw—"

"Well—"

"He'll be right back."

"Maybe I'd better call him back. I'm in a drugstore here and—"

"I have my orders, Mr. Shaw. If you'll give me that number, please."

"The number in the booth here is Circle eight, nine six three seven. I'll hang around for ten minutes or so, I guess, and have a cup of coffee." He hung up the phone and the newspaper fell from his pocket and flattened out on the floor showing the headline: MURDERS OF SENATOR AND DAUGHTER ENIGMA. Raymond picked the paper up slowly and returned it to his jacket pocket. He climbed on a stool at the soda fountain and waited for someone to come and take his order.

The agent on duty dialed a number rapidly. He got a busy signal. He waited painfully with his eyes closed, then he opened them and dialed again. He got a busy signal. He pulled his sleeve back from his wrist watch, stared at it for thirty seconds, then dialed again. The connection bubbled a through signal.

"Garden."

"This is Turtle Bay. Get me Marco. Red signal."

"Hold, please."

The booming voice of the platform speaker inside the arena was cut off from every amplifier throughout the Garden. The packed hall seemed, for an instant, like a silent waxworks packed with three thousand effigies. An urgent, new voice came pounding out the horns. It contrasted so much with the ribbon of pure silence that had preceded it, after two days of amplified fustian, that every delegate felt threatened by its urgency.

"Colonel Marco! Colonel Marco! Red signal! Red signal! Colonel Marco! Red signal!"

The voice cut itself off and another electronic flow of silence came through the system. Newspapermen immediately began to pressure the wrong officials about the significance of the interruption and the term *red signal,* and beginning with the first editions of the morning papers the term was printed again and again until it finally found itself on television variety shows as comedians' warning cries.

Marco sat backstage with an unleashed phone in his hand, within a semicircle of agents and police. Amjac was between earphones at one telephone monitor and Lehner was at the other. The recording machines were turning. Five minutes, eight seconds, had elapsed since Raymond had made his call. Marco dialed. He was sweating peanut butter.

The telephone rang in an empty booth. It rang again. Then again. A figure slumped into the seat to answer it. It was Raymond.

"Ben?" No other opening.

"Yes, kid."

"You read what happened?"

"Yes. I know. I know."

"How could anyone? How could it happen? Jocie—how could anyone—"

"Where are you, Raymond?" The men ringed around Marco seemed to lean forward.

"I think maybe I'm going crazy. I have the terrible dreams like you used to have and terrible things are all twisted together. But the craziest part is how anyone—could—Ben! They killed Jocie. Somebody *killed* Jocie!" The words came out hoarsely and on a climbing scale.

"Where are you, kid? We have to talk. We can't talk on the telephone. Where are you?"

"I have to talk to you. I have to talk to you."

"I'll meet you. Where are you?"

"I can't stay here. I have to get out. I have to get air."

"I'll meet you at the paper."

"No, no."

"In the Park, then."

"The Park?"

"The zoo, Raymond. On the porch of the cafeteria. O.K.?"

"O.K."

"Right away."

"They're inside my head, like you said."

"Get a cab and get up to the Park."

"Yes." Raymond hung up. Marco banged the phone down and wheeled in his swivel chair. Amjac and Lehner nodded at the same time. "The boy is in bad shape," Lehner said.

"I'll take him now," Marco said. "This has to move very normally. Raymond has to be allowed to feel safe, then he has to play solitaire, so this is all mine. Give me some cards."

Lehner took a pack of force cards out of a carton on the long work table supported by sawhorses and tossed them across the room to Marco. Lehner stuffed another pack into his pocket as a souvenir. A detail coming off duty straggled into the room. "Whatta you know?" the first man said. "They just handed the vice-presidency to that idiot Iselin." Marco grunted. He turned and nearly ran toward the Forty-ninth Street exit.

RAYMOND was sitting in the sooty sunlight with his back to the *arriviste* skyline of Central Park South, staring at a cup of coffee. Marco felt shock like a heavy hammer as he stared at him from a few feet off. He suddenly realized he had never seen Raymond unshaven before, or wearing a dirty shirt, or wearing clothes that could have been slept in for night after night. Raymond's face seemed to be falling into itself and it presented the kind of shock a small boy's face would bring if he had had all of his teeth extracted.

Marco sat down across from Raymond at the sturdy outdoor table. There were only eight or nine people on the long, broad terrace. Marco and Raymond had a lot of room to themselves. He put his hand on top of Raymond's dirty hand with the black rimmed fingers. "Hi, kid," he said almost inaudibly. Raymond looked up. His eyes glistened with wet. "I don't know what is happening to me," he said and Marco could almost see the ripping Raymond felt. Raymond's emotion was like that of a curate with his head filled with cocaine, or perhaps like that of a man after he has had acid thrown into his eyes. The grief that shone dully out of Raymond blocked out everything else within Marco's field of vision; it was blackness which threw back no reflection.

The seals in the large pool honked and splashed. Around the seal pond grew a moving garden of zoo-blooming balloons, their roots attached to bicycles and prams and small fists. The big cats were being fed somewhere in the area behind Marco and they were noisy eaters.

"They are inside my head like you said, aren't they, Ben?"

Marco nodded.

"Can they—can they make me do anything?"

Marco nodded less perceptibly.

"I have a terrible dream—oh, my God—I have a terrible dream that my mother and I—"

Raymond's eyes were so wild that Marco could not look at him. He shut his eyes and thought of the shapes of prayers. A rubber ball came bouncing then rolling along the stone terrace. It lodged against Marco's feet. A small boy with a comical face and hair like a poodle's came running after it. He held Raymond's arm as he bent down to get his ball, then ran away from them shouting at his friends.

"Who killed Jocie, Ben?"—and Marco could not answer him. "Ben, did I—did I kill Jocie? That could be, couldn't it? Maybe it was an accident, but they wanted me to kill Senator Jordan and—did I kill my Jocie?"

Marco could not watch this any longer. Mercifully, he said, "How about passing the time by playing a little solitaire?" and he slid the force deck across the table. He watched Raymond relax. Raymond got the cards out of the box and began to shuffle mechanically and smoothly.

Marco had to be sure that his red queen would command the authority to supersede all others. He had never been permitted to read Yen Lo's complete instructions for the operation of a murderer. Therefore, the force deck, which had been enlisted at first as a time-saver to bring the red queen into immediate play, was now seen by Marco as his insurance policy which had to be seven ways more powerful than the single queen of diamonds that the enemy had used. Every time Raymond's play showed the red queen, which was from the first card set down, he attempted reflexively to stop the play, Marco ordered him to play on, to lay out the full, upfaced seven stacks of solitaire. At last there was arrayed a pantheon of red queens in imperious row.

Where was Jocie? Raymond asked himself, far inside himself, as he stared at the advancing sweep of costumed monarchs. The seven queens commanded silence. They began to order him, through Marco, to unlock all of the great jade doors which went back, back, back, along an austere corridor in time to the old, old man with the withered, merry smile who said his name was Yen Lo and who promised him solemnly that in other lives, through which he would journey beyond this life, he would be spared the unending agony which he had found in this life. Where was Jocie? Mr. Gaines had been a good man but he had been told to make him dead. Amen. He had had to kill in Paris; he had killed in London by special appointment to the Queen of Diamonds, offices in principal cities. Amen. Where was Jocie? The tape recorder in the holster under Marco's arm revolved and listened. Raymond stared at the seven queens and talked. He told what his mother had told him. He explained that he had shot Senator Jordan and that—that he had—that after he had shot Senator Jordan he had—

Marco's voice slammed out at him, telling him he was to forget about what had happened at Senator Jordan's until he, Marco, told him to remember. He asked Raymond what he had been told to do in New York. Raymond told him.

In the end, when all Marco's questions had been answered, but not until the very end, did it become clear to Colonel Marco, what they would have to do. Marco thought of his father and his grandfather and of their Army. He considered his own life and its meaning. He decided for both of them what they would have to do.

They walked away from the terrace, past the seal pond, through the bobbing flowers in the garden of toy balloons. They walked past the bars marked YAK—POEPHAGUS GRUN-NIENS—CENT. ASIA and they moved out slowly through the gantlet of resters and lovers and dreamers toward the backside of General Sherman's bronze horse.

At Sixtieth Street, on Fifth Avenue, Marco tried to anticipate the changing of a traffic light. He stepped down from the curb two steps in front of Raymond, then turned to hurry Raymond along so that they could beat the light, when the Drive-Ur-Self car, rented by Chunjin, hit him. It threw him twelve feet and he lay where he fell. A crowd began to collect itself out of motes of sunlight. A foot policeman came running from the hotel marquee at Fifty-ninth Street because a woman had screamed like a crane. Chunjin leaned over and opened the door. "Get in, Mr. Shaw. Quickly, please." Raymond got into the car, carrying his satchel, and as the car zoomed off into the Park, he slammed the door. Chunjin left the Park at Seventy-second Street, crossed to Broadway, and started downtown. They did not speak until they reached the dingy hotel on West Forty-ninth Street when Chunjin gave him the key stamped 301, wished him good luck, shook his hand while he stared into Raymond's tragic, yellow eyes, told him to leave the car, and drove off, going west.

Raymond changed clothes in Room 301. He entered the Garden through a door marked Executive Entrance on the Forty-ninth Street side, at five forty-five, during the afternoon recess while the building held only five per cent of the activity it had seen one hour before. The candidate's acceptance speeches were scheduled to appear on all networks from ten to ten-thirty that night, and after that the campaign would start.

Raymond was dressed as he had been told to dress; as a priest, with a reversed stiff collar, a black suit, a soft, black hat, and heavy black shell eyeglasses. He smoked a large black cigar from the corner of his mouth and he carried a satchel. He looked overworked, preoccupied, and sour. Everybody saw him. No one recognized him. He walked across the main lobby just inside the Eighth Avenue gates and climbed the staircase slowly like a man on a dull errand. He kept climbing. When he could go no farther, he walked along behind the top tier of the gallery seats, now empty, not bothering to look down at the littered floor of the arena, six stories below him. Carrying the satchel, he went up the iron stepladder that was bolted to the wall, climbing twenty-two feet until he reached the catwalk that ran out at right angles from the wall and led to the suspended box that was a spotlight booth, used only for theatrical spectaculars. He let himself into the booth with a key, closing and locking the door behind him. He sat down on a wooden packing case, opened the satchel, took out a gun barrel, then the stock of a sniper's rifle, and assembled the gun with expert care. When he was satisfied with its connection, he took the telescopic sight out of its chamois case and, after polishing it carefully, mounted it on the piece.

XXIX

MARCO WAS fighting to kill time. He stalled at every possible chance as they tried to help him dress. He needed time for Raymond to find his position, for the inexorable, uncompromising television schedule to pull all of the counters into play. Marco thought about the face of John Yerkes Iselin and he made himself do everything more slowly.

His right arm was in full sling; right hand to the left shoulder. The right side of his face seemed to have come off. The skin was gone and under the snowy bandage it was as black as the far side of the moon. Four ribs had crumpled on the left side of his spine, and he was tightly taped. He was under semi-anesthesia to keep the pain under control, and it gave him everything on the outside in parts of fantasy and parts of reality. Two men were dressing him as rapidly as he would allow them to progress, although no one there could tell that he was stalling.

Amjac and Lehner squatted on the floor around a tape playback machine and the only sound in the room, beyond Marco's labored breathing and his quick, deep throat-sounds of pain, was the clear, impersonal sound of Raymond's voice, backed up by children's squeals and laughter, the roar of hungry cats, the honks and splats of seals, and the gentling undersound of two hundred red, green, and yellow balloons as they cut the air at a tenth of a mile per hour. Every man in the room was staring at the machine. It was saying:

"No, I don't think the priest's outfit is supposed to have any symbolic significance. My mother doesn't think that way. Primarily, it will be good camouflage. She may have arranged to have me caught after I kill him, when, I suppose, I will be exposed as a Communist with a tailor-made record as long as a hangman's rope. Then, of course, the choice of ecclesiastical costume will keep a lot of people enraged on still a different level, if they didn't happen to plan to vote for the dead candidate. If I am caught I am to state, on the second day, after much persuasion, that I was ordered to undertake the execution by the Kremlin. Mother definitely plans to involve them, but I don't think she will purposely involve me because she was really deeply upset and affected for the first time since I have known her when she discovered that they had chosen me to be their killer. She told me that they had lost the world when they did that and that when she and Johnny got into the White House she was going to start and finish a holy war, without ten minutes' warning, that would wipe them off the face of the earth, and that then we—I do not mean this country, I mean Mother and whoever she decides to use—will run this country and we'll run the whole world. She is crazy, of course. There will be a terrible pandemonium down in that arena after they are hit, and I am sure the priest's suit will help me to get away. I am to leave at once, but the rifle stays there. It's a Soviet issue rifle."

Marco's voice, from the tape, said, "Did you say after *they* are hit? Did you use the word 'they'?"

"Well, yes. I am ordered to shoot the nominee through the head and to shoot Johnny Iselin through the left shoulder, and when the bullet hits Johnny it will shatter a crystal compound which Mother has sewn in under the material which will make him look all soggy with blood. He won't be hurt because that whole area from his chin to his hips will be bullet-proofed. Mother said this was the part Johnny was actually born to play because he overacts so much and we can certainly use plenty of that here. The bullet's velocity will knock him down, of course, but he will get to his feet gallantly amid the chaos that will have broken out at that time, and the way she wants him to do it for the best effect for the television cameras and the still photographers is to lift the nominee's body in his arms and stand in front of the microphones like that because that picture will symbolize more than anything else that it is Johnny's party which the Soviets fear the most, and Johnny will offer the body of a great American on the altar of liberty, and as you know, as Mother says, there is nothing that has succeded in the history of politics like martyrdom, for now the people must rise and strike down this Communist peril which she can prove instantly lives within and amongst us all. Johnny will point that up in his speech he will make with the candidate in his arms. It is short, but Mother says it is the most rousing speech she has ever read. They have been working on that speech, here and in Russia, on and off, for over eight years. Mother will force some of the men on that platform to take the body away from Johnny because, after all, he's not Tarzan she said, then Johnny will really hit that microphone and those cameras, blood all over him, fighting off those who try to succor him, defending America even if it means his death, and rallying a nation of television viewers into hysteria and pulling that convention along behind him to vote him into the nomination and to accept a platform which will sweep them right into the White House under powers which will make martial law seem like anarchism, Mother says."

"When will you shoot the candidate, Raymond?" Marco's voice asked.

"Well, Mother wants him to be dead at about six minutes after he begins his acceptance speech, depending on his reading speed under pressure, but I will hit him right at the point where he finishes the phrase which reads: 'nor would I ask of any fellow American in defense of his freedom that which I would not gladly give myself—my life before my liberty.'"

"Where will you shoot from?"

"There is a spotlight booth that will not be in use. It's up under the roof of the Eighth Avenue side of the Garden. I haven't been in it, but Mother says I will have absolutely clear, protected shooting from it. She will seat Johnny on the platform directly behind the candidate, just a little to his left, so I'll be able to swing the sights and wing him with minimal time loss. That's about it. It's a very solid plan."

"They all are," Marco's voice said. "There are going to be one or two important changes, Raymond. Forget what your mother told you. This is what you are going to do."

There was a click. The tape in the playback machine rolled to a stop.

"What happened?" Amjac said quickly.

"The colonel stopped the machine," Lehner said, watching Marco.

"Come on," Marco said. "We have seconds, not minutes. Let's go." He started out of the room, forcing them to follow him.

"But what did you tell him, Colonel?"

"Don't worry," Marco said, walking rapidly. "The Army takes care of its own."

"You mean—Raymond?"

They crowded into the elevator at the end of the hospital corridor. "No," Marco answered. "I was thinking about two other things. About a General Jorgenson and the United States of America."

XXX

A HUSH FELL upon the delegations in the great hall as the Chairman announced that within a very few minutes their candidates would be facing the television cameras, when, for the first time together, eighty million American voters would see the next President and Vice-President of the United States standing before them. The convention thundered its approval. As they cheered the top brass of the party, made up of governors, national committeemen, fat cats, senators, and congressmen, were herded upon the platform, followed by the two nominees and their wives.

They moved with great solemnity. Senator Iselin and his wife seemed to be affected particularly. They were unsteady and extremely pale, which occasioned more than one delegate, newspaperman, committeeman, and spectator to observe that the vast dignity and the awful responsibility, truly the awesome meaning of that great office, had never failed to humble any man and that John Iselin was no exception, as he was proving up there now. When he sat down he was actually trembling and he seemed— he, of all people, whom audiences and speeches had stimulated all his life—nervous and apprehensive, even frightened. They could see his wife, a beautiful woman who was always at his side, a real campaigner and a fighter who, more than once, had looked subversion in the face and had stared it down, as she spoke to him steadily, in an undertone which was obviously too low-pitched and too personal for anyone to hear.

"Sit still, you son-of-a-bitch! He has never missed with a rifle in his life. Johnny! Damn it, Johnny, if you move you can get hurt. Give him a chance to sight you and to get used to this light. And what the hell are you sweating now for? You won't be hit until after the speech is under way. Did you take those pills? Johnny, did you? I knew it. I knew I should have stood over you and made you take those goddam pills." She fumbled inside her handbag. She worked three pills out of a vial and placed them together on the adhesive side of a piece of Scotch tape, within the purse. Very sweetly and with the graciousness of a Schrafft's hostess she gestured unobtrusively to a young man who was at the edge of the platform for just such emergencies and asked him for a glass of water.

When the water came, just as she got it in her hand, the nominee was on the air and his acceptance speech had begun. His voice was low but clear as he began to thank the delegations for the honor they had done him.

Only the speaker's platform was lighted. Three rows in front of the speaker, as he faced the darkness of the hall, one of the men of Marco's unit was crouched in the aisle, with walkie-talkie equipment. He spoke into the mouthpiece with a low voice, giving a running account of what was happening on the platform, and if the delegates seated near him thought of him at all, they thought he was on the air, although what he was saying would have mystified any radio audience.

"She just got a glass of water from the page. She is handling it very busily. She's doing something with the rim of it. I'm not sure. Wait. I'm not sure. I'm going to take a guess that she has stuck something on the rim of the glass—I even think I can see it—and she just handed the glass to Iselin."

On the platform, behind and to the left of the speaker, Raymond's mother said to Johnny, "The pills are on the edge of the glass. Take them as you drink. That's good. That's fine. Now you'll be O.K. Now just sit still, sweetheart. All you'll feel will be like a very hard punch on the shoulder. Just one punch and it's all over. Then you get up and do your stuff and we're home free, honey. We're in like Flynn, honey. Just take it easy. Take it easy, sweetheart."

MARCO, Amjac, and Lehner climbed the stairs. Lehner was carrying a walkie-talkie and mumbling into it. The nominee's speech was booming out of the speakers and Amjac was saying, as though in a bright conversation with nobody, O Jesus God, they were too late, they were too late. Marco moved clumsily under his bandages but he held the lead going up the stairs.

As they got to the top level they were scrambling and they started to run along behind the gallery seats toward the iron ladder as the nominee's voice reverberated all around them, saying: ". . . that which I would not gladly give myself—my life before my liberty," and Amjac was screaming, "Oh, my good God, no! No!" when they heard the first rifle shot crack out and echo. "No! No!" Amjac screamed, and the sounds were ripped out of his chest as though they were being sent on to overtake the bullet and deflect its course when the second shot ripped its sound through the air, then everything was drowned out by a great, enormous roar of shock and fear as comprehension of the meaning of the first shot reached the floor of the arena. The noise from the Garden floor was horrendous. Lehner stopped to crouch against the building wall, pressing the earphones to his ears, trying to hear the message from the man in front of the platform on the arena floor. "What? What? Louder. Aaaaaaah!" It was a wailed sigh. He dragged the earphones off his head, staring numbly at Amjac. "He shot Iselin, then he shot his mother. Dead. Not the nominee. Johnny and his wife are stone cold dead."

Amjac wheeled. "Colonel!" he shouted. "Where's the colonel?" He looked up and saw Marco moving painfully across the narrow catwalk toward the locked black box that was the spotlight booth. "Colonel Marco!" Amjac yelled. Marco turned slightly as he walked, and waved his left hand. It held a deck of playing cards. They watched him come to the door of the booth and kick at it gently.

When they reached the catwalk, Marco had disappeared into the booth. The door had closed again. Amjac started across the catwalk with Lehner behind him. They stopped short as the door opened and Marco came out. He couldn't close the door behind him because of the sling, but they could not see through the darkness inside. They backed up on the catwalk as he came toward them, and then they heard the third shot sound inside the booth—short, sharp, and clean.

"No electric chair for a Medal of Honor man," Marco said, and he began to pick his way painfully down the iron ladder listening intently for a memory of Raymond, for the faintest rustle of his ever having lived, but there was none.

ABOUT THE AUTHOR

RICHARD CONDON is the author of five novels, and is now busily at work on a sixth. All but one of his books have been made into movies; his fourth, *A Talent for Loving*, will shortly go into production, starring the Beatles.

Married and with two daughters, one of whom has recently made him a grandfather, Mr. Condon lives in Switzerland with his wife and an aging and aristocratic dachshund.